D0465554

ESSENTIAL
USA

1st Edition

Where to Stay and Eat
for All Budgets

Must-See Sights
and Local Secrets

Ratings You Can Trust

Fodor's Travel Publications   New York, Toronto, London, Sydney, Auckland
www.fodors.com

FODOR'S USA

Editors: Michael Nalepa, Paul Eisenberg, *lead editors*; Debbie Harmsen, Molly Moker, Jennifer Paull, Eric B. Wechter

Editorial Production: Tom Holton

Editorial Contributors: John Blodgett, Carissa Bluestone, Erin Byers Murray, Andrew Collins, Jennifer D'Anastacio, Michelle Delio, Jessica Norman Dupuy, T. D. Griffith, Amy Grisak, MiChelle Jones, Denise M. Leto, Susan MacCallum-Whitcomb, Piers Marchant, Russell McCulley, Gary McKechnie, Leslie Mizell, Reed Parsell, Steve Pastorino, Michael Ream, Susan Reigler, Sarah Richards, Swain Scheps, Eileen Robinson Smith, Judy Sutton Taylor, Kyle Wagner, Christine Vovakes, Bobbi Zane

Maps & Illustrations: Mark Stroud, David Lindroth and maps.com *cartographers*; Bob Blake Rebecca Baer and William Wu, *map editors*

Design: Fabrizio LaRocca, *creative director*; Guido Caroti, Siobhan O'Hare, *art directors*; Tina Malaney, Chie Ushio, Ann McBride, *designers*; Melanie Marin, *senior picture editor*; Moon Sun Kim, *cover designer*

Cover Photos: Statue of Liberty; Monument Valley, Arizona; and Washington Monument: Digital Vision/MediaBakery. Pumpkin Pie: Polka Dot/MediaBakery. Road sign in Amish Country: Thinkstock/MediaBakery. Trumpet: Frank-Peter Funke/Shutterstock. Antique car: Manfred Steinbach/Shutterstock. Las Vegas cowboy: Corbis.

Production/Manufacturing: Angela L. McLean

SPECIAL SALES

This book is available at special discounts for bulk purchases for sales promotions or premiums. Special editions, including personalized covers, excerpts of existing books, and corporate imprints, can be created in large quantities for special needs. For more information, write to Special Markets/Premium Sales, 1745 Broadway, MD 6-2, New York, New York 10019, or e-mail specialmarkets@randomhouse.com.

AN IMPORTANT TIP & AN INVITATION

Although all prices, opening times, and other details in this book are based on information supplied to us at press time, changes occur all the time in the travel world, and Fodor's cannot accept responsibility for facts that become outdated or for inadvertent errors or omissions. So **always confirm information when it matters**, especially if you're making a detour to visit a specific place. Your experiences—positive and negative— matter to us. If we have missed or misstated something, **please write to us**. We follow up on all suggestions. Contact the USA editor at editors@fodors.com or c/o Fodor's at 1745 Broadway, New York, NY 10019.

Be a Fodor's Correspondent

Your opinion matters. It matters to us. It matters to your fellow Fodor's travelers, too. And we'd like to hear it. In fact, we need to hear it.

When you share your experiences and opinions, you become an active member of the Fodor's community. That means we'll not only use your feedback to make our books better, but we'll publish your names and comments whenever possible. Throughout our guides, look for "Word of Mouth," excerpts of your unvarnished feedback.

Here's how you can help improve Fodor's for all of us.

Tell us when we're right. We rely on local writers to give you an insider's perspective. But our writers and staff editors—who are the best in the business—depend on you. Your positive feedback is a vote to renew our recommendations for the next edition.

Tell us when we're wrong. We're proud that we update most of our guides every year. But we're not perfect. Things change. Hotels cut services. Museums change hours. Charming cafés lose charm. If our writer didn't quite capture the essence of a place, tell us how you'd do it differently. If any of our descriptions are inaccurate or inadequate, we'll incorporate your changes in the next edition and will correct factual errors at fodors.com immediately.

Tell us what to include. You probably have had fantastic travel experiences that aren't yet in Fodor's. Why not share them with a community of like-minded travelers? Maybe you chanced upon a beach or bistro or B&B that you don't want to keep to yourself. Tell us why we should include it. And share your discoveries and experiences with everyone directly at fodors.com. Your input may lead us to add a new listing or highlight a place we cover with a "Highly Recommended" star or with our highest rating, "Fodor's Choice."

Give us your opinion instantly at our feedback center at www.fodors.com/feedback. You may also e-mail editors@fodors.com with the subject line "Essential USA Editor." Or send your nominations, comments, and complaints by mail to Essential USA Editor, Fodor's, 1745 Broadway, New York, NY 10019.

You and travelers like you are the heart of the Fodor's community. Make our community richer by sharing your experiences. Be a Fodor's correspondent.

Happy traveling!

Tim Jarrell, Publisher

CONTENTS

CONTENTS

ABOUT
THIS BOOK

Maps

The maps in this guide highlight many attractions that readers are encouraged to explore on their own. Unfortunately, space limitations preclude us from offering users of this guide full descriptions of every sight and property mentioned.

Our Ratings

As travelers we've all discovered a place so wonderful that its worthiness is obvious. And sometimes superlatives don't do that place justice: you just have to be there to know. These sights, properties, and experiences get our highest rating, **Fodor's Choice**, indicated by orange stars.

Black stars highlight sights and properties we deem **Highly Recommended**, places that our writers, editors, and readers praise again and again for consistency and excellence.

By default, there's another category: any place we include in this book is by definition worth your time, unless we say otherwise. And we will.

Disagree with any of our choices? Care to nominate a place or suggest that we rate one more highly? Visit our feedback center at www.fodors.com/feedback.

Budget Well

Hotel and restaurant price categories from ¢ to $$$$ are defined in each chapter. For attractions, we always give standard adult admission fees; reductions are usually available for children, students, and senior citizens. **AE, D, DC, MC, V** following dining and lodging listings indicate when American Express, Discover, Diner's Club, MasterCard, and Visa are accepted.

Restaurants

Unless we state otherwise, restaurants are open for lunch and dinner daily. We mention dress only when there's a specific requirement and reservations only when they're essential or not accepted.

Hotels

Hotels have private bath, phone, TV, and air-conditioning and operate on the European Plan (aka EP, meaning without meals), unless we specify that they use the Continental Plan (CP, with a continental breakfast), Breakfast Plan (BP, with a full breakfast), or Modified American Plan (MAP, with breakfast and dinner) or are all-inclusive (including all meals and most activities). We list facilities but not whether you'll be charged extra to use them.

Essentials

Please see the Essentials section in the back of the book for travel essentials for the entire area covered by the book.

Many Listings

★	Fodor's Choice
★	Highly recommended
✉	Physical address
�	Directions
⌂	Mailing address
☎	Telephone
🖷	Fax
⊕	On the Web
✎	E-mail
🖅	Admission fee
☉	Open/closed times
Ⓜ	Metro stations
⊟	Credit cards

Hotels & Restaurants

🏨	Hotel
⇥	Number of rooms
⚙	Facilities
†○†	Meal plans
✕	Restaurant
⟂	Reservations
⟍	Smoking
☖	BYOB
✕🏨	Hotel with restaurant that warrants a visit

Outdoors

⚐	Golf
⌂	Camping

Other

☾	Family-friendly
⇨	See also
✉	Branch address
☞	Take note

The Contiguous
United States

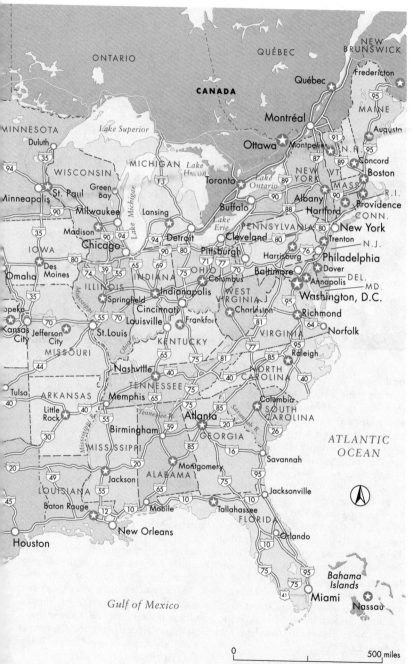

ONTARIO

QUÉBEC

NEW BRUNSWICK

Fredericton ★

CANADA

Québec ★

MAINE

95

MINNESOTA

Lake Superior

Duluth

Montréal ★

Augusta

94

35

WISCONSIN

MICHIGAN Lake Huron

Ottawa ★

Montpelier

N.H.

91

95

Concord

87

89

Minneapolis

St. Paul

Green Bay

Milwaukee

Lansing

Toronto

Lake Ontario

89

NEW YORK

VT.

Boston

MASS.

90

90

Buffalo

Albany

Hartford

Providence

R.I.

CONN.

88

90

Madison

90

94

Chicago

Lake Erie

Detroit

Cleveland

80

PENNSYLVANIA

80

New York

IOWA

35

Des Moines

80

94

Pittsburgh

76

Trenton

N.J.

Omaha

74

39

55

INDIANA

65

69

OHIO

71

77

Harrisburg

Philadelphia

Dover

DEL.

Springfield

Indianapolis

Columbus

70

70

Baltimore

Annapolis

MD.

ILLINOIS

55

70

Cincinnati

WEST VIRGINIA

95

Washington, D.C.

Topeka

70

Louisville

Frankfort

Charleston

81

Richmond

Kansas City

Jefferson City

St. Louis

KENTUCKY

64

Norfolk

MISSOURI

65

VIRGINIA

77

95

44

75

81

85

Raleigh

Nashville

40

40

NORTH CAROLINA

40

Tulsa

ARKANSAS

TENNESSEE

75

Memphis

65

75

85

Columbia

SOUTH CAROLINA

40

Little Rock

40

55

Birmingham

59

Atlanta

20

26

Savannah

30

MISSISSIPPI

20

85

GEORGIA

16

ATLANTIC OCEAN

49

Jackson

Montgomery

95

ALABAMA

LOUISIANA

55

65

75

Jackson ville

45

Baton Rouge

12

10

Mobile

10

Tallahassee ★

10

Houston

New Orleans

FLORIDA

Orlando

10

Gulf of Mexico

75

95

Bahama Islands

75

41

Miami

Nassau ★

0   500 miles

0   800 km

QUINTESSENTIAL USA

Road Trips

Right up there with baseball and apple pie, taking to the highway is an American tradition. If you've got enough time and enough gas money, you can reach any corner of the lower 48 (and Alaska, if you're really ambitious) by just hopping in the car and *going*. And most of us find out along the way that the old adage is true: It is the journey, not the destination. The experiences you have along the way—like buying a bag of pecans from a farm on a dusty Texas road, or watching a herd of antelope run across the Wyoming plains, or stumbling across great bluegrass in a Nashville bar, or having the best milkshake of your life in Hebron, Illinois—will stay with you longer than the tourist attractions at the end of the highway. More importantly, you'll see the real America.

Regional Delicacies

Every part of the U.S. claims to have fantastic food, and there are many debates to be settled. Like who has the best barbeque (Texas? Kansas City? Memphis? North Carolina?)? Is Chicago's deep-dish pizza better than New York's super-thin pies? Can Pacific Dungeness crab even hold a candle to Maine Coast lobster? And is it possible to decide on a top sandwich among the myriad hoagies, subs, muffulettas, heros that stretch from sea to shining sea? Mmmmm... research. While you're weighing in on these pressing matters, don't forget to sample the offerings at New Jersey's diners, San Antonio's Tex-Mex restaurants, Kansas City's beef palaces, Portland's locavore gastropubs, and South Carolina's calabash seafood. And don't forget to save some room for the pie (Key Lime, Georgia Pecan, Washington Apple...)

This is a huge, dramatically diverse country—more a continent than a nation. But no matter our differences, there are certain things that we're all looking for in a great American vacation . . . in addition to life, liberty, and the pursuit of happiness, of course.

Natural Wonders

Most of us live in urban or suburban areas, and escaping to a place without traffic jams and BlackBerries is often high on the vacation priority list. Thankfully, the U.S. is packed with jaw-dropping vistas, geological marvels, and proof that Mother Nature is indeed an artist—from Maine Coast's Acadia to California's Channel Islands, the National Park Service currently protects 391 swatches of the country (and counting). And while these pristine playgrounds are ideal starting points if you're trying to commune with the great outdoors, there are great natural spaces pretty much everywhere. From the rolling hills of western Iowa, to the rugged Oregon coast, to the vast nothingness of West Texas, to New York's Central Park, there's beauty around every corner. So get going, and recharge those batteries!

Vibrant Cities

Mark Twain said that there were only four unique American cities: Boston, San Antonio, San Francisco, and New Orleans. We're going to partially agree—these cities are among our favorites. But this list certainly has more than four members. We'd add America's unofficial capitol, New York, the most cosmopolitan city in the country. And Washington, DC, the actual capitol and chronicler of our nation's history, past, present, and future. And Chicago, where the skyscraper—and our modern concept of an urban landscape—was born. And tropical-hip Miami, beachy San Diego, haunted Savannah, decadent Las Vegas, star-struck Los Angeles, genteel Charleston, and crunchy Seattle. And we're definitely forgetting a few other notable burgs—this country is filled with them.

IF YOU LIKE

History

The United States may be a young country, but we've had an eventful 230+ years (in addition to the thousands of years of human history preceded the formation of the Union). Finding teachable moments on vacation is sometimes a tall order, but it's a little easier in these locales:

- **Washington, D.C.** This is the museum mother lode—from the amazing Smithsonian Institution to the hip International Spy Museum, there's a collection for everyone. Plus, DC is home to all three branches of the federal government, so you can sneak in a civics lesson.

- **Boston.** Even though the Declaration of Independence was signed in Philly, it's pretty easy to argue that America was born in Boston. Beantown is filled with opportunities to get in touch with your inner patriot.

- **Savannah and Charleston.** After the Civil War, Charleston could not afford to rebuild, and today the city is filled with restored historic homes, parts of the city feel like they're frozen in the 19th century. Savannahians surrendered to Sherman's fiery forces rather than see their beautiful city burned, and today the city is home to the nation's largest historic district.

- **The Black Hills of South Dakota.** The days of gold miners and gun fights may be over, but if you want to see what the Wild West was really like, head to Deadwood.

National Parks

Nothing brings a family together quite like a shared sense of wonder. The National Park Service oversees 391 natural and historical gems—so there are plenty of opportunities in every corner of the country to enjoy an awestruck moment with the ones you love.

- **Grand Canyon.** Nature's long-running work in progress both exalts and humbles the human spirit. Don't just peer over the edge, though—take the plunge into the canyon on a mule train, on foot, or on a rafting trip.

- **Yellowstone.** The oldest national park in the world covers some 3,845 square mi of beauty and wilderness. Best known for its gushing geysers (including Old Faithful) and flowing hot springs, Yellowstone is an eclectic mix of all that Mother Nature has to offer.

- **Yosemite.** Spectacular Half Dome, lofty Yosemite Falls, and mind-blowing views of the southern Sierra Nevada are a few reasons why this is one of America's most visited national parks. Yosemite has 800 mi of hiking trails in an area the size of Rhode Island—so lace up those boots, and get out there!

- **Southern Utah.** With five national parks—Arches, Bryce, Canyonlands, Capitol Reef, and Zion—southern Utah is filled with geological masterpieces, soaring arches, stunning rock windows, red rock canyons, alien landscapes, and breathtaking overlooks.

Good Eats

You can find great food in most parts of the U.S.—but a few areas stand out in our minds. Here are some of our favorite places to eat.

- **New Orleans.** The Big Easy has one of America's most distinct—and delicious—regional cuisines. From savory gumbo to intimidating muffulettas to melt-in-your-mouth beignets, it's hard not to have a dining epiphany eating in New Orleans.

- **New York.** Ethiopian? Check. Korean barbecue? Check. Malaysian, Scandinavian, and Turkish? Check, check, check. The possibilities are endless in the Big Apple. It's all here— and it's all good. Plus, most of America's top chefs have at least one NYC outpost. Hey, if you can make it here …

- **San Francisco.** The Bay Area is one of America's test kitchens—most trends that begin here quickly find their way east (and south, and north). The locavore movement, which focuses on incorporating the freshest local ingredients into dishes, began here and is thriving in restaurants across the city. Add San Francisco's close proximity to Napa and Sonoma Valleys, and you're going to have some memorable dining experiences.

- **Texas Hill Country.** OK, maybe this is an odd choice. But how can you argue against a steaming bowl of tortilla soup, a melt-in-your-mouth barbecue brisket sandwich, or sausage that rivals Germany's best? Washed down with a Shiner Bock and some Blue Bell ice cream, of course.

Slowing Down

If you don't need a vacation so much as an escape, head for one of the quieter corners of the U.S. Great for recharging your batteries, these places are not served by hourly direct flights, suffer from a distinct lack of Kinko's, and may have spotty cell phone service.

- **Maine Coast.** Windjammers, lobster pounds, lighthouses, and mile upon mile of rugged coastline. It takes a little effort to get up here, but it's worth it.

- **Western Montana.** Need a little space? Then you've come to the right place. Big Sky Country is filled with a lot of things—jaw-dropping vistas, crystal clear rivers, majestic peaks—but crowds of people isn't one of them.

- **The California Desert.** Your problems probably aren't going to follow you into the 120-degree, desolate blast furnace that is Death Valley. And if they do, they'll probably melt.

- **North Carolina's Outer Banks.** If you're looking for a chill beach vacation, you're found the right place. Spread out your towel, close your eyes, and listen to the waves. Instant Nirvana.

- **The Florida Keys.** Key West feels like the end of the world, and it's one of a handful of domestic destinations that actually feel like foreign locales. As you drive here from Miami, you'll pass over beautiful stretches of water and tiny spits of sand—and you'll be able to feel your blood pressure drop with each passing mile.

7 MISTAKES NOT TO MAKE ON YOUR NEXT FAMILY ROAD TRIP

You've no doubt thought of everything. The enormous suitcase that brained you when it slid from the closet is now nestled in the trunk, well-packed with your family's wardrobe for the week. Your kids have enough snacks to forestall whining for days if necessary. You spent the morning neatly stapling computer-generated directions for each leg of your trip. And if you drive at high speeds–with the flow of traffic, of course–you'll make the eight-hour drive in excellent time. So what are you missing?

Well, for starters, you've already made several mistakes that could turn your family car trip into a disaster.

Mistake #1: Packing the wrong bag

When you're driving, there's no advantage to consolidating your family's clothes in that indestructible bag you use for flying. Think nylon or canvas duffel bags–24 to 30 inches long–one for each person's things. You'll be carting more bags around, but you'll be able to put your hands on everything more quickly. Plus, repacking the trunk will be easier, especially if you're fitting small bags around a stroller and all those jugs of laundry detergent you bought.

Mistake #2: Altering meal times

A common road-trip blunder is disrupting your family's normal meal schedule. If you don't hit the road until late morning, there's a temptation to drive through lunch and snack your way to dinner. You know your kids will have no restraint when it comes to snacks, and neither will you. Plus, if after hours of gorging you make a spontaneous lunch stop, you'll be wolfing down food while your kids complain about not being hungry. And if lunch is thrown off, you'll all be out

of synch by dinner. By evening, your kids will be starving after both refusing to eat lunch and losing interest in the car snacks, and if it's later than you usually eat, dinner will be a miserable whinefest.

Solution: Keep it simple and eat all your meals at the usual times.

Mistake #3: Pacing the day badly

Nothing will sour a car trip faster than hitting the road at the wrong time. It's all-too-tempting to leave work at 4 or 5 p.m. on a Friday to get on the road for a weekend getaway. The good thing about this is that, regardless of their ages, your kids will immediately slide into comatose naps. The bad thing is that when you pull into your destination at 8 p.m. they'll be up, all night. A different tactic, hitting the road after 9 p.m. so that your kids will fall asleep and stay asleep works wonderfully—until you stop a few hours later. If they don't come to immediately, chances are they'll be wide awake by the time you've carried them inside.

Best bet: Sacrifice the evening escape and leave the following morning (or early enough the next afternoon so that a nap won't be disruptive) and ensure you're off the road for the day by dinnertime.

Mistake #4: Denying you could get lost

Computer-generated directions are nifty, but accurate to a fault; one wrong turn and they're next to useless. Bring a real road map. Also, invest in a portable GPS device or request one for your rental ($10 or less daily fee)–Hertz and Avis fleets are well-equipped with them. The first time a GPS generates an accurate course correction is the first time it pays for itself. Still, GPS isn't perfect. Like computer algorithms and your well-meaning

friend's husband, they can overcomplicate directions and, at times, fail to identify streets.

So pack the map no matter what.

Mistake #5: Driving like an idiot

We do stupid things on vacation that we don't do at home: skydiving, paying retail, eating organ meat we can't identify, and, curiously, driving more cavalierly than we normally do. This is a mistake no matter who's in the car, but the fact that the stakes are higher when you're driving with your family can't be overstated. One of the more perplexing things we do on the road is break traffic laws, making illegal turns or speeding down the highway because we're keeping up with the flow of traffic.

Sure, you can get away with it, and if you're a good driver you might rationalize the risk to your family. But don't underestimate the risk of being pulled over. Any leniency you might have been hoping for from that approaching highway patrolman will evaporate when he sees you have kids in the back.

Mistake #6: Not setting a budget for the little things

It's puzzling that many of us tirelessly research airfares, hotels, car rentals, and online coupon codes with the hope of saving a few dollars, yet when it comes to buying incidentals on the road, we're essentially careless. You wouldn't dream of giving your second grader a $50 weekly allowance at home. But for a week on the road, if you dare consider the sum of a pack of sour candies here, a souvenir pen there, a keychain for her BFF over in that store, and the other little things for which you're constantly breaking $5 bills, giving each kid a $50 allowance with a "once you spend it it's gone" proviso can end up being a good deal.

A debit scenario works equally well for grown-ups, too.

Mistake #7: Forgetting that the journey is the destination

If your goal is to get from point A to point B as quickly as possible, you probably shouldn't be traveling by car. One of the benefits of road trips is that you can pull over at the farm rather than give the kids a blurry glimpse of a cow; eat the best steak and eggs of your life at that nondescript roadside diner; and take that throwaway snapshot over by the guardrail that ends up being the quintessential photo of you and your daughter.

Hundreds of potentially undiscovered moments are around the next corner, which is why treating a drive as a means to an end rather t.han as part of your journey is the biggest mistake of all.

–Paul Eisenberg

GREAT ITINERARIES

BEST ROADTRIPS IN THE US

Jack Kerouac didn't take the Interstate. OK, maybe *On the Road* predates the U.S. Interstate Highway System, but that's beside the point. Kerouac still wouldn't have ridden these fast food outlet– and chain motel–crammed modern highways, even if he could have.

Four-lane Interstates are a fine choice when you need to get from Point A to Point B pronto, but for unforgettable road trips, try to get off the beaten path and take a ramble down one of America's older highways. Sure, there are stoplights and stop signs on these classic roads— but that means you'll need to slow down enough to actually *see* the area you're driving through. Hopefully you'll even get out of your car to experience some of the quirky local cultures, unique culinary traditions, and natural wonders that make this such a great country.

Every state boasts at least one distinctive road that tells a story about that place and its people. Most can be driven from start to finish in a day or two. (The Federal Highway Administration's National Scenic Byways Program has a great list at their website, www.byways.org.) Other famous historic roads actually still cross broad swatches of the country and can take weeks to travel. Here are a few of our favorites for great multi-state road trips.

Route 66

The Mother Road is America's most romanticized classic road. One of the greatest joys of this 2000+ mile journey from Chicago, Illinois to Santa Monica, California is the '50s time-warp you'll experience via the many kitschy roadside attractions, old diners, and motels that crop up in the middle of nowhere (often marked by huge elaborate neon signs)— as well as the seemingly endless but never boring "get your kicks on Route 66" nostalgia that is inseparably part of this road's ethos.

Only scattered segments of the old highway remain, but the remnants epitomize the classic American road trip. One of the longest surviving stretches of Route 66 starts in Arcadia, Oklahoma, just northeast of Oklahoma City (while you're here, look for the round red barn, a terrific little Route 66 museum and gift shop) and ends in Stroud, Oklahoma.

The drive in New Mexico between Gallup and Grants across the Zuni and Navajo Nation Indian Reservations (on what's now Highway 53) is also wonderful. Other high points include The Grand Canyon; the Cahokia Mounds in Collinsville, Illinois; Albuquerque, New Mexico; and the Gateway Arch in St. Louis, Missouri.

Route 66 is not shown on modern maps. Before you set off on your journey, visit www.national66.com to download meticulous turn-by-turn directions for the entire route.

The Pacific Coast Highway

One of the country's most scenic drives, this two-lane highway runs about 1,500 miles from the northwest tip of the United States at Olympic National Park almost all the way to the Mexican border. It's a feast for the senses, passing by (and through) forests, wilderness preserves, farmland, California wine country, and spiffy little seaside towns, and hugging gorgeous stretches of the coast.

A few caveats: the highway can get crowded—especially during the summer months—and drivers are often so amazed by the views that they forget to keep their eyes on the road. Drive carefully.

PCH highlights include redwood forests of Northern California; Big Sur (California); the views on the road between Florence and Lincoln City (Oregon) and from the scenic outlook at Cape Perpetu (just south of Yachats in Oregon); Hearst Castle in San Simeon (California); Point Lobos State Wildlife Reserve (just south of Carmel, California); and California's Carmel Valley vineyards (esp. Bernardus Winery and Talbotts Vineyards).

The Pacific Coast Highway is easy to follow; it's marked on maps as Route 1 in California and Route 101 farther north.

The Great River Road

The 3,000+ mile Great River Road follows the Mississippi River from its start as a cold, tiny, crystal-clear stream in northern Minnesota to its warm muddy merger with the Gulf Of Mexico in Venice, Louisiana.

Created in 1938 from a jumble of local-, state-, and federal roads, it's a picturesque and varied journey (parts of the route are comprised of well-maintained dirt and gravel roads) passing through forests, prairies, swamps, tiny towns, and bustling cities. Travelers have many opportunities to experience America's own music (the blues, jazz, zydeco, and rock-n-roll were all born along this highway) and sample unique regional tastes—wild rice and walleye in Minnesota, Maid-Rite loose meat sandwiches in Iowa, artisanal cheese in Wisconsin, BBQ in Memphis,

tamales in the Delta, and, of course, Creole and Cajun cooking in Louisiana.

Highlights along the Great River Road include the headwaters of the Mississippi at Lake Itasca State Park, Minnesota; Memphis, Tennessee (especially Sun Studios and Beale Street); The Mississippi Delta (especially Clarksville, Mississippi for blues fans); Vicksburg, Mississippi (for antebellum architecture aficionados); and New Orleans, Louisiana

If you're planning a trip along the Great River Road, check out www.experiencemississippiriver.com for more information.

U.S. Route 1

The northernmost part of what's now U.S. Route 1 dates back to at least 1636—when it took four days to make the 100-mile journey from Philadelphia to New York City. Today, this 2,425 mile circuit links Fort Kent, Maine, to Key West, Florida, traveling through a good chunk of America's history.

The road takes travelers though colonial New England, on to New York City, Philadelphia and Washington, D.C, then onto the US's oldest city (St. Augustine, Florida) and the thoroughly modern multicultural Miami, ending in ironically iconic Key West. Route 1 has some spectacular scenery (even the Great Dismal Swamp in southeastern Virginia/northeastern North Carolina is startlingly charming)—but it isn't always pretty, passing through plenty of urban blight and moldering towns that time forgot. That said, it's an endlessly fascinating highway—every bit of it has a story to tell.

The best sights along Route 1 include the Maine coastline; Okefenokee Swamp (Florida); the Florida Everglades; the Overseas Highway to the Florida Keys; the Masonic temple in Alexandria, Virginia; Washington D.C's museums and monuments; the Old Port section of Portland, Maine; New York City; and Old Town in St. Augustine.

—*Michelle Delio*

The Maine Coast

Old fishing shack, Portland

WORD OF MOUTH

"You absolutely MUST eat the Seafood Chowder at Gilbert's Chowder House in Portland in the Old Port area on the water. It is a very casual place, and the Super Seafood Chowder (that is the seafood chowder with double the seafood—it has clams, lobster, scallops and Maine shrimp in it) is so delicious . . . Portland is one of my favorite smaller cities. The Old Port is charming with cobblestone streets and fun little shops and great restaurants. Have fun. Maine is so beautiful!"

—skp

EXPLORING THE MAINE COAST

Portland is 110 mi north of Boston via I–93 and I–95. Camden is 80 mi northeast of Portland via I–295, U.S. 1, and ME–90. Acadia National Park is 170 mi from Portland via I–295, I–95, I–395, U.S. 1A, and U.S. 1.

By John Blodgett

Much of the appeal of the Maine Coast lies in its geographical contrasts, from its long stretches of swimming and walking beaches in the south to the cliff-edged, rugged rocky coasts in the north. And not unlike the physical differences of the coast, each town along the way reveals a slightly different character. But there's more than just the topography: fantastically fresh seafood, picturesque lighthouses, creative artisans, and down-to-earth people can all be found here.

The Maine Coast is generally divided into a number of regions. The Southern Coast is Maine's most visited region, stretching north from Kittery to just outside Portland. Despite the cold North Atlantic waters, beachgoers enjoy the area's miles of sandy expanses, which invite long walks and offer sweeping views of lighthouses, forested islands, and the wide-open sea.

Maine's largest and most cosmopolitan city, Portland deftly balances its historic role as a working—and still-thriving—harbor with its new identity as a center of sophisticated arts and shopping, innovative restaurants, and stylish accommodations.

North of Portland, from Brunswick to Monhegan Island, is the state's Mid-Coast region, where the craggy coastline swirls and winds its way around pastoral peninsulas.

The Penobscot Bay region combines lively coastal towns with dramatic natural scenery.

Mount Desert Island is home to Acadia National Park—Maine's most heavily visited attraction. Travelers come by the millions to climb (mostly by car) the miles of 19th-century carriage roads leading to the stunning peaks and vistas of the island's mountains.

It's a lot to take in, and pretty much impossible to visit each region all in one short trip. But that's OK, because the Maine Coast is the kind of place that you'll want to return to time and again.

WHO WILL ESPECIALLY LOVE THIS TRIP?

Shoppers: The Maine Coast has a surprisingly vibrant shopping scene, running the gamut from lobster T-shirt tourist traps to fine-art galleries, from local pottery studios to world-famous furniture makers. Many small-town Main streets have been rejuvenated, thanks to storefronts that cater to tourists.

History Buffs: It's rare to find a place where history is so alive. Classic sailing vessels known as Windjammers, complete with multiple and tall masts, still ply the waters off Penobscot Bay with tourists aboard; and many a historic home is still a home, or else a B&B, art gallery, or

TOP 5 REASONS TO GO

Freeport: Main Street is like one giant mall—anchored by the L.L. Bean mothership—except zoning laws ensure that the character and architecture of the street are maintained (witness the McDonald's located in a Victorian house, with a diminished logo and *without* a drive-thru).

Portland Head Light: The most familiar of Maine's 60-plus remaining lighthouses, it's accessible, photogenic, and historic. Watch tugboats head out to sea to escort large ships into Portland Harbor.

Acadia National Park: Maine has only one National Park, and it's regularly one of the most-visited in the United States. The scenic Loop Road leads all the way to the top of Cadillac Mountain, with 360-degree views of the surrounding coast. To head deeper into the park, walk along the Carriage Roads, built by John D. Rockefeller Jr.

Seafood: You should be sure to get some lobster while you're here, but you can also feast on clams, mussels, crabmeat, shrimp, scallops, halibut—the list seems to go on and on. You can't really go wrong, though—Maine seafood is about as fresh as it gets.

Sailing: No visit to the Maine Coast is complete without an ocean excursion, even if you don't leave the nearest bay. Take a ferry for an island tour, ride on a whale-watching boat, or sail aboard a grand old multimasted schooner from Maine's storied past.

museum. Speaking of museums, there is quite the variety here, from art to maritime to transportation to archaeological.

Photographers: It's a cliché, but true: the Maine Coast is postcard-perfect. Shutterbugs will find no shortage of subject matters here: classic sailboats, blazing foliage, historic architecture, the North Atlantic, and, of course, numerous lighthouses.

Families: Children are enthralled with the coast. Beachcombing is a ton of fun, even for adults (some beaches prohibit taking anything, so check the rules ahead of time). Tidal pools are also worth a look—they're often full of small, colorful snails called periwinkles. Large green spaces are ideal for unfurling a kite in the sea breezes, and in fall, watch your little ones' faces light up with wonder as they gaze at the blazing foliage.

WHEN IS THE BEST TIME TO VISIT?

Summer is the most popular time to visit Maine, with cooling summer breezes that come in off the water to offset what can sometimes be muggy weather. It's rarely hot for long, and generally comfortable so long as you bring a sweater or light jacket and rain gear just in case—plus insect repellent for when the pesky black flies are out.

The crowds diminish dramatically after Labor Day, which is one reason to consider a visit in fall; the other reason is the incredible foliage

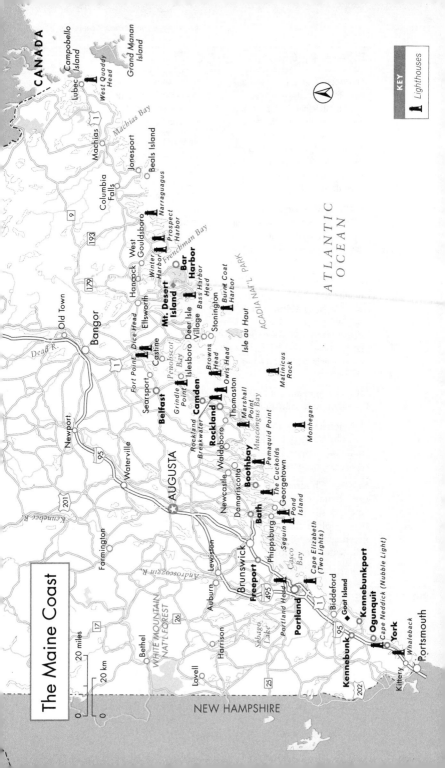

CLOSE UP

1

How to Snack

Foremost on the list of famous Maine foods, of course, is lobster, ideal at a pound and a quarter or a pound and a half. But there's more to Maine's seafood than this delectable shellfish. Clams, whether fried and dipped in tartar sauce, steamed and dipped in butter, or formed into a pattylike clamcake, are a delicacy. Crabmeat is particularly sweet, best served simply in a hot dog roll with lettuce and the barest amount of mayonnaise. The coast is peppered with little shacks and unpretentious restaurants like Red's Eats and Gilbert's Chowder House that serve seafood simply prepared, but for a more adventurous preparation try Street & Co. in Portland's Old Port.

Maine maple syrup is as delicious as Vermont's more famous brand. A sweet treat is soft maple candy, available at many tourist shops along the coast. Wild blueberries are harvested here; smaller and sweeter than those grown elsewhere, they're a popular ingredient in muffins, pancakes, pies, scones, jams, and more. French fries, sometimes made with Maine potatoes, are served with vinegar instead of ketchup in some beachfront eateries in the Old Orchard Beach area. And in fall you can pick your own apples—the tart McIntosh is a Maine favorite, and is often used to make cider and pies.

season, when crowds of leaf peepers flock to the state to see and photograph the rich reds, oranges, and yellows of trees preparing for the winter ahead (peak color is usually early-to-mid-October; check the state's Web site, www.maine.gov, for up-to-date information).

Winter brings even more solitude to the coast—this can be a very cozy time of year to stay at a B&B and perhaps go cross-country skiing or snowshoeing. Spring can be cool and wet right up until summer comes around again.

HOW SHOULD I GET THERE?

DRIVING

The major highways into Maine from the south are I-95, a toll road that provides relatively quick access to the coast until it passes Bangor, and U.S. 1, which mostly follows the coast itself. The latter is slower going, since it passes through countless towns and villages—but far more scenic and interesting.

FLYING

Major airports in Portland and Bangor offer relatively quick access to coastal areas. Bangor is closer to the Mid-Coast Region, but it tends to be more economical and convenient to fly into Portland, to the south. Bar Harbor has a small airport that is a quick flight from Portland. If you plan to spend most of your time along the Southern Coast, another option is to fly into Manchester, New Hampshire, or Boston, Massachusetts.

HOW DO I GET AROUND?

BY CAR

A handful of tour companies bring tourists to points along the coast via bus, but a car is the best way to explore the Maine Coast. You can enjoy the trip on your own schedule, and you can change your itinerary to follow your whims (coastal Maine towns have a way of drawing you in). If you fly to Maine, most car-rental agencies are clustered around the airports in Portland and Bangor, and in Manchester, New Hampshire, and Boston, Massachusetts.

WHERE SHOULD I FOCUS MY ENERGY?

If you're here for 1 day: Explore the galleries and shops of Portland's Old Port and walk among the architectural wonders of the Western Promenade. Then take a quick drive to Portland Head Light, returning to the Old Port for dinner.

If you're here for 2 days: Spend a second day in Portland to visit the Portland Museum of Art and, if you have children in tow, the Children's Museum of Maine. Take a Casco Bay Line's ferry to Peaks Island.

If you're here for 3 days: From Portland, drive to Freeport to spend the day shopping its myriad of shops, spending the most time in L.L. Bean's huge always-open store. If you want to take a retail break, visit nearby Wolfe's Neck Woods State Park.

If you're here for 4 days: Head north northeast to Bath, Maine's shipbuilding capital, and tour the Maine Maritime Museum. Continue on U.S. 1 north, through the towns of Wiscasset and Damariscotta, where you may find yourself pulling over frequently for outdoor flea markets or intriguing antiques shops.

If you're here for 5 days: Visit Camden and Rockland for the day, where historic homes are picture-perfect, windjammers ply the water, and nearby Mt. Battie offers sweeping views of it all. Be sure to visit Rockland's Farnsworth Art Museum and Wyeth Center.

If you're here for 6 days: From Camden, continue north along U.S. 1 to Acadia National Park on Mount Desert Island. Drive the Loop Road to the top of Cadillac Mountain and take in a panoramic view of much of Mid-Coast Maine. Take a driving tour of the many fine old mansions in nearby Bar Harbor.

If you're here for 7 days or more: From Bar Harbor you can drive north to Bangor and take I–95 to the Southern Coast, where York, York Village, Ogunquit, and the Kennebunks are all worth exploring.

WHAT ARE THE TOP EXPERIENCES?

Maritime History: Maine has arguably the richest Maritime history of any of the New England States. The state's shipbuilding heritage goes back more than 200 years, and even today small custom boatbuilders with international reputations can be found all along the coast.

1

The Maine Maritime Museum was built around the remnants of a 19th-century shipyard, and the Maine Lighthouse Museum celebrates the lighted towers that have protected sailors from the craggy coast since the 18th century. Visit just about any marina or working waterfront in the state, and you can see the entire spectrum of the boats that have made Maine famous, from graceful Friendship sloops to elegantly simple lobster boats to grand tall-masted Windjammers.

CLAIM TO FAME

Maine's coast is deceptively long. Measured in a straight line, it's roughly 230 mi—but when you factor in all the nooks, crannies, twists, and turns of the shoreline, it stretches to almost 3,500 mi in length! That's just longer than California's shoreline, and in the lower 48, only Louisiana and Florida surpass Maine.

Strolling: Even in Maine's larger cities you can encounter a relaxed way of life best suited for easy strolls, sightseeing, shopping, or simply meandering. Reid State Park has a wonderful sand beach and easy trails that follow the shoreline. Freeport's shopping district is so busy you have no choice but to walk (shoppers have the right of way here), but nearby quaint sidestreets recall the small city's roots. You can also walk the stone carriage roads of Acadia National Park (but keep an eye out for bicyclists). And if you visit Portland Head Light, bring a kite or a Frisbee along with your walking shoes.

Shopping: Maine has a well-established cottage industry of artisans who produce pottery, jewelry, glassware, and many other fine and often-whimsical items that are available for sale on location and at various outlets along the coast. Freeport, home of L.L. Bean, is a haven for outlet stores such as Cuddledown of Maine and the exquisite furniture showroom of Thos. Moser Cabinetmakers.

Dining: Maine restaurants run the gamut from humble seafood shacks, like Red's Eats, to award-winning establishments opened by top chefs, like Fore Street. Seafood plays a starring role in many places, but dining options are becoming increasingly eclectic and ethnic. Many chefs purchase locally grown meats, such as lamb, as well as organic produce and artisan cheeses and breads. Since Portland is Maine's largest city, it has the most varied dining scene—but there are fine options almost everywhere you go on the coast, even in the smallest villages.

BEST BETS

SIGHTS & TOURS

THE SOUTHERN COAST
The Yorks, Ogunquit & Wells. The Yorks—York Village, York Harbor, York Beach, and Cape Neddick—are typical of small-town coastal communities in New England and are smaller than most. Many of their nooks and crannies can be explored in a few hours. The beaches are the big attraction here.

Not unlike siblings in most families, the towns within this region reveal vastly different personalities. York Village and York Harbor abound with old money, picturesque mansions, impeccably manicured lawns, and gardens and shops that cater to a more staid and wealthy clientele. Continue along Route 1A from York Harbor to York Beach and soon all the pretense falls away like autumn leaves in a storm—it's family vacation time (and party time), with scores of T-shirt shops, ice-cream and fried-seafood joints, arcades and bowling, and motor court–style motels. North of York Beach, Cape Neddick blends back into more peaceful and gentle terrain, while Ogunquit is elegant high-spirited tourism to the hilt. Farther north on U.S. 1 is Wells, a town seemingly lost in the commercialism of the main route yet blessed with some of the area's best beaches.

> ### HISTORY YOU CAN SEE
>
> ■ Eastern Cemetery, on Portland's Congress Street, contains graves of settlers, soldiers, and Maine dignitaries that date back to the 18th Century.
>
> ■ Portland Head Light, one of the country's most iconic lighthouses, was commissioned by George Washington and was completed in early 1791.
>
> ■ Portland's Victoria Mansion is considered the finest example of its period left in the country.

The Kennebunks. The Kennebunks encompass Kennebunk, Kennebunk Beach, Goose Rocks Beach, Kennebunkport, Cape Porpoise, and Arundel. This cluster of seaside and inland villages provides a little bit of everything—salt marshes, sand beaches, jumbled fishing shacks, and architectural gems. Handsome white clapboard homes with shutters give Kennebunk, an early-19th-century shipbuilding center, a quintessential New England look. The many boutiques and galleries surrounding Dock Square draw visitors to Kennebunkport. People flock to Kennebunkport mostly in summer, but some come in early December when the Christmas Prelude is celebrated on two weekends. Santa arrives by fishing boat, and the Christmas trees are lighted as carolers stroll the sidewalks.

From Kennebunk, Route 35 south leads to Kennebunk's Lower Village. Continue south on Beach Avenue for Kennebunk Beach. To reach Kennebunkport from the Lower Village, head east on Route 9/Western Avenue and cross the drawbridge into Dock Square—technically, you're not in Kennebunkport until you cross that bridge. Continue east on Route 9, or take scenic Ocean Avenue and Wildes District Road to quiet Cape Porpoise. To access Goose Rocks Beach, continue east on Route 9, which is now called the Mills Road. Arundel is between Kennebunk and Kennebunkport.

GREATER PORTLAND

Fodor'sChoice **The Old Port.** A major international port and a working harbor since
★ the early 17th century, the Old Port bridges the gap between the city's historical commercial activities and those of today. It's home to fishing boats docked alongside whale-watching charters, luxury yachts, cruise ships, and oil tankers from throughout the globe. Busy Com-

mercial Street parallels the water and is lined with brick buildings and warehouses that were built following the Great Fire of 1866, and were intended to last for ages. In the 19th century, candle makers and sail stitchers plied their trades here; today, specialty shops, art galleries, and restaurants have taken up residence.

As with much of the city, it's best to park your car and explore the Old Port on foot. You can park at the city garage on Fore Street (between Exchange and Union streets) or opposite the U.S. Customs House at the corner of Fore and Pearl streets. A helpful hint: look for the PARK & SHOP sign on garages and parking lots and get one hour of free parking for each stamp collected at participating shops. Allow a couple of hours to wander at leisure on Market, Exchange, Middle, and Fore streets.

Portland Fish Exchange. For a lively and sensory-filled (you may want to hold your nose) glimpse into the Old Port's active fish business, take a free tour of the Portland Fish Exchange. Watch as the fishing boats unload their daily haul, the catch gets weighed in, and prices are settled through an auction process. It's a great behind-the-scenes view of this dynamic market. Auctions take place Sunday at 11 AM and Monday through Thursday at noon. ⊠*6 Portland Fish Pier* ☎*207/773–0017* ⊕*www.pfex.org* ▢*Free.*

★ **Portland Museum of Art.** Maine's largest public art institution has a number of strong collections, including fine seascapes and landscapes by Winslow Homer, John Marin, Andrew Wyeth, Edward Hopper, Marsden Hartley, and other painters. Homer's *Pulling the Dory* and *Weatherbeaten,* two quintessential Maine Coast images, are here; the museum owns and displays more than 20 other works by Homer. The Joan Whitney Payson Collection of impressionist and postimpressionist art includes works by Monet, Picasso, and Renoir. Harry N. Cobb, an associate of I. M. Pei, designed the strikingly modern Charles Shipman Payson building. ⊠*7 Congress Sq.* ☎*207/775–6148* ⊕*www.portland museum.org* ▢*$10, free Fri. 5–9* ⊘*Memorial Day–Columbus Day, Mon.–Thurs. and weekends 10–5, Fri. 10–9; Columbus Day–Memorial Day, Tues.–Thurs. and weekends 10–5, Fri. 10–9.*

Casco Bay Islands. The islands of Casco Bay are also known as the Calendar Islands because an early explorer mistakenly thought there was one for each day of the year (in reality there are only 140). These islands range from ledges visible only at low tide to populous Peaks Island, a suburb of Portland. Some islands are uninhabited; others support year-round communities as well as stores and restaurants. The brightly painted ferries of Casco Bay Lines are the islands' lifeline. There is frequent service to the most-populated ones, including Peaks, Long, Little Diamond, and Great Diamond. A ride on the bay is a great way to experience the dramatic shape of the Maine Coast while offering a glimpse of some of its hundreds of islands.

Casco Bay Lines (⊠*Maine State Pier, 56 Commercial St.* ☎*207/774– 7871* ⊕*www.cascobaylines.com*provides narrated cruises and transportation to Casco Bay Islands.

Fodor's Choice
★
Historic **Portland Head Light,** familiar to many from photographs and Edward Hopper's painting *Portland Head-Light (1927),* was commissioned by George Washington in 1790. The towering white stone lighthouse stands over the keeper's house, a white home with a blazing red roof. Besides a harbor view, its park has walking paths and picnic facilities. The keeper's house is now the Museum at Portland Head Light. The lighthouse is in Fort Williams Park, about 2 mi from the town center. *Museum ⊠1000 Shore Rd., Cape Elizabeth ☎207/799–2661 ⊕www.portlandheadlight.com ☜$2 ⊙Memorial Day–mid-Oct., daily 10–4; Apr., May, Nov., and Dec., weekends 10–4.*

Freeport. Those who flock straight to L.L. Bean and see nothing else of Freeport are missing out on some real New England beauty. The city's charming back streets are lined with historic buildings and old clapboard houses, and there's a pretty little harbor on the south side of the Harraseeket River. It's true, many who come to the area do so simply to shop—L.L. Bean is the store that put Freeport on the map, and plenty of outlets and some specialty stores have settled here. Still, if you choose, you can stay awhile and experience more than fabulous shopping; beyond the shops are bucolic nature preserves with miles of walking trails, well-maintained old homes, and plenty of places for leisurely ambling that don't require the overuse of your credit cards.

Fodor's Choice
★
Founded in 1912 as a mail-order merchandiser of products for hunters, guides, and anglers, **L.L. Bean** (⊠95 Main St., U.S. 1 ☎800/341–4341) attracts 3.5 million shoppers a year to its giant store (open 24 hours a day) in the heart of Freeport's shopping district. You can still find the original hunting boots, along with cotton, wool, and silk sweaters; camping and ski equipment; comforters; and hundreds of other items for the home, car, boat, and campsite.

THE MID-COAST

Bath. Along Front and Centre streets, in the heart of Bath's historic district are some charming 19th-century Victorian homes. Among them are the 1820 Federal-style Pryor House, at 360 Front Street, the 1810 Greek Revival–style mansion at 969 Washington Street, covered with gleaming white clapboards, and the Victorian gem at 1009 Washington Street, painted a distinctive shade of raspberry. All three operate as inns.

Bath has been a shipbuilding center since 1607. The venerable Bath Iron Works completed its first passenger ship in 1890 and is still building ships today, turning out frigates for the U.S. Navy.

★ In a cluster of buildings that once made up the Percy & Small Shipyard, the **Maine Maritime Museum** examines the world of shipbuilding and is open all year. A number of impressive ships, including the 142-foot Grand Banks fishing schooner *Sherman Zwicker,* are often on display in the port. Exhibits use ship models, paintings, photographs, and historical artifacts to tell the history of the region. From May to November, hour-long tours of the shipyard show how these massive wooden ships were built. You can watch boatbuilders wield their tools in the boat shop and learn about lobstering and its impact on the local culture. In summer boat tours sail the scenic Kennebec River. ✉243 *Washington St., Bath* ☎207/442–0961 ⊕*www.mainemaritimemuseum.org* ✆$10 ⊙*Daily 9:30–5.*

Wiscasset. Settled in 1663, Wiscasset sits on the banks of the Sheepscot River. It bills itself "Maine's Prettiest Village," and it's easy to see why: it has graceful churches, old cemeteries, and elegant sea captains' homes (many converted into antiques shops or galleries).

Pack a picnic and take it down to the dock, where you can watch the fishing boats or grab a lobster roll from Red's Eats or the lobster shack on the dock. Wiscasset has expanded its wharf, and this is a great place to catch a breeze on a hot day. U.S. 1 becomes Main Street, and traffic often slows to a crawl. If you park in town, you can walk to most galleries, shops, restaurants, and other attractions. ■TIP→ Try to arrive early in the morning to find a parking space—you'll likely have success if you try to park on Water Street rather than Main.

Boothbay. When Portlanders want a break from city life, many come north to the Boothbay region, which is made up of Boothbay proper, East Boothbay, and Boothbay Harbor. This part of the shoreline is a craggy stretch of inlets where pleasure craft anchor alongside trawlers and lobster boats. Commercial Street, Wharf Street, Townsend Avenue, and the By-Way are lined with shops and ice-cream parlors. You can browse for hours in the trinket shops, crafts galleries, clothing stores, and boutiques around the harbor. Excursion boats leave from the piers off Commercial Street. Boats to Monhegan Island are also available. Drive out to Ocean Point in East Boothbay for some incredible scenery.

PENOBSCOT BAY

Rockland. Though once merely a place to pass through on the way to tonier ports like Camden, Rockland now attracts attention on its own, thanks to this trio of attractions: the renowned Farnsworth Museum, the increasingly popular summer Lobster Festival, and the lively North Atlantic Blues Festival. The town's Main Street Historic District, with its Italianate, Mansard, Greek Revival, and Colonial Revival buildings, is on the National Register of Historic Places. Specialty shops and galleries line the main street, and at least one of the restaurants, Primo, has become nationally famous. Rockland has a growing popularity as a summer destination, but it's still a large fishing port and the commercial

> ### STRANGE BUT TRUE
>
> ■ Maine is so large that the other five New England States could fit within its boundaries.
>
> ■ Maine inventions include toothpicks, earmuffs, and a machine that makes doughnut holes.
>
> ■ Bangor claims to be the birthplace of Paul Bunyan, and some consider the 35-foot statue of the mythic lumberman to be life size.
>
> ■ The highest tides in the world occur at the Bay of Fundy off the far east corner of the state, where the waters typically rise and fall between 32 and 46 feet—sometimes as much as 50.

hub of this coastal area. You can find plenty of working boats moored alongside the yachts.

Rockland Harbor is the berth of more windjammer ships than any other port in the United States. The best place in Rockland to view these beautiful vessels as they sail in and out of the harbor is the mile-long granite breakwater, which bisects the outer portion of Rockland Harbor. To get there, go north on U.S. 1, turn right on Waldo Avenue, and right again on Samoset Road; go to the end of this short road.

Fodor's Choice
★ The **Farnsworth Art Museum** is one of the most important small museums in the country. The **Wyeth Center** is devoted to Maine-related works of the famous Wyeth family: Also on display are works by Fitz Hugh Lane, George Bellows, Frank W. Benson, Edward Hopper (his paintings of old Rockland are a highlight), Louise Nevelson, and Fairfield Porter. Works by living Maine artists are shown in the **Jamien Morehouse Wing.** The **Farnsworth Homestead,** a handsome circa-1852 Greek Revival dwelling that is part of the museum, retains its original lavish Victorian furnishings. ⊠ *16 Museum St., Rockland, 04841* 🕾 *207/596–6457* ⊕ *www.farnsworthmuseum.org* 🖃 *$10 for museum and Olsen House; $4 for Olsen House only* ⊙ *Daily 10 5.*

★ **Maine Lighthouse Museum.** The museum displays the largest collection of ⟳ the famed Fresnel lighthouse lenses to be found anywhere in the world as well as a collection of lighthouse artifacts and Coast Guard memorabilia. Sharing the same building is the Penobscot Bay Regional Chamber of Commerce, where tourists and visitors can pick up maps and area information. ⊠ *1 Park Dr., Rockland* 🕾 *207/594–3301* ⊕ *www.maine lighthousemuseum.com* 🖃 *$5* ⊙ *Weekdays 9–5, weekends 10–4.*

Camden. More than any other town along Penobscot Bay, Camden is the perfect picture-postcard of a Maine coastal village. "The Jewel of the Maine Coast" is the publicity slogan for Camden-Rockport-Lincolnville, and it's an apt description. Camden is famous not only for its geography but also for its large fleet of windjammers—relics and replicas from the age of sailing—with their romantic histories and great billowing sails. At just about any hour during the warm months, you're likely to see at least one windjammer tied up in the harbor. The excursions, whether for an afternoon or a week, are best from June through September.

The town's compact size makes it perfect for exploring on foot: shops, restaurants, and galleries line Main Street (U.S. 1), as well as side streets and alleys around the harbor. Especially worth inclusion on your walking tour is Camden's residential area. It's quite charming and filled with many fascinating old period houses from the time when Federal, Greek Revival, and Victorian architecture were the rage among the wealthy. Many of them now are B&Bs. The chamber of commerce, at the Public Landing, can provide you with a walking map.

Belfast. A number of Maine coastal towns, such as Wiscasset and Damariscotta, like to think of themselves as the prettiest little town in Maine, but Belfast may be the true winner of this title. It has a full variety of charms: a beautiful waterfront; an old and interesting main street climbing up from the harbor; a delightful array of B&Bs, restaurants, and shops; and a friendly population. The downtown even has old-fashioned street lamps, which set the streets aglow at night. If you like looking at old houses, many of which go all the way back to the Revolution and are in the Federal and Colonial style, just drive up and down some of the side streets.

ACADIA NATIONAL PARK & MOUNT DESERT ISLAND

Bar Harbor. A resort town since the 19th century, Bar Harbor is the artistic, culinary, and social center of Mount Desert Island. It also serves visitors to Acadia National Park with inns, motels, and restaurants. The island's unique topography was shaped by the glaciers of the most recent Ice Age. Around the turn of the last century—before the days of air-conditioning—the island was known as the summer haven of the very rich because of its cool breezes; lavish mansions were built throughout the island. Many of them were destroyed in a great fire that devastated the island in 1947, but many of those that survived have been converted into businesses. Shops are clustered along Main, Mount Desert, and Cottage streets. Take a stroll down West Street, a National Historic District, where you can see some fine old houses.

The island and its surrounding Gulf of Maine are home to a great variety of wildlife: whales, seals, eagles, falcons, ospreys, puffins (probably the most unusual-looking birds in the world), and denizens of the forest, such as moose, deer, foxes, coyotes, and black bears.

Acadia National Park. With more than 30,000 acres of protected forests, beaches, mountains, and rocky coastline, Acadia National Park is the second-most-visited national park in America; according to the national park service, more than 2.2 million people visit Acadia each year. The park holds some of the most spectacular scenery on the eastern seaboard: a rugged coastline of surf-pounded granite, and an interior graced by sculpted mountains, quiet ponds, and lush deciduous forests. Cadillac Mountain (named after an American Indian, not the car), the highest point of land on the Eastern Coast, dominates the park. Although it's rugged, Acadia National Park also has graceful stone bridges, horse-drawn carriages, and the elegant Jordan Pond House restaurant.

The 27-mi Park Loop Road provides an excellent introduction, but to truly appreciate the park, you must get off the main road and experience it by walking, biking, sea kayaking, or taking a carriage ride.

ACADIA NP ESSENTIALS

Admission Fee: $20 per vehicle for a seven-consecutive-day pass.

Admission Hours: 24 hours a day, year-round (roads often are closed in winter because of snow). Operating hours are 8 AM–4:30 PM April 15–October and until 6 PM. in July and August

Visitor Information: ✉ Acadia National Park, Box 177, Bar Harbor 04609 ☎ 207/288–3338 ⊕ www.nps.gov/acad.

If you get off the beaten path, you can find places you can have practically to yourself.

☾ At the Hulls Cove entrance to Acadia National Park, northwest of Bar Harbor on Route 3, the **Hulls Cove Visitor Center,** operated by the National Park Service, is a great spot to get your bearings. ⊠ *Park Loop Rd., Hulls Cove* ☎ *207/288–3338* ⊕ *www.nps.gov/acad* ☉ *Mid-June–Aug., daily 8–6; mid-Apr.–mid-June, Sept., and Oct., daily 8–4:30.*

The **Acadia National Park Headquarters** is on Route 233 in the park not far from the north end of Eagle Lake. It serves as the park's visitor center during the off-season.

> ### LIKE A LOCAL
>
> Maine has a distinctive native dialect, where yes is pronounced 'ayuh' and the alphabet seems to be missing the letter 'R.' For example, chowder is "chowdah," diner is "dinah," and lobster is "lobstah."
>
> Mainahs (also known as Mainiacs) are generally friendly and helpful, though often outwardly stoic. Still, people walking along the roadside will often wave when people drive by.
>
> Oh, and when you drive up the coast, you're really headed "Downeast."

WHERE TO EAT

WHAT IT COSTS				
¢	$	$$	$$$	$$$$
AT DINNER under $7	$7–$10	$11–$17	$18–$25	over $25

Restaurant prices are for a main course at dinner, excluding tax.

GREATER PORTLAND

$$$–$$$$
Fodor's Choice
★
✕ **Fore Street.** Two of Maine's best chefs, Sam Hayward and Dana Street, opened this restaurant in a renovated, airy warehouse on the edge of the Old Port (heating-oil delivery trucks once were parked here—honest). The menu changes daily to reflect the freshest local ingredients available. Every copper-top table in the two-level main dining room has a view of the enormous brick oven and hearth and the open kitchen, where sous-chefs seem to dance as they create entrées such as three cuts of Maine island lamb, Atlantic monkfish fillet, and breast of Moulad duckling. Desserts include artisanal cheeses. Reservations are recommended. ⊠ *288 Fore St.* ☎ *207/775–2717* ⊕ *www.forestreet.biz* ▤ *AE, MC, V* ☉ *No lunch.*

$$–$$$
★
✕ **Gilbert's Chowder House.** This is the real deal, as quintessential as Maine dining can be. Clam rakes, nautical charts, and a giant plastic marlin hang from the walls of this unpretentious waterfront diner. The flavors are from the depths of the North Atlantic, prepared and presented simply: fish, clam, and corn chowders; fried shrimp, haddock, clam strips, and extraordinary clam cakes. A chalkboard of daily specials is a must-read, and often features steamed mussels, oysters, and peel-and-eat shrimp. But don't miss out on the lobster roll—a toasted hot dog roll bursting with claw and tail meat unadulterated by mayo or other ingredients. It sits on a leaf of lettuce, but who needs more?

It's classic Maine, fuss-free and presented on a paper plate. ✉92 *Commercial St.* ☎*207/871–5636* ⊟*AE, MC, V.*

THE MID-COAST

$$–$$$$

Fodor'sChoice

★

✕**Cook's Lobster House.** Inhale the salt breeze as you cross the world's only cribstone bridge (designed so that water flows freely through gaps between the granite blocks) on your way south on Route 24 from Cook's Corner in Brunswick to this famous seafood restaurant 15 mi away, which began as a lobster shack on Bailey Island. Try the lobster casserole, or the delectable haddock sandwich. Several specialties come in smaller portions. Lobster dishes are at the $$$$ rating. Whether you choose inside or deck seating, you can watch the activity

---

ON THE WAY

Maine has many islands well off the coast that are reachable by ferry or boat. One of the most intriguing is **Monhegan Island,** about 10 mi off the Mid Coast town of Port Clyde. It's home to a thriving artist's colony, miles of hiking trails, and a quintessential Maine lobster fishing village.

Sebago Lake State Park borders Maine's second largest lake. The swimming here is excellent. From the quaint nearby town of Naples you can set sail on the Songo River Queen II, a stern paddle-wheel boat modeled after those that plyed the Mississippi River.

---

on the water: men checking lobster pots on the water and kayakers fanning across the bay. ✉*68 Garrison Cove Rd., Bailey Island* ☎*207/833–2818* ⊕*www.cookslobster.com* ⌔*Reservations not accepted* ⊟*D, MC, V* ⊗*Closed New Year's Day–mid-Feb.*

PENOBSCOT BAY

$$$–$$$$

Fodor'sChoice

★

✕**Marcel's.** If you're a serious gourmet and only have time to sample one dining experience in the Rockport-Rockland-Camden area, this lavish restaurant in the big Samoset Resort ought to be the one. Marcel's offers a fine array of Continental cuisine. Enjoy table-side preparation of a classic rack of lamb, châteaubriand, or Steak Diane while admiring the bay view. The menu includes a variety of Maine seafood and a fine wine list. The Sunday brunch buffet, with some of the finest seafood along the coast, is famous and draws a crowd. ✉*220 Warrenton St., off U.S. 1, Rockport* ☎*207/594–2511* ⌔*Reservations essential. Jacket required* ⊟*AE, D, DC, MC, V* ⊗*No lunch.*

ACADIA NATIONAL PARK & MOUNT DESERT ISLAND

$$$–$$$$

Fodor'sChoice

★

✕**Reading Room at the Bar Harbor Inn & Spa.** This elegant waterfront restaurant serves mostly Continental fare. Look for Maine specialties such as lobster pie and Indian pudding. There's live music nightly. When the weather is nice, what could be more romantic than dining out under the stars at the inn's Terrace Grille with the ships of beautiful Bar Harbor right at your feet? The natural thing to order here would be the Maine lobster bake with all the fixings. For something different, you might try the lobster stew, which is served in a bread bowl. The restaurant is also famous for its Sunday brunch, 11:30–2:30. ✉*Newport Dr., Bar Harbor 04609* ☎*207/288–3351 or 800/248–3351* ⊕*www.barharborinn.com* ⌔*Reservations essential* ⊟*AE, DC, MC, V* ⊗*Closed late Nov.–late Mar.*

WHERE TO STAY

WHAT IT COSTS				
	¢	$	$$	$$$	$$$$
FOR 2 PEOPLE	under $60	$60–$99	$100–$149	$150–$200	over $200

Hotel prices are for two people in a standard double room, excluding service charges and tax.

THE SOUTHERN COAST

$$$–$$$$

Fodor'sChoice

★

×🖼 **The Colony.** You can't miss this place—it's grand, white, and incredibly large, set majestically atop a rise overlooking the ocean. The hotel was built in 1914 (after its predecessor caught fire in 1898), and much of the splendid glamour of this earlier era remains. Many of the rooms in the main hotel (there are two other outbuildings) have breezy ocean views from private or semiprivate balconies. All are outfitted with antiques and hardwood floors; the bright white bed linens nicely set off the colors of the Waverly wallpaper. The restaurant ($$–$$$$) features New England fare, with plenty of seafood, steaks, and other favorites. The Colony is also Maine's first environmentally responsible hotel. ⊠ *Ocean Ave., Kennebunkport 04046* 🕾 *207/967-3331 or 800/552-2363* 🖷 *207/967-8738* ⊕ *www.thecolonyhotel. com/maine* 🛏 *124 rooms* ⃕ *In-room: no a/c (some), no TV (some), Wi-Fi. In-hotel: restaurant, room service, bar, pool, beachfront, bicycles, no-smoking rooms, some pets allowed* ⊟ *AE, MC, V* ☼ *Closed Nov.–mid-May* ⫶⦾⃒*BP.*

GREATER PORTLAND

$$$$

Fodor'sChoice

★

×🖼 **Harraseeket Inn.** Despite modern appointments such as elevators and whirlpool baths in some rooms, this 1850 Greek Revival home provides a pleasantly old-fashioned, country-inn experience just a few minutes' walk from L. L. Bean. Guest rooms have print fabrics and reproductions of Federal quarter-canopy beds. Ask for a second-floor, garden-facing room. The formal Maine Dining Room ($$$–$$$$) specializes in contemporary American regional (and organic) cuisine such as pan-roasted lobster and all-natural filet mignon. The casual yet excellent Broad Arrow Tavern ($$–$$$$) serves heartier fare and has a charming seasonal patio. Inn rates include a full buffet breakfast and afternoon tea. ⊠ *162 Main St., Freeport 04032* 🕾 *207/865-9377 or 800/342-6423* ⊕ *www.harraseeketinn.com* 🛏 *84 rooms* ⃕ *In-room: refrigerator (some), dial-up. In-hotel: 2 restaurants, pool, no-smoking rooms* ⊟ *AE, D, DC, MC, V* ⫶⦾⃒*BP.*

$$$–$$$$

Fodor'sChoice

★

🖼 **Pomegranate Inn.** The classic architecture of this handsome inn in the architecturally rich Western Promenade area gives no hint of the surprises within. Vivid hand-painted walls, floors, and woodwork combine with contemporary artwork, and the result is both stimulating and comforting. Rooms are individually decorated, and five have fireplaces. Room 8, in the carriage house, has a private garden terrace. ⊠ *49 Neal St., Portland 04102* 🕾 *207/772-1006 or 800/356-0408* ⊕ *www.pome granateinn.com* 🛏 *8 rooms* ⃕ *In-room: Wi-Fi. In-hotel: no elevator, no kids under 16, no-smoking rooms* ⊟ *AE, D, DC, MC, V* ⫶⦾⃒*BP.*

THE MID-COAST

$$–$$$$
★
🏨 **Harpswell Inn Bed & Breakfast.** The smell of the salt air greets you at this charming B&B on Lookout Point. The inn was originally the old cookhouse at Look Shipyard, where schooners and brigs were built around the time of the Civil War. Rooms are furnished with antiques, and many have fireplaces and balconies with a view of the sunset over Middle Bay. You can enjoy acres of oak-shaded lawns on the knoll overlooking the ocean. Ask the owners about their list of walking and hiking suggestions. The facility also rents out four cottages for $950–$1,400 a week. Pets are allowed in cottages; kids are best accommodated in suites or cottages. ⊠ *108 Lookout Point Rd., Harpswell 04079* ☎ *207/833–5509 or 800/843–5509* ⊕ *www.harpswellinn. com* 🛏 *9 rooms, 3 suites, 4 cottages* ⚡ *In-room: Wi-Fi (some), no a/c (some), no phone (some). In-hotel: no-smoking rooms, no elevator* ⊟ *D, MC, V* ⏐○⏐ *BP.*

PENOBSCOT BAY

$$$–$$$$
Fodor$Choice
★
🏨 **Norumbega.** The Norumbega is probably the most unusual-looking B&B you'll ever see. When you see this ivy-coated, gray stone castle, from the outside you may think, *Wow, Count Dracula would feel right at home here.* But inside it's cheerier, and elegant, with many of the antiques-filled rooms offering fireplaces and private balconies overlooking the bay. The inn was built in 1886 by local businessman and inventor (of duplex telegraphy) Joseph Stearns. Before erecting his home, he spent a year visiting the castles of Europe and adapting the best ideas he found. He named the castle after the original 17th-century name for what is now Maine, "Norumbega." The home was converted into a B&B in 1984 and has been named by the *Maine Times* as the most-photographed piece of real estate in the state. There are no ground-floor guest rooms, and no elevator. Pets are not allowed. ⊠ *63 High St., (U.S. 1), just a little north of downtown Camden, 04843* ☎ *207/236–4646 or 877/363–4646* ⊕ *www.norumbegainn.com* 🛏 *13 rooms* ⚡ *In-room: no a/c, dial-up, Wi-Fi. In-hotel: no-smoking rooms, no elevator* ⊟ *AE, DC, MC, V* ⏐○⏐ *BP.*

ACADIA NATIONAL PARK & MOUNT DESERT ISLAND

$$$–$$$$
Fodor$Choice
★
🏨 **Bar Harbor Inn & Spa.** Originally established in the late 1800s as a men's social club, this waterfront inn has rooms spread out over three buildings on well-landscaped grounds. Most rooms have gas fireplaces and balconies with great views. Rooms in the Oceanfront Lodge have private decks overlooking the ocean. Many rooms in the main inn have balconies overlooking the harbor. Should you need more room, there are also some two-level suites. A relatively new addition to the inn is a luxury spa, which offers everything from massages and mud wraps to aromatherapy and facials. The inn is a short walk from town, so you're close to all the sights, and a terrific restaurant, the Reading Room, is on-site *(⇨ see Where to Eat)*. ⊠ *Newport Dr., Bar Harbor 04609* ☎ *207/288–3351 or 800/248–3351* ⊕ *www.barharborinn.com* 🛏 *138 rooms, 15 suites* ⚡ *In-room: safe, refrigerator, DVD. In-hotel: 2 restaurants, pool, gym, no-smoking rooms* ⊟ *AE, DC, MC, V* ⊙ *Closed late Nov.–late Mar.* ⏐○⏐ *CP.*

SPORTS & THE OUTDOORS

GREATER PORTLAND

Maine Island Kayak Company (✉ *70 Luther St., Peaks Island* ☎ *207/766–2373 or 800/796–2313* ⊕ *www.maineislandkayak.com*)provides gear, instruction, and guidance.

L. L. Bean's year-round **Outdoor Discovery Schools** (✉ *Freeport* ☎ *888/552–3261* ⊕ *www.llbean.com/ods*) include half- and one-day classes, as well as longer trips that teach canoeing, shooting, photography, kayaking, fly-fishing, cross-country skiing, and other sports.

> **VITAL STATS:**
>
> - State Capitol: Augusta
> - State Motto: "Dirigo (I lead)"
> - State Flower: White Pine Cone
> - State Tree: White Pine
> - Highest Point: Katahdin, 5,268 feet
> - State Cat: Maine Coon Cat
> - How to say "yes": "Ayuh"

PENOBSCOT BAY

♺ **Maine Windjammer Association** (☎ *800/807–9463* ⊕ *www.sailmainecoast.com*) can set you up with a sailing excursion that very well may end up the highlight of your vacation.

ACADIA NATIONAL PARK & MOUNT DESERT ISLAND

Acadia Bike Rentals (✉ *48 Cottage St., Bar Harbor* ☎ *207/288–9605 or 800/526–8615*) rents mountain bikes good for negotiating the trails in Acadia National Park.

Acadia Outfitters (✉ *106 Cottage St., Bar Harbor* ☎ *207/288–8118*)rents canoes and sea kayaks. **Coastal Kayaking Tours** (✉ *48 Cottage St., Bar Harbor* ☎ *207/288–9605 or 800/526–8615*) conducts tours of the rocky coastline led by registered guides. **National Park Sea Kayak Tours** (✉ *39 Cottage St., Bar Harbor* ☎ *207/288–0342 or 800/347–0940*)leads guided kayak tours.

★ **Bar Harbor Whale Watch Co.** (✉ *1 West St., Bar Harbor* ☎ *207/288–2386*
♺ *or 800/942–5374)* ⊕ *www.whalesrus.com*) merged with the Acadian Whale Watcher to make one big company with four boats, one of them a 138-foot jet-propelled catamaran with spacious decks. In season the outfit also offers lobsters and seals cruises, a nature cruise, and puffins cruises. How likely are you to actually see a whale? Very. In fact, the company can practically guarantee it—they apparently have some sort of arrangement with the whales.

VISITOR INFORMATION

Maine Tourism Association & Visitor Information Center (✉ *U.S. 1 and I-95, Kittery 03904* ☎ *207/439–1319* ⊕ *www.mainetourism.com*).

Boston

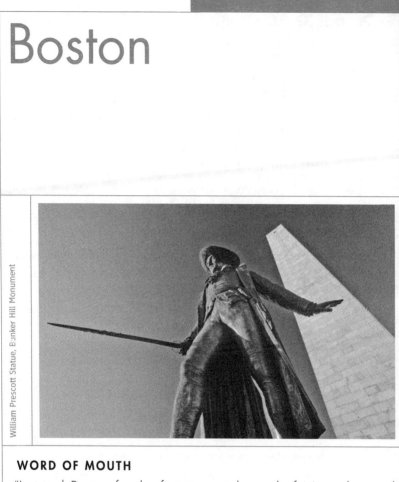

William Prescott Statue, Bunker Hill Monument

WORD OF MOUTH

"I visited Boston for the first time at the end of November and LOVED it. The history, architecture, food . . . terrific."

—lennyba

EXPLORING BOSTON

By Erin Byers
Murray

215 mi northeast of New York City via I–95; 106 mi south of Portland, ME via I–95 and I–93.

Once considered the "Hub of the Universe," Boston still clings to a pride it developed as the birthplace of America. There's history and culture at every turn here, permeating scholarly institutions, dining venues, successful sports teams, and cultural attractions. It's a city that thrives on change but strives to preserve its roots.

Visitors are typically awed by the concentration of historical sites clustered in the confines of downtown, while locals tend to incorporate history into their daily lives. Bostonians picnic in the same spot where Puritans once grazed their cattle, and still use the footpaths (now streets) laid out by their forefathers to get from neighborhoods like the vibrant South End, with its dynamic dining scene, to Cambridge's Harvard Square, where the "wicked sm-aht" kids congregate. Take your time getting to know any one of these areas, and you'll come to understand why many Bostonians still consider it the center of the world.

WHO WILL ESPECIALLY LOVE THIS TRIP?

Families: Kids-at-heart will have as much fun in Boston as actual kids. With plenty of family-friendly activities like the Children's Museum, Museum of Science, and whale-watching trips, and dining options like Legal Sea Foods, Boston is a great place to spend some quality time together (and you may be able to slip in a history lesson to boot).

History Buffs: From the Freedom Trail to the USS Constitution to the Old North Church, there's days of historic ground to cover here.

Sports Fans: Not to brag, but our baseball, football, and basketball teams are probably at the top of their games right now. Sit through a game, tour Fenway Park, or just hang out in one of our many sports bars for a few pints in the presence of Red Sox Nation.

Foodies: Thanks to a number of phenomenal, homegrown chefs, the independent restaurant scene is booming in Boston. Big-ticket destinations like Radius and No. 9 Park attract as many devotees as smaller dining rooms like Craigie Street Bistrot. And there's a style of cuisine for just about everyone.

WHEN IS THE BEST TIME TO VISIT?

Boston comes to life in spring and stays that way through fall, making April through October the ideal time to visit. Baseball games and outdoor festivals start in spring and carry on through summer. There are concerts on the Esplanade, harbor cruises, and plenty of options for outdoor dining. It's also the best time to visit the miles of picturesque coastline and nearby islands—just be sure to make reservations early, as hotels in and out of town fill up quickly. In fall the city and

TOP REASONS TO GO

The Freedom Trail: Walk along Paul Revere's fated path for a glimpse of living American history.

Cultural Encounters: Boston's world-class music scene includes Symphony Hall, several impressive collections of art and artifacts, and a vibrant and strongly supported local arts scene.

Red Sox Nation: Boston's baseball team is the one thing that will bring the entire city to its feet—or its knees. And with the Patriots and Celtics on tears of their own right now, Beantown may be the most dominant sporting town in the country.

Wicked Good Food: Independent restaurants owned by local chefs have put this city next to New York and San Francisco on the culinary map.

Harvard's Halls: The country's most well-regarded institution is also one of its oldest and most beautiful. From ivy-laced brick buildings to the namesake square on the edge of campus, you can see this must-visit neighborhood on a single, leisurely stroll.

surrounding region lights up with colorful foliage, making it one of the most popular times to visit.

A few times of year to watch out for are May, when colleges and universities host their graduations, and September, when the students return to campus. Accommodations and restaurant reservations are hard to come by during these time periods, especially in student-heavy areas like Harvard Square, Allston, Brighton, and Brookline. And though the wintertime might bring frigid temps, there are still plenty of opportunities for outdoor fun, like skating on the Frog Pond and trips to nearby ski resorts.

HOW SHOULD I GET THERE?

DRIVING

If you're driving to Boston, it's easily accessible from Interstate 95 North and South. Watch for signs that point you into Boston via Interstate 93, which runs directly into town and through the infamous Big Dig. From the West, Interstate 90 connects Boston to points across the country.

FLYING

Like most airports, Boston's Logan seems to be constantly undergoing construction, but it connects travelers to most domestic and international points. Just across the harbor from downtown, it's a quick, 10-minute drive into the city. Buses, the MBTA subway system, and ferries also travel to and from the airport frequently.

TRAIN

Boston's South Station is easily accessible on Amtrak; it's a stop on the high-speed Acela line, which runs down to Washington D.C. via New York and Philadelphia several times a day. For more information, go to www.amtrak.com.

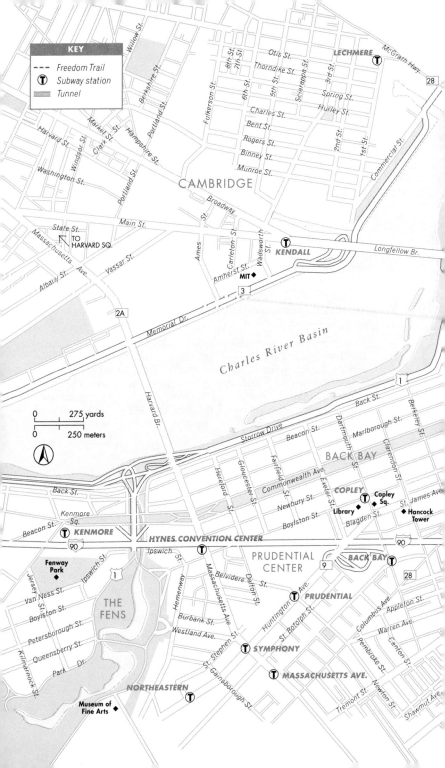

KEY

- - - Freedom Trail
Ⓣ Subway station
▒ Tunnel

Willow St.

Otis St.

Thorndike St.

Sciarappa St.

Spring St.

Hurley St.

LECHMERE Ⓣ

McGrath Hwy.

28

8th St.

7th St.

6th St.

5th St.

3rd St.

2nd St.

1st St.

Commercial St.

Fulkerson St.

Charles St.

Bent St.

Rogers St.

Binney St.

Munroe St.

Berkshire St.

Portland St.

Hampshire St.

Market St.

Clark St.

Windsor St.

Harvard St.

Washington St.

CAMBRIDGE

Broadway

Main St.

State St.

TO
HARVARD SQ.

Massachusetts Ave.

Vassar St.

Albany St.

Portland St.

St.

Ames St.

Carleton St.

Amherst St.

Wadsworth St.

MIT ◆

KENDALL Ⓣ

Longfellow Br.

3

2A

Memorial Dr.

Charles River Basin

1

Harvard Br.

0   275 yards
0   250 meters

Back St.

Berkeley St.

Storrow Drive

Beacon St.

Dartmouth St.

Marlborough St.

Clarendon St.

BACK BAY

Commonwealth Ave.

Fairfield St.

Gloucester St.

Hereford St.

Newbury St.

Exeter St.

COPLEY Ⓣ

Copley ◆
Sq.

Library ◆

St. James Ave.

Boylston St.

Blagden St.

Hancock ◆
Tower

Back St.

Kenmore
Sq.

Beacon St.

KENMORE Ⓣ

90

HYNES CONVENTION CENTER Ⓣ

Ipswich

90

PRUDENTIAL
CENTER

9

BACK BAY Ⓣ

28

Fenway
Park ◆

Ipswich St.

1

Van Ness St.

Jersey St.

Boylston St.

Petersborough St.

Queensberry St.

Park Dr.

Kilmarnock St.

THE
FENS

Hemenway St.

Massachusetts Ave.

Belvidere St.

Dalton St.

Burbank St.

Westland Ave.

Huntington Ave.

St. Botolph St.

PRUDENTIAL Ⓣ

Columbus Ave.

Appleton St.

Warren Ave.

St. Stephen St.

St. Gainsborough St.

SYMPHONY Ⓣ

MASSACHUSETTS AVE. Ⓣ

Pembroke St.

Canton St.

Tremont St.

Newton St.

Shawmut Ave.

NORTHEASTERN Ⓣ

Museum of
Fine Arts ◆

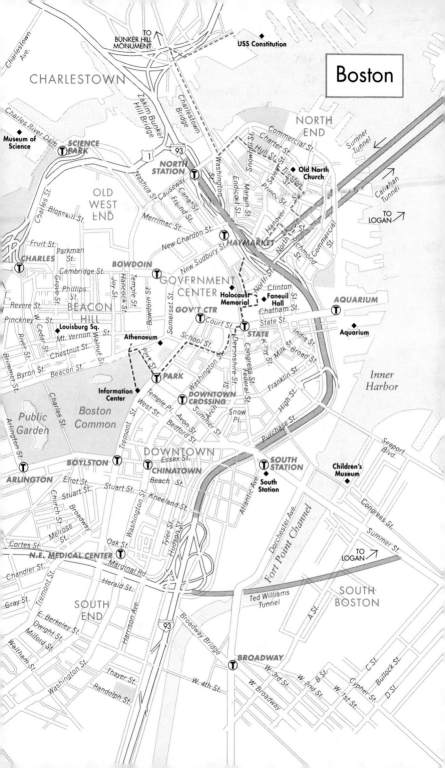

Boston

CHARLESTOWN

TO BUNKER HILL MONUMENT

USS Constitution

Charlestown Ave.

Charles River Dam

Museum of Science

SCIENCE PARK

Zakim Bunker Hill Bridge

Charlestown Bridge

NORTH END

Commercial St.

Charter St.

Hull St.

Snowhill St.

Salem St.

Tileston St.

Old North Church

Sumner Tunnel

Callahan Tunnel

TO LOGAN

NORTH STATION

Washington St.

Nashua St.

Causeway St.

Canal St.

Friend St.

Endicott St.

Hanover St.

March St.

Prince St.

North St.

Richmond St.

Commercial St.

OLD WEST END

Merrimac St.

New Chardon St.

HAYMARKET

New Sudbury St.

North St.

Clinton St.

Charles St.

Blossom St.

Fruit St.

Parkman St.

Cambridge St.

CHARLES

BOWDOIN

Hancock St.

Temple St.

Joy St.

Bowdoin St.

Somerset St.

GOVERNMENT CENTER

Holocaust Memorial

Faneuil Hall

Chatham St.

State St.

AQUARIUM

Aquarium

Phillips St.

Grove St.

Revere St.

Pinckney St.

W. Cedar St.

River St.

Byron St.

Brimmer St.

BEACON HILL

Louisburg Sq.

Mt. Vernon St.

Chestnut St.

Beacon St.

Walnut St.

Athenaeum

GOV'T CTR

Court St.

School St.

Devonshire St.

Congress St.

Federal St.

State St.

Milk St.

India St.

K St.

Broad St.

STATE

Franklin St.

High St.

PARK

Park St.

Tremont St.

West St.

Temple Pl.

DOWNTOWN CROSSING

Washington St.

Avon St.

Summer St.

Snow Pl.

Purchase St.

Inner Harbor

Information Center

Public Garden

Boston Common

Charles St.

Arlington St.

DOWNTOWN

Essex St.

Bedford St.

Arch St.

Seaport Blvd.

BOYLSTON

Eliot St.

Stuart St.

CHINATOWN

Beach St.

SOUTH STATION

South Station

Children's Museum

ARLINGTON

Church St.

Broadway

Melrose St.

Washington St.

Stuart St.

Kneeland St.

Atlantic Ave.

Dorchester Ave.

Fort Point Channel

Congress St.

Summer St.

Cortes St.

N.E. MEDICAL CENTER

Oak St.

Tyler St.

Hudson St.

Marginal Rd.

Herald St.

TO LOGAN

Ted Williams Tunnel

SOUTH BOSTON

Chandler St.

Gray St.

E. Berkeley St.

Dwight St.

Milford St.

Waltham St.

SOUTH END

Tremont St.

Washington St.

Harrison Ave.

Thayer St.

Randolph St.

Broadway Bridge

W. 4th St.

BROADWAY

W. 3rd St.

W. 2nd St.

W. 1st St.

W. Broadway

A St.

B St.

C St.

D St.

Bullock St.

Cypher St.

HOW DO I GET AROUND?

BY CAR

While having a car in Boston is convenient for day trips or traveling just outside the city, it's not necessary. In town, drivers are notoriously aggressive, parking can be hard to come by, and directional signage is somewhat less than helpful. If you do decide to drive here or rent a car, be prepared by carrying a detailed map and quarters for the parking meters. Try to avoid being on the road during large, city-wide events like the Boston Marathon or Red Sox game days.

BY SUBWAY

The "T," as the Massachusetts Bay Transportation Authority's subway system is affectionately known, connects most major parts of the city. Five lines run through town and into the outlying suburbs. The system of aboveground trolleys, underground trains, and buses will take you to every major point of interest.

BY TAXI

Cabs are available around the clock. Look for cab stands, which form lines at corners marked by signs in places like Harvard Square, around South Station, near Faneuil Hall Marketplace, and in the Theater District. Fares in Boston start at $1.75 and cost 30 cents for each $1/8$-mi thereafter.

WHERE SHOULD I FOCUS MY ENERGY?

If you're here for 1 day: Hit the Freedom Trail, which takes you past major sites in the downtown area including Charlestown, Faneuil Hall Marketplace, and the Boston Public Gardens. From there, explore the narrow cobblestone streets of Beacon Hill.

If you're here for 2 days: Cross the river and hit Cambridge. Start at Harvard Square, tour the campus, and then shop your way down to Central Square—or take a cab to Kendall Square for a look at the Massachusetts Institute of Technology.

If you're here for 3 days: Include a visit to the South End, where independent boutiques are nestled between fabulous restaurants. Stroll down Tremont Street before making your way to the art galleries on Harrison Avenue.

If you're here for 4 days: Take to the waters for a harbor cruise, or embark on a longer whale-watching expedition.

If you're here for 5 days: Drive up the coast to the North Shore and visit white-steeple waterfront towns like Gloucester, Salem, and Rockport.

If you're here for 6 days: Explore the southern coastline with a trip down to Plymouth, where you can tour Plimouth Plantation and the Mayflower II.

If you're here for 7 days or more: Take a drive to Cape Cod or a ferry ride out to the islands of Nantucket or Martha's Vineyard. *See Chapter 3, Cape Cod*

How to Snack

Boston's history is interwoven with the sea and everything that comes out of it. One of the city's easiest midday bolsters has always been a steaming bowl of New England chowder. A creamy pot of clams, potatoes, and various vegetables, it can range from thin and soupy to thick and hearty. **Turner Fisheries of Boston** (Westin Copley Place Boston, 10 Huntington Ave., Back Bay, 617/424-7425) has won Boston's annual Chowderfest so many times it's not allowed to compete anymore. **Legal Sea Foods** and **Neptune Oysters** are also solid options if you're in need of a midday break.

Fried clams and oysters may be the most popular take-away snacks at clam shacks like **No Name Restaurant,** but the lobster roll is by far the most famous. Made with chunks of lobster meat and either drizzled melted butter or a dab of mayo, the traditional version found around town is always served on a toasted bun. Pick them up at the deli counter at **James Hook Lobster Co.** (15-17 Northern Ave., Waterfront, 617/423-5500, www.jameshooklobster.com), sit down for a waterside view at the Barking Crab, or try an outstanding, but fancier version at **B&G Oysters** in the South End.

Although it has no relationship to seafood, the Fenway Frank is another Boston legend. Found mostly inside the walls of Fenway Park, the hot dogs served on steamed soft-sided buns can also be bought from vendors just outside the park along Yawkey Way and Lansdowne Street.

Bostonians are notorious for their obsession with ice cream, even in the dead of winter. A few spots remain at the top of every "Best Of" list, like **Christina's** (1255 Cambridge St., Cambridge, 617/492-7021), which serves not only an amazing variety of scoops but also has a tantalizing spice shop next door. There's also **Emack & Bolio's** (290 Newbury St., Back Bay, 617/247-8772) and **J.P. Licks** (659 Centre St., Jamaica Plain, 617/524-6720), which both have several locations and serve up huge helpings with every imaginable topping (plus milkshakes and sundaes).

WHAT ARE THE TOP EXPERIENCES?

The History: Few cities in this country offer as much historical bang for the buck. In one day, you can physically travel to dozens of spots where life-and-country-altering moments took place. Start by standing inside Faneuil Hall Marketplace, which (underneath the facade of several chain stores) gives a basic sense of life in 18th-century America. From here, walk along the Freedom Trail past most of the city's most entertaining historical highlights, like the Union Oyster House, the country's oldest restaurant (where John F. Kennedy's favorite booth is memorialized), and up to the Bunker Hill Monument. Stroll through the oldest public park in the U.S. and over to the Old South Meeting House, where the first rumblings of the Boston Tea Party were heard in 1773.

The Sporting Events: Boston may have been the red-headed stepchild of the sporting world as recently as 15 years ago, but the last six years have brought several championship titles for the Red Sox and the New

CLAIM TO FAME

Bostonians claim they have much to be proud of—and they enjoy bragging about these things. But it's the city's educational centers that seem to deserve the most attention. There are 27 universities inside Boston, bringing almost 200,000 students to town each year. Harvard is certainly one of the most famous, but it's also the oldest, having been founded in 1636. Harvard College, the undergraduate school, is filled with motivated, brilliant students that excitedly lead their own student programs and take advantage of the numerous research facilities on campus. The nearby Massachusetts Institute of Technology opened in the 1860s as an engineering and technology education center. Today it's a world-renowned institution, with seven Nobel Prize winners currently working on campus.

Across the river, Boston College, Boston University, Northeastern, and Emerson comprise the large liberal arts campuses. Intermingled among the city's neighborhoods, they are dynamic educational centers, each with its own unique personality and strengths. Boston College was one of the country's first Jesuit schools; it's now a diverse school open to all faiths. Boston University's campus is on the fringe of downtown, giving its 30,000 students easy access to a wide variety of theater, arts, and cultural experiences. Northeastern is focused on cooperative education, which gives students hands-on experience throughout their studies. Emerson, the most urban campus, keeps its focus squarely on the liberal arts. Music conservatories, graduate colleges, and law schools are also found here.

England Patriots—and there's promise of more to come. But we're a city that never forgets its past, which means there are plenty of places to relive it, like the Red Auerbach statue and bronze replica of Larry Bird's size 13 sneakers in Faneuil Hall, or at the Sports Museum of New England inside the TD Banknorth Garden (Use west premium seating entrance, 617/621-1234, www.sportsmuseum.org). Even a quick walk around Fenway Park (game day or not) can give visitors a sense of the pleasure—and agony—of being a New England sports fan.

The Food: The bean and the cod may have given Boston culinary clout in the old days, but today traditional seafood dishes are getting serious updates from the city's notable chefs. A trip here wouldn't be complete without a bowl of chowder, a side of baked beans, and a lobster roll. But don't stop there. Today's dining scene is all about homegrown chefs and ingredients, with most of the city's best restaurants (including Radius, No. 9 Park, Craigie Street Bistrot, and Oleana) are preparing world-class dishes. Fantastic oyster bars have popped up, as have well-priced French bistros and a dozen new steak houses. Keep your eye on that swinging door, because even the city's few celebrity chefs, like Ken Oringer of Clio and Ming Tsai of Blue Ginger, are in the kitchen almost every night.

The Water: Considering the city is bordered on almost every side by water, Boston and its residents have no choice but to take advantage of it (especially during the typically short summers). On the harbor, there's an almost constant display of tiny sailboats, ferries, massive tankers, and pleasure cruisers. A whale-watch trip gets you the best view of the harbor. The Charles is another hot spot for water fun, with rowers, individual sailors, and even Duck Tours constantly tackling the river. A few miles north or south of the city lay long stretches of New England's stunning beaches, and if you're up for a day trip, the islands of Nantucket and Martha's Vineyard offer a glimpse of the lives of high New England society.

The Neighborhoods: Boston is a walkable city of neighborhoods. So be sure to get away from the major historical monuments (and crowds), and discover Boston's real personality, which can be found along the hilly cobbled lanes of Beacon Hill or the trendy tree-lined streets of the South End. One of the best food tours in the city, Michele Topor's North End Market Tour (617/523–6032, www.micheletopor.com) goes through the North End, where Italian heritage is still alive and well—and usually sitting on lawn chairs along the streets. Venture out toward Brookline for a look at the stately homes that are the playground for wealthy Bostonians, or hang out in the coffee shops of Central Square for a glimpse of the punky, communal attitude that pervades Cambridge.

BEST BETS

SIGHTS AND TOURS

Fodor'sChoice
★
🌣
Boston Common. Nothing is more central to Boston than the Common, the oldest public park in the United States and undoubtedly the largest and most famous of the town commons around which New England settlements were traditionally arranged. Boston Common is not built on landfill like the adjacent Public Garden, nor is it the result of 19th-century park planning, as are Frederick Law Olmsted's Fens and Franklin Park; it started as 50 acres where the freemen of Boston could graze their cattle. (Cows were banned in 1830.) Dating from 1634, it's as old as the city around it. Latin names are affixed to many of the Common's trees; it was once expected that proper Boston schoolchildren be able to translate them. ⊠ *Bounded by Beacon, Charles, Tremont, and Park Sts., Beacon Hill* Ⓣ *Park St.*

Boston Common Visitor Information Center. This center, run by the Greater Boston Convention and Visitors Bureau, is on the Tremont Street side of Boston Common. It's well supplied with stacks of free pamphlets about Boston, including a useful guide to the Freedom Trail, which begins in the Common. ⊠ *147 Tremont St., Beacon Hill* ☎ *888/733–2678* ⊕ *www. bostonusa.com* ☉ *Weekdays 8:30–5, weekends 9–5* Ⓣ *Park St.*

Fodor'sChoice
★
🌣
Boston Public Garden. Although the Boston Public Garden is often lumped together with Boston Common, the two are separate entities with different histories and purposes and a distinct boundary between them at Charles Street. The central feature of the Public Garden is its irregularly shaped pond, intended to appear, from any vantage point along its banks,

much larger than its nearly 4 acres. The pond has been famous since 1877 for its foot-pedal-powered (by a captain) Swan Boats, which make leisurely cruises during warm months. They were invented by one Robert Paget, who was inspired by the swan-drawn boat that carries Lohengrin in the Wagner opera of the same name. (Paget descendants still run the boats.) The pond is favored by ducks and swans, and for the modest price of a few boat rides you can amuse children here for an hour or more. Near the Swan Boat dock is what has been described as the world's smallest suspension bridge, designed in 1867 to cross the pond at its narrowest point.

The park also contains a special delight for the young at heart; follow the children quack-quacking

HISTORY YOU CAN SEE

As the landing place of the Puritans and the launching point of the American Revolution, Boston is constantly referenced in history books. A few of the more notable events that took place here and nearby are the Salem Witch Trials, the Boston Massacre, the Boston Tea Party, and the battle of Bunker Hill. It's also the birthplace of notable political figures like Samuel Adams, Benjamin Franklin, John Adams, Susan B. Anthony, and John F. Kennedy. A walk through downtown will put you in contact with all of these major players through historical markers, preserved cemeteries, memorials—even pubs.

along the pathway between the pond and the park entrance at Charles and Beacon streets to the *Make Way for Ducklings* bronzes sculpted by Nancy Schön, a tribute to the 1941 classic children's story by Robert McCloskey. ⊠*Bounded by Arlington, Boylston, Charles, and Beacon Sts., Back Bay* ☎*617/522–1966* ⊕*www.swanboats.com* 🚣*Swan Boats $2.75* ☼*Swan Boats mid-Apr.–June 20, daily 10–4; June 21– Labor Day, daily 10–5; Labor Day–mid-Sept., weekdays noon–4, weekends 10–4* Ⓣ*Arlington.*

FodorsChoice ★ **Bunker Hill Monument.** Three misunderstandings surround this famous monument. First, the Battle of Bunker Hill was actually fought on Breed's Hill, which is where the monument sits today. (The real Bunker Hill is about ½ mi to the north of the monument; it's slightly taller than Breed's Hill.) Bunker was the original planned locale for the battle, and for that reason its name stuck. Second, although the battle is generally considered a colonial success, the Americans lost. It was a Pyrrhic victory for the British Redcoats, who sacrificed nearly half of their 2,200 men; American casualties numbered 400–600. And third: the famous war cry "Don't fire until you see the whites of their eyes" may never have been uttered by American Colonel William Prescott or General Israel Putnam, but if either one did shout it, he was quoting an old Prussian command made necessary by the notorious inaccuracy of the musket. No matter. The Americans did employ a deadly delayed-action strategy on June 17, 1775, and conclusively proved themselves worthy fighters, capable of defeating the forces of the British Empire.

In 1823 the committee formed to construct a monument on the site of the battle chose the form of an Egyptian obelisk. Architect Solomon Willard designed a 221-foot-tall granite obelisk, a tremendous feat of engineering for its day. The monument's zenith is reached by a flight of 294 steps. There's no elevator, but the views from the observatory are worth the effort of the arduous climb. A statue of Colonel Prescott stands guard at the base. In the lodge at the base, dioramas tell the story of the battle, and ranger-led talks are given on the hour. ☎617/242–5641 ⊕www.nps.gov/bost/historyculture/bhm.htm ⚏Free ⊗Lodge daily 9–5, monument daily 9–4:30 ⊤Community College.

Fodor'sChoice **Children's Museum.** Most children have so much fun here that they don't
★ realize they're actually learning something. Creative hands-on exhibits
☺ demonstrate scientific laws, cultural diversity, and problem solving. After completing a massive 23,000-square-foot expansion in 2007, the museum has updated a lot of its old exhibitions and added new ones, like the aptly named "Adventure Zone." Some of the most popular stops are also the simplest: bubble-making machinery, the two-story climbing maze, and "Boats Afloat," where children can float wooden objects down a 28-foot-long model of the Fort Point Channel. At the Japanese House you're invited to take off your shoes and step inside a two-story silk merchant's home from Kyoto. The "Boston Black" exhibit stimulates dialogue about ethnicity and community while children play in a Cape Verdean restaurant and the "African Queen Beauty Salon." In the toddler "Smith Family PlaySpace," children under three can run free in a safe environment. There's also a full schedule of special exhibits, festivals, and performances. ✉300 Congress St., Downtown ☎617/426–6500, 617/426–8855 recorded information ⊕www.bostonkids.org ⚏$9, Fri. 5–9 $1 ⊗Sat.–Thurs. 10–5, Fri. 10–9 ⊤South Station.

Fodor'sChoice **Fenway Park.** Fenway may be one of the smallest parks in the major
★ leagues (capacity almost 39,000), but it's one of the most beloved, despite its oddball dimensions and the looming left-field wall, otherwise known as the Green Monster. Parking is expensive and the seats are a bit cramped, but the air is thick with legend. ✉4 Yawkey Way, between Van Ness and Lansdowne Sts., The Fenway ☎617/267–1700 box office, 617/226–6666 tours ⊕http://boston.redsox.mlb.com ⚏Tours $12 ⊗Tours Mon.–Sat. 9–4, Sun. noon–4; on game days, last tour is 3 hrs before game time and lasts ½ hr.

Fodor'sChoice **Harvard Square.** Tides of students, tourists, political-cause proponents,
★ and bizarre street creatures are all part of the nonstop pedestrian flow
☺ at this most celebrated of Cambridge crossroads. Harvard Square is where Mass Ave., coming from Boston, turns and widens into a triangle broad enough to accommodate a brick peninsula (above the T station). The restored 1928 kiosk in the center of the square once served as the entrance to the MBTA station (it's now a newsstand). Harvard Yard, with its lecture halls, residential houses, libraries, and museums, is one long border of the square; the other three are comprised of clusters of banks and a wide variety of restaurants and shops. ⊕www.harvard square.com ⊤Harvard.

Fodor'sChoice **Holocaust Memorial.** At night, its six 50-foot-high glass-and-steel towers
★ glow like ghosts. During the day the monument seems at odds with the

CLOSE UP: Following the Freedom Trail

More than a route of historic sites, the Freedom Trail is a 2½-mi walk into history, bringing to life the events that exploded on the world during the Revolution. Its 16 way stations allow you to reach out and touch the very wellsprings of U.S. civilization. (And for those with a pinch of Yankee frugality, only three of the sites charge admission.) Follow the route marked on your maps, and keep an eye on the sidewalk for the red stripe that marks the trail.

It takes a full day to complete the entire route comfortably. The trail lacks the multimedia bells and whistles that are quickly becoming the norm at historic attractions, but on the Freedom Trail, history speaks for itself.

Begin at Boston Common. Get your bearings at the Visitor Information Center on Tremont Street, then head for the **State House,** Boston's finest piece of Federalist architecture. Several blocks away is the **Park Street Church,** whose 217-foot steeple is considered by many to be the most beautiful in all of New England.

Reposing in the church's shadows is the **Granary Burying Ground,** final resting place of Samuel Adams, John Hancock, and Paul Revere. A short stroll to Downtown brings you to **King's Chapel,** built in 1754 and a hotbed of Anglicanism during the colonial period. Follow the trail past the statue of Benjamin Franklin to the **Old Corner Bookstore** site, where Hawthorne, Emerson, and Longfellow were published. Nearby is the **Old South Meeting House,** where pretempest

arguments, heard in 1773, led to the Boston Tea Party. Overlooking the site of the Boston Massacre is the earliest-known public building in Boston, the **Old State House,** a Georgian beauty.

Cross the plaza to **Faneuil Hall** and explore its upstairs Assembly Room, where Samuel Adams fired the indignation of Bostonians during those times that tried men's souls. Find your way back to the red stripe and follow it into the North End.

Stepping into the **Paul Revere House** takes you back 200 years—here are the hero's own saddlebags, a toddy warmer, and a pine cradle made from a molasses cask. Nearby Paul Revere Mall is a tranquil rest spot. Next to the Paul Revere House is one of the city's oldest brick buildings, the **Pierce-Hichborn House.**

Next, tackle a place guaranteed to trigger a wave of patriotism: the **Old North Church** of "One if by land, two if by sea" fame—sorry, the 154 creaking stairs leading to the belfry are out-of-bounds for visitors. Then head toward **Copp's Hill Burying Ground,** cross the bridge over the Charles, and check out that revered icon the **USS Constitution,** "Old Ironsides."

The photo finish? A climb to the top of the **Bunker Hill Monument** for the incomparable vistas. Finally, head for the nearby Charlestown water shuttle, which goes directly to the downtown area, and congratulate yourself: you've just completed a unique crash course in American history.

18th-century streetscape of Blackstone Square behind it. Shoehorned into the north end of Union Park, the Holocaust Memorial is the work of Stanley Saitowitz, whose design was selected through an international competition; the finished memorial was dedicated in 1995. Recollections by Holocaust survivors are set into the glass-and-granite walls; the upper levels of the towers are etched with 6 million numbers in random sequence, symbolizing the Jewish victims of the Nazi horror. Manufactured steam from grates in the granite base makes for a particularly haunting scene after dark. ⊠ *Union St. near Hanover St., Government Center.*

Fodor'sChoice **Isabella Stewart Gardner Museum.**
★ A spirited young society woman, Isabella Stewart had come in 1860 from New York—where ladies were more commonly seen *and* heard than in Boston—to marry John Lowell Gardner, one of Boston's leading citizens. Through her flamboyance and energetic acquisition of art, "Mrs. Jack" promptly set about becoming the most un-Bostonian of the Proper Bostonians. When it came time finally to settle down with the old master paintings and Medici treasures she and her husband had acquired in Europe—with *her* money (she was heir to the Stewart mining fortune)—she decided to build the Venetian palazzo of her dreams in an isolated corner of Boston's newest neighborhood.

> **STRANGE BUT TRUE**
>
> One of the most infamous tragedies to occur in town was the great molasses flood of 1919. In the industrial North End on an unseasonably warm January day, a two-and-a-half million gallon tank of molasses owned by the United States Industrial Alcohol Company, ruptured, sending the sweet, sticky mess into the streets. Twenty-one people were killed from the explosion and aftermath, while building structures literally collapsed under the pressure of the viscous liquid. Some reported that a wall of molasses eight feet high charged the streets at 35 mi per hour.

In a city where expensive simplicity was the norm, Gardner's palazzo was amazing: a trove of paintings—including such masterpieces as Titian's *Rape of Europa,* Giorgione's *Christ Bearing the Cross,* Piero della Francesca's *Hercules,* and John Singer Sargent's *El Jaleo*—overflows rooms bought outright from great European houses. Spanish leather panels, Renaissance hooded fireplaces, and Gothic tapestries accent salons; eight balconies adorn the majestic Venetian courtyard. There's a Raphael Room, a Spanish Cloister, a Gothic Room, a Chinese Loggia, and a magnificent Tapestry Room for concerts, where Gardner entertained Henry James and Edith Wharton. Throughout the two decades of her residence, Mrs. Jack continued to build her collection under the tutelage of the young Bernard Berenson, who became one of the most respected art connoisseurs and critics of the 20th century.

An intimate restaurant overlooks the museum's garden, and in spring and summer tables and chairs spill outside. To fully conjure up the spirit of days past, try to attend one of the concerts still held from September to May (with a break for the holidays) in the Tapestry Room. A first-floor gallery has revolving exhibits of historic and contemporary art. ■ **TIP→ If you've visited the MFA in the past two days, there's a $2 discount to the admission fee. Also note that a charming quirk of the museum's admission policy waives entrance fees to anyone named Isabella, forever.** ⊠ *280 The Fenway, Fens* ☎ *617/566–1401, 617/566–1088 café* ⊕ *www.gardnermuseum.org* ⊠ *$12* ☯ *Museum Tues.–Sun. 11–5,* *open some holidays; café Tues.–Fri. 11:30–4, weekends 11–4. Weekend concerts at 1:30* ⊤ *Museum.*

Fodor'sChoice **Museum of Science.** With 15-foot
★ lightning bolts in the Theater of
Ⓒ Electricity and a 20-foot-long *Tyrannosaurus rex* model, this is just the place to ignite any child's scientific curiosity. Occupying a compound of buildings north of Massachusetts General, the museum sits astride the Charles River Dam. More than 550 exhibits cover astronomy, astrophysics, anthropology, progress in medicine, computers, the organic and inorganic earth sciences, and much more. The emphasis is on hands-on education. For instance, at the "Investigate!" exhibit children explore such scientific princi-

ples as gravity by balancing objects—there are no wrong answers here, only discoveries. Children can learn the physics behind everyday play activities such as swinging and bumping up and down on a teeter-totter in the "Science in the Park" exhibit. Other displays include "Light House," where you can experiment with color and light, and the perennial favorite, "Dinosaurs: Modeling the Mesozoic," which lets kids become paleontologists and examine dinosaur bones, fossils, and tracks. ⊠ *Science Park at Charles River Dam, Old West End* ☎ *617/723–2500* ⊕ *www.mos.org* 🖃 *$16* ☉ *July 5–Labor Day, Sat.–Thurs. 9–7, Fri. 9–9; Labor Day–July 4, Sat.–Thurs. 9–5, Fri. 9–9* ⊤ *Science Park.*

Fodor'sChoice **Old North Church.** Standing at one end of the **Paul Revere Mall** is a
★ church famous not only for being the oldest one in Boston (built in 1723) but for housing the two lanterns that glimmered from its steeple on the night of April 18, 1775. This is Christ Church, or the Old North, where Paul Revere and the young sexton Robert Newman managed that night to signal the departure by water of the British regulars to Lexington and Concord. Newman, carrying the lanterns, ascended the steeple (the original tower blew down in 1804 and was replaced; the present one was put up in 1954 after the replacement was destroyed in a hurricane) while Revere began his clandestine trip by boat across the Charles. ⊠ *193 Salem St., North End* ☎ *617/523–6676* ⊕ *www.old north.com* ☉ *Daily 9–5. Sun. services at 9 and 11* AM ⊤ *Haymarket, North Station.*

Fodor'sChoice **USS Constitution.** Better known as "Old Ironsides," the USS *Constitution*
★ rides proudly at anchor in her berth at the Charlestown Navy Yard.
Ⓒ The oldest commissioned ship in the U.S. fleet is a battlewagon of the old school, of the days of "wooden ships and iron men"—when she and her crew of 200 succeeded at the perilous task of asserting the sovereignty of an improbable new nation. Every July 4 and on certain

2

other occasions she's towed out for a turnabout in Boston Harbor, the very place her keel was laid in 1797.

The men and women who look after the *Constitution,* regular navy personnel, maintain a 24-hour watch. Sailors show visitors around the ship, guiding them to her top, or spar, deck, and the gun deck below. Another treat when visiting the ship is the spectacular view of Boston across Boston Harbor. ⊠*Charlestown Navy Yard, 55 Constitution Rd., Charlestown* ☎*617/242–5670* ⊕*www.ussconstitution.navy.mil* ☜*Free* ⊙*Apr. 7–Oct., Tues.–Sun. 10–4; Nov.–Apr. 6, Thurs.–Sun. 10–4; last tour at 3:30* Ⓣ*North Station.*

USS Constitution Museum. Artifacts and hands-on exhibits pertaining to the USS *Constitution* are on display—firearms, logs, and instruments. One section takes you step-by-step through the ship's most important battles. Old meets new in a video-game battle "fought" at the helm of a ship. ⊠*Adjacent to USS Constitution, Charlestown Navy Yard, Charlestown* ☎*617/426–1812* ⊕*www.ussconstitutionmuseum.org* ☜*Free* ⊙*May–Oct., daily 9–6; Nov.–Apr., daily 10–5* Ⓣ*North Station; MBTA Bus 92 to Charlestown City Sq. or Bus 93 to Chelsea St. from Haymarket; or Boston Harbor Cruise water shuttle from Long Wharf to Pier 4.*

WHERE TO EAT

WHAT IT COSTS IN BOSTON					
	¢	$	$$	$$$	$$$$
AT DINNER	under $8	$8–$14	$15–$24	$25–$32	Over $32

Prices are per person for a main course at dinner. Some restaurants are marked with a price range ($$–$$$, for example). This indicates one of two things: either the average cost straddles two categories, or if you order strategically, you can get out for less than most diners spend.

$$$$ ✕**Clio.** Years ago when Ken Oringer opened his snazzy leopard skin–
Fodor'sChoice lined hot spot in the tasteful boutique Eliot Hotel, the hordes were
★ fighting over reservations. Things have quieted down since then, but the food hasn't. Luxury ingredients pack the menu, from foie gras and tiny eels called elvers to the octopus sashimi and Kobe beef Oringer serves at Uni, the small but adventurous sushi bar set up in a side room off the main dining room. ⊠*Eliot Hotel, 370 Commonwealth Ave., Back Bay* ☎*617/536–7200* ⌂*Reservations essential* ▤*AE, D, MC, V* Ⓣ *Hynes/ICA.*

$$$$ ✕**No. 9 Park.** Chef Barbara Lynch's stellar cuisine draws plenty of well-
Fodor'sChoice deserved attention from its place in the shadow of the State House's
★ golden dome. Settle into the plush but unpretentious dining room and indulge in pumpkin risotto with rare lamb or the memorably rich prune-stuffed gnocchi drizzled with bits of foie gras. The wine list bobs and weaves into new territory but is always well chosen and the savvy bartenders are of the classic ilk, so you'll find plenty of classics and very few cloying, dessertlike sips here. ⊠*9 Park St., Beacon Hill* ☎*617/742–9991* ▤*AE, D, DC, MC, V* Ⓣ *Park St.*

$$$-$$$$ ✕ **Craigie Street Bistrot.** Buried away
★ on a residential street, this tiny bistro churns out outstanding dishes. Chef–owner Tony Maws is fanatical about fresh, local, and organic so he's in the kitchen every morning, prepping ingredients (which most likely came from the Harvard Square farmers' market or another local purveyor). His menu changes daily so options can range from a Spanish-style octopus to tender beef short ribs to pork done three ways. Sunday is Chef's Whim night, meaning you'll eat (and most likely love) whatever he feels like cooking for a discounted price. The mostly organic wine list focuses on France. ✉ 5 Craigie Circle, Cambridge ☎ 617/497–5511 ☐ AE, DC, MC, V ⊗ Closed Mon. No lunch ⓣ Harvard.

> ## ON THE WAY
>
> **Lincoln and Concord** are the sites of major Revolutionary War battles and were home to literary giants like Louisa May Alcott and Henry David Thoreau.
>
> **Newport, Rhode Island** is home to stately mansions built by New England's oldest and wealthiest families.
>
> **The Berkshires** make up a cultural hub two hours west of Boston; contemporary art museums and world-class music venues nestled are among rolling hills.

$$$-$$$$ ✕ **Radius.** Acclaimed chef Michael Schlow's notable contemporary
Fodor'sChoice French cooking lures scores of designer-clad diners to the Financial
★ District. The decor and menu are minimalist at first glance, but closer inspection reveals equal shares of luxury, complexity, and whimsy. Peruse the menu for such choices as roasted beet salad, a selection of ceviches, buttery Scottish salmon, or coconut panna cotta for dessert. It's a meal made for special occasions and business dinners alike. ✉ 8 High St., Downtown ☎ 617/426–1234 ⌕ Reservations essential ☐ AE, DC, MC, V ⓣ South Station.

$$-$$$$ ✕ **Blue Ginger.** Chef Ming Tsai's nimble maneuvers in the kitchen have
★ caught the nation's eye via a cable-TV cooking program, *Simply Ming,* and his many cookbooks, including the first, *Blue Ginger: East Meets West Cooking with Ming Tsai (1999).* Plan ahead (and make sure Tsai is there) to savor his Occident-meets-Asian cuisine. Top choices include roast-duck pot stickers with fresh pea salad and *sambal* (an Indonesian condiment of red chilies, onion, and lime) and tangerine-teriyaki wild salmon. There's no T stop anywhere nearby, but the 15-mi trip from downtown Boston is an easy jaunt west on the Massachusetts Turnpike to Route 16/Washington Street. ✉ 583 Washington St., Wellesley ☎ 781/283–5790 ☐ AE, MC, V ⊗ Closed Sun. No lunch Sat.

$$-$$$ ✕ **Legal Sea Foods.** What began as a tiny restaurant upstairs over a Cambridge fish market has grown to important regional status, with more than 20 East Coast locations, plus a handful of national ones. The hallmark is the freshest possible seafood, whether you have it wood grilled, in New England chowder, or doused with an Asia-inspired sauce. The smoked-bluefish pâté is delectable, and the clam chowder is so good it has become a menu staple at presidential inaugurations. A preferred-seating list allows calls ahead, and this location has private dining inside its beautiful, bottle-lined wine cellar. ✉ 26 Park Sq., The-

ater District ☎617/426–4444 ☜*Reservations not accepted* ▭*AE, D, DC, MC, V* Ⓣ *Arlington.*

$$–$$$ ✕**Neptune Oyster.** This tiny oyster bar, the first of its kind in the neighbor-
★   hood, has only six tables, but the long marble bar has extra seating for a dozen more and mirrors hang over the bar with handwritten menus. From there, watch the oyster shuckers as they deftly undo handfuls of bivalves. The *plateau di frutti di mare* is a gleaming tower of oysters and other raw-bar items piled over ice that you can order from the slip of paper they pass out listing each day's crustacean options. And the lobster roll, hot or cold, overflows with meat. Service is prompt even when it gets busy (as it is most of the time). Go early to avoid a long wait. ✉*63 Salem St., North End* ☎617/742–3474 ☜*Reservations not accepted* ▭*AE, DC, MC, V* Ⓣ *Haymarket.*

$$–$$$ ✕**Oleana.** Chef and owner Ana Sortun is one of the city's culinary trea-
Fodor'sChoice   sures—and so is Oleana. Here, flavors from all over the Middle East-
★   ern Mediterranean sing loud and clear, in the hot, crispy fried mussels starter, and in the smoky eggplant puree beside tamarind-glazed beef. Fish gets jacked up with Turkish spices, then grilled until it just barely caramelizes. In warm weather, the back patio is a hidden piece of uto-pia—a homey garden that hits the perfect note of casual refinement. ✉*134 Hampshire St., Cambridge* ☎617/661–0505 ☜*Reservations essential* ▭*AE, MC, V* ⊘*No lunch* Ⓣ *Central.*

$–$$ ✕**B & G Oysters, Ltd.** Chef Barbara Lynch (of No. 9 Park fame) has
Fodor'sChoice   made yet another fabulous mark on Boston with a style-conscious sea-
★   food restaurant that updates New England's traditional bounty with flair. Designed to imitate the inside of an oyster shell, the iridescent bar glows with silvery, candlelighted tiles and a sophisticated crowd. They're in for the lobster roll, no doubt—an expensive proposition at $24, but worth every cent for its decadent chunks of meat in a perfectly textured dressing. If you're sans reservation, be prepared to wait: the line for a seat can be epic. ✉*550 Tremont St., South End* ☎617/423–0550 ▭*AE, D, MC, V* Ⓣ *Back Bay/South End.*

¢–$$ ✕**Barking Crab Restaurant.** It is, believe it or not, a seaside clam shack plunk in the middle of Boston, with a stunning view of the downtown skyscrapers. An outdoor lobster tent in summer, in winter it retreats indoors to a warmhearted version of a waterfront dive, with chest-nuts roasting on a cozy woodstove. Look for the classic New England clambake—chowder, lobster, steamed clams, corn on the cob—or the spicier crab boil. ✉*88 Sleeper St., Northern Ave. Bridge, Waterfront* ☎617/426–2722 ▭*AE, DC, MC, V* Ⓣ *South Station.*

¢–$ ✕**No Name Restaurant.** Famous for not being famous, the No Name has
★   been serving fresh seafood, simply broiled or fried, since 1917. Once you find it, tucked off of New Northern Avenue (as opposed to Old Northern Avenue) between the World Trade Center and the Bank of America Pavilion, you can close your eyes and pretend you're in a little fishing village—it's not much of a stretch. ✉*15½ Fish Pier, off New Northern Ave., Waterfront* ☎617/338–7539 or 617/423–2705 ▭*AE, D, MC, V* Ⓣ *Courthouse.*

WHERE TO STAY

WHAT IT COSTS				
¢	$	$$	$$$	$$$$
FOR TWO PEOPLE	under $75	$75–$149	$150–$224	$225–$325	over $325

Prices are for two people in a standard double room in high season, excluding 12.45% tax and service charges.

$$$$
Fodor'sChoice
★
Fairmont Copley Plaza. For those who believe that too much of a good thing is just about right, the deliciously decadent, unabashedly romantic Fairmont lures. Richly decorated, and very ornate—we're talking cherubs on the ceiling here—this favors romance and tradition over sleek and modern. (Really love pampering? Stay on the Fairmont Gold floor, an ultradeluxe club level offering a dedicated staff, lounge, dining room, and library.) Shopping fanatics adore the close proximity to Newbury Street, the Prudential Center, and Copley Place. This 1912 landmark underwent a $34 million renovation in 2004, updating rooms with new classically inspired decor, marble bathrooms, and high-speed Internet access. The grand public spaces have mosaic floors, marble pillars, and high gilded ceilings hung with glittering chandeliers. The Oak Room restaurant matches its mahogany-panel twin in New York's Plaza Hotel; the equally stately—and tryst-worthy—Oak Bar has live music and one of the longest martini menus in town. ⊠*138 St. James Ave., Back Bay, 02116* ☎*617/267–5300 or 800/441–1414* 🖷*617/375–9648* ⊕*www.fairmont.com/copleyplaza* ⬓*366 rooms, 17 suites* ⬧*In-room: safe, refrigerator, Ethernet. In-hotel: restaurant, room service, bar, gym, laundry service, concierge, executive floor, public Wi-Fi, parking (fee), some pets allowed* ⊟*AE, D, DC, MC, V* ⊤*Copley, Back Bay/South End.*

$$$$
Fodor'sChoice
★
InterContinental Boston. Call it the anti-boutique hotel. Boston's new (2007), 424-room InterContinental Hotel, facing the harbor and the as-yet-unfinished Rose Kennedy Greenway—is housed in two opulent, 22-story towers wrapped in blue glass. In a nod to the city's history, the towers equal the height of the masts of the old tall ships, and the pewter bar in RumBa, the hotel's rum bar, would surely delight metalsmith Paul Revere. (It also harks back to Boston's connection with the rum trade.) Miel, the hotel's organic Provençal brasserie, is open 24/7. (Elsewhere in the city, good luck finding dinner after 9 PM.) Hallways are lined with Texan limestone, and lobbies are gleaming with Italian marble and leather—there's not a red brick in the place. Guest rooms are oversize, wired with the latest technology, and have wide-screen TVs, but best, perhaps, are the spalike bathrooms, done in mosaic tile and granite, with separate tubs and showers. Another drawing card here is the 6,600-square-foot spa and health club, and a pool that overlooks Atlantic Avenue and the Boston Fire Department. (Views on this side of the building will improve once they finish the Greenway.) Other features include a posh retail store and Sushi-Teq, a sushi-tequila restaurant with salsa dancers. Movers and shakers from local financial, real estate, and law firms of the Financial District make for a lively after-work scene

in the bars. ⊠*510 Atlantic Ave., Downtown, 02210* ☎*617/747–1000* 🖷*617/217–5020* ⊕*www.intercontinentalboston.com* ↩*424 rooms, 38 suites* ◌*In-room: safe, refrigerator, DVD, Wi-Fi. In-hotel: 2 restaurants, room service, bar, pool, gym, spa, laundry service, concierge, executive floor, public Wi-Fi, parking (fee)* ▤*AE, D, DC, MC, V.*

¢¢¢–$$$$ **Fodor'sChoice** ★ 🖥**Fifteen Beacon.** Although it's housed in an old (1903) beaux arts building, this boutique hotel is anything but stodgy. The tiny lobby is all black lacquer with bold splashes of red, brightened with recessed lighting and abstract art. Even the cage elevator is paneled in red leather. Just when you're thinking, "Hmm," you enter a guest room and go, "Ahh!" Rooms are done up in soothing-but-manly shades of cinnamon, taupe, and black, and each has a canopy bed, a gas fireplace, and surround-sound stereo. Fab little touches abound, like bath amenities from Newbury Street's Fresh, and little flat-screen TVs in the bathroom, plus huge mirrors and heated towel bars. A nearby health club is available to hotel guests, and the hotel's restaurant, the Federalist, is a favorite for fine dining. Tip: This is *the* place to be for Boston's Harborfest (July 4th) celebration, when guests can watch fireworks from the roof deck (open from Memorial Day to Labor Day). ⊠*15 Beacon St., Beacon Hill, 02108* ☎*617/670–1500 or 877/982–3226* 🖷*617/670–2525* ⊕*www.xvbeacon.com* ↩*58 rooms, 2 suites* ◌*In-room: safe, refrigerator, Ethernet. In-hotel: restaurant, room service, bar, gym, laundry service, concierge, parking (fee), some pets allowed* ▤*AE, D, DC, MC, V* ⊺*Government Center, Park St.*

$$–$$$ **Fodor'sChoice** ★ 🖥**Gryphon House.** Many of the suites in this four-story, 19th-century brownstone are thematically decorated; one evokes rustic Italy, another is inspired by neo-Gothic art. Among the many amenities—including gas fireplaces, wet bars, VCRs, CD players, and private voice mail—the enormous bathrooms with oversize tubs and separate showers are the most appealing. Even the staircase (there is no elevator) is extraordinary: a 19th-century wallpaper mural, *El Dorado*, wraps along the walls. Trompe-l'oeil paintings and murals by local artist Michael Ernest Kirk decorate the common spaces. Another nice touch: free passes to the Museum of Fine Arts and Isabella Stewart Gardner Museum. ⊠*9 Bay State Rd., Kenmore Sq., 02215* ☎*617/375–9003 or 877/375–9003* 🖷*617/425–0716* ⊕*www.gryphonhouseboston.com* ↩*8 suites* ◌*In-room: refrigerator, VCR, Ethernet, Wi-Fi. In-hotel: no elevator, public Internet, parking (no fee)* ▤*AE, D, MC, V* ⍾*CP* ⊺*Kenmore.*

VITAL STATS:

■ Boston's city motto is "God Be with Us as He Was with Our Fathers." (Ralph Emerson wrote a poem with this line as the subtitle.)

■ Boston built the first subway system in 1897—and some locals gripe that the trains look and feel that old, too.

■ Four U.S. presidents were born in Massachusetts's Norfolk County: John Adams, John Quincy Adams, John F. Kennedy, and George H.W. Bush.

■ The Fig Newton was named after nearby Newton, Massachusetts.

THE ARTS

Symphony Hall, one of the world's best acoustical settings—if not *the* best—is home to the Boston Symphony Orchestra (BSO) and the Boston Pops. The BSO is led by the incomparable James Levine, who's known for commissioning special works by contemporary composers, as well as for presenting innovative programs such as his two-year Beethoven/Schoenberg series. The Pops concerts, led by conductor Keith Lockhart, take place in May and June and around the winter holidays. The hall is also used by visiting orchestras, chamber groups, soloists, and many local performers. Rehearsals are sometimes open to the public, with tickets sold at a discount. ⊠ *301 Massachusetts Ave., Back Bay* ☎ *617/266–1492, 617/266–2378 recorded info* ⊕ *www. bostonsymphonyhall.org* Ⓣ *Symphony.*

SHOPPING

Pretty **Charles Street** is crammed beginning to end with top-notch antiques stores such as Judith Dowling Asian Art, Eugene Galleries, and Devonia as well as a handful of independently owned fashion boutiques whose prices reflect their high Beacon Hill rents. River Street, parallel to Charles Street, is also an excellent source for antiques. Both are easy walks from the Charles Street T stop on the Red Line.

Newbury Street (Ⓣ *Arlington, Copley, Hynes/ICA*) is Boston's version of New York's 5th Avenue. The entire street is a shoppers' paradise, from high-end names such as Brooks Brothers to tiny specialty boutiques such as Diptyque. Upscale clothing stores, up-to-the-minute art galleries, and dazzling jewelers line the street near the Public Garden. As you head toward Mass Ave., Newbury gets funkier and the cacophony builds, with skateboarders zipping through traffic and garbage-pail drummers burning licks outside the hip boutiques. The best stores run from Arlington Street to the Prudential Center.

VISITOR INFORMATION

Boston Common Visitor Information Center (⊠ *Tremont St. where the Freedom Trail begins, Downtown* ☎ *617/426–3115*).

Boston National Historical Park Visitor Center (⊠ *15 State St., Downtown* ☎ *617/242–5642* ⊕ *www.nps.gov/bost*).

Cambridge Tourism Office (⊠ *4 Brattle St., Harvard Sq., Cambridge* ☎ *800/862–5678 or 617/441–2884* ⊕ *www.cambridge-usa.org*).

Greater Boston Convention and Visitors Bureau (⊠ *2 Copley Pl., Suite 105, Back Bay* ☎ *888/733–2678 or 617/536–4100* 🖷 *617/424–7664* ⊕ *www.boston usa.com*).

Massachusetts Office of Travel and Tourism (⊠ *State Transportation Bldg., 10 Park Plaza, Suite 4510, Back Bay* ☎ *800/227–6277 or 617/973–8500* 🖷 *617/973–8525* ⊕ *www.massvacation.com*).

Cape Cod

WITH NANTUCKET & MARTHA'S VINEYARD

Nobska Lighthouse, Woods Hole

WORD OF MOUTH

"My husband and I rode the Cape Cod Trail from the start in Dennis to the National Seashore nonstop—lots of fun, and I believe you could stop for ice cream and snacks every two miles if you wanted!"

—JoyInVirginia

"I like Provincetown because the ocean is as much a part of the downtown as are the smells of garlic and wood fires."

—outofblue

www.fodors.com/forums

EXPLORING CAPE COD

By Andrew
Collins

50 mi southeast of Boston, via I–93 to Rte. 3; 60 mi east of Providence, RI, via I–195; 240 mi northeast of New York, NY, via I–95 to I–195; 370 mi southeast of Montréal via Rte. 35 to I–89 to I–93

The hook-shape Cape, comprising a 413-square-mi peninsula that juts into the Atlantic from southeastern Massachusetts, is divided into four geographical regions. The Upper Cape, the somewhat suburban region nearest the Bourne and Sagamore bridges, includes quiet Sandwich and Falmouth, the main ferry hub for Martha's Vineyard. On the Mid-Cape, you can find quiet, wooded hamlets—Barnstable, Yarmouth Port, Dennis—to the north along scenic Route 6A, which is rife with antiques shops and quaint inns. At the southern end, a family-oriented vibe prevails around Hyannis, South Yarmouth, and West Dennis, home to countless motels, restaurants, minigolf courses, and kid-friendly amusements (Hyannis is the main ferry departure point for Nantucket). The Lower Cape is really a microcosm of everything that is Cape Cod. Brewster is a continuation of the subtle, historic charms of Route 6A, while Harwich Port and Orleans both see some commercial exuberance—and excess—along Route 28 and Cape Cod's southern shore. Lightly developed Eastham is the gateway to Cape Cod National Seashore, and blue-blooded Chatham feels like a cross between the tony sections of Falmouth and Sandwich mixed with the restrained elegance of Nantucket. The narrow "forearm" of the Cape—less than 2 mi wide between Cape Cod Bay and the Atlantic Ocean in some spots—includes two of the Cape's least-developed areas, Wellfleet and Truro. U.S. 6 terminates in one of the world's great hubs of bohemian life, Provincetown, which ranks among the nation's leading gay vacation getaways. The Cape is also a stepping-off point for the charmed island summer vacation locales of Martha's Vineyard and Nantucket.

WHO WILL ESPECIALLY LOVE THIS TRIP?

Art & Antiques Shoppers: The Cape's off-the-beaten-path locale and glorious setting helped turn it into a prominent art colony in the mid-19th century. Today its concentration of art galleries is among the highest in the nation. And the Cape's prosperous history as a shipping and whaling center accounts for its plethora of fine antiques shops.

Bicyclists: Despite the heavy summertime traffic, the Cape is quite blessed with bike trails. Off-road, the sandy, pine needle–covered trails of miles of Outer Cape fire roads traverse the National Seashore on the ocean side, from Wellfleet all the way on up to Truro. The Cape's definitive route, the Cape Cod Rail Trail, offers a particularly memorable ride along 22-mi of paved right-of-way of the old Penn Central Railroad. And Falmouth's Shining Sea Trail offers an easy 3½-mi route along the coast, providing views of Vineyard Sound and dipping into oak and pine woods.

Boating & Fishing Enthusiasts: Surrounding the Cape and islands is nothing but pristine, fish-prolific seawater, the perfect milieu for boating or

TOP REASONS TO GO

The Beaches: Whether you explore the golden, dune-backed shore of Cape Cod National Seashore, the sheltered sands of Dennis and Barnstable, or the frothy ocean surf of the islands' southern shores, you can find enough beachfront here to keep you busy for months.

Country Inns: You'll find dozens of rambling, often historic B&Bs—many of them occupying former sea captain's homes—with glorious water views and museum-quality antiques.

The Great Outdoors: Numerous outfitters offer whale-watching and deep-sea-fishing charters, several parks and preserves contain pictur-esque hiking paths through gardens and woodlands, and bike paths lace the entire peninsula and the islands.

The Arts and Crafts: Creative spirits have long been drawn to the region's comparative isolation and inspired views, and you can browse their creations at countless galleries, many of them concentrated in Provincetown, Wellfleet, and on the islands.

The Food: It's not just casual lobster shacks and ice-cream stands around here—the Cape and islands abound with romantic, upscale eateries helmed by talented chefs preparing innovative seafood and regional American fare.

casting a line. Kayaking outfitters provide tours on Martha's Vineyard and in Barnstable and Yarmouth, and whale-watching boats leave regularly from Provincetown and Hyannis (both towns also have sunset and party cruises). Even just hopping the ferry out to or among the islands affords visitors a scenic change to commune with the sea and its expansive views.

Families: Cape Cod seems almost purpose-designed for families, and you can find plenty of kid-friendly accommodations and restaurants as well as all-ages activities throughout the region. The area with the strongest pull for families on the Cape is Route 28, from about Hyannis to Harwich Port, where you can find an especially high number of amusements and motor lodges geared toward families.

Gays & Lesbians: Provincetown, at the tip of the Cape, is one of the East Coast's leading lesbian and gay seaside destinations, and it also has a large year-round lesbian and gay community. Dozens of P-town establishments, from B&Bs to bars, cater specifically to lesbian and gay visitors, and all of the town's restaurants are gay-friendly; many are gay-owned and -operated. Hyannis has Cape Cod's sole gay bar outside P-town, but attitudes throughout Cape Cod tend to be extremely accepting and tolerant toward gays and lesbians.

Seafood Lovers: It should go without saying that a land named for a delicious type of fish would abound with opportunities to sample tasty seafood, and indeed, Cape Cod does not disappoint. Some of New England's most creative and talented chefs work in high-end restaurants on the Cape and the islands, but you can indulge in fresh local seafood and clambakes at seat-yourself shanties and even retail fish markets for a much lower price than their fine-dining counterparts.

How to Snack

The Cape, perhaps unsurprisingly, is known as much for seafood as for any other kind of taste treat, and there are a number of spots in the area that make for such perfect short-order snacks as lobster rolls, lobster bisque, clam rolls, and clam chowder. Try **Mac's Seafood** (Wellfleet Town Pier, Wellfleet, 508/349-0404), a takeout joint with perfect views of the sailboats and fishing trawlers in Wellfleet Harbor; **Sir Cricket's Fish and Chips** (Rte. 6A, near Stop & Shop, Orleans, 508/255-4453), a no-frills shanty in Orleans with tantalizing oyster rolls; **Osterville Fish Too** (275 Mill Way, Barnstable, 508/362-2295), a casual spot with an open-air deck overlooking Barnstable Harbor; **Baxter's Fish N' Chips** (Pleasant St., Hyannis, 508/775-4490), a quirky spot that's been doling out delicious short-order seafood since 1955; or **The Clam Shack** (227 Clinton Ave., Falmouth, 508/540-7758), known for its fried-seafood platters and hefty lobster rolls, plus a lovely location by Falmouth Harbor.

On Martha's Vineyard, your best bets for similarly enticing quick-bite seafood fare are **Net Result** (Tisbury Marketplace, 79 Beach Rd., Vineyard Haven, 508/693-6071) and **The Bite** (29 Basin Rd., Menemsha, 508/645-9239), in the picturesque fishing village of Menemsha. Nantucket's best bet for similar fare is **The Tavern** (1 Harbor Sq., Straight Wharf, 508/228-1266), at Straight Wharf in Nantucket Town—the water views from the deck make it especially pleasing.

WHEN IS THE BEST TIME TO VISIT?

Memorial Day through Labor Day (or, in some cases, Columbus Day) is high season on Cape Cod. In summer everything is open for business on the Cape, but you can also expect high-season evils: high prices, crowds, and traffic. The entire region, however—including the islands—-is becoming increasingly popular year-round.

The region enjoys fairly moderate weather most of the year, with highs typically in the upper 70s and 80s in summer, and in the upper 30s and lower 40s in winter. Snow and rain are not uncommon during the cooler months, and it can be windy any time of year, but even then the landscape here can be wonderfully dramatic.

HOW SHOULD I GET THERE?

BOAT

Ferries can play a significant role on the Cape, and a vital role in getting among the islands. **Bay State Cruise Company** (617/748-1428 *www. baystatecruisecompany.com*)and **Boston Harbor Cruises** (617/227-4321 or 877/733-9425 *www.bostonharborcruises.com*)both offer high-speed ferry service from Boston to Provincetown late spring to mid-October. Year-round, several companies offer year-round or seasonal ferry service between the Cape and Martha's Vineyard: **Hy-Line** (Ocean St. dock 508/778-2600 or 800/492-8082 *www.hy-linecruises.com*)Island Queen (Falmouth Harbor 508/548-

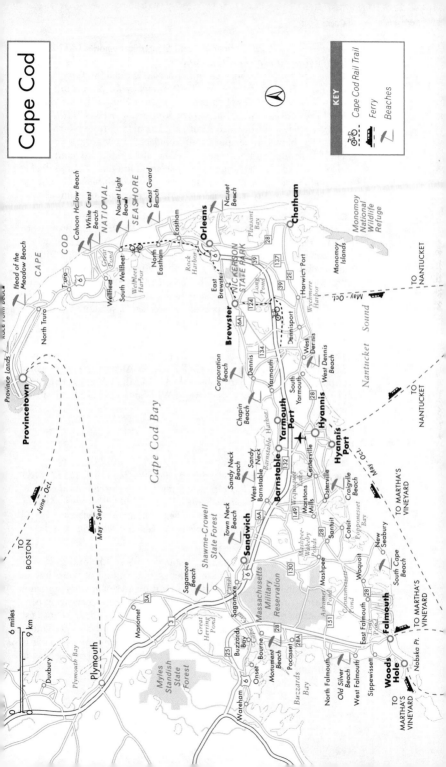

Cape Cod

KEY

🚲 Cape Cod Rail Trail

⛴ Ferry

Beaches

6 miles
9 km

TO BOSTON

Plymouth

Duxbury

Plymouth Bay

Manomet

Myles Standish State Forest

Wareham

Onset

Buzzards Bay

Bourne

Pocasset

Buzzards Bay

North Falmouth

West Falmouth

Sippewissett

Old Silver Beach

Monument Beach

Great Herring Pond

Sagamore

Sagamore Beach

Shawme-Crowell State Forest

Massachusetts Military Reservation

Ashumet Pond

Coonamesset Pond

East Falmouth

Falmouth

Woods Hole

Nobska Pt.

TO MARTHA'S VINEYARD

TO MARTHA'S VINEYARD

Mashpee-Wakeby Ponds

Mashpee

Waquoit

New Seabury

Cotuit

Santuit

Cataumet

Marstons Mills

Osterville

Centerville

Craigville Beach

Popponesset Bay

South Cape Beach

TO MARTHA'S VINEYARD

May-Oct.

Town Neck Beach

Sandwich

Sandy Neck Beach

West Barnstable

Sandy Neck

Barnstable Harbor

Barnstable

Yarmouth Port

Hyannis

Hyannis Port

TO NANTUCKET

Cape Cod Bay

Chapin Beach

Corporation Beach

Dennis

Yarmouth

South Yarmouth

West Yarmouth

Dennisport

West Dennis

West Dennis Beach

Harwich Port

Wychmere Harbor

Nantucket Sound

May-Oct.

TO NANTUCKET

Province Lands

Provincetown

June-Oct.

Head of the Meadow Beach

North Truro

Truro

CAPE COD

Great Pond

Wellfleet

South Wellfleet

Wellfleet Harbor

NATIONAL SEASHORE

Cahoon Hollow Beach

White Crest Beach

Nauset Light Beach

Coast Guard Beach

North Eastham

Eastham

Rock Harbor

Orleans

Nauset Beach

Pleasant Bay

Brewster

East Brewster

NICKERSON STATE PARK

Long Pond

Chatham

Monomoy National Wildlife Refuge

Monomoy Islands

May-Oct.

TO NANTUCKET

4800 ⊕www.islandqueen.com), and **Steamship Authority** (☎*508/477–8600 information and car reservations, 508/693–9130 on the Vineyard* ⊕*www.steamshipauthority.com*).Also, **New England Fast Ferry** (⊠*State Pier Ferry Terminal* ☎*866/683–3779* ⊕*www.nefastferry.com*)has seasonal service from New Bedford to Martha's Vineyard, and **Vineyard Fast Ferry** (⊠*Quonset Point, North Kingstown, RI* ☎*401/295–4040* ⊕*www.vineyardfastferry.com*)runs a seasonal ferry from North Kingstown, RI (between Newport and Providence) to Martha's Vineyard. The Steamship Authority and Hy-Line also run year-round ferries to Nantucket from Hyannis, and **Freedom Cruise Line** (⊠*Saquatucket Harbor, Harwich Port* ☎*508/432–8999* ⊕*www.nantucketislandferry.com*)runs seasonally from Harwich Port on the Cape to Nantucket.

CAR
Cape Cod is easily reached from Boston by Route 3 and Providence via I–195. Once you cross Cape Cod Canal, you're on the Cape, where you can take the main highway, U.S. 6, all the way to the tip. Without any traffic, it takes just about an hour to 90 minutes from Boston and Providence to reach the Upper (nearest to mainland Massachusetts) portion of the Cape, but keep in mind that delays onto and off the Cape are common all summer, especially on weekends, so allow an extra 30 to 60 minutes travel time.

PLANE
The major gateways to Cape Cod are Boston's Logan International Airport (BOS) and Providence's T. F. Green Airport (PVD). Smaller airports include the Barnstable (HYA), Martha's Vineyard (MVY), Nantucket (ACK), New Bedford (EWB), and Provincetown (PVC) municipal airports.

HOW DO I GET AROUND?

BY BUS
Cape Cod Regional Transit Authority (☎*508/790–2613 or 800/352–7155* ⊕*www.capecodtransit.org*)provides bus service throughout the Cape. **Martha's Vineyard Transit Authority** (*VTA* ☎*508/693–9940* ⊕*www.vineyardtransit.com*)and**Nantucket Regional Transit Authority (NRTA)** (☎*508/228–7025* ⊕*www.shuttlenantucket.com*)serve the islands.

BY CAR
Although traffic can be intense in summer, it's still helpful to have a car on the Cape, unless you're planning to spend all of your time in one community. Certain towns, such as Provincetown, Chatham, and Wellfleet are relatively easy to get around on foot. Also, cars are expensive to bring to Nantucket and Martha's Vineyard by ferry, so it's best just to rely on taxis and buses on the islands, or rent a car once you're there. Fall, winter, and spring, traffic subsides greatly and parking is easier—it makes more sense to use a car on the Cape and on the Islands at that time.

WHERE SHOULD I FOCUS MY ENERGY?

If you're here for 1 day: The Cape is sizable with much to see, so with just a day head to Provincetown via the ferry from Boston or by car up U.S. 6—stopping at a couple of interesting towns, such as Barnstable or Orleans. In Provincetown, partake of the many shops, galleries, and restaurants.

If you're here for 2 days: It's still best to base your operations in Provincetown, but spend the extra day exploring the dunes of Cape Cod National Seashore, and checking out the galleries and quirky shops of offbeat Wellfleet.

If you're here for 3 days: Add the charming, upscale town of Chatham to your itinerary, spending a night here at one of the historic inns and admiring the view from the iconic Chatham Light.

If you're here for 4 days: Spend two nights in Provincetown and two nights in Chatham, plan either a whale-watching cruise out of Provincetown, a guided boat trip to Monomoy National Wildlife Refuge from Chatham, or an excursion around local waters from Hyannis (not far from Chatham).

If you're here for 5 days: Add Falmouth to your plans, spending a night at one of the several fine inns downtown, and visiting Woods Hole, with its Oceanographic Institution, Marine Biology Laboratory, and National Marine Fisheries Service Aquarium.

If you're here for 6 days: From Falmouth, take the ferry to Martha's Vineyard, either spending a full day there touring the island or spending the night there.

If you're here for 7 days or more: With a week or more, you have time to spend at least five or six days on different parts of the Cape, and also spend a couple of days or more both on Martha's Vineyard and Nantucket.

CLAIM TO FAME

At the Baseball Hall of Fame in Cooperstown, New York, you can find a poster announcing a showdown between arch rivals Sandwich and Barnstable. The date? July 4, 1885. In the 100-plus years since that day, the Cape's ballplaying tradition has continued unabated, and if you're a sports fan, a visit to a Cape Cod Baseball League summer game is a must. To see a game on the Cape is to come into contact with baseball's roots. You'll remember why you love the sport and you'll have a newfound sense of why it became the national pastime.

WHAT ARE THE TOP EXPERIENCES?

The Beaches: Cape Cod has more than 150 beaches, enough to keep inveterate beachcombers happy—and covered in sand—all year long. Bay-side beaches generally have more temperate waters and gentler waves. South-side beaches, on Nantucket Sound, have rolling surf and, though still a bit chilly, are moderated by the Gulf Stream. Inland, you can find dozens of freshwater ponds, many with warm water and sandy beaches ideal for kids. The Cape Cod National Seashore offers the greatest "wow" factor: chilly water, serious surf, long and wide expanses of sand, magnificent dunes, and mesmerizing views.

Ice-Cream & Candy Shops: However you spend the day on Cape Cod— whether beachcombing or biking, sailing or sidewalk shopping—break up the action with a sweet treat from one of the region's many distinctive ice-cream and sweets shops. Avoid ubiquitous franchise operations, and try to stick with parlors selling homemade ice cream—there are plenty to choose from.

The Historic Inns: The Cape and islands are blessed with countless colonial and Victorian houses, many of them having been transformed into spectacular inns. In some cases you can only appreciate these establishments by spending the night, but others offer refined dining in beam-ceiling dining rooms with wide-plank floorboards and occasionally romantic views of the sea or a beguiling village center.

The Lighthouses: In addition to traditional Cape-style houses, Cape Cod is known for another distinctive architectural type: lighthouses. You can find them up and down the Cape and out on the islands, some still active, others decommissioned. Each has its own personality and profile. There's Highland Light in Truro, the Cape's oldest. Eastham's oft-photographed Nauset Light ranks among the most beautiful, and both Chatham Light and Falmouth's Nobska Light afford some of the best views. In Martha's Vineyard, be sure to journey out to Aquinnah Lighthouse, which stands atop a bluff above the beach and crashing surf. On Nantucket, there's Brand Point Light, built in 1902. It's definitely worth ascending any lighthouse open for tours .

BEST BETS

SIGHTS AND TOURS

CAPE COD

Fodor'sChoice **Art's Dune Tours** (⊠ *Commercial and Standish Sts., Downtown Center,* ★ *Provincetown* ☎ *508/487–1950* ⊕ *www.artsdunetours.com*)has been taking eager passengers into the dunes of Province Lands since 1946. Bumpy but controlled rides transport you through sometimes surreal sandy vistas peppered with beach grass and along shoreline patrolled by seagulls and sandpipers.

One of Yarmouth Port's most beautiful areas is Bass Hole, which ★ stretches from Homer's Dock Road to the salt marsh. **Bass Hole Boardwalk** ℭ (⊠ *Trail entrance on Center St. near Gray's Beach parking lot*)extends over a marshy creek; amid the salt marshes, vegetated wetlands, and upland woods meander the 2½-mi **Callery-Darling nature trails.**

Fodor'sChoice For nature enthusiasts, a visit to the **Cape Cod Museum of Natural His-** ★ **tory** is a must; it's just a short drive west from the heart of Brewster ℭ along Route 6A. The spacious museum and pristine grounds include guided field walks, a shop, a natural-history library, lectures, classes, nature and marine exhibits such as a working beehive, and a pond- and sea-life room with live specimens. ⊠*869 Main St. (Rte. 6A), West Brewster* ☎*508/896–3867, 800/479–3867 in Massachusetts* ⊕*www.ccmnh.org* 🎫*$8* ⊙*Oct.– Apr., Wed.–Sun. 11–3; Apr. and May, Wed.–Sun. 10–4; June–Sept., daily 10–4.*

Fodor's Choice

★

🔆

The Cape's most expansive national treasure, the 27,000-acre **Cape Cod National Seashore,** extends from Chatham to Provincetown, encompassing and protecting 30 mi of superb ocean beaches; great rolling dunes; swamps, marshes, and wetlands; pitch-pine and scrub-oak forest; all kinds of wildlife; and a number of historic structures. The seashore's **Salt Pond Visitor Center** (⊠*Doane Rd. off U.S. 6* ☎*508/255–3421* ⊕*www.nps.gov/caco*)is in Eastham, and the **Province Lands Visitor Center** (⊠*Race Point Rd., east of U.S. 6* ☎*508/487–1256*)is in Provincetown.

★ The famous view from **Chatham Light** (⊠*Main St. near Bridge St., West Chatham*)—of the harbor, the offshore sandbars, and the ocean beyond—justifies the crowds that gather to share it.

★ For a peek into the past, make a stop at **Hallet's,** a country drugstore preserved as it was in 1889 ⊠*139 Main St. (Rte. 6A), Yarmouth Port* ☎*508/362–3362* ⊙*Apr.–mid-Nov.; call for hrs.*

Fodor's Choice

★

🔆

Heritage Museums and Gardens, 100 beautifully landscaped acres overlooking the upper end of Shawme Pond, includes gardens and a café as well as an impressive complex of museum buildings with specialty collections ranging from cars to toys. The American History museum houses the Cape Cod Baseball League Hall of Fame. The art museum has a working 1912 Coney Island–style carousel that both adults and little ones can ride as often as they like. ⊠*67 Grove St., Sandwich* ☎*508/888–3300* ⊕*www.heritagemuseumsandgardens.org* 🎫*$12* ⊙*Apr.–Nov., daily 10–5; Nov.–Mar., call for very limited hrs.*

In Main Street's Old Town Hall, the **John F. Kennedy Hyannis Museum** explores JFK's Cape years (1934–63) through enlarged and annotated photographs culled from the archives of the JFK Library near Boston, as well as a seven-minute video narrated by Walter Cronkite. ⊠*397 Main St., Downtown Hyannis* ☎*508/790–3077* ⊕*www.jfkhyannis museum. org* 🎫*$5* ⊙*Memorial Day–Oct., Mon.–Sat. 9–5, Sun. noon–5; Nov.– early Dec. and mid-Feb.–mid-Apr., Thurs.–Sat. 10–4, Sun. noon–4. Closed Jan.*

HISTORY YOU CAN SEE

The Cape was the initial North American landing spot of the Pilgrims, who dropped anchor in Provincetown on Monday, November 21, 1620, after a difficult 63-day transatlantic voyage. While in the harbor the passengers signed the Mayflower Compact, the first document to declare a democratic form of government in America. One of the first things the ever-practical Pilgrims did was come ashore to wash their clothes, beginning the ages-old New England tradition of Monday wash day. They lingered for five weeks before moving on to Plymouth.

3

A trip to the Outer Cape isn't complete without a visit to the **Massachusetts Audubon Wellfleet Bay Wildlife Sanctuary,** an 1,100-acre haven for more than 250 species of birds attracted by the varied habitats found here. ⊠ *291 U.S. 6, South Wellfleet* ☎ *508/349–2615* ⊕ *www.wellfleetbay.org* ⚍ *$5* ⊘ *Trails daily 8* AM *–dusk; nature center late May–mid-Oct., daily 8:30–5; mid-Oct.–late May, Tues.–Sun. 8:30–5.*

Fodor'sChoice
★

Fodor'sChoice
★
Monomoy National Wildlife Refuge is a 2,500-acre preserve including the Monomoy Islands, a fragile 9-mi-long barrier-beach area south of Chatham. This is a quiet, peaceful place of sand and beach grass, tidal flats, dunes, marshes, freshwater ponds, thickets of bayberry and beach plum, and a few pines. ⊠ *Off Morris Island Rd., Morris Island, near Chatham* ☎ *508/945–0594* ⊕ *http://monomoy.fws.gov*

Fodor'sChoice
★
⚙
The compact **National Marine Fisheries Service Aquarium** displays 16 tanks of regional fish and shellfish in several rooms, cramped but nonetheless crammed with stuff to see. The top attraction is two harbor seals, on view in the outdoor pool near the entrance in summer; you can watch their feedings weekdays at 11 and 4. ⊠ *Albatross and Water Sts., Falmouth* ☎ *508/495–2267, 508/495–2001 recorded information* ⊕ *www.nefsc.nmfs.gov/nefsc/aquarium* ⚍ *Free* ⊘ *June–Aug., Tues.–Sat. 11–4; call for hrs off-season.*

★
The first thing you'll see in Provincetown is the **Pilgrim Monument.** This grandiose edifice commemorates the Pilgrims' first landing in the New World and their signing of the Mayflower Compact. ⊠ *High Pole Hill Rd.* ☎ *508/487–1310* ⊕ *www.pilgrim-monument.org* ⚍ *$7* ⊘ *Early Apr.–June and Sept.–Oct., daily 9–4:15; July and Aug., daily 9–6:15; Nov., weekends 9–4:15.*

Fodor'sChoice
★
Founded in 1914 to collect and show the works of artists with Provincetown connections, the **Provincetown Art Association and Museum** *(PAAM)* has a 1,650-piece permanent collection, displayed in changing exhibits that mix up-and-comers with established 20th-century figures. ⊠ *460 Commercial St., East End* ☎ *508/487–1750* ⊕ *www.paam.org* ⚍ *$3 donation suggested* ⊘ *Late May–early July and Sept., daily noon–5, also Fri. and Sat. 8* PM *–10* PM; *early July and Aug., daily noon–5 and 8* PM *–10* PM; *Oct.–May, Thurs.–Sun. noon–5.*

The **Sandwich Glass Museum,** with its 9,000 square feet of exhibits, has information about the history of the company, including an "ingredient room" showcasing a wide spectrum of glass colors along with the minerals added to the sand to obtain them, and an outstanding collection of blown and pressed glass in many shapes and shimmering hues. Glassmaking demonstrations are held in summer. ⊠*129 Main St., Sandwich Center* ☎*508/888–0251* ⊕*www.sandwichglassmuseum. org* ☜*$4.75* ☉*Apr.–Dec., daily 9:30–5; Feb. and Mar., Wed.–Sun. 9:30–4.*

Fodor'sChoice
★
☾
The **Thornton W. Burgess Museum** is dedicated to the Sandwich native whose tales of Peter Cottontail, Reddy Fox, and a host of other creatures of the Old Briar Patch have been part of children's bedtimes for decades. Storytelling sessions, often including the live animal that the Burgess story is about, take place regularly in July and August. In the Discovery Room, kids can use their imaginations in the prop-filled classroom. ⊠*4 Water St. (Rte. 130), Sandwich Center* ☎*508/888– 4668* ⊕*www.thorntonburgess.org* ☜*Donations accepted* ☉*May– Oct., Mon.–Sat. 10–4, Sun. 1–4.*

NANTUCKET
The **Maria Mitchell Association** (*MMA* ⊠*4 Vestal St., Nantucket Town* ☎*508/228–0898* ⊕*www.mmo.org*)leads marine-ecology field trips and nature and bird walks weekly in spring and early summer and three times a week from June through Labor Day.

★
☾
The **Nantucket Atheneum,** Nantucket's town library, is a great white Greek Revival building, with a windowless façade and fluted Ionic columns. Completed in 1847 to replace a structure lost to the 1846 fire, it's one of the oldest libraries in continuous service in the United States. ⊠*1 India St., Nantucket Town* ☎*508/228–1110* ⊕*www.nantucketatheneum.org* ☉*Late May–early Sept., Mon., Wed., Fri., and Sat. 9:30–5; Tues. and Thurs. 9:30–8; early Sept.–late May, Tues. and Thurs. 9:30–8, Wed., Fri., and Sat. 9:30–5.*

Fodor'sChoice
★
☾
Immersing you in Nantucket's whaling past with exhibits that include a fully rigged whaleboat and a skeleton of a 46-foot sperm whale, the **Whaling Museum**—a complex that includes a restored 1846 spermaceti candle factory—is a must-see. ⊠*13–15 Broad St., Nantucket Town* ☎*508/228– 1894* ☜*$15 or NHA Combination Pass* ☉*Jan.–mid-Apr., Fri.–Sun. 11–4; mid-Apr.–mid-May and mid-Oct.–mid-Dec., Thurs.–Mon. 11–4; mid-May–mid-Oct., Mon.–Wed., Fri.–Sun. 10–5, Thurs. 10–8.*

MARTHA'S VINEYARD
Fodor'sChoice
★
A National Historic Landmark, the spectacular **Aquinnah Cliffs** are dramatically striated walls of red clay; this is one of the island's major attractions.. ⊠*State Rd.*

☾
A National Historic Landmark, the **Flying Horses Carousel** is the nation's oldest continuously operating carousel; it was handcrafted in 1876 (the horses have real horse hair and glass eyes). ⊠*Oak Bluffs Ave., Oak Bluffs* ☎*508/693–9481* ☜*Rides $1.50, book of 8 tickets $10* ☉*Late May–early Sept., daily 10–10; Easter–late May, weekends 10–5; early Sept.–mid-Oct., weekdays 11–4:30, weekends 10–5.*

★
Stop at a complex of buildings and lawn exhibits that constitutes the **Martha's Vineyard Historical Society** to orient yourself historically before making your way around town. ⊠*Cooke and School Sts., Edgartown*

☎508/627–4441 ⊕www.marthasvineyardhistory.org ☒$7 ☉Mid-Mar.–mid-June and early Oct.–late Dec., Wed.–Fri. 1–4, Sat. 10–4; mid-June–early Oct., Tues.–Sat. 10–5; early Jan.–mid-Mar., Sat. 10–4.

Fodor'sChoice ★ The Trustees of Reservations' 14-acre **Mytoi** preserve is a serene, beautifully tended, Japanese-inspired garden with a creek-fed pool spanned by a bridge and rimmed with Japanese maples, azaleas, bamboo, and irises. ☒Dike Rd., [1//5] mi from intersection with Chappaquiddick Rd. ☎508/627–7689 ☒Free ☉Daily dawn–dusk.

★ Don't miss **Oak Bluffs Campground**, a 34-acre warren of streets tightly packed with more than 300 Carpenter Gothic Victorian cottages with wedding-cake trim, gaily painted in pastels. ☒Off Circuit Ave., Oak Bluffs ☎508/693–0525 ⊕www.mvcma.org/ ☒Tour $10.

★ A rich and expansive collection of flora and serene walking trails are the attractions of the **Polly Hill Arboretum**. Horticulturist and part-time Vineyard resident Polly Hill, now in her nineties, has over the years tended some 2,000 species of plants and developed nearly 100 species herself on her old sheep farm in West Tisbury. ☒809 State Rd., West Tisbury ☎508/693–9426 ⊕www.pollyhillarboretum.org ☒$5 ☉Grounds daily dawn–dusk. Visitor center late May–mid-Oct., daily 9:30–4; guided tours by appointment.

One of two lighthouses that mark the opening to Vineyard Haven Harbor, the 52-foot white-and-black West Chop Lighthouse was built of brick in 1838 to replace an 1817 wood building. E W. Chop Rd. (Main St.)

WHERE TO EAT

	WHAT IT COSTS				
	¢	$	$$	$$$	$$$$
RESTAURANTS	under $10	$10–$16	$16–$22	$22–$30	over $30

Restaurant prices are per person for a main course at dinner.

CAPE COD

$$$$
Fodor'sChoice
★
✗**Chillingsworth.** One of the crown jewels of Cape restaurants, Chillingsworth combines formal presentation with an excellent French menu and a diverse wine cellar to create a memorable dining experience. Super-rich risotto, roast lobster, and grilled Angus sirloin are favorites. Dinner in the main dining rooms is prix fixe and includes seven courses—appetizer, soup, salad, sorbet, entrée, "amusements," and dessert, plus coffee or tea. Less expensive à la carte options for lunch, dinner, and Sunday brunch are served in the more casual, patio-style Bistro. ☒2449 Main St. (Rte. 6A), East Brewster ☎508/896–3640 ⊕www.chillingsworth.com ☐AE, DC, MC, V ☉Closed Thanksgiving–mid-May.

$$$–$$$$
Fodor'sChoice
★
✗**Regatta of Cotuit.** It's worth driving out of your way to this refined restaurant in a handsomely restored cinnamon-hued stagecoach inn filled with wood, brass, and Oriental rugs. Chef Heather Allen turns out won-

LIKE A LOCAL

Great weather isn't always a sure thing on the Cape. But when the weather doesn't cooperate, do as the locals do:

■ Go storm-watching. If it's a windy, exciting storm, grab lunch at a waterfront restaurant and enjoy watching the dramatically crashing surf outside your window.

■ Sample some fine wines. In East Falmouth, Cape Cod Winery produces six well-respected wines.

■ Take a whale-watching trip. Two well-known Provincetown whale-

watching tour operators—Dolphin Fleet and Portuguese Princess—offer these trips rain or shine, as does Hyannis's Whale Watcher Cruises.

■ Go for a walk on the beach. You won't encounter big crowds, and you may see some interesting wildlife.

■ Take some pictures. Cape Cod offers plenty of intriguing photo-ops in the rain, from windswept sand dunes at Cape Cod National Seashore to dramatic street scenes in Provincetown and Dennis.

derfully inventive versions of classic regional American fare, such as foie gras and scallops with a port-wine reduction and tropical-fruit chutney. The signature premium fillet of buffalo tenderloin is prepared differently each night, with seasonal starches and vegetables. ⊠ *4631 Falmouth Rd. (Rte. 28), Cotuit* 🕾 *508/428–5715* ⊕ *www.regattaofcotuit.com* ⚑ *Reservations essential* ▤ *AE, MC, V.*

$$–$$$$ ✕ **Devon's.** This unassuming, tiny white cottage—with a dining room
Fodor'sChoice   that seats just 42 lucky patrons—serves up some of the best food in
★   Provincetown. Specialties from the oft-changing menu include pan-seared halibut with caramelized orange glaze, black rice, and sautéed beet greens; and free-range seared duck with a Syrah reduction, red-onion marmalade, and couscous primavera. Be sure to save some room for knockout dessert selections like blackberry mousse over ginger-lemon polenta cake with wildberry coulis. Devon's also serves up a terrific breakfast each day until 1 PM. ⊠ *401½ Commercial St., Provincetown* 🕾 *508/487–4773* ⊕ *www.devons.org* ⚑ *Reservations essential* ▤ *MC, V* ⦵ *Closed Wed. and Nov.–Apr.*

$$–$$$ ✕ **La Cucina Sul Mare.** Northern Italian and Mediterranean cooking is
Fodor'sChoice   the specialty at this classy, popular place. The staff is friendly and the
★   setting is both intimate and festive, if a bit crowded. Calamari, warm green salad with goat cheese and cranberries, a classic lemon chicken sautéed with shallots and capers, and a variety of specials—including plenty of local fresh fish—adorn the menu. The *zuppa de pesce,* a medley of seafood sautéed in olive oil and garlic and finished in a white wine herb-and-tomato broth, is a specialty. ⊠ *237 Main St. (Rte. 28), Falmouth* 🕾 *508/548–5600* ⚑ *No reservations* ▤ *AE, D, MC, V.*

$$–$$$ ✕ **Naked Oyster.** The big draw at this dapper restaurant with dark-
Fodor'sChoice   wood-paneled walls and soft lighting is the extensive list of weekly
★   changing specials, which truly show off the kitchen's estimable talents. You'll always find several raw and "dressed" oyster dishes (such as barbecue oysters on the half shell with blue cheese, caramelized onions,

and bacon) plus a nice range of salads and appetizers. Among the main dishes, consider the superb sliced duck breast with a port-wine and Rainier cherry sauce, or the sautéed shrimp in a piquant Thai peanut-cashew sauce over noodles. The oyster stew is also out of this world. ⊠*20 Independence Dr., off Rte. 132, Hyannis* ☎*508/778–6500* ⊟*AE, D, DC, MC, V* ⊗*No lunch weekends.*

> ## ON THE WAY
>
> **Plimoth Plantation:** One of America's most celebrated living-history museums, this painstakingly re-created village staffed by costumed "residents" tells the legacy of the Pilgrims. Warren Ave., Plymouth, 508/748–1622, www.plimoth.org., $21 admission.

$$–$$$
Fodor's Choice
★
✕**Pisces.** An intimate dining room inside a simple yellow house not far from the Harwich border, Pisces, as its name suggests, serves coastal-inspired fare—if it swims in local waters, you can probably sample it here. A rich chowder of lobster, butternut squash, and corn is a terrific way to start your meal. Move on to Mediterranean-style fisherman's stew in saffron-lobster broth, or roasted cod with a simple but flavorful dressing of tomatoes, capers, lemon, and olive oil. ⊠*2653 Main St., South Chatham* ☎*508/432–4600* ⊟*MC, V* ⊙*Closed Dec.–Mar. No lunch.*

$–$$$
Fodor's Choice
★
✕**Wicked Oyster.** In a rambling, gray clapboard house just off U.S. 6 on the main road into Wellfleet village, the Wicked Oyster serves up the most innovative fare in Wellfleet. Try the rosemary-and-scallion-crusted half rack of lamb over roasted-shallot-and-garlic potato salad, or the local mussels in tomato broth with smoky bacon, cilantro, jalapeño, and lime. Oyster stew and the Harry's Bar open-face burger (with caramelized onions, fresh mozzarella, and Worcestershire mayonnaise) are among the top lunch dishes. Breakfast is a favorite here—try the smoked salmon Benedict. ⊠*50 Main St., Wellfleet* ☎*508/349–3455* ⊟*AE, D, MC, V* ⊗*No dinner Wed.*

¢–$$$
Fodor's Choice
★
✕**Clem & Ursie's.** It's worth the short drive or long walk from downtown Provincetown to sample the tantalizing seafood prepared at this colorful café, grocery market, cocktail bar, and bakery. The mammoth menu touches on just about every kind of food from the ocean: tuna steaks, crab claws, squid stew, Japanese baby octopus salad, hot lobster rolls, lobster scampi. The Buffalo shrimp are addictive, and be sure to try the Portuguese clam pie. A nice range of nonfishy items is offered, too, from pulled-pork barbecue to bacon cheeseburgers—plus great desserts like pistachio cake and stuffed ice-cream sandwiches dipped in chocolate. ⊠*85 Shank Painter Rd., Provincetown* ☎*508/487–2333* ⊕*www.clemandursies.com* ⊟*MC, V* ⊙*Closed mid-Nov.–mid-Apr.*

$–$$
Fodor's Choice
★
✕**Cap'n Frosty's.** A great stop after the beach, this is where locals go to get their fried seafood. This modest joint has a regular menu that includes ice cream, a small specials board, and a counter where you order and take a number written on a french-fries box. The staff is young and hard working, pumping out fresh fried clams and fish-and-chips on paper plates. ⊠*219 Main St. (Rte. 6A), Dennis Village* ☎*508/385–8548* ⊿*Reservations not accepted* ⊟*MC, V* ⊙*Closed early Sept.–Mar.*

NANTUCKET

$$$–$$$$
FodorsChoice
★

✕**Straight Wharf.** This loftlike restaurant with harborside deck has enjoyed legendary status since the mid-'70s, when chef Marion Morash used to get a helping hand from culinary buddy Julia Child. The young couple who took over in 2006—Gabriel Frasca and Amanda Lydon—were fast-rising stars on the Boston restaurant scene, but their approach here is the antithesis of flashy. If anything, they have lent this venerable institution a more barefoot air, appropriate to the place and season—hurricane lamps lend a soft glow to well-spaced tables lined with butcher paper; dish towels serve as napkins. Intense champions of local produce and catches, Frasca and Lydon concoct stellar dishes like lobster-stuffed zucchini flowers with saffron–tomato vinaigrette, and line-caught swordfish in a vaguely Moroccan melange of golden raisins, pine nuts, and mint. ⊠ *6 Harbor Sq., Straight Wharf, Nantucket Town* ☎ *508/228–4499* ⊟*AE, MC, V* ⊘*Closed mid-Oct.–mid-May.*

MARTHA'S VINEYARD

$$$–$$$$
FodorsChoice
★

✕**Lure.** The airy restaurant at Winnetu Oceanside Resort draws plenty of discerning diners, including plenty of nonhotel guests, to sample some of the most exquisite and creatively prepared seafood on the island. It's the only dining room with a south-facing water view, and it's a stunning one at that. You won't find a better lobster dish on the island than Lure's tender butter-poached version topped with roasted corn and fava beans and served alongside buttery cornbread. Locally caught fluke with littleneck clams, leeks, smoked bacon, and a rich chowder broth is another star. Finish off with the molten Valhrona chocolate cake with vanilla ice cream and raspberry coulis. ⊠ *Katama Rd., Edgartown* ☎ *508/627–3663* ⊟*AE, D, MC, V* ⊘*No lunch.*

WHERE TO STAY

WHAT IT COSTS				
¢	$	$$	$$$	$$$$
HOTELS under $90	$90–$140	$140–$200	$200–$260	over $260

Hotel prices are for a standard double room, excluding 6% sales tax (more in some counties) and 1%–4% tourist tax.

CAPE COD

$$$$
FodorsChoice
★

✕🏠**Wequassett Inn Resort & Golf Club.** Twenty Cape-style cottages and an attractive hotel make up this traditionally elegant resort by the sea. On 22 acres of shaded landscape partially surrounded by Pleasant Bay, the Wequassett is an informally upscale resort. An attentive staff, evening entertainment, fun in the sun, and golf at the exclusive Cape Cod National Golf Club are just a few of the benefits you can count on at Wequassett. Chef Bill Brodsky's creative globally inspired cuisine graces the menus of the three restaurants—the star being the sophisticated 28 Atlantic ($$$–$$$$), which is one of the top destination restaurants on the Cape, serving such stellar creations as yellowfin and salmon tartare, and caramelized skate wing with beet-daikon-horseradish salad and watercress jus. ⊠*2173 Orleans Rd. (Rte. 28) 02633* ☎*508/432–5400*

or 800/225–7125 🖶 *508/432–5032*
⊕*www.wequassett.com* ⬅*102*
rooms, 2 suites ⭗*In-hotel: 3 res-*
taurants, room service, bar, tennis
courts, pool, gym, water sports,
children's programs, no elevator
🖃*AE, D, DC, MC, V* ⊘*Closed*
Nov.–Mar. ◉*FAP.*

VITAL STATS:

■ State Capital: Boston, founded in 1630, and 60 mi northwest of Cape Cod.

■ State Motto: Ense petit placidam sub libertate quietem (By the sword we seek peace, but peace only under liberty.)

■ State Fish: What else? Cod.

■ State Historical Rock: Plymouth Rock

$$–$$$$
Fodor'sChoice
★

✕ 🖼 **Belfry Inne & Bistro.** This delight-
ful one-of-a-kind inn comprises
a 1902 former church, an ornate
wood-frame Victorian, and an
1830 Federal-style house clustered
on a main campus. Room themes in
each building nod to their respec-
tive histories—the Painted Lady's charmingly appointed rooms, for
example, are named after former inhabitants. The luxurious rooms in
the Abbey, named for the six days of creation, have whirlpool tubs and
gas fireplaces, and are set along a corridor overlooking the restaurant
below. (If it's available, splurge on the Tuesday room—the incredible
stained-glass "compass" window will take your breath away.) The Bis-
tro ($$–$$$$) serves dazzling, globally inspired dishes ⊠*8 Jarves St.,
Sandwich 02563* 🕾*508/888–8550 or 800/844–4542* 🖶*508/888–3922*
⊕*www.belfryinn.com* ⬅*20 rooms* ⭗*In-room: no TV (some), Wi-Fi
(some), whirlpool tubs (some), fireplaces (some), massage. In-hotel: 2
restaurants, bar, no-smoking rooms, no elevator* 🖃*AE, D, DC, MC,
V* ◉*BP.*

$$–$$$$
Fodor'sChoice
★

🖼 **Orleans Inn.** This 1875 sea captain's mansion nearly met with the
wrecking ball before Ed Maas and his family took over the place in the
late '90s; today the Maas clan continues to run this bustling inn and
restaurant with warmth and enthusiasm. The imposing, turreted struc-
ture has two distinct faces: one turned toward a busy intersection and
a large shopping plaza, whereas the other looks longingly over tranquil
Town Cove. Rooms here are simply but charmingly appointed with
classic wood furniture and floral quilts on the beds; the larger water-
front suites have sitting areas and great views of the harbor. Common
areas include a kitchenette with a microwave and toaster oven and a
sitting room in the basement with a large TV and videos. The restau-
rant ($–$$$), which uses some creative ingredients in its traditional
standbys, serves up large portions of fish-and-chips, grilled sirloin, and
grilled salmon with orange-honey glaze. There's also an excellent Sunday brunch. ⊠*3 Old County Rd., Orleans 02653* ✒*Box 188, Orleans
02653* 🕾*508/255–2222 or 800/863–3039* 🖶*508/255–6722* ⊕*www.
orleansinn.com* ⬅*8 rooms, 3 suites* ⭗*In-room: VCR/DVD, fireplaces,
refrigerator, Wi-Fi. In-hotel: restaurant, bar, no-smoking rooms, no
elevator* 🖃*AE, MC, V* ◉*BP.*

$$$–$$$$
Fodor'sChoice
★

🖼 **Crowne Pointe Historic Inn and Spa.** Created meticulously from six dif-
ferent buildings, this inn has not left a single detail unattended. Period
furniture and antiques fill the common areas and rooms; a queen-size

bed is the smallest you'll find, dressed in 300-thread-count linens, with treats on the pillow for nightly turndown service. Many rooms have fireplaces. Penthouse suites have two floors of living space with a full kitchen, and many rooms have private balconies with water or town views. The grounds are accented with brick pathways, flowers, and trees. Start the day with a full, hot breakfast, then graze on freshly baked treats and wine and cheese in the afternoon—there's also an excellent restaurant, the Bistro at Crowne Pointe. ⊠*82 Bradford St., Provincetown 02657* ☎*508/487–6767 or 877/276–9631* 🖷*508/487–5554* ⊕*www.crownepointe.com* ⇋*37 rooms, 3 suites* ♿*In-room: kitchen (some), refrigerator, DVD, Ethernet, Wi-Fi (some). In-hotel: pool, spa, concierge, no elevator, laundry service, public Wi-Fi, airport shuttle* ☐*AE, D, MC, V* ⦿|*BP.*

$$ ⊞**Crow's Nest Resort.** Amid the mostly run-of-the-mill motels and cottage compounds along Route 6A in North Truro, this beautifully refurbished all-suites beachfront property stands head and shoulders above the rest. It's been around since the mid-1960s, but the rooms are refreshingly contemporary with tile and oak floors, modern kitchen appliances, light-wood furniture, and country quilts. Ground-floor units front an attractive wooden deck overlooking the bay, and upstairs units have private balconies with similar views. You can choose from studio, two-bedroom, and three-bedroom units, and all have full kitchens, fireplaces, Jacuzzi tubs, and washers and dryers. The resort also rents three attractive beachfront bungalows, called Crown's Nest Cottages, about a half-mile away. ⊠*496 Rte. 6A, Box 177, Truro 02652* ☎*508/487–9031 or 800/499–9799* ⊕*www.caperesort.com* ⇋*21 suites* ♿*In-room: kitchen, DVD, Ethernet. In-hotel: beachfront, no elevator* ☐*AE, MC, V* ⦿*Closed late Nov.–early Apr.*

FodorsChoice ★

NANTUCKET

$$$$ ⊞**Wauwinet.** This resplendently updated 1850 resort straddles a "haulover" poised between ocean and bay—which means beaches on both sides. Head out by complimentary van or launch to partake of utmost pampering. Optional activities include sailing, water-taxiing to a private beach along Coatue, and touring the Great Point nature preserve by Land Rover. Of course, it's tempting just to stay put, what with the cushy country-chic rooms and a splendid restaurant, Topper's. ⊠*120 Wauwinet Rd., Wauwinet* ⊡*Box 2580, Nantucket 02584* ☎*508/228–0145 or 800/426–8718* 🖷*508/228–7135* ⊕*www.wauwinet.com* ⇋*25 rooms, 5 cottages* ♿*In-room: safe, DVD, Wi-Fi. In-hotel: restaurant, room service, bar, tennis courts, spa, beachfront, bicycles, no elevator, concierge, town shuttle, no kids under 12, no-smoking rooms* ☐*AE, DC, MC, V* ⦿*Closed Nov.–Apr.* ⦿|*BP.*

FodorsChoice ★

MARTHA'S VINEYARD

$$$–$$$$ ✕⊞**Lambert's Cove Inn and Restaurant.** A narrow road winds through pine woods and beside creeper-covered stone walls to this posh, handsomely designed inn surrounded by gardens and old stone walls. The richly appointed rooms each have decorative schemes and antiques based on grand East Coast–resort towns. Those in the outbuildings are airy and a bit more contemporary, some with decks and porches. Guests receive

FodorsChoice ★

free passes to beautiful and private Lambert's Cove beach. Fireplaces and hardwood floors lend warmth to the stellar contemporary restaurant ✉*Off Lambert's Cove Rd.* 🏠*R.R. 1, Box 422, Vineyard Haven 02568* 📞*508/693–2298* 📠*508/693–7890* ⊕*www.lambertscoveinn. com* 🛏*17 rooms* ♿*In-room: DVD, Ethernet. In-hotel: restaurant, tennis court, pool, no elevator* ═*AE, MC, V* ⦿|*BP.*

SPORTS & THE OUTDOORS

Fodor'sChoice
★
Marconi Beach (✉*Off U.S. 6, Wellfleet*) charges $15 for daily parking or $45 for a season pass that provides access to all six National Seashore swimming beaches. There are lifeguards, restrooms, and outdoor showers from late June through early September.

Cape Outback Adventures (✉Truro 📞508/349–1617 or 800/864–0070 ⊕www.capeoutback.com) has friendly instruction and guided tours for kayakers, mountain bikers, and beginning surfers.

Fodor'sChoice
★
Race Point Beach (✉Race Point Rd., Provincetown, east of U.S. 6), one of the Cape Cod National Seashore beaches in Provincetown, has a wide swath of sand stretching far off into the distance around the point and Coast Guard station. Behind the beach is pure duneland, and bike trails lead off the parking lot. Parking is available, there are showers and restrooms, and lifeguards are stationed in season. From late June through early September, parking costs $15 per day, or $45 for a yearly pass good at all National Seashore beaches.

Fodor'sChoice
★
Nauset Light Beach (✉Off Ocean View Dr., South Wellfleet), adjacent to Coast Guard Beach, is a sandy beach backed by tall dunes, grass, and heathland. It has showers and lifeguards in summer. Nauset charges $15 daily per car; a $45 season pass admits you here and to the other five National Seashore swimming beaches.

On **Hyannis Whale Watcher Cruises** out of Barnstable Harbor, a naturalist narrator comments on whale sightings and the natural history of Cape Cod Bay. ✉Millway Marina, off Phinney's La., Barnstable 📞508/362–6088 or 888/942–5392 ⊕www.whales.net 💲$35 ⊙May–Oct.

VISITOR INFORMATION

Cape Cod Chamber of Commerce (📞508/862–0700 or 888/332–2732 ⊕ www.capecodchamber.org)
Martha's Vineyard Chamber of Commerce (📞 508/693–4486 or 800/505–4815 ⊕ www.mvy.com)
Nantucket Chamber of Commerce 📞 508/228–1700 ⊕ www.nantucket chamber.org

New York City

Times Square

WORD OF MOUTH

"We had a fabulous time in the big apple. In only 2½ days we managed to do some shopping in SoHo, walk through Tribeca, the Garment District . . . walk over the Brooklyn Bridge, coffee in Little Italy, stroll in Times Square, coffee at FIKA, browse in Rizzoli bookstore, walk in Central Park and through Upper West Side, breakfast on the Upper East Side, drink at the Carlyle Hotel, take in Mamma Mia! on Broadway, drinks and entertainment at the Carnegie Club and more."   —schnookies

EXPLORING NEW YORK CITY

225 mi northeast of Washington, DC, via MD–295, I–895, I–95, and New Jersey Turnpike; 215 mi southwest of Boston via I–90, I–84, I–91, and CT–15; and 95 mi northeast of Philadelphia via I–95 and New Jersey Turnpike.

By Michelle Delio

It's hard to believe our happy island nation, the city that never sleeps, is a mere 23.7 square mi total—only 13.4 mi long and 2.3 mi across at its broadest point. Locals often forget we're living on a smallish chunk of rock surrounded by water, so convinced are we that our beloved city—which drives us mad on a daily basis with her sounds, smells, crowds and craziness—is truly the center of the universe.

Uniquely American and simultaneously quite unlike anyplace else in the U.S, New York City has a culture, style, and spirit all its own. Home to 8,214,426 residents who represent every nation in the world, NYC is a fiercely multicultural capitol of finance, fashion, and publishing; boasts 19,000 restaurants and at least twice that many shops; has a lively theater district, arts, and music scene; and is home to more than a dozen world-class museums. Whatever you want, it's here. Prepare to be dazzled.

WHO WILL ESPECIALLY LOVE THIS TRIP?

Artsy types: Anyone who thinks a trip to a museum is a sensual pleasure, whose perfect Sunday is spent exploring art galleries, who loves big theatrical spectacles and music clubs ranging from refined to gritty will adore New York City.

Kids: The mummies at the Met, the sailboats and the zoo in Central Park, the bling of Times Square, and pretty much everything at the Museum of Natural History make the city a kiddie wonderland.

Foodies: Whether you love to sample the creations of some of the world's most exciting chefs, or long to taste authentic ethnic treats from around the world, Manhattan is the place to be.

And Everyone Else: New York City truly has something for everyone; except those hardy types who want to surf, ski, or hike backwoods trails on their holiday. Love fashion? Fascinated by power? Interested in history/architecture/popular culture/urban adventures? New York City is sure to delight you.

WHEN IS THE BEST TIME TO VISIT?

Autumn is beautiful in New York, with perfect temperatures and bright blue skies (many locals love this season the best). Fall also marks the opening of many cultural events and blockbuster museum shows. The holidays, from early December until New Year's Day, is also a very special time in New York, but hotels are insanely priced and the city can be very crowded—plan ahead if you're coming to visit during the festive season. Winter is quite cold and can be snowy, but it's a great time to

TOP 5 REASONS TO GO

Experiencing the energy: Nothing matches the rush of being a part of this huge, high-speed, open 24/7, creative madhouse.

Art, music, theater: Old, new, utterly outré, or classic, it's *all* here. The city's museums, galleries, and performance venues are home to things you've always wanted to experience in person—and things you probably never knew existed.

Food glorious food: New York is a buffet of world cuisine, making it an essential pilgrimage for foodies, and a delight to anyone who enjoys good eats.

People-watching: This is always a pleasure in NYC. You'll probably spot a few celebrities, but observing the locals and our many visitors is just as much fun. Grab a chair at a café, a bench at a park, or a space on the sidewalk, and enjoy watching the world dash by.

The shopping: Your credit card will probably melt from overuse, but hey, you only live once.

find hotel deals. Restaurants, museums, and theaters are at their least crowded (your best chance of getting a decently priced Broadway ticket to a top show is in January and February). Spring has a happy vibe; temperatures are moderate, and the city still isn't too crowded. Summer can be painfully hot, humid, and packed with teaming hordes of humanity, but there's also plenty of free entertainment (many cultural venues offer special performances in the city's parks).

In general, mid-September through October and May through mid-June are really wonderful times to visit NYC—the weather tends to be great for wandering around, and the crowds are manageable (…) but everyone should experience at least one Christmas season in the New York.

HOW SHOULD I GET THERE?

DRIVING

If you're coming from the north, take I–95 into the Bronx at 178th Street, then, depending on your initial destination, take either the FDR Drive (for the East Side of Manhattan) or the Westside Highway (West side of Manhattan). If you're coming in from the east, take I–87 through Queens and over the Triborough Bridge at 125th Street, which will connect you with the FDR Drive. Be aware that the highways surrounding the city are prone to major traffic jams from 8AM to 10 AM and 3PM to 6PM, as well as on the weekends (but they can also be crowded at pretty much any time). For a heads-up on road conditions as you approach the city, tune your AM radio to 1010 (WINS), a local all-news channel that offers regular traffic updates.

FLYING

Three major airports serve New York City: John F. Kennedy International Airport in Queens, about 15 mi (1 hour driving time) from Midtown Manhattan; LaGuardia Airport, also in Queens, about 8 mi (30 minutes) from Midtown; and Newark International Airport in New

Jersey, about 16 mi (45 minutes) from Midtown. Be aware that during rush hours (8 AM to 10 AM and 3 PM to 6 PM) it may take at least twice as long to travel to or from any of the airports. For information on transport options to and from all three airports, call Air-Ride (800/247–7433) for a recording that details bus and shuttle companies and private car services.

You can also grab an NYC-licensed cab at the airport. Fare from JFK to Manhattan is a flat rate of $45 (plus about $5 in tolls and a 15%–20% tip). Expect to pay $20–$30 plus about $4 in tolls (depending on the route) and a tip from LaGuardia. From Newark, the airport's cab dispatcher will provide you with a slip of paper with a flat rate ranging from $30 to $38 (not including $10 in tolls and tip), you'll need to tell the dispatcher precisely where you're headed in NYC (preferably the destination street and cross street information, rather than just a street address).

HOW DO I GET AROUND?

BY CAR

Driving Manhattan's crowded streets is about as much fun as chewing on tinfoil. Free parking is often impossible to find, and paid spots are insanely expensive. If you arrived in town by car, either stash it in your hotel's lot—and look for packages that include free parking, which can save you about $50 per night—or ask your hotel to recommend a good long-term lot. You'll often get a break on the cost of hourly parking if you park the car for a few days, but expect to spend at least $30 a day.

BY SUBWAY & BUS

Close to 5 million people ride New York City's 26 subway routes each day; another 2.4 million clamber onto the city's buses. The buses and subways are safe, reasonably prompt, and easy to navigate. For a complete rundown on how to use the city's transit services, costs, and route maps, visit www.mta.info, click on NYC Transit, then select Travel/Tourist Information from the menu. Note that public transit is packed between 8 AM and 9:30 AM and 4 PM and 6 PM, so plan your travels to avoid these times if you can.

BY TAXI

NYC's licensed street cabs are bright yellow and have a small sign—called a medallion—on the roof displaying the cab's unique identifying 4-digit number; the same set of numbers will also be painted on the door. These are the only cabs you should accept rides from on the street—nonlicensed "gypsy" cabs can be very expensive and are unregulated by the city.

When the number on the cab's roof medallion is lighted, the cab is available. Stand slightly off the curb in the street and stick out your arm to hail the cab. If another person is trying to hail a cab on the corner, it's considered polite to walk a block away or cross the street and try to hail a cab from there, or to wait until the first person gets a ride.

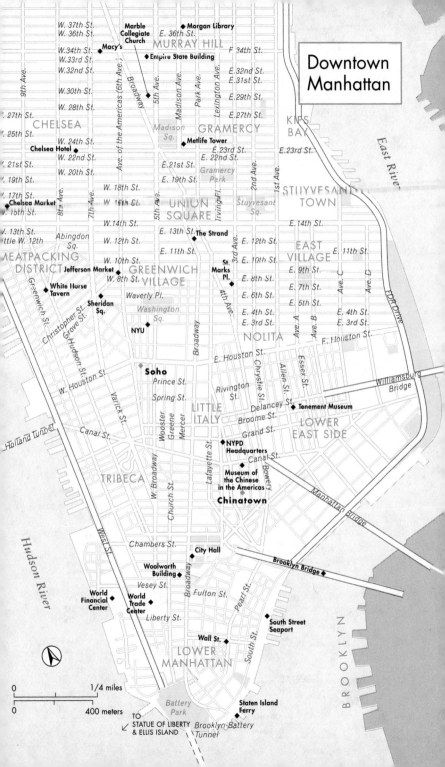

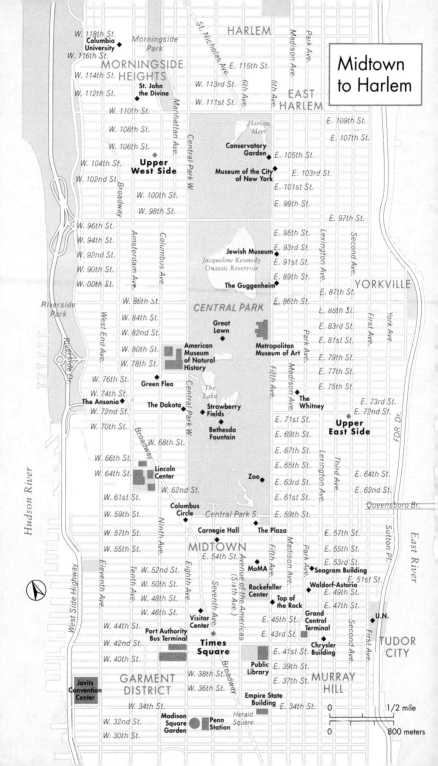

Midtown to Harlem

W. 118th St.
Columbia University
W. 116th St.

Morningside Park

HARLEM

E. 115th St.

W. 114th St.
MORNINGSIDE HEIGHTS

W. 113th St.

EAST HARLEM

W. 112th St.
St. John the Divine

W. 111th St.

W. 110th St.

E. 109th St.

E. 107th St.

W. 108th St.

Harlem Meer

W. 106th St.

Conservatory Garden

E. 105th St.

W. 104th St.
Upper West Side

Museum of the City of New York

E. 103rd St.

W. 102nd St.

E. 101st St.

W. 100th St.

E. 99th St.

W. 98th St.

E. 97th St.

W. 96th St.

E. 95th St.

W. 94th St.

Jewish Museum

E. 93rd St.

W. 92nd St.

Jacqueline Kennedy Onassis Reservoir

E. 91st St.

W. 90th St.

E. 89th St.

W. 00th St.

The Guggenheim

E. 87th St.

YORKVILLE

W. 86th St.

CENTRAL PARK

E. 86th St.

E. 85th St.

W. 84th St.

E. 83rd St.

W. 82nd St.

Great Lawn

E. 81st St.

W. 80th St.

American Museum of Natural History

Metropolitan Museum of Art

E. 79th St.

W. 78th St.

E. 77th St.

W. 76th St.

E. 75th St.

W. 74th St.
Green Flea

The Lake

W. 72nd St.
The Ansonia

The Dakota

The Whitney

E. 73rd St.

E. 72nd St.

W. 70th St.
Strawberry Fields

Upper East Side

E. 71st St.

Bethesda Fountain

E. 69th St.

W. 68th St.

E. 67th St.

E. 65th St.

W. 66th St.

Lincoln Center

E. 64th St.

W. 64th St.

Zoo

E. 63rd St.

E. 62nd St.

W. 62nd St.

E. 61st St.

W. 61st St.

Queensboro Br.

W. 59th St.
Columbus Circle

Central Park S.

E. 59th St.

W. 57th St.
Carnegie Hall

The Plaza

E. 57th St.

W. 55th St.
MIDTOWN

E. 55th St.

E. 54th St.

E. 53rd St.

W. 52nd St.
MoMA

Seagram Building

E. 51st St.

W. 50th St.
Rockefeller Center

Waldorf-Astoria

E. 49th St.

W. 48th St.
Top of the Rock

E. 47th St.

W. 46th St.

U.N.

Grand Central Terminal

Visitor Center

E. 45th St.

W. 44th St.

E. 43rd St.

Port Authority Bus Terminal

TUDOR CITY

W. 42nd St.
Times Square

Chrysler Building

E. 41st St.

W. 40th St.
Public Library

E. 39th St.

MURRAY HILL

W. 38th St.

E. 37th St.

GARMENT DISTRICT

Empire State Building

W. 36th St.

E. 34th St.

Javits Convention Center

W. 34th St.

0   1/2 mile

W. 32nd St.
Madison Square Garden

Penn Station

Herald Square

0   800 meters

W. 30th St.

Hudson River

Riverside Park

Riverside Dr.

West End Ave.

West Side Highway

Broadway

Amsterdam Ave.

Columbus Ave.

Central Park W.

Ninth Ave.

Tenth Ave.

Eleventh Ave.

Eighth Ave.

Seventh Ave.

Avenue of the Americas (Sixth Ave.)

Fifth Ave.

Madison Ave.

Park Ave.

Lexington Ave.

Third Ave.

Second Ave.

First Ave.

York Ave.

Sutton Pl.

FDR Dr.

East River

Manhattan Ave.

St. Nicholas Ave.

6th Ave.

5th Ave.

CLOSE UP

How to Snack

New York's street food has staved off many a hunger pang. "Dirty water" dogs (frankfurters, named for the clean-but-cloudy steaming water they float in on the carts), hot salted pretzels (smear them liberally with spicy mustard), ice cream, bagels and other pastries, falafels/kebobs/shawarma (spicy lamb), chili, nuts (try the honey-roasted peanuts), and fruit carts are all common on the city's busiest streets.

But for a real taste of New York, have a slice or two of our pizza, known for its thin, heat-blistered, hand-tossed crust topped sparingly with tomato sauce and melted mozzarella cheese. You can get a decent slice pretty much anywhere, but for a taste of true pizza perfection head to **John's** (*3 locations: 278 Bleecker St., 212/391–7560; 408 E. 64th, 212/980–4315; and our favorite, 260 W. 44th St., 212/243–1680*). **Lombardi's** (*32 Spring St., 212/941–7994*) is NYC's first pizzeria (it opened in 1905), and it still serves up some of the city's best slices. If you're uptown, head over to **Sal & Carmine's** (*2671 Broadway, between 101st St. and 102nd St., 212/663–7651*) to experience great pizza at a truly local joint. None of these slices really need further embellishment—but that doesn't stop New Yorkers from sprinkling red pepper flakes, garlic powder, or/and oregano on top before chowing down.

4

You can pay by credit or debit card using the swiper that's affixed to the screen on the back of the driver's seat, or by cash. The fare will be shown on the cab's meter, up front next to the driver, and is $2.50 as soon as you enter the car. There's a $0.40 for each "additional unit," which is calculated at one-fifth of a mile (when the taxicab is traveling) or every 60 seconds (when the cab is not in motion). Figure on about $8 for every 20 blocks. Pay the total that's shown on the meter, plus a 15%–20% gratuity. There are additional charges for trips outside the metropolitan area (and you'll pay any tolls as well), plus a night surcharge of $0.50 between 8 PM and 6 AM, and a peak hour weekday Surcharge of $1 weekdays between 4 PM and 8 PM.

WHERE SHOULD I FOCUS MY ENERGY?

If you're here for 1 day: Head downtown—walk along Wall Street to get a feel for the juice that runs NYC, then head over to South Street Seaport to glimpse the city's past as a bustling seaport. Pay your respects at Ground Zero.

If you're here for 2 days: Pick a museum—the Metropolitan or the Museum of Modern Art for adults, Natural History for kids—and spend as much time as you like exploring, with absolutely no intention of seeing it all. Then take in a Broadway show in the evening, or have a relaxed dinner at one of the city's fine restaurants.

If you're here for 3 days: After you've seen some of the real New York, you're ready to head to Times Square. It's utterly fabricated for tourists—the shopping and food are expensive and rather dull, and it's seriously crowded. Still it's worth seeing, just for the bright lights big city experience (for our money, it's a lot prettier at night).

If you're here for 4 days: Time to give your credit card a workout. Explore artisans' stalls at flea markets (check out Green Flea at Columbus between 76 & 77 streets, www.greenfleamarkets.com, Sunday only), the funky boutiques in the east and west villages, the world's largest department store (Macys, 151 W. 34th Street) and 5th Avenue from 50th to 59th streets—a very pricey shoppers' paradise.

If you're here for 5 days: Choose another of the city's big museums to explore, or spend some time at the smaller but just as fascinating Museum of the City of New York. Known for its quirky takes on local history, the photography shows are always worth seeing, as is the historic toy collection and Timescapes, a multimedia trip back into NYC's history.

If you're here for 6 days: Relax in Central Park: check out the zoo (64th Street and 5th Avenue), walk the paths, and enjoy the lush landscaping. One special spot to see is the Conservatory Garden (enter at 5th Avenue and 105th Street), which has plantings in the traditional styles of Italian, French, and English gardens.

If you're here for 7 days or more: Repeat whatever you've most enjoyed from your previous adventures, or explore an entirely new neighborhood. In the evening get a glorious farewell view of the city from the Top of the Rock.

WHAT ARE THE TOP EXPERIENCES?

The Museums: Within just one 30-block area (Museum Mile—5th Avenue from 82nd to 105th Street) there are nine world-class institutions and a dozen or so merely excellent ones. Resign yourself to the fact you aren't going to see it all, not even close. You can take in the highlights, though— the Egyptian gallery and the newly created Greek and Roman galleries at the Metropolitan, the Dinosaur and Ocean Life halls plus the Rose Center for Earth and Space at the Natural History Museum, and the fifth-floor masterpiece galleries at the Museum of Modern Art (MoMA).

The Neighborhoods: Walk 10 blocks in any direction in the city, and you're in a whole different world. Bustling Chinatown, artsy SoHo, the still-somewhat funky east and west villages, the ritzy Upper East Side, and the laid-back residential Upper West Side should be on your itinerary.

The Views: The Twin Towers may be gone, but the New York skyline remains beautiful. See it from 1,050 feet above on the Empire State Building's 86th-floor observatory—you can see up to 80 mi on a clear day. Or head to the Top of the Rock, where you get a 360-degree, unobstructed view from the 70th floor observatory, 850 feet above the ground. Having trouble choosing? The Empire State Building is great for daytime viewing, while the view from the Rock is spectacular at night.

The Icons: Wall Street, Rockefeller Center, Times Square, 5th Avenue—you've probably seen them many times before your first visit to NYC. They're all worth a visit, but the sentimental favorite has to be the Statue of Liberty. To see Lady Liberty, catch the ferry from Battery Park; the boats leave every half-hour between 9:30 AM and 3:40 PM. Your Liberty Island ticket also includes a stop at Ellis Island, once the arrival point for virtually every new arrival to the U.S. The Immigration Museum here really brings the experience alive—it's an absolute must-see. The Unexpected: Tucked away in odd corners of the city are things that many visitors never see, sites that would be the pride of other locales. Wandering around the city and finding these unhyped wonders is the best part of

> ### CLAIM TO FAME
>
> NYC offers something for everyone: restaurants that will please most fussy foodies, fabulous stores, awesome museums, brilliant theater, and a thriving arts scene. Locals are likely to point to the city's multicultural flavor, the open-minded attitudes and forthright nature of its inhabitants, and the wonders of their very own neighborhoods as the highlights of the city. To really experience New York, talk to its residents (we may bark but we don't bite), and ask them what you should see in their little piece of Manhattan. If you venture outside Times Square and Midtown, you'll begin to get a real feel for the city.

any NYC visit. For example, if you head uptown to Amsterdam Avenue and 112th Street, a quiet residential neighborhood, you'll find the Cathedral of St. John the Divine, the world's largest Gothic cathedral. Construction began in 1892 and is still underway. Neighborhood folks served as models for the carvings on the Cathedral's doors, and the inside of the church is home to more than a dozen unique altars. Then walk over to Riverside Drive and 122nd Street (6 blocks west and 10 north) to see Grant's Tomb, an elegant structure surrounded by exuberantly oddball mosaics created by a public works program in the 1970s.

BEST BETS

SIGHTS AND TOURS

★ **American Museum of Natural History.** The towering, spectacularly reassembled dinosaur skeletons that greet you when you enter this museum are practically worth the (suggested) price of admission. But there's tons more, including exhibits of ancient civilizations, animals both stuffed and living (don't miss the live Butterfly Conservatory October–May), a hall of oceanic creatures overlooked by a 94-foot model of a blue whale, and space shows at the adjoining Rose Center for Earth and Space. ⊠ *Central Park West at W. 79th St., Upper West Side* ☎ *212/769–5200* ⊕ *amnh.org* ⊠ *$20 suggested donation, includes admission to Rose Center for Earth and Space* ⊙ *Daily 10–5:45; Rose Center until 8:45 on Fri.* Ⓜ *Subway: B, C to 81st St.*

Fodor'sChoice **The Bronx Zoo.** When it opened its gates in 1899, the Bronx Zoo only
★ had 843 animals. But today, with 265 acres and more than 4,000 ani-
☺ mals (of more than 600 species), it's the largest metropolitan zoo in
the United States. Get up close and personal with exotic creatures in
outdoor settings that re-create natural habitats; you're often separated
from them by no more than a moat or wall of glass. ⊠ *Bronx River*
Pkwy. and Fordham Rd., Fordham ☎ *718/367–1010* ⊕ *www.bronx*
zoo.com 🖃 *Adults $14; free Wed., donation suggested; extra charge*
for some exhibits; parking $8 for cars ☉ *Apr.–Oct., weekdays 10–5,*
weekends 10–5:30; Nov.–Mar., daily 10–4:30; last ticket sold 30 min
before closing Ⓜ *Subway: 2 to E. Tremont/West Farms, then walk 2*
blocks to zoo's Wild Asia entrance; 5 to Pelham Pkwy., then walk
3 blocks west to Bronx Pkwy. entrance; Bx11 express bus to Bronx
Pkwy. entrance.

★ **Brooklyn Bridge.** "A drive-through cathedral" is how the critic James
Wolcott describes one of New York's noblest and most recognized landmarks, which spans the East River and connects Manhattan to the
heart of Brooklyn. A walk across the bridge's promenade—a boardwalk elevated above the roadway and shared by pedestrians, in-line
skaters, and bicyclists—takes about 40 minutes, from Manhattan's
civic center to the heart of Brooklyn Heights. It's well worth traversing
for the astounding views. The roadway is supported by a web of steel
cables, hung from the towers and attached to block-long anchorages
on either shore. Ⓜ *Subway: 4, 5, 6 to Brooklyn Bridge/City Hall; J, M,*
Z to Chambers St.

Fodor'sChoice **Central Park.** The literal and figurative center of Manhattan, Central
★ Park has 843 acres of meandering paths, tranquil lakes, ponds, and
open meadows. For equestrians, softball and soccer players, strollers,
ice- and roller skaters, rock climbers, bird-watchers, boaters, picnickers, and outdoor performers, it's an oasis of fresh air and greenery that
lets them forget—at least for a little while—the hustle and congestion
of the city.

Fodor'sChoice **Ellis Island.** Between 1892 and 1924, approximately 12 million men,
★ women, and children first set foot on U.S. soil at the Ellis Island federal immigration facility. By the time the facility closed in 1954, it
had processed ancestors of more than 40% of Americans living today.
The island's main building, now a national monument, reopened in
1990 as the Ellis Island Immigration Museum, containing more than
30 galleries of artifacts, photographs, and taped oral histories. The
centerpiece of the museum is the white-tile Registry Room (also known
as the Great Hall). It feels dignified and cavernous today, but photographs show that it took on a multitude of configurations through the
years, always packed with humanity undergoing one form or another
of screening. While you're there, take a look out the Registry Room's
tall, arched windows and try to imagine what passed through immigrants' minds as they viewed lower Manhattan's skyline to one side and
the Statue of Liberty to the other.

HISTORY YOU CAN SEE

The island's southernmost tip was once home to pirates, oyster fishermen, and all manner of rogues and revolutionaries, plus roaming packs of pigs that provided a primitive sanitation system. Flash forward to 1789, a year before New York City would lose its title as America's capital: George Washington was sworn in as the nation's first president at Federal Hall, the same spot where Congress would ratify the Bill of Rights two years later. Little evidence of this glorious federal past remains, but if you're in lower Manhattan you can still have a meal at **Fraunces Tavern** (*54 Pearl St. at Broad St., 212/425–1778*). Built in 1719 and converted to a tavern in 1763, it was the meeting place for the Sons of Liberty; in 1783 George Washington and his officers celebrated the British evacuation of New York in the Tavern. When you're done with your meal, head over to 85 Broad Street to see underground remains of another colonial tavern, the Lovelace, discovered during a construction project in 1980. (The tavern belonged to Francis Lovelace, New York's second British governor.)

Because there's so much to take in, it's a good idea to make use of the museum's interpretive tools. Check at the visitor desk for free film tickets, ranger tour times, and special programs. The audio tour is worth its $6 price: it takes you through the exhibits, providing thorough, engaging commentary interspersed with recordings of immigrants themselves recalling their experiences. Along with the Registry Room, the museum's features include the ground-level Railroad Ticket Office, which has several interactive exhibits and a three-dimensional graphic representation of American immigration patterns; the American Family Immigration Center, where you can search Ellis Island's records for your own ancestors (for a $5 fee); and, outside, the American Immigrant Wall of Honor, where the names of more than 500,000 immigrant Americans are inscribed along a promenade facing the Manhattan skyline. (For $100 you can add a family member's name to the wall.) ☎212/363–3200 Ellis Island, 212/561–4500 Wall of Honor information ⊕www.ellisisland.org ☜Free; ferry $11.50 round-trip ⊙ Daily 9–5; extended hrs in summer

Fodor'sChoice **Empire State Building.** From the 86th-floor observatory, which towers ★ 1,050 feet above the city, you can see up to 80 mi away on a clear ☾ day, and it's heated and air-conditioned, unlike the deck 16 stories further up. The views at night are equally dazzling, with the glittering city lights French architect Le Corbusier once called "a Milky Way come down to earth." If you're afraid of heights, gazing at the building from afar is nothing to sneeze at, either—especially after dark, when it's illuminated by colored lights that correspond to different holidays and causes (Go Yankees!). ☒350 5th Ave., at E. 34th St., Murray Hill☎212/736–3100 or 877/692–8439 ⊕www.esbnyc.com ☜$18 ⊙Daily 8 AM–2 AM; last elevator up leaves at 1:15 AM Ⓜ Subway: B, D, F, N, Q, R, V, W to 34th St./Herald Sq.

Fodor'sChoice **The Metropolitan Museum of Art.** The largest art museum in the West-
★ ern Hemisphere, the Met is—naturally—a mecca for art lovers of all
stripes. Treasures from all over the world and every era of human creativity comprise its expansive collection. It's easy to get dizzy, what
with all the Dutch Master canvases, bronze Rodins, and ancient Greek
artifacts—but if you need a breather, you can always retire to the Temple of Dendur or the rooftop café. ✉ *5th Ave. at 82nd St., Upper East
Side* ☎ *212/535-7710* ⊕ *www.metmuseum.org* ✉ *$20 suggested dona-
tion* ☉ *Tues.–Thurs. and Sun. 9:30–5:30, Fri. and Sat. 9:30–9* Ⓜ *Subway: 4, 5, 6 to 86th St.*

Fodor'sChoice **Museum of Modern Art.** Described as a "modernist dream world" after its
★ $425 million face-lift in 2004, the MoMA has since become as famous
for its architecture as for its collections. Yoshio Taniguchi, the Japanese
architect responsible for the redesign, created newly spacious, soaring-
ceilinged galleries suffused with natural light, where masterpieces like
Monet's *Water Lilies,* Picasso's *Les Demoiselles d'Avignon,* and Van
Gogh's *Starry Night* can get the oohs and aahs they deserve. The museum's restaurant next door, meanwhile, is nearly as breathtaking. ✉ 11
W. 53rd St., *between 5th and 6th Aves., Midtown East* ☎ 212/708–9400
⊕ *www.moma.org* ✉ *$20; children under 16 are free* ☉ *Sat.–Mon.,
Wed., and Thurs. 10:30–5:30, Fri. 10:30–8. Closed Tues.* Ⓜ *Subway: E,
V to 5th Ave./53rd St.; B, D, F, V to 47th–50th Sts./Rockefeller Center*

SoHo. The elegant cast-iron buildings, cobblestone streets, art galleries,
chic boutiques, and swanky hotels make this a wonderful area in which
to shop, drink, and dream of a more glamorous life.

Fodor'sChoice **Statue of Liberty.** Liberty Enlightening the World, as the statue is officially
★ named, was presented to the United States in 1886 as a gift from France.
The 152-foot-tall figure was sculpted by Frederic-Auguste Bartholdi and
erected around an iron skeleton engineered by Gustav Eiffel. It stands
atop an 89-foot pedestal designed by Richard Morris Hunt, with Emma
Lazarus's sonnet "The New Colossus" ("Give me your tired, your poor,
your huddled masses . . .") inscribed on a bronze plaque at the base.
Over the course of time, the statue has become precisely what its cre-
ators dreamed it would be: the single most powerful symbol of American ideals, and as such one of the world's great monumental sculptures.
Inside the statue's pedestal is a museum that's everything it should be:
informative, entertaining, and quickly viewed. Highlights include the
original flame (which was replaced because of water damage), full-scale
replicas of Lady Liberty's face and one of her feet, Bartholdi's alternative
designs for the statue, and a model of Eiffel's intricate framework.

You're allowed access to the museum only as part of one of the free
tours of the promenade (which surrounds the base of the pedestal) or
the observatory (at the pedestal's top). The tours are limited to 3,000
participants a day; to guarantee a place, particularly on the observatory tour, you should order tickets ahead of time—they can be reserved
up to 180 days in advance, by phone or over the Internet. Although
the narrow, double-helix stairs leading to the statue's crown have been
closed to visitors since 9/11, you get a good look at the statue's inner

structure on the observatory tour. From the observatory itself there are fine views of the harbor and an up-close (but totally uncompromising) glimpse up Lady Liberty's dress. If you're on one of the tours, you'll go through a security check more thorough than any airport screening, and you'll have to deposit any bags in a locker. Liberty Island has a pleasant outdoor café for refueling. ☎212/363–3200, 212/269–5755 *ferry information, 866/782–8834 ticket reservations* ⊕*www.statue reservations.com* ✆*Free; ferry $11.50 round-trip* ◷*Daily 9* AM*–5; extended hrs in summer.*

★ **Times Square.** Hands down, this is the most frenetic part of New York City, a cacophony of flashing lights, honking horns, and shoulder-to-shoulder crowds that many New Yorkers studiously avoid. But if you like sensory overload, the chaotic mix of huge underwear billboards, flashing digital displays, on-location television broadcasts, and outré street performers it will give you your fix. If you're a quieter sort, it will almost certainly give you a headache.

4

WHERE TO EAT

WHAT IT COSTS				
¢	$	$$	$$$	$$$$
AT DINNER	under $10	$10–$17	$18–$24	$25–$35	over $35

Price per person for a median main course or equivalent combination of smaller dishes. Note: if a restaurant offers only prix-fixe (set-price) meals, it has been given the price category that reflects the full prix-fixe price.

$$$$
NEW AMERICAN
Flatiron District
Fodor'sChoice
★

Eleven Madison Park. Under Swiss-born chef Daniel Humm, who was lured from San Francisco's Campton Place by restaurateur Danny Meyer, this art nouveau jewel overlooking Madison Park has become one of the city's most consistently exciting places to dine. Humm announces his lofty intentions with dishes like foie gras with golden raisin brioche and African kili pepper, butter-poached Scottish langoustines with carrot-orange nage, and Jamison Farm herb roasted lamb with tomato confit and niçoise olives. Don't forget your breakfast cake—a gift from the chef—as you walk out the door. ⊠*11 Madison Ave., at 24th St.* ☎*212/889–0905* ⊕*www.elevenmadisonpark.com* ⊜*Reservations essential* ⊟*AE, D, DC, MC, V* Ⓜ*Subway: N, R, W, 6 to 23rd St.*

$$$$
AMERICAN
Flatiron District

Gramercy Tavern. Danny Meyer's intensely popular restaurant tops many a New Yorker's favorite restaurant list. In front, the first-come, first-served tavern presents a lighter menu than the main dining room. The more formal dining room has a prix-fixe American menu; three courses at dinner is $82. Choose from seasonal dishes such as lightly smoked Spanish mackerel; grilled sturgeon with lemon fennel sauce; or stuffed meatball with fontina cheese. Meyer's restaurants—he owns several well-regarded eateries in the city—are renowned for their food and hospitality, and Gramercy Tavern sets the standard. ⊠*42 E. 20th St., between Broadway and Park Ave. S* ☎*212/477–0777* ⊕*www.gramercytavern.com* ⊜*Reservations essential for main dining room; reservations not accepted for the Tavern* ⊟*AE, DC, MC, V* Ⓜ*Subway: 6, R, W to 23rd St.*

STRANGE BUT TRUE

■ In the 1800s New York had several private firefighting forces that competed vigorously for work. They often paid street gangs to "protect" particular fire hydrants, barring other firefighters access to the water they needed to put out blazes. At the same time the city's two police forces, the Metropolitan and the Municipal, were engaged in frequent battles for control of the city's police stations. Criminals arrested by one force were often freed by the other.

■ The financial district's famous Charging Bull statue was a surprise present to the city from sculptor Arturo Di Modica, who left the 7,000-pound bronze statue under the Christmas tree in front of the New York Stock Exchange late in the evening of December 15, 1989. It was later relocated to Bowling Green after police complained it was blocking traffic in its original location. Since the city never commissioned it, the bull is still officially dubbed a "temporary installation."

¢¢¢¢ **Jean Georges.** This culinary temple focuses wholly on *chef celebre* Jean-
FRENCH   Georges Vongerichten's spectacular creations. Some approach the lim-
Upper West Side   its of the taste universe, like foie gras brûlée with spiced fig jam and
ice-wine verjus. Others are models of simplicity, like slow-cooked cod with warm vegetable vinaigrette. Exceedingly personalized service and a well-selected wine list contribute to an unforgettable meal. For Jean Georges on a budget, try the prix-fixe lunch in the front room, Nougatine. ⊠*1 Central Park W, at W. 59th St.* ☎*212/299–3900* ⊜*Reservations essential, jacket required* ⊟*AE, DC, MC, V* ☉*Closed Sun.* Ⓜ*Subway: A, B, C, D, 1, 2 to 59th St./Columbus Circle.*

$$$ **A Voce.** There's a warm glow in this 90-seat dining room, with its wal-
ITALIAN   nut floors and soft-green leather-top tables. Executive chef Andrew
Flatiron   Carmellini (from Café Boulud) has devised an Italian market–driven
Fodor's Choice   menu, and there's a congruently wide-ranging wine list. Duck meatballs
★   have a depth of flavor and texture that is not to be missed. Spaghetti all' Amatriciana is a piping-hot blend of spicy tomatoes, pancetta, and pecorino cheese, with truly *al dente* pasta. Red-wine-braised short ribs Piedmontese are partnered with fontina cheese potatoes. Chocolate bread pudding is not too sweet but rather complex, with roasted bananas along for the ride. In warm weather there's additional seating on the patio. ⊠*41 Madison Ave., between 25th and 26th Sts.* ☎*212/545–8555* ⊕*www.avocerestaurant.com* ⊟*AE, D, MC, V* Ⓜ*Subway: N, R to 23rd St.*

$$$ **Babbo.** After one bite of the ethereal homemade pasta or tender barbe-
ITALIAN   cued squab, you'll understand why it's so hard to get reservations at
Greenwich   Mario Batali's casually elegant restaurant. The complex and satisfying
Village   menu hits numerous high points, such as "mint love letters," ravioli
Fodor's Choice   filled with pureed peas, ricotta, and fresh mint, finished with spicy lamb
★   sausage ragu; and rabbit with Brussels sprouts, house-made pancetta, and carrot vinaigrette. Babbo is the perfect spot for a raucous celebratory dinner with flowing wine and festive banter. But be forewarned: if anyone in your party is hard of hearing, or bothered by loud rock music, choose someplace more sedate. ⊠*110 Waverly Pl., between*

MacDougal St. and 6th Ave. ☎*212/777–0303* ⊕*www.babbonyc.com* ✍*Reservations essential* ▤*AE, MC, V* ⊘*No lunch* Ⓜ*Subway: A, B, C, D, E, F, V to W. 4th St.*

$$$
AMERICAN
Flatiron District

Union Square Cafe. When he opened Union Square Cafe in 1985, Danny Meyer changed the American restaurant landscape. The combination of upscale food and unpretentious but focused service sparked a revolution. Today chef Carmen Quagliata still draws devotees with his crowd-pleasing menu. Wood paneling and white walls are hung with splashy modern paintings; in addition to the three dining areas, there's a long bar ideal for solo diners. The cuisine is American with a thick Italian accent: for example, the grilled, marinated filet mignon of tuna can land on the same table as creamy polenta with mascarpone. ✉*21 E. 16th St., between 5th Ave. and Union Sq. W* ☎*212/243–4020* ⊕*www. unionsquarecafe.com* ✍*Reservations essential* ▤*AE, D, DC, MC, V* Ⓜ*Subway: L, N, Q, R, W, 4, 5, 6 to 14th St./Union Sq.*

$$
BRASSERIE
SoHo

Balthazar. Even with long waits and excruciating noise levels, most out-of-towners agree that it's worth making reservations to experience restaurateur Keith McNally's flagship, a painstakingly accurate reproduction of a Parisian brasserie. Like the decor, entrées re-create French classics: Gruyère-topped onion soup, steak-frites, and icy tiers of crab, oysters, and other pristine shellfish. Brunch is one of the best in town—if you can get a table. The best strategy is to go at off-hours, or on weekdays for breakfast, to miss the crush of hungry New Yorkers. ✉*80 Spring St., between Broadway and Crosby St.* ☎*212/965–1785* ✍*Reservations essential* ▤*AE, MC, V* Ⓜ*Subway: 6 to Spring St.; N, R to Prince St.; B, D, F, V to Broadway–Lafayette.*

$$
ITALIAN
Lower East Side
Fodor'sChoice
★

'inoteca. The Italian terms on the menu may be a little daunting, but the food is not. An Italian small-plates concept with an excellent by-the-glass wine list, this rustic eatery is perpetually packed. Come for cheese and charcuterie plates, the famous truffled egg toast, and delicious panini sandwiches filled with cured meat, runny cheeses, and hot peppers. Fresh salads and creative entrées like polenta with braised escarole and pancetta, and braised chicken in a mushroom-chickpea sauce play supporting roles. ✉*98 Rivington St., at Ludlow St.* ☎*212/614–0473* ⊕*www.inotecanyc.com* ✍*Reservations not accepted* ▤*AE, MC, V* Ⓜ*Subway: F, J, M, Z to Delancey St.*

$$
ASIAN
East Village
Fodor'sChoice
★

Momofuku Ssam Bar. New York foodies have been talking about chef David Chang since he opened his first restaurant in 2004. Momofuku Ssam Bar, the wunderkind's much larger follow-up, is packed nightly with downtown diners cut from the same cloth as the pierced and tattooed waitstaff and cooks. The no-reservation policy means you'll likely have to wait for a chance to perch at the communal food bar and nibble on Chang's truly original small-plate cuisine. Dishes from the seasonally changing menu arrive like tapas for sharing. Although the chef works mostly with Asian flavors, his food is impossible to pigeon-hole. Chang's not-to-be-missed riff on a classic Chinese pork bun helped build his cult following. ✉*207 2nd Ave., at 13th St.,* ☎*212/254–3500* ✍*Reservations not accepted* ▤*AE, MC, V* Ⓜ*Subway: L to 1st Ave.*

$$ Tía Pol. This tiny, dark, out-of-the-way, but highly popular tapas bar is
SPANISH   usually packed, but there are good reasons for that: it's the best tapas
Chelsea   bar in town. The tables and stools are small and high, but the fla-
Fodor'sChoice   vors are enormous. One highly original tapa that everyone was talking
★   about is a signature here: bittersweet chocolate smeared on a baguette
disc and topped with real Spanish chorizo. Rough-cut potatoes are
deep-fried and served with a dollop of spicy aioli. You won't want
to share those. The pork loin, piquillo pepper, and mild tetilla cheese
sandwich is scrumptious, and so is the Galician octopus terrine. In
fact, everything on the menu is transporting and delicious. ⊠*205 10th
Ave., between 22nd and 23rd Sts.,* ☎*212/675–8805* ⚔*Reservations
essential for groups of 6-8* ⊟*AE, D, MC, V* ☉*No lunch* Ⓜ*Subway:
C, E to 23rd St.*

$ Fatty Crab. This rustic Malaysian cantina showcases the exciting cuisine
MALAYSIAN   of chef Zak Pelaccio, who spent years cooking at famous French restau-
West Village   rants before escaping to Southeast Asia, where he fell in love with the
Fodor'sChoice   flavors of the region. Start with the addictive watermelon-pickle-and-
★   crispy-pork salad, an improbable combination that is refreshing and
decadent. The can't-miss signature dish is chili crab—cracked Dunge-
ness crab in a pool of rich, spicy chili sauce, served with bread for
dipping. It's messy for sure, but worth rolling up your sleeves for. The
restaurant stays open until 4 AM Thursday through Saturday, making it
a late-night hangout for chefs and other folks in the restaurant industry.
⊠*643 Hudson St., between Gansevoort and Horatio Sts.,* ☎*212/352–
3590* ⊕*www.fattycrab.com* ⚔*Reservations essential* ⊟*AE, MC, V*
Ⓜ*Subway: A, C, E, L to 14th St.*

$ John's Pizzeria. The original John's, an institution on Bleecker Street
PIZZA   since 1929, is a perennial contender for best pizza pie in New York (as
GREENWICH   the famous sign on the window indicates, the place sells "no slices").
VILLAGE   At peak times you can find long lines on the sidewalk awaiting John's
scalding thin-crust pies generously appointed with the usual toppings.
Seated in a scuffed wood booth in the no-frills dining room, the only
decisions you'll have to make are what toppings to order and whether
you'd like an oversized shareable salad and a pitcher of beer. ⊠*278
Bleecker St., between 6th and 7th Aves.,* ☎*212/243–1680* ⚔*Reser-
vations not accepted* ⊟*No credit cards* Ⓜ*Subway: 1 to Christopher
St./Sheridan Sq.*1 to Christopher St.

$ Kampuchea Restaurant. Cambodian-born Ratha Chau, a former man-
CAMBODIAN   ager at the upscale French restaurant Fleur de Sel, is the driving force
Lower East Side   at this sophisticated Southeast Asian street-food spot. With exposed-
Fodor'sChoice   brick walls, elevated bar-style seating, and a well-planned wine list, it's
★   the most stylish noodle bar we've ever encountered. Start with grilled
corn lathered in coconut mayo, coconut flakes, and chili powder. The
unusual combination of flavors alerts your taste buds that they're in
for a wild ride. Follow it up with falling-off-the-bone grilled quail with
house-cured pickles or ginger-rubbed prawns. Don't miss Cambodian
savory crepes filled with Berkshire pork and chives. Then move on to
bountiful noodle dishes like chilled rice vermicelli with pork and Chi-
nese sausage, topped with a thick crown of herbs and bean sprouts, or
the hot filet mignon noodle soup with beef broth, peppercorn-encrusted

LIKE A LOCAL

We value speed and decisiveness here. Know what you want when you get to the head of the line, and place your order fast; if you dither, the people behind you and the folks behind the counter will get feisty. Don't block sidewalk traffic, move to the side if you need to check a map or tie your shoelace. Don't stop dead in front of doors, escalators, or elevators while you evaluate your next move; always keep the paths open for others. Watch how locals effortlessly weave around each other when they're walking—then give it a go, it's fun!

And please don't get upset if NYC-ers don't meet your eyes, greet you when you come in, or say a polite goodbye when you go. We're both giving you your space (in a city where we live packed so tightly together, not noticing others is a way of respecting others' privacy) and streamlining our interactions so everyone can keep moving. That being said, don't hesitate to ask us for help if you need it—we'll go out of our way to assist you. What may appear cold or even rude to you really isn't intended to be mean—it's just our way of getting through the day in a huge, crowded, crazy city.

fillet, and braised brisket. Finally, cool off with a refreshing glass of Riesling, and revel in the knowledge that you found one of New York's best hidden eats. ⊠*78 Rivington St., at Allen St.,* ☎*212/529–3901* ⊕*www.kampucheanyc.com* ⊟*AE, D, DC, MC, V* Ⓜ*F to Delancey St.; J, M, Z to Essex St.*

$
DELI
Lower East Side
Fodor's Choice
★

Katz's Delicatessen. Everything and nothing has changed at Katz's since it first opened in 1888, when the neighborhood was dominated by Jewish immigrants. The rows of Formica tables, the long self-service counter, and such signs as "send a salami to your boy in the army" are all completely authentic. What's different are the area's demographics, but all types still flock here for succulent hand-carved corned beef and pastrami sandwiches, soul-warming soups, juicy hot dogs, and crisp half-sour pickles. ⊠*205 E. Houston St., at Ludlow St.,* ☎*212/254–2246* ⊕*www.katzdeli.com* ⊟*AE, MC, V* Ⓜ*Subway: F, V to 2nd Ave.*

¢
FAST FOOD
Greenwich
Village
☾

Gray's Papaya. It's a stand-up, take-out dive. And, yes, limos do sometimes stop here for the legendary hot dogs. More often than not, though, it's neighbors or commuters who know how good the slim, traditional, juicy all-beef dogs are. Fresh-squeezed orange juice, a strangely tasty creamy banana drink, and the much-touted, healthful papaya juice are available along with more standard drinks, served up 24/7. You can find other Gray's Papaya outposts around the city, but this one's our favorite. ⊠*402 6th Ave., at W. 8th St.,* ☎*212/260–3532* ⚑*Reservations not accepted* ⊟*No credit cards* Ⓜ*Subway: A, C, E, F, S, V to W. 4th St.*

¢
VIETNAMESE
Chinatown
Fodor's Choice
★

Nha Trang. You can get a great meal for under $10 at this low-atmosphere Vietnamese restaurant in Chinatown. Start with crispy spring rolls, sweet-and-sour seafood soup, or shrimp grilled on sugarcane. For a follow-up, don't miss the thin pork chops, which are marinated in a sweet vinegary sauce and grilled until charred. Another favorite is deep-fried squid on shredded lettuce with a tangy dipping sauce. If the line is long, which it usually is, even with a second location around the corner, you may be asked to sit at a table with strangers. ⊠*87 Baxter St., between Bayard and Canal Sts.* ☎*212/233–5948* ▤*No credit cards* Ⓜ*Subway: 6, J, M, N, Q, R, W, Z to Canal St.* ⊠*148 Centre St., at Walker and White Sts.,* ☎*212/941–9292* ▤*No credit cards* Ⓜ*Subway: 6, J, M, N, Q, R, W, Z to Canal St.*

WHERE TO STAY

	WHAT IT COSTS				
	¢	$	$$	$$$	$$$$
FOR 2 PEOPLE	under $150	$150–$299	$300–$449	$450–$599	over $600

Prices are for a standard double room, excluding 13.625% city and state taxes.

$$$$ **Mandarin Oriental.** The Mandarin is the most exciting of the city's top-tier luxury hotels. Its cavernous lobby sizzles with energy from the 35th floor of the Time Warner Center. Here you can find two wonderful lounges, and the restaurant Asiate, from which to soak in the dramatic views above Columbus Circle and Central Park. On the higher floors, silk-encased throw pillows nearly cover the plush beds, and the marble ensconced bathrooms showcase Mandarin's mastery of luxury touches. That said, contrasted with the monumental frame created by floor-to-ceiling glass, and the view it presents, regular rooms feel small. Suites are really what set this hotel apart, by creating enough stage space to make the hotel's Asian-influenced decor, and the views, really kindle. The swimming pool has panoramic Hudson River vistas. The elaborate spa is the best in city. ⊠*80 Columbus Circle, at 60th St., Midtown West, 10023* ☎*212/805–8800* ☎*212/805–8888* ⊕*www.mandarinoriental.com* ➯*203 rooms, 46 suites* ♿*In-room: DVD, refrigerator, Ethernet. In-hotel: restaurant, room service, bar, pool, gym, spa, laundry service, concierge* ▤*AE, D, DC, MC, V* Ⓜ*Subway: A, B, C, D, 1 to 59th St./Columbus Circle.*

FodorsChoice ★

$$$ **Gramercy Park Hotel.** The GPH is on such a different plane of cool in comparison to all other NYC hotels, it might as well have its own hospitality category. Ian Schrager, who forged the boutique-hotel concept just over a decade ago, turned the design reins of this hotel over to famed painter and director Julian Schnabel. Embracing a spirit of High Bohemia, the property has a rock-and-roll baroque feel. You've just got to see it. Works by Cy Twombley, Andy Warhol, and Jean-Michel Basquiat aggressively decorate the lobby and the two exclusive, ground-level bars that have become key components in the city's nightlife. Only guests, however, enjoy access to the rooftop deck and its interesting lounges—no small privilege. Rooms are an assemblage of specific tastes: opulent velvets; studded leathers; moodily dark bathrooms and showers; photo prints from the famed Magnum collective. If it's your thing, you've just found your new favorite hotel. ⊠*2 Lexington Ave., at Gramercy Park, Gramercy Park, 10010* ☎*212/920–3300* ☎*212/673–5890* ⊕*www.gramercyparkhotel.com* ➯*140 rooms, 40 suites* ♿*In-room: safe, refrigerator, DVD, Ethernet. In-hotel: restau-*

FodorsChoice ★

ON THE WAY

Try your luck at **Atlantic City, New Jersey**. This onetime beach resort has been transformed into glitzy gambling town. It's no competition for Vegas, but it's a whole lot closer. A stroll along the casino-laden boardwalk is fun, and the Borgata hotel is home to an excellent Italian restaurant, Specchio. http://atlantic citynj.com.

Many residents of Manhattan envision the rest of the state as a vast undeveloped wilderness. This isn't true, of course, New York is home to thriving resort communities and even (gasp) other cities. If you want to grab a breath of truly fresh air and enjoy some stunning scenery, head upstate to the **Fingerlakes District**, filled with great vineyards, wonderful little inns, and terrific restaurants. Best bets: the towns of Geneva or Keuka. www.fingerlakes.org.

Mystic Seaport, Connecticut is a restored 1800s village, where you can explore a historic tall ship, visit a working shipyard, and experience life as it was once lived in a seafaring town along the Connecticut shore. The Seamen's Inne Restaurant & Pub serves excellent New England style lunches and dinners. www.mystic seaport.org.

rant, room service, bars, gym, laundry service, parking (fee), no-smok-ing rooms ☰AE, D, DC, MC, V Ⓜ Subway: 6 to 23rd St.

$$–$$$ **Hotel QT.** Giving budget a good name is this Times Square hotel by Andre Balazs, best known for the stylish Mercer Hotel. The unique lobby centers on a raised pool with peep-show-like windows that overlook the bar. Upstairs, rooms are modern, dorm-room in size, but have upscale hotel touches such as feather-pillow-topped mattresses, rain-head showers, and DVD players to accompany the flat-screen TVs. There's no work space, no bathtubs, and double rooms have bunk beds sprouting out of the wall; but you can't beat the price—rooms start at just $225, including continental breakfast—and the location is as central as they come. ⊠ 125 W. 45th St., between 5th and 6th Aves., Midtown West, 10036 ☎ 212/354–2323 📠 212/302–8585 ⊕ www. hotelqt.com ⇥ 139 rooms ⟋ In-room: safe, refrigerator, DVD, Wi-Fi. In-hotel: bar, pool, , gym, laundry service, some pets allowed, no-smok-ing rooms ☰ AE, DC, MC, V ⧖CP Ⓜ Subway: B, D, F, V to 42nd St.; 7 to 5th Ave.

$$ **The Hotel on Rivington.** THOR is a bolt of brazen lightning. The rooms have something completely original and breathtaking—when you hit a button on a remote control, your curtains slowly open to reveal floor-to-ceiling glass windows. Seen that trick before? Well, this is the only tall building around, and the views of the Lower East Side and Midtown are unadulterated New York. The bathrooms don't shy away from the scene either—you'll either want to shower with your glasses on, or you'll blush at being completely naked before the entire city (privacy curtains can be requested). It's a smash. Downstairs is quite possibly the buzzingest hotel bar in the city—this and the jumping restaurant are velvet-roped mayhem on weekends. (Staying here also gives you access to a small VIP bar next door.) The mezzanine bar–art library–

billiard room is a hangout you can call your own. ✉*107 Rivington St., between Ludlow and Essex Sts., Lower East Side, 10002* ☎*212/475–2600 or 800/915–1537* 📠*212/475–5959* ⊕*www.hotelonrivington. com* ↪*110 rooms* ⚐*In-room: safe, refrigerator, Ethernet, Wi-Fi. In-hotel: restaurant, room service, bar, laundry service, concierge, parking (fee), some pets allowed* ▭*AE, D, DC, MC, V* Ⓜ*Subway: F, J, M, Z to Delancey/Essex Sts.*

$$ 🔲 **The Mansfield.** The Mansfield has the best small details of any New York hotel. For instance, attractive key cards with old New York scenes, the lovely elongated leather guest services catalog, the gilt script font on a black leather privacy cards that read Kindly Service My Room. These touches might be gratuitous were it not that this thoughtfulness extends to every corner of the hotel. Built in 1904 as lodging for distinguished bachelors, this small, clubby property has an Edwardian sensibility from the working fireplace in the lounge to the lobby's coffered ceiling and marble-and-cast-iron staircase. The intimate M Bar, lined with books and leather banquettes, is one of the nicer hotel bars in the city. One quirk: standard rooms have much bigger bathrooms than suites, which are comically small. ✉*12 W. 44th St., between 5th and 6th Aves., Midtown West, 10036* ☎*212/944–6050 or 800/255–5167* 📠*212/764–4477* ⊕*www.mansfieldhotel.com* ↪*124 rooms, 25 suites* ⚐*In-room: safe, Wi-Fi. In-hotel: restaurant, room service, bar, laundry service, concierge, parking (fee), public Wi-Fi, public Internet, some pets allowed, no-smoking rooms* ▭*AE, D, DC, MC, V* Ⓜ*Subway: B, D, F, V to 42nd St.*

$–$$ **Herald Square Hotel.** Sculpted cherubs on the facade and vintage magazine covers adorning the common areas hint at this building's previous incarnation as *Life* magazine's headquarters. Rooms are basic and clean; all have TVs and phones with voice mail. There's no concierge and no room service, but the staff is friendly and nearby restaurants will deliver. A no-frills option, to be sure, but it's a great bargain for the convenient neighborhood. ✉*19 W. 31st St., between 5th Ave. and Broadway, Murray Hill, 10001* ☎*212/279–4017 or 800/727–1888* 📠*212/643–9208* ⊕*www.heraldsquarehotel.com* ↪*120 rooms* ⚐*In-room: safe, Wi-Fi. In-hotel: airport shuttle, public Internet, public Wi-Fi, some pets allowed* ▭*AE, D, MC, V* Ⓜ*Subway: B, D, F, N, Q, R, V, W to 34th St./Herald Sq.*

$–$$ **Hotel Beacon.** The Upper West Side's best buy for the price is three blocks from Central Park and Lincoln Center, and footsteps from Zabar's gourmet bazaar. All of the generously sized rooms and suites include marble bathrooms, kitchenettes with coffeemakers, pots and pans, stoves, and microwaves. Closets are huge, and some of the bathrooms have Hollywood dressing room–style mirrors. High floors have views of Central Park, the Hudson River, or the Midtown skyline; the staff here is especially friendly and helpful. The Hotel Beacon makes a nice choice to explore a different corner of New York in a safe, exciting residential neighborhood. Pros: Kitchenettes in all rooms; heart of UWS location; affordable. Cons: Slightly outdated rooms. ✉*2130 Broadway, at W. 75th St., Upper West Side, 10023* ☎*212/787–1100 or 800/572–4969* 📠*212/724–0839* ⊕*www.beaconhotel.com* ↪*120* *rooms, 110 suites* ⟨ *In-room: safe, kitchen, refrigerator. In-hotel: laundry facilities, parking (fee), no-smoking rooms* ▭*AE, D, DC, MC, V* Ⓜ*Subway: 1, 2, 3 to 72nd St.*

NIGHTLIFE & THE ARTS

THE ARTS

For opera, classical music, and dance performances, go to the box office or order tickets through the venue's Web site. For smaller performing-arts companies, including dance, music, and off-Broadway shows, also try **Ticket Central** (☎212/279–4200 ⊕*www.ticketcentral.com*). For Broadway (and some other big-hall events), sure bets are the box office of either **Telecharge** (☎212/239–6200 ⊕*www.telecharge.com*) or **Ticketmaster** (☎212/307–4100 ⊕*www.ticketmaster.com*). Virtually all larger shows are listed with one service or the other, but never both; specifying "premium" will help you get elusive—and expensive (upwards of $300–$400)—seats. A broker or your hotel concierge should be able to procure last-minute tickets, but be prepared to pay a steep surcharge.

■TIP→**Although most online ticket services provide seating maps to help you choose, the advantage of going to the box office is twofold: there are no add-on service fees, and a ticket seller can personally advise you about sight lines for the seat location you are considering.**

If you're in Midtown, inside the Times Square Visitors Center is the League of American Theatres and Producers' **Broadway Ticket Center** (✉*1560 Broadway, between W. 46th and W. 47th Sts Midtown West*☎*888/BROADWAY* ⊕*www.livebroadway.com* Ⓜ *1, 2, 3, 7, N, Q, R, W, S to 42nd St./Times Sq.; N, R, W to 49th St.*). Ticket hours are Monday–Saturday 9–7, Sunday 10–6. You can find a selection of discount vouchers here; it also serves as a one-stop shopping place for full-price tickets for most Broadway shows.

BROADWAY (AND OFF) AT A DISCOUNT

Some shows have front-row orchestra—or very rear balcony—"rush" seats available at a reduced price ($20–$25) on the day of the performance; you must go to the show's box office to buy them. The ⊕*www.broadwaybox.com* site provides a compilation of all discount codes available for a show. In some cases, as with all discount codes offered through the online subscriber services **TheaterMania** (⊕*www.theatermania.com*)and **Playbill** (⊕*www.playbill.com*) you must bring a printout of the offer to the box office, and make your purchase there.

For seats at 25%–50% off the usual price go to **TKTS** (✉*Duffy Sq., at W. 47th St. and Broadway, Midtown West* Ⓜ *1, 2, 3, 7, N, Q, R, W, S to 42nd St./Times Sq.; N, R, W to 49th St.; 1 to 50th St.* ✉*South St. Seaport, at Front and John Sts., Lower Manhattan* Ⓜ *2, 3, 4, 5, A, C, E, J, M, Z to Fulton St./Broadway-Nassau* ⊕*www.tdf.org*) At the Duffy Square location, there is a separate *play only* window. Check the electronic listings board near the ticket windows to mull over your choices while you're on line. Duffy Square hours are Monday–Saturday 3–8 (for evening performances); for Wednesday and Saturday matinees

CLOSE UP

What's Playing Where

New York is rich with easily accessible and comprehensive listings resources in both print and online formats. The *New York Times*'s (⊕ www.nytimes.com) listings are concentrated in its Thursday, Friday, and Sunday papers, as well as online. The *New Yorker* (⊕ www.newyorker.com) is highly selective, but calls attention to performances with its succinct reviews. It hits the stands on Monday. In *New York* magazine (⊕ www.nymag.com), also on newsstands on Monday, see "The Week" section for hot-ticket events. The freebie tabloid, the *Vil-* *lage Voice* (⊕ www.villagevoice.com), comes out on Wednesday; it has extensive listings—especially for theater, music, and dance—as well.

Online-only venues ⊕ www.nytheatre.com, ⊕ www.nyconstage.org, ⊕ www.tdf.org, and ⊕ www.broadway.com provide synopses, schedules when theaters are dark, accessibility info, run times, seating charts, and links to ticket purchases. (Tip: most of these also cover nontheater performances, but they do Broadway and off-Broadway best.)

10–2; for Sunday matinees 11–3; Sunday evenings 3–7. Seaport hours are Monday–Saturday 11–6, Sunday 11–4. With the exception of matinees at the Seaport location (they sell these for next-day performances), all shows offered are same day. Cash or traveler's checks *only at both locations.* ■TIP→Planning ahead? Their Web site notes whether shows are "frequently," "occasionally," or "never" available at their booths.

Fodor'sChoice **Carnegie Hall** (⊠ *881 7th Ave., at W. 57th St., Midtown West* ☎ *212/247–*
★ *7800* ⊕ *www.carnegiehall.org* Ⓜ *N, Q, R, W to 57th St.; B, D, E to 7th Ave.*) is one of the best venues—anywhere—to hear classical music. The world's top orchestras sound so good because of the incomparable acoustics of the fabulously steep Stern Auditorium. So do smaller ensembles and soloists such as soprano Renée Fleming. The subterranean **Zankel Hall,** which also has excellent acoustics, attracts performers such as the Kronos Quartet, Alarm Will Sound, and Youssou N'Dour. Many young talents make their New York debuts in the **Weill Recital Hall.**

★ **Lincoln Center for the Performing Arts** (⊠ *W. 62nd to W. 66th Sts., Broadway to Amsterdam Ave., Upper West Side* ☎ *212/546–2656* ⊕ *www.lincolncenter.org* Ⓜ *1 to 66th St./Lincoln Center*) is the city's musical nerve center, especially when it comes to classical music. Formal and U-shape, the massive Avery Fisher Hall presents the world's great musicians, and is home to the **New York Philharmonic** (☎ *212/875–5656* ⊕ *newyorkphilharmonic.org*), one of the world's finest symphony orchestras. Lorin Maazel conducts, from late September to early June. Bargain-price weeknight "rush hour" performances at 6:45 PM and Saturday matinee concerts at 2 PM are occasionally offered; orchestra rehearsals at 9:45 AM are open to the public on selected weekday mornings (usually Wednesday or Thursday) for $15. The **Chamber Music Society of Lincoln Center** (☎ *212/875–5788* ⊕ *www.chambermusicsociety.org*) performs in Alice Tully Hall, which—while updated for the 2008–09 season—is still considered to be as acoustically perfect as a concert hall can get. In August, Lincoln Center's longest-running classical series, the **Mostly Mozart Festival** (☎*212/875–5399*), captures the crowds.

NIGHTLIFE

Bowery Ballroom. This theater with art deco accents is the city's top midsize concert venue. Packing in the crowds here is a rite of passage for musicians on their way to stardom, including Nada Surf, Clap Your Hands Say Yeah!, and The Go! Team. You can grab one of the tables on the balcony or stand on the main floor. There's a comfortable bar in the basement. ⊠*6 Delancey St., between the Bowery and Chrystie St., Lower East Side10022* ☎*212/533–2111* ⊕*www.boweryballroom. com* Ⓜ*Subway: F, J, M to Delancey St.*

Fodor'sChoice ★ **Campbell Apartment.** Commuting professionals pack into this Grand Central Terminal bar on their way to catch trains home during the evening rush. One of Manhattan's more beautiful rooms, the restored space dates to the 1920s, when it was the private office of an executive named John W. Campbell. He knew how to live, and you can enjoy his good taste sipping a well-made cocktail from an overstuffed chair—if you avoid the evening rush. ⊠*15 Vanderbilt Ave. entrance, Grand Central Station, Midtown East10017* ☎*212/953–0409* ⊕*www.hospitality holdings.com* Ⓜ*Subway: 4, 5, 6, 7, S to 42nd St./Grand Central.*

Fodor'sChoice ★ **The Carlyle.** The hotel's discreetly sophisticated Café Carlyle hosts such top cabaret performers as Betty Buckley, Elaine Stritch, Barbara Cook, and Ute Lemper. Bemelmans Bar, with murals by the author of the *Madeline* books, features a rotating cast of pianist-singers. ⊠*35 E. 76th St., between Madison and Park Aves., Upper East Side,10021* ☎*212/744–1600* ⊕*www.thecarlyle.com* Ⓜ*Subway: 6 to 77th St.*

Four Seasons. New York City (and American) history is made here in Philip Johnson's landmark temple of modern design. Watch for politicos and media moguls in the Grill Room, or enjoy the changing foliage in the romantic Pool Room. ⊠*99 E. 52nd St., between Park and Lexington Aves., Midtown East10022* ☎*212/754–9494* ⊕*www.four seasonsrestaurant.com* Ⓜ*Subway: E, V to Lexington Ave./53rd St.; 6 to 51st St.*

Luna Park. This open-air café at the pavilion near the northern end of Union Square is a great place for a romantic date on a summer evening. Arrive before the 9-to-5 crowd to secure a seat beneath the strings of white lights. ⊠*50 E.17th St., between Broadway and Park Ave. S, Gramercy* ☎*212/475–8464* Ⓜ*Subway: 4, 5, 6, L, N, Q, R, W to 14th St./Union Sq.*

Fodor'sChoice ★ **Pravda.** Cocktails are the rule at this Eastern European–style bar. Choose from more than 70 brands of vodka, including house infusions, or opt for one of the house martinis. The cellarlike space, with an atmospheric vaulted ceiling, is illuminated with candles. Reserve a table for the Russian-inspired fare, especially on weekends. ⊠*281 Lafayette St., between Prince and E. Houston Sts., SoHo10012* ☎*212/226–4944* ⊕*www.pravdany.com* Ⓜ*Subway: B, D, F, V to Broadway–Lafayette St.; 6 to Bleecker St.*

Rainbow Room. On select Friday and Saturday evenings, this romantic institution on the NBC building's 65th floor opens its doors to the public for a dinner dance, where a revolving dance floor and big band orchestra delight those who like to swing-dance and tango. Call ahead for the dance schedule, or enjoy dinner and drinks at the Rainbow Grill any night of the week. The dress code is good news for those who like to play dress up: tuxedoes or suits for men, and cocktail dresses or evening gowns for women. ⊠ *30 Rockefeller Plaza, between 5th and 6th Aves., Midtown West* 10012 ☎ *212/632–5000* ⊕ *www.rainbowroom. com* Ⓜ *Subway: B, D, F, V to 47th–50th Sts./Rockefeller Center.*

Fodor's Choice **Village Vanguard.** This prototypical jazz club, tucked into a cellar in
★ Greenwich Village, has been the haunt of legends like Thelonious Monk, though today you might hear jams from the likes of Bill Charlap and Roy Hargrove, among other jazz personalities. Go on a Monday night to partake in a performance by the resident Vanguard Jazz Orchestra. ⊠ *178 7th Ave. S, between W. 11th and Perry Sts., Greenwich Village* 10014 ☎ *212/255–4037* ⊕ *www.villagevanguard.com* Ⓜ *Subway: A, C, E to 14th St.; L to 8th Ave.*

SHOPPING

Fodor's Choice **Barneys New York.** Barneys continues to provide the fashion-conscious
★ and big-budget shoppers with irresistible, must-have items at its uptown flagship store. The extensive menswear selection has a handful of edgier designers, though made-to-measure is always available. The women's department showcases cachet designers of all stripes, from the subdued lines of Armani and Jil Sander to the irrepressible Alaïa and Zac Posen. The shoe selection trots out Prada boots and strappy Blahniks; the cosmetics department will keep you in Kiehl's, Sue Devitt, and Frederic Malle; jewelry runs from the whimsical (Kazuko) to the classic (Ileana Makri). Expanded versions of the less expensive **Co-op** department occupy the old Barneys' warehouse space on West 18th Street and a niche on Wooster Street. ⊠ *660 Madison Ave., between E. 60th and E. 61st Sts., Upper East Side* ☎ *212/826–8900* Ⓜ *Subway: N, R, W, 4, 5, 6 to 59th St./Lexington Ave.* ⊠ *Barneys Co-op, 236 W. 18th St., between 7th and 8th Aves., Chelsea* ☎ *212/593–7800* Ⓜ *Subway: A, C, E to 14th St.* ⊠ *116 Wooster St., between Prince and Spring Sts., SoHo* ☎ *212/965–9964* Ⓜ *Subway: R, W to Prince St..*

Bloomingdale's. Only a few stores in New York occupy an entire city block; the uptown branch of this New York institution is one of them. The main floor is a crazy, glittery maze of mirrored cosmetic counters and perfume-spraying salespeople. Once you get past this dizzying scene, you can find good buys on designer clothes, bedding, and housewares. The downtown location is smaller, and has a well-edited, higherend selection of merchandise, so you can focus your search for that Michael Kors handbag or pricey pair of stilettos. ⊠ *1000 3rd Ave., main entrance at E. 59th St. and Lexington Ave., Midtown East* ☎ *212/705–2000* Ⓜ *Subway: N, R, W, 4, 5, 6 to 59th St./Lexington Ave.* ⊠ *504 Broadway, between Spring and Broome Sts., SoHo* ☎ *212/729–5900* Ⓜ *Subway: R, W to Prince St.*

Century 21. For many New Yorkers, this downtown fixture—right across the street from the former World Trade Center site—remains the mother lode of discount shopping. Four floors are crammed with

VITAL STATS:

■ State Capitol: As far as NYCers are concerned, "The City"—Manhattan—is the undisputed capital of the world. But we do grudgingly acknowledge the fact that Albany is the official New York state capital.

■ State Motto: "Excelsior!"—which apparently means "ever upward!" (Do feel free to holler our state motto really loudly the next time you're in an elevator.)

■ Official Fruit: New York's official fruit is the apple—but please don't call the NYC the Big Apple, absolutely no one does (unless they're being sarcastic or getting paid) except for the City's marketing people.

■ Official Insect: Our state insect is the nine-spotted ladybug (eight and seven spotters need not apply, we're very picky).

■ Official Animals: Few of us in the city have ever seen the state bird, the bluebird, or mammal, the beaver (though one was spotted swimming in the Bronx River in early 2007—the first NYC beaver sighting in 200 years). Many of us have happily consumed the state fish (Brook Trout, yum!). Hardly anyone knows (or cares) that the official state fossil is the Sea Scorpion, but it seems like a far more appropriate symbol for the indestructible and snarky spirit of this city than an apple or a beaver.

everything from Gucci sunglasses and half-price cashmere sweaters to Ralph Lauren towels, though you'll have to weed through racks of less-fabulous stuff to find that gem. The best bets in the men's department are shoes and the designer briefs; the full floor of designer women's wear can yield some dazzling finds, such as a Calvin Klein leather trench for less than $600 or a sweeping crinoline skirt from John Paul Gaultier. ■ TIP→ Since lines for the communal dressing rooms can be prohibitively long, you might want to wear a bodysuit under your clothes for quick, between-the-racks try-ons. ⊠ *22 Cortlandt St., between Broadway and Church St., Lower Manhattan* ☎*212/227–9092* Ⓜ *Subway: R, W to Cortlandt St.*

Fodor'sChoice **F.A.O. Schwarz.** A New York classic that's better than ever, this children's
★ paradise more than lives up to the hype. The ground floor is a zoo of extraordinary stuffed animals, from cuddly $20 teddies to towering, life-size elephants and giraffes (with larger-than-life prices to match). F.A.O. Schweets stocks M&Ms in every color of the rainbow; upstairs, you can dance on the giant musical floor keyboard, browse through Barbies wearing Armani and Juicy Couture, and design your own customized Hot Wheels car. ⊠ *767 5th Ave., at E. 58th St., Midtown East* ☎*212/644–9400* Ⓜ *Subway: 4, 5, 6 to E. 59th St.*

Museum of Modern Art Design and Book Store. The redesigned MoMA expanded its in-house shop with a huge selection of art posters and more than 2,000 titles on painting, sculpture, film, and photography. Across the street is the **MoMA Design Store** (⊠ *44 W. 53rd St., between 5th and 6th Aves., Midtown West* ☎ *212/767–1050* Ⓜ *Subway: E, V to 5th Ave./53rd St.*), where you can find Frank Lloyd Wright furniture reproductions, vases designed by Alvar Aalto, and lots of clever trinkets. The SoHo branch combines most of the virtues of the first two, although its book selection is smaller. ✉*11 W. 53rd Sts., between 5th and 6th Aves., Midtown West* ☎*212/708–9700* Ⓜ*Subway: E, V to 5th Ave./53rd St.* ✉*81 Spring St., between Broadway and Crosby St., SoHo* ☎*646/613–1367* Ⓜ*Subway: 6 to Spring St..*

Fodor'sChoice **The Strand.** The Broadway branch—a downtown hangout—proudly
★   claims to have "18 miles of books." Craning your neck among the tall-as-trees stacks will likely net you something from the mix of new and old. Rare books are next door, at 826 Broadway, on the third floor. The Fulton Street branch is near South Street Seaport; it's decidedly less overwhelming. ✉*828 Broadway, at E. 12th St., East Village* ☎*212/473–1452* Ⓜ*Subway: L, N, Q, R, W, 4, 5, 6 to 14th St./Union Sq.* ✉*95 Fulton St., between Gold and William Sts., Lower Manhattan* ☎*212/732–6070* Ⓜ*Subway: A, C, J, M, Z, 2, 3, 4, 5 to Fulton St./Broadway-Nassau*

Fodor'sChoice **Tiffany & Co.** The display windows can be soigné, funny, or just plain
★   breathtaking. Alongside the $80,000 platinum-and-diamond bracelets, a lot here is affordable on a whim—and everything comes wrapped in that unmistakable Tiffany blue. ✉*727 5th Ave., at E. 57th St., Midtown East* ☎*212/755–8000* Ⓜ*Subway: N, R, W to 5th Ave./59th St.*

VISITOR INFORMATION

Downtown Alliance (✉*120 Broadway, Suite 3340, between Pine and Thames Sts., Lower Manhattan, 10271* ☎*212/566–6700* ⊕*www.downtownny.com*).

Grand Central Partnership ☎*212/883–2420* (⊕*www.grandcentralpartnership. org*).

NYC & Company Convention & Visitors Bureau (✉*810 7th Ave., between W. 52nd and W. 53rd Sts., 3rd fl., Midtown West* ☎*212/484–1222* ⊕*www.nycvisit.com*).

Times Square Information Center (✉*1560 Broadway, between 46th and 47th Sts., Midtown West* ☎*212/768–1560* ⊕*www.timessquarenyc.org*).

Niagara Falls

WITH WESTERN NEW YORK

Horseshoe Falls

WORD OF MOUTH

"Make sure you stay in one of the hotels facing the falls on the Canadian side—we had a Sheraton with floor to ceiling views of the floodlit falls, a fireplace, Jacuzzi etc. And you can do the casino for a little mild amusement."

—nytraveler

EXPLORING NIAGARA FALLS

300 mi west of Albany via I–90; 400 mi northwest of New York City via I–80, I–81, and I–90.

By Sarah Richards

No photograph can capture the jaw-dropping beauty and absolute force of Niagara Falls. Though not among the world's highest waterfalls, the falls are, for sheer volume of water, unsurpassed at more than 750,000 gallons per second in summer. The falls spurred the invention of alternating electric current, and they run one of the largest hydroelectric developments in the world. They are a true natural wonder, even more amazing considering they're actually fueled by four of the Great Lakes—Superior, Michigan, Huron, and Erie—as they flow into the fifth, Ontario.

The falls are actually three cataracts: the American and Bridal Veil Falls in New York State, and the Horseshoe Falls in Ontario. On the American side, you can park in the lot on Goat Island near the American Falls and walk along the path beside the Niagara River, which becomes more and more turbulent as it approaches the big drop-off of just over 200 feet.

One highlight of the greater Niagara region is New York's second-largest city, Buffalo, which manages to maintain a quaint, "small town" feeling by hanging on to its distinct vibe—a product of its rich ethnic, cultural, and architectural history. Another jewel in western New York's crown is the Chautauqua-Allegheny region, 22 mi of soft hills, vineyards, and fish-filled lakes following the shores of Lake Erie. For most visitors, the main draw is the Chautauqua Institution, where an unusual mix of arts, education, religion, and recreation during a nine-week summer season is on offer. A final must-see in the region is Letchworth State Park, dubbed the "Grand Canyon of the East."

WHO WILL ESPECIALLY LOVE THIS TRIP?

Families: The young and young-at-heart love the falls, and all the amusements that go with them. The Niagara Power Project Visitors Center has interactive activities that are child-friendly; and the Aquarium of Niagara can be a delight for inquisitive minds. Marineland and Clifton Hill, on the other side of the border, cater to younger tourists.

Nature enthusiasts: Those looking for nature of a quieter variety find the unbridled beauty of Letchworth State Park a welcome respite. The oft-forgotten Chautauqua-Allegheny area is also pleasant, with rolling hills, wineries, and dense forests.

Couples: Romantic packages in hotels at Niagara Falls take full advantage of awe-inspiring views, enhanced by misty early mornings and grand after-dark illumination.

Gamblers: Try lady luck at either the Seneca Niagara Casino or across the border in Fallsview Casino Resort, where Vegas-style slots and card tables come complete with an all-you-can-eat buffet and cabaret show.

TOP 5 REASONS TO GO

Niagara Falls: Despite being one of the world's busiest destinations, the astounding beauty of the falls lives up to the hype.

Glitz & Kitsch: Cross the border to visit Ontario's gauche entertainment district, Clifton Hill; or splash out in the Vegas-style Fallsview Casino resort.

The Wright Stuff: Visit one of the largest collections of prairie-style architecture by the world-famous Frank Lloyd Wright in Buffalo.

Letchworth State Park: The area's lesser-known natural wonder is a giant canyon slicing through verdant splendor.

Chautauqua Institution: People gather from far and wide for this unique festival that touches on modern issues, such as politics, religion, and the arts.

WHEN IS THE BEST TIME TO VISIT?

In Niagara Falls, the high season runs from Memorial Day through Labor Day, when most cultural activities take place and the boat rides are operating. Summer temperatures range from 75°F to 85°F, with occasional light rainfall. The area near Niagara Falls is always misty, a natural refresher in the summertime and very hot, humid days are infrequent. Winter temperatures create ice-covered tree branches and rocks that sparkle, and the railings and bridges turn almost crystalline.

HOW SHOULD I GET THERE?

BUS
Greyhound and Trailways link the region with New York City and much of the rest of the state; stops include Buffalo and Niagara Falls. Tickets for the two bus lines are interchangeable.

DRIVING
Interstate 90, which extends from Seattle to Boston, passes through Buffalo.

FLYING
Buffalo Niagara International Airport (BNIA) is the main airport in the region. Continental and JetBlue Airlines fly direct from New York City.

TRAIN
Amtrak connects Buffalo and Niagara Falls with New York City.

HOW DO I GET AROUND?

BY CAR
From Buffalo, I–190 splits off from I–90; take it across Grand Island to the Robert Moses Parkway and into Niagara Falls. Another enjoyable route is the scenic New York State Seaway Trail, which traces the region's perimeter in the north and west along lakes Ontario and Erie.

Niagara Falls

Victoria Ave.

Roberts St.

Stanley Ave.

CANADA

Clifton Hill

Ferry St.

Niagara Pkwy.

ONTARIO

Murray St.

Niagara Falls
Casino Resort

Portage Rd.

Dunn St.

Stanley Ave.

Niagara River

Rainbow Br.

Prospect
Park

Prospect Point
Observation Tower

**American
Falls**

3

4

**Bridal Veil
Falls**

Luna Island

Pedestrian
Bridge

Green Island

American
Rapids Br.

Goat Island

Three Sisters
Islands

Horseshoe
Falls

Niagara Pkwy.

Niagara River

Robert Moses Pkwy.

Whirlpool St.

1

2

Pine Ave.

Walnut Av.

Main St.

Ferry Ave.

2nd St.

3rd St.

4th St.

5th St.

Niagara St.

1st Ave.

**Seneca
Niagara
Casino**

NEW YORK

Rainbow Blvd.

Buffalo Ave.

Robert Moses Pkwy.

TO
GRAND ISLAND

0   1/8 mile

0   200 meters

Marineland

How to Snack

Buffalo wings, deep-fried chicken wings coated in butter and cayenne, are the area's culinary claim to fame. In these parts, you can find them in nearly every bar or pub, but Anchor Bar & Restaurant claims to be the first.

Wings are traditionally served with celery sticks and bleu cheese dressing—one of those strange combinations that sounds disgusting, but just works for some reason. Be sure to at least try dunking one of your wings,

even if you don't normally like bleu cheese. Another option is to ask for a side of ranch dressing, which also pairs wonderfully with the wings' spicy coating.

Beef on weck, slow-roasted beef with fresh horseradish on a caraway seed roll was introduced by German immigrants in the late 1800s ("weck" is a shortened form of "kimmelweck"). Try it at Coles, one of Buffalo's hottest sandwich spots.

5

After enjoying the falls from the U.S. side, you may want to walk or drive across Rainbow Bridge to the Canadian side, where you can get a far view of the U.S. falls and a close-up of the Horseshoe Falls.

WHERE SHOULD I FOCUS MY ENERGY?

If you're here for 1 day: Don a rain slicker and take on the Falls on the *Maid of the Mist* boat tour.

If you're here for 2 days: If you've got a little more time, explore some of the other amusements in **Niagara Falls.**

If you're here for 3 days: Walk across the Rainbow Bridge for a view from the Canadian side.

If you're here for 4 days: Add a day-trip to Buffalo to view the Wright buildings.

If you're here for 5 days: Linger in Buffalo for a few more hours before moving on to the Chautauqua-Allegheny region.

If you're here for 6 days: Spend a day in Chautauqua.

If you're here for 7 days or more: Make a detour in Letchworth State Park before ending up back in Niagara Falls.

WHAT ARE THE TOP EXPERIENCES?

Buffalo Wings: Whether you like your deep-fried chicken wings "hot" or "suicidal," Anchor Bar & Restaurant is the best. If you're staying in Niagara Falls, count on Top of the Falls or Buzzy's for memorable wings.

Green space: The centerpiece of the nearly 15,000-acre expanse of Letchworth State Park is the 17-mi Genessee River Gorge, which has three large waterfalls and cliff walls that rise 600 feet. Take a breather in pleasant Chautauqua, a town that allows no automobile traffic—just the sounds of nature and pleasant townsfolk fill the silence.

Niagara Falls: Experiencing the spray of 750,000 gallons of water per second aboard the *Maid of the Mist*, armed with nothing but a yellow slicker—it's an exhilarating, not-to-be-missed experience.

Romance: Novelist Charles Dickens said of Niagara Falls, "I seemed to be lifted from the earth and to be looking into Heaven." Jerome Bonaparte (brother of Napoléon) was also taken by the beauty of the falls. He and his new bride stayed here for a week in 1803 during their honeymoon, sparking a tradition that still continues to this day.

> **HISTORY YOU CAN SEE**
>
> Architect buffs will be interested in touring the prairie-style Darwin D. Martin House Complex in Buffalo, commissioned in 1902. Also worth perusing on the vast estate are the Gardener's Cottage, the Walter V. Davidson House, the William R. Heath House, and a summer estate, Graycliff, built in 1926 atop a 70-foot-cliff overlooking Lake Erie.

BEST BETS

SIGHTS AND TOURS

NIAGARA FALLS, USA

★ **Aquarium of Niagara.** Dive into Niagara's other water wonder, a close encounter with more than 1,500 aquatic animals, including sharks, piranhas, sea lions, and moray eels. ⊠ *701 Whirlpool St.* ☎ *716/285–3575 or 800/500–4609* ⊕ *www.aquariumofniagara.org* ⊠ *$9* ☉ *Late May–early Sept., daily 9–7; early Sept.–late May, daily 9–5.*

Fodor's Choice *Maid of the Mist* **Boat Tour.** View the three falls from up close during a
★ spectacular 30-minute ride on this world-famous boat tour. Waterproof
☉ clothing is provided. To reach the boat launch on the New York side, take the elevator in the Prospect Point Observation Tower in Niagara Falls State Park down to the base. Call for special hours in summer and on holidays. ⊠ *Prospect Park, 151 Buffalo Ave.* ☎ *716/284–8897* ⊕ *www.maidofthemist.com* ⊠ *$12.50* ☉ *Apr.–late May and early Sept.–late Oct., weekdays 9:45–4:45, weekends 9:45–5:45; late May–mid-June, daily 9:45–5:45; mid-June–early Sept., daily 9:45–7:45.*

Niagara Falls State Park. Established in 1885 to protect the public's access to the land surrounding the falls, this is the oldest state park in the country. It was designed by noted landscape architect Frederick Law Olmsted, who also designed New York City's Central Park.

The mainland sites include a visitor center, an observation tower, and
★ a discovery center. The **Prospect Park Visitor Center** (⊠ *Center free, movie $2* ☉ *Daily 8–6*)is surrounded by gardens and has tourist information, exhibits, and a snack bar. The theater in the visitor center shows the giant-screen "thrill film" *Niagara: A History of the Falls*, which gets your attention with a virtual-reality helicopter simulator ride. The 282-foot-tall **Prospect Point Observation Tower** (⊠ *$1* ☉ *Late Mar.–Dec., daily 9–8*)offers dramatic views of all three falls. A glass-walled elevator takes you to

an observation deck high above the gushing waters. Take the elevator to the base of the tower for the *Maid of the Mist* boat tour. The **Niagara Gorge Discovery Center** (☎716/278–1070 ✉$3)explains, through interactive exhibits and a multiple-screen movie, the natural history of the Falls and the Niagara Gorge and their formation. **Goat Island** is a wonderful spot for a quiet walk and a close-up view of the rapids. The **Cave of the Winds Trip** (☎716/278–1730 ✉$10 ⊗*May–Oct., daily 9–8*), on Goat Island, gives you access to the base of Bridal Veil Falls. An

> ## LIKE A LOCAL
>
> With its close proximity to southwestern Ontario, many *Canadianisms* have transcended Niagara Falls and been incorporated into the vocabulary of many a western New Yorker. In addition vowel sounds are different in northern cities. A Buffalonian may tell you about the "busl wings" (as in the "best Buffalo wings") in the city and ask for a "cayeen of pop" ("a can of soda") to wash them down with.

elevator takes you down into the gorge, where you follow special walkways to an observation deck near the thundering waters—definitely close enough to get sprayed. Waterproof gear is provided. There are two main entrances (for cars) to the park, both off Robert Moses Parkway. The south entrance takes you over a bridge to Goat Island; the north entrance puts you near the visitors center. Goat Island has two parking areas, one near the American Falls.

Niagara Power Project Visitors Center. Niagara Falls generates power at one of the largest hydroelectric plants in the world. The visitor center, 4½ mi north of the Falls, has hands-on exhibits, including a working model of a hydropower turbine, computer games, and an explanation of how hydroelectric power is generated. Kids can play with 50 interactive exhibits. A 3-D photo display depicts the construction of the plant. ✉*5777 Lewiston Rd., Rte. 104* ☎*716/286–6661 or 866/697–2386* ⊕*www.nypa.gov* ✉*Free* ⊗*Daily 9–5.*

Seneca Niagara Casino. The Seneca Nation runs an 82,000-square-foot casino with more than 3,200 slot machines and 100 table games. ✉*310 4th St.* ☎*716/299–1100 or 877/873–6322* ⊕*www.snfgc.com* ✉*Free* ⊗*Daily 24 hrs.*

NIAGARA FALLS, CANADA

Marineland, a theme park with a marine show, wildlife displays, and rides, is 1½ km (1 mi) south of the falls. The daily marine shows includes performing killer whales, dolphins, harbor seals, and sea lions. Among the many rides is Dragon Mountain, the world's largest steel roller coaster. Marineland is signposted from Niagara Parkway or reached from the Queen Elizabeth Way by exiting at McLeod Road (Exit 27). ✉*8375 Stanley Ave.* ☎*905/356–9565* ⊕*www.marineland canada.com* ✉*C$33.95* ⊗*Late May–early Oct., daily 9–dusk.*

Clifton Hill is the most crassly commercial district of Niagara Falls. Sometimes referred to as "Museum Alley," this area includes more wax museums than one usually sees in a lifetime—and a House of Frankenstein Burger King. Attractions are typically open late (11 PM), with admission ranging from C$7 to C$13. They include the **Guinness Museum of World Records** (☎905/356–2299 ⊕*www.guinnessniagarafalls.com*);Ripley's Believe It or Not Museum and **Ripley's Moving Theatre** (☎905/356–2299 ⊕*www.ripleysniagara.com*), a 3-D movie, where you actually move with the picture (seats move in eight directions); and **Movieland Wax Museum** (☎905/358–3676 ⊕*www.cliftonhill.com/niagara_falls_attractions/movieland_wax_museum*), with such lifelike characters as Indiana Jones and Snow White. A six-story-high chocolate bar, at the base of Clifton Hill, marks the entrance to the **Hershey's World of Chocolate** (✉*5685 Falls Ave.* ☎*800/468–1714* ⊕*www.cliftonhill.com*). Inside are 7,000 square feet of milk shakes, fudge, truffles, cookbooks, and those trademark Kisses.

Niagara Fallsview Casino Resort, Canada's largest privately funded commercial development crowns the city's skyline overlooking the Niagara Parks with picture-perfect views of both falls. Within the C$1 billion, 30-story complex are a glitzy theater, spa, shops, 150 gaming tables, 3,000 slot machines, and plenty of restaurants. ✉*6380 Fallsview Blvd.* ☎*888/325–5788* ⊕*www.fallsviewcasinoresort.com* ⊙*Daily 24 hrs.*

BUFFALO, NEW YORK

★ **Albright-Knox Art Gallery.** The gallery's collections are especially rich in postwar American and European art, including Jackson Pollock, Jasper Johns, and Andy Warhol. On Sunday afternoons in July and August, free jazz performances are held on the massive front steps. ✉*1285 Elmwood Ave.* ☎*716/882–8700* ⊕*www.albrightknox.org* 🎟*$10* ⊙*Tues.–Thurs. and weekends 10–5, Fri. 10–10.*

The Darwin D. Martin House, part of the **Darwin D. Martin House Complex** in Buffalo's Parkside East Historic District, is considered one of the finest examples of a Wright prairie-style structure. Reservations are required; guided tours only. ✉*125 Jewett Pkwy., Buffalo* ☎*716/856–3858* ⊕*darwinmartinhouse.org* 🎟*$15* ⊙*By appointment.*

The Martins liked their Buffalo home so much that they also commissioned Wright to design their summer estate. The centerpiece of the 8½-acre **Graycliff** estate is the two-story main house, built in 1926. Its cantilevered balconies take advantage of its position atop a 70-foot-cliff overlooking Lake Erie. The property is about 13 mi south of Buffalo. ✉*6472 Old Lake Shore Rd., Derby* ☎*716/947–9217* ⊕*graycliff.bfn.org* 🎟*$25* ⊙*By appointment.*

LETCHWORTH STATE PARK

★ The Genesee River snakes its way through this 14,350-acre park, carving a 17-mi gorge with cliff walls that soar nearly 600 feet in some spots, which is why the park is often called the Grand Canyon of the East.

ON THE WAY

Lily Dale Assembly: Swing by the world's largest spiritualist community—an attractive colony of Victorian houses on the shores of Lake Cassadaga—if you're driving south to Chautauqua. From late June to Labor Day, there are workshops, medium readings, a research library, lectures, and a variety of recreational activities. ⊠5 Melrose Park, west of Rte 60, Lily Dale ☎716/595-8721 ⊕www.lilydaleassembly.com.

Luci-Desi Museum: On the way to Letchworth State Park, those who love Lucy may want to stop in her hometown, Jamestown, to visit this themed museum. ⊠212 Pine St. ☎716/484-0800 ⊕www.lucy-desi.com ⊠$6 ⊙Mon.-Sat. 10-5:30, Sun. 1-5.

Explore and More Children's Museum: Heading north from Letchworth State Park to Niagara Falls? Kids might enjoy a pause in East Aurora aka Toy Town, U.S.A., as it is home to both the headquarters of the Fisher-Price toy company and a unique toy museum. ⊠300 Gleed Ave. ☎716/655-5131 ⊕www.exploreandmore.org ⊠$5 ⊙Wed.-Sat. 10-5, Sun. noon-5.

The river spills over three large waterfalls—one 107 feet high—and the long and narrow park encompasses awesome rock formations and dense forest. Some 66 mi of trails are used for hiking, biking, horse-back riding, snowmobiling, and cross-country skiing. Many activities here center on water; you may go fishing, white-water rafting, or kayaking, or swim in one of two pools. ⊠1 Letchworth State Park, off I-390 Exit 7, Castile ☎716/493-3600 ⊕nysparks.state.ny.us ⊠Parking $6 daily Apr.-Oct. and weekends Dec.-Feb. ⊙Daily dawn-dusk.

CHAUTAUQUA

The Victorian splendor of this self-contained 856-acre village and cultural-education center on Chautauqua Lake attracts as many as 180,000 visitors each summer. It has small winding streets lined with gas lights and beautiful Victorian houses, which are often outfitted in bright colors, turrets, multiple gables, and gingerbread trim. It all began in 1874, when John Heyl Vincent, a Methodist minister, and Lewis Miller, an industrialist, set up a training center for Sunday-school teachers here. The **Chautauqua Institution** (⊠1 Ames Ave. ☎716/357-6250, 716/357-6200, or 800/836-2787 ⊕www.ciweb.org)rapidly grew into a summer-long cultural encampment. More than 2,000 events take place here from late June through August, including lectures, art exhibitions, outdoor symphonies, theater, dance performances, opera, and open-enrollment classes.

WHERE TO EAT

WHAT IT COSTS					
	¢	$	$$	$$$	$$$$
RESTAURANTS	under $8	$8–$14	$15–$21	$22–$30	over $30

Restaurant prices are for a main course at dinner (or at the most expensive meal served), excluding tax and tip.

NIAGARA FALLS, USA

$$$ ✕**Clarkson House.** This local institution occupies an antiques-filled 19th-century building. Cloth-covered tables contrast with hardwood floors and old wood beams. The menu blends contemporary, American, and Continental dishes; steaks—New York strip and Kobe flatiron among them—are a specialty. You have a large choice of starters, such as calamari and breaded oysters. Reservations are essential on weekends. ✉ *810 Center St., Lewiston* ☎ *716/754–4544* ⊟ *AE, MC, V* ⊘ *Closed Mon. No lunch.*

$$ ✕**Top of the Falls.** A panoramic way to dine, this spot, just feet from the brink of Niagara Falls, lives up to its name. The view is awesome, as is the thick New York strip steak. ✉ *Niagara Falls State Park, off Robert Moses Pkwy.* ☎ *716/278–0348* ⊟ *AE, D, MC, V* ⊘ *Closed Oct.–early May.*

$ ✕**Buzzy's New York Style Pizza & Buffalo Wings.** Buzzy's, an institution since 1953, serves 30 different pies, calzones, subs, and hoagies. For the adventurous eater, the chicken wings and chicken fingers—fresh, not frozen—come with blue-cheese dip and a choice of 10 sauces, including one called Suicide (the warning on the menu says it's "very hot"). ✉ *7617 Niagara Falls Blvd.* ☎ *716/283–5333* ⊟ *AE, MC, V.*

BUFFALO

$ ✕**Anchor Bar & Restaurant.** Anchor claims to have originated Buffalo

Fodor'sChoice   wings. Some people dispute that, but many come to sample the ground-

★   breaking invention in bar food. Try them "hot" for the full experience. A buffalo's head hanging on the wall is about all the atmosphere you need. ✉ *1047 Main St.* ☎ *716/886–8920* ⊟ *AE, D, DC, MC, V.*

$ ✕**Coles.** Sandwiches are a specialty of this restaurant, which was established in 1934. Among the mouthwatering favorites is the western New York special, "beef on weck"—sliced roasted beef on a caraway seed roll. Dinner choices include lobster ravioli in crab-vodka sauce and Gorgonzola-encased New York strip steak with wine sauce. The checkerboard floor, a long bar, and wooden booths are part of the charm of this casual place. ✉ *1104 Elmwood Ave.* ☎ *716/886–1449* ⊟ *AE, D, DC, MC, V.*

WHERE TO STAY

WHAT IT COSTS					
	¢	$	$$	$$$	$$$$
HOTELS	under $100	$100–$149	$150–$199	$200–$250	over $250

Hotel prices are for two people in a standard double room in high season, excluding tax.

NIAGARA FALLS, USA

$$ ✕⊡ **Red Coach Inn.** Established in 1923 and modeled after an old English inn, the sprawling Tudor-style building includes wood-burning fireplaces and a spectacular view of Niagara Falls' upper rapids. Luxurious touches include Frette robes, Bose stereos, and the champagne and cheese tray presented when you arrive. Dishes in the classy restaurant include slow-roasted prime rib and broiled 8-ounce lobster tail with black-pepper fettuccine. ⊠*2 Buffalo Ave., 14303* ☎*716/282–1459 or 866/719–2070* ⊕*www.redcoach.com* *2 rooms, 13 suites* ⌂*In-room: kitchen (some), refrigerator, VCR (some), dial-up. In-hotel: restaurant, room service, bar, laundry service, no-smoking rooms* ▭*D, MC, V* ⎪○⎪*CP.*

¢ ⊡ **Comfort Inn, The Pointe.** At the entrance to Niagara Falls State Park, this is the closest hotel to the falls in the United States. About half the rooms overlook the Niagara River on its breathtaking tumble. The rooms are standard, but with such scenery about 500 feet away you won't spend much time in them. ⊠*1 Prospect Pointe, 14303* ☎*716/284–6835 or 800/284 6835* 🖷*716/284–5177* ⊕*www.comfortinnthepointe.com* *116 rooms, 2 suites* ⌂*In-room: refrigerator (some), Wi-Fi. In-hotel: restaurant, laundry service, parking (no fee), no-smoking rooms* ▭*AE, D, DC, MC, V* ⎪○⎪*CP.*

NIAGARA FALLS, CANADA

$$$$ ✕⊡ **Niagara Fallsview Casino Resort.** The C$1 billion price tag of this

Fodor'sChoice
★
casino-resort means there are touches of luxury everywhere: natural light streams through glass domes and floor-to-ceiling windows, chandeliers hang in grand hallways, and frescoes lend an aristocratic feel. All bright and colorful rooms in this 30-story hotel tower overlook the Canadian or American Falls. The lavish buffet is excellent and reasonable (C$20 for dinner). ⊠*6380 Fallsview Blvd., L2G 7X5* ☎*905/358–3255 or 888/946–3255* 🖷*905/371–7952* ⊕*www.fallsviewcasinoresort.com* *283 rooms, 85 suites* ⌂*In-room: safe, kitchen (some). In-hotel: 3 restaurants, pool, gym, spa, concierge, laundry service, executive floor, public Internet, no-smoking rooms* ▭*AE, MC, V.*

$$ ⊡ **Sheraton on the Falls.** The first high-rise hotel you see as you're coming in on the Niagara Parkway, the Sheraton is a glistening behemoth, with rooms on 20 floors overlooking either the town or the falls. You can spend C$40 more per night to overlook the falls, but the view is truly spectacular. Rooms are large and sophisticated with king-size beds, sofas, electric fireplaces, floor-to-ceiling windows that include small doors you can open to hear the rush of the falls, and enormous marble bathrooms with Jacuzzi tubs. If you decide against a falls-view room, you can still get the panorama in the penthouse dining room. There's a Starbucks in the lobby and around the corner is the Clifton Hill tourist district. ⊠*5875 Falls Ave., L2G 3K7* ☎*905/374–4445 or 800/325–3535* 🖷*905/371–0157* ⊕*www.niagarafallshotels.com/sheraton* *320 rooms, 350 suites* ⌂*In-room: dial-up. In-hotel: restaurant, bar, pool, gym, concierge, laundry service, parking (fee), no-smoking rooms* ▭*AE, D, DC, MC, V.*

5

CHAUTAUQUA

$$$ 🏨 **The Spencer.** Rooms at this Victorian hotel are individually decorated and named for great authors. The Lord Byron room is decked out in regal red; the Isabel Allende room has leafy murals on the walls and a South America theme. Some rooms are small and cramped, whereas others are quite capacious. During the Chautauqua Institution season, the minimum required stay is a week. ✉ *25 Palestine Ave.* 🕾 *716/357–3785 or 800/398–1306* 🖷 *716/357–4733* ⊕ *www.thespencer.com* ⤵ *21 rooms, 5 suites* ⚲ *In-room: kitchen (some), VCR, Wi-Fi. In-hotel: no-smoking rooms* ▤ *No credit cards* ⃝ *CP.*

LETTWORTH STATE PARK

¢ 🏨 **Glen Iris Inn.** The country inn, part of Letchworth State Park, overlooks the Genesee River. Park founder William Pryor Letchworth had used the mansion as a retreat. It was turned into an inn in 1914. The interiors are decked out in Victorian style. Standard rooms are on the small side, with one double or two twin beds, but the suites are very spacious. The Cherry Suite has a whirlpool tub, a private porch with great views of the gorge, and striking chevron-patterned hardwood floors. The restaurant ($$–$$$; closed Nov.–late Mar.) serves American and Continental fare, such as baked salmon fillet in port sauce. ✉ *7 Letchworth State Park, Castile 14427* 🕾 *585/493–2622* 🖷 *585/493–5803* ⊕ *www.glenirisinn. com* ⤵ *12 rooms, 4 suites* ⚲ *In-room: no TV. In-hotel: restaurant, no-smoking rooms* ▤ *AE, D, MC, V* ⊙ *Closed Nov.–late Mar.*

> ### VITAL STATS
>
> ■ Niagara Falls attracts 12 million tourists each year.
>
> ■ Twenty percent of all the fresh water in the world lies in the Great Lakes Michigan, Huron, Superior, and Erie; all the outflow empties into the Niagara river and eventually cascades over Niagara Falls and into the fifth Great Lake, Ontario.
>
> ■ Until 1912—when the bridge broke and three tourists were killed—visitors were allowed to actually walk out onto the river's ice bridge and view the falls from below.

VISITOR INFORMATION

Buffalo Niagara Convention & Visitors Bureau (✉ *617 Main St., Suite 200, Buffalo 14203* 🕾 *800/283–3256* ⊕ *www.buffalocvb.org*).

Greater Niagara Region of New York State (⊕ *www.greaterniagarausa.com*).

Niagara Tourism & Convention Corp (✉ *345 3rd St., Suite 605, Niagara Falls 14303* 🕾 *716/282–8992 or 800/338–7890* ⊕ *www.niagara-usa.com*).

Philadelphia

WITH THE PENNSYLVANIA DUTCH COUNTRY

Boat House Row, Philadelphia

WORD OF MOUTH

"We loved Philadelphia! The history, architecture, ambiance, food–
all was above and beyond wonderful."

—SCannon

"But the 'must-sees' for one day could be so many things: I'd say
that the Liberty Bell/Independence Hall area would certainly be
among them . . . The Constitution Center is super and in that area
as well."

—Amy

EXPLORING PHILADELPHIA

95 mi southwest of Philadelphia via the New Jersey Turnpike and I-95; 140 mi northeast of Washington, DC, via MD–295, I–895, and I–95; 305 mi east of Pittsburgh via I–376 and I–76

By Piers
Marchant

"I'd like to see Paris before I die. Philadelphia will do."
—Mae West

Perhaps no other city in the country is as misunderstood as Philadelphia. Travelers who imagine a drab city filled with Rocky Balboa–type underdogs are surprised to find a vibrant, exciting, culturally rich, and expansive place brimming with history. As the birthplace to the country, the history of the U.S. is certainly celebrated here, from the Valley Forge Historical Park to the newly built Independence Mall. But there's also a more modern twist to Philadelphia culture—a stunning array of shops, restaurants, theaters, cafés, and galleries that can keep visitors busy for days.

A big sports town, Philly is also known for its die-hard fans, who flock to the city's four professional teams in droves—and, more often than not, drive home unhappy. But they can cushion the blow with a monstrous cheesesteak, washed down with a cold lager.

The city's main business–residential district, known, appropriately enough, as Center City, has been on an upswing for the better part of a decade, with newly constructed high-rises and condos constantly being erected to keep up with demand. And there's far more to Philly's neighborhood scene than Rittenhouse Square and Old City—two of the tonier and best-known areas. South Philly has come a long way since Rocky, there's a lot more going on here now than grey sweats-clad brawny boxers shuffling past trash fires.

WHO WILL ESPECIALLY LOVE THIS TRIP?

History Buffs: In addition to the aforementioned Independence Mall—which includes the Hall, Liberty Bell, the Visitor Center and the National Constitution Center—visitors can also check out the U.S. Mint and Franklin Court, where the home of Philadelphia's own Benjamin Franklin once stood.

Foodies: From lowbrow (cheesesteaks at Campo's) to highbrow (Coquilles Saint-Jacques rôties at Le Bec-Fin), Philadelphia is a food-lover's paradise. Here you can snag a world-class roast pork sandwich at Tony Luke's in South Philly, or enjoy award-winning homemade wild mushroom dumplings at Susanna Foo, on Philly's Restaurant Row, which is also home to ever-swank Rouge and extraordinary Alma de Cuba, among many notable others.

Sports Zealots: It's true that Philly has gone the longest without a championship of any city that has a team in all four major pro leagues—24 years and counting—but that does little to diminish the pride and enthusiasm of the city's great sports fans. Citizen's Bank Park, a newly built baseball-only park for the Phillies, sits adjacent to the equally new

TOP 5 REASONS TO GO

Boom!: No one anywhere loves fireworks more than the good citizens of Philadelphia. Independence Day is huge, naturally, and is spread out over several days, but New Year's fireworks are also a fixture.

More than just Cheesesteaks: Known for rolls filled with meat and cheese, Philly actually has an incredible assortment of excellent cuisine.

American Icons: The country was born here, and Independence Hall and the Liberty Bell still stand as monuments to our founding fathers.

Philadelphia Museum of Art: The PMA is, perhaps best known for having Rocky leap up its steps, but there's an amazing permanent collection inside.

Going Green: One of the largest municipal parks in the world, Fairmount Park offers acre after rolling acre of pristine beauty.

Lincoln Financial Field, home of the NFL's Eagles, and the Wachovia Center, where the NBA's 76ers and NHL's Flyers do business.

Sociologists: With its strong ties to history, Philly is a still largely a city of neighborhoods. From the huge population of Italians, Asians, and Latinos in South Philly to the predominantly African-American West Philly to the city's vibrant Chinatown, different cultures abound and flourish here.

Music Lovers: The world-class Philadelphia Orchestra plays in the gorgeous Kimmel Center; while the venerable Academy of Music, the former home of the Orchestra still hosts the Pennsylvania Ballet and the Opera Company. Fans of a less-classical nature can check out indie bands at the Trocadero and the North Star, or take in a show at the timeless Tower Theatre. Lovers of world-beat can head over to World Café Live; while jazz aficionados can take in some great music at Ortlieb's.

WHEN IS THE BEST TIME TO VISIT?

If you can brave the cold, the Mummer's Parade on New Year's Day is always a local highlight. Philly's answer to the Krewes of New Orleans, Mummers dress in outrageous, oft-feathered outfits and perform music and dances on and around their float as the parade makes its way down Broad Street.

Spring is long and pretty here. Before the summer heat and humidity creeps up, there are blossoming flowers and trees, and the temperature is just about perfect—this is a great time to take in the stunning array of flowers and fountains at Longwood Gardens. Summer, though hot, is the time to come to Philly for all things historic, including guided tours through Old City and Independence Mall, but especially for the massive Independence Day Celebration—actually a week of concerts, exhibitions, and fireworks galore.

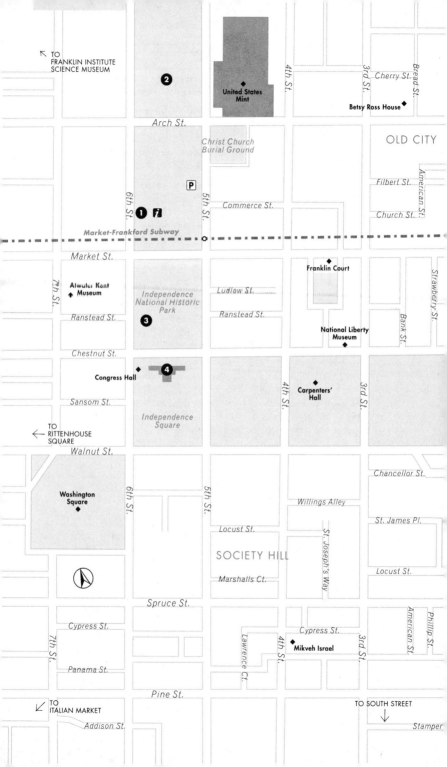

The Historic Area & Penn's Landing

Race St.

Front St.

◆ Elfreth's Alley

2nd St

Arch St.

Mascher St.

Cuthbert St.

Church St.

Market St.

Black Horse Alley [P]

Letitia

Front St.

Chestnut St.

Ionic St.

Gatzmer St. [P]

Sansom St.

2nd St

Walnut St.

Dock St.

38th Parallel Pl.

Dock St.

[P]

Spruce St.

Front St.

2nd St

Delancey St.

Pine St.

Pier 5

Pier 3

Delaware River

Delaware Expwy.

95

Christopher Columbus Blvd. (formerly Delaware Ave.)

PENN'S LANDING

FERRY DOCK

Independence Seaport Museum ◆

KEY

– · · – Market-Frankford Subway

[P] Parking

[i] Tourist Information

6

0 ——— 1/8 mile

0 ——— 200 meters

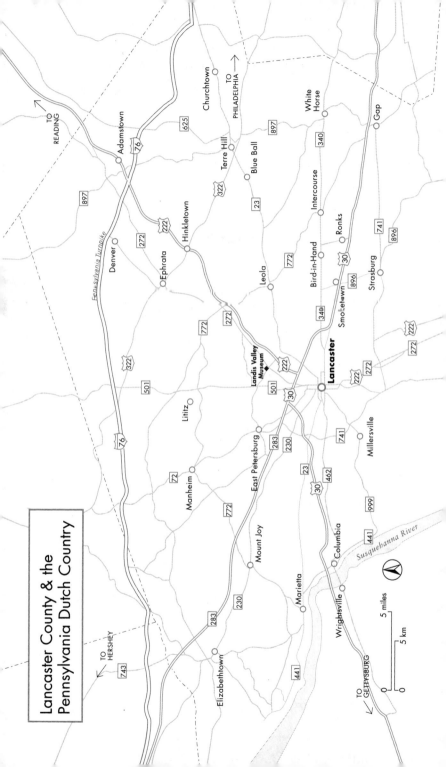

Lancaster County & the Pennsylvania Dutch Country

CLOSE UP

How to Snack

To a large degree, Philly might well be the snacking capital of the country. Consider some of the city's national foods: cheesesteaks, pretzels, water ice, hoagies, and Tastykakes. The cheesesteak, an institution here since it was created by Pat Olivieri and his brother Harry in the early 1930s, consists of thin-sliced steak, fried brown and topped with onions and cheese (often Cheez-Whiz) and sandwiched into a fresh hoagie roll. There are endless debates about where to get the best cheesesteak, but the most-famous locale is undoubtedly the corner of 9th and Passyunk, where arch-rivals **Pat's** (1237 E. Passyunk Ave., 215/468–1546) and **Geno's** (1219 S. 9th St., 215/389–0659) glare across the street at one another while serving thousands of sandwiches per week.

Fresh soft pretzels, another city staple, can be purchased at nearly every one of the street vendors throughout the city. For a real treat, though, head to one of the actual pretzel factories, like the **Philly Pretzel Factory** (7368 Frankford Ave., 215/338–5433), and get a hot, fresh pretzel slathered in mustard.

Water ice (invariably pronounced "wodder ice") is a frozen confection a bit like a sno-cone, only with real flavorings, which makes all the difference. Some of the best native water ice can be had at **John's Water Ice** (701 Christian St., 215/925–6955), a South Philly institution (though keep in mind that this seasonal treat won't be widely available during the colder months).

Hoagies are giant, long sandwiches that other cities call "subs," "heroes" or "grinders." They can be hot or cold, and are generally filled with meats and cheeses along with an assortment of condiments. **Sarcone's Deli** (734 S. 9th St., 215/922–1717) has a rep for being one of the top spots in the city to score the massive sandwich.

Finally, Tastykake is a local mass bakery, which makes ubiquitous cupcakes, cookies, brownies, pies, and cakes found throughout the area. Generally speaking, fresh-baked goods taste a lot better—but for quick, packaged treats, they can be truly addictive.

HOW SHOULD I GET THERE?

DRIVING

Philly is readily accessible via I–95 coming north from Maryland through Delaware or south from New York through New Jersey, though traffic can be intense during rush hours. From the west, the Pennsylvania Turnpike begins at the Ohio border and intersects the Schuylkill Expressway (I–76) at Valley Forge, with several exits in Center City. The Northeast Extension of the turnpike, renamed I–476, runs from Scranton to Plymouth Meeting, just north of Philadelphia. From the east the New Jersey Turnpike and I–295 access U.S. 30, which enters the city via the Benjamin Franklin Bridge, or New Jersey Route 42, which enters South Philadelphia near the stadiums via the Walt Whitman Bridge.

FLYING

All major airlines offer service to and from Philadelphia. Philadelphia International Airport is a hub for US Airways, which offers the most nonstop domestic flights. You can also find discounted airfares on Southwest Airlines and smaller carriers like Air Tran.

TRAIN

Coming into Philly by train is another good option, either via Amtrak, on one of the plentiful lines that run from Washington, DC, to New York, or, if you're coming from New Jersey, on New Jersey Transit trains, which are a good deal cheaper than the Amtrak options. Most likely, you will get into Philly's 30th Street Station, which is a beautiful, old building on the western edge of Center City. From there, you can easily take a taxi or subway to anywhere you want to go in the city.

HOW DO I GET AROUND?

BY CAR

Driving is certainly an option in the city, though you will probably need to park in a garage, as finding street parking can be daunting, especially in Center City. Outside Center City, the parking situation is much better, and you will definitely want to have a car if you intend to go to Longwood Gardens or Valley Forge.

In South Philly, the normal rules of parking go by the wayside, and natives have come up with creative means of keeping their cars handy—including staking out a spot in front of their house with traffic cones or plastic buckets, and parking in the meridian of the major two-way thoroughfares. Though these practices are looked upon as tradition in South Philly, and thus not ticketed, we suggest you don't try any of those maneuvers in Center City, where you will be towed in the blink of an eye.

BY SEPTA

SEPTA bus lines and trains are good ways to get around, though the subway system is limited to traveling on Broad and Market streets. All SEPTA commuter trains stop at 30th Street Station and connect to Suburban Station (16th St. and John F. Kennedy Blvd., near major hotels), and Market East Station (10th and Market Sts.), near the historic section and beneath the Gallery at Market East shopping complex.

BY TAXI

Taxis are popular modes of quick transport, and are easy to find throughout the city. The base fare is $2.70, with an additional $2.10 per mile thereafter. You can expect to pay between $7 and $12 for most fares between spots in Center City. There's a flat fee of $26.25 traveling to and from the airport in Center City.

CLAIM TO FAME

Philly is the true birthplace of the country. It was here some 230-odd years ago that Thomas Jefferson, Ben Franklin, John Adams, and the rest of the Second Continental Congress signed the Declaration of Independence, thereby declaring that this fledgling country was a sovereign nation from Great Britain. Philadelphia also served as the nation's first capital.

Philadelphians take their sports teams very seriously—and with a certain aggressiveness. The legend of Eagles' fans pelting Santa Claus with snowballs at the halftime of yet another blowout at the end of a particularly miserable Eagles' season is indeed true, though there were several mitigating factors (not the least of which was the PA announcer wishing everyone an overly cheery Merry Christmas on behalf of the Eagles and their employees). To Philly sports fans' chagrin the city has now gone the longest in the country without a championship in any of the four pro sports it supports.

WHERE SHOULD I FOCUS MY ENERGY?

If you're here for 1 day: For brief visits, you'll probably want to check out Independence Mall and the surrounding historic landmarks in Old City.

If you're here for 2 days: Include a visit to Rittenhouse Square, and enjoy the fine cuisine and shopping possibilities.

If you're here for 3 days: Get to the Philadelphia Museum of Art and take in the far-ranging permanent collection.

If you're here for 4 days: Hit Rocky's stomping grounds at the Italian Market, which features open-air vendors, and numerous bakeries, cheese shops, and butchers.

If you're here for 5 days: Check out Philly's Chinatown, filled with restaurants, merchants, and cafés representing many different kinds of Asian cuisine and culture.

If you're here for 6 days: Get outside the city and take in the floral splendor of Longwood Gardens and the historic majesty of Valley Forge.

If you're here for 7 days or more: Head out to the beautiful rolling hills of Lancaster County, home of a large population of Amish farms.

WHAT ARE THE TOP EXPERIENCES?

The Food: A couple of decades ago, Philly's culinary scene was dominated by Italian and French cooking, but now there are more choices and more possibilities than ever before. There are still a huge number of outstanding Italian and French restaurants, to be sure, but Latino, African, Mediterranean, and Asian places have popped up throughout the city. For a sense of the possibilities, you can swing by Reading Terminal Market, a giant, bustling mall of food stalls, produce stands, meat vendors, and culinary shops, filled with everything from cheesesteaks to Amish baked goods and produce to macrobiotic vegan options. One of Philly's little-known charms is the huge proliferation of BYOB places.

The Art: Besides the wondrous Philadelphia Museum of Art, there are many ways to explore visual arts in the city. Right near the PMA, on the Ben Franklin Parkway, is the Rodin Museum, which houses the largest collection of Auguste Rodin's work outside his native France. As far as private collections go, the Barnes Foundation, just outside the city (and soon to move near the PMA), offers a staggering number of priceless French impressionist, Postimpressionist, and early Modern works. For those with more literary tastes, the Rosenbach Museum has many interesting pieces, including original letters from Charles Dodgson, a lock of Charles Dickens' hair, and a splendid first edition of James Joyce's "Ulysses." Along the lines of art you can actually purchase, Old City has dozens of galleries displaying a wide range of works.

The History: No city in the country has more to do with the birth of our nation than Philadelphia, from Independence Hall, where the original Declaration of Independence was ratified, to the Liberty Bell, Philadelphia is filled with the founding history of our country. For a different angle, you can travel a short distance from the city to Valley Forge, where George Washington housed his battle-weary troops in the winter of 1777–78. Throughout the city, especially around Old City, you can find further evidence of Philly's unique participation in the history of the US, from Betsy Ross's home to Ben Franklin's Post Office.

The Architecture: Apart from all the Colonial homes in Old City, you can also find amazing old Victorians in West Philadelphia, as well as a fine example of Greek Revival in the Bank of Pennsylvania Building. Master architect Louis Khan was born and raised here, and designed several beautiful buildings—including the Richards Medical Center at the University of Pennsylvania. The Pennsylvania Academy of the Fine Arts is an ornate marvel, just north of City Hall, which is, in of itself, a gorgeous and stately construction in the dead center of the city. In the last 20 years, a massive eruption of modern skyscrapers have added to the Philly landscape, from the Towers at Liberty Place, to the brand-new construction of the Comcast Center, which at 975 feet, is now the tallest building in the city.

BEST BETS

SIGHTS AND TOURS

PHILADELPHIA

Fodor'sChoice ★ **Boathouse Row.** These architecturally varied 19th-century buildings—in Victorian Gothic, Gothic Revival, and Italianate styles—are home to the rowing clubs that make up the Schuylkill Navy, an association of boating clubs organized in 1858. ⊠ *Kelly Dr., E. Fairmount Park, Fairmount Park.*

★ **Chinatown.** Centered on 10th and Race streets two blocks north of Market Street, Chinatown serves as the residential and commercial hub of the city's Chinese community. Over the past 20 years, Chinatown's population has become more diverse, reflecting the increase in immigration from other parts of Southeast Asia. As a result the dining options are more varied; there now are restaurants serving authentic Vietnamese, Thai, Cambodian, and Burmese cuisine. One striking Chinatown site is the **Chinese Friendship Gate**, straddling 10th Street at Arch Street. ✉*9th to 11th Sts., Arch to Vine Sts., Chinatown* ⊕*www.phillychinatown.com.*

★ **Franklin Institute Science Museum.** ☾ Founded more than 175 years ago to honor Benjamin Franklin, the institute is a science museum that is as clever as its namesake, thanks to an abundance of dazzling hands-on exhibits. ✉*20th St. and Benjamin Franklin Pkwy., Logan Circle* ☏*215/448–1200* ⊕*www.fi.edu* ✆*$13.75–$18.75* ☾*Daily 9:30–5.*

HISTORY YOU CAN SEE

Being the birthplace of the nation and a major factor in the country's early years has left Philly with a nearly inexhaustible supply of historic touchstones. Independence Mall has Independence Hall, the Liberty Bell, and the National Constitution Center, all within a two-block radius. Right around the corner is the Franklin Court, built where Ben Franklin's house once stood. In the same immediate area, you can find the First Bank of Pennsylvania, as well as Christ Church, the Betsy Ross House, and Elfreth's Alley, the oldest continually occupied residential street in the U.S.

Fodor'sChoice **Independence Hall.** The birthplace of the United States, this redbrick ★ building with its clock tower and steeple is one of the nation's greatest icons. In this same room George Washington was appointed commander in chief of the Continental Army, Thomas Jefferson's eloquent Declaration of Independence was signed, and later the Constitution of the United States was adopted. From March through December and on major holidays, free, timed tickets from the visitor center are required for entry. Tickets also can be reserved by calling 800/967–2283 or by logging on to www.recreation.gov. ✉*Chestnut St. between 5th and 6th Sts., Historic Area* ☏*215/965–2305* ⊕*www.nps.gov/inde* ✆*Free* ☾*Daily 9–5.*

★ **Independence Visitor Center.** This is the city's official visitor center as well as the gateway to Independence National Historical Park. ✉*6th and Market Sts., Historic Area* ☏*215/965–7676 or 800/537–7676* ⊕*www.independencevisitorcenter.com* ☾*Sept.–June, daily 8:30–6; July and Aug., daily 8:30–7.*

★ **Italian Market.** It's more Naples than Philadelphia: vendors crowd the sidewalks and spill out onto the streets; live crabs and caged chickens wait for the kill; picture-perfect produce is piled high. You can find fresh pastas, cheeses, spices, meats, fruits and vegetables, and dry goods. ✉*9th St. between Washington Ave. and Christian St., Bella*

Vista/S. Philadelphia ⊕*www.phillyitalianmarket.com* ⊙*Tues.–Sat. 9–late afternoon, Sun. 9–12:30.*

★ **Liberty Bell.** In mid-2003 the bell moved to a new glass-enclosed pavilion with redbrick accents. Great care was taken to improve access to the bell and the view of its former home at Independence Hall, which is seen against the backdrop of the sky. ⊠*6th and Chestnut Sts., Historic Area* ☎*215/965–2305* ⊕*www.nps.gov/inde/liberty-bell.html* ◙*Free* ⊙*Daily 9–5.*

★ **Mütter Museum.** Skulls, antique microscopes, and a cancerous tumor removed from President Grover Cleveland's mouth in 1893 form just part of the unusual medical collection in the Mütter Museum, in the College of Physicians of Philadelphia, a few blocks south of the Please Touch Museum. ⊠*19 S. 22nd St., Rittenhouse Square* ☎*215/563–3737* ⊕*www.collphyphil.org* ◙*$12* ⊙*Mon.–Thurs. and weekends 10–5, Fri. 10–9.*

National Constitution Center. This 160,000-square-foot museum brings the U.S. Constitution alive through a series of highly interactive exhibits tracing the development and adoption of the nation's landmark guiding document. ⊠ *525 Arch St., Historic Area* ☎*215/409–6600* ⊕*www.constitutioncenter.org* ◙*$9* ⊙*Weekdays 9:30–5, Sat. 9:30–6, Sun. noon–5.*

Fodor's Choice **Philadelphia Museum of Art.** The city's premier cultural attraction is one
★ of the country's leading museums. You can enter the museum from the front or the rear; choose the front and you can run up the 99 steps made famous in the movie *Rocky*. The museum has several outstanding permanent collections: the John G. Johnson Collection covers Western art from the Renaissance to the 19th century; the Arensberg and A.E. Gallatin collections contain modern and contemporary works by artists such as Brancusi, Braque, Matisse, and Picasso. ⊠*26th St. and Benjamin Franklin Pkwy., Fairmount* ☎*215/763–8100* ⊕*www.phila museum.org* ◙*$10, Sun. pay what you wish* ⊙*Tues., Thurs., and weekends 10–5, Wed. and Fri. 10–8:45.*

Fodor's Choice **Reading Terminal Market.** One floor beneath the former Reading Railroad's
★ 1891 train shed, the sprawling market has more than 80 food stalls and other shops, selling items from hooked rugs and handmade jewelry to South American and African crafts. Here, amid the local color, you can sample Bassett's ice cream, Philadelphia's best; down a cheesesteak, a hoagie, a bowl of snapper soup, or a soft pretzel; or nibble Greek, Mexican, Thai, and Indian specialties. From Wednesday through Saturday the Amish from Lancaster County cart in their goodies, including Lebanon bologna, shoofly pie, and scrapple. ⊠*12th and Arch Sts., Market East* ☎*215/922–2317* ⊕*www.readingterminalmarket.org* ⊙*Mon.–Sat. 8–6, Sun. 9–4.*

Fodor's Choice **Rittenhouse Square.** Once grazing ground for cows and sheep, Philadel-
★ phia's most elegant square is reminiscent of a Parisian park. Until 1950 town houses bordered the square, but they have now been replaced on three sides by swank apartment buildings and hotels. If you want

to join the office workers who have lunch-hour picnics in the park, you can find many eateries along Walnut, Sansom, and Chestnut streets east of the square. Or you can dine alfresco at one of several upscale open-air cafés across from the square on 18th Street between Locust and Walnut. The term "Rittenhouse Row" describes the greater Rittenhouse Square area, bordered by Pine, Market, 21st, and Broad streets. ⌂ *Walnut St. between 18th and 19th Sts., Rittenhouse Square.*

South Street. Philadelphia's most bohemian neighborhood is crammed with craft shops and condom stores, coffee bars and tattoo parlors, ethnic restaurants, and New Age bookshops. At night it's crammed with people—those who hang out, and those who come to watch them, giving South Street the offbeat feel of Greenwich Village mixed with Bourbon Street. ⌂ *South St. from Front St. to about 10th St., Lombard St. to Bainbridge St., Society Hill/Queen Village* ⊕ *www.southstreet.com.*

> **VITAL STATS:**
>
> ■ City Population: 1,448,394 (as of 2006); 6th largest city in the country. State Capital: Harrisburg (population: 48,950; 10th largest city in Pennsylvania).
>
> ■ City Motto: "Philadelphia Maneto" (Let brotherly love endure).
>
> ■ Home to the nation's first: hospital (1751), university (1751), post office (1775), piano (1775), capital (1790), stock exchange (1790), bank (1791), art school (1805), zoo (1859), computer (1946).

★ **University Museum of Archaeology and Anthropology.** Rare treasures from the deepest jungles and ancient tombs make this one of the finest archaeological/anthropological museums in the world. ⌂ *33rd and Spruce Sts., University City* ☎ *215/898–4001* ⊕ www.upenn.edu/ museum ☒ *$8, free Sun.* ☉ *Labor Day–Memorial Day, Tues.–Sat. 10– 4:30, Sun. 1–5; Memorial Day–Labor Day, Tues.–Sat. 10–4:30.*

NEAR PHILADELPHIA

Fodor'sChoice **Barnes Foundation.** The Barnes Foundation's gallery art collection—one
★ of the world's greatest collections of impressionist and postimpressionist art—may move to a new building near the Rodin Museum in 2009. Until then you can see the Gauguins, Tintorettos, and Degases displayed as they have always been: wallpapered floor-to-ceiling and cheek-by-jowl alongside household tools, Amish chests, and New Mexican folk icons. Reservations are required, and should be made at least two months in advance for the busiest months of April, May, October, and November. ⌂ *300 Latches La., Merion* ☎ *610/667–0290* ⊕ *www. barnesfoundation.org* ☒ *$10* ☉ *Sept.–June, Fri.–Sun. 9:30–5; July and Aug., Wed.–Fri. 9:30–5.*

Fodor'sChoice There are few landmarks as touching as the **Gettysburg National Military**
★ **Park,** where General Robert E. Lee and his Confederate troops encountered the Union forces of General George Meade. There are more than 1,300 markers and monuments honoring the casualties of the battle in the 6,000-acre park. More than 30 mi of marked roads lead through the park, highlighting key battle sites. In the first week of July, Civil War

STRANGE BUT TRUE

Philly sports fans are a superstitious bunch, so the Curse of Billy Penn lives on in their fearful minds. High atop City Hall (548 feet tall) there stands a bronze statue of William Penn, the founder of both Philadelphia and the state of Pennsylvania. Under a gentlemen's agreement, it was decided that no building in the city would stand taller than the statue, which held true until 1987, when One Liberty Place rose up nearly 400 feet above Penn's head. To believers of the curse, the consequence of this architectural folly has been the complete dearth of professional team championships since the building was opened (though the city's last team championship was actually the 1983 76ers NBA championship). Two Liberty Place came soon after; the Comcast Center, under construction at this writing, will dwarf both Liberty Places, standing 975 feet from the ground. In an attempt to alleviate the curse, ironworkers allegedly affixed a small statue of William Penn to the highest steel beam in the building's construction.

reenactors dress in period uniforms and costumes to commemorate the three-day battle. ✉ *97 Taneytown Rd., Gettysburg* ☎ *717/334–1124* ⊕ *www.nps.gov/gett* ✉ *Free* ⊙ *Park roads 6 AM–10 PM.*

★ At **Hershey's Chocolate World**, a 10-minute automated ride takes you ☾ through the steps of producing chocolate, from picking the cocoa beans to making candy bars in Hershey's kitchens. This is the town's official visitor center, so you can get information while tasting your favorite Hershey confections and buying gifts in a spacious conservatory filled with tropical plants. ✉ *Park Blvd., Hershey* ☎ *717/534–4900* ⊕ *www.hersheypa.com* ✉ *Free* ⊙ *Daily, call for hours*

☾ At **Hersheypark** you can enjoy thrilling rides and socialize with 6-foot-tall Hershey Bars and Reese's Peanut Butter Cups. Touted as "the Sweetest Place on Earth," the park has more than 100 landscaped acres, with 60 rides, 5 theaters, and ZooAmerica, an 11-acre wildlife park with more than 200 animals. ✉ *Hersheypark Dr., Hershey, Rte. 743 and U.S. 422* ☎ *717/534–3090* ⊕ *www.hersheypa.com* ✉ *$43.95* ⊙ *Memorial Day–Labor Day, daily 10–10, some earlier closings; May and Sept., weekends only, call for hrs.*

★ **Valley Forge National Historical Park,** administered by the National Park Service, is the location of the 1777–78 winter encampment of General George Washington and the Continental Army. Stop first at the Valley Forge Welcome Center to see the 18-minute orientation film (shown every 30 minutes) and view exhibits. In summer you can take a narrated trolley tour for $15 person. A leisurely visit to the park takes no more than half a day. ✉ *Rte. 23 and N. Gulph Rd., Valley Forge* ☎ *610/783–1077* ⊕ *www.nps.gov/vafo* ✉ *Free* ⊙ *Park daily dawn–dusk; welcome center daily 9–5.*

PENNSYLVANIA DUTCH COUNTRY

The city of Lancaster has plenty to see and makes a good base for exploring the surrounding countryside. East of the city, between routes 340 and 23 in towns with names such as Intercourse, Blue Ball, Paradise, and Bird-in-Hand, lives most of Lancaster County's Amish community. Intercourse's odd name came from the Colonial term for intersection. At the intersection of routes 340 and 772, this town is a center of Amish life. Between Intercourse and up the road to Bird-in-Hand, the Amish way of life can be explored by observing their farms, crafts, quilts, and various educational experiences.

When you're visiting among the Amish, remember to respect their values. They believe that photographs and videos with recognizable reproductions of them violate the biblical commandment against making graven images. Out of respect, you should refrain from photographing the Amish.

Fodor'sChoice ★ A must-see in Lancaster City is the Romanesque **Central Market**. Constructed in 1889, it's the oldest continuously operating farmers' market in the country. ⊠ *Penn Sq., Lancaster* ☎ *717/291–4723* ⊙ *Tues. and Fri. 6–4, Sat. 6–2.*

6

The **Historic Lancaster Walking Tour** is a 90-minute stroll through the heart of this old city by costumed guides who impart anecdotes about notable points of interest. ⊠ *S. Queen and Vine Sts.* ☎ *717/392–1776* ⊠ *$7* ⊙ *Apr.–Oct., Tues., Fri., and Sat. at 10 and 1, Sun., Mon., Wed., and Thurs. at 1; Nov.–Mar., by reservation.*

Not far from Central Market, the **Lancaster Quilt & Textile Museum** has a breathtaking display of Amish quilts and other textiles. ⊠ *37 Market St., Lancaster* ☎ *717/299–6440* ⊕ *www.lancasterheritage.com* ⊠ *$6* ⊙ *Tues.–Sat. 10–5* ⊙ *Closed Sun.*

Fodor'sChoice ★ The **Landis Valley Museum** is an open-air museum of Pennsylvania German rural life and folk culture before 1900. You can visit more than 15 historical buildings, from a farmstead to a country store, with costumed guides providing interesting bits of history. There are demonstrations of skills such as spinning and weaving, pottery making, and tinsmithing. ⊠ *2451 Kissel Hill Rd., Lancaster, off Oregon Pike, Rte. 272* ☎ *717/569–0401* ⊕ *www.landisvalleymuseum.org* ⊠ *$9* ⊙ *Mar.–Dec., Mon.–Sat. 9–5, Sun. noon–5.*

WHERE TO EAT

	WHAT IT COSTS				
	¢	$	$$	$$$	$$$$
AT DINNER	under $8	$8–$14	$14–$20	$20–$26	over $26

Prices are for one main course at dinner.

PHILADELPHIA

$$$$ ✕**City Tavern.** You can time-travel to the 18th century at this authentic re-creation of historic City Tavern, where the atmosphere suggests that founding fathers such as John Adams, George Washington, Thomas Jefferson, and the rest of the gang *might* have supped here (they didn't; the restaurant was built under the supervision of the National Park Service in 1994, to the specifications of the original 1773 tavern). The food—West Indies pepper-pot soup, Martha Washington's turkey stew, honey pecan roast duckling—is prepared from enhanced period recipes and served on handsome Colonial-patterned china or pewter. Happily all is not authentic—the restaurant makes good use of refrigeration and electricity. Reservations are recommended. ⊠ *138 S. 2nd St., Old City* ☎ *215/413–1443* ▤ *AE, D, DC, MC, V.*

$$$$ ✕**Lacroix.** Eyebrows lifted when young, gastronomically adventurous
Fodor's Choice Matthew Levin took over from legendary Jean-Marie Lacroix, but he
★   has proven himself to be a worthy successor, even earning the elusive four-bell rating from the *Inquirer's* cranky Craig LaBan. Levin mixes cutting-edge techniques with quality ingredients for inventive, sometimes playful, dishes—smoked black codfish with a smattering of pop rocks; nori-crusted rib eye; shellfish soup with toffee. Combined with a 500-plus-label cellar of high-end bottles and a gorgeous dining room overlooking Rittenhouse Square, a meal here is guaranteed to be one of your most memorable. There's also the $52 blowout Sunday brunch—a tremendous value. ⊠ *210 W. Rittenhouse Sq., Rittenhouse Square* ☎ *215/790–2533* ⟁ *Reservations essential. Jacket required* ▤ *AE, D, DC, MC, V.*

$$$$ ✕**Le Bec-Fin.** A few years ago, Georges Perrier took the Versailles-style
Fodor's Choice decor down to a 19th-century Parisian salon motif and the servers' uni-
★   forms down from tuxedoes to blazers. This loosening up at the front of the house had no effect on whatever's happening in the kitchen. This outpost of cuisine from Lyon continues to set a stratospherically high standard for Philadelphia, and there's still sufficient acclaim to require an advance reservation of a month or more to garner a table on Saturday night. The popular *galette de crab* (a sublime crab cake) is a signature appetizer. Do save room for the magnificent dessert cart—as much as you can eat is included in the prix-fixe. If dinner is out of your price range, Le Bar Lyonnais—down a flight of stairs from the main dining room—is a small, charming space that features the chef's specialty dishes for entrées that range $15–$40. ⊠ *1523 Walnut St., Center City* ☎ *215/567–1000* ⟁ *Reservations essential. Jacket required* ▤ *AE, D, DC, MC, V* ⊘ *Closed Sun.*

$$-$$$$ ✕**Morimoto.** Stunningly expensive
Fodor'sChoice dishes created by celebrity chef
★ Masaharu Morimoto (of the Food
Network's *Iron Chef*) are served in
an elegant, slightly futuristic set-
ting. Tables and benches are made
of hard white plastic and the ceiling
is undulating bamboo. *Omakase*
(tasting menus), $40–$80 at lunch
and $80–$120 at dinner, are well
worth the expense. Authentic and
creative à la carte dishes include
toro (tuna) with caviar and wasabi.
Reservations are recommended.
✉*723 Chestnut St., Historic Area*
☎*215/413–9070* ▭*AE, D, DC,
MC, V* ☾*No lunch weekends.*

¢–$ ✕**Continental Restaurant & Martini Bar.**
Fodor'sChoice Light fixtures fashioned like olives
★ pierced with toothpicks are a tip-off to the theme at this cool water-
ing hole. It's installed in a classic diner shell in the center of Old City's
action. This is the first of Stephen Starr's trendy restaurants, where he
serves lively (but not outré) food to people who know how to enjoy it.
Don't miss the addictive Szechuan french-fried potatoes with hot-mus-
tard sauce and the crispy calamari salad. ✉*138 Market St., Old City*
☎*215/923–6069* ▭*AE, DC, MC, V.*

ON THE WAY

Lancaster County: Known pri-
marily as the best-known home
of Amish people in the country,
Lancaster, due west of Philadel-
phia, is also a scenic country idyll,
with rolling hills, abundant trees,
and lots of all-butter Amish treats
for sale.

Delaware Water Gap: One of the
better recreational areas on the
East Coast, the DWG cuts through
a mountain ridge and has ample
hiking, fishing, canoeing, and
kayaking opportunities.

6

WHERE TO STAY

	WHAT IT COSTS				
	¢	$	$$	$$$	$$$$
FOR 2 PEOPLE	under $90	$90–$139	$140–$189	$190–$240	over $240

Prices are for a standard double room.

PHILADELPHIA

$$$$ 🏨**Four Seasons.** On the outskirts of the finance district, this landmark
Fodor'sChoice is within walking distance of the Philadelphia Museum of Art and
★ the department stores along Walnut Street. Furnishings are in the for-
mal Federal style. The staff indulges you (with in-room exercise equip-
ment and nonallergenic pillows), your children (with milk and cookies
at bedtime), and your pet (with fresh-baked dog biscuits and bottled
water served in a silver bowl). Other amenities include complimen-
tary limousine service within Center City. Rooms on the hotel's north
side offer the best views of the Greek Revival public library and fam-
ily court, Logan Circle, and the Cathedral of Saints Peter and Paul.
The Fountain Restaurant is one of the best in town and the Swann
Lounge one of the liveliest at cocktail time. ✉*1 Logan Sq., Benjamin
Franklin Parkway/Museum Area,19103* ☎*215/963–1500 or 800/332–*

3442 ⌂*215/963–9506* ⊕*www.fourseasons.com/philadelphia* ⤴*364 rooms, 102 suites* ⎕*In-room: safe, refrigerator, Ethernet, dial-up, Wi-Fi (some). In-hotel: 2 restaurants, room service, bar, pool, gym, spa, concierge, parking (fee), some pets allowed, no-smoking rooms* ⊟*AE, D, DC, MC, V.*

$$$$ ⊡**Park Hyatt Philadelphia at the Bellevue.** A Philadelphia institution for
Fodor's Choice almost a century, the elegant Bellevue sparkles. The spacious rooms,
★ done in bright prints, have the high ceilings and moldings typical of older buildings. The posh restaurant, called XIX, has views of the city from its 19th-floor perch; the Barrymore Room, topped by a 30-foot stained-glass dome, is great for tea and cocktails. The hotel's lower floors have been transformed into a shopping center with stores like Tiffany and Ralph Lauren. ⊠*Broad and Walnut Sts., Center City,19102* ☏*215/893–1234 or 800/233–1234* ⌂*215/732–8518* ⊕*www. parkhyatt.com* ⤴*172 rooms, 13 suites* ⎕*In-room: safe, refrigerator, DVD, Ethernet, dial-up. In-hotel: restaurant, room service, bar, pool, spa, concierge, laundry service, parking (fee), public Internet, public Wi-Fi, no-smoking rooms* ⊟*AE, D, DC, MC, V.*

$$$$ ⊡**The Rittenhouse.** This small luxury hotel takes full advantage of its
★ location on Rittenhouse Square; the restaurant and many of the rooms
☽ overlook the city's famous park. The staff, among the nicest in the city, greets you with a glass of champagne, chocolate-covered strawberries and, if you have children, a "treasure chest" of toys. The 33-story building's sawtooth design gives the guest rooms unusual shapes, with nooks and alcoves. Each room has a large marble bathroom with a glass-enclosed shower and television; many also have whirlpool tubs. The management is deeply involved in community affairs, and promotes local artists at the third-floor Satellite Gallery, and with the placement of original art throughout the hotel. The restaurant, Lacroix, puts a sumptuous French spin on local ingredients. ⊠*210 W. Rittenhouse Sq., Rittenhouse Square,19103* ☏*215/546–9000 or 800/635–1042* ⌂*215/732–3364* ⊕*www.rittenhousehotel.com* ⤴*87 rooms, 11 suites* ⎕*In-room: kitchen (some), Ethernet, dial-up, Wi-Fi. In-hotel: 3 restaurants, room service, bar, pool, gym, spa, concierge, laundry service, public Internet, public Wi-Fi, parking (fee), some pets allowed, no-smoking rooms* ⊟*AE, D, DC, MC, V.*

VISITOR INFORMATION

Greater Philadelphia Tourism Marketing Corporation (☏*800/537–0776* ⊕*www.gophila.com*).

Pennsylvania Dutch Convention & Visitors Bureau (⊠*501 Greenfield Rd., Lancaster,17601* ☏*717/299–8901 or 800/735–2629* ⊕*www.padutchcountry.com*).

Pennsylvania Office of Travel and Tourism (☏*800/847–4872* ⊕*www.visitpa. com*).

Washington, D.C.

Thomas Jefferson Memorial

WORD OF MOUTH

"Has anyone mentioned that you should NOT MISS the National Archives? . . . It is just a really incredible thing to see an actual copy of the Declaration of Independence. When we took our kids the first time (probably 15 years ago), it wasn't even in the hermetically sealed, raise it up once an hour contraption that they later put it in for safety (from people and pollution). Regardless, it's a must-see."

—dmlove

EXPLORING WASHINGTON, D.C.

225 mi southwest of New York City via I–95 and Maryland Rte. 295 (Baltimore-Washington Pkwy.); 141 mi southwest of Philadelphia via I–95 and Maryland Rte. 295 (Baltimore-Washington Pkwy.); 400 mi northeast of Charlotte, NC, via I–85, I–95, and I–395;250 mi southeast of Pittsburgh via I–376, I–76, I–70, I–270, I–495, and the George Washington Memorial Pkwy.

Political persuasions and feelings about the federal government aside, there's no denying that Washington, D.C. is a must-do family vacation. No place in America offers parents more teachable moments per square mile, and even the most jaded child will struggle to act disinterested when they're standing underneath the Capitol Rotunda or looking out from the steps of the Lincoln Memorial.

D.C. is a cosmopolitan city, and its myriad attractions don't begin and end with the Mall. Massachusetts Avenue's Embassy Row is packed with the diplomatic outposts of dozens of nations, from Australia to Lesotho to Zambia. The city's upper northwest corner is home to Washington National Cathedral—the sixth largest in the world. Posh Georgetown is filled with upscale boutiques; busy Dupont Circle has a funky, urban feel; charming Eastern Market is a perfect place to while away a Saturday morning; and hip Adams-Morgan is home to offbeat shops and great ethnic eats. You can hear dozens of different languages spoken on Washington's streets—and have the opportunity to try cuisines you may never have encountered before (Ethiopian anyone?). And of course, there's always a chance you'll bump into a famous politician (you may not pass the president on the street, but it's not uncommon to see the commander-in-chief's motorcade).

WHO WILL ESPECIALLY LOVE THIS TRIP?

History Buffs: Washington, D.C. is steeped in history—and continues to produce historic moments on a daily basis. It's hard to walk down a block in the city without passing something of note, and the density increases the closer you move toward Capitol Hill. The city is also home to the nation's attic, the Smithsonian—the largest museum collection in the world—and dozens of other top-notch cultural institutions, including the National Archives, home to the *actual* Declaration of Independence, Constitution, and Bill of Rights.

Families: The possibilities for together time are limitless in D.C. From exploring the Smithsonian's treasures, to trying new ethnic cuisines, to learning about the Constitution by reading the original, you'd need to try really hard to run out of things to do with your kids here. D.C is an extremely compact city, so you're never too far from your next attraction—or, if you stay in the District, your hotel room for that mid-afternoon nap.

Walkers: Though it has a great public transit system, D.C. is a pedestrian's paradise. A good chunk of the city is protected green space. The Mall—America's front yard—may be one of the nicest places in the

TOP 5 REASONS TO GO

The Monuments & Memorials: Many things in life don't live up to the hype—but that list doesn't include watching a Vietnam vet making a rubbing at the Wall, gazing out on a sea of gravestones at Arlington National Cemetery, or reading Lincoln's Second Inaugural Address under the nighttime gaze of the president's statue.

The Museums: The Smithsonian—the nation's attic—is huge. It would literally take you weeks to tour all of the museums in this fantastic, free collection. But D.C. has many other heavy hitters outside of the world's largest museum complex, including the Corcoran Art Gallery, the International Spy Museum, the National Archives, the National Gallery of Art, the United States Holocaust Memorial Museum, and the Phillips Collection.

The Capitol: It's so much bigger and more beautiful in person. Just as the Constitution is a living document, this is a living building—if you have the time, try to see Congress in session so you can experience part of the slow process of debate, insult, and wrangling that eventually produces our nation's laws.

The Food: The old "melting pot" analogy really fits Washington well. In addition to sophisticated bistros and hip New American spots, D.C. has excellent Vietnamese, Ethiopian, Thai, Middle Eastern, Chinese, Moroccan, Malaysian . . . and pretty much any other ethnic eats you might be craving.

The Neighborhoods: Each area of the city has a clearly defined personality, and some, like Capitol Hill, Georgetown, Dupont Circle, and Adams Morgan, feel like small towns.

country to go for a stroll. Washington also has a fantastic collection of strollable neighborhoods, including Georgetown, Dupont Circle, Woodley Park, the U Street Corridor, Adams-Morgan, Capitol Hill, and Cleveland Park.

WHEN IS THE BEST TIME TO VISIT?

Washington has two delightful seasons: spring and autumn. In spring, the city's ornamental fruit trees—including the famous cherry trees near the Jefferson Memorial—are budding, and its many gardens are in bloom. By autumn, most of the summer crowds have left and you can enjoy the sights in peace. Summers can be uncomfortably hot and humid. Winter weather is mild by East Coast standards, but a handful of modest snowstorms each year bring this southern city to a standstill.

HOW SHOULD I GET THERE?

DRIVING

Interstate 95 skirts D.C. as part of the Beltway, the six- to eight-lane highway that encircles the city. The eastern half of the Beltway is labeled both I–95 and I–495; the western half is just I–495. If you're coming from the south, take I–95 to I–395 and cross the 14th Street Bridge to

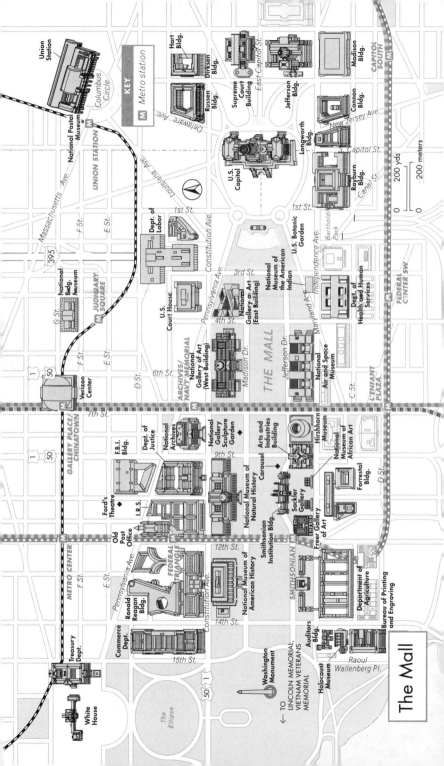

The Mall

14th Street in the District. From the north, stay on I–95 South. Take the exit to Washington, which will place you onto the Baltimore–Washington (B–W) Parkway heading south. The B–W Parkway will turn into New York Avenue, taking you into downtown Washington, D.C.

Interstate 66 approaches the city from the southwest. You can get downtown by taking I–66 across the Theodore Roosevelt Bridge to Constitution Avenue.

Interstate 270 approaches Washington, D.C. from the northwest before hitting I–495. To get downtown, take I–495 east to Connecticut Avenue south, toward Chevy Chase.

FLYING

The major gateways to D.C. are Ronald Reagan Washington National Airport (DCA) in Virginia, 4 mi south of downtown Washington; Dulles International Airport (IAD), 26 mi west of Washington, D.C.; and Baltimore/Washington International–Thurgood Marshall Airport (BWI) in Maryland, about 30 mi to the northeast.

Reagan National Airport is closest to downtown D.C. and has a metro stop in the terminal; East Coast shuttles and shorter flights tend to fly in and out of this airport. Dulles is configured primarily for long-haul flights. BWI offers blended service, with its many gates for no-frills Southwest Air, as well as international flights. Although metro doesn't serve Dulles and BWI, there's affordable and convenient public transportation to and from each airport. Prices vary between each of the three area airports so be sure to compare fares before booking your flights.

TRAIN

More than 80 trains a day arrive at Washington, D.C.'s Union Station, which is a few blocks northeast of the Capitol Building. Amtrak's regular service runs from D.C. to New York in 3¼–3¾ hours and from D.C. to Boston in 7¾–8 hours. Acela, Amtrak's high-speed service, travels from D.C. to New York in 2¾–3 hours and from D.C. to Boston in 6½ hours.

Two commuter lines—Maryland Rail Commuter Service (MARC) and Virginia Railway Express (VRE)—run to the nearby suburbs. They're cheaper than Amtrak, but they don't run on weekends.

Amtrak has both reserved and unreserved trains available. If you plan to travel during peak times, such as a Friday night or near a holiday, you'll need to get a reservation and a ticket in advance. Some trains at nonpeak times are unreserved, with seats assigned on a first-come, first-served basis.

HOW DO I GET AROUND?

BY CAR

Driving in Washington can be a headache. Traffic is usually congested, and the road layout is designed for frustration, with one-way streets popping up at just the wrong moment. Once you've reached your des-

CLOSE UP

How to Snack

It can be pretty hard to track down a decent bite to eat when you're touring the mall—especially if hot dogs, soft pretzels, an ice cream from a cart aren't going to cut it. Most of the museums' cafeterias have mediocre fare at sky-high prices—with the exception of the Museum of the American Indian's **Mitsitam Café** and the National Gallery's **Pavilion Cafè**. Venture a few blocks from the throngs of tourists, though, and you can find some better grub. The food courts at the **Old Post Office Pavilion** (1100 Pennsylvania Ave. NW, between 11th and 12th Sts.), the **Ronald Reagan Building and International Trade Center** (1300 Pennsylvania Ave. NW, between 13th and 14th Sts.), and **Union Station** (Columbus Circle at Massachusetts Ave. and 1st St.) offer dozens of excellent choices. **Pennsylvania Avenue SE,** between 2nd and 4th streets, has plenty of pubs, cafès, and sandwich shops.

tination, the real challenge begins: Washington may be the most diffi-cult city in America to find a place to park. All of which means, if you have a car, you'd be wise to leave it at your hotel and use public-transit whenever possible. If you do decide to drive, take a deep breath, and be aware of the following peculiarities of D.C.'s civic design:

The city is divided into the four quadrants of a compass (NW, NE, SE, SW), with the U.S. Capitol at the center. Because the Capitol doesn't sit in the exact center of the city (the Washington Monument does), Northwest is the largest quadrant. The boundaries are North Capitol Street, East Capitol Street, South Capitol Street, and the National Mall. That's where street addresses start and climb as you move up the numbers and alphabet.

Numbered Streets & Lettered Streets: Within each quadrant, numbered streets run north to south, and lettered streets run east to west (the letter J was omitted to avoid confusion with the letter I). The streets form a fairly simple grid—for instance, 900 G Street NW is the intersection of 9th and G streets in the northwest quadrant of the city. Likewise, if you count the letters of the alphabet, skipping J, you can get a good sense of the location of an address on a numbered street. For instance, 1600 16th Street NW is close to Q Street, Q being the 16th letter of the alphabet if you skip J.

Avenues on the Diagonal: As if all this weren't confusing enough, Major Pierre L'Enfant, the Frenchman who originally designed the city, threw in diagonal avenues recalling those of Paris. Most of D.C.'s avenues are named after U.S. states.

BY METRO & BUS

The Washington Metropolitan Area Transit Authority operates a network of subway lines (known locally as the metro) and bus routes throughout D.C. Most popular tourist attractions are near metro stops, though certain areas are only accessible by bus, most notably Georgetown and Adams-Morgan.

Metro fares depend on the distance traveled. Fares range from $1.35 to $3.90 during morning and evening rush hour and after 2 AM, and from $1.35 to $2.35 at all other times. Bus fares are $1.25 (exact change only) for regular routes, and $3 for express routes. Transfers between buses are free; transfers from the metro to the bus take 90 cents off your bus fare. One-day passes are available for $3 on buses and $6.50 on the metro. For fare information, route maps, and trip planning help, visit www.wmata.com or call 202/637–7000 (the Web site's Metro Trip Planner is especially helpful, offering detailed point-to-point directions).

BY TAXI

If you take a cab in D.C., you'll notice the taxis don't have fare meters. That's because D.C. operates on a zone system, with the fare depending on the number of zones traveled through. Extra passengers with the same origin and destination increase the fare by $1.50 each; passengers sharing a cab but riding to different destinations pay full fare, regardless of how many people are in the cab. For more information about this often-confusing system, visit http://dctaxi.dc.gov.

WHERE SHOULD I FOCUS MY ENERGY?

If you're here for 1 day: If you have a day or less (and even a dollar or less!) in D.C. your sightseeing strategy is simple: take the metro to the Smithsonian stop and explore the area around the Mall.

If you're here for 2 days: Continue to explore the Mall, where you can check out the museums and monuments that were probably a prime motivation for your coming to Washington in the first place. Take time out for a walk from the Washington Monument to the Lincoln Memorial and around the Tidal Basin, where you can see the Jefferson Memorial and the FDR Memorial, and take a leisurely paddleboat ride around the cherry trees.

If you're here for 3 days: Make this your day on Capitol Hill, where you'll have the option of visiting the Capitol, the U.S. Botanic Gardens, the Library of Congress, the Supreme Court, and the Folger Shakespeare Library.

If you're here for 4 days: Head to the National Zoo and say good morning to the pandas. Then hop on the metro to Dupont Circle for lunch. Walk west on P Street NW to Georgetown, where you can shop, admire the architecture, and people-watch through the afternoon. Another option is to head to the International Spy Museum, which tends to be less crowded after 2 PM.

If you're here for 5 days: Spend the morning at Arlington National Cemetery, one of the Washington area's most moving experiences. A short detour north of the cemetery brings you to the Marine Corps War Memorial (the "Iwo Jima"). In the afternoon, head across town to the neighborhoods of Adams-Morgan and Dupont Circle, both of which have unusual shops, restaurants, and clubs.

CLAIM TO FAME

Washingtonians are certifiably sports crazy. Where else but D.C. would a mediocre team with an offensive name be the most valuable sports franchise in the NFL? Loyal Redskins fans are extremely passionate, selling out every game and wearing burgundy and gold from September to December.

Washingtonians also have a new sports passion—baseball—though the currently uninspiring Nationals aren't nearly as exciting as the drama over their stadium. The new sports complex, which opened on the Anacostia waterfront in 2008, was a pet project of former mayor Anthony Williams and Major League Baseball. The $611 million project was opposed by many residents and City Council members, who thought taxpayers would be contributing too much money for insufficient financial return. Those who supported the project have wanted a baseball team back in D.C. since the Washington Senators' 1971 departure (that team is now the Texas Rangers).

If you're here for 6 days: Take the metro or drive to Old Town Alexandria, which is filled with restored 18th- and 19th-century homes, churches, and taverns, as well as lots of great small restaurants, boutiques, and antique dealers. Mount Vernon, George Washington's estate, is an 8 mi drive south of Alexandria.

If you're here for 7 days or more: Spend some additional time exploring the Mall's many treasures, or head to Annapolis, Maryland, a nautical paradise filled with gorgeous boats, delicious seafood, cute shops, and one of the country's largest assemblages of 18th-century architecture (including more than 50 buildings that predate the Revolutionary War).

WHAT ARE THE TOP EXPERIENCES?

Getting a Civics Lesson: Don't be content to look at the outside of D.C.'s government edifices—get inside and see some action. Contact your representative or senator (well) before your trip to arrange to see the houses of Congress (and floor debate) and the White House. If you're more of a last-minute type, you can arrange a Capitol building tour the morning of your visit, ditto to see all or part of a Supreme Court session (when the court is not hearing arguments, there are hourly tours on a first-come, first-served basis).

D.C. at Night: Washington's mall and monuments are majestic by day, but you should also visit them after the sun goes down. The floodlighted Capitol cuts a stark white contrast to the night sky—and seems even more imposing than it does in sunlight. The golden glow from the Lincoln Memorial will draw you inside to visit the Great Emancipator's statue and read his words etched on the walls, and the nearby Vietnam Veterans Memorial—sobering during the day—is even more wrenching in the darkness. And if you find yourself driving out of the District on the Arlington Memorial Bridge at night, look up; the flickering light on the hilltop is the eternal flame of JFK's grave in Arlington National Cemetery.

The Cherry Blossoms: Every spring, usually from late March to mid-April, Washington's famous cherry trees burst into white and pink bloom, and shake the city out of winter's grip. The trees—decedents of 3,020 originally given to Washington by Tokyo, Japan—look like ground-level cartoon clouds when they flower. Toward the end of the magnificent display, the blossoms drop from the branches, creating snowstorms of petals. Most of the cherry trees are planted around the Tidal Basin, near the Washington Monument, and in East Potomac Park (also referred to as Haines Point). For more information, visit www.nationalcherry blossomfestival.org.

The Air and Space Museum: Scanning the soaring lobby of the world's most popular museum, you can take in the entire history of human flight in about 30 seconds—from the Wright Flyer, to the Spirit of St. Louis, to the sound-barrier-breaking X-1, to Apollo 11, to Space-ShipOne. It goes without saying that kids love this place. Admission is free, so even if you only have five minutes, this is a can't-skip stop.

BEST BETS

SIGHTS AND TOURS

NEIGHBORHOODS

Fodor's Choice ★ **The Mall.** This expanse of green, which stretches due west from the Capitol to the Washington Monument, is lined on the north and south by some of America's finest museums, almost all of which are free. Lindbergh's Spirit of St. Louis, some of Andy Warhol's soup cans, the Hope Diamond, Julia Child's kitchen, a tyrannosaurus rex, and myriad other modern and classical artifacts await you. Of course, the 300-foot-wide Mall is more than just a front yard for museums: it's a picnicking park and a running path, an outdoor stage for festivals and fireworks, and America's town green.

Fodor's Choice ★ **Georgetown.** The capital's wealthiest neighborhood (and one that's attractive to architecture buffs) is always hopping, even if most of its once unique merchants have given way to stores and eateries found at malls around the country. Restaurants, bars, nightclubs, and boutiques cluster along Wisconsin and M streets. Washington Harbour is a riverfront development of restaurants, offices, apartments, and upscale shops; Georgetown Park is a multilevel shopping extravaganza; and Georgetown University is the oldest Jesuit school in the country. Dumbarton Oaks's 10 acres of formal gardens provide one of the loveliest spots in Washington. With its cobblestone side streets and many nooks and crannies, this is one of D.C.'s best neighborhoods for a good stroll.

Fodor's Choice ★ **Dupont Circle.** Fashionable, vibrant Dupont Circle has a cosmopolitan air owing partly to its many restaurants, shops, and specialty bookstores. It's also home to the most visible segment of Washington's gay community. This neighborhood is especially popular in the warmer months, when 17th Street becomes a scene—witnessed by drinkers

HISTORY YOU CAN SEE

The city that calls to mind politicking, back-scratching, and delicate diplomatic maneuvering is itself the result of a compromise. Tired of its nomadic existence after having set up shop in eight locations, Congress voted in 1785 to establish a permanent federal city. Northern lawmakers wanted the capital on the Delaware River, in the North; Southerners wanted it on the Potomac, in the South. A deal was struck when Virginia's Thomas Jefferson agreed to support the proposal that the federal government assume the war debts of the colonies if New York's Alexander Hamilton and other Northern legislators would agree to locate the capital on the banks of the Potomac. George Washington himself selected the site of the capital, a diamond-shape, 100-square-mi plot that encompassed the confluence of the Potomac and Anacostia rivers, not far from his estate at Mount Vernon.

To give the young city a head start, Washington included the already thriving tobacco ports of Alexandria, Virginia, and Georgetown, Maryland, in the District of Columbia. In 1791 Pierre-Charles L'Enfant, a French engineer who had fought in the Revolution, created the classic plan for the city (which explains why parts of D.C. look quite European).

It took the Civil War—and every war thereafter—to energize the city, by attracting thousands of new residents and spurring building booms that extended the capital in all directions. Streets were paved in the 1870s, and the first streetcars ran in the 1880s. Memorials to famous Americans such as Lincoln and Jefferson were built in the first decades of the 20th century, along with the massive Federal Triangle, a monument to thousands of less-famous government workers.

and diners enjoying the strip's countless outdoor eating and drinking establishments—and the round green in the middle of Dupont teems with sunbathers, chessmasters, and musicians. The exclusive Kalorama neighborhood to the northwest is a peaceful, tree-lined enclave filled with embassies and luxurious homes.

★ **Capitol Hill.** The Capitol, where the Senate and the House have met since 1800, along with the Supreme Court and the Library of Congress, dominate this neighborhood. But the Hill is more than just the center of government. There are charming residential blocks of Victorian row houses here filled with young hill staffers, who have attracted a fine assortment of restaurants, bars, and shops. Union Station, Washington's train depot, has vaulted and gilded ceilings, arched colonnades, statues of Roman legionnaires, a shopping mall, and a movie theater multiplex.

★ **Adams-Morgan.** One of Washington's most ethnically diverse and interesting neighborhoods, bohemian Adams-Morgan holds many offbeat restaurants and shops, and a brash and amazingly diverse bar-and-club scene.

★ **U Street Corridor.** The revival of U Street NW in the 1990s turned the area into a provocative spot for anyone looking for cutting-edge shopping, welcoming restaurants, and live music. For Washington's African-Americans, the glory of U Street never went away. Signs of its longevity include the elegant Duke Ellington mural above the 13th Street exit of the U Street Metro stop, as well as the restoration of the vaudeville-era Lincoln Theater, and an influx of new businesses.

MUSEUMS

Corcoran Gallery of Art. The Corcoran is Washington's largest non-Federal art museum, as well as its first art museum. Founded "for the purpose of encouraging American Genius," the Corcoran's extensive collection of 16,000 works of 18th-, 19th-, and 20th-century American art, represents most significant American artists, as well as a fine collection of European art. ⊠*500 17th St. NW, White House area* ☎*202/639–1700* ⊕*www.corcoran.org* ☞*$14* ☾*Sun., Mon., and Wed. 10–6, Thurs. 10–9, Fri. and Sat. 10–5.* Ⓜ*Farragut W or Farragut N.*

Fodor'sChoice
★ **International Spy Museum.** Cryptologists, masters of disguise, and former CIA, FBI, and KGB operatives are among the advisers of this museum, which displays the world's largest collection of spy artifacts. These artifacts range from the coded letters of Revolutionary War über-spy Benedict Arnold, to the KGB's lipstick pistol, to high-tech 21st-century espionage toys, showcased with theatrical panache in a five-building complex (one, the Warder-Atlas Building, held Washington's Communist party in the 1940s). ⊠*800 F St. NW, East End* ☎*202/393–7798* ⊕*www.spymuseum.org* ☞*$16, children $13* ☾*Apr.–Oct., daily 9–8; Nov.–Mar., daily 10–6; hrs subject to change; check Web site before visiting* Ⓜ*Gallery Pl./Chinatown.*

National Air and Space Museum. This is the world's most visited museum, attracting 9 million people annually to the world's largest collection of historic aircraft and spacecraft. Its 23 galleries tell the story of aviation from the earliest human attempts at flight to supersonic jets and spacecraft. For more giant jets and spaceships, visit the **National Air and Space Museum Steven F. Udvar-Hazy Center,** at Washington Dulles International Airport in northern Virginia. A shuttle bus runs from the museum entrance on the Mall to the outdoor center, where you can see a Concorde, the space shuttle *Enterprise,* and the *Enola Gay* (which in 1945 dropped on Japan the first atomic devices to be used in war). ⊠*Independence Ave. and 6th St. SW, The Mall* ☎*202/357–1729, 202/357–1686 movie information, 202/357–1729 TDD* ⊕*www.nasm.si.edu* ☞*Free, IMAX $8.50, planetarium $8.50* ☾*Daily 10–5:30* Ⓜ*Smithsonian.*

National Archives. The National Archives are at once monument, museum, and the nation's memory. Headquartered in a grand marble edifice on Constitution Avenue, the National Archives and Records Administration is charged with preserving and archiving the most historically important U.S. government records. Its 8 billion paper records and 4 billion electronic records date back to 1775. The star attractions, which draw millions of reverential viewers every year, are the Declaration of Independence, Constitution, and Bill of Rights. ⊠*Constitution Ave. between 7th and 9th Sts. NW, The Mall* ☎*202/501–5000,*

202/501–5205 tours ⊕www.nara.gov ⊠Free ⊙Apr.–Labor Day, daily
10–9; Labor Day–Mar., daily 10–5:30; tours weekdays at 10:15 and
1:15 ⓜArchives/Navy Memorial.

Fodor'sChoice **National Gallery of Art, West Building.** The two buildings of the National
★ Gallery hold one of the world's foremost collections of paintings,
sculptures, and graphics, from the 13th to the 21st centuries. If you
want to view the museum's holdings in (more or less) chronological
order, it's best to start your exploration in the West Building. The only
painting by Leonardo da Vinci on display in the Western Hemisphere,
Ginevra de'Benci is the centerpiece of the collection's comprehensive
survey of Italian Renaissance paintings and sculpture. The gallery of
gorgeous French Impressionist masterworks by superstars such as
Claude Monet, Auguste Renoir, and Edgar Degas, is unmissable. ⊠The
Mall ☎202/737–4215, 202/842–6176 TDD ⊕www.nga.gov ⊠Free
⊙Mon.–Sat. 10–5, Sun. 11–6 ⓜArchives/Navy Memorial

Fodor'sChoice **National Gallery of Art, East Building.** The East Building opened in 1978
★ in response to the changing needs of the National Gallery, especially
its growing collection of modern art. Masterpieces from every famous
name in 20th century art—Pablo Picasso, Jackson Pollock, Piet Mon-
drian, Roy Lichtenstein, Joan Miró, Georgia O'Keeffe, and dozens of
others—fill the galleries. ⊠Constitution Ave. between 3rd and 4th Sts.
NW, The Mall ☎202/737–4215, 202/842–6176 TDD ⊕www.nga.gov
⊠Free ⊙Mon.–Sat. 10–5, Sun. 11–6 ⓜArchives/Navy Memoria.l

Fodor'sChoice **National Museum of African Art.** Opened in 1987, this unique under-
★ ground building houses galleries, a library, photographic archives,
☪ and educational facilities. Its rotating exhibits present African visual
arts, including sculpture, textiles, photography, archaeology, and modern art. Long-term installations explore the sculpture of sub-Saharan
Africa, the art of Benin, the pottery of Central Africa, the archaeology of the ancient Nubian city of Kerma, and the artistry of everyday
objects. ⊠950 Independence Ave. SW, The Mall ☎202/633–1000,
202/357–1729 TDD ⊕www.nmafa.si.edu ⊠Free ⊙Daily 10–5:30
ⓜSmithsonian.

Fodor'sChoice **National Museum of American History.** The 3 million artifacts in the coun-
★ try's largest history museum explore America's cultural, political, technical, and scientific past, with holdings as diverse and iconic as the desk
on which Thomas Jefferson wrote the Declaration of Independence, the
top hat Abraham Lincoln was wearing the night he was assassinated,
and Judy Garland's ruby slippers from The Wizard of Oz. The original Star-Spangled Banner: the 15-stripe and 15-star American flag that
flew over Fort McHenry during the British bombardment of Baltimore
Harbor in 1814, and inspired Francis Scott Key to write the national
anthem, is the centerpiece of the museum's vast collections. ⊠Constitu-
tion Ave. and 14th St. NW, The Mall ☎202/633–1000, 202/357–1729
TDD ⊕www.americanhistory.si.edu ⊠Free ⊙Daily 10–5:30; call for
hrs of Hands on History and Hands on Science rooms ⓜSmithsonian
or Federal Triangle

Fodor's Choice
★ **National Museum of the American Indian.** The Smithsonian's newest museum opened in 2004 and is the first national museum devoted entirely to Native American artifacts, presented from a Native American perspective. ⊠*4th St. and Independence Ave. SW* ☎*202/633–1000* ⊕*www.americanindian.si.edu* 🎫*Free* ⊗*Daily 10–5:30* Ⓜ*L'Enfant Plaza*

Fodor's Choice
★ **National Museum of Natural History.** This is one of the great natural history museums in the world. The giant dinosaur fossils, glittering gems, creepy-crawly insects, and other natural delights—124 million specimens in all—attract nearly 6 million visitors annually. ⊠*Constitution Ave. and 10th St. NW, The Mall* ☎*202/633–1000, 202/357–1729 TDD* ⊕*www.mnh. si.edu* 🎫*Free, IMAX $8* ⊗*Museum daily 10–5:30; Discovery Room Tues.–Fri. noon–2:30, weekends 10:30–3:30; free passes for Discovery Room distributed during regular museum hrs near Discovery Room door* Ⓜ*Smithsonian or Federal Triangle*

> ### STRANGE BUT TRUE
>
> D.C.'s license plates read "Taxation Without Representation." And that's not a joke! At this writing, the city's residents did not have a voting member in the United States Congress (a deal was to give the liberal district a full-fledged representative in exchange for giving conservative Utah an extra House member was passed in the house—but failed in the senate—in 2007). D.C. does have a delegate in the House, Eleanor Holmes Norton—but she can't vote for legislation. The district does have a representative in the electoral college, though, so they do help select the president.

Fodor's Choice
★ **Phillips Collection.** The first permanent museum of modern art in the country, the masterpiece-filled Phillips Collection is unique both in origin and content.At the heart of the collections are impressionist and modern masterpieces by Pierre-Auguste Renoir, Vincent van Gogh, Paul Cézanne, Edgar Degas, Pablo Picasso, Paul Klee, and Henri Matisse. ⊠*1600 21st St. NW, Dupont Circle* ☎*202/387–2151* ⊕*www.phillipscollection.org* 🎫*Free for permanent collection on weekdays; admission varies on weekends and for special exhibitions* ⊗*Oct.–May, Tues., Wed., Fri., and Sat. 10–5, Thurs. 10–8:30, Sun. noon–7; June–Sept., Tues., Wed., Fri., and Sat. 10–5, Thurs. 10–8:30, Sun. noon–5* Ⓜ*Dupont Circle*

Fodor's Choice
★ **United States Holocaust Memorial Museum.** This museum's permanent exhibition tells the stories of the millions of Jews, Gypsies, Jehovah's Witnesses, homosexuals, political prisoners, the mentally ill, and others killed by the Nazis between 1933 and 1945. The exhibitions are detailed and graphic; the experiences memorable and powerful. Timed-entry passes (distributed on a first-come, first-served basis at the 14th Street entrance starting at 10 AM or available in advance through tickets.com) are necessary for the permanent exhibition. ⊠*100 Raoul Wallenberg Pl. SW, enter from Raoul Wallenberg Pl. or 14th St. SW, The Mall* ☎*202/488–0400, 800/400–9373 tickets.com* ⊕*www.ushmm.org* 🎫*Free* ⊗*Daily 10–5:30* Ⓜ*Smithsonian.*

MONUMENTS & MEMORIALS

Fodor's Choice ★ **Arlington National Cemetery.** More than 250,000 American war dead, as well as many notable Americans (among them Presidents William Howard Taft and John F. Kennedy, General John Pershing, and Admiral Robert E. Peary), are interred in these 612 acres across the Potomac River from Washington, established as the nation's cemetery in 1864. Tourmobile tour buses leave every 15–20 minutes from just outside the visitor center April through September, daily 8:30–26:30, and October through March, daily 8:30–24:30. You can buy tickets here for the 40-minute tour of the cemetery, which includes stops at the Kennedy grave sites, the Tomb of the Unknowns, and Arlington House. ⊠ *West end of Memorial Bridge, Arlington, VA* ☎*703/607–8000* ⊕*www.arlingtoncemetery.org* ⊟*Cemetery free, parking $1.25 per hr. Tourmobile $6* ⊙*Apr.–Sept., daily 8–7; Oct. –Mar., daily 8–5* Ⓜ*Arlington Cemetery.*

Fodor's Choice ★ **Lincoln Memorial.** Many consider the Lincoln Memorial the most inspiring monument in Washington, but that hasn't always been the case: early detractors thought it inappropriate that a president known for his humility should be honored with what amounts to a grandiose Greek temple. The memorial was intended to be a symbol of national unity, but over time it has come to represent social justice and civil rights. In its shadow, Americans marched for integrated schools in 1958, rallied for an end to the Vietnam War in 1967, and laid wreathes in a ceremony honoring the Iranian hostages in 1979. It may be best known, though, as the site of Martin Luther King Jr.'s "I Have a Dream" speech. ⊠ *West end of Mall* ☎*202/426–6895* ⊕*www.nps.gov/linc* ⊟*Free* ⊙*Open 24 hrs; staffed daily 8 am–midnight* Ⓜ*Foggy Bottom.*

Fodor's Choice ★ **National World War II Memorial.** Dedicated just before Memorial Day in 2004, this symmetrically designed monument honors the 16 million Americans who served in the armed forces, the more than 400,000 who died, and all who supported the war effort at home. An imposing circle of 56 granite pillars, each bearing a bronze wreath, represents the U.S. states and territories of 1941–45. Four bronze eagles, a bronze garland, and two 43-foot-tall arches inscribed with "Atlantic" and "Pacific" surround the large circular plaza. The roar of the water comes from the Rainbow Pool, here since the 1920s but newly renovated as the centerpiece of the memorial. There are also two fountains, and two waterfalls. ⊠*17th St., at east of Washington Monument* ⊕*www.wwiimemorial. com* ⊟*Free* ⊙*Open 24 hrs* Ⓜ*Smithsonian.*

Fodor's Choice ★ **Thomas Jefferson Memorial.** Jefferson had always admired the Pantheon in Rome, so the Jefferson Memorial's architect, John Russell Pope, drew on it for inspiration. The memorial's bronze statue of Jefferson, standing on a 6-foot granite pedestal, looms larger than life. ⊠*Tidal Basin, south bank* ☎*202/426–6821* ⊕*www.nps.gov/thje* ⊟*Free* ⊙*Daily 8 am–midnight* Ⓜ*Smithsonian.*

Fodor's Choice ★ **Vietnam Veterans Memorial.** "The Wall," as it's commonly called, is one of the most visited sites in Washington. The names of more than 58,000 Americans who died in the Vietnam War are etched in its black granite panels, creating a somber, dignified, and powerful memorial. ⊠*Consti-*

LIKE A LOCAL

Happy Hour on the Hill: At 6 PM on a weekday evening, bars in D.C. are hopping like it's Saturday night. The happy hour culture here is strong, as government employees, lawyers, and other city workers unwind or network over half-price beers, rail drinks, and pub grub. For the quint-essential D.C. happy hour experi-ence, throw on something business casual and head to the Hill- no one will know you're not a Congressional staffer.

Dine on Ethiopian Food: The District's many Ethiopian expats have introduced the community to their unique African cooking. The best restaurants, such as Dukem and Meskerem, are in the U Street and Adams-Morgan neighborhoods. Meat and vegetarian dishes are ladled onto a large round of spongy injera bread, and diners eat with their hands, ripping off pieces of bread to scoop up the delectable stews.

Where else can you play with your food in public?

Hang Out on U Street: You won't find many tourists in the U Street neighborhood, and many locals have only recently discovered the area. During the day, browse through the unique boutiques that line 14th and U Streets NW, or read the Washing-ton CityPaper at one of the many cafés. In the evening, select from trendy or ethnic restaurants, hang out at a local bar like the Chi Cha Lounge, or catch live music at the 930 Club or Bohemian Caverns.

Catch a Flick: A typical Saturday night's dinner and a movie gets a lit-tle more exciting in D.C. The art deco Uptown Theater in Cleveland Park is an old-school movie house with the largest screen in town. The American City Diner farther up Connecticut Avenue shows movie classics from the '40s through '60s while custom-ers chow down on diner fare.

7

tution Gardens, 23rd St. and Constitution Ave. NW ☎202/634–1568 ⊕www.nps.gov/vive ⊒Free ⊗24 hrs; staffed daily 8 am–midnight Ⓜ Foggy Bottom.

Fodor'sChoice
★ **Washington Monument.** At the western end of the Mall, the 555-foot, 5-inch Washington Monument punctuates the capital like a huge excla-mation point. Inside, an elevator takes you to the top for a bird's-eye view of the city. ⊠Constitution Ave. and 15th St. NW ☎202/426–6841, 877/444–6777 for advance tickets ⊕www.nps.gov/wamo, www. recreation.gov for advance tickets ⊒Free; $2 service fee per advance ticket ⊗Daily 9–5 Ⓜ Smithsonian.

OFFICIAL WASHINGTON

Fodor'sChoice
★ **The Capitol.** Beneath its magnificent dome, the day-to-day business of American democracy takes place. To see the Capitol you're required to go on a 30- to 40-minute tour conducted by the Capitol Guide Service. The first stop is the Rotunda, followed by the National Statuary Hall, the Hall of Columns, the old Supreme Court Chamber, the crypt (where there are exhibits on the history of the Capitol), and the gift shop. Note that you don't see the Senate or House chambers on the tour—you'll need to contact your senator or representative in advance to arrange to see congress in session. ⊠East end of Mall ☎202/224–4048, 202/225–

6827 recorded updates, 202/224–4049 TDD ⊕www.aoc.gov, www. senate.gov, www.house.gov ☎*Free* Ⓜ*Capitol S or Union Station.*

Fodor's Choice ★ **The Supreme Court.** The court convenes on the first Monday in October and hears cases until April. There are usually two arguments a day at 10 and 11 in the morning, Monday through Wednesday, in two-week intervals. On mornings when court is in session, two lines form for people wanting to attend. The "three-to-five-minute" line shuttles you through, giving you a quick impression of the court at work. The full-session line gets you in for the whole show. If you want to see a full session, it's best to be in line by at least 8:30. The Washington Post carries a daily listing of what cases the court will hear. In May and June the court takes to the bench Monday morning at 10 to release orders and opinions. Sessions usually last 15 to 30 minutes and are open to the public. When court isn't in session, you can hear lectures about the court, typically given every hour on the half hour from 9:30 to 3:30. ✉*1 1st St. NE, Capitol Hill* ☎*202/479–3000* ⊕*www.supremecourtus. gov* ☎*Free* ☉*Weekdays 9–4:30; court in session Oct.–June* Ⓜ*Union Station or Capitol S.*

Fodor's Choice ★ **The White House** America's most famous house is open to visitors, but getting in requires planning. You'll need to contact your representative or senator—arrangements are made through their offices. To visit in spring or summer, you should make your request about six months in advance. For a January visit, a month might suffice. Non-U.S. citizens make arrangements through their embassy. You also need a group of 10 or more in order to visit. Don't have 10? The office of your representative or senator may be able to place you with another group. Before your visit, you'll be asked for the names, birthdates, and social security numbers of everyone in your group, and you'll be told where to meet and what you can bring. On the morning of your tour, call the White House Visitors Office information line, 202/456–7041. Tours are subject to last-minute cancellation. Arrive 15 minutes early. Your group will be asked to line up in alphabetical order. Everyone 15 years or older must present photo ID. Going through security will probably take as long as the tour itself: 20 to 25 minutes. ✉*1600 Pennsylvania Ave. NW* ☎*202/208–1631, 202/456–7041 24-hr info line* ⊕*www. whitehouse.gov* ☎*Free; reservations required* ☉*Tours Tues.–Sat. 7:30–12:30* Ⓜ*Federal Triangle, Metro Center, or McPherson Sq.*

Fodor's Choice ★ **Washington National Cathedral.** Like its 14th-century Gothic counterparts, the stunning National Cathedral (officially the Cathedral Church of St. Peter and St. Paul) has a nave, flying buttresses, transepts, and vaults that were built stone by stone. It's the sixth largest cathedral in the world. ✉*Wisconsin and Massachusetts Aves. NW, Upper Northwest* ☎*202/537–6200, 202/537–6207 tour information* ⊕*www.cathedral.org/cathedral* ☎*Suggested tour donation $3* ☉*Weekdays 10–5, Sat. 10–4, Sun. 8–6:30 (8–2:45 for worship only). Tours Mon.–Sat. 10–4, every 30 min. Gardens open dawn–dusk* Ⓜ*Cleveland Park or Tenleytown. Take any 30 bus series.*

WHERE TO EAT

WHAT IT COSTS				
¢	$	$$	$$$	$$$$
AT DINNER under $10	$10–$17	$18–$25	$26–$35	over $35

Price per person for an average main course or equivalent combination of smaller dishes. Note: if a restaurant offers only prix-fixe (set-price) meals, it has been given the price category that reflects the full prix-fixe price.

$$$$
AMERICAN
Downtown
Fodor's Choice
★

CityZen. The Mandarin Hotel's rarefied dining room has fast become a destination for those serious about food. In a glowing space with soaring ceilings, chef Eric Zeibold, formerly of Napa Valley's famed French Laundry, creates luxe fixed-price meals from the finest ingredients. Unexpected little treasures abound, such as scrambled eggs with white truffles shaved at the table and buttery miniature Parker House rolls. Main courses could include black bass over caramelized cauliflower and braised veal shank with potato gnocchi, and desserts such as Meyer lemon soufflé seem spun out of air. A three-course meal is $75, and the tasting menus run $90–$105. ⊠ *Mandarin Oriental, 1330 Maryland Ave. SW, Downtown* ☎ 202/787–6868 △ *Reservations essential* ⊟ *AE, D, DC, MC, V* ⊘ *Closed Sun. and Mon. No lunch.*

$$–$$$$
AMERICAN
Georgetown

1789. This dining room with Early American paintings and a fireplace could easily be a room in the White House. But all the gentility of this 19th-century town house–restaurant is offset by the down-to-earth food on the menu, which changes daily. The soups, including the seafood stew, are flavorful. Rack of lamb and fillet of beef are specialties, and the seafood dishes are excellent. Service is fluid and attentive. Bread pudding and crème brûlée are sweet finishes. ⊠ *1226 36th St. NW, Georgetown* ☎ 202/965–1789 △ *Reservations essential. Jacket required* ⊟ *AE, D, DC, MC, V* ⊘ *No lunch.*

$$–$$$$
CONTINENTAL
Downtown

Caucus Room. Here's the quintessential Washington political restaurant. The limited partnership that owns it includes a Democratic super-lobbyist and a former Republican National Committee chairman. The dark wood and rich leather within make it perfect for business lunches or dinners, and the many private dining rooms are popular for political fund-raising events. The menu changes about three times a year, but you can count on prime meats, and seafood dishes including sea bass and seared tuna. ⊠ *401 9th St. NW, Downtown* ☎ 202/393–1300 ⊟ *AE, D, DC, MC, V* ⊘ *Closed Sun. No lunch weekends* Ⓜ *Navy Archives.*

$$–$$$$
NEW
AMERICAN
Dupont Circle
Fodor's Choice
★

Komi. Johnny Monis, the young, energetic chef–owner of this small, personal restaurant, offers one of the most adventurous dining experiences in the city. The five-course prix-fixe is $74 and showcases contemporary fare with a distinct Mediterranean influence. Star plates include fresh sardines with pickled lemons, suckling pig over apples and bacon with polenta, and mascarpone-filled dates with sea salt. ⊠ *1509 17th St., Dupont Circle* ☎ 202/332–9200 △ *Reservations essential* ⊟ *AE, D, MC, V* ⊘ *Closed Sun. and Mon. No lunch* Ⓜ *Dupont Circle.*

$–$$$
AMERICAN
Downtown

Old Ebbitt Grill. People flock here to drink at the several bars, which seem to go on for miles, and to enjoy well-prepared buffalo wings, hamburgers, and Reuben sandwiches. The Old Ebbitt also has Wash-

7

ON THE WAY

Alexandria, Virginia is across the Potomac and 7 mi downstream from Washington. As a commercial port, it competed with Georgetown in the days before Washington was a city. It's now a "big" small town loaded with historic homes, shops, and restaurants.

Annapolis, Maryland's capital, is a popular destination for seafood lovers and boating fans. Warm, sunny days bring many boats to the City Dock, where they're moored against a background of waterfront shops and restaurants. The city has one of the country's largest assemblages of 18th-century architecture, with more than 50 pre–Revolutionary War buildings. Its nautical reputation is enhanced by the presence of the U.S. Naval Academy.

Three splendid examples of plantation architecture remain on the Virginia side of the Potomac, 16 mi south of the District. **Mount Vernon** (South end of George Washington Parkway, Mount Vernon, VA, 703/780-2000, www.mounvernon. org), the most-visited historic house in America, was the home of George Washington; **Woodlawn** (9000 Richmond Hwy., Mount Vernon, VA, 703/780–4000, www.woodlawn1805. org) was the estate of Washington's step-granddaughter; and **Gunston Hall** (10709 Gunston Rd., Mason Neck, VA, 703/550–9220, www.gunstonhall.org) was the residence of George Mason, a patriot and author of the document on which the Bill of Rights was based.

ington's most popular raw bar, which serves farm-raised oysters. Pasta is homemade, and daily fresh fish or steak specials are served until 1 AM. Despite the crowds, the restaurant never feels cramped, thanks to its well-spaced, comfortable booths. ■ TIP→ Service can be slow at lunch; if you're in a hurry, try the café-style Ebbitt Express next door. ⊠ 675 15th St. NW, Downtown ☎ 202/347–4800 ☐ AE, D, DC, MC, V Ⓜ Metro Center.

¢–$ **2 Amys.** Judging from the long lines here, the best pizza in D.C. is
PIZZA uptown. Simple recipes allow the ingredients to shine through at this
Glover Park Neapolitan pizzeria. You may be tempted to go for the D.O.C. pizza
Fodor'sChoice (it has Denominazione di Origine Controllata approval for Neapolitan
★ authenticity), but don't hesitate to try the daily specials. Roasted peppers with anchovies and deviled eggs with parsley-caper sauce have by now become classics. At busy times, the wait for a table can exceed an hour. ⊠ 3715 Macomb St. NW, Glover Park ☎ 202/885–5700 ⚊ Reservations not accepted ☐ MC, V ⊗ No lunch Mon.

¢–$ **Ben's Chili Bowl.** Long before U Street became hip, Ben's was serving chili.
AMERICAN Chili on hot dogs, chili on Polish-style sausages, chili on burgers, and
U Street just plain chili. Add cheese fries if you dare. The faux-marble bar and shiny red vinyl stools give the impression that little has changed since the 1950s, but turkey and vegetarian burgers and meatless chili are a nod to modern times. Ben's closes at 2 AM Monday through Thursday, at 4 AM on Friday and Saturday, and at 8 PM Sunday. Southern-style breakfast is served from 6 AM weekdays and from 7 AM on Saturday. ⊠ 1213

U St. NW, U Street corridor ☎202/667–0909 ⊟*No credit cards* Ⓜ*U Street/Cardozo.*

$
AFRICAN
U Street

Etete. The best of the city's Ethiopian restaurants, Etete doesn't hold back on the spices. Savory pastries known as *sambusas* are filled with fiery lentils, and ginger brightens a stew of vegetables. The sharing of dishes and the mode of eating—rather than using utensils diners tear off pieces of a spongy pancakelike bread to scoop up stews and sautées—make for exotic and adventurous dining at this style-conscious eatery. ⊠*1942 9th St. NW, U Street* ☎202/232–7600 ⊟*AE, D, DC, MC, V* Ⓜ*U St./African-American Civil War Memorial/Cardozo.*

¢
AMERICAN
Georgetown
☺

Five Guys. One of the quirky traditions of this homegrown fast-food burger house is to note on the menu board where the potatoes for that day's fries come from, be it Maine, Idaho, or elsewhere. The place gets just about everything right: from the grilled hot dogs and hand-patted burger patties—most folks get a double—to the fresh hand-cut fries with the skin on and the high-quality toppings such as sautéed onions and mushrooms. Add an eclectic jukebox to all of the above and you've got a great burger experience. ⊠*1335 Wisconsin Ave. NW, Georgetown* ☎202/337–0400 ⊟*MC, V.*

WHERE TO STAY

7

WHAT IT COSTS				
	¢	$	$$	$$$	$$$$
FOR 2 PEOPLE	under $125	$125–$210	$211–$295	$296–$399	over $400

Prices are for a standard double room in high season, excluding room tax (14.5% in D.C., 12.5% in MD, and 10.15% in VA).

$$$$
Fodor'sChoice
★
☺

Four Seasons Hotel. Having completed a whopping $40 million renovation in 2005, the Four Seasons has reasserted its role as Washington's leading hotel. Impeccable service and a wealth of amenities have long made this a favorite with celebrities, hotel connoisseurs, and families. Luxurious, ultramodern rooms offer heavenly beds, flat-screen digital TVs with DVD players, and French limestone or marble baths with separate showers and sunken tubs. A 2,000-piece original art collection graces the walls, and a walk through the corridors seems like a visit to a wing of the MoMA or the Met. The formal Seasons restaurant offers traditional dishes with an elegant twist, as well as a popular Sunday brunch. The sophisticated spa here is one of the best in town. ⊠*2800 Pennsylvania Ave. NW, Georgetown, 20007* ☎202/342–0444 or 800/332–3442 📠*202/944–2076* ⊕*www.fourseasons.com/washington* ⌨*160 rooms, 51 suites* ⌂*In-room: safe, Ethernet. In-hotel: restaurant, room service, bar, pool, gym, concierge, children's programs (ages 5–16), parking (fee), some pets allowed* ⊟*AE, D, DC, MC, V* Ⓜ*Foggy Bottom.*

$$$
Fodor'sChoice
★

Hay-Adams Hotel. Two famous Americans—statesman John Hay and historian Henry Adams—once owned homes on the site where this Italian Renaissance mansion now stands, next to Lafayette Park and the White House. The elegant boutique hotel offers outstanding personalized service, and the White House views from rooms on the sixth, seventh, and eighth floors are stunning. Other rooms, dressed in beige and pale sage green, face St. John's church or the interior, and are less expensive. The Lafayette serves exquisite American cuisine, and the hotel's bar is one of the most sophisticated you will find anywhere. ⊠ *1 Lafayette Sq. NW, Downtown 20006* ☎ *202/638–6600 or 800/424–5054* 🖷 *202/638–2716* ⊕ *www.hayadams.com* 📨 *125 rooms, 20 suites* ♿ *In-room: refrigerator (some), Wi-Fi. In-hotel: restaurant, room service, bar, concierge, laundry service, parking (fee), some pets allowed* ☐ *AE, D, DC, MC, V* Ⓜ *McPherson Sq. or Farragut N.*

$$$ **Hotel George.** Rooms at this cool **Fodor's**Choice boutique hotel offer duvet-covered ★ beds with the softest Egyptian cotton sheets, granite-topped desks, silkscreen prints, CD players, and seating areas with a lounge chair and ottoman. Most have marble bathrooms and terry robes, and each room comes with a complimentary in-room television "yoga program" (mat, block, and strap provided). Portraits of America's first president, by Andy Warhol protégé Steve Kaufman, adorn public areas. Bistro Bis serves updated versions of classic French dishes. ⊠ *15 E St. NW, Capitol Hill 20001* ☎ *202/347–4200 or 800/576–8331* 🖷 *202/347–4213* ⊕ *www.hotelgeorge.com* 📨 *139 rooms* ♿ *In-room: Ethernet, refrigerator. In-hotel: restaurant, room service, bar, gym, concierge, laundry service, parking (fee), some pets allowed* ☐ *AE, D, DC, MC, V* Ⓜ *Union Station.*

$–$$$ **Hotel Madera.** The unique Hotel Madera sits in a quiet part of town **Fodor's**Choice southwest of Dupont Circle. Innovative guest rooms with art nouveau ★ styling have CD players, complimentary high-speed or wireless Internet access, and minibars. Extra-spacious "specialty rooms" are decorated in rich earthy tones with finer furnishings, although the bathrooms remain small. The adjoining American bistro, Firefly, has a massive fake oak tree in the center of its dining room. The tree is hung with candles that resemble flickering fireflies. ⊠ *1310 New Hampshire Ave. NW, Dupont Circle, 20036* ☎ *202/296–7600 or 800/368–5691* 🖷 *202/293–2476* ⊕ *www.hotelmadera.com* 📨 *82 rooms* ♿ *In-room: safe, kitchen (some), Wi-Fi. In-hotel: restaurant, bar, parking (fee), pets allowed* ☐ *AE, D, DC, MC, V* Ⓜ *Dupont Circle.*

VITAL STATS:

■ Population, city: 571,000

■ Population, metro area: 5,162,029

■ Land area, city: 61 square mi

■ Nicknames: The District, D.C., Inside the Beltway

■ Natural hazards: Lobbyists, motorcades, lack of congressional representation

■ Major industries: Government, law, tourism, high-tech, higher education

■ Official motto: Justitia omnibus (justice for all)

■ Official food: The half-smoke, a large, smoked link sausage most famously found at Ben's Chili Bowl on U Street.

NIGHTLIFE & THE ARTS

Fodor's Choice ★ **John F. Kennedy Center for the Performing Arts.** On the bank of the Potomac River, the gem of the D.C. arts scene is home to the National Symphony Orchestra, the Washington Ballet, and the Washington National Opera. It also pulls the best out-of-town acts, regardless of medium.On the Millennium Stage in the center's Grand Foyer, you can catch free performances almost any day at 6 PM. ■TIP➔On performance days, a free shuttle bus runs between the Center and the Foggy Bottom/GWU Metro stop. ⊠*New Hampshire Ave. and Rock Creek Pkwy. NW, Foggy Bottom* ☎*202/467–4600 or 800/444–1324* ⊕*www.kennedy-center. org* Ⓜ*Foggy Bottom/GWU.*

Fodor's Choice ★ **Smithsonian Institution** Jazz, musical theater, and popular standards are performed in the National Museum of American History. In the museum's third-floor Hall of Musical Instruments, musicians occasionally play period instruments from the museum's collection. The Smithsonian's annual Folklife Festival, held on the Mall, highlights the cuisine, crafts, and day-to-day life of several different cultures. The Smithsonian Associates sponsors programs that offer everything from a cappella groups to Cajun Zydeco bands; all events require tickets, and locations vary. ⊠*1000 Jefferson Dr. SW, The Mall* ☎*202/357–2700, 202/633-1000 recording, 202/357–3030 Smithsonian Associates* ⊕*www.si.edu* Ⓜ*Smithsonian.*

SHOPPING

The Capitol Hill area's redbrick **Eastern Market** houses farmers, flower vendors, craftspeople, and other merchants who sell their fresh produce and handcrafted wares to locals and tourists alike. Although the main building was gutted in a fire in April 2007, the outdoor flea market continues to bustle on weekends. At this writing, the market building was undergoing a $30 million renovation, and indoor vendors were being housed in a temporary structure. ⊠*7th and C Sts. SE, Capitol Hill* Ⓜ*Eastern Market or Union Station.*

You might call **Dupont Circle** a younger, less staid version of Georgetown—almost as pricey but with more apartment buildings than houses. Its many restaurants, offbeat shops, and specialty book and record stores give it a cosmopolitan air. ⊠*Connecticut Ave. between M and S Sts.* Ⓜ*Dupont Circle.*

Although **Georgetown** is not on a metro line and parking is difficult at best, people still flock here, keeping it D.C.'s favorite shopping area. This is also the capital's center for famous residents, as well as being a hot spot for restaurants, bars, and nightclubs. ■TIP➔The nearest Metro, Foggy Bottom/GWU, is a 10- to 15-minute walk from the shops. Most stores lie to the east and west on M Street and to the north on Wisconsin. A few chic, independent shops can be found just south of the library on Wisconsin Avenue. ⊠*Intersection of Wisconsin Ave. and M St., Georgetown* Ⓜ*Foggy Bottom/GWU.*

7

SPORTS & THE OUTDOORS

☾ **National Zoo.** The National Zoo's pandas are stars, and their many fans cluster around their bamboo-filled compound. Carved out of Rock Creek Park, the zoo is a series of rolling, wooded hills that complement the many innovative compounds showing animals in their native settings. ✉*3001 Connecticut Ave. NW, Woodley Park* ☎*202/673–4800 or 202/673–4717* ⊕*www.si.edu/natzoo* ✉*Free, parking $16* ☾*May–mid-Sept., daily 6* AM*–8* PM*; mid-Sept.–Apr., daily 6–6. Zoo buildings open at 10 and close before zoo closes* Ⓜ*Cleveland Park or Woodley Park/Zoo.*

Fodor'sChoice **United States National Arboretum.** During azalea season (mid-April
★ through May), this 446-acre oasis is a blaze of color. In early summer, clematis, peonies, rhododendrons, and roses bloom. At any time of year, the 22 original Corinthian columns from the U.S. Capitol, re-erected here in 1990, are striking. ✉*3501 New York Ave. NE, Northeast* ☎*202/245–2726* ⊕*www.usna.usda.gov* ✉*Free* ☾*Arboretum and herb garden daily 8–5, bonsai collection daily 10–3:30* Ⓜ*Weekends only, Union Station, then X6 bus (runs every 40 min); weekdays, Stadium/Armory, then B2 bus to Bladensburg Rd. und R St.*

☾ **Rock Creek Park.** The 1,800 acres surrounding Rock Creek have provided a cool oasis for D.C. residents ever since Congress set them aside for recreational use in 1890. Bicycle routes and hiking and equestrian trails wind through the groves of dogwoods, beeches, oaks, and cedar, and 30 picnic areas are scattered about. ☎*202/282–1063 park information.*

☾ **Tidal Basin.** This placid pond was part of the Potomac until 1882, when portions of the river were filled in to improve navigation and create additional parkland. At the **boathouse** (☎*202/479–2426*), on the northeast bank of the Tidal Basin, you can rent paddleboats during the warmer months. Rental cost is $8 per hour for a two-person boat, $16 per hour for a four-person boat. The boathouse is open from mid-March through October from 10 to 6. The Tidal Basin's cherry trees are now the centerpiece of Washington's two-week **Cherry Blossom Festival,** held each spring since 1935. The festivities are kicked off by the lighting of a ceremonial Japanese lantern that rests on the north shore of the Tidal Basin, not far from where the first tree was planted. The trees are usually in bloom for about 10–12 days in late March or early April. ✉*Bordered by Independence and Maine Aves., The Mall* Ⓜ*Smithsonian.*

VISITOR INFORMATION

D.C. Visitor Information Center (✉*1300 Pennsylvania Ave. NW, Washington, DC, 20004* ☎*202/328–4748* ⊕*www.dcvisit.com*).

Washington, DC Convention and Tourism Corporation (☎*202/789–7000 or 800/422–8644* ⊕*www.washington.org*).

North Carolina's Outer Banks

Cape Hatteras Lighthouse

WORD OF MOUTH

"Weather in the OBX is great to the end of September, except for the occasional hurricane system. My understanding is that "high season" ends mid-August because in NC children return to school from summer vacation at that time. There is not a lot of nightlife in the OBX, though more so in Nags Head and Kitty Hawk, less so in Duck and Corolla. But the beaches are nice and the water is warm."

—nohomers

EXPLORING NORTH CAROLINA'S OUTER BANKS

195 mi west of Raleigh, NC, via US–64; 325 mi south of Baltimore via I–95 and US–64; 600 mi northeast of Atlanta via I–95 and US–64.

By Leslie Mizell

Although there's plenty to do in North Carolina's Outer Banks and the area's historical roots run deep, vacationing here isn't about rushing from a landmark to a museum or from one activity to the next. Wide expanses of sand and broad sea horizons invite you to pull up a chair, lay down a towel, or just curl your toes in the sand. Turn off your cell phone. Use your feet instead of your car. Try to get in synch with the slow roll of the Atlantic's waves, and listen to the birds, and the wind. And above all, relax and slow down.

A trip here is a feast for all five senses, filled with sun and sand, seafood and iced tea, kites and lighthouses, salt breezes and shag music. Maybe the *real* reason people slow down when they arrive is just to make every minute here last as long as possible.

WHO WILL ESPECIALLY LOVE THIS TRIP?

Sun-Worshippers: With 100 mi of public and private beaches, it's easy to find a stretch of sand to call your own on the Outer Banks.

Anglers: Fishermen (and women) can ply fresh- or salt water and fish from charter boats, piers, or shore. Your haul could include bluefish, speckled trout, striped bass, croaker, or small sharks—maybe even a 1,000-pound Atlantic Blue Marlin (the International Gamefish Association says the Outer Banks and the Virgin Islands are the best places in the U.S. to hook one of these massive fish).

Families: When they stop to catch their breath after camping, biking, kayaking, or swimming, you can take the kids to an aquarium, an outdoor drama, or to watch the hang-gliders on Jockey's Ridge.

Daredevils: The Outer Banks is a tranquil place, but thrill-seekers can still find plenty here to keep their adrenaline flowing. Visitors can find experts to teach them hang-gliding or parasailing, or kayak along the coast and the Outer Banks' many waterways.

Wedding parties: Couples from all 50 states get married along these barrier islands—there's even an Outer Banks Wedding Association to help with the tough decisions. (Should you get married on a beach or in a garden, at sunrise or sunset?)

WHEN IS THE BEST TIME TO VISIT?

To take full advantage of everything the Outer Banks has to offer, you should plan your vacation for peak season, which is between Memorial Day and Labor Day. There are more crowds and traffic, but everything will be open and in full swing. After a full day at the beach, you can

TOP 5 REASONS TO GO

Water, water everywhere: Rolling waves, rippling inlets, glassy lakes, waving salt marshes—the landscape variety lets you choose your own adventure, whether it's boating, trekking, sunning, or simply observing. With 900 square mi of water, this is the third largest estuary system in the world.

Don't skimp on the shrimp: A myriad of seafood restaurants offer everything from Lowcountry fare—fried fish and cornbread, shrimp and grits—to elegant haute cuisine creations.

The lost colony: Sometime between 1587 and 1590, 90 English settlers, including Virginia Dare, the first European baby born in the New World, disappeared from Roanoke Island without a trace, save one clue—the word "Croatoan" carved into a post. Their story is presented both through historical context and dramatic speculation in Manteo.

Lighting the darkness: The five operational lighthouses in the Outer Banks have individual personalities, from the masculine elegance of Currituck's brick facade to the iconic spiral of Hatteras.

Pirate lore and hidden booty: The Graveyard of the Atlantic is littered with shipwrecks, many of them popular dive sites. Hidden treasure still lies beneath the shifting sands here—Blackbeard's Queen Anne's Revenge, wrecked in 1718, was just discovered in 1996.

take in the absorbing The Lost Colony or an evening of minor league baseball with the Outer Banks Daredevils.

The mid-July temperature averages a toasty 90, with fierce humidity. If "sultry" isn't one of your favorite words, consider visiting in spring or fall instead. There are bargains to be had for traveling in the low-season—primarily in lodging—and although some restaurants will be closed, you'll still be able to enjoy a good meal.

If you visit December to February, however, you'd better pack in *all* your supplies, since most businesses are locked down during this time. You'll likely have your pick of deserted beaches, but the mixture of sand and wind can be literally abrasive during this time.

HOW SHOULD I GET THERE?

DRIVING

The Outer Banks are not accessible by Interstate. To get here, you must either cross bridges from the mainland on U.S. 158 (from the north) or U.S. 64 (from the west) or take ferries from Swan Quarter or Cedar Island after long mainland drives farther south.

FLYING

The closest large commercial airports are Raleigh-Durham, a five-hour drive, and Norfolk International in Virginia, a 1½ hour drive. Charter service is also available at Dare County Regional Airport.

8

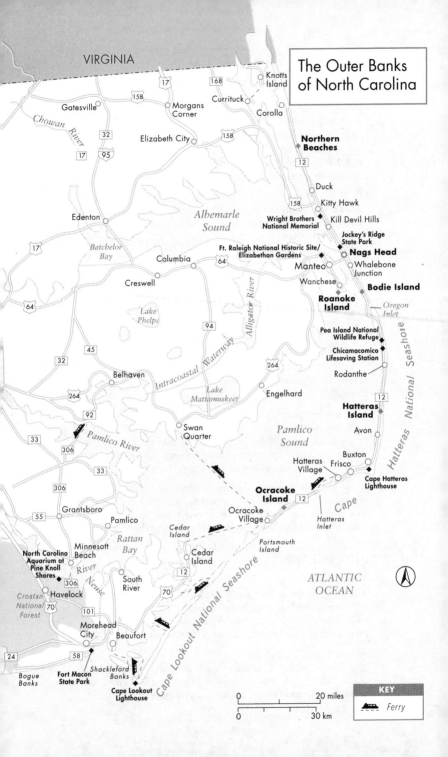

The Outer Banks
of North Carolina

VIRGINIA

Knotts
Island

Currituck

Corolla

Gatesville

Morgans
Corner

Elizabeth City

**Northern
Beaches**

Chowan River

Duck

158

Kitty Hawk

*Albemarle
Sound*

Wright Brothers
National Memorial

Kill Devil Hills

Jockey's Ridge
State Park

Edenton

Ft. Raleigh National Historic Site/
Elizabethan Gardens

Nags Head

*Batchelor
Bay*

Columbia

Manteo

Whalebone
Junction

Creswell

Wanchese

Bodie Island

**Roanoke
Island**

*Oregon
Inlet*

*Lake
Phelps*

Pea Island National
Wildlife Refuge

Chicamacomico
Lifesaving Station

Alligator River

Rodanthe

Belhaven

Intracoastal Waterway

*Lake
Mattamuskeet*

Engelhard

**Hatteras
Island**

Avon

Pamlico River

Swan
Quarter

*Pamlico
Sound*

Buxton

Hatteras
Village

Frisco

Cape Hatteras
Lighthouse

Grantsboro

Pamlico

**Ocracoke
Island**

Ocracoke
Village

Cape

Minnesott
Beach

*Rattan
Bay*

Cedar
Island

*Hatteras
Inlet*

North Carolina
Aquarium at
Pine Knoll
Shores

River

Cedar
Island

*Portsmouth
Island*

South
River

**ATLANTIC
OCEAN**

*Croatan
National
Forest*

Havelock

Neuse

Morehead
City

Beaufort

*Bogue
Banks*

Fort Macon
State Park

*Shackleford
Banks*

Cape Lookout National Seashore

Cape Lookout
Lighthouse

Hatteras National Seashore

KEY
Ferry

0 _____ 20 miles

0 _____ 30 km

How to Snack

CLOSE UP

Although plenty of famous food items have originated in North Carolina—Krispy Kreme Doughnuts, Pepsi-Cola, Texas Pete hot sauce, and Cheerwine (a cherry-flavor soda) among them—the Outer Banks isn't the sight of any truly groundbreaking culinary creations. But walk down the street in any of its small towns on a humid summer night, and you can see one foodstuff over and over again: ice cream. Whether it's stuffed in cups, ladled into shakes, or balanced on cones, it's the dessert that people here like to end their days with.

There are also snacks from the sea (after all, this is the coast). Raw bars serve oysters and clams on the half shell; seafood houses sell fresh crabs (soft shells in the early summer season) and whatever local catch—tuna,

wahoo, mahimahi, mackerel, shrimp—has been hauled in that day. Increasingly, highly trained chefs are settling in the region and diversifying menus. Fish dishes—broiled, fried, grilled, or steamed—are listed alongside entrées fusing Asian flavors and traditional Southern ingredients such as black-eyed peas.

Although it's not a snack, per se, the scuppernong grape has an increasing importance to the state. The native grapes, named for the Scuppernong River, were first cultivated in the 17th century. They're an acquired taste—the skin and meat are tart, but the juice between the two is delicious. Several vineyards grow scuppernongs in the sandy coastal soil, some from vines thought to be 400 years old.

HOW DO I GET AROUND?

8

BY BIKE

This simple mode of transportation will allow you to skip the traffic on Highway 12 and work up an appetite for (and work off the calories from) fried shrimp and hushpuppies. Rental shops are commonplace throughout the Outer Banks.

BY BOAT

Seagoing folks can travel the Intercoastal Waterway west of the Outer Banks and dock at nearly 150 marinas here.

BY CAB & LIMO

Beach Cabs, based in Nags Head, has 24-hour cab service from Norfolk to Ocracoke and all the little towns in between. The Connection has a shuttle service with passenger vans large enough for families, their camping equipment, surfboards, and bikes. The Outer Banks Limo Service, headquartered in Kill Devil Hills, serves the Norfolk International Airport and runs around the clock.

BY CAR

You can travel the region from the south end by taking a car ferry to Ocracoke Island or, as in the following route, from the north end. Driving the 120-mi stretch of Route 12 from Corolla to Ocracoke can be managed in a day, but be sure to allow plenty of time in summer to wait for the ferry connecting the islands and for exploring the undeveloped

CLAIM TO FAME

The Outer Banks have a stormy past, and each hurricane erodes a little more from these fragile barrier islands. Called "the Graveyard of the Atlantic," strong currents and fierce weather in this area have sent more than 2,000 ships to Davy Jones's Locker since 1526.

The U.S.S. Monitor, the first ironclad ship commissioned by the U.S. Navy, was swamped and sank off North Carolina on New Year's Eve 1862, with 16 of 62 crewman still aboard. The ship was found again in 1973 off Cape Hatteras. Although declared a National Landmark, her propeller, steam engine, and revolving gun turret have been raised and are on display.

Even more exciting, though, is the discovery of Blackbeard's flagship vessel, the Queen Anne's Revenge, in 20 feet of water in Beaufort Inlet—a find verified on the 278th anniversary of Blackbeard's death (November 22, 1996). Wrecked in 1718, she continues to be studied, and artifacts are still being brought up from her resting place.

You can learn more about one of the world's most treacherous stretches of coastline at the Graveyard of the Atlantic Museum (59200 Museum Dr., Hatteras, 252/986-2995, www. graveyardoftheatlantic.com) in Hatteras Village.

beaches, historic lighthouses, and small beach communities stretched along the national seashores. Mile markers (MM) indicate addresses for sites where there aren't many buildings.

WHERE SHOULD I FOCUS MY ENERGY?

If you're here for 1 day: During a quick trip, visit the Wright Brothers National Museum for a little taste of history in the morning. Spend the afternoon on the beach, with a quick trip to Jockey Ridge—the largest sand dune system in the Eastern U.S.—to watch the hang-gliders . . . or join them.

If you're here for 2 days: Include a visit to Manteo to see the 10-acre Elizabethan Gardens and to learn about the Lost Colony; catch Pulitzer Prize–winning playwright Paul Green's outdoor drama, *The Lost Colony,* performed at night during the summer.

If you're here for 3 days: Visit North Carolina's most famous lighthouse, the Hatteras Light, then check out the shopping in Nag's Head.

If you're here for 4 days: Spend the morning on a tour of Fort Macon in the Fort Macon State Park, then the afternoon at the North Carolina Aquarium at Pine Knoll Shores.

If you're here for 5 days: Commune with the nature in Pea Island National Wildlife Refuge, home to more than 365 species of birds. Walking trails and an observation tower help you spot wildlife. And across the street from the visitor center, you can see a genuine shipwreck.

HISTORY YOU CAN SEE

Outer Banks residents take great pride in their "First in Flight" moniker, and they won't hesitate to threaten fisticuffs with folks from Ohio who claim the title. (The Wright Brothers lived in the Buckeye State and experimented and built their airplane in their Dayton bicycle shop, but it *flew* in North Carolina.)

The Wright Brothers National Memorial, in Kill Devil Hills, includes the 60-foot granite pylon that marks the spot where Orville and Wilbur began experimenting with their glider; actual models of their 1902 glider and 1903 flying machine are on display. You can also build and fly your own paper airplane to see how aerodynamics work.

Outside, the steady winds that drew the brothers to North Carolina are still blowing strong.

If you're here for 6 days or more: Get out on the water. Hone your kayaking skills, head out on a fishing charter, or dive to a sunken shipwreck.

If you're here for 7 days or more: Slow down and explore at a more leisurely pace—relaxing, after all, is the main point of a vacation here.

WHAT ARE THE TOP EXPERIENCES?

The Food: Although there are plenty of upper-scale restaurants along the Outer Banks—a surprising number of Yankee chefs have retired here—to experience the full flavor of the area, you have to get your fingers wet. Peel your own shrimp right from the pot, crack your own crab, and fight with your table over who gets the last deep-fried hushpuppy.

The Festivals: The Outer Banks' wide range of events will keep you hopping during the peak summer season, but there's plenty of fun in the spring and fall, too. For example, a reenactment of the 1862 Battle of Roanoke Island takes place in March, and breezy kite festivals take to the sky in April, June, July, and October in Jockey's Ridge State Park. The birthday of the Lost Colony's lost child is celebrated at the Virginia Dare Faire in August, while Blackbeard and his ilk are honored with September's Pirate Festival. The year wraps with the Annual Celebration of the Wright Brothers First Flight in December.

The History: The Outer Banks' dark and mysterious past stretches back to 1585, when a group of British settlers landed . . . and later disappeared and became the infamous "Lost Colony." The Graveyard of the Atlantic stole plenty of other lives and ships, and the pirates that trolled her shores left their own grisly mark as well. The Civil War impacted the area as well, but less than 50 years later two brothers from Ohio would give the Outer Banks its true claim to fame: the Wright Brothers managed to fly their powered, heavier-than-air machine for as long as 59 seconds on a windy December 17, 1903, at Kitty Hawk.

STRANGE BUT TRUE

■ Dare County covers 800 square mi in North Carolina—391 land, and 409 water.

■ The Cape Hatteras Lighthouse is, at 208 feet, the tallest brick lighthouse in the U.S.

■ *The Lost Colony* is the oldest outdoor drama in the country. More than 4 million people have seen the play, which has been performed at Roanoke Island's Waterside Theater since 1937.

■ The post office changed the town of Chicamacomico's name to Rodanthe in 1874 because its name was too difficult to spell. But the U.S. Lifesaving Service (which eventually became the Coast Guard) resurrected the name when it opened a lifesaving station there. Chicamacomico may mean "sinking sand" or "wild turkeys" in the Algonkian language.

■ Legend has it that the wild horses—sometimes called "banker horses"—found around Corolla and on Ocracoke are descendants of the mustangs that washed ashore following the wreck of a Spanish galleon.

The Music: On the coast, it's all about beach music. The regional style that's sometimes acrimoniously claimed by both North and South Carolina is a 4/4 blend of swing, blues, jazz, and rock 'n' roll. Upbeat tunes by artists such as the Coasters, Sam Cooke, the Drifters, Ben E. King, the Platters, and the Tams helped generations of beachgoers "shag" dance. Although the music has lost ground after a 1980s revival, it still has plenty of devotees.

BEST BETS

SIGHTS AND TOURS

★ The **Wright Brothers National Memorial,** a 60-foot granite monument that resembles the tail of an airplane, stands as a tribute to Wilbur and Orville Wright. The two bicycle mechanics from Ohio took to the air here on December 17, 1903. You can see a replica of the *Flyer* and stand on the spot where it made four takeoffs and landings, the longest flight a distance of 852 feet. Exhibits and an informative talk by a National Park Service ranger bring the event to life. ⊠ *U.S. 158 between MM 7 and MM 8, 5 mi south of Kitty Hawk, Kill Devil Hills* ☎ *252/441–7430* ⊕ *www.nps. gov/wrbr* ☞ *$3* ☉ *Sept.–May, daily 9–5; June–Aug., daily 9–6.*

⟳ **Jockey's Ridge State Park** has 420 acres that encompass the tallest sand dune on the East Coast (about 90 to 110 feet), although it has lost some 22 feet since the 1930s thanks to the million visitors a year who carry sand away on their shoes and clothes. The climb to the top is a challenge; nevertheless, it's a popular spot for hang gliding, kite flying, and sand boarding. ⊠ *U.S. 158, MM 12* ☎ *252/441–7132* ⊕ *www.ils. unc.edu/parkproject* ☞ *Free* ☉ *Daily 8–dusk.*

★ The lush **Elizabethan Gardens** are a 10 acre re-creation of 16th-century English gardens, established as an elaborate memorial to the first English colonists. Walk through the brick and wrought-iron entrance to see antique statuary, wildflowers, rose gardens, and a sunken garden, all impeccably maintained by the Garden Club of North Carolina. ✉ *1411 National Park Dr., 3 mi north of downtown Manteo* ☎ *252/473–3234* ⊕ *www.elizabethangardens. org* ✍ *$8* ☾ *Dec.–Feb., daily 10–4; Mar. and Nov., daily 9–5; Apr., May, Sept., and Oct., daily 9–6; June–Aug., Mon.–Sat. 9–8, Sun. 9–7.*

LIKE A LOCAL

Driving along Highway 12, you'll notice that almost every car has an oval decal with a stark "OBX" printed on it. This nickname for the Outer Banks grew so popular that the residents asked the North Carolina Department of Motor Vehicles to use the three-letter prefix on their license plates. Unfortunately the DMV printed only 9,999 tags (OBX-0000 through OBX-9999), leaving the rest of the populace out of luck. Residents voiced their displeasure, and the state continued with OBX-10000.

Coquina Beach, in the Cape Hatteras National Seashore, is considered by locals to be the loveliest beach in the Outer Banks. Free parking, public changing rooms, showers, and picnic shelters are available. ✉ *Off Rte. 12, MM 26, 8 mi south of U.S. 158.*

Bodie Island Lighthouse designer Dexter Stetson is also the brains behind the Cape Hatteras lighthouse, which explains why the two look so much alike. Bodie, with its fat (22-feet tall) black-and-white horizontal stripes, stands 156 feet tall and is capped by a black cast-iron lantern. The current lighthouse was completed in 1872 and is in the midst of a two-part renovation that won't be complete until 2009. ■ TIP➔ Only the lower level, keeper's house, and museum can be toured; visitors will have to make a return trip to climb the 214 steps to the top. ✉ *1401 National Park Dr.* ☎ *252/473–2111 or 252/441–5711* ⊕ *www.nps. gov/caha/bdlh.htm* ✍ *Free* ☾ *Memorial Day–Labor Day, daily 9–6; Labor Day–Thanksgiving, daily 9–5.*

Pea Island National Wildlife Refuge is made up of more than 5,800 acres of marsh on the Atlantic flyway. To bird-watchers' delight more than 365 species have been sighted from its observation platforms and spotting scopes, including threatened peregrine falcons and piping plovers. A visitor center on Route 12 has an information display and maps of the two trails. ■ TIP➔ Remember to douse yourself in bug spray, especially in spring. Guided canoe tours are available for a fee. ✉ *Pea Island Refuge Headquarters, Rte. 12, 5 mi south of Oregon Inlet* ☎ *252/987–2394* ⊕ *http://peaisland.fws.gov* ✍ *Free* ☾ *June–Aug., daily 9–5; Mar.–May and Sept.–Nov., daily 9–4; Dec.–Feb., hrs vary, call ahead.*

The restored 1911 **Chicamacomico Lifesaving Station** (pronounced "chik-a-ma-*com*-i-co") is now a museum that tells the story of the brave people who manned 24 stations that once lined the Outer Banks. ✉ *Off Rte. 12 at MM 39.5, Rodanthe* ☎ *252/987–1552* ✍ *$5* ☾ *Mid-Apr.–Nov., weekdays noon–5.*

ON THE WAY

USS *North Carolina* Battleship Memorial. In Wilmington you can take a self-guided tour of a ship that participated in every major naval offensive in the Pacific during World War II. Exploring the floating city, with living quarters, a post office, chapel, laundry, and even an ice-cream shop, takes about two hours. (A climb down into the ship's interior is not for the claustrophobic.) The ship can be reached by car or by taking the river taxi from Riverfront Park, Memorial Day through Labor Day, at a cost of $2 per person. Battleship Rd., junction of U.S. 74/76 and U.S. 17 and 421, west bank of Cape Fear River, Downtown Wilmington, 910/251–5797, www.battleshipnc.com.

The Futuro House—which looks like an alien spacecraft—was designed by Finnish architect Matti Suuronen in 1968 and sold over the next decade. There's one in Frisco, NC.

★ **Cape Hatteras Lighthouse** was the first lighthouse built in the region, autho-
☺ rized by Congress in 1794 to help prevent shipwrecks. The original structure was lost to erosion and Civil War damage; this 1870 replacement is, at 208 feet, the tallest brick lighthouse in the world. In summer the principal keeper's quarters are open for viewing, and you can climb the 257 steps (12 stories) to the viewing balcony. ■TIP➔ **Children under 42 inches in height aren't allowed in the lighthouse.** Offshore lie the remains of the USS *Monitor,* a Confederate ironclad ship that sank in 1862. ✉*Off Rte. 12, 30 mi south of Rodanthe, Buxton* ☎*252/995–4474* ⊕*www.nps.gov/caha* ✉*Visitor center and keeper's quarters free, lighthouse tower $6* ☼*Visitor center and keeper's quarters: daily 9–5. Lighthouse tower: Apr.–mid-Oct., daily 10–5.*

Ocracoke Island **beaches** are among the least populated and most beautiful on the Cape Hatteras National Seashore. Four public access areas have parking as well as off-road vehicle access. ✉*Off Rte. 12.*

Look out from the **Ocracoke Pony Pen** observation platform at the descendants of the Banker Ponies that roamed wild before the island came under the jurisdiction of Cape Hatteras National Seashore. The park service took over management of the ponies in 1960 and has helped maintain the population of about 30 animals; the wild herd once numbered nearly 500. All the animals you see today were born in captivity and are fed and kept on a 180-acre range. Legends abound about the arrival of the island's Banker Ponies. Some believe they made their way to the island after the abandonment of Roanoke's Lost Colony. Others believe they were left by early Spanish explorers or swam to shore following the sinking of the *Black Squall,* a ship carrying circus performers. ✉*Rte. 12, 6 mi southwest of Hatteras-Ocracoke ferry landing.*

Built in 1823, **Ocracoke Lighthouse** is the second oldest operating lighthouse in the U.S. (Sandy Hook, New Jersey, has the oldest). It was first fueled by whale oil, then kerosene, and finally electricity. ■TIP➔ **The squat whitewashed structure, 75 feet tall, is unfortunately not open to the public for climbing—although it's a photographer's dream.** ✉*Off Rte.*

12, Live Oak Rd., Ocracoke Village ⊕www.nps.gov/caha/ ocracokelh.htm.

When the original red-and-white-stripe 1812 lighthouse proved too short and unstable, the 1859 **Cape Lookout Lighthouse** was built to replace it. This 169-foot lighthouse withstood retreating Confederate troops' attempts to blow it up to keep it out of Union hands (they stole the lens instead). With its white-and-black diamond markings, the beacon continues to function as a navigational aid. A small museum inside the visitor center on Harkers Island tells the story of the lighthouse from its first incarnation in 1812. From there you must take a ferry to get to the lighthouse.

VITAL STATS:

■ State capital: Raleigh

■ State motto: Esse quam videri ("To be, rather than to seem")

■ State flower: Dogwood

■ State tree: Longleaf pine

■ State salt water fish: Red Drum (also known as the Channel bass)

■ State historical boat: Shad boat

■ State dog: Plott Hound

■ State vegetable: Sweet potato

■ State fruit: Scuppernong grape

■ State carnivorous plant: Venus Flytrap

■ State popular dance: Shag

The tower is undergoing renovation and is open infrequently. ⊠*Core Banks* ☎*252/728–5766 for climb reservations* ⊕*www.nps.gov/calo* ⊠*Free.*

★ The centerpiece of **Fort Macon State Park** is the 1834 pentagon-shape for-
☾ tress used first to protect the coast against foreign invaders and pirates, then against Yankees during the Civil War. You can explore on your own or take a guided tour. The 365-acre park set in a maritime forest also offers picnicking areas, hiking trails, a mile-long beachfront with a large bathhouse and refreshments, and summer concerts. Rangers offer a wide selection of nature talks and walks, including Civil War weapons demonstrations, bird or butterfly hikes, and beach explorations. Follow the boardwalk over the dunes to the beach, which, due to strong currents, has lifeguards on duty June through Labor Day from 10 to 5:45. A bathhouse locker costs $4. ⊠*East end of Rte. 58, Bogue Banks, 3 mi south of Morehead City, Atlantic Beach* ☎*252/726–3775* ⊕*http://ils. unc.edu/parkproject* ⊠*Free* ☾*Fort: daily 9–5:30. Grounds Apr., May, and Sept., daily 8–7; June–Aug., daily 8–8; Oct.–Mar., daily 8–6.*

Fodor's Choice Exhibits at the **North Carolina Aquarium at Pine Knoll Shores** include jelly-
★ fish; river otters; and a 306,000-gallon, 60-foot long Living Shipwreck
☾ of a German submarine sunk off the North Carolina coast in 1942. There's a large selection of lectures, walks, excursions, and camps. You can take a nighttime stroll on the beach looking for loggerhead turtles, kayak the Theodore Roosevelt Natural Area, and take a wildlife tour of the Rachel Carson National Estuarine Reserve. Kids will love seeing the aquarium menagerie getting fed or spending a night at a slumber party in the Living Shipwreck exhibit. ☎*252/247–4003, 866/294–3477 for activities* ⊠*U.S. 58, Atlantic Beach* ⊕*www.ncaquariums.com* ⊠*$8* ☾*Daily 9–5.*

8

★ **Fort Raleigh National Historic Site** is a restoration of the original 1585
earthworks that mark the beginning of English-colonial history in
America. ■TIP→Be sure to see the orientation film and then take a
guided tour of the fort. A nature trail through the 513-acre grounds
leads to an outlook over Roanoke Sound. Native American and Civil
War history is also preserved here. *The Lost Colony (⊠1409 U.S.
64/264 ☏252/473–3414 or 800/488–5012 ⊕www.thelostcolony.org
✉$16)*, Pulitzer Prize–winner Paul Green's drama, was written in
1937 to mark the 350th birthday of Virginia Dare. Except from 1942
to 1945, it has played every summer since in Fort Raleigh National
Historic Site's Waterside Theatre. It reenacts the story of the first colonists, who settled here in 1587 and mysteriously vanished. Cast alumni
include Andy Griffith and Lynn Redgrave. Reservations are essential.
⊠*National Park Dr., off U.S. 64/264, 3 mi north of downtown Manteo* ☏*252/473–5772* ⊕*www.nps.gov/fora* ✉*Free* ⊙*Sept.–May, daily
9–5; June–Aug., daily 9–6.*

WHERE TO EAT

WHAT IT COSTS					
	¢	$	$$	$$$	$$$$
RESTAURANTS	under $7	$7–$11	$12–$16	$17–$22	over $22

Restaurant prices are for a main course at dinner.

$$$$ ✕**Windmill Point.** The menu changes here, but you can always count on
Fodor'sChoice the signature seafood trio: a choice of any combination of three fish.
★ You can have it lightly poached or grilled, and topped with roasted red
pepper and capers, or shredded cucumber and dill, or a pineapple salsa.
Beef, poultry, pasta, and vegetarian selections are always available, and
there's a kids' menu as well. Brunch is served weekends from 10 to 4.
The restaurant has stunning views of the sound at sunset, eye-catching
memorabilia from the luxury liner SS *United States,* and, yes, a real
windmill. ⊠*U.S. 158, MM 16.5* ☏*252/441–1535* ▤*AE, D, MC, V.*

$$$–$$$$ ✕**Blue Point Bar & Grill.** This upscale spot with an enclosed porch over-
★ looking Currituck Sound is as busy as a diner and as boldly colorful—
with a red, black, and chrome interior. The menu mixes Southern style
with local seafood, including the ever-popular she-crab soup, a thick
and rich concoction made with cream, sherry, herbs, Old Bay season-
ing, and, of course, female crab. Brunch is served Sunday. ⊠*1240
Duck Rd., Duck* ☏*252/261–8090* ⊠*Reservations essential* ▤*AE,
D, MC, V.*

$$–$$$$ ✕**Owens' Restaurant.** Inside an old Nags Head–style clapboard cottage,
Fodor'sChoice this old-fashioned coastal restaurant has been in the same family and
★ location since 1946. Stick with the seafood or chops, at which they
excel. Miss O's crab cakes are ever-popular, as is the filet mignon topped
with lump crabmeat and asparagus béarnaise sauce. Pecan-encrusted
sea scallops are plump and tender. The 16-layer lemon and chocolate
cakes are delicious. In summer arrive early and expect to wait. ⊠*U.*

S. 158, MM 16.5, Nags Head ☎*252/441–7309* ⌘*Reservations not accepted* ⊟*AE, D, MC, V* ☽*Closed Jan. and Feb. No lunch.*

$$–$$$$ ✕**The Pelican Restaurant and Patio Bar.** This 19th-century harborfront home in a grove of twisted oak trees has a patio next to an outdoor bar; many people take a seat here and don't leave for a long while. Jumbo shrimp stuffed with cream cheese and jalapeño peppers and lump crab cakes are two of the most requested food items. "Shrimp Hour," which is really two hours every day (3 to 5), draws crowds because large steamed shrimp sell for 15¢ each here. The Pelican also serves breakfast until 11 AM. ✉*305 Irvin Garrish Hwy., Ocracoke* ☎*252/928–7431* ⊟*AE, D, MC, V.*

¢–$$$ ✕**Full Moon Café.** Colorful stained-glass panels hang in the large front
★ windows of this wonderfully cheerful bistro renovated from a gas station. The herbed hummus with roasted pita is fantastic, as are the crab cakes and baked crab-dip appetizer. Other choices include salads, veggie wraps, Cuban-style enchiladas, burgers of all kinds, and a dozen innovative and hearty sandwiches. ✉*207 Queen Elizabeth Ave., Manteo* ☎*252/473–6666* ⊟*AE, D, MC, V.*

$–$$$ ✕**Tides.** South of the entrance for the Cape Hatteras Lighthouse, this place is popular for its well-prepared food and homey manner. In addition to offering the usual seafood—try the shrimp gumbo—the menu has chicken and ham. It's also a popular breakfast spot. ✉*Rte. 12, Buxton* ☎*252/995–5988* ⊟*MC, V* ☽*Closed Dec.–early Apr. No lunch.*

¢–$ ✕**Sam & Omie's.** This no-nonsense niche is named after two fishermen who were father and son, and it's the oldest restaurant in the Outer Banks. Fishing illustrations hang on the walls, and Merle Haggard plays in the background. It's open daily 7 to 7, serving every imaginable kind of seafood, and then some. Try the fine marinated tuna steak, Cajun tuna bites, or frothy crab-and-asparagus soup. The chef has been using the same recipe for the she-crab soup for 22 years; locals love it. ■TIP➜ Diehard fans claim that Sam & Omie's serves the best oysters on the beach. ✉*U.S. 158, MM 16.5* ☎*252/441–7366* ⌘*Reservations not accepted* ⊟*D, MC, V* ☽*Closed Dec.–Feb.*

WHERE TO STAY

WHAT IT COSTS				
¢	$	$$	$$$	$$$$
HOTELS under $70	$70–$110	$111–$160	$161–$220	over $220

Hotel prices are for two people in a standard double room in high season.

$$$$ ✕🏨**The Sanderling Resort & Spa.** A remote beach, 5 mi north of Duck,
★ is a fine place to be pampered, go swimming, play tennis, or enjoy a round of golf. A 3-mi nature trail winds through the adjacent Pine Island Bird Sanctuary; the concierge can help arrange kayak tours and other activities. Sanderling has three inn buildings plus villas, all with the mellow look of old Nags Head. Whirling ceiling fans, wicker furniture, and bright tones make the rooms casual and summery. The formal, dinner-only Left Bank restaurant ($$$$) has a wall of win-

8

dows overlooking Currituck Sound. Crab cakes, roast duckling, or fricassee of shrimp may be on the seasonal menu. The resort-casual Lifesaving Station ($–$$$$), in a restored 1899 lifesaving station, serves breakfast, lunch, and dinner and includes a second-floor lounge. ⊠ *1461 Duck Rd., Duck 27949* ☏ *252/261–4111 or 800/701–4111* 🖷 *252/261–1638* ⊕ *www.sanderlinginn.com* ↪ *88 rooms, 29 studios, 4 villas* ♿ *In-room: kitchen (some), refrigerator (some), VCR, Wi-Fi. In-hotel: 2 restaurants, room service, bar, tennis courts, pool, gym, spa, bicycles, laundry service* ▤ *AE, D, MC, V* ⏹ *BP.*

$$$–$$$$ ✕▦ **Tranquil House Inn.** This charming 19th-century-style inn sits water-
★ front, a few steps from shops, restaurants, and the Roanoke Island Festival Park. The mood of the individually decorated rooms is one of classic, clean lines, and muted colors; some have comfy sitting areas. Complimentary wine and cheese are served in the evening. The popular restaurant, 1587 ($$$–$$$$), is known for its chop-house-style cuts and inventive entrées, such as Asian tuna over shrimp-fried rice or grilled porkloin on kahlua mashed sweet potatoes. ⊠ *405 Queen Elizabeth Ave., Box 2045, Manteo 27954* ☏ *252/473–1404 or 800/458–7069* 🖷 *252/473–1526* ⊕ *www.1587.com* ↪ *8 rooms* ♿ *In-hotel: restaurant, bicycles, no-smoking rooms* ▤ *AE, D, MC, V* ⏹ *BP.*

$–$$$ ▦ **First Colony Inn.** Stand on the verandas that encircle this old, three-
Fodor's Choice story, cedar-shingle inn and admire the ocean views. Two rooms have
★ wet bars, kitchenettes, and whirlpool baths; others have four-poster or canopy beds, handcrafted armoires, and English antiques. All rooms contain extras, such as heated towel bars. In fall and winter Nature Conservancy birding weekends include excursions to the Pea Island Wildlife Refuge. ⊠ *6720 S. Virginia Dare Trail, 27959* ☏ *252/441–2343 or 800/368–9390* 🖷 *252/441–9234* ⊕ *www.firstcolonyinn.com* ↪ *26 rooms* ♿ *In-room: kitchen (some). In-hotel: restaurant, pool, no-smoking rooms* ▤ *AE, D, MC, V* ⏹ *BP.*

VISITOR INFORMATION

Dare County Tourist Bureau (⊠ *704 S. U.S. 64/264, Box 399, Manteo 27954* ☏ *252/473–2138 or 800/446–6262* ⊕ *www.outerbanks.org*).

Hatteras Island Welcome Center (⊠ *Rte. 12, Buxton* ☏ *No phone*).

National Park Service, Cape Lookout National Seashore (⊠ *131 Charles St., Harkers Island 28531* ☏ *252/728–2250* ⊕ *www.nps.gov*).

National Park Service's Group Headquarters (⊠ *1401 National Park Dr., Manteo* ☏ *252/473–2111 24 hrs* ⊕ *www.nps.gov*).

National Park Service Superintendent (⊠ *Rte. 1, Box 675, Manteo 27954*).

Outer Banks Welcome Center on Roanoke Island (⊠ *1 Visitors Center Circle, Manteo 27954* ☏ *877/298–4373*).

Charleston & Savannah

WITH THE SOUTH CAROLINA & GEORGIA LOWCOUNTRY

Drayton Hall, Charleston

WORD OF MOUTH

We spent a lot of time just wandering [in Charleston]. We found it very easy to orient ourselves and not have to rely on the map to get everywhere. I think our favorite walks were south of Broad along Meeting and the other little side streets. Peeking at private homes & their impeccable gardens was such a treat!

–ATtravel

EXPLORING CHARLESTON & SAVANNAH

Charleston is 320 mi east of Atlanta via I–20 and I–26; 208 mi south-east of Charlotte via I–77 and I–26; 110 mi northeast of Savannah via I–95 and I–526; 985 mi south of Boston via I–95 and I–26; and 379 mi north of Orlando via I–95 and Hwy. 17N.

By Eileen Robinson Smith

Few places on this planet are as endowed with natural beauty as the Lowcountry of South Carolina and Georgia. The region's miles of pristine beaches, subtropical vegetation, and stretches of golden marshlands with waist-high grasses are as evocative and poetic as the tendrils of silver Spanish moss that adorn its centuries-old live oaks. A warm, primal sensuality seems to permeate everything. And when the nocturnal fog rolls in, it gives rise to the preternatural tales that southern children are raised on.

Its historic cities are a main draw for travelers. They wander through Charleston's historic district, scanning the skyline for the spires and steeples of some 180 churches punctuate the low skyline. Horse-drawn carriages pass centuries old mansions and well tended courtyard gardens. A southern charmer, Charleston has consistently won awards as the most mannerly city in the country.

Savannah, with the nation's largest historic district, has become wildly popular since John Berendt's tell-all book *Midnight in the Garden of Good and Evil*. The story is a testimony to the eccentricities that can flourish in this hothouse environment, as well as the legendary hospitality and tolerance of Savannhians.

WHO WILL ESPECIALLY LOVE THIS TRIP?

Couples: If you're looking for a quiet, romantic getaway, this is the place. The area is a big draw for inquisitive, well-traveled adults who want to immerse themselves in the natural beauty, charm, architecture, and history of the Old South.

Foodies: Charleston has a growing reputation as a food destination, and creative, contemporary restaurants have sprung up throughout the Lowcountry. Seafood- and soul-food lovers will not be disappointed.

Families: There's plenty here for kids to see and do. Charleston is home to the Children's Museum of the Lowcountry, the South Carolina Aquarium, and Waterfront Park. Many area hotels have pools, and there are glorious beaches. The island resorts have great children's programs. Hilton Head has countless activities for young visitors, including nocturnal turtle nesting walks.

WHEN IS THE BEST TIME TO VISIT?

Charleston has been likened to Camelot, especially during spring festivals like the Spoleto Festival and the BBT Food + Wine Festival. This is peak season in Charleston, Beaufort, and Savannah—the weather is

TOP 5 REASONS TO GO

Lowcountry cuisine. The Lowcountry at large is known for its distinctive southern fare. Charleston has become a culinary destination, with talented chefs who offer innovative twists on the region's traditional cuisine.

Spoleto Festival USA. The most magical time in "Camelot" is the 17-days in May and June when this internationally heralded performing arts festival enlivens the entire city of Charleston with a flood of indoor and outdoor performances, including opera, music, dance, and theater.

Savannah Music Festival. Georgia's acclaimed festival runs for 18 days beginning in mid-March, with multiple performances daily at downtown venues; there's something magical for everyone.

African-American Heritage. Attractions like Charleston's Old Slave Mart; the York W. Bailey Museum, with its displays on sea Island blacks, at St. Helena's Penn Center; and Gullah tours explaining the language and culture and the slaves' role in the Union army give tremendous insight into the struggles and triumphs of blacks in the Lowcountry.

The inimitable beauty of the Lowcountry. From subtropical islands and beaches to the restored historic districts of some of America's most gorgeous cities, lovely things are all around you in the Lowcountry.

sunny, but not steamy hot. The azaleas bloom as early as March, followed by magnolias, camellias, and other subtropical flowers.

Summer is hot and humid, and hotel rates drop down in the cities; this is the time for beach fun on the barrier sea-islands. On Hilton Head and the Golden Isles, the high season follows typical beach-town cycles, with May through August and holidays year-round being the busiest and most costly (though weekend bookings are fairly strong until the end of November). Winter is when you'll find the best prices there.

Late fall and early spring are ideal for visiting Georgia's coastal isles. By February, temperatures often reach into the 70s, while nights remain cool, which keeps the bugs at bay. By May, deerflies and mosquitoes swarm the coast and islands. Although the more populated localities spray, do bring repellants along as well.

In September the Carolina sun starts to cool, and in Charleston the fall brings the Candlelight Tours of Homes and Gardens. The holiday season here has as much Christmas spirit as a Dickensonian novel, and shopping is a pleasure. Historic homes are dressed in their holiday best.

HOW SHOULD I GET THERE?

BUS

Greyhound Bus stops in Charleston, Beaufort, Savannah, and Brunswick. The Lowcountry Regional Transportation Authority has a bus that leaves Beaufort in the morning for Hilton Head that costs $2.25. Exact change is required. This same company has a van that, with 24-

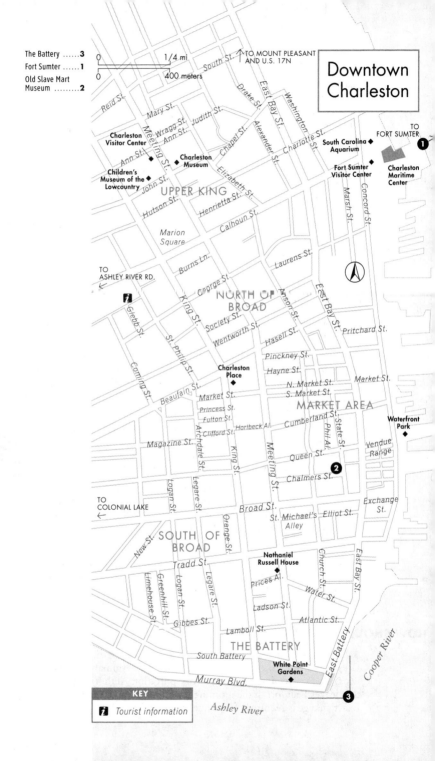

The Battery **3**
Fort Sumter **1**
Old Slave Mart
Museum **2**

0 ⌊_____⌋ 1/4 mi
0 ⌊_____⌋ 400 meters

↑ TO MOUNT PLEASANT
AND U.S. 17N

Downtown Charleston

TO FORT SUMTER

South St.

Reid St.

Mary St.

Drake St.

East Bay St.

Washington St.

Charlotte St.

Charleston
Visitor Center

Wragg St.
Ann St.
Judith St.

Chapel St.

Alexander St.

South Carolina
Aquarium

Charleston
Museum

Children's
Museum of the
Lowcountry

John St.

Elizabeth St.

Fort Sumter
Visitor Center

Charleston
Maritime
Center

1

Meeting St.

UPPER KING

Hutson St.

Henrietta St.

Calhoun St.

Marsh St.

Concord St.

Marion
Square

Burns Ln.

Laurens St.

TO
ASHLEY RIVER RD.
←

George St.

NORTH OF
BROAD

East Bay St.

Glebb St.

King St.

Jason St.

St. Philip St.

Society St.

Wentworth St.

Hasell St.

Pritchard St.

Coming St.

Pinckney St.

Hayne St.

Charleston
Place

N. Market St.
S. Market St.

Market St.

Beaufain St.

Market St.

Princess St.

Fulton St.

Clifford St.

Horlbeck Al.

Cumberland St.

State St.

Phil Al.

MARKET AREA

Waterfront
Park

Magazine St.

Archdale St.

King St.

Meeting St.

Queen St.

Vendue
Range

Logan St.

Legare St.

Chalmers St.

2

TO
COLONIAL LAKE
←

Broad St.

St. Michael's
Alley

Elliot St.

Exchange
St.

New St.

SOUTH OF
BROAD

Orange St.

Tradd St.

Nathaniel
Russell House

Prices Al.

Church St.

Water St.

East Bay St.

Limehouse St.

Greenhill St.

Logan St.

Legare St.

Ladson St.

Gibbes St.

Atlantic St.

Lamboll St.

THE BATTERY

South Battery

White Point
Gardens

East Battery

Cooper River

Murray Blvd.

3

Ashley River

KEY

ℹ️ *Tourist information*

hour notice, will pick you up at your hotel and drop you off at your destination for $3. You can request a ride weekdays 7 AM to 10 AM or 12:30 PM to 3 PM.

DRIVING
Interstate 26 traverses South Carolina from northwest to southeast and terminates at Charleston; U.S. 17, the coastal road, also passes through the city. Interstate 526, also called the Mark Clark Expressway, runs primarily east–west, connecting the West Ashley area, North Charleston, Daniel Island, and Mount Pleasant; it's a fast track from the airport to Highway 17 south.

In Savannah I–95 slices north–south along the eastern seaboard, intersecting 10 mi west of town with east–west Interstate 16, which deadends in downtown Savannah. U.S. 17, the Coastal Highway, also runs north–south through town. U.S. 80, which connects the Atlantic to the Pacific, is another east–west route through Savannah.

FLYING
Charleston International Airport, about 12 mi west of downtown, is served by American Eagle, Continental, Delta, United Express, Northwest, US Airways and now AirTran Airways. Wings Air, a commuter airline that flies to and from Atlanta, operates out of Mount Pleasant Regional Airport and the Charleston Executive Airport.

Savannah has service by AirTran, American Eagle, Continental Express, Northwest Airlink, Delta Air Lines, Delta Connection, Independence Air, Northwest Airlink, and United Express. Savannah/Hilton Head International Airport has 40-plus daily nonstop flights. It's 18 mi west of downtown.

TRAIN
Amtrak has service to Charleston from such major cities as New York, Philadelphia, Washington, Richmond, Savannah, and Miami. The Amtrak station is somewhat isolated and not pretty, but a visible police presence means there are few reports of crime in the area. Taxis meet every train; a ride to downtown averages $25.

The Savannah Amtrak station is about 6 mi from downtown, 45 minutes to Hilton Head.

HOW DO I GET AROUND?

BY BOAT & FERRY
The Charleston Water Taxi is a delightful way to travel between Charleston and Mount Pleasant. Some people take the $8 round-trip journey just for fun. It departs from the Charleston Maritime Center, half a block south of Adger's Wharf. Charleston is also a highly rated port of embarkation for several cruise ship lines.

Belles Ferry provides a regular service from the City Hall dock in the Historic District to the Westin Savannah Harbor Golf Resort & Spa at the Convention Center, on Hutchinson Island. Ferries are part of the transit system and run daily 7 AM to 11 PM with departures every 10 to

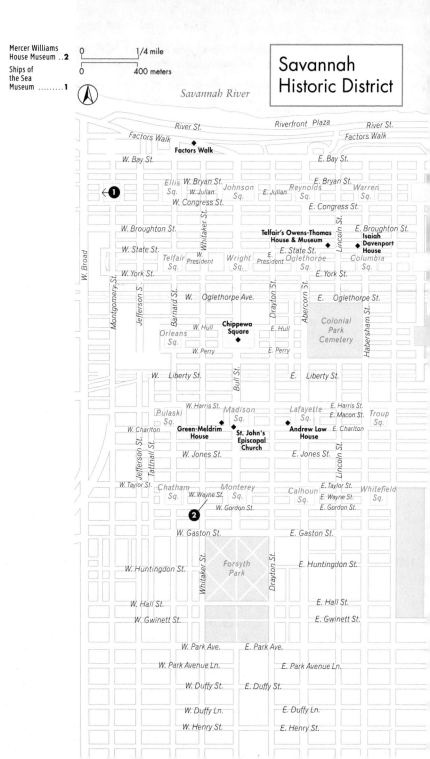

Mercer Williams House Museum ..**2**

Ships of the Sea Museum **1**

0   1/4 mile

0   400 meters

Savannah Historic District

Savannah River

River St.   Riverfront Plaza   River St.

Factors Walk   Factors Walk

W. Bay St.   E. Bay St.

Ellis W. Bryan St.   *Johnson*   *Reynolds*   *Warren*
Sq. W. Julian   *Sq.* E. Julian *Sq.*   *Sq.*

W. Congress St.   E. Congress St.

W. Broughton St.   E. Broughton St.

Telfair's Owens-Thomas   **Isaiah**
House & Museum   **Davenport**
W. State St.   E. State St.   **House**

Telfair W.   *Wright* E. Oglethorpe *Columbia*
Sq. *President* *Sq.* *President* *Sq.* *Sq.*

W. York St.   E. York St.

W.   Oglethorpe Ave.   E.   Oglethorpe St.

Orleans W. Hull **Chippewa** E. Hull   *Colonial*
Sq.   **Square**   *Park*
                                                    Cemetery
W. Perry   E. Perry

W.   Liberty St.   E.   Liberty St.

W. Harris St. *Madison*   *Lafayette*   E. Harris St.
               Sq.   *Sq.*   E. Macon St. *Troup*
Pulaski   *Sq.*
Sq.
W. Charlton **Green-Meldrim** **Andrew Low** E. Charlton
             House **St. John's** **House**
                        Episcopal
                        Church
W. Jones St.   E. Jones St.

W. Taylor St. *Chatham* *Monterey* *Calhoun* E. Taylor St. *Whitefield*
               Sq. W. Wayne St. *Sq.* *Sq.* E. Wayne St. *Sq.*
                        W. Gordon St.   E. Gordon St.

W. Gaston St.   E. Gaston St.

W. Huntingdon St.   *Forsyth*   E. Huntingdon St.
                        Park

W. Hall St.   E. Hall St.

W. Gwinett St.   E. Gwinett St.

W. Park Ave.   E. Park Ave.

W. Park Avenue Ln.   E. Park Avenue Ln.

W. Duffy St.   E. Duffy St.

W. Duffy Ln.   E. Duffy Ln.

W. Henry St.   E. Henry St.

How to Snack

Boiled peanuts are a big-time snack in the Lowcountry. Street vendors in downtown Charleston sell the tasty snack (they're more visible during festivals). Just outside the city limits, farm stands selling produce cook up boiled peanuts as well. If you see men tending big, steaming vats near the side of the road, pull over and buy a brown bag full.

Benne wafers and pecan pralines are two other traditional Lowcountry treats. Benne is the African word for sesame seeds (considered good luck), which are scattered within these thin, sweet cookies. Pecan pralines can be found at several different shops in the market notably **Market Street Sweets** (⊠ *100 N. Market St., Market area* ☎ *843/722-1397*) for the melt-in-your-mouth pralines and fudge.The 24-hour **Harris Teeter** (⊠ *290 E. Bay St., Market area* ☎ *843/722-6821*), one of the best local supermarkets, carries Charleston foodstuffs.

When you're walking around Charleston, take a break with an icy treat at **Paolo's Gelato Italiano** (⊠ *41 John St., Upper King* ☎ *843/577-0099*). Fla-

vors include various fruits as well as traditional flavors like pistachio. They also serves crepes covered with delicious sauces.

In Savannah the best place for an ice-cream soda is **Leopold's** (⊠ *212 E. Broughton St., Historic District* ☎ *912/234-4442*), a local institution since 1919. It's currently owned by Stratton Leopold, grandson of the original owner and a Hollywood producer whose films include *Mission Impossible 3, The General's Daughter,* and *The Sum of All Fears.* Movie paraphernalia makes for an entertaining addition to the selection of ice creams and sorbets. Famed lyricist Johnny Mercer was a faithful customer.

Byrd Cookie Company & Gourmet Marketplace (⊠ *6700 Waters Ave., Highland Park* ☎ *912/355-1716*), founded in 1924, sells picture tins of Savannah and gourmet foodstuffs like condiments and dressings. It's the best place to get benne wafers and trademark Savannah cookies, which are also sold in numerous gift shops around town.

9

15 minutes. The crossing takes two minutes and costs $1 round-trip (in exact change). Guests staying in the convention district ride for free.

BY BUS

The Charleston Area Regional Transportation Authority, the city's public bus system, takes passengers around the city and to the suburbs. Bus 11, which goes to the airport, stops at the Mary Street parking garage, and costs $1.50. CARTA operates DASH, which runs buses that look like vintage trolleys along three downtown routes. A single ride is $1.25, and a day-long pass is $4. You should have exact change.

Chatham Area Transit (CAT) operates buses in Savannah and Chatham County Monday through Saturday from 6 AM to 11 PM, Sunday from 9 to 7. Some lines may stop running earlier or may not run on Sunday. The CAT Shuttle operates throughout the Historic District and is free. For other Savannah buses, the fare is $1.

CLAIM TO FAME

Charleston boomed with the plantation economy in the years before the Civil War. South Carolina's rice, indigo, and cotton crops produced an extraordinary concentration of wealth—much of it built upon the backs of slaves. Seeking a social and cultural lifestyle to match its financial success, the plantocracy entertained itself in style. The city was also renowned for its talented goldsmiths, silversmiths, gunsmiths, tobacconists, brewers, and cabinet-makers. More than 200 private residences were built during this period, and the city was one of the top shopping places in North America.

Remarkably there's still a 300-acre historic district downtown, which is comprised of centuries-old homes. To observe the city's pride and joy walk down to the Battery, South of Broad. This area showcases handsome mansions surrounded by elaborate gardens. Several of the city's lavish house museums call this famously affluent neighborhood home. The look is reminiscent of the West Indies, since in the late 17th century, many early British colonists came to Charleston after first settling on Barbados and other Caribbean isles.

Savannah, America's "Southern Treasure," captivates, intrigues, surprises, and romances visitors with her gracious hospitality and subtle eccentricities. She is known for her timeless beauty and seductive charms. The people here are as warm as the climate, and entertaining comes naturally. Paula Deen, the southern cuisine queen of Food Network fame, is a Savannah girl who raised her two handsome sons on her brand of home cooking. (They now have their own Food Network show as well.) With her thick southern accent and earthiness, Deen often cooks at various historic venues like Tybee Island's Fort Pulaski. She has her own restaurants here, notably the Lady & Sons, where tourists line up for the buffet of local specialties.

BY CAR

Driving in Charleston is quite pleasant; what is considered rush hour here compares favorably to that of any major metropolis. Parking garages, both private and municipal, are throughout the city, and streets are punctuated with meters. Know that the meter maids are among the most efficient city employees. (After 6 and on weekends—no worries.) You may want to keep your car parked if you stay in the historic district and just walk everywhere in your most comfortable shoes. On foot you can explore the sunlighted alleys and admire the courtyard gardens.

In Savannah patrollers are quick to dole out parking tickets. Tourists may purchase two-day parking passes ($8) at the Savannah Visitors Center and at some hotels and inns. Passes are valid in metered spots as well as in the city's lots and garages; they allow parkers to exceed the time limit in time-limit zones.

BY TAXI

Fares within Charleston average about $5 per trip. As a rule, you can't hail a cab—you'll have to call for one. Reputable companies include Safety Cab and Yellow Cab, which are available 24 hours a day. These cabs are metered with a $2 minimum and each additional mile is $1.75. Charleston Black Cab Company, which has London-style taxis with uniformed drivers, line up near Charleston Place. Classier, they are understandably more expensive. They will take you anywhere in the downtown peninsula for $10. A ride to Kiawah or Seabrook Islands is $75 plus at Kiawah, a $10 gate fee. It's recommended that you call 24 hours in advance to reserve a black cab, whenever possible. Another option is Charleston Rickshaw Company—they'll pedal you anywhere in the historic district for $7 to $12.

In Savannah, AAA Adam Cab Co. is a reliable 24-hour taxi service. Calling ahead for reservations could yield a flat rate. Yellow Cab Company is another dependable taxi service. Standard taxi fare is $1.50 a mile. The standard flat rate between the Historic District and the airport is $25, which can rise to as much as $38 if you're staying in Savannah's South Side.

WHERE SHOULD I FOCUS MY ENERGY?

If you're here for 1 day: Take a carriage ride to both see Charleston's historic sights, shop, visit Fort Sumter, and browse the French Quarter art galleries. Dine at a renowned restaurant, and follow with a nightcap and a dance at a music venue.

If you're here for 2 days: Spend 24 hours or more on Hilton Head, particularly if you're a golfer.

If you're here for 3 days: Add an additional day in Charleston and visit one of her historic plantations. Then go kayaking in the ocean or creeks, or bike the world's largest single-span bridge to the town of Mount Pleasant. Take a water taxi back downtown.

If you're here for 4 days: Spend a day wandering through Savannah's historic district. Have a memorable dinner in a former historic home, followed by some fun in the bars on River Street or the smokin' jazz clubs.

If you're here for 5 days: Add a day in Beaufort, SC a diminutive city with many of the same appealing characteristics of Charleston. Visit its historic sites or cross the bridge to the sea islands and learn more about African-American history.

If you're here for 6 days: Spend an additional day in Savannah and play beach bum at Tybee Island (definitely see the lighthouse). Stay on island for cocktails and a dose of fresh seafood. Once you're back downtown, take in a piano bar.

If you're here for 7 days or more: Explore the Golden Isles. Each has its own endearing personality, everything from subtropical-rusticity to five-star comfort.

HISTORY YOU CAN SEE

Charleston was founded in 1670, and it's the oldest city between Virginia and Florida. Immigrants, like the French Hugenots, flocked here initially for religious freedom.

The city has one of the country's most colorful histories. It played a pivotal role in the American Revolution, as depicted in Mel Gibson's feature film, The Patriot. Later, the first shots of the Civil War were fired here at Fort Sumter.

Charleston persevered through the poverty following the Civil War, and despite natural disasters like fires, earthquakes, and hurricanes, many of Charleston's earliest public and private buildings still stand. And thanks to a rigorous preservation movement

and strict Board of Architectural Review, the city's new structures blend with the old ones.

In Savannah the oldest and most beloved section is the Historic District, which houses the city's 22 beautiful squares and many of its accommodations, restaurants, and shops. Included in this area is the National Historic Landmark District—2.5 square mi bears the highest historic district-level designation awarded by the National Park Service. Also within the Historic District area are two neighborhoods on the National Register of Historic Places—the Victorian District, which is just south of the Landmark District, and the Thomas Square Streetcar Historic District.

WHAT ARE THE TOP EXPERIENCES?

Coastal Cuisine. The Lowcountry from Charleston to Savannah is known for its distinctive, regional fare. Entertaining is one of Savannah's favorite customs, and food is deeply embedded in Lowcountry tradition, reflecting the area's ethnic population and quirky persona. Local favorites range from the seafood delicacies of the coast to downhome, southern-fried cooking to contemporary, innovative twists on the traditional cuisine. In sea-side shacks and fishing camps, teaming platters of fresh seafood are blended with Caribbean spices.

Festivals. The region's major internationally recognized festivals such as Spoleto Festival, U.S.A. and the Savannah Musical Festival deserve their recognition. Yet, some of the smaller fests give a real insight into what makes the Lowcountry tick—without the lines and bumped-up hotel rates. Ask tourism offices for their calendar of events, and you'll be amazed—there are festivals celebrating everything from oysters to rice to watermelon.

Tours, tours & more tours. There's an amazing array of tours available in the Lowcountry, including horse carriage tours, ghost walks, Civil War and Gullah tours, and dolphin-watching excursions. Savannah favorites are the guided walks that follow the book, "Midnight in the Garden of Good and Evil" and tour of some of the scene locations.

The sporting life on Hilton Head. Visitors to HH can bike and beachcomb miles of ocean sand, horseback ride, sail, swing on an internationally known PGA golf course, hit a few balls with a former Wimbledon champion at his tennis academy—or simply watch several major sporting events.

BEST BETS

SIGHTS AND TOURS

CHARLESTON

FodorsChoice ★ **Battery.** From the intersection of Water Street and East Battery you can look east toward the city's most photographed mansions; look west for views of Charleston Harbor and Fort Sumter. Walk south along East Battery to White Point Gardens, where the street curves and becomes Murray Boulevard. ⊠ *East Bay St. and Murray Blvd., South of Broad*

★ **Fort Sumter National Monument.** The first shot of the Civil War was fired at Fort Sumter on April 12, 1861. After a 34-hour battle, Union forces surrendered the fort, which became a symbol of Southern resistance. The Confederacy held it, despite almost continual bombardment, from August of 1863 to February of 1865. When finally evacuated, the fort was a heap of rubble. Today the National Park Service oversees it. The **Fort Sumter Liberty Square Visitor Center,** next to the South Carolina Aquarium, contains exhibits on the Civil War. This is a departure point for ferries headed to the island where you find Fort Sumter itself. ⊠ *340 Concord St., Upper King* ☎ *843/577–0242* 🎫 *Free* ☉ *Daily 8:30–5.* Rangers conduct guided tours of the restored **Fort Sumter.** To reach the fort you have to take a ferry; boats depart from Liberty Square Visitor Center and from Patriot's Point in Mount Pleasant. There are six crossings daily between mid-March and mid-August. The schedule is abbreviated the rest of the year, so call first. ⊠ *Charleston Harbor* ☎ *843/577–0242* ⊕ *www.nps.gov/fosu* 🎫 *Fort free; ferry $14* ☉ *Apr.– early Sept., daily 10–5:30; early Sept.–Mar., daily 10–4.*

The Old Slave Mart Museum has reopened after many years of planning. It operated as an auction house from 1859 until the South was defeated in the Civil War. It's the only known extant building used as a slave auction gallery in South Carolina. Slaves stood on 3-foot-high tables so that they could be viewed. Now the museum has an impressive, permanent exhibition that features first the orientation area. The domestic slave trade is explained within the greater historical context of slavery in the rest of the South and an overview of the trans-Atlantic slave trade is given. An architectural side-bar, using visual and archival documentation, details the site's changing footprint over time. ⊠ *6 Chalmers St., the cobblestone street, Market area* ☎ *843/958–6467* 🎫 *$7* ☉ *Mon.–Sat. 9–5.*

9

STRANGE BUT TRUE

■ Charlestonian Anne Bonnet was America's first female pirate, teaming with Blackbeard, Gentleman Stede Bonnet, and Calico Jack.

■ The world's first successful submarine attack occurred in Charleston harbor in 1864 when the Confederate submarine H. L. Hunley sank the Union warship Housatonic. A replica of the Hunley can be seen at the Charleston Museum.

■ The Pirates' House, a famous Savannah restaurant, was actually a tavern frequented by pirates who sailed the Caribbean in 1794. Events at the Pirates' House were the inspiration for Robert Lewis Stevenson's novel Treasure Island.

■ James L. Pierpont (1822–93) is reputed to have written the Christmas classic Jingle Bells in Savannah. A native of Medford, Massachusetts, Pierpont became music director of Savannah's Unitarian church in the 1850s.

SAVANNAH

The Mercer-Williams House Museum   (✉ *430 Whitaker St.* ☎ *912/236–6352* ⊕ *www.mercerhouse.com* ✎ *$12.50* ☉ *10:30–4:30, Sun. noon–4*), known for its "Midnight in the Garden of Good and Evil" fame, was designed for General Hugh W. Mercer, great grandfather of singer–songwriter Johnny Mercer. The construction was begun just before the Civil War. This redbrick Italianate mansion became Jim Williams's Taj Mahal. In 1969 he was one of Savannah's earliest and most dedicated private restorationists. He bought the then vacant house and began a two-year restoration. He's the main character in the book and here he ran a world-class antiques dealership and held *the* Christmas party of the season. Williams himself died here of a heart attack in 1990, near the very spot where his sometime house mate, Danny Hansford, succumbed to gunshot wounds. The house is now open to the public.

The Ships of the Sea Museum. William Jay designed this house for merchant prince William Scarbrough, one of the principal investors in the S.S. Savannah, the first steam vessel to cross the Atlantic. This maritime museum houses a large collection of ship models, artifacts, and memorabilia representing man's 2,000-year quest to conquer the sea. ✉ *41 Martin Luther King Jr. Blvd., Historic District* ☎ *912/232–1511* ⊕ *http://shipsofthesea.org* ✎ *$8* ☉ *Tues.–Sun. 10–5.*

Tybee Island. *Tybee* is an Indian word meaning "salt." The Yamacraw Indians came to this island in the Atlantic Ocean to hunt and fish, and legend has it that pirates buried their treasure here. The island is about 5 mi long and 2 mi wide, with seafood restaurants, chain motels, condos, and shops—most of which sprang up during the 1950s and haven't changed much since. The entire expanse of white sand is divided into a number of public beaches, where you can shell and crab, charter fishing boats, and swim. **Tybee Island Lighthouse and Museum** (✉ *Off U.S. 80 at Fort Screven, 30 Meddin Dr.* ☎ *912/786–5801* ⊕ *www.tybeelighthouse. org* ✎ *$6* ☉ *Mon., Wed., and Sun. 9–5:30*)has been well restored; the

Head Keeper's Cottage is the oldest building on the island, and should be on your list. The Lighthouse has been the guardian of the Savannah River since 1736. The existing 154-foot-tall lighthouse was rebuilt in 1887. The museum was built in 1897 as a coastal artillery battery on Tybee Island. It features exhibits of early life on the Island, Indian and Civil War weaponry and dolls. Kids will enjoy the **Marine Science Center** (⊠ *1510 Strand Ave.* ☎ *912/786–5917*), which houses local marine life such as the Ogeechee corn snake, turtles, and American alligator. Tybee Island is 18 mi east of Savannah; take Victory Drive (U.S. 80), sometimes called Tybee Road, onto the island. Nearby, the misnamed Little Tybee Island, actually larger than Tybee Island, is entirely undeveloped.

WHERE TO EAT

WHAT IT COSTS					
	¢	$	$$	$$$	$$$$
RESTAURANTS	under $7	$7–$11	$12–$16	$17–$22	over $22

Restaurant prices are for a main course at dinner.

CHARLESTON

$$$$ ✕**Charleston Grill.** Bob Waggoner's groundbreaking New South cuisine
Fodor's Choice is now served in a dining room highlighted by pale wood floors, flow-
★ ing drapes, and elegant Queen Anne chairs. A jazz ensemble adds a hip, yet unobtrusive, element. The "new" Grill is more relaxed than its previous incarnation, so as to attract a younger and more vibrant clientele. The affable and highly talented chef raised the culinary bar in this town, and continues to provide what many think of as its highest gastronomic experience. He employs only the best produce, like the organic vegetables used in the golden beet salad. The menu is now in four quadrants: simple, lush (foie gras and other delicacies), cosmopoli-tan, and southern. A nightly tasting menu is a way to taste it all. Master pastry chef Vinzenze Ascabacher sends out divine creations like praline parfait. Sommelier Rick Rubel has 1,300 wines in his cellar, with 25 of them served by the glass. ⊠ *Charleston Place Hotel, 224 King St., Market area* ☎ *843/577–4522* ⌔ *Reservations essential* ▤ *AE, D, DC, MC, V* ⊘ *No lunch.*

$$$–$$$$ ✕**High Cotton.** Lazily spinning paddle fans, palm trees, and brick walls
★ create a plantation ambience. The chef combines wonderful flavors and flawless presentation for memorable meals. His take on foie gras, for example, is a terrine with port-wine cherry chutney. You can feast on bourbon-glazed pork and white-cheddar grits. The chocolate souf-flé with blackberry sauce and the praline soufflé are both remarkable. Sunday brunch is accompanied by musicians who sweeten the scene. At night the bar is enlivened with jazz. The latter serves as a meeting place for singles. ⊠ *199 E. Bay St., Market area* ☎ *843/724–3815* ⌔ *Reser-vations essential* ▤ *AE, D, DC, MC, V* ⊘ *No lunch weekdays.*

$–$$ ✕**Five Loaves Cafe.** At this café tucked in the back of Millennium Music, the food is as fresh as that sold at the farmers market in nearby Marion Square. Each day there are five new soups—if you're lucky, one of them

9

will be pureed eggplant. A favorite is the spinach salad with grilled polenta croutons, fresh mozzarella, and toasted almonds. The mix-and-match lunch options are ideal, particularly for small appetites. For $7.50 you can choose a cup of soup or a small salad and half a sandwich. Everything is super healthful (if you can forgo the sinful desserts). ⊠ *372 King St., Upper King* ☎ *843/805–7977* ⊠ *1055 Johnnie Dodds Blvd., Suite 50, Mount Pleasant* ☎ *843/937–1043* ⊟ *AE, DC, MC, V.*

SAVANNAH

$$$–$$$$ ✕ **Sapphire Grill.** Savannah's young and restless pack this trendy haunt nightly. Chef Chris Nason focuses his seasonal menus on local ingredients, such as Georgia white shrimp, crab, and fish. The Grill features succulent choices of steak, poultry, and fish, with a myriad of interesting à la carte accompaniments such as jalapeño tartar, sweet soy-wasabi sauce, and lemongrass butter. Vegetarians will delight in the elegant vegetable presentations—perhaps including roasted sweet onions, spicy peppers, rice-marinated watercress, or fried green tomatoes with grilled ginger. Chocoholics should try the delicious, potent chocolate flan. ■ TIP→ **Downstairs the decor is hip with gray brick walls alongside those painted a deep sapphire and a stone bar; upstairs is quieter and more romantic.** ⊠ *110 W. Congress St., Historic District* ☎ *912/443–9962* ⌂ *Reservations essential* ⊟ *AE, D, DC, MC, V* ⊙ *No lunch.*

$$–$$$$ ✕ **Georges' of Tybee.** There's a romantic ambience in this upscale restaurant with a warmly lighted interior, a lovely stone fireplace, and dark rose-painted walls. Chef Robert Wood puts a refreshing spin on favorites such as a grilled rack of lamb, served with spinach, olives, and mushrooms tossed with Israeli couscous and apricot and fig chutney. The sautéed black grouper is a treat, served over bamboo rice with Asian slaw and coconut curry. ■ TIP→ **The restaurant's beachfront sister, North Beach Grill, is way more casual, serving burgers by day and jerk chicken and pork in the evening.** ⊠ *1105 E. U.S. 80, Tybee Island* ☎ *912/786–9730* ⊟ *AE, MC, V* ⊙ *Closed Mon. No lunch.*

$$–$$$$ ✕ **Olde Pink House.** This pink-brick Georgian mansion was built in 1771 for James Habersham, one of the wealthiest Americans of his time, and the old-time atmosphere comes through in the original Georgia pine floors of the tavern, the Venetian chandeliers, and the 18th-century English antiques. The she-crab soup with sherry is a light but flavorful version of a Lowcountry specialty. Regional ingredients find their way into many of the dishes, including the black grouper stuffed with blue crab and served with a Vidalia onion sauce. ⊠ *23 Abercorn St., Historic District* ☎ *912/232–4286* ⊟ *AE, MC, V* ⊙ *No lunch.*

LIKE A LOCAL

The Lowcountry was once studded with some of the largest plantations in the south, which were worked by African slaves. The slaves developed a patois that became known as Gullah, a mélange of African dialects and English, which had a lyrical rhythm. There are a number of African-Americans, particularly on the sea islands, the islands off Beaufort, and a small group on Hilton Head, who strive to keep the Gullah language alive. In the Charleston area, Alphonso Brown conducts tours highlighting the Gullah culture and traditions (843/763-7551, www.gullahtours.com).

WHERE TO STAY

WHAT IT COSTS				
¢	$	$$	$$$	$$$$

	¢	$	$$	$$$	$$$$
HOTELS	under $70	$70–$110	$111–$160	$161–$220	over $220

Hotel prices are for two people in a standard double room in high season.

CHARLESTON

$$$$ 🖼 **HarbourView Inn.** Ask for a room facing the harbor and you can gaze down at the landmark pineapple fountain in Waterfront Park. Calming earth tones and rattan soothe and relax; four-poster beds and sea-grass rugs complete the Lowcountry look. Some of the rooms are in a former 19th-century shipping warehouse with exposed brick walls, plantation shutters, and whirlpool tubs. Afternoon wine and cheese and evening milk and cookies are included. ⊠ *2 Vendue Range, Market area, 29401* ☎ *843/853–8439 or 888/853–8439* 📠 *843/853–4034* ⊕ *www. harbourviewcharleston.com* 🛏 *52 rooms* 🚭 *In-room: refrigerator, Wi-Fi. In-hotel: concierge, public Internet, no-smoking rooms* ▤ *AE, D, DC, MC, V* ⏍ *BP.*

$$$$ 🖼 **Market Pavilion Hotel.** The melee of one of the busiest corners in the
Fodor's Choice city vanishes as soon as the uniformed bellman opens the lobby door to
★ dark, wood-panel walls, antique furniture, and chandeliers hung from high ceilings. It resembles a grand hotel from the 19th century, and you feel like visiting royalty. Get used to being pampered—smartly attired bellmen and butlers are quick at hand. Rooms are decadent with French-style chaises and magnificent marble baths. One of Charleston's most prestigious fine-dining spots, Grill 225, is here. ■ **TIP→ Join sophisticated Charlestonians who *do* cocktails and apps at the rooftop Pavilion Bar.** ⊠ *225 E. Bay St., Market area, 29401* ☎ *843/723–0500 or 877/440–2250* 📠 *843/723–4320* ⊕ *www.marketpavilion.com* 🛏 *61 rooms, 9 suites* 🚭 *In-room: Ethernet. In-hotel: restaurant, bar, pool, concierge, public Internet, no-smoking rooms* ▤ *AE, D, DC, MC, V* ⏍ *EP.*

INNS, B&BS & GUESTHOUSES

To find rooms in homes, cottages, and carriage houses, contact **Historic Charleston Bed and Breakfast** (⊠ *60 Broad St., South of Broad* ☎ *843/ 722–6606* ⊕ *www.historiccharlestonbedandbreakfast.com*).

$$$$ 🖼 **Governors House Inn.** This quintessential Charleston lodging radiates
★ 18th-century elegance. Its stately architecture typifies the grandeur, romance, and civility of the city's bountiful colonial era. A National Historic Landmark, it's filled with antiques and period reproductions in the public rooms and the high-ceiling guest rooms. The best (its honeymoon material) is the Rutledge Suite, a legacy to the original owner, Governor Edward Rutledge. Nice touches include a proper afternoon tea. ⊠ *117 Broad S., South of Broad, 29401* ☎ *843/720–2070 or 800/720–9812* 📠 *843/805–6549* ⊕ *www.governorshouse.com* 🛏 *7 rooms, 4 suites* 🚭 *In-hotel: concierge, no-smoking rooms* ▤ *AE, MC, V* ⏍ *BP.*

9

ON THE WAY

From Charleston go over the magnificent Arthur Ravenel Jr. Bridge and drive along U.S. 17N, through and beyond Mount Pleasant, to find the **basket ladies** weaving beautiful sweetgrass, pine-straw, and palmetto-leaf baskets at their rickety roadside stands. Baskets typically cost less on this stretch than in downtown Charleston, and each purchase supports the artisans, whose numbers are dwindling.

The ruins of **Sheldon Church**, built in 1753, make an interesting stop if you're driving from Charleston to Beaufort, or from Beaufort to Edisto Island. The church burned down in 1779 and again in 1865. Only the brick walls and columns remain, but on any given Saturday you can see a wedding in progress. ⊠ *18 mi northwest of Beaufort.*

Hunting Island State Park has nature trails and about 3 mi of public beaches—some dramatically and beautifully eroding. The 1,120-foot-long fishing pier is among the longest on the East Coast. You can climb the 181 steps of the Hunt-

ing Island Lighthouse (built in 1859 and abandoned in 1933) for sweeping views. The nature center has exhibits, an aquarium, and lots of turtles. A stroll along the marsh boardwalk is to be at one with nature. The park is 18 mi southeast of Beaufort via U.S. 21; call for cabin and camping reservations. ⊠ *1775 Sea Island Pkwy., off St. Helena Island, Hunting Island* ☏ *843/838–2011* ⊕ *www.southcarolinaparks. com* ⊠ *$2* ⊙ *Park Apr.–Oct., daily 6 AM–9 PM; Nov.–Mar., daily 6–6. Lighthouse daily 11–4.*

In Savannah, **Factors Walk,** a network of iron crosswalks, connects Bay Street with the multistory buildings that rise up from the river level; iron stairways descend from Bay Street to Factors Walk. The area was originally the center of commerce for cotton brokers, who walked between and above the lower cotton warehouses. Cobblestone ramps lead pedestrians down to River Street. ■ **TIP→ These are serious cobblestones, so wear comfortable shoes.** ⊠ *Bay St. to Factors Walk, Historic District.*

SAVANNAH

$$$–$$$$
★ **Ballastone Inn.** This sumptuous inn occupies an 1838 mansion that once served as a bordello. Rooms are handsomely furnished, with luxurious linens on canopy beds, antiques and fine reproductions, and a collection of original framed prints from *Harper's* scattered throughout. On the garden level, rooms are small and cozy, with exposed brick walls, beam ceilings, and, in some cases, windows at eye level with the lush courtyard. Most rooms have working gas fireplaces, and three have whirlpool tubs. ■ **TIP→ Afternoon tea and free passes to a nearby health club are included.** ⊠ *14 E. Oglethorpe Ave., Historic District, 31401* ☏ *912/236–1484 or 800/822–4553* ☐ *912/236–4626* ⊕ *www. ballastone.com* ⊅ *16 rooms, 3 suites* ♨ *In-room VCR. In-hotel: bicycles* ☐ *AE, MC, V* ⦿ *BP.*

$$–$$$$
★ **Mulberry Inn.** This 1860s livery stable later became a cotton warehouse and then a Coca-Cola bottling plant. Gleaming heart-pine floors and antiques, including a handsome English grandfather clock and an

exquisitely carved Victorian mantel, make it unique. The pianist hitting the keyboard of a baby grand every afternoon adds to the elegant flair. The café is a notch nicer than most other Holiday Inn restaurants. An executive wing, at the back of the hotel, is geared to business travelers. ⊠*601 E. Bay St., Historic District, 31401* ☎*912/238–1200 or 877/468–1200* 🖷*912/236–2184* ⊕*www.savannahhotel.com* ⋖*145 rooms, 24 suites* ♿*In-room: VCR, dial-up. In-hotel: restaurant, bar, pool, gym, public Wi-Fi* ⊟*AE, D, DC, MC, V* ⦿*EP.*

COASTAL ISLES

$$$$
FodorsChoice
★

The Cloister. One of the region's grand dames, when this legendary hotel had begun to look like tattered aristocracy, the owners tore it down, saving only some of the facades. The result is a Mediterranean-style resort complemented by semi-tropical landscaping. There are all the luxuries you would expect like pampering service, elegant, over-size accommodations, a sprawling two-story spa, as well as those that are a wonderful surprise, like the bi-level water garden. The Beach Club was the last of the buildings to be razed, making way for a set of beachfront suites. If you can't afford to stay here, reserve a table at the award-winning Georgian Room. Come early enough to take an aperitif in the main salon and delight in the pianist's repertoire. ⊠*Sea Island, GA 31522* ☎*912/638–3611 or 866/465–3563* ⊕*www.seaisland.com* ⋖*153 rooms, 3 suites* ♿*In-room: safe, dial-up, in-room Wi-Fi. In hotel: 4 restaurants, bars, golf courses, tennis courts, pools, beachfront, water sports, children's programs (ages 3–19)* ⊟*AE, D, DC, MC, V* ⦿*EP.*

$$$–$$$$
FodorsChoice
★

Main Street Inn & Spa. This Italianate villa has stucco facades ornamented with lions' heads, elaborate ironwork, and shuttered doors. Staying here is like being a guest at a rich friend's estate. Guest rooms have velvet and silk brocade linens, feather duvets, and porcelain and brass sinks. An ample breakfast buffet is served in a petite, sunny dining room. In the afternoon there's complementary gourmet coffee and homemade cookies in the formal garden. The spa offers excellent treatments ranging from traditional Swedish to Indian Kyria massages. ⊠*2200 Main St., North End, Hilton Head, SC 29926* ☎*843/681–3001 or 800/471–3001* 🖷*843/681–5541* ⊕*www.mainstreetinn.com* ⋖*33 rooms* ♿*In-hotel: pool, spa, no-smoking rooms* ⊟*AE, D, MC, V* ⦿*BP.*

9

SHOPPING

CHARLESTON

The Market area is a cluster of shops and restaurants centered around the **Old City Market** (⊠*E. Bay and Market Sts., Market area*). Sweetgrass basket weavers work here, and you can buy the resulting wares. **King Street** is the major shopping street in town. Lower King (from Broad to Market streets) is lined with high-end antiques dealers. Middle King (from Market to Calhoun streets) is a mix of national chains like Banana Republic and Pottery Barn. Upper King (from Calhoun Street to Cannon street) is the up-and-coming area where fashionistas like the alternative shops like Putumayo. Shopping uptown has never been better. Check it out: www.upperkingdesigndistrict.com.

VITAL STATS:

- Boiled peanuts are the official snack of South Carolina.

- South Carolina is the palmetto state.

- The Shag is South Carolina's state dance. (It's best done to Carolina beach music, which originated in Myrtle Beach; the northern equivalent is the Bop.) With the Shag, the foot movements are more detailed and the man is "the peacock." Shag clubs exist from Charleston to MB.

- Georgia's State Amphipian: Green Tree Frog. You can hear them croaking at night, particularly in the wetlands, know in previous decades as the Georgia swamps.

- The Right Whale (not the left) is the state's marine mammal.

- "Georgia On My Mind" is the state song. It was performed on March 7, 1979, before the State Legislature by Georgia native, Ray Charles.

SAVANNAH

Although Savannah's 1870s open **City Market** was razed years ago, city fathers renovated four blocks, over three years, to capture the authentic atmosphere and character of its bustling origins. The market features artists working in their lofts and exhibits of works for sale. Already a lively destination with open-air cafés, theme shops, stores offering crafts, accessories, and gifts, and jazz clubs, this popular pedestrian-only area is becoming the ever more vibrant, youthful heart of Savannah's Historic District. ⊠*Bordered by Barnard, Congress, and Bryan Sts., Historic District* ☎*912/232–4903 for current events* ⊕*www.savannahcitymarket.com.*

VISITOR INFORMATION

The **Charleston Visitor Center** (⊠*375 Meeting St., Upper King* ⊡*423 King St., 29403* ☎*843/853–8000 or 800/868–8118* ⊕*www.charlestoncvb.com*) is housed in a restored 1856 railroad warehouse.

Savannah Area Convention & Visitors Bureau (⊠*101 E. Bay St., Historic District, 31401* ☎*912/644–6401 or 877/728–2662* 🖷*912/944–0468* ⊕*www.savannahvisit.com*).

Savannah Area Welcome Center (⊠*301 Martin Luther King Blvd., 31401* ☎*912/944–0455* 🖷*912/786–5895* ⊕*www.savannahvisit.com*).

Welcome Center of Hilton Head (⊠*100 William Hilton Pkwy., 29938* ☎*843/689–6302 or 800/523–3373* ⊕*www.hiltonheadisland.org*).

Orlando & the Space Coast

Kennedy Space Center, Cape Canaveral

WORD OF MOUTH

"WDW is not for wimps, and not for those not willing to plan ahead and plan a lot. We're all athletic and in shape (runners, dancers, etc.) but 3–4 back-to-back days in the parks is a body beating. You will easily walk between 7–15 miles a day, especially if using fast passes, zipping back and forth. Totally worth it though."

—ellen_griswold

EXPLORING ORLANDO & THE SPACE COAST

Orlando's attractions are about 75 mi east of Tampa via I–4; 55 mi southwest of Daytona Beach via I–4; and 60 mi due west from Cocoa Beach via State Road 528. Cocoa Beach is 135 mi east of Tampa via I–4 and the Beachline Expressway; and 166 mi south of Jacksonville via I–95 and State Road 528.

By Gary
McKechnie

Orlando is almost synonymous with urban sprawl and whether you love it or hate it, what's undeniable is that part of that sprawl includes several of the world's top tourist attractions drawing 50 million people a year. We suggest you find a way to love it. And while the theme parks would rather have you think otherwise, they are only part of the deal: Orlando has worthy attractions on International Drive, theme restaurants, stand-alone elaborate hotels, dinner shows, and other sources of nighttime fun.

But if after a few days you begin to regret that Orlando traded in much of its natural environment for a collection of hotels and man-made attractions, know that that's where the Space Coast is different. Granted, the top attraction is the decidedly not-occurring-in-nature Kennedy Space Center, and the coast isn't always pristine—especially in downtown Cocoa and along the busy tourist strip near highways 520 and A1A—but the amount of preserved land and waterways is unusually generous for Central Florida.

WHO WILL ESPECIALLY LOVE THIS TRIP?

Families: If your family is bored on an Orlando vacation, then call Dr. Phil and request some family counseling. In Orlando, the problem is never having too little to do.

Space Junkies: There isn't anywhere else on earth where you can get as close to the history of the American space program than on the Space Coast. From the earliest launches to the giant leaps between Mercury, Gemini, Apollo, Skylab, and the space shuttle program, this is space fan central.

Nature Lovers: From New Smyrna Beach on the north and Titusville to the south, the Canaveral National Seashore includes 24 mi of ocean-front, which is the longest undeveloped stretch of beach on Florida's east coast. And because the Kennedy Space Center needs this area of Florida coastline, it will never be turned into a paved collection of towering condos. An even larger spread of preserved land can be found at KSC's neighbor, the Merritt Island National Wildlife Refuge, an extraordinarily wonderful 140,000 acres of marshes, estuaries, scrub pine, dunes, and hardwood hammocks that serve as a migratory route along the Great Florida Birding Trail.

The Stressed: It'd be a shame to go to Orlando to completely relax, but it can be done if you're willing to ignore the theme parks and activities and devote your vacation to lazing by the pool, visiting nearby natural springs, shopping on Winter Park's ritzy Park Avenue, or submitting

TOP 5 REASONS TO GO

Walt Disney World: Four of the world's leading theme parks—as well as golf courses, resorts, and dinner shows—are right here.

SeaWorld: A dependable theme park with an aquatic slant. Slower-paced, but manageable in a day or less and filled with fun.

Universal Orlando: Although they're not related, the parks here—Universal Studios and Islands of Adventure—could be Disney's mischievous little brother.

Kennedy Space Center: Quite simply, it's America's portal into the heavens.

Cocoa Beach: Crisp, clean sands make this one of Florida's finest beaches. A perfect place to savor a quiet and tranquil day.

yourself to the luxuries of its plentiful, pampering spas. Over on the coast, you can make it a real vacation by doing something different: absolutely nothing. Rent an oceanfront room, unfold a beach chair, set up an umbrella, then read a book or take a nap to the sounds of the lapping waves.

WHEN IS THE BEST TIME TO VISIT?

In Orlando the quietest months at the theme parks are October (school's just started), February (just before Spring Break) and May (just before summer vacation). After that, summer hits the ground running and families descend in droves. At the attractions, despite sweltering, humid days and abnormally long lines, people are still packing parking lots and waiting in line just to sit in a flying elephant.

On the Space Coast, space enthusiasts may want to schedule their vacation to coincide with the schedule of an upcoming launch. Spring Breakers won't mind that the high season—roughly February through April—can be more crowded; they're just happy to be on a beach. Although the summer sun can bake an unsuspecting sunbather in a few hours, the heat is tempered by the perpetual breeze blowing in from the sea—sometimes a bit too much. Hurricane season lasts from the beginning of June to the end of November and can affect either region.

In Orlando the summer season sees daytime highs in the 90s, lows rarely falling below 70, and extreme humidity pushing the daytime heat index above 100 degrees. Stick around until January, and you'll appreciate average nighttime lows in the 50s and highs that climb to a pleasing 72.

On the Space Coast, from November to the end of February, the temperature averages a low of 53 and high of 74, from May through the end of August, the average low is 70 and the average high reaches 89.

10

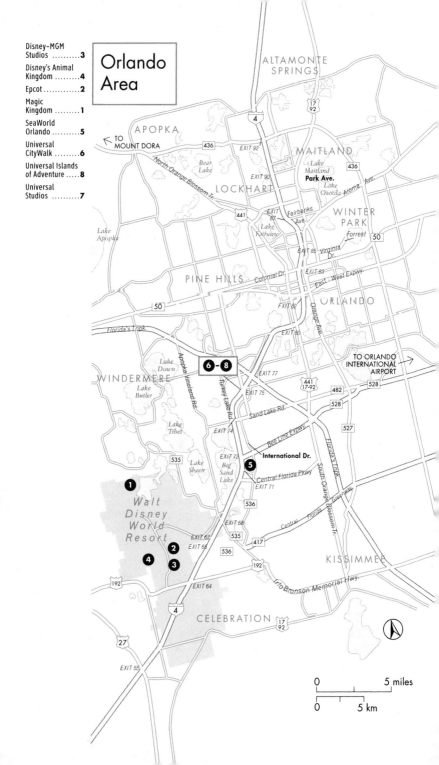

Orlando Area

HOW SHOULD I GET THERE?

FLYING

Assuming you're going to arrive in Orlando, chances are you'll land at the Orlando International Airport. It's at the junction of three major roads that can get you wherever you need to be: State Road 528 (aka the Beachline Expressway) heads east to the Space Coast and west to the Florida Turnpike and I–4, which is the gateway to Walt Disney World and Universal Orlando.

DRIVING

State Road 417 (aka the Greene Way) is a toll road that will one day encircle Orlando, and it also leads southwest to Walt Disney World and the Kissimmee-St. Cloud resort area. The last major road at OIA is State Road 436 but, unless you're going to the eastern or northern suburbs of Orlando, you won't find much use for it.

If you're planning to reside at the beach for a few days, the Beachline Expressway to State Road 520 and southeast to the coast is usually clear sailing. While you're there, if you plan a tour of the Atlantic Coast, Interstate 95 runs north-south, which makes reaching the Space Coast from Daytona-New Smyrna a snap. Likewise, I–95 makes it a fairly straight shot from every eastern seaboard city from Miami on up.

HOW DO I GET AROUND?

BY CAR

A car is far and away the best way to travel in and around Orlando.

BY BUS

Orlando's public transportation system is Lynx, a bus system that operates throughout the wide-ranging metropolitan area. The fare is $1.75 per ride, and $14 for a seven-day pass. For visitors, the I-Ride Trolley provides a convenient service with routes throughout the International Drive attractions area. Fares are $1, and $3 for a day pass.

On the coast, Space Coast Area Transit is the provider of local bus service. The fare is $1.25 for adults, 60 cents for senior citizens, people with disabilities, or students with valid ID cards. Route 9 runs north and south along the beach, Route 4 east and west between the Merritt Square Mall and Cocoa Beach.

10

WHERE SHOULD I FOCUS MY ENERGY?

If you're here for 1 day: You should never come to Orlando for just one day. If you do, go straight to the Magic Kingdom. Before departing the next morning, kick yourself for staying just one day.

If you're here for 2 days: Give the competition a chance: go over to Universal Studios. It'll be a study in contrasts as you compare this "theme park delinquent" with your day at the Magic Kingdom.

If you're here for 3 days: Take a break and hit Cocoa Beach. Family-friendly beaches are found miles north and south of highways 520 and A1A.

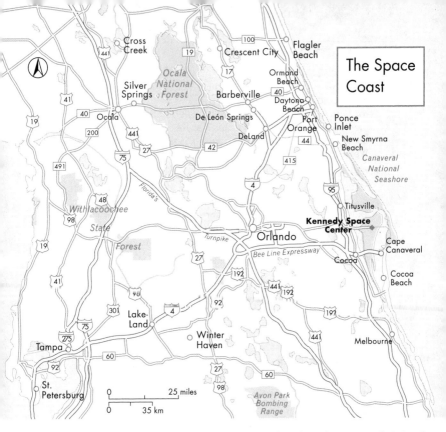

There are also miles of undisturbed beaches along the Canaveral National Seashore. Wrap up the day dining (or fishing) at the Cocoa Beach Pier.

If you're here for 4 days: Head back to Orlando to see SeaWorld, one of the nicest, most tranquil theme parks in America.

If you're here for 5 days: Take a break and hit some of Orlando's shopping malls and outlet centers.

If you're here for 6 days: Pick another of Disney's theme parks: Epcot, Disney's Hollywood Studios, or Disney's Animal Kingdom. Do your homework ahead of time and see which one appeals to you; if you're planning on doing more than one Disney park, know that the price per day per person drops the longer you visit.

If you're here for 7 days or more: Wrap up any loose ends by visiting your favorites, and then packing your bags and stepping aboard a cruise ship at Port Canaveral and departing for another week in the Caribbean.

WHAT ARE THE TOP EXPERIENCES?

Magic and Animal Kingdoms: Obviously, if it weren't for the theme parks there would be far fewer reasons to visit Orlando. The original, Walt Disney World's Magic Kingdom, was modeled after Disneyland. While

How to Snack

Food throughout Central Florida is the same as anywhere else—unless you're dining at the Lone Cabbage Fish Camp. Florida 'Cracker' food is based on rudimentary ingredients that the pioneers ate, and that includes delicacies like swamp cabbage and possum. Thankfully, those aren't on the menu here, but a few of the holdouts—gator tail and frog legs—are.

There's no "right" way to dine on any of these, but there is a right to wonder what they'll taste like. Gator tail—usually breaded and deep-fried—tastes like chicken. On the other hand, frog legs taste like . . . chicken. The hardest part about eating frog legs is that they look precisely like frog legs, so if you can convince yourself that you're not eating an amphibian, you'll be better off

it holds true to the theme park pioneer, it also adds the mixed blessing of size, with a larger castle as well as more and, some believe, better attractions. While Disney Hollywood Studios and EPCOT pack appeal, Disney's Animal Kingdom, which captures the essence of Asian and African wildlife and culture, is arguably the most low key and under-appreciated of all of Orlando's theme parks.

Space: There's a reason why marketers dubbed this the Space Coast: It's where the nation focused its attention when America was challenging the Soviet Union in the Space Race. In less than a decade, NASA went from exploding rockets on the launch pad to putting a man on the moon. It was an incredible pairing of science, technology, competition, and American spirit that helped overcome those challenges and put the nation in a lead it has never relinquished. While the glory days are past, there is still a sense of history in the making when you watch kids at Kennedy Space Center absorbing the images of rockets and astronauts and realizing that one day, one of them may be traveling to Mars.

Shopping: Although you can always buy anything from an astronaut pen to a surfboard on the Space Coast, the best shopping by far is in Orlando. In addition to the billions of Disney souvenirs, there are massive outlet malls selling cut-rate name-brand items. Granted, outlets don't necessarily mean bargains anymore (if they ever did), but that doesn't stop the faithful from making a day of it. Not everything in Orlando is designed for modest budgets. At the quite upscale Mall at Millennia, for instance, you can drop in at Rocks Fine Jewelry and buy a lovely Jacob Tourbillion wristwatch—for a modest $750,000.

Nature: The Canaveral National Seashore's 24 mi of shoreline is the longest stretch of undeveloped public beach on Florida's east coast, and its neighbor, the Merritt Island National Wildlife Refuge, encompasses a terrifically impressive 140,000 acres that includes a beautifully tended wildlife loop that circles through the backwoods and presents a view of Florida that would be familiar to the Timucua tribes that lived here 7,000 years ago. On assorted nature tours you can see small, undis-

10

CLAIM TO FAME

■ What do you do with the old city hall when you want to build a new city hall? You blow it up—which is what happened in 1992 and was recorded for posterity for the closing scene spliced into Lethal Weapon 3. That's just one thing locals like to talk about. Of course, in conversation they'll also talk about how, in the 1990s, Orlando became the Liverpool of America as it churned out an assembly line of boy bands including N'Sync, the Backstreet Boys, C-Note, US 5, and O-Town. Actually, Orlando didn't churn out the groups. That distinction goes to impresario Lou Pearlman who, in 2007, was arrested for operating one of the largest Ponzi schemes in history. At last count, he had acquired, lost, or hidden more than $500 million in investors' funds.

■ Orlando can be a fantasyland, but the Space Coast is sprinkled with some of that pixie dust. While locals are all proud of the fact that NASA couldn't accomplish any launches without their help, what they may be even more proud of is the fact that I Dream of Jeannie was based here. Granted, Barbara Eden only filmed one show here (when she and Major Nelson were married), but it is a point of pride that Cocoa Beach was her home when she wasn't living in a bottle.

■ Aside from the fact that it's the sister city of Kyustendil, Bulgaria, Cocoa Beach is also pleased to be the uncontested "Small Wave Capital of the World," a distinction that serves Ron Jon Surf Shop quite well, and also helped make local resident Kelly Slater eight-time world champion.

turbed islands and explore hidden lagoons that are home to an amazing menagerie of wildlife such as dolphins, amberjack, mackerel, herons, egrets, osprey, and eagles.

BEST BETS

SIGHTS AND TOURS

ORLANDO

Fodor'sChoice ★ **The Magic Kingdom.** What most people imagine to be Walt Disney World—the Magic Kingdom—actually is a small, but emblematic, part of it. For many of those who have grown up with Cinderella, Snow White, Peter Pan, Dumbo, and Pinocchio, it's a magical place. It's the site of such world-famous attractions as Space Mountain, Pirates of the Caribbean, Splash Mountain, and "it's a small world," as well as new thrills like Stitch's Great Escape and Mickey's Philharmagic. *Take the Magic Kingdom–U.S. 192 exit (Exit 64) off I–4.*

Fodor'sChoice ★ **Epcot.** Designed to promote enthusiasm for discovery and learning, WDW's Epcot is a sweeping combination of amusement park and world's fair. In Future World, the focus inside 10 landmark pavilions is on the fascinating discoveries of science and technology. Don't miss the funny, often startling, 3-D film and special-effects attraction *Honey, I Shrunk* *the Audience,* and if you can handle an intense simulation blast-off, try out the Mission: SPACE ride to Mars. In the second major area of Epcot, the World Showcase, you can tour 10 different countries without the jet lag. *Take the Epcot–Downtown Disney exit (Exit 67) off I–4.*

★ **Disney–MGM Studios.** This is Disney's re-creation of Hollywood as it might have been in the good old days. Amazing attractions are the key to "The Studios'" success: there's the Rock 'n' Roller Coaster Starring Aerosmith, the Twilight Zone Tower of Terror, the classic Great Movie Ride, and two stunt shows. Other not-to-be-missed attractions include the closing show, *Fantasmic!,* and the Magic of Disney Animation. *Take the Disney–MGM Studios exit (Exit 64) off I–4,*

Fodor'sChoice **Disney's Animal Kingdom.** In the center of the park, the huge, sculpted
★ Tree of Life rises 145 feet, towering over all the other trees in the park. Walkways encircle the tree, leading to attractions, including a water ride, a safari ride, and several shows in the Asia, Africa, and Dinoland areas of the park. With a 100-acre savanna and wildlife preserve, the Animal Kingdom is the largest of all the Disney parks. *Take the Disney's Animal Kingdom exit (Exit 65) off I–4.*

★ **Universal Studios.** Universal's classic theme park pays tribute to the movie business with well-designed street scenes from Hollywood and New York, and rides devoted to making you feel like you're actually in a movie. Look for The Mummy Returns and Shrek 4-D, as well as *Back to the Future*—The Ride and *Men In Black:* Alien Attack. *Near intersection of I–4 and Florida's Tpke. Heading eastbound on I–4, take Exit 75A. Heading west on I–4, take Exit 74B and follow signs.*

★ **Islands of Adventure.** If you have teenagers or adult thrill seekers in your party, do not miss a day here. It has absolutely the best roller coasters in central Florida, and the fantastical designs of its five lands give Disney a run for the money. The screamfest begins at the Incredible Hulk Coaster and continues at the double coaster known as Dueling Dragons. People are still shrieking like babies at the Amazing Adventures of Spider-Man 3-D show. There are plenty of ways to get soaked, too: Dudley Do-Right's Ripsaw Falls is a flume ride with a serious drop and a splash landing that even gets onlookers wet. Little ones have a land all to themselves: Seuss Landing, where they can enter the world of *One Fish, Two Fish, Red Fish, Blue Fish* and *The Cat in the Hat.* All in all, they've done it all—and they've done it all right. *Near intersection of I–4 and Florida's Tpke. Heading east on I–4, take Exit 75A; heading west, take Exit 74B.*

10

★ **Universal CityWalk.** With nightspots ranging from a red-hot Latin music club to a cool and smooth jazz lounge, the CityWalk entertainment complex has enough diversity to please any couple or family. Clubgoers should check out "the groove" nightclub or Latin Quarter, and bar hoppers should make it to Jimmy Buffett's Margaritaville. When deciding between here and Disney's Pleasure Island, keep in mind that each is equally entertaining, but CityWalk's $9.49 admission is less than half of Disney's $21 cover.

HISTORY YOU CAN SEE

How do you transform cattle pastures and swamps and orange groves into the world's most popular vacation destination? You get Walt Disney to buy it.

Already stung by the fact that his limited finances didn't allow him to buy more land to buffer the seedy attractions that bordered his beloved Disneyland, Walt Disney began scouting for a new location—one that would provide him with the "blessing of size."

His new Disneyland had to be in a temperate climate, provide plentiful land, and be easily accessible. Eventually, he narrowed his vision to Florida and, in November 1963, he flew over Bay Lake, saw an old fishing camp on an island, and said, "That's it! That's Tom Sawyer's Island!"

Adding to Walt's excitement was its location—right near a new highway, Interstate 4, and the nearby Florida Turnpike.

Now he just had to find out who owned the land and how much it cost. For ranchers and fishermen, the land didn't mean much to them at the time—but the situation might have been different if they'd known Walt was the buyer. To avoid skyrocketing prices, Disney created dummy corporations like the Latin-American Development and Managers Corporation and the Reedy Creek Ranch Corporation to approach landowners. By May 1965 Orlando's Sentinel Star realized that a mysterious buyer had spent $1.5 million on two large tracts of land in neighboring Osceola County. Now speculation hit full speed. Was it the government? An aerospace company? An automobile factory? More than 27,000 acres had been sold—but no one knew who had bought it.

On a press trip in California that November, Orlando reporter Emily Bavar met Walt Disney and asked if he was the mystery buyer. His denial—filled with facts and figures about why he would never be interested in Orlando—told Bavar that he knew a lot more about a place he professed was of no interest to him. She broke the story, and on November 15, 1965, Walt along with his brother–chief financial officer Roy held a press conference to announce the arrival of "Disneyland East."

Fodor's Choice
★
SeaWorld Orlando. It's the animals who are the stars here. Sleek dolphins perform like gymnastic champions, and orcas sail through the air like featherweight Nijinskys. The world's largest zoological park, SeaWorld is devoted to mammals, birds, fish, and reptiles that live in the oceans and their tributaries. Every attraction is designed to explain the marine world and its vulnerability to human use. Yet the presentations are always enjoyable, and almost always memorable. The highlight is Shamu Stadium, where you can see Shamu and his sidekicks propel their trainers high up into the air.

As of this writing, a SeaWorld–operated water park, **Aquatica**, was slated to open across the street from SeaWorld in 2008.

SPACE COAST

Fodor'sChoice The must-see **Kennedy Space Center Visitor Complex.** The fact that Ameri-
★ ca's space missions launch from here is almost as impressive as the fact
that some folks figured out how to incorporate a tourist attraction into
what is really a top secret, well-guarded military base. But they did,
and that's good for you because this place contains the greatest collection of space history and memorabilia in the United States. Must-sees
include the Rocket Garden, and, on the other side of the Visitor Complex, the Astronaut Memorial, a 35 ton, 42 x 50-foot "space mirror"
of polished black granite etched with the names of America's 24 fallen
astronauts. Opened in 2007, the Shuttle Launch Experience re-creates
the sensation of lift-off with a rattling, vertical lift off that includes
the five g's that astronauts feel as they go from zero to 18,000 mi per
hour. The preshow video, starring Space Shuttle Commander Charlie
Bolden is as great as the ride itself. Also worthy is the daily Astronaut
Encounter, which includes a Q&A with an actual NASA astronaut.
For an even closer encounter, Lunch with an Astronaut ($22.92 adults,
$15.99 children) gives you time to pepper an actual space explorer
with every question you can imagine and, no, you won't be dining on
freeze-dried food and Tang. Interactive programs make for the best
experiences here, but if you want a low-key overview of the facility
(and if the weather is foul) take the bus tour, included with admission. Buses depart every 15 minutes, and you can get on and off any
bus whenever you like. ⊠*S.R. 405, Kennedy Space Center* ☎*321/449–
4444* ⊕*www.kennedyspacecenter.com* ✉*General admission includes
bus tour, IMAX movies, Visitor Complex shows and exhibits, and the
Astronaut Hall of Fame, $38* ☉*Space Center opens daily at 9, closing
times vary according to season (call for details), last regular tour 3 hrs
before closing; closed certain launch dates.*

WHERE TO EAT

WHAT IT COSTS				
¢	$	$$	$$$	$$$$
AT DINNER under $8	$8–$15	$15–$20	$20–$30	over $30

Prices are per person for a main course at dinner, excluding tax and tip.

10

ORLANDO

$$$$ ✕**Victoria and Albert's.** At this Disney fantasy, you're served by "Victo-
Fodor'sChoice ria" and "Albert," who recite the menu in tandem. There's also a som-
★ melier to explain the wine pairings. Everyone, of course, is dressed in
period Victorian costumes. This is one of the plushest fine-dining experiences in Florida: a regal meal in a lavish, Victorian-style room. The
seven-course, prix-fixe menu ($100; wine is an additional $55) changes
daily. Appetizer choices might include Iranian caviar, veal sweetbreads,
or artichokes in a mushroom sauce; entrées may be Kobe beef with
celery-root puree or veal tenderloin with cauliflower-and-potato puree.
The restaurant also features a vegetarian menu with exotics such as
rutabaga Napoleon with melted leeks and ramps. For most of the year,

there are two seatings, at 5:45 and 9. In July and August, however, there's generally just one seating—at 6:30. The chef's table dinner event is $165 to $235 (with wine pairing) per person. Make your reservations 90 days in advance. ⊠ *Grand Floridian* ☎ *407/939–3463* ⌒ *Reservations essential. Jacket required* ☰ *AE, MC, V* ⊘ *No lunch.*

$$$–$$$$ ✕ **Emeril's.** The popular eatery is a culinary shrine to Emeril Lagasse,
★ the famous Food Network chef who occasionally appears here. The menu changes frequently, but you can always count on New Orleans treats like andouille sausage, shrimp, and red beans appearing in some form or fashion. Entrées may include andouille-crusted redfish with crispy shoestring potatoes; milk-fed veal with shrimp, artichoke hearts, and a mustard hollandaise sauce; and grilled beef fillet with bacon mashed potatoes and buttermilk-breaded onion rings. The wood-baked pizza, topped with exotic mushrooms, is stellar. Save room for Emeril's ice-cream parfait—banana-daiquiri ice cream topped with hot fudge, caramel sauce, walnuts, and a double-chocolate-fudge cookie. ⊠ *6000 Universal Blvd., at Universal Orlando's City Walk* ☎ *407/224–2424* ⌒ *Reservations essential* ☰ *AE, D, MC, V.*

$$–$$$$ ✕ **California Grill.** The view of the surrounding Disney parks from this
★ rooftop restaurant is as stunning as the food, especially at night, when you can watch the nightly Magic Kingdom fireworks from the patio. Start with the brick-oven flatbread with grilled duck sausage or the *unagi* (eel) sushi. For a main course, try the oak-fired beef fillet with three-cheese potato gratin and tamarind barbecue sauce, or the seared scallops with risotto, baby carrots, and crustacean butter sauce. Good dessert choices include the orange crepes with Grand Marnier custard, raspberries, and blackberry coulis and the butterscotch, orange, and vanilla crème brûlée. ⊠ *Contemporary Resort, Titusville* ☎ *407/939–3463* ☰ *AE, MC, V.*

SPACE COAST

$–$$$$ ✕ **Dixie Crossroads.** This sprawling restaurant is always crowded and fes-
★ tive, but it's not just the setting that draws the throngs; it's the seafood. The specialty is the difficult-to-cook rock shrimp, which is served fried or broiled. Other standouts include clam strips, all-you-can-eat catfish, and famous corn fritters. Often the wait for a table can last 90 minutes, but if you don't have time to wait, you can order takeout or eat in the bar area. ⊠ *1475 Garden St., Titusville, 2 mi east of I–95 Exit 220* ☎ *321/268–5000* ⌒ *Reservations not accepted* ☰ *AE, D, DC, MC, V.*

$ ✕ **Lone Cabbage Fish Camp.** The word *rustic* doesn't even begin to describe this down-home, no-nonsense restaurant (translation: you eat off paper plates with plastic forks) housed in a weathered old clapboard shack along with a bait shop and airboat tour company. Set your calorie counter for plates of catfish, frogs' legs, turtle, and alligator (as well as burgers and hot dogs). Dine inside or on the outdoor deck overlooking the St. Johns River. Who knows, you might even see your dinner swimming by. And don't miss Lone Cabbage's world-famous fish fry the first and third Sunday of every month. ⊠ *8199 Rte. 520 , Cocoa* ☎ *321/632–4199* ⌒ *Reservations not accepted* ☰ *AE, MC, V.*

STRANGE BUT TRUE

■ It was in 1973 at a convention of newspapers editors at Disney's Contemporary Hotel that Richard Nixon famously declared "I am not a crook."

■ After being trapped playing cheap juke joints for unappreciative audiences in Orlando, Ray Charles wanted to get far, far away. He headed for Seattle, and a brilliant career

■ Jack Kerouac wrote the Dharma Bums and The Beat Generation while living in Orlando between the fall of 1957 and the spring of 1958.

■ Flowing off the coast of Cape Canaveral, the Gulf Stream is an ocean river roughly 1,000 times larger than the Mississippi River. It runs from the Gulf of Mexico to Europe.

■ The Lizard King, Jim Morrison, is from Melbourne, Florida.

■ More dangerous to swimmers than sharks are "rip currents," where receding waves break through a sandbar and create a powerful, narrow current that can pull you out to sea. If you're caught in a riptide, stay calm and swim parallel to the shore until you're out of the force of the flow before trying to swim to shore.

WHERE TO STAY

WHAT IT COSTS				
¢	$	$$	$$$	$$$$
FOR 2 PEOPLE under $80	$80–$140	$140–$220	$220–$280	over $280

Prices are per night for a standard double room in high season, excluding taxes and service charges.

ORLANDO

$$$$ **Grand Floridian Resort & Spa.** On the shores of the Seven Seas Lagoon,
Fodor's Choice this red, gable-roof Victorian is all delicate gingerbread, rambling
★ verandas, and brick chimneys. It's Disney's flagship resort: add a dinner or two at Victoria and Albert's or Cítricos and you may spend more in a weekend here than on your mortgage payment—but you'll have great memories. Although you won't look out of place walking through the lobby in flip-flops, afternoon high tea and a pianist playing nightly in the lobby are among the high-scale touches. The Mouseketeer Clubhouse on the ground floor offers children's programs until midnight daily. ☎ 407/824–3000 ⇨ 900 rooms, 90 suites ⏶ In-room: safe, Ethernet, Wi-Fi. In-hotel: 5 restaurants, room service, tennis courts, pools, gym, spa, beachfront, concierge, children's programs (ages 4–12), laundry facilities, laundry service, executive floor, no-smoking rooms ☰ AE, D, DC, MC, V.

$$–$$$$ **Nickelodeon Family Suites by Holiday Inn.** The Nickelodeon theme
★ extends everywhere, from the suites, where separate kids' rooms have
☺ bunk beds and SpongeBob wall murals, to the two giant pools built up like water parks. Kids will look forward to wake-up calls from Nickelodeon stars, character breakfasts, and live entertainment. You can

10

LIKE A LOCAL

Aside from random "y'all's," folks in Orlando talk pretty much like everyone else. Where the language is more distinct is on the Space Coast, where surfers will have a better time understanding you when you drop in a few of these terms.

- Amped: Charged up; stoked
- Bail: To jump off a board for your own safety
- Clucked: When you fear a particularly large wave
- Fluff: The misty spray off the lip of a wave
- Gnarly: Quite awesome—and intimidating
- Goofy Foot: A surfer who rides with his right foot forward
- Grommet: An adolescent surfer
- Hiddie: Hideous
- Kook: A poseur; an unskilled surfer
- Local: A surfer who's on the waves almost every day

- Noodle: Absolutely exhausted
- Pearl: When the nose of your board dips into the water (from pearl diving)
- Rip: Surfing to the maximum of your ability
- Squid: An unlikable individual
- Scabbed: Getting hurt by hitting a rock or reef
- Shred: Executing a series of rapid, repeated turns
- Sick: A particularly impressive display of skill or surfing conditions
- Snake: Stealing a wave from the surfer in front of you
- Stoked: Incredibly enthused
- Swish: A fearful surfer
- Tube: When a wave completely encloses itself and creates a cylinder where the surfer rides
- Wahine: A young female surfer

choose between one-, two-, and three-bedroom suites, with or without full kitchens. ⊠*14500 Continental Gateway, I–4 Exit 67, Orlando 32821* ☎*407/387–5437 or 866/462–6425* ⊕*www.nickhotels.com* ⟿*800 suites* ⚷*In-room: safe, kitchen (some), refrigerator, Ethernet. In-hotel: 3 restaurants, room service, pools, 9-hole golf course, gym, children's programs (ages 4–12), laundry facilities, laundry service, public Wi-Fi, no-smoking rooms* ⊟*AE, D, DC, MC, V.*

$$–$$$$ ⛺**Wilderness Lodge.** The architects outdid themselves with this seven-
FodorsChoice   story hotel modeled after the majestic turn-of-the-20th-century lodges
★   of the American Northwest. The five-story lobby, supported by towering tree trunks, has an 82-foot-high, three-sided fireplace made of rocks from the Grand Canyon and lighted by enormous tepee-shape chandeliers. Two 55-foot-tall hand-carved totem poles complete the illusion. Rooms have leather chairs, patchwork quilts, cowboy art, and a balcony or a patio. The hotel's showstopper is its Fire Rock Geyser, a faux Old Faithful, near the large pool, which begins as an artificially heated hot spring in the lobby. This hotel is a good option if you're a couple without kids looking for more serenity than is found at Disney's other hotels. ☎*407/824–3200* ⟿*728 rooms, 31 suites* ⚷*In-room: safe, Ethernet. In-hotel: 3 restaurants, room service, pool, beachfront, bicycles, children's programs (ages 4–12), laundry facilities, laundry*

service, concierge, executive floor, public Wi-Fi, no-smoking rooms ⊟*AE, D, DC, MC, V.*

$$–$$$

Fodor'sChoice

★

🖼**Royal Pacific Resort.** The entrance—a footbridge across a tropical stream—sets the tone for the South Pacific theme of this hotel, which is on 53 acres planted with tropical shrubs and trees, most of them palms. The focal point is a 12,000-square-foot, lagoon-style pool, which has a small beach and an interactive water play area. Indonesian carvings decorate the walls everywhere, even in the rooms, and Emeril Lagasse's restaurant, Tchoup Chop, draws crowds. The hotel hosts Polynesian-style luaus every Saturday. ⊠*6300 Hollywood Way, Univeral Orlando, 32819* ☎*407/503–3000 or 800/232–7827* ⊕*www.universalorlando. com* ↪*1,000 rooms, 113 suites* ♿*In-room: safe, VCR, Ethernet. In-hotel: 3 restaurants, room service, bars, pool, gym, children's programs (ages 4–14), laundry facilities, laundry service, executive floor, public Wi-Fi, no-smoking rooms, some pets allowed (fee)* ⊟*AE, DC, MC, V.*

SPACE COAST

$–$$

🖼**Holiday Inn Cocoa Beach Oceanfront Resort.** When two adjacent beach hotels were redesigned and a promenade park landscaped between them, the Holiday Inn Cocoa Beach Resort was born. Hit hard by the 2004 hurricanes, the oceanfront property underwent a multimillion-dollar renovation, with a complete exterior makeover and updates to guest rooms and meeting rooms. Standard rooms are modern, and designed in bright tropical colors. Suites and villas have a Key West feel, with louvered doors and rattan ceiling fans. Lodging options include standard and king rooms; oceanfront suites, which have a living room with sleeper sofa; villas; or bi-level lofts. Kids are given the royal treatment, with specially designed KidsSuites that feature bunk beds and video games and a pirate-ship pool with water-blasting cannons. ⊠*1300 N. Atlantic Ave., Cocoa Beach 32931* ☎*321/783–2271 or 800/206–2747* 🖷*321/784–8878* ⊕*www.hicocoabeachhotelsite. com* ↪*500 rooms, 119 suites* ♿*In-room: safe, kitchen (some), refrigerator (some), Wi-Fi. In-hotel: restaurant, bars, tennis courts, pool, gym, beachfront, laundry facilities, laundry service, executive floor, parking (no fee)* ⊟*AE, DC, MC, V.*

$

★

🖼**Wakulla Suites Resort.** This kitschy two-story motel in a converted 1970s apartment building is clean and comfortable and just off the beach. Some rooms are a block away from the water, and a few are just a walk down the boardwalk. The bright rooms are fairly ordinary, decorated in tropical prints. Completely furnished five-room suites, designed to sleep six, are great for families; each includes two bedrooms and a living room, dining room, and fully equipped kitchen. ⊠*3550 N. Atlantic Ave., Cocoa Beach 32931* ☎*321/783–2230 or 800/992–5852* 🖷*321/783–0980* ⊕*www.wakullasuites.com* ↪*117 suites* ♿*In-room: kitchen, Wi-Fi. In-hotel: restaurant, pool, no elevator, laundry facilities, laundry service, parking (no fee), no-smoking rooms* ⊟*AE, D, DC, MC, V.*

10

ON THE WAY

Ocala. You have to get off the major highways—Highway 441 and I-75—to really see Ocala. It's one of the top horse breeding regions in America, where rolling hills and picturesque ranches are akin to the bluegrass areas of Kentucky. Silver Springs, the state's first tourist attraction, is here and still going strong.

Mount Dora. Approximately 25 mi northwest of Orlando, this charming New England–style village has a wonderful collection of antiques shops, galleries, boutiques, sidewalk cafés, and bookstores.

Daytona Beach. For years, the beach here was the main attraction. Now NASCAR racing is in the lead, with the Daytona International Speedway's Daytona 500, Pepsi 400, and assorted races and events throughout the year injecting an estimated $3 billion per year into the local economy.

NIGHTLIFE & THE ARTS

ORLANDO

Many Disney clubs are at **Pleasure Island,** a 6-acre after-dark entertainment complex connected to the rest of Downtown Disney by footbridges. Despite its location on Disney property, the entertainment has real grit and life. In addition to seven clubs and an Irish pub, you can find a few restaurants and shops. A pay-one-price admission gets you into all the clubs and shows. ⊠ *Off Buena Vista Dr., Downtown Disney* ☎ *407/934–7781 or 407/824–4500* ☞ *Pay-one-price admission to clubs $20.95 plus tax, shops and restaurants open to all 10:30–7* ☉ *Clubs daily 7 pm–2 am; shops and restaurants daily 10:30 am–2 am.*

Downtown Disney West Side is a pleasingly hip outdoor complex of shopping, dining, and entertainment. A 24-screen AMC cinema shows first-run movies.

Fodor'sChoice ★ **Cirque du Soleil** (☎ *407/939–7600*)starts at 100 mph and accelerates from there. It's 90 minutes of extraordinary acrobatics, avant-garde staging, costumes, choreography, and a grand finale that'll make you double-check Newton's laws of motion. Shows featuring 72 performers are scheduled twice daily, five days a week (call for current performance schedule).Adjacent to the **House of Blues** (☎ *407/934–2583*)restaurant,

Fodor'sChoice ★ which itself showcases cool blues starting at 11, HOB's up-close-and-personal concert venue presents local and nationally known artists playing everything from reggae to rock to R&B. ⊠ *Off Buena Vista Dr., Downtown Disney* ☎ *407/824–4321 or 407/824–2222.*

SPACE COAST

Stretching far over the Atlantic, the **Cocoa Beach Pier** (⊠ *401 Meade Ave.* ☎ *321/783–7549* ⊕ *www.cocoabeachpier.com*)is an everyday gathering spot as well as a beachside grandstand for space-shuttle launches. There are several souvenir shops, bars, and restaurants, as well as a bait-and-tackle shop. It costs $3 to park here, and another

$1 for access to the fishing part of the pier that dangles 800 feet out into the Atlantic.

SHOPPING

ORLANDO

★ **Prime Outlets Orlando.** Two malls and four annexes make Prime Outlets Orlando the area's largest collection of outlet stores. One of the best places to find deals is Off 5th, the Saks Fifth Avenue Outlet. ✉ *5401 W. Oak Ridge Rd., at northern tip of International Dr.* ☎ *407/352–9600* ⊕ *www.primeoutlets.com* ⊗ *Mon.–Sat. 10–9, Sun. 10–6.*

Mall at Millenia (✉ *4200 Conroy Rd.* ☎ *407/363–3555* ⊗ *Mon.–Sat. 10–9:30, Sun. 11–7*) has high-end designers like Gucci, Dior, Burberry, Chanel, Jimmy Choo, Hugo Boss, Cartier, and Tiffany, plus Anthropologie, Neiman Marcus, Bloomingdale's, Bang & Olufsen, and Orlando's only Apple store. It's easy to reach: take Exit 78 off Interstate 4.

SPACE COAST

Perhaps Cocoa's most interesting feature is restored **Cocoa Village.** Within the cluster of restored turn-of-the-20th-century buildings and cobblestone walkways, you can enjoy several restaurants, indoor and outdoor cafés, snack and ice-cream shops, and more than 50 specialty shops and art galleries. To get to Cocoa Village, head east on Route 520—named King Street in Cocoa—and when the streets get narrow and the road curves, make a right onto Brevard Avenue; follow the signs for the free municipal parking lot. ✉ *S.R. 520 and Brevard Ave.* ☎ *321/631–9075* ⊕ *www.cocoavillage.com* 🖾 *Free* ⊗ *Hrs vary by store.*

Fodor's Choice With a giant surfboard and an aqua, teal, and pink art deco facade,
★ **Ron Jon Surf Shop** (✉ *4151 N. Atlantic Ave., Rte. A1A* ☎ *321/799–8888* ⊕ *www.ronjons.com*) takes up nearly two blocks along A1A. What started in 1963 as a small T-shirt and bathing-suit shop has evolved into a 52,000-square-foot superstore that's open every day 'round the clock. The shop has water-sports gear as well as chairs and umbrellas for rent, and sells every kind of beachwear, surf wax, plus the requisite T-shirts and flip-flops. For up-to-the-minute surfing conditions, call the store and press 3 and then 7 for the **Ron Jon Surf and Weather Report.**

10

SPORTS & THE OUTDOORS

SPACE COAST

★ Miles of grassy, windswept dunes and a virtually empty beach await you at **Canaveral National Seashore,** a remarkable 57,000-acre park with 24 mi of undeveloped coastline spanning from New Smyrna to Titusville. Stop at any of the six parking areas and follow the wooden walkways to the beach. Ranger-led weekly programs include canoe trips and sea-turtle talks. At the northern end of the Seashore and the southernmost tip of New Smyrna Beach is **Apollo Beach** (☎ *386/428–3384*). In addition to typical beach activities (lifeguards are on duty May 30–September 1), visitors can also ride horses here (with a permit), hike self-guided trails, and tour the historic Eldora Statehouse.

⊠*7611 S. Atlantic Ave.* ☏*321/267–1110* ⊕*www.nps.gov/cana* 🎟*$3 per person* ☉*Nov.–Mar., daily 6–6; Apr.–Oct., daily 6 am–8 pm.*

VITAL STATS

■ On March 3, 1845, Florida became the 27th state in the Union.

■ Nickname: the Sunshine State.

■ State shell: horse conch.

■ State tree: sabal palm.

■ State flower: orange blossom.

■ State beverage: orange juice.

■ State rock: moon rock.

■ State freshwater mammal: manatee.

■ State saltwater mammal: dolphin.

■ State cat: Florida panther.

Fodor'sChoice ★ If you prefer wading birds over waiting in line, don't miss the 140,000-acre **Merritt Island National Wildlife Refuge,** which adjoins the Canaveral National Seashore. It's an immense area dotted by brackish estuaries and marshes and patches of land consisting of coastal dunes, scrub oaks, pine forests and flatwoods, and palm and oak hammocks. A 20-minute video about refuge wildlife and accessibility—only 10,000 acres are developed—can help orient you. You might take a self-guided tour along the 7-mi **Black Point Wildlife Drive.** On the **Oak Hammock Foot Trail,** you can see wintering migratory waterfowl and learn about the plants of a hammock community. If you exit the north end of the refuge, look for the **Manatee Observation Area** just north of the Haulover Canal (maps are at the visitor center). They usually show up in spring and fall. The refuge is closed four days before a shuttle launch. ⊠*Rte. 402, across Titusville causeway* ☏*321/861–0667* ⊕*www.fws.gov/merrittisland* 🎟*Free* ☉*Daily dawn–dusk; visitor center weekdays 8–4:30, weekends 9–5 (Nov.–Mar.).*

VISITOR INFORMATION

Cocoa Beach Convention and Visitor's Bureau (⊠*400 Fortenberry Rd., Merritt Island 32952* ☏*321/454–2022 or 877/321–8474* ⊕*www.cocoabeach.com*).

SeaWorld Information (☏*407/351–3600 or 888/800–5447* ⊕*www.seaworld.com*)

Universal Information (☏*407/363–8000 TDD* ⊕*www.universalorlando.com*).

Universal Resort reservations (☏*888/273–1311*).

WDW Information (☏*407/824–4321, 407/827–5141 TDD*). **WDW Resort Reservations** (☏*407/934–7639*). **WDW Dining reservations** (☏*407/939–3463*).

Miami & the Florida Keys

Art Deco District, Ocean Drive, Miami Beach

WORD OF MOUTH

"The club scene in South Beach is ever-changing and getting a little past its 'That's so hot' stage, so don't be too intimidated. You DO want to dress a bit flashily for the better places, certainly, but don't go too over the top."

—rjw_lgb_ca

"The Beach at Bahia Honda is the best in the Keys. In fact, it is one of the nicest beaches I have ever visited."

—CarolSchwartz

www.fodors.com/forums

EXPLORING MIAMI & THE FLORIDA KEYS

Downtown Miami is 652 mi southeast of Pensacola; 231 mi southeast of Orlando; 54 mi north of Key Largo; and 153 mi northeast of Key West

By Susan MacCallum-Whitcomb

Miami is hot—and we're not just talking about temperature. Anyone who watches TV is familiar with the city's classic images: glass-skinned skyscrapers, towering palms, a plethora of yachts, and a population so stylish that even crime scene investigators look fabulous. On top of that, Miami lays claim to the country's most celebrated strand, South Beach, as well as intriguing neighborhoods like Little Havana and Coral Gables.

Moreover, Miami offers easy access to both the Everglades and the Florida Keys, an 800-island archipelago filled with contradictions. Years of geographic isolation allowed tropical flora to flourish on the Keys—and enabled locals to nurture a distinctive culture. Unfortunately, the area's popularity has impacted both, so the Keys now have a split personality. On one hand they are a reef-rimmed wilderness populated by free-spirited folks; on the other they're a relatively mainstream realm comprised of minimalls and trailer parks. Avoiding the latter can be hard, but the charm of the former is ample reward.

WHO WILL ESPECIALLY LOVE THIS TRIP?

Hedonists: Interested in preening poolside and power shopping by day then strutting supermodel-style through A-list restaurants and clubs by night? You can do all that without leaving South Beach. In the Keys—where Jimmy Buffett, not Gianni Versace, is the style icon—the pleasures are simpler. Even the well-heeled shed their shoes and hoist pitchers of margaritas.

Arts Lovers: The Carnival Center (home to the Florida Grand Opera, Miami City Ballet, and New World Symphony) is the jewel in Miami's cultural crown. But events like the International Film Festival and Art Basel also register on culture vultures' radar. The Keys, long a haven for artsy types, have their own thriving scene—albeit on a more intimate scale.

Families: Despite the attention paid to G-strings, this area also has real G-rated appeal. Attractions like Miami's Children's Museum, Seaquarium, and MetroZoo draw kids in droves; as do educational (and sometimes kitschy) Everglades excursions. Keys highlights include family-oriented resorts and dolphin programs, like the one run by the Dolphin Research Center.

Outdoor Adventurers: Beyond the bright lights, nature beckons. After all, Miami is the only city in the U.S. with—count 'em—two national parks (Everglades and Biscayne) in its backyard. And if that isn't enough to impress fresh air fans, the Keys contain the world's third largest coal reef. So the eco-opportunities are endless.

TOP 5 REASONS TO GO

Blissful Beaches: Sybaritic South Beach is a magnet for see-and-be-seen types; while Robinson Crusoe wannabes gravitate to isolated keys that fulfill their castaway fantasies.

Miami Beach's Art Deco Delights: The world's largest concentration of Art Deco edifices is here; and the Art Deco District—with more than 800 buildings of significance—has earned a spot on the National Register of Historic Places.

Kicking Back in the Keys: Some dream of "sailing away to Key Largo," others of "wasting away again in Margaritaville." In any case, the Flor-

ida Keys have become synonymous with relaxation and a come-as-you-are, do-as-you-please vibe.

Ethnic Enclaves: Wander into some Miami neighborhoods, and you might think you've entered a foreign country. Influxes of immigrants (many hailing from Spanish-speaking nations) make this one of America's most ethnically diverse cities.

The Everglades: Covering mainland Florida's southern tip, the "River of Grass" is home to 2,000 species of plants, 700 of fish, 400 of birds, and 100 of mammals (and lots of bugs).

WHEN IS THE BEST TIME TO VISIT?

Traditionally, high season starts with the run-up to Christmas and extends through Easter. Snowbirds migrate down then to escape frosty weather back home, and festival goers flock in for major events (such as Art Basel or the Orange Bowl). Moreover, winter is *the* time to visit the Everglades. Temperatures and mosquito activity are lower—as are water levels, making wildlife easier to spot.

Bargains, conversely, are easier to find during fall and spring shoulder seasons. Costs drop even further during Miami's hot, humid summer. This period is increasingly popular on the Keys because temps are usually 10°F cooler than on the mainland, with substantially less rain. (The Keys get around 30 inches annually, compared with 55 to 60 in Miami.)

Summer sojourners in either destination should expect afternoon lightning and accompanying thundershowers. Also note that hurricane season officially runs from June 1 to November 30. Severe storms can dampen your plans, disrupt public services, or worse. If you're advised about a hurricane watch before departing, consider postponing your trip.

HOW SHOULD I GET THERE?

DRIVING

I–95 is the major expressway connecting South Florida with points north. State Road 836 is the major east-west expressway; it connects to Florida's Turnpike, State Road 826, and I–95. Seven causeways link Miami and Miami Beach: I–195 and I–395 are the most convenient. Continuing on to the Keys means traversing the 110-mi Overseas Highway, also known as U.S. 1. It's notable for its views, its bridges (43 all told), and its peak-time traffic jams.

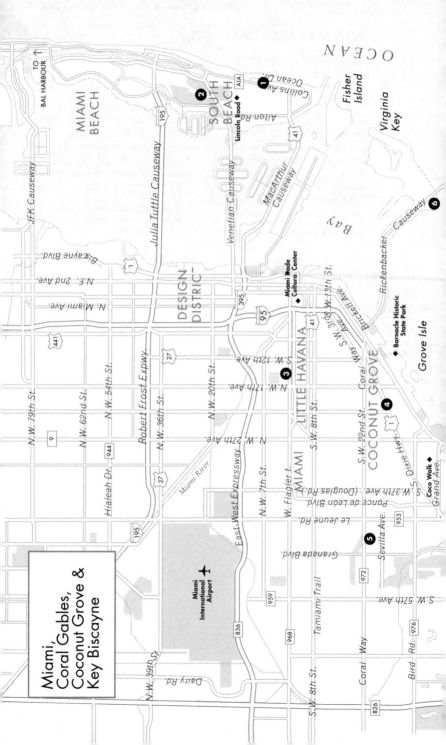

Miami,
Coral Gables,
Coconut Grove &
Key Biscayne

OCEAN

Fisher
Island

Virginia
Key

Grove Isle

Rickenbacker Causeway

Bay

MacArthur
Causeway

Venetian Causeway

MIAMI
BEACH

SOUTH
BEACH

Lincoln Road ◆

Collins Av.
Ocean Dr.

A1A

TO
BAL HARBOUR

JFK Causeway

Julia Tuttle Causeway

195

41

DESIGN
DISTRICT

Miami Dade
Cultura Center ◆

Barnacle Historic
State Park ◆

Coco Walk ◆

COCONUT GROVE

LITTLE HAVANA

MIAMI

Miami River

Miami
International
Airport

East-West Expressway

Robert Frost Expwy

Biscayne Blvd.

N.E. 2nd Ave.

N. Miami Ave.

N.W. 79th St.

N.W. 62nd St.

N.W. 54th St.

N.W. 36th St.

N.W. 20th St.

N.W. 27th Ave.

N.W. 17th Ave.

S.W. 12th Ave.

S.W. 8th St.

S.W. 22nd St.

S. Dixie Hwy.

Coral Way

S. Bayshore Dr.

Brickell Ave.

S.W. 3rds.

S.W. 13th St.

Hialeah Dr.

N.W. 7th St.

W. Flagler t.

Ponce de León Blvd.
(Douglas Rd.)

Le Jeune Rd.

Sevilla Ave.

Granada Blvd.

Tamiami Trail

S.W. 8th St.

Coral Way

Bird Rd.

S.W. 57th Ave.

S.W. 37th Ave.
Grand Ave.

Dairy Rd.

N.W. 39th St.

9

944

441

27

27

195

836

959

968

972

953

976

826

41

95

395

1

1

1

27

❶
❷
❸
❹
❺
❻

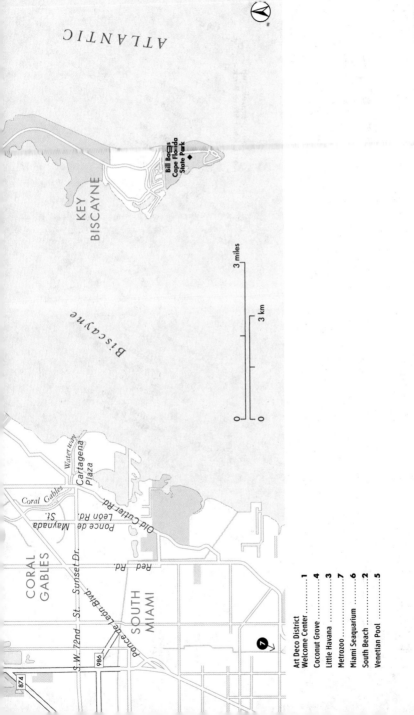

ATLANTIC

KEY BISCAYNE

Bill Baggs
Cape Florida
State Park

Biscayne

Coral Gables

Waterway

Cartagena
Plaza

Ponce de León Rd.

Old Cutler Rd.

CORAL
GABLES

S. W. 72nd. St.

Sunset Dr.

Ponce de León Blvd.

Maynada St.

Red Rd.

SOUTH
MIAMI

986

874

3 miles

3 km

0   0

The Florida Keys

TO MIAMI

Card Sound Bridge

905

905A

Barnes Sound

1

Key Largo Hammock

Key Largo

Royal Palm Visitor Center ◆

Ernest F. Coe Visitor Center ◆

Everglades National Park

9336

Whitewater Bay

Flamingo

Cape Sable

Florida Bay

John Pennekamp Coral Reef State Park

Tavernier

Plantation Key

Windley Key

Islamorada

Upper Matecumbe Key

Lignumvitae Key

Lower Matecumbe Key

Indian Key

Fiesta Key

Long Key

Conch & Duck Keys

Grassy Key

Marathon Airport

Vaca Key

Marathon

Seven Mile Bridges

1

Pigeon Key

Bahia Honda State Park

No Name Key

National Key Deer Refuge

Big Pine Key

Little Torch Key

Summerland Key

Ramrod Key

Cudjoe Key

Sugarloaf Key

Saddlebunch Keys

Big Coppitt Key

Boca Chica Key

Stock Island

Key West

Key West International Airport

Gulf of Mexico

Straits of Florida

ATLANTIC OCEAN

20 miles

30 km

FLYING

Miami International Airport (305/876–7000, www.miami-airport.com), 7 mi west of Downtown, is one of the world's busiest airports. Some 30 million people pass through annually, and more than 80 airlines serve 150 cities from here. If you're destined for the north side of Miami-Dade, consider less-crowded Fort Lauderdale International Airport (866/435–9355, www.broward.org). Key West has its own airport (305/296–7223, www.keywestinternationalairport.com). However, flights here are among the most frequently cancelled, due to high fuel costs and low passenger counts.

TRAIN/BUS/BOAT

Amtrak (800/872 7245, www.amtrak.com) serves Miami from 500 destinations, and interstate Greyhound buses (800/231–2222, www.greyhound.com) stop at four area terminals. Greyhound also runs a Keys shuttle, departing three or four times daily from MIA. Traveling by sea? Both Miami and Key West are busy cruise ship ports. The former handles 3.5 million passengers annually, and the latter welcomes 660,000 each year. Another marine option is Key West Express (866/593-3779, www.seakeywestexpress.com), a high-speed catamaran service that connects the Conch Republic to Marco Island, Fort Myers Beach, and Miami.

HOW DO I GET AROUND?

BY CAR

Though some major attractions—like South Beach and Key West's Old Town—beg to be explored on foot, you'll need wheels to see many sites. So drive down in your own vehicle or rent one upon arrival. (Rentals are readily available, as are taxis for those who loath to take the wheel.) When you long to feel the wind in your hair, upgrade to a convertible: it's the classic choice for cruising SoBe. Alternately, dump the car and opt for two-wheel transportation. In Miami Beach (where traffic gets congested) and Key West's Old Town (where parking is at a premium), scooter rentals are popular.

BY PUBLIC TRANSIT

Metro-Dade Transit (305/770–3131, www.miamidade.gov/transit) maintains 60-plus bus routes in Miami-Dade County and charges a $1.50 fare. Other mainland alternatives include Metrorail, which extends west to Hialeah and south to Kendall; or Tri-Rail, which has commuter stations throughout Dade, Broward, and Palm Beach Counties. On the islands, Key West Transit (305/809–3910, www.keywestcity.com) offers bus service in Key West itself and as far north as Marathon. One-way fares are $1 to $2.

WHERE SHOULD I FOCUS MY ENERGY?

If you're here for 1 day: Start in South Beach. After ohhing and ahhing over art deco architecture, park yourself to ogle the parade of "beautiful people" along Ocean Drive or join them by browsing Lincoln

How to Snack

Culinary critics get tongue-tied trying to come up with superlatives to describe Greater Miami's food scene. Who can blame them? Restaurants have innovative menus prepared by big-name chefs in world-class settings (Azul, Table 8). But some of the tastiest offerings are quick nibbles that will simultaneously satisfy your hunger and give you a crash course in local culture. The best place for a snack attack is Little Havana. You can make a meal out of tapas-style treats at neighborhood restaurants, or simply sample what's being served by street vendors. Visitors with delicate palettes should skip the *chicharrones* (deep-fried pork skin) in favor of *masitas de puerco fritas* (deep-fried pork meat); or order old standbys such as tamales, empanadas, churros, plantain chips, and made-to-order Cubano sandwiches. They're easy as pie to find. And speaking of pie . . . don't forget the Keys' quintessential dessert. A classic Key Lime Pie balances sweetness (be it from whipped cream or meringue topping) with a mouth-puckering tartness that comes courtesy of the namesake tiny, extra-sour limes. To be authentic, however, the custard inside must be yellowish. (If you're served a garish green slice, send it back.) One good place to taste the real deal is the Blond Giraffe, a bakery-cum-coffee shop with seven locations in Key West, Marathon, and South Miami.

Road Mall. Later merengue over to Little Havana, epicenter of Miami's Cuban community.

If you're here for 2 days: You're on vacation, so follow your bliss. Explore Coconut Grove or Coral Gables. Shop 'til you drop at Bal Harbour, the Village of Merrick Park and the über-trendy Miami Design District. Hit the links, play tennis, cast a line, or just catch some rays.

If you're here for 3 days: No trip to South Florida is complete without seeing the Everglades, and Miami is a logical launch pad. If you've never watched an alligator eat marshmallows or experienced an airboat ride, here's your chance. Afterward swing down to the Keys, overnighting in Key Largo.

If you're here for 4 days: Get up early for the 100-mi drive to Key West. You can make a suitably sandy pit stop at Bahia Honda State Park (it's a great place to take a swim or walk) and still be in Key West early enough to pay your regards to "Papa."

If you're here for 5 days: Spend the morning exploring Old Town. Active types can follow up with a moped tour of the island or snorkeling around Fort Zachary Taylor. After scoping out the parrotfish, return to town and join local "Parrotheads" in a Jimmy Buffett sing-a-long.

If you're here for 6 days: If you had a long night, sleep in; then hit Duval Street for last-minute souvenir shopping. When retracing your route to Miami, stop at John Pennekamp or Bill Baggs State Park for a final taste of the life aquatic before heading home.

CLAIM TO FAME

Lots of destinations have sun and sand. What sets this one apart is its attitude: a special outlook on life that is, in a word, "exuberant." Give residents of this region the slimmest excuse to party and there's no holding them back. Witness Carnaval Miami in Little Havana, which involves 10 days of irresistible hip-swiveling, salsa-spiced action (to say nothing of the world's longest conga line); or Art Deco Weekend in South Beach, when even normally staid architecture buffs turn Ocean Drive into a massive street fair. Things get crazier still on the Keys, where a packed calendar of outlandish events culminates with Key West's Fantasy Fest: an over-the-top Halloween extravaganza that attracts 70,000 revelers. (FYI: timid types need not apply.) Yet Key West is also a place where simple sunsets warrant a celebration, which is precisely why jugglers, clowns, and assorted eccentrics ritually gather in Mallory Square to applaud Mother Nature's nightly light show. Such enthusiasm is hard to resist. So relax and embrace it!

If you're here for 7 days or more: Do all of the above . . . only more slowly. Vacations here are as much about lifestyle as locale, so it's important that you give yourself time to enjoy it.

WHAT ARE THE TOP EXPERIENCES?

SoBe It: Over the past 20 years, no American beach has generated as much buzz as the one that hugs Ocean Drive. Fringed with palms, backed by art deco architecture, and pulsating with urban energy, South Beach is simply *the* hippest place to soak up some sun. It's also a glam place to dance by moonlight. The SoBe crowd has elevated clubbing to an art form—they often keep grooving until 5AM.

Livin' La Vida Local: In Little Havana, a 3.3-square-mi neighborhood just west of Downtown, salsa tunes blare and the smell of spicy chorizo fills the air. (You can get a good whiff of tobacco, too, due to cigar makers who hand roll their products here.) Little Havana's heart is Calle Ocho (8th Street); the commercial thoroughfare hosts the pre-Lenten Carnaval Miami. It's as close as you'll get to Cuba without running afoul of the law.

Call of the Wild: Miami and Key West are ideal habitats for party animals. However, there are other kinds of wildlife in South Florida. Take the Everglades, where indigenous critters like alligators, Florida panthers, and cottonmouth snakes can add bite to your trip. For an up-close look, thrill seekers can careen through the grassy water at 40 mph in an airboat. Purists, alternately, can placidly kayak inside the boundaries of Everglades National Park. Just remember to keep your hands in the boat!

Finding Nemo: The Keys' aquarium-clear waters are populated by 40 species of coral and more than 600 of fish, which means divers and snorkelers can spot purple sea fans, blue tangs, yellow-tailed snappers, and more. Locals debate the premier place for viewing them, but John Pennekamp Coral Reef State Park is high on everyone's list. Underwater outings organized by park concessionaires let you put your best flipper forward.

Who's Your Papa? Ask that question around Key West and the answer will invariably be "Ernest Hemingway." The iconic author lived and worked here for 11 years. Today, touring his former home and favorite haunts seems mandatory. To fully understand the Importance of Being Earnest, though, come in July for Hemingway Days. Events include a marlin tournament, mock bull running, and a look-alike contest featuring bushy-bearded Papa impersonators.

BEST BETS

SIGHTS AND TOURS

MIAMI & MIAMI BEACH

Art Deco District Welcome Center. Run by the Miami Design Preservation League, the center provides information about the buildings in the district. Several tours—covering Lincoln Road, Española Way, North Beach, and the entire Art Deco District, among others—start here. ⊠ *1001 Ocean Dr., at Barbara Capitman Way (10th St.), South Beach* ☎ *305/531-3484* ⊕ *www.mdpl.org* 🖳 *Tours $20* ☉ *Sun.–Thurs. 10– 7, Fri. and Sat. 10–6.*

Coconut Grove. Eclectic and intriguing, Miami's Coconut Grove can be considered the tropical equivalent of New York's Greenwich Village. A haven for writers and artists, the neighborhood has never quite outgrown its image as a small village. For blocks in every direction, students, honeymooning couples, families, and prosperous retirees flow in and out of a mix of galleries, restaurants, bars, bookstores, comedy clubs, and theaters.

★ **Little Havana.** First settled en masse by Cubans in the early 1960s, after that country's Communist revolution, Little Havana is a predominantly working-class area and the core of Miami's Hispanic community. The main commercial zone is bounded by Northwest 1st Street, Southwest 9th Street, Ronald Reagan Avenue (Southwest 12th Avenue), and Teddy Roosevelt Boulevard (Southwest 17th Avenue). Calle Ocho (Southwest 8th Street) is the axis of the neighborhood. Some of the restaurants host traditional flamenco performances and Sevillaña *tablaos* (dances performed on a wood-plank stage, using castanets), and some clubs feature recently arrived Cuban acts. Intimate neighborhood theaters host top-notch productions ranging from Spanish classics to contemporary satire.

★ **Metrozoo.** One of the few zoos in the United States in a subtropical
☉ environment, the 290-acre Metrozoo is state of the art. Inside the cageless zoo, some 800 animals roam on islands surrounded by moats. ⊠ *12400 S.W. 152nd St.* ☎ *305/251-0400* ⊕ *www.miamimetrozoo.*

com 🖳*$11.50, 45-min tram tour $2.50* ⊙*Daily 9:30–5:30; last admission at 4.*

🔄 **Miami Seaquarium.** This classic but aging visitor attraction stages shows with sea lions, dolphins, and Lolita the killer whale. Discovery Bay, an endangered mangrove habitat, is home to indigenous Florida fish and rays, alligators, herons, egrets, and ibis. The big draw, though, is the Swim with Our Dolphins program. ✉*4400 Rickenbacker Causeway, Virginia Key, Miami* ☎*305/361–5705* ⊕*www.miamiseaquarium.com* 🖳*$32, dolphin swim program $189, parking $7* ⊙*Daily 9:30–6, last admission at 4:30; dolphin swim daily at 8:30, noon, and 3:30.*

Fodor'sChoice **South Beach.** The hub of South Beach is the 1-square-mi Art Deco Dis-
★ trict, fronted on the east by Ocean Drive and on the west by Alton Road. (The area is now distinguished as the nation's first 20th-century district to be listed on the National Register of Historic Places, with 800 significant buildings making the roll.) Life along Ocean Drive now unfolds 24 hours a day. Beautiful people pose in hotel lounges and side-walk cafés, tanned cyclists zoom past palm trees, and visitors flock to see the action. On Lincoln Road café crowds spill onto the sidewalks, weekend markets draw all kinds of visitors and their dogs, and thanks to a few late-night lounges the scene is just as alive at night.

Fodor'sChoice **Venetian Pool.** Sculpted from a rock quarry in 1923 and fed by arte-
★ sian wells, this 825,000-gallon municipal pool remains quite popular because of its theme architecture—a fantasized version of a waterfront Italian village. ✉*2701 De Soto Blvd., at Toledo St., Coral Gables* ☎*305/460–5356* ⊕*www.venetianpool.com* 🖳*Apr.–Oct., $9; Nov.–Mar., $6, free parking across De Soto Blvd.* ⊙*June–Aug., weekdays 11–7:30, weekends 10–4:30; Sept. and Oct., Apr., and May, Tues.–Fri. 11–5:30, weekends 10–4:30; Nov.–Mar., Tues.–Fri. 10–4:30, weekends 10–4:30.*

OUTSIDE MIAMI

★ **Biscayne National Park.** Occupying 173,000 acres along the southern portion of Biscayne Bay, south of Miami and north of the Florida Keys, this national park is 95% under water, and its altitude ranges from 4 feet above sea level to 60 feet below. Contained within it are four distinct zones, which from shore to sea are mangrove forest along the coast, Biscayne Bay, the undeveloped upper Florida Keys, and coral reefs. You can take a glass-bottom-boat ride to see this underwater wonderland, but you really have to snorkel or scuba dive to appreciate it fully.

★ Biscayne National Park's **Dante Fascell Visitor Center** has a wide veranda with views across mangroves and Biscayne Bay. Among the facilities are the park's canoe and tour concessionaire, restrooms with showers, a ranger information area, a gift shop, and vending machines. This is the only area of the park accessible without a boat. ✉*9700 S.W. 328th St., Homestead* ☎*305/230–7275* ⊕*www.nps.gov/bisc* 🖳*Free* ⊙*Daily 9–5.*

Fodor'sChoice ★ **Everglades National Park.** The best way to experience the real Everglades is to get your feet wet either by taking a walk in the muck, affectionately called a "slough slog," or by paddling a canoe into the maze of mangrove islands to stay in a backcountry campsite. You can also take a boat tour in Everglades City or Flamingo, ride the tram or bike the loop road at Shark Valley, or walk the boardwalks that extend out from the main park road. Admission to Everglades National Park's two pay gates (main entrance and Shark Valley) is valid at both entrances for seven days. The main park road (Route 9336) travels from the main visitor center to Flamingo, across a section of the park's eight distinct ecosystems: hardwood hammock, freshwater prairie, pinelands, freshwater slough, cypress, coastal prairie, mangrove, and marine-estuarine.

> ### HISTORY YOU CAN SEE
>
> **Get Wrecked:** In Florida Keys National Marine Sanctuary and Biscayne National Park, archaeological artifacts compete with marine life for divers' attention. The former boasts nine wrecks; the latter has five.
>
> **Feel Fortified:** Fort Zachary Taylor, focal point of Key West's eponymous Historic State Park, is a mid-19th century military installation that played significant roles in both the Civil and Spanish-American Wars. Take a ranger-led tour; then retire to the park's beach for sunning and swimming—it's the best one in town.

Fodor'sChoice ★ Ⓒ Numerous interactive exhibits and films make the Everglades' **Ernest F. Coe Visitor Center** a worthy and important stop during your tour of the region. ⊠ *11 mi southwest of Homestead on Rte. 9336* ☎ *305/242–7700* ⊕ *www.nps.gov/ever* ◨ *Park $10 per vehicle, $5 per pedestrian, bicycle, or motorcycle* ☉ *Daily 8–5; hrs sometimes shortened in off-season.*

A must for anyone who wants to experience the real Everglades, the
★ **Royal Palm Visitor Center** permits access to the Anhinga Trail boardwalk, where in winter spying alligators congregating in watering holes is almost guaranteed. ⊠ *4 mi west of Ernest F. Coe Visitor Center on Rte. 9336* ☎ *305/242–7700* ☉ *Daily 8–4.*

THE KEYS

Fodor'sChoice ★ Sun-soaked, 524-acre **Bahia Honda State Park** sprawls across both sides of the highway, giving it 2½ mi of fabulous white sandy coastline—three beaches in all—on both the Atlantic Ocean and the Gulf of Mexico. It's regularly declared the best beach in Florida, and you'll be hard-pressed to argue: the sand is baby-powder soft, and the aqua water is warm, clear, and shallow, with mild currents. ⊠ *MM 37, OS, 36850 Overseas Hwy., 33043* ☎ *305/872–2353* ⊕ *www.floridastateparks. com* ◨ *$3.50 for 1 person, $6 per vehicle for 2 people, plus 50¢ per additional person; $1.50 per pedestrian or bicyclist* ☉ *Daily 8–dusk.*

★ Ⓒ The **Dolphin Research Center** is home to a colony of dolphins and sea lions. The not-for-profit organization has tours, narrated programs every 30 minutes, and several programs that allow interaction with dolphins in the water (Dolphin Encounter) or from a submerged platform

(Dolphin Splash). ⊠*MM 59, BS* ⊕*Box 522875, Marathon Shores 33052* ☎*305/289–1121 general information, 305/289–0002 interactive program information* ⊕*www.dolphins.org* ☎*Tours $19.50, Dolphin Splash $130, Dolphin Encounter $180, Trainer for a Day $650* ⊙*Daily 9–4:30; walking tours daily at 10, 11, 12:30, 2, 3:30, 4:30.*

★ **Ernest Hemingway Home & Museum.** Guided tours of Ernest Hemingway's home are full of anecdotes about the author's life in the community and his household quarrels with wife Pauline. While living here between 1931 and 1942, Hemingway wrote about 70% of his life's work, including *For Whom the Bell Tolls.* Few of the family's belongings remain, but photographs help illustrate his life, and scores of descendants of Hemingway's cats have free rein of the property. ⊠*907 Whitehead St., Key West* ☎*305/294–1136* ⊕*www.hemingwayhome.com* ☎*$10* ⊙*Daily 9–5.*

Fodor'sChoice Best diving and snorkeling sites in the Sunshine State? **John Pennekamp**
★ **Coral Reef State Park** is on everyone's list of faves. This underwater gem
♺ encompasses 78 square mi of coral reefs, sea-grass beds, and mangrove swamps. Its reefs contain 40 of the 52 species of coral in the Atlantic Reef System and more than 650 varieties of fish. ⊠*MM 102.5, OS, Box 487, 33037* ☎*305/451–1202* ⊕*www.floridastateparks.org/pennekamp/default.cfm* ☎*$3.50, or $6 per vehicle for 2 people plus 50¢ each additional person; $1.50 per pedestrian or bicyclist; $29–$50 for dive and snorkel tours; $22 for glass-bottom-boat tours* ⊙*Daily 8–dusk.*

WHERE TO EAT

WHAT IT COSTS					
	¢	$	$$	$$$	$$$$
AT DINNER	under $10	$10–$15	$15–$20	$20–$30	over $30

Prices are per person for a main course at dinner.

MIAMI

$$$–$$$$ ✕**Nemo.** The SoFi (South of Fifth Street) neighborhood may have
Fodor'sChoice emerged as a South Beach hot spot, but Nemo's location is not why
★ this casually comfortable restaurant receives raves. It's the menu, which often changes but always delivers, blending Caribbean, Asian, Mediterranean, and Middle Eastern influences and providing an explosion of cultures in each bite. Popular appetizers include garlic-cured salmon rolls with tobiko caviar and wasabi mayo, and crispy prawns with spicy salsa cruda. Main courses might include wok-charred salmon or grilled Indian-spice pork chop. Hedy Goldsmith's funky pastries are exquisitely sinful. Bright colors and copper fixtures highlight the tree-shaded courtyard. ⊠*100 Collins Ave., South Beach* ☎*305/532–4550* ☐*AE, DC, MC, V.*

$$–$$$$ ✕**Chispa.** Meaning "spark" in Spanish, Chispa indeed sparkles. Chef
Fodor'sChoice Robbin Haas has taken command of the open kitchen, basing the
★ menu on a melting pot of Latin flavors that reflects Miami's population. *Cazuelitas* let you have smaller portions as appetizers—from

STRANGE BUT TRUE

Tan-gible Proof: Again proving that "Necessity is the Mother of Invention," a Miami Beach pharmacist named Benjamin Green created the first suntan lotion in 1944. Presumably tired of turning red, Mr. Green cooked up the first batch on his stove and called the concoction . . . Coppertone.

Paging All Writers: Ten Pulitzer Prize winners (among them Ernest Hemingway, Tennessee Williams, and Truman Capote) have resided in the Keys. Living legends with homes here include crime writer Carl Hiaasen and songwriter Jimmy Buffett.

Famous Last Words: Headstones in City Cemetery (Key West's 20-acre graveyard) underscore the locals' quirky sensibility. One for a wayward husband reads "Now I know where he's sleeping at night." Another for a reformed privateer proclaims he was a "good citizen for 65 of his 108 years."

mussels with chipotle chili to Spanish *cava* (sparkling wine) fondue. Ceviches are assertively marinated, croquettes melt in your mouth, and skeptics can have flatbreads with various toppings (read: pizzas). Share plates and platters of grilled shrimp or suckling pig before guava cheesecake or churros with chocolate sauce. Exotic drinks are served at the 40-foot bar, and leather banquettes, Bahama shutters, and colorful Cuban tiles complete the hacienda feel. ⊠ *225 Altara Ave., Coral Gables* ☎ *305/648–2600* ⊟ *AE, MC, V.*

$–$$ ✕ **Big Pink.** The decor in this innovative diner may remind you of a
Fodor's Choice roller-skating rink—everything is pink Lucite, stainless steel, and campy
★ (think sports lockers as decorative touches). And the menu is a virtual book, complete with table of contents. But the food is solidly all-American, with dozens of tasty sandwiches, pizzas, turkey or beef burgers, and side dishes, each and every one composed with gourmet flair. Customers comprise club kids and real kids, who alternate, depending on the time of day—Big Pink makes a great spot for brunch—but both like to color with the complimentary crayons. ⊠ *157 Collins Ave., South Beach* ☎ *305/532–4700* ⊟ *AE, MC, V.*

$–$$ ✕ **Havana Harry's.** When Cuban families want a home-cooked meal but
Fodor's Choice don't want to cook it themselves, they come to this spacious, airy res-
★ taurant. In fact, you're likely to see whole families here, from babes in arms to grandmothers. The fare is traditional Cuban: the long thin steaks known as *bistec palomilla*, roast chicken with citrus marinade, and fried pork chunks; contemporary flourishes—mango sauce and guava-painted pork roast—are kept to a minimum. Most dishes come with white rice, black beans, and a choice of ripe or green plantains. The sweet ripe ones offer a good contrast to the savory dishes. This is an excellent value. ⊠ *4612 Le Jeune Rd., Coral Gables* ☎ *305/661–2622* ⊟ *AE, MC, V.*

THE KEYS

$$–$$$$ ✕**Alice's Key West Restaurant.** A rather plain-Jane storefront gives way
Fodor'sChoice to a warm and cozy dining room, where chef–owner Alice Weingarten
★ works whimsical creations that are very far from plain. Color, zing,
and spice are Weingarten's main ingredients. Take the tuna tartare
tower: it's spiced with a garlic-chili paste, topped with tomato-ginger
jam, and served between crisp wonton wafers. The Brazilian churrasco
pan-seared skirt steak is served with garlicky chimichurri sauce and
green chili and manchego cheese mashed potatoes. Or, try the Asian-
spiced wild boar baby back ribs or the marinated ostrich. It's open for
breakfast and lunch, too; end your Duval Crawl here for a breakfast
of eggs, fries, and toast for as little as $4. ⊠1114 Duval St., Key
West ☎305/292–5733 ⊕www.aliceskeywest.com ☐AE, D, MC, V
⊗No lunch.

WHERE TO STAY

WHAT IT COSTS					
	¢	$	$$	$$$	$$$$
FOR 2 PEOPLE	under $150	$150–$199	$200–$299	$300–$400	over $400

Prices are for two people in a standard double room in high season, excluding
12.5% city and resort taxes.

MIAMI

$$$$ 🏨**Delano Hotel.** "I am the movie director of the clients of this hotel.
Fodor'sChoice They are the actors, not the spectators—never!" Never was "never" so
★ visionary. When you stay at the Delano today, 20 years after designer
Philippe Starck uttered these words to *Vanity Fair* about his brainchild
hotel, you're still within the spectacle of glamour. The Delano was a
pioneer that defined what Miami hotels were to become. And here you
can still live the fantasy: catwalk through massive, white, billowing
drapes, and try to act casual while celebs, models, and moguls gather
beneath cabanas and pose by the pool. A rooftop bathhouse and solar-
ium, an airy lobby lounge (the Rose Bar), and the fabulous Blue Door
restaurant complete the picture. ⊠1685 Collins Ave., South Beach
33139 ☎305/672–2000 or 800/555–5001 ☐305/532–0099 ⊕www.
delano-hotel.com ⌫184 rooms, 24 suites ⌂In-room: safe, refrigera-
tor, Wi-Fi. In-hotel: 2 restaurants, room service, bars, pool, gym, spa,
beachfront, laundry service, concierge, public Wi-Fi, parking (fee), no-
smoking rooms ☐AE, D, DC, MC, V.

$$$–$$$$ 🏨**Biltmore Hotel.** Built in 1926, this landmark hotel has had several
Fodor'sChoice incarnations over the years—including a stint as a hospital during
★ World War II—and has changed hands more than a few times. Through
it all, this grandest of grande dames remains an opulent reminder of
yesteryear, with its palatial lobby and grounds, enormous pool, and dis-
tinctive 315-foot tower, which rises above the canopy of trees shading
Coral Gables. Fully updated, the Biltmore has on-site golf and tennis,
a spa and fitness center, extensive meeting facilities, and the celebrated
Palme d'Or restaurant. ⊠1200 Anastasia Ave., Coral Gables, 33134

11

☎*305/445–1926 or 800/727–1926* 🖷*305/913–3159* ⊕*www. biltmorehotel.com* ↩*241 rooms, 39 suites* ♿*In-hotel: 4 restaurants, bars, golf course, tennis courts, pool, gym, spa, public Internet* ▤*AE, D, DC, MC, V.*

$–$$$$
Fodor's Choice
★

🏨**Sagamore.** This super-sleek all-white hotel in the middle of the action looks and feels more like a Chelsea art gallery, filled with brilliant contemporary art. Its restaurant, Social Miami, is one of the hottest reservations in town. With all the mind-bending hipness, you might expect some major flaw, like small rooms, but in fact they're all suites here, and some of the largest on the strip, starting at 525 square feet. All have full kitchens with big fridges, mini ovens, microwaves, and dishwashers. You can also expect huge flat-screen TVs

LIKE A LOCAL

Considering that more than 57% of Greater Miami's population is Hispanic or Latino, it only seems natural that Spanish words would pepper everyday conversation. So it might be prudent for the linguistically challenged to practice saying *por favor* (please), *gracias* (thank you), and *muy caliente* (very hot) before arriving.

Key West natives may call you "Bubba," but they call themselves "Conchs." It's particularly important to get the pronunciation right (conk, rhymes with plonk) during April's Conch Republic Celebration when the "island nation" of Key West asserts its sovereignty.

and whirlpool baths. Hallways have artists' quotes lining the halls, and public restrooms have video installations. The poolside duplex bungalows make posh party pads on weekend nights, when the Sagamore is *the* place to be in all of Miami (no surprise there). ⊠*1671 Collins Ave., South Beach, 33139* ☎*305/535–8088* 🖷*305/535–8185* ⊕*www. sagamorehotel.com* ↩*93 suites* ♿*In-room: safe, kitchen, refrigerator, Wi-Fi. In-hotel: restaurant, room service, bars, pool, spa, beachfront, laundry service, concierge, parking (fee), no-smoking rooms* ▤*AE, D, DC, MC, V.*

OUTSIDE MIAMI

$$$
Fodor's Choice
★

🏨**Marquesa Hotel.** In a town that prides itself on its laid-back luxe, this complex of four restored 1884 houses stands out. Guests—typically shoeless in Marquesa robes—relax among richly landscaped pools and peaceful gardens (you're asked to turn off your cell phones in common areas) against a backdrop of steps rising to the villalike suites. Elegant rooms surround a courtyard and have antique and reproduction furnishings, creamy-white and aqua fabrics, and marble baths. The lobby resembles a Victorian parlor, with antiques, Audubon prints, flowers, and photos of early Key West. The clientele is well traveled and affluent 40- to 70-year-olds, mostly straight, but the hotel is very gay-friendly. ⊠*600 Fleming St., Key West 33040* ☎*305/292–1919 or 800/869–4631* 🖷*305/294–2121* ⊕*www.marquesa.com* ↩*27 rooms* ♿*In-room: safe, dial-up. In-hotel: restaurant, room service, pools, spa, bicycles, no elevator, laundry service, concierge, public Wi-Fi* ▤*AE, DC, MC, V.*

NIGHTLIFE & THE ARTS

MIAMI

Fodor'sChoice ★ **Cameo.** Sophisticated and fun, this newly renovated disco-era-inspired club combines sleek with a state-of-the-art light and sound system to dazzle the senses. ✉ *1445 Washington Ave., South Beach* ☎ *305/532–2667.*

Fodor'sChoice ★ **Pearl.** An airy space lab of white and orange bathed in lavender light, this restaurant-cum-nightclub overlooks the ocean and is next door to Nikki Beach Club. ✉ *1 Ocean Dr., South Beach* ☎ *305/538–1111.*

Fodor'sChoice ★ **SkyBar at the Shore Club.** Splendor-in-the-garden is the theme at this haute spot by the sea, where multiple lounging areas are joined together. ✉ *1901 Collins Ave., South Beach* ☎ *305/695–3100.*

Fodor'sChoice ★ **Tobacco Road.** Opened in 1912, this classic holds Miami's oldest liquor license: No. 0001! This is the hangout of grizzled journalists, bohemians en route to or from nowhere, and club kids seeking a way station before the real parties begin. ✉ *626 S. Miami Ave., Downtown* ☎ *305/374–1198.*

KEY WEST

Capt. Tony's Saloon (✉ *428 Greene St.* ☎ *305/294–1838*) was the original Sloppy Joe's in the mid-1930s, when Hemingway was a regular. Later, a young Jimmy Buffett sang here and made this Key's watering hole famous in his song "Last Mango in Paris." Bands play nightly.

Belly up to the bar for a cold mug of the signature Hog's Breath Lager at the infamous **Hog's Breath Saloon** (✉ *7400 Front St.* ☎ *305/296–4222*), a must-stop on the Key West bar crawl. Live entertainment plays daily 10 AM–2 AM.

There's more history and good times at **Sloppy Joe's** (✉ *201 Duval St.* ☎ *305/294–5717*), the successor to a famous 1937 speakeasy named for its founder, Captain Joe Russell. Decorated with Hemingway memorabilia and marine flags, the bar is popular with travelers and is full and noisy all the time.

SHOPPING

MIAMI

Fodor'sChoice ★ **South Beach–Lincoln Road Mall.** This eight-block-long pedestrian mall is home to more than 150 shops, 20-plus art galleries and nightclubs, about 50 restaurants and cafés, and the renovated Colony Theatre. Do as the locals do, and meander along "the Road" day or night, stopping for refreshment at one of the top-flight bistros or open-air eateries. ✉ *Lincoln Rd. between Alton Rd. and Washington Ave., South Beach, Miami Beach* ☎ *305/672–1270.*

★ **Miami Design District.** Miami is synonymous with good design, and this visitor-friendly shopping district is an unprecedented melding of public space and the exclusive world of design. Covering a few city blocks around N.E. 2nd Avenue and N.E. 40th Street, the Design

District contains more than 200 showrooms and galleries, including Kartell, Ann Sacks, Poliform, and Luminaire. ⊠*N.E. 36th St. to N.E. 42nd St. between N.E. 2nd Ave. and N. Miami Ave., Design District, Miami* ⊕*www.miami designdistrict.net.*

THE KEYS

Duval Street. Key West's unabashedly trashy commercial strip can look like a mini–Las Vegas, with ubiquitous T-shirt shops and tour shills substituting for casinos. If you elbow your way through the gawking day-trippers, you can find colorful local art; all things key lime; a handful of boutiques carrying designer labels; and the raunchiest T-shirts, thongs, and costumes in the civilized world.

ON THE WAY

Redland: This agriculture enclave lies 40 minutes south of Miami. Top stops for gallivanting gourmets include Robert is Here, an oversize fruit stand; the Fruit & Spice Park, with 500 varieties of fruit, nut, and spice trees; and Schnebly Winery, which makes vino from mangos and other locally grown goodies.

Dry Tortugas National Park: 70 mi off Key West, this seven-island park is known to history buffs as the site of Fort Jefferson, one of the largest coastal forts ever built. (Dr. Samuel Mudd was imprisoned here for his role in the Lincoln assassination.)

SPORTS & THE OUTDOORS

MIAMI

FodorśChoice ★ The stretch of beach along **Ocean Drive**—primarily the 10-block stretch from 5th to 15th streets—is one of the most talked-about beachfronts in America. The beach is wide, white, and bathed by warm aquamarine waves. ⊠*Ocean Dr., between 1st and 22nd Sts., South Beach, Miami Beach* ☎*305/673–7714.*

FodorśChoice ★ Beyond Key Biscayne's commercial district, at the southern tip of the island, is **Bill Baggs Cape Florida State Park,** a natural oasis with an excellent swimming beach. The 410-acre park has a restored lighthouse, 18 picnic shelters, and a casual seafood restaurant. ⊠*1200 S. Crandon Blvd., Key Biscayne* ☎*305/361–5811 or 305/361–8779* 🗨*$1 per person on foot, bike, motorbike, or bus; $5 per vehicle up to 8 people* ☉*Daily 8–dusk, lighthouse tours Thurs.–Mon. 10 and 1.*

VISITOR INFORMATION

Florida Keys & Key West Visitors Bureau (⊠*402 Wall St., Box 1146, Key West, 33041* ☎*800/352–5397* ⊕*www.fla-keys.com*).

Florida Tourism Industry Marketing Corporation (Visit Florida) (☎*888/7FLA-USA automated* ⊕*www.visitflorida.com*).

Greater Miami Convention & Visitors Bureau (⊠*701 Brickell Ave., Suite 2700, Miami 33131* ☎*305/539–3000, 800/933–8448 in U.S.* ⊕*www.gmcvb.com*).

Kentucky Bluegrass Country

Keeneland Track, Lexington

WORD OF MOUTH

"We visited the Kentucky Horse Park this past July . . . The highlight for us was the thoroughbred Walk of Fame where they bring out the famous retired horses. Also, there is a live show with different breeds and they allow you to get up and touch the horses after the performances. My suggestion would be to go early, as soon as they open in the morning to avoid the crowds and the heat. Also, bring a picnic lunch."

—offlady

EXPLORING KENTUCKY BLUEGRASS COUNTRY

90 mi south of Cincinnati via I–71 and I–75; 375 mi southeast of Chicago via I–65 and I–64; 380 mi north of Atlanta via I–75; 490 mi west of Richmond via I–64.

By Susan Reigler

Postcard views along America's superhighways are rare, but that's exactly what travelers zipping along Interstate Highways 64 and 75 in central Kentucky see. For many miles, the routes are bounded by rolling, fenced pastures of emerald green bluegrass where Kentucky's famous Thoroughbred racehorses graze. In the distance are the graceful outlines of owners' mansions—and the equally expensive equine residences. (Most barns in horse country are climate-controlled.)

Visitors to Kentucky will find ample opportunities to interact with the horses. You can attend horse racing in Lexington or Louisville, visit museums dedicated to horses, or just enjoying the horse-rich scenery while driving along quieter roads, including Old Frankfort Pike, which meanders between farmsteads. Along with the history and the scenery, you can find charming hostelries where guests are pampered and award-winning restaurants that incorporate regional ingredients—including Kentucky's famed bourbon—in sophisticated dishes.

WHO WILL ESPECIALLY LOVE THIS TRIP?

Horse Lovers: The world's greatest population density of pedigreed racehorses lives on more than 460 farms in the area surrounding Lexington. A visit to the **Kentucky Horse Park** is essential for equine fans.

History Buffs: Elegant antebellum houses have become museums open to visitors. Tour the former homes of Henry Clay (Ashland), Mary Todd Lincoln (Mary Todd Lincoln House), George Rogers Clark (Locust Grove), and other prominent figures in Kentucky history.

Foodies: The state's award-winning restaurants include Lilly's in Louisville, Jonathan at Gratz Park in Lexington, and the Holly Hill Inn in Midway. Whiskey lovers should tour (and taste) at the Woodford Reserve bourbon distillery near Versailles.

Families: The Horse Park is a great place to take kids, and though they're too young to place bets, children are welcome at Churchill Downs and Keeneland racecourses. Other attractions like the Gorilla Forest and the Islands at the Louisville Zoo, as well as several great museums, will keep children (and adults) enthralled.

WHEN IS THE BEST TIME TO VISIT?

Springtime in the Kentucky Bluegrass is stunning. The pastures are deep green, bordered by blooming dogwoods and redbuds in all their white and pink glory. Foals born the previous winter frolic near their mothers in the pastures. You might hit a rainy day or two, but warm, sunny days are frequent, and the chilly nights are great for sleeping. Fall is also a fine season, and you'll be rewarded with colorful foliage

TOP 5 REASONS TO GO

Horse Farm Scenery: Tree-shaded lanes wind though some of the world's most beautiful landscape, home to the elegant Thoroughbreds who graze on the state's famous namesake bluegrass.

Kentucky Derby Festival: Three weeks of nonstop partying lead up to the first Saturday in May and the Greatest Two Minutes in Sports.

One-of-a-Kind Museums: You can find the world's largest baseball bat at the Louisville Slugger Museum and tiny, priceless bibelots at the Headley-Whitney Museum.

Kentucky Haute Cuisine: The region's chefs use locally produced Southern ingredients in tried-and-true dishes and contemporary creations.

Relaxing Getaways: Pamper yourself with a stay in one of Kentucky's historic bed-and-breakfasts or hotels.

12

along the country lanes. Summer, especially July, August, and most of September, can be hot and humid. If your winter visit coincides with an inch or two of snow, the horse farms will be every bit as beautiful as any other time of year—and bourbon's legendary warming properties will be especially welcome. The Kentucky Derby Festival is held in the two weeks prior to Derby Day (the first Saturday in May) at Churchill Downs in Louisville. The annual international cross-country and steeplechase Rolex Three-Day Event is also held during the later part of April at the Kentucky Horse Park outside Lexington.

HOW SHOULD I GET THERE?

DRIVING

Several interstate highways converge in Kentucky, and automobile access to the central portion of the state is excellent. I–64 passes straight through the center of Bluegrass Country, running east to west. Access from north or south is along I–75, which intersects with I–64 at Lexington. Take I–64 exits 58 or 65 for access to horse country drives. Exits 113 and 115 on the merged I–64/75 will take you into downtown Lexington. I–64 passes through downtown Louisville; the 3rd Street exit (5C) gives the best access to downtown attractions.

FLYING

Two airports—and virtually every American airline—serve central Kentucky. Louisville International Airport is just south of the city's downtown. Blue Grass Airport, with considerably fewer flights than Louisville, serves Lexington. The two cities are an hour apart by car.

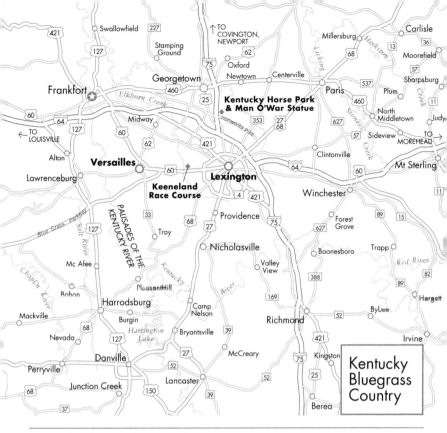

HOW DO I GET AROUND?

BY BICYCLE

If you ride, bring your bike to the Bluegrass. Many of the rolling, two-lane roads that run along the horse farm boundaries are favorite routes for cyclists.

BY CAR

The bus systems of both Louisville and Lexington are limited, and cabs are usually found only around hotels or airports. Traveling by car is the easiest and best way to get around both cities and the surrounding countryside. Downtown Lexington traffic always seems slow, so allow plenty of time to get to your destinations. Interstate traffic around Louisville gets heavy during the morning and evening commutes.

WHERE SHOULD I FOCUS MY ENERGY?

If you're here for 1 day: If your time is limited and you want a flavor of horse country, take one of the daylong van tours of horse farms and **Keeneland** race course that depart from downtown Lexington hotels.

If you're here for 2 days: Spend a morning at the **Kentucky Horse Park**, enjoy lunch in nearby Lexington, and meander along the roads around

How to Snack

CLOSE UP

The denizens of central Kentucky don't really snack. They tend to savor sit-down lunches and dinners, very much in keeping with the region's small city, semi-rural pace of life. Naturally, an important component of dining and entertaining is the "sippage." Given the ready supply of corn for fermenting and white oak for making barrels, Kentucky became an important whiskey-making center early in its history. By law bourbon is distilled from fermented grain that must be at least 51% corn. Other grains in the formula (the "mash bill") are barley and rye or wheat; wheated bourbons tend to be fruitier, while those containing rye are spicier. After fermentation, the whiskey must be aged in charred, never-before-used white oak barrels for at least two years. (Most are aged for five to seven years.)

Bourbon is definitely the state beverage. Locals drink it before dinner with a splash of water ("bourbon and branch"), or in cocktails such as the Old Fashioned (invented in Louisville in the 19th century) or the Manhattan. Favorite brands are Woodford Reserve, Maker's Mark, and Buffalo Trace. After dinner, high-proof bourbons with multiple layers of flavors are savored in snifters. Pappy Van Winkle, Wild Turkey Russell's Reserve, and Booker's are among the best; a drop or two of water releases their complex bouquets.

By the way, you can be instantly marked as a "foreigner" if you go into a bar or restaurant and order a mint julep—outside of Derby weekend, no one touches the drink. Kentuckians know not to ruin good bourbon with mint-infused sugar syrup and too much crushed ice. In fact, all the juleps served at Churchill Downs are made with Early Times, which is technically not "bourbon" but "Kentucky whiskey" since it's aged in *used* oak barrels.

the horse farms in the afternoon. (This could be an alternate one-day itinerary, too.)

If you're here for 3 days: Visit the **Headley-Whitney Museum** and lunch and shop along Main Street in nearby **Midway.**

If you're here for 4 days: Tour a couple of the historic homes in or near Lexington, such as Ashland, the Hunt-Morgan House, the Mary Todd Lincoln House, or White Hall.

If you're here for 5 days: Take a bourbon distillery tour at Woodford Reserve.

If you're here for 6 days: Head to Louisville and visit the Kentucky Derby Museum at Churchill Downs and watch some races if you are visiting during the spring or fall race meets.

If you're here for 7 days or more: Linger in Louisville to see attractions such as the Louisville Slugger Museum and Locust Grove and check out the city's restaurant scene.

CLAIM TO FAME

The horse-racing tradition is the state's most famous, and Kentuckians are justly proud of it. Great Thoroughbreds foaled in Kentucky include Man O' War, Citation, and Seattle Slew. Slew, who was purchased for a mere $17,000 at the Keeneland yearling sales, went on to win the Triple Crown in 1977 and command million of dollars in stud fees. (The horse racing and breeding business amounts to a multi*billion* dollar industry in the state.)

You can see evidence of the love of horses everywhere, from street names (Man O' War Boulevard is a major Lexington thoroughfare) to statues. Colorfully painted, life-size horses are fixtures of street art in Louisville and Lexington. Shops sell hundreds of equine-inspired items,

from jewelry and clothing to art and hand-painted furniture. Louisville's Kentucky Derby Festival easily rivals New Orleans' Mardi Gras as a community party, kicking off with the country's largest fireworks display, "Thunder Over Louisville." It continues for two weeks with a hot air balloon race, a marathon, a steamboat race, the Pegasus Parade, dozens of charity balls, and thousands of private parties. (Don't worry, if you're in town during this time, you'll get invitations to at least half a dozen.)

Outside of Louisville, the Governor of Kentucky hosts a Derby Breakfast on the grounds of the state capitol, and many Derby Eve balls are held on the horse farm estates around Lexington.

WHAT ARE THE TOP EXPERIENCES?

The Horses: In many ways, Kentucky is the Horse capital of the World. Not only does it have the largest number of horse farms, it is also, of course, the home of the Kentucky Derby, run the first Saturday in May at Louisville's Churchill Downs. As you might expect, America's longest continuously held sporting event is seeped in tradition, (the first Derby was in 1875), so if you're ever going to drink a mint julep, do it on Derby Day.

The History: Kentucky became a state in 1790, while Washington was president. It was an important area in the establishment of the United States west of the Appalachians and was hotly contested during the Civil War. Birthplace of both Abraham Lincoln and Jefferson Davis, it was a slave state that never seceded from the Union. Both leaders had ties to the Bluegrass—Lincoln courted his wife in her Lexington home, and Davis attended Lexington's Transylvania University. Senator Henry Clay made his home in Lexington, as did his cousin, the colorful emancipationist and newspaper publisher, Cassius Marcellus Clay.

Food & Drink: There's much, much more to Kentucky cuisine than fried chicken. (Though the true, panfried version is one of America's great dishes.) Sample traditional favorites such as salty, smoke-cured country ham, flavorfully sweet Bibb lettuce, cheddar grits, panfried quail, and, in season, venison. The must-have dessert is bread pudding with bourbon sauce. Many restaurants serve a mix of the classic dishes and updates that incorporate regional delicacies. Think you don't like fried chicken livers? You may reassess when you encounter them bathed in a lemony cream sauce. More and more wineries are springing up on the sites of former tobacco farms; several are in the Bluegrass and offer tours, concerts, and tastings. And speaking of tastings, treat yourself to a snifter of really fine bourbon as an after-dinner drink. Virtually all of the region's better restaurants have extensive lists, and the staff can give you advice on selection.

Southern Hospitality: At the historic hotels and bed-and-breakfasts of Louisville, Lexington, and the countryside in between, you'll be greeted as a long-lost relative, not a mere guest. The emphasis on service is very apparent here. In many of the B&Bs (many of which overlook the horse farms), it's likely that

> **HISTORY YOU CAN SEE**
>
> Kentucky was the 15th state and the first west of the Appalachians. General George Rogers Clark, who founded Louisville, was responsible for capturing the Northwest Territory from the British during the Revolutionary War. Frontiersman Daniel Boone traversed the state, and there are many historic markers in Kentucky about his activities. Driving around the countryside, you can come across many 18th and 19th century stone or brick buildings—even a few log cabins. Most of the historic home museums in the region are linked to important Civil War era figures, such as Lincoln and members of the Clay family.

you'll be sleeping in an antique bed. Breakfasts, cooked to order by the hosts, are so filling that you may need to skip lunch.

BEST BETS

SIGHTS AND TOURS

Ashland. This 18-room brick mansion was the country home of Senator Henry Clay and his family for more than four decades. The tour highlights antebellum Kentucky plantation life and the political achievements of Clay, who served both in the U.S. House of Representatives (as Speaker) and in the U.S. Senate. ⊠ *120 Sycamore Rd., Lexington* ☎ *859/266–8581* ⊕ *www.henryclay.org* 🕙 *$7* ⊙ *Feb., weekends by appointment; Mar., Nov., and Dec., Tues.–Sat., 10–4, Sun. 1–4; Apr.–Oct., Mon.–Sat. 10–4, Sun. 1–4.*

★ **Bluegrass Tours.** Lexington's oldest tour company takes visitors to horse farms, Keeneland racetrack, and historic venues in Lexington. It's an excellent introduction to the area, especially if you only have a day or two in the region. ⊠ *817 Enterprise Dr., Lexington* ☎ *800/755–6956* ⊕ *www.bluegrasstours.com* 🕙 *$26* ⊙ *Daily tours at 9:30 and 1:30. Must be booked at least three days in advance.*

Fodor's Choice ★ **Churchill Downs and the Kentucky Derby Museum.** Exhibits here recount the history of America's oldest sporting event and include a surround-sound film of the race. Admission includes a tour of the historic racetrack; in summer visitors can tour the stable areas as well. The café overlooks a paddock occupied by a retired racehorse. ✉ *704 Central Ave., Louisville* ☎ *502/637–1111* ⊕ *www.derbymuseum.org* 🎫 *$10* 🕐 *Mar. 15–Nov. 30, Mon.–Sat. 8–5, Sun. 11–5; Dec. 1–Mar. 14, Mon.–Sat. 9–5, Sun. 11–5.*

Equus Run Vineyards. Thirty-five rolling acres are planted in several kinds of grapes, but you won't mistake this for Napa Valley. As the name suggests, horses are grazing in the Bluegrass pasture just over the fence. ✉ *1220 Moore's Mill Rd., Midway* ☎ *859/846–9463* ⊕ *www.equusrunvineyards.com* 🎫 *Free; additional charge for concerts* 🕐 *Nov.–Mar., Tues.–Sat. 11–5; Apr.–Oct., Tues.–Sat. 11–7.*

> **STRANGE BUT TRUE**
>
> Why are there so many horse farms in the Bluegrass? It's the soil. Limestone makes up the geological underpinning of central Kentucky. The mineral found in limestone is calcium carbonate, and when water comes in contact with the rock, it gradually wears away the surface, releasing calcium into the topsoil and the stream water. So the bluegrass on which the horses are grazing and the water they're drinking is rich in the mineral they need to develop strong bones in their long, fragile racing legs.

Headley-Whitney Museum. George W. Headley was a prominent designer of jewelry and small decorative art objects known as bibelots. Dozens of his pieces are on display here in a museum on his former estate. ✉ *4435 Old Frankfort Pike, Lexington* ☎ *859/255–6653* ⊕ *www.headley-whitney.org* 🎫 *$7* 🕐 *Tues.–Fri. 10–5, weekends noon–5.*

Hunt-Morgan House. John Wesley Hunt, the first millionaire west of the Appalachians, built this Federal-style house in Lexington's Gratz Park district in the early 1800s. His grandson, John Hunt Morgan was a Confederate cavalry officer. Family furniture decorates the house, which also has a small Civil War museum. ✉ *201 N. Mill St., Lexington* ☎ *859/233–3290* 🎫 *$7* 🕐 *Mar.–Nov., Wed.–Fri 1–5, Sat. 10–4, Sun. 1–4.*

Fodor's Choice
★ **Kentucky Horse Park.** Tour the International Museum of the Horse, run in cooperation with the Smithsonian Institution. In addition to viewing the many exhibits on the ancient relationship between people and horses, you'll also be able to get close to real horses. There's a Parade of Breeds, horse-drawn carriage rides, and a 45-minute trail ride around the park—suitable even for those who've never ridden before. The park also houses the American Saddlebred Museum (that's the breed used for dressage). Tours of nearby horse farms are available for an extra fee. ✉ *4089 Iron Works Pike, Lexington* ☎ *859/233–4303* ⊕ *www.kyhorsepark.com* 🎫 *$15* 🕐 *Mar. 15–Oct. 31, daily 9–5; Nov. 1–Mar. 14, Wed.–Sun. 9–5.*

Locust Grove. This redbrick Georgian plantation house was built around 1790 by William and Lucy Croghan, who was George Rogers Clark's sister (the Revolutionary War hero and founder of Louisville lived here during the last nine years of his life). The 55-acre grounds include eight outbuildings and restored gardens; the last tour departs at 3:30. ✉ *561 Blankenbaker La., Louisville* ☎ *502/897–9845* ⊕ *www.locustgrove.org* 🎫 *$6* 🕐 *Mon.–Sat., 10–4:30, Sun. 1–4:30.*

★ **Louisville Slugger Museum & Factory.** You can't miss this place—a seven-story baseball bat leans against the building housing the museum and bat factory. (An appropriately sized baseball is imbedded in one window of the plate glass factory next door, too.) Step up to the plate at the very scary virtual pitching diamond. Autographed bats of virtually every baseball great are also on display. ⊠*800 W. Main St., Louisville* ☎*502/588-7228* ⊕*www. sluggermuseum.org* ⊠*$9* ⊙*Mid-Aug.–June 30, daily Mon.–Sat. 9–5, Sun. noon–5; July 1–mid-Aug., daily Mon.–Sat. 9–6, Sun. noon–6.*

Louisville Zoo. More than 1,300 animals from around the world live here in landscaped settings. The Gorilla Forest, home to Lowland Gorillas, is an award-winning exhibit; birds will perch on your shoulder at Lorikeet Landing. Other zoo residents include polar bears, lions, tigers, penguins, timber wolves, and Komodo dragons. ⊠*1100 Trevilian Way, Louisville* ☎*502/459-2181* ⊕*www.louisvillezoo.org* ⊠*$12* ⊙*Mar.–June, daily 10–5; July and Aug., Sun.–Wed. 10–5, Thurs.–Sat. 10–8; Sept.–Feb., daily 10–4.*

Mary Todd Lincoln House. This two-story Georgian house, built from 1803 to 1806, was originally an inn. Abraham Lincoln courted Mary Todd, who lived here with her parents, when he came to visit Kentucky friends. This was the first historic site to be restored in honor of a First Lady. ⊠*578 W. Main St., Lexington* ☎*859/233-9999* ⊕*www. mtlhouse.org* ⊠*$7* ⊙*Mar. 15–Nov. 30, Mon.–Sat. 10–4.*

★ **Woodford Reserve Distillery.** Limestone buildings dating from the early 19th century have been restored to operation for distilling, aging, and bottling Woodford Reserve bourbon. At the end of the distillery tour, guests 21 and over can sample the whiskey. ⊠*7855 McCracken Pike, Versailles* ☎*859/879-1812* ⊕*www.woodfordreserve.com* ⊠*$5* ⊙*Apr.–Oct., Tues.–Sat. 9–5, Sun. 12:30–4:30.*

WHERE TO EAT

	WHAT IT COSTS			
	¢	$	$$	$$$	$$$$
AT DINNER	under $8	$8–$12	$13–$18	$19–$25	over $25

Prices are per person for a main course at dinner.

$$$$ ✕**Holly Hill Inn.** Chef–owner Ouita Michel uses locally grown meats and produce to create her five-course prix-fixe menus. These change every two weeks and may be Southern, French, Southwestern or any cuisine that strikes her fancy. The restaurant has multiple dining rooms in an old Southern mansion with a wraparound porch, where alfresco dining is offered in summer. Wine pairings are available for an additional charge. ⊠*426 N. Winter St., Midway* ☎*859/846–4732* ✍*Reservations required* ▭*AE, MC, V* ⊘*Closed Mon. and Tues.*

$$$–$$$$ ✕**Jonathan at Gratz Park.** Linen-covered tables in the formal dining room add to the old-world charm of this restaurant, but the wood-paneled bar with roaring fireplace feels cozier. Be sure to start your meal with fried green tomatoes, a Southern classic. Entrées include blackened salmon with crawfish corn pudding, and a bacon-wrapped filet mignon with bourbon demi glace. ⊠*120 W. 2nd St., Lexington* ☎*859/252–4949* ▭*AE, MC, V* ⊘*Closed Mon.*

$$$–$$$$ ✕**Lilly's.** Chef–proprietor Kathy Cary is Kentucky's most honored chef. She emphasizes local ingredients in dishes with Southern and Continental influences; her creations range from Kentucky tapas (a changing selection of light bites) to a nightly version of veal scallopine (sauces and sides change). The contemporary purple and deep green dining rooms will make you feel like you're dining in an elegant private home. ⊠*1147 Bardstown Rd., Louisville* ☎*502/451–0447* ✍*Reservations required* ▭*AE, MC, V* ⊘*Closed Sun. and Mon.*

$$–$$$$ ✕**Limestone.** High-end comfort food is served up here, including the excellent braised beef short ribs with smoky beans and collard greens. Grilled chops or fish come with sides such as crawfish corn pudding or the "grits du jour." Both the wine and bourbon lists are excellent. ⊠*10001 Forest Green Blvd., Louisville* ☎*502/426–7477* ▭*AE, D, MC, V* ⊘*No dinner Sun.*

$$–$$$$ ✕**Merrick Inn.** In an antebellum farmhouse that was the center of a horse farm, the Merrick Inn's dining rooms are filled with antiques. Southern fried chicken, pork tenderloin, and rainbow trout are traditional favorites here; there's also a selection of steaks, and lobster tail is available. Old-fashioned desserts include peach Melba. ⊠*3380 Tates Creek Rd., Lexington* ☎*859/269–5417* ▭*AE, MC, V* ⊘*Closed Sun.*

$–$$$$ ✕**Bourbons Bistro.** If you want to learn more about Kentucky's amber elixir, this is the place to come—they have virtually every bourbon currently in production (more than 120 or them). Tasting flights are available. The menu, which ranges from burger to sea bass, includes Southern favorites like pan seared pork chop and bacon-wrapped scallops. Naturally, bourbon is an ingredient in many dishes. ⊠*2255 Frankfort Ave., Louisville* ☎*502/894–8838* ▭*AE, MC, V.*

WHERE TO STAY

	WHAT IT COSTS IN U.S. DOLLARS				
	¢	$	$$	$$$	$$$$
FOR 2 PEOPLE	under $75	$75–$125	$126–$175	$176–$225	over $225

Prices are for a standard double room for two during peak season

12

ON THE WAY

Abraham Lincoln's Birthplace National Historic Site. The 16th president was born in a one-room log cabin here on his parents' Kentucky farm on February 12, 1809. A replica log cabin is preserved inside a stone memorial reached by climbing 56 steps, one for each year of Lincoln's life. The visitor center has a series of exhibits, including a short film about the Great Emancipator. 2995 Lincoln Farm Road (U.S. 31 E), Hodgenville, 270/358-3137. Free. Open daily. Labor Day–Memorial Day: 8 AM–4:45PM; Memorial Day–Labor Day: 8 AM–6:45 PM

Mammoth Cave National Park. A variety of guided tours of different portions of the 365-mi cave system are available. They emphasize geology, history, or animal life. Casual visitors to serious spelunkers are accommodated. 1 Mammoth Cave Pkwy., Mammoth Cave, 270/758-2180. Cave tours, $5–$48. Open daily.

$$–$$$$ 🛏️**Bed & Breakfast at Silver Springs Farm.** This place is the ultimate Bluegrass B&B—your horse can spend the night in the on-site barn while you sleep in the handsome, 1880 Federal-style farmhouse. The B&B is on 21 picturesque acres near the Kentucky Horse Park. ⊠3710 Leestown Pike, Lexington, 40511 ☎859/255–1784 ⊕www.bbsilver springsfarm.com ➦3 rooms ⚷In-room: no phone, VCR, Wi-Fi. In-hotel: no elevator, restaurant (breakfast only), parking (no fee), some pets allowed, no kids under 12, no-smoking rooms ⊟MC, V.

$$–$$$$ 🏨**Gratz Park Inn.** This small, European-style hotel is on the edge of historic Gratz Park. The Federalist–Georgian architecture and decor are inviting, and the house reportedly is home to a friendly ghost. ⊠120 W. 2nd St., Lexington, 40507 ☎800/752–4166 ⊕www.gratzparkinn. com ➦44 rooms ⚷In-room: refrigerator (some), Ethernet. In-hotel: restaurant, bar, room service, laundry service, concierge, parking (no fee), no-smoking rooms ⊟AE, D, DC, MC, V.

$$–$$$$ 🏨**Seelbach Hilton Hotel.** Seven U.S. presidents and such notables as gangster Al Capone, the Duchess of York, and author F. Scott Fitzgerald (who set a scene in *The Great Gatsby* here) have stayed at this historic hotel, which celebrated its 100 anniversary in 2005. Check out the live jazz in the bar off the lobby before retiring to your four-poster for the night. ⊠500 S. 4th St., Louisville, 40202 ☎502/585–3200 ⊕www. seelbachhilton.com ➦321 rooms ⚷In-room: refrigerator (some), Ethernet. In-hotel: 3 restaurants, 2 bars, room service, gym, spa, laundry service, concierge, airport shuttle, parking (fee), some pets allowed, no-smoking rooms ⊟AE, D, DC, MC, V.

$–$$ 🏨**Brown Hotel.** Opened in 1923, this grand-but-intimate hotel has a gilded second-floor lobby that gleams with marble and polished wood. Rooms are furnished with fine reproductions and luxurious bedding. A special Louisville dish, the Hot Brown, was invented here—you can order the turkey/bacon/cheese sandwich–casserole hybrid from room service. ⊠335 W. Broadway, Louisville, 40202 ☎502/583–1234 ⊕www.brownhotel.com ➦293 rooms ⚷In-room: refrigerator (some), VCR (some), Ethernet. In-hotel: 3 restaurants, 2 bars, room *service, gym, laundry service, concierge, public Wi-Fi, airport shuttle, parking (fee), some pets allowed, no-smoking rooms* ▭AE, D, DC, MC, V.

VISITOR INFORMATION

Kentucky Department of Tourism ☎ *800/225-8747* ⊕ *www.kentuckytourism.com.*

Lexington Convention and Visitors Bureau ☎ *800/845-3959* ⊕ *www.visitlex.com.*

Louisville Convention and Visitors Bureau ☎ *800/626-5646* ⊕ *www.gotolouisville.com.*

VITAL STATS

■ State Name: Accounts of the origin vary, but most agree that Kentucky is an Indian name—possibly Wyandot for "Land of Tomorrow" or Iroquois for "Land of Meadows."

■ State Song: "My Old Kentucky Home," composed by Stephen Collins Foster, was supposedly inspired by visits to his Kentucky cousins in Bardstown.

■ Greatest Paradox: Kentucky Is the world's largest producer of bourbon, distilling about 95% of the supply—but almost half of the state's 120 counties are dry.

Tennessee

Great Smoky Mountains National Park

WORD OF MOUTH

"Check out what's playing at the Bluebird Cafe [in Nashville]. Always entertaining and always reasonably priced. You'll see quality live acts that you won't find anywhere else in the country for that value. They have a website, and you can book advance tickets over the web."

—stumpworks73

EXPLORING TENNESSEE

Nashville is 249 mi northwest of Atlanta via I–75 and I–24; 174 mi southwest of Louisville, KY, via I–65; 306 mi southeast of St. Louis via I–64, I–57, and I–24; and 214 mi northeast of Memphis via I-40.

By MiChelle Jones

Historically, Tennessee embodies a courageous pioneer spirit, harkening back to the days when settlers fed up with colonial life in Virginia and North Carolina crossed the mountains and settled in what is now Knoxville.

There are three stars in the Tennessee state flag, each representing one of the distinct regions of the state: East Tennessee, Middle Tennessee, and West Tennessee. These three areas differ not only in landscape—mountains and heavily forested hillsides in the east, rolling hills in the middle, and flat, fertile land in the west—but also in the attitudes of the residents and the ambience of the cities and towns found there.

Memphis is about as far west as you can get in the state, tucked into the southwest corner on the eastern banks of the Mississippi River. The colorful history of the Delta region, along with flavorful barbecue and soulful music give Memphis a unique atmosphere. Nashville, in the middle of the state, is the center of state government, a hub of the nation's health-care industry and home to several universities and colleges—and the laid-back heart of the country music industry. Natural beauty abounds in the eastern part of the state, where the Great Smoky Mountains cross over into North Carolina.

WHO WILL ESPECIALLY LOVE THIS TRIP?

Music Buffs: Whether you consider Memphis the "home of the blues" or the "birthplace of rock 'n' roll," there's no denying that the city has had a lasting effect on the music (and larger culture) of the world. Blues lovers should gravitate to Beale Street's clubs, while Elvis fans will want to make a pilgrimage to Graceland. Country music fans should head to Nashville for visits to the Ryman Auditorium, the Grand Ole Opry, and the Country Music Hall of Fame.

Families: Take the kids camping or hiking in the one of Tennessee's many national, state, and municipal parks. Or, learn about sea life during a visit to Chattanooga's Tennessee Aquarium (⊠*1Broad St., 37402* ☎*800/262–0695* ⊕*www.tnaqua.org*)or Gatlinburg's Ripley's Aquarium of the Smokies (⊠*88 River Rd. 37738* ☎*865/430–8808* ⊕*www.ripleysaquariumofthesmokies.com*). You can also squeeze in a history lesson at Nashville's Tennessee State Museum (⊠*505 Deaderick St., Downtown, 37243* ☎*615/741–2692 or 800/407–4324* ⊕*www.tnmuseum.org*)or Memphis' Fire Museum, but the ultimate kid-friendly museum experiences may be Nashville's Adventure Science Museum (⊠*800 Fort Negley Blvd., 37203* ☎*615/862–5160* ⊕*www.adventuresci.com*)and the Memphis Children's Museum (⊠*2525 Central Ave., Midtown, 38104* ☎*901/458–2678 or 901/320–3170* ⊕*www.cmom.com*).

TOP 5 REASONS TO GO

Music: Whether your taste leans toward blues, early rock 'n' roll, or soul, Memphis is not to be missed. Nashville, aka Music City USA, is the home to the mother church of country music and a thriving music publishing industry.

History: Tennessee has played a key role in our nation's history: it's seen everything from trailblazing pioneers to Civil War battles to WPA projects (such as the Tennessee Valley Authority) to civil rights events. The state is peppered with battlefields, dams, national parks, and other sites that are testaments to this rich legacy.

Culture: The state is chock-full of galleries and craft workshops, performing arts companies, and museums filled with historical artifacts and great works of art.

Nature: The Great Smoky Mountains form Tennessee's eastern border, and the Mississippi River forms the western border. In between there are lakes, rivers, waterfalls, and limestone bluffs galore for outdoor enthusiasts.

Food: Memphis is the barbecue capital of the state, though you can find excellent 'cue all over Tennessee. You can also find the ubiquitous "meat-and-three" plates throughout the state.

Civil War Buffs: There's no shortage of battlefields and sites to explore in Tennessee, including Stones River National Battlefield (⊠*3501 Old Nashville Hwy., 37129* ☎*615/794-0903* ⊕*www.nps.gov/stri*)in Murfreesboro and Franklin's Carnton Plantation (⊠*1345 Carnton La., 37064* ☎*615/794–0903* ⊕*www.carnton.org*), which served as a Confederate field hospital during the bloody Battle of Franklin.

Nature Lovers: With the Smoky Mountains on one end of the state, wetland areas of the Mississippi River on the other; and valleys, lakes, rocky cliffs, and woodlands sprinkled throughout, Tennessee is a nature lover's paradise. Hiking, camping, hunting, boating, and fishing are popular pastimes here.

Homes and Garden Devotees: If you find yourself addicted to HGTV (whose headquarters are in Knoxville) and home interiors magazines, you can find plenty to see in Tennessee. Belle Meade Plantation (⊠*5025 Harding Rd., Belle Meade, 37205* ☎*615/356–0501* ⊕*www. bellemeadeplantation.com*)and Cheekwood Botanical Garden and Museum of Art are in Nashville; the Hermitage, the home of Andrew Jackson, is just east of Nashville; and Memphis is home to the Woodruff-Fontaine House (⊠*680 Adams Ave., 38105* ☎*901/526–1469* ⊕*www.woodruff-fontaine.com*)and the Dixon Gallery and Gardens. You might also consider Elvis's Graceland worthy of a visit—after all, it's now on the National Register of Historic Places.

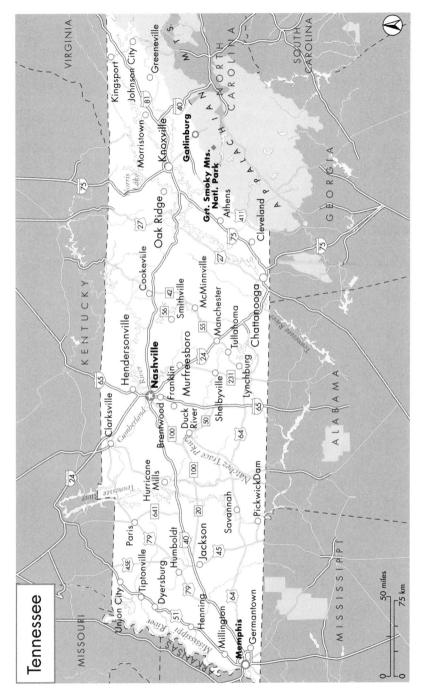

Tennessee

50 miles
75 km

WHEN IS THE BEST TIME TO VISIT?

During the height of summer, Tennessee is hot and humid—especially in July and August (though it's cooler in the mountains). The best times to visit Tennessee are early spring, when temperatures are pleasantly mild and everything seems to be in bloom, and during the long autumn, which begins in late September and lasts well into November. Shorts and short sleeves can often be worn until late October, and fall colors are especially vivid from late September through late October (later in drier years). Winter in the mountains and January through February can be rather cold in the middle part of the state, but overall, the climate here is relatively mild year-round.

Festivals are held throughout the year, mostly during the warmer months. Major events include Awesome April in Nashville, a month packed with events such as the Country Music Marathon, Tin Pan South Songwriters Festival, Gospel Music Association Gospel Week and the Dove Awards, Nashville Film Festival, and the CMT Music Awards. The Memphis International Film Festival also takes place in April; in May, the city also hosts the World Championship Barbecue Cooking Contest and the Beale Street Music Festival.

In June country music fans descend on Nashville for the CMA Music Festival, while rock fans gather on a farm in Manchester (about 60 mi southeast of Nashville) for four days of the Bonnaroo Music and Arts Festival. Elvis fans head to Memphis in droves to pay tribute to the king during Elvis Week in August.

HOW SHOULD I GET THERE?

DRIVING
Tennessee is bordered by eight states (Kentucky, Virginia, North Carolina, Georgia, Alabama, Mississippi, Arkansas and Missouri), making it incredibly accessible by car. I–40 traverses the state, connecting it to North Carolina in the east and Arkansas in the west. I–65 runs north and south through Tennessee, leading to Indiana to the north and Alabama to the south. Georgia lies to the southeast via I–24.

FLYING
Flying into Tennessee is also easy. Nashville International Airport is served by the major carriers, as is Memphis International Airport.

HOW DO I GET AROUND?

BY CAR
Unless your trip is focused on one city, you'll probably need a car to get around. In congested downtown areas, you may have to search for a parking garage—but in general it's easier to park here than, say, Chicago's Loop.

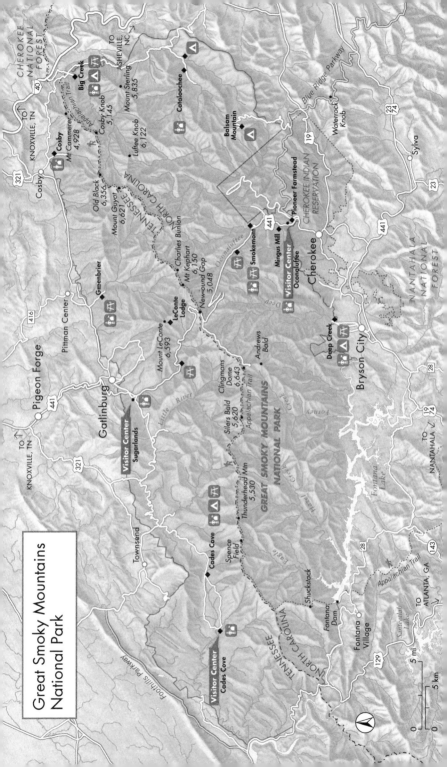

Great Smoky Mountains National Park

How to Snack

CLOSE UP

13

Everyone knows you can find good barbecue in Tennessee, but you'll have to decide whether you're a "wet" or "dry" fan. Wet (heavy on thick sauce) is good, but try a rack of ribs dry-rubbed with spice ("dry" is a bit of a misnomer, as sauce is involved) and you may just switch sides. Corky's does both, visit them in Memphis (5259 Poplar Ave., East Memphis ☎ 901/685–9744 ⊕ www. corkysbbq.com)or in Brentwood, just south of Nashville (✉ 100 Franklin Rd., 37027 ☎ 615/373–1020 ⊕ www. corkysbrentwood.com).

Another staple of Tennessee cuisine is the "meat-and-three," or meat and three vegetables. This being the South, "vegetables" can mean anything from turnip greens, squash, and black-eyed peas to macaroni-and-cheese. Order a piece of cornbread (sweet or nonsweet) or a biscuit on the side. And to drink? You can't get more down-home than a tall glass of iced tea, *sweet* tea, of course. You can sample this cuisine all over Tennessee; in Nashville try Sylvan Park (✉ 4502 Murphy Rd. ☎ 615/292–9275)or Swett's (✉ 2725 Clifton Ave. ☎ 615/329–4418 ✉ Farmers Market, 900 8th Ave. N ☎ 615/742–0699), for a soul food version. In Memphis grab a table at the Four-Way (✉ 998 Mississippi Blvd. ☎ 901/507–1519)or stop by Alcenia's (✉ 317 N. Main St., Pinch District, 38103 ☎ 901/523–0200).

BY TAXI

Average cab fare in Memphis is about $1.50 per mi. In Nashville, the meter starts at $3 ($4.50 at the airport), with $1 charge per extra person and $2 for each additional mi.

BY TROLLEY

Trolleylike vehicles in Nashville and Chattanooga travel limited tourist routes.

Gatlinburg's trolleys are color-coded by route and vehicle, and run on an environmentally friendly mix of B20 bio-diesel. You'll probably want to park your car once you reach the city. This is a very small place, directions and locations are given by traffic light number. Fares: 50 cents on Red, Blue and Purple routes; $1 on the Yellow, Pink. Exact change is required.

Meanwhile Memphis has real trolleys, refurbished antique specimens that run along three routes: Main Street, Madison Avenue, and the Riverfront Loop. The base fare is $1. Details are available at www. matatransit.com.

WHERE SHOULD I FOCUS MY ENERGY?

If you're here for 1 day: Hit Nashville. Spend the day in the downtown area visiting museums and shops, and hanging out at Riverfront Park overlooking the Cumberland River.

If you're here for 2 days: If you're not staying at Nashville's Gaylord Opryland Hotel, by all means go check it out. The indoor landscaping and sheer scale of the complex are amazing. There are many dining options, and there's an outlet center with an IMAX theater across the street.

If you're here for 3 days: Take a trip out to the Hermitage, home of Andrew Jackson, or stay in town for a visit to Cheekwood Botanical Garden and Museum of Art, a historic house and art museum.

If you're here for 4 days: Drive three hours west to Memphis and experience Beale Street, visit the National Civil Rights Museum, and see the mighty Mississippi.

If you're here for 5 days: Spend the night in Memphis at the Peabody Hotel (or at least watch the daily Duck March) and see the city via the South Main Trolley Tour (☎*901/274–6282* ⊕*www.matatransit.com*), or a Heritage Tour concentrating on African-American history (☎*901/527–3427* ⊕*www.heritagetoursmemphis.com*).

If you're here for 6 days: Take a trip to the other end of the state for a day in Chattanooga.

If you're here for 7 days or more: Head to the Gatlinburg/Pigeon Forge area to enjoy the beauty of the Smoky Mountains

WHAT ARE THE TOP EXPERIENCES?

The Music: Blues lovers should gravitate to Beale Street's clubs, and also tour the W.C. Handy Museum (⊠*352 Beale St., at 4th St., Beale Street Historic District, 38103* ☎*901/527–3427 or 901/522–1556*), home of the man who wrote "Memphis Blues," the first published blues song. Elvis fans will want to spend a lot of time at Graceland, especially during Elvis week in mid-August, and Sun Studio, where he cut his first record. Also in Memphis, two museums explore soul music, Soulsville: The Stax Records Museum and the Memphis Rock 'n' Soul Museum. Over in Nashville, country music steals the show, and even nonfans will enjoy the near acoustic perfection of the Ryman Auditorium, the Grand Ole Opry, and the Country Music Hall of Fame. The Musician's Hall of Fame (⊠*301 6th Ave. S, Downtown* ☎*615/244–3263* ⊕*www.musicianshalloffame.com*) pays tribute to the session players, as well as big-name musicians who recorded the sounds we all love.

Nashville: If you think Nashville has only music to offer, you're in for a surprise. This is the state capital, and you should check out the capitol building while you're here, even if it's just a glance from Bicentennial Capitol Mall State Park (⊠*600 James Robertson Pkwy., Downtown* ☎*615/741–5280*). Afterward, stop in the nearby Farmers Market (⊠*600 James Robertson Pkwy., Downtown, 37208* ☎*615/741–5280*)for a quick snack. Make your way over to 2nd Avenue and Lower Broadway, a tourist haven with shops, restaurants, and clubs. Next, walk over the Shelby Street Pedestrian Bridge (have someone take your picture with the skyline in the background) for an up-close look at LP Field, home of the Tennessee Titans (⊕*www.titansonline.com*)and site of the annual Music City Bowl. If you have time, drive across one of the bridges spanning the Cumberland River to see lovingly restored

CLAIM TO FAME

Tennessee is known for many things, not the least of which are certain forms of music and a particular way of preparing pork. But the state is also known for horses and liquor (what, you thought those things only came from Kentucky?)—specifically Tennessee Walking Horses and Jack Daniel's Whiskey.

Gentle-natured Tennessee Walking Horses provide a smooth ride courtesy of their distinctive rolling gait. The horses actually have three "speeds": a flat-foot walk, a running walk, and a canter. And though they're often associated with shows—particularly the 11-day Tennessee Walking Horse National Celebration that draws nearly 250,000 people to Shelbyville each year—these are also working horses. Tennessee Walking Horses are ridden by policemen, cattle ranchers, and trail explorers. According to the Shelbyville Chamber of Commerce, the breed's gene pool draws from: "Thoroughbreds from Virginia and England, Morgans from Vermont, American Saddlebreds from Kentucky, and Standard breeds from Ohio and the Midwest. Also included, more distantly, are the Canadian and Narraganset Pacers and Arabians."

To visit horse farms in the area, contact the Shelbyville Chamber of Commerce (☎ 931/684–3482 ⊕ www.shelbyvilletn.com). You can also learn more at the Tennessee Walking Horse Museum (☎ 931/759–5747), on the town square in neighboring Lynchburg.

You may also want to visit Lynchburg for another reason—the town is home to the Jack Daniel's Distillery (✉ 280 Lynchburg Hwy, 37352 ☎ 931/759-4221 ⊕ www.jackdaniels.com), where visitors can learn about the distillery's legendary founder and the production of the world-famous beverage. You can't sample the Tennessee Sippin' Whiskey on the premises, however—ironically, tiny Moore County has been dry since Prohibition.

When you're in Lynchburg, be sure to stop by Miss Mary Bobo's Boarding House (✉ South Main St. ☎ 931/759–6319), where Mr. Daniel used to dine, for great Southern cuisine. If you love barbecue, there are plenty of options here as well, especially if you're here on the fourth Saturday of October for the annual Jack Daniel's World Championship Invitational Barbecue.

old houses in East Nashville. Drive through the historic campus of Fisk University (✉ 1000 17th Ave. N, 37208 ☎ 615/329–8500 ⊕ www. fisk.edu), home of the Fisk University Singers. Architecture, as well as art buffs, will want to visit the Frist Center for the Visual Arts (take a peek into Union Station next door). On the way to Cheekwood, where the extensive grounds should satisfy any horticulturist, drive through Vanderbilt University's tranquil campus. Finish the day with live music at the Bluebird Cafè or the Station Inn (✉ 402 12th Ave. S, 37203 ☎ 615/255–3307 ⊕ www.stationinn.com)for bluegrass.

Great Smoky Mountains: The Great Smoky Mountains are a beautiful, impressive sight in any season—and a designated International Biosphere Reserve (and how many of those have you seen?). Leaf peepers should plan to visit the mountains in mid-September though October for brilliant bursts of gold, orange, and red. Created in 1934 as a WPA project with workers from the Civilian Conservation Corps, Great Smoky Mountains National Park (☎865/436–1200 ⊕www.nps.gov/grsm) is the most visited of our national parks. The Appalachian Trail runs through the park, which is divided between Tennessee (244,000 acres) and North Carolina (276,000 acres). For those who require more "civilized" accommodation than the park's 10 campgrounds and 100 "primitive" campsites, nearby Gatlinburg is the place to stay. By the way, the area got its name from the blue-mist often seen hovering near the mountaintops.

Gatlinburg: A favorite getaway for Tennesseans, tiny Gatlinburg has around 400 shops, 15 wedding chapels (as a wedding location, it's second only to Las Vegas), and up-close views to Great Smoky Mountain National Park. During a weekend here, visit Ripley's Aquarium of the Smokies, play around at the Gatlinburg Municipal Golf Course in nearby Pigeon Forge (⊠Dollywood Ave., 37208 ☎800/231–4128 or 865/453–3912 ⊕www.gatlinburg-tennessee.com/golf.html), and indulge your passion for traditional crafts at the Great Smoky Arts & Crafts Community (☎800/565–7330 ⊕artsandcraftscommunity.com), or the Arrowmont School of Arts and Crafts (⊠556 Parkway, 37738 ☎865/436–5860 ⊕www.arrowmont.org), founded in 1912. Visitors can also take an Alpine tram to the top of Mt. Harrion or ski, snowboard, and ice skate at Ober Gatlinburg (⊠1001 Parkway, 37738 ☎865/436–5423 ⊕www.obergatlinburg.com); night skiing is offered January through February.

Festivals: There are festivals celebrating everything from Moon Pies and RC Cola (June in Bell Buckle) to Tennessee Walking Horses (late August in Shelbyville) in Tennessee. Gatlinburg kicks off spring with the Spring Wildflower Pilgrimage featuring tours, lectures, hikes, etc. In May, Memphis holds an annual Canoe & Kayak Race (actually it's about 500 races), the Tennessee Renaissance Festival takes place in Triune (about 25 mi south of Nashville), the Iroquois Steeplechase is run in Nashville, and Gatlinburg's Scottish Festival and Games in mid-May honor the Scotch-Irish immigrants who settled the mountain areas of North Carolina and Tennessee. Uncle Dave Macon Days, held in Murfreesboro in July, celebrates traditional music and old-fashioned activities like a "motorless" parade. Come fall there's the Memphis Music and Heritage Festival in September, along with county fairs scattered across the state and the Tennessee State Fair (☎615/862–8980 or 615/862–8993 ⊕www.tennesseestatefair.org) in Nashville. In October Nashville hosts the Grand Ole Opry Birthday Bash, Native American Indian Association PowWow, and Oktoberfest. Holiday events begin in November, with more than 2 million lights at Nashville's Gaylord Opryland Hotel's A Country Christmas and Gatlinburg's Winterfest Celebration, which features trolley tours of the mountain town decked out in thousands upon thousands of lights.

HISTORY YOU CAN SEE

The Civil War ravaged Tennessee like no other state except Virginia, and Tennessee was one place where brother literally fought brother, and neighbor fought neighbor. Geography and politics dictated that the state would be a major battlefield. Military campaigns consisted mainly of Federal thrusts southward and Confederate attempts to stop them. The major battles of Fort Donelson (near Dover), Shiloh (near Savannah, at the Tennessee River, near the Mississippi border), Stones River (Murfreesboro), Chickamauga (Georgia), and Chattanooga, and the less violent but important Tullahoma Campaign, all fit this pattern. Two exceptions were the Confederate advance to Knoxville in late 1863 and the Confederate army's brief return to Middle Tennessee in late 1864.

In the 20th century, components for the Manhattan Project's atomic bomb were built in Oak Ridge, in the eastern part of the state; you can learn more at that city's American Museum of Science & Energy (⊠ 300 S. Tulane Ave., 37830 ☎ 865/576-3200 ⊕ www.amse.org).

13

BEST BETS

SIGHTS AND TOURS

NASHVILLE

Fodor's Choice ★ Thirty acres of gardens at the **Cheekwood Botanical Garden and Museum of Art** showcase annuals, perennials, and seasonal wildflowers. The museum, in a carefully restored neo-Georgian mansion, has a permanent exhibition that shows American art to 1945, while the "Temporary Contemporary" gallery presents local and national artists. A collection of Fabergé pieces—including three Imperial Easter Eggs—from the Matilda Geddings Gray Foundation will be displayed at Cheekwood for the next several years. ⊠ 1200 Forrest Park Dr., Belle Meade ☉ Tues.–Sat. 9:30–4:30, Sun. 11–4:30; open Memorial Day and Labor Day. ☎ 615/356–8000 ⊕ www.cheekwood.org 🖘 $10.

Fodor's Choice ★ **Country Music Hall of Fame and Museum.** This tribute to country-music's finest, among them Hank Williams, Loretta Lynn, Patsy Cline, and Johnny Cash, reopened in 2001 in a new facility across from the Gaylord Entertainment Center. A block long, the museum contains plaques honoring country greats, a two-story wall with every gold and platinum country record, a theater that screens a digital film on the industry, not to mention Elvis Presley's solid-gold 1960 Cadillac limo. A digital film presentation surveys country music around the world. ⊠ 222 5th Ave. S, Downtown, 37203 ☎ 615/416–2001 ⊕ www.countrymusichalloffame. com 🖘 $17.95 ☉ Daily 9–6; except Tuesday in Jan. and Feb., when museum is closed.

Fodor's Choice ★ ☾ **Frist Center for the Visual Arts.** This art gallery boasts 24,000 square feet of exhibit space and hosts first-class exhibitions of paintings, sculpture, and other visual art. The historic building, with its original art deco exterior, was formerly Nashville's downtown post office. In its current incarnation, it houses art galleries, a children's discovery gallery, a 250-seat auditorium, gift shop, café, art workshops, and an art resource center. ⊠ *919 Broadway, Downtown, 37203* 🖀 *615/244–3340* ⊕ *www.fristcenter.org* 🖃 *$8.50* ⊙ *Mon.–Wed. and Sat. 10–5:30, Thurs. and Fri. 10–9, Sun. 1–5:30.*

★ **Grand Ole Opry.** This enormously popular radio show, performed in the Grand Ole Opry House, has been broadcasting country music for more than 70 years. You can see superstars, legends, and up-and-coming stars on this stage. The Opry seats about 4,400 people and is broadcast live on WSM AM 650 every Tuesday (7 PM), Friday (8 PM), and Saturday (6:30 and 9:30 PM); buy tickets ($34.50–$47.50) well in advance, particularly during CMA Music Festival week in June. ⊠ *2804 Opryland Dr., 37214* 🖀 *615/889–6611, 800/733–6779 ticket information* ⊕ *www.opry.com.*

★ **Ryman Auditorium and Museum.** A country-music shrine, the Ryman Auditorium and Museum was home to the Grand Ole Opry from 1943 to 1974 and is listed on the National Register of Historic Places. The auditorium seats 2,000 for live performances of classical, jazz, pop, gospel, and, of course, country. Self-guided tours include photo-ops on the legendary stage, and a stroll through the museum, with its photographs and memorabilia of past Ryman Auditorium performances. Visitors may also take the backstage tour of dressing rooms and more otherwise off-limits areas. ⊠ *116 5th Ave. N, Downtown, 37219* 🖀 *615/889–6611 tickets* ⊕ *www.ryman.com* 🖃 *Tours $12.50; main- and backstage tour $16.25* ⊙ *Daily 9–4; call for show schedules and ticket prices.*

★ **The Hermitage.** The life and times of Andrew Jackson, known as Old Hickory, are reflected with great care at this house and museum. Jackson built the mansion on 600 acres for his wife, Rachel, for whose honor he fought and won a duel; both are buried here in the family graveyard. By the 1840s, more than 140 African-American slaves lived and worked on the Hermitage Plantation, and archaeological digs have uncovered the remains of many slave dwellings. The Andrew Jackson Center, a 28,000-square-foot museum, visitor center, and education center, contains many Jackson artifacts never before exhibited. Mansion tours are led by costumed guides, while tours of the grounds are self-guided. Wagon tours are offered April through October. The Garden Gate Café, a museum store, and the Hermitage Garden Shop are also on the grounds. The Hermitage is 12 mi east of Nashville; take I–40E to exit 221A (Hermitage exit). From I–65 North, take Exit 92, (Old Hickory Boulevard South exit). ⊠ *4580 Rachel's La., Hermitage 37076* 🖀 *615/889–2941* ⊕ *www.thehermitage.com* 🖃 *$15* ⊙ *Apr. 1–Oct. 15, daily 8:30–5; Oct. 16–Mar. 31, daily 9–4:30 except 3rd wk in January, when museum is closed.*

MEMPHIS

Graceland, the estate once owned by Elvis Presley, is 12 mi south of Downtown. A guided tour of the mansion, which Elvis bought in 1957 at age 22, as well as the adjoining automobile museum reveals the spoils of stardom. Graceland might be the only colonial suburban home on record to have a jungle room, a pink Cadillac, and close to 700,000 guests annually. Elvis is buried outside the mansion, and tours conclude with many fans leaving tokens at his gravesite. Reservations are recommended, especially in August during "Elvis Week." ✉ *3717 Elvis Presley Blvd., South Haven, 38116* ☎ *901/332-3322 or 800/238-2000* ⊕ *www.elvis.com* 🎟 *Mansion $27, all attractions $32* ⊙ *Closed Tues. Nov.–Mar.*

STRANGE BUT TRUE
Reelfoot Lake, in the western part of the state, was created during a series of earthquakes along the New Madrid fault line between December 1811 and March 1812. These same earthquakes also reversed the flow of the Mississippi River and caused entire forests to sink into the ground, creating new swamps and lakes. Marshy Reelfoot Lake is only about 5.2 feet deep, and looks more like something found in Louisiana than Tennessee.

13

★ **Memphis Rock 'n' Soul Museum.** In the shadow of the FedEx Forum just off Beale Street, this museum showcases Memphis as musical mecca, tracing the history of legendary performers who poured into Memphis and made everlasting contributions to blues, rock 'n' roll, and other musical forms. Several jukeboxes give visitors the opportunity to listen to the hits that originated in Memphis. ✉ *191 Beale St., at 3rd St., 38103* ☎ *901/205-2533* ⊕ *www.memphis rocknsoul.org* 🎟 *$10* ⊙ *Daily 10–7.*

☾ Memphis begins at the Mississippi River, which is celebrated in a 52-acre river park on **Mud Island** (☎ *901/576–6595 or 800/507–6507* ⊕ *www.mudisland.com*). A footbridge and monorail at 125 North Front Street get you to the island, where the five-block **River Walk** replicates the Mississippi's every twist, turn, and sandbar from Cairo, Illinois, to New Orleans, Louisiana. Also in the park is the **Mississippi River Museum** (🎟 *$8* ⊙ *Closed Mon.*), featuring a simulated Civil War gunboat battle. The park also has pedal boat and bicycle rentals and numerous gift shops.

Fodor's Choice
★

South of Downtown, the motel in which Dr. Martin Luther King Jr. was assassinated in 1968 has been transformed into the **National Civil Rights Museum,** an outstanding facility that documents the civil rights movement through exhibits and clever audiovisual displays. ✉ *450 Mulberry St., Downtown, 38103* ☎ *901/521–9699* ⊕ *www.civilrights museum.org* 🎟 *$12* ⊙ *Mon.–Sat. 9–5, Sun. 1–5; open 1 hr later daily June–Aug.* ⊙ *Closed Tues.*

Soulsville: Stax Museum of American Soul Music. Look for the marquee reading SOULSVILLE U.S.A., and listen for the sounds of soul icons like Otis Redding, Isaac Hayes, and Aretha Franklin as you approach the former home of Stax Records, rebuilt from the ground up to look as it did during the label's heyday in the 1960s and early '70s. Inside, it's wall-to-wall music—along with a history of Stax, from its beginnings as a home base for local musicians to an international sensation. ✉ *926 E. McLemore Ave., 38106* ☎ *901/946-2535* ⊕ *http://staxmuseum.com* 🎟 *$10.*

Sun Studio. Sam Phillips' modest studio is the birthplace of rock 'n' roll, where Elvis Presley, Jerry Lee Lewis, B.B. King, Carl Perkins, Johnny Cash, and Roy Orbison, among others, launched their careers. Tours are given every 30 minutes beginning at 10 AM. The studio is seven blocks east of Downtown. ⊠*706 Union Ave., Downtown, 38103* ☏*901/521–0664 or 800/441–6249* ⊕*www.sunstudio.com* ☞*$9.50* ⊙*Daily 10–6.*

WHERE TO EAT

WHAT IT COSTS IN U.S. DOLLARS				
¢	$	$$	$$$	$$$$
Restaurants	under $10	$10–$19	$20–$29	$30–$40	over $40

Prices are for per person, for a main course at dinner.

NASHVILLE

$$$–$$$$ ★ ✕ **Capitol Grille and Oak Bar.** This charming restaurant in downtown's historic Hermitage Hotel serves cuisine with a regional flair, including seafood and Black Angus beef. The Capitol Grille is consistently ranked as one of Nashville's top restaurants by local food reviewers; one described it as serving "opulent food." Breakfast, lunch, and dinner are served; there's a brunch on Sunday. ⊠*231 6th Ave. N, 37219* ☏*615/345–7116* ⊕*www.thehermitagehotel.com* ⊟*AE, DC, MC, V.*

$$$–$$$$ ✕ **The Stockyard.** Housed in an authentic former stockyard (that's an auction house for livestock), the Stockyard restaurant is something of a Nashville institution. An antique building in the heart of the historic district, the restaurant boasts three complete floors of authentic Old Nashville ambience—antique furniture and wallpaper, plus top-drawer dining. ⊠*901 2nd Ave. N, 37201* ☏*615/255–6464* ⊕*www. stock-yardrestaurant.com* ⊟*AE, D, DC, MC, V* ⊙*No lunch.*

$–$$$ ✕ **Mad Platter.** This local favorite in historic downtown Nashville blends traditional gourmet with California cuisine, using locally available ingredients from the nearby farmers' market. The baked salmon with red grapes and feta cheese, rack of lamb, and bananas Foster are favorites. It's a popular spot for power lunches by day, but jazz music transforms the cozy 18th-century brownstone into a romantic nook at night. ⊠*1239 6th Ave. N, 37208* ☏*615/242–2563* ⊠*Reservations essential* ⊟*AE, D, DC, MC, V* ⊙*No lunch Sat.–Mon.*

$–$$ ★ ✕ **Sunset Grill.** Seafood, pastas, steaks, and vegetarian specials highlight the menu of this inventive restaurant. A good entrée choice is Voodoo pasta with andouille sausage, chicken, and shrimp in a roasted pepper sauce served over Cajun-spiced fettuccine. There's sublime homemade sorbet to finish your meal and 70 wines are served by the glass. A special late-night menu is served from 10 PM (midnight on weekends) until closing at 1:30 AM. ⊠*2001-A Belcourt Ave., Hillsboro Village, 37212* ☏*615/386–3663* ⊕*www.sunsetgrill.com* ⊟*AE, D, DC, MC, V* ⊙*No lunch weekends.*

¢–$ ✕ **Pancake Pantry.** This Nashville institution is the place to go for breakfast. It's a favorite with locals, students, and celebrities. Breakfast is the specialty, with 20 kinds of pancakes and homemade syrups, but there are soups and sandwiches for lunch. Get there by 8:15 weekdays to avoid lines; but be prepared to wait on weekends. ⊠*1796 21st Ave. S, Hillsboro Village, 37212* ☎*615/383–9333* ⚲*Reservations not accepted* ⊟*AE, D, DC, MC, V* ⊘*No dinner.*

¢ ✕**Elliston Place Soda Shop.** Come to this old-fashioned soda shop for great burgers, frothy ice-cream sodas, and delicious chocolate shakes. ⊠*2111 Elliston Pl., Elliston Place, 372103* ☎*615/327–1090* ⊟*MC, V* ⊘*Closed Sun.*

13

$$$$ ✕**Chez Philippe.** This Memphis institution serves sophisticated dishes in
★ an ornately decorated dining room Downtown. Nightly creations might include beef tenderloin, or Chilean snapper with portobello mushrooms on a horseradish reduction. Desserts include baked Alaska (sponge cake topped with ice cream and meringue, then baked) and crème brûlée. Afternoon tea is served Tuesday through Saturday from 2 to 3, but you'll need to make a reservation 24 hours in advance. ⊠*Peabody Hotel, 149 Union Ave., Downtown* ☎*901/529–4188 Jacket required* ⊟*AE, DC, MC, V* ⊘*Closed Sun. and Mon. No lunch.*

$–$$$ ✕**Paulette's.** This Overton Square classic, located in a half-timbered
★ house with an elegantly appointed dining room, serves delicious crepes (try the hot chocolate dessert crepe) and salads and excellent grilled chicken, salmon, and swordfish. ⊠*2110 Madison Ave., Overton Square* ☎*901/726–5128* ⊟*AE, D, DC, MC, V.*

¢–$$ ✕**Alfred's on Beale.** Not surprisingly, music is the theme at this busy restaurant on Beale Street, the city's bluesy entertainment district. Up to 500 people can be accommodated inside and on the two-story outdoor patio. Southern plate lunches, burgers, pork chops, pasta, catfish, and barbecued ribs make up the comforting menu. The kitchen is open until 3 AM; on weekends the bar serves until 5 AM. Bands play Thursday through Sunday, and there's karaoke Monday through Wednesday. ⊠*197 Beale St.* ☎*901/525–3711* ⊟*AE, D, DC, MC, V.*

¢–$ ✕**Charlie Vergos' Rendezvous.** They sell plenty of dry-style barbecued ribs in this downtown restaurant in an 1890 building, in an alley just north of the Peabody Hotel. A diverse group chows down in the antiques- and collectibles-filled basement dining room, and the service is among the most efficient in town. The menu also includes shoulder sandwiches, pork loin, chicken, and a shrimp skillet. ⊠*52 S. 2nd St.* ☎*901/523–2746* ⊟*AE, D, MC, V* ⊘*Closed Sun. and Mon. No lunch Tues.–Thurs.*

WHERE TO STAY

	WHAT IT COSTS IN U.S. DOLLARS				
	¢	$	$$	$$$	$$$$
FOR 2 PEOPLE	under $75	$75–$125	$126–$175	$176–$225	over $225

Prices are for two people in a standard double room in high season.

ON THE WAY

In the southeastern corner of the state, just a brief drive from Atlanta and accessible via I-24, Chattanooga bills itself as "a great city by nature." Kids, railroad fans, and Civil War buffs can find plenty to do in this town, whether visiting the 24-acre Chattanooga Choo Choo hotel and convention complex (⊠ *1400 Market St., 37402* ☎ *800/872-2529* ⊕ *www. choochoo.com*), taking the Lookout Mountain Incline Railway (the world's steepest), or spending time in the Tennessee Aquarium or the Hunter Museum of American Art.

Franklin and Murfreesboro. Civil war battlefields, a historic town square,

Middle Tennessee State University, and two large shopping malls await visitors to the two communities. Carnton Plantation (featured in Tennessee native Robert Hicks' best-selling novel, Widow of the South), the former home of Robert and Carrie McGavock, is the site of the largest privately owned Confederate cemetery in the country, where those killed in the Battle of Franklin are buried. Other Civil War sites in the area include Stones River National Battlefield. Franklin is south of Nashville, via I-65; Murfreesboro is southeast of Nashville, via I-24.

NASHVILLE

$$$$ ⊞**Gaylord Opryland Resort and Convention Center.** This massive plantation-
★ style hotel complex adjacent to Opryland has a 2-acre glass-walled conservatory filled with 10,000 tropical plants and a sky-lighted indoor area with water cascades and a half-acre lake. Some rooms have private balconies overlooking the spectacular atrium. The 18-hole golf course was designed by Larry Nelson. ⊠ *2800 Opryland Dr., 37214* ☎ *615/889–1000* ☎ *615/871–7741* ⊕ *www.gaylordhotels.com/gaylordopryland* ᖩ *2,716 rooms, 165 suites* ⑂ *In-room: ethernet, Wi-Fi. In-hotel: 7 restaurants, pools, gym, public Wi-Fi* ≡ *AE, D, MC, V.*

$$$$ ⊞**The Hermitage Hotel.** Everything here is luxurious, from the large
Fodor'sChoice rooms to the plush robes and the public restrooms. This hotel offers a
★ pampering package for pets, so it should come as no surprise that the concierge service here promises to address *any* request. The on-site restaurant is the much-heralded Capitol Grille. ⊠ *231 6th Ave. N, Downtown, 37214* ☎ *615/244–3121 or 888/888–9414* ☎ *615/254–6909* ⊕ *www.thehermitagehotel.com* ᖩ *122 rooms, 11 suites* ⑂ *In-room: Wi-Fi. In-hotel: room service, bar, gym, laundry service, airport shuttle, some pets allowed, no-smoking rooms* ≡ *AE, D, DC, MC, V.*

$$-$$$ ⊞**Union Station Hotel.** A luxury hotel located in the renovated 1900
Fodor'sChoice train station from which it takes its name. The lobby maintains the lofty
★ dimensions of the original train shed, and architectural details abound throughout the hotel. Rooms have Herman Miller Aeron desk chairs, plush robes, and, in some cases, marble soaking tubs. ⊠ *1001 Broadway, Downtown, 37203* ☎ *615/726–1001 or 877/999–3223* ☎ *615/248–3554* ⊕ *www.unionstationhotelnashville.com* ᖩ *125 rooms, 12 suites* ⑂ *In-room: Wi-Fi. In-hotel: room service, bar, pool, laundry service, airport shuttle, no-smoking rooms* ≡ *AE, D, DC, MC, V.*

MEMPHIS

$$$$
Fodor'sChoice
★

☷ **Peabody Hotel.** Even if you're not staying here, it's worth a stop to see this 12-story downtown landmark, built in 1925. The lobby has the original stained-glass skylights and the travertine-marble fountain that is home to the hotel's resident ducks. (The ducks parade to the fountain at 11 AM, and they depart the fountain at 5 PM.) The rooms are decorated in a variety of period styles. ✉ *149 Union Ave., Downtown, 38103* ☎ *901/529–4000 or 800/732–2639* 🖷 *901/529–3600* ⊕ *www.peabodymemphis.com* ⇋ *464 rooms, 15 suites* ♿ *In-hotel: 4 restaurants, pool, gym* ⊟ *AE, D, DC, MC, V* ⦿ *BP (some).*

$$$–$$$$

☷ **Memphis Marriott Downtown.** Relax and listen to the grand piano that's played in the greenery-filled lobby of this sophisticated high-rise. The 19-story hotel is next to the Downtown Convention Center. ✉ *250 N. Main St., 38103* ☎ *901/527–7300* 🖷 *901/526–1561* ⊕ *www.marriott.com* ⇋ *600 rooms, 10 suites* ♿ *In-room: refrigerator (some), ethernet. In-hotel: restaurant, bar, public Wi-Fi, pools, whirlpool, sauna, gym, executive floor, parking (fee)* ⊟ *AE, D, DC, MC, V.*

$–$$$

☷ **Hampton Inn and Suites at Peabody Place.** Completely renovated in a traditional style in 2007. Many of the rooms have views of Beale Street. ✉ *175 Peabody Pl., 38103* ☎ *901/260–4000* 🖷 *901/260–4050* ⇋ *144 rooms, 35 suites* ⊕ *www.hampton-inn.com* ♿ *In-room: refrigerator (some). In-hotel: pool, laundry service* ⊟ *AE, D, DC, MC, V* ⦿ *CP.*

NIGHTLIFE & THE ARTS

NASHVILLE

At the famous **Bluebird Cafe** (✉ *4104 Hillsboro Rd., Green Hills, 37215* ☎ *615/383–1461* ⊕ *www.bluebirdcafe.com*), country singers try out their latest material.

Exit/In (✉ *2208 Elliston Pl., Elliston Place, 37203* ☎ *615/321–4400*) showcases the most cutting-edge blues and rock bands from the United States and beyond. Groove to the music in an unpretentious atmosphere.

The **Grand Ole Opry** (✉ *2804 Opryland Dr., 37214* ☎ *615/889–6611, 800/733–6779 ticket information* ⊕ *www.opry.com*)has packed in the crowds on Friday and Saturday nights since 1925. Show times are Tuesday at 7 PM, Friday at 8 PM, and Saturday at 6:30 PM and 9:30 PM.

The **Tennessee Performing Arts Center** (✉ *505 Deaderick St., Downtown, 37243* ☎ *615/782–4000, 615/255–2787 tickets* ⊕ *www.tpac.org*), known as TPAC, is the venue for performances by the **Nashville Ballet** (☎ *615/297–2966* ⊕ *www.nashvilleballet.com*), **Nashville Opera** (☎ *615/832–5242* ⊕ *www.nashvilleopera.org*), and **Tennessee Repertory Theatre** (☎ *615/244–4878* ⊕ *www.tnrep.org*). The center's Andrew Jackson Hall also hosts touring Broadway shows.

In the **District**, check out the **Wild Horse Saloon** (✉ *120 2nd Ave. N 37201* ☎ *615/902–8200* ⊕ *www.wildhorsesaloon.com*), which offers daily dance lessons and live performances. All ages are welcome until 10 PM.

13

VITAL STATS:

- During the War of 1812 so many Tennesseans answered native son Gen. Andrew Jackson's call to serve that the state acquired the sobriquet "The Volunteer State."

- Total area: 42,146 square mi
- Length: 440 mi
- Width: 120 mi
- State bird: Mockingbird
- State folk dance: Square Dance
- State gem: Tennessee Pearl

- State horse: Tennessee Walking Horse
- State insects: Firefly and Honeybee
- State tree: Tulip Poplar
- State wildflower: Passion Flower
- State wild animal: Raccoon
- Lowest point in Tennessee: The Mississippi River at 175 feet.
- Highest point in Tennessee: Clingmans Dome in Great Smoky Mountains National Park at 6,643 feet

MEMPHIS

Among the offerings of Beale Street's three blocks of music clubs, one of the most popular is **B. D. King's Blues Club** (⊠ *143 Beale St., Beale Street Historic District, 38103* ☏ *901/524–5464* ⊕ *http://memphis.bbking-clubs.com*), where B. B. himself occasionally performs, as do numerous top blues bands.

The **Orpheum Theatre** (⊠ *203 S. Main St., Downtown, 38103* ☏ *901/525–3000 or 901/525–7800* ⊕ *www.orpheum-memphis.com*)is a restored 1920s movie house that hosts touring Broadway shows as well as performances by Opera Memphis and Ballet Memphis.

VISITOR INFORMATION

Chattanooga Area Convention & Visitors Bureau (☏ *800/322–3344 or 423/756–8687* ⊕ *www.chattanoogafun.com*)

Great Smoky Mountains National Park (☏ *865/436–1200* ⊕ *www.nps.gov/grsm*)

Gatlinburg Visitors & Convention Bureau (☏ *800/568–4748* ⊕ *www.gatlinburg.com*)

Memphis Convention and Visitors Bureau (☏ *901/543–5300* ⊕ *www.memphistravel.com*)

Nashville Convention and Visitors Bureau (☏ *800/657–6910* ⊕ *www.visitmusiccity.com*)

The Ozarks

WITH BRANSON, MO

Ozark Mountains, Arkansas

WORD OF MOUTH

"They [the Ozarks] are beautiful in the spring and fall. The winding, twisting roads lead to some spectacular views when you get to the top of a ridge . . . [Eureka Springs] is full of beautiful Victorian homes (most are open to the public) . . . The live music shows [in Branson] are pure enjoyment. There is a wide range of entertainment. From country, to gospel, to Andy Williams, or even Yakov, you will have fun. Branson offers something for everyone. There are three great fishing lakes, lots of arts and crafts, and beautiful scenery."   —L. Vermeis

EXPLORING THE OZARKS

Branson, Missouri, is 253 mi southwest of St. Louis via I–44 and U.S. Rte. 65; 211 mi southeast of Kansas City via U.S. Rte. 71, Missouri Rte. 7, Missouri Rte. 13, I–44, and U.S. Rte. 65; 301 mi northwest of Memphis via I–40 and U.S. Rte. 65; and 475 mi northeast of Dallas via U.S. Rte. 75, U.S. Rte. 69, the Indian National Turnpike, U.S. Rte. 75, I–44, and U.S. Rte. 65

By Michael
Ream

The gentle peaks and rolling valleys of the Ozarks have long lured vacationers to southern Missouri and northern Arkansas with the promise of scenic beauty and outdoor recreation. Extending roughly from the Missouri River to the Arkansas River and covering nearly 50,000 square mi, the wooded heights are not really mountains at all, but rather a series of plateaus carved by erosion.

Though it's largely a rural area, some parts of the Ozarks can become overrun with visitors, particularly in the summertime. Canoers and kayakers seek out an endless number of spots for paddling and floating; the Buffalo National River, in northern Arkansas, is one of the most popular destinations. Of course, the ultimate tourist destination in the Ozarks is Branson, which attracts millions of visitors who come to sample the long lineup of entertainment extravaganzas—including a number of shows featuring aging country and pop music stars—crowded along the town's main drag. More traditional Ozarks music can be found in the tiny Arkansas hamlet of Mountain View, which lies in a valley and can be reached by driving twisty hilltop roads.

WHO WILL ESPECIALLY LOVE THIS TRIP?

Music Fans: Branson and Mountain View both offer visitors (each in their own unique way) the chance to see some classic American music. Some may be put off by Branson's gaudy version of entertainment, but seeing a show here is an All-American experience you won't soon forget. In Mountain View the folk shows present a more traditional form of music and Ozarks culture.

Outdoor Enthusiasts: Paddlers and hikers will be in paradise: the Ozarks offers so many winding rivers, streams, and hiking trails that it's impossible to list them all. Notable is the Buffalo National River, and the wide array of trails in the Ozark National Forest and Mark Twain National Forest.

History Buffs: Several Civil War battlefields can be found in both southern Missouri and northern Arkansas, and the area was also a hotbed for bushwhackers who marauded through the valleys and communities caught on the ragged edge of the war. In addition, historical attractions in Branson and Mountain View give visitors a close-up look (and sometimes hands-on demonstrations) of the area's early settlers' lifestyles.

Families: Away from its flashy entertainment emporiums, Branson offers attractions that will thrill and delight children, primarily at the amuse-

TOP 5 REASONS TO GO

Branson: There's perhaps no better place to see country music stars and old pop stars from the '50s than in this city's over-the-top—sometimes schlocky—entertainment revues.

Mountain View: For a more home-spun musical experience, head to this town, where traditional folk music is presented in an intimate theater setting.

Buffalo National River: Gliding past the unspoiled banks and through the canyons of this natural treasure is pure bliss—even when you're maneuvering between other canoes and kayaks.

Springfield: An urban oasis hidden among typical roadside gas stations and fast-food joints, the largest city in the Ozarks offers an array of dining options and a true downtown for strolling and shopping.

Fayetteville: This quintessential college town has a vibrant arts scene and a charming downtown square full of independent shops and restaurants.

14

ment parks Silver Dollar City and Celebration City. Mountain View has a crafts village, with demonstrations about pioneer life in the Ozarks.

WHEN IS THE BEST TIME TO VISIT?

The best times to visit the Ozarks are spring and fall, when the weather tends toward the mild, with cool breezes blowing through the peaks and hollows. Despite the high elevation, it can be hot and unpleasant in the summer, and 90° temperatures and high humidity are often the norm in July and August. Winters are generally mild, with brisk but not freezing temperatures—although ice storms and occasional small amounts of snow are not unheard of, which can make driving on mountain roads hazardous. Parts of the Ozarks lie on the edge of "Tornado alley," which is on alert for twisters from late spring through fall.

The majority of Branson's theaters are open from March until early December, and some remain open year-round. While many visitors come between spring and late summer, the town goes all out for Christmas and draws many visitors in November and December. Folk music shows at the Ozark Folk Center in Mountain View run from mid-April until about November 1.

HOW SHOULD I GET THERE?

DRIVING

Many of the main towns in the Ozarks are fairly easy to reach via car: I–44 (Old route 66) skirts the northern edge of the Ozarks, passing through the sprawling city of Springfield, which serves as a jumping-off point to Branson, 40 mi to the south. I–540 goes straight through the Ozarks in northwest Arkansas, with exits in the university town of Fayetteville and the booming cities of Springdale and Rogers, before heading north toward Missouri and an intersection with I–44. The

How to Snack

Ozarks culinary mainstays are barbecue and catfish. These humble, tasty foods can be found throughout the region: every good-size town seems to have at least one of each type of restaurant, with the food included in the restaurant's name, such as "Catfish Hole" or "Smokey's Barbecue." It's hard to go wrong with a simple roadside restaurant—just look for pickup trucks in the parking lot and no-frills decor inside, and you'll probably be eating well.

The catfish is almost always served deep-fried, although it can be found broiled in some restaurants. The boneless filets come heaped high on the plate—often as part of an all-you-can-eat selection—and can be eaten without utensils. High-fat, high-calorie side dishes generally include coleslaw, hush puppies, and french fries (If you don't like deep-fried foods, dining in

the Ozarks is going to be a bit of a challenge.) More exotic side dishes include fried okra, a green vegetable with a unique flavor hidden inside its crunchy shell.

Ozarkers are passionate about their barbecue, and the region lies smack in the middle of the revered barbecue axis of Texas/Kansas City/Memphis. The sweet, smoky smell of a barbecue smoker—a black or silver kettle that often juts out the side or back of the restaurant, usually next to a woodpile used to feed the fire—is a sign that you've found a serious barbecue place. While ribs can certainly be found in most 'cue joints, true aficionados go for the pulled pork—meat that is smoked, sometimes for hours, then shredded. Sauces range from the mildly spicy to the blisteringly hot—be sure to ask about the heat when placing an order.

eastern half of the Ozarks, which includes Mountain View, located deep within hilly hollows, is a bit more of a trip: From I–40 or I–540, several national and state highways cross the Ozarks, twisting through the peaks and hollows. A good road map is essential, and be sure to stay alert, as the roads snake around cliffs and rock faces.

FLYING

Two decent-size airports serve the Ozarks. Springfield-Branson National Airport offers direct flights from several cities, including Atlanta, Chicago, Dallas, and Denver, while fast-growing Northwest Arkansas Regional Airport, about 10 mi off I–540 near Rogers and Bentonville, has flights from those same cities, plus New York, Washington D.C., Los Angeles, Houston, and several other cities.

HOW DO I GET AROUND?

BY CAR

A car is by far the best way to get around the Ozarks. The area is remote, with virtually no transportation options other than private automobiles. Many cities and attractions are miles apart, separated by twisty mountain roads. That said, some of the more popular places in the Ozarks, such as Branson, can have traffic jams as bad as those in big cities. Loads of tour buses pour into Branson from spring to fall,

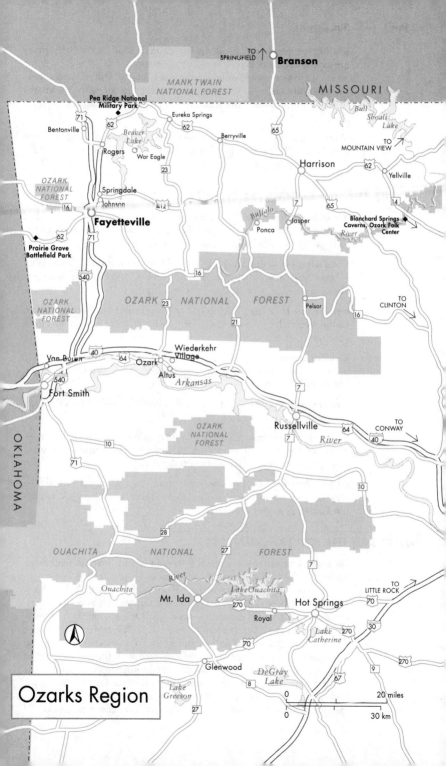

Ozarks Region

MISSOURI

TO SPRINGFIELD ↑ **Branson**

MANK TWAIN NATIONAL FOREST

Pea Ridge National Military Park

Bentonville

71

62

Eureka Springs

62

Berryville

65

Bull Shoals Lake

TO MOUNTAIN VIEW

Beaver Lake

Rogers

War Eagle

Harrison

62

Yellville

OZARK NATIONAL FOREST

23

Springdale

Johnson

412

7

65

14

16

Fayetteville

71

Buffalo River

Jasper

Blanchard Springs Caverns, Ozark Folk Center

62

Ponca

Prairie Grove Battlefield Park

540

16

OZARK NATIONAL FOREST

OZARK NATIONAL FOREST

23

21

Pelsor

16

TO CLINTON

40

Wiederkehr Village

Ozark

Altus

Arkansas

7

Van Buren

64

540

Fort Smith

OZARK NATIONAL FOREST

Russellville

64

TO CONWAY

40

10

7

River

71

10

OKLAHOMA

OUACHITA NATIONAL FOREST

28

27

7

Ouachita River

Lake Ouachita

TO LITTLE ROCK

Mt. Ida

Hot Springs

70

270

Royal

Lake Catherine

270

30

70

9

270

Glenwood

8

DeGray Lake

67

Lake Greeson

27

0

0

20 miles

30 km

jostling for space along the town's single main road. Fortunately, maps are available that point out some of the lesser used side roads—ask for one at a visitors' center, of which there are several. Out in the countryside, a good road map is invaluable for navigating along the backroads to get to some of the more scenic, off-the-beaten-path places.

BY TAXI

Shuttles and taxis can be useful for getting around Branson, although they need to be ordered in advance from hotels. Rates range $6–$20, depending on how far you're going.

WHERE SHOULD I FOCUS MY ENERGY?

If you're here for 1 day: Check out Branson. See a show (or two) and drop in on one of the city's amusement parks or the Shepherd of the Hills complex for a look at traditional Ozarks life.

If you're here for 2 days: Take a short hop from Branson to Springfield, and stroll the downtown streets of this urbane city. Grab lunch or dinner at one of Springfield's excellent restaurants.

If you're here for 3 days: Take a float trip on the Buffalo National River. Camp overnight, or head back early to Fayetteville for dinner in the charming college town.

If you're here for 4 days: Head over to Mountain View to hear some authentic folk music and experience pioneer life in the Ozarks at the Ozark Folk Center.

If you're here for 5 days: Visit a Civil War battlefield—Wilson's Creek in Missouri, or Pea Ridge in Arkansas.

If you're here for 6 days: Slip on your hiking boots for a day in the Ozark National Forest or Mark Twain National Forest, where trails wind through some spectacular mountain scenery.

If you're here for 7 days or more: Hit some of the sites just outside the Ozarks, such as the Harry S Truman Birthplace and George Washington Carver National Monument.

WHAT ARE THE TOP EXPERIENCES?

The Music: One of the most popular live music and entertainment destinations in the United States, Branson packs visitors into its more than 50 theaters to hear internationally famous performers, including Andy Williams, Mickey Gilley, and Yakoff Smirnoff, as well as popular variety shows based on everything from classic Ozarks comedy to American icons like Dick Clark and Lawrence Welk. It's unabashedly hokey, over-the-top, and soaked with nostalgia for "The good ol' days"—and audiences love it. Performances are delivered with the highest level of professionalism from singers, dancers, and musicians who know how to entertain their fans. Over on the other side of the Ozarks, the Ozark Folk Center in Mountain View presents acoustic sets in its lone theater, where the stage is likely to include traditional instruments like the

CLAIM TO FAME

The word "Ozarks" for many conjures up the image of the hillbilly. Shiftless, lazy, poor, illiterate, and armed with a shotgun as he goes to inspect his moonshine still, this classic American folk character has endured in American popular culture, even as it has become outdated and condescending.

The view of Ozarkers as backward and rustic emerged out of the area's geographic history: landlocked and far from major transportation routes, the Ozarks were always remote and isolated, leading to a rough-hewn, frontier culture of self-reliance and ignorance of the outside world. The hillbilly character became popular with the "Arkansas Traveler," a popular song and then stage performance that began in the mid-1800s, depicting an outsider riding his horse through Arkansas and encountering a local woodsman who spoke in a rough, backcountry dialect.

The "Arkansas Traveler" caricature inspired a popular newspaper column that in turn spawned additional pop culture takes on the hillbilly and homespun Ozarks folk in general, including the "Lum N' Abner" radio show, which was one of the most popular radio programs nationwide for nearly 25 years, from the 1930s to the 1950s. More contemporary versions of the hillbilly could be seen in the comic strips "Snuffy Smith" and "Lil' Abner," the latter of which even led to a theme park in the Ozarks that eventually closed in the early 1990s. One of Branson's first shows, opened in the late 1950s, featured the "Baldknobbers," comedic versions of the hillbilly; it's still running today.

The Shepherd of the Hills, which provides something of an antidote to the cartoonish portrayal of the hillbilly, has been in production in Branson for nearly 50 years. Based on an extremely popular book first published in the early 20th century, it tells the story of stoic, independent hill people in the Branson area. The self-reliance of many early settlers is also on display in craft villages at Silver Dollar City in Branson and the Ozark Folk Center in Mountain View. Today the descendents of early settlers, many of whom remain in remote, isolated areas, continue to make a living adapting their skills to the modern world.

Interestingly, there's actually some pride in the old caricatures, with area high school football teams nicknamed "Hillbillies" or "Mountaineers" that feature logos of mountain men with floppy hats, pipes, and shotguns.

14

dulcimer and songs that have been passed down through generations of Ozarks mountain folk.

The Culture: Re-created villages at attractions in Branson and Mountain View present the sights, sounds, and tastes experienced by Ozarks settlers, and old-time crafts like candlemaking, glass-blowing, and black-smithing are demonstrated. Of course, for a true taste of the Ozark way of life, hop onto one of the back roads for a drive through picturesque mountain villages. Stop off for a meal in a café, or browse in old general stores that have been around since this area was a remote, rugged outpost on the American frontier. And for a more detailed look at the culture of the earlier people of the Ozarks—and how some of the enduring (and often negative) stereotypes formed—can be seen at the Shiloh Museum of Ozark History in Springdale, Arkansas.

The Outdoors: Hiking, canoeing, and kayaking enthusiasts may think they've reached nirvana when they explore the soft peaks and deep hollows of the Ozarks. Ozark and Mark Twain National Forests each contain a seemingly endless number of trails, while rivers and streams curl their way for miles through woods and canyons formed by erosion. Most notable is the Buffalo National River, in northern Arkansas, where canoers and kayakers can spend anywhere from a day to more than a week gliding past towering bluffs, banks lined with seasonal wild flowers, and wildlife.

> **HISTORY YOU CAN SEE**
>
> Missouri had the third highest number of Civil War actions (behind Virginia and Tennessee), and two major sites are in the Ozarks area of the state: Wilson's Creek National Battlefield, just outside of Springfield, and Battle of Carthage State Historic Site near Joplin. The Arkansas Ozarks saw a fair share of fighting, too, and an excellent view of a pivotal battle can be seen at Pea Ridge Military Park, just south of the Missouri state line in northwest Arkansas.

The History: Union and Confederate troops fought for control of the Ozarks during the Civil War, with notable battles taking place at Pea Ridge National Military Park in Arkansas (15930 U.S. Hwy. 62, 10 mi northeast of Rogers, Garfield, Arkansas, 479/451–8122, www.nps.gov/peri) and Wilson's Creek National Battlefield in Missouri (6424 W. Farm Rd. 182, 10 mi southwest of Springfield, Republic, Missouri, 417/732–2662, www.nps.gov/wicr). Both feature exhibits on the Civil War and its impact on the area. Just a few hours from the Ozarks is the Missouri–Kansas border, which was an infamously lawless region in the years before the war that occasionally exploded in conflict between marauding gangs of Jayhawkers and Bushwhackers. The Bushwhacker Museum in Nevada, Missouri, gives a short presentation on this unique slice of history (212 W. Walnut St., 417/667–9602, www.bushwhacker.org).

BEST BETS

SIGHTS AND TOURS

Fodor's Choice **BRANSON**

★ Love it or hate it, Branson is a uniquely American place. Clustered along U.S. Route 76—or Country Music Boulevard—are a sampling of Branson's nearly 50 famous theaters, which offer up popular musical revues. With more theater seats than Broadway and Las Vegas, Branson packs in visitors from all over, who come to town to see superstars such as Mickey Gilley, Larry Gatlin, and Mel Tillis, as well as family acts—some of which have been entertaining for generations. The music is primarily recycled "oldies," and shows are very wholesome (with God and patriotism playing a significant role in most productions).

★ **Shepherd of the Hills Historic Homestead and Outdoor Theatre.** In operation since 1960, the show here tells the story of the settlers who first came to the Ozarks in the 1800s—with a cast of 90 people and live animals on a football-size field. An adjoining re-created homestead gives you a chance to further explore the lives of the story's characters. ⊠*5586 W. Hwy. 76* ☎*417/334–4191 or 800/653–6288* ⊕*www.theshepherd ofthehills.com* ⊠*Theater: $32; homestead tour: $12* ⊗*May–Dec.; call for individual show dates and times.*

★ **Silver Dollar City.** This classic old-fashioned amusement park is a few miles outside of Branson. It has several roller coasters, as well as rides for very young children. There's also an 1880s craft village with more than 100 different crafters, including glassblowers, wood- and metal workers, bakers, and candlemakers, as well as numerous food stalls. ⊠*399 Indian Point Rd.* ☎*800/475–9370* ⊕*www.silverdollarcity.com* ⊠*$48* ⊗*Mar.–Dec.; call for hrs.*

14

The World's Largest Titanic Museum Attraction. This one's hard to miss: a half-size model of the famous doomed ship protrudes from a replica iceberg on Branson's main drag. Inside is a fascinating look at the "practically unsinkable" craft, from its design and construction to its ill-fated voyage. Some exhibits are interactive, giving you the opportunity to stroll outside the Titanic in the moonlight or see what it felt like to stand on the upended decks as it went down. ⊠*3235 W. Hwy. 76, Country Blvd.* ☎*417/334–9500 or 800/381–7670* ⊕*www.titanic branson.com* ⊠*$19* ⊗*Daily 9–5.*

SPRINGFIELD

A longtime pit stop for travelers along Route 66 (And now I–44), Springfield, the largest city in the Ozarks, maintains a cluster of gas stations and chain motels just off the highway—but it also has a vibrant urban core. It's not easy to find (it's several miles from the interstate, on the south side of Springfield's old downtown), but if you seek it out you can find a neighborhood filled with coffeehouses, a used bookstore, and trendy nightclubs and restaurants.

Discovery Center. Kids will love this hands-on science museum just outside downtown, which includes exhibits on energy, flight, and technology; a high-wire bike ride; and an immersion cinema, with interactive films on wildlife and other subjects. ⊠*438 St. Louis St.* ☎*417/862–9910* ⊕*www.discoverycenter.org* ⊠*$7; additional charge for some exhibits* ⊗*Tues.–Thurs. 9–5, Fri. 9–8, Sat. 10–5, Sun. 1–5.*

Fodor'sChoice **MOUNTAIN VIEW**

★ Mountain View is the anti-Branson. Although it's also a small, remote, mountain town where the main draw is music, Mountain View takes a slower, more down-home approach. The center of traditional Ozark Mountain Music, Mountain View sits in a windswept valley reached by twisting mountain roads that wind their way through the surrounding bucolic countryside. Sandstone buildings line Main Street, including the courthouse, where musicians have traditionally gathered on the front lawn and surrounding side streets to pluck away on guitars, dulcimers, and other old-time instruments.

★ **The Ozark Folk Center.** This is the place to see traditional Ozarks music and culture. A 1,000-seat auditorium showcases "unplugged" concerts of traditional folk, roots, and country music by both area musicians and national acts—Ricky Skaggs, Marty Stuart, and Del McCoury, among others, have played here. Instruments may include guitar, banjo, fiddle, mandolin, dulcimer, and spoons, and many shows also feature mountain-style jig dances. An adjoining crafts village has numerous demonstrations and daytime programs recalling 19th-century pioneer life in the Ozarks. The center also has a restaurant and motel-style rooms for overnight stays. ⊠ *1032 Park Ave.* ☎ *870/269–3851* ⊕ *www.ozarkfolkcenter.com* ✉ *Music Auditorium: $10; Crafts Village: $10; combination tickets available* ☉ *Mid-Apr.–Nov. 1; call for dates and times.*

> **STRANGE BUT TRUE**
>
> One of the more odd destinations in the Ozarks is the town of Eureka Springs, Arkansas, accessible via winding mountain roads near the Missouri border. In the mid- to late 19th century, the town was a popular destination for those who believed in the healing powers of the water that bubbled up from natural springs in the area. Today the town is an eccentric mixture of traditional Ozarks mountain culture, bohemian artiness, Victorian architecture, Christian fundamentalism, and alternative spirituality (numerous New Age practitioners who have set up shop here).

FAYETTEVILLE

The cultural center of northwest Arkansas, Fayetteville is home to the flagship campus of the University of Arkansas and a large performing arts center. A popular farmer's market brings crowds to a charming downtown square, where the lack of parking and numerous ethnic restaurants make it feel like a much bigger city. Nearby Dickson Street is the main student drag, where bars and shops are being crowded out by new condominiums that are an indication of the region's growing prosperity.

Shiloh Museum of Ozark History. Several miles north of Fayetteville in the Ozarks boomtown of Springdale, this museum tells the story of the settlement and growth of northwest Arkansas, through a re-created homestead showcasing the hardscrabble life of early residents and displays on the fruit and poultry industries that led it to the region's current status as an economic powerhouse. Outside is a reconstructed pioneer village featuring a barn and general store. ⊠ *118 W. Johnson Ave.* ☎ *479/750–8165* ⊕ *www.springdaleark.org/shiloh* ✉ *Free* ☉ *Weekdays 10–5.*

Fodor'sChoice **BUFFALO NATIONAL RIVER**

★ Winding nearly 150 mi from the Boston Mountains until it flows into the White River high in the Ozarks, the Buffalo passes by some of the country's most pristine scenery. Sandstone and limestone bluffs soar more than 400 feet in parts of the river, creating virtual canyons. Black bear, bobcat, and mink have all been spotted in the area, as well as herds of elk, which can be easily sighted near some stretches of the river.

Hiking, hunting, and fishing are all popular, but the true draw for locals and visitors is a float trip, with canoes and kayaks perfectly tailored for the many long, lazy stretches of river. While some parts—particularly the upper Buffalo—have whitewater stretches that should be attempted only by experienced paddlers, most sections are made for laid-back floats that require no more than basic paddling skills. The park office has information on local outfitters who run float trips, as well as tips for a successful float. There's also a visitor center at Tyler Bend on U.S. Highway 65 between the towns of Gilbert and St. Joe. Some parts of the river can get crowded, especially on weekends in spring and early summer. Numerous individual and group campsites are along the river. The small town of Jasper is a popular staging point for float trips, and has restaurants and lodgings.

14

Fodor's Choice ★ **OZARK & MARK TWAIN NATIONAL FORESTS**
Covering nearly 3 million acres, the Ozark National Forest in northern Arkansas and the Mark Twain National Forests in southern and central Missouri offer unparalleled backcountry adventure. Endless hiking trails crisscross the peaks, woods, and valleys, including the 165 mi Ozark Highlands Trail, which may rival the Appalachian Trail for rugged hiking through undisturbed wilderness. (It's also possible to hike short portions of this trail.) For longer hikes or extended trips in the woods it's a good idea to check with area ranger stations before you set out, and make sure you have a good map. (Maps are usually available at ranger stations.) Canoeing, kayaking, caving, mountain biking, and horseback riding are also popular activities, and backcountry camping is allowed on most forest service land. Several state parks are in or near the forests, and lodging options abound, from primitive campsites to fully equipped cabins with kitchens and bathrooms.

WHERE TO EAT

	WHAT IT COSTS IN U.S. DOLLARS				
	¢	$	$$	$$$	$$$$
Restaurants	under $10	$10–$19	$20–$29	$30–$40	over $40

Prices are per person for a main course at dinner.

BRANSON

$$–$$$$
Fodor's Choice ★
✕ **Candlestick Inn.** Perched on a bluff overlooking downtown Branson and Lake Taneycomo, this cozy, narrow room bookended by fireplaces is a throwback to an earlier era of elegant dining. Since opening in 1962 the restaurant has been known for its steaks and prime rib, and the menu also includes champagne-battered lobster and tournedos of beef and wild mushroom with Maytag bleu cheese. The famous Candlestick Cupcake is the signature desert. ⊠ *127 Taney St.* ☎ *417/334–3633* ⊟ *AE, D, DC, MC, V* ⊗ *Closed Mon. and Tues. No lunch.*

SPRINGFIELD

$–$$$ ✕**Fire & Ice.** Locals flock to this
★ hip dining room in the Oasis Hotel
and Convention Center just off
I–44. An ice bar runs the length of
the open kitchen, and dishes are
served by black-clad waitstaff. Din-
ners begin with bread served with
pomegranate papaya and garlic
herb butters. A delicious salmon
in raspberry vodka sauce shares
menu space alongside all-American
entrées with innovative twists, such
as pork chops with chipotle gin-
ger barbecue sauce, and meat loaf
with applewood smoked bacon
and roasted tomato espagnole.
On Wednesday the menu includes
cashew chicken, which was first
served in Springfield by executive
chef Wing Yee Leong's father and
remains a local favorite. ✉*2546
N. Glenstone* ☎*417/522–7711* ▭*AE, D, DC, MC, V* ☾*Closed Sun.*

> **LIKE A LOCAL**
>
> One thing visitors will notice
> in the Ozarks is the odd pro-
> nunciation of certain words. If
> you're used to hearing the state
> pronounced "Mis-sour-EE," you
> may be surprised to hear some
> natives say "Mis-sour-AH." Bolivar,
> Missouri, is "BAWL-i-var," while
> out on the edge of the Ozarks,
> Nevada, Missouri is "Ne-VAY-da,"
> and nearby El Dorado Springs is
> "El Dor-AY-duh." (On the other
> side of the state, New Madrid is
> "New MAD-rid.") This may be due
> to early settlers' Deep South
> origins—or it might simply be a
> case of Ozark quirkiness.

MOUNTAIN VIEW

¢–$$$ ✕**Tommy's Famous.** This laid-back, family-owned pizza and barbe-
cue joint is just past the courthouse and downtown. Pizza toppings
include pesto and shiitake mushrooms. They also serve excellent ribs
and calzones with a variety of fillings. ✉*Carpenter and West Main
St.* ☎*870/269–3278* ▭*No credit cards* ☾*No lunch.*

FAYETTEVILLE

¢–$ ✕**Hugo's.** You descend a sidewalk staircase just off the Fayetteville town
★ square to enter this funky subterranean bar and grill that's popular
with students and locals. You can't go wrong with the burgers, especially the "Bleu Moon," with melted blue cheese. The menu also has
more offbeat pub grub, such as quiche Lorraine and a cheese board
that can include camembert, edam, and port wine cheddar. The fried
catfish po' boy is a true taste of the Ozarks. ✉*25½ N. Block Ave.*
☎*479/521–7585* ▭*AE, D, MC, V* ☾*Closed Sun.*

WHERE TO STAY

WHAT IT COSTS IN U.S. DOLLARS					
	¢	$	$$	$$$	$$$$
FOR 2 PEOPLE	under $75	$75–$125	$126–$175	$176-$225	over $225

Prices are for two people in a standard double room in high season.

BRANSON

$–$$$$
Fodor'sChoice
★

Hilton Branson Convention Center. Towering over downtown and the new Branson Landing complex, this hotel is a step up from typical Branson lodging options. Rooms are sleek and stylish, with retro lounge chairs, flat-screen televisions, and floor-to-ceiling windows. A sweeping staircase descends from the mezzanine restaurant to the lobby, which includes several sitting areas clustered around a stone fireplace. (A smaller boutique hotel, the Hilton Promenade at Branson Landing, is one block away.) ⊠*200 E. Main St., 65616*☎*417/336–5400 or 417/336–5500* ⊕*www.hilton.com* ⋧*290 rooms* ⌂*In-room: safe, kitchen (some), refrigerator, Ethernet, Wi-Fi, In-hotel· restaurant, room service, bar, pools, gym, laundry service, concierge, public Internet (fee), public Wi-Fi, parking (fee), some pets allowed (fee), no-smoking rooms* ▤*AE, D, DC, MC, V.*

14

SPRINGFIELD

$–$$$
★

University Plaza Hotel & Convention Center. A short distance from downtown restaurants and nightlife (a downtown shuttle is available), this high-rise hotel features a skylighted atrium, with a fountain flanking the lobby bar. ⊠*333 John Q. Hammonds Pkwy.,* ☎*417/864–7333* ⊕*www.upspringfield.com* ⋧*271 rooms* ⌂*In-room: kitchen (some), refrigerator (some), Ethernet, Wi-Fi. In-hotel: restaurant, bar, pools, gym, laundry facilities, public Internet, public Wi-Fi, parking (no fee), some pets allowed (fee)* ▤*AE, D, MC, V.*

MOUNTAIN VIEW

¢–$$
★

Wildflower Bed & Breakfast. This rambling old house sits just behind Mountain View's courthouse square. The interior is light and breezy, and all rooms have private bath and television. Book far ahead for summer weekend stays. ⊠*100 Washington St., 72560*☎*870/269–4383 or 800/591–4879* ⊕*www.wildflowerbb.com* ⋧*6 rooms* ⌂*In-room: no phone, kitchen (some), refrigerator (some), VCR (some), Wi-Fi. In-hotel: no elevator, public Wi-Fi, no-smoking rooms* ▤*AE, D, MC, V.*

FAYETTEVILLE

$–$$$

Inn at Carnall Hall. This converted dorm on the University of Arkansas campus still retains a few touches of its former life, but the interiors would be largely unrecognizable to former undergrads. Stylish furniture and flat-screen televisions complement high-ceilinged guest rooms, some of which have whirlpool tubs and gorgeous views of the older buildings on the university quad. The wraparound porch and fireplace in the lobby provide a relaxing, homey feel. ⊠*465 N. Arkansas Ave., 72701*☎*479/582–0400 or 800/295–9118* ⊕*www.innatcarnallhall. com* ⋧*49 rooms* ⌂*In-room: refrigerator (some), Ethernet (some), Wi-Fi. In-hotel: restaurant, room service, bar, laundry service, public Internet, parking (no fee), no-smoking rooms* ▤*AE, D, DC, MC, V.*

NIGHTLIFE & THE ARTS

For information on show schedules and tickets, as well as maps of area attractions, check out one of Branson's visitor centers at the intersection of U.S. Highway 65 and Missouri Highway 160 north of Branson,

ON THE WAY

William J. Clinton Presidential Center. Perched on the banks of the Arkansas River in downtown Little Rock, the museum and library reviews the career of the 42nd president, with video and interactive exhibits, as well as a full-scale replica of the Oval Office. ⊠ *1200 President Clinton Ave., Little Rock AR 72201* 🕾 *501/374-4242* ⊕ *www.clintonpresidentialcenter.org* 🎫 *$7* 🕙 *Mon.–Sat. 9–5, Sun. 1–5.*

George Washington Carver National Monument. Carver was raised on this farm, and developed his lifelong interest in botany and other sciences here. The on-site museum features extensive and detailed exhibits on Carver's work with the peanut and other plants, and tells his remarkable life story—from slavery to an esteemed career as a scientist and professor. ⊠ *5646 Carver Rd., Diamond, MO 64840* 🕾 *417/325-4151* ⊕ *www.nps.gov/gwca* 🎫 *free* 🕙 *Daily 9–5.*

and at the intersection of U.S. Highway 65 and Missouri Highway 248 in town. You can also call 800/214–3661 or 417/334–4084, or log onto explorebranson.com. Be aware that several shows and attractions are closed from January until March.

VISITOR INFORMATION

Arkansas Department of Parks & Tourism (⊠ *1 Capitol Mall, Little Rock, AR, 72201* 🕾 *501/682-7777* ⊕ *www.arkansas.com*).

Branson Lakes Area Chamber of Commerce and Convention & Visitors Bureau (⊠ *Box 1897, Branson, MO, 65615* 🕾 *417/334-4084* ⊕ *www.explorebranson.com*).

Buffalo National River (⊠ *402 N. Walnut St., Harrison, AR, 72601* 🕾 *870/741-5443* ⊕ *www.nps.gov/buff*).

Fayetteville Visitors Bureau (⊠ *21 S. Block Ave., Suite 100, Fayetteville, AR, 72701* 🕾 *479/521-5776 or 800/766-4626* ⊕ *www.experiencefayetteville.com*).

Mark Twain National Forest (⊠ *401 Fairgrounds Rd., Rolla, MO, 65401* 🕾 *573/364-4621* ⊕ *www.fs.fed.us/r9/forests/marktwain*).

Missouri Division of Tourism (⊠ *Box 1055, Jefferson City, MO, 65102* 🕾 *573/751-4133 or 800/519-2100* ⊕ *www.visitmo.com*).

Mountain View Chamber of Commerce (⊠ *Court Square, Box 133, Mountain View, AR, 72560* 🕾 *870/269-8068 or 888/679-2859* ⊕ *www.ozarkgetaways.com*).

Ozark National Forest (⊠ *605 W. Main St., Russellville, AR, 72801* 🕾 *479/964-7200* ⊕ *www.fs.fed.us/oonf/ozark/*).

Springfield Convention & Visitors Bureau (⊠ *815 E. St. Louis St., Springfield, MO, 65806* 🕾 *417/881-5300 or 800/678-8767* ⊕ *www.springfieldmo.org*).

New Orleans

Mardi Gras

WORD OF MOUTH

"New Orleans is a city with a lot of character. I found it very different from almost every other American city I have been to and I have been to nearly 40 states in the country. With the weather and the old city street layout (and the buildings), it really comes across as a European city . . . One fine night, steamboat Natchez was playing (rather loud!!) Dukes of Dixieland off its speakers and complete with whistles, horns, and changing lights. It really was quite magical."

–ComfyShoes

www.fodors.com/forums

EXPLORING NEW ORLEANS

195 mi west of Pensacola, FL, via I–10; 350 mi east of Houston via I–10; 400 mi south of Memphis via I–55; 460 mi southwest of Atlanta via I–85 and I–65

By Russell McCulley

"It has been said that a Scotchman has not seen the world until he has seen Edinburgh; and I think that I may say that an American has not seen the United States until he has seen Mardi-Gras in New Orleans."

—Mark Twain, 1859

Mark Twain called New Orleans one of four unique American cities, a distinction that the Crescent City still deserves today. This is a vibrant, colorful, over-the-top place, a city of excess filled with music, food, drink, and fun. The calendar is packed with festivals celebrating everything from jazz to gumbo to Tennessee Williams, but spontaneous parties can pop up at any time, for *any* reason—people even dance in the street after funerals here.

And while this party atmosphere was once the dominant image associated with the city, today Hurricane Katrina is the first thing that comes to mind when people think of New Orleans. The city was crippled by the storm, and though it's still not back to 100%—whole neighborhoods are gone, and the residents who remain are fighting hard to rebuild their homes—the heart of New Orleans remains. It beats a little stronger each month. Today there are more restaurants in the city than before Katrina, and almost as many hotel rooms. The most popular parts of the city—the French Quarter and the Garden District—are completely up and running, filled with unusual sights, opulent hotels, delicious food, and soul-stirring music. So come on down for a visit. You'll help this historic city get back on its feet and, more importantly, you'll find out what Mark Twain was talking about.

WHO WILL ESPECIALLY LOVE THIS TRIP?

People-Watchers: Think America is becoming too homogenous? Then you haven't been to Louisiana recently. Stroll down Bourbon Street at 2 AM, join a dance party in Cajun Country, or take a swamp tour. You'll definitely meet people here who you wouldn't encounter anywhere else in America.

Live Music Lovers: Jazz was born here, and America's only homegrown musical art form continues to thrive in New Orleans. Hear it at classic spots like Preservation Hall or the Palm Court Jazz Café, or countless venues around the city.

Foodies: New Orleans is packed with great restaurants, like Commander's Palace and Brennan's, where you don't so much have a meal as an experience. For more modest (but no less delicious) fare, grab a po'boy at Johnny's, a muffuletta from Central Grocery, or tuck into a plate of beignets at the most quintessential New Orleans dining destination of them all—Café du Monde.

TOP 5 REASONS TO GO:

Mardi Gras: The quintessential party in America's party town.

French Quarter Strolls: Walking amid the city's historic buildings, you'll meet buskers and drunks, artists and ghosts. It's one of the most intriguing neighborhoods in the country.

All That Jazz: Entire chapters of America's musical history were written here—and you can still see some of the country's best artists perform here in incredibly intimate settings.

Soul Food: Eating in New Orleans is like going on a taste safari. There's Creole, Cajun, and southern comfort food, as well as ethnic eats and countless fusion cuisines.

Cajun Culture: It's alive and well in South Louisiana's smaller burgs, where locals celebrate their heritage in food, song, and other occasionally odd ways (like doing the Saturday morning two-step at Fred's Lounge in Mamou).

15

Families: Don't wince, there's plenty to see and do here if you have kids in tow. The city has fantastic museums, the Aquarium of the Americas and Audubon Zoo, fabulous parks, and more colorful attractions (and people) than you can shake a stick at. (One of our favorites is Blaine Kern's Mardi Gras World.) Just steer clear of Bourbon Street at night—unless you're prepared to answer a lot of uncomfortable questions from your five-year-old.

History Buffs: With so much historic architecture—and residents who guard their traditions like family heirlooms—New Orleans feels like a living museum. There's much here for anyone interested in the nation's history, from lovingly restored plantations and French Quarter town homes to the impressive National World War II Museum in the Warehouse District.

WHEN IS THE BEST TIME TO VISIT?

The best time to visit New Orleans is early spring. Days are pleasant, except for seasonal cloudbursts, and nights are cool. The azaleas are in full bloom, and the city bustles from one outdoor festival to the next. May through September is hot and humid—but most hotels and restaurants are air-conditioned, and in July and August, hotel prices are lower. June through September are the months to watch for heavy rains and occasional hurricanes; weather can be capricious, but generally pleasant, in October and November. Although winters are mild compared with those in northern climes, the high humidity can really put a chill in the air December through February.

New Orleans is nothing if not festive, and festivals play an important role in the city's cultural and entertainment calendars. Some of the more significant events include the Mardi Gras celebrations and the Jazz & Heritage Festival, which runs from late April to early May. Smaller festivals held throughout the year may not be quite as showy as

Fat Tuesday, but they often give visitors a better understanding of New Orleans than the better-publicized, star-studded events.

HOW SHOULD I GET THERE?

DRIVING
If you're driving, it's easy to get to New Orleans. Interstate 10 runs from Florida to California and passes directly through the city (from up north, take I–55). To get to the CBD (Central Business District), exit at Poydras Street near the Louisiana Superdome. For the French Quarter, look for the Orleans Avenue/Vieux Carré exit.

FLYING
Since Katrina, flights in and out of Louis Armstrong New Orleans International Airport are at about 70% of prehurricane levels. Several carriers offer nonstop flights, but despite the airport's name, international flights are routed through other U.S. hubs. Try to book as early as you can—flights tend to fill up, and the longer you wait, the more you can expect to pay. This is especially true for popular weekends like Mardi Gras and Jazz Fest.

TRAIN
Three Amtrak lines serve New Orleans: the Crescent, with daily service from New York City; the City of New Orleans, which travels to and from Chicago daily; and the Sunset Limited, which makes a stop in New Orleans three times a week on its Orlando-to-Los Angeles route. The Sunset Limited, in particular, is plagued by frequent delays, so plan accordingly.

HOW DO I GET AROUND?

BY CAR
Having a car in New Orleans is no problem—except at Mardi Gras and during other special events, including the Sugar Bowl (around New Year's) and the Bayou Classic (Thanksgiving weekend). During these times, some streets in the French Quarter and CBD are closed to traffic. At all times of the year, carefully read street signs in the French Quarter and CBD; tickets are quickly written, and towings are frequent. For excursions to surrounding Plantation Country and Cajun Country, you'll definitely need a set of wheels.

BY STREETCAR
Inside New Orleans, the riverfront streetcar covers a 2-mi route along the Mississippi River, connecting major sights from the end of the French Quarter (Esplanade Avenue) to the New Orleans Convention Center (Julia Street), with nine stops along the way. This streetcar operates 7 AM to 10:30 PM, passing each stop every 30 minutes. The famous St. Charles Avenue streetcar line runs from Canal Street—the border between the French Quarter and the CBD—to the corner of Carrollton and Claiborne avenues, via the Garden District and Uptown. The line was shut down after Hurricane Katrina, but had resumed partial service at this writing; it's expected to be fully operational by summer

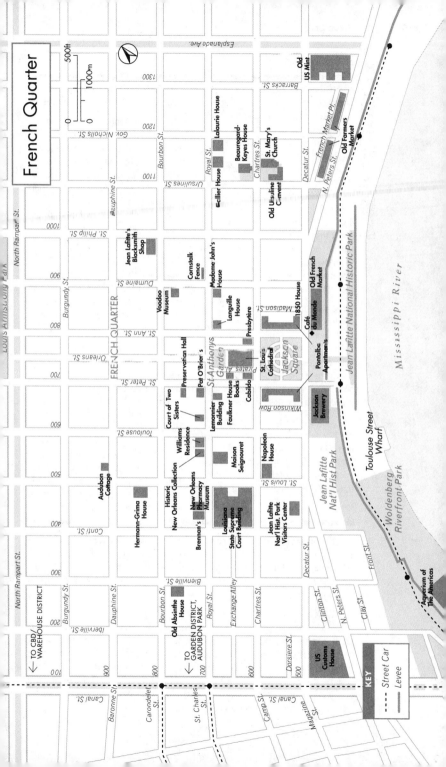

French Quarter

500 ft

1000 m

Esplanade Ave.

1300

1200

Gov. Nicholls St.

Bourbon St.

1100

Royal St.

Lalaurie House

Beauregard-Keyes House

St. Mary's Church

Barracks St.

Old US Mint

French Market Pl.

Old Farmers Market

Decatur St.

North Rampart St.

Louis Armstrong Park

St. Philip St.

1000

Burgundy St.

900

Dauphine St.

Ursulines St.

Chartres St.

Gallier House

Old Ursuline Convent

N. Peters St.

Jean Lafitte's Blacksmith Shop

Dumaine St.

Cornstalk Fence

Madame John's House

Voodoo Museum

Longuille House

Presbytère

800

St. Ann St.

Madison St.

1850 House

Café du Monde

Old French Market

Jean Lafitte National Historic Park

Mississippi River

FRENCH QUARTER

Orleans St.

700

St. Anthony's Garden

St. Louis Cathedral

Preservation Hall

Pat O'Brien's

Jackson Square

Pontalba Apartments

Pirate's Alley

Cabildo

Faulkner House Books

St. Peter St.

600

Toulouse St.

Court of Two Sisters

Williams Residence

Lemonnier Building

Wikinson Row

Jackson Brewery

Toulouse Street Wharf

Woldenberg Riverfront Park

500

Audubon Cottage

Maison Seignouret

Napoleon House

St. Louis St.

Jean Lafitte Nat'l Hist Park

Conti St.

400

Hermann-Grima House

Historic New Orleans Collection

New Orleans Pharmacy Museum

Brennan's

Louisiana State Supreme Court Building

Jean Lafitte Nat'l Hist. Park Visitors Center

Decatur St.

Front St.

Aquarium of The Americas

North Rampart St.

← TO CBD/ WAREHOUSE DISTRICT

Iberville St.

Burgundy St.

200

Dauphine St.

Bourbon St.

Old Absinthe House

← TO GARDEN DISTRICT, AUDUBON PARK

Bienville St.

Royal St.

Exchange Alley

Chartres St.

Clinton St.

N. Peters St.

Clay St.

300

Baronne St.

100

Canal St.

Caronelet St.

St. Charles St.

Canal St.

Camp St.

Magazine St.

US Customs House

Dorsiere St.

500

600

700

800

900

KEY

--- Street Car

— Levee

CLOSE UP

How to Snack

New Orleans boasts some superb fine dining establishments—including a few that have been around for more than a century—but people here are just as proud of the simple fare that has fueled the working classes for generations. You can get a plate of red beans and rice most any day, but it's traditionally served on Monday (and still shows up as the Monday special on many café menus). Legend has it that Monday was set aside for laundry, so home cooks needed something they could throw in a pot and forget about while they went about the laborious task of washing.

While the origins of the muffuletta sandwich are debatable, there's no doubt about the durability of this gut-busting sandwich. Locals and visitors alike queue up at **Central Grocery** for whole- or half-muffulettas, Italian bread loaves stuffed with ham, salami, provolone, and a layer of olive salad.

The po'boy—sliced meat, fried seafood, or even fried potatoes crammed into a loaf of French bread and slathered in mayonnaise or gravy—is another must-try for visitors, who throng **Mother's** (*401 Poydras St.,* *504/523-9656*) and **Johnny's** (*511 St. Louis St., 504/524-8129*) at lunchtime.

Crawfish are another regional specialty. The little crustaceans turn up in elegant Creole dishes such as etouffe and bisque, but are best served boiled with potatoes, onions, and incendiary spices, ready for sloppy snacking. During peak season, from late January through June, boiled crawfish turn up on many menus—even in bars, where you're likely to find a big portable cauldron set up on the sidewalk.

Napoleon House Bar and Café (*500 Chartres St., 504/524-9752*) serves a respectable jambalaya, the Cajun spin on paella made famous in the eponymous Hank Williams song.

For sweets, it's hard to beat the beignets at **Café du Monde,** where the fried French-style "doughnuts" come dusted in powdered sugar and accompanied by chicory-laced café au lait. And then there's the praline, traditionally a wafer of sugar, butter, cream, and pecans, now available in nontraditional flavors such as chocolate, coconut, peanut butter, and rum. They're available in shops all over the French Quarter, some of which offer a view of the candy chef in action.

2008. A third streetcar line runs along Canal Street several blocks from the river to City Park and passes every 12 minutes. One-way fare is $1.25 (exact change); one-day and three-day visitor passes are available at $5 and $12, respectively, for unlimited rides. Children up to two years old ride free.

BY TAXI

Cabs are metered at $2.50 minimum for two passengers, plus $1 for each additional passenger, $1 for fuel allowance, and $2 per mile. You can hail cabs in some of the busier areas (try Decatur Street or Canal Street), or call one. If you need a cab from a major event, call and have one pick you up a few blocks away (so you aren't stuck sitting in the congestion once your ride shows up). During Mardi Gras, it can be extremely difficult to get a cab.

WHERE SHOULD I FOCUS MY ENERGY?

If you're here for 1 day: If your visit is brief, focus your attention on the French Quarter, in the heart of the city, which you can easily see in a day.

If you're here for 2 days: Include a visit to the Garden District, filled with elegant homes, and do some shopping on Magazine Street.

If you're here for 3 days: Check out the Warehouse District, packed with art galleries, restaurants, and a handful of fine museums.

If you're here for 4 days: Include a guided Katrina Tour to visit the Lower Ninth Ward and other areas of the city hit hard by the storm, or arrange a swamp tour for a glimpse of Louisiana's wilder side.

If you're here for 5 days: Visit Blaine Kern's Mardi Gras World.

If you're here for 6 days: Venture outside New Orleans to Plantation Country and tour a few grand antebellum estates.

If you're here for 7 days or more: Spend at least one night in Cajun Country to dine and party with people who love to do both.

WHAT ARE THE TOP EXPERIENCES?

The Food: New Orleans has absorbed culinary influences from all over the world and distilled them into what may be the country's most distinctive regional cuisines. A quick crash course: at the top of the food pyramid, so to speak, sits Creole, which blends classic French techniques with south Louisiana's ridiculously bountiful seafood harvest. Cajun cuisine, another big component of New Orleans–style dining (if you want to start an argument, ask a group of locals where to get the best bowl of gumbo), is Caribbean and West African–influenced soul food. Beyond these two culinary traditions is a wealth of local delights: overstuffed po'boys, olive salad–laden muffuletta sandwiches, red beans and rice, beignets and café au lait, and flaming bananas Foster. You'll quickly learn why eating is one of New Orleans visitors'—and locals'—favorite pastimes.

The Music: Prepare to be blown away by the amount of good local music on tap, any night and in just about any neighborhood. While some of the city's most noteworthy musicians—from Louis Armstrong to Harry Connick Jr. and Marsalis brothers Wynton and Branford—sought fame and fortune elsewhere, quite a few elder statesmen (and women) who have spent their careers in New Orleans. Jazz gets most of the attention, but scratch around the city's club scene and you can find much more: rhythm and blues, funk, roots rock, zydeco, and even a little country. Clubs tend to be intimate and informal, and crowds are lively.

The Festivals: Pick a weekend; chances are, there's a festival happening in or near New Orleans. Carnival, several days of pageantry, debauchery, and just plain silliness that culminate on Mardi Gras day, is the Big One. The New Orleans Jazz and Heritage Festival, in late April and early May, runs a close second. If you want to avoid big crowds, there are countless smaller festivals like the Tennessee Williams Literary Festival, the French Quarter Festival, and celebrations dedicated to everything from tomatoes and gumbo to the lowly mirliton, or chayote.

The Architecture: Few other American cities have preserved as much of their bricks-and-mortar history as New Orleans—and not just in the French Quarter, although that's a good place to start. With some buildings dating back to the late 18th century, the Quarter's stately Jackson Square, delicate wrought-iron balconies, and leafy courtyards reflect centuries of French, Spanish, and Caribbean influences. The mansions of St. Charles Avenue and the oak-shaded Garden District, the distinctive shotgun houses scattered throughout the Faubourg Marigny, opulent plantation homes—even the city's crumbling, aboveground cemeteries—are also worth a look.

BEST BETS

SIGHTS & TOURS

Aquarium of the Americas. The museum has four major exhibit areas—the Amazon Rain Forest, the Caribbean Reef, the Mississippi River, and the Gulf Coast—all of which have fish and animals native to that environment. A special treat is the Seahorse Gallery, which showcases seemingly endless varieties of these beautiful creatures. The aquarium's spectacular design allows you to feel part of the watery worlds by providing close-up encounters with the inhabitants.

Fodor'sChoice
★

Woldenberg Riverfront Park, which surrounds the aquarium, is a tranquil spot with a view of the Mississippi. Package tickets for the aquarium and a river cruise are available outside the aquarium. You can also combine tickets for the aquarium and the **Entergy IMAX Theater,** a river cruise, and the **Audubon Zoo** in a package, or take the river cruise by itself. Note that the zoo cruise halts operation for several weeks around December each year for maintenance. ⊠ *1 Canal St., French Quarter* ☎ *504/581–4629 or 800/774–7394* ⊕ *www.auduboninstitute. org* ⊠ *Aquarium $17.50; combination ticket with IMAX $22.50; combination ticket for aquarium, zoo, and round-trip cruise $41* ☉ *Aquarium Tues.–Sun. 10–5; hrs are subject to change, so check Web site or call before visiting.*

★ **French Market.** The sounds, colors, and smells here are alluring: street performers, ships' horns on the river, pralines, muffulettas, sugarcane, and Creole tomatoes. Originally a Native American trading post, later a bustling open-air market under the French and Spanish, the French Market historically began at Café du Monde and stretched along Decatur and North Peters streets all the way to the downtown edge of the Quarter. Today the market's graceful arcades have been mostly enclosed and filled with shops and eateries, and the fresh market has been pushed several blocks downriver, under sheds built in 1936 as part of a Works Progress Administration project. This area of the French Market, which begins at Ursulines Street and contains a

CLAIM TO FAME

New Orleans' chief selling point may be the fact that it's so unlike any other place in America. Few other cities have retained as distinctive a culture, from the street music of brass bands to the Creole-Cajun cuisine that graces the city's tables. Then there's the backdrop: whether it was the result of neglect or thoughtful preservation, the city has managed to hold onto a tremendous amount of its architectural heritage, not only in the French Quarter and Garden District but throughout its neighborhoods. The *laissez-faire* attitude that prevails in New Orleans is reflected in its relaxed attitudes toward work and play (with Mardi Gras and 24-hour bars being the most obvious examples) as well as a general tolerance for people who fall well outside the mainstream. Since 2005, of course, New Orleans may be best known for Hurricane Katrina and the horrors that storm wrought; even years later, recovery still consumes much of daily life here. But there are a lot of proud locals who are determined to rebuild, while fiercely protecting the traditions and attractions that make city special.

15

large **flea market** as well as a farmers' market area and its own praline and food stands, was slated for major renovation even before Katrina tore away its awnings and the 2005 hurricane season devastated the farming communities that provided its produce. The new renovated French Market is not only a great place to shop for cheap souvenirs, sunglasses, or beads, but a vibrant farmers' market as well. ⊠ *Decatur St., French Quarter* ⊙ *Daily 6–6; hrs may vary depending on season and weather.*

★ **Jackson Square.** Surrounded by historic buildings and filled with plenty
☺ of the city's atmospheric street life, the heart of the French Quarter is today a beautifully landscaped park. Originally called the Place d'Armes, the square was founded in 1718 as a military parade ground. It was also the site of public executions carried out in various styles, including burning at the stake, beheading, breaking on the wheel, and hanging. A **statue of Andrew Jackson,** victorious leader of the Battle of New Orleans in the War of 1812, commands the center of the square; the park was renamed for him in the 1850s. The words carved in the base on the cathedral side of the statue—THE UNION MUST AND SHALL BE PRESERVED—are a lasting reminder of the federal troops who occupied New Orleans during the Civil War and who inscribed them. President George W. Bush made a major address to the nation here after Katrina, in which he celebrated the importance of the city in the history of the country and the federal government's commitment to its recovery.

Among the notable buildings around the square are **St. Louis Cathedral** and **Faulkner House.** Two Spanish colonial–style buildings, the **Cabildo** and the **Presbytère,** flank the cathedral. The handsome rows of brick apartments on each side of the square are the **Pontalba Buildings.** The park is landscaped in a sun pattern, with walkways set like rays streaming out from the center, a popular garden design in the royal court of King Louis XIV, the Sun King. In the daytime dozens of artists hang their paintings on the park fence and set up outdoor studios where they work on canvases or offer to draw portraits of passersby. These artists are easy to engage in conversation and are knowledgeable about many aspects of the Quarter and New Orleans. You can also be entertained by musicians, mimes, tarot-card readers, and magicians who perform on the flagstone pedestrian mall surrounding the square, many of them day and night. ⊠ *French Quarter* ⊙ *Park daily 8 AM–dusk; flagstone paths on park's periphery open 24 hrs.*

Fodor's Choice ★ **Bourbon Street.** Ignore your better judgment and take a stroll down Bourbon Street, past the bars, restaurants, music clubs, and novelty shops that have given this strip its reputation as the playground of the

HISTORY YOU CAN SEE

When Thomas Jefferson negotiated the Louisiana Purchase with Napoleon Bonaparte, he was really after New Orleans, a strategic post near the mouth of the Mississippi River. Throughout the 19th century, the port city blossomed into one of the nation's largest and most significant, a beneficiary of the cotton industry and brisk international trade (much of it, tragically, built on the backs of slaves). New Orleans' heyday is long past, but many visible remnants of its Colonial and Antebellum past remain, from the French Quarter to the elegant plantation homes dotting the Mississippi.

South. The bars of Bourbon Street were among the first businesses of the city to reopen after the storm; catering to the off-duty relief workers, they provided a different form of relief. On most nights, the crowds remain lighter here than in recent years, but the spirit of unbridled revelry is back in full swing. The noise, raucous crowds, and bawdy sights are not family fare; if you go with children, do so before sundown. Although the street is usually well patrolled, it's wise to stay alert to your surroundings. The street is blocked to make a pedestrian mall at night; often the area is shoulder to shoulder, especially during major sports events and Mardi Gras.

★ **Jean Lafitte National Park Visitor Center.** This center has free visual and sound exhibits on the customs of various communities throughout the state, as well as information-rich daily history tours of the French Quarter. The one-hour daily tour leaves at 9:30 AM; tickets are handed out one per person (you must be present to get a ticket), beginning at 9 AM, for that day's tours only. Arrive at least 15 minutes before tour time to be sure of a spot. The office also supervises and provides information on Jean Lafitte National Park Barataria Unit, a nature preserve (complete with alligators) across the river from New Orleans, and the Chalmette Battlefield, where the Battle of New Orleans was fought in the War of 1812. Each year in January, near the anniversary of the battle, a reenactment is staged at the Chalmette site. ⊠ *419 Decatur St., French Quarter* ☎ *504/589–2636* ⊙ *Daily 9–5.*

Fodor's Choice ★ **National World War II Museum.** The former National D-Day Museum was renamed in 2006 to reflect the full scope of its exhibits. The brainchild of historian and writer Dr. Stephen Ambrose, who taught for many years at the University of New Orleans until his death in 2002, this moving, well-executed examination of World War II covers far more ground than simply the 1944 D-Day invasion of Normandy. The seminal moments are re-created through propaganda posters and radio clips from the period; biographical sketches of the military personnel involved; a number of short documentary films (including one bitterly sad film on the Holocaust, featuring interviews with survivors); and collections of weapons, personal items, and other artifacts from the war. The exhibits occupy a series of galleries spread through the interior of a huge warehouse space. One spotlighted exhibit, in a large, open portion of the warehouse near the entrance, is a replica of the Higgins boat troop landing craft, which were manufactured in New Orleans. ⊠ *925 Magazine St., main entrance on Andrew Higgins Dr., Warehouse District* ☎ *504/527–6012* ⊕ *www.ddaymuseum.org* ⊠*$14* ⊘ *Tues.–Sun. 9–5.*

Fodor'sChoice ★ **Garden District.** With its beautifully landscaped gardens surrounding elegant antebellum homes, the Garden District lives up to its name. Although very few buildings in the neighborhood are open to the public on a regular basis, enjoying the sights from outside the cast-iron fences surrounding their magnificent estates is well worth the visit.

15

The Garden District is divided into two sections by Jackson Avenue. Upriver from Jackson is the wealthy **Upper Garden District,** where the homes are meticulously kept up. Below Jackson, the Lower Garden District is rougher in areas, though the homes here are often structurally just as beautiful and are increasingly being restored. Still, the streets are less well patrolled and best toured during the day. **Magazine Street,** lined with antiques shops, boutiques, restaurants, and coffeehouses, serves as a southern border to the Garden District. As part of the "high ground" of the city, it too escaped flooding from Katrina and reopened quickly following the storm; its charm and vivacity is well worth a visit. St. Charles Avenue forms the northern border. The historic St. Charles Streetcar is a fun and leisurely way to see the sights along the avenue on the way from downtown.

Fodor'sChoice ★ **The St. Charles Avenue streetcar** provides a wonderful way to take in the neighborhood. In the early 1900s streetcars were the most prominent mode of public transit and ran on many streets. Today, streetcars operate here, along the riverfront, and along Canal Street. ■ TIP→ **Avoid rush hours—from 7 to 9 and 3 to 6—or you may have to stand still much of the way and will not be able to enjoy the scenery.** The ride on the streetcar from Washington Avenue, in the center of the Garden District, to Louisiana Avenue takes about 30 minutes (considerably more during rush hour).

★ ℭ **Audubon Park.** Formerly the plantation of Etienne de Boré, the father of the granulated sugar industry in Louisiana, **Audubon Park** is a large, lush stretch of green between St. Charles Avenue and Magazine Street, continuing across Magazine Street to the river. Designed by John Charles Olmsted, nephew of Frederick Law Olmsted (who laid out New York City's Central Park), it contains the world-class **Audubon Zoo**; a 1.7-mi track for running, walking, or biking; picnic and play areas; a golf course; a tennis court; and a river view. Calm lagoons wind through the

STRANGE BUT TRUE

To its credit—or detriment, depending on your point of view—the Puritan work ethic has never gained much of a foothold in New Orleans. Even the captains of industry here largely put aside business for a couple of weeks each year to become captains of secretive Mardi Gras krewes, donning elaborate costumes, parading the streets atop floats, and tossing trinkets to the less fortunate rabble below.

By Fat Tuesday, virtually the entire city has shut down; the mayor cedes power to the King of the Krewe of Rex, who orders all citizens to set aside work and devote the day to merriment. There have been interruptions (as during World War II, when parades took a hiatus) and attempts at reform (a city ordinance in the early 1990s forced the old-line krewes to integrate or lose their parading permits). But the celebration has endured—even Hurricane Katrina didn't derail Mardi Gras.

park, harboring egrets, catfish, and other indigenous species. The park and zoo were named for the famous ornithologist and painter John James Audubon, who spent many years working in and around New Orleans. None of the original buildings from its former plantation days remain; in fact, none of the buildings that housed the 1884–85 World's Industrial and Cotton Centennial Exposition, which was held on these acres and gave New Orleans its first international publicity after the Civil War, have survived. The only reminder of this important event in New Orleans's history is Exposition Boulevard, the street address assigned to houses that front the park along the downtown side.

If time permits, you may want to venture beyond the zoo, cross the railroad tracks, and stroll along **Riverview Drive,** a long stretch of land behind the zoo that is part of Audubon Park, on the levee overlooking the Mississippi River. This area is referred to as "The Fly" by locals, after a butterfly-shape building that was torn down here some years ago, and it's a popular place for picnics and pickup sports. The river lookout includes Audubon Landing, where the *John James Audubon* cruise boat (nicknamed "the zoo cruise" because it travels between the Aquarium of the Americas downtown and the zoo) docks, and a landscaped walkway. ⊠*6500 Magazine St., Uptown* ☎*504/586–8777* ⊕*www.auduboninstitute.org* ☜*Park free; zoo $12.50, zoo cruise $17, combination ticket for zoo and Aquarium of the Americas $22.50, combination ticket for cruise, zoo, and aquarium $38.25* ☼*7-mi river ride to French Quarter and Canal St. daily at 11, 1, 3, and 5.*

Fodor'sChoice
★
☾
Blaine Kern's Mardi Gras World. Blaine Kern has for many years been the best-known artist and creator of Mardi Gras floats; he often personally conducts tours through this one-of-a-kind facility. You can watch the artists and builders at work, view a film about Mardi Gras, and buy Carnival memorabilia in the gift shop. A photo of you with one of the giant figures used on the floats makes a terrific souvenir, and there's a chest full of costumes for children to try on. A free shuttle van takes you from the ferry to Mardi Gras World; otherwise, an

enjoyable 10-minute walk along the levee gets you here. (Note: At this writing, there were rumors that Mardi Gras World might move. Please confirm the current location before your visit.) ⊠ *233 Newton St., Algiers Point* ☎ *504/362–8211* ⊕ *www.mardigrasworld.com* ⊠ *$13.50 includes cake and coffee* ⊙ *Daily 9:30–4:30.*

OUTSIDE NEW ORLEANS

Fodor'sChoice
★
The South's largest plantation house, **Nottoway**, should not be missed. Built in 1857, the mansion is a gem of Italianate style. With 64 rooms, 22 columns, and 200 windows, this white castle (the town of White Castle was named for it) was the crowning achievement of architect Henry Howard. It was saved from destruction during the Civil War by a Northern officer (a former guest of the owners, Mr. and Mrs. John Randolph). An idiosyncratic layout reflects the individual tastes of the original owners and includes a grand ballroom, famed in these parts for its crystal chandeliers and hand-carved columns. You can stay here overnight, and a formal restaurant serves lunch and dinner daily. ⊠ *30970 Rte. 405, 70 mi west of New Orleans* ☎ *225/545–2730 or 866/527–6884* ⊕ *www.nottoway.com* ⊠ *$10* ⊙ *Daily 9–5.*

15

WHERE TO EAT

WHAT IT COSTS					
	¢	$	$$	$$$	$$$
AT DINNER	under $9	$9–$16	$17–$25	$26–$35	over $35

Restaurant prices are for a main course at dinner, excluding sales tax of 9.5%.

$$$–$$$$
★
✗ **Brennan's.** Lavish breakfasts are what first put Brennan's on the map. They're still a big draw from morning to night on two floors of luxuriously appointed dining rooms in a gorgeous 19th-century building. The best seats include views of the lush courtyard and fountain. For breakfast, eye-opening cocktails flow freely, followed by poached eggs sandwiched between such treats as hollandaise, creamed spinach, artichoke bottoms, and Canadian bacon; all are listed with suggested wines. Headliners at lunch or dinner include textbook versions of oysters Rockefeller and seafood gumbo, and bananas Foster, which was created here. Looking for consistency? Chef Lazone Randolph has been creating culinary delights in Brennan's kitchen for more than 40 years. The wine list is a stunner, both in quantity and quality. ⊠ *417 Royal St., French Quarter* ☎ *504/525–9711* ⟋ *Reservations essential* ▭ *AE, D, MC, V.*

$$$–$$$$
Fodor'sChoice
★
✗ **Commander's Palace.** No restaurant captures New Orleans's gastronomic heritage and celebratory spirit as well as this one, long considered the grande dame of New Orleans's fine dining. The post-Katrina renovation has added new life, especially upstairs, where the Garden Room's glass walls have marvelous views of the giant oak trees on the patio below; other rooms promote conviviality with their bright pastels. The menu's classics include foie-gras-and-rabbit pie; a spicy and meaty turtle soup; terrific grilled veal chops with grits; and a wonder-

LIKE A LOCAL

"You want that dressed, dawlin'?" Order a po'boy, and you'll likely be faced with that question. "Dressed" simply means with mayo, lettuce, and tomato. And the term of endearment is one of the city's more charming customs: don't be surprised if someone much younger than you calls you "baby," even if it's a meter maid scolding you for parking illegally.

If someone giving you directions tells you to cross the "neutral ground,"

fear not: they're not referring to a DMZ but the median on one of the city's wide boulevards.

You'll often hear locals greeting each other with a cheery "Where y'at?" This is not to be taken literally; it's the equivalent of "how are you doing?" and has given rise to a slangy description of natives, "Yats," who speak with the peculiarly Brooklynesque accent of working class New Orleans.

ful sautéed Gulf fish coated with crunchy pecans. Among the addictive desserts is the bread-pudding soufflé. Weekend brunches are a New Orleans tradition. Jackets are preferred at dinner. ☒ *1403 Washington Ave., Garden District* ☎ *504/899–8221* ♣ *Reservations essential* ▭ *AE, D, DC, MC, V.*

$$$ ✕ **August.** If the Gilded Age is long gone, someone forgot to tell the
Fodor'sChoice folks at August, whose main dining room shimmers with masses of
★ chandelier prisms, thick brocade fabrics, and glossy woods. Service is anything but stuffy, however, and chef John Besh's modern technique adorns every plate. Nothing is mundane here: handmade gnocchi with blue crab and winter truffle shares menu space with Texas wild boar, pheasant, "sugar and spice" duckling, and even a slow-cooked venison. The sommelier is happy to confer with you on the hefty, but surprisingly affordable, wine list. ☒ *301 Tchoupitoulas St., CBD* ☎ *504/299–9777* ♣ *Reservations essential* ▭ *AE, MC, V* ☉ *Closed Sun. No lunch Sat.*

$–$$$ ✕ **Galatoire's.** Galatoire's has always epitomized the old-style French-
Fodor'sChoice Creole bistro. Many of the recipes date to 1905. Fried oysters and
★ bacon en brochette are worth every calorie, and the brick-red rémoulade sauce sets a high standard. Other winners include veal chops in béarnaise sauce, and seafood-stuffed eggplant. The setting downstairs is a single, narrow dining room lighted with glistening brass chandeliers; bentwood chairs and white tablecloths add to its timelessness. You may reserve a table in the renovated upstairs rooms, though the action is on the first floor, where partying regulars inhibit conversation but add good people-watching entertainment value. Friday lunch starts early and continues well into early evening. A jacket is required. ☒ *209 Bourbon St., French Quarter* ☎ *504/525–2021* ▭ *AE, D, DC, MC, V* ☉ *Closed Mon.*

¢–$ ✕ **Central Grocery.** This old-fashioned Italian grocery store produces
Fodor'sChoice authentic muffulettas, one of the gastronomic gifts of the city's Italian
★ immigrants. Good enough to challenge the po'boy as the local sandwich champs, they're made by filling round loaves of seeded bread with

ham, salami, mozzarella, and a salad of marinated green olives. Sandwiches, about 10 inches in diameter, are sold in wholes and halves. You can eat your muffuletta at a counter, or get it to go and dine on a bench on Jackson Square or the Moon Walk along the Mississippi riverfront. The Grocery closes at 5:30 PM. ⊠ *923 Decatur St., French Quarter* ☎ *504/523–1620* ⊟ *D, MC, V* ☼ *No dinner.*

¢–$ ✕ **Johnny's Po'boys.** Strangely enough, good po'boys are hard to find in
★ the French Quarter. Johnny's compensates for the scarcity with a cor-
☼ nucopia of them, even though the quality is anything but consistent, and the prices are somewhat inflated for the tourist trade. Inside the soft-crust French bread come the classic fillings, including lean boiled ham, well-done roast beef in garlicky gravy and crisply fried oysters or shrimp. The chili may not cut it in San Antonio, but the red beans and rice are the real deal. The surroundings are rudimentary. It's open until around 4 PM daily. ⊠ *511 St. Louis St., French Quarter* ☎ *504/524–8129* ⊟ *No credit cards* ☼ *No dinner.*

¢ ✕ **Café du Monde.** No trip to New Orleans is complete without a cup
Fodor'sChoice of chicory-laced café au lait and addictive sugar-dusted beignets in this
★ venerable Creole institution. The tables under the green-and-white striped awning are jammed at every hour with locals and tourists feasting on powdery doughnuts and views of Jackson Square. The magical time to go is just before dawn, when the bustle subsides and you can hear the birds in the crepe myrtles across the way. Four satellite locations (Riverwalk Marketplace in the CBD, Lakeside Shopping Center in Metairie, Esplanade Mall in Kenner, and Veterans Boulevard in Metairie) are convenient but lack the character of the original. ⊠ *800 Decatur St., French Quarter* ☎ *504/525–4544* ⊟ *No credit cards.*

WHERE TO STAY

	WHAT IT COSTS			
	¢	$	$$	$$$	$$$$
2 PEOPLE	under $100	$100–$149	$150–$199	$200–$275	over $275

Prices are for two people in a standard double room in high season, excluding 13% city and state taxes.

$$$$ 🏨 **Harrah's New Orleans Hotel.** One of the newest entrants into the
Fodor'sChoice local hotel market is also one of the most luxurious. Directly across the
★ street from Harrah's New Orleans casino, this 26-story hotel is richly appointed with marble floors, exquisite chandeliers, plush furnishings, and artwork selected and installed by local gallery owner Arthur Roger. High-profile chef Todd English's lobby-level restaurant, Riche, features strictly French cuisine, and big-name local entertainers headline "528," an adjacent jazz club nightly. Guest rooms are larger than the local norm and have extras like refrigerators, high-definition televisions, cordless phones, and Wi-Fi. A four-block promenade featuring shops, private party spaces, and live entertainment areas is connected to the hotel. ⊠*Poydras St. at Fulton St., CBD, 70130* ☎*504/533–6000 or 800/847–5299* 🖷*504/593–8010* ⊕*www.harrahs.com* 🛏*450 rooms,*

15

ON THE WAY

If you're driving into New Orleans from the west, you'll likely be crossing the 18-mi I-10 bridge over the Atchafalaya River Basin, more than a half-million acres of sparsely populated bottomland and swamp. It's a scenic stretch and a popular place for guided swamp tours, home to gators and Louisiana black bears and an important stop on the North American bird migration route.

Mark Twain hated it, but the castlelike Old State Capitol in Baton Rouge—not far from the Huey P. Long–commissioned skyscraper that replaced it is a good starting point for exploring that city's revitalized downtown. The refurbished building houses a museum dedicated to Louisiana political history—a subject that makes for quite a colorful collection.

Coming into New Orleans from the North, you pass near a number of towns that don't quite fit into the Cajun Country or plantation trail categories, but make worthwhile stops nonetheless: Potchatoula, for antiques shopping or the town's annual Strawberry festival; Covington, for its scenic downtown and arts and crafts; and Mandeville, on the northern shore of Lake Pontchartrain, which was a summertime refuge for prosperous New Orleanians back in the steamboat era.

---

81 suites & In room: refrigerator, Wi-Fi. In-hotel: restaurant, bar, pool, gym, spa, concierge, laundry service ▤AE, D, DC, MC, V.

$$$$

Fodor'sChoice

★

The Ritz-Carlton New Orleans. The Ritz occupies the artfully converted, historic Maison Blanche department store building with a luxurious hotel reminiscent of old New Orleans. Rooms are furnished with local antiques, and feature oversize marble bathrooms, and plush linens. The Club Floor has 75 rooms, including one suite, with a concierge and a private lounge. The expansive lobby, adorned in carefully selected fine art and upscale furnishings found in traditional New Orleans homes, opens onto a luxurious courtyard. The hotel's recently opened dining room, Mélange, offers re-creations of signature dishes from high-profile restaurants throughout the city. The hotel, within walking distance of most attractions and minutes from the Convention Center, borders the French Quarter and faces the CBD. ⊠*921 Canal St., French Quarter, 70112* ☎*504/524–1331* 🖷*504/524–7675* ⊕*www.ritzcarlton.com* 🛏*527 rooms, 38 suites & In-hotel: restaurant, bars, spa, parking (fee)* ▤*AE, D, DC, MC, V.*

$$$–$$$$

Fodor'sChoice

★

Monteleone Hotel. The grande dame of French Quarter hotels—with its ornate baroque facade, liveried doormen, and shimmering lobby chandeliers—was built in 1886 and renovated in 2004. A stellar addition is the full-service Spa Aria. Rooms are extra large and luxurious, with rich fabrics and a mix of four-poster beds, brass beds, and beds with traditional headboards. Junior suites are spacious; sumptuous VIP suites come with extra pampering. The slowly revolving Carousel Piano Bar *(⇨Nightlife)* in the lobby is a local landmark, and the first-rate dinner in the hotel's Hunt Room Grill is one of the city's best-kept secrets. There's live jazz every night in the lounge. ⊠*214 Royal St., French Quarter, 70130* ☎*504/523–3341 or 800/535–9595*

504/528–1019 ⊕*www.hotelmonteleone.com* 🛏*600 rooms, 55 suites* ⚐*In-room: Wi-Fi. In-hotel: 3 restaurants, bar, pool, gym, spa, concierge, public Wi-Fi* ⊟*AE, D, DC, MC, V.*

$$–$$$$ 🖼 **Hotel Maison de Ville.** This small romantic hotel lies in seclusion amid
Fodor'sChoice   the hustle and bustle of the French Quarter. Tapestry-covered chairs, a
★   gas fire burning in the sitting room, and antiques-furnished rooms all
contribute to a 19th-century atmosphere. Some rooms are in former
slave quarters in the courtyard; others are on the upper floors of the
main house. Breakfast is served on a silver tray, and port and sherry
are available in the afternoon. For a special hideaway, book one of
the hotel's Audubon Cottages. ✉*727 Toulouse St., French Quarter,
70130* 📠*504/561–5858 or 800/634–1600* 📠*504/528–9939* ⊕*www.
maisondeville.com* 🛏*14 rooms, 2 suites, 7 cottages* ⚐*In-room: Wi-
Fi. In-hotel: pool, parking (fee), no kids under 12* ⊟*AE, D, DC, MC,
V* ⧉*CP.*

15

NIGHTLIFE & THE ARTS

Fodor'sChoice   **Lafitte's Blacksmith Shop.** Probably the most photographed building in
★   the Quarter after St. Louis Cathedral, this atmospheric piano bar in an
18th-century cottage recently underwent renovations that critics say
left the exterior, with its coyly artificial "crumbling" plaster, reeking of
Disneyland-style architectural kitsch. The rustic and candle-lit interior
is as appealing as ever, though, and the small outdoor patio has banana
trees and a sculpture by the late Enrique Alferez, whose work decorates
City Park. ✉*941 Bourbon St., French Quarter* 📠*504/522–9397.*

★   **Pat O'Brien's.** Pat O's, heavily dependent on the tourism and convention
trade, struggled to regain its bearings after Hurricane Katrina disrupted
the city's hospitality trade. But the venerable bar has bounced back,
gradually expanding its hours and entertainment in the popular piano
bar to the right of the St. Peter Street entrance. Sure, it's touristy, but
worth a visit for its friendly staff, easy camaraderie among patrons, and
the lush patio out back, which is heated in winter. ✉*718 St. Peter St.,
French Quarter* 📠*504/525–4823.*

Palm Court Jazz Café. Banjo player Danny Barker immortalized this res-
taurant in his song "Palm Court Strut." The best of traditional New
Orleans jazz is presented in this classy setting with tile floors, exposed
brick walls, and a handsome mahogany bar. There are decent crea-
ture comforts here; regional cuisine is served, and you can sit at the
bar and rub elbows with local musicians. There's a wide selection of
records, tapes, and CDs on sale here. ✉*1204 Decatur St., French
Quarter* 📠*504/525–0200.*

Fodor'sChoice   **Preservation Hall.** The jazz tradition that flowered in the 1920s is
★   enshrined in this cultural landmark by a cadre of distinguished New
Orleans musicians, most of whom were schooled by an ever-dwindling
group of elder statesmen who actually played with Louis Armstrong
et al. There's limited seating on benches—many patrons end up squat-
ting on the floor or standing in back—and no beverages are served or
allowed. Nonetheless, the legions of satisfied customers regard an eve-
ning here as an essential New Orleans experience. Cover charges range

VITAL STATS:

■ As of late 2007, the population of New Orleans was hovering at about 300,000—roughly two-thirds what it was before Hurricane Katrina.

■ At 450 feet, Louisiana's State Capitol building in Baton Rouge, the brainchild of Gov. Huey P. Long, is the tallest in the U.S.

■ The St. Charles Avenue streetcar has been running in one form or another—from locomotives to mule-drawn cars to the electric-powered cars used today—since 1835, making it the oldest continually used transit line in the country.

■ Unlike the other 49 states, Louisiana is divided into parishes, not counties.

■ Le Petit Theatre du Vieux Carre, founded in 1916, is the country's oldest community theater.

■ The Louisiana Catahoula Leopard Dog, also known as the Catahoula Cur, is the state's official dog. The breed's roots go back to the 16th century and the "war dogs" that accompanied the Spanish explorer Hernando De Soto.

■ The official colors of Mardi Gras—purple, green, and gold—represent justice, faith, and power, respectively, and were introduced by the Krewe of Rex in 1892 (appropriately, their theme that year was "Symbolism of Colors").

from $8 to $20 for special appearances. ⊠726 St. Peter St., French Quarter ☎504/522–2841 or 504/523–8939.

FodorsChoice **Maple Leaf.** The phrase "New Orleans institution" gets thrown around
★ a lot, but this place deserves the title. It's wonderfully atmospheric, with pressed-tin walls and a lush tropical patio, and one of the city's best venues for blues, New Orleans–style R&B, funk, zydeco, and jazz. On Sunday, the bar hosts the South's longest-running poetry reading. It's a long haul from the French Quarter, but worth the trip, especially if combined with a visit to one of the restaurants clustered near this commercial stretch of Oak Street. ⊠8316 Oak St., Uptown ☎504/866–9359.

VISITOR INFORMATION

Louisiana Office of Tourism ⌂ Box 94291, Baton Rouge, LA 70804-9291 ☎800/633–6970 ⊕www.louisianatravel.com.

New Orleans Convention & Visitors Bureau ⊠2020 St. Charles Ave., 70130 ☎800/672–6124 or 504/566–5011 ⊕www.neworleanscvb.com.

New Orleans Multicultural Tourism Network ⊠1520 Sugar Bowl Dr., 70112 ☎800/725–5652 or 504/523–5652 ⊕www.soulofneworleans.com.

The Texas Hill Country

WITH SAN ANTONIO AND AUSTIN

Texas Hat Shop, Fredericksburg

WORD OF MOUTH

" . . . if you're on Main Street, stop in at the Fredericksburg Winery. It is on the edge of the main drag. For a very reasonable price, you can get a flight consisting of up to five wines. And the winemakers were very entertaining in explaining the differences, etc. They have a wonderful orange muscat."

—sarge56

EXPLORING THE TEXAS HILL COUNTRY

Fredericksburg, TX is 78 mi west of Austin via U.S. 290; 70 mi northwest of San Antonio via I–10 and U.S. Highway 87; 263 mi northwest of Houston via I–10 and U.S. Highway 87; and 271 mi southwest of Dallas via I–35 and U.S. Highway 290

By Jessica Norman Dupuy

The word "Texas" evokes images of wild prairies, ranches, and the Rio Grande winding through a desert populated with cacti and cowboy clones of John Wayne—or oil barons like J.R. Ewing living in plantation-style mansions in suburban Dallas. But the Lone Star State is a much more than the sum of its Western- and pop culture stereotypes—it's a broad, diverse place filled with natural wonders, sophisticated cities, culinary treasures, historic towns, and vibrant arts and nightlife scenes.

Texas's number-one regional treasure, the Hill Country, is between two thriving, centrally located cities—artsy, left-wing Austin and internationally infused San Antonio. It's an area filled with rolling hills and placid lakes, charming towns, and independent wineries. The area has a dozen or more towns—Fredericksburg is the most popular with tourists—but its defining feature is the land itself. The Hill Country is etched with dramatic slopes of rocky terrain, wide-open vistas displaying an endless horizon of blue sky, and roads that seemingly go on forever. Graying cedar posts wrapped in rusty barbed wire meander about a rough-hewn landscape contrasted with rugged mesquite-plagued pastures and fields of vibrant wildflowers (especially colorful and fragrant come spring, when the famous bluebonnets blanket the hills). Majestic Cypress trees shade idyllic spring-fed rivers, while sprawling-armed oak trees cool the facades of weather-worn ranch houses.

WHO WILL ESPECIALLY LOVE THIS TRIP?

Sunday Drivers: Some of the most spectacular views of the Hill Country can be experienced from the seat of a car—or the back of a Harley, if you prefer. With countless ups and downs, Ranch Road 337 from Medina to Vanderpool is especially great for motorcycles. For an added treat, end this picturesque drive by spending a few hours at Lost Maples State Park, to the north on Ranch Road 187. A second option is Bandera to Kerrville via State Highway 16. Though State Highway 173 is a more direct route between the two towns, Highway 16 offers a more worthwhile experience with tight, winding passages and steep climbs—take precautions if you're prone to motion sickness. If you're in Fredericksburg, then Ranch Road 1376 from Fredericksburg to Boerne makes for an excellent drive (be sure to stop in Luckenbach for some great live music—you never know who's going to stop here and play a set).

Music Lovers: The Hill Country is where the vibrant Tejano music, made popular by the late Selena, got its start. Fans of this music genre—as well as just about every other kind of beat—gravitate to central Texas for the annual big-town events like Austin's South By Southwest and Austin City Limits Music Festivals, as well as for the year-round enter-

TOP 5 REASONS TO GO:

Fredericksburg: There's a little something for everyone along this peaceful town's Main Street. An afternoon here will likely net a collection of shopping bags, a hearty German meal, and a few samplings of German beer and Texas wine.

Wine: Take a journey down the Texas Wine Trail and taste for yourself why some critics see a robust and full-bodied viticultural future for the Hill Country.

Gruene: This tiny town packs quite a punch. Grab a burger and a cold beer, and watch the sun set on the Guadalupe River at the Gristmill before heading to the famed Gruene Hall to catch an evening show.

Enchanted Rock State Park: Interested in scaling the face of a massive 1,825-foot-tall pink rock (or at least seeing one in person)? Then head to this excellent state park, where camping, hiking, and rock climbing are other popular pursuits.

Austin & San Antonio: Texas's capital is known for the pulsating sounds of 6th Street, a buzzing arts scene, some of the best live music in the country (including the massive South By Southwest festival), and its friendly, laid-back, liberal population (the city's unofficial motto is "Keep Austin Weird"). Tourist mecca San Antonio boasts the colorful and lively Riverwalk, the legendary Alamo, and a myriad of family-fun spots like Sea World and Six Flags Fiesta Texas.

16

tainment at legendary small-town venues, such as Luckenbach and Gruene Hall. Several music giants past and present call this area home, including songwriters Robert Earl Keen and Willie Nelson and rock-'n'-roll legend Stevie Ray Vaughan.

Foodies: San Antonio and Austin are home to some amazing Tex-Mex, barbecue, and fine dining experiences. Among the best for Tex-Mex are Polvo's in Austin, and Rosario's and Mi Tierra in San Antonio. Barbecue bests are spread all over: the Salt Lick in Driftwood, Cooper's in Llano, and Rudy's in a number of locations between Austin and San Antonio. You won't find much haute cuisine on the Hill Country back-roads, but Fredericksburg is home to a few upscale restaurants, including August E's and Rebecca's Table. The Hill Country is filled with casual places serving down-home and ethnic fare, from German-influenced entrées at New Braunfels' October Wurstfest and Fredericksburg's Oktoberfest, to the handmade gorditas from Mason's family-run Santo's Taqueria y Cantina.

Wine Enthusiasts: Think you have to go to Napa to sample good wine? You may be surprised at what's in store for you here. Vintners across the Hill Country are abuzz with hearty blends of wine created from the fruits of the region's arid limestone earth. It's the same type of soil you'd find in northwest Italy and southern Spain and France, where revered names such as Chateauneuf-du-Pape stake their claim. The best times to tour Hill Country wineries are spring—especially during Austin's Texas Hill Country Wine and Food Festival in April—and fall, when the vineyards turn deep colors and the festival calendar is packed with events like the Fredericksburg Food & Wine Fest, the Gruene Music & Wine Fest, and the San Antonio New World Wine & Food Festival.

Nature Lovers: Birders looking to check a few native and migratory species off of their "life list" should visit Lost Maples and Pedernales State parks or take a kayak trip down the Llano River from Mason County, where they'll spy everything from herons and hawks to flycatchers. Traversing the southern part of the region and heading north on U.S. Highway 281 to Marble Falls and west on FM 1431, rock lovers find an abundance of geological formations ranging from fossil-rich limestone to magnificent outcrops of granite. Also hiding in the Hill Country are a number of caves, including the Eckert James River Cave outside of Mason, the Old Tunnel Wildlife Management Area outside of Fredericksburg, and Austin's own man-made cave, South Congress bridge, home to millions of Mexican Free-tailed bats during their migratory and mating seasons.

WHEN IS THE BEST TIME TO VISIT?

There really isn't a bad time to visit the Hill Country. Winters are mild, with days averaging about 50°. Summers—undeniably the high season—are extremely warm in July in August, with temperatures averaging about 85°–90° (many days the mercury tops 100°, especially in San Antonio, which is hotter and more humid than most of the Hill Country). Summertime visitors beat the heat with cool activities like floating (tubing) the Guadalupe River, taking a dip in the ice-cold Krause Springs (34 mi west of Austin in Spicewood), and diving into the blue-lagoon-like Hamilton Pool (30 mi southwest of Austin via Highway 71 and Farm Road 3238).

Though the summer heat doesn't really break until late October (sometimes even later), fall festivities are well under way by mid-September with the Austin City Limits Music Festival, a terrific way to see the "Live Music Capital" at its best. As the weather cools, the Hill Country comes alive with food and wine festivals, such as New Braunfels' Wurstfest and Fredericksburg's Octoberfest, both delivering plenty of beer and German sausage.

Hill Country winters are fairly mild, dipping below freezing in the evenings, but often remaining above freezing for the majority of the season. Though late winter can feel cold and desolate, the festive holiday season transforms many small towns into Dickensian portraits filled with Christmas carolers, flickering lights, and main street parades. Flyfishers find fantastic winter action in the region's many rainbow trout-stocked lakes and rivers.

By early March outdoor enthusiasts are ready to hike Enchanted Rock and bike the Hill Country's back roads. This is also the wildflower season—brilliant red Indian paintbrushes, yellow brown-eyed Susans, and the state's famed bluebonnets flourish in fields all along the roadside.

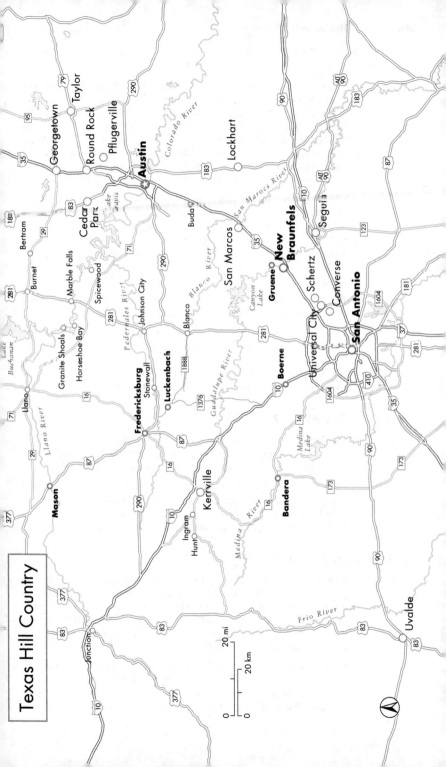

Texas Hill Country

HOW SHOULD I GET THERE?

DRIVING

Centrally located in Texas, you can access the Hill Country from I–35 or I–10, coming from the north and south or east and west, respectively. The area's gateway cities are Austin and San Antonio. Between these two hubs on I–35 lie New Braunfels, Gruene, and San Marcos. Running north and south through the Hill Country is U.S. Highway 281, which intersects with I–10 West and San Antonio, and can be reached from Austin via State Route 71 or U.S. Highway 290; the latter traverses the region from east to west.

Interstate 35 marks the Hill Country's eastern border, while San Antonio's State Loop 1604 notes the southern limit. The northern border is ambiguous but generally includes everything south of Lake Buchanan and along State Highway 29. The western border is also open to interpretation, but is best followed along U.S. Highway 83 from Junction to Uvalde.

FLYING

The main airports for the Hill Country are San Antonio International Airport and Austin's Bergstrom International Airport.

To drive to the Hill Country from Austin's airport, follow U.S. Highway 290 West until the terrain changes from flat to steep and rolling (pretty easy—when you see the hills, you'll know you've arrived). From San Antonio, U.S. Highway 281 North and I–10 West will both take you straight into the heart of the Hill Country.

HOW DO I GET AROUND?

This is the land of the open road—there are no trains, buses, or subways. The best, and really the *only* way to access the Hill Country is by car (or by motorcycle, which is an increasingly popular method).

The towns are all small enough that parking is not a problem. And though it's not encouraged, you're generally safe leaving your car unlocked—locals often joke that they can spot an out-of-towner when they hear the "beep" of a car alarm locking a vehicle.

WHERE SHOULD I FOCUS MY ENERGY?

If you're here for 1 day: Most visitors head to San Antonio or Austin, and you could easily spend a day (or a week!) in either. But if you want to see the heart of Hill Country, go to Fredericksburg. Steeped in German heritage, this tiny town is filled with great restaurants and fun shops. It's also the beginning of the Texas Wine Trail, and just a few miles from musical wonderland Luckenbach.

If you're here for 2 days: Spend more time in Fredericksburg, as there's quite a bit to do. Or, if you want a change of scenery and love to shop, take Comfort on for an afternoon. Be sure to grab lunch at High's (⊠*726 High St.* ☎*830/995–4995*)—the soups, sandwiches, and pas-

CLOSE UP

How to Snack

Strolling Fredericksburg's Main Street amid the myriad shops, you may need a **German sweet pretzel** to tide you over before your next meal. Though not the simplest thing to eat, the pastry dough is a bit crumbly (almost like sweet pie crust) and is sprinkled with pecans, cinnamon, and a sweet, sugary icing. Fresh pretzels are made daily at the Old German Bakery and the Fredericksburg Bakery, as are savory Kolaches—thin German sausages encased in a sweet, doughy bread. It's difficult to find these tasty snacks in every Hill Country town, but in Boerne, the Bear Moon Bakery is sure to have fresh ones on hand.

At fall festivals such as **Wurstfest** and **Octoberfest**, the average attendee is carrying a beer in one hand and a warm German sausage wrap in the other. Vendors can be found throughout the festivals on the main grounds doling them out by the dozens. Spicy German mustard makes a better wrap, and some vendors will include sauerkraut as an added bonus.

Of course, you can't forget Tex-Mex fare. Although chips and salsa are the standard table offering when seated at a Tex-Mex restaurant, **nachos** make a more substantial, and decidedly more rewarding snack. Nachos are strictly fried tortilla chips toasted with cheddar cheese (sometimes Monterrey Jack as well), and served with slices of pickled jalepeños. But most Tex-Mex restaurants and taco stands will sell nachos *compuestos*, which adds piles of refried beans, guacamole, and sometimes sour cream onto the crisp, cheesy snacks. Though it's a pretty simple order, not all nachos are created equal, and Texans are as partial to their favorite Tex-Mex joint as Chicagoans are to their favorite deep-dish pizza purveyor. A couple of safe bets in the Hill Country are **Maudie's** *nachos compuestas* in Austin, **Mamacita's** *nachos de queso* (with cheese) in Kerrville and Fredericksburg, and **La Fogata's** *nachos rancheros de carne* (layered with thick strips of beef fajita meat) in San Antonio.

16

tries are fabulous! Or, if you'd rather soak up some history, head to Stonewall and visit the Lyndon B. Johnson National Historic Park and the Lyndon B. Johnson State Park.

If you're here for 3 days: Add a day in Mason. Rich in history, the town has a lovely downtown square—and some fantastic fly-fishing along the Llano River.

If you're here for 4 days: Check out Cascade Caverns and Boerne's Main Street for shopping and great food at Cypress Grille.

If you're here for 5 days: Take the long way on State Highway 16 to pay homage to the Cowboy Capital, otherwise known as Bandera. It's a beautiful drive, and once you arrive, you may find a horse or two parked outside of Arkey Blue's Silver Dollar bar.

If you're here for 6 days: If you're here in late fall, travel in the direction of Vanderpool and on toward Lost Maples State Park, where the changing leaves are not to be missed. If it's summer, hit the Highland

Lakes. Take U.S. Highway 281 North to Marble Falls and treat yourself to a night at the Horseshoe Bay Resort Marriott Hotel.

If you're here for 7 days or more: If it's warm, keep touring the lakes, including Lake Buchanon and Lake Travis. If it's not, explore Boerne and the Old Tunnel Wildlife Management Area bat cave. Continue east to Gruene for a spin on the legendary floors of Gruene Hall. When your trip's over, stop in Driftwood (if you're flying out of Austin) for a Texas-size helping of the Hill Country's finest barbecue at the Salt Lick.

WHAT ARE THE TOP EXPERIENCES?

The Food: Though you can find anything from thick, juicy burgers to elegantly pan-seared escolar here, the predominant culinary influence in many Hill Country towns is German (especially in Fredericksburg, New Braunfels, and Boerne). Meat lovers will find that true bliss comes from Texas pit-smokers in the form of brisket, sausage, smoked-turkey, and ribs. Barbecue has quite a reputation in the Hill Country, with the best bets being Cooper's in Llano and the Salt Lick in Driftwood (on the outskirts of Austin). Tex Mex also permeates the region, particularly in and around San Antonio.

The Festivals: From German-influenced fall festivals in Fredericksburg and New Braunfels, to spring's Austin City Limits Music Festival and Fiesta in San Antonio, to summer's Peach Jamboree in Fredericksburg, there's a lot of celebrating going on in the Hill Country. The Lakefest drag boat races take place in August in Marble Falls, and Christmas lighting festivals and parades take place in every town around the holidays. Oh, and don't forget that October is Texas Wine Month.

The Music: It's impossible to escape the strong musical influence of this region—and how the different cultures have influenced each other. For instance, the cheerful tones of the accordion, originally popular in German polka-style music, are now frequently used in the widely popular Mexican-influenced Tejano music. More prevalent in the Hill Country are the soulful and often humorous chords strummed by Texas singer-songwriters (the style is pretty eclectic, but you'll usually hear some folk, a dash of country, and a bit of rock 'n' roll—accompanied by thoughtful lyrics). From Gruene Hall to Luckenbach and the honky-tonk bars of Bandera, poets such as Robert Earl Keen, Bruce and Charlie Robison, Lyle Lovett, the Dixie Chicks, and Willie Nelson have all taken center stage in these parts.

The History: Six national flags have flown over the Lone Star State, and many of the state's early turbulent transitions took place in and near Austin, San Antonio, and the Hill Country. The most notable historical marker is of course San Antonio's Alamo, which you should definitely tour if you're visiting the city. But if you have time, be sure to explore the other four 18th-century Spanish missions along San Antonio's Mission Trail.

CLAIM TO FAME

The emerging Hill Country wine scene has added a level of credibility and sophistication to the area's fine dining (in addition to a remarkable number of great vintages). You can find more than Merlot and Chardonnay here, including Malbec, Muscat, Viognier, Riesling—even several renditions of the Texas version of Port. Visit www.texaswinetrail.com to plot your course (there's more information at www.gotexanwine.org, which also includes information on Texas wineries outside the Hill Country).

Music is as ingrained in the culture of this region as the twisting roots of cedar trees that dig deep into the Hill Country's limestone soil. And while Austin, the self-proclaimed "Live Music Capital of the World,"

gets a lot of the attention, you can find talented troubadours throughout the region. Wherever you are, ask around—chances are someone's playing somewhere in town that night. If the stages are all dark, head out to Luckenbach, a Texas Institution where there's always someone strummin' something.

But the Hill Country's biggest draw by far is the quiet escape it offers. Life slows to a more relaxed pace here, and the pleasant environment is echoed in the friendly faces you'll meet in the regions' small towns. So take a deep breath, and enjoy. As Texas singer-songwriter Robert Earl Keen says, "Feels so good, feelin' good again."

16

BEST BETS

SIGHTS AND TOURS

HILL COUNTRY

★ **Enchanted Rock State Natural Area.** Protruding from the earth in the form of a large pink dome, Enchanted Rock looks like something from another planet. This Precambrian granite formation rises 1,825 feet, and its bald vastness can be seen from miles away. Arrive early, park officials close the park to protect the resources once parking lots reach capacity. ⊠ *16710 RR 965, Fredericksburg* ☎ *325/247–3903* ⊕ *www. tpwd.state.tx.us/spdest/findadest/parks/enchanted_rock* ☜ *$6.*

Fodor's Choice **Luckenbach.** Luckenbach isn't just some fabled small Texas town roman-
★ ticized by classic Country singers Willie Nelson and Waylon Jennings. Luckenbach is a state of mind. Whether you're a fan of country music or not, you haven't officially been to Luckenbach without grabbing an ice-cold brew, listening to whomever may be strumming the guitar on stage, and picking up a souvenir bumper sticker for the road. ⊠ *412 Luckenbach Town Loop, off RR 1376, Luckenbach.*

Natural Bridge Caverns. Guides will take you on an incredible journey underground at the largest known cavern in Texas, which has ½ mi of paved trails. The brave of heart shouldn't miss the flashlight tour of the Jaremy Room, a 120-foot-deep chamber known for its soda straws and delicate formations. ⊠ *26495 Natural Bridge Caverns Rd., North of San Antonio, I–35 exit 175, Natural Bridge Caverns Rd./FM*

3009 ☎*210/651–6101* ⊕*www.naturalbridgecaverns.com* ◱*$16.95* ⊙*Daily; call for hrs.*

Llano River. Though the Guadalupe River has received much acclaim for its vast angling opportunities, the Mason County side of the Llano River is a little slice of heaven for fly-fishers. Large outcrops of granite protrude from the river depths creating easy navigable rapids and great deep pools. Some of the river is wade-able, but a kayak or canoe is advised.

Schlitterbahn. This 65-acre waterpark and resort in nearby New Braunfels features more than 40 rides and family activities spread over 6 areas. ⊠*Off I–35 in New Braunfels, between San Antonio and Austin, Exit 184 or 190B* ☎*830/625–2351* ⊕*www.schlitterbahn.com* ◱*$35* ⊙*Late Apr.–mid-Sept.; call for hrs.*

WINERIES

★ Becker Vineyards (⊠464 Becker Farms Rd., Stonewall, 78671 ☎830/644–2681 ⊕www.beckervineyards.com).Bell Mountain Vineyards (⊠463 Bell Mountain Rd., Willow City, 78675 ☎830/685–3297 ⊕www.bellmountainwine.com).Comfort Cellars (⊠723 Front St., Comfort, 78013 ☎830/995–3274 ⊕www.comfort-cellars.com).Driftwood Vineyards (⊠4001 Elder Hill Rd., CR 170, Driftwood, 78619 ☎512/858–9667 ⊕www.driftwoodvineyards.com).Dry Comal Creek (⊠1741 Herbein Rd., New Braunfels, 78132 ☎830/885–4121 ⊕www.drycomalcreek.com).Fall Creek Vineyards (⊠1820 CR 222, Tow, 78672 ☎325/379–5361 ⊕www.fcv.com).Flat Creek Estate (⊠24912 Singleton Bend E, Marble Falls, 78654 ☎512/267–6310 ⊕www.flatcreekestate.com).Grape Creek Vineyards (⊠97 Vineyard La., Stonewall, 78671 ☎830/644–2710 ⊕www.grapecreek.com). Sandstone Cellars (⊠211 San Antonio St., Mason, 76856 ☎325/347–9463 ⊕www.sandstonecellarswinery.com).Sister Creek Vineyards (⊠1142 Sisterdale Rd., RR 1376, Sisterdale, 78006 ☎830/324–6704 ⊕www.sistercreekvineyards.com). Torre Di Pietra Vineyards (⊠10915 E. U.S. Hwy. 290, Fredericksburg, 78624 ☎830/644–2829 ⊕www.texashillcountrywine.com).

AUSTIN

Fodor's Choice **Bob Bullock Texas State History Museum.** Four blocks north of the capitol,
★   this museum hosts exhibitions of archaeological objects, documents,
Ꮯ   and other materials from regional museums throughout the state and also presents historical and educational programs; it's a great overview of Lone Start State history. ⊠*1800 N. Congress Ave., Austin, 78701* ☎*512/936–8746* ⊕*www.thestoryoftexas.com* ◱*Museum $5.50, IMAX $7* ⊙*Mon.–Sat. 9–6, Sun. noon–6.*

★ Downtown Austin is dominated by the impressive **Texas State Capitol** (⊠*1100 Congress Ave., Austin, 78701* ☎*512/463–0063*). Built in 1888 of Texas pink granite, it's even taller than the U.S. Capitol (yes, everything *is* bigger in Texas). Be sure to catch one of the free historical tours, offered 8:30–4:30.

The stately capitol is seated at the north end of **Congress Avenue,** while at the south end—specifically, under the Congress Avenue bridge—is a colony of more than one million Mexican free-tailed bats. The nocturnal critters swarm into town every evening at dusk from May until October.

LIKE A LOCAL

Texans use the word "y'all" a lot. You'll hear it in pretty much any type of conversation, and you'll likely incorporate it into your vocabulary before heading home. (It really is a useful word, and it sounds so nice—at least when Texans say it.) There are a few other sayings and pronunciations that are unique to the Lone Star State:

■ "He's all hat and no cattle": Used to describe someone who is all talk and no action.

■ "This ain't my first rodeo": I wasn't born yesterday.

■ "You can put your boots in the oven, but that don't make them biscuits": Say what you want, but that doesn't make it true.

■ "We've howdied, but we ain't shook yet": We've made a brief acquaintance, but have not been formally introduced.

■ Burnet: "Burn it"

■ Pedernales: "Pur-dah-nallis"

■ Guadalupe: "Gwaa-dah-loop"

■ Manchaca: "Man-shack"

■ San Felipe: "San Fill-a-pee"

Fodor's Choice
★ The **University of Texas** campus flanks the capitol's north end. The campus is home to Austin's new showcase museum, the **Blanton Museum of Art** (✉ *Martin Luther King Jr. Blvd. and Congress St., Austin, 78701* ☎ *512/471–7324* ⊕ *www.blantonmuseum.org* ✍ *$5*), formerly the Huntington Art Gallery. The Blanton, the largest university art museum in the country, holds one of the largest private collections of old master paintings and drawings in the country. The artifacts and voluminous documents on exhibit at UT's **Lyndon Baines Johnson Library and Museum** (✉ *2313 Red River St., Austin, 78705* ☎ *512/721–0200* ⊕ *www.lbjlib. utexas.edu* ✍ *Free* ◷ *Daily 9–5*) provide some insight into the 36th president's mind and motivations, and though his foibles are downplayed, a clear sense of the man—earthy, conniving, sensitive, and wry—emerges.

The **Lady Bird Johnson Wildflower Center** (✉ *4801 LaCrosse Ave., Austin 78739* ☎ *512/292–4100* ⊕ *www.wildflower.org* ✍ *$7* ◷ *Tues.–Sat. 9–5:30, Sun. noon–5:50*) includes a 43-acre complex sponsored by Lady Bird Johnson and has educational programs and extensive plantings of wildflowers that bloom year-round. It's closed Monday.

★ **Zilker Park.** The former site of temporary Franciscan missions in 1730 ☼ and a former American Indian gathering place is now Austin's everyday backyard park. The 351-acre site along the shores of Lake Austin includes **Barton Springs Pool**, numerous gardens, a meditation trail, and a Swedish log cabin dating from the 1840s. Canoe rentals are available for the hour or day (⊕ www.zilkerboats.com). In March the park hosts a kite festival. During spring months concerts are held in the park's Beverly S. Sheffield Zilker Hillside Theater, a natural outdoor amphitheater beneath a grove of century-old pecan trees; in July and August, musicals and plays take over. ✉ *2201 Barton Springs Rd.* ☎ *512/974–6700 parks dept., 512/477–5335 for the Hillside Theater* ⊕ *www.ci.austin. tx.us/zilker* ✍ *Free; parking $3 per vehicle* ◷ *Daily dawn–dusk.*

16

SAN ANTONIO

Fodor's Choice
★
At the heart of San Antonio, the **Alamo** (⊠*Alamo Plaza* ☎*210/225–
1391* ⊕*www.thealamo.org* ✉*Free* ⊗*Mon.–Sat. 9–5:30, Sun. 10–
5:30*), originally a Franciscan mission, stands as a repository of Texas
history, a monument to the 189 volunteers who died there in 1836
during a 13-day siege by the Mexican dictator, General Antonio López
de Santa Anna.

★
Except for the Alamo, all of San Antonio's historic missions consti-
tute **San Antonio Missions National Historical Park** (⊠*2202 Roosevelt Ave.*
☎*210/932–1001* ⊕*www.nps.gov/saan* ✉*Free* ⊗*Daily 9–5*). Established along the San Antonio River in the 18th century, the missions
stand as reminders of Spain's most successful attempt to extend its
New World dominion northward from Mexico. All of the missions
are active parish churches, and all are beautiful, in their own ways.
Start your tour at the stunning **Mission San José** (⊠*6701 San Jose Dr.*
☎*210/922–0543*), the "Queen of Missions," where a National Park
Service visitor center illuminates the history of the missions. San José's
outer wall, Native American dwellings, granary, water mill, and workshops have been restored. Here you can pick up a map of the **Mission
Trail** that connects San José with the other missions. **Mission Concepción**
(⊠*807 Mission Rd., at Felisa St.* ☎*210/534–1540*)is known for its
frescoes.**Mission San Juan** (⊠*9101 Graf Rd.* ☎*210/534–0749*), with
its Romanesque arches, has a serene chapel.**Espada** (⊠*10040 Espada
Rd.* ☎*210/627–2021*), the southernmost mission, includes an Arab-
inspired aqueduct that was part of the missions' famous *acequia* water
management system.

Fodor's Choice
★
San Antonio's **River Walk** (⊕*www.thesanantonioriverwalk.com*), or
Paseo del Rio, is the city's (and the state's) leading tourist attraction.
Built a full story below street level, it comprises about 3 mi of scenic stone pathways lining both banks of the San Antonio River as it
flows through downtown. In some places the walk is peaceful and
quiet; in others it's a mad conglomeration of restaurants, bars, hotels,
and strolling mariachi bands, all of which can also be seen from river
taxis and charter boats. To book a narrated boat tour contact **Rio San
Antonio Cruises** (☎*210/244–5700 or 800/417–4139* ⊕*www.riosan
antonio.com* ✉*$7.75*); they also offer charter dinner cruises. Try
to take your trip near twilight, when the sounds and light begin to
soften.The historic **Arneson River Theatre** (☎*210/207–8610* ⊕*www.
lavillita.com/arneson*) is an outdoor music and performing arts venue
in the heart of La Villita. Audience members sit in outdoor tiered seating on the river's edge and watch performers on the small stage, which
is across the San Antonio River.

★
☺
The University of Texas's **Institute of Texan Cultures** (⊠*801 S. Bowie St.*
☎*210/458–2300* ⊕*www.texancultures.utsa.edu* ✉*$7* ⊗*Tues.–Sat.
10–6, Sun. noon–5*) is an interactive museum focusing on the 30 ethnic
groups who have made Texas what it is today. The museum is closed
Monday.

FodorsChoice Once a farmers market, **Market Square–El Mercado** (✉*Bordered by W.* ★ *Commerce St., Santa Rosa St., Dolorosa St., and I–35* ☎*210/207–8600* ⊕*www.marketsquaresa.com*)is now a bustling marketplace filled with stores and street vendors selling a wide array of goods from Mexico, from pottery to blankets to jewelry. Enjoy the music of roaming mariachis and the delicious foods offered at stalls along the way, and pick up some *pan dulce* (sweet bread) at the famed Mi Tierra Mexican Restaurant and Bakery, open 24 hours a day.

WHERE TO EAT

WHAT IT COSTS IN U.S. DOLLARS				
	¢	$	$$	$$$	$$$$
AT DINNER	under $10	$10–$19	$20–$29	$30–$40	over $40

Prices are per person for a main course at dinner.

HILL COUNTRY

FREDERICKSBURG

¢–$ ✕**Hondo's.** Named for John Russell "Hondo" Crouch, self-proclaimed ★ Mayor of Luckenbach, this local "dive" is becoming something of a legend in itself. If the live music and Texas country decor isn't entertaining enough, the menu certainly is. From the "What's David Smokin' Plate" of finger-lickin' fabulous barbecue, to the "Supa Chalupa Salad," everything about this place radiates good old-fashioned fun. The half-pound doughnut burgers, made in the shape of a donut, are excellent—especially the "Blue Ribbon Barbecue Bacon Burger." The baked Frito chili pie is heaven in a skillet. ✉*312 W. Main St.* ☎*830/997–1633* ▭*AE, D, MC, V.*

MARBLE FALLS

$–$$$ ✕**Cafè 909.** This little urban-esque cafè with muted exposed brick walls, FodorsChoice a long, thin bar, and a cozy New York–size dining room offers a little ★ bit of Dallas chic, with a dash of relaxed Hill Country charm. Chef-owner Mark Schmidt has a penchant for marrying bold flavors with fairly standard fare. Take for instance the plump and savory seared Dayboat scallops resting atop a bed of shortrib-braised farruto (sort of like risotto) accented with fiery horseradish and crème fraiche. Be sure to end the meal with a few spoonfuls of the frozen pistachio parfait—a cloudlike, creamy treat complimented by a decadent burnt honey caramel and crushed pistachios. ✉*909 2nd St., 78654* ☎*830/693–2126* ▭*AE, D, MC, V.*

DRIFTWOOD

¢–$ ✕**The Salt Lick.** If you see smoke rising while driving along FM 1826, FodorsChoice don't be alarmed. It's just the siren song of Driftwood, a barbecue bea-★ con calling you to the perpetually smoking pits, long picnic tables, and dance hall–style compound of the Salt Lick. On weekends—particularly when the Longhorns are at home—this family-friendly hot spot is tough to get into. But it's always worth the wait. Bring your own

16

cooler of beer, and sit beneath the sprawling oaks. You'll be joined by locals and travelers from miles around waiting to feast on perfectly smoked brisket, beautifully basted baby back ribs, vinegary German potato salad and cole slaw, and enough soft white bread to sop up a gallon of the secret sauce. Oh, and did we mention the sausage? Get some of that, too. ⊠ *18001 FM 1826, Driftwood* ☎ *512/858–4959* ▤ *No credit cards.*

AUSTIN

$–$$$$

Fodor'sChoice

★

✕**Jeffrey's.** Executive chef Alma Alcocer holds court at this fine-dining institution in the historic Clarksville area downtown, where the menu of "contemporary Texas cuisine" changes regularly. Expect complex dishes that combine Latin and Southwestern flavors with standbys from more Continental traditions. Start with crispy oysters on yucca chips with habanero-honey aioli, then move on to the balsamic duck and shrimp with baby vegetables, apples, and Roquefort cheese for an entrée. The sophisticated wine list is carefully selected. Cozy alcoves, a romantic atmosphere, and consistently attentive service make for a memorable evening. ⊠ *1204 W. Lynn St., Austin, 78703* ☎ *512/477–5584* ⊕ *www.jeffreysofaustin.com* ▤ *AE, D, DC, MC, V* ⊗ *No lunch.*

$–$$$

★

✕**Fonda San Miguel.** This celebrated villa-style North Loop spot combines sophisticated ambience with a seasonal menu of authentic Mexican classics. Start with quesadillas layered with poblano, chicken, or mushrooms; or go light with ceviche Veracruzano (with chiles, onion, tomato, and spices). Continue with a multilayered dish like the *ancho relleno* San Miguel—a roasted pepper stuffed with chicken, capers, raisins, and olives and topped with cilantro cream—or try the *pollo pibil,* chicken baked in a banana leaf. Shrimp dishes are extraordinary. Yes, most of it is pricey for what you get, but we feel the lovely, romantic atmosphere makes up for it. The extravagant Sunday brunch is the quintessential upscale Austin weekend breakfast. ⊠ *2330 W. North Loop Blvd., Austin, 78756* ☎ *512/459–4121* ⊕ *www.fondasanmiguel. com* ▤ *AE, D, DC, MC, V* ⊗ *No lunch.*

$–$$$

Fodor'sChoice

★

✕**Lamberts.** On an up-and-coming block near City Hall, Lamberts draws businessmen, Web types, trenchermen, and foodies for its "fancy barbecue," aka stylish twists on Texas classics. You know this isn't your father's barbecue joint when you hear Belle & Sebastian on the speakers instead of LeAnn Rimes or Merle Haggard. Chimay beer is available *on draft,* and the Frito pie costs $10 and contains goat cheese. Appetizers range from Asian-style crispy wild-boar ribs to broiled Gulf oysters with apple-smoked bacon. Desserts, like lemon chess pie with

ON THE WAY

Barbecue lovers should make a point to visit the tiny town of Lockhart, southeast of Austin, where fantastic German-style oak-smoked barbecue awaits at the famed **Kreuz Market** (⊠ *619 N. Colorado St.* ☎ *512/398–2361* ⊕ *www.kreuzmarket.com*). Here the brisket is sinfully juicy and tender enough to cut with a plastic fork. The Kreuz family is so proud of their 'cue method—used for more than a century—that they don't serve barbecue sauce (trust us, this stuff is so good it doesn't need sauce getting in the way).

blueberry sauce, are tangy-sweet and satisfying. They even make a decent cappuccino. Service is competent and cheerful. The restaurant is housed in a historic two-story 1873 brick building; the front room has whitewashed brick, green leatherette '60s banquettes, and a bar serving top single-malt Scotches. The second floor has a bar with a few tables and a stage where bands play the nights away. ⊠*401 W. 2nd St., Austin, 78701* ☎*512/494–1500* ⊕*www.lambertsaustin.com* ▤*AE, D, DC, MC, V.*

SAN ANTONIO

$–$$$$ ✗**Citrus.** This über-cool restaurant at the Hotel Valencia overlooks the
★ River Walk and serves New American and Spanish-influenced cuisine. Their creative paella and pasta bar (you choose the ingredients) is popular at lunch, while dinner fare ranges from hickory-plank-roasted redfish to honey-orange-glazed duck. Executive chef Jeff Balfour puts on a pretty good show with fresh produce and a diverse repertoire. An extensive wine list and creative cocktails make it a one-stop shop for an evening's enjoyment. ⊠*150 E. Houston St.* ☎*210/230–8412* ▤*AE, D, DC, MC, V.*

$–$$$ ✗**Biga on the Banks.** Like Texas, enthusiastic chef Bruce Auden's menu
Fodor'sChoice is big and eclectic, and the dining atmosphere manages to be both big-
★ ger than life and romantic. Dishes change daily to take advantage of the freshest food available, ranging from seared red grouper grits to 11-spice axis venison chops. Don't skip out of dessert, which may be the best in town: the sticky toffee pudding is a must. This is one of the best spots for a leisurely dinner on the River Walk, if you can get a reservation. ⊠*203 S. St. Mary's St.* ☎*210/225–0722* ▤*AE, D, DC, MC, V.*

¢–$$ ✗**Mi Tierra Café and Bakery.** In the heart of Market Square lies one of
Fodor'sChoice San Antonio's most venerable culinary landmarks. Opened in 1941 as
★ a place for early-rising farmers to get breakfast, Mi Tierra is now a 24-hour traditional Mexican restaurant, bakery, and bar. Its hallmark breakfasts are served all day, and the *chilaquiles famosas*—eggs scrambled with corn tortilla strips and topped with *ranchero* sauce (similar to salsa) and cheese—are alone worth coming back for again and again. Truly memorable tacos, enchiladas, chalupas, and house specialties, all made from fresh ingredients, are served at lunch and dinner. The giant, carved oak bar serves up aged tequilas, authentic margaritas, draught beer, and mixed drinks. The bakery has an enormous selection of *pan dulces* (Mexican pastries) and excellent coffee. ⊠*218 Produce Row, Market Square* ☎*210/225–1262* ⌂*Reservations not accepted* ▤*AE, D, DC, MC, V.*

WHERE TO STAY

	WHAT IT COSTS IN U.S. DOLLARS				
	¢	$	$$	$$$	$$$$
FOR 2 PEOPLE	under $75	$75–$125	$126–$175	$176–$225	over $225

Prices are for a standard double room for two during peak season, excluding tax and service charges.

16

HILL COUNTRY

MEDINA

$$$$ Escondida Resort. Nestled within this rural, rugged, cowboy country
Fodor'sChoice lies a pristine Mexican-style villa offering privacy and tranquility in one
★ of the few luxury accommodations in the Hill Country. The stately villa
fashioned with stucco, river stone, and exposed timber is reminiscent of
Spanish architecture, but resolutely unique to the rugged Texas region,
is concealed between a cluster of towering hill tops with winding hiking trails and is hugged by the idyllic aquamarine Wallace Creek with
pools created by hand-laid river stone dams. As if the serene surroundings weren't enough to invite a stay here, each of the 10 guest rooms is
outfitted with elegant hardwood and iron furniture with leather chairs
and subtle Mexican tile accents. The cloudlike comfort of triple-sheeted
iron-framed beds makes leaving your room each morning a difficult
feat. The on-site chef prepares hearty, home-style dinners each evening
including appetizers, beer, and wine and a gourmet hot breakfast each
morning. Don't leave without treating yourself to a massage from one
of the spa's excellent therapists. ⊠ *23670 State Hwy. 16 N, 78055*
☎ *888/589–7507* ⊕ *www.escondidaresort.com* ⇆ *10 rooms* △ *In-
hotel: refrigerator, DVD, Wi-Fi, Ethernet. In-hotel: no kids under 21,
some pets allowed* ⊟ *AE, D, MC, V* ⧖ *AI.*

BOERNE

$$–$$$$ ✕ Ye Kendall Inn. Built in 1859 as Boerne's stagecoach stop, this inn,
★ prominently situated in the town square along Cibolo Creek, is a state
and national historic landmark. The main lodge of this 9-acre property
features 22-inch hand-cut limestone walls and airy porches giving an
authentic Hill Country feel. Beyond the main house is a collection of
fully restored cottages—there's even a 19th-century chapel that serves
as a lovely bridal suite. Each of the 36 rooms, suites, or cottages are
uniquely decorated with vintage pieces as well as modern luxuries.
Dinner at the acclaimed Limestone Grill is a must. The inn recently
opened a full service Aveda Spa on the premises. ⊠ *128 W. Blanco,
78006* ☎ *800/364–2138 or 830/249–2138* ⊕ *www.yekendallinn.com*
⇆ *36 rooms* △ *In-room: Wi-Fi. In hotel: restaurant, bar, spa, gym*
⊟ *AE, D, MC, V* ⧖ *EP.*

MARBLE FALLS

$$$$ Horseshoe Bay Resort Marriott Hotel. This isn't your typical Marriott
Fodor'sChoice experience. The views of the glimmering fingers of Lake LBJ weaving
★ between the dramatic slopes of the hills are breathtaking. Every room
features a view of something spectacular and the lush, and tropical-
meets-Hill-Country-rustic landscape is inviting. Despite the rustic feel
of the region, modern amenities here include access to three champi-
onship golf courses, a full-service spa, clay- and hard-surface tennis
courts, room service, and an upscale restaurant and bar. ⊠ *200 Hi
Circle N, Horseshoe Bay, 78657* ☎ *830/598–8600* ⊕ *www.horseshoe
baymarriott.com* ⇆ *349 rooms* △ *In room: refrigerator, Ethernet, Wi-
Fi. In-hotel: 3 pools, laundry facilities, airport shuttle (fee), children's
program, spa, gym, some pets allowed* ⊟ *AE, D, MC, V* ⧖ *EP.*

AUSTIN

$$$$
Fodor's Choice
★

⌂ Driskill Hotel. There may be glitzier hotels in Austin, but the Driskill is the undisputed grande dame, and its staff works hard to maintain the property's pristine reputation. The historic Renaissance Revival edifice, fronting Congress Avenue, was built in 1886 by cattle baron Jesse Driskill. The lobby is highlighted by vaulted ceilings, beautiful columns, and chandeliers. Each room is decorated with original art and rich fabrics. The entire effect is expansive (and expensive) old-fashioned luxury, and the style is Texas to the core. The acclaimed Driskill Grill restaurant and delightfully restored 1886 Café and Bakery are both worth a visit—even if you're not staying at the hotel. The elegant bar (with frequent live piano music) has long attracted Austin's movers, shakers, and wannabes. ✉ 604 Brazos St., Austin, 78701 ☎ 512/474–5911 or 800/252–9367 🖷 512/474–2214 ⊕ www.driskillhotel.com ✦ 176 rooms, 13 suites ⌂ In-hotel: restaurant, room service, bar, parking (no fee) ▭ AE, D, DC, MC, V.

> ### VITAL STATS
>
> - State Capital: Austin
> - State Flower: Bluebonnet
> - State Flying Mammal: Mexican Free-tailed Bat
> - State Dish: Chili (made without beans)
> - Texas derives its name from the Caddo American Indian word *tay shas*, or *tejas*, meaning friend.
> - Six national flags have flown over the state of Texas: Spain, France, Mexico, Republic of Texas, United States, and the Confederate States.
> - Texas is the second largest state after Alaska.

16

$$–$$$$
★

⌂ Barton Creek Resort & Spa. This recreational resort sits on 4,000 acres of Texas Hill Country just west of Austin. You can find four championship golf courses, a European-style spa, meeting facilities, four restaurants, and just about every other amenity you'd expect at a major resort. Standard guest rooms have a king- or two queen-size beds, a bath and a half, study desks with data ports, an armoire with a TV, and a well-stocked minibar, and many also have panoramic views of the surrounding countryside. ✉ 8212 Barton Club Dr., Austin, 78735 ☎ 512/329–4000 or 800/336–6158 ⊕ www.bartoncreek.com ✦ 300 rooms ⌂ In-room: Wi-Fi. In-hotel: 4 restaurants, bar, golf courses, tennis courts, pool, spa, public Internet, public Wi-Fi ▭ AE, D, MC, V.

SAN ANTONIO

$$$$
Fodor's Choice
★

⌂ La Mansion del Rio. Gorgeous, even inspirational, Spanish-style luxury rooms and suites set this enormous hotel apart from the rest of the River Walk. Inside and out it's replete with Mediterranean tiles, archways, and soft wood tones. Rooms are equipped with data ports, and most have balconies or verandas. ✉ 112 College St., 78205 ☎ 210/225–2581 or 800/292–7300 🖷 210/226–0389 ⊕ www.lamansion.com ✦ 337 rooms ⌂ In-room: dial-up. In-hotel: 2 restaurants, room service, bar, pool, airport shuttle, some pets allowed ▭ AE, D, DC, MC, V.

$$$–$$$$
★

⌂ Menger Hotel. Since its 1859 opening, the Menger has lodged, among others, Robert E. Lee, Ulysses S. Grant, Theodore Roosevelt, Oscar

Wilde, Sarah Bernhardt, and Roy Rogers and Dale Evans. Guests appreciate the charming three-story Victorian lobby, sunny dining room, flowered courtyard, and four-poster beds (in the oldest part of the hotel only). ⊠*204 Alamo Plaza, 78205* ☎*210/223–4361 or 800/345–9285* 🖨*210/228–0022* ⊕*www.mengerhotel.com* ↝*316 rooms* ⌂*In-room: dial-up. In-hotel: restaurant, room service, bar, pool, gym, parking (no fee)* ⊟*AE, D, DC, MC, V.*

NIGHTLIFE & THE ARTS

AUSTIN

Numerous traveling and homegrown bands play nightly in Austin's music venues, many of which are clustered around downtown's **6th Street**, between Red River Street and Congress Avenue. The **Warehouse District** (around 4th Street) and the newer **2nd Street District** (which runs between San Antonio Street and Congress Avenue for two blocks north of the river) cater to a more mature crowd. **South Congress** or "SoCo" also has a lively scene.

Fodor'sChoice
★   The **South by Southwest Festivals and Conferences** (usually shortened to SXSW) are a huge music, film, and interactive event held every March at venues in and around Austin.

★   **Antone's** (⊠*213 W. 5th St., Austin, 78701* ☎*512/320–8424 recording, 512/263–4146 information* ⊕*www.antones.net*)is a local musical institution, booking legendary blues and funk acts.

★   The coolest club in this very cool city? We're not absolutely sure, but a prime contender is the **Belmont** (⊠*305 W. 6th St., Austin, 78701* ☎*512/457–0300* ⊕*www.thebelmontaustin.com*).

Fodor'sChoice
★   Rustic, quirky, and no bigger than your parents' basement, the smoky, no-frills **Continental Club** (⊠*1315 S. Congress Ave., Austin, 78704* ☎*512/441–2444* ⊕*www.continentalclub.com/Austin.html*)is one of Austin's signature entertainment spaces.

VISITOR INFORMATION

Texas Tourism (☎*800/888–8839* ⊕*www.traveltex.com*)

Chicago

Lake Shore Park

WORD OF MOUTH

"Chicago is such a wonderful city and has so much to offer. Go to the top of the John Hancock building, which has an incredible view of the city and the lake from its observation deck."

—lisa

EXPLORING CHICAGO

90 mi south of Milwaukee via I–94; 180 mi west of Indianapolis via I–90 and I–65; 220 mi east of Iowa City via I–88 and I–80.

By Judy Sutton Taylor

The Windy City, the Second City, the City of Big Shoulders, My Kind of Town, Hog Butcher Capital to the World—Chicago might as well be called the City of Nicknames. This plethora of monikers proves that Chicago has something for everyone—it's a proud, down-to-earth, Midwestern city that easily rivals the global greats when it comes to culture and sophistication.

Chicago's charm is indisputable—the impeccably clean streets, the alluring mix of lush parks, Lake Michigan, and slick skyscrapers. But it's got a gritty side, too—you're never far from the sound of a screeching El train, and plenty of factories and blue collar bars dot the stunning architectural landscape. This is a city of contrasts: some of the most rabid sports fans in the country coexist with culture vultures who spend their free time gallery hopping or attending the opera. You can sample an international array of street food or sit down to a multicourse meal at some of the country's best restaurants; check out edgy, groundbreaking theater or productions bound for Broadway, and shop for the toniest brands or scour ethnic enclaves for killer bargains.

WHO WILL ESPECIALLY LOVE THIS TRIP?

Foodies. Chicago has a Little Italy, Koreatown, Greektown, and *two* Chinatowns. It's famous for gut-busting deep-dish pizza, Italian beef sandwiches, and hot dogs. And for the white tablecloth crowd there's the nouvelle cuisine at Charlie Trotter's, stunning and sophisticated Mexican at Frontera Grill/Topolobampo, the seasonal contemporary American perfection at blackbird, and the groundbreaking multicourse sensory experience at Alinea, named the best restaurant in the country by Gourmet magazine in 2006.

Families. Together-time in Chicago is easy. There are, of course, the museums and cultural institutions—the Shedd Aquarium, Field Museum (home to Sue, the world's largest and most complete T. rex skeleton), Adler Planetarium, and the Art Institute of Chicago (named "the Most Kid-Friendly Museum in the Country" by Child magazine)—all grouped conveniently close to one another. Then there's Millennium Park, with its spitting fountains, and Navy Pier, home to the Chicago Children's Museum, a giant Ferris Wheel, and loads of other G-rated merriment. Throw in the free Lincoln Park Zoo and more than 500 parks, and you'll find no shortage of things to do with wee ones in tow.

Architecture buffs. Following the Great Fire of 1871, a who's who of soon-to-be greats took the city's blank slate and made it into something spectacular. Daniel Burnham, Mies van der Rohe, H.H. Richardson, Skidmore, Owings & Merrill, and, of course, Frank Lloyd Wright all made their marks on the reborn metropolis. The Chicago Architecture

TOP 5 REASONS TO GO

Lake Michigan. "Cooler by the lake" is an oft-used weather term wisely adapted by local marketing types to describe how everything is just a little bit nicer in the environs of the city's stunning lakefront.

The Magnificent Mile. Four lavish malls and more than 460 stores along the stretch of Michigan Avenue that runs from the Chicago River to Oak Street makes the Mag Mile one of the best shopping strips in the world.

Wrigley Field. It doesn't matter if the Cubs are winning (and let's be honest, they're probably not), a trip to the "Friendly Confines" is a history lesson, sociological study, and all-around perfect way to spend a summer afternoon in Chicago.

Deep dish pizza. Critics scoff and say it's more quiche than pizza, but forget the technicalities and grab a knife and fork to dig into the city's famously cheesy creation

Summer in the City. Locals like to say that if Chicago summers—filled with legendary street fairs, sidewalk café dining, and frolicking on the lakefront—lasted all year long, the whole world would want to move here.

Foundation offers excellent walking, bus, and boat tours throughout the city—be sure to take one.

Music Lovers. You'll hear quintessential Chicago blues at clubs like the Checkerboard Lounge and B.L.U.E.S., and jazz standards at Andy's and Green Mill. But this is also home to an active indie rock scene—Smashing Pumpkins, Wilco, and Liz Phair are among the locals who've made it big.

Sports fans. The Chicago Bears haven't won a Super Bowl since 1985, and the cursed Chicago Cubs haven't scored a World Series championship since way back in 1908. But the fans for these teams—as well as the White Sox, NBA's Bulls and NHL's Blackhawks—pack the stands and always make the best of it, with a wait-until-next-year sense of eternal hope and undying loyalty.

WHEN IS THE BEST TIME TO VISIT?

June, September, and October are normally mild and sunny. November through March, temperatures range from crisp to positively bitter; April and May can fluctuate between cold/soggy and bright/warm; and July and August can be perfect summer months or pack the double-whammy of high heat and stifling humidity.

Locals like to say that the only thing certain about Chicago's weather is that it will change. If you head here in the warmer months, you'll be able to catch some outdoor festivals; during the holiday season, the city is decked out in lights. It's also worth keeping in mind that more than 1,000 conventions and trade shows come to Chicago each year, and when the bigger ones—like the National Restaurant Association show in May and the International Housewares Association show in

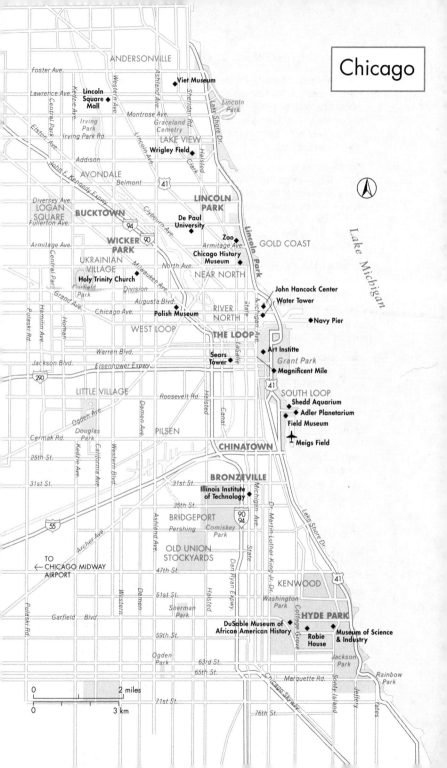

Chicago

Lake Michigan

ANDERSONVILLE

Foster Ave.
Lawrence Ave.
◆ Lincoln Square Mall
Montrose Ave.
Irving Park
Irving Park Rd.
Addison
Belmont

◆ Viet Museum

Graceland Cemetery
LAKE VIEW
◆ Wrigley Field

AVONDALE

41

LOGAN SQUARE
Diversey Ave.
Fullerton Ave.
BUCKTOWN
Armitage Ave.
WICKER PARK
UKRAINIAN VILLAGE
◆ Holy Trinity Church
Division
Augusta Blvd.
Chicago Ave.
◆ Polish Museum

LINCOLN PARK
De Paul University ◆
Zoo ◆
Armitage Ave.
Chicago History Museum ◆
NEAR NORTH

GOLD COAST

John Hancock Center ◆
Water Tower ◆

RIVER NORTH
◆ Navy Pier

WEST LOOP
THE LOOP
Warren Blvd.
Jackson Blvd.
Eisenhower Expwy.
Sears Tower ◆
◆ Art Institte
Grant Park
◆ Magnificent Mile

290

LITTLE VILLAGE
Roosevelt Rd.
PILSEN
Ogden Ave.
Cermak Rd.
Douglas Park
26th St.
31st St.

41
SOUTH LOOP
◆ Shedd Aquarium
◆ Adler Planetarium
◆ Field Museum
✈ Meigs Field

CHINATOWN

BRONZEVILLE
◆ Illinois Institute of Technology
35th St.
BRIDGEPORT
Pershing
Comiskey Park
90 94
OLD UNION STOCKYARDS
TO ← CHICAGO MIDWAY AIRPORT
47th St.
51st St.
Sherman Park
KENWOOD
41
Washington Park

Garfield Blvd.
59th St.
Ogden Park
63rd St.
65th St.
71st St.
76th St.

HYDE PARK
◆ DuSable Museum of African American History
◆ Robie House
◆ Museum of Science & Industry
Jackson Park
Rainbow Park

0 ___ 2 miles
0 ___ 3 km

March—are here, you may be hard-pressed to find a hotel room or snag a dinner reservation at popular restaurants.

HOW SHOULD I GET THERE?

DRIVING

There are several main arteries that lead directly to Chicago: I–90, which runs from Seattle to Boston, runs right through downtown Chicago, where it partners up with I–94, another east-west interstate that runs from Michigan to Montana, to form the Kennedy Expressway. I–55 starts in Louisiana and ends in Chicago, where the portion of the freeway is known as the Stevenson Expressway.

FLYING

Chicago is serviced by two major airports. O'Hare International Airport (ORD) is on the northern tip of the city and is a major international hub as well as one of the busiest (and delay-prone) airports in the country. Midway Airport (MDW) is a smaller airport on the city's south side, served mostly by discount airlines. Both airports are easily reached by the city's El trains.

HOW DO I GET AROUND?

BY CAR

Having a car in Chicago can be more of a liability than an asset. Traffic is often heavy, on-street parking can be nearly impossible to find, parking lots are expensive, and congestion—especially during rush hours—can create frustrating delays. Plus, there's seemingly never-ending construction on the major roads and highways. (Local joke: Chicago only has two seasons: winter and construction.) Cars are best used only for trips to the outlying suburbs and areas not easily accessible by public transportation.

BY PUBLIC TRANSPORTATION

The Chicago Transit Authority (CTA) operates rapid-transit trains and buses. Chicago's rapid-transit train system is known as the El (short for elevated, because parts of the tracks run above ground on an elevated platform). Each of the eight lines has a color name as well as a route name (for example, Brown/Ravenswood). Most rapid-transit lines operate 24 hours, though some stations are closed at night. The El, though very crowded during rush hours and plagued by continuous construction and service delays, is the quickest way to get around.

Northbound and southbound buses generally stop on every other corner, eastbound and westbound buses generally stop on every corner. Schedules vary depending on the time of day and route; service is less frequent on weekends and off-hours.

Payment is either by cash or by transit cards, which are available at train stations and some grocery stores and currency exchanges. The basic fare for rapid transit trains is $2 when paying cash or using a transit card, and transfers are free. For buses, the cost is $2 when paying in cash and $1.75 when using a transit card. Transfers—which can be used twice within a two-hour period—are 25 cents when using a transit card; no transfers are issued when paying cash.

You can also purchase a $5, one-day Visitor Pass that offers 24 hours of unlimited CTA use (discounts are available for multiday passes). These passes are sold at hotels, museums, and other tourist spots.

BY TAXI

You can hail a cab on just about any busy street in Chicago; hotel door-men will get one for you as well. Cabs aren't all yellow anymore, and, in some cases, may be minivans. Chicago taxis are metered, with fares beginning at $2.25 upon entering the cab and $1.90 for each additional mile. There's also a charge of $1 for the first additional passenger and 50 cents for each additional passenger after that.

WHERE SHOULD I FOCUS MY ENERGY?

If you're here for 1 day: If you're only here for a short visit, stick to the Michigan Avenue portion of the downtown Loop neighborhood, where you can visit Millennium Park and the Art Institute of Chicago.

If you're here for 2 days: Venture out around the Magnificent Mile shopping district, and stop for a drink at the top of the John Hancock Building to take in the sweeping views. Then gallery hop in nearby River North or the West Loop and have dinner at one of the trendy restaurants along Randolph Street.

If you're here for 3 days: Add the Museum Campus into the mix, which includes the Adler Planetarium, Shedd Aquarium, and Field Museum, plus stunning lakefront scenery.

If you're here for 4 days: Check out the Chicago Architecture Foundation's array of top-notch boat, bus, and walking tours.

If you're here for 5 days: Take in a Cubs baseball game from the bleachers at Wrigley Field, or visit one of the city's many jazz and blues clubs—some have daytime shows.

If you're here for 6 days: Venture into some of Chicago's diverse neighborhoods: hipster havens Wicker Park and Bucktown; leafy, upscale Lincoln Park; and historic Bronzeville and Hyde Park, home to the University of Chicago and Frank Lloyd Wright's Robie House.

If you're here for 7 days or more: Hang out at the lakefront with the locals: sunbathe or play volleyball on the beach, rent rollerblades or a bicycle, join a pick-up soccer match, or just sit back at a café and people-watch.

WHAT ARE THE TOP EXPERIENCES?

The Festivals. Chicago festivals range from local neighborhood parties to citywide extravaganzas. People fly into town for the biggies like the Chicago Blues Festival (312/744–3315, www.chicagobluesfestival.org)

How to Snack

Pizza, hot dogs, and Italian beef sandwiches are considered Chicago's holy trinity. Long before the local dining scene was all gussied up with boldface-named chefs and swanky hot spots, Chicago perfected hearty, gut-busting food for the average Joe.

The founders of both Pizzeria Uno and Lou Malnati's both lay claim to creating the deep dish-style pizza the city is famous for, made in a two-inch high pan with tomato sauce on top of the thick layers of cheese and toppings. Try them both and see which you like best.

The iconic Chicago-style hot dog got its start at the 1893 World's Fair Columbian Exposition. Two immigrants from Austria and Hungary hawked a beef frankfurter sandwiched in a steamed bun piled high with mustard, relish, onion, tomato, dill pickle, hot peppers and celery salt—that is, "dragged through the garden" in today's lingo. One thing that remains strictly forbidden, though, is ketchup. Sample Chicago-style dogs drive-in style at Superdawg, with a side of attitude at Weiner's Circle, or along with more exotic encased meats at Hot Doug's.

Italian beef sandwiches are the creation of Chicago's Italian immigrants, who happily adapted to the locally abundant meat supply to produce this now-classic local staple. The two-fister stuffs an Italian roll with thin slices of sirloin, top round, or bottom round that's wet-roasted and dripping in a spiced broth. The whole thing is topped with hot giardiniera, a spicy relish of Serrano peppers, diced carrots, cauliflower, celery, and olives in oil. If you order the sandwich "wet," it'll come with an extra ladle of juice and an extra stack of napkins; if you order a cheesy beef, they'll melt a slice or two of mozzarella over the whole mess. Locals crowd both Mr. Beef and Al's No. 1 Italian Beef to satisfy their cravings.

17

---

in Grant Park in early June, and Taste of Chicago (312/744–3315), also in Grant Park for 10 days around July 4. But neighborhood street festivals also offer great people watching opportunities and a variety of fried doughs if you're in town between June and September. Other noteworthy festivals include the Chicago Jazz Festival during Labor Day Weekend in Grant Park, Halsted Market Days in the Lakeview neighborhood every August, and the Magnificent Mile Lights Festival, which kicks off the holiday season each November with a parade and the illumination of more than one million lights on Michigan Avenue.

The Food. You could spend weeks in Chicago and barely scratch the surface of the city's amazing culinary offerings. The collective appetite champions both haute and street cuisine, but mediocrity—at any price level—just doesn't fly here. The city is home to more than 7,000 restaurants, and many of the most exciting ones to open in the past several years have been in residential neighborhoods, from Alinea in Lincoln Park to Green Zebra in Ukrainian Village and HotChocolate in Bucktown.

The Architecture. Every great city has great buildings, but Chicago *is* its great buildings. Everything Chicagoans do is framed by some of the

CLAIM TO FAME

Chicagoans are a proud lot—they don't take the Second City title lightly. Many residents unabashedly consider this the best city in America, and they point to peaceful Lake Michigan as the city's crown jewel. Bikers, dog walkers, boaters, and runners crowd the lakefront on warm days; in winter the lake is equally beautiful, with icy towers formed from frozen sheets of water.

But Chicago is most of all a city of neighborhoods. Each neighbor-hood in the city has its own flavor, reflected in its architecture, public art, restaurants, and businesses, and most have their own summer or holiday festivals. You can take a trip around the globe without leaving Chicago by visiting Little Italy, the Swedish neighborhood of Andersonville, the Mexican enclave of Pilsen/Little Village, and Devon Avenue, which transitions from Indian to Pakistani to Russian Orthodox Jewish communities within a few blocks.

most remarkable architecture anywhere. From the sky-scraping of its tall towers to the horizontal sweep of its Prairie School designs, Chicago's built environment is second to none.

The Museums. Chicago's museums are the cultural heart of the city—so vital that the mayor rerouted Lake Shore Drive to create a verdant Museum Campus for the Adler Planetarium, Shedd Aquarium, and Field Museum. Treasures in Chicago's museums include Grant Wood's iconic painting American Gothic at the Art Institute; "Sue," the largest T. rex ever discovered, at the Field Museum; and the only German U-boat captured during World War II, at the Museum of Science and Industry.

BEST BETS

SIGHTS AND TOURS

★ **Adler Planetarium and Astronomy Museum.** Navigate your way through the solar system with interactive and state-of-the-art exhibits that appeal to planetarium traditionalists as well as technology-savvy kids and adults. ✉1300 S. Lake Shore Dr., South Loop ☎312/922–7827 ⊕www.adler planetarium.org/ 🖃$16 museum admission and 1 show, $20 museum admission and 2 shows. Free Mon. and Tues. Jan., Feb., Oct., and Nov. Discount weeks throughout year ☉ 9:30 AM–4:30 PM (except 1st Fri. of month when open until 10 PM); summer hrs 9:30 AM–6:30 PM (except 1st Fri. of month when open until 10 PM).

Fodor'sChoice **Art Institute of Chicago.** Some of the world's most famous paintings are
★ housed in this museum, including an incredibly strong collection of impressionist and Postimpressionist paintings, with seminal works by Monet, Renoir, Gauguin, and Van Gogh, among others. Some of these images are so familiar in popular culture, that when you see the originals at the museum, it's like meeting a dear pen pal face-to-face for the first time. A few of the museum's best-known paintings in the perma-

nent collection are Grant Wood's American Gothic, Edward Hopper's Nighthawks, Pablo Picasso's The Old Guitarist, and Georges Seurat's A Sunday Afternoon on La Grande Jatte-1884. ⊠111 S. Michigan Ave., *South Loop* ☎312/443–3600 ⊕www.artic.edu/aic ⊠$12 ⊙Mon.– Wed. and Fri. 10:30–4:30, Thurs. 10:30–8, weekends 10–5.

Chicago Children's Museum. "Hands-on" is the operative concept for this brightly colored Navy Pier anchor. Kids play educational video games, climb through multilevel tunnels, run their own TV stations, and, if their parents allow it, get soaking wet. ⊠*Navy Pier, 700 E. Grand Ave., Near North* ☎312/527–1000 ⊕*www.chichildrensmuseum. org* ⊠$8, *free Thurs. 5–8* PM *and 1st Mon. of month for children 15 and younger* ⊙*Sun.–Wed. and Fri. 10* AM–5 PM, *Thurs. and Sat. 10* AM–8 PM.

★ **Chicago History Museum.** The museum went through a major overhaul in late 2006 when it changed its name from the Chicago Historical Society in honor of its 150th birthday. The new permanent sights include a Costume and Textile Gallery and the exhibit entitled "Chicago: Crossroads of America," which demystifies historic tragedies like the Great Chicago Fire and Haymarket Affair. ⊠*1601 N. Clark St., Lincoln Park* ☎312/642–4600 ⊕*www.chicagohistory.org* ⊠$12, *Mon. free* ⊙*Mon.–Wed., Fri., and Sat. 9:30–4:30, Thurs. 9:30–8, Sun. noon–5.*

Chinatown. "Compact commotion" best describes Chicago's Chinatown, a neighborhood packed with restaurants and shops. Tour the historic commercial district along Wentworth and Archer avenues and you might just forget you're in a Midwestern city. South of the Prairie Avenue district, where Wentworth Avenue and Cermak Road/22nd Street meet, is the entrance to Chinatown. Our favorite part about Chinatown is the plethora of gift shops spilling over with eye candy in **Chinatown Square** (on bustling Archer Avenue), and the mouthwatering smells from the area's many restaurants and bakeries.

Farther north, **Devon Avenue** is where Chicagoans go when they crave Indian food, or, as the avenue moves west, a good Jewish challah. The Indian restaurants and shops start popping up just east of Western Avenue. Besides authentic, inexpensive Indian and Pakistani food, you find the latest Bollywood flicks, electronics, jewelry, and beautifully embellished saris and fabrics. Restaurants and stores change over rapidly, however, so if the place you're looking for has closed, simply step into the next alluring spot you find. At Talman Avenue, the multicultural wares transform to Jewish specialties. There are butchers and bakers and windows decorated with Russian newspapers and handmade *matrioshkas* (nesting dolls), evidence of this section's concentration of Russian Jews.

★ **DuSable Museum of African American History.** The DuSable is a colorful— and haunting—exploration of the African-American experience, set alongside the lagoons of Washington Park. There are handwritten lyric sheets from Motown greats, letters and memorabilia of scholar W.E.B. DuBois and poet Langston Hughes, and a significant African-American art collection. The most moving exhibit is one on slavery; the poignant,

HISTORY YOU CAN SEE

The modern skyscraper hails from Chicago, and at one time the Sears Tower was the tallest building in the world. It's now been trumped by several higher structures in Southeast Asia (though at 1,451 feet it remains the tallest building in the United States). Not far behind it are two other local skyscrapers: the Aon Center (1,136 feet) and the John Hancock Center (1,127 feet), which come in after the Empire State Building at number three and number four, respectively. The 1896 Haymarket Riot, where 11 people were killed in a melee sparked by protests for the legalization of an eight-hour workday, took place in Chicago's West Loop.

The event led to the creation of May Day, a worker's holiday still observed the first day in May throughout much of Europe. A memorial sculpture is near the intersection of Randolph and Des Plaines Streets. Notorious depression-era bank robber John Dillinger was shot and killed outside the Biograph Theater (2433 N. Lincoln Ave.) in Lincoln Park, home today to the Victory Gardens Theater Company. "The whole world was watching" the 1968 Democratic National Convention in Chicago on television when clashes between anti-war protesters and local police erupted into violence, later resulting in the infamous Chicago Eight conspiracy trials.

disturbing artifacts include rusted shackles used on slave ships. ⊠*740 E. 56th Pl., Hyde Park* ☎*773/947–0600* ⊕*www.dusablemuseum.org* ☜*$3, free Sun.* ☉*Tues.–Sat. 10–5, Sun. noon–5.*

Fodor'sChoice **Field Museum.** More than 6 *acres* of exhibits fill this gigantic world-
★ class museum, which explores cultures and environments from around the world. Interactive exhibits examine such topics as the secrets of Egyptian mummies, the people of Africa and the Pacific Northwest, and the living creatures in the soil. The Field's dinosaur collection is one of the world's best. You can't miss 65-million-year-old "Sue," the largest and most complete Tyrannosaurus rex fossil ever found—it's on permanent exhibit in the lobby. ⊠*1400 S. Lake Shore Dr., South Loop* ☎*312/922–9410* ⊕*www.fieldmuseum.org* ☜*$12* ☉*Daily 9* AM–*5* PM; *last admission at 4* PM.

Grant Park. Two of Chicago's greatest treasures reside in Grant Park—the Art Institute and Buckingham Fountain. Bordered by Lake Michigan to the east and a spectacular skyline to the west, the ever-popular Grant Park hosts many of the city's outdoor events, including the annual Taste of Chicago, a vast picnic featuring foods from more than 70 restaurants. The event precedes a fireworks show around July Fourth. The fountain is a wonderful place to people-watch.

★ The centerpiece of Grant Park is the gorgeous, tiered **Buckingham Fountain** (⊠*Between Columbus and Lake Shore Drs. east of Congress Plaza*), which has intricate designs of pink-marble seashells, water-spouting fish, and bronze sculptures of sea horses. It was patterned after a fountain at Versailles but is about twice as large as its model. See it in all its glory between May 1 and October 1, when it's elaborately illuminated at night and sprays colorfully lighted waters. ⊠*South Loop* ☎*312/747–1534.*

On Carpenter Street between Randolph Street and Washington Boulevard is **Harpo Studios** (⊠*1058 W. Washington Blvd., West Loop* ☎*312/591–9222* ⊕*www.oprah.com*), the taping site for Oprah Winfrey's talk show. The studio isn't open to tours, and tickets to the show can be near-impossible to score, so a stop here isn't much more than a fun photo op. However, if you're a die-hard Oprah fan and want to attempt to get tickets, here's what you need to know: The show books audiences only for the current and following month. When you call—and if you're lucky enough to get through—a staffer will give you the taping schedule and a list of available dates. You can reserve up to four seats for any one taping (all attendees must be at least 18). If you can't get tickets in advance, check the Web site for occasional last-minute tickets via e-mail.

★ **Historic Water Tower.** This famous Michigan Avenue structure, completed in 1867, was originally built to house a 137-foot standpipe that equalized the pressure of the water pumped by the similar pumping station across the street. Oscar Wilde uncharitably called it "a castellated monstrosity" studded with pepper shakers. Nonetheless, it remains a Chicago landmark and a symbol of the city's spirit of survival following the Great Chicago Fire of 1871. ⊠*806 N. Michigan Ave., at Pearson St., Near North* ☎*Free* ⊙*Mon.–Sat. 10–6:30, Sun. 10–5.*

17

★ **John G. Shedd Aquarium.** Take a plunge into an underwater world at the world's largest indoor aquarium. Built in 1930, the Shedd is one of the most popular aquariums in the country, housing more than 8,000 aquatic animals in realistic waterscapes. ⊠*1200 S. Lake Shore Dr., South Loop* ☎*312/939–2438* ⊕*www.sheddaquarium.org* ☎*$23 all-access pass* ⊙*Memorial Day–Labor Day, daily 9–6, Thurs. until 10; Labor Day–Memorial Day, weekdays 9–5, weekends 9–6.*

Fodor's Choice ★ **John Hancock Center.** Designed by the same team that designed the Sears Tower (Skidmore, Owings & Merrill), this multi-use skyscraper is distinguished by its tapering shape and the enormous X braces, which help stabilize its 100 stories. Packed with retail, parking, offices, a restaurant, and residences, it has been likened to a city within a city. Impressive from any angle, it offers mind-boggling views from a 94th floor observatory (as with the Sears Tower, you can see to four states on clear days). For anyone afflicted with vertigo, a sensible option is a seat in the bar of the 95th floor Signature Room. ⊠*875 N. Michigan Ave., Near North* ☎*312/751–3681* ⊕*www.hancock-observatory.com and www.johnhancockcenterchicago.com* ☎*Observatory $10* ⊙*Daily 9 AM–11 PM; last ticket sold at 10:45 PM.*

★ **Lincoln Park.** When you get to Lincoln Park, just north of Old Town, don't be confused: the neighborhood near the southern part of the city's oldest and most popular lakefront park also bears its name. Lincoln Park—the *park*—today extends from North Avenue to Hollywood Avenue. The neighborhood adjacent to the original park, bordered by Armitage Avenue on the south, Diversey Parkway on the north, the lake on the east, and the Chicago River on the west, also became known as Lincoln Park. In some ways Lincoln Park today epitomizes all the things that people love to hate about yuppified urban areas: stratospheric housing prices, teeny boutiques with big-attitude salespeople, and plenty of fancy-schmancy coffee shops, wine bars, and cafés. That said, it's also got some of the prettiest residential streets in the city, that gorgeous park, a great nature museum, and a thriving arts scene.

Lincoln Park Zoo. Lions, gorillas, and bears, oh my! At this urban zoo, you can face-off with lions (separated by a window, of course) outside the Lion House, watch 24 gorillas go ape in the Great Ape House, or watch some rare and endangered species of bears, such as the spectacle bear (named for the eyeglasslike markings around its eyes). ⊠*2200 N. Cannon Dr., Lincoln Park* ☎*312/742–2000* ⊕*www.lpzoo.com* ⊡*Free* ⊙*Daily 9–5.*

FodorśChoice **Millennium Park.** The Bean, the fountains, the Disney-esque music pavil-
★ ion—all the pieces of this new park quickly stole the hearts of Chicagoans and visitors alike.

The showstopper here is Frank Gehry's stunning **Jay Pritzker Pavilion.** Dramatic ribbons of stainless steel stretching 40 feet into the sky look like petals wrapping the music stage. The sound system, suspended by a trellis that spans the great lawn, gives concert-hall sound outside.

Hot town? Summer in the city? Cool off by letting George W. spit on you. Okay, it's just a giant image of him and a bunch of other faces rotating through on two huge (read: 50-foot-high) glass block–tower fountains. The genius behind the **Crown Fountain,** Spanish sculptor Jaume Plensa, made an opening where the mouths are on the photos, and water comes shooting out at random intervals. Kids love it, and we feel like kids watching it. It's at the southwest corner of the park.

You've seen the pictures. Now go, take your own. The **Cloud Gate sculpture,** otherwise known as "the Bean," awaits your delighted *ooohs* and *aaahs* as you stand beneath its gleaming seamless polished steel. It's between Washington and Madison streets.

In summer the carefully manicured plantings in the **Lurie Garden** bloom; in winter the **McCormick Tribune Ice Rink** is open for public skating. ⊠*Bounded by Michigan Ave., Columbus Dr., Randolph Dr., and Monroe St., Loop* ⊕*www.millenniumpark.org* ⊡*Free* ⊙*Daily 6 AM–11 PM.*

Museum of Contemporary Art. A group of art patrons who felt the great Art Institute was unresponsive to modern work founded the MCA in 1967, and it's remained a renegade art museum ever since. The MCA's growing 7,000-piece collection, which includes work by René Magritte, Alexander Calder, Bruce Nauman, Sol LeWitt, Franz Kline, and June Leaf, makes up about half the museum. The other half is dedicated to temporary exhibitions. ⊠*220 E. Chicago Ave., Near North* ☎*312/280–2660* ⊕*www.mcachicago.org* ⊡*$10, free Tues.* ⊙*Tues. 10 AM–8 PM, Wed.–Sun. 10 AM–5 PM.*

STRANGE BUT TRUE

- In 2006 the Chicago City Council banned the sale of foie gras—goose or duck liver made by force-feeding the birds—because the delicacy is considered inhumane. The controversial ban is loathed by many city chefs, who get around the law by offering it as a side dish free of charge.

- Jackson Park, on Chicago's South Side, has a notable parrot population. It all started back during the World's Columbian Exposition of 1893, when parrots were imported for an exhibit. The Exposition left, but the parrots stayed and seem to brave the cold winters just fine.

- In 1945, William Sianis, the owner of the Billy Goat Tavern, bought two tickets to one of the 1945 Cubs-Tigers World Series games: one for him, and one for his goat. The goat was turned away, Sianis cursed the Cubs, and they have not won a World Series since.

- The widely retold story that the Great Chicago Fire of 1871—which destroyed four square miles of the city—was started by a cow kicking over a lantern in Catherine O'Leary's barn, is a myth. A reporter later admitted he made it up because it made colorful copy.

Fodor'sChoice ★ **Museum of Science and Industry.** The beloved MSI is one of the most visited sites in Chicago, and for good reason. The sprawling open space has 2,000 exhibits on three floors, with new exhibits being added constantly. The museum's high-tech interior is hidden by the classical-revival exterior; it was designed in 1892 by D.H. Burnham & Company as a temporary structure to house the Palace of Fine Arts for the World's Columbian Exposition. It's the fair's only surviving building. ⊠ *5700 S. Lake Shore Dr., Hyde Park* ☎ *773/684–1414* ⊕ *www.msi chicago.org* ⊠ *$11; museum and Omnimax admission $17; parking $12* ⊙ *Memorial Day–Labor Day, Mon.–Sat. 9–5:30, Sun. 11–5:30; Labor Day–Memorial Day, Mon.–Sat. 9:30–4, Sun. 11–4.*

★ **National Museum of Mexican Art.** Formerly the Mexican Fine Arts Museum Center, this sparkling site, the largest Latino museum in the country, is half art museum, half cultural exploration. After the big downtown museums, this is the one you shouldn't miss. Galleries house impressive collections of contemporary, traditional, and meso-American art from both sides of the border, as well as vivid exhibits that trace immigration woes and political fights. Every fall the giant Day of the Dead exhibit stuns Chicagoans with its altars from artists across the country. ⊠ *1852 W. 19th St., Pilsen* ☎ *312/738–1503* ⊕ *www.national museumofmexicanart.org* ⊠ *Free* ⊙ *Tues.–Sun. 10–5.*

Fodor'sChoice ★ **Navy Pier.** Yes, it's a little schlocky, but Navy Pier is fun, especially for families. Everyone can fan out to shop in the mall, play minigolf in the Crystal Ballroom in winter, see a movie at the IMAX Theater, or explore the Chicago Children's Museum. Plus, there's a stained-glass museum, a maze, and a 3-D ride that whizzes through scenes of Chicago. Meet up later at the Ferris wheel for a photo op or just settle

17

LIKE A LOCAL

■ Bleacher Bums: Regulars who sit in the bleachers at Wrigley Field.

■ Boul Mich: Tongue-in-cheek nickname for the high-end Magnificent Mile on Michigan Avenue.

■ Brat: Short for bratwurst, a staple at sporting events and tailgating parties. Pronounced "braht."

■ Cheesehead: What the locals call people from Wisconsin.

■ Chicagoland: Chicago and the surrounding suburbs.

■ Come with: Chicagoans tend to leave off the "us" or "me —for example, "We're going to a party. Do you want to come with?"

■ Gapers: Drivers who slow down traffic to look an accident. You'll hear about "gapers blocks" or "gapers delays" on traffic reports.

■ The "L": Nickname for the city's public train system, short for "elevated." Even though most of the system is above ground, the term is used even when the train goes underground.

■ Pop: A soft drink, like Coca-Cola—don't use the word "soda" here.

■ Trixie: A jabbing nickname for the young, ex-sorority types who live in and around the Lincoln Park neighborhood. (Their lesser-known male counterparts are referred to as "Chads.")

on the pier with a drink and enjoy the view. ⊠ *600 E. Grand Ave.* ☎ *800/595–7437 or 312/595–7437* ⊕ *www.navypier.com*

Robie House. Frank Lloyd Wright's Prairie-style masterpiece, built in 1909 for inventor and businessman Frederick C. Robie, is one of the most remarkable designs in modern American architecture. Study the exterior to see the horizontal lines, from the brickwork and the limestone sills to the sweeping roofs, which Wright felt reflected the prairies of the Midwest. A cantilevered roof provides privacy while allowing in light. Like most of Wright's buildings, it seems compact from the outside, but inside it's a complex, fully thought-out maze of 174 art glass windows. ⊠ *5757 S. Woodlawn Ave., Hyde Park* ☎ *773/834–1847* 🎫 *$12* ☉ Tour weekdays at 11, 1, and 3; weekends every ½-hr 11–3:30.

Fodor'sChoice **Rookery.** This 11-story structure, with its eclectically ornamented ★ facade, got its name from the pigeons and politicians who roosted at the city hall that once stood on this site. Designed in 1885 by Burnham & Root, who used both masonry and the more modern steel-frame construction, the Rookery was one of the first buildings in the country to feature a central court that brought sunlight into interior office spaces. Frank Lloyd Wright, who kept an office here for a short time, renovated the two-story lobby and light court, eliminating some of the ironwork and terra-cotta and adding marble scored with geometric patterns detailed in gold leaf. ⊠ *209 S. LaSalle St., Loop.*

Fodor'sChoice **Sears Tower.** In Chicago, size matters. This soaring 110-story skyscraper, ★ designed by Skidmore, Owings & Merrill in 1974, was the world's tall-☾ est building until 1996 when the Petronas Towers in Kuala Lumpur,

Malaysia, claimed the title. However, the folks at the Sears Tower are quick to point out that Petronas counts its spire as part of the building. If you were to measure the 1,450-foot-high Sears Tower in terms of highest occupied floor, highest roof, or highest antenna, the Sears Tower would win hands down. Those bragging rights aside, the **Skydeck** is really something to boast about. Enter on Jackson Boulevard to take the ear-popping ride to the 103rd-floor observatory. ✉*233 S. Wacker Dr.; for Skydeck, enter on Jackson Blvd. between Wacker Dr. and Franklin St., Loop* ☎*312/875–9696* ⊕*www.the-skydeck.com* 🎫*$12* ☉*Apr.–Sept., daily 10–10; Oct.–Mar., daily 10–8.*

Fodor'sChoice
★

Wrigley Field. The Friendly Confines, as it's known, was built in 1914, which makes it the second-oldest ballpark in the country. Ticket prices to a game can range from $10 to $70. (Don't expect to score tickets on short notice, though; games sell out early in the season.) The Cubs offer 90-minute tours that provide an insider's look at 90 years of Wrigley history. Tickets are $25 per person, and you must book in advance. ✉*1060 West Addison St., at corner of Addison St. and Clark St., Wrigleyville* ☎*773/404–2827* ⊕*http://chicago.cubs.mlb.com.*

TOURS

The **ArchiCenter of the Chicago Architecture Foundation** (✉*224 S. Michigan Ave., Loop* ☎*312/922–3432* ⊕*www.architecture.org* ☉*Sun.–Fri. 9:30–6, Sat. 9–6*) conducts excellent, docent-led boat tours of the Loop. Our favorites are the "Early Skyscrapers" tour and the "Modern and Beyond" tour. The ArchiCenter also has walking and bus tours and hosts exhibitions, lectures, and discussions.

Watch the panoply of Chicago's magnificent skyline slide by from the decks of *Chicago's First Lady* or *Chicago's Little Lady,* the fleet of the **Chicago Architecture Foundation River Cruise.** Make reservations in advance for the popular 90-minute tours. **Ticketmaster** (☎*312/902–1500* ⊕*www.ticketmaster.com/illinois*) sells tickets by phone, online, and at the Hot Tix booth in the Chicago Water Works Visitor Center. Ticketmaster fees apply at these outlets. You can also purchase tickets at the *Chicago's First Lady* ticket window or at the Chicago ArchiCenter (✉ *224 S. Michigan Ave.*). ✉*Southeast corner of Michigan Ave. Bridge* ☎*847/358–1330* ⊕*www.cruisechicago.com* 🎫*$26 Mon.–Thurs., $28 Fri.–Sun.* ☉*May–Oct., daily; Nov., weekends.*

WHERE TO EAT

	WHAT IT COSTS				
	¢	$	$$	$$$	$$$$
FOR 1 PERSON	under $10	$10–$18	$19–$27	$28–$36	over $36

Prices are per person for a typical main course or equivalent combination of smaller dishes. Note: if a restaurant offers only prix-fixe (set-price) meals, it has been given the price category that reflects the full prix-fixe price.

$$$$
CUTTING-EDGE
Lincoln Park
Fodor'sChoice
★

✕**Alinea.** Believe the hype and book well in advance. Chicago's most exciting restaurant—hidden in a bunkerlike building on a residential block—demands an adventurous spirit, an ample appetite, and a serious commitment of time and money. If you have four hours and $300 to spare, the 23-course tasting menu is the best way to experience young whiz Grant Achatz's stunning cutting-edge food. The gastronomic roller coaster (there's also a less pricey 12-course version) takes you on a journey through intriguing aromas, visuals, flavors, and textures. Buttery duck with extruded mango puree arrives perched on a pillow that emits juniper-scented air. A black truffle–bon bon explodes in your mouth when you bite. Brown butter turned into powder accompanies a skate fish fillet. Though some dishes—they range in size from one to four bites—may look like science projects, there's nothing gimmicky about the endless procession of bold and elegant tastes. The hours fly by in the windowless bi-level dining room, aided by the effortless service and muted decor. ⊠ *1723 N. Halsted St.* ☎ *312/867–0110* ⌂ *Reservations essential* ☰ *AE, D, DC, MC, V* ⊘ *Closed Mon. and Tues. No lunch.*

$$$$ ★
NEW AMERICAN
Lincoln Park

✕**Charlie Trotter's.** Plan well in advance to dine at top toque Charlie Trotter's namesake (or call the day of and hope for a cancellation). One of the nation's most acclaimed chefs, Trotter prepares his menus daily from the best of what's available globally. The results are daring, multi-ingredient dishes that look like art on a dinner plate. Menus follow a multicourse, $155 degustation format ($130 for the vegetarian version). For a worthwhile splurge, order the wines-to-match option. This temple of haute cuisine occupies a stately Lincoln Park town house. ⊠ *816 W. Armitage Ave.* ☎ *773/248–6228* ⌂ *Reservations essential. Jacket required* ☰ *AE, DC, MC, V* ⊘ *Closed Sun and Mon. No lunch.*

$$$
NEW AMERICAN
West Loop
Fodor'sChoice
★

✕**Green Zebra.** Chef Shawn McClain of Spring fame took the vegetable side dish and ran it up the marquee. The result gives good-for-you veggies the star treatment in a sleek shop suave enough to attract the likes of Gwyneth Paltrow. All dishes are small and change seasonally. You might see roast beets with horseradish foam or sunchoke raviolis with melted goat cheese and hazelnuts. One chicken and one fish dish make do for carnivores. ⊠ *1460 W. Chicago Ave.* ☎ *312/243–7100* ☰ *AE, D, DC, MC, V* ⊘ *Closed Mon.*

$$$
AMERICAN
Lincoln Park
Fodor'sChoice
★

✕**North Pond.** A former Arts and Crafts–style warming house for ice-skaters at Lincoln Park's North Pond, this gem-in-the-woods fittingly champions an uncluttered culinary style. Talented chef Bruce Sherman emphasizes organic ingredients, wild-caught fish, and artisanal farm products. Menus change seasonally, but order the Midwestern favorite walleye pike if available. Like the food, the wine list seeks out small American craft producers. The food remains top-notch at lunch but the scene, dense with strollers and high chairs, is far from serene. ⊠ *2610 N. Cannon Dr.* ☎ *773/477–5845* ☰ *AE, D, DC, MC, V* ⊘ *Closed Mon. No lunch Oct.–May.*

ON THE WAY

The **Birthplace of Ernest Hemingway** is just a stone's throw from Chicago in the nearby suburb of **Oak Park**. You can tour the three-story Queen Anne Victorian (339 N. Oak Park Ave., 708/848–2222, www. hemingway.org) and affiliated **Ernest Hemingway Museum** (200 N. Oak Park Ave.) seven days a week.

Just over the Wisconsin border in the city of Kenosha (65 mi to the north) is the quirky **Mars Cheese Castle** (2800 120th Ave., Kenosha, 262/859–2244, www.marscheese. com), a tavern, restaurant, and gift shop where you can sample local brews and find all manner of Dairy State–made delicacies.

About 200 mi south of Chicago is **Springfield,** the state capital of Illinois and home to the **Abraham Lincoln Presidential Library and Museum** (112 N. 6th St., 800/610–2094, www.alplm.org)

$$
NEW AMERICAN
West Loop
Fodor'sChoice
★

✕**Avec.** Go to this Euro-style wine bar when you're feeling gregarious; the rather stark space only has seating for 55 people, and it's all at communal tables. The results are loud and lively, though happily the shareable fare—a mix of homemade charcuterie, Mediterranean, and American dishes from a wood-burning oven—is reasonably priced. It's as popular as its next-door neighbor Blackbird (and run by the same forces), and only early birds are guaranteed tables. The doors open at—yikes!—3:30 PM. ⊠615 W. Randolph St. ☎312/377–2002 ⊟AE, D, DC, MC, V ⊘No lunch.

$$ ★
MEXICAN
River North

✕**Frontera Grill.** Devotees of chef–owner Rick Bayless queue up for his distinct fare at this casual restaurant, brightly trimmed in Mexican folk art. Bayless annually visits Mexico with the entire staff in tow. Servers, consequently, are encyclopedic on the food, typified by trout in yellow mole, red chili-marinated pork, and black-bean tamales filled with goat cheese. The reservation policy is tricky: they're accepted for parties of five or more, though smaller groups can phone in the same day. Otherwise, make like most and endure the two-margarita wait. ⊠445 N. Clark St. ☎312/661–1434 ⊟AE, D, DC, MC, V ⊘Closed Sun. and Mon.

$ ★
BURGER
Near North

✕**Billy Goat Tavern.** The late comedian John Belushi immortalized the Goat's short-order cooks on *Saturday Night Live* for barking, "No Coke! Pepsi!" and "No fries! Cheeps!" at customers. They still do the shtick at this subterranean hole-in-the-wall favored by reporters posted nearby at the *Tribune* and the *Sun-Times*. Griddle-fried "cheezborgers" are the featured chow, and people-watching the favored sport. ⊠430 N. Michigan Ave., lower level ☎312/222–1525 ⊟No credit cards.

$
Fodor'sChoice
★
ITALIAN
River North

✕**Pizzeria Uno.** Chicago deep-dish pizza got its start here in 1943, and both local and out-of-town fans continue to pack in for filling pies. Housed in a Victorian brownstone, Uno offers a slice of old Chicago in dim paneled rooms with reproduction light fixtures. Spin-off Due down the street handles the overflow. Plan on two thick, cheesy slices or less as a full meal. This is no quick-to-your-table pie, so do order

17

salads and be prepared to entertain the kids during the inevitable wait. ✉*29 E. Ohio St.* ☎*312/321–1000.*

¢ ✕**Hot Doug's.** Don't tell the zealots who have made Hot Doug's famous that these are *just* hot dogs—these "encased meats" go beyond your standard Vienna wiener. The gourmet purveyor wraps buns around chipotle chicken sausage, smoked crawfish and pork sausage with spicy remoulade, and even rabbit sausage. Make the trek on a Friday or Saturday, when the artery-clogging duck-fat fries are available. The clientele is a curious mix of hungry hard-hats and serious foodies, neither of which care about the lack of frills. ✉*3325 N. California Ave.* ☎*773/751–1500* ⊟*No credit cards* ۞*Closed Sun. No dinner.*

HOT DOGS
Lake View
Fodor's Choice
★
۞

¢ ★ ✕**Mr. Beef.** A Chicago institution for two-fisted Italian beef sandwiches piled with red peppers and provolone cheese, Mr. Beef garners citywide fans from area hard-hats to restaurateurs and TV personalities. Service and setting—two indoor picnic tables and a dining rail—are fast-food no-nonsense. This workingman's favorite, go figure, located near River North's art galleries. ✉*666 N. Orleans St.* ☎*312/337–8500* ⊟*No credit cards* ۞*Closed Sun. No dinner.*

AMERICAN
River North

WHERE TO STAY

WHAT IT COSTS					
	¢	$	$$	$$$	$$$$
FOR 2 PEOPLE	under $110	$110–$219	$220–$319	$320–$419	over $420

Prices exclude service charges and Chicago's 15.4% room tax

$$$$ 🏨 **Drake Hotel.** Built in 1920, the grande dame of Chicago hotels presides over the northernmost end of Michigan Avenue. The lobby, inspired by an Italian Renaissance palace, is all deep-red walls and glimmering crystal. The sounds of a fountain and harpist beckon at Palm Court, a traditional setting for afternoon tea. There's live jazz in the **Coq d'Or** most nights and the **Cape Cod Room** serves to-die-for crab cakes. The downsides? No swimming pool (a bummer for the price you're paying) and some rooms are tiny. ✉*140 E. Walton Pl., Near North, 60611* ☎*312/787–2200 or 800/553–7253* 🖷*312/787–1431* ⊕*www.thedrakehotel.com* 🛏*535 rooms, 55 suites* ♿*In-room: safe, Ethernet, dial-up, refrigerator. In-hotel: 4 restaurants, room service, bar, gym, concierge, laundry service, public Wi-Fi, parking (fee), no-smoking rooms* ⊟*AE, D, DC, MC, V.*

★

$$$$ 🏨 **Peninsula Chicago.** On weekend nights the Peninsula's soaring lobby lounge becomes a chocolate fantasia, centered on an overflowing chocolate buffet. The hotel, committed to keeping its guests well fed and well rested, is also home to one of the city's most creative restaurants (Avenues) along with a lavish and popular afternoon tea. One of only three branches in the United States of the venerable Hong Kong–based Peninsula chain, its comfortable rooms feature plush pillow-top beds, Wi-Fi, and state-of-the-art bedside consoles that control both the TV and "do not disturb" light. The rooftop lap pool is enclosed in a Zen

Fodor's Choice
★

VITAL STATS:

- Chicago's name comes from a Potawatomi Indian word meaning "wild onion" or "skunk." When Indians first arrived, the future home of America's third-largest city was a patch of rotting marshland onions.

- The title "Windy City" was given to Chicago by New York Sun editor Charles Dana in 1893. He was tired of listening to long-winded local politicians.

- The world's longest street is Chicago's Western Avenue.

- After the Great Chicago Fire in 1871, the debris was dumped into Lake Michigan. The area of downtown Chicago east of Michigan Avenue was built on the resulting landfill.

- Every year for St. Patrick's Day the city dyes the Chicago River green.

aerie offering stunning views over the city. Make time to enjoy the property's award-winning spa. ⊠*108 E. Superior St., Near North, 60611* ☎*312/337–2888 or 866/288–8889* ⬛*312/751–2888* ⊕*www. chicago.peninsula.com* ⤳*339 rooms, 83 suites* ♿*In-room: refrigerator, safe, DVD, Ethernet, Wi-Fi. In-hotel: 4 restaurants, room service, bar, pool, gym, spa, concierge, laundry service, parking (fee), no-smoking rooms, some pets allowed* ▭*AE, D, DC, MC, V.*

$$$

Fodor's Choice

★

🏨 Hotel Burnham. Making creative use of a city landmark, this hotel is housed in the famed 13-story Reliance Building, which D.H. Burnham & Company built in 1895. The refurbished interior retains such original details as Carrara marble wainscoting and ceilings, terrazzo floors, and mahogany trim. Guest rooms, which were once the building's offices, are compact. But we'll overlook the lack of wiggle room thanks to perks like the "pillow library," which offers anything from firm to hypoallergenic pillows. On the ground floor, the intimate Atwood Cafe has a stylish mahogany bar and serves contemporary American fare, including its popular potpies. ⊠*1 W. Washington St., Loop, 60602* ☎*312/782–1111 or 877/294–9712* ⬛*312/782–0899* ⊕*www.burn hamhotel.com* ⤳*103 rooms, 19 suites* ♿*In-room: Wi-Fi, refrigerator. In-hotel: restaurant, room service, bar, gym, concierge, laundry service, public Wi-Fi, parking (fee), some pets allowed* ▭*AE, D, DC, MC, V.*

Fodor's Choice

★

$$$

🏨 The James Hotel. If you don't get the hint from the bustling bar scene spilling into the lobby or the antique suitcases stacked as an art piece near the elevator, the James further announces its hipster pedigree when you enter your room. Pre-programmed alt-rock plays on the iPod-ready stereo system perched on the bar beneath the ready-to-party bottles (not minis) of vodka, whiskey, and rum. Some rooms feature not one but two flat-screen TVs, not to mention Kiehl's bath products and design-conscious furnishings like platform beds and full-length lean-to mirrors. The relatively hands-off service is fitting enough—for a party hotel. ⊠*55 E. Ontario St., at Rush St., Near North, 60611* ☎*312/337–1000* ⊕*www.jameshotels.com/chicago* ⤳*297 rooms* ♿*In-room: refrigerator, safe, Wi-Fi. In-hotel: restaurant, room service, bar, gym, spa, concierge, laundry service, public Wi-Fi, parking (fee), no-smoking rooms, some pets allowed* ▭*AE, D, DC, MC, V.*

17

NIGHTLIFE & ENTERTAINMENT

THE ARTS

★ **Hubbard Street Dance Chicago** (☎312/850–9744 ⊕*www.hubbardstreet dance.com*), Chicago's most notable success story in dance, exudes a jazzy vitality that has made it extremely popular. The style mixes classical-ballet techniques, theatrical jazz, and contemporary dance.

★ **Lookingglass Theatre Company.** Gawk at offbeat and fantastically acrobatic performances inside the belly of the Chicago Water Works building. The company's physically and artistically daring works incorporate theater, dance, music, and circus arts. ☎312/337–0665 ⊕*www. lookingglasstheatre.org*.

★ **Lyric Opera of Chicago.** The big voices of the opera world star in these top-flight productions. This is one of the top two opera companies in America today. Don't worry about understanding German or Italian; English translations are projected above the stage. All of the superb performances have sold out for more than a dozen years, and close to 90% of all Lyric tickets go to subscribers—the key to getting in is to call the Lyric in early August when individual tickets first go on sale. ☎312/332–2244 ⊕*www.lyricopera.org* ⊗*Sept.–Mar.*

Fodor'sChoice **Steppenwolf.** The alumni roster speaks for itself: John Malkovich, Gary
★ Sinise, Joan Allen, and Laurie Metcalf all honed their chops with this troupe. The company's trademark cutting-edge acting style and consistently successful productions have won national acclaim. ☎312/335– 1650 ⊕*www.steppenwolf.org*.

NIGHTLIFE

The famous Chicago bar scene known as **Rush Street** has faded into the mists of time, although the street has found resurgent energy with the opening of a string of upscale restaurants and outdoor cafés. For the vestiges of the old Rush Street, continue north to trendy **Division Street** between Clark and State streets. The crowd here consists mostly of suburbanites and out-of-towners on the make.

Fodor'sChoice **Second City** (✉1616 N. Wells St., Near North ☎312/337–3992), an
★ institution since 1959, has served as a launching pad for some of the hottest comedians around. Alumni include Dan Aykroyd and the late John Belushi. Funny, loony skit comedy is presented on two stages, with a free improv set after the show every night but Friday.

VISITOR INFORMATION

Chicago Convention and Tourism Bureau (✉2301 S. Lake Shore Dr., 60616 ☎312/567–8500 or 877/244–2246 ⊕www.choosechicago.com).

Chicago Water Works (✉163 E. Pearson St., at Michigan Ave. ☎877/244–2246 ⊕www.877chicago.com ⊗Daily 7:30–7).

Minneapolis & St. Paul

WITH THE MALL OF AMERICA

Mary-Tyler-Moore-Statue, Nicollet Mall, Minneapolis

WORD OF MOUTH

"Minneapolis is fun…walk up and down Nicollet Mall (downtown), get over to the Uptown area (funky, artsy, south of downtown), and then walk over to the lakes: Harriet, Calhoun . . . lots of walkers, bikers, windsurfers, rollerbladers. In St. Paul, walk up and down Summit and Grand Ave. . . . lots of interesting mansions and shopping. . . . Cafe Latte is a good spot for a salad/sandwich/soup/latte/DESSERT."

—Colette

EXPLORING MINNEAPOLIS & ST. PAUL

407 mi northwest of Chicago via I–94; 336 mi northwest of Milwaukee, WI, via I–94; 243 mi north of Des Moines, IA, via I–35; 240 mi southeast of Fargo, ND, via I–94.

By Jennifer
D'Anastasio

Minnesotans may be too nice to claim the Twin Cities as the "Minne-Apple," rivaling New York City, but there's a reason the name stuck. The Cities offer an extensive repertoire of cultural events, putting it on par with other major destinations around the U.S. In fact Minneapolis has more theater seats per capita than any other U.S. city, only beat by the true Big Apple.

The year 2005 ushered in a cultural rebirth for the Twin Cities, beginning with Swiss architects Jacques Herzog and Pierre de Meuron's bold aluminum addition to the acclaimed modern art Walker Art Center. The following year the downtown Minneapolis Central Library opened in a light-filled space designed by Cesar Pelli, and the venerable Guthrie Theater relocated to a dramatic structure on the Mississippi River by renowned French architect Jean Nouvel. Not to be left out of the action, the Minneapolis Institute of Arts recently expanded with a Michael Graves–designed new wing.

Whether you're looking for highbrow sophistication or a quiet picnic on the Chain of Lakes, the Twin Cities has something for everyone.

WHO WILL ESPECIALLY LOVE THIS TRIP?

Foodies: Restaurants dish innovative cuisine with local ingredients, which has its challenges in winter, to say the least. Parsnips anyone? Don't let that fool you, the Twin Cities is one very serious food town with many establishments gaining national recognition and racking up James Beard nominations. Farmers' markets, many featuring local organic food, dot the summer landscape.

Shoppers: Three words: Mall Of America. Need we say more? Maybe one more thing: no sales tax on clothing. In all seriousness, there are more than 500 stores in the enclosed shopping center, ranging from the everyday department store to luxe boutiques such as Chanel (inside Nordstrom) and Burberry. For more unique shops, head to Uptown Minneapolis or Grand Avenue in St. Paul.

Families: The Twin Cities perennially tops lists as a great place to raise children, which stands to reason there's an abundance of family fun to be enjoyed here. Kids can learn while having fun at the Minnesota Children's Museum and Historic Fort Snelling. Outdoor activities such as walking around Lake Calhoun, Minnehaha Park, and Como Park Zoo are always crowd pleasers.

Architecture Buffs: Just to get you started, there's Frank Gehry's Weisman Art Museum, Michael Graves's new wing at the Minneapolis Institute of Arts, Jacques Herzog and Pierre de Meuron's Walker Art Center expansion, and Jean Nouvel's Guthrie Theater. And those are just the modern marvels.

TOP 5 REASONS TO GO

Theater: The Guthrie Theater tops the best-of-the-best list, garnering international acclaim as one of three theaters around the U.S. to attract London's Royal Shakespeare Company. The Hennepin Avenue Theatre District brings Broadway to Minneapolis, or for something different, try one of the many experimental theaters.

Architecture: Between the world-class architects who have added their modern designs and the old art deco preserved in the historic landmarks, architecture lovers will have a full itinerary.

Mall of America: The largest enclosed mall in the nation.

Minneapolis Sound: Prince, the Replacements, Soul Asylum, Atmosphere—these local musicians define the genre that has been reproduced by artists across the country. Local darlings Bob Dylan and Mason Jennings round out that sweet Twin Cities noise.

Chain of Lakes: Minnesota isn't called the Land of 10,000 Lakes for nothing. Rent a canoe at Lake Calhoun and disappear for the day. Enjoy an outdoor concert at Lake Harriet, or head out to Lake Minnetonka for the ultimate boating experience.

WHEN IS THE BEST TIME TO VISIT?

Summer showcases all the best that the Twin Cities has to offer—local farmers' markets, flowers in full bloom, water activities on the nearly 10,000 lakes in the surrounding area, outdoor dining and music options, festivals . . . you get the idea. Too bad summer is also one of the briefest seasons. The weather can get hot and humid, although more often than not summers are sunny and pleasant. Fall brings beautiful foliage—take a scenic drive to capture the changing colors of the season. If you must come in winter, the miles-long enclosed skyway system in both downtowns will allow you to park, go to lunch, shop, and see a show, all while never setting a foot out in the blistery cold. For those brave enough for the challenge, several winter events, including downtown's Holidazzle Parade and St. Paul's Winter Carnival, almost make the cold weather bearable.

Summer brims with endless local festivals but the most celebrated are the Minnesota State Fair (www.mnstatefair.org) and the Uptown Art Fair (www.uptownminneapolis.com/art-fair). Both events take place in August. The Uptown Art Fair in Minneapolis draws more than 400 exhibitors with art ranging from jewelry to pottery to abstract sculptures. Prices tend to lean toward the serious art set, but there are still some affordable bargains to be found. The Minnesota State Fair heralds the end of the summer for many Minnesotans. Running at the end of August through Labor Day, it's something that cannot be adequately explained, just an experience to behold. Some highlights include foods of all kind on-a-stick and/or deep-fried, several animal barns, blue ribbon winners for baking, art exhibits, and national music acts.

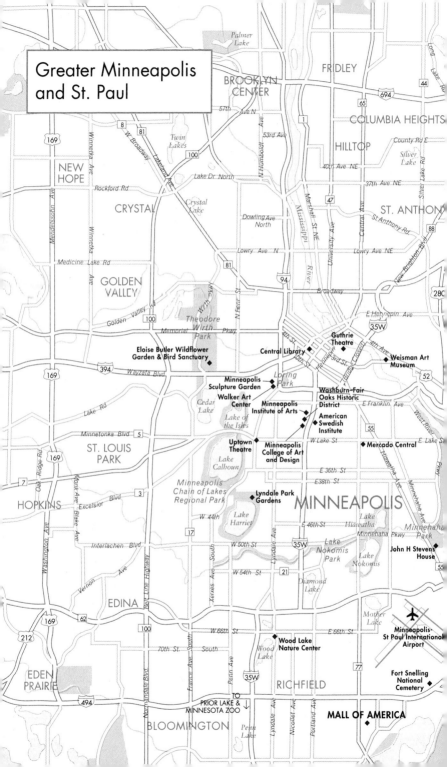

Greater Minneapolis and St. Paul

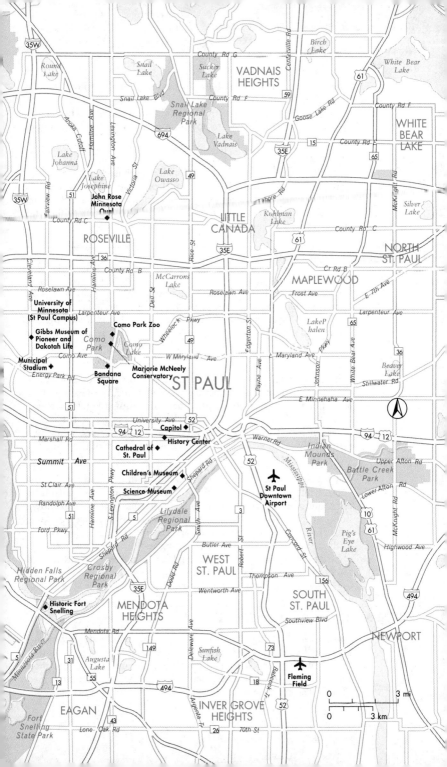

HOW SHOULD I GET THERE?

DRIVING

Interstate 94 runs from Michigan through North Dakota, passing through Chicago, Milwaukee, and the Twin Cities. For downtown St. Paul, exit at 5th Street. For downtown Minneapolis, exit at 11th Street. Be warned, the highways are not a fun place to be during rush hour, especially I–94.

FLYING

The Minneapolis/St. Paul International airport is close to the Cities and offers many direct flights to and from major destinations. The airport serves as a hub for Northwest Airlines. The Light Rail runs from the airport into downtown Minneapolis as well as to the Mall of America.

HOW DO I GET AROUND?

BY BUS/LIGHT RAIL

Public buses canvas the Cities during the day with limited service in the evenings. One-way fare is $1.50 (nonrush hour) and a one-day pass is available at $6 for unlimited rides. The light rail provides convenient but limited service from downtown Minneapolis to the airport and the Mall of America.

BY CAB

Cabs are popular in downtown areas and more sparse elsewhere in the Cities. You can hail a cab after major sporting, theater, and music events or head toward one of the many downtown hotels that have cab stands. Always be prepared to call one just in case. Reliable companies include Yellow Cab (☎612/824–4000) and Red & White Taxi (☎612/871–1600). Cabs have a minimum of $5 per ride.

BY CAR

Getting around the Twin Cities is easiest with a car and will allow you the farthest reach of activities. Avoid rush hour for optimal driving conditions (and four-wheel drive is a blessing in the winter snow). Both downtowns have ample parking garages and metered parking, but keep alert for the one-way streets. Note that the popular Nicollet Mall, downtown Minneapolis's shopping and eating hub, is open only to buses and cabs, and use caution on Hennepin Avenue, another main artery in downtown Minneapolis that is one-way in some areas. The I–94 Lyndale/Hennepin exit to Uptown can also be tricky.

WHERE SHOULD I FOCUS MY ENERGY?

If you're here for 1 day: Even with a brief visit, you can still fall in love with the Twin Cities by focusing on downtown Minneapolis. Check out the Walker Art Center and adjacent sculpture garden, then shop and dine your way down Nicollet Mall. See a show at the acclaimed Guthrie Theater or in the Hennepin Avenue Theatre District.

How to Snack

The Twin Cities are not identified by one particular type of food or cuisine, despite the Scandinavian roots and predominantly Lutheran background. However, two specialties that appear frequently on many restaurant menus are walleye (the state fish) and wild rice soup, a favorite among locals.

In summer locals comb the Twin Cities' farmers markets, which offer an embarrassment of riches—fresh, local, and oftentimes organic fruits and vegetables in addition to artisanal cheeses and meats. The Minneapolis Farmers Market is the largest, open daily mid-April through mid-November (312 E. Lyndale Ave., www.mplsfarmersmarket.com). The St. Paul Farmers' Market sells only local produce and goods weekend mornings, April through November

(290 E. 5th St., www.stpaulfarmersmarket.com). The Mill City Farmers' Market is the newest of the bunch and the innovation of local celebrity chef Brenda Langton. The market promises only local and organic products every Saturday morning from mid-May through mid-October (Chicago Ave. and 2nd St. S, between Guthrie Theater and Mill City Museum, www.millcityfarmersmarket.org).

Finally if you happen to visit the Minnesota State Fair, you can't get more local than food-on-a-stick. Nearly all of the fair food is designed to be eaten while walking around. Although corn on the cob is classic, there are some more innovative choices. Deep-fried Snickers bar, anyone?

If you're here for 2 days: Spend a day exploring Lake Calhoun and Uptown. They're within walking distance of each other, and Uptown's funky-fun restaurants and shops are nicely contrasted with Lake Calhoun's serenity.

18

If you're here for 3 days: Head to the Mall of America for all the shopping and eating you could want under one roof.

If you're here for 4 days: Add St. Paul to the itinerary. You'll have the best experiences in its neighborhoods. Tour the historic homes on Summit Avenue and explore the urban shopping and eating on Grand Avenue (between Dale Street and Lexington Avenue). Nearby Cathedral Hill on Selby Avenue is anchored by the Cathedral of St. Paul and offers stellar neighborhood dining and shopping options.

If you're here for 5 days: Check out another museum or two: Minneapolis Institute of Arts, Science Museum of Minnesota, Minnesota Children's Museum(☎651/225–6000 ⊕*www.mcm.org*), Minnesota History Center, or the Weisman Art Museum. Learn some history at Historic Fort Snelling (☎612/726–1171 ⊕*www.mnhs.org*) or take a fun St. Paul Gangster Tour (☎651/292-1220).

If you're here for 6 days: For some outdoor enjoyment, add Como Park Zoo and Conservatory or Minnehaha Park to your itinerary.

If you're here for 7 days or more: Head out to under-the-radar neighborhoods Northeast Minneapolis and the University of Minnesota's Dinkytown for unique shops and restaurants. Wander over to "the U's"

CLAIM TO FAME

Local celebrities include Garrison Keillor of Prairie Home Companion fame; Prince, who got his start at First Avenue in downtown Minneapolis; Charles Schulz, creator of the Peanuts cartoon strip; and even Bob Dylan, who technically hails from Hibbing, Minnesota. The opening credits of the 1970s sitcom The Mary Tyler Moore Show features Mary tossing her hat on Nicollet Mall, a pedestrian-only thoroughfare in downtown Minneapolis. A statue commemorating this event sits right outside Macy's.

Sports teams are also a sense of pride for the Twin Cities. Although the Minnesota Twins baseball team last won a World Series in 1991, fans still hold the Twins in high esteem and couldn't be more proud of today's team. St. Paul was recently christened Hockeytown USA in 2007 by Sports Illustrated for its devotion to the Minnesota Wild hockey team. With Wisconsin nearby, the rivalry between Minnesota Vikings and Green Bay Packers fans is legendary, even penetrating outside of football circles.

gorgeous campus and Stadium Village area to get your "Ski-U-Mah" on. Stop at the Frank Gehry–designed Weisman Art Museum while you're there.

WHAT ARE THE TOP EXPERIENCES?

Cultural events overload: Museums? Check. Two of the best include the world-class modern art museum the Walker Art Center and the Minneapolis Institute of Arts. Theatre? Check. The Hennepin Avenue Theatre District offers Broadway shows in addition to the esteemed productions the Guthrie Theater puts on. Music? Check. The Cities draw national acts and gave plenty of musicians their start (Prince, The Replacements, Soul Asylum, and Bob Dylan, to name a few). Sports? Check. For now, the Minnesota Vikings and University of Minnesota Gophers football teams and the Minnesota Twins baseball team all share the Hubert H. Humphrey Metrodome(⊠ *900 S. 5th St., Minneapolis* ☏ *612/332–0386* ⊕ *www.msfc.com*). The Minnesota Wild hockey team plays in St. Paul's Xcel Energy Center(⊠ *317 Washington St., St. Paul* ☏ *651/989–5151* ⊕ *www.xcelenergycenter.com*) and the Minnesota Timberwolves basketball team plays at the Target Center (⊠ *600 1st Ave. N, Minneapolis* ☏ *612/673–1600* ⊕ *www.targetcenter.com*).

Shop till you drop: The Mall of America is ground zero for shoppers visiting the Twin Cities. Appropriately nicknamed the Megamall, it has more than 500 stores, an aquarium, and amusement park. To experience more local flavor, venture beyond the mall to some of the Cities' best neighborhood boutiques. Unique shops dot Hennepin Avenue in Minneapolis' Uptown area, southwest of the city's downtown. Grand Avenue in St. Paul is home to several one-of-a-kind shops, particularly the strip between Dale Street and Lexington Avenue. Still looking for more? Consider the neighborhoods of Highland Park and St.

Anthony Park in St. Paul and the Warehouse District and North Loop in Minneapolis.

Exploring outdoors: Perhaps given the cold winter temperatures, Minnesotans cherish the all-too-brief outdoor summer weather even more than their Midwest counterparts. Take a summers day stroll through Como Park Zoo and Conservatory. Picnic near Minnehaha Falls in Minnehaha Park or nosh some tasty fish tacos at the Park's inexpensive restaurant Sea Salt Eatery (4825 Minnehaha Ave., 612/721–8990, www.seasalteatery.com). End the day walking around Lake Calhoun with Minneapolis locals. The summer also brings various street fairs and local farmers' markets. August offers two of the best outdoor festivals, the Uptown Art Fair and the Minnesota State Fair.

STRANGE BUT TRUE

■ In the late 1990s Minnesotans elected Governor Jesse "The Body" Ventura, a one-time pro-wrestler from the Independence Party of Minnesota.

■ Minnesota has two towering Paul Bunyan statues (in Bemidji and Brainerd) that claim the rightful birthplace of the fictional lumberjack and his blue ox.

■ Minnesota's slogan "Land of Ten Thousand Lakes" isn't quite accurate. At last count, the state had more than 11,800 lakes (10 acres or larger) according to the Minnesota Department of Natural Resources.

Architectural wonders: The Twin Cities offers several architectural must-sees, both modern and historical. Whereas St. Paul is Romanesque sandstone mansions and the iconic Cathedral of St. Paul, Minneapolis is through and through modern with a smattering of the historic preserved. The architectural biggies of Minneapolis have received national coverage, bringing a sense of pride to the locals. To cover your bases, check out the IDS Center, Walker Art Center, Guthrie Theater, Minneapolis Central Library and Weisman Art Museum.

Local food: The Twin Cities' restaurant scene has changed dramatically in recent years, thanks in part to several nationally recognized chefs who are challenging the local palate with culinary wonders. Two celebrity chefs with culinary outfits in Minneapolis include Wolfgang Puck's 20.21 in the Walker Art Center and Jean Georges Vongerichten's Chambers Kitchen in the Chambers boutique hotel. The growing immigrant population has introduced ethnic food to the Twin Cities' cuisine; head to 17-block Eat Street (⊠ Nicollet Ave. from Grant to 29 St.) for the best slice of authenticity.

History 101: Interested in learning more about the mighty Mississippi River and the two towns linked by it? Start with Historic Fort Snelling, a living-history park with 1820s fort life reenactments. Also check out the Minnesota History Center in St. Paul. The kid-friendly center houses Minnesota-related exhibits in addition to a research library and museum store. The Mill City Museum (704 S. 2nd St., 612/341–7555, www.millcitymuseum.org) provides a good overview of the proud past of a productive milling town.

18

BEST BETS

SIGHTS AND TOURS

MINNEAPOLIS

★ The **Minneapolis Institute of Arts** (⊠*2400 3rd Ave. S, Whittier, Minne-*
☺ *apolis* ☎*612/870–3131* ⊕*www.artsmia.org* 🖅*Free, except special
exhibits* ⊙*Tues., Wed., Fri., Sat. 10–5, Thurs. 10–9, Sun 11–5; closed
Mon.*), displays more than 80,000 works from every age and culture,
including French Impressionists, rare Chinese jade, and a photography collection from 1863 to the present. The building also houses the
Children's Theatre Company.

★ **Nicollet Mall,** a mile-long pedestrian shopping strip, runs from Washing-
☺ ton Avenue S to Grant Street E, with an extensive system of skyways
connecting its many shops. It's home to the new Cesar Pelli–designed
Minneapolis Central Library (⊠*300 Nicollet Mall, Downtown, Minneapolis* ☎*612/630–6000* ⊙*Tues., Thurs. 10–8, Wed., Fri., Sat. 10–6).*
The modern, light-filled structure houses a significant children's collection, a teen library center, and a coffee shop.

Fodor's Choice The **Walker Art Center** has an outstanding collection of 20th- and 21st-
★ century American and European sculpture, prints, and photography, as
well as traveling exhibits and national and international acts. Adjacent
to the museum is the **Minneapolis Sculpture Garden** (🖅*Free*), the nation's
largest outdoor urban sculpture garden. ⊠*1750 Hennepin Ave., Lor-
ing Park, Minneapolis* ☎*612/375–7600* ⊕*www.walkerart.org* 🖅*$8,
free Thurs. evenings and 1st Sat. of month* ⊙*Tues., Wed., Sat., Sun.
11–5, Thurs. and Fri. 11-9; closed Mon.*

Fodor's Choice **Uptown** (⊠*Centered at intersection of Lake St. and Hennepin Ave.,
★ Minneapolis* ⊕*www.uptownminneapolis.com*) is a funky enclave of
unique shops, restaurants, and bars. The one-room **Uptown Theatre**
(⊠*2906 Hennepin Ave.* ☎*612/825–6006*) is the place to catch independent and foreign-language films.Nearby, **Lake Calhoun** is often
packed with jogging and rollerblading locals, or people just looking
for a quiet spot to read or enjoy a spectacular sunset.

The most talked-about building on campus is the **Weisman Art Museum**
(⊠*University of Minnesota, 333 E. River Rd., University, Minneapolis*
☎*612/625–9494* ⊕*www.weisman.umn.edu* 🖅*Free* ⊙*Tues., Wed.,
Fri. 10–5, Thurs. 10–8, weekends 11–5*), designed by famed avant-
garde architect Frank Gehry. The permanent collection includes works
and installations by American pop artists and modernists like Andy
Warhol, Roy Lichtenstein, and Georgia O'Keeffe.

ST. PAUL

Fodor's Choice The **Cathedral of St. Paul** (⊠*239 Selby Ave., Cathedral Hill, St. Paul*
★ ☎*651/228–1766*), a classic Renaissance-style domed church in the
style of St. Peter's in Rome, lies ¼ mi southwest of the capitol. Inside
are beautiful stained-glass windows, statues, paintings, and other works
of art, as well as a small historical museum on the lower level.

○ **Como Park** (✉*N. Lexington Ave., at Como Ave., Como, St. Paul*) has picnic areas, walking trails, playgrounds, and swimming facilities. **Como Park Zoo** (☎*651/487–8201* ⊕*www.comozooconservatory.org*) is home to large cats, land and water birds, primates, and aquatic animals. The adjacent **Como Park Conservatory,** in a domed greenhouse, has sunken gardens, a fern room, biblical plantings, and seasonal flower shows.

○ Interactive exhibits at the **Minnesota History Center** show the story of the state from the perspectives of Native Americans, explorers, and settlers. A research library and museum store are on-site. ✉*345 Kellogg Blvd. W., St. Paul* ☎*651/296–6126 or 800/657–3773* ⊕*www.mnhs.org* 🎟*$8* ⊙*Closed Mon. Sept.–June.*

○ The **Science Museum of Minnesota** (✉*120 W. Kellogg Blvd., Downtown* ☎*651/221–9444* ⊕*www.smm.org* 🎟*$9.50, films extra* ⊙*Mon.–Sat. 8:30–10, Sun. 8:30–7*) has exhibits on archaeology, technology, and biology and many hands-on exhibits for kids. In the **McKnight Omnitheater** 70mm films are projected overhead on a massive tilted screen.

★ St. Paul's **Summit Avenue,** which runs 4½ mi from the cathedral to the Mississippi River, has the nation's longest stretch of intact residential Victorian architecture. F. Scott Fitzgerald was living at 599 Summit in 1919 when he wrote *This Side of Paradise.*

WHERE TO EAT

	WHAT IT COSTS				
	¢	$	$$	$$$	$$$$
AT DINNER	under $8	$8–$12	$13–$18	$19–$25	over $25

Prices are per person for a main course at dinner.

MINNEAPOLIS

$$$$ ✕ **Chambers Kitchen.** Not your run-of-the-mill hotel restaurant, Cham-
★ bers is helmed by celebrity chef Jean Georges Vongerichten. The menu dazzles with seared duck and other artful selections, just like the eclectic works that adorn the hotel's walls. ✉*Chambers Hotel, 901 Hennepin Ave., Minneapolis* ☎*612/767–6979* ⌁*Reservations essential* ▤*AE, D, DC, MC, V.*

18

$$$–$$$$
★
✕ **D'Amico Cucina.** From the gleaming white linens to the marble floors and leather chairs, this is a haute place. The seasonal menu has a modern Italian accent and includes artistically presented pastas. ⊠ *Butler Sq., 100 N. 6th St., Downtown, Minneapolis* ☎ *612/338–2401* ⚐ *Reservations essential* ▭ *AE, D, DC, MC, V* ⊙ *Closed Sun.*

$$$–$$$$
Fodor'sChoice
★
✕ **La Belle Vie.** A must-stop for serious foodies, La Belle Vie's elegant atmosphere and unparalleled service perennially send it to the top of the Twin Cities' best dining lists (it's also garnered national recognition). The restaurant offers a five- or eight-course tasting menu as well as many à la carte items. ⊠ *510 Groveland Ave., Minneapolis* ☎ *612/874–6440* ⚐ *Reservations essential* ▭ *AE, D, DC, MC, V.*

$$$–$$$$
Fodor'sChoice
★
✕ **Restaurant Alma.** This off-the-beaten-path contemporary eatery is firmly nestled at the top of the list for best dining in the Twin Cities. Exposed ceilings still manage to feel cozy in this multilevel space. Order the three-course tasting menu that changes seasonally, or select from à la carte options. ⊠ *528 University Ave. S.E., Minneapolis* ☎ *612/379–4909* ⊕ *www.restaurantalma.com* ⚐ *Reservations essential* ▭ *AE, MC, V.*

$$$–$$$$
★
✕ **20.21.** Wolfgang Puck crafts beautiful culinary delights, right at home among the Walker Art Center's collection of 20th- and 21st-century art. Don't miss the chocolate spoon, cube, and cherry dessert—an edible imitation of the famous Spoonbridge and Cherry sculpture in the garden adjacent to the Walker. ⊠ *1750 Hennepin Ave., Minneapolis* ☎ *612/253–3410* ⊕ *www.wolfgangpuck.com* ⚐ *Reservations essential* ▭ *AE, D, DC, MC, V* ⊙ *Closed Mon.*

$–$$$$
✕ **112 Eatery.** This small, urban bistro, which serves upscale comfort food, is one of *the* restaurants in Minneapolis. The *tres leches* (three milks) cake is splendid, and the joint's open late. ⊠ *112 N. 3rd St., Minneapolis* ☎ *612/343–7696* ▭ *AE, D, DC, MC, V* ⊙ *No lunch.*

$$$
Fodor'sChoice
★
✕ **Chino Latino.** Street food from hot zones around the equator is how this restaurant describes its unique cuisine, served family-style. There's also a sushi bar and imaginative drink list, including the Chinopolitan, a cosmo garnished with dry ice. Don't forget your hearing aid, because this place is a scene all week long, especially during happy hour. ⊠ *2916 Hennepin Ave. S, Minneapolis* ☎ *612/824–7878* ⚐ *Reservations essential* ▭ *AE, D, DC, MC, V* ⊙ *No lunch.*

$$$
✕ **Cosmos.** This sexy restaurant in the Graves 601 Hotel has received national attention over the years, and serves contemporary fare worthy of a stopover. You may end up lingering in the trendy lounge when you're done eating. ⊠ *601 1st Ave. N., Minneapolis* ☎ *612/312–1168* ⚐ *Reservations essential* ▭ *AE, D, DC, MC, V.*

ST. PAUL

$$$$ ✕ **W.A. Frost and Company.** In this romantic Victorian house, each dining
★ room has a fireplace, Oriental rugs, and marble-topped tables. Country French and Mediterranean flavors predominate the cuisine. The
menu changes seasonally. ✉ *374 Selby Ave., St. Paul* ☎ *651/224–5715*
⊕ *www.wafrost.com* ⬚ *Reservations essential* ▤ *AE, D, DC, MC, V.*

$$–$$$$ ✕ **Pazzaluna.** A floor-to-ceiling mural of the face of Botticelli's Venus
overlooks this artfully designed trattoria, which manages to be busy
and tranquil at once. Pazzaluna stakes its reputation on innovative
dishes such as the *fritto misto* (fried calamari and vegetable strips) but
brings panache to standards like handmade fettuccine in a Bolognese
meat sauce. ✉ *360 St. Peter St., Downtown* ☎ *651/223–7000* ⊕ *www.
pazzaluna.com* ▤ *AE, D, DC, MC, V.*

$$$ ✕ **Heartland.** The contemporary Midwestern menu changes nightly at
★ this arts and craft decked restaurant. The adjoining wine bar also serves
tantalizing regional cuisine. ✉ *1806 St. Clair Ave., St. Paul* ☎ *651/699–
3536* ⊕ *www.heartlandrestaurant.com* ⬚ *Reservations essential* ▤ *D,
DC, MC, V* ⊙ *Closed Mon.*

$ ✕ **Cafe Latté.** This ever-popular Grand Avenue haunt is three restau-
Fodor'sChoice rants in one: a cafeteria-style deli, a pizza and wine bar, and a delec-
★ table patisserie—quite possibly the best desserts in town. Don't miss
the turtle cake or one of 30 cheesecakes. ✉ *850 Grand Ave., St. Paul*
☎ *651/224–5687* ⊕ *www.cafelatte.com* ▤ *AE, D, MC, V.*

¢–$ ✕ **Mickey's Diner.** On the National Register of Historic Places, this quint-
⊙ essential 1930s diner is accented with lots of chrome and vinyl. Sit at the
lunch counter or in one of the few tiny booths to enjoy stick-to-your-ribs
fare; breakfast is the most popular meal of the day. ✉ *36 W. 7th St., at
St. Peter St., Downtown, St. Paul* ☎ *651/222–5633* ▤ *D, MC, V.*

18

WHERE TO STAY

	WHAT IT COSTS IN U.S. DOLLARS				
	¢	$	$$	$$$	$$$$
FOR 2 PEOPLE	under $75	$75–$125	$126–$175	$176–$225	over $225

Prices are for a standard double room for two during peak season.

MINNEAPOLIS

$$$–$$$$ ▥ **Chambers Hotel.** Eclectic art adorns the gleaming white walls of this
ultrahip and trendy boutique hotel in the downtown Theatre District,
giving off a cosmopolitan, mod feel. The hotel's swanky restaurant,
celebrity chef Jean Georges Vongerichten's Chambers Kitchen, serves
artful fare. ✉ *901 Hennepin Ave., Minneapoli,s 55403* ☎ *612/767–
6900* ⊕ *www.chambersminneapolis.com* ⬙ *60 rooms* ⬚ *In room:
refrigerator, Wi-Fi. In hotel: restaurant, room service, bars, gym, laun-
dry service* ▤ *AE, D, DC, MC, V.*

$$$–$$$$ ▥ **Graves 601 Hotel.** This fashionable boutique hotel, steps away from
Fodor'sChoice the bustling Warehouse District, is a sleek, serene environment. A trendy
★ lounge and AAA Four Diamond restaurant complete the package.

⊠*601 1st Ave. N, Minneapolis, 55403* ☎*612/677–1100* ⊕*www. graves601hotel.com* ⤶*255 rooms, 6 suites* ⌂*In room: refrigerator, Ethernet. In hotel: restaurant, room service, bar, gym, laundry service* ▭*AE, D, DC, MC, V.*

$$$–$$$$ 🏠 **Nicollet Island Inn.** This charming 1893 limestone inn is on Nicollet Island in the middle of the Mississippi River, with downtown Minneapolis on one shore and the Riverplace and St. Anthony Main on the other. There's early-American reproduction furniture in the rooms, some of which have river views. ⊠*95 Merriam St., Downtown, Minneapolis, 55401* ☎*612/331–1800* ⊕*www. nicolletislandinn.com* ⤶*24 rooms* ⌂*In-room: Ethernet. In-hotel: restaurant, room service, bar, pool, gym, laundry service, parking (no fee), no pets allowed* ▭*AE, D, DC, MC, V.*

> ## ON THE WAY
>
> The magnificent **Mississippi River** starts humbly as a trickle of water, barely 20 feet wide. The headwaters of the Mississippi are in Itasca State Park in Park Rapids (36750 Main Park Dr., Park Rapids, MN, 218/266–2100).
>
> Laura Ingalls Wilder fans can delight in Walnut Grove, the site of the **Laura Ingalls Wilder Museum**. The museum is devoted to the children's book author and the television series Little House on the Prairie. (800/528–7280, www.walnutgrove.org). Just outside of town is the Ingallses' original dugout site along Plum Creek.

$$$–$$$$ 🏠 **Westin Minneapolis.** Minneapolis's historic Farmers & Mechanics
★ Bank was transformed into this luxurious hotel without losing the original woodwork, marble staircase, and light fixtures in the bank lobby. The building's two original vaults are now a meeting room and a wine vault. ⊠*88 S. 6th St., Minneapolis, 55402* ☎*612/333–4006* ⊕*www.westin.com/minneapolis* ⤶*214 rooms, 19 suites* ⌂*In-room: refrigerator, Wi-Fi. In-hotel: restaurant, bar, pool, gym, laundry service* ▭*AE, D, DC, MC, V.*

$$–$$$$ 🏠 **The Grand Hotel Minneapolis.** This boutique hotel, in the heart of the
★ Business District, offers traditional rooms with crown molding, an on-site spa, and complimentary access to a 58,000 square foot gym. The hotel's restaurant, Martini Blu, serves excellent sushi. ⊠*615 2nd Ave. S, Minneapolis, 55402* ☎*612/288–8888* ⊕*www.grandhotelminneapolis. com* ⤶*140 rooms, 19 suites* ⌂*In-room: Wi-Fi. In hotel: restaurant, bar, pool, spa, gym, laundry service* ▭*AE, D, DC, MC, V.*

ST. PAUL

$$$ 🏠 **Saint Paul Hotel.** This 12-story, marble-pillared 1910 landmark on
★ Rice Park has been a stopover for presidents, heads of state, and celebrities. It's within 7 blocks of the Ordway Center for the Performing Arts, the Civic Center, and the Children's Museum. Rooms are traditional in style. ⊠*350 Market St., St. Paul, 55102* ☎*651/292–9292 or 800/292–9292* ⊕*www.stpaulhotel.com* ⤶*255 rooms* ⌂*In-room: ethernet. In-hotel: 2 restaurants, bar, laundry service* ▭*AE, D, DC, MC, V.*

VITAL STATS:

- State capital: St. Paul
- Mottos: Land of Ten Thousand Lakes
- Nickname: Gopher State
- Unofficial insect: mosquito
- Unofficial food: anything on a stick at the Minnesota State Fair, hotdish (casserole), walleye, wild rice
- Five largest cities: Minneapolis: 387,711; St. Paul: 287,385; Rochester: 90, 515; Duluth: 85,889; Bloomington: 84,347. (According to the Minne-

sota State Demographic Center 2005 estimates)
- Length of Mississippi River in Minnesota: 680 mi
- Winter survival mechanism: extensive heated downtown skyway system
- Famous Minnesotans: Bob Dylan, F. Scott Fitzgerald, Judy Garland, Jean Paul Getty, Hubert H. Humphrey, Garrison Keillor, Prince, Jessica Lange, Sinclair Lewis, Charles A. Lindbergh Jr., Walter Mondale, and Charles Schulz.

NIGHTLIFE & THE ARTS

For restaurants (including a Hard Rock Café), bars and clubs, a video arcade, and a movie theater under one roof, check out **Block E** on Hennepin Avenue in downtown Minneapolis. The **Shout House** (⊠*650 Hennepin Ave* ☎*612/337–6700*) dueling piano bar is always packed. The big Warehouse District clubs are right down the street.

★ The **Dakota Jazz Club and Restaurant** (⊠*1010 Nicollet Mall, Downtown, Minneapolis* ☎*612/332–1010* ⊕*www.dakotacooks.com*) is one of the best jazz bars in the Midwest, with some of the Twin Cities' finest performers.

★ The intimate **Fine Line Music Café** (⊠*318 1st Ave. N, Downtown, Minneapolis* ☎*612/338–8100* ⊕*www.finelinemusic.com*) gets you up close and personal to locally and nationally known rock musicians.

Fodor's Choice ★ The iconic **First Avenue & Seventh Street Entry** (⊠*701 1st Ave. N, Downtown, Minneapolis* ☎*612/332–1775* ⊕*www.first-avenue.com*) is where locals go to hear top rock groups and to get their groove on. Prince played as a regular at the club in the '80s, and it was featured in his movie *Purple Rain.*

Fodor's Choice ★ The **Guthrie Theater** (⊠*818 S. 2nd St., Downtown, Minneapolis* ☎*877/447–8243* ⊕*www.guthrietheater.org*) has a repertory company praised for its balance of classic and avant-garde productions.

The acclaimed **Minnesota Orchestra** (⊕*www.minnesotaorchestra.org*) performs in **Orchestra Hall** (⊠*1111 Nicollet Mall, Downtown, Minneapolis* ☎*612/371–5656*).

The **Ordway Center for the Performing Arts** (⊠*345 Washington St., Rice Park, St. Paul* ☎*651/224–4222* ⊕*www.ordway.org*) is home to the **St. Paul Chamber Orchestra** (⊕*www.thespco.org*), the **Minnesota Opera**

18

(⊕ *www.mnopera.org*), and other performing-arts groups. Broadway shows also stop here.

The **Orpheum** and **State Theatres** (⊠ *910 and 805 Hennepin Ave., Downtown, Minneapolis* ☎ *612/339–7007* ⊕ *www.hennepintheatredistrict. org*) stage Broadway productions and national acts.

Trendy bars and fun restaurants scattered around **Uptown's** main intersection at Lake Street and Hennepin Avenue are always rocking with nightlife debauchery. Try especially hot spots **The Independent** (⊠ *Calhoun Square, 3001 Hennepin Ave., Minneapolis* ☎ *612/378–1905*) and **Chino Latino** (⊠ *2916 Hennepin Ave., Minneapolis* ☎ *612/824–7878*).

SHOPPING

Gaviidae Common (⊠ *655 Nicollet Mall, Downtown, Minneapolis*), has three levels of upscale shops, including Neiman Marcus and Saks Fifth Avenue's discount outlet, Off Fifth. Kiddie-corner is **Macy's**, the city's largest department store.

Fodor'sChoice
★
☯
Appropriately nicknamed the Megamall, the **Mall of America** (⊠ *24th Ave. S. and Killebrew Dr., Bloomington* ☎ *952/883–8800* ⊕ *www. mallofamerica.com*) has more than 500 stores and an aquarium, movie theater, and amusement park.

★ Visit more than 40 (mostly) one-of-a-kind, hip urban shops in **Uptown** (⊠ *Lake St. and Hennepin Ave., Uptown, Minneapolis*), with a smaller shopping center on Calhoun Square.

Victoria Crossing (⊠ *870 Grand Ave., Grand Avenue, St. Paul*) is a collection of small shops and specialty stores among the 200-plus stores on the 2½-mi-long **Grand Avenue.** Down the road is **Just Truffles** (⊠ *1363 Grand Ave.* ☎ *651/690–0075*) an artisanal chocolatier that concocted a special truffle for Luciano Pavarotti.

SPORTS & THE OUTDOORS

Fodor'sChoice
★
☯
Southwest of downtown Minneapolis is the **Chain of Lakes** (⊕ *www. minneapolisparks.org*), popular with locals for walking, jogging, rollerblading, biking, fishing, and canoeing. Lake of the Isles, Lake Calhoun, and Lake Harriet are always popular in good weather.

☯ **Minnehaha Park** (⊠ *Minnehaha Pkwy. and Hiawatha Ave., Minneapolis*) is the site of Minnehaha Falls, which was made famous by Longfellow's *Song of Hiawatha.* Minnehaha Parkway follows Minnehaha Creek, providing miles of jogging, biking, and in-line-skating trails.

VISITOR INFORMATION

Meet Minneapolis (☎ *612/767–8000* ⊕ *www.minneapolis.org*)

St. Paul RiverCentre Convention and Visitors Authority (☎ *800/627–6101* ⊕ *www.stpaulcvb.org*)

South Dakota's Black Hills

WORD OF MOUTH

"Mount Rushmore must be seen at day and at night, as the nighttime view has massive spotlights on the faces and patriotic music, as I recall. The Crazy Horse Monument is also an interesting stop. It is a work in progress for over 50 years now. "

–jeff

EXPLORING SOUTH DAKOTA'S BLACK HILLS

609 mi west of Minneapolis via 35W North and I–90; 406 mi north of Denver via I–25, U.S. 85, U.S. 18, and SD 79; 372 mi southeast of Billings, MT, via I–90; 351 mi southwest of Bismarck, ND, via I–94, U.S. 85, and I–90.

By T.D. Griffith   Arguably one of the most scenic areas in the nation, the Black Hills of South Dakota were the last region in the U.S. to be mapped. For many travelers, it remains one of the overlooked jewels of the West. Comprised of some of the oldest mountains in the world, the Black Hills are, in fact, a mix of lush green forests, open mountain prairies, creek-carved canyons, and crystal-clear lakes encompassing more than 1.2 million acres—an area roughly the size of Delaware.

Today the Black Hills welcome more than 3 million annual visitors from around the globe who come to see one of the highest concentrations of parks, monuments, and memorials anywhere in the world. Nowhere else will you find the majesty of a mountain memorial commemorating the birth, growth, preservation, and development of the United States a few miles from another mountain carving in-progress that pays tribute to the indigenous peoples who first populated the Great Plains. When coupled with an abundance of free-roaming wildlife, history and mystery, scenic drives, outdoor adventure, and a plethora of public and private attractions, the Black Hills remain one of America's great secrets in travel.

WHO WILL ESPECIALLY LOVE THIS TRIP?

Adventure Addicts: While sightseeing in the Black Hills is outstanding, the opportunity for outdoor adventure here is even better. Bike or hike the 109-mi Mickelson Trail, wet a dry-fly in Spearfish Canyon, ski Terry Peak, and snowmobile on 340 mi of groomed trails on a network ranked among the best in the nation.

Families: This isn't Disney World—in a good way. From the majesty of Mount Rushmore to lesser-known treasures like the Mammoth Site, Crazy Horse Memorial, Reptile Gardens, and Bear Country USA, the Black Hills are among the best and most affordable family destinations anywhere.

History Buffs: Every town has a museum, but few places have as rich and colorful a past as the Black Hills. From legendary Lakota warriors and famed cavalry soldiers to Wild West gunfighters and celebrated gold strikes in places like Deadwood and Lead, this is the place where history *really* happened.

Writers, Photographers & Artists: There are subjects waiting to be photographed, painted, or written about all across this ancient mountain range. Many American luminaries, including Mark Twain, Frank Lloyd Wright, and Theodore Roosevelt, were drawn to the Black Hills, and the characters, climate and countryside still attract their contempo-

TOP 5 REASONS TO GO

Parks & Monuments: Crowned by Mount Rushmore National Memorial, this region is home to one of the highest concentrations of parks, monuments, and memorials in the U.S.

America's Outback: With more than a million acres of creek-carved canyons and emerald forests, this may be the last, best place to hide.

History & Mystery: As the last region of the U.S. to be mapped, the Black Hills are home to countless legends, from a vast underground wilderness to Native American culture and cowboy lore.

Family Attractions: There may be no better place to reconnect with your spouse or children than the Black Hills, host to dozens of great family adventures that won't wound your wallet.

The Call of the Wild: From the buffalo herds of Custer State Park to the mountain lions that wander the region, the Black Hills are home to an incredible array of free-roaming wildlife, including elk, deer, pronghorn, Rocky Mountain goats, Bighorn sheep, coyotes, and raptors.

raries today—including actor Kevin Costner, writer David Milch, and watercolorist Jon Crane.

WHEN IS THE BEST TIME TO VISIT?

The ideal time to visit the Black Hills is during the summer months—except during the first full week of August, when a half-million motorcycle enthusiasts flock to the annual Sturgis Motorcycle Rally and fill virtually every hotel and motel room and campground between Sundance, WY, and Wall, SD. Summer days can be warm, but numerous caves and 18 peaks exceeding 7,000 feet allow visitors to escape to cooler temperatures. Nights are generally cool, particularly in the mountains. Spring and early summer are marked by late snows and frequent afternoon thunderstorms.

19

Shoulder- and off-season lodging is less expensive than during the height of the summer season. September and October are excellent months to visit the Black Hills, with warm days and mild nights, changing leaves, and the annual Custer State Park Buffalo Roundup, held the first Monday in October. Skiers and snowmobilers are attracted to the heavy snowfalls of February, March and April, particularly in the northern Hills where room rates can be as low as $30 per night.

HOW SHOULD I GET THERE?

BUS
Greyhound Lines provides national service out of Rapid City.

DRIVING
More than three-quarters of the visitors to the Black Hills arrive by private vehicle. Most motorists arrive via I-90, which connects Rapid City to Sioux Falls and Billings. From the south, visitors can get to the

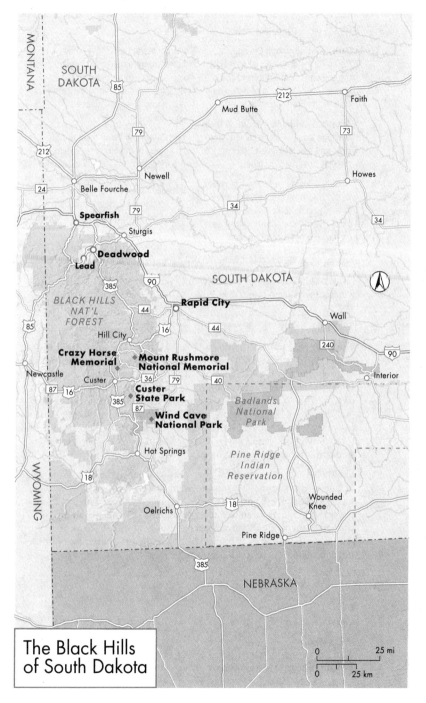

MONTANA

SOUTH
DAKOTA

[85]

[212] — Mud Butte — Faith

[79] [73]

[212] — Howes

[24] — Belle Fourche

Spearfish [79] — Sturgis [34]

[34]

Deadwood
Lead [385] [90]

SOUTH DAKOTA

*BLACK HILLS
NAT'L
FOREST* [44] — **Rapid City**

Wall

[85] [16] — Hill City [44]

[240]

**Crazy Horse
Memorial** ◆ **Mount Rushmore
National Memorial** [90]

Newcastle — Custer [36] [79] [40]

[87] [16] **Custer
State Park** ◆

[385]

[87] ◆ **Wind Cave
National Park** *Badlands
National
Park*

Interior

Hot Springs

*Pine Ridge
Indian
Reservation*

WYOMING

[18]

Wounded
Knee

Oelrichs [18]

Pine Ridge

[385]

NEBRASKA

The Black Hills
of South Dakota

0   25 mi

0   25 km

CLOSE UP

How to Snack

Like neighboring Wyoming, the Black Hills are not known for culinary diversity, and no matter where you go in this part of the world, beef is king. Nevertheless, thanks to a growing population and increasing numbers of visitors, the area is beginning to see more dining options.

Rapid City and Spearfish have an abundance of national chain restaurants, and both communities have local eateries that specialize in Continental, contemporary, Native American, Italian, and traditional American cooking. Although dining in Deadwood's casinos often involves an all-you-can-eat buffet, the tiny town also claims some of the best-ranked restaurants in South Dakota.

Don't be afraid to try wild game dishes. Buffalo, pheasant, and elk are relatively common ingredients in the Black Hills.

Black Hills via U.S. highways 79, 85, or 18. From the north, most drivers arrive via U.S. Highway 85.

FLYING

It's never been easier to get to the Black Hills by air. Rapid City Regional Airport ranks among the fastest growing in the U.S., with multiple daily connections to several major hubs. Delta Air provides a connection to the Black Hills from Salt Lake City, Northwest Airlines offers service from Minneapolis, United Airlines flies from Denver and Chicago O'Hare, Frontier flies direct to Denver, and Allegiant Air has nonstop flights from Las Vegas and Phoenix. For current flight info visit airline websites or www.rapairport.org.

HOW DO I GET AROUND?

19

BY BIKE

More adventurous travelers can embark on a two-wheeled tour of the Black Hills via the 109-mi Mickelson Trail (⊕*www.ridethetrail.com*), which runs the length of the Black Hills from north to south. This splendid option incorporates more than 100 converted railroad bridges and four tunnels along the route. Although the grade seldom exceeds 4%, parts of the trail are strenuous. A $2 day pass lets you hike or bike on the trail ($10 for an annual pass); passes are available at self-service stations along the trail, at some state park offices, and through the South Dakota Game, Fish, and Parks website (⊕*www.state.sd.us/gfp*). A portion of the trail is open for snowmobiling in winter.

BY CAR

Unless you come to the Black Hills on an escorted package tour, a car is essential. I–90 cuts directly through South Dakota from east to west, connecting the northern towns of Spearfish, Sturgis, and Deadwood (which lies about 8 mi off the interstate) with Rapid City. From there the interstate turns straight east, passing Wall and Badlands National Park on its way to Sioux Falls.

Minor highways of importance include U.S. 385, which connects the interior of the Black Hills from south to north, and U.S. 16, which winds south of Rapid City toward Mount Rushmore and Crazy Horse Memorial. Highway 44 is an alternate route between the Black Hills and the Badlands.

Roads are generally numerous and well-maintained, and navigation is easy. Towns with services are plentiful, so you won't need to worry about how much gas you've got in your tank or where you'll be able to find a place to stay the night. Rapid City, the largest community in the region, is the most popular base for exploration of the Black Hills. The northern towns of Deadwood and Spearfish, as well as the central and southern communities of Hill City, Custer, and Hot Springs, also are good options.

WHERE SHOULD I FOCUS MY ENERGY?

If you're here for 1 day: If your visit is brief, start your Black Hills visit at the Journey Museum *(222 New York St., Rapid City, SD 57701, 605/394–6923, www.journeymuseum.org)* in Rapid City, then drive 24 mi to Mount Rushmore National Memorial with a stop in Hill City to peruse its art galleries.

If you're here for 2 days: Include a half-day visit to Crazy Horse Memorial, and a scenic drive on Iron Mountain Road and the Needles Highway, with a lunch or dinner break at Sylvan Lake Lodge.

If you're here for 3 days: Spend a day in the northern Black Hills, with a stop at the High Plains Western Heritage Center *(825 Heritage Dr., Spearfish, SD 57783, 605/642–9378, www.westernheritagecenter. com)*, a drive through Spearfish Canyon, a stop at the Homestake Visitor Center *(160 W. Main St., Lead, 57754, 605/584–3110, www.home staketour.com)* in Lead, and an overnight in Deadwood.

If you're here for 4 days: Explore Custer State Park by hiking to the top of Harney Peak, stopping for lunch at the State Game Lodge, then driving the Wildlife Loop or taking the Buffalo Jeep Safari right in to the herds.

If you're here for 5 days: Take in the southern Black Hills by touring Wind Cave National Park or Jewel Cave National Monument, the Mammoth Site, the Black Hills Wild Horse Sanctuary *(12 mi south of Hot Springs off U.S. Hwy. 71, 800/252–6652, www.wildmustangs. com)* and, if time allows, a swim at Evans Plunge *(1145 N. River St., Hot Springs, SD 57747, 605/745–5165, www.evansplunge.com)*.

If you're here for 6 days: Stop at the Wall Drug Store *(510 Main St., Wall, SD 57790, 605/279–2175, www.walldrug.com)* for great doughnuts and flapjacks, then tour the Minuteman Missile National Historic Site *(21280 SD Hwy. 240, Philip, SD 57567, 605/433–5552, www.nps. gov/mimi)* before taking a short hike in Badlands National Park.

If you're here for 7 days or more: Hang out in Rapid City, visit the Prairie Edge Trading Company and Gallery, eat lunch next door at the

Firehouse Brewing Co., play one of the outstanding local golf courses, call on the creatures on Dinosaur Hill, check out the life-size bronzes on the City of Presidents tour *(631 Main St., Rapid City, SD 57702, 605/342–7272),* or relax along the banks of Rapid Creek.

WHAT ARE THE TOP EXPERIENCES?

Taking in Mount Rushmore's Majesty. There may be no better way to start a day than breakfast with the presidents at Mount Rushmore National Memorial. The colossal carving is best viewed in morning light, followed by a leisurely stroll up the Avenue of Flags where the Grand View Terrace affords a commanding view of the granite visages of Washington, Jefferson, Lincoln, and Theodore Roosevelt. If you're not an early riser, check out Mount Rushmore's nightly program with a ranger talk, film and the enhanced lighting of the memorial, which ranks as the National Park Service's most popular interpretive program.

CLAIM TO FAME

When world-renowned sculptor Gutzon Borglum visited the Black Hills in 1927 and suggested that its pine-clad cliffs would be ideal for sculpting a monument to the American spirit, most locals thought he was either under-medicated or over-medicated. But in six and a half years of work that occurred over a 14-year period, Borglum and his rag-tag assemblage of drill-dusty, out-of-work, hardrock miners molded a mountain into one of the world's most enduring icons. Today, America's Shrine of Democracy attracts nearly 3 million visitors each year.

Watching a Work in Progress. You'd be hard-pressed to find a place with one mountain memorial completed and one in progress. But, just down the road from Mount Rushmore visitors find Crazy Horse Memorial, a tribute to the legendary Lakota leader and all North American Indian tribes. While visiting Crazy Horse, it's not uncommon to witness a massive dynamite blast that removes tons of rock in the "carving" of this, the world's largest work of art in the making.

19

Going Underground. In an age when satellites can read a license plate from space and most of the world's topography has been mapped, the underground wilderness of caves represents one of the earth's last uncharted territories. The Black Hills are home to numerous private cave attractions, as well as two National Park Service units dedicated to preserving these outstanding natural resources. Wind Cave National Park and Jewel Cave National Monument offer cave tours for virtually every skill level and there, in the darkness, visitors discover exceedingly rare specimens found nowhere else on the globe.

Traveling Back in Time. Walking the brick-lined streets of Deadwood, you'd swear you had stepped into the past. Once known as the wildest and wickedest town in the West, in a place fueled by gold, guns, and greed, the Deadwood of today is decidedly more visitor-friendly. Legalized gaming has stimulated a transformation and resulted in more than $200 million in historic preservation projects. High on a hill above town, you'll find Deadwood's own Boot Hill, where Wild Bill Hickok, Calamity Jane, and other western legends are permanent residents.

BEST BETS

SIGHTS AND TOURS

Fodor'sChoice **Mount Rushmore National Memorial.** At Mount Rushmore, one of the
★ nation's most famous sights, 60-foot-high likenesses of Presidents
George Washington, Thomas Jefferson, Abraham Lincoln, and Theodore Roosevelt grace a massive granite cliff, which, at an elevation of
5,725 feet, towers over the surrounding countryside and faces the sun
most of the day. Start your day with breakfast with the presidents, and
allow two hours to tour the memorial. The memorial is equally spectacular at night in June through mid-September, when a special lighting
ceremony dramatically illuminates the carving. ⊠*24 mi southwest of
Rapid City via U.S. 16 and U.S. 16A.*.

The **Mount Rushmore Information Center,** between the park entrance and
the Avenue of Flags, has a small exhibit with photographs of the presidents' faces as they were being carved. There's also an information desk
here, staffed by rangers who can answer questions about the memorial or the surrounding Black Hills. A nearly identical building across
from the information center houses restrooms, telephones, and soda
machines. ⊠*Beginning of Ave. of Flags* ☎*605/574–3198* ⊕*www.
nps.gov/moru* ⊠*Free; parking $10* ◎*May–Sept., daily 8* AM*–10* PM;
Oct.–Apr., daily 8–5.

Fodor'sChoice **Crazy Horse Memorial.** Designed to be the world's largest sculpture, the
★ tribute to Crazy Horse, the legendary Lakota leader who helped defeat
General Custer at the Little Bighorn, is a work in progress. So far the
warrior's head has been carved out of the mountain, and the head of
his horse is starting to emerge; when work is under way you can expect
to witness frequent blasting. Self-taught sculptor Korczak Ziolkowski
conceived this memorial to Native American heritage in 1948, after
Chief Henry Standing Bear told him that "the red man would like the
white man to know that he has heroes, too." Following Ziolkowski's
death in 1982, his family took on the project. The completion date is
unknown, since activity is limited by weather and funding. Near the
work site stands an exceptional orientation center, the Indian Museum
of North America, Ziolkowski's studio/home and workshop, indoor
and outdoor sculpture galleries, and a restaurant. ⊠*15 mi southwest
of Mount Rushmore National Memorial via Hwy. 244 and U.S. 16.*
☎*605/673–4681* ⊕*www.crazyhorse.org* ⊠*$10 per adult or $24 per
carload for more than 2 adults* ◎*May–Sept., daily 8* AM*–9* PM; *Oct.–
Apr., daily 8–4:30.*

★ **Custer State Park.** Down the road less traveled, in 71,000-acre Custer
State Park, scenic backcountry is watered by crisp, clear trout streams.
Elk, antelope, deer, mountain goat, bighorn sheep, mountain lion, wild
turkey, prairie dog, and one of the largest herds of bison in the world
walk the pristine land. Some of the most scenic drives in the country roll
past fingerlike granite spires and panoramic views. Each year at the CSP
Buffalo Roundup and Arts Festival, thousands of spectators watch the
park's 1,450 bison thunder through the hills at the start of a Western-

HISTORY YOU CAN SEE

Following a series of engagements that marked the Plains Indian Wars, in December 1890, remnants of the 7th Cavalry (the same regiment wiped out at the Battle of the Little Bighorn in 1876) confronted Min-niconjou Sioux Chief Big Foot and his band of 350 men, women, and children near Wounded Knee Creek southeast of the Black Hills. On the morning of December 28, 500 soldiers surrounded the Indian camp and prepared to disarm the Indians. When a shot rang out, the soldiers responded with a barrage of bullets, including hundreds of rounds from rapid-fire Hotchkiss guns. In a matter of minutes, about 200 Indians were killed, and the bodies of unarmed women and children were later found as far away as 3 mi from the initial confrontation. Twenty-five of the military men were dead.

While 23 Medals of Honor were awarded to soldiers for "valor" shown in the carnage, both whites and their Indian brethren were incensed by the massacre. The Battle of Wounded Knee signaled the end of America's Indian Wars, the closing of nation's "last frontier" and, most significantly, the final stanza of nearly 400 years of unrelenting war against the indigenous people of the Americas.

theme art and food expo. ⊠ *U.S. 16A, 4 mi east of Custer* ☎ *605/255–4515* ⊕ *www.custerstatepark.info* ⊠ *$2.50–$23* ⊗ *Year-round.*

Fodor'sChoice ★ **Deadwood.** Its brick-paved streets plied by old-time trolleys, illuminated by period lighting, and lined with original Victorian architecture, Deadwood today owes much of its historical character to casinos. In 1989 South Dakota voters approved limited-stakes gaming for the town, on the condition that a portion of revenues be devoted to historic preservation. Since then, more than $200 million has been dedicated to restoring and preserving this once infamous gold-mining boomtown, which has earned distinction as a National Historic Landmark. ⊠ *42 mi northwest of Rapid City via I-90 and U.S. 14A.*

Mammoth Site. During the construction of a housing development in 1974, earthmoving equipment uncovered this sinkhole where giant mammoths supposedly came to drink, got trapped, and died. To date, 55 of the fossilized woolly beasts have been unearthed since digging began, and most can be seen in-situ. You may watch the excavation in progress and take guided tours. The last tour begins one hour prior to closing. ⊠ *1800 Hwy. 18 Truck Rte. U.S. 18, 15 mi south of Wind Cave National Park, Hot Springs* ☎ *605/745–6017 or 800/325–6991* ⊕ *www.mammothsite.com* ⊠ *$7.50* ⊗ *Daily; hrs vary, call ahead.*

★ ☺ **Reptile Gardens.** On the bottom of a valley between Rapid City and Mount Rushmore is western South Dakota's answer to a zoo. In addition to the world's largest private reptile collection, the site also has a raptor rehabilitation center. No visit is complete without watching some alligator wrestling or letting the kids ride the giant tortoises. ⊠ *8955 S. U.S. 16, Rapid City* ☎ *605/342–5873* ⊕ *www.reptile gardens.com* ⊠ *$12* ⊗ *Memorial Day–Labor Day, daily 8–7.*

19

☺ **Bear Country U.S.A.** A unique drive-through wildlife park featuring the largest collection of privately owned North American wildlife in the world, including black bears, elk and wolves. There's also a walk-through wildlife center. ⊠ *13820 S. U.S. 16, Rapid City* ☎ *605/343–2290* ⊕ *www.bearcountryusa.com* ⊠ *$15* ⊙ *May–Nov., daily 8–7.*

WHERE TO EAT

	WHAT IT COSTS				
	¢	$	$$	$$$	$$$$
RESTAURANTS	under $7	$7–$10	$11–$15	$16–$22	over $22

Restaurant prices are for a main course at dinner, excluding sales tax of 4%–7%.

$$$–$$$$
Fodor's Choice
★
✕ **Enigma.** The Rapid City Radisson's signature restaurant is known as "Enigma," and there's certainly some mystery in how a bistro in the middle of America offers fare you'd more commonly find in London, Vienna, or Milan. Chefs Gunter Schnopp of Austria and Benjamin Klinkel, a Casper, WY, native, have extensive culinary backgrounds that include stops in Austria, Germany, Turkey, Spain and Italy. European influences are apparent in their remarkable menu. ⊠ *Radisson Hotel, 445 Mount Rushmore Rd., Rapid City* ☎ *605/348–8300* ⊟ *AE, MC, V.*

$$$–$$$$
Fodor's Choice
★
✕ **Roma's Ristorante.** Search the West and you'd be hard-pressed to discover a restaurant more inviting than Roma's in Spearfish. Airy and open, this fine establishment is housed in an 1893 sandstone building a block off the main drag. Roma's signature dishes include smoked pheasant ravioli, traditional lasagna and the carbonara, as well as the house-baked bread and the house salad with balsamic vinaigrette topped with goat cheese. But diners also will discover an exceptional blend of chicken dishes, pastas, steaks, seafood, and vegetarian selections. ⊠ *701 5th St., Spearfish* ☎ *605/722–0715* ⊟ *AE, MC, V.*

$$$–$$$$
Fodor's Choice
★
✕ **Sage Creek Grille.** With its unique blend of local dishes, the Sage Creek Grille has evolved into one of the most popular restaurants in the southern Black Hills. Opened in 1999 by owner–chef Nancy Gellerman, the 50-seat restaurant touts exceptional nightly specials and all cuts of South Dakota certified steaks, as well as a pan-seared buffalo tenderloin that you'll remember long after the Black Hills fade away in your review mirror. The menu changes every three weeks. ⊠ *611 Mt. Rushmore Rd., Custer* ☎ *605/673–2424* ⊟ *AE, MC, V.*

$$–$$$$
★
✕ **Deadwood Thymes Bistro.** Across from the historic courthouse, away from the Main Street casinos, this bistro has a quieter, more intimate feel than other town restaurants—and the food is among the best. The menu changes frequently, but expect dishes like brioche French toast, salmon quiche, Parisian grilled ham and Swiss, Thai burrito with peanut sauce, and lamb chops marinated in white wine and mustard and served with parsley-gin sauce. The wine list features imports, and desserts are incredible. You might find raspberry cheesecake or chocolate angel food cake with a whiskey-bourbon sauce. ⊠ *87 Sherman St., Deadwood* ☎ *605/578–7566* ⊟ *MC, V.*

STRANGE BUT TRUE

■ Had they been carved from head to toe, the four presidents on Mount Rushmore would have stood 465 feet tall.

■ Each day during the annual Sturgis Motorcycle Rally—the world's largest such gathering—city crews haul off more garbage to the local landfills than do New York City crews following the New Year's Eve celebration in Times Square.

■ Crazy Horse Memorial, a massive mountain carving in-progress in the Black Hills, will result in the largest work of art on earth. By comparison, the four faces of Mount Rushmore would fit in the horse's head.

■ In 125 years of sweat and toil, hardrock miners at Lead's Homestake Gold Mine carved out shafts as deep as 8,000 feet below the surface, where the rock is 135 degrees.

■ Jewel Cave and Wind Cave, both in the Black Hills, rank as the second and third longest caves in the world—but explorers have no idea how long they truly are.

■ Bison once blanketed the Great Plains—there were once 60 million of the shaggy beasts. By 1889 less than 1,000 buffalo were left in the U.S. Thanks to the efforts of South Dakotans like Fort Pierre rancher Scotty Phillips, the American bison was saved from extinction and now nibble buffalo grass from Arizona to Alaska.

■ South Dakota averages 10 people per square mile. But, in the remote locations of northwestern South Dakota, population is measured in square miles per person.

■ With the admission of Alaska and Hawaii to the Union in 1959, the U.S. Coast & Geodetic Survey officially designated a point 20 mi north of Belle Fourche, on the northern foothills of the Black Hills, as the "Geographic Center of the Nation."

■ Thanks to the Great Lakes of Missouri River, South Dakota has more miles of shoreline than Florida.

19

$$–$$$$ ✕**Firehouse Brewing Company.** Brass fixtures and firefighting equipment ornament the state's first brewpub, located in a 1915 firehouse. The five house-brewed beers are the highlight here, and the menu includes such hearty pub dishes as pastas, salads, and gumbo. Thursday nights buffalo prime rib is the specialty. Kids' menus are available. ⊠*610 Main St., Rapid City* ☎*605/348–1915* ⊕*www.firehousebrewing.com* ⌲*Reservations not accepted* ⊟*AE, D, DC, MC, V* ⊘*No lunch Sun.*

$–$$$ ✕**Deadwood Social Club.** On the second floor of historic Saloon No. 10,
Fodor'sChoice   this warm restaurant surrounds you with wood and old-time photo-
★   graphs of Deadwood's past. Light jazz and blues play over the sound system. The decor is Western, but the food is northern Italian, a juxtaposition that keeps patrons coming back. The menu stretches from wild-mushroom pasta-and-seafood nest with basil cream to chicken *piccata* (sautéed and served with a lemon and parsley sauce) and melt-in-your-mouth Black Angus rib eyes. The wine list had nearly 200 selections at last count. Reservations are a good idea. ⊠*657 Main St., Deadwood* ☎*605/578–1533* ⊟*AE, MC, V.*

WHERE TO STAY

	WHAT IT COSTS				
	¢	$	$$	$$$	$$$$
HOTELS	under $70	$70–$109	$110–$159	$160–$220	over $220

Hotel prices are for two people in a standard double room in high season, excluding service charges and 5%–10% tax.

$–$$$$ ⚏ **Radisson Hotel Rapid City/Mount Rushmore.** Murals of the surrounding landscape and a large Mount Rushmore mosaic in the marble floor distinguish the lobby of this nine-floor hotel in the heart of downtown Rapid City. Decorated in gold and beige, the rooms here are unremarkable, with one exception: most feature Sleep Number beds, whose comfort level can be adjusted by users. The popular accommodation stands between the interstate and U.S. 16, the highway that leads into the southern Black Hills and Mount Rushmore. ✉ *445 Mt. Rushmore Rd., Rapid City, 57701* ☎ *605/348–8300* 🖷 *605/348–3833* ⊕ *www.radisson.com/rapidcitysd* ♜ *176 rooms, 5 suites* ♿ *In-hotel: pool, gym, public Wi-Fi, no-smoking rooms* ⊟ *AE, D, DC, MC, V.*

$–$$$$ ⚏ **Sylvan Lake Resort.** This spacious stone-and-wood lodge in Custer
★   State Park affords fantastic views of pristine Sylvan Lake and Harney
♺   Peak beyond. The rooms in the lodge are large and modern, and there are rustic cabins, some with fireplaces, scattered along the cliff and in the forest. The Lakota Dining Room has an exceptional view of the lake; its lovely veranda constructed of native stone is the perfect place to sip tea and watch the sunrise. On the menu are buffalo selections and rainbow trout. You can canoe, fish, and swim in the lake, and numerous hiking trails make this a great choice for active families. ✉ *16 mi east of Custer on U.S. 16A, Hill City* 🖅 *HC 83, Box 74, Custer, 57730* ☎ *605/574–2561 or 800/658–3530* 🖷 *605/574–4943* ⊕ *www.custerresorts.com* ♜ *35 rooms, 31 cabins* ♿ *In-hotel: restaurant, no-smoking rooms* ⊟ *AE, D, MC, V* ☾ *Closed Oct.–Mother's Day.*

$$$ ⚏ **Spearfish Canyon Lodge.** About midway between Spearfish and Dead-
Fodor'sChoice   wood, near the bottom of Spearfish Canyon, this lodge-style hotel com-
★   mands some of the best views in the Black Hills. Limestone cliffs rise nearly 1,000 feet in all directions. The rush of Spearfish Falls is only a ¼-mi hike away, while the gentle flow of Roughlock Falls is a mile-long hike through pine, oak, and aspen from the lodge's front door. Rooms are furnished in natural woods, and fabrics are dark maroon and green. ✉ *10619 Roughlock Falls Rd., Lead, 57754* ☎ *877/975–6343 or 605/584–3435* 🖷 *605/584–3990* ⊕ *www.spfcanyon.com* ♜ *54 rooms* ♿ *In-room: Ethernet. In-hotel: no elevator, restaurant, room service, bar, laundry facilities, no-smoking rooms* ⊟ *AE, D, MC, V.*

$$–$$$ ⚏ **Audrie's Bed & Breakfast.** This secluded, romantic B&B, set in a thick
★   woods 7 mi west of Rapid City, is filled with Victorian antiques. Suites, cottages, and creek-side cabins sleeping two come with old-world furnishings, fireplaces, private baths, hot tubs, and big-screen TVs. Bicycles and fishing poles can be obtained free from the office. ✉ *23029 Thunderhead Falls Rd., Rapid City 57702* ☎ *605/342–7788* ⊕ *www.audriesbb.com* ♜ *2 suites, 7 cottages and cabins* ♿ *In-hotel: no eleva-*

ON THE WAY

If you're traveling to the Black Hills from the east, at least 100 billboards will alert you to your pending arrival at the Wall Drug Store near the Badlands, about 55 mi east of Rapid City. It all began with the offer of free ice water, but has evolved into a third generation attraction that commands an entire block.

The landscape of Badlands National Park east of the Black Hills is other-worldly, with 244,000 acres of ragged ridgelines and sawtooth spires that make it look like the surface of the moon. Best seen at sunup or dusk, the 32-mi Badlands Loop Road is well worth the drive.

The Black Hills spill over the South Dakota state line into extreme northeastern Wyoming, where you'll discover Devils Tower National Monument (Near Hulett, WY, 307/467–5283, www.nps.gov/deto),

the first such monument established in the U.S. The trading post outside the park's entrance is worth a stop, as is the monument's visitor center. A gentle walking path surrounds the geologic up-thrust made famous in the movie Close Encounters of the Third Kind.

If your route to the Black Hills takes you through Montana, a stop at the Little Bighorn Battlefield National Monument (Exit 510 off I–90, Crow Agency, 59022–0039, 406/638–3204, www.nps.gov/libi) south of Hardin, MT, is a must. The park memorializes one of the final armed efforts of the Plains Indian tribes to preserve a way of life and marks the spot where, in 1876, 263 soldiers of the U.S. Army's 7th Cavalry led by Lt. Col. George Armstrong Custer, met their deaths at the hands of several thousand Cheyenne and Lakota warriors.

tor, bicycles, no-smoking rooms, no kids under 21 ⊟*No credit cards* ⊠|*BP.*

$–$$$ 🏨 **Bullock Hotel.** A casino occupies the main floor of this meticulously restored, pink-granite hotel, which was built by Deadwood's first sheriff, Seth Bullock, in 1895. Rooms are furnished in Victorian style with reproductions of the original furniture. You can order a steak or hamburger at the casual downstairs restaurant ($–$$). ⊠*633 Main St., Deadwood, 57732* ☎*605/578–1745 or 800/336–1876* 🖷*605/578–1382* ⊕*www.historicbullock.com* 🛏*29 rooms, 7 suites* ♿*In-hotel: restaurant, room service, bar, no-smoking rooms* ⊟*AE, D, MC, V.*

19

NIGHTLIFE & THE ARTS

Fodor'sChoice ★   Billing itself as a "museum with a bar," the **Old Style Saloon No. 10** (⊠*657 Main St., Deadwood* ☎*605/578–3346*) is littered with thousands of artifacts, from vintage photos and antique lighting to a stuffed two-headed calf and the chair in which Wild Bill Hickok was supposedly shot. A reenactment of his murder takes place four times daily in summer. At night come for some of the region's best bands, lively blackjack tables, and quiet bartenders who cater to noisy customers.

SPORTS & THE OUTDOORS

The Black Hills are filled with tiny mountain creeks, especially on the wetter western and northern slopes, that are ideal for fly-fishing. Rapid Creek, which flows down from the Central Hills into Pactola Reservoir and finally into Rapid City, is a favorite fishing venue for the city's anglers, both because of its regularly stocked population of trout and for its easy accessibility (don't be surprised to see someone standing in the creek casting a line as you drive through the center of town on Highway 44). Also popular are nearby Spearfish, Whitewood, Spring, and French creeks, all within an hour's drive of Rapid City.

VITAL STATS

■ Size: 77,123 square mi, with an average of 10 people per square mi.

■ Capital: Pierre (pronounced peer)

■ Official Sport: Rodeo

■ Population: 754,844 (2000 Census)

■ Official Nickname: The Mount Rushmore State

■ State Slogan: Great Faces. Great Places.

■ State Animal: Coyote

■ State Tree: Black Hills spruce

■ State Fossil: Triceratops

Although they'll take you on a guided fly-fishing trip any time of the year, the folks at **Dakota Angler and Outfitter** (⊠ *513 7th St., Rapid City* ☎ *605/341–2450*) recommend fishing between April and October. The guides lead individuals and groups on half- and full-day excursions, and they cater to all skill levels.

VISITOR INFORMATION

Badlands National Park (⌖ *Box 6, Interior, 57750* ☎ *605/433–5361* ⊕ *www. nps.gov/badl*)

Black Hills, Badlands and Lakes Association (⊠ *1851 Discovery Circle, Rapid City, 57701* ☎ *605/355–3600* ⊕ *www.blackhillsbadlands.com*).

Black Hills Central Reservations (⊠ *68 Sherman St., Suite 206, Deadwood, 57732* ☎ *866/329–7566* ⊕ *www.blackhillsvacations.com*).

Black Hills National Forest (⊠ *1019 N. 5th St., Custer, 57730* ☎ *605/673–9200* ⊕ *www.fs.fed.us/r2/blackhills*).

Deadwood Area Chamber of Commerce & Visitor Bureau (⊠ *735 Main St., Deadwood, 57732* ☎ *605/578–1876 or 800/999–1876* ⊕ *www.deadwood.com*).

Rapid City Chamber of Commerce and Convention & Visitors Bureau (⊠ *Civic Center, 444 N. Mt. Rushmore Rd., Box 747, Rapid City, 57709* ☎ *605/343–1744 or 800/487–3223* ⊕ *www.visitrapidcity.com*).

South Dakota Department of Tourism (⊠ *711 E. Wells Ave., Pierre, 57501* ☎ *605/773–3301* ⊕ *www.travelsd.com*).

Wind Cave National Park (⊠ *U.S. 385 (Box 190), Hot Springs, 57747* ☎ *605/745–4600* ⊕ *www.nps.gov/wica*)

Western Montana

Piegan Pass, Glacier National Park

WORD OF MOUTH

"Glacier NP is of course beautiful. Don't miss Going to the Sun Road, the only road across the park. MANY hiking opportunities, if U like that. For a relatively quick hike that will get you some beautiful views and, if UR lucky, close up mountain goat sightings, take the trail behind the Logan Pass Visitors Center. It's pretty obvious, but just ask inside and they'll point it out."

—outwest713

EXPLORING WESTERN MONTANA

Missoula is 475 mi east of Seattle via I–90; 525 mi north of Salt Lake City via I–15 and I–90; and 715 mi west of Rapid City, SD, via I–90

By Amy Grisak   Montana is a dichotomy of sorts. On one hand, it's distinctly wild. There are huge expanses of rugged country where you can hike for days without seeing a soul. It's a place to discover how beautiful the night sky can be and what "dark" truly is in the absence of glimmering city lights. It's also a place where you'll be inclined to take deep breaths because the air is shockingly fragrant and clean. And whether you prefer taking a quiet stroll through a meadow of stunning wildflowers or careening down the powdered slopes, there's an outdoor activity for you here—Montana is a place to shed your daily routine and renew your relationship with the natural world.

On the other hand, you don't have to own a pair of hiking boots to love it here. There are festivals throughout the year celebrating everything from Rocky Mountain Oysters to the brilliant display of the tamaracks changing color in autumn, and cultural events showcase the outstanding talent of new and old residents alike. It's a welcoming place because people want to be here and love to share the state with others.

WHO WILL ESPECIALLY LOVE THIS TRIP?

Wildlife-Watchers: Western Montana, particularly the northwest region, is one of the few places where the top predators—grizzlies, wolves, and mountain lions—are present. Although these stealthy hunters can be elusive, herds of elk, deer, bighorn sheep, and mountain goats are often visible from the highways.

Families: If you're looking to pry the children away from the television or computer, Northwest Montana is the perfect place to capture their attention. Hike with the youngsters and see how many ground squirrels you can count in a day, or take them fishing in one of the crystal clear lakes or rivers. A Carousel for Missoula (⊠ *101 Carousel Dr., Missoula* ☎*406/549–8382* ⊕*www.carrousel.com*) is a favorite for kids of any age, or rent bicycles for either the community trail systems such as the north and south side trails along the Clark Fork River or the Kim Williams Trail that takes hikers through Hellgate Canyon in Missoula.

History Buffs: Even though Montana isn't a very old state (it joined the Union in 1889), it has a rich and entertaining past. Butte, once the "Richest Hill on Earth," is filled with mining history detailing the cutthroat politics of the time and the hazardous mining practices. There are also many points of interest from the Lewis and Clark Expedition, including campsites along the Clark Fork River and Lolo Pass in the Missoula area.

Fly-Fishermen: The Missouri and Madison Rivers are renowned for big rainbows and brown trout, and there are plenty of outfits to show you the ropes and help you gear up for a first-rate fishing excursion.

TOP 5 REASONS TO GO

Glacier National Park: The only place in the lower 48 states where glaciers still exist in the high mountain valleys. Be ready to be dazzled by stunning scenery and abundant wildlife.

Cowboys & Cowgirls: If you're a wrangler at heart this is where you can ride the range and experience the lifestyle of working ranches. "Another day at the office" never looked so good.

Groovy Missoula: Inhabited by an eclectic mix of writers, artists, and creative folks, this college town is the epicenter of culture in Montana.

World-Class Fishing: Whether wading in the rivers, or trolling the deep, cold lakes, Montana's fish are big, hungry, and looking for a fight.

Getting Away from It All: Roughly 40% of the state is public land, giving you plenty of room to roam, and there are many areas where you couldn't use a cell phone even if you wanted.

Adrenaline Junkies: If you're looking for a rush, pick your poison: kayak or raft on Class IV+ rapids on the rivers after the spring runoff; parasail on Flathead Lake; ski black diamonds at Big Mountain, Big Sky, or Snowbowl; mountain bike on extreme terrain; or jump out of a perfectly good airplane at Lost Prairie in Kila.

WHEN IS THE BEST TIME TO VISIT?

The best time to be here is during September after Labor Day. There are fewer tourists, everything is still open, and the trails are relatively clear of snow. (Sometimes early storms will dump a foot or more at higher elevations.) The days are ideal with moderate temperatures and blue skies—perfect for enjoying the mountains. And the nights have that cozy autumn nip in the air.

There are plenty of cultural events to balance the outdoor activities including First Friday Gallery Nights (☎406/543–4238 ⊕www. missouladowntown.com) in Missoula; recitals from the Glacier Symphony and Chorale (✉Box 2491, Kalispell, 59903 ☎406/257–3241 ⊕www.glaciersymphonychorale.org); and the Taste of Whitefish (☎406/862–3501 ⊕www.whitefishchamber.com), the place to be for foodies to sample the Northwest's finest cuisine. Farmers' Markets continue throughout the month, and are excellent places to find fresh, local food, unique arts and crafts, as well as some of the more interesting and eclectic residents.

HOW SHOULD I GET THERE?

DRIVING

State and federal highways are generally well-maintained, although mountain ranges, lakes, and rivers sometimes require longer routes to circumvent than you'd think. Be aware that some roads are closed once

20

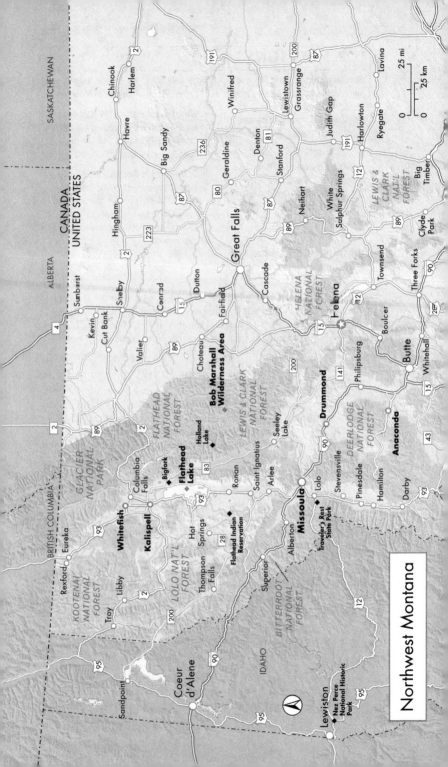

Northwest Montana

SASKATCHEWAN

ALBERTA

BRITISH COLUMBIA

CANADA
UNITED STATES

IDAHO

GLACIER NATIONAL PARK

KOOTENAI NATIONAL FOREST

FLATHEAD NATIONAL FOREST

LOLO NAT'L FOREST

BITTERROOT NATIONAL FOREST

LEWIS & CLARK NATIONAL FOREST

DEERLODGE NATIONAL FOREST

HELENA NATIONAL FOREST

LEWIS & CLARK NAT'L FOREST

Bob Marshall Wilderness Area

Flathead Indian Reservation

Sandpoint

Coeur d'Alene

Lewiston

Nez Perce National Historic Park

Rexford
Eureka
Libby
Troy

Whitefish
Kalispell
Columbia Falls
Bigfork
Flathead Lake

Hot Springs
Thompson Falls
Superior
Alberton
Missoula
Traveler's Rest State Park
Lolo
Stevensville
Florence
Pinesdale
Hamilton
Darby

Holland Lake
Seeley Lake
Roman
Saint Ignatius
Arlee
Drummond
Philipsburg
Anaconda
Butte
Whitehall

Kevin
Sunburst
Cut Bank
Shelby
Valier
Conrad
Dutton
Fairfield
Choteau

Chinook
Harlem
Havre
Big Sandy
Hingham

Winifred
Geraldine
Denton
Stanford
Lewistown
Grassrange
Lavina
Judith Gap
Harlowton
Ryegate

Great Falls
Cascade
Neihart
White Sulphur Springs
Helena
Townsend
Three Forks
Boulder
Clyde Park
Big Timber

25 mi
25 km

the snow flies, and the mountain passes can be treacherous compared to the lower elevations in winter. Always be prepared with proper clothing, water, and food, regardless of the season.

Highway 2 (called the Hi-line) is a pleasant two-lane road along the northern part of the state taking you along the southern boundary of Glacier National Park, through the Flathead Valley and eventually to Idaho. Interstate 90 connects the larger cities of Bozeman, Butte, and Missoula, while Helena and Great Falls can be reached off I–15.

FLYING

Flying into Montana can be tricky during the height of the season because there are limited flights into all of the larger airports in Kalispell, Missoula, and Bozeman. Delta, Northwest, and United are the major airlines that fly into Western Montana. Book your flights well in advance for travel during the busy summer months, as well as the winter when the ski hills attract snow lovers.

TRAIN TRAVEL

Amtrak's Empire Builder parallels Highway 2, allowing passengers to disembark at any of the smaller towns in eastern Montana, and travels along the southern boundary of Glacier National Park. You can stop at East Glacier at the Izaak Walton Inn (⊠*290 Izaak Walton Inn Rd.* ☎*406/888–5700* ⊕*www.izaakwaltoninn.com*) in Essex, or continue to either the West Glacier or Whitefish depots before heading to Seattle.

HOW DO I GET AROUND?

BY CAR

There's a lot of ground to cover in Montana, and distance is typically discussed in time instead of miles. Interstate 90 begins in Billings in the southeast section of the state and travels 142 mi (229 km) to Bozeman; it's 82 mi (132 km) from Bozeman to Butte and another 120 mi (193 km) to Missoula. The most direct route from Missoula to the Flathead is the 115 mi (185 km) of Highway 93 along the west shore of Flathead Lake. Be aware that it fluctuates between a two- and four-lane road along the way making it notorious for accidents; hence the bumper sticker "Pray for Me, I Drive 93." Driving in Montana is almost a necessity since there's limited train and bus travel, and most towns are too far apart for a cab ride . . . if there's even one in town. Pedestrian and bicycle traffic is hit and miss in some areas. Helena, Whitefish, Missoula, and Bozeman have quaint downtown areas with shops and restaurants, but box stores and strip malls are popping up outside of town.

Speed limits are no longer "reasonable and prudent," and it's best to follow the posted limits not only to avoid a ticket, but to watch for hapless critters. Most of Montana is free range for livestock, which means if you hit a cow or a horse you're responsible for reimbursement to the rancher.

Southwest Montana

How to Snack

To truly experience Western Montana, you have to indulge in a huckleberry treat. There's something for every taste including outstanding huckleberry milkshakes, pies, candy, and fudge at the **Huckleberry Patch in Hungry Horse** (Box 1, Hungry Horse, 59919 ☎ 406/387–5000 ⊕ www.huckleberrypatch.com). Or there's even huckleberry wine from **Flathead Lake Winery** (✉ 29 Golden Eagle St., Columbia Falls, 59912 ☎ 406/387–9466 ⊕ www.flatheadlakewinery.com), and Wild Huckleberry beer at **Great Northern Brewery** (✉ 2 Central Ave., Whitefish, 59937 ☎ 406/863–1000).

Starting around the third week of August, stop along any of the small fruit stands along Flathead Lake (although more on the east side) to purchase a bag of freshly picked Lambert cherries. The temperate microclimate along the big lake is ideal for growing these sweet cherries, which are worth the drive from anywhere in the state. If you aren't in the Flathead during cherry season, check out the Farmers' Markets in Missoula and Bozeman.

Pasties (pronounced pass-tees) were a traditional meal found in the lunch box of many miners back in the day, particularly the Cornish workers in Butte. This is a meat pie made with steak, onions, and potatoes baked in folded-over pie dough. It can be served as a smaller version for an appetizer, or smothered in chili or gravy. Try **Joe's Pasty Shop** (✉ 1641 Grand Ave., Butte, 59701 ☎ 406/723–9071), **Park Street Pasties** (✉ 800 West Park, Butte ☎ 406/782–6400) or **Gamer's Café** (✉ 15 West Park, Butte ☎ 406/723–5453).

Forget an energy bar, you can't hit the dusty trails without a stash of jerky to sustain you. **M&S Meats** in Rollins on the west shore of Flathead Lake (✉ 86755 Hwy. 93 S, Rollins, 59931 ☎ 406/844–3414 ⊕ www.msmeats.com) has an exceptional selection of buffalo jerky, as well as a wide selection of sausages, salamis, and cheeses. **Chalet Market** in Belgrade (✉ 6410 Jackrabbit La., Belgrade, 59714 ☎ 800/752–1029 ⊕ www.chaletmarket.com) can also set you up with beef and wild game jerky, snack sticks, and even elk summer sausage.

If you're looking for a hearty deli sandwich, a scrumptious sweet roll, or a bag of some of the best flour in the world, find one of the **Wheat Montana** stores (✉ 10778 Hwy. 287, Three Forks, 59752 ☎ 800/535–2798 ⊕ www.wheatmontana.com). The original deli in Three Forks is near the farm, which is listed in the Guinness Book of World Records for producing a loaf of bread from field to oven in 8 minutes, 13 seconds. There are also stores in Kalispell, Polson, Missoula, Bozeman, and Great Falls.

20

BY JAMMER OR SHUTTLE BUS

The historic Red "Jammer" Buses in Glacier National Park have tours over Going-to-the-Sun Road, as well as along the southern boundary on Highway 2 and up to Waterton Lakes National Park in Alberta. Reservations are available through Glacier Park Inc. (☎ 406/892–2525 ⊕ www.glacierparkinc.com). Travelers and hikers can also pick up the free park service shuttle. Starting points are at the new Apgar Transit

CLAIM TO FAME

Both loved and feared, the grizzly is the icon of the West, and northwestern Montana has the largest population in the Lower Forty-eight. Glacier National Park is the hot spot, and it's rare a season passes without at least one mauling due to a surprise encounter. However the large omnivores in this region primarily subsist on vegetation and the occasional carcass, and are more likely to avoid you before you even spot them. The best time to see grizzlies is in spring when they are on the move looking for calories any way they can find them. Scope out avalanche slopes and open meadows where new greenery is prevalent, and watch for dark forms traveling across the snow.

The huckleberry, a tart, wild cousin of the blueberry, is king in Western Montana. Huckleberries cannot be cultivated domestically, and only thrive in the acidic, sandy loam of the mountains. Harvesting hucks begins most years in late July, and will last until a hard freeze usually at the end of September. Pickers arrive from far and wide to set up camp since they can pocket thousands of dollars each season selling them to restaurants and roadside stands. Retail prices range $30–$50 per gallon depending on the year, but it's well worth it if you're not equipped to hike into remote locations and compete with the bears that love them as much as you do.

Center and St. Mary Visitor Center. There are 16 stops within the park, and riders can get on or off the shuttle at any point of the route. No reservations are required (☎ *406/888–7800* ⊕ *www.nps.gov/glac*).

WHERE SHOULD I FOCUS MY ENERGY?

"If you're here for 1 day: Leave early and travel Going-to-the-Sun Road in Glacier National Park before breakfast. The views along the way and the opportunity to spot wildlife are worth missing some sleep.

If you're here for 2 days: Ride the gondola to the summit of Big Mountain in Whitefish, (☎ *406/862–2900* ⊕ *www.bigmtn.com*) and hike the Danny On Trail back down.

If you're here for 3 days: Enjoy a leisurely drive along either shore of Flathead Lake stopping along the way to take photos of osprey, deer, and tremendous scenic views of the Mission Mountains. Spend the afternoon floating the Clark Fork River and Alberton Gorge with Montana River Guides near Missoula.

If you're here for 4 days: Take the 52-mi round-trip train excursion from Anaconda to Butte on the elegant Copper King Express (✉ *300 W. Commercial Ave., Anaconda, 59711* ☎ *406/563–5458* ⊕ *www. copperkingexpress.com*) for a rolling history lesson of the wild and wooly mining era. Then try your hand at panning for sapphires at Gem Mountain (✉ *3835 Skalkaho Rd., Philipsburg, 59858* ☎ *406/859–4367* ⊕ *www.gemmtn.com*) in nearby Philipsburg.

If you're here for 5 days: Spend a day fly-fishing on the Beaverhead River trying to outwit the big rainbows and brown trout.

HISTORY YOU CAN SEE

Well before white people started moving west, the Native American tribes occupied the area of Montana. The feared Blackfeet nation, "Lords of the Plains," encompassed a large section of Northcentral Montana, including land that is now part of Glacier National Park. The Salish, Kootenai Tribes, and Kalispel were in the western region with the Pend o'Reille around Flathead Lake.

After a handful of Nez Perce men killed white settlers in 1877, while the tribe was being relocated against their will, Chief Joseph decided to take his people to Canada instead of the intended reservation in Idaho to avoid retaliation from the U.S. Calvary. During their flight, the Calvary caught up with the 800 Nez Perce camped at Big Hole, killing 87. The Cavalry lost 28 of their own men. Chief Joseph fled east through Yellowstone, and eventually was apprehended within 40-mi of the Canadian Border in the Bear

Paw Mountains east of Havre. This is where Chief Joseph uttered the profound words, "Hear me, my chiefs. I am tired. My heart is sick and sad. From where the sun now stands, I will fight no more forever."

In 1805 Lewis and Clark and the Corps of Discovery entered Montana and encountered a number of challenges to their goal of identifying a water route to the Pacific Ocean. The five waterfalls on the Missouri River near Great Falls proved insurmountable, forcing the group to portage around them. Lewis had a run-in with the Blackfeet, killing one of the warriors causing them to further distrust the encroaching Americans, and the entire party nearly met their demise tackling the mountains near Lolo Pass. There are still many spots where Lewis and Clark enthusiasts can visit former campsites and significant areas along Highway 2 and Interstate 90.

If you're here for 6 days: Tour the Museum of the Rockies in Bozeman to learn about Montana's prehistoric past, then go for a soak in the Bozeman Hot Springs (✉ *81123 East Gallatin Rd.* ☎ *406/586–6492*).

If you're here for 7 days or more: Drive back to the Flathead Valley on Highway 89 along the Rocky Mountain Front, and spend some time in Choteau (☎ *800/823–3866* ⊕ *www.choteaumontana.com*). From there you can explore the eastern edge of the Bob Marshall Wilderness Area (✉ *1935 3rd Ave. E, Kalispell, 59901* ☎ *406/758–5200* ⊕ *www. fs.fed.us/r1*), Egg Mountain (one of the premier paleontological sites in the world) and the Nature Conservancy's Pine Butte Swamp Preserve (⊕ *HC 58, Box 34B, Choteau, 59422* ☎ *406/466–5526* ⊕ *www. nature.org*).

20

WHAT ARE THE TOP EXPERIENCES?

The Mountains: Montana means "mountainous" in Spanish, and the mountains are still the state's primary draw. When you're traveling from the east across the enormous expanse of prairie, the Rocky Mountains are an impressive sight even from more than 100 mi away. The Rockies aren't a single set of mountains; they're a series of ranges

STRANGE BUT TRUE

■ The **Dumas Brothel** (✉ *45 East Mercury* ☎ *406/494-6908* ⊕ *www. thedumasbrothel.com*)in Butte began business in 1890, and ended its reign as the country's longest running parlor house in 1982. It's now a museum paying homage to Butte's salacious past and is rumored to have spirits of the red light district haunting its halls.

■ According to local legend there's a creature similar to the Loch Ness Monster in Flathead Lake. It was first sighted in 1889 when a steamer captain thought the large object was another boat, and there have been

similar claims from reputable people ever since.

■ The **House of Mystery** (✉ *7800 Hwy. 2 E, Columbia Falls* ☎ *406/892-1210* ⊕ *www.mon tanavortex.com*)along Highway 2 in Columbia Falls claims to have several vortexes (a natural, swirling field of force) that seemingly skew gravity and defy the laws of nature. For instance, people appear to shrink or grow by simply walking along the level platform, and many perceive a sense of increased energy. It was a sacred area for many of the Indian tribes, and offerings of tobacco and sweet grass continue to this day

that, at times, appear unending. For many, their mystical grandeur is irresistible. If you're able, venture into the mountains by foot or on horseback.

The Rivers: If the mountains are Montana's backbone, the rivers provide the life-force of water to the region, and like everything else in the state, they change dramatically with the seasons. In spring, they're roiling with melt-off from the snow-packed mountains, enticing whitewater enthusiasts to tackle rapids with names like Bonecrusher, Boateater, and Fang. But by late summer many are gentle channels where anglers wade and kids float in inner tubes. The Madison, Missouri, and Clark Fork rivers are only a few of the world-class trout fisheries in the state. Fly-fishermen appear on the waters along with the various insect hatches beginning in March and April, but typically taper off during the heat of July and August before improving again in September when the water temperature cools.

The Wildlife: Montana is where the deer and the antelope roam, along with bears, mountain lions, wolves, bison, elk, and a whole bunch of other critters. Montana has the most diverse wildlife in the country, and they're relatively easy to find. Head to the mountains to see bighorn sheep and mountain goats, along with interesting smaller creatures like pica and hoary marmots, which prefer the subalpine regions. Elk can be found in open parks and grasslands; moose like to hang out in wetlands and groves where browse is abundant, and deer are all over the place, from the mountains to downtown Helena. To see or photograph the animals, it's best to start looking early in the morning before they bed down out of sight for the day.

Creative Cuisine: No longer is iceberg lettuce the standard salad green; now innovative culinary artists create outstanding cuisine with Montana flair. More and more chefs are stepping up and offering upscale fare that still maintains the Montana tradition of simple, hearty food with a creative twist. Think ample portions of Montana-raised beef with local, seasonal produce at some of the best restaurants. Bison and trout, as well as huckleberries and Flathead cherries also find their way into the cuisine giving a nod to the state's ample natural resources.

The People: Sit down with a group of locals, and you never know who you might meet. Montana lures the wealthy and influential, as well as the free-spirits, academics, and hard-working blue collar folks. Such diversity makes for lively discussions when it comes to environmental issues, private property rights, and Montana's hunting and fishing heritage so it's best to feel out the sentiment of the group before offering an opinion.

BEST BETS

SIGHTS AND TOURS

★ **Big Hole National Battlefield.** In 1877 Nez Perce warriors in central Idaho killed some white settlers as retribution for earlier killings by whites. Knowing the U.S. Army would make no distinction between the guilty and innocent, several hundred Nez Perce fled, beginning a 1,500-mi, five-month odyssey that has come to be known as the Nez Perce Trail. The fugitives engaged 10 separate U.S. commands in 13 battles and skirmishes. One of the fiercest of these was at Big Hole, where both sides suffered serious losses. From here the Nez Perce headed toward Yellowstone. The Big Hole battlefield remains as it was when the battle unfolded; tepee poles erected by the park service mark the site of a Nez Perce village and serve as haunting reminders of what transpired here. Big Hole National Battlefield is one of 38 sites in four states that make up the **Nez Perce National Historic Park** (☎208/843–3155 ⊕*www. nps.gov/nepe*), which follows the historic Nez Perce Trail. ⊠*Hwy. 43, 10 mi west of Wisdom; 87 mi southwest of Butte via I–90 west, I–15 south, and Hwy. 43 west* ☎406/689–3155 ⊕*www.nps.gov/biho* ⊠*Free* ⊙*May–Labor Day, daily 9–6; Labor Day–Apr., daily 10–5.*

★ In their travels on the Missouri River, Lewis and Clark made note of towering limestone cliffs. **Gates of the Mountains** (⊠*Off I–15, 20 mi north of Helena* ☎406/458–5241 ⊕*www.gatesofthemountains.com* ⊙*Memorial Day–mid-Sept.*) boat tours take you past these same great stone walls, which rise 1,200 feet above the river.

Fodor's Choice ★ **Going-to-the-Sun Road.** This magnificent, 50-mi highway—a National Historic Civil Engineering Landmark—crosses the crest of the Continental Divide at Logan Pass and traverses the towering Garden Wall. The Federal Highway Administration and the park have embarked on a multiyear road rehabilitation, which will see this narrow, curving highway undergo structural repair. A shuttle system is provided by the National Park Service to decrease the amount of traffic during the construction.

20

Fodor's Choice ★ ☺ **Jewel Basin Hiking Area** (⊠ *10 mi east of Bigfork via Hwy. 83 and Echo Lake Rd. to Jewel Basin Rd. (No. 5392))* provides 35 mi of well-maintained trails among 27 trout-filled alpine lakes. You'll find the nearest phone and hearty to-go trail lunches at the Echo Lake Cafe at the junction of Highway 83 and Echo Lake Road. The **Swan Lake Ranger District Office** (⊠ *200 Ranger Station Rd.* ☎ *406/837-7500*) in Bigfork sells hiking maps.

Fodor's Choice ★ ☺ **Museum of the Rockies.** Here you can find a celebration of the history of the Rockies region, with exhibits ranging from prehistory to pioneers, plus a planetarium with laser shows. Most renowned is the museum's Siebel Dinosaur Complex housing one of the world's largest dinosaur fossil collections along with the largest known T-rex skull, a Mesozoic Media Center, and a Hall of Giants complete with sound effects. Children love the hands-on science activities in the Martin Discovery Room and the outdoors Tensley Homestead, with home-crafts demonstrations, including butter churning, weaving, and blacksmithing. May through mid-September, sheep, donkeys, and horses graze among the tall pasture grasses of the homestead. ⊠ *600 W. Kagy Blvd., Bozeman, south end of university campus* ☎ *406/994-3466* ⊕ *www.museumoftherockies.org* ⊞ *$8 museum and planetarium combo ($10 summer), $5 planetarium laser shows* ☉ *Mon.–Sat. 9–5, Sun. 12:30–5; Memorial Day–Labor Day, daily 8–8.*

☺ **Rocky Mountain Elk Foundation Wildlife Visitor Center.** The new visitor center features natural-history displays (including hands-on displays for kids), films, art, taxidermied animals, a world-record-size pair of elk antlers and an outdoor nature trail. The foundation works to preserve wild lands for elk and other wildlife; since 1984, the nonprofit organization has saved almost 5 million acres from development. ⊠ *5705 Grant Creek Rd., Missoula; look for the big bronze elk* ☎ *406/523-4500 or 800/225-5355* ⊕ *www.rmef.org* ⊞ *Donations accepted* ☉ *Jan. 1–Memorial Day, weekdays 8–5, Sat. 10–5; Memorial Day–Dec. 30, weekdays 8–6, weekends 9–6.*

☺ **Traveler's Rest State Park.** This park includes a Lewis and Clark camp on a floodplain overlooking Lolo Creek. The explorers stayed here from September 9 to 11, 1805, and again from June 30 to July 3, 1806. Archaeologists in 2002 found evidence of a latrine and a fire hearth, making this one of only a few locations with a physical record of the expedition's camp. Tepee rings suggest that Native Americans used the riverside location, too. Self guided tours meander through cottonwoods and the historic campsite. Daily interpretive presentations and guided tours run during the summer, on the hour between 11 and 3. Talks such as "Go Griz . . . PLEASE . . . Go!," "The Modern Day Journey" and several others have special aspects to interest the kids. ✉ *6550 Mormon Creek Rd., south of Lolo, ¼ mi west of U.S. 93, Lolo* ☎ *406/273–4253* ⊕ *www.travelersrest.org* ✍ *$2* ⊙ *Memorial Day weekend–Labor Day, daily 8–8; Labor Day–Memorial Day, Mon.–Fri. 9–4, Sat.–Sun. 12-4.*

WHERE TO EAT

	WHAT IT COSTS				
	¢	$	$$	$$$	$$$$
RESTAURANTS	under $7	$7–$11	$11–$16	$16–$22	over $22

Restaurant prices are for a main course at dinner.

$$–$$$$
★
✕ **Capers.** Known as the place to go for upscale dining as Café Max for more than a decade, the owners decided it was time for a change to provide more moderately priced meals with the same delicious flare. The revamped menu still offers upscale fare, such as the grilled Montana buffalo tenderloin or melt-in-your-mouth seared ahi, but includes a less pricey, but equally impressive cheeseburger (made with local beef) or vegetarian lasagna. They also have an outstanding wine and a surprisingly varied selection of local and imported beer. ✉ *121 Main St., Kalispell* ☎ *406/755–7687* ▤ *AE, MC, V* ⊙ *Closed Mon.*

$$–$$$$
Fodor's Choice
★
✕ **Lolo Creek Steakhouse.** For a real taste of Montana, head for this steak house in a rustic log structure 8 mi south of Missoula, in Lolo. The dining room has a hunting-lodge atmosphere, replete with taxidermied wildlife on the walls. Although most diners opt for one of their signature sirloins—cooked over a crackling open-pit barbecue and available in three sizes—there are other well-prepared meat, chicken, and seafood dishes from which to choose. ✉ *6600 U.S. 12 W, Lolo* ☎ *406/273–2622* ▤ *AE, D, MC, V* ⊙ *Closed Mon. No lunch.*

$$–$$$$
★
✕ **Montana Ale Works.** A cavernous brick building, the former Northern Pacific Railroad depot houses a brewery, a full bar, and a restaurant with outdoor dining in summer. In addition to the 37 beers on tap, the Ale Works serves bison burgers, baked pasta dishes, Caribbean and Spanish dishes, and nightly specials such as fresh-grilled yellowfin tuna and blue marlin. ✉ *611 E. Main St., Bozeman* ☎ *406/587–7700* ▤ *AE, D, MC, V* ⊙ *No lunch.*

$$–$$$$
✕ **On Broadway.** Wooden booths, discreet lighting, and brick walls contribute to the comfortable ambience at this Italian-fusion restaurant. Popular dishes include rib-eye steak and pasta puttanesca (sautéed Greek olives, artichoke hearts, red bell peppers, red onions, capers, and pine nuts tossed in linguine). When the state legislature is in session, representatives make this a boisterous place. ✉ *106 Broadway, Helena* ☎ *406/443–1929* ✍ *Reservations not accepted* ▤ *AE, D, MC, V* ⊙ *Closed Sun. No lunch.*

20

ON THE WAY

Montana Dinotrail (⊕ www.mtdinotrail.org): Scattered from east to west, with several exhibits along the Hi-line, there are fifteen active digs, field stations or interpretive centers dedicated to Montana's rich dino history.

Lewis and Clark Interpretive Center (✉ 4201 Giant Springs Rd., Great Falls 59405 ☎ 406/727–8733 ⊕ www.fs.fed.us/r1/lewisclark/lcic): Above the Missouri River in Great Falls, the Interpretive Center will give you a new appreciation of what the explorers witnessed when they came to a series of five waterfalls in this part of their journey. Tour the facility, listen to the knowledgeable interpreters, or stroll along the 24 mi of the River's Edge Trail (⊕ www.thetrail.org)along the Missouri.

Little Bighorn Battlefield National Monument (⌂ Box 39; Crow Agency, 59022 ☎ 406/638–3204 ⊕ www.nps.gov/libi): The area where Lt. Colonel George Armstrong Custer and five companies of soldiers met their demise against Lakota and Cheyenne warriors is a poignant landmark in the history of the West. The monument is open throughout the year, and there are interpretive talks in summer at the visitor center.

WHERE TO STAY

WHAT IT COSTS					
	¢	$	$$	$$$	$$$$
HOTELS	under $70	$70–$109	$110–$159	$160–$220	over $220

Hotel prices are for two people in a standard double room in high season, excluding service charges and a 7% bed tax.

$$$$ 🏠 **The Bar W.** Just a short drive north of Whitefish, the Bar W is a playground for horse people and outdoor recreation enthusiasts. You can ride the nearby trails or in the indoor arena, watch trainers work with horses, or take lessons themselves. For the nonequine-minded, there are unlimited hiking opportunities, fishing in their private pond, badminton, archery and more. The rooms are simple and comfortable with a distinct Western flair. The cabin overlooks pasture and the nearby woods, and it's not uncommon to sit on the deck and watch deer and other wildlife. Pros: They provide horse boarding, so you can bring your own to ride the 3000-plus acres on forest service land, or train them at one of their clinics. They're a great facility for business or family gatherings with lots of activities and plenty of room. ✉ 2875 Hwy. 93 W, Whitefish, 59937 ☎ 406/863–9099 or 888/828–2900 🖷 406/863–9500 ⊕ www.thebarw.com ⇆ 6 rooms, 1 cabin ᇈ In cabin: refrigerator, microwave. In lodge: public Wi-Fi, no elevator ▤ AE, D, MC, V ⍣ BP.

$–$$$ 🏠 **Toad Hall Manor Bed and Breakfast.** Built as a private home in the
Fodor'sChoice early 1990s, this mansion has an historic feel thanks to hardwood
★ accents, marble tile, and a classic redbrick exterior. Each of the four guest rooms is named after a character from Kenneth Grahame's *The Wind in the Willows*. The ground-floor Papa Otter's Place, with its

Victorian-style furnishings, marble-accented Jacuzzi, and French doors opening to a private garden, probably offers the best value. Sir Badger's Suite, which takes up the entire fifth floor with two bedrooms, a two-person Jacuzzi, walk-in closet, and loft-style windows, ranks as the most luxurious option. ⊠*1 Green La., Butte 59701* ☎*406/494–2625 or 866/443–8623* 🖶*406/494–8025* ⊕*www.toadhallmanor.com* 🛏*4 rooms* ♿*In-hotel: no-smoking rooms, public Internet, elevator* ☰*AE, D, MC, V* 🍴❘*BP.*

$$ 🏊 **Fairmont Hot Springs Resort.** This resort between Anaconda and Butte
☺ is a great option if you have children. Although not much to look at, the Fairmont has naturally heated indoor and outdoor swimming pools, a 350-foot waterslide, a playground, and a wildlife zoo in a beautiful setting. There's also an 18-hole golf course on the grounds. ⊠*1500 Fairmont Rd., Fairmont, 59711* ☎*406/797–3241 or 800/332–3272* 🖶*406/797–3337* ⊕*www.fairmontmontana.com* 🛏*153 rooms, 23 suites* ♿*In-room: Wi-Fi. In-hotel: restaurant, bar, golf course, tennis courts, pools, casino, no-smoking rooms* ☰*AE, D, MC, V.*

¢–$$ ✕🏊 **Chico Hot Springs Resort & Day Spa.** During the gold rush of the 1860s,
★ a miner noted that he "washed [his] dirty duds" in the hot-springs water near the Yellowstone River. Soon a series of bathhouses sprang up, attracting people to the medicinal waters. The Chico Warm Springs Hotel opened in 1900, drawing famous folks such as painter Charlie Russell (1864–1926) to the 96°F–103°F pools. The hotel is surrounded by two large outdoor soak pools, a convention center, and upscale cottages that open to views of 10,920-foot Emigrant Peak and the Absaroka-Beartooth Wilderness beyond. The dining room (3$–4$) is considered among the region's best for quality of food, presentation, and service. Pine nut–encrusted halibut with fruit salsa and gorgonzola filet mignon are among the biggest draws. ⊠*1 Old Chico Rd., Pray, 59065* ☎*406/333–4933 or 800/468–9232* 🖶*406/333–4694* ⊕*www.chicohotsprings.com* 🛏*82 rooms, 4 suites, 16 cottages* ♿*In-room: no a/c (some), kitchen (some), refrigerator (some), no TV, dial-up. In-hotel: restaurant, room service, bar, pool, spa, no elevator, some pets allowed* ☰*AE, D, MC, V.*

SPORTS & THE OUTDOORS

★ The folks at **Adventure Cycling** (⊠*150 E. Pine St., Missoula* ☎*406/721–1776 or 800/755–2453* ⊕*www.adv-cycling.org*) in downtown Missoula have good suggestions for nearby bike routes and an extensive selection of regional and national bike maps for sale. You can find bikes to rent or buy, cycling accessories, and cross-country ski gear at **Open Road Bicycles & Nordic Equipment** (⊠*517 S. Orange St., Missoula* ☎*406/549–2453*).

The name of Lone Peak, the mountain that looms over the isolated community beneath Big Sky, is a good way to describe **Big Sky Ski and Summer Resort,** one of the most remote major ski resorts in the country. Here you can ski a true wilderness. Yellowstone National Park is visible from the upper mountain ski runs, as are 11 mountain ranges in three states. ⊠*1 Lone Mountain Trail, Box 160001, Big Sky 59716; 43 mi*

20

VITAL STATS:

- State Nickname: The Treasure State; Big Sky Country.

- State Motto: Oro y Plata (Gold and Silver).

- State Gem: Yogo sapphire, found only in Montana and rarer than diamonds.

- Montana is the fourth largest state in land area.

- There are more than twice as many cows as people in Montana.

- The headwaters of the Missouri River, which ultimately converges with the Mississippi in St. Louis, begin in Three Forks.

- At 201 feet (61 m) the Roe River in Great Falls is the shortest river in the world. It runs between Giant Springs and the Missouri River.

- The temperature at Rogers Pass bottomed out at -70°F on January 20, 1954—the coldest temperature recorded in the Contiguous United States.

southwest of Bozeman via I–90, then U.S. 191 ☎406/995–5000 or 800/548–4486 ⊕ *www.bigskyresort.com.*

Fodor'sChoice Raft and kayak adventures with **Montana River Guides** (⊠*Sawmill Gulch*
★ *Rd., 35 minutes west of Missoula on I–90, Exit 70 at Cyr, cross Cyr Bridge, turn left on Sawmill Gulch and look for yellow rafts* ☎406/273–4718 or 800/381–7238) splash down the Blackfoot and Bitterroot rivers and the rowdy Alberton Gorge of the Clark Fork River.

★ **Swan Mountain Outfitters** have trail rides in Glacier National Park, as well as in the Swan and Mission Mountains. Trips range from one hour to all day, and can accommodate most riding levels. No riders over 250 pounds. Reservations are essential. ✍*Box 5081, Swan Lake59911* ☎877/888–5557, 800/919–4416 in winter ⊕*www.swanmountain outfitters.com* ✉*$32 for an hour, $135 for a full day* ☉*Mid-May–mid-Sept.* ☰*MC, V.*

★ **Tom's Fishing and Bird Hunting Guide Service** (⊠*3460 St. Ann St., Butte* ☎406/723–4753 or 800/487–0296) arranges float and wade trips for blue-ribbon trout fishing.

VISITOR INFORMATION

Glacier National Park (✍*Box 128, West Glacier, MT, 59936* ☎*406/888–7800* ⊕ *www.nps.gov/glac).*

Montana Bed & Breakfast Association (☎*406/582–8440* ⊕ *www.mtbba. com).*

Montana Dude Ranchers' Association (✍*Box 589, Manhattan, MT, 59741* ☎*888/284–4133* ⊕*www.montanadra.com).*

Montana Innkeepers Association (☎*406/449–8408* ⊕*www.montanainnkeep ers.com).*

Travel Montana (⊠*301 S. Park, Helena, 59620* ☎*406/841–2870 or 800/847–4868* ⊕ *www.visitmt.com).*

Yellowstone National Park

WITH GRAND TETON NATIONAL PARK

Beauty Pool, Yellowstone National Park

WORD OF MOUTH

"We were in YNP & GTNP this past September and had a wonderful trip. Tons of wildlife, little or no crowds, and the weather was nice, leaves golden and red, even got a little snow."

—BayouGal

EXPLORING YELLOWSTONE & GRAND TETON

320 mi north of Salt Lake City via I–15 and U.S. 20; 75 mi southeast of Bozeman, MT, via I–90 and U.S. 89

By Steve Pastorino

Much more than just America's first National Park, Yellowstone is the quintessential example of the nation's natural splendor. Remote as it may be, millions have been drawn here by the park's incomparable combination of pure beauty, rugged wilderness, abundant wildlife, and intense geothermal activity for the past 130 years. The park, along with nearby Grand Teton National Park, makes this northwestern corner of Wyoming a haven for backcountry wanderers and backseat explorers alike. The parks are a veritable gold mine of national treasures, with ecosystems as rich as any in the world.

WHO WILL ESPECIALLY LOVE THIS TRIP?

Families: A summer trip to Yellowstone is a rite of passage for families. Kids revel at seeing their first bear and bison, "roughing it" in moderately priced cabins, and pursuing their Junior Ranger badges. They'll sleep soundly as they drift off to the sound of bugling elk.

Snowmobilers: In a controversial but popular move, the National Park Service opens many of Yellowstone's 300-plus mi of roads to "over snow" travel from Christmas to mid-March each year.

Anglers: The parks' 2,000-plus mi of streams and countless lakes are home to several types of trout, grayling, and mountain whitefish. There are popular fishing spots accessible from Yellowstone's Grand Loop Road, but fly-fishermen in tie-filled vests are common on park hiking trails in search of backcountry hot spots.

Wolf-Watchers: The reintroduction of the American wolf to Yellowstone in the 1990s has spawned a new generation of wildlife watchers. Virtually any day of the year, you can encounter spotting scope-armed volunteers in Lamar Valley or Hayden Valley.

Mountaineers: Grand Teton National Park offers nine peaks higher than 12,000 feet, with a certain smugness reserved by those who have climbed their way to Grand Teton's 13,770-foot summit. Yellowstone's highest point, Eagle Peak, is only 11,358 feet, but the Absaroka and Gallatin ranges both offer 10,000-foot peaks reachable by earnest hikers without special gear or overnight camping.

WHEN IS THE BEST TIME TO VISIT?

There are two distinct seasons in Yellowstone. The park's roads are open to cars from May to early November only, and to over-snow travel (snowmobiles, snow coaches, and skis) from late December to March. The park is closed during the shoulder seasons.

It's a matter of preference and experience whether you decide to brave the crowds and traffic in summer or the frigid temperatures in winter. You can find peace and tranquility almost any day of the year in Yel-

TOP 5 REASONS TO GO

Bison. Bison are just one of many species (including elk and wolf) that roam as freely here today as they did in pre-Columbian times. Seemingly docile, the buffalo will make your heart race if you catch them racing across Lamar Valley in a stampede.

Old Faithful. Is there a natural landmark in the U.S. that's more identifiable than this geyser? Stay in the park and visit at night to avoid the crowds, and you can enjoy a surreal, personal geyser encounter.

Yellowstone Lake. You can fish, boat, kayak, stargaze, and bird-watch on warm days in the short summer season—just don't plan to stray too far into the frigid water from the black obsidian beaches. At West Thumb, you can combine geyser watching and with a lakeside stroll (or approach by canoe or kayak).

1,000-plus Miles of Trails. Whether you hope to summit a 13,000-foot peak, follow a trout-filled creek, descend 1,000-plus feet into Grand Canyon of the Yellowstone, or find peace and silence just a half-mile off the road, Yellowstone and Grand Teton have a path for you to tread.

Teton's Peaks. Rising above ritzy Jackson and tranquil National Elk Refuge, the Tetons' three tallest peaks tower over the valley and provide inspiration to about 4,000,000 visitors each year. Grand Teton is the highest, at 13,770 feet above sea level.

lowstone—you just have to wander off the well-worn roads, especially in summer.

Snake River float season is in full swing in July and August in the Grand Tetons, but the crowds are at their height then as well. June and September are good choices. Winter is another beast altogether—during this time Teton Village and Jackson are mobbed with skiers and snowmobilers.

HOW SHOULD I GET THERE?

DRIVING

The interstate highway system does not go directly to Yellowstone or Grand Teton. Yellowstone is nearly 55 mi from I–90 (turn south at Livingston, MT, which is 117 mi west of Billings, MT, and 26 mi east of Bozeman, MT) and 115 mi from I–15 (you'll leave the interstate in Idaho Falls, ID). It's no wonder that Yellowstone is considered one of the most remote places in the continental United States. Still, hundreds of thousands of cars make the pilgrimage here each summer. Those who make the trek are immediately rewarded at any of the park's five entrances with a feast of sights, from the animal-rich Madison Valley at the popular west entrance, to the travertine terraces of Mammoth Hot Springs in the north and the stunning peaks of the east and northeast entrances.

If you're driving east from Idaho Falls, you'll arrive at Grand Teton before Yellowstone. You'll continue north through Jackson Hole from Jackson, WY, paralleling the Teton range to the west and crossing the National Elk Refuge.

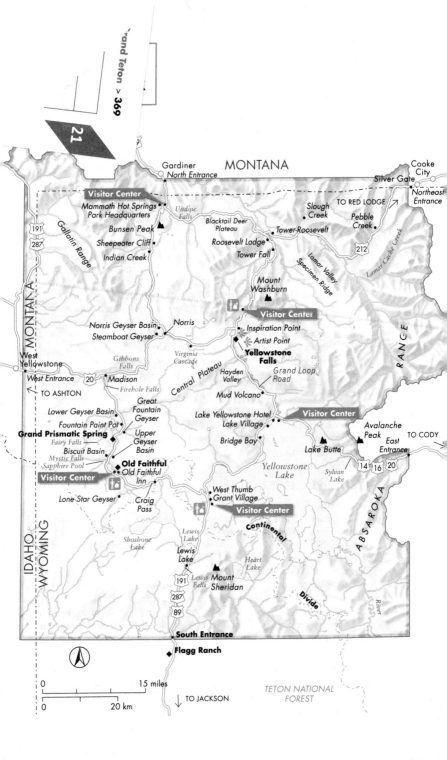

Grand Teton › 369

21

Gardiner
North Entrance

MONTANA

Cooke
City

Silver Gate

Northeast
Entrance

Visitor Center

Mammoth Hot Springs
Park Headquarters

Undine
Falls

Slough
Creek

TO RED LODGE

Pebble
Creek

Bunsen Peak

Blacktail Deer
Plateau

Tower-Roosevelt

Sheepeater Cliff

Roosevelt Lodge

Indian Creek

Tower Fall

Gallatin Range

Lamar Valley

Lamar Cache Creek

212

191
287

Mount
Washburn

Specimen Ridge

RANGE

MONTANA

Norris Geyser Basin

Norris

Visitor Center

Steamboat Geyser

Inspiration Point

Artist Point

West
Yellowstone

Virginia
Cascade

Yellowstone
Falls

West Entrance

20

Madison

TO ASHTON

Gibbons
Falls

Firehole Falls

Central Plateau

Hayden
Valley

Grand Loop
Road

Lower Geyser Basin

Great
Fountain
Geyser

Mud Volcano

Fountain Paint Pot

Grand Prismatic Spring

Upper
Geyser
Basin

Lake Yellowstone Hotel
Lake Village

Visitor Center

Avalanche
Peak

TO CODY

Fairy Falls

Biscuit Basin

Mystic Falls
Sapphire Pool

Old Faithful

Bridge Bay

Lake Butte

East
Entrance

Visitor Center

Old Faithful
Inn

Yellowstone
Lake

14 16 20

Sylvan
Lake

Lone Star Geyser

Craig
Pass

West Thumb
Grant Village

ABSAROKA

Visitor Center

Lewis
Falls

Continental

Shoshone
Lake

Lewis
Lake

Heart
Lake

Lewis Lake

IDAHO

WYOMING

191
287
89

Lewis
Falls

Mount
Sheridan

Divide

River

South Entrance

Flagg Ranch

0   15 miles

0   20 km

TETON NATIONAL
FOREST

↓ TO JACKSON

How to Snack

CLOSE UP

21

Save money and precious time in the park by packing in as much of your food as you can. There are nearly 50 picnic areas in Yellowstone and 11 in Grand Teton, all with tables and pit toilets and some with grills or fire pits. Most are alongside the parks' major roads. (Be sure to journey inward a bit after you eat—walking a few hundred yards from pavement greatly increases your chances of seeing wildlife.)

Most Yellowstone General Stores have a small grocery section, including fruits, vegetables, dairy products, meat, alcohol, and packaged goods—just don't expect to find many choices or bargains. Yellowstone has more than a dozen restaurants, grills, cafés, and delis, but they're all operated by the same two concessionaires. One flavorful constant in the park is hand-dipped ice cream, which although pricey, satisfies many campers as they emerge from the backcountry.

Outside Yellowstone, many restaurants in gateway communities offer a "box lunch" for day-trippers into the park; **Ernie's Deli & Bakery** (*406 Hwy. 20, West Yellowstone; 406/646–9467*) in West Yellowstone may have the best. If you're approaching from the south in mid- to late-summer, you can purchase fresh fruit from roadside stands in Idaho.

If you're in the mood for more than a snack, try dining at Grand Teton's **Jackson Lake Lodge Mural Room** beneath its 700-square-foot Carol Roters mural. Outside the park, try **The Bunnery** (*130 N. Cache St., Jackson; 307/733–5474*) for breakfasts and sandwiches made on great bread, or the burgers and sourdough pancakes at **Jedediah's House of Sourdough** (*135 E. Broadway Ave., Jackson; 307/733–5671*).

FLYING

Skywest flies daily to West Yellowstone, MT, (WYS) from Salt Lake City during the summer. Jackson, WY, (JCA) and Bozeman, MT, (BZN) are farther from the park entrances but offer more service from more destinations.

SNOWCOACH & SNOWMOBILE

In winter various concessionaires run over-snow vehicles to Old Faithful from West Yellowstone and Mammoth Hot Springs. A limited number of private snowmobiles are allowed, but only with a park-approved guide; there are also restrictions on engine types.

HOW DO I GET AROUND?

BY BOAT

Motorized and nonmotorized boats are allowed in both National Parks, although permits are required for both. Motorized boats are allowed on Jenny, Jackson, and Phelps lakes in Grand Teton; and on Yellowstone and Lewis lakes in Yellowstone. Kayakers and canoeists also enjoy paddling these waters, but the Lewis Lake Channel to Shoshone Lake is the only river where boats are allowed in Yellowstone. Every

CLAIM TO FAME

Old Faithful attracts virtually every one of the park's 3 million-plus annual visitors to view its eruptions, which take place about every 90 minutes. The Upper Geyser Basin, which includes Old Faithful, is the single greatest concentration of geysers in the world—and approximately 50% of the world's hydrothermal features are clustered within the park's boundaries.

Geysers are just one of the park's hydrothermal features. Travertine terraces (like at Mammoth Hot Springs) form when thermal waters rise through limestone carrying high amounts of dissolved carbonate, which is released as carbon dioxide and calcium carbonate (the chalky white rock). Mudpots are gassy, bubbling pools of cloudy acidic water; the Fountain Paintpots are a particularly fascinating group. Hot springs, like the immense Grand Prismatic, are pools where heated water cools at the earth's surface, often in an array of colors caused by microscopic organisms.

Grand Teton's most photographed features are the mountains, which rise up abruptly from Jackson Hole. Go closer to explore Jenny Lake, Jackson Lake, and the Snake River—these waters are home to cutthroat trout, rare birds, and other animals both large and small.

variety of nonmotorized boat (kayak, canoe, inflatable, etc.) is seen on the Snake River (which runs higher and faster in early summer).

BY CAR

The Grand Loop Road is a figure-eight that takes drivers to more than a half-dozen developed visitor centers in Yellowstone National Park in summer. It's hard to get lost. Five entrance roads feed the Grand Loop.

The Jackson Hole Highway (U.S. 89/191) runs the entire length of Grand Teton National Park; Teton Park Road takes you closer to Jenny Lake and the mountains.

WHERE SHOULD I FOCUS MY ENERGY?

If you're here for 1 day: Head to Yellowstone, where Old Faithful, the historic Old Faithful Inn, and the nearby geyser basins trump everything else. Also check out Madison and Firehole valleys, where you're likely to see wildlife.

If you're here for 2 days: Grand Canyon of the Yellowstone offers another timeless vista. From Old Faithful drive counterclockwise and see Fishing Bridge, the Lake Hotel, and the wildlife-rich Hayden Valley. Spend a few hours on one of the parks wonderful trails.

If you're here for 3 days: Explore one of the wildlife-rich valleys (Hayden, Lamar, Firehole, or Madison) at dawn or dusk, and be on the lookout for bears, wolves, owls, and eagles. Scale a modest peak like Avalanche, Bunsen, or Washburn.

If you're here for 4 days: Spend a day in a less-traveled area, like Slough Creek, Shoshone Lake, or Pelican Valley (Yellowstone) or String Lake

Trail or Death Canyon Trail (Grand Teton). B
camping under a bright canopy of stars.

If you're here for 5 days: Discover your inner geologist with
of geysers, fumaroles, hot springs, and mudpots. Start at
Hot Springs and descend the northwest portion of the Grand
Road to Roaring Mountain, Norris & Madison geyser basins, and
Artists' Paintpots.

If you're here for 6 days: While away the afternoon on the porch at the
Lake Lodge or the second floor of the Old Faithful Inn. Then, for dinner, treat yourself to fine dining at the Lake.

If you're here for 7 days or more: Experienced campers should plunge
into either park's backcountry for off-the-map waterfalls, geysers and, of
course, up-close encounters with abundant wildlife. If you've had enough
of the great outdoors, head to Jackson, WY, and do some shopping.

WHAT ARE THE TOP EXPERIENCES?

Yellowstone's Old West Dinner Cookout. The Old West comes to life
as horses transport you 3 mi and 100 years back in time for steak-
and-beans cookout. You'll almost expect John Wayne to come riding around the bend. Intrepid urban cowboys ride ponies from the
Roosevelt Corral—while the more cautious types clamber in on an
old horse-drawn wagon. ✉ *Xanterra Parks & Resorts* ☉ *866-439-7375*
☉ *summer only.*

Snake River Float. Ride the high fast river early in the season, or enjoy a
melancholy float in late summer. Either way, you'll be treated to stunning views of 12,000-plus-foot peaks, wading wildlife, and graceful
raptors soaring high overhead. Multiple outfitters will handle all the
logistics; most pick up their clients at the float-trip parking area near
Moose Visitor Center. Don't forget a permit—it's $10 to raft for the
entire season, or $5 to raft for seven days.

Mammoth Hot Springs. This thriving park community is just inside the
Yellowstone boundaries near Gardiner, MT. Stroll the grounds of Ft.
Yellowstone, which may remind you of West Point or an eastern prep
school. Then, traverse the travertine terraces of the hot springs, which
look a lot like a moonscape. You can swim in "Boiling River" (a place
where a large hot spring flows into the Gardner River), stride the 45th
parallel at the base of the hill from town, or hike into the backcountry
in minutes on the Beaver Falls Trail. Mammoth Hotel is the only Yellowstone property open in both summer and winter (like all park lodging, it's closed for about a month in fall and spring) year-round.

Lose Yourself in Backcountry. Both Grand Teton and Yellowstone are best
enjoyed away from the masses. No matter how much time you have in
the parks, allot a few hours (or days!) to some of America's finest hiking
terrain. Descend 1,000 feet to the Yellowstone River, or climb double
that height to any number of peaks. Listen for creaking lodgepole pine,
dribbling creeks, or chattering rodents—and revel in a silence broken

U CAN SEE

first national
wonders
to conserve
a's wild places.
S. Grant signed the
nal Park Protec-
on March 1, 1872,
headwaters of the
er. is hereby reserved
and w..... from settlement, occupancy, or sale. and dedicated and set apart as a public park or pleasuring-ground for the benefit and enjoyment of the people."

Since Yellowstone was administered ineffectively by the U.S. Army for much of the next four decades, Washington created the National Park Service in 1916 "to conserve the scenery and the natural and historic objects and the wildlife therein and to provide for the enjoyment of the same in such manner. as will leave them unimpaired for the enjoyment of future generations."

National Park Mountain is a peak visible on the west horizon of Yellowstone's volcanic crater (called the caldera). There is an oft-repeated story that members of the 1870 Washburn expedition gazed upon the peak as they sat at a well-marked spot near the present-day Madison Ranger Station. They discussed protecting the lands as a park, rather than exploiting them—and much credit (including a plaque on site) is given to them for the National Park concept. This legend has recently been revealed to be a myth. The name of the peak, however, remains unchanged.

only by your footsteps. (Bring bear spray for worst-case scenarios, and keep a safe distance from the elk, bear, and bison you may chance upon in a wooded thicket.)

Grand Lodges. It's appropriate that America's first national park, Yellowstone, has one of the National Park Service's architectural gems—Old Faithful Inn. The prototype stone-and-wood construction spawned a generation of "parchitecture" buildings that fit in with their natural surroundings. The eight-story lobby of lodgepole pine, with its soaring stone fireplace and ornate iron fixtures, is an American treasure. Stop in for a meal or tour (given daily in summer) even if you're not staying there.

BEST BETS

SIGHTS AND TOURS

YELLOWSTONE

Fodor'sChoice
★ On a busy day in summer, maybe six parties will fill out the trail register at the **Avalanche Peak** trailhead, so you won't have a lot of company on this hike. Yet many say it's one of the best kept secrets in the park. Starting across from a parking area on East Entrance Road, the difficult 4-mi, four-hour round-trip climbs 2,150 feet to the peak's 10,566-foot summit, from which you can see the rugged Absaroka Mountains running north and south. Look around the talus and tundra near the top of the peak for alpine wildflowers and butterflies. Don't try this trail

before late June or after early September—it may be covered in snow. Also, rangers discourage hikers from attempting this hike in September or October due to bear activity. Whenever you decide to go, carry a jacket: the winds at the top are strong. ⊠ *2 mi east of Sylvan Lake on north side of East Entrance Rd..*

★ **Canyon Visitor Center.** This new building has elaborate, interactive exhibits for adults and kids. The focus here is volcanoes and earthquakes, but there are also exhibits on Native Americans and park wildlife as well. The video entitled "Water, Heat & Rock" is a riveting look at the geo- and hydrothermal basis for the park. As with all visitor centers, you can obtain park information, backcountry camping permits, etc. The adjacent bookstore, operated by the Yellowstone Association, is the best in the park with guidebooks, trail maps, gifts and hundreds of books on the park, its history, and the science surrounding it. ⊠ *Canyon Village* ☎ *307/242-2552* ☉ *Late May–Aug., daily 8–7; Sept., daily 8–6; Oct., daily 9–5. .*

Fodor'sChoice **Grand Canyon of the Yellowstone.** This stunning canyon is 23 mi long, but ★ there's only one trail from rim to base. As a result, a majority of park visitors clog the north and south rims to see Upper and Lower Falls. To compound problems, park officials will completely close North Rim Road in 2008 for construction. Popular north rim scenic stops Grand View, Lookout Point, Inspiration Point, and Brink of the Lower Falls may be reachable only by foot, if at all. Check with park officials for the latest updates.

Unless you're up for the six-hour strenuous hike called Seven Mile Hole, you have no choice but to join the crowds on the rims to see this natural wonder. The red-and-ochre canyon walls are topped with emerald-green forest. It's a feast of color. Also look for ospreys, which nest in the canyon's spires and precarious trees. ⊠ *Canyon.*

Mammoth Hot Springs is known for its massive natural terraces, where mineral water flows continuously, building an ever-changing display. You will almost always see elk grazing in the area. Mammoth Hot Springs is also headquarters for Yellowstone National Park. In the early days of the park, it was the site of Fort Yellowstone, and the brick buildings constructed during that era are still used for various park activities. The Albright Visitor Center has information and displays about the park history, including reproductions of original Thomas Moran paintings, created on an 1871 government expedition to the area, which made the broader public aware of Yellowstone's beauty and helped lead to its establishment as a national park. There's a complete range of visitor services here as well. There are lots of steps on the lower terrace boardwalks, so plan to take your time here.

Fodor'sChoice **Old Faithful.** Yellowstone's most predictable big geyser—although not ★ its largest or most regular—sometimes reaches 180 feet, but it averages ☉ 130 feet. Sometimes it doesn't shoot as high, but in those cases the eruptions usually last longer. The mysterious plumbing of Yellowstone has lengthened Old Faithful's cycle somewhat in recent years, to every 94 minutes or so. To find out when Old Faithful is likely to erupt, check at the visitor center, or at any of the lodging properties in the area. The 1-mi hike to Observation Point yields a unique view—from above—of the geyser and its surrounding basin. ✉*Southwest segment, Grand Loop Rd.*

Fodor's Choice ★ **Slough Creek Trail,** starting at Slough Creek Campground, climbs steeply along a historic wagon trail for the first 1½ mi before reaching expansive meadows and prime fishing spots, where moose are common and grizzlies occasionally wander. From this point the trail, now mostly level, meanders another 9½ mi to the park's northern boundary. Anglers absolutely rave about this trail. ✉*7 mi east of Tower-Roosevelt off Northeast Entrance Rd..*

Ⓒ **West Thumb Geyser Basin.** The primary Yellowstone caldera was created by a volcanic eruption 640,000 years ago, but West Thumb came about much more recently, 150,000 years ago, as the result of a another volcanic eruption. This unique geyser basin is the only place to see active geothermal features in Lake Yellowstone. Two boardwalk loops are offered—take the longer one to see features like "Fishing Cone" where fishermen used to catch fish, pivot, and drop their fish in boiling water for cooking—without ever taking it off the hook. It's particularly popular for winter visitors who take advantage of the nearby warming hut and a stroll around the geyser basin before continuing their trip via snow coach or snowmobile. ✉*Grand Loop Rd., 22 mi north of South Entrance. .*

Fodor's Choice ★ Ⓒ Operated by **Xanterra,** tours on historic White Motors' 14-passenger buses are the most elegant way to see and learn about the park. Eight of the 70-year-old vehicles were restored at a cost of more than $2 million and reintroduced to rave reviews in 2007. The soft-top convertibles allow you to bask in the sun if it's warm enough—and keep you plenty warm when it's not. Well-trained guides amuse and educate you through more than a dozen itineraries ranging from one hour to all day long. Prices range from $12.50 to $87 for adults with discounts for children. Reservations are essential. ☎*307/344–7901* ⊕*www.travelyellowstone.com.*

Fodor's Choice ★ If you're interested in having a park expert, whether a naturalist, geologist, or wildlife specialist accompany you, the **Yellowstone Association Institute** offers daylong hiking excursions; multiday "Lodging and Learning" trips geared around hikes, some of them designed for families (there are age restrictions on some trips); and full-blown backcountry backpacking trips. The association also offers courses on topics

---

STRANGE BUT TRUE

There are 16 ways to die in Yellowstone that are more common than bear attacks, including death by drowning, horse-and-buggy accidents, fire, lightning strikes, Indian attacks, and falling ice. The five deaths by bear attacks in the park's history do outnumber deaths by falling rocks, though. You can read more in Lee Whittlesey's Death in Yellowstone.

A robotic submarine often patrols Yellowstone Lake in summer. Operated by scientists at the University of Wisconsin, it has discovered canyons nearly 400 feet deep and water temperatures of more than 250 degrees.

ranging from nature writing to wolf biology. Taught by college professors or other experts, most courses are for people age 18 and older. ⌂ *Box 117, Yellowstone National Park, WY82190* ☎*307/344–2293* ⊠*307/344–2486* ⊕*www.yellowstoneassociation.org* ✉*From $80 for one-day trips to $1,000-plus for 5-night trips including lodging.*

★ **Yellowstone Lake Scenic Cruises,** run by Xanterra Parks & Resorts, oper-
☼ ates the *Lake Queen II* from out of Bridge Bay Marina on Yellowstone Lake. The one-hour cruises make their way to Stevenson Island and then return to Bridge Bay. Boats depart throughout the day. ⊠*Bridge Bay Marina* ☎*307/344–7311* ✉*$11.25* ☉*June–mid-Sept., daily.*

Yellowstone Wilderness Outfitters is exclusively dedicated to trips inside Yellowstone National Park (no elk-hunting trips here). Multitalented guide Jett Hitt (he has a doctorate in music composition and wrote the violin concerto Yellowstone for Violin and Orchestra) leads trips ranging from half- and full-day family rides to 3- to 10-day pack trips in every area of the park. Trips may feature wildlife biologists and lecturers. ⌂ *Box 745, Yellowstone NP, WY82190* ☎*406/223–3300* ⊕*www.yellowstone.ws* ✉*From $110 for half-day trips up to $2,400 for multiday trips.*

GRAND TETON

★ **Jenny Lake Trail.** You can walk to Hidden Falls from Jenny Lake ranger
☼ station by following the mostly level trail around the south shore of the lake to Cascade Canyon Trail. Jenny Lake Trail continues around the lake for 6½ mi. It's an easy trail—classed here as moderate because of its length—that will take you two to three hours. You can walk through a lodgepole pine forest, have expansive views of the lake and the land to the east, and hug the shoulder of the massive Teton range itself. Along the way you're likely to see elk, pikas, golden mantle ground squirrels, a variety of ducks and water birds, plus you may hear elk bugling, birdsong, and the chatter of squirrels. ⊠*S. Jenny Lake Junction, ½ mi off Teton Park Rd., 8 mi north of Moose Junction.*

★ **National Elk Refuge.** More than 7,000 elk spend winter in the National
☼ Elk Refuge, which was established in 1912 to rescue starving herds. The animals migrate to the refuge grounds in late fall and remain until early spring. Trumpeter swans live here, too, as do bald eagles, coyotes, and wolves. In winter you can take a wagon or sleigh ride through the herd. In summer migration means that there are fewer big-game animals here, but you likely can see waterfowl and you can also fish on the refuge. ⊠*2820 Rungius Rd., Jackson* ☎*307/733–9212* ✉*Sleigh rides $13* ☉*Year-round; sleigh rides mid-Dec.–Mar.*

WHERE TO EAT

	WHAT IT COSTS				
	¢	$	$$	$$$	$$$$
RESTAURANTS	under $8	$8–$12	$13–$20	$21–$30	over $30

Restaurant prices are per person for a main course at dinner

YELLOWSTONE

$$–$$$$ ✕ **Lake Yellowstone Hotel Dining Room.**

Fodor'sChoice   Opened in 1893 and renovated by
★   Robert Reamer beginning in 1903,
this double-colonnaded dining room
off the hotel lobby is the most ele-
gant dining experience in the park.
This dining room is an upgrade from
Old Faithful Inn in every way—ser-
vice, china, view, menu sophistica-
tion, and even the quality of the
crisp salads. Arrive early and enjoy
a beverage in the airy sunroom. The
menu includes elk medallions, buf-
falo prime rib, and fettuccine with
wild smoked salmon. The wine
list features California, Oregon,
and Washington—and ranges as
high as a $120 bottle of Mondavi
Reserve Cabernet. ⌖ *Lake Village
Rd.* ☎ *307/344–7311* ⌖ *Reserva-
tions essential* ☰ *AE, D, DC, MC,
V* ⊘ *Closed early Oct.–mid-May.*

$–$$$ ✕ **Old Faithful Inn Dining Room.** Set just behind the lobby, the original din-
ing room—designed by Robert Reamer in 1903 and expanded by him
in 1927—has lodgepole-pine walls and ceiling beams and a giant volcanic rock fireplace graced with a contemporary painting of Old Faithful
by the late Paco Young. A buffet offers quantity over quality: bison,
chicken, shrimp, two salads, two soups, and a dessert. You're better off
choosing from nearly a dozen entrées, including grilled salmon, French-
baked chicken, prime rib, and bison rib eye. Save room for a signature
dessert such as the Caldera, a chocolate truffle torte with a "molten"
middle. The most extensive wine list in the park offers more than 50 (all
American) choices. ⌖ *Old Faithful Village* ☎ *307/344–7311* ⌖ *Reservations essential* ☰ *AE, D, DC, MC, V* ⊘ *Closed late Oct.–early May.*

$ ✕ **Wild West Pizzeria.** Good pizza seems to taste better in mountain
★   resort towns—and Wild West is no exception. The crisp crust, flavor-
☺   ful sauce, and "celebrity" frontier combinations work. The "Sitting
Bull" features Italian pepperoni, sausage, and salami—plus Canadian
Bacon. The "Calamity Jane" is topped with white sauce, mushrooms,
artichoke hearts, minced garlic, and fresh tomatoes. Beer is poured in
the adjacent Strozzi's Bar, but you can bring it into the pizzeria. ⌖ *14
Madison Ave.,* ☎ *406/646–4400* ☰ *MC, V.*

GRAND TETON

$$$$ ✕ **Jenny Lake Lodge Dining Room.** Elegant yet rustic, this is Grand Teton
★   National Park's finest dining establishment, with jackets required for
men. The menu is ever changing and offers fish, pasta, chicken, and
beef; the wine list is extensive. Dinner is prix-fixe; lunch is à la carte.
⌖ *Jenny Lake Rd., 2 mi off Teton Park Rd., 12 mi north of Moose*

Junction ☎*307/733–4647 or 800/628–9988 Jacket required* ✍*Reservations essential* 🞎*AE, MC, V* ◷*Closed early Oct.–late May.*

$$–$$$ ✕**Jackson Lake Lodge Mural Room.** The ultimate park dining experience
Fodor'sChoice is found in this large room that gets its name from a 700-square-foot
★ mural painted by Western artist Carl Roters. The mural details an 1837 Wyoming mountain man rendezvous and covers two walls of the dining room. Select from a menu that includes trout, elk, beef, and pasta. The cedar plank salmon is a great choice, or try a buffalo steak. The tables face tall windows affording a panoramic view of Willow Flats and Jackson Lake to the northern Tetons. ✉*U.S. 89/191/287, ½ mi north of Jackson Lake Junction* ☎*307/543–2811 Ext. 1911 or 800/628–9988* 🞎*AE, MC, V* ◷*Closed mid-Oct.–late May.*

WHERE TO STAY

WHAT IT COSTS

	¢	$	$$	$$$	$$$$
HOTELS	under $50	$50–$100	$101–$150	$151–$200	over $200
CAMPING	under $10	$10–$17	$18–$35	$36–$49	over $50

Restaurant prices are per person for a main course at dinner.

YELLOWSTONE

$$$–$$$$ 🞎**Lake Yellowstone Hotel.** More Kennebunkport than Western, this
★ distinguished hotel is the park's oldest. Dating from 1891 the white-and-pastel color edifice has maintained an air of refinement that Old Faithful Inn can't (due to its throngs of tour buses packed with visitors). Just off the lobby a spacious sunroom offers priceless views of Lake Yellowstone at sunrise or sunset. It's also a great place to play cards, catch up on a newspaper from the gift shop, or just soak up the grandeur of a 117-year-old National Historic Landmark. Note the tile-mantel fireplace, the etched windows of the gift shop, and the bay windows. Rooms have white wicker furnishings, giving them a light, airy feeling; some have lake views. ✉*Lake Village Rd.* ☎*307/344–7901* 🖷*307/344–7456* ⊕*www.travelyellowstone.com* ➱*194 rooms* ☘*In-room: no a/c, no TV. In-hotel: Restaurant, bar, no-smoking rooms* 🞎*AE, D, DC, MC, V* ◷*Closed early Oct.–mid-May.*

$–$$$$ 🞎**Old Faithful Inn.** This National Historic Landmark has been a favorite
Fodor'sChoice of five generations of park visitors. The "Old House" was originally
★ built in 1904. The lobby features a 76-foot-high, 8-sided fireplace;
☘ bright-red iron-clad doors and two balconies (open to the public) as well as a fantasylike "treehouse" of platforms, ladders, and dormer windows high above the foyer. Believe it or not, you can stay in 1904-era rooms with thick wood timber walls and ceilings for under $100—if you're willing to forsake a private bathroom. Rooms with bathrooms in either the "Old House" or the "modern" wings, built in 1913 and 1927, can rent for over $200—especially if they have geyser views. Renovations will continue in 2008, but shouldn't compromise one of America's most distinctive buildings. ✉*Old Faithful Village*

ON THE WAY

It's the least used entrance to Yellowstone, but the Northeast Entrance can be reached by the spectacular **Beartooth Scenic Byway** between Red Lodge and Cooke City.

Buffalo Bill Historical Center. With five museums and a research library under one roof, this complex is well worth the stop as you approach Yellowstone from the east. Western art, firearms, Plains Indians, natural history, and the complex's namesake, Buffalo Bill Cody are featured. *720 Sheridan Ave., Cody, WY; 307/587–4771; www.bbhc.org.*

Some of America's best cross-country skiing takes place at **Rendezvous Ski Trails** in West Yellowstone. Its 22 mi of trails of groomed trails are home to various ski festivals and races.

Jackson, WY, is a booming community of 7,000 people at the southern end of the Grand Tetons. Its raised wooden sidewalks and old-fashioned storefronts maintain a historical feel—belied by the seven-figure residential real estate prices.

☎307/344–7901 ♨307/344–7456 ⊕*www.travelyellowstone.com* ♥*327 rooms, 6 suites* ⚒*In-room: no a/c, no phone (some), no TV. In-hotel: Restaurant, bar, no-smoking rooms* ▭*AE, D, DC, MC, V* ♥*Closed late Oct.–early May.*

$$–$$$ · **Fodor's Choice** · ★ · ⊞**Bar N Ranch.** A deluxe option for the increasing number of affluent anglers, hunters, and visitors to West Yellowstone, this supersize bed-and-breakfast combines Midwestern hospitality of its Chicago-born owners with big-timber architecture and a frontier feel. Seven rooms in the main lodge (above a spacious living room and the community's finest restaurant), plus seven stand-alone cabins sleep from two to eight. It's 6 mi from the entrance to Yellowstone National park on a 200-acre ranch that first welcomed visitors in 1906. ⊠*890 Buttermilk Creek Rd., West Yellowstone, MT59758* ☎*406/646–0300* ♨*406/646–0301* ⊕*www.bar-n-ranch.com* ♥*14 rooms* ⚒*In-Room: No a/c, no phones, refrigerators, DVD player, Wi-Fi. In-hotel: no elevator, restaurant, bar, pool, public Wi-Fi, public Internet, some pets allowed, no-smoking rooms.* ⦿|*BP* ▭*AE, D, MC, V* ♥*No lunch.*

GRAND TETON

$$$$ · ★ · ⊞**Wort Hotel.** The locals have been gathering at this Jackson landmark half a block from Town Square since the early 1940s, and you can view the history of Jackson in the photos and clippings posted in the lobby. The spacious rooms have lodgepole furniture and comfortable armchairs. Junior suites have large sitting areas. ⊠*50 N. Glenwood St., Jackson, 83001* ☎*307/733–2190 or 800/322–2727* ♨*307/733–2067* ⊕*www.worthotel.com* ♥*59 rooms, 4 suites* ⚒*In-hotel: restaurant, room service, bar* ▭*AE, D, MC, V.*

$–$$$ · **Fodor's Choice** · ★ · ⊞**Moulton Ranch Cabins.** Along Mormon Row these cabins stand a few dozen yards south of the famous Moulton Barn, which you see on brochures, jigsaw puzzles, and photographs of the park. The land was once part of the T. A. Moulton homestead, and the cabins are still owned by the Moulton family. The quiet property has views of the Teton and the

Gros Ventre ranges, and the owners can regale you with stories about early homesteaders. There's a dance hall in the barn, making this an ideal place for family and small group reunions. No smoking on the premises. ⊠*Off Antelope Flats Rd., U.S. 26/89/191, 2 mi north of Moose Junction* ☎*307/733–3749 or 208/529–2354* ⊕*www.moulton ranchcabins.com* ⥽*5 units* ♿*In-room: kitchen (some). In-hotel: no-smoking rooms* ▤*MC, V* ☉*Closed Oct.–May. No Sun. check-in.*

SPORTS & THE OUTDOORS

YELLOWSTONE

Free Heel and Wheel, just outside Yellowstone's West Entrance, rents bikes and dispenses advice, and sells hiking and cross-country skiing gear. The staff here can also recommend road cycling routes inside and outside the park. Rates: $8 per hour, $25 per day including helmet and water bottle. ⊠*40 Yellowstone Ave., West Yellowstone, MT* ☎*406/646–7744* ⊕*www.freeheelandwheel.com.*

★ **Xanterra Parks & Resorts.** Yellowstone's in-park concessionaire provides one- and two-hour horse rides in Canyon Village, Mammoth Hot Springs, and Tower-Roosevelt. Reservations are recommended. Xanterra also offers horseback or wagon rides to an Old West cookout site for a steak dinner. Advance reservations are required. ☎*307/344–7311* ⊕*www.travelyellowstone.com* ⊠*$37, 1-hr rides, $57 2-hr rides; $56–$79, Old West Cookouts.*

Gunsel Horse Adventures. Since 1968 this South Dakota–based outfitter has provided 4-, 7-, or 10-day excursions into Yellowstone's backcountry. The trips are a great way to see moose, bear, deer, elk, and wolves. ☎*605/343–7608* ⊕*www.gunselhorseadventures.com* ⊠*$250 per day; $1,400–$1,500 multiday trips.*

Rimrock Dude Ranch. Outfitter Gary Fales has been leading multiday pack trips into Yellowstone for decades, operating out of this ranch west of Cody. Regular trips include treks between the Cody area and Jackson. Trips last a week and include backcountry camping, fishing, hiking, and horseback activities. All food and camping items are provided. ☎*307/587–3970* ⊕*www.rimrockranch.com* ⊠*$1,475 per person.*

GRAND TETON

Fodor'sChoice ★ Skiers and snowboarders love **Jackson Hole Mountain Resort,** one of the great skiing experiences in America. There are literally thousands of routes up and down the mountain, and not all of them are hellishly steep, despite Jackson's reputation. ⊠*Box 290, Teton Village, 83025* ☎*307/733–2292 or 800/333–7766* ⊕*www.jacksonhole.com.*

Teton Mountain Bike Tours. Mountain bikers of all skill levels can take guided half-, full-, or multiday tours with this company into both Grand Teton and Yellowstone national parks, as well as to the Bridger-Teton and Caribou–Targhee national forests. ⌂*Box 7027, Jackson, 83002* ☎*307/733–0712 or 800/733–0788* ⊕*www.wybike.com* ⊠*$55–$125 for half- to full-day trips; multiday trips $379–$400 per day* ☉*May–Sept.*

Exum Mountain Guides. You can find a variety of climbing experiences here, ranging from one-day mountain climbs to ice climbing to backcountry adventures on skis and snowboards. ⌂ *Box 56, Moose, 83012* ☎ *307/733–2297* ⊕ *www.exumguides.com* ✉ *One-day climbs $200–$340, climbing schools $105–$170* ⊘ *Year-round.*

Grand Teton Lodge Company. The park's major concessionaire operates guided Jackson Lake fishing trips that include boat and tackle, and guided fly-fishing trips on the Snake River. (They also rent motorboats, rowboats, and canoes.) Make reservations at the activities desks at Colter Bay Village or Jackson Lake Lodge, where trips originate. ✉ *Colter Bay Marina or Jackson Lake Lodge* ☎ *307/543–3100 or 800/628–9988* ⊕ *www.gtlc.com* ✉ *$130–$375 and up* ⊘ *June–Sept.*

VITAL STATS

■ Stunning Biodiversity: Yellowstone is home to 61 species of mammals and 322 recorded species of birds.

■ Most Controversial Animal: The National Park Service reintroduced 31 wolves to Yellowstone in the '90s despite "over my dead body" threats from local ranchers. (Livestock losses have been much lower than previously feared.)

■ Best Legacy: The John D. Rockefeller Jr. Memorial Parkway, which connects Yellowstone and Grand Teton national parks, commemorates Rockefeller's generous donations of lands to the National Park System.

VISITOR INFORMATION

Grand Teton National Park. ⌂ *Box 170, Moose, WY, 83012* ☎ *307/739–3300, 307/739–3400 TTY* ⊕ *www.nps.gov/grte.*

Jackson Chamber of Commerce ⌂ *Box 550, Jackson, WY, 83001* ☎ *307/733–3316* 🖷 *307/733–5585* ⊕ *www.jacksonholechamber.com.*

Jackson Hole Chamber of Commerce (✉ *990 W. Broadway, Box E, Jackson, WY, 83001* ☎ *307/733–3316* 🖷 *307/733–5585* ⊕ *www.jacksonholeinfo.com).*

West Yellowstone Chamber of Commerce (✉ *30 Yellowstone Ave., West Yellowstone, MT, 59758* ☎ *406/646–7701* 🖷 *406/646–9691* ⊕ *www.westyellowstonechamber.com).*

Yellowstone National Park ⌂ *Box 168, Mammoth, WY, 82190* ☎ *307/344–7381, 307/344–2386 TDD* 🖷 *307/344–2005* ⊕ *www.nps.gov/yell.*

The Colorado Rockies

WITH DENVER AND BOULDER

Coyote pups, Rocky Mountain National Park

WORD OF MOUTH

"You might find that Denver has more to offer in the way of nightlife and restaurants, but Boulder is well worth seeing and exploring. If the weather cooperates, you could go hiking in the Flatirons, the hills above the city, spend time on the Pearl St. Mall, a pedestrian shopping area, visit a very cool restaurant, the Dushanbe Teahouse . . . The 16th St. Mall is the heart of downtown [Denver] with shopping and restautant. Lower Downtown (LoDo) is where the action is with lots of bars and clubs."

—tekwriter

EXPLORING THE COLORADO ROCKIES

Denver is 70 mi north of Colorado Springs via I–25; 383 mi north of Santa Fe via I–25; 565 mi east of Salt Lake City via I–15 and I–70; 612 mi west of Kansas City via I–70; and 915 mi southwest of Minneapolis via I–35 and I–70

By Kyle Wagner

With an average of 320 days of sun a year, a unique blend of Old West quirks combined with contemporary urban amenities, and enough outdoor opportunities to keep even the most avid enthusiast endlessly occupied, the Queen City of the Plains makes good on her promise to serve as a gateway to the West. Visit Denver, also called the Mile High City, and enjoy world-renowned art and science museums, performing arts venues that rival those on the coasts, champion-caliber sports teams, and restaurants and shops that have garnered wide acclaim.

Or venture farther into the Colorado Rockies—perhaps to Boulder, 30 mi north, where the upscale collegiate atmosphere absorbs and reflects the energy from the power elite, latter-day hippies, and retirees who have swelled this former bedroom community into a vibrant metropolis that still manages to retain its small-town feel. Another 30 mi northwest sits Rocky Mountain National Park, a year-round mecca for outdoor activities that include hiking through alpine forests, bird-watching in wildflower-dotted meadows, cross-country skiing around hundreds of miles of trails, and racing snowmobiles across untracked, freshly fallen powder. If you're pressed for time, you can easily drive through the park to experience its magnificent snow-capped peaks and catch a glimpse of the many species of wildlife inhabiting its 265,770 acres.

WHO WILL ESPECIALLY LOVE THIS TRIP?

Outdoors Enthusiasts: You can't go more than 10 feet in the Denver metro area without bumping into someone dressed for outdoor success, and they are all too happy to point you in the right direction for adventures of your own. Need a few ideas? Hike around Red Rocks Amphitheatre to get a look at the famous red rock, or stroll around Chautauqua Park and the Flatirons in Boulder. And the possibilities are endless in nearby Rocky Mountain National Park.

Beer Lovers: From the Great American Beer Fest held each October to the fact that there seems to be a microbrewery or brewpub on every block, fans of fermented grain will find plenty to toast in a city that eagerly promotes its beer heritage. Stop by Wynkoop Brewing Company, Denver's first brewpub, and check out the annual winners of the "Beer Drinker of the Year" award—and consider tossing your hat into the ring.

Old West Aficionados: For many folks, Denver still is the Old West. A meal at the Buckhorn Exchange, a trip to the National Western Stock Show, a stroll through the historic neighborhoods, as well as LoDo and Larimer Square, and a stop by the Brown Palace may be all it takes to recapture that place in time. Need more? Camp overnight in

TOP 5 REASONS TO GO

LoDo, Larimer Square & the 16th Street Mall: These three connected, walkable areas of Denver (LoDo is the term locals use for "Lower Downtown") can be seen in a day but are home to a lifetime's worth of history, shops, dining, and people-watching opportunities.

National Western Stock Show: Grab your pardner and bust out of the post-holiday blues in January by participating in two weeks of galavantin' Western-style, with rodeo events, livestock sales, and plenty of good eats.

Microbrews: Colorado is rich with beer history. Not only is Coors brewed here, but the Denver metro area boasts one of the highest con-centrations of microbreweries and brewpubs in the country. The city also hosts the annual Great American Beer Festival.

The Great Outdoors: Stick to the many miles of paved paths in the Denver area, or go off-road with your bike, hike the foothills, kayak along the Platte River at the edge of downtown, strap on your Nordic skis and glide through Rocky Mountain National Park . . . the choices seem-ingly are endless, and the weather almost always cooperates.

Pearl Street: Boulder's hip, hap-pening hub is packed with shops, restaurants, galleries, and more, with an inviting vibe and entertainment provided by traveling buskers.

Rocky Mountain National Park and fall asleep to the sound of howl-ing coyotes.

Foodies: Denver and Boulder offer an astounding variety of cuisines, including Mexican (LoLa Mexican Seafood), Vietnamese (New Sai-gon), Japanese (Sushi Den), and Italian (Luca d'Italia), and the number of nationally recognized restaurants (Boulder's Frasca Food & Wine, Denver's Restaurant Kevin Taylor) has increased dramatically in the past decade.

Families: In addition to sporting one of the top amusement parks in the country at Elitch Gardens, Denver boasts the world-class Denver Zoo and Downtown Aquarium, the Denver Museum of Nature & Science, and other kid-friendly museums. And, of course, with all of the out-door pursuits available, it's also one of the healthiest places to bring your family.

WHEN IS THE BEST TIME TO VISIT?

The peak times for a Rocky Mountain visit are summer and early fall, before the snow flies in earnest—unless, of course, you're planning to head to the mountains for winter sports. The metro area is normally hit with one quick snowfall sometime in September or October; warm days return through late October or early November, when winter begins to get serious. With the exception of late August, when the tem-peratures can sit in the upper 90s or even hit 100, summers are dry and tolerably warm, with temperatures dropping by 10 degrees for every 1,000 or so feet you climb.

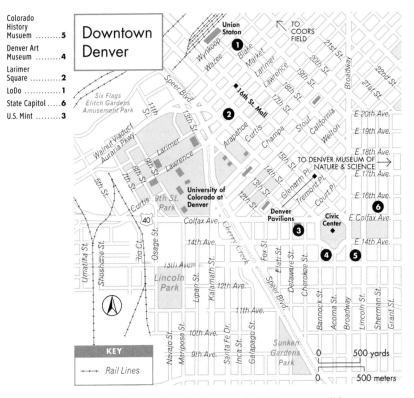

Be aware that even though winter technically starts much later, a snow-storm can hit as early as the first week of September and as late as the last week in May; it's always wise to pack at least one warm piece of clothing during this time period. And remember that the Rocky Mountain region is dry, dry, dry—so start drinking water the moment you arrive.

Denver sees a lot of convention and business traffic during the week, so downtown hotel rates drop on the weekends. Summertime finds a festival happening somewhere in the city proper nearly every week, beginning with Cinco de Mayo on May 5, a celebration commemorating Mexico's success over the French in 1862. An enormous arts gathering called the Capitol Hill People's Fair takes place in June, and the last true hurrah of summer is the smorgasbord of food and music that is Labor Day weekend's Taste of Colorado.

HOW SHOULD I GET THERE?

DRIVING
Approaching from the West means you'll be navigating the sometimes tedious and, in inclement weather, treacherous mountains. The main veins for getting around are the east-west Interstate 70 and north-south Inter-

state 25; exit I–70 onto I–25 to drop into the heart of the city via multiple exits, most notably Speer Boulevard, which runs diagonally alongside the city, as well as the Cherry Creek and Platte River Valley areas.

FLYING

With its meringuelike peaked roof crafted to duplicate a mountain range, Denver International Airport (DEN) is one of the most recognizable airports in the world. Once you land, the trip into the city, 15 mi southwest, usually takes about a half hour. To get into downtown from the airport, you can rent a car at the convenient Rental Car Center or take a shuttle (many hotels offer them free; you can also use a service, such as Super Shuttle, for about $19 per person), hop on a bus using RTD's SkyRide ($8–$10 one way), or take a limo or taxi (about $55–$100, depending on your final destination) from the transportation center just outside baggage claim.

TRAIN

A trip by train into Union Station in LoDo is the slowest way to get to Denver, but certainly the most evocative of the Old West. Most trains are run by Amtrak, although several luxury train companies have popped up, as well. Amtrak's California Zephyr is the most economical and convenient of the train options into Denver; it takes 17 hours to make the trip from Chicago to Denver, or 30 hours to travel from San Francisco, with several stops en route.

HOW DO I GET AROUND?

BY BUS

In downtown Denver, a free shuttle-bus service operates continually from 5 AM until 1:35 AM from one end of the 16th Street Mall to the other, stopping every block. The region's public bus service, RTD, is comprehensive, with routes throughout the metropolitan area; the service also links Denver to Boulder. You can buy bus tokens at grocery stores or pay with exact change on the bus. Fares vary according to time and zone. Within the city limits, buses cost $1.75 ($15.75 for 10-ride ticket book).

BY CAR

If you plan to spend much time outside downtown, a car is advised (although Denver has one of the best city bus systems in the country, and taxis are readily available). Getting from Denver to Boulder can be a quick trip (30 minutes) or a slow slog (an hour or more) up U.S. 36, especially during rush hour, but the bus travels there as well.

BY TRAIN

RTD's Light Rail train service links southwest and northeast Denver and the south suburbs with downtown. Local fares within two zones are $1.75 one-way ($15.75 for a 10-ride ticket book).

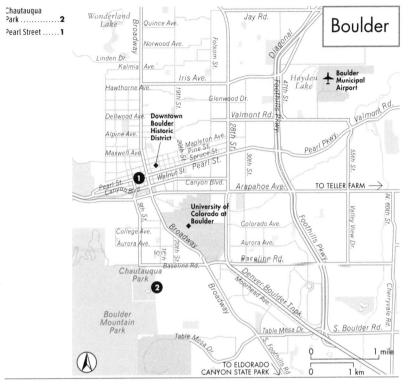

WHERE SHOULD I FOCUS MY ENERGY?

If you're here for 1 day: If this is a quick visit, focus on getting around downtown; wander around LoDo, Larimer Square, and along the 16th Street Mall.

If you're here for 2 days: Include Capitol Hill and as many of its offerings as possible: the Denver Art Museum, the Colorado History Museum *(1300 Broadway, 303/866–3682, www.coloradohistory.org)* or the U.S. Mint *(320 W. Colfax Ave., 303/405–4761, www.usmint.gov).* At night, catch a performance at the Denver Performing Arts Complex.

If you're here for 3 days: If the weather is nice and if you have kids or love amusement parks, add a trip to Elitch Gardens (the Downtown Aquarium is another great option if it's not so nice out), or try to catch a Rockies game at Coors Field. There's also the Denver Zoo and Denver Museum of Nature & Science, and the urban oasis that is City Park.

If you're here for 4 days: Head up to Boulder to explore Pearl Street, with groovy shops, galleries, and outstanding dining options strung along a wide pedestrian mall, or get some exercise in picturesque Chautauqua Park.

CLOSE UP

How to Snack

The 16th Street Mall in Denver makes it easy to grab a quick bite as you sightsee downtown; the pedestrians-only stretch is lined with hot dog carts and vendors purveying everything from cheesesteak sandwiches and boxed lunches to hot soups and homemade ice cream. Green chili, a thick gravy of pork cooked down with chiles, and tacos are a popular fast meal throughout the metro area, as are other forms of fast-casual Mexican; neighborhood taquerias and burrito joints are as common and well attended as churches and bars in other cities. Artisan cheese shops have popped up around town, offering pasteurized and unpasteurized goodies from all over the globe, along with gourmet condiments, baked goods and other items needed to pull off an impromptu picnic as well as a limited amount of prepared foods; some of the more well-known establishments include the **Truffle** (2906 E. 6th Ave., 303/322-7363) between downtown and Cherry Creek and **St. Kilian's** (3211 Lowell Blvd., 303/477-0374) in the Highland neighborhood.

The need for an expanded selection of prepared dishes and organic produce has prompted the opening of several more comprehensive food markets: **Marczyk Fine Foods** (770 E. 17th Ave., 303/894-9499) is a locally owned establishment that specializes in upscale cooked dishes and sous-vide sides (vacuum-packed foods that stay fresh longer), with a well-varied wine shop attached; and **Cook's Fresh Market** (1600 Glenarm Pl., 303/893-2277) on the 16th Street Mall, offers cheeses, a large organic produce section, imported foods, and made-to-order sandwiches that can be eaten at prime people-watching tables on the Mall. Up in Boulder, the massive **Whole Foods** (2905 Pearl St., 303/545-6611) still holds sway in terms of top-notch organic and prepared foods, and its convenient location makes popping in as you head through town a snap.

Farmers' markets run from April through October in Denver on Market Street downtown, in Cherry Creek and City Park, and at the edge of Pearl Street in Boulder and downtown in Estes Park.

If you're here for 5 days: Drive over to Rocky Mountain National Park, where the animals still outnumber the people, and check out the easy, 1-mi Sprague Lake hike.

If you're here for 6 days: Spend some time in Estes Park, RMNP's front door, a small Western town that boasts the historic Stanley Hotel.

If you're here for 7 days or more: Consider a trip to a mountain resort to bike, hike, rock or ice climb, ski, or snowboard.

WHAT ARE THE TOP EXPERIENCES?

The Culture: Once mocked as a cow town, today Denver is considered to be a "now" town, where Broadway shows are premiered outside of New York, the Colorado Ballet keeps everyone on their toes at the Denver Center for the Performing Arts, films are screened at such glitzy events as the Starz Denver Film Festival each November, and major art exhibits move through the newly expanded Denver Art Museum, designed by world-renowned architect Daniel Libeskind. In addition to the mainstream offerings, the area also features multiethnic options, including Museo de Las Americas *(861 Santa Fe Dr., 303/571–4401, www.museo.org)*, a well-regarded tribute to Latino contributions to the region's culture, and the Black American West Museum and Heritage Center *(3091 California St., 303/292–2566, www.blackameri canwestmuseum.com)*, devoted to the history of black cowboys and blacks in the military.

The Great Outdoors: Denver has one of the top urban bike trail systems, with more than 850 mi of paved off-road paths. The off-off-road stuff is pretty impressive, too—within 15 minutes of the city limits (and even closer if you're in Boulder), you can sail your mountain bike down sweet singletrack in the most varied terrain imaginable, from smooth, open-space plains rides to breezy, alpine technical trails. Kayaking can be found right along the Platte River near REI's flagship store (no surprise that this is where they set up shop), and hiking trails abound at destinations such as Red Rocks Amphitheatre, just west of the city, and Boulder's Chautauqua Park and Eldorado Canyon State Park (also a top spot for kayaking and rock climbing). And of course there's Rocky Mountain National Park yet, a magical place where hundreds of thousands of acres yield up mile upon mile of trail ideal for trekking year-round—in boots during warm weather and on skis and snowshoes when the cold sets in.

The Microbrews: It's a rare bar or eatery that doesn't offer some locally brewed product in these parts. Colorado has the second-highest number of breweries in the country (California is number one) and the highest number of microbreweries per capita; the Rockies Brewing Company, one of the first in the country, began production in 1979 and is still going strong. Most folks say the water makes the difference—pure snow melt flowing down from the mountains doesn't need much filtering, and a clean taste means brewers don't need to mess much with the rest of the ingredients. There's something for every palate, from pale ales to stout stouts, including a chili-infused brew at Wynkoop Brewing Company—Denver's first brewpub, which was opened by Denver Mayor John Hickenlooper (it's a wicked elixir that some swear by, while others claim it's an acquired taste). A note of caution: alcohol's effects are stronger at high altitudes, so plan accordingly.

CLAIM TO FAME

Part of Jack Kerouac's classic Beat tome "On the Road" is set in Denver, with its famous passage about arriving in the Queen City of the Plains. "I stumbled along with the most wicked grin of joy in the world, among the bums and beat cowboys of Larimer Street." Main character Dean Moriarty was based on Neal Cassady, who grew up on the street and befriended the writer. Kerouac, who owned a house in Lakewood at one point, spent time in many places around the city, including the still-hopping LoDo jazz club El Chapultepec and the ever-popular burger joint My Brother's Bar, one of the oldest bars in the city.

The Food: The Denver metro area's culinary scene is ethnically diverse and constantly evolving, incorporating a blend of cuisines from the large influx of people who moved to the city from Mexico, California, Texas, the Southwest, and the Midwest, as well as from other countries. Neighborhoods continue to reflect immigrant populations that may not still be predominant; for instance, North Denver is still a stronghold for Italian food, while Federal Boulevard offers Vietnamese and Chinese restaurants that slowly are being outnumbered by Mexican offerings. Green chile—always spelled with an "e" and referring to a pork-chile stew—continues to be a local favorite; it's best smothered on a giant burrito. Red sauce Italian, authentic Vietnamese, and superb sushi, long the top takes on ethnic eats, are slowly being overtaken by seasonal menus that focus on local ingredients, cooked by chefs who are becoming nationally recognized. The area also has a huge number of steak houses, many of which serve another famous Colorado product: bison. If you're up to the challenge, you can also sample some of the West's most famous oddities—delicacies such as Rocky Mountain oysters (bull's testicles) and rattlesnake cakes, along with a wide variety of game.

22

BEST BETS

SIGHTS AND TOURS

ROCKY MOUNTAIN NATIONAL PARK

Fodor's Choice ★ **Rocky Mountain National Park.** Anyone who delights in alpine lakes, mountain peaks, and an abundance of wildlife—not to mention dizzying heights—should consider Rocky Mountain National Park. Here, a single hour's drive leads from a 7,800-foot elevation at park headquarters to the 12,183-foot apex of the twisting and turning Trail Ridge Road. More than 350 mi of hiking trails take you to the park's many treasures: meadows flushed with wildflowers, cool dense forests of lodgepole pine and Engelmann spruce, and the noticeable presence of wildlife, including elk and bighorn sheep. ✉ *1000 U.S. 36, Estes Park, CO, 80517-8397* ☎ *970/586-1206* ⊕ *www.nps.gov/romo.*

DENVER

BUS TOURS **Actually Quite Nice Brew Tours'** 23-seat Brewmobile hauls beer aficionados to the best microbreweries in Metro Denver, which it touts as the "Napa Valley of Brewing."

Gray Line offers the usual expansive and exhaustive coach tours of anything and everything, from shopping in Cherry Creek to visiting Rocky Mountain National Park. Fees range $35–$95.

Contacts **Actually Quite Nice Brew Tours** (☎ *303/431–1440*). **Gray Line** (☎ *800/348–6877* ⊕ *grayline.com*).

WALKING TOURS **Lower Downtown District, Inc.,** runs guided tours of historic Denver. Self-guided walking-tour brochures are available from the Denver Metro Convention and Visitors Bureau.

Contacts **Lower Downtown District, Inc.** (☎ *303/628–5428*).

Fodor's Choice **Denver Art Museum.** Unique displays of Asian, pre-Columbian, Spanish
★ Colonial, and Native American art are the hallmarks of this model
☾ of museum design. Among the museum's regular holdings are John
DeAndrea's sexy, soothing, life-size polyvinyl painting *Linda* (1983);
Claude Monet's dreamy flowerscape *Le Bassin des Nympheas* (1904);
and Charles Deas' red-cowboy-on-horseback *Long Jakes, The Rocky
Mountain Man* (1844). The works are thoughtfully lighted, though
dazzling mountain views through hallway windows sometimes steal
your attention away. Imaginative hands-on exhibits and video corners
will appeal to children; the Adventures in Art Center has hands-on art
classes and exploration for children and adults. With the opening of
the $90.5 million Frederic C. Hamilton building in October 2007, the
museum doubled in size. Designed by architect Daniel Libeskind, who
was selected to design the World Trade Center site in Manhattan, the
addition prompts debate: some to say the glass and titanium design has
ruined the view, while others think the building is a work of art in its
own right. ✉ *100 W. 14th Ave. Pkwy., Civic Center* ☎ *720/865–5000*
⊕ *www.denverartmuseum.org* ✉ *$13, free Sat. for Colorado residents*
☾ *Tues., Thurs., Sat. 10–5, Fri. 10–10, Sun. noon–5.*

Fodor's Choice **Denver Museum of Nature & Science.** Over the past 100 years, the museum
★ has amassed more than 775,000 objects, making it the largest natural
☾ history museum in the western United States. It houses a rich combination of traditional collections—dinosaur remains, animal dioramas,
a mineralogy display, an Egyptology wing—and intriguing hands-on
exhibits. The massive complex also includes an IMAX movie theater and the Gates Planetarium. ✉ *2001 Colorado Blvd., City Park*
☎ *303/322–7009 or 800/925–2250* ⊕ *www.dmns.org* ✉ *Museum
$10, IMAX $8; $15 for combined pass* ☾ *Daily 9–5, IMAX shows at
6 and 7:40* PM *on Fri. and Sat.*

Fodor's Choice **Larimer Square.** Larimer Square is on the oldest street in the city, immor-
★ talized by Jack Kerouac in his seminal book, *On the Road.* It was
saved from the wrecker's ball by a determined preservationist in the
1960s, when the city went demolition-crazy in its eagerness to present
a more youthful image. Much has changed since Kerouac's wander-
ings, as Larimer Square's rough edges have been cleaned up in favor
of upscale retail and chic restaurants. The Square has become a serious late-night party district thanks to spillover from the expanded
LoDo neighborhood and Rockies fans flowing out from the baseball
stadium. ✉ *Larimer and 15th Sts., LoDo* ☎ *303/685–8143* ⊕ *www.
larimersquare.com.*

★ **LoDo.** The Lower Downtown Historic District, the 25-plus square-block
area that was the site of the original 1858 settlement of Denver City,
is nicknamed LoDo. It's home to art galleries, chic shops, nightclubs,
and restaurants ranging from Denver's most upscale to its most down-
home. Since the early 1990s, LoDo has metamorphosed into the city's
cultural center, thanks to its resident avant-garde artists, retailers, and
loft dwellers who have taken over the old warehouses and redbricks.

The handsome **Coors Field** (⊠*Blake and 20th Sts., LoDo*), home of baseball's Colorado Rockies, has further galvanized the area. Its old-fashioned brick and grillwork facade, ornamented with 41 blue, green, and white terra-cotta columbines (the state flower), was designed to blend in with the surrounding Victorian warehouses. As with cuddly Wrigley Field, on the north side of Chicago, Coors Field has engendered a nightlife scene of sports bars, restaurants, and dance clubs. ⊠*From Larimer St. to South Platte River, between 14th and 22nd Sts., LoDo* ⊕*www.lodo.org.*

★ **16th Street Mall.** Outdoor cafés and tempting shops line this pedestrians-only 12-block thoroughfare, shaded by red-oak and locust trees. You can find Denver's best people-watching here, with more than 1,000 chairs set out along its length for taking in the sights. Catch one of the free shuttle buses that run the length of downtown. ⊠*From Broadway to Wynkoop St., LoDo.*

State Capitol. Built in 1886, the capitol was constructed mostly of materials indigenous to Colorado, including marble, granite, and rose onyx. Especially inspiring is the gold-leaf dome, a reminder of the state's mining heritage. ⊠*200 E. Colfax Ave., Capitol Hill* ☎*303/866–2604, 303/866–3834 for dome tours* ⊕*www.Colorado-dome.org* ⊠*Free* ⊙*Bldg., weekdays 7–5:30. Tours, Sept.–May, weekdays 9–2:30; June–Aug., weekdays 9–3:30.*

BOULDER

Pearl Street, between 8th and 20th streets, is the city's hub, an eclectic collection of classy boutiques, consignment shops, eccentric bookstores, art galleries, cafés, bars, and restaurants. A few national chains have hung out their signs among the home-grown businesses along the four-block pedestrian mall, but beyond 11th Street to the west and 15th Street to the east, the milieu evokes the early days of the Pearl Street Mall.

★ For the prettiest views of town, follow Baseline Drive (west from Broadway) up to **Chautauqua Park** (⊠*900 W. Baseline Rd.*), site of the Colorado Music Festival, and a favorite oasis of locals on weekends. Continue farther up Flagstaff Mountain to Panorama Point and Boulder Mountain Park, where people jog, bike, and climb.

★ **Eldorado Canyon State Park,** with its awe-inspiring canyon of steep walls and pine forests, offers outdoor activities for everyone—even birdwatchers and artists. Kayakers get adrenaline rushes on the rapids of

---

HISTORY YOU CAN SEE

Denver was founded in 1858 during the Gold Rush. The settlement was part of the Kansas Territory, and originally was called Denver City after the Territory's governor, James W. Denver. When Colorado was admitted to the Union in 1876 (its nickname is the "Centennial state"), Denver dropped the "City" and was named the capital.

The gold-leaf dome on Denver's circa-1886 State Capitol Building pays tribute to the city's mining heritage. And if you want to see more precious metals, stop in at the city's U.S. Mint, where most U.S. coin currency is made.

South Boulder Creek, while rock climbers scale the world-renowned, vertical, granite canyon walls. Picnickers can choose from 42 spots, and anglers' catches average 8 inches. Hikers have 12 mi of trails to wander. ⊠ *Drive south on Broadway (Hwy. 93) 3 mi to Eldorado Canyon Dr. (Rte. 170). The paved road ends at village of Eldorado Springs. Drive through town to park entrance* ☎ *303/494–3943* ⊕ *www.parks.state. co.us* ⌦ *$7 per vehicle.*

WHERE TO EAT

	WHAT IT COSTS				
	¢	$	$$	$$$	$$$$
AT DINNER	under $8	$8–$12	$13–$18	$19–$25	over $25

Prices are per person for a main course at dinner, excluding sales tax of 4%.

DENVER

$¢$¢ ✕ **Mizuna.** Chef–owner Frank Bonanno knows how to transform but-
Fodor's Choice ter and cream into comforting masterpieces at this cozy, charming eat-
★ ery with warm colors and intimate seating. His menu is reminiscent of California's French Laundry, with quirky dishes such as "liver and onions" (foie gras and a sweet-onion tart), and his Italian heritage has given him the ability to work wonders with red sauce, such as in his inimitable ragú. Be sure to try the griddle cakes for dessert, and expect to be served by the most professional staff in town. ⊠ *225 E. 7th Ave., Central Denver, 80203* ☎ *303/832–4778* ⌲ *Reservations essential* ⊟ *AE, DC, MC, V* ⊘ *Closed Sun. and Mon. No lunch.*

$$$$ ✕ **Restaurant Kevin Taylor.** Elegant doesn't do justice to this restaurant's
Fodor's Choice dining room, a classy, soothing room done in tones of gold and hunter
★ green. Exclusive upholstery, flatware, and dishes add to the upscale attitude, as does the formal service style and a pricey but top-shelf wine list. The contemporary menu has an updated Mediterranean bent underscored by French techniques, with such classics as braised short ribs sharing space with antelope strudel and black truffle baked potatoes. The tasting menu, geared to theatergoers heading to the Denver Performing Arts Complex a block away, gives a rare chance to try chef Taylor's eclectic creations, and the stone-lined wine cellar makes for intimate private dining. ⊠ *1106 14th St., Downtown, 80202* ☎ *303/820–2600* ⌲ *Reservations essential* ⊟ *AE, DC, MC, V* ⊘ *Closed Sun. No lunch.*

$$$–$$$$ ✕ **Rioja.** When chef Jennifer Jasinski left Panzano to open her own
★ place, Denver nearly salivated with anticipation over what she would do. Rioja is the result of Jasinski's intense attention to detail, a tribute to Mediterranean food with contemporary flair, with special focus on Spain and Italy. Her partners in this venture are all women: Beth Gruitch runs the front of the house while sous chef Dana Rodriguez helps in the back, and together this trio makes Gorgonzola ravioli with sugary pears and walnuts in browned butter sing, and crispy angel hair–wrapped shrimp so well melded you can't tell where pasta ends and shrimp begins. Check out the smoked salmon galette and the French

STRANGE BUT TRUE

Denver lays claim to several odd inventions, chief among them the Denver boot, a bizarre car-immobilization contraption that looks like a big yellow lock. The device was created by a Denverite during World War II to keep people from stealing tires to sell (the price of rubber was extremely high at the time); in 1955, the boot came back as a way to halt scofflaws.

Denver also vies for bragging rights to the cheeseburger—in 1935, Louis Ballast received a patent for the tasty item after he accidentally spilled cheddar on his grill at the long-gone Humpty-Dumpty Drive-In on Speer Boulevard. The Denver omelet is another delicious local concoction, with green peppers, onions, diced ham, and cheese mixed into eggs. There are many theories for its inception, but the favored explanation is that Chinese cooks on the railroads put the egg creation on bread (the Western sandwich) as a way to appease workers unwilling to swallow egg foo yong.

toast at brunch. The restaurant is hip and artsy, with exposed brick and blown-glass lighting, arched doorways and textured draperies. The wine list presents riojas galore, and is very well priced for Larimer Square. ⊠*1431 Larimer St., Larimer Square* ☎*303/820–2282* ⚓*Reservations essential* ▭*AE, DC, MC, V.*

$$–$$$$ ✕**Vesta Dipping Grill.** Both the remodeled building and the interior space
★ designed to house this modern grill, named after Vesta, the Roman hearth goddess, have won national architectural awards, and it's easy to see why: The sensual swirls of fabric and copper throughout the room make diners feel as though they're inside a giant work of art, and the clever, secluded banquettes are among the most sought-after seats in town. The menu is clever, too, and the competent grill masters in the kitchen put out expertly cooked meats, fish, and vegetables, all of which can be paired with some of the three-dozen dipping sauces that get their inspiration from chutneys, salsas, mother sauces, and barbecue. The wine list is as cool as the clientele. ⊠*1822 Blake St., LoDo* ☎*303/296–1970* ⚓*Reservations essential* ▭*AE, D, DC, MC, V* ⊗*No lunch.*

¢–$ ✕**My Brother's Bar.** Drop by one of Denver's oldest bars to listen to classical music while inhaling a giant, juicy burger that comes with a plastic tub full of condiments. Laid-back and filled with locals, the inside dining room competes with the fence-lined back patio for popularity, and the beer list is invitingly large. This is one of Denver's most beloved late-nighters, too, serving food until 1:30 AM. ⊠*2376 15th St., Downtown* ☎*303/455–9991* ⚓*Reservations not accepted* ▭*MC, V* ⊗*Closed Sun.*

BOULDER

$$$$ ✕**Flagstaff House.** Sit on the patio at one of Colorado's finest restau-
★ rants and drink in the sublime views of Boulder from the side of Flagstaff Mountain. Executive Chef Mark Monette has fresh fish flown in daily, grows some of the herbs for his cuisine, and is noted for his

exquisite combinations of ingredients—some organic—and fanciful, playful presentations. The menu changes daily, but sample inspirations include ruby red trout with salmon and scallops in caviar butter and watercress sauce; buffalo filet mignon and foie gras Wellington; and Tasmanian king salmon with spicy mustard glaze. The wine list is remarkably comprehensive. ☒*1138 Flagstaff Rd.* ☏*303/442–4640* ⚄*Reservations essential no shorts, t-shirts, or athletic attire* ☰*AE, D, DC, MC, V* ☉*No lunch.*

$$-$$$$ ✕**L'Atelier.** Chef Radek Cerny, who trained with Paul Bocuse, creates
★ delicious French meals lightly influenced by Spanish cuisine. Seafood entrées are his forté, and the red Tasmanian crab salad with oranges is a wonderful starter before an entrée of duck breast rose with cherries. Be sure to save a crust of bread to use as a sippet in the savory sauces before ending with a crunchy florentine garnished with fresh berries. The knowledgeable servers can pair a wine with your meal from the extraordinary wine list that covers all price ranges and vintages. The restaurant is elegant but not ostentatious, with light woods, warm colors, white linens, and Riedel stemware. ☒*1739 Pearl St.* ☏*303/442–1233* ☰*AE, D, MC, V* ☉*No lunch weekends.*

$-$$ ✕**Boulder Dushanbe Teahouse.** Unique to Colorado, this teahouse is a gift
Fodor'sChoice from Boulder's sister city, Dushanbe, Tajikistan. Tajik artisans hand
★ crafted the building in a traditional style that includes ceramic Islamic art and a carved, painted ceiling. The menu presents a culinary cross section of the world; your meal could include such dishes as Spanish seafood paella, Burmese coconut curry, or Tabrizi *kooftah* balls (Persian meatballs with dried fruits, nuts, and herbs in a tomato sauce). The house-tea gingerbread is a favorite. Relax during high tea at 3 PM (reservations required) with one of more than 80 varieties of tea. Creekside patio tables have views of Central Park. Brunch is served on weekends. ☒*1770 13th St.80302* ☏*303/442–4993* ☰*AE, D, MC, V.*

WHERE TO STAY

WHAT IT COSTS					
	¢	$	$$	$$$	$$$$
FOR 2 PEOPLE	under $80	$80–$120	$121–$170	$171–$230	over $230

Prices are for two people in a standard double room in high season, excluding service charges and 10.75% tax.

DENVER

$$$$ 🏨**Brown Palace.** This grande dame of Colorado lodging has hosted pub-
Fodor'sChoice lic figures from President Eisenhower to the Beatles since it first opened
★ its doors in 1892. The details are exquisite: a dramatic nine-story lobby is topped with a glorious stained-glass ceiling, and the Victorian rooms have sophisticated wainscoting and art deco fixtures. The hotel pays equal attention to modern necessities, such as high-speed Web access and cordless telephones. The Churchill cigar bar sells rare cigars and single-malt scotches. In 2005 a $2 million spa was added (in a space that originally held a spa when the hotel first opened), with Swiss showers

and a natural rock waterfall that draws from the hotel's artesian well. ⌂*321 17th St., Downtown, 80202* ☎*303/297–3111 or 800/321–2599* ⊕*www.brownpalace.com* ⬮*230 rooms, 25 suites* ⬮*In-room: refrigerator (some), VCRs (some), Ethernet. In-hotel: 4 restaurants, room service, bars, gym, spa, concierge, laundry service, public Wi-Fi, parking (fee), no-smoking rooms* ⊟*AE, D, DC, MC, V.*

22

$$$–$$$$
★
🖼 **Hotel Monaco.** Celebrities and business travelers check into this hip property, which occupies the historic 1917 Railway Exchange Building and the 1937 Art Moderne Title Building, for the modern perks and art deco–meets–classic French style. The unabashedly colorful guest rooms, in vivid reds and yellows, have original art, custom headboards, glass-front armoires, and CD players. The service is similarly a cut above: room service is available around the clock, pets are welcome, and guests without pets are given the complimentary company of a goldfish. The hotel's mascot, a Jack Russell terrier named Lily Sopris, is one of Denver's best-known canines. ⌂*1717 Champa St., Downtown, 80202* ☎*303/296–1717 or 800/397–5380* ⊕*www.monaco-denver. com* ⬮*157 rooms, 32 suites* ⬮*In-room: refrigerator, Ethernet, Wi-Fi. In-hotel: restaurant, room service, bar, gym, spa, concierge, laundry service, public Internet, parking (fee), some pets allowed, no-smoking rooms* ⊟*AE, D, DC, MC, V.*

$$–$$$
Fodor'sChoice
★
🖼 **Oxford Hotel.** During the Victorian era this hotel was an elegant fixture on the Denver landscape, and civilized touches like complimentary shoe shines, afternoon sherry, and morning coffee remain. The charming and comfortable rooms are furnished with French- and English-period antiques and the Cruise Room bar re-creates an art deco ocean liner. Art galleries are nearby. The popular McCormicks Restaurant ($$$) serves excellent seafood and a delicious Sunday brunch. ⌂*1600 17th St., LoDo, 80202* ☎*303/628–5400 or 800/228–5838* ⊕*www. theoxfordhotel.com* ⬮*80 rooms* ⬮*In-room: VCRs (some), Ethernet, Wi-Fi. In-hotel: restaurant, room service, bars, gym, spa, public Wi-Fi, parking (fee), no-smoking rooms* ⊟*AE, D, DC, MC, V.*

BOULDER

$$$
★
🖼 **The Bradley Boulder Inn.** Elegant and contemporary, this downtown inn has a spacious great room with warm tones and an inviting stone fireplace. Local artwork is on display throughout. Each room is individually decorated, but all have flat-screen TVs, 400 thread-count cotton duvets and bed linens, and Aveda products. Some rooms have Jacuzzi tubs, fireplaces, and/or balconies. Breakfasts feature fresh fruit parfaits, French toast casserole, quiche, and excellent coffee. ⌂*2040 16th St., 80302* ☎*303/545–5200 or 800/858–5811* ⊕*www.the brad leyboulder.com* ⬮*12 rooms* ⬮*In-room: DVD, ethernet, Wi-Fi. In-hotel: no elevator, parking (no fee), no kids under 12, no-smoking rooms.* ⊟*AE, MC, V* ⍟*BP.*

$$$
Fodor'sChoice
★
🖼 **Hotel Boulderado.** The gracious lobby of this elegant 1909 beauty has a soaring stained-glass ceiling, and the mezzanine beckons with romantic nooks galore. When choosing a room, opt for the old building, with spacious quarters filled with period antiques and reproductions. The new wing is plush and comfortable but has less Victorian character. Rooms with mountain views are available on request. The restaurant,

ON THE WAY

Mesa Verde National Park. The dwellings of the Ancestral Puebloan people, also known as the Anasazi, are well worth the 266-mi drive southwest from Denver (35 mi west of Durango), if only to imagine a way of life unlike anything you've ever seen before—elaborate homes built into precarious cliffs, surrounded by stunning canyons. U.S. 160, 970/529–4465, www.nps.go/meve.	**Great Sand Dunes National Park & Preserve.** Located 212 mi southwest of Denver, these dramatic, 750-foot-high sand dunes cover 55 square mi. You can camp next to or on them, snowboard them, wade in the Medano Creek that runs next to them during nondrought times, or just sit for hours and watch as their shapes shift with the Sangre de Cristo Mountains rising in the background to the east. 11500 Rte. 150, Mosca, 719/378–2312, www.nps.gov/grsa.

Q's ($$$$), serves stylish contemporary American cuisine. The Catacombs Blues Bar is always hopping and has live music three nights a week. Guests have access to the nearby health club, One Boulder Fitness. The downtown hotel is one block from the Pearl Street Mall. ✉*2115 13th St., 80302* ☎*303/442–4344 or 800/433 4344* ⊕*www. boulderado.com* ⇆*160 rooms* ⌂*In-room: Wi-Fi. In-hotel: 3 restaurants, bars, public Wi-Fi, no-smoking rooms* ▤*AE, D, DC, MC, V.*

NIGHTLIFE & THE ARTS

DENVER

★ The **Denver Performing Arts Complex** is a huge, impressively high-tech group of theaters connected by a soaring glass archway to a futuristic symphony hall. The complex, which occupies a four-block area, hosts more events than any other performing arts center in the world. ✉*Box office, 14th and Curtis Sts.,* LoDo ☎*303/893–4000* ⊕*www. denvercenter.org.*

The **Wynkoop Brewing Co.** (✉*1634 18th St.,* LoDo ☎*303/297–2700*)is now more famous for its owner—Denver Mayor John Hickenlooper—than for its brews, food, or ambience. But it remains one of the city's best-known bars—a relaxing, slightly upscale, two-story joint filled with halfway-decent bar food, the usual pool tables, and games and beers of all types. It has anchored LoDo since it was a pre-Coors Field warehouse district.

El Chapultepec (✉*1962 Market St.,* LoDo ☎*303/295–9126*)is a cramped, fluorescent-lighted, bargain-basement Mexican dive. Still, the limos parked outside hint at its enduring popularity: this is where Ol' Blue Eyes used to pop in, and where visiting musicians, including the Marsalis brothers, continue to jam after hours.

Of Denver's numerous smoky hangouts, the most popular is the regally restored **Bluebird Theater** (✉*3317 E. Colfax Ave., Capitol Hill*

☎303/322–2308), which showcases local and national acts, emphasizing rock, hip-hop, ambient, and the occasional evening of cinema.

BOULDER

Fodor's Choice ★ CU's Mary Rippon Outdoor Theater is the venue for the annual **Colorado Shakespeare Festival** (☎303/492–0554 ⊕*www.coloradoshakes.org*), presenting the bard's comedies and tragedies from early July to mid-August.

SHOPPING

DENVER

In a pleasant, predominantly residential neighborhood 2 mi from downtown, the **Cherry Creek** shopping district has retail blocks and an enclosed mall.

Fodor's Choice ★ **Tattered Cover.** A must for all bibliophiles, the Tattered Cover may be the best bookstore in the United States, not only for the near-endless selection of volumes (more than 400,000 on two floors at the new Colfax Avenue location and 300,000 in LoDo) and helpful, knowledgeable staff, but also for the incomparably refined atmosphere. ⊠*2526 E. Colfax Ave., Capitol Hill* ☎*303/322–7727* ⊠*1628 16th St., LoDo* ☎*303/436–1070.*

★ **REI.** Denver's REI flagship store's 94,000 square feet are packed with all stripes of outdoors gear and some special extras: a climbing wall, a mountain-bike track, a white-water chute, and a "cold room" for gauging the protection provided by coats and sleeping bags. ⊠*1416 Platte St., Jefferson Park* ☎*303/756–3100.*

BOULDER

Fodor's Choice ★ Boulder's **Pearl Street Mall** (⊠*Pearl St. between 11th and 15th Sts.*)is a shopping extravaganza, with upscale boutiques, art galleries, bookstores, shoe shops, and stores with home and garden furnishings. Street musicians and magicians, caricaturists, and buskers with lovebirds are magnets for locals and visitors.Stroll along **Twenty-Ninth Street** (⊠*29th St. between Arapahoe Ave. and Pearl St.*), Boulder's newest area to shop, and pick up a pair of shoes, some outdoor gear, a funny greeting card, or a present to bring home for your pooch. The mall has plenty of nationally known clothiers, a bookstore, a stationer, coffee shops, and eateries.**University Hill** (or "the Hill"), centered around 13th Street between College Avenue and Pennsylvania Street, is a great place for hip duds, new and used CDs, and CU apparel.

SPORTS & THE OUTDOORS

DENVER

The **Denver Parks Department** (☎720/913–0696 ⊕*www.denvergov.org/Parks*)has suggestions for bicycling and jogging paths throughout the metropolitan area's 250 parks, including the popular Cherry Creek and Chatfield Reservoir State Recreation areas. With more than 400 mi of off-road paths in and around the city, cyclists can move easily between urban and rural settings.

*Fodor's*Choice ★ Fifteen miles southwest of Denver, **Red Rocks Park and Amphitheatre** is a breathtaking, 70-million-year-old wonderland of vaulting oxblood-and-cinnamon-color sandstone spires. The outdoor music stage is in a natural 9,000-seat amphitheater (with perfect acoustics, as only nature could have designed). The Trading Post loop hiking trail, at 6,280 feet, is 1.4 mi long and quite narrow with drop-offs and steep grades. Allow about two hours. The trail closes one-half hour before sunset. The park is open from 5 AM to 11 PM daily. 🕈 *I-70 west to exit 259, turn left to park entrance* ⊠ *Morrison* ⊕ *www.redrocksonline.com.*

> **VITAL STATS**
>
> ■ State motto: Nil sine numine, "Nothing without providence"
>
> ■ State flower: Rocky Mountain columbine
>
> ■ State fossil: Stegosaurus
>
> ■ State folk dance: The square dance
>
> ■ State song: "Where the Columbines Grow," written and composed by A.J. Flynn
>
> ■ State song #2: "Rocky Mountain High," lyrics by John Denver, music by Mike Taylor

BOULDER

☾ At the southeast end of Lake Granby, the **Indian Peaks Wilderness Area** is great for hiking. The area around the Monarch Lake is popular with families for the selection of trails and the views of the Indian Peaks and the Continental Divide. Trails range in distance from 1.5 to 10.8 mi one-way. You can get a day pass ($5) from the staff or at the self-serve pay station. ⊠ *Sulphur Ranger District, Arapaho National Forest* ☎ *970/887–4100* ⊕ *www.fs.fed.us/r2/arnf/.*

With a 1,600-foot vertical drop (the longest run is 3 mi), **Eldora Mountain Resort** has 53 trails, 12 lifts, and 680 acres; 25 mi (40 km) of groomed Nordic track; and four terrain parks accommodating different ability levels for snowboarders and skiers. ⊠ *5 mi west of Nederland off Hwy. 119* ☎ *303/440–8700* ⊕ *www.eldora.com* 🎿 *$59* ☾ *Mid-Nov.–mid-Apr., weekdays 9–4; weekends and holidays 8:30–4.*

VISITOR INFORMATION

Denver Metro Convention and Visitors Bureau (⊠ *1600 California St., LoDo, Denver, 80202* ☎ *303/892–1112 or 800/393–8559* ⊕ *www.denver.org*).

Boulder Convention & Visitors Bureau (⊠ *2440 Pearl St., Boulder, 80302* ☎ *303/442–2911 or 800/444–0447* ⊕ *www.bouldercoloradousa.com*).

Santa Fe, Taos & Albuquerque

Taos, New Mexico

WORD OF MOUTH

"Definitely go to a pueblo! Preferably after visiting the Cultural Center in Albuquerque."

—laurieb_nyny

"Santa Fe is a compact and easy town to walk, so I wouldn't worry about a bus tour. Pick up a tourist map and you should be fine."

—beachbum

EXPLORING SANTA FE, TAOS & ALBUQUERQUE

Santa Fe is 400 mi south of Denver, via I–25; Albuquerque is 460 mi northeast of Phoenix, via I–17 to I–40; Santa Fe is 60 mi northeast of Albuquerque via I–25; Taos is 70 mi northeast of Santa Fe via U.S. 285 and Hwy. 68.

By Andrew Collins

New Mexico has always marched to its own beat. It's only been a part of the Union since 1912. It has the highest percentage of Hispanic Americans in the country, and the second-highest percentage of Native Americans. In no other state in the contiguous United States will you encounter such a wholly distinct culture, especially in terms of art, music, and food. The North-Central part of the state, sometimes referred to as the northern Rio Grande Valley, captures much of the state's essence—it's home to New Mexico's most-visited cities and town: Santa Fe, the state capital; Taos, the town with the state's highest mountain peaks; and Albuquerque, the state's most populous city and also its transportation and economic hub.

It's in the Rio Grande Valley that indigenous people have lived in pueblos for centuries, where Spanish conquistadors first established settlements in the 1500s, and where entrepreneurs from the United States first traveled for trade purposes in the mid-19th century along the Old Santa Fe Trail. From Albuquerque to Taos, along a roughly 125-mi stretch of the Rio Grande, you can encounter some of the state's—and the nation's—most spectacular high-desert and mountain scenery, most esteemed art museums and galleries, and swankiest small hotels and country inns, most of them clad in the distinctive adobe-brick facing for which the region is famous.

WHO WILL ESPECIALLY LOVE THIS TRIP?

Artists & Art Collectors: New Mexico draws all kinds of vibrant spirits who visit, revisit, and relocate, but the state is particularly a magnet for artists. Santa Fe, with its dozens of prestigious galleries and art museums, claims the third-largest art market in the nation, after New York City and Los Angeles. The much-smaller town of Taos claims a similarly exciting gallery scene, and countless small villages in the northern Rio Grande Valley—from Abiqui (where Georgia O'Keeffe lived) and to Madrid (pronounced Mad-drid), hold studio tours once or twice a year, when local artists open their home studios to the public.

Hikers: Six national forests cover many thousands of acres around New Mexico, as do 34 state parks and a number of other national and state monuments and recreation areas, many of them in the Albuquerque, Santa Fe, and Taos corridor. The ski areas make for great mountaineering during the warmer months, and the state's many Indian ruins are also laced with trails. Highlights in this area include Kasha-Katuwe Tent Rocks National Monument, with its short hike past bizarre rock formations; Wheeler Peak, the state's highest point at 13,161 feet, which rewards visitors with stunning views of the Taos Ski Valley; and

TOP 5 REASONS TO GO

The Art Scene: Santa Fe all by itself has one of the most vibrant and prolific art-gallery scenes in the country—throw in the many galleries in Taos and the emerging scene in Albuquerque, and you have an art lover's paradise.

Adobe Inns and B&Bs: North-Central New Mexico abounds with cozy, thick-walled adobe accommodations. Many have rooms or private casitas containing beam ceilings, wood-burning kiva (beehive-shape) fireplaces, and colorful tile work.

The Great Outdoors: Mountainous, pristine, and sparsely populated northern New Mexico ranks among the nation's most stunning landscapes, a land of first-rate hiking, skiing, mountain-biking, white-water rafting, and wildlife-watching.

The Tri-Cultural History: In no other state will you find such a distinctive heritage, reflected in everything from art and architecture to music and food. Three cultures have deep roots: New Mexico has been home to indigenous inhabitants for more than 1,000 years; Spanish conquistadors settled here in the late 1500s; and Anglo traders arrived via the Old Santa Fe Trail in the mid-19th century.

The Food: New Mexico has its own brand of local cuisine, blending indigenous and Spanish recipes and ingredients, with an emphasis on fiery hot green and red chilies. Many contemporary chefs have given the region's culinary scene an inventive spin in recent years.

Albuquerque's challenging La Luz Trail, which climbs 9 mi (and an elevation of more than 3,000 feet) to Sandia Crest.

Skiers: Taos Ski Valley is distinctive not only for its expert slopes but also because it's one of the world's few resorts that does now allow snowboarding. Also close to Taos, there's Angel Fire Resort, which is nestled in the Sangre de Cristos. Santa Fe Ski Area offers a nice range of beautifully groomed trails and spectacular views, and there's also fine skiing at the underrated Pajarito Mountain Ski Area in Los Alamos, and at affordable Sandia Peak Ski area, just outside Albuquerque.

Photographers: New Mexico's spectacular landscapes and crystal-clear atmosphere can help just about any amateur with a decent camera produce professional-quality photos. Many of the common scenes around the state seem tailor-made for photography sessions: terra-cotta-hued adobe buildings against azure blue skies, souped-up low-rider automobiles cruising along wide-open highways, rustic fruit and chili stands by the side of the road. In summer, dramatic rain clouds contrasted with vermillion sunsets create memorable images. Come fall, shoot the foliage of cottonwood and aspen trees, and in winter, the state's snow-capped mountains cut a dashing figure.

Progressive Minds: The communities along the northern Rio Grande Valley, from Albuquerque clear up to Taos, have long been a haven of unconventional, open-minded, and spiritually inclined travelers. New Agers have long appreciated the area's ethereal scenery and weather

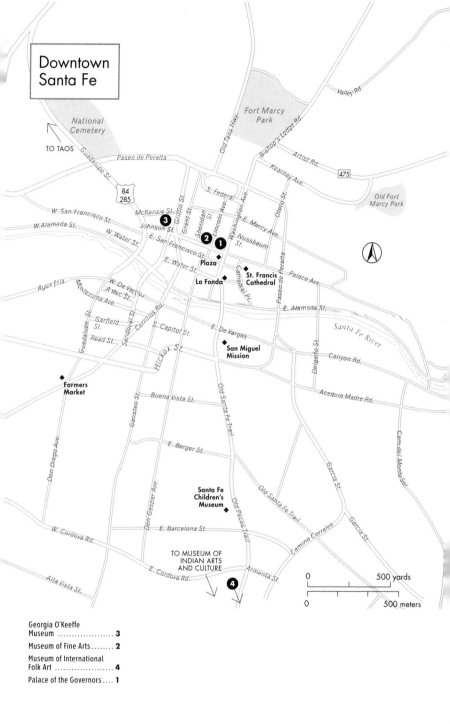

Downtown Santa Fe

National Cemetery

TO TAOS

Fort Marcy Park

Valley Rd.

Bishop's Lodge Rd.

Artist Rd.

475

Old Fort Marcy Park

Paseo de Peralta

Old Taos Hwy.

Kearney Ave.

84 285

Guadalupe St.

W. San Francisco St.

McKenzie St.

S. Federal St.

Griffin St.

Grant St.

Sheridan St.

Lincoln Ave.

Washington Ave.

E. Marcy Ave.

Grant St.

W. Alameda St.

Johnson St.

E. San Francisco St.

3

2

1

Nussbaum St.

W. Water St.

W. De Vargas St.

E. Water St.

Plaza

La Fonda

St. Francis Cathedral

Garfield Pl.

Palace Ave.

Paseo de Peralta

Agua Fria

A Vec St.

Montezuma Ave.

Garfield St.

Sandoval St.

Cerrillos Rd.

S. Capitol St.

E. De Vargas

E. Alameda St.

Santa Fe River

Guadalupe St.

Read St.

Hickox St.

San Miguel Mission

Delgado St.

Canyon Rd.

Farmers Market

Buena Vista St.

Gallisteo St.

Old Santa Fe Trail

Acequia Madre Rd.

Cam. del Monte Sol

Don Diego Ave.

Don Gaspar Ave.

E. Berger St.

Santa Fe Children's Museum

Old Pecos Trail

Old Santa Fe Trail

Garcia St.

Garcia St.

W. Cordova Rd.

E. Barcelona St.

Camino Corrales

Armenta St.

4

TO MUSEUM OF INDIAN ARTS AND CULTURE

E. Cordova Rd.

Alta Vista St.

| 0 | 500 yards |
| 0 | 500 meters |

and rich ties to indigenous culture and spirituality. Gays and lesbians have been drawn to the area for decades, staying in the numerous gay-friendly B&Bs. And politically, Santa Fe, Taos, and Albuquerque have earned a reputation for liberal views and social awareness that's unusual compared with many other parts of the Southwest.

(Fiery) **Food Lovers:** In a land where the official state question, "red or green?," refers to which color chili you favor with your meal, it's easy to see that New Mexicans take eating—and chilies—seriously. Food has become one of the great draws in Santa Fe, Taos, and Albuquerque, and talented, creative chefs now helm the top restaurants in these parts, dreaming up inventive renderings of New Mexico cuisine.

WHEN IS THE BEST TIME TO VISIT?

The cool, dry climates of Santa Fe and Taos are a lure in summer, as is the skiing in Taos and Santa Fe in winter. Christmas is a wonderful time to be in New Mexico because of Native American ceremonies as well as the Hispanic religious folk plays, special foods, and musical events. Santa Fe is at its most festive at this time, with incense and piñon smoke sweetening the air and the darkness of winter illuminated by thousands of farolitos. These glowing paper-bag lanterns line walkways, doorways, rooftops, and walls. With glowing lights reflected on the snow, Santa Fe is never lovelier.

Most ceremonial dances at the pueblos occur in summer, early fall, and at Christmas and Easter. Other major events—including the Santa Fe Opera, Chamber Music Festival, and Indian and Spanish markets—are geared to the heavy tourist season of July and August. The Santa Fe Fiesta and New Mexico State Fair in Albuquerque are held in September, and the Albuquerque International Balloon Fiesta in October.

Hotel rates are generally highest during the peak summer season but fluctuate less than those in most major resort areas. If you plan to come in summer, be sure to make reservations in advance. You can avoid the heaviest crowds by coming in spring or fall.

HOW SHOULD I GET THERE?

DRIVING
North-Central New Mexico is relatively isolated, a full day's drive from major metro areas in the neighboring states of Arizona, Utah, Colorado, Oklahoma, and Texas. Unless you're a big fan of long road-trips (the scenery getting here is spectacular, especially coming from Arizona, Utah, and Colorado), it generally makes the most sense to fly here.

FLYING
The region's main air gateway is Albuquerque International Sunport (ABQ), which is served by virtually all of the nation's major domestic airlines as well as some smaller regional ones; there are direct flights from all major West Coast and Midwest cities and a number of big East

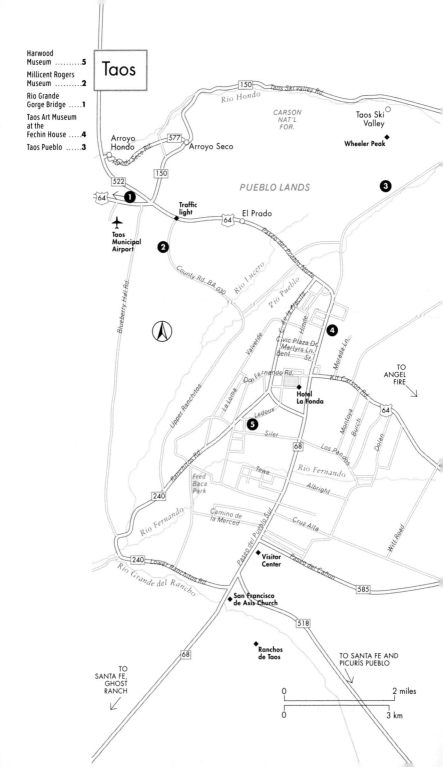

Taos

Harwood
Museum

150   Taos Ski Valley Rd.

Rio Hondo

CARSON NAT'L FOR.

Taos Ski Valley

577

Arroyo Hondo

Hondo Seco Rd.

Arroyo Seco

Wheeler Peak

522

150

PUEBLO LANDS

3

64

1

Traffic light

64   El Prado

Taos Municipal Airport

2

County Rd. BA-030

Rio Lucero

Paseo del Pueblo Norte

Rio Pueblo

Blueberry Hill Rd.

Te Vista Martin

Hinde

4

Civic Plaza Dr.
Martyrs Ln.

Bent St.

Morada Ln.

TO ANGEL FIRE

Valverde

Don Fernando Rd.

Kit Carson Rd.

64

Upper Ranchitos

La Loma

Hotel La Fonda

Montoya

Burch

Dolan

Ledoux

5

Siler

68   Los Pandos

Ranchitos Rd.

Tewa

Rio Fernando

Fred Baca Park

Albright

240

Witt Road

Camino de la Merced

Paseo del Pueblo Sur

Cruz Alta

Rio Fernando

240   Lower Ranchitos Rd.

Visitor Center

Paseo del Cañon

Rio Grande del Rancho

585

San Francisco de Asis Church

518

68

Ranchos de Taos

TO SANTA FE AND PICURÍS PUEBLO

TO SANTA FE, GHOST RANCH

0   2 miles

0   3 km

CLOSE UP

How to Snack

In a state with plenty of open ranching land and an appreciation for no-nonsense, home-style eating, it's no surprise that locals debate intensely about where to find the best burger in town.

In New Mexico the preferred meal is a green-chili cheeseburger—a culinary delight that's available just about anyplace that serves hamburgers. Burgers served in tortillas or sopaipillas also earn plenty of kudos, and increasingly, you can find establishments serving terrific buffalo, lamb, turkey, and even tuna and veggie burgers. You don't have to dine at a no-frills fast-food shack to find a great burger, but it does tend to be these informal, quirky establishments that cultivate the most loyal following. Try these favorites:

With about 75 locations throughout the state, the New Mexico chain

Blake's Lotaburger (www.lotaburger.com) has become a cult favorite for its juicy Angus beef burgers. Just order at the counter, take a number, and wait for your meal (which is best accompanied by a bag of seasoned fries). A friendly and funky little roadhouse about a 15-minute drive south of Santa Fe, Bobcat Bite is a much-loved source of outstanding green-chili burgers. Loyalists order them rare. Feasting on a burger at the Mineshaft Tavern (2846 Hwy. 14, Madrid, 505/473-0743) is a big reason to stop in the tiny village of Madrid, as you drive up the fabled Turquoise Trail from Albuquerque to Santa Fe. This rollicking old bar serves particularly hefty and filling patties. Albuquerque's Casa de Benavidez has long captured the fancies of burger aficionados with its delicious burger wrapped inside a fluffy sopaipilla.

Coast cities. From here it's an easy 60-minute drive to Santa Fe, or a 2½-hour drive to Taos (shuttle services are available).

TRAIN

Amtrak *(800/872–7245, www.amtrak.com)* makes stops in the small town of Lamy (near Santa Fe) and downtown Albuquerque on its Southwest Chief run between Chicago and Los Angeles.

HOW DO I GET AROUND?

BY CAR

A car is your best way to get around the region, whether traveling among North-Central New Mexico's main cities, or even exploring them in depth. You can see much of downtown Santa Fe and Taos on foot or using buses, but in Albuquerque, a car is really a necessity for any serious touring and exploring.

WHERE SHOULD I FOCUS MY ENERGY?

If you're here for 1 day: With just a day, spend your time in the heart of Santa Fe, exploring the Plaza and the top museums around it, the Palace of the Governors, the Museum of Fine Arts, and the Georgia O'Keeffe Museum.

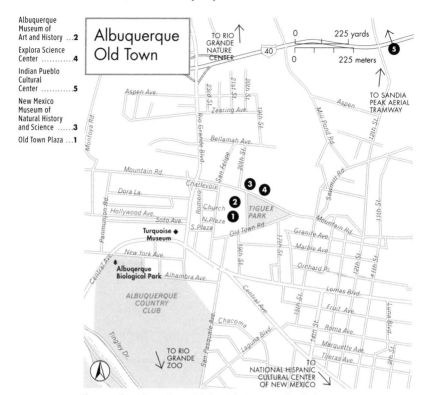

If you're here for 2 days: Stick with Santa Fe both days, using your second day to wander the art galleries and shops along Canyon Road, one or two of the museums at Museum Hill (if time is short, make it the Museum of International Folk Art), and take in a hike at the Randall Davey Audubon Center or up near the Santa Ski Basin.

If you're here for 3 days: Spend a night in Taos, taking a full day to get here via the spectacular High Road from Santa Fe—stop in Chimayó for lunch and a bit of shopping, as well as visiting the famed El Santuario de Chimayó.

If you're here for 4 days: Spend two nights in Taos, two in Santa Fe. With the extra time in Taos, visit Taos Pueblo, the Millicent Rogers Museum, the Harwood Museum, and the shops around Taos Plaza

If you're here for 5 days: Add a night in Albuquerque, giving yourself time to explore the Old Town area, tour the Albuquerque Museum of Art and History, and check out the city's vibrant Nob Hill district.

If you're here for 6 days: Give yourself two full nights in Albuquerque, using the extra time to take the Sandia Peak Aerial Tramway, visit the Anderson-Abruzzo International Balloon Museum, and travel the Turquoise Trail between here and Santa Fe, making a stop in the village of Madrid to shop for art and crafts.

CLAIM TO FAME

The one aspect of local pride that seems to surprise most visitors is the degree to which people here seem to cherish living on unpaved roads. In fact, Santa Fe has a higher percentage of unpaved roads than any other U.S. capital city. In Taos, you can find that the vast majority of roads outside the main commercial areas are unpaved, and this is doubly true for the many small villages and towns strung along the roads between Taos and Santa Fe, and even down toward Albuquerque.

In Albuquerque itself, paved roads are actually the norm, but up in the most exclusive sections of the city's Northeast Heights area, yet again, it's common to find roads without pavement. So what gives? Many people in these parts have horses, which are much happier trotting on dirt than pavement. But more often, dirt roads are associated with living off the beaten path—they underscore the insularity, long history, rural character, and outdoorsy nature of the Rio Grande Valley.

If you're here for 7 days or more: With at least a week, you can spend at least two or three days in Albuquerque and Taos, and three to five days in Santa Fe, exploring not only the major sights in each community but also some of the fascinating villages and attractions reached on easy day-trips from these three communities, such as Abiquiú, Los Alamos, and Bandelier National Monument.

WHAT ARE THE TOP EXPERIENCES?

Peak Moments: With nearly 50 peaks towering higher than 12,000 feet, New Mexico is truly a wonderland for people who love to play in the mountains. The southern spine of the Rocky Mountain range, known as the Sangre de Cristos, runs right down through the center of the state, looming over Taos and Santa Fe. The stunning Sandia Mountains face the city of Albuquerque, and similarly beautiful peaks of the Jémez Mountains overlook Los Alamos.

Art Museums: Outside of major urban centers like New York, Chicago, and Washington, DC, the Rio Grande Valley offers perhaps the best selection of truly stellar art museums in the country. It's here over the past century or so that literally thousands of professional artists have honed their craft, and in museums in Santa Fe, Taos, and Albuquerque (recommendations follow in "Best Bets") you can admire the works of not just local masters but major international talents.

Pueblos & Indigenous Sites: Nowhere in the United States will you find communities that have been continuously inhabited for a longer period than the oldest pueblos of New Mexico, Acoma, and Taos. Acoma, which you can reach as a side trip from Albuquerque, has been a living, working community for more than 1,000 years—the cliff-top city here is perhaps the most dramatically situated pueblo in the state, and a must-see attraction. Taos Pueblo also dates back more than a millennium.

BEST BETS

SIGHTS AND TOURS

ALBUQUERQUE

Fodor's Choice **Albuquerque Museum of Art and History.** This modern structure, which
★ underwent a spectacular 40,000-square-foot expansion in 2004, houses
the largest collection of Spanish-colonial artifacts in the nation, along
with relics of the city's birth and development. The centerpiece of the
colonial exhibit is a pair of life-size models of Spanish conquistadors
in original chain mail and armor. The sculpture garden contains 45
works by 20th-century southwestern artists that include Glenna Goo-
dacre, Michael Naranjo, and Luís Jiménez. ⊠*2000 Mountain Rd. NW,
Old Town* ☎*505/243–7255* ⊕*www.albuquerquemuseum.com* ☞*$4*
☉*Tues.–Sun. 9–5.*

☼ **Explora Science Center.** Albuquerque's cultural corridor received another
jewel in 2003, when this imaginatively executed science museum
opened right across from the New Mexico Museum of Natural History
and Science. Explora bills itself as an all-ages attraction, but there's no
question that many of the hands-on exhibits—from a high-wire bicycle
to kinetic sculpture display—are geared especially to children. ⊠*1701
Mountain Rd. NW, Old Town* ☎*505/224–8300* ⊕*www.explora.mus.
nm.us* ☞*$7* ☉*Mon.–Sat. 10–6, Sun. noon–6.*

★ **Indian Pueblo Cultural Center.** The multilevel semicircular design at this
☼ museum was inspired by Pueblo Bonito, the prehistoric ruin in Chaco
Canyon in northwestern New Mexico. In the upper-level alcove, each of
the state's 19 pueblos has a space devoted to its particular arts and crafts.
Lower-level exhibits trace the history of the Pueblo people. Youngsters
can touch Native American pottery, jewelry, weaving, tools, and dried
corn at the Hands-On Corner and also draw petroglyph designs and
design pots. ⊠*2401 12th St. NW, Los Duranes* ☎*505/843–7270 or
800/766–4405* ⊕*www.indianpueblo.org* ☞*$6* ☉*Daily 9–5.*

Fodor's Choice **National Hispanic Cultural Center of New Mexico.** A showcase for Latino
★ culture and genealogy in Albuquerque's old Barelas neighborhood,
this dramatic, contemporary space contains several art galleries and
performance venues, a 10,000-volume genealogical research center
and library, a restaurant, and a television studio. ⊠*1701 4th St. SW,
at Bridge St., Barelas* ☎*505/246–2261* ⊕*www.nhccnm.org* ☞*$3*
☉*Tues.–Sun. 10–5.*

☼ **New Mexico Museum of Natural History and Science.** The world of wonders
at Albuquerque's most popular museum includes the simulated volcano
(with a river of bubbling hot lava flowing beneath the see-through glass
floor), the frigid Ice Age cave, and the world-class dinosaur exhibit
hall. The Evolator—short for Evolution Elevator—a six-minute high-
tech ride, uses video, sound, and motion to whisk you through 35
million years of New Mexico's geological history. ⊠*1801 Mountain
Rd. NW, Old Town* ☎*505/841–2800* ⊕*www.nmnaturalhistory.org*
☞*Museum $6, DynaTheater $6, planetarium $6; combination ticket*

for any 2 attractions $11, for any 3 attractions $16 ⊙ *Daily 9–5.*

Fodor'sChoice ★ **Old Town Plaza.** An oasis of tranquility, the plaza is filled with shade trees, wrought-iron benches, a graceful white gazebo, and strips of grass. Roughly 200 shops, restaurants, cafés, galleries, and several cultural sites in *placitas* (small plazas) and lanes surround Old Town Plaza. The scents of green chili, enchiladas, and burritos hang in the air. During fiestas Old Town comes alive with mariachi bands and dancing señoritas. Event schedules and maps, which contain a list of public restrooms, are available at the **Old Town Visitors Center** (✉ *303 Romero St. NW, Old Town* ☎ *505/243–3215*), across the street from San Felipe de Neri Catholic Church. Center is open daily, typically 9–4:30 but usually a bit later in summer.

Established in 1706, Albuquerque's bustling Old Town has been a center of commerce and social life ever since. Most of the historic adobe buildings on the Plaza contain shops, galleries, and restaurants today, but you can escape from the crowds in the tranquil San Felipe de Neri Catholic Church, erected in 1793.

★ **Sandia Peak Aerial Tramway.** Tramway cars climb 2.7 mi up the steep western face of the Sandias, giving you a close-up view of red rocks and tall trees—it's the world longest aerial tramway. From the observation deck at the 10,378-foot summit you can see Santa Fe to the northeast and Los Alamos to the northwest.

✉ *10 Tramway Loop NE, Far Northeast Heights* ☎ *505/856–7325* ⊕ *www.sandiapeak.com* 🎫 *$15* ⊙ *Memorial Day–Labor Day, daily 9–9; Sept.–May, daily 9–8.*

SANTA FE

★ **Georgia O'Keeffe Museum.** One of many East Coast artists who visited New Mexico in the first half of the 20th century, O'Keeffe returned to live and paint here, eventually emerging as the demigoddess of Southwestern art. ✉ *217 Johnson St.* ☎ *505/995–1000* ⊕ *www.okeeffemuseum.org* 🎫 *$8, free Fri. 5–8* PM ⊙ *Daily Sat.–Thurs. 10–5, Fri. 10–8.*

Fodor'sChoice ★ **Museum of Fine Arts.** Designed by Isaac Hamilton Rapp in 1917, the museum contains one of America's finest regional collections. It's also one of Santa Fe's earliest Pueblo Revival structures, inspired by the adobe structures at Acoma Pueblo. The 8,000-piece permanent collection, of which only a fraction is exhibited at any given time, emphasizes the work of regional and nationally renowned artists, including the early Modernist Georgia O'Keeffe. ✉ *107 W. Palace Ave.* ☎ *505/476–5072* ⊕ *www.mfasantafe.org* 🎫 *$8, 4-day pass $18 (good at all 5 state museums in Santa Fe), free Fri. 5–8* PM ⊙ *Tues.–Thurs. and weekends 10–5, Fri. 10–8.*

Fodor'sChoice ★ ☾ **Palace of the Governors.** A humble-looking one-story adobe on the north side of the Plaza, the palace, built circa 1610, is the oldest public building in the United States. Renovations are ongoing to convert the palace into a house-museum; call ahead before you go to determine if you'll

STRANGE BUT TRUE

Although elementary-school text-books tend to devote more attention to the Pilgrims of Massachusetts, it's settlers from Spain who first settled the New World, and developed cities in what is now the United States. St. Augustine, Florida, is actually considered to be America's oldest permanent settlement, it having been founded in 1565. But Santa Fe is the second-oldest, dating to 1608 or so (there's some debate over the exact year).

Santa Fe, Taos, and Albuquerque are distinctive in a number of ways. At 7,000 feet above sea level, Santa Fe is the highest state capital city in the nation. Taos is unusual for being home to both a village and building—Taos Pueblo—that's been inhabited continuously for more than 1,000 years. And among Albuquerque's claims to fame, it's home to the world's longest aerial tramway (which runs up to the peak of the Sandia Mountains) .

have access to the building. Dozens of Native American vendors gather daily under the portal of the Palace of the Governors to display and sell pottery, jewelry, bread, and other goods. ⊠ *Palace Ave., north side of Plaza* ☎ *505/476–5100* ⊕ *www.palaceofthegovernors.org* 🖾 *$8, 4-day pass $18 (good at all 5 state museums in Santa Fe), free Fri. 5–8* ⏰ *Tues.–Thurs. and weekends 10–5, Fri. 10–8.*

SANTA FE AREA

Bandelier National Monument, named after author and ethnologist Adolph Bandelier (his novel *The Delight Makers* is set in Frijoles Canyon), contains 23,000 acres of backcountry wilderness, waterfalls, and wildlife. Sixty miles of trails traverse the park. *10 mi south of Los Alamos via NM 501 south to NM 4 east; 40 mi north of Santa Fe via U.S. 285/84 north to NM 502 west to NM 4 west.* ☎ *505/672–0343* ⊕ *www.nps. gov/band* 🖾 *$10 per vehicle, good for 7 days* ⏰ *Late May–early Sept., daily 8–6; early Sept.–Oct. and Apr.–late May, daily 8–5:30; Nov.–Mar., daily 8–4:30.*

Fodor'sChoice
★
El Santuario de Chimayó, a small frontier adobe church, has a fantastically carved and painted wood altar and is built on the site where, believers say, a mysterious light came from the ground on Good Friday in 1810 and where a large wooden crucifix was found beneath the earth. The chapel sits above a sacred *pozito* (a small hole), the dirt from which is believed to have miraculous healing properties. Dozens of abandoned crutches and braces placed in the anteroom—along with many notes, letters, and photos—testify to this. The Santuario draws a steady stream of worshippers year-round—Chimayó is considered the Lourdes of the Southwest. ⊠ *Signed lane off CR 98* ☎ *505/351–4889* ⊕ *www.arch diocesesantafe.org/AboutASF/Chimayo.html* 🖾 *Free* ⏰ *June–Sept., daily 9–5; Oct.–May, daily 9–4.*

TAOS

Harwood Museum. The Pueblo Revival former home of Burritt Elihu "Burt" Harwood, a dedicated painter who studied in France before moving to Taos in 1916, is adjacent to a museum dedicated to the works of local artists. Traditional Hispanic northern New Mexican artists, early art-colony painters, post–World War II modernists, and contemporary artists such as Larry Bell, Agnes Martin, Ken Price, and Earl Stroh are represented. ✉ *238 Ledoux St.* ☎ *505/758–9826* ⊕ *www.harwoodmuseum.org* ⌨ *$7, $20 with Museum Association of Taos combination ticket* ☉ *Tues.–Sat. 10–5, Sun. noon–5.*

23

Fodor'sChoice **Taos Art Museum at the Fechin House.** The interior of this extraordinary
★ adobe house, built between 1927 and 1933 by Russian émigré and artist Nicolai Fechin, is a marvel of carved Russian-style woodwork and furniture that glistens with an almost golden sheen. Fechin constructed it to showcase his daringly colorful paintings. The house has hosted the Taos Art Museum since 2003, with a collection of paintings from more than 50 Taos artists. ✉ *227 Paseo del Pueblo Norte* ☎ *505/758–2690* ⊕ *www.taosartmuseum.org* ⌨ *$8, $20 with Museum Association of Taos combination ticket* ☉ *Tues.–Sun. 10–5.*

Rio Grande Gorge Bridge. It's a dizzying experience to see the Rio Grande 650 feet underfoot, where it flows at the bottom of an immense, steep rock canyon. In summer the reddish rocks dotted with green scrub contrast brilliantly with the blue sky, where you might see a hawk lazily floating in circles. The bridge is the second-highest expansion bridge in the country. ✉ *U.S. 64, 12 mi west of town.*

Millicent Rogers Museum. More than 5,000 pieces of spectacular Native American and Hispanic art are on display here. Among the pieces are baskets, blankets, rugs, kachina dolls, carvings, paintings, rare religious artifacts, and most significantly, jewelry. Docents conduct guided tours by appointment, and the museum hosts lectures, films, workshops, and demonstrations. ✉ *1504 Millicent Rogers Rd., from Taos Plaza head north on Paseo del Pueblo Norte and left at sign for CR BA030, also called Millicent Rogers Rd. or Museum Rd.* ☎ *505/758–2462* ⊕ *www. millicentrogers.com* ⌨ *$7, $20 with Museum Association of Taos combination ticket* ☉ *Apr.–Sept., daily 10–5; Nov.–Mar., Tues.–Sun. 10–5.*

Fodor'sChoice **Taos Pueblo.** For nearly 1,000 years the mud-and-straw adobe walls of
★ Taos Pueblo have sheltered Tiwa-speaking Native Americans. A United
☾ Nations World Heritage Site, this is the largest collection of multistory pueblo dwellings in the United States. ✉ *Head to right off Paseo del Pueblo Norte just past Best Western Kachina Lodge* ☎ *505/758–1028* ⊕ *www.taospueblo.com* ⌨ *Tourist fees $10. Guided tours by appointment. Still-camera permit $5; note: cameras that may look commercial, such as those with telephoto lenses, might be denied a permit; video-camera permit $5.* ☉ *Mon.–Sat., 8–4:30, Sun. 8:30–4:30. Closed for funerals, religious ceremonies, and for 2-month quiet time in late winter or early spring, and last part of Aug.; call ahead before visiting at these times.*

WHERE TO EAT

ALBUQUERQUE

$$–$$$$ ✕**Bien Shur.** The panoramic city and
Fodor'sChoice   mountain views are part of the draw
★   at this fine restaurant on the top floor
of the stunning seven-story Sandia
Casino complex, but Bien Shur is
also one of the most sophisticated
restaurants in the city. Even if you're
not much for gambling, it's worth
coming here for chef Salim Khoury's
superbly crafted contemporary fare.
⊠*Sandia Resort & Casino, Tramway Rd. NE just east of I–25, Far Northeast Heights* ☎*505/796–7500* ⊕*www.sandiacasino.com* ⊟*AE, D, MC, V* ☾*Closed Mon. and Tues. No lunch.*

$$–$$$ ✕**Artichoke Cafe.** Locals praise the Artichoke for its service and French,
Fodor'sChoice   contemporary American, and Italian dishes prepared, whenever pos-
★   sible, with organically grown ingredients. Specialties include house-
made ravioli stuffed with ricotta and butternut squash with a white
wine, sage, and butter sauce; and pan-seared sea scallops wrapped in
prosciutto with red potatoes, haricots vert, and wax beans. The appe-
tizers are so tasty you may want to make a meal out of them. ⊠*424 Central Ave. SE, Downtown* ☎*505/243–0200* ⊕*www.artichokecafe. com* ⊟*AE, D, DC, MC, V* ☾*Closed Sun. No lunch Sat.*

¢–$$ ✕**Monica's El Portal.** Locals in the know favor this rambling, assuredly
authentic New Mexican restaurant on the west side of Old Town over
the more famous, though less reliable, standbys around Old Town
Plaza. If you've never had *chicharrones* (fried pork skins), try them here
with beans stuffed inside a flaky sopaipilla. Or consider the traditional
blue-corn chicken or beef enchiladas, and the savory green-chili stew.
⊠*321 Rio Grande Blvd. NW, Old Town* ☎*505/247–9625* ⊟*AE, D, MC, V* ☾*Closed Mon. No dinner weekends.*

TAOS

$$–$$$$ ✕**De La Tierra.** This chic spot presents daring globally influenced cui-
sine. Top starters include smoked trout with horseradish-cognac
cream, and blue-corn calamari. Among the mains, try the molas-
ses-marinated quail with a parsnip cake and dried-blueberry sauce,
or pan-roasted lamb with asiago, grilled asparagus, and sage bread
pudding. Tequila-lime pie with white-chocolate–ancho chili crust and
prickly pear syrup makes for a happy ending. ⊠*317 Kit Carson Rd., El Monte Sagrado Resort* ☎*505737–9855* ⊕*www.elmontesagrado. com* ⊟*AE, D, DC, MC, V.*

$$–$$$$ ✕**Joseph's Table.** Locally renowned chef Joseph Wrede has moved
Fodor'sChoice   around the area a bit in recent years, but has settled into what he does
★   best—overseeing his own swank yet friendly restaurant in the La Fonda
Hotel on the Taos Plaza. The masterpiece here is pepper-crusted elk ten-

derloin with foie gras and truffle demi-glace. ⊠ *108 A S. Taos Plaza, La Fonda Hotel* ☎ *505/751–4512* ⊕ *www.josephstable.com* ▭ *AE, D, DC, MC, V.*

¢ ✗**Orlando's.** This family-run local favorite may be packed during peak hours, while guests wait patiently to devour favorites such as *carne adovada* (red chili–marinated pork), blue-corn enchiladas, and scrumptious shrimp burritos. You can eat in the cozy dining room, outside on the front patio, or call ahead for takeout if you'd rather avoid the crowds. ⊠ *114 Don Juan Valdez La., off Paseo del Pueblo Norte* ☎ *505/751–1450* ▭ *No credit cards* ⊗ *Closed Sun.*

23

WHERE TO STAY

ALBUQUERQUE

$$–$$$$
Fodor'sChoice
★

🏨**Sandia Resort & Casino.** Completed in early 2006 after much anticipation, this seven-story casino resort has set the new standard for luxury in Albuquerque. Ceramic bath tiles, walk-in showers with separate tubs, 32-inch plasma TVs, handcrafted wooden furniture, louvered wooden blinds, and muted, natural color palettes lend elegance to the spacious rooms, most of which have sweeping views of the Sandia Mountains or the Rio Grande Valley. The 700-acre grounds include a superb golf course and an amphitheater that hosts top-of-the-line music and comedy acts. The casino is open 24 hours. ⊠ *Tramway Rd. NE just east of I-25, Old Town, 87122* ☎ *505/796–7500 or 800/526–9366* ⊕ *www. sandiacasino.com* ⇄ *198 rooms, 30 suites* ♿ *In-room: Wi-Fi. In-hotel: 4 restaurants, room service, bars, golf course, pool, gym, spa, laundry service, parking (no fee).*

$$–$$$
🏨**Embassy Suites Hotel Albuquerque.** This swanky new all-suites high-rise with a striking contemporary design sits on a bluff alongside I-40, affording guests fabulous views of the downtown skyline and vast desert mesas to the west, and the verdant Sandia Mountains to the east. ⊠ *1000 Woodward Pl. NE, 87102 Downtown* ☎ *505/245–7100 or 800/362–2779* 🖷 *505/247–1083* ⊕ *embassysuites.hilton.com* ⇄ *261 suites* ♿ *In-room: refrigerator, Wi-Fi. In-hotel: restaurant, bar, parking (no fee)* ▭ *AE, D, MC, V* ⦿*BP.*

SANTA FE

$$$$
🏨**Inn of the Anasazi.** Unassuming from the outside, this first-rate boutique hotel is one of Santa Fe's finest, with superb architectural detail. Each room has a beamed viga-and-latilla ceiling, kiva-style gas fireplace, antique Indian rugs, handwoven fabrics, and organic toiletries (including sunblock). Other amenities include full concierge services, twice-daily maid service, exercise bikes upon request, and a library. An especially nice touch in this desert town are the humidifiers in each guest room. ⊠ *113 Washington Ave., 87501* ☎ *505/988–3030 or 800/688–8100* 🖷 *505/988–3277* ⊕ *www.innoftheanasazi.com* ⇄ *57 rooms* ♿ *In-room: safe, VCR, Wi-Fi. In-hotel: restaurant, bar, parking (fee), some pets allowed (fee)* ▭ *AE, D, DC, MC, V.*

$$
Fodor'sChoice
★

🏨**Hotel Santa Fe.** Picuris Pueblo has controlling interest in this handsome Pueblo-style three-story hotel on the Guadalupe District's edge and a short walk from the Plaza. The light, airy rooms and suites are traditional Southwestern, with locally handmade furniture, wooden blinds, and Pueblo paintings; many have balconies. The hotel gift shop, Santa Fe's only tribally owned store, has lower prices than many nearby retail stores. The 35 rooms and suites in the posh Hacienda wing have corner fireplaces and the use of a London-trained butler. Amaya is one of the better hotel restaurants in town. ⊠ *1501 Paseo de Peralta, 87505* ☎ *505/982–1200 or 800/825–9876* 🖷 *505/984–2211* ⊕ *www.hotelsantafe.com* ⤵ *40 rooms, 91 suites* ⌂ *In-hotel: restaurant, bar, pool, concierge, laundry service, parking (no fee)* ☰ *AE, D, DC, MC, V.*

> **ON THE WAY**
>
> **Las Vegas:** No, not that Las Vegas. New Mexico has its very own little city of Las Vegas, a quiet, scenic, and historic community about 65 mi northeast of Santa Fe via I-25. With one of the state's best-preserved historic plazas and a number of offbeat shops, galleries, and restaurants, this is an enchanting detour.

TAOS

$$$$
Fodor'sChoice
★

🏨 **El Monte Sagrado.** Pricey but classy, El Monte Sagrado is an ecosensitive New Age haven offering all manner of amenities, from alternative therapies like milk-and-honey body wraps to cooking and wine classes. A short drive away, the property has an expansive ranch property that's available for you to explore on horseback or on foot. Suites and casitas are accented with exotic themes. The on-site restaurant, De la Tierra, serves daring cuisine. ⊠ *317 Kit Carson Rd., 87571* ☎ *505/758–3502 or 800/828–8267* 🖷 *505/737–2980* ⊕ *www.elmontesagrado.com* ⤵ *18 suites, 18 casitas* ⌂ *In-room: kitchen (some), refrigerator (some), VCR, Wi-Fi. In-hotel: 2 restaurants, room service, bar, pool, gym, spa, bicycles, concierge, children's programs (ages 4–12), laundry service, some pets allowed (fee)* ☰ *AE, D, DC, MC, V.*

$$–$$$$
Fodor'sChoice
★

🏨 **Hacienda del Sol.** Frank Waters wrote *People of the Valley* here— other guests have included Willa Cather and D.H. Lawrence. Most of the rooms contain kiva fireplaces, Southwestern handcrafted furniture, and original artwork, and all have CD players. Certain adjoining rooms can be combined into suites. Breakfast is a gourmet affair that might include banana pancakes or stuffed French toast. Perhaps above all else, the "backyards" of the rooms and the secluded outdoor hot tub have a view of Taos Mountain so idyllic it can evoke tears of joy from even the most cynical of travelers. ⊠ *109 Mabel Dodge La., Box 177, 87571* ☎ *505/758–0287 or 866/333–4459* 🖷 *505/758–5895* ⊕ *www. taoshaciendadelsol.com* ⤵ *11 rooms* ⌂ *In-room: refrigerator (some), no TV* ☰ *AE, D, MC, V* ⏀*BP.*

SHOPPING

ALBUQUERQUE

Funky **Nob Hill** (⊠ *Central Ave. from Girard Blvd. to Washington St.*), just east of University of New Mexico and anchored by old Route 66, pulses with colorful storefronts and kitschy signs. Many of the best shops are clustered inside or on the blocks near Nob Hill Business

Center, an art deco structure containing several intriguing businesses and La Montañita Natural Foods Co-op.

Weyrich Gallery (✉ *2935–D Louisiana Blvd. NE, Uptown* ☎ *505/883–7410*) carries distinctive jewelry, fine art, Japanese tea bowls, woodblocks, hand-color photography, and other largely Asian-inspired pieces.

Gertrude Zachary (✉ *1501 Lomas Blvd. NW, Old Town* ☎ *505/247–4442* ✉ *3300 Central Ave. SE, Nob Hill* ☎ *505/766–4700* ✉ *416 2nd St. SW, Old Town* ☎ *505/244–1320*) dazzles with its selection of Native American jewelry. A second branch, at 416 2nd Street, carries antiques.

23

SANTA FE

*Fodor's*Choice
★ **Gerald Peters Gallery** (✉ *1011 Paseo de Peralta* ☎ *505/954–5700*) is Santa Fe's leading gallery of American and European art from the 19th century to the present. It has works by Max Weber, Albert Bierstadt, the Taos Society, the New Mexico Modernists, and Georgia O'Keeffe, as well as contemporary artists.

Monroe Gallery (✉ *112 Don Gaspar Ave.* ☎ *505/992–0800*) showcases works by the most celebrated black-and-white photographers of the 20th century, from Margaret Bourke-White to Alfred Eisenstaedt.

Nambé Outlets (✉ *104 W. San Francisco St.* ☎ *505/988–3574* ✉ *924 Paseo de Peralta* ☎ *505/988–5528*) carries the classic metal bowls, vases, and candlesticks made by the acclaimed artisans of the Nambé Pueblo, just north of town; lead crystal, lighting, and porcelain are also sold.

TAOS

J.D. Challenger Gallery (✉ *221 Paseo del Pueblo Norte* ☎ *505/751–6773 or 800/511–6773*) is the home base of personable painter J.D. Challenger, who has become famous for his dramatically rendered portraits of Native Americans from tribes throughout North America.

Country Furnishings of Taos (✉ *534 Paseo del Pueblo Norte* ☎ *505/758–4633*) sells folk art from northern New Mexico, handmade furniture, metalwork lamps and beds, and colorful accessories.

SPORTS & THE OUTDOORS

ALBUQUERQUE

*Fodor's*Choice
★ There are several reliable companies around metro Albuquerque that offer ballooning tours. A ride will set you back about $160–$180 per person. One of the best outfitters in town is **Rainbow Ryders** (☎ *505/823–1111 or 800/725–2477* ⊕ *www.rainbowryders.com*).

☼ **Rio Grande Nature Center State Park.** Along the banks for the Rio Grande, this year-round 170-acre refuge in a portion of the Bosque is the nation's largest cottonwood forest. If bird-watching is your thing, you've come to the right place. The park has active programs for adults and children and trails for biking, walking, and jogging. ✉ *2901 Candelaria*

Rd. NW, North Valley ☎ *505/344–7240* ⊕ *www.nmparks.com* 🖺 *$1; grounds free* ⊙ *Nature Center daily 10–5, park daily 8–5.*

VITAL STATS:

■ State Capital: Santa Fe, founded in 1608, and 60 mi northeast of Albuquerque

■ State Motto: It Grows As It Goes

■ State Bird: Roadrunner

■ State Tree: Piñon pine

■ State Flower: Yucca

■ State Song: O, Fair New Mexico

SANTA FE

Spurring off the Dale Ball trail system, the steep but rewarding (and dog-friendly) **Atalaya Trail** runs from the visitor parking lot of St. John's College (off of Camino de Cruz Blanca, on the East Side) up a winding, ponderosa pine–studded trail to the peak of Mt. Atalaya, which affords incredible 270-degree views of Santa Fe. The nearly 6-mi round-trip hike climbs a nearly 2,000 feet (to an elevation of 9,121 feet), so pace yourself.

Ski Santa Fe (⊠ *End of NM 475, 18 mi northeast of downtown* ☎ *505/982 4429, 505/983–9155 conditions* ⊕ *www.skisantafe.com*), open roughly from late November through early April, is a fine, mid-size operation that receives an average of 225 inches of snow a year and plenty of sunshine. Snowboarders are welcome, and there's the Norquist Trail for cross-country skiers.

TAOS

Los Rios Anglers (⊠ *226–C Paseo del Pueblo Norte* ☎ *505/758–2798 or 800/748–1707*) is a fly-fisherman's haven for fly rods, flies, clothing, books, instruction, and guide service to local streams.

Paradise Balloons (☎ *505/751–6098* ⊕ *www.taosballooning.com*) will thrill you with a "splash and dash" in the Rio Grande River as part of a silent journey through the 600-foot canyon walls of Rio Grande Gorge.

VISITOR INFORMATION

Albuquerque Convention and Visitors Bureau (☎ *505/842–9918 or 800/284–2282* ⊕ *www.itsatrip.org*).

New Mexico Department of Tourism (☎ *505/827–7400 or 800/733–6396 Ext. 0643* ⊕ *www.newmexico.org*).

Santa Fe Convention and Visitors Bureau (☎ *505/955–6200 or 800/777–2489* ⊕ *www.santafe.org*).

Taos Chamber of Commerce (☎ *505/758–3873 or 800/732–8267* ⊕ *www.taosguide.com*).

Salt Lake City

Mormon Tabernacle Choir, Salt Lake City

WORD OF MOUTH

"SLC has a fascinating history . . . you can spend the entire day at Temple Square, if you care about history . . . Go up immigration Canyon, as far as the snow allows, or Parleys, for some great views. Go to Trolley Square for some fun shopping, or the State Capitol . . ."

—clarasong

EXPLORING SALT LAKE CITY

420 mi northeast of Las Vegas via I–15; 535 mi west of Denver via I–25 and I–80; 660 mi north of Phoenix via I–17, U.S. 89, and I–15; 340 mi southeast of Boise via I–84 and I–15; and 520 mi west of Reno via I–80.

By John Blodgett

Sitting at the foot of the rugged Wasatch Mountains and extending to the south shore of the Great Salt Lake, Salt Lake City is unique among American cities. There are few other places where you can enjoy urban pleasures and, within 20 minutes, hike a mountain trail or rest by a rushing stream.

The city is an important western center for business, medicine, education, and culture; and the Church of Jesus Christ of Latter-day Saints (LDS), as the Mormon faith is officially called, is headquartered in Salt Lake City's Temple Square. High-rise hotels punch the skyline, restaurants serve up a myriad of flavors, fashionable retail enclaves are popping up all around town, and nightlife is surprisingly vibrant. Increased commitment to the arts from the public and private sectors has created a cultural scene as rich as what you'd find in a city twice Salt Lake's size.

Despite its population of roughly 180,000, Salt Lake City feels like a small city. Wide streets and an efficient mass transit system make it easy to get around. The heart of Salt Lake's social, religious, and political institutions can be found within a few blocks of Temple Square downtown.

WHO WILL ESPECIALLY LOVE THIS TRIP?

Outdoorsy Folks: Salt Lake City spreads directly from the shadows of the Wasatch Mountains. With peaks surpassing 10,000 feet in elevation, this mountainous area is host to recreationists of all bents: rock climbers, skiers, snowboarders, snowshoers, ice climbers, mountain bikers, road bikers, backpackers, and more.

Mormons: Salt Lake City has been the center of the Mormon universe since 1847, after members of the Church of Jesus Christ of Latter-day Saints were driven west from points in Illinois and Missouri. Temple Square in downtown Salt Lake City attracts Mormons from all over the world.

Families: A strong, loving family is important to Mormons, and as a result Utah is a family-friendly state filled with kid-friendly attractions. Kids will love the Utah's Children's Museum and Clark Planetarium, both located in the Gateway, and moms and dads will enjoy themselves as well.

Amateur Genealogists: Thanks to the Church of Jesus Christ of Latter-day Saints' focus on genealogy, Salt Lake City has some of the world's greatest resources for researching your family history. You need not be a Mormon to access the massive stores of family information at the Family History Museum near Temple Square.

TOP 5 REASONS TO GO

Temple Square: When Mormon pioneer leader Brigham Young first entered the Salt Lake Valley, he chose this spot at the mouth of City Creek Canyon for the headquarters of the Mormon Church, a role the city maintains to this day. The Temple took 40 years to build.

Skiing: There are four ski resorts within 45 minutes of downtown Salt Lake City: Brighton and Solitude up Big Cottonwood Canyon, and the famous neighbors Snowbird and Alta up Little Cottonwood Canyon. (Note that Alta does not allow snowboarders.)

Hiking: It's rare for a city the size of Salt Lake to be nestled up against a towering mountain range, and residents take advantage by hiking the many nearby trails. The Bonneville Shoreline Trail is quick to access, easy to hike, and offers wide-open views of the Salt Lake Valley. For a more challenging hike with both mountain and city views, Mt. Olympus is a local favorite.

Biking: The Wasatch Front, directly east of Salt Lake City, attracts cyclists of all styles and abilities. Professional and expert road bikers work out their lungs of steel by climbing Big and Little Cottonwood canyons, while Mill Creek, Emigration, and City Creek canyons also provide great workouts. Mountain bikers frequent the Bonneville Shoreline Trail and a number of interlocking trails off Mill Creek Canyon.

Access to Adventure: Part of Salt Lake City's attraction is that it serves as an excellent base for exploring all corners of Utah, plus areas of Idaho, Wyoming, and Colorado.

24

WHEN IS THE BEST TIME TO VISIT?

Spring and summer are wonderful times to visit Salt Lake City. The winter's smoggy inversion is lifted, the trees fill with green, and the sun shines bright and warm from a clear, deep blue sky. It's a perfect time of year to walk around the sights and sites of downtown, such as Temple Square, and to head off into the nearby Wasatch Mountains for hiking or mountain biking. Of course, come winter the Salt Lake area is paradise for skiers, snowshoers, and snowboarders.

HOW SHOULD I GET THERE?

BUS

Greyhound Lines runs several buses each day to Salt Lake's terminal. The company also serves Provo, Ogden, Tremonton, Green River, Logan, Brigham City, and St. George.

DRIVING

Two major highways offer direct access to Salt Lake City, making it easy to get here by car. From the north and south, take I–15; from east and west, I–80. If you're coming from Denver, take I–70 west to Route 6 north to reach I–15 in Spanish Fork, about an hour south of Salt Lake City.

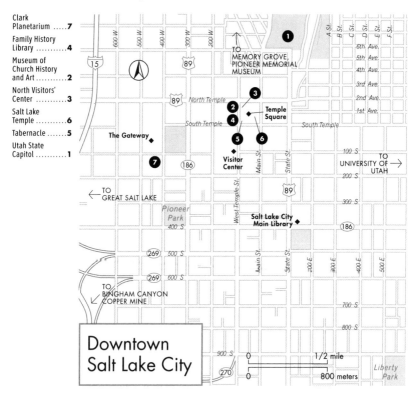

Downtown
Salt Lake City

FLYING

The major gateway to Utah is Salt Lake City International Airport. Salt Lake City is approximately 16 hours from Sydney, 12 hours from London, 3 hours from Dallas, 5 hours from New York, 4 hours from Chicago, 3¾ hours from Los Angeles, and 1½ from Las Vegas.

TRAIN

Amtrak connects Utah to both coasts and many major American cities, with trains that stop in Salt Lake City, Ogden, Provo, Helper, Green River, and St. George.

HOW DO I GET AROUND?

BY CAR

You'll need a car in Salt Lake City. Public transportation exists, but it mainly caters to commuters, not tourists.

Highway travel around Salt Lake is usually quick and easy, though construction can sometimes throw you for a loop. From I–80, take I–15 north to 600 South Street to reach the city center. Salt Lake City's streets are extra wide and typically not congested; most are two-way. Expect heavy traffic weekdays between 6 AM and 10 AM and again

CLOSE UP

How to Snack

Utahns love their ice cream, and there's no shortage of places to get a scoop—or three—in Salt Lake City. Local chain **Nielsen's Frozen Custard** is locally famous for its "concrete": frozen custard mixed with natural flavoring. (Think a real thick and delicious—and huge—shake that you eat with a spoon.)

The downtown area is also home to numerous popular sidewalk taco stands, where you can usually pick up two authentic tacos with all the fixin's for about a buck-fifty.

Tony Caputo's Market and Deli and **Cucina Deli** are fine places to get a to-go lunch for touring downtown or relaxing at Liberty Park. Or try a lean and delicious buffalo burger at the **Buffalo Point** lunch spot on Antelope Island.

24

between 4 PM and 7 PM. To encourage carpooling, some freeways have special lanes for so-called high-occupancy vehicles (HOV)—cars carrying more than one passenger.

WHERE SHOULD I FOCUS MY ENERGY?

If you're here for 1 day: Spend your first day visiting Temple Square, shopping the Gateway, and taking in a show at Clark Planetarium.

If you're here for 2 days: Visit Red Butte Garden & Arboretum and This Is the Place Heritage Park in the foothills of Salt Lake, then tour the Kearns Mansion or the Pioneer Memorial Museum.

If you're here for 3 days: A short 20 minutes away is Great Salt Lake State Park Marina, where you can see what it feels like to float in water three times heavier than freshwater. Then head to Antelope Island State Park.

If you're here for 4 days: On the University of Utah campus, visit the Utah Museum of Natural History and the Utah Museum of Fine Arts. Finish the day with a shopping trip to Trolley Square.

If you're here for 5 days: Start the morning with a walk or jog through Liberty Park and visit Tracy Aviary. Then head to the Bingham Canyon Copper Mine.

If you're here for 6 days: Start with a walk in Memory Grove, then visit any of the sights you didn't have time for the rest of the week. If it's winter and you haven't done so already, hit the slopes!

If you're here for 7 days or more: Check out a portion of the Pony Express Trail.

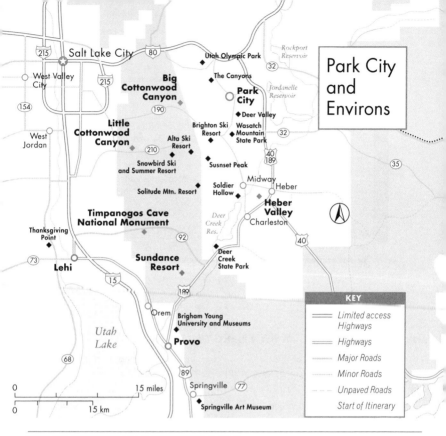

215 Salt Lake City 80

Park City and Environs

KEY

═══	Limited access Highways
───	Highways
·······	Major Roads
-------	Minor Roads
- - -	Unpaved Roads
········	Start of Itinerary

Utah Olympic Park
The Canyons
Rockport Reservoir
Jordanelle Reservoir
Park City
Deer Valley
Big Cottonwood Canyon
Brighton Ski Resort
Wasatch Mountain State Park
Little Cottonwood Canyon
Alta Ski Resort
Snowbird Ski and Summer Resort
Susnset Peak
Midway Heber
Soldier Hollow
Solitude Mtn. Resort
Heber Valley
Timpanogos Cave National Monument
Deer Creek Res.
Charleston
Thanksgiving Point
Sundance Resort
Deer Creek State Park
Lehi
Orem
Brigham Young University and Museums
Utah Lake
Provo
Springville
Springville Art Museum

West Valley City
West Jordan

0   15 miles
0   15 km

WHAT ARE THE TOP EXPERIENCES?

Visiting Temple Square: This is the heart and the world headquarters of the Church of Jesus Christ of Latter-day Saints, but you need not be Mormon to enjoy walking the grounds and touring the various buildings (though only Mormons with a Temple Recommend can enter the sacred Salt Lake Temple). In spring, summer, and even fall it's known for its wonderful flowers; come Christmas the trees blaze with thousands of decorative lights. Get your bearings at the North Visitors' Center, then head to the Tabernacle, home to the Mormon Tabernacle Choir, which was recently renovated. Check out the Family History Library, which has millions of genealogical records that anyone can research.

Hitting the Slopes: If ever an outdoor activity was synonymous with Utah, skiing is it. The bulk of the state's resorts, known for the fluffy powder that falls upward of 500 to 600 and more inches a year, are within a comfortable drive from the Salt Lake airport. Of these, the closest are Brighton, Solitude, Snowbird, and Alta. You can rent equipment at Utah Ski & Golf, or plan an entire ski vacation at Alta Vacation, Ski the Rockies, or Snow Ventures.

Visiting the Great Salt Lake: No visit to Utah is quite complete without a trip to the Great Salt Lake. Because the lake is so shallow, an inch or two of change in the lake's depth translates into yards of sticky mud between the sandy beach and water deep enough to float in. In late spring the brine flies can be atrocious in some parts, but this shouldn't keep you from taking a cruise on the lake or visiting Antelope Island State Park, the best way to experience the lake, where the shore dynamics are much different. Birds of many different feathers flock here at all times of the year, and Antelope Island's resident herd of bison is a popular attraction.

Eating Well: Salt Lake City has an excellent dining scene that keeps getting better as experienced chefs

24

flock here to open restaurants with mountain views. Long regarded as the best restaurant in the city, Metropolitan has a modern vibe, an extensive wine list, and impeccable presentation. Squatter's Pub Brewery is the place where locals bring visiting family and friends. Over at the Bayou, you can find Cajun-inspired fare, plus a few hundred types of beer. Mole and other classic Mexican fare takes center stage at the always-crowded Red Iguana, while Mazza Middle Eastern Cuisine recently added a second location to better serve fans of its lamb, chicken, and kebab dishes.

BEST BETS

SIGHTS AND TOURS

★ **Bingham Canyon Copper Mine.** This enormous open-pit mine measures nearly 2½ mi across and ¾ mi deep—the result of removing 5 billion tons of rock. Since operations began nearly 90 years ago by the Kennecott Utah Copper company, about 17 million tons of copper have been produced. At the visitor center, exhibits and multimedia presentations explain the history and present-day operation of the mine. Outside, trucks the size of dinosaurs and cranes as tall as apartment buildings continue to reshape the mountain. ✉*Rte. 48, Copperton* ☎*801/252–3234* ⊕*www.kennecott.com* ✉*$5 per vehicle* ☉*Apr.–Oct., daily 8–8.*

★ **Clark Planetarium.** The Hansen Dome Theatre and 3-D IMAX Theatre comprise this Salt Lake County facility in the Gateway Mall. The Star Theatre uses state-of-the-art technology to simulate three-dimensional flights through space. Hands-on exhibits and science paraphernalia fill the "Wonders of the Universe" Science Store. ✉*110 S. 400 West St., Downtown* ☎*801/456–7827* ⊕*www.clarkplanetarium.org* ✉*Star Show $8, IMAX $8, combination tickets $13* ☉*Daily 10:30* AM*—end of last show.*

Family History Library. Genealogy is important to Mormons. This library houses the world's largest collection of genealogical data. Mormons and non-Mormons alike come here to do research. ⊠ *35 N. West Temple, Temple Square* ☎ *801/240–2584 or 800/346–6044* ⊕ *www.lds.org* 🗺 *Free* ⊙ *Mon. 8–5, Tues.–Sat. 8* AM–*9* PM.

★ **Great Salt Lake State Park.** The Great Salt Lake is eight times saltier than the ocean and second only to the Dead Sea in salinity. What makes it so briny? There's no outlet to the ocean, so salts and other minerals carried by rivers and streams become concentrated in this enormous evaporation pond. Ready access to this wonder is possible at Great Salt Lake State Park, 16 mi west of Salt Lake City, on the lake's south shore.

> **HISTORY YOU CAN SEE**
>
> The little-visited Pioneer Memorial Museum is an absolute gem for history buffs. Near the Utah State Capitol, the museum has an extensive collection of pioneer-era artifacts and photographs (if you find an image of an ancestor, staff will print you a copy for just a few dollars). Pioneer history also comes alive at This is the Place Heritage Park, where volunteers dress in period clothing and give tours of a replica pioneer village.

The picnic beaches on Antelope Island State Park are the best places to float. If you can't take the time to get to Antelope Island, however, you can walk down the boat ramp at the Great Salt Lake State Marina and stick your legs in the water to experience the unique sensation of floating on water that won't let you sink. Your feet will bob to the surface and you will see tiny orange brine shrimp floating with you. At the marina, you can make arrangements for group or charter sails. Trips take from one to six hours, and there's a range of reasonable prices to match; some include meals. **Salt Island Adventures** (☎ *801/252–9336* ⊕ *www.gslcruises.com*) runs cruises year-round. ⊠ *Frontage Rd., 2 mi east of I–80 Exit 104, Salt Lake City* ☎ *801/250–1898* 🗺 *$2* ⊙ *Daily 7* AM–*10* PM.

Memory Grove. Walk the quiet street, free from traffic, that runs through the park or take one of many trails near City Creek. Monuments to veterans of war are found throughout this grove. You can hike, jog, or bike part or all of the paved road that is closed to cars on odd-numbered days along **City Creek Canyon.**

Museum of Church History and Art. The museum houses a variety of artifacts and works of art relating to the history and doctrine of the Mormon faith, including personal belongings of church leaders Joseph Smith, Brigham Young, and others. There are also samples of Mormon coins and scrip used as standard currency in Utah during the 1800s, and beautiful examples of quilting, embroidery, and other handwork. Upstairs galleries exhibit religious and secular works by Mormon artists from all over the world. ⊠ *45 N. West Temple, Temple Square* ☎ *801/240–4615* ⊕ *www.lds.org* 🗺 *Free* ⊙ *Weekdays 9–9, weekends 10–7.*

North Visitors' Center. The history of the Mormon Church and the Mormon pioneers' trek to Utah is outlined in displays and a 53-minute film here.

⊠*50 W. North Temple, Temple Square* ☎*801/240–4872* ⊕*www. lds.org* ☜*Free* ⊗*Daily 9–9.*

Salt Lake City Tours provides tours of Salt Lake City; most tours include lunch at Brigham Young's historic living quarters. (⊠*3359 S. Main St., Downtown* ☎*801/534–1001* ⊕*www.saltlakecitytours.org*).

Pioneer Memorial Museum. The West's most extensive collection of settlement era relics, many of which relate to Mormon pioneers, fills 38 rooms—plus a carriage house—on four floors. Displays include clothing, furniture, tools, wagons, and carriages. ⊠*300 N. Main St., Capitol Hill* ☎*801/532–6479* ☜*Free, donations accepted* ⊗*Mon.–Sat. 9–5 year-round; June–Aug. Sun. 1–5.*

★ **Red Butte Garden and Arboretum.** With more than 100 acres of gardens ⟳ and undeveloped acres, the grounds here provide many pleasurable hours of strolling. Lectures on everything from bugs to gardening in arid climates, workshops, and concerts are presented regularly. The Summer Concert Series is adored by city residents and attracts musicians such as John Hiatt and Greg Brown. ⊠*300 Wakara Way, east of Foothill Dr., University of Utah* ☎*801/581–4747* ⊕*www.redbutte garden.org* ☜*$6* ⊗*May–Aug., Mon.–Sat. 9–9, Sun. 9–5; Sept. and Apr., Mon.–Sat. 9–7:30, Sun. 9–5; Oct.–Mar., daily 10–5.*

Fodor'sChoice **Salt Lake Temple.** Brigham Young chose this spot for a temple as soon ★ as he arrived in the Salt Lake Valley in 1847, but work on the building didn't begin for another six years. Built of blocks of granite hauled by oxen and train from Little Cottonwood Canyon, the Mormon Temple took 40 years to the day to complete. Its walls are 16 feet thick at the base. Off-limits to all but faithful Mormons, the temple is used for marriages, baptisms, and other religious functions. ⊠*South Temple and Main St., Temple Square* ☎*No phone* ⊕*www.lds.org* ⊗*Not open to public.*

★ **Tabernacle.** The Tabernacle is best known as the home of the famous Mormon Tabernacle and its impressive organ. Visitors can tour the Tabernacle and hear organ recitals daily. ⊠*50 W. North Temple, Temple Square* ☎*801/240–4872* ⊕*www.lds.org* ☜*Free.*

Utah Heritage Foundation offers the most authoritative tours of Salt Lake's historic sights. (⊠*485 Canyon Rd., Temple Square* ☎*801/533–0858* ⊕*www.utahheritagefoundation.com*).

⟳ **Utah Children's Museum.** The museum's goal is to "create the love of learning through hands-on experience," and that's exactly what it does at its Discovery Gateway location at the Gateway. Children can pilot a jetliner, draw with computers, dig for mammoth bones, or lose themselves in the many other interactive exhibits. ⊠*444 W. 100 South St., Downtown* ☎*801/328–3383* ⊕*www.childmuseum.org* 🖃*$9.50* ⊗*Mon., Fri. 10–9; Tues.–Thurs., Sat. 10–6, Sun. noon–6.*

★ **Utah Museum of Fine Arts.** Because it encompasses 74,000 square feet and more than 20 galleries, you'll be glad this facility has a café and a sculpture court—perfect places to rest. Special exhibits are mounted regularly, and the vast permanent collection includes Egyptian, Greek, and Roman relics; Italian Renaissance and other European paintings; Chinese ceramics and scrolls; Japanese screens; Thai and Cambodian sculptures; African and Latin American artworks; Navajo rugs; and American art from the 17th century to the present. ⊠*410 Campus Center Dr., University of Utah* ☎*801/581–7332* ⊕*www.utah.edu/ umfa* 🖃*$5* ⊗*Tues.–Fri. 10–5, Wed. 10–8, weekends 11–5.*

☉ **Utah Museum of Natural History.** Exhibits focus on the prehistoric inhabitants of the Colorado Plateau, the Great Basin, and other Southwestern locations. Utah's dry climate preserved for centuries not only the structures of these peoples, but also their clothing, foodstuffs, toys, weapons, and ceremonial objects. In the basement are thousands of dinosaur fossils, dominated by creatures from the late Jurassic period, many from the Cleveland-Lloyd quarry in central Utah. ⊠*1390 E. Presidents Circle, University of Utah* ☎*801/581–6927* ⊕*www.umnh. utah.edu* 🖃*$6* ⊗*Mon.–Sat. 9:30–5:30, Sun. noon–5.*

★ **Utah State Capitol.** In 1912, after the state reaped $800,000 in inheritance taxes from the estate of Union Pacific Railroad president Edward Harriman, work began on the Renaissance Revival structure that tops Capitol Hill. From the exterior steps you get a marvelous view of the entire Salt Lake Valley. In the rotunda beneath the 165-foot-high dome a series of murals, commissioned as part of the WPA project during the Depression, depicts the state's history. ⊠*400 N. State St., Capitol Hill* ☎*801/538–1563.*

WHERE TO EAT

	WHAT IT COSTS				
	¢	$	$$	$$$	$$$$
AT DINNER	under $8	$8–$12	$13–$18	$19–$25	over $25

Restaurant prices are per person for a main course at dinner, excluding sales tax of 7.6%

$$–$$$$ ✕**Metropolitan.** From its inventive cuisine to its minimalist design, **Fodor's Choice** owner Karen Olson's restaurant is chic in every way. Menus veer from ★ Asian-fusion to regional Rocky Mountain fare. You can usually walk in and get a seat at the curved bar or a bar table and order from a small bistro menu. But for the full experience, reserve a table and put yourself in the culinary team's capable hands with the daily tasting menu. Service here borders on choreography—synchronized, yet unobtrusive. The wine list is the best in the city. ⊠*173 W. Broadway, Downtown,*

84101 ☎801/364–3472 🖃AE, D, MC, V ☯Closed Sun. No lunch.

$–$$$$ ✕**Cucina Toscana.** One of the city's
★ most bustling trattorias is tucked into the corner of a renovated brick Firestone Tire shop. The menu of house-made pastas includes hand-made spinach and ricotta filled ravioli and handmade gnocchi. Handmade tiramisu is a favorite dessert. The deco-style pressed-tin ceiling, open kitchen, bas-relief trim, and banquette seating, create an urban, artsy atmosphere, which complements the top-notch service, food, and wines. ✉307 W. Pierpont Ave., Downtown ☎801/328–3463 🖃AE, D, MC, V ☯Closed Sun.

$–$$$ ✕**Mazza Middle Eastern Cuisine.** Authentic and affordable Middle Eastern food in a casual order-at-the-counter setting is what Mazza is all about. The homemade falafel, stuffed grape leaves, lamb, chicken and beef kebabs, and an assortment of side dishes are all fresh and tasty. So are the sweets, such as the honey-drenched baklava. ✉1515 S. 1500 East St., East Side ☎801/484–9259 🖃AE, D, MC, V ☯Closed Sun.

$–$$ ✕**The Bayou.** You can find more than 200 microbrews, both bottled and
★ on tap, at chef-owner Mark Alston's lively bar and restaurant. There's also a full bar and wine list. The menu offers everything from Cajun specialties such as jambalaya and étouffée to blackened seafood and a terrific, garlicky hamburger with sweet-potato fries. Live jazz, pool tables, and a clean, brick design creates a casual, high-energy (and often crowded) atmosphere. It's a private club, so visitors must pay $4 for a temporary membership. ✉645 S. State St., Downtown ☎801/961–8400 🖃AE, D, MC, V ☯No lunch weekends.

$–$$ ✕**Red Iguana.** This lively Mexican restaurant is staffed with a warm
Fodor'sChoice and accommodating crew, serving the best house-made moles and
★ chile verde in town. They pour premium margaritas and good Mexican beers, and always keep the salsa and chips coming. Expect a wait almost always. This is a great place to stop on your way to or from the airport if you don't want to take the freeway. ✉736 W. North Temple, 84116 ☎801/322–1489 🖃AE, D, DC, MC, V.

$ ✕**Cucina Deli.** Locals flock to this neighborhood café and take-away food market for the creative salads and colorful entrées displayed like jewels in glass cases. Most people order a sampler of three or four salads, such as orzo with mint, feta, chicken, and artichoke hearts; or wild rice–based concoctions. Also on the menu are house-made soups, generous deli sandwiches, and hot entrées such as meat loaf and mashed potatoes. Big windows and warm mustard and terra-cotta tones are reminiscent of a Tuscan-style café, with seating indoors and out. ✉1026 E. 2nd Ave., The Avenues ☎801/322–3055 🖃AE, D, DC, MC, V.

ON THE WAY

One of the best-preserved sections of the original **Pony Express Trail** is the 133-mi section through the desert of west-central Utah. It starts at Camp Floyd–Stagecoach Inn State Park in Fairfield and ends in Ibapah near the Utah–Nevada border. Stone pillars with metal plaques mark the route that starts and ends on pavement, then becomes a dirt road for 126 mi that is passable when dry. A brochure describing the major stops along the trail is available from the U.S. Bureau of Land Management's Salt Lake Field Office.	**Antelope Island State Park** is the most developed and scenic spot in which to experience the Great Salt Lake. Hiking and biking trails crisscross the island, and you can go saltwater bathing at several beach areas. (Since the salinity level of the lake is always greater than that of the ocean, the water is extremely buoyant.) The island has historic sites, as well as desert wildlife and birds in their natural habitat—though the most popular inhabitants here are a herd of more than 500 bison.

WHERE TO STAY

WHAT IT COSTS					
	¢	$	$$	$$$	$$$$
FOR 2 PEOPLE	under $70	$70–$110	$111–$150	$151–$200	over $200

Hotel prices are for two people in a standard double room in high season, excluding taxes of 10.1% to 11.2%

$$$$
Fodor'sChoice
★

The Grand America Hotel. With its white Bethel granite exterior, this 24-story luxury hotel dominates the skyline a few blocks south of downtown. Inside the beveled-glass and brass doors, you step into a world of Italian marble floors and walls and pure old-world style—think English wool carpets, French furniture and tapestries, and colorful Murano-glass chandeliers. The posh guest rooms average 700 square feet. Most have views and small balconies. This is a great place to sit back with room service and revel in some pampering. The big outdoor pool and indoor spa are among the best in the city. ⊠ *555 S. Main St., Downtown 84111* ☎ *801/258–6000 or 800/621–4505* ⊞ *801/258–6911* ⊕ *www.grandamerica.com* ⟋ *386 rooms, 389 suites* ⚲ *In-room: safe, kitchen (some), refrigerator (some), DVD, VCR, Ethernet. In-hotel: restaurant, room service, 2 bars, 2 pools, gym, spa, laundry service, concierge, executive floor, public Internet, public Wi-Fi, parking (fee), no-smoking rooms* ⊟ *AE, D, DC, MC, V* ⦿ *EP.*

$$$–$$$$
Fodor'sChoice
★

Hotel Monaco Salt Lake City. This swank hotel is ensconced in a former bank, distinguished by an exterior decorated with classical cornices and cartouches. Inside, the look and feel are sophisticated, eclectic, and upbeat. Rooms offer extras such as big fringed ottomans, oversize framed mirrors and beds, and lots of pillows. And, there are special rooms for especially tall folks, with extra-long beds. Bambara Restaurant, on the ground level (under separate management), is one of the city's most celebrated dining spots. ✉ *15 W. 200 South St., Downtown, 84101* ☎ *801/595–0000 or 800/805–1801* 🖷 *801/532–8500* ⊕ *www.monaco-saltlakecity.com* ⇆ *187 rooms, 38 suites* ✑ *In-room: safe, Ethernet, Wi-Fi. In-hotel: restaurant, room service, bar, gym, concierge, laundry service, parking (fee)* ⊟ *AE, D, DC, MC, V.*

$$–$$$ 🏨 **Inn on the Hill.** This turn-of-the-
★ 20th-century Renaissance Revival mansion makes a striking impression with its red rock exterior and bold painted trim. Inside, it's like stepping into the just-polished parlor and living rooms of a private home, replete with stained-glass windows. Rooms are eclectic in style, with historic Utah themes. All are very cushy, with big bathtubs and fireplaces. ✉ *225 N. State St., Capitol Hill, 84103* ☎ *801/328–1466* 🖷 *801/328–0590* ⊕ *www.inn-on-the-hill.com* ⇆ *6 rooms, 6 suites* ✑ *In-room: refrigerator (some), VCR (some), Ethernet (some). In-hotel: no elevator, public Internet, public Wi-Fi, no kids under 14, no-smoking rooms* ⊟ *AE, MC, V* ⍟ *BP.*

VITAL STATS

- State Capitol: Salt Lake City
- State Insect: Honey Bee
- State Motto: "Industry"
- State Cooking Pot: Dutch Oven
- State Emblem: Beehive
- Unofficial State Condiment: Fry sauce (ketchup mixed with mayo)
- Highest Point: King's Peak, 13,528 feet
- Lowest Point: Beaver Dam Wash, 2,350 feet
- Favorite Invective: Oh my heck

24

NIGHTLIFE & THE ARTS

Fodor's Choice Rub shoulders with the "beautiful people" in Park City during Rob-
★ ert Redford's **Sundance Film Festival** (✉ *Box 684429, Park City 84068* ☎ *435/658–3456* ⊕ *www.sundance.org*) or come to three venues in downtown Salt Lake City. The festival has more than 100 screenings in Salt Lake City at the Tower Theatre, Broadway Center Theatre, and Rose Wagner Performing Arts Center. Buy tickets ahead online, or purchase day-of-show tickets, if available, at the theaters.

Fodor's Choice The **Mormon Tabernacle Choir** (✉ *Temple Sq.* ☎ *801/240–4150* ⊕ *www.*
★ *mormontabernaclechoir.org*), which includes men and women of all ages from around the Intermountain region, performs sacred music, with some secular—classical and patriotic—works.

SPORTS & THE OUTDOORS

Fodor's Choice When it comes to skiing, **Alta Ski Area** is widely acclaimed for both what
★ it has and what it doesn't have. What it has is perhaps the best snow anywhere in the world—up to 500 inches a year, and terrain to match it. What it doesn't have is glitz and pomp—and snowboarders (they're not allowed). ✉ *Box 8007, 84092* ☎ *801/359–1078, 801/572–3939 snow report* ⊕ *www.alta.com* ⇆ *2,020-feet vertical drop; 2,200 skiable acres; 25% novice, 40% intermediate, 35% advanced; 2 high*

speed quads, 3 triple chairs, 3 double chairs ⬛Lift tickets $59; Alta Snowbird One Pass $79.

★ **Snowbird Ski and Summer Resort** has plenty of powder-filled chutes, bowls, and meadow areas. Snowbird's signature 125-passenger tram takes you from the base all the way to the top in one fell swoop for a leg-burning top to bottom run of more than 3,000 vertical feet. The terrain here is weighted more toward experts—35% of Snowbird is rated black-diamond—and if there's a drawback to this resort it's a lack of beginner terrain. ⊠*Hwy. 210, Box 929000, Snowbird, 84092* ☎*801/933–2222, 800/232–9542 lodging reservations, 801/933–2110 special events, 801/933–2100 snow report* 🖷*801/947–8227* ⊕*www. snowbird.com* ⌕*3,240-feet vertical drop; 4,700 skiable acres; 27% novice, 38% intermediate, 35% advanced; 125-passenger tram, 4 quad lifts, 6 double chairs, and a skier tunner with surface lift* ⬛*Lift tickets $69 tram and chairs, $59 chairlift only; Alta Snowbird One Pass $79.*

With the perfect combination of all the fluffy powder of Alta and Snowbird and all the quiet charm many large resorts have left behind,
A **Brighton Ski Resort** is a favorite among serious snowboarders and out-on-the-edge skiers. Its expert terrain and new renegade image notwithstanding, this is still a great place for families, with ideal beginner and intermediate terrain. ⊠*12601 Big Cottonwood Rd., Brighton, 84121* ☎*801/532–4731, 800/873–5512, 800/873–5512 snow report* 🖷*435/649–1787* ⊕*www.brightonresort.com* ⌕*1,745-feet vertical drop; 1050 skiable acres; 21% beginner, 40% intermediate, 39% advanced/expert; 4 high-speed quad chairs, 1 fixed grip quad, 1 triple chair* ⬛*Lift tickets $53.*

★ Since the early 1990s the base of **Solitude Mountain Resort** has grown into a European-style village with lodges, condominiums, a luxury hotel, and award-winning restaurants, but downhill skiing and snowboarding are still the main attractions. ⊠*12000 Big Cottonwood Canyon, Solitude, 84121* ☎*801/534–1400, 800/748–4754, 801/536–5774 Nordic Center, 801/536–5777 snow report* 🖷*435/649–5276* ⊕*www.skisolitude. com* ⌕*2,047-feet vertical drop; 1,200 skiable acres; 20% beginner, 50% intermediate, 30% advanced; 1 high-speed quad chairs, 2 quad chair, 1 triple chairs, 4 double chairs* ⬛*Lift tickets $55.*

VISITOR INFORMATION

Salt Lake Convention and Visitors Bureau (⊠*90 S. West Temple, Downtown, 84101* ☎*801/534–4900, 800/541–4955* ⊕*www.saltlake.org*).

Utah Travel Industry (⊠*300 N. State St., Capitol Hill, 84114* ☎*801/538–1030 or 800/200–1160* ⊕*www.utah.com*).

Southern Utah

WITH ARCHES, BRYCE CANYON, CANYONLANDS, CAPITOL REEF, AND ZION NATIONAL PARKS

Bryce Amphitheater, Bryce Canyon National Park

WORD OF MOUTH

"You can't really go wrong with the Utah parks . . . Arches and Canyonlands are hard to beat. Moab has plenty of lodging and restaurants. Zion and Bryce are equally as good, with Lodging inside the park if that interests you. You could possibly sneak in a day or 2 at Capital reef with either one of these options."

—spirobulldog

EXPLORING SOUTHERN UTAH

220 mi (Capitol Reef), 310 mi (Zion) south of Salt Lake City via I–15, I–70, and local roads; 160 mi (Zion), 450 mi (Arches) northeast of Las Vegas via I–15, I–70, and local roads; 350 mi (Arches), 640 mi (Zion) west of Denver via I–15, I–70, and local roads

By John Blodgett

Southern Utah is unique—nowhere else in the country do five national parks exist in such close proximity. What's fascinating is that each one is quite different from the others. From southwest to southeast, they are Zion, with sheer cliffs that drop 2,000 feet or more; Bryce Canyon (actually an amphitheater), with its bright orange hoodoos; Capitol Reef, a 100-mi fold in the earth; Canyonlands, segmented into three distinct regions by deep canyons formed by the Colorado and Green Rivers; and Arches, containing the largest concentration of natural arches in the world (and some pretty funky formations to boot).

It's a lot to take in, and it's pretty much impossible to do all of them justice in one short trip. But that's OK, because Southern Utah is the kind of place that keeps drawing people back time and again for adventure and exploration.

WHO WILL ESPECIALLY LOVE THIS TRIP?

Outdoor Enthusiasts: Southern Utah's national parks offer something for adventurers of every ability level. Hiking is by far the most popular activity, and it's wise to consult with a ranger ahead of time to discuss trip length, level of difficulty, and the likelihood of flash flooding (not as much an issue at Bryce as at the lower elevation parks). Rafting is especially popular along the Green and Colorado rivers inside (and outside) Canyonlands.

Archaeology Buffs: Ancient Indian tribes made their homes in many of the canyons of Southern Utah. The Horseshoe Canyon section of Canyonlands has some especially wonderful examples of rock art, including the famed Great Gallery. You can occasionally spot granaries on some of the steep alcoves and cliffs, and you can also find evidence of the early pioneers who first settled (or tried to settle) these often arid lands.

Photographers: You definitely won't have to look hard for photo ops in Southern Utah. In Arches, the often snow-covered 12,000-foot La Sal Mountains are a contrasting backdrop for the park's Navajo sandstone formations. The bright orange hoodoos of Bryce make obvious subjects, but try to photograph them at sunrise or sunset when the colors are richest. And few vistas can rival the southward view from Grand View Point Overlook in Canyonlands' Island in the Sky district.

Families: There are plenty of things to enjoy with your children in each of Utah's five national parks. Most parks have a junior ranger program, as well as educational visitor centers. (Zion's visitor center and the Zion Human History Museum are two of the most informative sites of all Southern Utah's parks.) All parks have kid-friendly—some ranger-led—and other programs suitable for families.

TOP 5 REASONS TO GO

The Subway: Formed by millennia of running water, this route in the Zion backcountry is attempted only by the sturdiest of canyoneers—who often must proceed through chest-deep water, holding their backpacks above their heads.

Thor's Hammer: The most fancifully named of Bryce's limestone hoo-doos, this formation was shaped by years and years of erosion.

Cathedral Valley: Exploring the backcountry of Capitol Reef is a spir-itual experience—silent, uncrowded, and beneath massive stone forma-tions that are stained by the golden light of the setting sun.

Island in the Sky: From here you can take in all of sprawling Canyon-lands, from deep river-carved gorges to mazelike canyons to tall rock formations.

Delicate Arch: The most famous arch in Arches graces one of Utah's license plates.

25

WHEN IS THE BEST TIME TO VISIT?

Ask five different people when you should visit Utah's five national parks, and you'll get five different answers. It really depends on what you want to do—and how well you tolerate extremes in weather. June, July, and August are especially hot in Arches, Canyonlands, and Capi-tol Reef, but this just means that many people don't stray far from their air-conditioned vehicles or tour buses (or go rafting to cool off). April, May, September, and even early October can be very comfortable times for exploring. It's less crowded during this time, perfect for mountain biking or hiking; campers delight in the warm, comfortable nights. In winter, December through March, you can find even fewer people. Bryce is at the highest elevation, and therefore the coldest. It's also the snowiest, which attracts snowshoers and cross-country skiers.

There's more than weather to consider when timing a visit to Southern Utah. Understandably, most local festivals and events occur during the warmest months—such as Moab's Jeep Safari (near Arches and Can-yonlands), golfing (Zion), and the funky Bicknell Film Festival (Capitol Reef). Summer is also the high season for shopping, as many places close during the off-season.

HOW SHOULD I GET THERE?

DRIVING

If you're driving into Southern Utah from the Salt Lake City area, start by taking I–15 south. From there take Route 6 southeast to I–70 east, and then Route 191 south to access Arches and Canyonlands. Or, continue south on I–15 until I–70 east for Capitol Reef via Route 40, or for Bryce via Route 89 and then Route 12. Zion is best reached by leaving I–15 for Route 9 farther south. There are plenty of backways to and from each park as well, so if you feel like exploring, get a good map or atlas and hit the road.

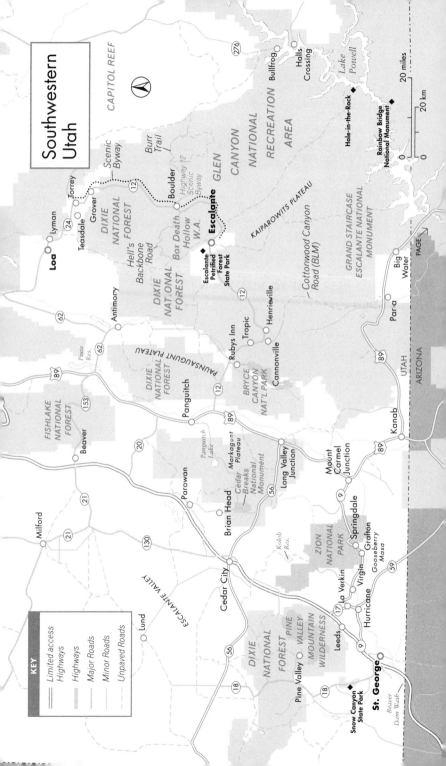

Southwestern Utah

CAPITOL REEF

276

Bullfrog

Halls
Crossing

Lake
Powell

Hole-in-the-Rock

Rainbow Bridge
National Monument

20 miles

20 km

GLEN CANYON NATIONAL RECREATION AREA

Burr
Trail

Scenic
Byway

12

Boulder

Highway #12
Scenic
Byway

24

Torrey

Lyman

Loa

Grover

Teasdale

DIXIE NATIONAL FOREST

Hell's
Backbone
Road

Box Death
Hollow
W.A.

Escalante

KAIPAROWITS PLATEAU

DIXIE
NAT.ONAL
FOREST

Antimory

Escalante Petrified
Forest
State Park

62

12

Henrieville

Cottonwood Canyon
Road (BLM)

GRAND STAIRCASE
ESCALANTE NATIONAL
MONUMENT

Big
Water

Para

PAGE

Piute
Res.

62

89

FISHLAKE
NATIONAL
FOREST

153

Beaver

20

PAUNSAUGUNT PLATEAU

Panguitch

Rubys Inn

Tropic

Cannonville

BRYCE
CANYON
NAT'L PARK

12

89

DIXIE
NATIONAL
FOREST

Parowan

Panguitch
Lake

Markagunt
Plateau

Cedar
Breaks
National
Monument

Long Valley
Junction

56

Kanab

89

UTAH
ARIZONA

21

Milford

130

Cedar City

Brian Head

Kolob
Res.

ZION
NATIONAL
PARK

Mount
Carmel
Junction

9

89

ESCALANTE VALLEY

Lund

56

DIXIE
NATIONAL
FOREST

PINE
VALLEY
MOUNTAIN
WILDERNESS

Pine Valley

Leeds

La Verkin

Virgin

Springdale

Grafton

Gooseberry
Mesa

59

18

St. George

Snow Canyon
State Park

Beaver
Dam Wash

9

Hurricane

17

KEY

Limited access
Highways

Highways

Highways

Major Roads

Minor Roads

Unpaved Roads

CLOSE UP

How to Snack

In the small town of Bicknell, about 25 minutes north of Capitol Reef, the Sunglow Cafè proudly serves home-made Pinto Bean and Pickle pies (they taste a lot better than they sound). Stop in for a slice, or take a whole pie (or two) to go. The Pinto Beans are full of carbs, perfect fuel for a hike.

Jerky—long slices of seasoned meat that have been dehydrated for preservation—is another popular treat here, and also good to take along on a hike.

Almost every gas station and grocery store sells it, but keep an eye out for local roadside vendors who sell it as fresh as it can be.

Beef and turkey are popular, but you can make jerky out of pretty much any type of meat. You may come across more exotic offerings, including elk and buffalo.

25

FLYING

Many visitors choose to fly into Las Vegas, especially to reach Zion and Bryce. Salt Lake City and Denver are other options, but you'll have a longer drive ahead once you touch down.

HOW DO I GET AROUND?

BY CAR

Various tour companies—from inside and outside Utah—bring tourists to each of the five national parks via bus tours, but a car is by far the best way to explore Southern Utah (especially with children in tow). You can enjoy the trip on your own schedule, and you can change your itinerary on the fly. An SUV or four-wheel-drive vehicle will help you get off the beaten path, but don't underestimate the skill and experience it takes to drive into the backcountry—and the exorbitantly high cost of a tow if you get stranded.

WHERE SHOULD I FOCUS MY ENERGY?

If you're here for 1 day: If your visit is brief, you'll probably spend much of your time in or near your vehicle. Choose either Arches or Bryce, which have scenic drives that access many major overlooks and rock formations.

If you're here for 2 days: From Arches, check out Canyonlands' Island in the Sky district and spend some time in Moab. From Bryce, head to Zion via the Zion–Mt. Carmel tunnel—a narrow 1.1-mi journey through rock (RVs must arrange an escort from a ranger for a fee). Overnight in Springdale.

If you're here for 3 days: Spend some time hiking (there are casual strolls if you're not up for a strenuous trail).

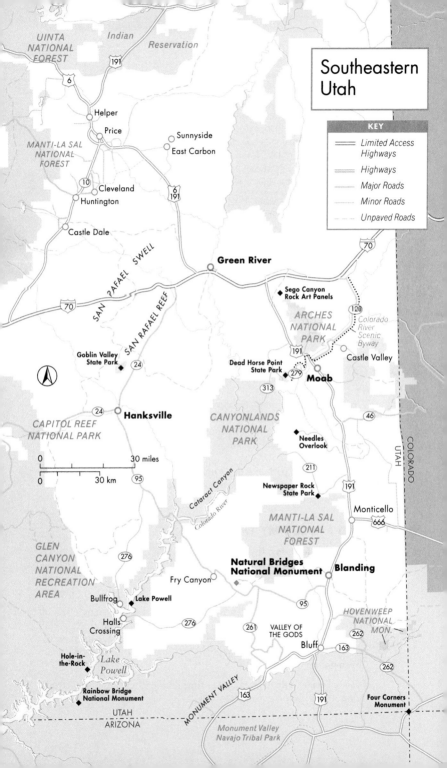

Southeastern Utah

KEY

═══	*Limited Access Highways*
───	*Highways*
───	*Major Roads*
‑‑‑	*Minor Roads*
‑ ‑ ‑	*Unpaved Roads*

UINTA NATIONAL FOREST

Indian Reservation

191

6

Helper

Price

MANTI-LA SAL NATIONAL FOREST

Sunnyside

East Carbon

10

Cleveland

Huntington

6
191

Castle Dale

SAN RAFAEL SWELL

Green River

SAN RAFAEL REEF

70

Sego Canyon Rock Art Panels

ARCHES NATIONAL PARK

128

Colorado River Scenic Byway

Goblin Valley State Park

24

Dead Horse Point State Park

191

Castle Valley

279

Moab

313

CAPITOL REEF NATIONAL PARK

24

Hanksville

CANYONLANDS NATIONAL PARK

46

Needles Overlook

211

0 _____ 30 miles
0 _____ 30 km

95

Cataract Canyon

Colorado River

Newspaper Rock State Park

191

Monticello

666

GLEN CANYON NATIONAL RECREATION AREA

MANTI-LA SAL NATIONAL FOREST

276

Natural Bridges National Monument

Blanding

Fry Canyon

95

Bullfrog

Lake Powell

Halls Crossing

276

261

VALLEY OF THE GODS

HOVENWEEP NATIONAL MON.

262

Hole-in-the-Rock

Lake Powell

Bluff

163

262

Rainbow Bridge National Monument

UTAH
ARIZONA

MONUMENT VALLEY

163

191

Four Corners Monument

UTAH | COLORADO

Monument Valley Navajo Tribal Park

CLAIM TO FAME

Having five national parks in such close proximity is enough of a reason to feel boastful, but there are other aspects of Southern Utah in which locals take justifiable pride. Originally created for off-road motorcyclists, Moab's Slickrock Trail has long reigned as the center of the mountain biking universe. Bikers can roll along the Navajo sandstone for miles, and there's a practice loop for novices. Kanab, south of Zion and Bryce, is known as "Little Hollywood" for all of the movies—mostly westerns—that have been filmed in the vicinity. Clint Eastwood's "The Outlaw Josey Wales" was the last film shot in a town site built near the ruins of the pioneer town Paria. The home and studio of Maynard Dixon, famed painter of western landscapes, is north of Kanab in the tiny town of Mt. Carmel; tours are given between May and October. Edward Abbey wrote his seminal Desert Solitaire while he was a ranger at Arches. Published in 1968, it established Abbey as an outspoken critic of industrialism, commercialism, and the desecration of wilderness.

25

If you're here for 4 days: Take a scenic flight out of either Bryce or Moab airport, then spend some time shopping and dining in Springdale or Moab.

If you're here for 5 days: If you're in the Moab area, consider camping on Days 4 and 5 so you can hike in the Needles District of Canyonlands. If you've checked out Bryce and Zion, head to Capitol Reef and take the scenic drive before dining in Torrey.

If you're here for 6 days: Head to one of the parks you haven't visited yet.

If you're here for 7 days or more: You can divide a weeklong trip among all five national parks (though keep in mind that you may be doing a lot of driving). Another option is to focus on fewer parks—say two or three—and explore each one more in depth by hiking, camping, rafting, mountain biking, and horseback riding.

WHAT ARE THE TOP EXPERIENCES?

Rockreation: Geology is one of Southern Utah's main draws. The landscape here is shaped and colored by rock: the reddish Entrada sandstone and the beige Navajo sandstone, both rippling and rolling in formation; bright orange limestone that has eroded into hoodoos; and the white of bentonite clay that colors them thar hills. In parts of Zion, the asphalt you drive upon is tinted red to better fit in with the surroundings. The Green River's green color comes from dissolved mineral solids; the Colorado River, whether placid or roiling, is a deep brown. Watch for the play of colored light upon the ground at sunrise or sunset. There is no place on earth quite like Southern Utah, which is why many European and Asian tourists flock to this area at every time of the year. When you're here, whether by foot or bike or horseback, make sure to experience the rock.

HISTORY YOU CAN SEE

In 1869 John Wesley Powell and nine other brave men embarked on a 1,000-mi river journey that would take them through Utah on the Green and Colorado rivers, all the way to Arizona's Grand Canyon. The expedition explored what had until then been uncharted territory, opening up the west for further settlement.

Ten years later, Mormon pioneers, trying to find a shortcut to a proposed settlement, reached a crack in the canyon rim above the Escalante River near its confluence with the Colorado River. For three cold winter months, 250 men, women, and children—along with 83 wagons and more than 1,000 head of cattle—waited as the hole was enlarged with pickaxes, shovels, and limited explosives. Once it was wide enough, the entire expedition had to descend the 2,000 feet to the river—with an average grade of 25 degrees (45 degrees in some places). The Hole-in-the-Rock, as it came to be called, is visible at the end of a 45-mi graded dirt road leading southeast out of Escalante.

Hiking: A car will let you cover a lot of ground in a short time, but don't be fooled—you'll miss a lot of Southern Utah if you don't get out to explore, no matter how slowly you drive. There are trails for hikers and walkers of every ability level, places where you can spot elusive flowers, scurrying lizards (don't worry, they aren't poisonous), soaring Peregrine falcons, and the looks of wonder on the faces of your companions. Make sure to dress appropriately (for the heat or the cold, depending on the time of year and time of day) and bring along plenty of water even when the temps go down (it's dry out here). Look for printed trail maps in any visitor center, or talk with a ranger for guidance—who knows, you might get a secret trail tip or two.

History: Hundreds of years have passed since the last Native Americans made their homes in the canyons of Southern Utah, but their presence is still palpable. For every readily accessible rock art panel—like the petroglyphs along the Fremont River in Capitol Reef—there are numerous less visible examples of ancient artwork in the backcountry, along with granaries and the remnants of other structures. There's plenty of pioneer and modern human history, too, including the collapsing winch atop Cable Mountain in Zion more than 2,000 feet above the floor of Zion Canyon (it was used to lower wood used to building homes and other structures).

Photography: Make sure your camera's memory cards are suitably large—or bring plenty of film if you haven't yet gone digital. Southern Utah is a color photography paradise in any season, and not just in the national parks. Entrada sandstone is a deep, rich red, Navajo sandstone an almost golden beige, the limestone at Bryce is an otherworldly orange; and all are intensified at sunset. The colored rock is beautiful at sun rise, too, and when reflected in river water.

BEST BETS

SIGHTS AND TOURS

★ **Anasazi State Park.** Anasazi is a Navajo word interpreted to mean "ancient enemies." What the Anasazi called themselves we will never know, but their descendants, the Hopi people, prefer the term ancestral Puebloan. This state park is dedicated to the study of that mysterious culture, with a largely unexcavated dwelling site, an interactive museum, and a reproduction of a pueblo. ✉ *460 N. Hwy. 12, Boulder* ☎ *435/335–7308* ⊕ *www.state parks.utah.gov* 💲 *$3 per person* 🕐 *Memorial Day–Labor Day, daily 8–6; Labor Day–Memorial Day, daily 9–5.*

Courthouse Wash. Although this rock-art panel fell victim to a sad and unusual case of vandalism in 1980, when someone scoured the petroglyphs and pictographs that had been left by four cultures, you can still see ancient images if you take a short walk from the parking area on the left-hand side of the road. ✉ *U.S. 191, about 2 mi south of Arches National Park entrance.*

Dead Horse Point State Park. One of the finest state parks in Utah overlooks a sweeping oxbow of the Colorado River, some 2,000 feet below, and the upside-down landscapes of Canyonlands National Park. Dead Horse Point itself is a small peninsula connected to the main mesa by a narrow neck of land. As the story goes, cowboys used to drive wild horses onto the point and pen them there with a brush fence. Some were accidentally forgotten and left to perish. Facilities at the park include a modern visitor center and museum, a 21-site campground with drinking water, and an overlook. ✉ *34 mi west from Moab at end of Rte. 313* ☎ *435/259–2614, 800/322–3770 for campground reservations* ⊕ *www.stateparks.utah.gov* 💲 *$7 per vehicle* 🕐 *Daily 8–6.*

The **Dixie National Forest** (✉ *1789 N. Wedgewood La., Cedar City* ☎ *435/865–3700* ⊕ *www.fs.fed.us/dxnf*) administers an area encompassing almost 2 million acres, stretching 170 mi across southwestern Utah, and containing 26 designated campgrounds. The forest is popular for such activities as horseback riding, fishing, and hiking.

★ **Edge of the Cedars State Park.** Tucked away on a backstreet in Blanding is one of the nation's foremost museums dedicated to the ancestral Puebloan Indians. The museum displays a variety of pots, baskets, spear points, and such. Interestingly, many of these artifacts were donated

STRANGE BUT TRUE

In 1934 20-year-old Everett Reuss, an artist and poet, left his well-to-do family and disappeared into the wilderness near Escalante. His burros and some of his gear were found in a box canyon, but he was never heard from again.

Nearby, the town of Paria never quite took hold, due to the Paria River's flooding. Founded in 1865, the original townsite is now a crumbling ghost town. A replica western town was built nearby and used in television shows and movies—but it too eventually succomed to flood waters. A replica of the replica has since been constructed in the name of tourism.

25

by pot hunters—archaeological looters. Behind the museum, you can visit an actual Anasazi ruin. ✉ *660 W. 400 North St., Blanding* ☎ *435/678–2238* ⊕ *www.state parks.utah.gov* ✉ *$6 per vehicle* ◷ *May–Sept., daily 9–6; Oct.–Apr., daily 9–5.*

Created to protect a huge repository of fossilized wood and dinosaur bones, **Escalante Petrified Forest** ★ **State Park** has two short interpretive trails to educate visitors. There's an attractive swimming beach at the park's Wide Hollow Reservoir, which is also good for boating, fishing, and birding. ✉ *710 N. Reservoir Rd., Escalante* ☎ *435/826–4466* ⊕ *www.stateparks.utah.gov* ✉ *$5* ◷ *Daily*

Fodor's Choice **Grand Staircase–Escalante National Monument.** In September 1996 Presi-
★ dent Bill Clinton designated 1.7 million acres in south-central Utah as the Grand Staircase–Escalante National Monument, the first monument to be administered by the Bureau of Land Management instead of the National Park Service. Its three distinct sections—the Grand Staircase, the Kaiparowits Plateau, and the Canyons of the Escalante—offer remote backcountry experiences hard to find elsewhere in the lower 48. Waterfalls, Native American ruins and petroglyphs, shoulder-width slot canyons, and improbable colors all characterize this wilderness. Straddling the northern border of the monument, the small towns of Escalante and Boulder offer access, information, outfitters, lodging, and dining to adventurers. The highway that connects them, Route 12, is one of the most scenic stretches of road in the Southwest.

All of the landscape in this part of the country is strange and surreal, ★ but **Goblin Valley State Park** takes the cake as the weirdest of all. As the name implies, the area is filled with hundreds of gnomelike rock formations. Colored in a dramatic orange hue, the goblins especially delight children. Short, easy trails wind through the goblins, and there's a small, but dusty, campground with modern restrooms and showers. ✉ *Rte. 24, 12 mi north of Hanksville* ☎ *435/564–3633* ⊕ *www.state parks.utah.gov* ✉ *$6 per vehicle* ◷ *Daily 8–dusk.*

Fodor's Choice Keep your camera handy and steering wheel steady along **Highway 12**
★ **Scenic Byway** between Escalante and Loa, near Capitol Reef National Park. Though the highway starts at the intersection of U.S. 89, west of Bryce Canyon National Park, the stretch that begins in Escalante is one of the most spectacular. The road passes through Grand Staircase–Escalante National Monument and on to Capitol Reef along one of the most scenic stretches of highway in the United States. Be sure to stop at the scenic overlooks; almost every one will give you an eye-

popping view. Don't get distracted, though; the paved road is twisting and steep, and at times climbs over a hogback with sheer drop-offs on both sides.

While en route to southeastern Utah in 1879, Mormon pioneers chipped and blasted a narrow passageway in solid rock, through which they lowered their wagons. The **Hole-in-the-Rock Trail**, now a 60-mi gravel road, leads south from Route 12, east of Escalante, to the actual hole-in-the-rock site in Glen Canyon Recreation Area. Much of the original passageway has been flooded by the waters of Lake Powell.

John Wesley Powell River History Museum. Here you can see what it was like to travel down the Green and Colorado rivers in the 1800s. A series of interactive displays tracks the Powell Party's arduous, dangerous 1869 journey. The center also houses the River Runner's Hall of Fame, a tribute to those who have followed in Powell's wake. An art gallery reserved for works thematically linked to river exploration is also on-site. ⊠ *885 E. Main St., Green River* ☎ *435/564-3427* ⌨ *$7 per person, children 3–12 $1, $7 per family* ☉ *Apr.–Oct., daily 8–7; Oct.–Mar., daily 9–5.*

Fodor'sChoice

Natural Bridges National Monument. When visitor Elliot McClure came to Natural Bridges National Monument in 1931, the road in was so bad his car slowly disintegrated. First his headlights fell off. Next, his doors dropped off. Finally, his bumpers worked loose, and the radiator broke away. Today a drive to the three stone bridges is far less hazardous. All roads are paved and a scenic 9-mi route takes you to stops that overlook Sipapu, Owachomo, and Kachina bridges. There's also a 13-site primitive campground. Natural Bridges is a drive of about 100 mi southwest from the Needles District of Canyonlands National Park. ⊠ *Rte. 275 off Rte. 95* ☎ *435/692–1234* ⊕ *www.nps.gov/nabr* ⌨ *$6 per vehicle* ☉ *Daily 7 AM–dusk.*

★ **Newspaper Rock Recreation Site.** One of the West's most famous rock-art sites, this large panel contains Native American etchings that accumulated on the rock over the course of 2,000 years. Apparently, early pioneers and explorers to the region named the site Newspaper Rock because they believed the rock, crowded with drawings, constituted a written language with which early people communicated. Archaeologists now agree the petroglyphs do not represent language. This is one of many "newspaper rocks" throughout the Southwest. ⊠ *Rte. 211, about 15 mi west of U.S. 191.*

San Rafael Swell. About 80 mi long and 30 mi wide, this massive fold and uplift in the Earth's crust rises 2,100 feet above the desert. The Swell, as it's known locally, is northeast of Capitol Reef, between Interstate 70 and Highway 24. You can take photos from several viewpoints. ⊠ *BLM San Rafael Resource Area, 900 North and 700 East, Price* ☎ *435/637–4584* ⊕ *www.ut.blm.gov.*

Red Navajo sandstone mesas and formations are crowned with black lava rock, creating high-contrast vistas from either end of **Snow Canyon State Park.** From the campground you can scramble up huge sandstone

25

ON THE WAY

■ About 150 mi south of Salt Lake City, the Utah Territorial Statehouse in Fillmore, off I–15, is Utah's oldest government building. Fillmore was the original capital of what was then Utah Territory, but the building saw only one year's use before Salt Lake City became the capital in 1856.

■ The last standing fort built by Mormon pioneers, Cove Fort, near the junction of I–15 and I–70, is on the way to Bryce and Capitol Reef. Built in 1867 to protect traveling settlers from Indians, Cove Fort has been restored and now operates as a state historic site.

■ When iron deposits were discovered in Southern Utah in the late 1840s, Mormon leader Brigham Young assembled people to colonize what was called the Iron Mission. The original foundry still stands in Old Iron Town, west of what is now Cedar City.

mounds and overlook the entire valley. ⊠ *1002 Snow Canyon Dr., Ivins* ☎ *435/628–2255* ⊕ *www.stateparks.utah.gov* ☎ *$5* ☉ *Daily.*

WHERE TO EAT

	WHAT IT COSTS				
	¢	$	$$	$$$	$$$$
AT DINNER	under $8	$8–$12	$13–$20	$21–$30	over $30

Restaurant prices are per person for a main course at dinner, excluding sales tax and tip.

$$–$$$$ ✕ **Milt's Stage Stop.** This dinner spot in beautiful Cedar Canyon is known
★ for its 12-ounce rib-eye steak, prime rib, fresh crab, lobster, and shrimp dishes. In winter deer feed in front of the restaurant as a fireplace blazes away inside. A number of hunting trophies decorate the rustic building's interior, and splendid views of the surrounding mountains delight patrons year-round. ⊠ *Cedar Canyon, 5 mi east of town on Rte. 14, Cedar City* ☎ *435/586–9344* ⊟ *AE, D, DC, MC, V* ☉ *No lunch.*

$$–$$$ ✕ **Bit & Spur Restaurant and Saloon.** This restaurant has been a legend in
Fodor'sChoice Utah for more than 25 years. The house favorites menu lists familiar
★ Southwestern dishes like flautas verde, but the kitchen also gets creative. Try the chili-rubbed *bistec asado* or pasta with rosemary cream sauce. When the weather is nice, arrive early so you can eat outside and enjoy the lovely grounds and views. ⊠ *1212 Zion Park Blvd., Springdale* ☎ *435/772–3498* ⊕ *www.bitandspur.com* ⊟ *AE, D, MC, V* ☉ *No lunch.*

$$–$$$ ✕ **Cafe Diablo.** This popular Torrey restaurant keeps getting better, and
Fodor'sChoice indeed is one of the state's best. Saltillo-tile floors and matte-plaster
★ white walls are a perfect setting for the Southwestern art that lines the walls in this intimate restaurant. Innovative Southwestern entrées include fire-roasted pork tenderloin, artichoke and sun-dried tomato

tamales, and local trout crusted with pumpkin seeds and served with a cilantro-lime sauce. The rattlesnake cakes, made with free-range desert rattler and served with ancho-rosemary aioli, are delicious. ⊠ *599 W. Main St. (Hwy. 24), Torrey* ☎ *435/425–3070* ⊕ *www.cafediablo.net* ⊟ *AE, D, MC, V* ⊘ *Closed mid-Oct.–mid-Apr. No lunch.*

$$–$$$
★
×**Center Café.** This little jewel in the desert has a courtyard for outdoor dining. The mood inside is Spanish Mediterranean, made even more lovely by the fireplace. From grilled Black Angus beef tenderloin with caramelized onion and Gorgonzola, or roasted eggplant lasagna with feta cheese and Moroccan olive marinara, there's always something here to make your taste buds go "ah." This treasure has been named "Best Restaurant in Southern Utah" more than once. Be sure to ask for the impressive wine list. ⊠ *60 N. 100 West, Moab* ☎ *435/259–4295* ⊟ *D, MC, V* ⊘ *Closed Dec. and Jan. No lunch.*

$–$$$
Fodor'sChoice
★
×**Hell's Backbone Grill.** The owners use only local organic foods that are historically relevant to the area, so you might find buffalo and corn-meal-molasses and pecan skillet trout on the menu. Native American, Western range, Southwestern, and Mormon pioneer recipes inspire the chef. Salads might contain strawberries, jicama, pine nuts, and dried corn. ⊠ *20 N. Rte. 12, in Boulder Mountain Lodge, Box 1428, Boulder, 84716* ☎ *435/335–7464* ⊕ *www.hellsbackbonegrill.com* ⊟ *DC, MC, V* ⊘ *Closed mid-Nov.–Feb. No lunch.*

¢–$$
×**Fosters Family Steakhouse.** With a stone fireplace and picture windows, Fosters is a clean, relatively quiet, modern steak house, and one of the most pleasant restaurants in the area. The menu features prime rib, steaks, and basic chicken and seafood dishes. Beer is the only alcohol served. ⊠ *Rte. 12, 2 mi west of junction with Rte. 63, Bryce Canyon National Park* ☎ *435/834–5227* ⊟ *AE, D, MC, V* ⊘ *Closed Mon.–Thurs. in Jan.*

¢–$
★
×**Bear Paw Coffee Company.** The menu is full of flavor, with elements of Southwestern, Tex-Mex, American, and Italian cuisines all represented, but breakfast is the star of the show here (and served all day, every day). The coffee is hot, the teas loose, the juice fresh, and the servers smiling. Home brewers (of coffee and tea, that is) can get their fresh beans and leaves here, too. ⊠ *75 N. Main St., St. George* ☎ *435/634–0126* ⊟ *AE, D, MC, V* ⊘ *No dinner.*

WHERE TO STAY

	WHAT IT COSTS				
	¢	$	$$	$$$	$$$$
FOR 2 PEOPLE	under $50	$50–$100	$101–$150	$151–$200	over $200

Hotel prices are for two people in a standard double room in high season, excluding taxes and service charges.

$$$$
Fodor'sChoice
★
Red Mountain Spa. Near the mouth of redrock-wonder Snow Canyon and next to lava fields, this fit and active resort is a source of rejuvenation. Breakfast and lunch buffets list the nutritional contents for each food item, while dinner is a more traditional sit-down experience. But

it's not just about the food—there are fitness classes, hikes, Yoga, and far more activities that leave you with a healthy glow when you depart. The place bustles at 6 AM as people go to breakfast before heading off on a hike. ✉ *1275 E. Red Mountain Circle, Ivins 84738* ☎ *435/673–4905 or 800/407–3002* 🌐 *redmountainspa.com* *82 rooms, 24 suites* *In-room: safe, Ethernet. In-hotel: 2 restaurants, tennis court, pools, gym, spa, water sports, bicycles, no elevator, laundry facilities, concierge, public Internet, airport shuttle, some pets allowed, no kids under 12, no-smoking rooms* ▭ *AE, D, MC, V* *FAP.*

$$$$ ★ **Sorrel River Ranch.** This luxury ranch about 24 mi from Arches National Park is the ultimate getaway. On the banks of the Colorado River, all rooms offer either a river view or mountain view. No matter which way you look in a landscape studded with towering red cliffs, buttes, and spires, the vista is spectacular. Rooms are furnished with hefty log beds, tables, and chairs, along with Western art and Native American rugs. Some of the bathtubs even have views of the river and sandstone cliffs. For an extra cost, you can choose to relax in the spa with aromatherapy and a pedicure, go river rafting or mountain biking, or take an ATV out for a spin. ✉ *Mile marker 17.5, Rte. 128, Box K, Moab, 84532* ☎ *435/259–4642 or 877/359–2715* *435/259–3016* 🌐 *www.sorrelriver.com* *27 suites, 32 rooms* *In-room: kitchen, VCR (some), Wi-Fi. In-hotel: no elevator, restaurant, tennis court, pool, gym, laundry facilities, no-smoking rooms* ▭ *AE, MC, V.*

$$$ ★ **Red Cliffs Adventure Lodge.** You can have it all at this gorgeous, classically Western property. The Colorado River rolls by right outside your door, canyon walls reach for the sky in all their red glory, and you can gaze at it all from your private riverfront patio. Rooms are decidedly Western in flavor, with log furniture, lots of wood and saltillo tile. Added attractions include an on-site winery, a movie memorabilia museum, and guided rafting, hiking, biking, and horseback-riding adventures into the desert. You can hook up to high-speed Internet in your room. ✉ *Milepost 14, Rte. 128, Moab, 84532* ☎ *435/259–2002 or 866/812–2002* 🌐 *www.redcliffslodge.com* *100 rooms, 1 suite* *In-room: kitchen, VCR, Ethernet. In-hotel: no elevator, restaurant, room service, pool, gym, laundry facilities* ▭ *AE, D, MC, V.*

$$ Fodor'sChoice ★ **Bryce Canyon Lodge.** A few feet from the amphitheater's rim and trailheads is this rugged stone-and-wood lodge. You have your choice of suites on the lodge's second level, motel-style rooms in separate buildings (with balconies or porches), and cozy lodgepole-pine cabins, some with cathedral ceilings and gas fireplaces. Reservations are hard to come by, so call several months ahead. Horseback rides into the park's interior can be arranged in the lobby. Reservations are essential for dinner at the lodge restaurant. ✉ *Bryce Canyon National Park; 2 mi south of park entrance, 84717* ☎ *435/834–5361 or 888/297–2757* *435/834–5464* 🌐 *www.brycecanyonlodge.com* *70 rooms, 3 suites, 40 cabins* *In-room: no a/c, no TV. In-hotel: restaurant, no-smoking rooms* ▭ *AE, D, DC, MC, V* *Closed Nov.–Mar.*

$$ ★ **Escalante's Grand Staircase Bed & Breakfast Inn.** Rooms have skylights, tile floors, log furniture, and murals reproducing area petroglyphs. You can relax on the outdoor porches or in the library, or make use

of the rental bikes to explore the adjacent national monument. ✉ *280 W. Main St., Box 657, Escalante 84726* ☎ *435/826–4890 or 866/826–4890* ⊕ *www.escalan tebnb.com* 🛏 *8 rooms* ⚐ *In-room: no a/c, no phone, no TV, Wi-Fi. In-hotel: no elevator, public Wi-Fi, no kids under 12, no-smoking rooms* ⊟ *AE, D, MC, V* ⏏ *BP.*

VITAL STATS

- State Insect: Honey Bee
- State Motto: "Industry"
- State Cooking Pot: Dutch Oven
- State Emblem: Beehive
- Unofficial State Condiment: Fry sauce (ketchup mixed with mayo)
- Unofficial State Casserole: Funeral potatoes (similar to pota-toes au gratin; often served at funerals)
- Highest Point: King's Peak, 13,528 feet
- Lowest Point: Beaver Dam Wash, 2,350 feet
- Favorite Invective: Oh my heck

$–$$ 🏨 **Desert Rose Inn and Cabins.** Bluff's
Fodor's Choice largest motel is truly a rose in the
★ desert. It's an attractive log-cabin-style structure with a front porch that gives it a nostalgic touch, and all rooms are spacious and clean with uncommonly large bathrooms. The cabins have small refrigerators and microwaves. ✉ *701 W. Main St., U.S. 191, Bluff, 84512* ☎ *435/672–2303 or 888/475–7673* 🖷 *435/672–2217* ⊕ *www.desertroseinn.com* 🛏 *30 rooms, 6 cabins* ⚐ *In-room: refrigerator (some), Wi-Fi. In-hotel: no elevator, laundry facilities* ⊟ *AE, D, MC, V.*

SPORTS & THE OUTDOORS

ARCHES NATIONAL PARK

★ **Delicate Arch Trail.** To see the park's most famous freestanding arch up close takes some effort. The 3-mi round-trip trail ascends a steep slick-rock slope that offers no shade—it's very hot in summer. What you find at the end of the trail is, however, worth the hard work. You can walk under the arch and take advantage of abundant photo ops, especially at sunset. In spite of its difficulty, this is a popular trail. Allow from one to three hours for this hike, depending on your fitness level and how long you plan to linger at the arch. The trail starts at Wolf Ranch. ✉ *13 mi from park entrance, 2.2 mi off main road.*

Fodor's Choice **Devils Garden Trail.** If you want to take a longer hike in the park, head
★ out on this network of trails, where you can see a number of arches. You will reach Tunnel and Pine Tree arches after only 0.4 mi on the gravel trail, and Landscape Arch is 0.8 mi from the trailhead. Past Landscape Arch the trail changes dramatically, increasing in difficulty with many short, steep climbs. You will encounter some heights as you inch your way across a long rock fin. The trail is marked with rock cairns, and it's always a good idea to locate the next one before moving on. Along the way to Double O Arch, 2 mi from the trailhead, you can take short detours to Navajo and Partition arches. A round-trip hike to Double O takes from two to three hours. For a longer hike, include Dark Angel and/or return to the trailhead on the primitive loop. This is a difficult route through fins with a short side trip to Private Arch. If

you hike all the way to Dark Angel and return on the primitive loop, the trail is 7.2 mi round-trip. Allow about five hours for this adventure, take plenty of water, and watch your route carefully. ⊠ *18 mi from park entrance on main road.*

★ **Windows Trail.** One of everyone's favorite stops in the park also gives
☾ you an opportunity to get out and enjoy the desert air. Here you can see three giant openings in rock and walk on a trail that leads you right through the holes. Allow about an hour on this gently inclined 1-mi round-trip hike. ⊠ *On main road, 9½ mi from park entrance.*

BRYCE CANYON NATIONAL PARK

Bryce Canyon Airlines & Helicopters. For a once-in-a-lifetime view of Bryce Canyon National Park, join professional pilots and guides for a helicopter ride over the park. Flights depart from Ruby's Inn Heliport. You can swoop over the amphitheater for as long as 15 minutes to more than an hour. Small airplane tours and charter services are also available. ☎ *435/834–5341* ⊕ *www.rubysinn.com/bryce-canyon-airlines.html* ⊠ *$55–$225.*

Fodor's Choice **Canyon Trail Rides.** Via horse or mule descend to the floor of the Bryce
★ Canyon amphitheater. Most who take this expedition have no riding experience, so don't hesitate to join in. A two-hour ride ambles along the amphitheater floor to the Fairy Castle before returning to Sunrise Point. The half-day expedition follows Peekaboo Trail, winds past the Fairy Castle and the Alligator, and passes the Wall of Windows before returning to Sunrise Point. To reserve a trail ride, call or stop by their desk in the lodge. ⊠ *Bryce Canyon Lodge* ☎ *435/679–8665.*

Fodor's Choice **Fairyland Loop Trail.** Hike into whimsical Fairyland Canyon on this stren-
★ uous but uncrowded 8-mi trail. It winds around hoodoos, across trickles of water, and finally to a natural window in the rock at Tower Bridge, 1½ mi from Sunrise Point and 4 mi from Fairyland Point. The pink-and-white badlands and hoodoos surround you the whole way. Allow four to five hours round-trip. You can pick up the loop at Fairyland Point or Sunrise Point. ⊠ *Fairyland Point, 1 mi off main park road, 1 mi south of park entrance; Sunrise Point, 2 mi south of park entrance.*

★ **Navajo Loop Trail.** A steep descent via a series of switchbacks leads to Wall Street, a narrow canyon with high rock walls and towering fir trees. The northern end of the trail brings Thor's Hammer into view. Allow one to two hours on this 1½-mi trail. ⊠ *Sunset Point, 2 mi south of park entrance.*

CANYONLANDS NATIONAL PARK

Fodor's Choice **Mesa Arch Trail.** By far the most popular trail in the park, this 2/3-mi
★ loop acquaints you with desert plants and terrain. The highlight of the hike is a natural arch window perched over an 800-foot drop below. The vistas of the rest of the park are nothing short of stunning. ⊠ *6 mi from Island in the Sky Visitor Center.*

Tag-A-Long Expeditions. This company holds more permits with the National Park Service and has been taking people into the white water of Cataract Canyon and Canyonlands longer than any other outfitter in Moab. They also run four-wheel-drive expeditions into the back-country of the park as well as calm-water excursions on the Colorado River. They are the only outfitter allowed to take you into the park via both water and 4x4. Trips run from half day to six days in length. ⊠*452 N. Main St., Moab* ☎*435/259–8946 or 800/453–3292* ⊕*www. tagalong.com.*

Fodor'sChoice ★ **White Rim Road.** Mountain bikers all over the world like to brag that they've ridden this 112-mi road around Island in the Sky. The trail's fame is well-deserved: it traverses steep roads, broken rock, and ledges as well as long stretches that wind through the canyons and look down onto others. There's always a good chance you'll see bighorn sheep here, too. Permits are not required for day use, but if you're biking White Rim without an outfitter you'll need careful planning and backcountry reservations (make them as far in advance as possible through the reservation office, 435/259–4351). Information about permits can be found at www.nps.gov/cany. There's no water on this route. White Rim Road starts at the end of Shafer Trail near Musselman Arch. ⊠*Off main park road about 1 mi from entrance, then about 11 mi on Shafer Trail; or off Potash Rd. (Rte. 279) at Jug Handle Arch turnoff about 18 mi from U.S. 191, then about 5 mi on Shafer Trail, Island in the Sky.*

CAPITOL REEF NATIONAL PARK

Fodor'sChoice ★ **Capitol Gorge Trail and the Tanks.** Starting at the Pioneer Register, about a mile from the Capitol Gorge parking lot, is a trail that climbs to the Tanks. After a scramble up about 0.2 mi of steep trail with cliff drop-offs, you can look down into the Tanks and can also see a natural bridge below the lower tank. Including the walk to the Pioneer Register, allow an hour or two for this interesting little hike. ⊠*At end of Scenic Dr., 9 mi south of visitor center.*

★ ☾ **Cohab Canyon Trail.** Children particularly love this trail for the geological features and native creatures, such as rock wrens and Western pipistrelles (canyon bats), that you see along the way. One end of the trail is directly across from the Fruita Campground on Scenic Drive, and the other is across from the Hickman Bridge parking lot. The first ¼ mi from Fruita is pretty strenuous, but then the walk becomes easy except for turnoffs to the overlooks, which are strenuous but short. Along the way you'll find miniature arches, skinny side canyons, and honeycombed patterns on canyon walls where the wrens make nests. The trail is 3.2 mi round-trip to the Hickman Bridge parking lot. The Overlook Trail adds 2 mi to the journey. Allow one to two hours to overlooks and back; allow two to three hours to Hickman Bridge parking lot and back. ⊠*About 1 mi south of visitor center on Scenic Dr., or about 2 mi east of visitor center on Hwy. 24.*

Fodor'sChoice ★ **Hickman Bridge Trail.** This trail is a perfect introduction to the park. It leads to a natural bridge of Kayenta sandstone, which has a 135-foot opening carved by intermittent flash floods. Early on, the route climbs a set of steps along the Fremont River, and as the trail tops out onto a bench, you'll find a slight depression in the earth. This is what remains of an ancient Fremont pit house, a kind of home that was dug into the ground and covered with brush. The trail splits, leading along the right-hand branch to a strenuous uphill climb to the Rim Overlook and Navajo Knobs. Stay to your left to see the bridge, and you'll encounter a moderate up-and-down trail. As you continue up the wash on your way to the bridge, you'll notice a Fremont granary on the right side of the small canyon. Allow about 1½ hours to walk the 2-mi round-trip. The walk to the bridge is one of the most popular trails in the park, so expect lots of company along the way. ✉ *Hwy. 24, 2 mi east of visitor center.*

ZION NATIONAL PARK

Fodor'sChoice
★

Angels Landing Trail. Truly one of the most spectacular hikes in the park, this trail is an adventure for those not afraid of heights. On your ascent you must negotiate Walter's Wiggles, a series of 21 switchbacks built out of sandstone blocks, and traverse sheer cliffs with chains bolted into the rock face to serve as handrails. In spite of its hair-raising nature, this trail attracts many people. Small children should skip it, however, and older children should be carefully supervised. Allow 2½ hours round-trip if you stop at Scout's Lookout, and four hours if you keep going to where the angels (and birds of prey) play. ✉ *Zion Canyon Scenic Drive, about 4½ mi north of Canyon Junction, Zion National Park.*

Fodor'sChoice
★

Canyon Overlook Trail. It's a little tough to locate this trailhead, but you'll find it if you watch for the parking area just east of Zion–Mount Carmel tunnel. The trail is moderately steep but only 1 mi round-trip; allow an hour to hike it. The overlook at trail's end gives you views of the West and East Temples, Towers of the Virgin, the Streaked Wall, and other Zion Canyon cliffs and peaks. ✉ *Rte. 9, east of Zion–Mount Carmel Tunnel.*

VISITOR INFORMATION

Arches National Park ✉ *N. U.S. 191, Moab, UT, 84532* 🕾 *435/719–2299, 435/719–2200, 435/719–2391 for the hearing-impaired* ⊕ *www.nps.gov/arch.*

Bryce Canyon National Park (✑ *Box 170001, Bryce Canyon, 84717* 🕾 *435/834–5322* 🖷 *435/834–4102* ⊕ *www.nps.gov/brca).*

Canyonlands National Park ✉ *2282 W. Resource Blvd., Moab, UT, 84532* 🕾 *435/719–2313, 435/259–4351 Backcountry Reservation Office* ⊕ *www.nps.gov/cany.*

Capitol Reef National Park ✉ *HC 70 Box 15, Torrey, UT, 84775* 🕾 *435/425–3791* ⊕ *www.nps.gov/care.*

Moab Area Travel Council ✉ *Main and Center Sts., Box 550, Moab, 84532* 🕾 *435/259–8825 or 800/635–6622* ⊕ *www.discovermoab.com.*

Zion National Park (✉ *Springdale, UT, 84767-1099* 🕾 *435/772–3256* ⊕ *www.nps.gov/zion).*

Grand Canyon National Park

Grand Canyon National Park

WORD OF MOUTH

". . . We watched the changing colors on the buttes and in the canyon depths as the sun set on the Grand Canyon. We finally headed indoors, not wanting the day to end."

–Gilbert56

EXPLORING GRAND CANYON NATIONAL PARK

81 mi north of Flagstaff via U.S. 180; 231 mi north of Phoenix via I–17

When it comes to the Grand Canyon, there are statistics, and there are sensations. While the former are impressive—the canyon measures an average width of 10 mi, stretches 277 mi, and is a mile deep—they don't truly prepare you for that initial encounter. Seeing the canyon for the first time is an astounding experience, even for the most jaded travelers. Some call the experience spiritual, and the term "Grand" will probably seem completely insufficient after a visit. There are just so few places on earth like this, where you can feel the immensity of the world around you.

The National Park is unparalleled on so many levels—biologically, historically, and recreationally. The canyon provides a record of three of the four eras of geological time, and reveals prehistoric traces of human adaptation to an unforgiving environment; you can see first-hand evidence of things you learned in history and science classes. The Grand Canyon is also home to several major ecosystems, five of the world's seven life zones, three of North America's four desert types, and all kinds of rare, endemic, and protected plant- and animal species.

WHO WILL ESPECIALLY LOVE THIS TRIP?

Explorers: Grand Canyon National Park offers a wealth of opportunities for adventure, and countless opportunities to discover its natural beauty by air, land, and sea. The Rim Trail is one of the most popular in the South Rim, as it includes several historical landmarks. Take a mule ride with Grand Canyon National Park Lodges to gain a different perspective on the terrain. In the North Rim, try the Widforss Trail, which provides lovely views of autumn foliage. Along the West Rim, don't forget to check out the new Skywalk to experience a view of the canyon unlike any other.

History Buffs: While most trips to the Grand Canyon last a mere four hours, serious travelers will linger to truly experience the beauty of the area. Most of the Canyon's lodging and camping, restaurants, museums and stores are in the South Rim, so plan accordingly. Stop by the Kolb Studio to view exhibitions of painting, pottery, and crafts. The Lookout Studio offers excellent views as well as a chance to experience the architecture of Mary Jane Colter, whose mark on northern Arizona is almost unmatched. The Powell Memorial is the site where Grand Canyon National Park was dedicated. In the North Rim, don't miss the Grand Canyon Lodge, which is on the National Register of Historic Places. Enjoy views of the canyon through plate glass windows while National Park Service employees lecture on geology and history.

Thrill Seekers: Extreme sports enthusiasts can definitely get their fill in Grand Canyon National Park. The Clear Creek Trail is one of the most

TOP 5 REASONS TO GO

The Significance: The Grand Canyon makes pretty much every list of "must-see" travel spot in the world. It's unlike anything else.

Mother Nature: Painted desert, sandstone canyon walls, pine and fir forests, mesas, plateaus, volcanic features, the Colorado River, streams, and waterfalls make for an awe-inspiring journey.

The Adventures: There's no better place for outdoors enthusiasts to hike, bike, fish, camp, ride mules, whitewater raft, cross-country ski, or snowshoe.

No Report Cards: Children of all ages get a world-class education during park-sponsored nature walks and interpretive programs.

Planes, Trains & Automobiles . . . & Mules: Experience the canyon by every mode of transportation, from above by plane, by below by boat, and even from the back of a mule.

difficult in the South Rim. Be sure to bring enough water and energy foods for this multiday trip; drinking water in the creek is usually available, but should be treated. For a fun—and bumpy—experience, take an off-road journey with Grand Canyon Jeep Tours. In the North Rim, experienced hikers may dare to test the North Kaibab Trail. Only open from May through October, experts recommend allowing four days to complete the hike. One of the most popular thrill-seeking adventures is also in the North Rim: white-water rafting, offered by more than a dozen companies. Most trips start at Lees Ferry, which is a few miles below the Glen Canyon Dam near Page.

WHEN IS THE BEST TIME TO VISIT?

There's no bad time to visit the canyon, though the busiest times of year are summer and spring break. Visiting during these peak seasons, as well as holidays, requires patience and a tolerance for crowds. Note that weather can change on a whim in this exposed high-desert region. And remember that you cannot visit the North Rim in winter due to weather conditions and road closures.

The best time of day to see the canyon is before 10 AM and after 2 PM, when the angle of the sun brings out the colors of the rock, and clouds and shadows add dimension. Plan ahead, especially if you want to go down the canyon on a mule: mule rides require at least a six-month advance reservation, and up to one or two year's notice for the busy season (they can be reserved up to 23 months in advance). For camping and lodging in the park, reservations are also essential; they're taken up to 13 months in advance. If you visit in May, you can enjoy Williams Rendezvous Days. A black powder shooting competition, 1800s-era crafts, and a parade fire up Memorial Day weekend in honor of Bill Williams, the town's namesake mountain man. 928/635–4061, www.williamschamber.com.

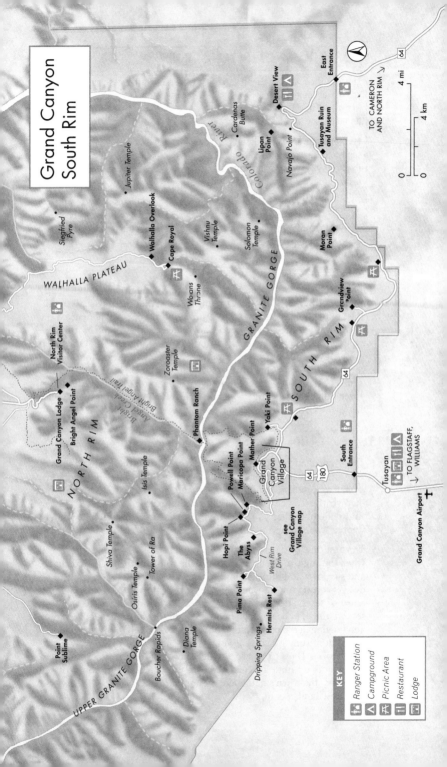

Grand Canyon South Rim

KEY

- Ranger Station
- Campground
- Picnic Area
- Restaurant
- Lodge

Colorado River

Cardenas Butte

Desert View

East Entrance

TO CAMERON AND NORTH RIM →

64

Tusayan Ruin and Museum

Lipan Point

Navajo Point

Moran Point

GRANITE GORGE

Vishnu Temple

Solomon Temple

Woans Throne

Jupiter Temple

Siegfried Pyre

Walhalla Overlook

Cape Royal

WALHALLA PLATEAU

North Rim Visitor Center

Grandview Point

SOUTH RIM

Zoroaster Temple

Phantom Ranch

Bright Angel Trail

Bright Angel Point

Grand Canyon Lodge

NORTH RIM

Isis Temple

Yaki Point

64

Mather Point

Maricopa Point

Powell Point

Grand Canyon Village

see Grand Canyon Village map

Shiva Temple

Tower of Ra

Osiris Temple

Hopi Point

The Abyss

West Rim Drive

64

180

South Entrance

Tusayan

TO FLAGSTAFF, WILLIAMS →

Pima Point

Hermits Rest

Dripping Springs

Diana Temple

Boucher Rapids

Point Sublime

UPPER GRANITE GORGE

Grand Canyon Airport

4 mi

4 km

0   0

How to Snack

CLOSE UP

Inside the park, particularly in Grand Canyon Village in the South Rim, you can find a range of fare from cafés to elegant restaurants. Foodies, be fore-warned: fine dining is not a draw here. If your tastes lean toward finer fare, make reservations at El Tovar at least a month in advance. Otherwise, stop by the Canyon Village Marketplace for provisions you can even pick up backpacking supplies here.

When hiking, always plan accordingly and bring water and energy-supplying foods. There's only one restaurant in the North Rim, but the North Rim General Store has groceries and sundries.

The best picnic spots in the park include Buggeln, 15 mi east of Grand Canyon Village on Desert View Drive, Cape Royal, 23 mi south of the North Rim's visitor center, Grandview Point, 12 mi east of the Village on Desert View Drive, and Point Imperial, 11 mi northeast of the North Rim's visitor center.

In September take in the Grand Canyon Music Festival, three weekends of "mostly chamber" music that fills the Shrine of Ages at Grand Canyon Village. 928/638–9215 or 800/997–8285, grandcanyonmusicfest.org.

26

HOW SHOULD I GET THERE?

BUS

Greyhound Lines provides bus service to Williams, Flagstaff, and King-man. Schedules change frequently; call or check the Web site for infor-mation. *800/231–2222, www.greyhound.com.*

DRIVING

If you're driving to Arizona from the east, or coming up from the southern part of the state, the best access to the Grand Canyon is from Flagstaff. You can take U.S. 180 northwest (81 mi) to Grand Canyon Village on the South Rim. Or, for a scenic route with stopping points along the canyon rim, drive north on U.S. 89 from Flagstaff, turn left at the junction of AZ 64 (52 mi north of Flagstaff), which merges with U.S. 180 at Valle, and proceed north and west for an additional 57 mi until you reach Grand Canyon Village on the South Rim.

To visit the North Rim of the canyon, proceed north from Flagstaff on U.S. 89 to Bitter Springs. Then take U.S. 89A to the junction of AZ 67. Travel south on AZ 67 for approximately 40 mi to the North Rim, which is 210 mi from Flagstaff.

If you're crossing Arizona on Interstate 40 from the west, your most direct route to the South Rim is on AZ 64 (U.S. 180), which runs north from Williams for 58 mi to Grand Canyon Village.

FLYING

North Las Vegas Airport in Las Vegas is the primary air hub for flights to Grand Canyon Airport. Several carriers fly to the Grand Canyon Airport from Las Vegas, including Air Vegas, Scenic Airlines, and Vision Air. You can also make connections into the Grand Canyon

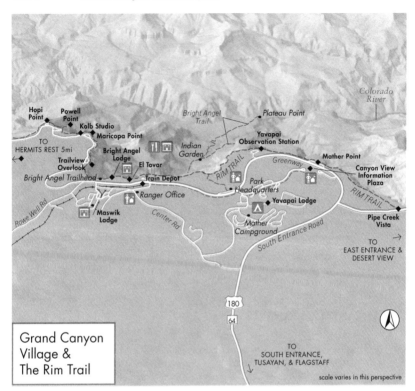

Grand Canyon
Village &
The Rim Trail

from Sky Harbor International Airport in Phoenix. Most travelers, however, choose to reach the canyon by car.

TRAIN
The Grand Canyon Railway offers a fun excursion from Williams to the South Rim, but it's more of a tourist experience rather than a mode of transportation. Williams Depot, 233 N. Grand Canyon Blvd. at Fray Marcos Blvd., Williams; 800/843–8724, www.thetrain.com.

HOW DO I GET AROUND?

BY CAR
Most of Arizona's scenic highlights are many miles apart, and a car is essential for touring the state. (However, you won't really need one if you're planning to visit only the Grand Canyon's South Rim.)

The South Rim is open to car traffic year-round, though access to Hermits Rest is limited to shuttle buses from March through November. Parking is free once you pay the $25 park entrance fee, but it can be hard to find a spot. Try the large lot in front of the general store near Yavapai Lodge or the Maswik Transportation Center lot. If you visit from October through April, traffic will be lighter and parking less of a problem.

CLAIM TO FAME

The Grand Canyon is, after all, the Grand Canyon—the entire thing is pretty much a claim to fame. But human progress and ingenuity recently made its mark in the canyon's West Rim, where the Hualapai Tribe has opened the Skywalk (Eagle Point, 877/716-9378, www.destinationgrandcanyon.com). This cantilever-shape glass bridge is suspended 4,000 feet above the Colorado River and the canyon floor, extending 70 feet from the edge—talk about a cliffhanger! Located at Eagle Point, the Skywalk is approximately 10 feet wide; the bridge's deck, made of tempered glass several inches thick, has 5-foot glass railings on each side. A nearby visitor center features souvenir shops, bars, and restaurants, including the high-end Skywalk Café, which has an outdoor patio and rooftop seating on the edge of the canyon.

The experience is a little pricey—packages that include the Skywalk start at $74.95 per person.

Grand Canyon National Park is most crowded near the entrances and in Grand Canyon Village, as well as on the scenic drives, especially the 25-mi Desert View Drive. To avoid crowds, go farther into the canyon, and try the mostly paved Rim Trail.

The more remote North Rim is off limits during winter. From mid-October (or the first heavy snowfall) through mid-May, there are no services, and Highway 67 south of Jacob Lake is closed.

BY SHUTTLE

In summer South Rim roads are congested, and it's easier, and sometimes required, to park your car and take the free shuttle. Running from one hour before sunrise until one hour after sunset, shuttles arrive every 15 to 30 minutes. The roughly 30 stops are clearly marked throughout the park.

There are three free shuttle routes in the Grand Canyon: the Hermits Rest Route operates March through November, between Grand Canyon Village and Hermits Rest. The Village Route operates year-round in the village area; it provides the easiest access to the Canyon View Information Center. The Kaibab Trail Route goes from Canyon View Information Center to Yaki Point, including a stop at the South Kaibab Trailhead.

Xanterra Transportation Company offers 24-hour taxi service at Grand Canyon Airport, Grand Canyon Village, and the nearby village of Tusayan. Taxis also make trips to other destinations in and around Grand Canyon National Park.

WHERE SHOULD I FOCUS MY ENERGY?

If you're here for 1 day: Head to the South Rim, and make the most of your time by stopping at the Information Plaza and using the shuttle to see as many points of interest as possible. Cap the day off by watching the sunset at Hermits Rest, and enjoy dinner at the El Tovar Hotel.

HISTORY YOU CAN SEE

In the mid-19th century, much of today's southwest United States was ceded to the U.S after the war with Mexico, and Army surveyors were sent out to map this new Southwestern territory. In 1857 Lieutenant Joseph Ives explored the Grand Canyon region; in 1858 he drafted a report that called the area "valueless" and a "profitless locality." Less than 10 years later, Major John Wesley Powell and his team became the first men to journey along the Colorado River through the Grand Canyon. Powell later founded the U.S. Geological Survey and negotiated treaties between Native American tribes and the government. By the turn of the century, the Grand Canyon was an established tourist area. The El Tovar Hotel opened in 1905 and was the inspiration for future National Parks buildings that matched their surrounding environments. The Grand Canyon was made a National Park in 1919.

If you're here for 2 days: See some additional points of interest in the South Rim, including Grandview Point and Tusayan Ruin and Museum. Stay at the historic El Tovar Hotel and shop for souvenirs in the village.

If you're here for 3 days: Spend more time exploring Desert View Drive. Stop by Grand Canyon Airport and enjoy a view of the canyon by plane or helicopter, or hike a trail such as Bright Angel.

If you're here for 4 days: Expand your itinerary to include time in Grand Canyon West. Take a Hummer tour or enjoy a boat ride on the Colorado River. Enjoy Hualapai tacos at the Hualapai Lodge's Diamond Creek Restaurant.

If you're here for 5 days: If you're not visiting in winter, head for the North Rim on your fourth day and enjoy popular trails such as Transept and Cliff Springs.

If you're here for 6 days: Expand your journey to include day trips of the surrounding area, such as Sedona or Flagstaff. Explore historic Route 66 to get the full northern Arizona treatment.

If you're here for 7 days or more: Travel at a more relaxed pace, taking more time to savor nature's beauty during your visit. Cap off your Grand Canyon journey by driving Cape Royal Road for 11 mi to Point Imperial. At 8,803 feet, it's the highest vista at the Canyon.

WHAT ARE THE TOP EXPERIENCES?

Visiting the South Rim: Most visitors come to the South Rim. You'll need to spend several days here to appreciate this magnificent place. Grand Canyon Village is here, and thus so are most of the park's historic hotels, museums, stores, and restaurants. Open year-round, this area offers the quintessential Grand Canyon experience from the El Tovar to the Bright Angel Trail and tours by Jeep or air. To get away from the crowds and truly appreciate the canyon, take a hike either into the canyon or around the rim and enjoy the sound of (relative) silence.

Hiking Bright Angel Trail: If you hike one trail during your visit, make it this one. Relatively friendly to beginners, this well-maintained South Rim trail is also one of the most scenic hiking paths to the bottom of the canyon. Plan on spending six to nine hours to complete the hike to Plateau Point. Bright Angel Trail is the easiest of all the footpaths into the canyon, but because the climb out from the bottom is an ascent of 5,510 feet, the trip should be attempted only by those in good physical condition—it should be avoided in midsummer, due to the extreme heat. The top of the trail, a tight set of switchbacks called Jacob's Ladder, can be icy in winter. Originally a bighorn sheep path and later used by the Havasupai, the trail was widened late in the 19th century for prospectors and is now used for both mule and foot traffic.

> **STRANGE BUT TRUE**
>
> ■ Each year more than 400 search-and-rescue operations are conducted at the park. Most are the result of unprepared hikers who aren't physically capable of handling the trails, or who don't pack sufficient food and water.
>
> ■ Even beasts of burden have their limits the park's mules can only accommodate a 200-pound load.

26

Solitude at the North Rim: Significantly cooler than the South Rim (it's 1,000 feet higher), the North Rim has many fewer visitors—and also amenities— but the views are spectacular. The area is off-limits in the winter months, so it's wise to plan your trip accordingly. This is an area for roughing it—lodging is limited, and hiking boots and camping gear are recommended. If you make it here, plan on hiking the Kaibab Forest. Mule rides are available, too.

Scenic Drives: Experience the beauty of northern Arizona on one or more of several scenic drives in the area. In the South Rim, drive Hermit Road. The Santa Fe Company built Hermit Road, formerly known as West Rim Drive, in 1912 as a scenic tour route. Ten overlooks dot this 8-mi stretch, each worth a visit. The road is filled with hairpin turns, so make sure you adhere to posted speed limits. From March through November, Hermit Road is closed to private auto traffic because of congestion; during this period, a free shuttle bus will carry you to all the overlooks.

In the North Rim, venture on Highway 67. Open mid-May through mid-October (sometimes until Thanksgiving), the two-lane paved road climbs 1,400 feet in elevation as it passes through the Kaibab National Forest. Point Imperial and Cape Royal can be reached by spurs off this scenic drive running from Jacob Lake to Bright Angel Point. Outside of the canyon, drive U.S. 89. This road north from Cameron, AZ, offers fantastic views of the Painted Desert, which eventually gives way to sandstone cliffs that run for miles. Brilliantly hued and ranging in color from light pink to deep orange, the Echo Cliffs rise to more than 1,000 feet in many places. They are essentially devoid of vegetation, but in a few high places, thick patches of tall cottonwood and poplar trees, nurtured by springs and water seepage from the rock escarpment, manage to thrive. At Bitter Springs, Aria., 60 mi north of Cameron, U.S. 89A branches off from U.S. 89, running north and providing views of Marble Canyon, the geographical beginning of the Grand Canyon. Like the Grand Canyon, Marble Canyon was formed by the Colorado River. Traversing a gorge nearly 500 feet deep is Navajo Bridge, a narrow steel span built in 1929 and listed on the National Register of Historic Places. Formerly used for car traffic, it now functions only as a pedestrian overpass.

> **PETS IN THE CANYON**
>
> Pets are allowed in Grand Canyon National Park; however, they must be on a leash at all times. With the exception of service animals, pets are not allowed below the rim or on park shuttles. A kennel near the Maswik Lodge houses cats and dogs. It's open daily 7:30 AM–5 PM (928/638–0534). Reservations are strongly recommended.

BEST BETS

SIGHTS AND TOURS

Grandview Point. At an elevation of 7,496 feet, the view from here is one of the finest in the canyon. To the northeast is a group of dominant buttes, including Krishna Shrine, Vishnu Temple, Rama Shrine, and Shiva Temple. A short stretch of the Colorado River is also visible. Directly below the point, and accessible by the steep and rugged Grandview Trail, is Horseshoe Mesa, where you can see the ruins of Last Chance Copper Mine. ⊠ *About 12 mi east of Grand Canyon Village on Desert View Dr.*

★ **Hermits Rest.** This westernmost viewpoint and Hermit Trail, which descends from it, were named for "hermit" Louis Boucher, a 19th-century French-Canadian prospector who had a number of mining claims and a roughly built home down in the canyon. Views from here include Hermit Rapids and the towering cliffs of the Supai and Redwall formations. The stone building at Hermits Rest sells curios and refreshments. ⊠ *About 8 mi west of Hermit Road Junction on Hermit Rd.*

Kolb Studio. Built in 1904 by the Kolb brothers as a photographic workshop and residence, this building provides a view of Indian Gardens, where, in the days before a pipeline was installed, Emery Kolb descended 3,000 feet each day to get the water he needed to develop his prints. Kolb was doing something right; he operated the studio until he died in 1976 at age 95. The gallery here has changing exhibitions of paintings, photography, and crafts. There's also a bookstore. ⊠ *Grand Canyon Village, near Bright Angel Lodge* ⊗ *Daily 8–6.*

★ **Mather Point.** You'll likely get your first glimpse of the canyon from this viewpoint, one of the most impressive and accessible on the South Rim. Named for the National Park Service's first director, Stephen Mather, this spot yields extraordinary views of the Grand Canyon, including deep into the Inner Gorge and numerous buttes: Wotan's Throne,

Brahma Temple, and Zoroaster Temple, among others. The Grand Canyon Lodge, on the North Rim, is almost directly north from Mather Point and only 10 mi away—yet you have to drive 215 mi to get from one spot to the other. ✉ *Near Canyon View Information Plaza.*

TRAILS

Fodor'sChoice ★ **Bright Angel Point.** The trail, which leads to one of the most awe-inspiring overlooks on either rim, starts on the grounds of the Grand Canyon Lodge and runs along the crest of a point of rocks that juts into the canyon for several hundred yards. The walk is only ½ mi round-trip, but it's an exciting trek accented by sheer drops on each side of the trail. In a few spots where the route is extremely narrow, metal railings ensure visitors' safety. The temptation to clamber out to precarious perches to have your picture taken could get you killed—every year several people die from falls at the Grand Canyon. ✉ *North Rim Dr., Grand Canyon.*

★ **Bright Angel Trail.** Well-maintained, this is one of the most scenic hiking paths from the South Rim to the bottom of the canyon (9 mi each way). Rest houses are equipped with water at the 1½- and 3-mi points from May through September and at Indian Garden (4 mi) year-round. Water is also available at Bright Angel Campground, 9¼ mi below the trailhead. Plateau Point, about 1½ mi below Indian Garden, is as far as you should attempt to go on a day hike; plan on spending six to nine hours. Bright Angel Trail is the easiest of all the footpaths into the canyon, but because the climb out from the bottom is an ascent of 5,510 feet, the trip should be attempted only by those in good physical condition and should be avoided in midsummer due to extreme heat. The top of the trail, a tight set of switchbacks called Jacob's Ladder, can be icy in winter. Originally a bighorn sheep path and later used by the Havasupai, the trail was widened late in the 19th century for prospectors and is now used for both mule and foot traffic. Hikers going downhill should yield to those going uphill. Also note that mule trains have the right-of-way—and sometimes leave unpleasant surprises in your path.

Fodor'sChoice ★ **Rim Trail.** The South Rim's most popular walking path is the 13-mi (one-way) Rim Trail, which runs along the edge of the canyon from Mather Point (the first overlook on Desert View Drive) to Hermits Rest. This walk, which is paved to Maricopa Point, visits several of the South Rim's historic landmarks. Allow anywhere from 15 minutes to a full day; the Rim Trail is an ideal day hike, as it varies only a few hundred feet in elevation from Mather Point (7,120 feet) to the trailhead at Hermits Rest (6,640 feet). The trail also can be accessed from the major viewpoints along Hermit Road, which are serviced by shuttle buses during the busy summer months.

AIR TOURS

★ Flights by plane and helicopter over the canyon are offered by a number of companies, departing for the Grand Canyon Airport at the south end of Tusayan. Prices and lengths of tours vary, but you can expect to pay about $109–$120 per adult for short plane trips and approximately $130–$235 for brief helicopter tours.

ON THE WAY

London Bridge: Like antiquing? Check out London Bridge—yes that London Bridge—in Lake Havasu City. The bridge was moved stone-by-stone to the U.S. after Robert McCulloch, founder of Lake Havasu City, submitted a $2.4 million winning bid in 1968. It cost $7 million to move, and the process took three years.

Route 66: If you're up for a road trip, what better route to travel than historic Route 66? Head to Holbrook, about 90 mi east of Flagstaff on I-40, to experience the ultimate in Route 66 kitsch. Remnants of the "Mother Road" can be found all over

town. If you're planning an overnight stay, check out the iconic Wigwam Motel, which is on the National Register of Historic Places. 711 W. Hopi Dr., Holbrook, 928/524–3048.

Hoover Dam: You've seen one of Mother Nature's master works, so why not check out one of mankind's biggest creations? Hoover Dam, near the Arizona–Nevada border on U.S. Highway 93, is a far trek from the canyon—some 250 mi—but it's a great diversion if a trip to Las Vegas is in your plans (the dam is about 30 mi southeast of the city). 702/494-2517, www.usbr.gov/lc/hooverdam.

OUTFITTERS &
EXPEDITIONS
Companies worth noting are **Air Grand Canyon** (⊠ *Grand Canyon Airport, Tusayan* ☎ *928/638–2686 or 800/247–4726* ⊕ *www.airgrandcanyon.com*), **Grand Canyon Airlines** (⊠ *Grand Canyon Airport, Tusayan* ☎ *928/638–2407 or 866/235–9422* ⊕ *www.grandcanyonairlines.com*), **Grand Canyon Helicopters** (⊠ *Grand Canyon Airport, Tusayan* ☎ *928/638–2764 or 800/541–4537* ⊕ *www.grandcanyonhelicoptersaz.com*), **Maverick-AirStar Helicopters** (⊠ *Grand Canyon Airport, Tusayan* ☎ *928/638–2622 or 800/962–3869* ⊕ *www.maverick.com*), and **Papillon Grand Canyon Helicopters** (⊠ *Grand Canyon Airport, Tusayan* ☎ *928/638–2419 or 800/528–2418* ⊕ *www.papillon.com*).

JEEP TOURS

Grand Canyon Jeep Tours & Safaris. If you'd like to get off the pavement and see parts of the park that are accessible only by dirt road, a jeep tour can be just the ticket. From March through October, Grand Canyon Outback leads daily, 1½- to 4½-hour, off-road tours within the park, as well as in Kaibab National Forest. The rides are bumpy and are not recommended for people with back injuries. Combo tours adding helicopter and airplane rides are available. ⌂ *Box 1772, Grand Canyon 86023* ☎ *928/638–5337 or 800/320–5337* ⊕ *www.grandcanyonjeeptours.com* 🖃 *$45–$199* ☰ *AE, MC, V* ⌕ *Reservations essential.*

MULE TOURS

★ **Grand Canyon National Park Lodges Mule Rides.** These trips delve into the canyon from the South Rim. Riders must be at least 55 inches tall, weigh less than 200 pounds, and understand English. Children under 15 must be accompanied by an adult. Riders must be in fairly good physical condition, and pregnant women are advised not to take these trips. The all-day ride to Plateau Point costs $142.21 (box lunch included). An overnight with a stay at Phantom Ranch at the bottom of the canyon is $369.54 ($651.80 for two riders). Two nights at Phantom

Ranch, an option available from November through March, will set you back $517.82 ($879.63 for two). Meals are included. ⌂ *6312 S. Fiddlers Green Circle, Suite 600, N. Greenwood Village, CO 80111* ☎ *303/297–2757 or 888/297–2757* 🖷 *303/297–3175* ⊕ *www.grand canyonlodges.com* ⊙ *May–Sept., daily.*

BUS TOURS

Xanterra Motorcoach Tours. Narrated by knowledgeable guides, tours include the Hermits Rest Tour, which travels along the old wagon road built by the Santa Fe Railway; the Desert View Tour, which glimpses the Colorado River's rapids and stops at Lipan Point; and Sunrise and Sunset Tours. ⌂ *6312 S. Fiddlers Green Circle, Suite 600, N. Greenwood Village, CO 80111* ☎ *303/297–2757 or 888/297–2757* ⊕ *www.grandcanyonlodges.com* 🖳 *$13.50 to $38 per person; children 16 and younger free when accompanied by a paying adult.*

TRAIN TOURS

★ The **Grand Canyon Railway,** first established in 1901 and reopened in 1989, transports passengers in railcars that date from the 1920s. The scenic, narrated train ride (2¼ hours each way) runs from the Williams Depot to the South Rim of the Grand Canyon. The vintage 1923 train travels 65 mi through prairie, ranch, and national park land to the log-cabin train station in Grand Canyon Village. You won't see the Grand Canyon from the train, but you can walk or catch the shuttle at the restored, historic Grand Canyon Railway Station. On board, Wild West characters entertain. Specialty tours include the Polar Express, a wintertime train ride that has often been sold out. If you have a pet, it can stay at the Pet Resort while you ride the train. ✉ *Williams Depot, 233 N. Grand Canyon Blvd. at Fray Marcos Blvd.* ☎ *800/843–8724 railway reservations and information* ⊕ *www.thetrain.com* 🖳 *$60–$155 round-trip, not including 9.525% tax and national park entrance fee. Youth and child rates available* ⊙ *Departs daily from Williams between 8:30 and 10:30 AM, depending on season, and from South Rim between 3 and 4:30 PM.*

RAFTING TRIPS

Fodor'sChoice Those who have taken a white-water raft trip down the Colorado River
★ often say it is one of their most memorable life experiences. Most trips begin at Lees Ferry, a few miles below the Glen Canyon Dam near Page. There are tranquil half- and full-day float trips from the Glen Canyon Dam to Lees Ferry, as well as raft trips that run from 7 to 18 days. Many of these voyages end at Phantom Ranch at the bottom of the Grand Canyon at river mile 87. You'll encounter some good white water along the way, including Lava Falls, listed in the *Guinness Book of World Records* as "the fastest navigable white water stretch in North America."

Sixteen companies (at the time of this writing) offer motorized and oar-powered excursions, but reservations for raft trips (excluding smooth-water, one-day cruises) often need to be made more than six months in advance. Prices for river-raft trips vary greatly, depending on type and length. Half-day trips on smooth water run as low as $62 per adult,

$52 for children. Trips that negotiate the entire length of the canyon and take as long as 12 days can cost more than $3,000.

OUTFITTERS &
EXPEDITIONS

Reputable outfitters include **Arizona River Runners** (☎602/867–4866 or 800/477–7238 ⊕www.raftarizona.com), **Canyoneers, Inc.** (☎928/526–0924, 800/525–0924 outside Arizona ⊕www.canyoneers.com), **Diamond River Adventures, Inc.** (☎928/645–8866 or 800/343–3121 ⊕www.diamondriver.com), **Grand Canyon Expeditions Company** (☎435/644–2691 or 800/544–2691 ⊕www.gcex.com), **Tour West, Inc.** (☎801/225–0755 or 800/453–9107 ⊕www.twriver.com), and **Wilderness River Adventures** (☎928/645–3279 or 800/992–8022 ⊕www.riveradventures.com).

Arizona Raft Adventures (✉4050 E. Huntington Rd., Flagstaff 86004 ☎928/526–8200 or 800/786–7238 🖷928/526–8246 ⊕www.azraft.com) organizes 6- to 16-day paddle and/or motor trips for all skill levels. Trips, which run $1,600 to $3,450, depart April through October.

WHERE TO EAT

WHAT IT COSTS					
	¢	$	$$	$$$	$$$$
AT DINNER	under $8	$8–$12	$13–$20	$21–$30	over $30

Prices are per person for a main course at dinner, excluding taxes and tip.

$–$$$ ✕**Arizona Room.** The canyon views from this casual Southwestern-style steak house are the best of any restaurant on the South Rim. The menu includes chicken, steak (there's good prime rib), and seafood (including salmon), as well as vegetarian options. It's open for lunch 11:30–3 and for dinner starting at 4:30; seating is first-come, first-served, so arrive early to avoid the crowds. ✉Bright Angel Lodge, West Rim Dr., Grand Canyon Village ☎928/638–2961 ⌲Reservations not accepted ☰AE, D, DC, MC, V ⊙Closed Jan.–mid-Feb.

$–$$$
Fodor's Choice
★

✕**El Tovar Dining Room.** Modeled after a European hunting lodge, this rustic 19th-century dining room built of hand-hewn logs is worth a visit. Breakfast, lunch, and dinner are served beneath the beamed ceiling. The cuisine is modern Southwestern, and the menu includes such dishes as sautéed rainbow trout served with a wild rice salad and grilled New York strip steak with buttermilk-cornmeal onion rings and pepper jack au gratin potatoes. It's the best restaurant for miles. ✉El Tovar Hotel, West Rim Dr., Grand Canyon Village ☎303/297–2757, 888/297–2757 reservations only, 928/638–2961 ⌲Reservations essential ☰AE, D, DC, MC, V.

$–$$$
★

✕**Grand Canyon Lodge Dining Room.** The historic lodge has a huge, high-ceilinged dining room with spectacular views and very good food; you might find pork medallions, red snapper, and spinach linguine with red clam sauce on the dinner menu. It's also open for breakfast and lunch. ✉Grand Canyon Lodge, Bright Angel Point (North Rim) ☎928/638–2611 ⌲Reservations essential ☰AE, D, DC, MC, V ⊙Closed mid-Oct. to mid-May.

$-$$ ✗**Pancho McGillicuddy's.** Established
★ in 1893 as the Cabinet Saloon, this
restaurant is on the National Register of Historic Places. Gone are the
spittoons and pipes—the smoke-
free dining area now has Mexican-
inspired decor and such specialties
as "armadillo eggs," the local name
for deep-fried jalapeños stuffed
with cheese. Other favorites include
fish tacos, buzzard wings—better
known as hot wings—and pollo
verde (chicken breasts smothered
in a sauce of cheese, sour cream,
and green chilies). The bar has TVs
tuned to sporting events and pours
more than 30 tequilas. ✉*141 Railroad Ave., Williams* ☎*928/635–
4150* ▤*AE, D, MC, V.*

¢-$$ ✗**Cruisers Café 66.** Talk about
FodorsChoice nostalgia. Imagine your favorite
★
☺

> **VITAL STATS**
>
> ■ Nearly 5 million visitors come to the park each year.
>
> ■ 630 mi of trails traverse the canyon (51 are maintained).
>
> ■ Mules are used to deliver mail to Havasupai, at the bottom of the canyon.
>
> ■ Marble Canyon got its name from its thousand-foot-thick seam of marble and for its walls that have eroded to display a glass-like, polished finish.
>
> ■ Eighty-eight mammal species, 300 bird species, 24 types of lizards, and 24 kinds of snakes inhabit Grand Canyon National Park

26

'50s-style, high school hangout—with cocktail service. Good burgers,
salads, and malts are family-priced, but a choice steak is available,
too, for $30. Stuffed buffalo, a large mural of the town's heyday along
the "Mother Road," and historic cars out front make this a Route 66
favorite. Kids enjoy the relaxed atmosphere and jukebox tunes. ✉*233
W. Rte. 66, Williams* ☎*928/635–2445* ▤*AE, DC, MC, V.*

¢-$ ✗**Maswik Cafeteria.** You can get a burger or Mexican fare at this food
court. ✉*Maswik Lodge, Grand Canyon Village* ☎*928/638–2961*
⌦*Reservations not accepted* ▤*AE, D, DC, MC, V.*

WHERE TO STAY

WHAT IT COSTS				
¢	$	$$	$$$	$$$$
FOR 2 PEOPLE	under $50	$50–$100	$101–$150	$151–$200	over $200

Prices are for two people in a standard double room in high season, excluding taxes and service charges.

$$-$$$$ ▦**El Tovar Hotel.** A registered National Historic Landmark, El Tovar
FodorsChoice was built in 1905 of Oregon pine logs and native stone. The hotel's
★ proximity to all of the canyon's facilities, its European hunting-lodge
atmosphere, and its renowned dining room make it the best place to
stay on the South Rim. It's usually booked well in advance (up to 13
months ahead), though it's easier to get a room during winter months.
Three suites and several rooms have canyon views (these are booked
early), but you can enjoy the view anytime from the cocktail-lounge
back porch. ✉*West Rim Dr., Grand Canyon Village* ✉*Box 699,
Grand Canyon 86023* ☎*303/297–2757, 888/297–2757 reservations*

only, 928/638–2961 🖷*303/297–3175 reservations only* ⊕*www.grand canyonlodges.com* 🛏*70 rooms, 12 suites* ⟡*Restaurant, room service, refrigerators, cable TV, bar, a/c, no smoking* ▤*AE, D, DC, MC, V.*

$–$$ 🍴**Bright Angel Lodge.** Famed architect Mary Jane Colter designed
☉   this 1935 log-and-stone structure, which sits within a few yards of the canyon rim and blends superbly with the canyon walls. It offers a similar location to El Tovar for about half the price. Accommodations are in motel-style rooms or cabins. Lodge rooms don't have TVs, and some rooms do not have private bathrooms. Scattered among the pines, 50 cabins, some with fireplaces, have TVs and private baths. Expect historic charm but not luxury. The Bright Angel Dining Room serves family-style meals all day and a Warm Apple Grunt dessert large enough to share. The Arizona Room serves dinner only. Adding to the experience are an ice-cream parlor, gift shop, and small history museum with exhibits on Fred Harvey and Mary Jane Colter. ✉ *West Rim Dr., Grand Canyon Village* ⌂*Box 699, Grand Canyon 86023* ☎*303/297–2757, 888/297–2757 reservations only, 928/638–2961* 🖷*303/297–3175 reservations only* ⊕*www.grandcanyonlodges.com* 🛏*39 rooms, 6 with shared toilet and shower, 13 with shared shower; 50 cabins* ⟡*Restaurant, coffee shop, bar, Internet room, shop, no a/c, no TV in some rooms.* ▤*AE, D, DC, MC, V.*

$–$$ 🍴**Grand Canyon Lodge.** This historic property, constructed mainly in
Fodor'sChoice   the 1920s and '30s, is the premier lodging facility in the North Rim
★   area. The main building has limestone walls and timbered ceilings. Lodging options include small, rustic cabins; larger cabins (some with a canyon view and some with two bedrooms); and newer, traditional motel rooms. You might find marinated pork kebabs or linguine with cilantro on the dining room's dinner menu ($–$$$). Dining room reservations are essential and should be made as far in advance as possible. ✉*Hwy. 67, North Rim, Grand Canyon National Park 86052* ☎*303/297–2757, 888/297–2757 reservations only, 928/638–2611* 🖷*303/297–3175 reservations only* ⊕*www.grandcanyonnorthrim. com* 🛏*44 rooms, 157 cabins* ⟡*Cafeteria, dining room, bar, shop, laundry facilities, no a/c, no room TVs, no-smoking rooms* ▤*AE, D, MC, V* ☾*Closed mid-Oct.–mid-May.*

VISITOR INFORMATION

Grand Canyon Chamber of Commerce (☎*928/638–2901* ⊕*www.grandcanyon chamber.com*).

Grand Canyon National Park (☎*928/638–7888 recorded message* 🖷*928/638– 7797* ⊕*www.nps.gov/grca*).

Grand Canyon National Park Lodges (☎*303/297–2757* 🖷*303/297–3175* ⊕*www.grandcanyonlodges.com*).

North and South Rim Camping (☎*800/365–2267* ⊕*http://reservations.nps. gov/index.cfm*).

Phoenix

WITH SCOTTSDALE, TEMPE & THE VALLEY OF THE SUN

Hole-in-the-Rock, Papago Park

WORD OF MOUTH

Don't miss Old Town Scottsdale. There are tons of shops and galleries! Also, the hike up Camelback Mountain is intense but the view is well worth it!

—Kerry392

EXPLORING PHOENIX

372 mi east of Los Angeles via I0-10; 113 mi north of Tucson via I–10; 225 mi south of the Grand Canyon via I–17.

With more than 325 days of sun a year, Mother Nature plays a central part of life in Phoenix, located in an area lovingly referred to as the Valley of the Sun. The mascot of Arizona State University? The Sun Devil. The vehicle of choice? A convertible. The center of your backyard? A swimming pool.

Some 4 million people call the Phoenix area home and largely credit its weather for their excellent quality of life. This same weather made the northern tip of the Sonoran Desert so inhospitable for centuries—until the arrival of air-conditioning changed the landscape of the entire Southwest in the mid-20th century.

For decades, the vast horizon, breathtaking sunsets, and dramatic summer monsoon showers have been transforming visitors briefly escaping the cold into residents who worship the sun. Today the Valley is in its next generation of growth, with a burgeoning interest in the culinary arts, an active nightlife and arts community, and state-of-the art recreation and sports facilities.

WHO WILL ESPECIALLY LOVE THIS TRIP?

Sports Fans: With weather so hospitable to recreation, it's no wonder Phoenix is a sports mecca. Start the year off right with the FBR Open, known as one of the rowdiest stops on the PGA Tour. In spring head to the ballpark for Major League Baseball's Cactus League Spring Training (12 teams call Arizona home each year before opening day). The University of Phoenix Stadium, home to the NFL's Arizona Cardinals, is an architectural marvel (it has a retractable room *and* field). And don't forget the true local passion: the high-flying Phoenix Suns, led by two-time league MVP Steve Nash, keep the Valley on the edge of its collective seat each spring during the playoffs.

Golfers: In Phoenix golf is more of a passion than mere game. With more golf courses in town than McDonald's restaurants, it's easy to understand the degree to which golf is revered in the Valley. Be prepared: tee times are competitive—and pricey—in cooler spring, fall, and winter months. Serious golfers start their days before dawn in summer to take advantage of the temperature and the bargains.

Nature Lovers: There's nothing quite like a sunset in Phoenix. Imbued with hues of red, orange, and purple, the sky puts on a splendid show over the Valley each night. You can also discover Mother Nature's beauty by hiking up Camelback Mountain or in the McDowell Mountains, heading north and taking a Jeep tour of Sedona, or by visiting the Desert Botanical Gardens to see the area's unique flora.

Western Enthusiasts: Although it's often most associated with luxury living, Scottsdale calls itself "The West's Most Western Town." Both personalities fit—you won't have to look hard to find opportunities to

TOP 5 REASONS TO GO

Fun in the Sun: There's a reason locals call Phoenix "The Valley of the Sun." With more than 325 sunny days in the year, most residents forget where they last left their umbrella.

Fore!: Golfers visit Phoenix in droves for the chance to play on one—or more—of the area's 200-plus courses.

Pampering Paradise: The Valley isn't just about the outdoors. World-class spas are found in nearly every corner of the metro area, providing luxurious escapes and massaging your cares away.

Native Traditions: From exploring the Heard Museum in the heart of the city to taking a day trip north to Sedona, discover the Native American culture and art that make the Valley so special.

See & Be Seen: Discover the luxe life in Scottsdale, where locals shop by day and party the night away.

purchase boots and spurs, take a ride on horseback, and don a cowboy hat. Then head south to Rawhide to get a taste for yesteryear's West. And don't forget to shop in Old Town for a perfect souvenir, perhaps Native American jewelry accented with turquoise.

WHEN IS THE BEST TIME TO VISIT?

As they say here, "it's a dry heat." While Phoenix is in the desert, it's a common misconception that mercury always hovers near the 100-degree mark. Of course, the days can be uncomfortable from June through October, but air-conditioning (and perhaps a shopping excursion or hour-long massage) solves most climate-related quandaries. The best weather, by far, is from late January through early May, when it seems like every car on the street is a convertible and the smells of fresh orange blossoms permeate the air. Be sure to check out the FBR Open and the Cactus League if you're in town at this time. The best deals are to be had in summer, when resorts slash their rates. In fall check out the state fair in October and Zoo Lights at the Phoenix Zoo in November and December.

HOW SHOULD I GET THERE?

DRIVING

As a city that was born in the 1950s and enjoyed its growth in the '80s and '90s, Phoenix was designed for the open road. The area is best toured by car—very purposeful urban planning has produced wide roads and a simple gridlike city design, and it's very easy to get around town. Interstates 10 and 17 run through the center of the city. Road conditions in Phoenix are usually ideal—there are very few weather-related closures—but be sure to plan accordingly if you're traveling to or from northern Arizona's high country and ski slopes.

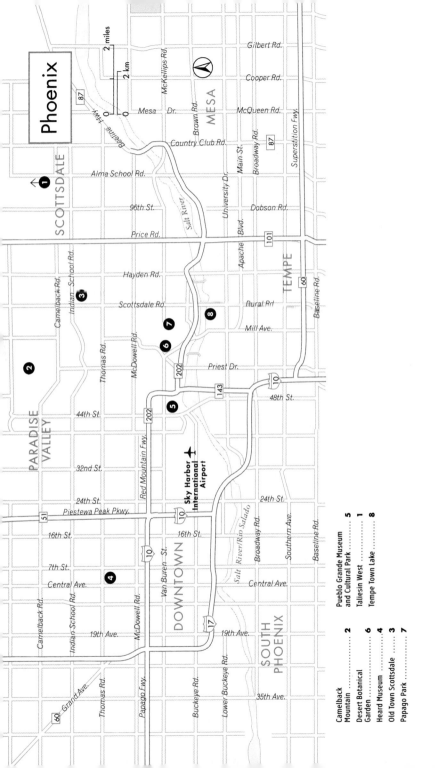

Phoenix

87

2 miles
2 km
0

SCOTTSDALE

Beeline Hwy.

McKellips Rd.

Gilbert Rd.

Cooper Rd.

MESA

Mesa   Dr.

Brown Rd.

McQueen Rd.

Country Club Rd.

87

Main St.

Broadway Rd.

Superstition Fwy.

Alma School Rd.

96th St.

University Dr.

Dobson Rd.

Salt River

Price Rd.

101

Apache Blvd.

TEMPE

60

Baseline Rd.

Camelback Rd.

Indian School Rd.

Hayden Rd.

❸

Scottsdale Rd.

Rural Rd

❽

❼

Mill Ave.

Thomas Rd.

McDowell Rd.

❻

202

PARADISE
VALLEY

❷

Priest Dr.

143

10

44th St.

202

❺

48th St.

Red Mountain Fwy.

32nd St.

Sky Harbor
International
Airport

24th St.

24th St.

51

Piestewa Peak Pkwy.

16th St.

16th St.

Salt River/Rio Salado

Broadway Rd.

Southern Ave.

Baseline Rd.

7th St.

10

Central Ave.

❹

Central Ave.

Camelback Rd.

Indian School Rd.

McDowell Rd.

Van Buren St.

DOWNTOWN

SOUTH
PHOENIX

19th Ave.

19th Ave.

17

Buckeye Rd.

Lower Buckeye Rd.

60

Grand Ave.

Thomas Rd.

Papago Fwy.

35th Ave.

Camelback
Mountain **2**

Desert Botanical
Garden **6**

Heard Museum **4**

Old Town Scottsdale **3**

Papago Park **7**

Pueblo Grande Museum
and Cultural Park **5**

Taliesin West **1**

Tempe Town Lake **8**

How to Snack

Phoenix is not a pedestrian city, so don't expect to find hot dog stands on Downtown corners. But that doesn't mean snacking is out of the question.

For some of the best people-watching in town, stop by the **Coffee Plantation** at Biltmore Fashion Park.

For picnic fare, or just a decent lunch on the patio, check out any of the Valley's **AJ's Fine Foods** locations. The gourmet grocer of Phoenix, AJ's

prides itself on its deli and wine offerings. There's also a decent floral shop in each location.

If you're looking for breakfast fare, find the nearest **Chompie's** (*9301 E. Shea Blvd., Scottsdale, 480/860–0475, www.chompies.com*), which serves—by far—the best bagels in town.

FLYING

Sky Harbor International Airport is one of the busiest in the nation; it's a hub for several carriers, including Southwest and US Airways. The airport is centrally located, and it's approximately 20 minutes from most destinations in the city. Many hotels and resorts offer shuttle services to and from Sky Harbor. If you plan on renting a car at the airport, it's best to reserve ahead of time— particularly in spring.

27

TRAIN

Although Amtrak does have a stop in Phoenix, the train is not a recommended method of travel in the Valley. Light Rail will begin to carry passengers in 2008–09, but it will be several years before the system can accommodate cross-town traffic.

HOW DO I GET AROUND?

BY CAR

Having a car in Phoenix is a requirement. The Valley is vast—Phoenix is the nation's fifth-largest city—and stretches more than 50 mi from end to end. Navigating the area is relatively simple, and new highways make exploring even easier. Most all north–south streets are numbered (7th Street, 7th Avenue) and east–west streets are named (Glendale Road, Camelback Road). Downtown Phoenix, Scottsdale, and Tempe are pedestrian-friendly, but take note: outside of a brief stroll in these areas, no one walks anywhere in the Valley.

WHERE SHOULD I FOCUS MY ENERGY?

If you're here for 1 day: For a brief visit, stay in Scottsdale, where you can enjoy the best Phoenix has to offer, both day and night.

If you're here for 2 days: No trip to Phoenix is complete without authentic Mexican food. Head to one of the area's best Mexican eateries, such as Carolina's or Los Dos Molinos, and enjoy a Phoenix original, a chimichanga.

If you're here for 3 days: Take in the history and culture of Central Phoenix, from the Heard Museum to Encanto and Willo, two of Phoenix's historic districts. Stop for lunch at My Florist café just blocks away.

If you're here for 4 days: Two words: tee time. And if your partner isn't interested, be sure to book an appointment at the hotel spa. You'll both be pleased.

If you're here for 5 days: Enjoy the great outdoors by taking a hike on one of the area's famous trails, such as Camelback Mountain. For less exertion, take a hot air balloon trip to see the beauty of the Valley from above.

If you're here for 6 days: Plan an excursion north to Sedona, where you can discover the beauty of northern Arizona's red rocks. Be sure to take a Jeep tour to get the complete Sedona experience.

If you're here for 7 days or more: Discover some of Phoenix's hidden treasures, such as the Tovrea Castle *(5041 E. Van Buren St., Phoenix, 602/256–3220)* or Arcosanti, and savor some of the area's signature restaurants, perhaps Tarbell's or Pizzeria Bianco.

WHAT ARE THE TOP EXPERIENCES?

The Wild, Wild West: From an afternoon of horseback riding to an evening filled with great entertainment at Rawhide, you can satisfy your inner cowboy in the Valley. Old Town Scottsdale provides the right combination of Western authenticity and cowboy kitsch, while downtown Phoenix's Wells Fargo History Museum lets you see first-hand what life was like in the 1800s.

A New Culinary Vocabulary: Visitors quickly become conversational in Mexican food after a trip to Phoenix. By the time your journey ends, you'll know whether you crave machaca or carne asada, or if you're brave enough to tackle the hatch chile. And no two Mexican restaurants are the same. The daring should check out Los Dos Molinos, which serves some of the spiciest food in town. The traditional should visit the birthplace of the chimichanga, Macayo's *(4001 N. Central Ave., Phoenix; 602/264–6141),* or Carolina's, home to some of the best tortillas in town. And foodies can't miss Richardson's Cuisine of New Mexico *(1582 E. Bethany Home Rd., Phoenix, 602/265–5886),* which provides a finer-dining approach to Mexican cuisine.

The Links: For a tour of Phoenix's premier courses, look no further than the Arizona Biltmore Country Club, the Phoenician, and Troon North. If you're traveling on a budget, fret not. Check out Arizona State University's Karsten Golf Course, where the Sun Devils practice, or Encanto Park, one of Phoenix's historic parks. Always book your tee times early, particularly during cooler months.

The Open Road: With near year-round sunshine, open highways, magnificent horizons and spellbinding mountains, Phoenix is the perfect site for a road trip. Drive from one corner of the Valley to another, taking in Superstition Mountain and the McDowell Mountains—be sure to head west while the sun sets. Travel north of the Valley to the cooler temperatures of Flagstaff and Prescott, or head to Sedona to view some of nature's masterpieces. If you're feeling nostalgic, you can even take a detour on historic Route 66 in Flagstaff.

Girls' Excursions: With dozens of spas at your disposal—some of the best include the Aji at Sheraton Wild Horse Pass, the Alvadora at Royal Palms, and the Sanctuary at Sanctuary Camelback Mountain—Phoenix is ready to provide an escape that will put any Chick Flick to shame. With breathtaking mountain views, luxurious cabanas, and services fit for royalty, Valley spas take pampering to a new level. (Hollywood celebrity spottings are not uncommon here). Make reservations early, particularly in spring and fall, many resorts offer hugely discounted packages in summer.

BEST BETS

SIGHTS AND TOURS

Fodor'sChoice
★
☺
Heard Museum. Pioneer settlers Dwight and Maie Heard built a Spanish colonial–revival building on their property to house their collection of Southwestern art. Today the staggering collection includes such exhibits as a Navajo hogan, an Apache wickie-up (a temporary Native American structure, similar to a lean-to, constructed from branches, twigs, and leaves, sometimes covered with hides), and rooms filled with art, pottery, jewelry, katsinas, and textiles. The Heard also actively supports and displays pieces by working Indian artists. A fabulous new long-term exhibition entitled Home: Native People In the Southwest, opened in 2005. Annual events include the Guild Indian Fair & Market and the World Championship Hoop Dance Contest. Children enjoy the interactive art-making exhibits. ■TIP➜**The museum also has an incredible gift shop with authentic, high-quality goods purchased directly from native artists.** There's a museum satellite branch in Scottsdale that has rotating exhibits, and another in the West Valley featuring some of the Heard's permanent collection as well as rotating exhibits. ⊠*2301 N. Central Ave., Central Phoenix* ☎*602/252–8848* ⊕*www.heard.org* ⊠*$10* ☉*Daily 9:30–5* ⊠*Heard Museum West: 16126 N. Civic Center Plaza, West Valley Surprise* ☎*623/344–2200* ⊠*$5* ☉*Tues–Sat. 9:30–5* ⊠*Heard Museum North: 32633 N. Scottsdale Rd., North Scottsdale* ☎*602/488–9817* ⊠*Suggested $3 donation* ☉*Mon–Sat. 10–5:30.*

Fodor'sChoice
★
☺
Desert Botanical Garden. Opened in 1939 to conserve and showcase the ecology of the desert, these 150 acres contain more than 4,000 different species of cacti, succulents, trees, and flowers. A stroll along the ½-mi-long Plants and People of the Sonoran Desert trail is a fascinating lesson in environmental adaptations; children enjoy playing the self-guiding game "Desert Detective." Specialized tours are available at an extra cost; check the Web for times and prices. ⊠*1201 N. Galvin Pkwy., Papago Salado, Phoenix* ☎*480/941–1225* ⊕*www.dbg.org* ⊠*$10* ☉*Oct.–Apr., daily 8–8; May–Sept., daily 7 AM–8 PM.*

27

☺ **Papago Park.** An amalgam of hilly desert terrain, streams, and lagoons, this park has picnic ramadas, a golf course, a playground, hiking and biking trails, and even large-mouth bass and trout fishing. (An urban fishing license is required for anglers age 15 and over.) The hike up to landmark **Hole-in-the-Rock** (a natural observatory used by the native Hohokam to devise a calendar system) is steep and rocky, and a much easier climb up than down. **Governor Hunt's Tomb,** the white pyramid at the top of Ramada 16, commemorates the former Arizona leader and provides a lovely view. ✉ *625 N. Galvin Pkwy., Papago Salado, Phoenix* ☎ *602/256–3220* ☞ *Free* ☉ *Daily 6 AM–11 PM.*

Fodor's Choice
★
☺ **Pueblo Grande Museum and Cultural Park.** Phoenix's only national landmark, this park was once the site of a 500-acre Hohokam village supporting about 1,000 people and containing homes, storage rooms, cemeteries, and ball courts. Three exhibition galleries hold displays on the Hohokam culture and archaeological methods. View the 10-minute orientation video before heading out on the ½-mi Ruin Trail past excavated mounds and ruins that give a hint of Hohokam savvy: there's a building whose corner doorway was perfectly placed to watch the summer-solstice sunrise. Children particularly like the hands-on, interactive learning center. Guided tours by appointment only. ✉ *4619 E. Washington St., Papago Salado* ☎ *602/495–0901* ⊕ *www.pueblogrande. com* ☞ *$2, free Sun.* ☉ *Mon.–Sat. 9–4:45, Sun. 1–4:45.*

★ **Old Town Scottsdale.** "The West's Most Western Town," this area has rustic storefronts and wooden sidewalks; it's touristy, but the closest you'll come to experiencing life here as it was 80 years ago. High-quality jewelry, pots, and Mexican imports are sold alongside kitschy souvenirs. ✉ *Main St. from Scottsdale Rd. to Brown Ave., Downtown Scottsdale.*

Fodor's Choice
★
Taliesin West. Ten years after visiting Arizona in 1927 to consult on designs for the Biltmore hotel, architect Frank Lloyd Wright chose 600 acres of rugged Sonoran Desert at the foothills of the McDowell Mountains as the site for his permanent winter residence. Wright and apprentices constructed a desert camp here using organic architecture to integrate the buildings with their natural surroundings. In addition to the living quarters, drafting studio, and small apartments of the Apprentice Court, Taliesin West has two theaters, a music pavilion, and the Sun Trap—sleeping spaces surrounding an open patio and fireplace. Five guided tours are offered, ranging from a one-hour "panorama"

tour to a three-hour behind-the-scenes tour, with other tours offered seasonally. (In 2005, after a major renovation, Wright's living quarters were opened for the first time to the public. They include a living space and a private bedroom and work space.) Today the site is a National Historic Landmark and still an active community of students and architects. Times vary, so call ahead; all visitors must be accompanied by a guide. ✉ *12621 Frank Lloyd Wright Blvd., North Scottsdale* ☎ *480/860–2700* ⊕ *www.franklloydwright.org* 🕮 *$18–$45* 🕐 *Sept.– June, daily 8:30–5:30; July and Aug., Thurs.–Mon. 8:30–5:30.*

🕙 **Tempe Town Lake.** Town Lake is the newest addition to the growth of Tempe and attracts college students and Valley residents of all ages. Little ones enjoy the Splash Playground, and fishermen appreciate the rainbow trout–stocked lake. **Rio Lago Cruises** rents boats and has a selection of short cruise options. ✉ *990 W. Rio Salado Pkwy., between Mill and Rural Aves. north of Arizona State University* ☎ *480/517– 4050 Rio Lago Cruises* ⊕ *www.tempe.gov/lake and www.riolago cruise.com.*

★ **Camelback Mountain & Echo Canyon Recreation Area** (✉ *Tatum Blvd. and McDonald Dr., Paradise Valley* ☎ *602/256–3220 Phoenix Parks & Recreation Dept.*) has intermediate to difficult hikes up the Valley's most outstanding central landmark.

WHERE TO EAT

27

WHAT IT COSTS				
	¢	$	$$	$$$	$$$$
AT DINNER	under $8	$8–$12	$13–$20	$21–$30	over $30

Prices are per person for a main course. The final tab will include sales tax of 8.1% in Phoenix, 7.95% in Scottsdale.

$$$–$$$$ ✕ **House of Tricks.** There's nothing up the sleeves of Robert and Robin
★ Trick, who work magic on the eclectic menu that emphasizes the freshest available seafood, poultry, and fine meats, as well as vegetarian selections. One of the Valley's most unique dining venues, the restaurant encompasses a 1920s home and a separate brick- and adobe-style house originally built in 1903, adjoined by an intimate wooden deck and outdoor patio shaded by a canopy of grapevines and trees. At lunch you can't go wrong with the quiche of the day. ✉ *114 E. 7th St., Tempe* ☎ *480/968–1114* ▭ *AE, D, MC, V* 🕐 *Closed Sun.*

$$–$$$$ ✕ **Christopher's Fermier Brasserie & Paola's Wine Bar.** Chef Christopher Gross serves simple, delicious French brasserie fare using the freshest ingredients and produce from local farmers. Wine director Paola Gross offers more than 100 wines by the glass and stocks an excellent selection of cigars. Thursday to Saturday from 10 PM to midnight, you'll love the inexpensive "Leftovers from the Kitchen" specials. ✉ *Biltmore Fashion Park, 2584 E. Camelback Rd., Camelback Corridor* ☎ *602/522–2344* ▭ *AE, D, DC, MC, V.*

$$–$$$$ ✕**Don & Charlie's.** A favorite with major-leaguers in town for spring training, this venerable chophouse specializes in prime-grade steak and baseball memorabilia—the walls are covered with pictures, autographs, and uniforms. The New York sirloin, prime rib, and double-thick lamb chops are a hit; sides include au gratin potatoes and creamed spinach. ⊠*7501 E. Camelback Rd., Central Scottsdale* ☎*480/990–0900* ▤*AE, D, DC, MC, V* ⊙*No lunch.*

$$–$$$$ ✕**Roaring Fork.** Elk-antler chande-
Fodor'sChoice liers, earth-tone fabrics and leath-
★ ers, barbed-wire accessories, and a buffalo skull above the bar add up to a comfortable, rustic restaurant named after the river that winds past Aspen in Colorado. Creations

> **HISTORY YOU CAN SEE**
>
> Many history buffs aren't aware, but the Civil War was fought in Arizona, too. The site of the westernmost battle of the war, Picacho Peak, is off Interstate 10 approximately one hour south of Phoenix between Casa Grande and Tucson. During the battle, Union and the Confederate soldiers fought for 90 minutes on April 15, 1862; three Union soldiers died. Today, **Picacho Peak State Park** is known for its brilliant spring wildflowers, and visitors can pursue more peaceful pastimes, like camping and hiking the park's trails. *Exit 219 off Interstate 10, 520/466–3183*

include a pork porterhouse steak and fork-barbecued gulf shrimp on lobster, alongside such mouthwatering side dishes as stone-ground chili cheese grits and green-chili macaroni. The reasonably priced saloon menu is served in the bar from 4 to 7 PM Monday to Saturday. ⊠*Finova Building, 4800 N. Scottsdale Rd., Central Scottsdale* ☎*480/947–0795* ⩜*Reservations essential* ▤*AE, D, DC, MC, V* ⊙*No lunch.*

$$–$$$$ ✕**Tarbell's.** Cutting-edge cuisine is the star at this sophisticated bistro. The grilled salmon glazed with a molasses-lime sauce and served on a crispy potato cake is a long-standing classic; the focaccia with red onion, Romano cheese, and roasted thyme with hummus is excellent; and imaginative designer pizzas are cooked in a wood-burning oven. Your sweet tooth won't be disappointed by Tarbell's warm, rich, chocolate cake topped with pistachio ice cream. Hardwood floors, copper accents, and a curving cherrywood and maple bar create a sleek, cosmopolitan look, favored by Biltmore golfers. ⊠*3213 E. Camelback Rd., Camelback Corridor* ☎*602/955–8100* ⩜*Reservations essential* ▤*AE, D, DC, MC, V* ⊙*No lunch.*

$$–$$$ ✕**Barrio Cafe.** Owners Wendy Gruber and Silvana Salcido Esparza
★ have taken Mexican cuisine to a new level. Expect guacamole prepared tableside and modern Mexican specialties such as *cochinita pibil,* slow-roasted pork with red achiote and sour orange, and *chiles en Nogada,* a delicious traditional dish from Central Mexico featuring a spicy poblano pepper stuffed with fruit, chicken, and raisins. The flavor-packed food consistently draws packs of people but you can drink in the intimate atmosphere—and a specialty margarita—while you wait for a table. ⊠*2814 N. 16th St., Downtown Phoenix* ☎*602/636–0240* ⩜*Reservations not accepted* ▤*AE, MC, V* ⊙*Closed Mon.*

$–$$ ✕**Los Dos Molinos.** In a hacienda that belonged to silent-era movie star
★ Tom Mix, this fun restaurant focuses on New Mexican–style Mexican

food. That means *hot*. New Mexico chilies form the backbone and fiery breath of the dishes, and the green-chili enchilada and beef taco are potentially lethal. The red salsa and enchiladas with egg on top are excellent. There's a funky courtyard where you can sip potent margaritas while waiting for a table. This is a must-do dining experience if you want authentic New Mexican–style food, but be prepared to swig lots of water. ✉8646 S. Central Ave., South Phoenix ☎602/243–9113 ⌑Reservations not accepted ⊟AE, D, DC, MC, V ⊘Closed Sun. and Mon. ✉260 S. Alma School Rd., Mesa ☎480/969–7475 ⌑Reservations not accepted ⊟AE, D, DC, MC, V ⊘Closed Sun. and Mon.

¢–$$ ✕**La Grande Orange.** This San Francisco–inspired store and eatery sells

Fodor's Choice artisanal nosh and novelty items, along with a formidable selection

★ of wines. Valley residents flock here to feast on mouthwatering sandwiches, pizzas, salads, and decadent breads and pastries. The small tables inside fill up quickly at breakfast and lunch but there's also seating on the patio. Try the Commuter Sandwich on a homemade English muffin or the delicious French pancakes with a Spanish latte that might be the most memorable cup of *jose* you'll ever have. ✉4410 N. 40th St., Central Phoenix ☎602/840–7777 ⊟AE, MC, V.

¢–$$ ✕**Nello's.** Leave it to two brothers from Chicago to come up with some of the best pizza in the Valley. The motto is "In Crust We Trust," and Nello's excels in both thin-crust and deep-dish pies. Try traditional varieties heaped with homemade sausage and mushrooms, or go vegetarian with the spinach pie. Pasta entrées are very good, too, and the family-style salads are inventive and fresh. ✉8658 E. Shea Blvd., North Scottsdale ☎480/922–5335 ⊘Closed Mon. ✉2950 S. Alma School Dr., Mesa ☎480/820–5995 ⊘Closed Mon. ✉1806 E. Southern Ave., Tempe ☎480/897–2060 ⊘Closed Mon. No lunch Sun. ✉4710 E. Warner Rd., Ahwatukee, Phoenix ☎480/893–8930 ⊘Closed Mon. No lunch Sun. ⊟AE, MC, V.

¢ ✕**Carolina's.** This small, nondescript restaurant in South Phoenix makes

★ the most delicious, thin-as-air flour tortillas imaginable. In-the-know locals and downtown working folk have been lining up at Carolina's for years to partake of the homey, inexpensive Mexican food. The tacos, tamales, burritos, flautas, and enchiladas are served on paper plates. ✉1202 E. Mohave St., South Phoenix ☎602/252–1503 ⊟AE, D, DC, MC, V ⊘Closed Sun. Dinner on weekdays only until 7:30 PM and Sat. until 6 PM ✉2126 E. Cactus Rd., North Central Phoenix ☎602/275–8231 ⊟AE, D, DC, MC, V ⊘Closed Sun.; dinner on weekdays only until 7:30 PM and Sat. until 6 PM.

WHERE TO STAY

	WHAT IT COSTS				
	¢	$	$$	$$$	$$$$
FOR 2 PEOPLE	under $100	$100–$150	$151–$225	$226–$350	over $350

Prices are for a standard double in high season.

STRANGE BUT TRUE

- Arizona doesn't observe Daylight Savings Time.

- It's illegal to walk through a hotel lobby in Phoenix with spurs on.

- The largest Wurlitzer pipe organ in the world is at Organ Stop Pizza in Mesa.

- It's against the law to refuse a person a glass of water in Arizona.

- Rockers Alice Cooper and Stevie Nicks call Phoenix home.

- Some scenes from "Bill and Ted's Excellent Adventure" were filmed at

Phoenix's Metrocenter Mall and Coronado High School in Scottsdale.

- South Mountain Park covers 20,000 acres; it's the world's largest municipal park.

- Phoenix is one of only 13 cities with teams in all four major sports leagues: Arizona Cardinals (NFL), Arizona Diamondbacks (MLB), Phoenix Coyotes (NHL), and Phoenix Suns (NBA).

- In 1981 Arizona native Sandra Day O'Connor was the first woman appointed to the U.S. Supreme Court.

$$$$

Fodor's Choice

★

🖼 **Arizona Biltmore.** Designed by Frank Lloyd Wright's colleague Albert Chase McArthur, the Biltmore has been Phoenix's premier resort since it opened in 1929. The lobby, with its stained-glass skylights, wrought-iron pilasters, and cozy sitting alcoves, fills with piano music each evening. Guest rooms are spacious, with Southwestern-print fabrics and Mission-style furniture. Accommodating staff are unobtrusive. The Biltmore sits on 39 impeccably manicured acres of cool fountains, open walkways, and colorful flower beds. ⊠*2400 E. Missouri Ave., Camelback Corridor, 85016* 🕾*602/955–6600 or 800/950–0086* 🖷*602/381–7600* ⊕*www.arizonabiltmore.com* 🛏*739 rooms, 72 villas* ⌂*In-room: safe, Ethernet, Wi-Fi (some), refrigerator. In-hotel: 4 restaurants, bar, tennis courts, pools, gym, spa, bicycles, concierge, children's programs (ages 6–12), laundry service, parking (no fee), no-smoking rooms*🚭*AE, D, DC, MC, V.*

$$$$

★

☘

🖼 **Fairmont Scottsdale Princess.** Home of the Tournament Players Club Stadium golf course and the FBR Phoenix Open, this resort covers 450 breathtakingly landscaped acres of desert. Willow Stream Spa, one of the top spa spots in the country, has a dramatic rooftop pool and kids love the fishing pond and water slides. Rooms are done in Southwestern style and service is what you'd expect at a resort of this caliber: excellent and unobtrusive. Even pets get the royal treatment: a specially designated pet room comes with treats and turndown service. ⊠*7575 E. Princess Dr., North Scottsdale, 85255* 🕾*480/585–4848 or 800/344–4758* 🖷*480/585–0091* ⊕*www.fairmont.com* 🛏*458 rooms, 119 casitas, 72 villas, 2 suites* ⌂*In-room: safe, dial-up (some). In-hotel: 5 restaurants, bars, golf courses, tennis courts, pools, gym, spa, children's programs (ages 6–12), parking (no fee), no-smoking rooms, some pets allowed*🚭*AE, D, DC, MC, V.*

$$$$

Fodor's Choice

★

☘

🖼 **The Phoenician.** In a town where luxurious, expensive resorts are the rule, the Phoenician still stands apart, primarily in the realm of service. The gilded, marbled lobby with towering fountains is the backdrop for the $25 million fine art collection. Large rooms, in the main building and outer-lying casitas are decorated with elegant 1960s furniture and have private patios and oversize marble bathrooms. There's a secluded tennis garden and 27 holes of premier golf. The Centre for Well Being Spa has a meditation atrium and a pool lined with mother-of-pearl tiles where you can drift off to another world. Afterward, you can take in a sophisticated afternoon tea, or save your energy and money for a night at Mary Elaine's ($$$$), one of the finest (and most expensive) restaurants in the state. ⊠ *6000 E. Camelback Rd., Camelback Corridor, 85251* ☎*480/941–8200 or 800/888–8234* 🖷*480/947–4311* ⊕*www. thephoenician.com* 🛏*574 rooms, 73 suites* ⚷*In-room: safe, refrigerator (some), dial-up, Ethernet. In-hotel: 6 restaurants, bars, room service, golf courses, tennis courts, pools, gym, children's programs (ages 5–12), parking (no fee), no-smoking rooms, public Wi-Fi* ▤*AE, D, DC, MC, V.*

$$$$
Fodor'sChoice
★
🖭**Royal Palms Resort & Spa.** Once the home of Cunard Steamship executive Delos T. Cooke, this Mediterranean-style resort has a stately row of the namesake palms at its entrance, courtyards with fountains, and individually designed rooms. Deluxe casitas are all different, though they follow one of three elegant styles—trompe l'oeil, romantic retreat, Spanish colonial. The restaurant, T. Cook's ($$$–$$$$), is renowned and the open-air Alvadora Spa, featuring 7 new spa suites, seems like it has every imaginable amenity, including an outdoor rain shower. In 2007 the resort unveiled its new Montavista collection of rooms, and suites featuring fireplaces and luxury amenities. ⊠*5200 E. Camelback Rd., Camelback Corridor, 85018* ☎*602/840–3610 or 800/672–6011* 🖷*602/840–6927* ⊕*www.royalpalmshotel.com* 🛏*76 rooms, 62 suites, 44 casitas* ⚷*In-room: safe, refrigerator, Ethernet, Wi-Fi. In-hotel: restaurant, room service, bar, pool, gym, spa, laundry service, parking (fee), no-smoking rooms* ▤*AE, D, DC, MC, V.*

$$$–$$$$
Fodor'sChoice
★
🖭**Sanctuary on Camelback Mountain.** This luxurious boutique hotel is the only resort on the north slope of Camelback Mountain. Secluded mountain casitas are painted in desert hues and feature breathtaking views of Paradise Valley. Chic spa casitas surround the pool and are outfitted with contemporary furnishings and private patios. Bathrooms are travertine marble with elegant sinks and roomy tubs. For those who enjoy going *eau* and even *au naturel*, some suites have outdoor tubs. An infinity-edge pool, Zen meditation garden, and Asian-inspired Sanctuary Spa make this a haven for relaxation. The hotel's restaurant, elements ($$$), is the hotspot for cocktails at sunset. ⊠*5700 E. McDonald Dr., Paradise Valley 85253* ☎*480/948–2100 or 800/245–2051* 🖷*480/483–7314* ⊕*www.sanctuaryaz.com* 🛏*98 casitas* ⚷*In-room: kitchen (some), refrigerator (some), dial-up, Ethernet, Wi-Fi. In-hotel: restaurant, room service, bar, tennis courts, pools, gym, spa, parking (no fee), no-smoking rooms, no elevator, public Wi-Fi* ▤*AE, D, DC, MC, V.*

$$–$$$$
☺
🖭**Crowne Plaza San Marcos Golf Resort.** When it opened in 1912, the San Marcos was the first golf resort in Arizona and it's still one of the state's most treasured landmarks. Now part of the Crowne Plaza family, the palm-studded, mission-style San Marcos has undergone luxury

27

LIKE A LOCAL

Phoenix visitors take heed: someone is watching your car. Camera devices are mounted on several streetlights and select freeways to catch speeders and red-light runners, and their locations are constantly changing. You may think you've gotten away with a few miles over the limit—only to return home to find a ticket waiting for you.

Left-turn lane confusion causes many accidents in the Valley. Each individual jurisdiction varies: in some, the left turn arrow precedes the green light; in others, it follows the green light. Be aware that yellow lights tend to be shorter here than

most drivers are accustomed to—be prepared for sudden stops, and watch intersections for red-light runners who cross right after the light changes.

Weekdays 6 AM to 9 AM and 4 PM to 6 PM in Downtown Phoenix, the center or left-turn lanes on the major surface arteries of 7th Street and 7th Avenue become one-way traffic-flow lanes between McDowell Road and Dunlap Avenue. These specially marked lanes are dedicated to north–south traffic (into downtown) in the morning and to south–north traffic (out of downtown) in the afternoon.

upgrades to keep it on par with the competition, while maintaining its historic beauty and charm. Improvements include the Images day spa and restyled rooms with pillow-top mattresses, high-thread-count sheets, and down-filled duvets. Each room and suite has either a balcony or patio and the quiet, single-level golf-course casitas offer patios with "*Fore!*-star" views. ■TIP➔The resort operates an on-site Starbucks and there's great nearby shopping and dining. ⊠ *One San Marcos Pl., Chandler 85225* ☎*480/812–0900* 🖷*480/899–5441* ⊕*www.sanmarcosresort. com* ⌲*238 rooms, 45 casitas, 12 suites* ⚖*In-room: Ethernet, dial-up. In-hotel: 2 restaurants, room service, bars, golf course, pools, spa, parking (no fee), no-smoking rooms* ▭*AE, D, DC, MC, V.*

$$–$$$$ 🏨**Hyatt Regency Scottsdale at Gainey Ranch.** When you stay here, it's ☾ easy to imagine that you're relaxing at an oceanside resort instead of the desert. Shaded by towering palms, with manicured gardens and paths, the property has water everywhere—a large pool area has a beach, a three-story waterslide, waterfalls, and a lagoon. The two-story lobby, filled with Native American art, opens to outdoor conversation areas where fires burn in stone fireplaces on cool nights. Large rooms have balconies or patios. Three golf courses at nearby Gainey Ranch Golf Club will suit any duffer's fancy. Spa Avania aims to soothe the soul, while kids get their kicks at Camp Hyatt. ⊠ *7500 E. Doubletree Ranch Rd., North Scottsdale, 85258* ☎*480/444–1234 or 800/233–1234* 🖷*480/483–5550* ⊕*www.scottsdale.hyatt.com* ⌲*461 rooms, 7 casitas, 22 suites* ⚖*In-room: dial-up, Ethernet, Wi-Fi. In-hotel: 4 restaurants, bars, golf courses, tennis courts, pools, gym, spa, bicycles, children's programs (ages 3–12), executive floor, parking (no fee), no-smoking rooms* ▭*AE, D, DC, MC, V.*

$$–$$$$ 🏨**JW Marriott Desert Ridge Resort & Spa.** Arizona's largest resort has an ☾ immense entryway with floor-to-ceiling windows that allow the sand-

stone lobby, the Sonoran Desert, and the resort's amazing water features to meld together in a single prospect. Four acres of water fun include the popular "lazy river," where you can flop on an inner tube and float the day away. Young 'uns love the Kokopelli Kids program, while adults can rejuvenate at Revive Spa or tee off at the on-site golf courses. Each elegantly decorated room offers a balcony or patio. ⊠*5350 E. Marriott Dr., North Central Phoenix, 85054* ☎*480/293–5000 or 800/835–6206* 🖶*480/293–3600* ⊕*www.jwdesertridgeresort.com* 🛏*869 rooms, 81 suites* ♿*In-room: safe, refrigerator (some), Ethernet, dial-up. In-hotel: 9 restaurants, room service, bars, golf courses, tennis courts, pools, spa, bicycles, children's programs (ages 4–12), no-smoking rooms* 🚭*AE, D, DC, MC, V.*

NIGHTLIFE & THE ARTS

Fodor's Choice
★
🕙
Rawhide Western Town and Steakhouse at the Wildhorse Pass (⊠*5700 W. North Loop Rd., Gila River Indian Community, Chandler* ☎*480/502–5600* ⊕*www.rawhide.com*) moved from Scottsdale in 2006, and now calls the 2,400-acre master-planned Wild Horse Pass Development in the Gila River Indian Community, home. Large portions of the original Rawhide were moved to the new site, including the legendary steakhouse and saloon, Main Street and all of its retail shops, and the Six Gun Theater. Exciting additions include canal rides along the Gila River Riverwalk, train rides, and a Native American village honoring the history and culture of the Akimel O'othom and Pee Posh Tribes.

AZ88 (⊠*7353 Scottsdale Mall, Scottsdale Civic Center, Scottsdale* ☎*480/994–5576*) is great for feasting on huge portions of great food and lavish quantities of liquor, but also for feasting your eyes on the fabulous people who flock here on weekend nights to see and be seen.

★ **Jade Bar** (⊠*5700 E. McDonald Dr., Sanctuary on Camelback Resort, Paradise Valley* ☎*480/948–2100*) has spectacular views of Paradise Valley and Camelback Mountain, an upscale modern bar lined with windows, and a relaxing fire-place-lighted patio.

★ **Axis/Radius** (⊠*7340 E. Indian Plaza Rd., Central Scottsdale, Scottsdale* ☎*480/970–1112*) is the dress-to-impress locale where you can party at side-by-side clubs connected by a glass catwalk.

Myst (⊠*7340 E. Shoeman La., North Scottsdale, Scottsdale* ☎*480/970–5000*) is an ultraswanky dance club where you can sip cocktails in a sunken lounge or hang out at the white-hot Milk Bar adorned with white leather seating and an all-white bar. Upstairs is the private VIP lounge, complete with sky boxes overlooking the dance floor.

SHOPPING

★ **Biltmore Fashion Park** (⊠*24th St. and Camelback Rd., Camelback Corridor* ☎*602/955–8400*) has a posh, parklike setting. Macy's, Saks Fifth Avenue, and Borders are the anchors for more than 70 stores and upscale shops, such as Betsey Johnson and Cartier. It's accessible from the Camelback Esplanade and the Ritz Carlton by a pedestrian tunnel that runs beneath Camelback Road.

27

ON THE WAY

Yuma Territorial Prison: Incarceration in 1876 wasn't pretty, and one afternoon at the Yuma Territorial Prison will drive that fact home. One of the oddest stops along Interstate 8 in Yuma, the prison is a state historic park and open for tours. You may claim your high school was a prison, but take note: Yuma High School actually used the prison's buildings from 1910 to 1914. 1 Prison Hill Rd., Yuma, off I-8 and Giss Pkwy., 928/783-4771.

Arcosanti: A self-sustaining habitat created by Italian architect Palo Soleri, there's no place in the world like Arcosanti. Envisioned as a place where architecture and ecology could function in symbiosis, the community's artisans make and sell fantastic copper goods, including wind chimes. 65 mi north of Phoenix off I-17 at Cordes Junction, 928/632-7135, www.arcosanti.org.

Snoopy Rock: Phoenix might have Camelback Mountain, but Sedona has Snoopy Rock. Off Arizona State Route 179 on Schnebly Hill Road (about 115 mi south of Phoeniz), this formation looks like the famed Peanuts beagle lying atop red rock instead of his doghouse. You can distinguish the formation from several places around town.

The Borgata (⌧6166 N. Scottsdale Rd., Central Scottsdale, Scottsdale), an outdoor re-creation of the Italian village of San Gimignano, with courtyards, stone walls, turrets, and fountains, is a lovely setting for browsing upscale boutiques or just sitting at an outdoor café.

★ **Kierland Commons** (⌧Greenway Pkwy. at Scottsdale Rd., North Scottsdale, Scottsdale ☎480/348-1577), next to the Westin Kierland Resort, is one of the city's newest shopping areas. "Urban village" is the catchphrase for this outdoor pedestrian mall with restaurants and upscale chain retailers, among them J. Crew and Tommy Bahama.

★ **Mill Avenue Shops** (⌧Mill Ave., between Rio Salado Pkwy. and University Dr., Downtown, Tempe ☎480/967-4877), named for the landmark Hayden Flour Mill, is an increasingly commercial area, but it's still a fun-filled walk-and-shop experience. Directly west of the Arizona State University campus, Mill Avenue is an active melting pot of students, artists, residents, and tourists. Shops include Borders, Urban Outfitters, a few remaining locally owned clothing and curio stores, and countless bars and restaurants. The Valley Art Theater is a Mill Avenue institution and Tempe's place for indie cinema. Twice a year (in early December and March–April), the Mill Avenue area is the place to find indie arts and crafts when it hosts the Tempe Festival of the Arts.

★ **Old Town Scottsdale** (⌧Bordered by Goldwater Blvd., Brown Ave., 5th Ave., and 3rd St., Downtown, Scottsdale ☎800/737-0008) is the place to go for authentic Southwest-inspired gifts, clothing, art, and artifacts. Despite its massive modern neighbors, this area and its merchants have long respected and maintained the single-level brick storefronts that embody Scottsdale's upscale cowtown charm. More than 100 businesses meet just about any aesthetic want or need, including Gilbert Ortega, one of the premiere places for fine Native American jewelry and art. Some of Scottsdale's best restaurants are also tucked in this pleasing maze of merchants.

★ **Scottsdale Fashion Square** (✉ *Scottsdale and Camelback Rds., Central Scottsdale, Scottsdale* ☎ *480/949–0202*) has a retractable roof and many specialty shops unique to Arizona. There are also Nordstrom, Dillard's, Neiman Marcus, Macy's, Juicy Couture, Anthropologie, Z Gallerie, Louis Vuitton, Tiffany, and Arizona's only Gucci store. A huge food court, restaurants, and a cineplex complete the picture.

SPORTS & THE OUTDOORS

GOLF

Arizona has more golf courses per capita than any other state west of the Mississippi River, making it one of the most popular golf destinations in the United States. It's also one of Arizona's major industries, and greens fees can run from $35 at a public course to more than $500 at some of Arizona's premier golfing spots. New courses seem to pop up monthly: there are more than 200 in the Valley (some lighted at night), and the PGA's Southwest section has its headquarters here. Call well ahead for tee times during the cooler months. In summer fees drop dramatically and it's not uncommon to schedule a round before dawn.

■ **TIP→** **Some golf courses offer a discounted twilight rate—and the weather is often much more amenable at this time of day.** Check course Web sites for discounts before making your reservations. Also, package deals abound at resorts as well as through booking agencies like **Arizona Golf Adventures** (☎ *877/841–6570* ⊕ *www.azteetimes.com*), who will plan and schedule a nonstop golf holiday for you. For a copy of the *Arizona Golf Guide,* contact the **Arizona Golf Association** (☎ *602/944–3035 or 800/458–8484* ⊕ *www.azgolf.org*).

Fodor'sChoice **ASU Karsten Golf Course** (✉ *1125 E. Rio Salado Pkwy., Tempe* ☎ *480/921–
★ 8070* ⊕ *www.asukarsten.com*) is the Arizona State University 18-hole golf course where NCAA champions train. Greens fees are between $30 and $105.

Fodor'sChoice **Gold Canyon Golf Club** (✉ *6100 S. King's Ranch Rd., Gold Canyon
★ ☎ 480/982–9449 or 800/624–6445* ⊕ *www.gcgr.com*), near Apache Junction in the East Valley, offers fantastic views of the Superstition Mountains and challenging golf. Greens fees range from $74 to $189.

Fodor'sChoice **Troon North** (✉ *10320 E. Dynamite Blvd., North Scottsdale, Scottsdale
★ ☎ 480/585–7700* ⊕ *www.troonnorthgolf.com*) is a challenge for the length alone (7,008 yards). The million-dollar views add to the experience at this perfectly maintained 36-hole course. Greens fees are $75 to $295.

BASEBALL

Today the **Cactus League** consists of 12 major-league teams (9 in the Valley and 3 in Tucson). Ticket prices are reasonable, around $7 to $8 for bleacher seats to $15 for reserved seats. Many stadiums have lawn-seating areas in the outfield, where you can spread a blanket and bring a picnic. Cactus League stadiums are more intimate than big-league parks, and players often come right up to the stands to say hello and to sign autographs. Special events such as fireworks nights, bat and T-shirt giveaway nights, and visits from sports mascots add to the festive feeling during spring training.

Tickets for some teams go on sale as early as December. Brochures listing game schedules and ticket information are available on the Cactus League's Web site (⊕ *www. cactus-league.com*). During the regular major-league season, the hometown **Arizona Diamondbacks** (⊕ *www.azdiamondbacks.com*) play on natural grass at Chase Field, formerly Bank One Ballpark (BOB), in the heart of Phoenix's Copper Square (the team does spring training in Tucson). The

VITAL STATS

■ Phoenix is the nation's fifth-largest city, with 1.4 million residents; the greater Phoenix area has a population of nearly 3.8 million.

■ Phoenix has an average annual rainfall of 7.66 inches.

■ Arizona is home to 23 Native American reservations representing 21 different tribes.

■ State Nickname: Grand Canyon State

■ State Flower: Saguaro Cactus Blossom

■ State Gem: Turquoise

■ State Neckware: Bola tie

stadium is a technological wonder; if the weather's a little too warm outside, they close the roof, turn on the gigantic air-conditioners, and keep you cool while you enjoy the game. You can tour the stadium, except on afternoon-game days and holidays.

VISITOR INFORMATION

Arizona Office of Tourism (☎ *602/364–3730 or 888/520–3444* ⊕ *www.arizona guide.com*).

Greater Phoenix Convention and Visitors Bureau (☎ *602/254–6500* ⊕ *www. phoenixcvb.com*).

Native American Tourism Center (✉ *4130 N. Goldwater Blvd., Phoenix* ☎ *480/945–0771* 🖶 *480/945–0264*).

Scottsdale Convention and Visitors Bureau (☎ *480/421–1004 or 800/782–1117* ⊕ *www.scottsdalecvb.com*).

Las Vegas

The Las Vegas Strip

WORD OF MOUTH

"Vegas has changed enormously in the 10 years I've been visiting, and not always for the better. The growth in huge, corporate resorts means the personal touch is being forgotten. For all that, it's still the most jaw-dropping, ridiculous, fun place to visit. Would I go every year? No. Would I go every two years? Actually, yes."

–GrahamC

EXPLORING LAS VEGAS

By car, Las Vegas is 2,500 mi from Hoboken, NJ (Birthplace of Frank Sinatra) via Chicago, Omaha, & Denver; 1,850 mi from Louisville, KY (Birthplace of Hunter S. Thompson) via St Louis & Topeka; 2,500 mi from Norfolk, VA (Birthplace of Wayne Newton) via Memphis, Amarillo, & Flagstaff; 260 mi from Pasadena, CA (Birthplace of Stacey Augmon) via Barstow; 2,150 mi from Steubenville, OH (Birthplace of Dean Martin) via St. Louis, & Kansas City; and 1,700 mi from Tupelo, MS (Birthplace of Elvis Presley) via Little Rock, & Albuquerque. By air, Las Vegas is 7,700 mi from Luxor, Egypt; 7,900 mi from Mandalay, Burma; 5,800 mi from Monte Carlo, Monaco; 5,400 mi from Paris, France; and 5,900 mi Venice, Italy

By Swain
Scheps

Washington, D.C., may be America's seat of power, but if you want its seat of promise, it just might reside in the land of oversize coin cups in slot pits, where particular ATMs only dispense $100 bills and all-you-can-eat buffets challenge you to eat your weight in jumbo shrimp, Alaskan crab legs, and prime rib. And the promise takes many forms, 24/7. Whether you go for the volcanic excess and passionate consumerism of the Strip, the more humble (but still neon-bathed) downtown experience, or the grittier locals joints, Las Vegas promises wealth, excitement, and a temporary sense of importance to all who visit.

For the millions of visitors who make the trek to Las Vegas every year, the city offers an ever-increasing array of sights, sounds, and experiences to play on their unsatisfied needs. We desire travel to exotic locales, so we stay in a hotel modeled after one, like the Mirage or the Venetian. We want to experience adventure, so we play casino games: a good adrenaline proxy for physical risk. Just for a moment we want to own and consume finer things than we have, so we visit opulent restaurants and visit any of several concentrations of high-end shopping districts, looking to buy items that would be just beyond our reach back in the "real" world.

Beyond and to some degree within the spectacle, the people of Las Vegas are quintessentially American. It shines through in the out-of-staters who settled in Southern Nevada for a million different reasons over the years, who deal blackjack and drive cabs. But also evident is the melting pot; Las Vegas is the city on the hill for immigrants from all over the world. For visitors and many locals as well, Las Vegas knows what you want and doles it out in spades. It's both exotic and comfortably familiar at the same time. But the city goes beyond merely reflecting American tastes and ideals; it consumes, amplifies, and blasts them out at high volume.

WHO WILL ESPECIALLY LOVE THIS TRIP?

Groups: You don't have to be on a bachelor or bachelorette party to have fun here. Any excuse that brings together a loosely connected group of people ready to have a good time will do. Friendships get

TOP 5 REASONS TO GO

The Spectacle: In the old days, reason one would be gaming, but these days you can gamble—in one form or another—in nearly every state in the union. Las Vegas is a place you must see even if you've never rolled dice in your life outside of that Yahtzee game that ended in tears at your 4th grade birthday party.

The Adrenaline. The variety of gambling and entertainment outlets, the level of stakes, the quality of dealers, the sheer numbers of players at the tables, and the overall energy radiating from the Strip and its environs makes Vegas a unique kind of rush.

The People: They're sometimes beautiful and famous, sometimes they're middle-of-the-road, and sometimes they're beyond description. But no matter what they're always fascinating to observe. It's not just a people-watcher's paradise, Vegas provides a fantastic opportunity to interact. Belly up to a craps table and you'll see why.

The Food: The days of the $4.95 steak dinner are over. But that's a good thing; in their place have come scores of world-class restaurants of all cuisines. And you don't have to go to a five-star restaurant to get excellent chow; some folks swear the casino coffee shops and taco stands offer the best grub in the city. And, friends, you can take a pass on some of the buffets, but don't pass them all. The dinner buffet at the Bellagio is a triple threat: classy, plentiful, and good.

The Smiles: When people go to Las Vegas they come alive, because the city provides so many opportunities to become a slightly different person. You'll rarely get reminders of your daily routine, because the sometimes flamboyant, sometimes seedy Vegas is like nowhere else you've ever been. And that's precisely the idea.

28

cemented (and occasionally severed), love blossoms (and occasionally wilts), but the stories of your trip will echo for a long time.

Couples: Yes, couples—real life, thought-they-knew-everything-about-each-other couples. And it's not so he can play golf at the 18-hole, 6,994 yard par-71 Bali Hai Golf Club while she's miles away shopping at Fashion Outlets Las Vegas in Primm, NV. Playing a game together like Blackjack spurs stress-free interaction that is hard to come by in other environments. You'll remember that it's fun to have fun together.

Singles: Vegas used to be a city where men outnumbered women by a wide margin. No more. Vegas is as much of a hook-up town as there is anywhere. Try the pool at the Hard Rock Hotel on a Saturday afternoon if you're on the prowl. Or make friends playing Blackjack at the Party Pit at Harrah's. At night, dress to impress and you just might get in to Pure in Caesar's Palace where you can dance the night away.

Serious Gamblers: You won't find higher stakes anywhere in the United States. And if your goal is to play poker for 55 out of the 60 hours you're in town, there's a seat open for you right now at the Bellagio Poker Room among others. Nevada's also the only state in the union with legal sports betting, and you'll love picking the point spreads, then kicking back in a comfy chair to watch the games at places like the Mandalay Bay Race and Sports Book.

Foodies: Southern Nevada has a high concentration of fine restaurants with some world-famous chefs. Have a pizza by Wolfgang Puck at the Venetian's Postrio. But gustatory pleasures can be found off the Strip, too, like Nora's Wine Bar.

Sun Worshippers: Vegas gets 300 days of sun a year, so rain checks are rare at the local golf courses. A quick trip out of the city limits and you can find yourself rock climbing, hiking, or exploring a ghost town. Or if you'd prefer a more leisurely approach to your vacation, the swimming pools at the megaresorts offer everything from swim-up gambling to poolside cabanas.

Shutterbugs: Sure there's the gaudy architecture and volcanic spectacles of the Las Vegas Strip. But don't let your f-stop there. Get out of town to the stunning environs; just over the hills are mountains, forests, nature preserves, lakes, dams, and wildlife.

Families: You might occasionally be forced to cover their eyes and ears, but the underage crowd loves the video game arcades, and the wide variety of roller coasters like X-Scream atop the Stratosphere.

WHEN IS THE BEST TIME TO VISIT?

First-time visitors tend to gravitate to the Strip, and that means a lot of walking. If you go in the summer, be prepared to face the dry afternoon heat, which can climb into the low 100s. Wear sunscreen and drink lots of water. If you can't stand the heat, the only shot you have to get out of the kitchen is to go between October and April.

At no time of year is weather in Las Vegas particularly bad. Sure it gets hot in the summer, and winter nights can get downright cold. But if you prepare well, and bring clothes that suit your planned activities, you'll be fine.

If you suffer from agoraphobia (fear of crowds) you should consider an alternate destination entirely. You will wait in lines and bump shoulders with others no matter when you go. The only hint of "quiet time" to be had is in the middle of the week. If you're able to take off work, you'll get cheaper flights, better hotel rates, and lower minimum bets at the tables.

On the other hand, if you want to spin up the excitement meter as high as it can go, travel to Las Vegas on New Years Eve, St. Patrick's Day, or during one of the long summer-holiday weekends (Memorial Day, July 4, Labor Day). You may have to fight for space at a craps table, but once you're in there and rolling dice, you'll be at the center of your own little party.

Big crowds gravitate to Las Vegas for headline sporting events, and the hotels will usually take advantage of the surges with higher rates.

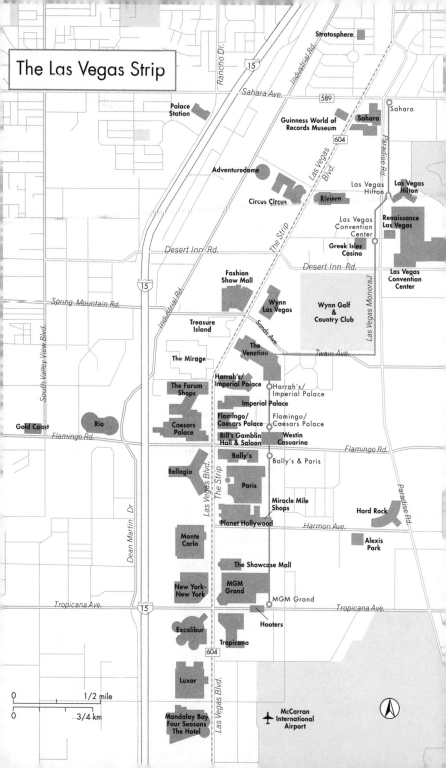

Booking early may save you heartburn on a busy weekend, but it's not likely to save you much money.

Any NFL playoff weekend will fill the casinos with jersey-wearing yahoos, culminating in Superbowl Sunday in early February. NASCAR visits Las Vegas in spring, bringing race fans out of the woodwork and into the casinos and restaurants. College basketball's March Madness is sure to swell the casinos as do the NBA playoffs in May and June. Then there are the headline boxing matches—if there is such a thing anymore—along with the Super Bowl in early February. Another big event is December's National Finals Rodeo—the "Super Bowl" of the bull-riding set.

It's not just sports enthusiasts that can affect your stay in Las Vegas. The city is a prime destination for conventions and exhibitions, and when the big ones roll through town, they bring exhibitors and visitors that crowd the hotels and restaurants. In its heyday, Comdex brought a quarter of a million people to town, but that show is no longer an annual Vegas tradition. These days it's the Consumer Electronics Show that brings the most visitors to Vegas, drawing more than 100,000 people in for its week's run of showing off the newest in personal gadgetry.

HOW SHOULD I GET THERE?

DRIVING

There's nothing quite like a road trip to Vegas. Opportunities abound for fun along the way, whether you're traveling the old Route 66 from somewhere in the heartland, driving through the Mojave desert from Los Angeles, or finding your way to Vegas from points farther. If you can time it right, the night approach is magical. After twisting through darkened mountain passes and driving across vast salt flats, the first hint of Las Vegas is an unearthly glow rising from the distant desert horizon, which at last gives way to a carnival of twinkling neon as you see the city for the first time from across the valley.

Las Vegas is a drivable weekend destination for residents of Southern California and Arizona. Los Angelenos will take I–15 through Barstow. Phoenix residents don't have the luxury of a straight shot to Las Vegas. The best they can do is wind through the notoriously dangerous U.S. 93 that makes its way through Wikieup before meeting I–40.

If you're coming from farther away, you'd better plan on staying the night somewhere. For those approaching from the east on I–40, why not take a moment to contemplate your life at the South Rim of the Grand Canyon? Or if you're coming from the northwest down I–15, clear your head for a night at St. George, Utah, on the edge of the stunning Zion National Park.

FLYING

Las Vegas is served by most of the major domestic carriers through McCarran International Airport, the sixth busiest airport in the U.S., which sits on the east side of the south end of the Strip. Scheduled

How to Snack

When in Vegas you're at the hub of a glorious food galaxy. It's akin to New York City because you're always within a few yards and a few minutes of a hot meal 24 hours a day. But just because Las Vegas is home to award-winning eateries doesn't mean visitors have to make every meal a sit-down event.

Newer hotels offer the spectrum of fast-food options inside the facilities. The Starbucks phenomenon has fully penetrated the casino scene, and if your hotel doesn't have the name brand, there will be some analog serving lattes and bagels over a countertop. Most Strip and Downtown resort hotels offer several typecast restaurants, including a high-end continental joint, perhaps a steak house, and/or some kind off yummy ethnic chow. In addition, snackers will almost always find a 24-hour coffee shop to keep you knee deep in breakfast food, sandwiches, and desserts. **Mr. Lucky's 24/7 Café** at the Hard Rock Hotel (*4455 Paradise Rd., 702/693–5000*) is the best in the city, offering a diverse menu to table and counter customers. The similarly named but unrelated **24/7** at the Palms (*4321 W Flamingo Rd., 702/942–7777*) is worth the side trip off the Strip for the meat loaf alone.

If your goal is to get local fare, you'll need to remove yourself from within 100 yards of any neon whatsoever. Las Vegas has great restaurants, but they're strictly for the tourists. Las Vegas is an immigrant city, with a fifth of the populace being foreign-born, so try the ethnic fare. **Nora's Wine Bar & Osteria** is a modern Italian experience with a live jazz trio on weekends and a special computer-controlled wine-serving system to complement the Sicilian accented menu. Locals also turn to **Mimmo Ferraro's Italian** for a quieter night out. **Big Mama's Rib Shack** (*2230 W. Bonanza, 702/597–1616*) is a not-so-well-kept secret a few miles outside of Downtown, offering much more than yummy hickory-cooked barbeque; there are creole items (red beans and rice) and authentic Georgia soul food (chitlins), too. The strong Far East influence can be felt in the Las Vegas gastronomic scene at locals favorites **Joyful House**—the best Cantonese food in the state—and the nontraditional **Firefly**, a tapas house blending Asian, Spanish, and Latin influences. Vegetarians, as is their lot in life, must often find Indian food for a full vegetarian menu. In Las Vegas that means **Shalimar**. For dessert, you can't go wrong at **Luv It Frozen Custard**.

28

flights and charters also flow through McCarran from several different countries including Mexico, Canada, and scattered cities in Europe.

Most passengers have to deal with a brief tram ride between the main terminal and the gate complexes. If you're flying in at the start of a busy weekend the taxi line snakes through the loading zone and can look daunting to a weary traveler anxious to hit the tables. The good news is that it moves pretty fast. Limousines and hotel shuttles (both direct and indirect) are available as well.

Getting out of Las Vegas has its challenges as well. Monday usually sees a mass exodus of weekend visitors, which can clog even the most efficient ticketing and airport security operations. You can do yourself

CLAIM TO FAME

Oh boy. If you don't know what the Las Vegas claim to fame is, perhaps a trip to Poughkeepsie is more your speed.

The town may exude promise, but it was built on sin. Consider that the basic premise of the city's slogan, "What happens here, stays here" is that you're good-naturedly encouraged to lie about your trip should anyone ask about it. And there's a reason for that: what happens here usually stays there because it's likely illegal where you live. While bars all across America are closing at 1 or 2 AM, alcohol consumption in Las Vegas continues into the breakfast hours completely unhindered. If you're thinking about getting married, the waiting period in this state is exactly the length of time it takes you to fill out the appropriate forms.

And let's get this straight: prostitution, while legal in some parts of Nevada, is not legal in Las Vegas, despite all the advertising for, well, sex in the city.

Debauchery and matrimony aside, the main course in this town is, of course, gambling. Every light hanging from all the magnificent buildings, as well as every fountain, pirate ship, and volcano is paid for with gamblers' losses in games of chance. In fact most of the public works in the state of Nevada could be described the same way. The limits are higher than just about anywhere else, and the range of bets you can make is broader as well, from card games to sporting events two continents away to the outcome of elections. Gambling makes Vegas go.

several favors to make life easier: use electronic ticketing and check-in, be aware of security regulations when you pack your bag, and get to the airport two hours early.

TRAIN
Train travel is seriously underrated in this age of instant gratification and impatience. Since you're breaking some rules on this trip, why not take a little extra time in getting there by hopping on Amtrak's Southwest Chief? Rolling between Los Angeles and Chicago, the Chief stops in Needles, California, where Amtrak provides connecting bus service to both Laughlin and Las Vegas. Nothing could be finer.

HOW DO I GET AROUND?

Las Vegas is a walking town. You can find broad sidewalks, escalators, and moving walkways all over town. In addition, the Strip has recently sprouted a series of pedestrian bridges to make it easier than ever to cross the busy intersections and get to the next megaresort. Just be aware that distances can be deceiving. It may well seem like you're just next door to Caesar's Palace, but by the time you find your way out of your own hotel, walk along the busy sidewalks of the Strip, and travel the long moving sidewalks leading into Caesar's, you'll find 20 minutes have elapsed.

When your dogs give out, you can take the monorail or taxis to your next destination. Or better yet, maybe you're lucky enough to be staying at a hotel with a luxury spa, like the Spa Wynn Las Vegas, where you can treat your aching feet to a deep tissue massage.

BY CAR

If you've driven into town, or gotten a rental at the airport, a car can come in handy in Las Vegas. Parking at the casinos is usually free and plentiful. Just beware of the Strip at night; it can turn into a parking lot of bass thumpers, cruisers, and gawkers. Stick to the routes behind the casinos if you know what's good for you.

A car is great if you're interested in getting off the Strip, out of Downtown, and into the more welcoming locals' scene that you can find at the Suncoast or the Station casinos, where the tables are friendlier, the rooms cheaper, and the scene less ostentatious. There are also fancy resorts on the outskirts, like the Red Rock Casino Resort Spa where low-lying A-listers (*cough* George Clooney *cough*) are sometimes seen.

And there's plenty to do well outside of town, so take full advantage of your automotive resources by exploring the magnificent countryside around Las Vegas. There's more to it than desert scrub. Consider one of several government-operated nature preserves and parks like Mt. Charleston or Red Rock Canyon, just west of town. Take the tour at Hoover Dam, or rent a boat at Lake Mead. In the winter months you can even go skiing in Lee Canyon at Las Vegas Ski and Snowboard Resort.

BY MONORAIL

The Las Vegas monorail opened in 2004 and runs along 4 mi of track from the MGM Grand to stops at Bally's, Flamingo, and Harrah's before taking a jog to the east and stopping at stations near the Convention Center, Las Vegas Hilton, and the Sahara. This is by no means the scenic route, as the train runs along the backside of the hotels rather than the Strip. You may save some time, but it doesn't come cheap. A one-way ticket is $5, regardless of your entry and exit point. Discounts are available if you buy in bulk.

There is talk of extending the monorail to Downtown via the Stratosphere tower, and another link will take passengers to the airport. But for now, those projects are on ice until the monorail crowd works out funding details.

BY TAXI

This isn't New York, so don't think you can hail a cab standing on any street corner. Taxis are no longer permitted to pick up or drop off passengers on the Strip, the place you're most likely to discover an intense dislike of walking. If you're on the Strip and need a cab, just walk into the nearest hotel. Almost all of them have clearly marked taxi stands where an attendant will hail a waiting cab on your behalf. (Be polite: give him or her a buck.) Rates are reasonable given the level of convenience, but visit a cash machine before you hop in, as most Las

HISTORY YOU CAN SEE

Unexpectedly, perhaps, the city has several fine collections of art, artifacts, and culturally important pieces. Consider the masters on display at the Guggenheim Hermitage Collection at the Venetian or the Bellagio Gallery of Fine Art, showing the works of Faberge, Warhol, and Picasso, to name a few.

If you're after local flavor, you can get a whiff of Vegas's history by going downtown, where the original casinos stood. Outside of town, Lake Mead and Hoover Dam are each amazing landmarks as well as living reminders of the great public works projects of the New Deal. Boulder City, originally a temporary village created for the workers on the dam in the 1930s, thrives today and has an interesting Hoover Dam Museum, detailing the history of that project and its effect on the area. A dam tour, into the bowels of the turbines and spillways is well worth the history buff's time, too, and kids love it.

Vegas cabs inexplicably don't take plastic. Taxi-stand lines can get long on weekend nights, so if you have a tight itinerary and the economics make sense, you might consider arranging a car service of some kind through your hotel concierge.

WHERE SHOULD I FOCUS MY ENERGY?

If you're here for 1 day: Try the spicy scrambled eggs for brunch at the Mesa Grill at Caesar's Palace to get you started off right. Then make a complete lap of Las Vegas Blvd, North to the Wynn, then South to the Mandalay and Luxor, drinking in the sights and sounds of the Strip.

If you're here for 2 days: Catch a show if you're in town for a night. Even during the weekdays you can see some great standing acts, like comic magician Mac King at Harrah's, or a Broadway-lite show like the Producers at Paris Las Vegas.

If you're here for 3 days: You'll be here long enough to get a good feel for what a Vegas all-nighter is really like, so belly up to a midnight card game at Hard Rock Hotel, then sleep it off in a poolside Cabana. By the third day you shouldn't even have to use your Blackjack crib sheet anymore.

If you're here for 4 days: The Main Street Experience downtown is a (mostly) wholesome spot for people weary of the crowds on the Strip. Take the time to learn a more challenging table game like Craps or Pai Gow. It helps when you're playing at lower stakes at the El Cortez Hotel downtown as you suck in that authentic Vegas vibe.

If you're here for 5 days: See some of the countryside. Tour the Hoover Dam just south of town and spend some time at Boulder Beach on Lake Mead. When night falls, pick out a Cirque du Soleil show to see; there are at least five to choose from on most nights. We recommend Mystere at Treasure Island.

If you're here for 6 days: Why not see the weirder side of Las Vegas? Go bowling at the Suncoast Hotel, then consider the nuclear option: the Atomic Testing Museum. Head out west to spend a night at the Little A'Le'Inn on Highway 375 in Lincoln County, better known as the Extraterrestrial Highway for its history of UFO sightings and proximity to the ever-spooky Area 51.

If you're here for 7 days or more: Surely you can't gamble for a week straight, right? Drive out to the new glass-floored Grand Canyon Skywalk. It extends 70 feet out over the gorge, providing you an unobstructed view a mile straight down. Follow that up with a night in Laughlin, the mini-Vegas on the Arizona border with a charm and style all its own.

WHAT ARE THE TOP EXPERIENCES?

The Football Weekend: For the true pigskin faithful, there are few better places to spend a fall weekend than in the loving embrace of a Las Vegas sports book, with a fist full of betting slips to invest you in the gridiron events like never before. Surrounded by boisterous fans, colossal video screens, and clockwork cocktail waitresses, you'll think you've died and gone to your living room . . . in heaven. Football contests make ideal anchor events for groups traveling together; a moment when everyone can pause for two hours together of screaming at professional athletes. Make plans to get into town Friday evening, and don't even think about leaving before Tuesday morning so you don't miss any of the college or NFL action. You can't go wrong camping out at the Mandalay Bay sports book with plenty of cushy lounge chairs and a snack bar within arm's reach. If you're traveling with a crowd, Paris and Red Rocks have hundreds of seats with individual TVs. Pick your month wisely and you'll get a bonus; September and October has baseball, and November and beyond have basketball.

Celeb Sightings: Actors, rock stars, and athletes are people, too, (sort of) and they are drawn to Southern Nevada for the same Dionysian reasons everyone else is: the resorts are palatial, the gambling is a rush, the restaurants are exceptional, and there's always another party to attend. Besides, Vegas offers the ideal setting for a famous person to be rich and famous, with its crowds of onlookers just dying to gawk at somebody of interest. So if you're on a first-name basis with your favorite stars (you know: Brad, Angelina, Leonardo) or perhaps your subscription to People just expired, head to Sin City and play a game of "I Spy: Celebrity Challenge." Start at the Hard Rock Hotel and count Baldwin brothers in the Circle Bar or over tuna tataki at Nobu. Then jump in a cab and head to any watering hole at the HRH's archrival across town: the Palms. If you time it just right, you can catch a Hilton-sister centered squabble just as dessert arrives at spectacular Alizé, with its unbroken view of the valley from 55 floors up. And in case you were worried, the well-known and well-born don't restrict themselves to off-strip locations either. You'll practically have to fight through the reality TV stars at Caesar's Palace famous Forum Shops, where Spago is as

28

STRANGE BUT TRUE

- Las Vegas is making dramatic changes to its image and appeal. Fewer than 1 visitor in 10 actually comes to Las Vegas for the purpose of gambling.

- All the same, 87% of visitors to Las Vegas report they gambled when they were there.

- The average bankroll for Las Vegas gamblers is about $600.

- Gambling was illegal in Las Vegas between 1910 and 1931.

- Las Vegas was recently voted the "meanest city in america" toward homeless people.

- The Stratosphere Tower is the tallest building west of the Mississippi River.

- The high-end suite atop the Hard Rock Hotel has its own bowling lane.

- New York City may never sleep, but Las Vegas is one of two major cities in the country with no closing laws. The other? New Orleans.

- If you're at the casino sports book hoping to bet on the local teams, you can forget it. Casinos don't offer bets for or against UNLV, and if a professional sports league plays an exhibition game in Vegas, that game will not be available for betting.

good a place to spend your 15 minutes as any. And if you're willing to dive deep into the A-list scene, Vegas nightclubs and boogie joints are always awash in rockers and athletes on steroid suspension. Boy-banders are known to congregate at Treasure Island's Tangerine, and then go right upstairs to ultrahip sushi and gathering spot Social House. Or you can always try the hottest clubs in town: Pure at Caesar's Palace, or Tao at Mandalay Bay. Since you're on a first name basis with the stars, you should have no trouble getting in!

Bachelor/Bachelorette Party: For the soon-to-be-wed, Las Vegas offers an unforgettable opportunity for making a final stand in the name of bachelor- or bachelorette-hood. Forget the celebrities; for this one weekend, you're the star. But before we get too deep into the fantasy, keep in mind that the friends who volunteered to come with you aren't coming for you, they're coming for Vegas. There's something for everyone in your pack, but at the same time it's the perfect destination for group activities: lounge together, eat together, and play together in any of the activities readymade for a group of six to eight people. If you're all staying at a full-service resort hotel like Bellagio or Venetian, nobody has to stray very far to get exactly what they want, be it food, shopping, spa services, or something else. That gives prenuptial parties a sense of cohesion that isn't available in New Orleans, Miami, or New York. Boys can be boys at the local golf courses (among other manly activities). Girls can be girls at any of a dozen deluxe spas, like Spa Wynn. If titillation is the order of the day, girls will enjoy their time watching Thunder from Down Under, the male revue at Excalibur. The bachelor party will, in all likelihood, choose to skip the PG-13 rated dance reviews and head straight to Spearmint Rhino, an international-chain topless joint. Then there's the over-the-top side of Las Vegas that can contribute to the party getting really out of hand: the guys might do something extreme like Flyaway Indoor Skydiving *(702/731–4768)* or get after-hours pedicures at AMP

Salon (the Palms) by lingerie-clad technicians (all on the up-and-up, we assure you). Meanwhile, the ladies might take a pole-dancing lesson, or take a shopping detour at Serge's Showgirl Wigs *(953 Sahara Ave., 702/732–1015)*. Both parties might wind up at the Palms' in-house Hart & Huntington Tattoo parlor *(702/942–7040)* for a permanent reminder of this weekend. Anything is possible.

BEST BETS

TOURS

Gray Line. Several bus companies offer Las Vegas city and neon-light tours, but Gray Line is among the best; excursions may take you into Red Rock Canyon, Lake Mead, Colorado River rafting, Hoover Dam, and Valley of Fire; longer trips go to different sections of the Grand Canyon.(☎*702/384–1234 or 800/634–6579* ⊕*www.graylinelasvegas.com*).

Helicopter Tours. Helicopters do two basic tours in and around Las Vegas: a brief flyover of the Strip and a several-hour trip out to the Grand Canyon and back.

Operators Maverick Helicopters Tours (☎*702/261-0007 or 888/261-4414* ⊕*www.maverickhelicopter.com*). **Papillon Grand Canyon Helicopters** (☎*702/736-7243 or 888/635-7272* ⊕*www.papillon.com*). **Sundance Helicopters** (☎*702/736-0606 or 800/653-1881* ⊕*www.helicoptour.com*).

Monorail. Begun in 1995 and greatly expanded in 2004, the monorail stretches from MGM Grand, on the south, to the Sahara, to the north, with several stops in between, and makes the 4-mi trip in about 14 minutes. To head farther south to Mandalay Bay, walk across the Strip and pick up the small, free monorail at the Excalibur. To the north, a downtown monorail extension is in the planning stages but completion is several years away. Also, although it's a fairly short walk (10 minutes tops) between the Mirage and Treasure Island casinos, you can also get between them on the free tram that runs roughly every 10 to 15 minutes, 9 AM–1 AM.

The monorail runs Monday–Thursday 7 AM–2 AM, Friday–Sunday 7 AM–3 AM. Fares are $5 for one ride, $9 for two rides, $35 for 10 rides, $15 for a one-day pass, and $40 for a three-day pass. You can purchase tickets at station vending machines or in advance online. (☎*702/699-8200* ⊕*www.lvmonorail.com*).

WHERE TO EAT

	WHAT IT COSTS				
	¢	$	$$	$$$	$$$$
AT DINNER	under $10	$10–$20	$20–$30	$30–$40	over $40

Prices are per person for a main course at dinner.

28

LIKE A LOCAL

With so many casinos, Las Vegas is home to a thousand and one words, customs, and mores that stem from the business and the insane volumes of cash that change hands between tourists and the house every minute of every day. You'll observe casino personnel performing odd rituals with their hands to "show" anyone watching them they aren't stealing.

And that's just the beginning. The gambling scene can feel a little like a club you don't belong to sometimes; especially if you've never played before. But don't worry, you'll pick it up fast. Here are some quick tips for getting along in a Las Vegas casino:

■ Don't cheat—yes it's possible, and yes, you can get into big trouble for it.

■ Don't chat—if you're at a table game, using a cellular phone or handheld device will get you booted from the table.

■ Don't hand money to dealers. Nobody in Vegas can take money directly from your hand, so when you want to buy chips, put your bills down on the table halfway between you and the casino employee.

■ Do your homework. If you don't have a chance to learn how to play your game of choice prior to arrival, make your first foray at a less-crowded table, where the dealer will have time to explain what's happening to you.

■ Don't linger: if you're not enjoying yourself, if you don't like the dealer or the people you're playing next to, or if you think they don't like you. Just get up and leave.

$$$$ ✗ **Alex.** Super chef Alessandro Stratta serves his high-end French Riviera cuisine to the well-heeled at this drop-dead-gorgeous dining room,
Fodor's Choice   reached via a grand staircase. Stratta's four-course prix-fixe menu
★   ($145) and seasonal tasting menu ($325, with wine pairings) are not for the meek of wallet, but the artfully presented food here absolutely delivers. Specialties include foie gras ravioli in a truffle bouillon with duck confit salad and wild turbot with salsifis (an herb whose edible root has an oysterlike taste), black truffles, almonds, and a red wine sauce. Dessert tends toward the fanciful, including a wonderful chocolate-banana malt with caramel–and–macadamia brittle ice cream. This is one Vegas restaurant you might want to dress your best for—jackets aren't required but are suggested. ⊠ *Wynn Las Vegas, 3131 Las Vegas Blvd. S, North Strip* ☎ *702/248–3463* ⊲ *Reservations essential* ⊟ *AE, D, DC, MC, V* ⊗ *Closed Mon. No lunch.*

$$$$ ✗ **Aureole.** Celebrity chef Charlie Palmer re-created his famed New
★   York restaurant for Mandalay Bay. He and designer Adam Tihany added a few playful, Las Vegas–style twists: a four-story wine tower, for example, holds 10,000 bottles that are reached by "wine fairies" who are hoisted up and down via a system of electronically activated pulleys. Seasonal specialties on the fixed-price menu might include French onion soup with foie gras, truffles, and Sonoma squab topped with seared foie gras and served in a preserved-cherry jus. For dessert try innovative offerings like citrus-scented cheesecake with huckleberry compote or crème brûlée ice cream with maple–brown sugar sauce.

✉ *Mandalay Bay Resort & Casino, 3950 Las Vegas Blvd. S, South Strip* ☎ *702/632–7401* ✎ *Reservations essential* 🍴 *AE, D, DC, MC, V* ⊘ *No lunch.*

$$$$ ✗ **Delmonico Steakhouse.** Hammy showbiz chef Emeril Lagasse gives the
★ New Orleans touch to this big city–style steak house at the Venetian. Enter through 12-foot oak doors; you can find a subdued modern interior that creates a feeling of calm, and friendly but professional staff members who set you at ease. Consider the classic steak tartare with Dijon emulsion or the panfried oysters with shrimp, mushrooms, and spinach pasta for starters, and such entrées as grilled rack of lamb with parsnip potatoes and port wine–cherry reduction, or the tender bone-in rib steak. Don't miss the apple–and–cheddar cheese bread pudding for dessert. ✉ *Venetian Resort-Hotel-Casino, 3355 Las Vegas Blvd. S, Center Strip* ☎ *702/733–5000* ✎ *Reservations essential* 🍴 *AE, D, DC, MC, V.*

$$$$ ✗ **Le Cirque.** This sumptuous restaurant, a branch of the New York
Fodor's Choice City landmark, is one of the city's best. The mahogany-lined room
★ is all the more opulent for its size: in a city of mega-everything, Le Cirque seats only 80 under its drooping silk-tent ceiling. Even with a view of the hotel's lake and its mesmerizing fountain show, you'll only have eyes for your plate when your server presents dishes such as the roasted venison loin, braised rabbit in Riesling, or grilled monkfish tournedos. The wine cellar contains about 1,000 premium selections representing every wine-producing region of the world. Although men aren't required to wear a jacket and tie, most do. ✉ *Bellagio Las Vegas, 3600 Las Vegas Blvd. S, Center Strip* ☎ *702/693–8100* ✎ *Reservations essential* 🍴 *AE, D, DC, MC, V* ⊘ *No lunch.*

$$$$ ✗ **Picasso.** This restaurant, adorned with the artist's original works,
★ raised the city's dining scene a notch when it opened. Although it's still much adored, some believe it may be resting a bit on its laurels, and that chef Julian Serrano doesn't change his menu often enough. The artful, innovative cuisine is based on French classics but also has strong Spanish influences. Appetizers on the seasonal menu might include warm quail salad with sautéed artichokes and pine nuts or poached oysters with osetra caviar and vermouth sauce. Sautéed medallions of fallow deer, roasted milk-fed veal chop, or roasted almond–and–honey crusted pigeon might appear as entrée choices. Dinners are prix fixe, with four- or five-course menus. ✉ *Bellagio Las Vegas, 3600 Las Vegas Blvd. S, Center Strip* ☎ *702/693–8105* ✎ *Reservations essential* 🍴 *AE, D, DC, MC, V* ⊘ *Closed Tues. No lunch.*

$$$–$$$$ ✗ **André's French Restaurant.** This second location of André's French Res-
★ taurant serves food that's as excellent as that at the downtown original but in a more spectacular room packed with lavish Louis XVI furnishings. Specialties here include filet mignon tartare prepared tableside with potato pancakes and arugula salad, and seared venison loin with crème fraîche polenta, Napa cabbage, Granny Smith apples, and bing cherry chutney. A clubby cigar bar has an amazing selection of ports. (⇨ *André's French Restaurant in Downtown.*) ✉ *Monte Carlo Resort and Casino, 3770 Las Vegas Blvd. S, South Strip* ☎ *702/798–7151* ✎ *Reservations essential* 🍴 *AE, DC, MC, V* ⊘ *No lunch.*

28

ON THE WAY

Always worth the stop, the South Rim of the **Grand Canyon** sits about an hour north of the freeway in Arizona. Visitors can take a quick view of the gorge at the visitor center, or take part in any number of more exciting activities, like camping, mule rides, or guided tours.

If **Meteor Crater** was in Ohio it would be front-page news, but because this 50,000-year-old hole-in-the-ground happens to be right next to the world's most famous hole in the ground (see above), it gets forgotten. About 30 mi east of Flagstaff, all 4,000 feet wide and 550 feet deep of the Crater sits right off I–40, making it much more convenient than the Grand Canyon for a quick stop.

Route 66 came closest to Las Vegas between Barstow, then Needles, California to Oatman and Kingman, Arizona. Adventurers can go out and find pieces of the original two-lane road. Art, photographs, Americana, and other wonders await at Barstow's relatively new Route 66 "Mother Road" Museum *(760/255–1890).* Oatman offers a mining town-turned-offbeat tourist trap feel, and comes complete with burros, saloons, and staged gunfights.

$$–$$$$ ✕ **Eiffel Tower Restaurant.** The must-do restaurant of Paris Las Vegas is a
★ room with a view, all right—it's about a third of the way up the hotel's half-scale Eiffel Tower replica, with views from all four glassed-in sides (request a Strip view when booking for the biggest wow factor—it overlooks the fountains at Bellagio, across the street). But patrons are often pleasantly surprised that the food here measures up to the setting. The French-accented menu includes appetizers of cold smoked salmon, sea scallops, and Russian caviar. On the entrée list, you find Atlantic salmon in pinot noir sauce, lobster thermidor, roasted rack of lamb Provençal, and filet mignon in mushroom sauté. ⊠ *Paris Las Vegas, 3655 Las Vegas Blvd. S, Center Strip* ☎ *702/948–6937* ⌛ *Reservations essential* ☰ *AE, D, DC, MC, V.*

$$–$$$$ ✕ **Nobu.** Chef Nobu Matsuhisa has replicated the decor and menu of
★ his Manhattan Nobu in this slick restaurant with bamboo pillars, a seaweed wall, and birch trees. Imaginative specialties include spicy sashimi, monkfish pâté with caviar, sea-urchin tempura, and scallops with spicy garlic. For dessert there's a warm chocolate soufflé. ⊠ *Hard Rock Hotel and Casino, 4455 Paradise Rd., Paradise Road* ☎ *702/693–5000* ☰ *AE, D, DC, MC, V* ⊙ *No lunch.*

$–$$$$ ✕ **Spago Las Vegas.** His fellow chefs stood by in wonder when Wolf-
★ gang Puck opened this branch of his famous Beverly Hills eatery in the culinary wasteland that was Las Vegas in 1992, but Spago Las Vegas has become a fixture in this ever-fickle city, and it remains consistently superb. The less expensive Café, which overlooks the busy Forum Shops at Caesars, is great for people-watching; inside, the dinner-only Dining Room is more intimate. Both menus are classic Puck. In the Café, sample white-bean cassoulet with chicken sausage and whole-grain mustard. Top picks in the Dining Room include porcini mushroom ravioli with Muscovy duck confit and white-truffle foam, and coriander-crusted yellowfin tuna with a lemongrass, coconut, and

sea urchin sauce. ⊠*Forum Shops at Caesars, 3500 Las Vegas Blvd. S, Center Strip* ☎*702/369–6300* ⊟*AE, D, DC, MC, V.*

$$–$$$ ✗**Verandah.** Informal, peaceful, and refined, this beautifully decorated
★ though somewhat overlooked gem at the Four Seasons offers the perfect antidote to the noisier and flashier restaurants elsewhere at Mandalay Bay. It's easy to carry on a conversation outside on the tropically landscaped terrace or inside the dining room with its muted colors and candlelit tables. Service here rivals any in town, and the presentation and quality of the innovative dishes leaves nothing to be desired, especially considering the comparatively reasonable prices. You might start with the smoked salmon–and–potato galette with celery-root rémoulade and lemon essence, followed by mushroom-truffle gnocchi with broad beans or pistachio-crusted New Zealand snapper with roasted corn, pearl pasta, and citrus sauce. Many of Mandalay Bay's best restaurants don't serve breakfast or lunch—Verandah does an admirable job with both. ⊠*Four Seasons Hotel, 3960 Las Vegas Blvd. S, South Strip* ☎*702/632–5000* ⊟*AE, D, DC, MC, V.*

$–$$$ ✗**Mon Ami Gabi.** This French-inspired steak house that first earned
★ acclaim in Chicago has became much beloved here in Vegas. It's the rare restaurant with sidewalk dining on the Strip—enjoy the views of nearby casinos and the parade of curious passersby. For those who prefer a less lively environment, a glassed-in conservatory just off the street conveys an outdoor feel, and still-quieter dining rooms are inside, adorned with chandeliers dramatically suspended three stories above. The specialty of the house is steak frites, offered four ways: classic, au poivre, bordelaise, and Roquefort. The skate with garlic fries and caper-lemon butter is also excellent. This place is a favorite for Sunday brunch. ⊠*Paris Las Vegas, 3655 Las Vegas Blvd. S, Center Strip* ☎*702/944–4224* ⊟*AE, D, DC, MC, V.*

¢–$ ✗**'Wichcraft.** Skip the drab fast-food court at MGM and grab a bite at this futuristic space with marble-top café tables, vibrant lime-green walls, and blond-wood floors. The creative sandwiches include Sicilian tuna with fennel, black olives, and lemon juice on a baguette, and meat loaf with bacon, cheddar, and tomato relish on a roll. It's a great option for breakfast, too—try a roll stuffed with a fried egg, bacon, blue cheese, and greens. Although it's possible to make this an early dinner option, keep in mind that it closes at 6 on weekdays, 8 on Friday and Saturday. ⊠*MGM Grand Hotel and Casino, 3799 Las Vegas Blvd. S, South Strip* ☎*702/891–3166* ⌕*Reservations not accepted* ⊟*AE, D, DC, MC, V.*

28

WHERE TO STAY

WHAT IT COSTS				
¢	$	$$	$$$	$$$$
FOR 2 PEOPLE under $60	$60–$129	$130–$200	$200–$270	over $270

All prices are for a standard double room, excluding 10% tax.

$$-$$$$　　Bellagio Las Vegas. This is a hard place to land good deals, although
Fodor's Choice　it never hurts to check the hotel's Web site for specials: rates average
★　$250 to $300 much of the year, but during slower weeks you can usu-
ally snag a room for around $170 to $180 (competitive in comparison
with other high-end Strip properties). If it's pampering you're after, stay
in the Spa Tower, which has impressive rooms and suites as well as an
expanded full-service spa and salon—suites have steam showers and
soaking tubs. Rooms in the original hotel tower are super snazzy, with
luxurious fabrics and Italian marble. Elegant Italian provincial furni-
ture surrounds either a single king-size bed or two queen-size beds. Bel-
lagio has one of the higher staff-to-guest ratios in town, which results
in visibly more solicitous service than you might expect at such an
enormous property. Because this is an adult-oriented resort, few of its
amenities are geared toward kids. ✉ *3600 Las Vegas Blvd. S, Center
Strip, 89109* ☎ *702/693–7111 or 888/987–6667* ⊕ *www.bellagio.com*
⤶ *3,421 rooms, 512 suites* ☰ *AE, D, DC, MC, V.*

$$-$$$$　　Hard Rock Hotel. It's impossible to forget you're in the Hard Rock,
★　no matter where you go in this rock-fixated joint: even the hall carpet-
ing is decorated with musical notes. The rooms are large, with sleek
furnishings, Bose CD stereos, and flat-screen plasma TVs that show
continuous music videos on one channel. Some beds have leather head-
boards, bathrooms have stainless-steel sinks, and the double French
doors that serve as floor-to-ceiling windows actually open. The Hard
Rock's pool area—a tropical beach–inspired oasis with a floating bar,
private cabanas, and poolside blackjack—is a favorite filming location
for MTV and popular TV shows. Very crowded (but fun) public areas
offer plenty of opportunities for people-watching. It's possible to score
reasonable rates here on weeknights—the Hard Rock has definitely lost
a bit of its arrogance, thanks to all those competing hipster-infested
hotels in town, and works harder to please guests. The Rock Spa is one
of the coolest places in town to get a massage. ✉ *4455 Paradise Rd.,
Paradise Road, 89109* ☎ *702/693–5000 or 800/473–7625* ⊕ *www.
hardrockhotel.com* ⤶ *583 rooms, 64 suites* ☰ *AE, D, DC, MC, V.*

$$-$$$$　　Red Rock Casino Resort Spa. Opened in 2006 on the western edge of
★　Las Vegas suburbia, near Red Rock canyon, is this swanky golden-
age Vegas throwback—there are crystal chandeliers throughout (an
interesting contrast to earthy sandstone walls and teak-marble floors),
a large pool area, a 16-screen movie theater, a vast selection of excel-
lent restaurants (some with outdoor patios), and rooms with floor-
to-ceiling glass windows and 42-inch TVs. An early 2007 expansion
added another 450 rooms. The sports book has its own VIP area and
three video walls that can combine into one huge screen. ✉ *11011
W. Charleston Blvd., Summerlin, 89011* ⤶ *805 rooms, 45 suites*
☎ *702/797–7777 or 866/767–7773* ⊕ *www.redrocklasvegas.com*
☰ *AE, D, DC, MC, V.*

$$-$$$$　　Venetian. Some of the Strip's largest and plushest suites are found
Fodor's Choice　at this elegant, gilded resort that's a hit with foodies, shoppers, and
★　high rollers. It's all about glitz and wow effect here, which makes it a
popular property if you're celebrating a special occasion or looking for
the quintessential over-the-top Vegas experience. The 700-plus-square-
foot guest quarters, richly adorned in a modified Venetian style, have

a sunken living room with dining table and convertible sofa, walk-in closets, separate shower and tub, three telephones (including one in the bathroom), and 27- or 36-inch TVs. The even posher Venezia Tower has a concierge floor, private entrance, fountains, and gargantuan suites with mosaic walls, vaulted ceilings, and carved marble accents. Service here, at one time a bit uneven, has improved markedly in recent years. ⊠*3355 Las Vegas Blvd. S, Center Strip, 89109* ☎*702/414–1000 or 888/883–6423* ⊕*www.venetian.com* ◪*4,027 suites* ▤*AE, D, DC, MC, V.*

$$–$$$$
Fodor'sChoice
★
Wynn Las Vegas. Decked out with replicas of pieces from Steve Wynn's acclaimed art collection, the princely rooms, averaging a whopping 650 square feet, offer spectacular views through wall-to-wall floor-to-ceiling windows. Rest your head at night on custom pillow-top beds with 320-thread-count linens, and stay plugged into the world with cordless phones—bedside drapery and climate controls are another nice touch. The superposh Tower Suites Parlor and Salon units have use of a separate pool and lanai and have such opulent amenities as granite wet bars, separate powder rooms, 42-inch flat-screen TVs, and walk-in closets. Even relatively minor touches, such as richly appointed armchairs with ottomans and giant, fluffy Turkish towels, speak to the sheer sumptuousness of this place. ⊠*3131 Las Vegas Blvd. S, Center Strip, 89109* ☎*702/770–7100 or 888/320–9966* ⊕ *www.wynnlas vegas.com* ◪*2,359 rooms, 357 suites* ▤*AE, D, DC, MC, V*

$–$$$$
Golden Nugget Hotel and Casino. New owners took over the Golden Nugget in 2003 and again in 2005; since that time, the place has continued to rank as downtown's leading property, although it doesn't have quite the flair it did back when Steve Wynn operated it. Among its neighbors, the hotel has the biggest and best pool. The well-kept rooms are modern and comfortable, with desks, high-speed Internet, armoires, and marble bathrooms. Casino policies are inconsistent, but a popular permanent poker room is likely to last. ⊠*129 E. Fremont St., Downtown, 89101* ☎*702/385–7111 or 800/634–3454* ⊕*www. goldennugget.com* ◪*1,805 rooms, 102 suites* ▤*AE, D, DC, MC, V.*

$–$$$$
★
Mandalay Bay. The main hotel at the Mandalay Bay Resort & Casino (THEhotel and the Four Seasons are the others) is the least fabulous of the three, but it's still a first-rate property with cavernous rooms. Bathrooms have understated, elegant stone floors and counters as well as deep soaking tubs with separate showers. The breezy, low-key decor is luxurious without being overbearing. ⊠*3950 Las Vegas Blvd. S, South Strip, 89119* ☎*702/632–7777 or 877/632–7700* ⊕*www.mandalay bay.com* ◪*3,215 rooms, 1,100 suites* ▤*AE, D, DC, MC, V.*

$–$$$$
★
☾
Monte Carlo Resort and Casino. The Strip could use more places like this: it's handsome but not ostentatious, and they haven't skimped on the rooms, which are outfitted with elegant cherrywood furnishings. If you have kids, it's a good alternative to Excalibur: family-friendly perks include a kiddie pool and a mini-"water park." There's a decent selection of restaurants (among them, Andre's) and the casino is so orderly you can follow a carpeted "road" from one end to the other. The pool was handsomely renovated in 2006. ⊠*3770 Las Vegas Blvd. S, South*

28

VITAL STATS:

■ Las Vegas is home to 538,653 people plus about a million and a half more outside the city limits.	more than 5,000 people move there every month.
■ The city is disproportionately foreign-born with 20% of citizens hailing from outside the country as opposed to 12% nationally.	■ The valley was discovered by Europeans by a Spanish Expedition in 1826 that noted the many springs in the area. Mormon missionaries moved in before the Civil War and the city was incorporated in 1905 after it had become an important railroad center.
■ MGM Grand is the world's largest hotel in terms of rooms. Luxor is third. (In case you're wondering, some hotel in Thailand is second.)	
■ Las Vegas is one of the fastest-growing cities in the United States;	■ Las Vegas averages 294 days of sun per year with an average daytime high of 80°.

Strip, 89109 ☎*702/730–7777 or 888/529–4828* ⊕*www.montecarlo. com* 🛏*2,743 rooms, 259 suites* ▭*AE, D, DC, MC, V.*

NIGHTLIFE & THE ARTS

Fodor's Choice **Body English.** An increasingly competitive nightclub environment sent
★ Hard Rock reps scouring Europe's hottest nightspots in search of a winning design to replace the previous dance emporium. The chosen theme seems to be "1970s decadent English rock aristocracy's living room," and it works. As wallflowers swill brandy, very sexy singles gyrate on the dance floor under a huge crystal chandelier said to be valued at $250,000. Meanwhile, you can find celebs (and there tend to be a lot of them, depending on the event—one time we were there, Jenna Jameson and Jenny McCarthy were purring at each other) hang out in VIP areas that overlook the action. Sunday night is when the grooviness soars for the weekly party night. ⊠*Hard Rock Hotel and Casino, 4455 Paradise Rd., Paradise Road* ☎*702/693–5000.*

★ **Crown & Anchor Pub.** Not far from the Strip, this friendly British-style pub caters to the university crowd. Grab a Guinness, Newcastle, or Blackthorn Cider from the very, very, very extensive drinks menu, play a game of darts, or settle in and grab some grub. ⊠*1350 E. Tropicana Ave., University District* ☎*702/739–8676* ⊕*www.crownandanchorlv.com.*

Fodor's Choice **Mix at THEhotel.** Floor-to-ceiling windows, an appealing curved bar, an
★ equally appealing staff—what could top all that? An outdoor deck that offers stunning views of the Strip, that's what. At this spot atop THEhotel at Mandalay, even the glass-walled restrooms give you a window onto the city. Black leather accented by red lighting creates a hipper-than-thou vibe. ⊠*Mandalay Bay Resort & Casino, 3590 Las Vegas Blvd. S, South Strip* ☎*877/632–9500.*

Fodor's Choice **Peppermill's Fireside Lounge.** Many visitors to Sin City looking for a bit
★ of ring-a-ding-ding leave disappointed, finding the frequently swinging wrecking ball has left behind little but massive movie-set-like resort-casinos to dominate the landscape. But benign neglect has preserved this

shagadelic lounge, one of the town's truly essential nightspots. Near the old Stardust Hotel, this evergreen ironic-romantic getaway serves food, but what you're really here for is the must-see-to-believe firepit, the crazy waitress outfits, and the lethally alcoholic Scorpion cocktail. The Pep showed up in the Martin Scorsese film *Casino.* ⊠ *2985 Las Vegas Blvd. S, Center Strip* ☎ *702/735–7635* ⊕ *www.peppermilllasvegas.com.*

Fodor'sChoice **PURE.** Although other clubs are newer and flashier, PURE still takes
★ the cake for best all-around shake appeal. In addition to its super-cool Tuesday night party and alluring crowd, it's got a secret weapon in its outdoor terrace, one complete with waterfalls, private cabanas, dance floor, and a view that places you not high above but right in the middle of the action on the Strip. Indoor types party in a cream-color main room or in the smaller Red Room, which is a special VIP area. For the deejay mavens out there, red-hot spinmeister (and former Nicole Richie beau) DJ AM is in residence. It connects to the fabulous Pussycat Dolls Lounge if you need a breather. ⊠ *Caesars Palace, 3500 Las Vegas Blvd. S, Center Strip* ☎ *702/731–7873.*

SHOPPING

BEST MALLS

★ **Fashion Show Mall.** It's impossible to miss this swanky, fashion-devoted mall due to one big element: The Cloud, a futuristic steel shade structure that looms high above the mall's entrance. Ads and footage of the mall's own fashion events are continuously projected onto the eye-catching architecture (think Times Square à la Las Vegas). The inside of the mall is sleek, spacious, and airy, a nice change from some of the claustrophobic casino malls. The mall delivers on its name—fashion shows are occasionally staged in the Great Hall on an 80-foot-long catwalk that rises from the floor. ⊠ *3200 Las Vegas Blvd. S, North Strip* ☎ *702/369–8382* ⊕ *www.thefashionshow.com.*

Fodor'sChoice The **Forum Shops at Caesars** resemble an ancient Roman streetscape,
★ with immense columns and arches, two central piazzas with fountains, and a cloud-filled ceiling with a sky that changes from sunrise to sunset over the course of three hours. The Festival Fountain (in the west wing of the mall) puts on its own show every hour on the hour daily starting at 10 AM: a robotic, pie-eyed Bacchus hosts a party for friends Apollo, Venus, and Mars, complete with lasers, music, and sound effects; at the end, the god of wine and merriment delivers—what else?—a sales pitch for the mall. The "Atlantis" show (in the east wing) is even more amazing: Atlas, king of Atlantis, can't seem to pick between his son, Gadrius, and his daughter, Alia, to assume the throne. A struggle for control of the doomed kingdom ensues amid flame and smoke. ⊠ *Caesars Palace, 3500 Las Vegas Blvd. S, Center Strip* ☎ *702/896–5599 Appian Way, 702/893–4800 Forum Shops* ⊕ *www.forumshops.com.*

Fodor'sChoice **The Venetian.** The **Grand Canal Shoppes** are *the* most elegant—and
★ fun—shopping experience on the Strip. Duck into shops like Burberry or Lladró as you amble under blue skies alongside a Vegas-ified Grand Canal. Eventually, all the quaint bridges and walkways lead you to

28

St. Mark's Square, which is full of little gift-shop carts and street performers. If you're loaded down with bags, hail a gondola—it's one of the kitschiest experiences in any of the megamalls ($15 per person). ⊠ *Venetian Resort-Hotel-Casino, 3355 Las Vegas Blvd. S, Center Strip* ☎ *702/733–5000* ⊕ *www.venetian.com.*

SPORTS & THE OUTDOORS

GOLF

Bali Hai Golf Club. The calling card of this 7,002-yard par-71 is its convenience to the Strip; the tee for the first hole is a few minutes' walk from the Mandalay Bay. Greens fees start at around $200 for the twilight specials, and well North of $325 on weekends. *5160 Las Vegas Blvd. S.,* ☎ *888/427–6678* ⊕ *www.balihaigolfclub.com.*

★ **Reflection Bay Golf Club.** Fifteen miles from the Strip and minutes from the Hyatt resort, the 7,261-yard par-72 Jack Nicklaus–designed Reflection Bay has a beautiful location fronting Lake Las Vegas, with 10 mi of lakefront beach. Weekday greens fees are $275; $295 on weekends. Twilight rates are $160 weekdays and $180 weekends. Guests at Lake Las Vegas hotels pay about $60 less per round ⊠ *75 MonteLago Blvd., Henderson* ☎ *702/740–4653* ⊕ *www.lakelasvegas.com.*

VISITOR INFORMATION

Las Vegas Advisor (☎ *702/252–0655* ⊕ *www.lasvegasadvisor.com*).

Las Vegas Convention and Visitors Authority (☎ *702/892–0711 or 877/847–4858* ⊕ *www.visitlasvegas.com*).

Nevada Commission on Tourism (☎ *775/687–4322 or 800/638–2328* ⊕ *www.travelnevada.com*).

The California Deserts

WITH DEATH VALLEY, PALM SPRINGS, JOSHUA TREE NATIONAL PARK & THE MOJAVE DESERT

Death Valley

WORD OF MOUTH

"We loved the Mojave Desert Drive through Kelso—an old railway transit stop with great atmosphere, and the sand dunes and volcanic areas along the way. We met a group of twenty or so cowboys, proper cowboys with horses and lassos and big hats, waiting for their HELICOPTER to find a burro in the dunes."

—Carrabella

EXPLORING THE CALIFORNIA DESERTS

Palm Springs is 109 mi east of Los Angeles via I–10 and CA Rte. 111; 142 mi northeast of San Diego via I–15, I–215, CA Rte. 60, I–10, and CA Rte. 111; 282 mi southwest of Las Vegas via I–15, I–215, CA Rte. 60, I–10, and CA Rte. 111; and 265 mi west of Phoenix via I–10

By Bobbi Zane

The arid land that occupies more than half of Southern California is one of the most strikingly beautiful places in the United States. A diverse place, the desert stretches from the Colorado River in the east to the mile-high mountains that surround Los Angeles in the west. North to south, the desert extends from the southern Sierra Nevada to the Mexican border. This chapter covers three distinct desert destinations: Death Valley National Park, Mojave National Preserve, and Joshua Tree National Park/Palm Springs Desert Resorts area.

WHO WILL ESPECIALLY LOVE THIS TRIP?

Desert rats: Campers, rock-climbers, hikers, nature lovers, stargazers and other outdoor enthusiasts find endless attractions in the desert, wherever they go. Bask in the vivid desert scenery at Artists Point, or take in the top-to-bottom view of Mount Whitney and Badwater in Death Valley. Gear up for the challenges of some of the best rock climbing in the world at Echo Rock or Saddle Rock in Joshua Tree, or explore the world beneath the desert at Mitchell Caverns in the Mojave Preserve.

Art lovers: Palm Springs is packed with examples of mid-century modern architecture and design; enthusiasts can find Eames chairs, Melmac dinnerware, and cruiser bikes at small, historic lodgings such as the Albert Frey–designed Movie Colony Hotel or the Orbit In. The Palm Springs Art Museum holds large collections of modern and art glass, including works by Dale Chihuly.

Gays and lesbians: Palm Springs has a large resident gay population, and the city has cultivated an extremely welcoming atmosphere for well-heeled gay and lesbian visitors. There's great nightlife, a sense of community, and gay-oriented events such as the annual Dinah Shore Weekend and the White Party.

Stargazers: The Palm Springs area is still a hideout for Hollywood celebrities and wealthy business people. These folks, who value privacy above all, frequently lock themselves behind gates in massive residential complexes in Rancho Mirage and Indian Wells. But some can be spotted in restaurants, bars, and cruising Palm Canyon Drive during the weekly Village Fest. Also look for celebs during the annual Palm Springs Film Festival held in January.

Snowbirds: Endless sunshine and the opportunity to play golf or a round of tennis every day at world-class resorts lure long-term visitors from the cold Midwest and Canada for stays in second homes or time shares in Palm Desert, Rancho Mirage and La Quinta.

TOP 5 REASONS TO GO

Stunning Desert Scenery: Get off the freeway and you'll soon be surrounded by a vibrant wilderness that goes on as far as you can see. Imagine you're a 49er crossing this land—not knowing where you are, or when you'll get to the end of it.

Star Gazing. The desert's clear dark skies put on a stellar show every night. And if stars of the Hollywood type interest you more, you can spot them in Palm Springs restaurants, shops, and hotels.

Play Hard. There's no better place to fine-tune your golf game than on one of the 100-plus golf courses in the Palm Springs area.

Shop Until You Drop. The beautiful people shop the nooks and crannies of Palm Desert's El Paseo, seeking the latest fashions, decor, and gifts. Everybody shops the Village Fest in Palm Springs, a weekly street fair where you can find one-of-a-kind items.

Get Pampered. Indulge in an evening spa treatment for two by candlelight under the stars.

WHEN IS THE BEST TIME TO VISIT?

The season, January through April, is definitely the best time to visit the desert—particularly Palm Springs and neighboring cities. The weather is perfect, the nightlife is at its liveliest, and the restaurants are packed. The Palm Springs Film Festival, held in January, offers a chance to hobnob with film celebs.

Following late winter rains, the desert puts on its brilliant annual wildflower display starting in March. Colors begin in the low-lying areas of Death Valley and the Coachella Valley surrounding Palm Springs. As the desert heats up, the display travels to the higher elevations of Joshua Tree National Park and the Mojave Preserve.

The ultrahot summer, when temperatures can soar to 120°F or higher, is a busy time in some desert destinations—particularly Death Valley National Park. Most of the rest of the desert takes a summer break; many attractions operate with reduced hours or stay open into the evening, restaurants close or deeply discount their menus, lodgings offer huge discounts, and park campgrounds have lots of open spaces.

Fall, from October through December, is a delightfully uncrowded shoulder season, when prices are still down in most expensive hotels and restaurants. Typically the weather is cooler, as the sun moves lower in the sky, casting a golden glow over the mountains at dawn and dusk.

29

HOW SHOULD I GET THERE?

DRIVING

Both Death Valley National Park and the Mojave National Preserve are best accessed via I–15, which runs between the Las Vegas and the Los Angeles areas. For those driving from Las Vegas, Death Valley is 182 mi west of Primm on the Nevada state line via I–15 and north on

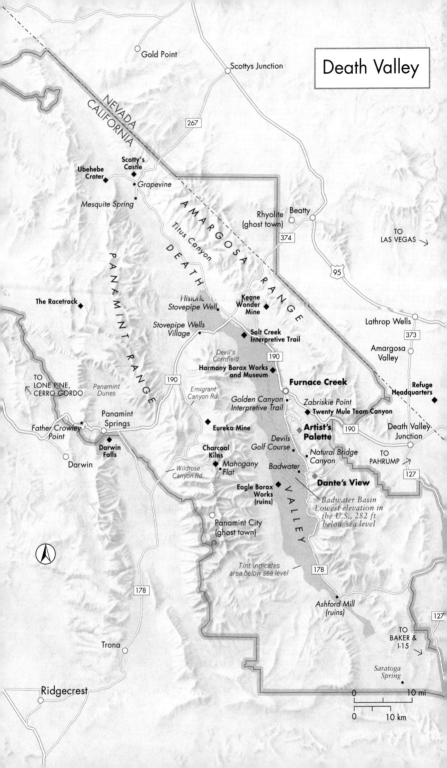

Death Valley

Gold Point

Scottys Junction

NEVADA
CALIFORNIA

267

Ubehebe
Crater

Scotty's
Castle

Grapevine

Mesquite Spring

Rhyolite
(ghost town)

Beatty

374

TO
LAS VEGAS →

95

AMARGOSA RANGE

DEATH

Titus Canyon

The Racetrack

PANAMINT RANGE

Historic
Stovepipe Well

Keane
Wonder
Mine

Lathrop Wells

373

Stovepipe Wells
Village

Salt Creek
Interpretive Trail

190

Amargosa
Valley

Devil's
Cornfield

Harmony Borax Works
and Museum

Furnace Creek

Refuge
Headquarters

TO
LONE PINE,
CERRO GORDO →

Panamint
Dunes

190

Emigrant
Canyon Rd.

Golden Canyon
Interpretive Trail

Zabriskie Point

Twenty Mule Team Canyon

Father Crowley
Point

Panamint
Springs

Eureka Mine

Artist's
Palette

190

Death Valley
Junction

Darwin
Falls

Darwin

Charcoal
Kilns

Mahogany
Flat

Devils
Golf Course

Natural Bridge
Canyon

Badwater

TO PAHRUMP →

127

Wildrose
Canyon Rd.

Eagle Borax
Works
(ruins)

Dante's View

Panamint City
(ghost town)

Badwater Basin
Lowest elevation in
the U.S. 282 ft
below sea level

178

Tint indicates
area below sea level

DEATH VALLEY

178

Ashford Mill
(ruins)

127

Trona

TO
BAKER &
I-15 →

Saratoga
Spring

Ridgecrest

0   10 mi

0   10 km

How to Snack

CLOSE UP

With a few exceptions, snacking is not a way of life in the Palm Springs area, long known among visitors and residents alike as a culinary wasteland. For the most part, cuisine takes second place to the "scene." But you can find plenty of tributes to one of the world's oldest cultivated foods: this is the only region in the U.S. where the humble date grows. Locals concerned with maintaining their buff bodies rarely eat the high-sugar morsels, but you can pick up boxes of chocolate-covered or walnut-stuffed Medjools, and organic date rolls in many area shops. Cafés throughout the region also offer date shakes and date ice cream. To get the full story, visit **Oasis Date Gardens** in Thermal and take a tour.

Tiny, bite-size hamburgers called "sliders" are served up at lunchtime at **Tylers** in the heart of Palm Springs. This walk-up place is very popular with locals, who will stand in line for 15 or 20 minutes to place an order. Get here before noon to reduce your wait time and snag a spot at one of the outdoor tables. Locals also swear by Tylers potato salad and coleslaw.

If you're headed for Death Valley or the Mojave Preserve, you'll find slim pickings when it comes to road food. Exceptions are the **Bagdad Café**, about 15 mi east of Barstow on historic U.S. 66 (Old National Trails Highway), and **The Mad Greek**, a walk-up just off the freeway in Baker.

California Highway 127 and Highway 190. From the Los Angeles/San Diego areas, the most direct route is I–15 east to State Highway 127; the distance from Los Angeles is 288 mi and 407 mi from San Diego.

The Mojave National Preserve can be accessed from the Baker exit off I–15, about 180 mi east of downtown Los Angeles and about 50 mi west of Primm, Nevada.

The Palm Springs area is about 90 mi east of the Los Angeles/Orange County areas via I–10. From San Diego take I–15 north to Riverside and connect with State Highway 60, then head east to catch I–10 to Palm Springs.

Caution: Traffic can back up for hours on both I–15 and I–10, especially on Sunday afternoons and around holiday weekends.

FLYING
Major airlines serve Palm Springs International Airport, about 2 mi from downtown; in some cases, you'll need to change planes in Los Angeles or Las Vegas. Cabs and rental cars are readily available.

HOW DO I GET AROUND?

BY BUS
SunBus, operated by the SunLine Transit Agency, serves the entire Coachella Valley—including Palm Springs—from Desert Hot Springs to Mecca. Fares are $1 or less.

29

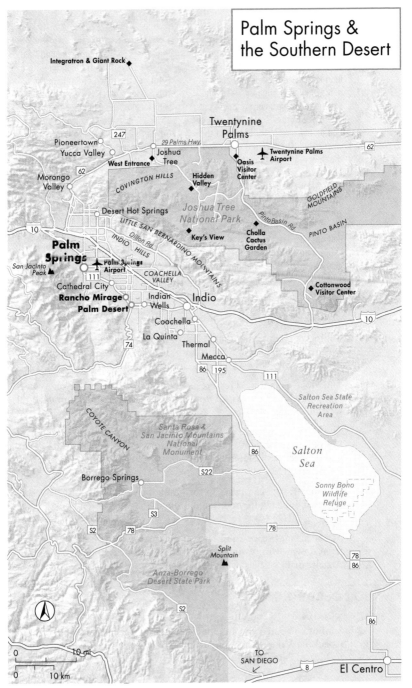

Palm Springs & the Southern Desert

Integratron & Giant Rock

247

Pioneertown
Yucca Valley

29 Palms Hwy.

Twentynine Palms

62

West Entrance

Joshua Tree

Twentynine Palms
Airport

62

Morongo
Valley

COVINGTON HILLS

Hidden
Valley

Oasis
Visitor
Center

Desert Hot Springs

Joshua Tree
National Park

GOLDFIELD
MOUNTAINS

10

LITTLE SAN BERNARDINO MOUNTAINS

Pinto Basin Rd.

PINTO BASIN

Key's View

Cholla
Cactus
Garden

Dillon Rd.

**Palm
Springs**

INDIO HILLS

San Jacinto
Peak

111

Palm Springs
Airport

COACHELLA
VALLEY

Cottonwood
Visitor Center

Cathedral City
Rancho Mirage
Palm Desert

Indian
Wells

Indio

10

Coachella

La Quinta

74

Thermal

Mecca

86   195

111

Salton Sea State
Recreation
Area

COYOTE CANYON

Santa Rosa &
San Jacinto Mountains
National
Monument

Salton
Sea

86

S22

Sonny Bono
Wildlife
Refuge

Borrego Springs

S3

S2

78

78

Split
Mountain

78

86

Anza-Borrego
Desert State Park

S2

86

0   10 mi
0   10 km

TO
SAN DIEGO

8

El Centro

BY CAR

Distances are so great in the desert that driving is the only practical way to get around. The exception is in the urban Palm Springs resorts area, where the SunBus provides good public transportation throughout the Coachella Valley. The desert national parks do not operate shuttle services for visitors.

Be sure to heed official warnings about road conditions—off the main highways, many roads are unimproved and require four-wheel-drive vehicles. They're also subject to flooding—even when the storm is not overhead.

WHERE SHOULD I FOCUS MY ENERGY?

If you're here for 1 day: On a one-day trip to Palm Springs from Los Angeles, you can get a great view from the top of the Palm Springs Tramway, stroll the Starwalk along Palm Canyon Drive, and—if you've made reservations—catch a retro show at the Follies or Buddy Greco's Supper Club.

If you're here for 2 days: If you're here for two days, add a half-day or longer loop through Joshua Tree National Park, where you can crawl through the rocks at Hidden Valley, admire the Joshua trees and the panorama from Keys View, possibly spot a coyote or big horn sheep, or glimpse the hardships of pioneer life on the Keys Ranch tour. When you're done, you'll still have time to indulge with treatment at the Spa Hotel.

If you're here for 3 days: Visit Death Valley National Park. Spend a day at Scotty's Castle and go on the Living History tour before returning to your hotel. Along the way you can also walk the Salt Creek Interpretive Trail and search for the rare desert pupfish. You'll also have time to visit at Dante's Point and to take a spin along colorful Artists Dr.

If you're here for 4 days: If you add a fourth day, you'll have time to see the Devil's Golf Course and the Harmony Borax Works and Museum, or you can treat yourself to a guided horseback ride or hayride offered at Furnace Creek Ranch.

If you're here for 5 days: Add a side trip to the Mojave National Preserve, before or after your visit to Death Valley. Be sure to see Kessler Peak and the Lava Tube, Teutonia Peak, and the Cinder Cone Lava Beds.

If you're here for 6 days: If you have six days, expand your visit to Mojave to include take a tour of Mitchell Caverns and explore the Kelso Dunes.

If you're here for 7 days or more: Spending a week or longer in the Southern California desert will give you an opportunity to explore the many hiking and nature trails throughout the region. Or you can indulge yourself at one of the posh resorts: Furnace Creek Ranch in Death Valley; La Quinta Resort and Club and Rancho Las Palmas in Rancho Mirage; or the over-the-top Parker in Palm Springs.

29

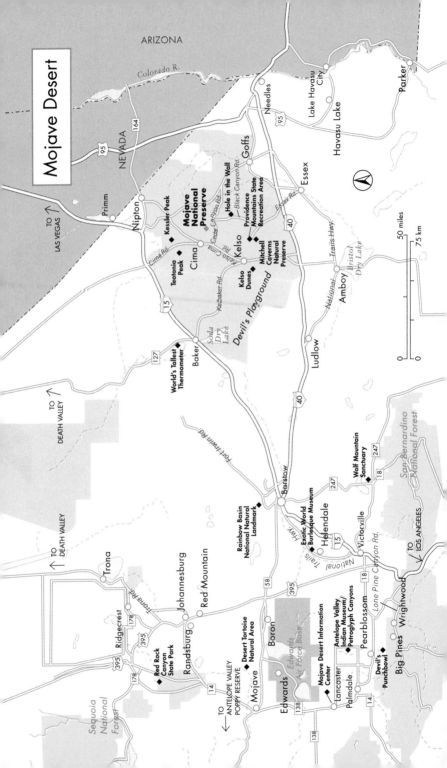

Mojave Desert

ARIZONA

Colorado R.

NEVADA

95

164

95

TO
LAS VEGAS

Primm

Nipton

Kessler Peak

Mojave
National
Preserve

Hole in the Wall

Goffs

Essex

Black Canyon Rd.

Eagle Canyon Rd.

Providence
Mountains State
Recreation Area

40

Essex Rd.

Needles

Lake Havasu
City

Havasu Lake

Parker

95

Cima Rd.

Teotonia
Peak

Cima

Kelso-Cima Rd.

Kelbaker Rd.

Kelso

Mitchell
Caverns Natural
Preserve

Kelso
Dunes

National Trails Hwy.

Bristol
Dry Lake

Amboy

Devil's Playground

50 miles

75 km

127

World's Tallest
Thermometer

Baker

Soda
Dry
Lake

15

Ludlow

40

TO
DEATH VALLEY

Fort Irwin Rd.

Barstow

247

Wolf Mountain
Sanctuary

18

San Bernardino
National Forest

247

Rainbow Basin
National Natural
Landmark

Exotic World
Burlesque Museum

Helendale

15

Victorville

18

Lone Pine Canyon Rd.

TO
DEATH VALLEY

Trona

Johannesburg

Red Mountain

National Trails Hwy.

395

58

TO
LOS ANGELES

Wrightwood

Big Pines

Ridgecrest

395

178

Randsburg

178

14

Red Rock
Canyon State Park

Sequoia
National
Forest

Trona Rd.

Desert Tortoise
Natural Area

Boron

Edwards
Air Force Base

395

Antelope Valley
Indian Museum/
Petroglyph Canyons

18

Pearblossom

Devil's
Punchbowl

TO
ANTELOPE VALLEY
POPPY RESERVE

Mojave

Mojave Desert Information
Center

Lancaster

138

Edwards

Palmdale

14

138

CLAIM TO FAME

Palm Springs has promoted its relationship with the Hollywood crowd since the early days of the movies—1926, to be exact, when Frank Capra checked into the La Quinta Hotel for a few weeks of seclusion so he could write "It Happened One Night." The hotel, much changed over the years, still hangs its hat on that connection.

Other celebrities followed Capra's lead. Many—including Frank Sinatra, Liberace, Bob Hope, Desi Arnaz, and Lucille Ball—maintained second homes in the desert. The current glitterati still make the trek from Hollywood to enjoy a few days of fun in the sun. California's Governor Arnold Schwarzenegger and wife Maria Shriver have been spotted in the gardens of what is now La Quinta Resort. Palm Springs area cities continue to honor their beloved stellar residents by naming streets in their honor: Bob Hope Drive, Frank Sinatra Drive, and Dinah Shore Drive. The Eisenhower Hospital is named for President Dwight Eisenhower, who spent his retirement years in the desert. Former First Lady Betty Ford, who retired to the desert at the end of her husband President Gerald Ford's term, established her substance abuse recovery center at the hospital.

WHAT ARE THE TOP EXPERIENCES?

The Vistas: Views in the Southern California desert seem to stretch forever, always eventually ending at a mountain range. An ever-changing palette of hues includes white, black, and all the colors of the rainbow; the best times to experience desert color are at dawn or dusk.

Beating the Cold: A visit to the desert in winter will mess with your seasonal senses. You can play a round of golf in the morning, then lounge around the pool and catch some rays (and get a nice tan) before playing a few sets of tennis in the afternoon. Outdoor dining is de rigueur most mornings and afternoons. The winter weather here is also perfect for hiking in the hills, biking along the avenues, or strolling though mostly outdoor El Paseo shopping area. Some spas even have outdoor treatment areas.

Indulging: You'll be well taken care of at 24 luxurious resorts in the Palm Springs area. With beautifully appointed rooms with all the must-have amenities, staffs that are at your beck and call, sublime spas, delicious dining, and nightly entertainment, you won't be left wanting for much. Savor the ultimate indulgence—an evening soak or treatments outdoors on a starry, starry night. Resorts and small hotels offer after-dark spa services for one or two, some combining a soak and a happy hour.

Golfing Where the Pros Play: The desert floor is carpeted with legendary golf courses, holes routinely visited by PGA pros like Tiger Woods and Phil Mickelson. Although it may be difficult to get tee-times, it's possible to hit the links at tournament courses like La Quinta/PGA West and Westin Mission Hills Golf Resort. Public and semi-private courses can be more accessible and less expensive; they include Indian Canyon

29

Golf Resort and Tahquitz Creek Palm Springs. Many hotels also can arrange tee-times for you. And if you want to rub elbows with a legend, drop into Arnold Palmer's restaurant La Quinta any night—you just might encounter the pro himself.

BEST BETS

SIGHTS AND TOURS

DEATH VALLEY NATIONAL PARK

★ **Artist's Palette.** So called for the brilliant colors of its volcanic deposits, this is one of the most magnificent sights in Death Valley. ✉ *11 mi south of Furnace Creek, off Badwater Rd.*

Fodor's Choice **Dante's View.** The view here is astounding: you can see the highest and
★ lowest spots in the contiguous United States from the same vantage point. ✉ *Dante's View Rd. off Hwy. 190, 35 mi from Badwater, 20 mi south of Twenty Mule Team Canyon.*

Fodor's Choice **Keane Wonder Mine.** The tram towers and cables from the old mill used
★ to process gold from Keane Wonder Mine are still here, leading up to the crumbling mine, which is a steep 1-mi hike up the mountain. ✉ *Access road off Beatty Cutoff Rd., 17½ mi north of Furnace Creek.*

★ **Scotty's Castle.** This Moorish-style mansion, begun in 1924 and never
🍼 completed, takes its name from Walter Scott, better known as Death Valley Scotty. Costumed rangers re-create life at the castle circa 1939. Try to arrive for the first tour of the day to avoid a wait, which can be up to two hours. ✉ *Scotty's Castle Rd., Hwy. 267, 53 mi north of Salt Creek Interpretive Trail* ☎ *760/786–2392* ⊕ *www.nps.gov/deva* 💲*$11* 🕙 *Daily 8:30–5, tours daily 9–5.*

VISITOR **Beatty Information Center.** ✉ *Rte. 95, 120 mi north of Las Vegas* ☎ *775/*
CENTERS *553–2200* ⊕ *www.nps.gov/deva* 🕙 *Daily 8–6.*

Furnace Creek Visitor Center and Museum. ✉ *Hwy. 190, 30 mi northwest of Death Valley Junction* ☎ *760/786–3200* ⊕ *www.nps.gov/deva* 🕙 *Daily 8–6.*

PALM SPRINGS

Fodor's Choice A trip on the **Palm Springs Aerial Tramway** provides a 360-degree view
★ of the desert through the picture windows of rotating tram cars. The
🍼 2½-mi ascent through Chino Canyon, the steepest vertical cable ride in the United States, brings you to an elevation of 8,516 feet in less than 20 minutes. ✉ *1 Tramway Rd.* ☎ *760/325–1391 or 888/515–8726* ⊕ *www.pstramway.com* 💲*$22; ride-and-dine package $34* 🕙 *Tram cars depart at least every 30 min from 10 AM weekdays and 8 AM weekends; last car up leaves at 8 PM, last car down leaves Mountain Station at 9:45 PM.*

★ The **Palm Springs Art Museum** and its grounds hold several wide-ranging collections of contemporary and traditional art displayed in bright, open galleries, with daylight streaming through huge skylights. ✉ *101*

HISTORY YOU CAN SEE

With one of the largest concentrations of modern architecture in the world, Palm Springs displays a distinctive style, known as Desert or Palm Springs Modernism. Its signature is simple, single-story buildings inspired by vast expanses of desert sand, surrounded by towering mountains, and set against a clear blue sky.

Some of the world's most forward-looking architects designed and constructed buildings around Palm Springs between 1940 and 1970, and modernism became an ideal fit for desert living, because it minimizes the separation between indoors and outdoors. See-through houses with glass exterior walls are

common. Oversize flat roofs provide shade from the sun, and many buildings' sculptural forms reflect nearby landforms.

Most obvious to visitors are portions of the Palm Springs Aerial Tramway complex, designed and built in the 1960s by Swiss-born Albert Frey. A Palm Springs resident for more than 60 years, Frey also designed the indoor–outdoor City Hall, Fire Station #1, and numerous houses.

The **Palm Springs Modern Committee** publishes a map and driving guide to 52 historic buildings, which is available for $5 at either of the Palm Springs Visitor Information Centers or at ⊕ www.psmodcom.com.

Museum Dr. ☎ *760/325–7186* ⊕ *www.psmuseum.org* ✉ *$12.50 Oct.– May, $3 June–Sept.; free Thurs. 4–8 during Village Fest* ☉ *Oct.–May, Tues., Wed., and Fri.–Sun. 10–5, Thurs. noon–8; June–Sept., Wed. and Fri.–Sun. 10–5, Thurs. noon–8.*

Stop at the **Palm Springs Visitor Information Center,** near the tramway, for information on sights to see and things to do in the area. ✉ *2901 N. Palm Canyon Dr.* ☎ *760/778–8418 or 800/347–7746* ⊕ *www.palm-springs. org* ☉ *Weekdays 9–5.*

29

A stroll down shop-lined Palm Canyon Drive will take you along the **Palm Springs Starwalk** (✉ *Palm Canyon Dr., around Tahquitz Canyon Way, and Tahquitz Canyon Way, between Palm Canyon and Indian Canyon Drs.*), where nearly 200 bronze stars are embedded in the sidewalk (à la the Hollywood Walk of Fame).

Fodor'sChoice
★

Palm Springs holds one of the largest collections of homes and public buildings designed by the famed Desert Moderne architects of the 1950s, Albert Frey, Richard Neutra, and William F. Cody. You can see many of these beauties on tours assembled by the cities of Palm Springs and Palm Desert; the **Palm Springs Visitor Center** (✉ *2901 N. Palm Canyon Dr., Palm Springs* ☎ *760/318–6118* ⊕ *www.palm-springs.org*) also offers three-hour tours to these mid-century landmarks (you can also pick up a copy of *Palm Springs: Brief History and Architectural Guide* here. If you'd rather go it alone, pick up a map and guide to

★ more than 40 distinctive mid-century buildings at the **Palm Desert Visitor Center** (✉ *72–567 Hwy. 111, Palm Desert* ☎ *760/568–5240* ⊕ *www. palm-desert.org*).

PALM DESERT

★ Come eyeball-to-eyeball with wolves, coyotes, mountain lions, chee-
☺ tahs, bighorn sheep, golden eagles, warthogs, and owls at the **Living
Desert Zoo and Gardens.** Easy- to challenging scenic trails traverse 1,200
acres of desert preserve populated with plants of the Mojave, Colorado, and Sonoran deserts in 11 habitats. ⊠*47–900 Portola Ave.*
☎*760/346–5694* ⊕*www.livingdesert.org* ☜*$8.75 mid-June–Aug.;
$12 Sept.–mid-June* ☉*Mid-June–Aug., daily 8–1:30; Sept.–mid-June,
daily 9–5.*

JOSHUA TREE NATIONAL PARK

Cholla Cactus Garden. This stand of bigelow cholla (sometimes called
jumping cholla, since its hooked spines seem to jump at you) is best
seen and photographed in late afternoon, when the backlit spiky stalks
stand out against a colorful sky. ⊠*Pinto Basin Rd., 20 mi north of
Cottonwood Visitor Center.*

Hidden Valley. This legendary cattle-rustlers hideout is set among big
boulders, which kids love to scramble over and around. ⊠*Park Blvd.,
14 mi south of West Entrance.*

★ **Keys View.** At 5,185 feet, this point affords a sweeping view of the
Coachella Valley, the mountains of the San Bernardino National Forest,
and—on a rare clear day—Signal Mountain in Mexico. ⊠*Keys View
Rd., 21 mi south of West Entrance.*

VISITOR
CENTERS **Cottonwood Visitor Center.** ⊠*Pinto Basin Rd.* ☎*No phone* ⊕*www.nps.
gov/jotr* ☉*Daily 8–4.*

Joshua Tree Visitor Center. ⊠*6554 Park Blvd.* ☎*760/367–5500* ⊕*www.
nps.gov/jotr* ☉*Daily 8–5.*

Oasis Visitor Center. ⊠*74485 National Park Dr., Twentynine Palms*
☎*760/367–5500* ⊕*www.nps.gov/jotr* ☉*Daily 8–4:30.*

MOJAVE NATIONAL PRESERVE

The 1.4 million acres of the Mojave National Preserve hold a surprising abundance of plant and animal life—especially considering their
elevation (nearly 8,000 feet in some areas).

★ As you enter the preserve from the south, you'll pass miles of open
scrub brush, Joshua trees, and beautiful red-black cinder cones before
encountering the **Kelso Dunes** (⊠*Kelbaker Rd., 90 mi east of I–15 and
14 mi north of I–40* ☎*760/928–2572, 760/733–4040, or 760/252–
6100* ⊕*www.nps.gov/moja*). These perfect, pristine slopes of gold-
white sand cover 70 square mi, often reaching heights of 500 to 600
feet. You can reach them via a ½-mi walk from the main parking area.
North of the dunes, in the town of Kelso, is the Mission revival–style
Kelso Depot Information Center, flanked by three swaying palm trees. The
Depot's Beanery restaurant features the same historic menu that refu-
eled weary passengers and rail workers. Primitive campsites are available at no charge near the dunes' main parking area.

☺★ The National Park Service administers most of the Mojave preserve,
but **Providence Mountains State Recreation Area** is under the jurisdiction

of the California Department of Parks. The visitor center has views of mountain peaks, dunes, buttes, crags, and desert valleys. At **Mitchell Caverns Natural Preserve** (🎫 *$4*) you have a rare opportunity to see all three types of cave formations—dripstone, flowstone, and erratics—in one place. The year-round 65°F temperature provides a break from the desert heat. Tours, the only way to see the caverns, are given weekdays at 1:30 and weekends at 10, 1:30, and 3. Arrive a half-hour before tour time to secure a spot. Between late May and early September, tours are given only on weekends at 1:30. ⊠ *Essex Rd., 16 mi north of I-40* 🕾 *760/928–2586* ⊕ *www.parks.ca.gov* ⊙ *Visitor center May–Sept., Fri. and Sat. 9–4.*

WHERE TO EAT

WHAT IT COSTS					
	¢	$	$$	$$$	$$$$
RESTAURANTS	under $8	$8–$12	$13–$20	$21–$30	over $30

Restaurant prices are per person for a main course at dinner.

29

DEATH VALLEY NATIONAL PARK

$$$
Fodor's Choice
★

✕ **Inn Dining Room.** Fireplaces, beamed ceilings, and spectacular views provide a visual feast to match the inn's ambitious menu. Dishes may include such desert-theme items as rattlesnake empanadas and crispy cactus, and simpler fare such as cumin-lime shrimp, lamb, and New York strip steak. An evening dress code (no jeans, T-shirts, or shorts) is enforced. Lunch is served October–May only, but you can always have afternoon tea, an inn tradition since 1927. Breakfast and Sunday brunch are also served. ⊠ *Furnace Creek Inn Resort, Hwy. 190, Furnace Creek* 🕾 *760/786–2345* ⊕ *www.furnacecreekresort.com* ⌖ *Reservations essential* ☐ *AE, D, DC, MC, V* ⊙ *No lunch June–Sept.*

PALM SPRINGS

$$$$
★

✕ **Le Vallauris.** Le Vallauris, in the historic Roberson House, is popular with ladies who lunch, all of whom get a hug from the maître d'. The menu changes daily, and each day it's handwritten on a white board. Lunch entrées may include perfectly rare tuna niçoise salad, or grilled whitefish with Dijon mustard sauce. Dinner might bring a sublime smoked salmon, sautéed calves' liver, or roasted quail with orange sauce or rack of lamb. Service is beyond attentive. The restaurant has a lovely tree-shaded garden. On cool winter evenings, request a table by the fireplace. ☒ *385 W. Tahquitz Canyon Way* ☎ 760/325–5059 ☝ *Reservations essential* ☰ *AE, D, DC, MC, V* ⊘ *No lunch Wed.–Sat. in July and Aug.*

$$$–$$$$ ✕ **Copley's on Palm Canyon.** Chef Manion Copley is cooking up the most innovative cuisine in the desert, drawing fans region-wide. Start with such appetizers as roasted beet and warm goat cheese salad or perfectly grilled charred prawns and scallops. Oh My Lobster Pot Pie is the biggest hit on an entrée menu that features unusual seafood. And save room for Copley's sweet and savory servings of herb ice cream. The rustic, casual eatery is in a hacienda that was once owned by Cary Grant. Service is pleasant and friendly. ☒ *621 N. Palm Canyon Dr.* ☎ 760/327–9555 ☰ *AE, D, DC, MC, V* ⊘ *Closed Mon. No lunch.*

LIKE A LOCAL

Glitterati driving directions: To get to the Westin Hotel, go down Bob Hope, take a left at Frank (Sinatra), go past Gerry (Ford), and make a left at Dinah (Shore).

Kickin' it Old School. Senior moments populate much of the entertainment here. You'll hear endless jokes about the pains of getting old, being old, or even knowing someone who's old enough to collect Social Security.

Early-bird dining. Many locals take advantage of discounts offered to early diners by restaurants, and it's a good plan for visitors as well.

JOSHUA TREE NATIONAL PARK

$–$$ ✕ **Pappy & Harriet's Pioneertown Palace.** Smack in the middle of a Western-movie-set town is this Western-movie-set saloon, where you can have dinner, dance to live country-and-western music, or just relax with a drink at the bar. The food ranges from Tex-Mex to Santa Maria barbecue to steak and burgers—no surprises but plenty of fun. It may be in the middle of nowhere, but you'll need reservations for dinner on weekends. ☒ *53688 Pioneertown Rd., Pioneertown* ☎ 760/365–5956 ⊕ *www.pappyandharriets.com* ☰ *AE, D, MC, V* ⊘ *No lunch Mon.–Wed.*

MOJAVE NATIONAL PRESERVE

¢–$ ✕ **Bagdad Café.** Tourists from all over the world flock to the site where ★ the 1988 film of the same name was shot. Built in the 1940s, this Route 66 eatery serves a home-style menu of burgers, chicken-fried steak, and seafood. An old Airstream trailer from the movie sits outside the café. ☒ *46548 National Trails Hwy., Newberry Springs* ☎ 760/257–3101 ⊕ *www.bagdadcafeusa.com* ☰ *AE, MC, V.*

¢–$ ✕ **Emma Jean's Hollandburger Cafe.** This circa-1940s diner sits right on ★ U.S. Historic Route 66 and is favored by locals for its generous portions and old-fashioned home cooking. Try the biscuits and gravy, chicken-fried steak, or the famous Trucker's Sandwich, chock-full of roast beef, bacon, chilies, and cheese. ☒ *17143 D St.* ☎ 760/243–9938 ☰ *AE, MC, V* ⊘ *Closed Sun. No dinner.*

WHERE TO STAY

WHAT IT COSTS				
¢	$	$$	$$$	$$$$

	¢	$	$$	$$$	$$$$
HOTELS	under $50	$50–$100	$101–$150	$151–$200	over $200
CAMPING	under $10	$10–$17	$18–$35	$36–$49	over $50

Hotel prices are per night for two people in a standard double room in high season, excluding taxes and service charges. Camping prices are for a standard (no hookups, pit toilets, fire grates, picnic tables) campsite per night.

DEATH VALLEY NATIONAL PARK

¢¢¢¢ ✗ 🏨 **Furnace Creek Inn.** Built in 1927, this adobe-brick-and-stone lodge is nestled in one of the park's greenest oases. A warm mineral stream gurgles across the property, and its 85°F waters feed into a swimming pool. The rooms are decorated in earth tones, with old-style furnishings. The top-notch Furnace Creek Inn Dining Room ($$$) serves desert-theme dishes such as rattlesnake empanadas and crispy cactus, as well as less exotic fare such as cumin-lime shrimp, lamb, and New York strip steak. Afternoon tea has been a tradition since 1927. ⊠ *Furnace Creek Village, near intersection of Hwy. 190 and Badwater Rd.* 🏠 *Box 1, Death Valley, 92328* ☎ *760/786–2345* 🖷 *760/786–2361* ⊕ *www.furnacecreekresort.com* ➳ *66 rooms* ⚬ *In-room: dial up. In-hotel: restaurant, room service, bar, tennis courts, pool* ⊟ *AE, D, DC, MC, V* ☺ *Closed mid-May–mid-Oct.*

Fodor's Choice
★

$–$$ 🏨 **Stovepipe Wells Village.** If you prefer quiet nights and an unfettered view of the night sky and nearby sand dunes, this property is for you. No telephones break the silence here, and only the deluxe rooms have televisions and some refrigerators. Rooms are simple yet comfortable and provide wide-open desert vistas. The Toll Road Restaurant serves American breakfast, lunch, and dinner favorites, from omelets and sandwiches to burgers and steaks. RV campsites with full hookups ($23) are available on a first-come, first-served basis. ⊠ *Hwy. 190, Stovepipe Wells* 🏠 *Box 559, Death Valley, 92328* ☎ *760/786–2387* 🖷 *760/786–2389* ⊕ *www.stovepipewells.com* ➳ *83 rooms* ⚬ *In-room: no phone (some), refrigerator (some). In-hotel: restaurant, bar, pool, no-smoking rooms, some pets allowed* ⊟ *AE, D, MC, V.*

PALM SPRINGS

$$$$ 🏨 **The Parker Palm Springs.** A cacophony of color, flashing lights, and over-the-top contemporary art assembled by New York designer Jonathan Adler, this is the hippest hotel in the desert, appealing to a young L.A.-based clientele. When you arrive, a greeter will whisk you from your car to your room to complete registration; the stroll takes you through a brilliant desert garden. You may find relaxation around the pools, if nowhere else—pulsating music fills the air throughout the resort. Rooms have textured sisal floor coverings, exotic woven fabrics in bright reds and browns, and leather seating. All have private balconies or patios (with hammocks) that are secluded behind tall shrubs. The clubby restaurant, Mister Parker's ($$$$), will delight any well-heeled carnivore. ⊠ *4200 E. Palm Canyon Dr., 92264* ☎ *760/770–5000 or*
★

29

800/543–4300 📠*760/324–2188* *⊕www.theparkerpalmsprings.com* 🛏*133 rooms, 12 suites* ♿*In-room: safe, refrigerator, DVD, Wi-Fi. In-hotel: 2 restaurants, room service, bar, tennis courts, pools, gym, spa, bicycles, concierge, laundry service, parking (no fee), no-smoking rooms* ☐*AE, D, DC, MC, V.*

\$\$\$\$ 🛏 **★ The Viceroy Palm Springs.** The first thing that strikes you at the Viceroy is its bright, sunny white-and-yellow ambience, reminiscent of a sun-filled desert day. Guest rooms for two and villas for three or more are spread out over four tree-shaded acres, where secluded nooks and blue-and-white-striped cabañas beg chic bikini-clad guests to hole up with a good book and a glass of the inn's delicious iced tea. The tranquil inn, just a short walk from Palm Canyon Drive, is home to the stylish eatery Citron, which is decorated with larger-than-life-size photos of Marilyn Monroe and Clark Gable. The inn is exceptionally canine friendly—they even offer dog-walking services. ✉*415 S. Belardo Rd., 92262* ☎*760/320–4117 or 800/327–3687* 📠*760/323–3303* *⊕www.viceroypalmsprings.com* 🛏*43 rooms, 16 suits* ♿*In-room: safe, kitchen (some), refrigerator, Wi-Fi, Ethernet. In hotel: no elevator, restaurant, room service, bar, pools, gym, spa, bicycles, public Internet, parking (fee), some pets allowed, no-smoking rooms* ☐*AE, D, MC, V*

TWENTYNINE PALMS

\$–\$\$\$ ✕🛏 **29 Palms Inn.** The funky 29 Palms is the lodging closest to the entrance to Joshua Tree National Park. The collection of adobe and wood-frame cottages, some dating back to the 1920s and 1930s, is scattered over 70 acres of grounds that are popular with birds and bird-watchers year-round. Innkeeper Jane Smith's warm, personal service more than makes up for the cottages' rustic qualities. Ranging from pasta to seafood, the contemporary fare at the inn's convivial restaurant (\$\$) is more sophisticated than its Old West appearance might suggest. ✉*73–950 Inn Ave., 92277* ☎*760/367–3505* 📠*760/367–4425* *⊕www.29palmsinn.com* 🛏*18 rooms, 5 suites* ♿*In-room: no a/c (some), no phone. In hotel: no elevator, restaurant, pool, public Wi-Fi, parking, some pets allowed, no-smoking rooms* ☐*AE, D, DC, MC, V* ❘◎❘*CP.*

ON THE WAY

The Cabazon Dinosaurs. Dino and Rex, two life-size dinosaur statues guard the Morongo Casino, off I–10 west of Palm Springs.

Calico Early Man Archaeological Site. This dig has produced nearly 12,000 stone tools that are said to be 200,000 years old, contradicting the dominant theory that humans populated North America as recently as 13,000 years ago. Off I–15, Minneola Rd. exit, 760/254–2248, call for tour schedule.

Baker Thermometer. This roadside curiosity's 134-foot height pays homage to the U.S. record high U.S. 134°F temperature recorded in Death Valley on July 10, 1913. 72157 Baker Blvd., Baker.

JOSHUA TREE NATIONAL PARK

$ 🏕 **Black Rock Canyon Campground.** Set among juniper bushes, cholla cacti, and other desert shrubs, Black Rock Canyon is one of the prettiest campgrounds in Joshua Tree. South of Yucca Valley, it's the closest campground to most of the desert communities. Located on the California Riding and Hiking Trail, it has facilities for horses and mules. ✉ *Joshua Lane, south of Hwy. 62 and Hwy. 247* ☎ *760/367–5500, 800/365–2267 for reservations* ⊕ *www.recreation.gov* ⇗ *100 sites* ⬧ *Flush toilets, dump station, drinking water, fire pits, picnic tables, ranger station* ⊟ *D, MC, V* ☺ *Year-round.*

NIGHTLIFE & THE ARTS

PALM SPRINGS

In late March, when the world's finest female golfers hit the links for the Annual LPGA Kraft Nabisco Championship in Rancho Mirage, thousands of lesbians converge on Palm Springs for a four-day party popularly known as **Dinah Shore Weekend–Palm Springs** (⊕ *www.clubskirts. com*). The **White Party** (☎ *323/944–0051 for tickets*), held on Easter weekend, draws tens of thousands of gay men from around the country to the Palm Springs area for a round of parties and gala events.

In mid-January the **Palm Springs International Film Festival** (☎ *760/322–2930 or 800/898–7256* ⊕ *www.psfilmfest.org*) brings stars and more than 150 feature films from 25 countries, plus panel discussions, short films, and documentaries, to the McCallum and other venues.

The Spanish-style **Historic Plaza Theatre** (✉ *128 S. Palm Canyon Dr.* ☎ *760/327–0225*) plays host to the hottest ticket in the desert, the **Fabulous Palm Springs Follies** (⊕ *www.palmspringsfollies.com*), which mounts 10 weekly sell-out performances November through May. The vaudeville-style revue, about half of which focuses on mid-century nostalgia, stars extravagantly costumed, retired (but very fit) showgirls, singers, and dancers.

29

SPORTS & THE OUTDOORS

DEATH VALLEY NATIONAL PARK

Fodor's Choice ★ ☺   **Darwin Falls.** This lovely 2-mi round-trip hike rewards you with a refreshing waterfall surrounded by thick vegetation and a rocky gorge. No swimming or bathing is allowed, but it's a beautiful place for a picnic. Adventurous hikers can scramble higher toward more rewarding views of the falls. ✉ *Access 2-mi graded dirt road and parking area off Hwy. 190, 1 mi west of Panamint Springs Resort.*

★ **Natural Bridge Canyon.** The somewhat rough 2-mi access road has interesting geological features in addition to the bridge itself. It's ½-mi round-trip. ✉ *Access road off Badwater Rd., 15 mi south of Furnace Creek.*

Fodor's Choice ★   **Keane Wonder Mine.** Allow two hours for the 2-mi round-trip trail that follows an out-of-service aerial tramway to this mine. The way is steep, but the views of the valley are spectacular. Do not enter the tunnels or hike beyond the top of the tramway—it's dangerous. The trailhead is 2 mi down an unpaved and bumpy access road. ⊠ *Access road off Beatty Cutoff Rd., 17½ mi north of Furnace Creek.*

PALM SPRINGS

Palm Springs is host to more than 100 golf tournaments annually. The Palm Springs Desert Resorts Convention and Visitors Bureau **Events Hotline** (☏ *760/770–1992*) lists dates and locations. **Palm Springs TeeTimes** (☏ *760/324–5012*) can match golfers with courses and arrange tee times. You can book tee times online (⊕ *www.palmspringsteetimes.com*).

> **VITAL STATS:**
>
> ■ Days of sun per year: 350
> ■ Average July high: 107
> ■ Average July low: 77
> ■ Average December high: 70
> ■ Average December low: 43
> ■ Average rainfall: 3.38 inches per year.

JOSHUA TREE NATIONAL PARK

★ **Mastodon Peak Trail.** Some boulder scrambling is required on this 3-mi hike up 3,371-foot Mastodon Peak, but the journey rewards you with stunning views of the Salton Sea. The peak draws its name from a large rock formation that early miners believed looked like the head of a prehistoric behemoth. ⊠ *Cottonwood Spring Oasis.*

Fodor'sChoice **Ryan Mountain Trail.** The payoff for hiking to the top of 5,461-foot Ryan
★ Mountain is one of the best panoramic views of Joshua Tree. You'll need two to three hours to complete the 3-mi round-trip. ⊠ *Ryan Mountain parking area, 16 mi southeast of West Entrance or Sheep Pass, 16 mi southwest of Oasis Visitor Center.*

Fodor'sChoice With an abundance of weathered igneous boulder outcroppings, Joshua
★ Tree is one of the nation's top winter climbing destinations and offers a full menu of climbing experiences—from bouldering for beginners in the Wonderland of Rocks to multiple-pitch climbs at Echo Rock and Saddle Rock. The best-known climb in the park is Hidden Valley's Sports Challenge Rock.

VISITOR INFORMATION

Death Valley National Park ⟐ *Box 579, Death Valley, 92328* ☏ *760/786–2331, 760/786–3225 TDD* 📠 *760/786–3283* ⊕ *www.nps.gov/deva.*

Joshua Tree National Park ⊠ *74485 National Park Dr., Twentynine Palm, 92277* ☏ *760/367–5500* 📠 *760/367–6392* ⊕ *www.nps.gov/jotr.*

Mojave National Preserve ⊠ *2701 Barstow Rd., Barstow, 92311* ☏ *760/252–6100* ⊕ *www.nps.gov/mojav.*

Palm Springs Visitor Information Center (⊠ *2901 N. Palm Canyon Dr., 92262* ☏ *800/347–7746* ⊕ *www.palm-springs.org*).

Los Angeles & San Diego

WITH DISNEYLAND

Silver Strand State Beach, San Diego

WORD OF MOUTH

"The Zoo (in my opinion) is a must! It was our favorite part of the trip. . . . We LOVED San Diego and decided that it was the city of friendly people as everyone was so nice."

—travelmonkey

" When we were there [at the Getty Center], the place was crawling with families picnicking . . . The galleries are varied, the views are spectacular, and the gardens are wonderful."

—happytrailstoyou

www.fodors.com/forums

EXPLORING LOS ANGELES & SAN DIEGO

Los Angeles is 121 mi northwest of San Diego via I–5; 382 mi southeast of San Francisco via I–80, I–580, and I–5; and 271 mi southwest of Las Vegas via I–15 and I–10.

By Jennifer Paull & Bobbi Zane

Los Angeles is as much a fantasy and a state of mind as it is a physical city. The capital-I Industry (that is, film and television) constantly radiates images of the sun-soaked basin, giving a cinematic glow to the beaches and high-rises, surfers and face-lifters, shopping strips and barrios. So many L.A. places have been seen on screens that you may find yourself in a constant state of semi-déja-vu. Are you ready for your close-up?

Massive freeways snake through the hundreds of miles that make up the city's urban sprawl. In fact, some places that people think of as quintessentially L.A. are independent cities, like posh Beverly Hills and the oceanfront communities of Santa Monica and Malibu. Los Angeles is also known for its astonishing cultural diversity, as arrivals from 140 other countries join its population of 4 million. No single neighborhood fully embodies L.A. It's in the mix and the contrasts that you can find the city's character.

San Diego, another jump down the coastline, has a distinctly different feel than L.A. and Orange County. Founded as the first European settlement in California, it has strong historical ties in its Old Town district and Victorian-era Gaslamp Quarter. It's a terrific place to bring children, since it has three outstanding animal parks, low-key beaches, and a bustling waterfront.

WHO WILL ESPECIALLY LOVE THIS TRIP?

Families: All those beaches and boardwalks are only the beginning of the kid-friendly attractions in this area. You could go all out and spend the day at the Disneyland Resort, or keep it simple with a trip to a terrific park, like L.A.'s Griffith Park or San Diego's Balboa Park. Want to get a close-up look at a manatee or a panda? Head to the supersized San Diego Zoo, San Diego Wild Animal Park, or SeaWorld San Diego for awesome animal-spotting. Many of SoCal's cultural hotspots, like the Getty Center, have special childrens' programs. Remember to plan ahead to keep the freeway time at a minimum!

Cultural Explorers: Check out the neighborhoods throughout SoCal for ethnic diversity and dining—you can find one-of-a-kind shopping experiences, and you can get an earful of some of the 86 different languages spoken here. In L.A., you can easily hit three ethnic neighborhoods that are in close proximity to each other (and downtown)—Chinatown, Little Toyko, and Olvera Street. In Orange County's Westminster, Little Saigon boasts the largest concentration of Vietnamese in the U.S., and San Diego supports a large community of Pacific Islanders—who naturally gravitate to the city's fabulous beaches.

TOP 5 REASONS TO GO

Hollywood. Look inside the heart of world entertainment. Hit this part of L.A. for celebrity sightings, the Walk of Fame, TV show tapings, and glitterati-filled restaurants and nightclubs.

Eating well. From In-N-Out Burger to Wolfgang Puck's Spago to fish tacos, you won't have a hard time finding fantastic eats in SoCal—including the freshest seafood and almost any ethnic cuisine.

Hitting the beach. Grab a towel and get some sand in your shoes—Southern California's beaches are great for swimming, surfing, sunbathing, fishing, running—or just people-watching.

Disneyland and more. The mouse still knows how to show visitors to America's oldest theme park a good time. You'll also have a blast at Knott's Berry Farm, Universal Studios Hollywood, SeaWorld San Diego, the San Diego Zoo and Wild Animal Park, and Legoland California.

Roots that run deep. Explore Spanish missions, adobe homes, and 19th-century ships in some of the state's—and the nation's—oldest communities.

Outdoor Enthusiasts: Despite urban congestion, you can find large open spaces throughout SoCal. Griffith Park in L.A. and Balboa Park in San Diego hold golf courses, tennis courts, walking and running trails, and hiking paths that lead to great views. L.A.'s Santa Monica Mountains support state and national parks, where you can hike, camp, and explore. If you're in San Diego, join the locals who jog the trails through Mission Gorge Regional Park and along the shoreline of Mission Bay. And, of course, no matter where you are, you won't be too far from some great beaches.

Fashionistas: You can find gorgeous designer fashions and accessories in Beverly Hills, South Coast Plaza Shopping Mall, and San Diego's Fashion Valley. But they cost way, way less when you get them at L.A.'s Fashion District, where most shops are open to the public on Saturday.

30

WHEN IS THE BEST TIME TO VISIT?

Coastal Southern California has one of the best year-round climates in the world. From midsummer through fall, there's usually very little rain and low humidity; the Pacific Ocean breezes keep things from getting too hot. Although fog tends to hang around the coast in spring and early summer (locals call it "June gloom"), summer brings the most visitors to the area. That's when everyone heads outdoors for concerts, plays, dining alfresco, sailing, and hiking. In summer, San Diego attractions—including SeaWorld and the zoo—put on nighttime light shows. Pasadena's major annual event, the Tournament of Roses Parade and football game, takes place every New Year's Day, frequently against a backdrop of an azure sky with snow-covered mountains in the distance.

HOW SHOULD I GET THERE?

DRIVING

All three of these areas are best explored by car—driving is virtually a necessity within the cities, and it's the best way to get between them. Within California, Los Angeles is about 400 mi south of San Francisco Bay area cities and Sacramento in the Central Valley, via I–5; from Las Vegas the trip is about 300 mi via I–15. Orange County destinations are about 35 mi south of downtown Los Angeles via I–5; San Diego is another 120 mi farther south via I–5.

It's possible to take the legendary coastal route Highway 1, otherwise known as the Pacific Coast Highway (PCH), between L.A., Orange County, and San Diego—but this is a much slower route.

FLYING

A major hub for most domestic and international airlines, Los Angeles is served by several airports, including Los Angeles International Airport (LAX). Bob Hope Airport (BUR) in Burbank is convenient and sometimes less expensive for visitors to central Los Angeles, Hollywood, San Fernando Valley, and Pasadena. Long Beach Airport (LGB) is a handy hub for central Los Angeles and north Orange County. John Wayne Airport Orange County (SNA) in Santa Ana is a good choice for visiting coastal Orange County and the northern portions of San Diego County. San Diego International Airport (SAN) is a short drive or shuttle bus ride from downtown.

TRAIN

Amtrak provides frequent service between L.A.'s Union Station and San Diego via Orange County, where there are stops in Fullerton and Anaheim. It's a comfortable and scenic two-hour trip, affording a great ocean view as the train hugs the beach in the southern half of the journey.

HOW DO I GET AROUND?

BY CAR

SoCal is the car culture capital of the world, and it's a good idea to have a car to get around. All of Southern California was built with the automobile in mind. Traffic, particularly during long morning and evening rush hours, can be agonizingly slow, but most drivers are courteous. Streets and freeways are wide and well marked, with electronic signs that update drivers to time and distance to upcoming intersections. Talk radio stations throughout the region broadcast traffic updates frequently throughout the day and night. With the exception of downtown Los Angeles and San Diego, parking is relatively easy to find.

BY PUBLIC TRANSIT

L.A.'s Metro Rail covers a limited amount of ground, but what service it offers is convenient, largely safe, inexpensive, and frequent. The underground Red Line is most useful for visitors, as it runs from downtown's Union Station through Mid-Wilshire, Hollywood, and Universal City on its way to North Hollywood, stopping at some major tourist spots en route. The monorail-like Gold Line connects Union Station

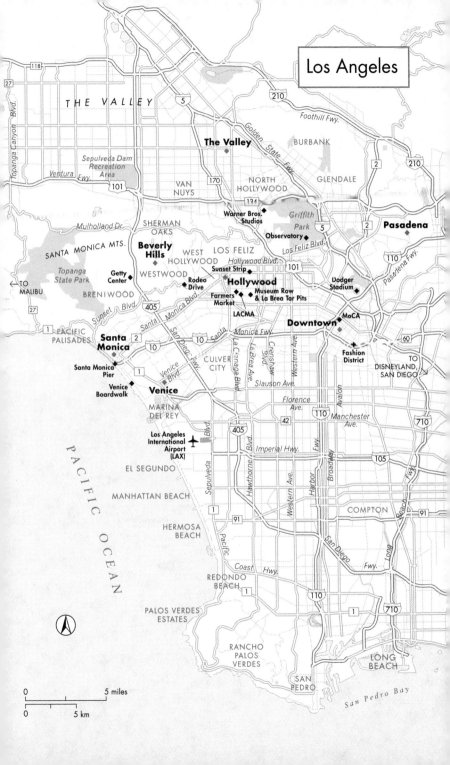

Los Angeles

THE VALLEY

118

27

Topanga Canyon Blvd.

5

210

Foothill Fwy.

Golden State Fwy.

Ventura Fwy.

Sepulveda Dam Recreation Area

101

The Valley

BURBANK

GLENDALE

NORTH HOLLYWOOD

VAN NUYS

170

SHERMAN OAKS

134

2

210

Mulholland Dr.

Warner Bros. Studios

Griffith Park

2

Pasadena

SANTA MONICA MTS.

Beverly Hills

WEST HOLLYWOOD

LOS FELIZ

Observatory

Los Feliz Blvd.

5

110

Pasadena Fwy.

Topanga State Park

← TO MALIBU

27

BRENIWOOD

Getty Center

WESTWOOD

Rodeo Drive

Sunset Strip

Hollywood Blvd.

Hollywood

101

Dodger Stadium

Sunset Blvd.

405

Farmers Market

Museum Row & La Brea Tar Pits

Santa Monica Blvd.

LACMA

Downtown

MoCA

Santa Monica Fwy.

1

PACIFIC PALISADES

Santa Monica

2

10

10

Monica Fwy.

Fashion District

60

TO DISNEYLAND, SAN DIEGO

Santa Monica Pier

Venice Blvd.

La Cienega Blvd.

La Brea Ave.

Crenshaw Blvd.

Western Ave.

Avalon

710

Venice Boardwalk

1

Venice

CULVER CITY

Slauson Ave.

MARINA DEL REY

Florence Ave.

42

110

Manchester Ave.

Sepulveda Blvd.

405

Los Angeles International Airport (LAX)

Imperial Hwy.

Hawthorne Blvd.

Harbor Fwy.

Broadway

105

EL SEGUNDO

MANHATTAN BEACH

Western Ave.

COMPTON

91

HERMOSA BEACH

1

91

San Diego Fwy.

Long Beach Fwy.

PACIFIC OCEAN

Pacific Coast Hwy.

REDONDO BEACH

1

110

710

PALOS VERDES ESTATES

1

RANCHO PALOS VERDES

SAN PEDRO

LONG BEACH

San Pedro Bay

0   5 miles

0   5 km

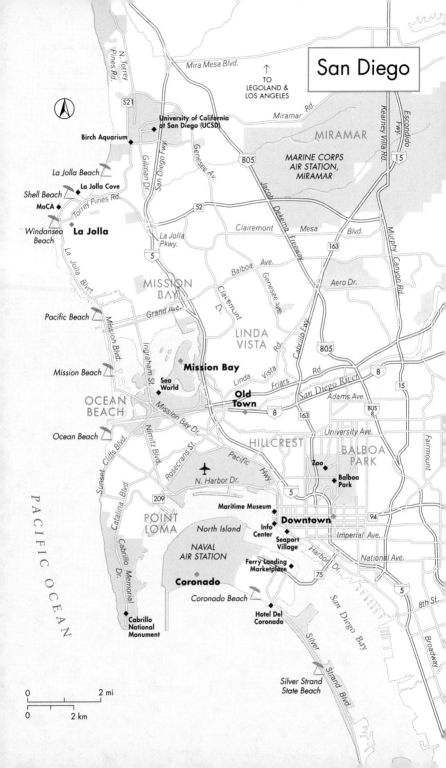

CLOSE UP

How to Snack

As the hot dog is to Chicago, the burger is to L.A. It's said that the drive-in burger joint was invented in Los Angeles, probably to meet the demands of an ever-mobile car culture. You can find signature burgers in fancy restaurants, beachside shacks, and take-out chains—it's one of the few common denominators in this town.

In-N-Out Burger is one of the most popular and ubiquitous chains. The made-to-order burgers are a highlight of the fast-food scene; for the "secret" menu of specialty orders, check out the company's Web site. **Tommy's** sells a wonderfully sloppy chili burger (wash one down with a Hawaiian Punch—we have no idea why this combo works, but it does). For a time-warp experience, hit the **Apple Pan** for a cheddar-topped burger; the place hasn't changed much since 1947. Newcomer **The Counter** is quickly opening multiple locations; it puts together all sorts of patties and toppings, including some very untraditional choices.

L.A.'s Japanese and Chinese places are also great places to snack. This is one of the best places to eat sushi outside of Japan; there are plenty of high-end sushi bars in town but you should check out the area around **Sawtelle Boulevard** for low-key spots for a quick bite. In **Monterey Park** you can nab a seat in a Hong Kong–style dim sum palace. And don't overlook the landmark **Farmers Market**, which is crammed with good eats from all over. Whether you're craving a muffaletta sandwich or a fresh doughnut, you can find it here.

The fish taco reigns supreme in the San Diego area. Actually, it's an import from Baja California where the taco stands spring up on street corners. **Rubio's**, a local fast-food chain, claims to serve up an authentic version: fried chunks of fish along with a creamy coleslaw stuffed into a tortilla, topped with salsa.

and Pasadena. Other lines, such as the Green and Blue lines, are primarily for commuter service.

Metro Rail costs $1.25 plus 25¢ per transfer, or $3 for an all-day pass. Tickets are sold through vending machines in the stations. It's on an honor system, so you won't need to go through turnstiles. Trains operate from roughly 4:30 AM to 12:30 AM, every 5 to 15 minutes.

30

Orange County's public transportation system is not very thorough or convenient—not a practical choice for visitors. San Diego has a better network, particularly with its bright orange trolleys that connect sights in the Gaslamp Quarter and Old Town.

WHERE SHOULD I FOCUS MY ENERGY?

If you're here for 1 day: If you have just one day to spend in Southern California, you'll need to make a choice, depending on where you arrive. If your flight lands at LAX or San Diego, your best bet may be taking a full or half-day city tour—you'll avoid the hassle of renting a car and navigating unfamiliar territory. If your layover is in Orange County, you can squeeze a quick trip to Disneyland in one day.

If you're here for 2 days: Two days will give you time to combine culture with some Hollywood haunts. Start with a morning tour of the J. Paul Getty Center in Brentwood, a travertine and marble-clad campus with visual surprises around every corner. Spend the afternoon exploring the West Side, shopping in Beverly Hills, or cruising West 3rd Street, where the Farmer's Market and the Grove beckon with great food and even better shopping. On Day 2 head for Hollywood and Highland, where you can see where the Academy Awards are handed out, walk in the footsteps of famous stars at Grauman's Chinese Theater next door, and stroll the Hollywood Walk of Fame. Afternoon options include a tour of the Hollywood Bowl or a visit to Universal Studios Hollywood.

If you're here for 3 days: A third day gives you a chance to go behind the scenes. See a television show taping, tour Paramount Studios, check out the museums on Museum Row: the Los Angeles County Museum of Art and the Page Museum at the LaBrea Tar Pits. Or spend an afternoon at the beach. If you're going south to Disneyland, plan to get an early start on your last day in LA.

If you're here for 4 days: You can see Disneyland in a day, especially if it's not a crowded summer day, but for the full effect plan to spend two days here. It will allow you to visit both Disneyland and California Adventure parks, dine in Downtown Disney and maybe take a quick drive to the coast.

If you're here for 5 days: Head south and spend some time in San Diego. If you have young children, don't miss Legoland California in Carlsbad along the way.

If you're here for 6 days: Spend Day 6 in San Diego at the Wild Animal Park, about a 30-minute drive from downtown, or if you don't want to drive, see the pandas at the Zoo in Balboa Park.

If you're here for 7 days or more: On your seventh day you can visit with Shamu, ride Shipwreck Rapids, or march with the penguins at Sea World San Diego.

WHAT ARE THE TOP EXPERIENCES?

Going Wild. Get up close and personal with mother nature at the San Diego Wild Animal Park, where animals appear to roam freely across 1,800 acres. Enclosures reflect natural habitats in Africa, Asian plains and swamps, and the Australian rain forests. The giraffes are friendly, and seem to enjoy tottering on their long legs to snatch snacks from a visitor. Visit the park in spring, and you're likely to see many young animals, including short-legged giraffes, hippos, and rhinos. You can also walk through a huge aviary, meet an endangered California condor, explore botanical gardens, visit a growing herd of elephants, and see cheetahs take off at breakneck speed.

Bobsledding. The Matterhorn at Disneyland is one of the park's original rides from 1955. Don't miss riding the bobsled as it twists, turns, and spirals down the snowy mountain. Newer rides may offer more thrills and chills, but the sled ride always has a long line. For bigger thrills you can also take a spin on Space Mountain and Splash Mountain.

Stargazing two ways. Peer through the telescopes at the recently renovated Griffith Park Observatory *(2800 E. Observatory Rd., Los Angeles, CA 90027, 213/473–0800)*; clear summer nights are your best times for seeing Saturn's rings or Jupiter's moons. Or you can take in the entire Universe at one of the daily sky shows presented at the Samuel Oschin Planetarium, considered the finest planetarium in the world. Perched atop the southern slope of Mount Hollywood, just above the Los Feliz neighborhood at 1,134 feet above sea level, the observatory is visible from many locations in the Los Angeles basin. It's a national leader in public astronomy, and one of SoCal's most popular attractions.

Staring out to sea. Southern California's Pacific views are as good as they get. La Jolla Cove is a standout vantage point along the 100-plus mi of coastline that run between San Diego and Los Angeles. Take in the vista from the manicured park that overlooks the water; on a clear day you'll feel like you can see forever. At low tide, you can walk down to the surf line and explore the tide pools and cliff caves. If you like to dive, this is one of the great places to explore underwater—it's protected as part of the San Diego–La Jolla Underwater Park Ecological Reserve.

BEST BETS

SIGHTS AND TOURS

LOS ANGELES

Fodor'sChoice **Farmers Market & The Grove.** The saying "Meet me at 3rd and Fair-
★ fax" has become a standard line for generations of Angelenos who ate, shopped, and spotted the stars who had drifted over from the studios for a breath of unpretentious air. The market now includes 110 stalls and more than 20 counter-order restaurants, plus the landmark 1941 Clock Tower. In 2002 a massive expansion called The Grove opened; this highly conceptualized outdoor mall has a Euro spin, with cobblestones, marble mosaics, and pavilions. ⊠*Farmers Market, 6333 W. 3rd St.; The Grove, 189 The Grove Dr., Fairfax District* 🕾*323/933–9211 Farmers Market, 323/900–8080 The Grove* ⊕*www.farmersmarketla. com* 🕙*Farmers Market weekdays 9–9, Sat. 9–8, Sun. 10–9; The Grove Mon.–Thurs. 10–9, Fri. and Sat. 10–10, Sun. 11–7.*

Fodor'sChoice **The Getty Center.** With its curving walls and isolated hilltop perch, the
★ Getty Center resembles a pristine fortified city of its own. You may have
☾ been lured up by the beautiful views of L.A. (on a clear day stretching all the way to the Pacific Ocean), but the architecture, uncommon gardens, and fascinating art collections will be more than enough to capture and hold your attention. Notable among the paintings are Rembrandt's *The*

30

Abduction of Europa, Van Gogh's *Irises*, Monet's *Wheatstack, Snow Effects*, and *Morning*, and James Ensor's *Christ's Entry into Brussels*. ■ TIP→On-site parking is subject to availability and usually fills up by late afternoon on holidays and summer weekends, so try to come early in the day. ✉*1200 Getty Center Dr., Brentwood* ☎*310/440–7300* ⊕*www.getty.edu* 🖃*Free, parking $8* ☉*Tues.–Thurs. and Sun. 10–6, Fri. and Sat. 10–9.*

FodorsChoice **Getty Villa Malibu.** The antiquities here are astounding, but on a first visit
★   even they take a backseat to their environment. This megamansion sits on some of the most valuable coastal property in the world. Modeled after an Italian country home, the Villa dei Papiri in Herculaneum, the Getty Villa includes beautifully manicured gardens, reflecting pools, and statuary. ■ TIP→Make reservations well in advance since this is one L.A. hot spot with long-term popularity, and talking your way in is out of the question. ✉*17985 Pacific Coast Hwy., Pacific Palisades* ☎*310/440–7300* ⊕*www.getty.edu* 🖃*Free, reservations required. Parking $8, cash only* ☉*Wed.–Sun. 11–4.*

★ **Grauman's Chinese Theatre.** A place that inspires the phrase "only in Hollywood," this fantasy of Chinese pagodas and temples has become a shrine to stardom. Although you have to buy a movie ticket to appreciate the interior trappings, the courtyard is open to the public, though weekend tours are also available. Here you can find those oh-so-famous cement hand- and footprints. ✉*6925 Hollywood Blvd., Hollywood* ☎*323/461–3331, 323/463–9576 for tours* ⊕*www.manntheatres.com.*

★ **Hollywood & Highland.** Now an extremely busy tourist attraction (read: not a lot of locals), this hotel-retail-entertainment complex was a dramatic play to bring glitz, foot traffic, and commerce back to Hollywood. A Metro Red Line station provides easy access to and from other parts of the city, and there's plenty of underground parking accessible from Highland Avenue. ✉*Hollywood Blvd. and Highland Ave., Hollywood* ⊕*www.hollywoodandhighland.com* 🖃*Parking $2 with validation* ☉*Mon.–Sat. 10–10, Sun. 10–7.*

★ **Hollywood Sign.** With letters 50 feet tall, Hollywood's trademark sign can be spotted from miles away. ⊕*www.hollywoodsign.org.*

★ **Hollywood Walk of Fame.** Along Hollywood Boulevard runs a trail of affirmations for entertainment-industry overachievers. On this mile-long stretch of sidewalk, inspired by the concrete handprints in front of Grauman's Chinese Theatre, the names are embossed in brass, each at the center of a pink star embedded in dark-gray terrazzo. Contact the **Hollywood Chamber of Commerce** (✉*7018 Hollywood Blvd.* ☎*323/469–8311* ⊕*www.hollywoodchamber.net*) for celebrity-star locations and information on future star installations.

★ **Kodak Theatre.** Follow the path of red-carpet Hollywood royalty to the home of the Academy Awards. While taking a half-hour tour of this famous setting isn't cheap, it's a worthwhile expense for movie buffs who just can't get enough insider information. ✉*6801 Hollywood Blvd., Hollywood* ☎*323/308–6300* ⊕*www.kodaktheatre.com* 🖃*$15.*

Fodor'sChoice ★ **Los Angeles County Museum of Art (LACMA).** Since it opened in 1966, LACMA has assembled a vast, encyclopedic collection of more than 150,000 works from around the world; its collection is widely considered the most comprehensive in the western United States. ⊠ *5905 Wilshire Blvd., Miracle Mile* ☎ *323/857-6000* ⊕ *www.lacma. org* ☜ *$7, free 2nd Tues. of month* ☉ *Mon., Tues., and Thurs. noon–8, Fri. noon–9, weekends 11–8.*

Fodor'sChoice ★ **The Museum of Contemporary Art (MOCA).** The MOCA's permanent collection of American and European art from 1940 to the present divides itself between three spaces: this linear red-sandstone building at California Plaza, the **Geffen Contemporary,** in nearby Little Tokyo, and the satellite gallery at W. Hollywood's **Pacific Design Center.** ⊠ *250 S. Grand Ave., Downtown* ☎ *213/626-6222* ⊕ *www.moca.org* ☜ *$8, free on same day with Geffen Contemporary admission and on Thurs.* ☉ *Mon. and Fri. 11–5, Thurs. 11–8, weekends 11–6.*

CLAIM TO FAME
L.A. is the entertainment capital of the world. But it's home to the nation's first freeway (the Pasadena Freeway). Fine examples of every architectural movement since 1900 abound, including the Arts and Crafts cottages and bungalows in Pasadena, the many ornate art deco movie palaces built in the 1920s and early '30s in downtown L.A., the mid-century modern structures exemplified by the theme building at LAX and the Los Angeles County Museum of Art, and present-day marvel the Frank Gehry–designed Walt Disney Concert Hall. Oh, and the Port of Los Angeles is the busiest cargo port in the nation.

Fodor'sChoice ★ **The Music Center.** L.A.'s major performing-arts venue since its opening in 1964, the Music Center is also now Downtown's centerpiece. Home to the Los Angeles Philharmonic, the Los Angeles Opera, the Center Theater Group, and the Los Angeles Master Chorale, the Music Center is also a former site of the Academy Awards. The crown jewel of the Music Center is the **Walt Disney Concert Hall,** designed by Frank Gehry. ⊠ *135 N. Grand Ave., at 1st St., Downtown* ☎ *213/972-7211, 213/972-4399 for tour information* ⊕ *www.musiccenter.org* ☜ *Free* ☉ *Free tours Tues.–Fri. 10–1:30, Sat. 10–noon.*

30

★ ☻ **Olvera Street.** As the major draw of the oldest section of the city, known as **El Pueblo de Los Angeles,** Olvera Street has come to represent the rich Mexican heritage of L.A. The street is a vibrant marketplace where vendors sell puppets, leather goods, sandals, serapes (woolen shawls), and handicrafts from stalls that line the center of the narrow street. For information, stop by the **Olvera Street Visitors Center** (⊠ *622 N. Main St., Downtown* ☎ *213/628-1274* ⊕ *www.olvera-street.com*), in the Sepulveda House, a Victorian built in 1887 as a hotel and boardinghouse. The center is open Monday–Saturday 10–3. Free 50-minute walking tours leave here at 10, 11, and noon Tuesday–Saturday.

Fodor'sChoice ★ **Paramount Pictures.** With a history dating to the early 1920s, this studio was home to some of Hollywood's most luminous stars, including Rudolph Valentino, Mae West, Mary Pickford, and Lucille Ball, who filmed episodes of *I Love Lucy* here. The lot still churns out memorable movies and TV shows, including *Forrest Gump*, *Titanic*, and *Star Trek*. You can take a studio tour (reservations required) led by friendly guides who walk and trolley you around the back lots. You can also be part of an audience for a live TV taping. Tickets are free; call for listings and times. ⊠ *5555 Melrose Ave., Hollywood* ☎ *323/956–1777* ⊕ *www.paramount.com* ☎ *Tours $35.*

Fodor'sChoice
★ **Rodeo Drive.** The ultimate shopping indulgence—Rodeo Drive is one of Southern California's bona fide tourist attractions; here you can shop for five-digit jewelry or a $35 handbag. At the southern end of Rodeo Drive (at Wilshire Boulevard) is **Via Rodeo,** a curvy cobblestone street designed to resemble a European shopping area or a Universal Studio backlot—take your pick. ⊠ *Beverly Hills.*

> ## HISTORY YOU CAN SEE
>
> The La Brea Tar Pits contain bones and fossils of extinct animals such as saber-toothed tigers, mammoths, and eagles that roamed the Los Angeles basin between 40,000 and 10,000 years ago, during the last Ice Age. Since 1906 more than a million bones have been recovered, representing 231 species of vertebrates, plus insects, birds, and other creatures. Excavations continue to this day; you can see the volunteer diggers at work in Pit 91 during the summer months and watch paleontologists cleaning and cataloging the bones and other items at the laboratory in the adjacent Page Museum in Hancock Park.

Santa Monica Pier. Souvenir shops, a psychic adviser, arcades, eateries, and **Pacific Park** are all part of this truncated pier at the foot of Colorado Boulevard below Palisades Park. The pier's trademark 46-horse Looff Carousel, built in 1922, has appeared in several films, including *The Sting.* Free concerts are held on the pier in summer. ⊠ *Colorado Ave. and ocean, Santa Monica* ☎ *310/458–8900* ⊕ *www.santamonicapier.org* ☎ *Rides $1* ⊙ *Carousel May–Sept., Tues.–Fri. 11–9, weekends 10–9; Oct.–Apr., Thurs.–Sun., hrs vary.*

★ **Sunset Strip.** For 60 years the Hollywood nighttime crowd has headed for the 1¾-mi stretch of Sunset Boulevard between Crescent Heights Boulevard on the east and Doheny Drive on the west, known as the Sunset Strip. Parking and traffic around the Strip can be tough on weekends, but the time and money may be worth it if you plan to make the rounds—most clubs are within walking distance of each other.

Fodor'sChoice
★ **Venice Boardwalk.** "Boardwalk" may be something of a misnomer—it's really a five-block section of paved walkway—but this L.A. mainstay delivers year-round action. Bicyclists zip along and bikini-clad rollerbladers attract crowds as they put on impromptu demonstrations, vying for attention with magicians, fortune-tellers, a chain-saw juggler, and sand mermaids.

Warner Bros. Studios. If you're looking for a more authentic behind-the-scenes look at how films and TV shows are made, head to this major studio center. There aren't many bells and whistles here, but you'll get a much better idea of production work than you will at Universal Studios. ■TIP➔The two-hour tours involve a lot of walking, so dress comfortably and bring plenty of sunscreen. Reservations are required. Call at least one week in advance and ask about provisions for people with disabilities; children under 8 are not admitted. Tours are given at least every hour, more frequently from May to September. ⊠ *3400 W. Riverside Dr., Burbank* ☎ *818/972–8687* ⊕ *www.wbsf.com* ✉ *$42* ☉ *Weekdays 8:30–4.*

ORANGE COUNTY

Fodor'sChoice ★ **Disneyland** and Disney's **California Adventure** (both in nearby Anaheim) are open daily, 365 days a year; hours vary, depending on the season. If you plan to visit for more than a day, you can save money by buying three-, four-, and five-day Park Hopper tickets that grant same-day "hopping" privileges between Disneyland and Disney's California Adventure. Disneyland is about a 30-mi drive from either LAX or downtown. From LAX, follow Sepulveda Boulevard south to the I–105 freeway and drive east 16 mi to the I–605 north exit. Exit at the Santa Ana Freeway (I–5) and continue south for 12 mi to the Disneyland Drive exit. Follow signs to the resort. From downtown, follow I–5 south 28 mi and exit at Disneyland Drive. ⊠ *1313 Harbor Blvd., Anaheim* ☎ *714/781–4565* ⊕ *www.disneyland.com.*

Disneyland Resort Express offers daily nonstop bus service between LAX, John Wayne Airport, and Anaheim. Reservations are not required. The cost is $19 one way for adults, $16 for children. (☎ *714/978–8855* ⊕ *www.airportbus.com*).

Downtown Disney is a 20-acre promenade of dining, shopping, and entertainment that connects the Disneyland Resort hotels and theme parks. ⊠ *Disneyland Dr. between Ball Rd. and Katella Ave., Anaheim* ☎ *714/300–7800* ⊕ *www.disneyland.com* ✉ *Free* ☉ *Daily 7 AM–2 AM; hrs at shops and restaurants vary.*

★ ☉ **Knott's Berry Farm.** This 160-acre amusement park complex has 100-plus rides, dozens of restaurants and shops, and even a brick-by-brick replica of Philadelphia's Independence Hall. While it has some good attractions for small children, the park is best known for its roster of awesome thrill rides. The park is open June–mid-Sept., daily 9 am–midnight; mid-Sept.–May the park usually opens at 10 and closes between 5 and 8 on weekdays, and between 10 and midnight weekends. Knott's is an easy 10-minute drive from Disneyland or a 30-minute drive from downtown Los Angeles. Take I–5 to Beach Boulevard and head south 3 mi; follow the park entrance signs on the right. ⊠ *8039 Beach Blvd., Buena Park ✛ Between La Palma Ave. and Crescent St., 2 blocks south of Hwy. 91* ☎ *714/220–5200* ⊕ *www.knotts.com.*

SAN DIEGO

Fodor'sChoice ★ **Balboa Park.** Overlooking downtown and the Pacific Ocean, 1,200-acre Balboa Park is the cultural heart of San Diego, where you can find most of the city's museums and its world-famous zoo. Most first-time visitors see only these attractions, but Balboa Park is really a series of botanical gardens.

30

STRANGE BUT TRUE

■ The 50-foot-high Hollywood sign, illuminated at night and visible from many places in the Los Angeles basin, was originally erected on Mt. Lee in 1923 to promote a real estate venture; it read "Hollywood-land." Over the years the sign was vandalized, altered, spray-painted, renovated, and reduced to Hollywood. It's now secured to deter intruders.

■ The Cobb salad (a concoction of finely chopped lettuce, tomatoes, bacon, chicken, avocado, Roquefort cheese, hard-cooked eggs, and chives) was created by the Brown Derby restaurant owner Bob Cobb

as a midnight snack for Sid Grauman one night in 1937. The salad became an instant hit; variations are served in restaurants around the world.

■ Gunslinger Wyatt Earp was well known to San Diegans in the late 1800s. Not long after he survived the Gunfight at OK Corral in Tombstone, Arizona, Earp and his wife Josie moved to a booming San Diego, where they gambled heavily, invested in real estate, and operated saloons in the rough and tumble downtown area that was then known as the Stingaree district. It's now part of the Gaslamp Quarter.

★ ☺ **Cabrillo National Monument.** This 160-acre preserve marks the site of the first European visit to San Diego, made by 16th-century explorer Juan Rodríguez Cabrillo (circa 1498–1543). Government grounds were set aside to commemorate his discovery in 1913, and today the site, with its rugged cliffs and shores and outstanding overlooks, is one of the most frequently visited of all the national monuments. ⌂ *1800 Cabrillo Memorial Dr., Point Loma* ☎ *619/557–5450* ⊕ *www.nps.gov/cabr* ☑ *$5 per car, $3 per person entering on foot or by bicycle, entrance pass allows unlimited admissions for 1 wk from date of purchase; free for Golden Age and Golden Access passport and National Parks Pass holders* ☺ *Park daily 9–5:15.*

Fodor'sChoice ★ **Gaslamp Quarter Historic District.** The 16½-block national historic district contains most of the Victorian-style buildings that rose in San Diego after Alonzo Horton arrived in 1867, bent on supplanting San Diego's Old Town with a new downtown closer to the waterfront. The majority of the quarter's landmark buildings are on 4th and 5th avenues, between Island Avenue and Broadway. For additional information about the historic area, call the **Gaslamp Quarter Association** (☎ *619/233–5227*) or log on to their Web site www.gaslamp.org. ⌂ *Between 4th and 6th Aves., from Broadway to Harbor Dr.*

★ **Horton Plaza.** Downtown's centerpiece is the shopping, dining, and entertainment mall that fronts Broadway and G Street from 1st to 4th avenues and covers more than six city blocks. A collage of pastels with elaborate, colorful tile work on benches and stairways, banners waving in the air, and modern sculptures marking the entrances, Horton Plaza rises in uneven, staggered levels to six floors; great views of downtown from the harbor to Balboa Park and beyond can be had here. ☎ *619/238–1596* ⊕ *www.westfield.com/hortonplaza.*

International Visitor Information Center. One of the two visitor information centers operated by the San Diego Convention and Visitors Bureau (the other is in La Jolla), this is the best resource for information on the city. It's just across from Broadway Pier. ✉ *1040 W. Broadway, at Harbor Dr.* ☎ *619/236–1212* ⊕ *www.sandiego.org* ⊙ *June–Sept., daily 9–5; Oct.–May, daily 9–4.*

Fodor'sChoice
★ **La Jolla.** La Jollans have long considered their village to be the Monte Carlo of California, and with good cause. Its coastline curves into natural coves backed by verdant hillsides covered with homes worth millions. Prospect Street and Girard Avenue, the village's main drags, are lined with expensive shops and office buildings. Through the years the shopping and dining district has spread to Pearl and other side streets.

Fodor'sChoice
★
♻ **Legoland California,** the centerpiece of a development that includes resort hotels and a designer discount shopping mall, offers a full day of entertainment for pint-size fun-seekers and their parents. ✉ *1 Legoland Dr.* ✛ *Exit I–5 at Cannon Rd. and follow signs east ¼ mi, Carlsbad* ☎ *760/918–5346* ⊕ *www.legolandca.com* ✑ *$57* ⊙ *Hrs vary; call for information.*

Fodor'sChoice
★
♻ **Maritime Museum.** A must for anyone with an interest in nautical history, this collection of six restored and replica ships affords a fascinating glimpse of San Diego during its heyday as a commercial seaport. If you crave more than a dockside experience, you can take to the water in the museum's other sailing ship, the *Californian,* a replica of a 19th-century revenue cutter that patrolled the shores of California. ✉ *1492 N. Harbor Dr., Embarcadero* ☎ *619/234–9153* ⊕ *www.sdmaritime.org* ✑ *$12 includes entry to all ships* ⊙ *Daily 9–8, until 9 PM in summer.*

Fodor'sChoice
★
♻ **San Diego Zoo.** Balboa Park's—and perhaps the city's—most famous attraction is its 100-acre zoo, and it deserves all the press it gets. Nearly 4,000 animals of some 800 diverse species—including the zoo's famous pandas—roam in hospitable, expertly crafted habitats that replicate natural environments as closely as possible. ✉ *2920 Zoo Dr., Balboa Park* ☎ *619/234–3153, 888/697–2632 giant panda hotline* ⊕ *www.sandiegozoo.org* ✑ *$22.75 includes zoo, Children's Zoo, and animal shows; $33 includes above, plus guided bus tour, unlimited express bus rides, and round-trip Skyfari Aerial Tram rides; zoo free for children under 12 in Oct.; $59 pass good for admission to zoo and San Diego Wild Animal Park within 5 days* ⊙ *Mid-June–Labor Day., daily 9–9; Labor Day–Mid-June, daily 9–4; Children's Zoo and Skyfari ride generally close 1 hr earlier.*

Fodor'sChoice
★
♻ **SeaWorld San Diego.** One of the world's largest marine-life amusement parks, SeaWorld is spread over 189 tropically landscaped bay-front acres. ✉ *500 Sea World Dr., near west end of I–8, Mission Bay* ☎ *800/257–4268* ⊕ *www.seaworld.com* ✑ *$56; parking $10 cars, $6 motorcycles, $15 RVs and campers; 1-hr behind-the-scenes walking tours $12 extra* ▭ *AE, D, MC, V* ⊙ *Daily 10–dusk; extended hrs in summer.*

30

WHERE TO EAT

	WHAT IT COSTS			
	¢	$	$$	$$$	$$$$
RESTAURANTS	under $7	$7–$12	$13–$22	$23–$32	over $32

Dining prices are per person for a main course or equivalent combination of smaller plates (e.g., tapas, sushi), excluding sales tax.

LOS ANGELES

$$$$
Fodor'sChoice
★
✕**CUT.** In a true collision of artistic titans, celebrity chef Wolfgang Puck presents his take on steak house cuisine in a space designed by Getty Center architect Richard Meier. Its contemporary lines and cold surfaces recall little of the home comforts of this beloved culinary tradition. And like Meier's design, Puck's fare doesn't dwell much on the past, and a thoroughly modern crab Louis is the closest thing to nostalgia on the menu. Playful dishes like bone marrow flan take center stage before delving into genuine Japanese Kobe beef or a perfect dry-aged hunk of Nebraskan sirloin that proves the Austrian-born superchef understands our quintessentially American love affair. ✉ *Regent Beverly Wilshire, 9500 Wilshire Blvd., Beverly Hills* ☎ *310/276–8500* ☛ *Reservations essential* ▤ *AE, D, DC, MC, V* ⊘ *Closed Sun. No lunch.*

$$$$
Fodor'sChoice
★
✕**Valentino.** Renowned as one of the country's top Italian restaurants, Valentino has a truly awe-inspiring wine list. With nearly 2,500 labels consuming 89 pages, backed by a cellar overflowing with 100,000 bottles, this restaurant is nothing short of heaven for serious oenophiles. In the 1970s, suave owner Piero Selvaggio introduced L.A. to his exquisite modern Italian cuisine, and he continues to impress guests with dishes like wild boar–filled pasta with black truffles and almonds, a garlicky veal chop with a rich *fonduta* of Parmigiano-Reggiano, and sautéed branzino with lemon emulsion. Prix-fixe menus begin at a reasonable $45. A recent addition to this exalted venue is a more casual wine and carpaccio bar. ✉ *3115 Pico Blvd., Santa Monica* ☎ *310/829–4313* ☛ *Reservations essential* ▤ *AE, DC, MC, V* ⊘ *Closed Sun. No lunch Sat. and Mon.–Thurs.*

$$$–$$$$
Fodor'sChoice
★
✕**Mori Sushi.** Only a small fish logo identifies the facade of this restaurant, but many consider it the best sushi bar in L.A. and Morihiro Onodera one of the great sushi masters in America. The austere whitewashed space stands in contrast to the chef's artful presentations of pristine morsels of seafood, all served on ceramic plates he makes himself. Allow him to compose an entire meal for you—although this can be an expensive proposition—and he'll send out eye-popping presentations of sushi or sashimi accented with touches of rare sea salts, yuzu, and freshly ground wasabi, as well as intricately conceived salads, housemade tofu, and soups. ✉ *11500 Pico Blvd., West L.A.* ☎ *310/479–3939* ▤ *AE, MC, V* ⊘ *Closed Sun. No lunch Sat.*

$$$–$$$$
Fodor'sChoice
★
✕**Patina.** In a bold move, chef–owner Joachim Splichal moved his flagship restaurant from Hollywood to downtown's striking Frank Gehry–designed Walt Disney Concert Hall. His gamble paid off— the contemporary space, surrounded by a rippled "curtain" of rich walnut, is an elegant, dramatic stage for the acclaimed restaurant's

contemporary French cuisine. Specialties include copious amounts of foie gras, caramelized halibut with mushroom ragout, roasted squab in chocolate sauce, and a formidable *côte de boeuf* for two, carved tableside. Finish with a hard-to-match cheese tray (orchestrated by a genuine *maître fromager*) and sensual desserts. ⊠ *Walt Disney Concert Hall, 141 S. Grand Ave., Downtown* ☏213/972–3331 ⓐ *Reservations essential* ⊟AE, D, DC, MC, V ⊘ *No lunch weekends.*

$$$–$$$$ ✕ **Spago Beverly Hills.** The famed
Fodor's Choice flagship restaurant of Wolfgang
★ Puck, Mr. Celebrity Chef himself, is justifiably a modern L.A. classic. The illustrious restaurant centers on a buzzing outdoor courtyard shaded by 100-year-old olive trees. From an elegantly appointed table inside, you can glimpse the exhibition kitchen and, on occasion, the affable chef-owner greeting his famous friends. The people-watching here is worth the price of admission, but the clientele is surprisingly inclusive, from the biggest Hollywood stars to Midwestern tourists to foodies more preoccupied with vintages of Burgundy than with faces from the cover of *People*. The daily-changing menu could offer *côte de boeuf* with Armagnac-peppercorn sauce, Cantonese-style duck, or some traditional Austrian specialties. Acclaimed pastry chef Sherry Yard works magic with everything from a sophisticated tart inspired by the Twix candy bar to an Austrian *kaiserschmarrn* (crème fraîche pancakes with fruit). ⊠*176 N. Cañon Dr., Beverly Hills* ☏*310/385–0880* ⓐ*Reservations essential* ⊟*AE, D, DC, MC, V* ⊘*No lunch Sun.*

$$–$$$$ ✕ **Musso & Frank Grill.** Liver and onions, lamb chops, goulash, shrimp Louis salad, gruff waiters—you can find all the old favorites here in Hollywood's oldest restaurant. A film-industry hangout since it opened in 1919, Musso & Frank still welcomes the working studio set to its maroon faux-leather booths. Great breakfasts are served all day, but the kitchen's famous "flannel cakes" (pancakes) are served only until 3 PM. ⊠*6667 Hollywood Blvd., Hollywood* ☏*323/467–7788* ⊟*AE, DC, MC, V* ⊘*Closed Sun. and Mon.*

$$ ✕ **Pizzeria Mozza.** Part of the long-awaited venture from *Iron Chef*
Fodor's Choice Mario Batali and celebrated bread maker Nancy Silverton (founder
★ of L.A.'s La Brea Bakery and Campanile), this casual venue gives new-found eminence to the humble "pizza joint." With traditional Mediterranean items like white anchovies, lardo, squash blossoms, and Gorgonzola, Mozza's pies—thin-crusted delights with golden, blistered edges—are much more Campania than California, and virtually every one is a winner. Utterly simple salads sing with vibrant flavors thanks to

---

LIKE A LOCAL

To get around on LA's freeway system, you've got to know the lingo. Odd numbered interstates run north and south (I-5 and I-15), evens run east and west (I-10 and I-8); and most freeways have highway numbers and names. I-5 is known as the Santa Ana Freeway in most of Los Angeles and Orange Counties, but it becomes the San Diego Freeway where it joins the 405 in Irvine (the San Diego Freeway in L.A. and Orange Counties). Freeway intersections have their own names, such as the Orange Crush (Highway 57 and I-5) and the Colossus of Roads (Highway 110, Highway 91, and I-405).

30

superb market-fresh ingredients, and daily specials include crisp duck legs with lentils and *Saba* (a balsamic-like vinegar), or fennel sausage with rapini. Like the menu, the wine list is both interesting and affordable. For more serious dining, try their other collaboration, Osteria Mozza, next door. ⊠*641 N. Highland Ave., Hollywood* ☎*323/297–0101* ⚷*Reservations essential* ⊟*AE, MC, V.*

¢–$$ ✕**Roscoe's House of Chicken 'n Waffles.** Okay, the name of this casual eat-
★   ery may sound a little weird, but don't be put off. Roscoe's is *the* place
☾   for real down-home Southern cooking. Just ask the patrons, who drive from all over L.A. for Roscoe's bargain-price fried chicken, wonderful waffles (which, by the way, turn out to be a great partner for fried chicken), buttery chicken livers, and grits. Although Roscoe's has the intimate feel of a smoky jazz club, those musicians hanging out here are just taking five. ⊠*1514 N. Gower St., Hollywood* ☎*323/466–7453* ⚷*Reservations not accepted* ⊟*AE, D, DC, MC, V.*

¢   ✕**The Apple Pan.** A burger-insider haunt since 1947, this unassuming
Fodor'sChoice   joint with a horseshoe-shape counter—no tables here—turns out one
★   heck of a good burger topped with Tillamook cheddar, plus a hickory burger with barbecue sauce. You'll also find great fries and, of course, an apple pie good enough to name a restaurant after (although many regulars argue that the banana cream deserves the honor). Be prepared to wait. ⊠*10801 W. Pico Blvd., West L.A.* ☎*310/475–3585* ⚷*Reservations not accepted* ⊟*No credit cards* ☾*Closed Mon.*

¢   ✕**Pink's Hot Dogs.** Orson Welles ate 18 of these hot dogs in one sitting,
★   and you, too, will be tempted to order more than one. The chili dogs
☾   are the main draw, but the menu has expanded to include a Martha Stewart Dog (a 10-inch frank topped with mustard, relish, onions, tomatoes, sauerkraut, bacon, and sour cream). Since 1939 Angelenos and tourists alike have been lining up to plunk down some modest change for one of the greatest guilty pleasures in L.A. Pink's is open until 3 AM on weekends—expect long lines even then. ⊠*709 N. La Brea Ave., Beverly–La Brea* ☎*323/931–4223* ⚷*Reservations not accepted* ⊟*No credit cards.*

SAN DIEGO

$$$–$$$$ ✕**1500 Ocean.** The new fine-dining restaurant at Hotel Del Coronado
Fodor'sChoice   offers a memorable evening that showcases the best organic and natu-
★   rally raised ingredients the Southland has to offer. Chef Jason Shaeffer, who honed his technique as opening sous chef at Thomas Keller's famed New York restaurant, Per Se, presents sublimely subtle dishes such as buffalo mozzarella with baby artichokes, oyster gratin, lamb porterhouse with black olives, and pan-roasted sea bass with chickpea *panisse* (similar to polenta). The interior, at once inviting and elegant, evokes a posh cabana, while the terrace offers ocean views. An excellent international wine list and equally clever desserts and artisanal cheeses complete the experience. ⊠*Hotel Del Coronado, 1500 Orange Ave., Coronado* ☎*619/522–8490* ⊟*AE, D, DC, MC, V* ☾*No lunch.*

$$$–$$$$ ✕**George's California Modern.** Formerly George's at the Cove, a $2.6
Fodor'sChoice   million makeover brought a new name and sleek updated look to this
★   eternally popular restaurant overlooking La Jolla Cove. Hollywood types and other visiting celebrities can be spotted in the sleek main

STREET SCENE, SOCAL STYLE

Los Angeles has some interesting neighborhoods that put to rest the old saying, "nobody walks in L.A." These days you can see people on the streets hoofing it from one trendy shop to a chic restaurant or café morning, noon, and night. Surprisingly, Hollywood Boulevard is one of the places to go for all-day and most of the night entertainment. Park at the Hollywood and Highland Center, and start your haunt. The open-air complex is lined with hot shops and cool cafés; it offers a perfect frame to photograph the Hollywood sign, and you can bowl (sometimes with the stars) at the Lucky Strike Lanes. Dining options here include Wolfgang Puck's Vert (French brasserie), Shabu Shabu (Japanese hot pot and sushi) and the Grill on Hollywood. If you're a fan of the late night's Jimmy Kimmel Live TV show, you'll recognize El Capitan Theater and Disney's Soda Fountain and Studio Store across the street. A stroll along Hollywood Boulevard and the side streets lead to a clutch of new bars and lounges that have entertainment. Currently popular are Three Clubs, the Beauty Bar (manicures available) where the edgy people hang, and Rockbar, owned by rockers Tommy Lee and Dave Navarro. Since the Valley is where Hollywood works, you're most likely to spot celebrities along Ventura Boulevard in Studio City from Laurel Canyon to Coldwater Canyon Boulevard, also an avenue where casual walking is best, with beckoning shops, a selection of eateries, and familiar faces. You might spot one going in or out of one of two delis, Jerry's Famous Deli (open 24 hours) or Art's Delicatessen. Fancier places like Pinot Bistro, Marrakesh, and Le Pain Quotidien draw Hollywood types as well. Fans of "The Tonight Show with Jay Leno" will recognize the Universal Studios CityWalk; Jay does stand-ups from the outdoor entertainment and nightlife complex about once a week or so. The complex holds bars, restaurants, movie theaters, and shops, and it's always hopping well into the night.

dining room with its wall of windows. Simpler, more casual preparations of fresh seafood, beef, and lamb reign on the new menu chef Trey Foshee enlivened with seasonal produce from local specialty growers. Give special consideration to imaginatively garnished, citrus-cured yellowtail, succulent garlic-roasted chicken, chickpea-crusted petrale sole, and spice-braised Duroc pork shoulder. For more informal dining and a sweeping view of the coast try the rooftop Ocean Terrace ($–$$). ⊠ *1250 Prospect St., La Jolla* ☎ *858/454–4244* ⚏ *Reservations essential* ☰ *AE, D, DC, MC, V* ☯ *No lunch.*

$$$–$$$$ ✕ **Rainwater's on Kettner.** San Diego's premier homegrown steak house ★ also ranks as the longest running of the pack, not least because it has the luxurious look and mood of an old-fashioned Eastern men's club. The cuisine is excellent: open with the signature black bean soup with Madeira. Continue with the tender, expertly roasted prime rib, superb veal's liver with onions and bacon, broiled free-range chicken, fresh seafood, or the amazingly succulent pork chops, all served in vast portions with plenty of hot-from-the-oven corn sticks on the side. The prime steaks sizzle, as does the bill. The well-chosen wine list has pricey

30

but superior selections. ✉*1202 Kettner Blvd., Downtown* ☎*619/233–5757* ⊟*AE, MC, V* ⊗*No lunch weekends.*

$$$–$$$$ ✕**Tapenade.** Named after the delicious Provençal black olive–and–
Fodor's Choice anchovy paste that accompanies the bread here, Tapenade specializes in
★ the cuisine of the south of France—although that cuisine has lost some of its weight in the trip across the Atlantic. It now matches the unpretentious, light, and airy room, lined with 1960s French movie posters, in which it is served. Fresh ingredients, a delicate touch with sauces, and an emphasis on seafood characterize the menu, which changes frequently. If you're lucky, it may include boar stewed in red wine (possibly the single best entrée in San Diego), lobster in a lobster-corn sauce flavored with Tahitian vanilla, pan-gilded sea scallops, and desserts like chocolate fondant. The two-course "Riviera Menu" served at lunch for $19.95 is a fabulous steal. ✉*7612 Fay Ave., La Jolla* ☎*858/551–7500* ⊟*AE, DC, MC, V* ⊗*No lunch weekends.*

$$–$$$ ✕**Rama.** Gauzy draperies and a rock wall flowing with water create a
Fodor's Choice dreamy rain-forest effect in the back room of this excellent newcomer
★ to the Gaslamp Quarter's booming restaurant row. One of the best Thai restaurants in San Diego, Rama combines professional service with a kitchen that understands the subtle demands of spicing the myriad dishes. The tart, pungent, spiced-to-order (as everything can be) *talay* (seafood soup—it literally means "ocean") pairs well with a crispy duck salad as a light meal for two. Dozens of curries and stir-fries take the taste buds on exciting adventures in flavor. The front dining room is now a private club; as a result, reservations are advised. ✉*327 4th Ave., Gaslamp Quarter* ☎*619/501–8424* ⊟*AE, D, DC, MC, V.*

$–$$ ✕**Hash House A Go Go.** Expect to wait an hour or more for weekend
Fodor's Choice breakfast at this trendy Hillcrest eatery, whose walls display photos of
★ farm machinery and other icons of middle America, but whose menu takes an up-to-the-minute look at national favorites. At breakfast, huge platters carpeted with fluffy pancakes sail out of the kitchen and return empty in a matter of moments, while at noon, customers favor the overflowing chicken potpies crowned with flaky pastry. The parade of old-fashioned good eats continues at dinner with hearty meat and seafood dishes, including the grand sage-flavored fried chicken, bacon-flavored waffles, and hot maple syrup combinations. A Las Vegas developer was so smitten with Hash House that he persuaded them to branch out to his home town. ✉*3628 5th Ave., Hillcrest* ☎*619/298–4646* ⊟*AE, MC, V.*

¢–$$$ ✕**Baja Lobster.** To experience something akin to dining in Puerto Nuevo,
Fodor's Choice Baja California—the famed lobstering village south of the border—
★ head to this excellent but quite informal eatery, easily reached from I–5. Local lobsters are split and lightly fried, served with family-style portions of fresh flour tortillas, creamy beans crammed with flavor, and well-seasoned rice. Although lobsters are the big catch, steak and chicken options are on the menu, too, and there's full bar service. A pair of high-quality shrimp tacos costs just $5.95. Note that a similarly named chain, Rockin' Baja Lobster, is not related to Baja Lobster. ✉*1060 Broadway, Chula Vista* ☎*619/425–2512* ⊟*MC, V.*

WHERE TO STAY

WHAT IT COSTS					
	¢	$	$$	$$$	$$$$
HOTELS	under $75	$75–$124	$125–$199	$200–$325	over $325

Hotel prices are for two people in a standard double room in high season.

LOS ANGELES

$$$$
Fodor'sChoice
★

Hotel Bel-Air. In a wooded canyon with lush gardens and a swan-filled lake, the Hotel Bel-Air's fairy-tale luxury and seclusion have made it a favorite of discreet celebs and royalty for decades. Bungalow-style rooms feel like fine homes, with country-French, expensively upholstered furniture in silk or chenille; many have hardwood floors. Several rooms have wood-burning fireplaces (the bell captain will build a fire for you). Eight suites have private outdoor hot tubs. Complimentary tea service greets you upon arrival; enjoy it on the terrace warmed by heated tiles. A pianist plays nightly in the bar. The hotel's excellent restaurant spills into the garden and a heated, vine-draped terrace. ⊠ *701 Stone Canyon Rd., Bel Air 90077* ☎*310/472–1211 or 800/648–4097* 🖷*310/476–5890* ⊕*www.hotelbelair.com* 🛏*52 rooms, 39 suites* △*In-room: safe, refrigerator, DVD, VCR, Ethernet, Wi-Fi. In-hotel: restaurant, room service, bar, pool, gym, concierge, laundry service, public Internet, public Wi-Fi, parking (no fee), some pets allowed, no-smoking rooms* ⊟*AE, DC, MC, V.*

$$$$
Fodor'sChoice
★

Peninsula Beverly Hills. They seem to think of everything at this French Riviera–style palace. It's a favorite of Hollywood boldface names, but all kinds of visitors consistently describe their stay as near perfect—though very expensive. Rooms overflow with antiques, artwork, and marble; high-tech room amenities are controlled by a bedside panel. Service is exemplary and always discreet. Soak up the sun by the fifth-floor pool with its fully outfitted cabanas or sip afternoon tea in the living room under ornate chandeliers. Belvedere, the hotel's flower-filled restaurant, is a lunchtime favorite for film-business types. A complimentary Rolls Royce is available for short jaunts in Beverly Hills. ⊠*9882 S. Santa Monica Blvd., Beverly Hills 90212* ☎*310/551–2888 or 800/462–7899* 🖷*310/788–2319* ⊕*www.peninsula.com* 🛏*166 rooms, 36 suites, 16 villas* △*In-room: safe, refrigerator, DVD, VCR, Ethernet, Wi-Fi. In-hotel: restaurant, room service, bar, pool, gym, spa, concierge, laundry service, public Wi-Fi, parking (fee), some pets allowed, no-smoking rooms* ⊟*AE, D, DC, MC, V.*

$$$$
Fodor'sChoice
★

Shutters on the Beach. Set right on the sand, this gray-shingle inn has become synonymous with in-town escapism. Guest rooms have those namesake shutter doors, pillow-top mattresses, and white built-in cabinets filled with art books and curios. Bathrooms are luxe, each with a whirlpool tub, a raft of bath goodies, and a three-nozzle, glass-walled shower. While the hotel's service gets mixed reviews from some readers, the beachfront location and show-house decor make this one of SoCal's most popular luxury hotels. ⊠*1 Pico Blvd., Santa Monica 90405* ☎*310/458–0030 or 800/334–9000* 🖷*310/458–4589* ⊕*www.*

30

ON THE WAY

Mount Palomar Observatory. Set atop Palomar Mountain, the observatory houses the 200-inch Hale Telescope, as well as other telescopes used in cutting-edge celestial research. The small museum here holds photos of some of these discoveries, as well as shots taken by NASA's Hubbell Space Telescope and from recent NASA-European Space Agency missions to Mars and Saturn. *Hwy. S6, north off Hwy. 76, east of I–15, Palomar Mountain, 760/742–2119, www.astro.caltech. edu/palomar. Free. Observatory* open for self-guided tours daily, 9–4, except Dec. 24 and 25.

Watts Towers. This complex of 17 sculptural towers, created by Italian immigrant Simon Rodia, is listed on the National Register of Historic Places. Rodia, who lived in the neighborhood, spent 30 years building the towers—some as tall as 100 feet—using castoff materials such as broken glass, sea shells, pottery, and ceramic tiles. *1765 E. 107th St., Los Angeles, CA 90002, 213/847–4646, open Fri.–Sun., admission $7.*

shuttersonthebeach.com ⤴*186 rooms, 12 suites* ⌂ *In-room: safe, refrigerator, DVD, Ethernet, Wi-Fi. In-hotel: 2 restaurants, room service, bar, pool, gym, spa, beachfront, bicycles, concierge, laundry service, public Wi-Fi, parking (fee), no-smoking rooms* ☰*AE, D, DC, MC, V.*

$$$
Fodor'sChoice
★
Millennium Biltmore Hotel. One of downtown L.A.'s true treasures, the gilded 1923 beaux arts masterpiece exudes ambience and history. The lobby (formerly the Music Room) was the local headquarters of JFK's presidential campaign, and the ballroom hosted some of the earliest Academy Awards. These days, the Biltmore hosts business types drawn by its central downtown location, ample meeting spaces, and services such as a well-outfitted business center that stays open 24/7. Some of the guest rooms are small by today's standards, but all have classic, formal furnishings, shuttered windows, and marble bathrooms. Stay on the Club Level for excellent views and complimentary breakfast and evening cocktails. And bring your bathing suit for the vintage tiled indoor pool and adjacent steam room. ✉*506 S. Grand Ave., Downtown, 90071* ☎*213/624–1011 or 800/245–8673* 📠*213/612–1545* ⊕*www.millenniumhotels.com* ⤴*683 rooms, 56 suites* ⌂ *In-room: Ethernet. In-hotel: 3 restaurants, room service, bars, pool, gym, concierge, laundry service, executive floor, public Internet, public Wi-Fi, parking (fee), no-smoking rooms* ☰*AE, D, DC, MC, V.*

$–$$
Fodor'sChoice
★
The Standard, Downtown LA. Built in 1955 as Standard Oil's company's headquarters, the building was completely revamped under the sharp eye of owner André Balazs. The large guest rooms are practical and funky: all have orange built-in couches; windows that actually open; and platform beds. Bathrooms have extra-large tubs. The indoor–outdoor rooftop lounge has a preening social scene and stunning setting, but be prepared for some attitude at the door. Daytime traffic, the nightly bar scene and 24/7-open coffee shop make some rooms noisy. Rudy's barbershop on the ground floor specializes in updated do's. ✉*550*

S. Flower St., Downtown, 90071 ☎*213/892–8080* 🖷*213/892–8686*
⊕*www.standardhotel.com* ⬎*205 rooms, 2 suites* ⎈*In-room: safe,
refrigerator, DVD, Ethernet. In-hotel: restaurant, room service, bars,
pool, gym, concierge, laundry service, parking (fee), some pets allowed,
no-smoking rooms* ☰*AE, D, DC, MC, V.*

ORANGE COUNTY

$$$$
Fodor'sChoice
★
Disney's Grand Californian. The newest of Disney's Anaheim hotels,
this Craftsman-style luxury property has guest rooms with views of the
California Adventure park and Downtown Disney. They don't push the
Disney brand too heavily; rooms are done in dark woods with amber-
shaded lamps and just a small Bambi image on the shower curtain.
Restaurants include the Napa Rose dining room and Storytellers Cafe,
where Disney characters entertain children at breakfast. Of the three
pools, the one shaped like Mickey Mouse is just for kids, plus there's an
evening child activity center and portable cribs in every room. Room-
and-ticket packages are available; the hotel has its own entry gate to
California Adventure. The new Mandara spa has a couple's suite with
Balinese-inspired art and textiles. ⊠*1600 S. Disneyland Dr., Disneyland Resort, 92803* ☎*714/956–6425* 🖷*714/300–7701* ⊕*www.
disneyland.com* ⬎*701 rooms, 44 suites* ⎈*In-room: safe, refrigerator,
Ethernet. In-hotel: 2 restaurants, room service, bars, pools, gym, concierge, children's programs (ages 5–12), laundry service, parking (fee),
no-smoking rooms* ☰*AE, D, DC, MC, V.*

SAN DIEGO

$$$$
Fodor'sChoice
★
U.S. Grant. Stepping into the regal U.S. Grant not only puts you in
the lap of luxury, but also back in San Diego history; the 98-year-old
building is on the National Register of Historic Sites. A 2006 remodel
reintroduced the hotel's original grandeur and opulence. The lobby is
a confection of luxurious French fabrics, crystal chandeliers, and Italian Carrara–marble floors. Guests sip tea and martinis here Thursday
through Sunday afternoons. The rooms feature custom Italian linens,
opera lighting, and original French and Native American artwork, and
the sunny baths are elegantly designed with marble tile shower enclosures and stone sinks. The Grant Grill restaurant reopened in January
2007, boasting a fusion of grilled specialties and fresh regional cuisine.
The venue's 1940s-style New York decor has a glamorous appeal with
African mahogany walls and plush seating. ⊠*326 Broadway, Downtown 92101* ☎*866/837–4270 or 800/237–5029* 🖷*619/239–9517*
⊕*www.usgrant.net* ⬎*270 rooms, 47 suites* ⎈*In-room: safe, Ethernet, Wi-Fi. In-hotel: restaurant, room service, bar, gym, laundry service, concierge, public Wi-Fi, airport shuttle, parking (fee), no-smoking
rooms* ☰*AE, D, DC, MC, V.*

$$$$
Fodor'sChoice
★
Westgate Hotel. A nondescript, modern high-rise near Horton Plaza
hides what must be the most opulent hotel in San Diego. The lobby,
modeled after the anteroom at Versailles, has hand-cut Baccarat chandeliers. Rooms are individually furnished with antiques, Italian marble
counters, and bath fixtures with 24-karat-gold overlays. From the ninth
floor up the views of the harbor and city are breathtaking. Afternoon
tea is served in the lobby to the accompaniment of piano and harp

30

music. The San Diego Trolley stops right outside the door. ✉*1055 2nd Ave., Gaslamp Quarter 92101* ☎*619/238–1818, 800/221–3802, 800/522–1564 in CA* 🖷*619/557–3737* ⊕*www.westgatehotel.com* ↩*223 rooms* ⌂*In-room: dial-up. In-hotel: 2 restaurants, room service, bar, gym, spa, bicycles, concierge, airport shuttle, parking (fee), no-smoking rooms* ▭*AE, D, DC, MC, V.*

$$$–$$$$
Fodor's Choice
★
🖵**Hotel Del Coronado.** The Victorian-styled "Hotel Del," along 28 oceanfront acres, is as much of a draw today as it was when it opened in 1888. The resort is always alive with activity, as guests—including U.S. presidents, European royalty, and celebrities—and tourists marvel at the fanciful architecture, surrounding sparkling sand, and gorgeous ocean views. About half of the resort's accommodations are in the more charming, original Victorian building, where each room is unique in size and footprint. Rooms in the California Cabana buildings and Ocean Towers, built in the mid-1970s, have just completed a Williams-Sonoma–style makeover with new bathrooms and more contemporary furnishings. These setups are closer to the pool and the beach, making them a good option for families with children. In 2007 the property added several luxury enhancements, including a new spa with an infinity pool and Beach Village: 78 lavish beachfront villas and cottages that feature fully equipped kitchens, fireplaces, spa-style baths with soaking tubs, Bose sound systems, and private ocean-view terraces. A new signature restaurant, 1500 Ocean, serves southern coastal cuisine in an elegant beachfront cabana setting. ✉*1500 Orange Ave., Coronado 92118* ☎*800/468–3533 or 619/435–6611* 🖷*619/522–8262* ⊕*www.hoteldel.com* ↩*757 rooms, 65 suites, 43 villas, 35 cottages* ⌂*In-room: safe, refrigerator (some), Ethernet. In-hotel: 6 restaurants, room service, bars, pools, gym, spa, beachfront, water sports, bicycles, children's programs (ages 4–12), laundry service, concierge, airport shuttle, parking (fee), no-smoking rooms* ▭*AE, D, DC, MC, V.*

$$$
Fodor's Choice
★
🖵**La Valencia.** This pink Spanish-Mediterranean confection drew Hollywood film stars in the 1930s and '40s with its setting and views of La Jolla Cove. Many rooms, although small, have a genteel European look, with antique pieces and richly colored rugs. The personal attention provided by the staff, as well as the plush robes and grand bathrooms, make the stay even more pleasurable. The hotel is right in the middle of the shops and restaurants of La Jolla village. Rates are lower if you're willing to look out on the village rather than the ocean. Be sure to stroll the tiered gardens in back. ✉*1132 Prospect St., La Jolla 92037* ☎*858/454–0771 or 800/451–0772* 🖷*858/456–3921* ⊕*www. lavalencia.com* ↩*91 rooms, 9 suites, 15 villas* ⌂*In-room: safe, DVD. In-hotel: 3 restaurants, room service, bar, pool, gym, beachfront, bicycles, laundry service, concierge, parking (fee), no-smoking rooms* ▭*AE, D, MC, V.*

NIGHTLIFE & THE ARTS

LOS ANGELES

Hollywood and West Hollywood, where hip and happening nightspots liberally dot Sunset and Hollywood boulevards, are the epicenter of L.A. nightlife. While the ultimate in velvet-roped vampiness and glamour used to be the Sunset Strip, in the past couple of years the glitz has definitely shifted to Hollywood Boulevard and its surrounding streets. West Hollywood's Santa Monica Boulevard bustles with gay and lesbian bars and clubs. For less conspicuous—and congested—alternatives, check out the events in downtown L.A.'s performance spaces and galleries. Silver Lake and Echo Park are best for boho bars and live music clubs.

> **JOIN THE STUDIO AUDIENCE**
>
> **Audiences Unlimited** (⊠ *100 Universal City Plaza, Bldg. 153, Universal City 91608* ☎ *818/506-0043* ⊕ *www.tvtickets.com*) helps fill seats for television programs (and sometimes for televised award shows). The free tickets are distributed on a first-come, first-served basis. Shows that may be taping or filming include *King of Queens*. Note: you must be 16 or older to attend a television taping.

For a thorough listing of local events, www.la.com and *Los Angeles Magazine* are both good sources. The Calendar section of the *Los Angeles Times* (⊕ *www.calendarlive.com*) also lists a wide survey of Los Angeles arts events, especially on Thursday and Sunday, as do the more alternative publications, *LA Weekly* and *Citybeat Los Angeles* (both free, and issued every Thursday). Call ahead to confirm that what you want to see is ongoing.

SAN DIEGO

The Gaslamp, along with neighboring downtown and the emerging East Village (where the baseball stadium opened in 2004), is where you can find the most popular—and expensive—bars and clubs, many of them cultivating a see-and-be-seen vibe. The beach areas offer a more casual atmosphere. The dance clubs and bars of Pacific Beach and Mission Beach appeal to a casually dressed, college-age crowd. The Uptown district around Hillcrest is the heart of San Diego's gay nightlife and home to a few coffeehouses where conversation is the entertainment.

Check the *Reader,* San Diego's free alternative newsweekly (it comes out every Thursday), for the lowdown on nightlife. *San Diego CityBeat* is another free paper that has a great nightlife section. And be sure to consult *San Diego* magazine's "Restaurant & Nightlife Guide" for further ideas. Also, the *San Diego-Union Tribune* publishes a weekly (Thursday) entertainment insert, *Night and Day.*

SPORTS & THE OUTDOORS

LOS ANGELES

Los Angeles County beaches (and state beaches operated by the county) have lifeguards on duty year-round, with expanded forces during the summer. Public parking is usually available, though fees can be as

30

much as $8; in some areas, it's possible to find free street and highway parking. Both restrooms and beach access have been brought up to the standards of the Americans with Disabilities Act. Generally, the northernmost beaches are best for surfing, hiking, and fishing, and the wider and sandier southern beaches are better for tanning and relaxing. ■TIP➡Almost all are great for swimming, but beware: pollution in Santa Monica Bay sometimes approaches dangerous levels, particularly after storms. Call ahead for **beach conditions** (☎310/457–9701) or go to www.watchthewater.com for specific beach updates.

Fodor'sChoice **Robert H. Meyer Memorial State Beach.** Part of Malibu's most beautiful
★ coastal area, this beach is made up of three minibeaches: El Pescador, La Piedra, and El Matador—all with the same spectacular view. Scramble down the steps to the rocky coves where nude sunbathers sometimes gather—although in recent years, police have been cracking down. "El Mat" has a series of caves, Piedra some nifty rock formations, and Pescador a secluded feel; but they're all picturesque and fairly private. ■TIP➡One warning: watch the incoming tide and don't get trapped between those otherwise scenic boulders. ⊠32350, 32700, and 32900 PCH, Malibu ☎818/880–0350 ☞Parking, 1 roving lifeguard unit, restrooms.

★ **Santa Monica State Beach.** It's the first beach you'll hit after the Santa Monica Freeway (I–10) runs into the PCH, and it's one of L.A.'s best known. Wide and sandy, Santa Monica is *the* place for sunning and socializing: be prepared for a mob scene on summer weekends, when parking becomes an expensive ordeal. Swimming is fine (with the usual poststorm pollution caveat); for surfing, go elsewhere. For a memorable view, climb up the stairway over the PCH to Palisades Park, at the top of the bluffs. Summer-evening concerts are often held here. ⊠1642 Promenade, PCH at California Incline, Santa Monica ☎310/305–9503 ☞Parking, lifeguard (year-round), restrooms, showers.

Venice City Beach. The surf and sand of Venice are fine, but the main attraction here is the boardwalk scene, which is a cosmos all its own—with fire-eating street performers, vendors hawking everything from cheap sunglasses and aromatherapy oils, and bicep'ed gym rats lifting weights at legendary Muscle Beach. Go on Saturday or Sunday afternoon for the best people-watching experience. There are also swimming, fishing, surfing, basketball (it's the site of some of L.A.'s most hotly contested pickup games), racquetball, handball, and shuffleboard. You can rent a bike or some in-line skates and hit the Strand bike path. ⊠West of Pacific Ave., Venice ☎310/577–5700 ☞Parking, restrooms, food concessions, showers, playground.

★ **Redondo Beach.** The Redondo Beach Pier marks the starting point of this wide, sandy, busy beach along a heavily developed shoreline community. Restaurants and shops flourish along the pier, excursion boats and privately owned crafts depart from launching ramps, and a reef formed by a sunken ship creates prime fishing and snorkeling conditions. If you're adventurous, you might try to kayak out to the buoys and hobnob with pelicans and sea lions. A series of free rock and jazz concerts takes place at the pier every summer. ⊠ *Torrance Blvd. at Catalina Ave., Redondo Beach* ☎ *310/372–2166* ☞ *Parking, lifeguard (year-round), restrooms, food concessions, showers.*

SAN DIEGO

Water temperatures are generally chilly, ranging from 55°F to 65°F from October through June, and 65°F to 75°F from July through September. For a surf and weather report, call 619/221–8824. For a general beach and weather report, call 619/289–1212. Pollution, which has long been a problem near the Mexican border, is inching north and is generally worse near river mouths and storm drain outlets. The weather page of the *San Diego Union-Tribune* includes pollution reports along with listings of surfing and diving conditions.

Lifeguards are stationed at city beaches from Sunset Cliffs up to Black's Beach in the summertime, but coverage in winter is provided by roving patrols only. Pay attention to signs listing illegal activities; undercover police often patrol the beaches, carrying their ticket books in coolers. Glass containers are prohibited on all San Diego beaches if their purpose is to carry drinks, and fires are allowed only in fire rings or elevated barbecue grills. Alcoholic beverages—including beer—are completely banned on some city beaches; on others you are allowed to partake from noon to 8 PM. Imbibing in beach parking lots, on boardwalks, and in landscaped areas is always illegal. Although it may be tempting to take a starfish or some other sea creature as a souvenir from a tide pool, it upsets the delicate ecological balance and is illegal, too.

★ **Coronado Beach.** With the famous Hotel Del Coronado as a backdrop, this stretch of sandy beach is one of San Diego County's largest and most picturesque. Parking can be difficult on the busiest days. There are plenty of restrooms and service facilities, as well as fire rings. *From the bridge, turn left on Orange Ave. and follow signs, Coronado.*

★ **Mission Beach.** San Diego's most popular beach draws huge crowds on hot summer days. The 2-mi-long stretch extends from the north entrance of Mission Bay to Pacific Beach. A wide boardwalk paralleling the beach is popular with walkers, joggers, roller skaters, bladers, and bicyclists. Toward its north end, near the Belmont Park roller coaster, the beach narrows and the water becomes rougher; the crowds grow thicker and somewhat rougher as well. For parking, your best bets are the two big lots at Belmont Park. ⊠ *Exit I–5 at Grand Ave. and head*

30

west to Mission Blvd. Turn south and look for parking near roller coaster at West Mission Bay Dr., Mission Beach.

Fodor'sChoice **La Jolla Cove.** This is one of the prettiest spots on the West Coast. A
★ palm-lined park sits on top of cliffs formed by the incessant pounding of the waves. At low tide the tide pools and cliff caves provide a destination for explorers. Divers, snorkelers, and kayakers can explore the underwater delights of the San Diego–La Jolla Underwater Park Ecological Reserve. The cove is also a favorite of rough-water swimmers. ⊠*Follow Coast Blvd. north to signs, or take La Jolla Village Dr. Exit from I–5, head west to Torrey Pines Rd., turn left, and drive downhill to Girard Ave. Turn right and follow signs, La Jolla.*

★ **La Jolla Shores.** On summer holidays all access routes are usually closed,
☾ so get here early—this is one of San Diego's most popular beaches. The lures are an incredible view of La Jolla peninsula, a wide sandy beach, an adjoining grassy park, and the most gentle waves in San Diego. In fact, several surf schools teach here and kayak rentals are nearby. A concrete boardwalk parallels the beach. Arrive early to get a parking spot in the lot at the foot of Calle Frescota. ⊠*From I–5 take La Jolla Village Dr. west and turn left onto La Jolla Shores Dr. Head west to Camino del Oro or Vallecitos St. Turn right, La Jolla.*

VISITOR INFORMATION

Anaheim-Orange County Visitor and Convention Bureau (⊠*Anaheim Convention Center, 800 W. Katella Ave., Anaheim, 92802*☏*714/765-8888* ⊕*www.anaheimoc.org*).

California Office of Tourism (☏*916/444-4429 or 800/862-2543* ⊕*gocalif.ca.gov*).

L.A. Inc./The Convention and Visitors Bureau (☏*213/624-7300 or 800/228-2452* ⊕*www.lacvb.com*).

San Diego Convention & Visitors Bureau (☏*619/232-3101* ⊕*www.sandiego.org*).

San Diego Convention & Visitors Bureau International Visitor Information Center (☏*619/236-1212* ⊕*www.sandiego.org*).

San Diego Visitor Information Center (☏*619/276-8200 for recorded information* ⊕*www.infosandiego.com*).

Yosemite National Park

WITH SEQUOIA & KINGS CANYON NATIONAL PARKS

Half Dome, Yosemite National Park

WORD OF MOUTH

Take the hiker's bus to Glacier Point and walk back down the Panorama Trail. If you want a longer hike, you can hike up the John Muir Trail to Glacier Point and back down the Panorama Trail. Fantastic views all the way down.

—maj

EXPLORING YOSEMITE

Yosemite is 214 mi east of San Francisco via I–80, I–580, I–205, and Hwy. 120; 330 mi northeast of Los Angeles via I–5, Hwy. 99, and Hwy. 41

By Constance Jones and Reed Parsell

You can lose your perspective in Yosemite National Park. This is a land where everything is big. Really big. There are big rocks, big trees, and big waterfalls. The park has been so extravagantly praised and so beautifully photographed that some people wonder if the reality can possibly measure up. For almost everyone, it does. Here, you can remember what breathtaking really means. With 1,189 square mi of parkland—94.5% of it undeveloped wilderness accessible only to the backpacker and horseback rider—Yosemite is a nature lover's wonderland. Wander through this world of wind-warped trees, scurrying animals, and bighorn sheep, and you'll come away with a distinct sense of peace and solitude.

Not far from Yosemite are the silent giants of Kings Canyon and Sequoia national parks. Surrounded by vast granite canyons and towering snowcapped peaks, they strike awe in everyone who sees them. No less than famed naturalist John Muir proclaimed the sequoia tree "the most beautiful and majestic on Earth." The two parks share a boundary and are administered together. They encompass 1,353 square mi, with topography that ranges from the western foothills at an elevation of 1,500 feet to the towering peaks of the Great Western Divide and the Sierra Crest. The Kings River cuts a swath through the backcountry and over the years has formed a granite canyon that, in places, towers nearly 4,000 feet above the canyon floor. Mt. Whitney, at 14,494 feet the highest peak in the contiguous United States, is the crown jewel of the eastern side.

WHO WILL ESPECIALLY LOVE THIS TRIP?

Photographers: Ansel Adams, the 20th-century's greatest visual chronicler of the American West, cut his photographic teeth as a teenager in Yosemite. As a young man his congressional testimony helped establish Kings Canyon and Sequoia as national parks. The natural wonders Adams had to work with—towering trees, stunning monoliths, and cascading waterfalls—remain much as they were in his day—although keeping people and automobiles out of your field of focus is more challenging than it was back then.

Hikers & backpackers: Strolling in Yosemite Valley is a visually stunning if physically tame exercise. If you want to really work up a sweat, try trekking up and down some nearby trails like Bridalveil Fall, steeper Vernal Fall, and challenging Half Dome. Backpacking through Tuolumne Meadows brings wildflowers and, most likely, wildlife into closer view. In Sequoia National Park, the 350-step stairway up Moro Rock is on the National Register of Historic Places; it spills out onto a ledge with a spectacular, 360-degree view.

TOP 5 REASONS TO GO

Yosemite Valley: In the southern third of the park, east of the High Sierra, beats Yosemite's heart. This is where you can find the park's most famous sights and biggest crowds.

Glacier Point: Take in the entire Yosemite Valley with one glance; it's about 16 hilly, twisting miles east of Wawona Road (Route 41).

Wawona & Mariposa Grove: Yosemite's southeastern tip holds Wawona, with its grand old hotel and pioneer history center, and the Mariposa Grove of Big Trees, filled with giant sequoias.

Giant Forest-Lodgepole Village: The most heavily visited area of Sequoia National Park contains major sights such as Giant Forest, General Sherman Tree, Crystal Cave, and Moro Rock.

A grander-than-Grand Canyon: Drive the twisting Kings Canyon Scenic Byway down into the jagged, granite Kings River Canyon—deeper in parts than the Grand Canyon.

Lodge Enthusiasts: The Ahwahnee Hotel & Dining Room in Yosemite Valley dates from the 1920s and sets the standard for luxury accommodations in the region. The Wawona Hotel & Dining Room is four decades older and less majestic, but charms visitors with whitewashed buildings and like the Ahwahnee is listed as a National Historic Landmark. South of Yosemite the Tenaya Lodge is disconcertingly modern in appearance but offers total comfort for its overnighters; the Wuksachi Village Lodge has spectacular views and Sequoia's only upscale restaurant.

WHEN IS THE BEST TIME TO VISIT?

The best times to visit Yosemite are from mid-April through Memorial Day and from mid-September through October, when the park is only moderately busy and the days usually are sunny. During the extremely busy summer season—especially July 4 weekend—you may experience delays at the entrance gates that approach an hour. If you can only make it here in the warmest months, try to visit midweek. In winter heavy snows occasionally cause road closures, and tire chains or four-wheel drive may be required on the roads that remain open.

Kings Canyon and Sequoia are at their best in the early fall, when temperatures are moderate and crowds are thin, and when the Kings Canyon Scenic Byway and road to Mineral King are still open. Summertime can draw hoards of tourists to see the giant sequoias, and the few, narrow roads mean congestion at peak holiday times. By contrast, in wintertime you may feel as though you have the parks all to yourself—but many attractions are not accessible without snowshoes and an enormous amount of determination and time.

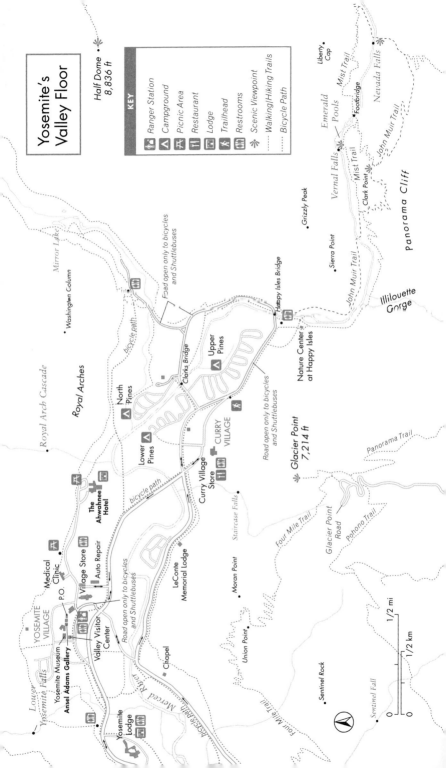

Yosemite's Valley Floor

KEY

🛖 Ranger Station
⛺ Campground
🏕 Picnic Area
🍴 Restaurant
🏠 Lodge
🥾 Trailhead
🚻 Restrooms
✳ Scenic Viewpoint
‑ ‑ ‑ Walking/Hiking Trails
······ Bicycle Path

Half Dome •
8,836 ft

Liberty •
Cap
Nevada Falls ✳
Mist Trail
Footbridge
John Muir Trail
Emerald
Pools
Vernal Falls ✳
Mist Trail
Clark Point
John Muir Trail
Panorama Cliff
Grizzly Peak •
Sierra Point •
John Muir Trail
Illilouette
Gorge

Mirror Lake
Washington Column •
bicycle path
Royal Arch Cascade
Royal Arches
Road open only to bicycles and Shuttlebuses
Clarks Bridge
North Pines ⛺
Upper Pines ⛺
Lower Pines ⛺
Happy Isles Bridge
Nature Center at Happy Isles 🛖
Road open only to bicycles and Shuttlebuses
CURRY VILLAGE
Curry Village Store 🍴🚻
🥾
Glacier Point ✳
7,214 ft

The Ahwahnee Hotel 🏕🚻
bicycle path
LeConte Memorial Lodge
Staircase Falls
Moran Point •
Panorama Trail
Glacier Point Road
Four Mile Trail
Pohono Trail

Medical Clinic 🏕
Village Store 🚻
Auto Repair
P.O.
YOSEMITE VILLAGE
Yosemite Museum
Ansel Adams Gallery
Valley Visitor Center
Lower Yosemite Falls
Yosemite Falls
Yosemite Lodge 🏠🚻
Road open only to bicycles and Shuttlebuses
Bicycle Path
Merced River
Chapel
Union Point •
Sentinel Rock •
Four Mile Trail
Sentinel Fall

0   1/2 km
0   1/2 mi

CLOSE UP

How to Snack

31

In Yosemite National Park, ready-made picnic lunches are available at Ahwahnee and Wawona with advance notice. Otherwise you can stop at the Food Court at Yosemite Lodge for a prepackaged salad or sandwich, or at grocery stores in the village to pick up supplies. There are 13 designated picnic areas around the park; restrooms and grills or fire grates are available only at those in the valley. Primo picnic places include Cathedral Beach, underneath spirelike Cathedral Rocks; Church Bowl, behind the Ahwahnee Hotel; the El Capitan picnic area; Sentinel Beach, alongside a running creek; and Yellow Pine, named for the towering trees that cluster on the banks of the Merced River.

In Sequoia National Park, Crescent Meadow is an area near Moro Rock at which the tables are under giant sequoias. Drinking water and restrooms are available, as they also are at Foothills Picnic Area near the south entrance. Near the Route 180 entrance to Kings Canyon National Park, Big Stump is the only picnic area whose road is plowed in the wintertime. Good summertime spots are at Columbine, near Grant Grove Visitor Center; and Grizzly Falls, a few miles west of the Cedar Grove entrance. To save money, purchase your picnic supplies in Fresno, Merced, or one of the smaller towns close to the parks' borders.

HOW SHOULD I GET THERE?

DRIVING

To get to Yosemite from the major California cities, work your way north or south, then over to Highway 99. Take Route 120 east to the Big Oak Flat entrance, or west to the Tioga Pass entrance (summer to late fall only); Route 140 east to the Arch Rock entrance; or Route 41 to the south entrance. From Reno or Las Vegas, you can reach Yosemite during the nonwinter months from Highway 395, one of the country's most underrated scenic roadways. Kings Canyon National Park is 53 mi east of Fresno on Route 180, and Sequoia National Park is 36 mi east of Visalia on Route 198—neither park can be driven to from the east.

FLYING

Fresno Yosemite International Airport is also the nearest airport to Kings Canyon and Sequoia national parks. Alaska, Allegiant, American, America West, Continental, Delta, Frontier, Hawaiian, Horizon, Mexicana, Northwest, United Express, and US Airways fly there. Reno-Tahoe and Sacramento international airports are several hours' drives from Yosemite, Sequoia, and Kings Canyon, but are served by many airlines; Mammoth-Yosemite Airport, just west of its namesake national park, primarily welcomes charter flights.

TAKING THE TRAIN OR BUS

Amtrak offers train and bus service from the Bay Area and Sacramento. Greyhound is another option (though somewhat less plush).

VIA Adventures operates five daily buses from Merced to Yosemite Valley; the trip is about 2½ hours and costs roughly $20 round-trip.

The Yosemite Area Regional Transportation System (YARTS) connects with Amtrak and Greyhound routes in Merced.

HOW DO I GET AROUND?

BY CAR

Unless you have super-strong legs and a fearless personality, bicycling will not get you far in these expansive, mountainous parks. The only legitimate transportation options are an automobile, RV, or motorcycle—except within Yosemite Valley, which is serviced by a free year-round shuttle-bus service.

WHERE SHOULD I FOCUS MY ENERGY?

If you're here for 1 day: Spend the day exploring Yosemite Valley, including a refreshing jaunt up to Vernal Fall.

If you're here for 2 days: Drive out to Glacier Point, for a bird's-eye view of the valley. Use binoculars to check out the brave Half Dome hikers. If you have time, squeeze in a drink at the Wawona Hotel and a scamper through Mariposa Grove of Big Trees.

If you're here for 3 days: Do all of the above, and spend more time appreciating the valley's main attractions, including Yosemite Village, Ansel Adams Gallery, and the re-created Ahwahneechee Village. Also add a stroll down the Bridalveil Fall trail.

If you're here for 4 days: Take a long—but wondrous—drive up the Generals Highway, through Kings Canyon and Sequoia national parks.

If you're here for 5 days: While you're in Sequoia and Kings Canyon, head to Mineral King and drive along the Kings Canyon Scenic Byway (both only open in summer).

If you're here for 6 days: Check out Tuolumne Meadows in east-central Yosemite, with its myriad hiking and backpacking possibilities.

If you're here for 7 days or more: Spend some more time exploring some of the parks' less-visited attractions, like Hetch Hetchy in Yosemite and Cedar Grove in Kings Canyon.

WHAT ARE THE TOP EXPERIENCES?

Enjoying the View: Some of Yosemite's signature attractions are distinctive domed mountains, including El Capitan, the largest exposed-granite monolith in the world; Half Dome, which rises to 8,842 feet; Glacier Point, which looms 3,214 feet above the valley; and Sentinel Dome, whose views are similar to those at Glacier Point. The park also has a host of spectacular waterfalls, including Vernal Fall (317 feet), Nevada Fall (594 feet), Bridalveil Fall (620 feet), Ribbon Fall (1,612 feet), and Yosemite Falls, at 2,425 feet—the highest waterfall in North America and the fifth-highest in the world. May is the best month to see waterfalls at their fullest.

Tree Huggin': Pop on your wide-angle lens and get ready to crane your neck a lot in Mariposa Grove of Big Trees, Yosemite's largest grove of giant sequoias. The Grizzly Giant, the oldest tree there, is estimated to be 2,700 years old. For the maximum big-tree experience, take the Generals Highway to the Wolverton Road turnoff to reach Sequoia National Park's General Sherman Tree, the world's largest living tree, estimated to be 2,100 years old. Nearby, the Giant Forest Museum has outstanding exhibits on the ecology of the giant sequoia. Grant Grove, also in Sequoia, contains the General Grant Tree, the world's third-largest, which is also known as the nation's Christmas tree. King Canyon's Redwood Mountain Grove, accessible only by foot or horseback, is the largest grove of giant sequoias in the world.

CLAIM TO FAME
When someone asks you, "What's the big deal about Kings Canyon and Sequoia national parks," you can simply reply, "just the largest living things on the planet." The park's *Sequoiadendron giganteum* trees are not as tall as the coastal redwoods (*Sequoia sempervirens*), but they're more massive and, on average, older. Exhibits at the visitor centers explain why these trees can live so long and grow so big, as well as the special relationship between these trees and fire (their thick, fibrous bark helps protect them from flames and insects, and their seeds can't germinate until they first explode out of a burning pinecone).

Lodge Hopping: It may be hard to believe, but some of Yosemite's top attractions are man-made. The Ahwahnee Hotel, a stately lodge of granite and concrete beams, perfectly complements Yosemite Valley's natural majesty. Take time to visit the immense parlors with walk-in hearths and priceless, antique Native American rugs and baskets. The park's first lodge, the Wawona Hotel, is a fine example of Victorian resort architecture—a blend of rusticity and elegance. It's an excellent place to stay or to stop for lunch. When you're done, visit the Ansel Adams Gallery, where you can find original and reproduction prints by the bearded master. Or visit the Ahwahneechee Village, a re-creation of a Native American village as it might have appeared in 1872; markers explain the lifestyle of Yosemite's first residents.

Taking Scenic Drives: Route 41 provides great views and stopover points en route to Yosemite Valley. Along the way heading north, you'll encounter a turnoff to Mariposa Grove of Big Trees, the Wawona Hotel, a turnoff for Glacier Point, and a tunnel that has a jaw-dropping view of the valley on its opposite end. Also in Yosemite, Tioga Road is a summer-only, high-country blacktop that will reward you with gorgeous alpine scenery, including crystal-blue lakes, grassy meadows dotted with wildflowers, and high-alpine peaks. The Kings Canyon Scenic Byway winds along the powerful Kings River, below towering granite cliffs and past two tumbling waterfalls in the Kings River Canyon. Generals Highway, which connects the two southern national parks, is a narrow, twisting road that runs past the region's major attractions, including Lost Grove, the General Sherman Tree, and the Giant Forest Museum.

HISTORY YOU CAN SEE

The Miwok, the last of several Native American peoples to inhabit the Yosemite area (they were forced out by gold miners in 1851), named the Yosemite Valley *Ahwahnee*, which is thought to mean "the place of the gaping mouth." Abraham Lincoln established Yosemite Valley and the Mariposa Grove of Giant Sequoias as public land in 1864, when he deeded the land to the state of California. This grant was the first of its kind in America, and it laid the foundation for the establishment of national and state parks. The high country above the valley, however, was not protected. John Muir, concerned about the destructive effects of over-grazing on subalpine meadows, rallied together a team of dedicated supporters and lobbied for expanded protection of lands surrounding Yosemite Valley. As a result of their efforts, Yosemite National Park was established by Congress on October 1, 1890.

BEST BETS

SIGHTS AND TOURS

YOSEMITE NATIONAL PARK

Ansel Adams Gallery. This shop displays and sells original and repro-duction prints by the master Yosemite photographer, as well as work by other landscape photographers. Its elegant camera shop conducts photography workshops and sometimes holds private showings of fine prints on Saturdays. ⊠ *Northside Dr., Yosemite Village* ☎ *209/372–4413 or 888/361–7622* ⊕ *www.anseladams.com* 🖃 *Free* ☉ *Apr.–Oct., daily 9–6; Nov.–Mar., daily 9–5.*

★ **Ansel Adams Photo Walks.** Photography enthusiasts shouldn't miss these two-hour guided camera walks offered by professional photographers. Some walks are hosted by the Ansel Adams Gallery, others by Delaware North Corporation; meeting points vary. All are free, but participation is limited—call up to 10 days in advance or visit the gallery. In-depth information about the walks can be found at www.anseladams.com. ☎ *209/372–4413 or 800/568–7398* ⊕ *www.yosemitepark.com* 🖃 *Free* ⚠ *Reservations essential.*

Fodor'sChoice **Ahwahnee Hotel.** Built in 1927, this stately lodge of granite-and-concrete
★ beams stained to look like redwood is a perfect man-made comple-ment to Yosemite's natural majesty. Even if you aren't a guest, take time to visit the immense parlors with walk-in hearths and priceless, antique Native American rugs and baskets. The dining room, its high ceiling interlaced with massive sugar-pine beams, is extraordinary. Din-ner is formal; breakfast and lunch are more casual. ⊠ *Ahwahnee Rd., about ¾ mi east of Yosemite Valley Visitor Center, Yosemite Village* ☎ *209/372–1489.*

31

Ahwahneechee Village. Tucked behind the Valley Visitor Center, a short loop trail of about 100 yards circles through a re-creation of an Ahwahneechee Native American village as it might have appeared in 1872, 21 years after the Native Americans' first contact with Europeans. Markers explain the lifestyle of Yosemite's first residents. Allow 30 minutes to see it all. ⊠ *Northside Dr., Yosemite Village* 🖾 *Free* ⊙ *Daily dawn–dusk.*

Fodor'sChoice **El Capitan.** Rising 3,593 feet—more than 350 stories—above the Val-
★ ley, El Capitan is the largest exposed-granite monolith in the world. It's almost twice the height of the Rock of Gibraltar. Look for climbers scaling the vertical face. ⊠ *Off Northside Dr., about 4 mi west of Valley Visitor Center*

Fodor'sChoice **Glacier Point.** A Yosemite hot spot for its sweeping, bird's-eye views,
★ Glacier Point looms 3,214 feet above the valley. From the parking area, walk a few hundred yards and you can see waterfalls, Half Dome, and other mountain peaks. It's a tremendous place to watch the sun set. Glacier Point is also a popular hiking destination. You can make the strenuous hike up, or take a bus ($15) to the top and hike down. The bus runs June through October, weather permitting; call 209/372–1240 for schedules. ⊠ *Glacier Point Rd., 16 mi northeast of Rte. 41.*

Fodor'sChoice **Half Dome.** Though you may have seen it on countless postcards and
★ calendars, it's still arresting to see Half Dome, the Valley's most recognizable formation, which tops out at an elevation of 8,842 feet. The afternoon sun lights its face with orange and yellow shades that are reflected in the Merced River; stand on the Sentinel Bridge at sunset for the best view.

Hetch Hetchy Reservoir. The Hetch Hetchy Reservoir, which supplies water and hydroelectric power to San Francisco, is about 40 mi from Yosemite Valley. Some say John Muir died of heartbreak when this grand valley was dammed and flooded beneath 300 feet of water in 1913. Almost from the start, environmental groups such as the Sierra Club have lobbied the government to drain the reservoir; in 2006 the State of California issued a report stating that restoration of the valley is feasible. ⊠ *Hetch Hetchy Rd., about 15 mi north of Big Oak Flat entrance station.*

Fodor'sChoice **Mariposa Grove of Big Trees.** Mariposa is Yosemite's largest grove of giant
★ sequoias. The Grizzly Giant, the oldest tree here, is estimated to be 2,700 years old. You can visit the trees on foot or, in summer, on a one-hour tram tour. If the road to the grove is closed in summer—which happens when Yosemite is crowded—park in Wawona and take the free shuttle (9 AM to 4:30 PM) to the parking lot. The access road to the grove may also be closed by snow for extended periods from November to mid-May; you can still usually walk, snowshoe, or ski in. ⊠ *Rte. 41, 2 mi north of South entrance station.*

★ **Tuolumne Meadows.** The largest subalpine meadow in the Sierra, at 8,600 feet, is a popular way station for backpack trips along the Sierra-scribing Pacific Crest and John Muir trails. No wonder: the cracklingly clear air

BEARS

The Sierra Nevada is home to thousands of bears, and you should take all necessary precautions to keep yourself—and the bears—safe. Bears that acquire a taste for human food can become very aggressive and destructive and often must be destroyed by rangers. The national parks' campgrounds and some campgrounds outside the parks provide food-storage boxes that can keep bears from pilfering your edibles (portable canisters for backpackers can be rented in most park stores). It's imperative that you move all food, coolers, and items with a scent (including toiletries, toothpaste, chewing gum, and air fresheners) from your car (including the trunk) to the storage box at your campsite; day-trippers should lock food in bear boxes provided at parking lots. If you don't, a bear may break into your car by literally peeling off the door or ripping open the trunk, or it may ransack your tent. The familiar tactic of hanging your food from high tree limbs is not an effective deterrent, as bears can easily scale trees. In the Southern Sierra, bear canisters are the only effective and proven method for preventing bears from getting human food.

and dramatic sky above the river-scored valley can make even the most jaded heart soar. The colorful wildflowers peak in mid-July and August. Tioga Road provides easy access to the high country, but the highway closes when snow starts to fall, usually in mid-October. ⊠ *Tioga Rd., Rte. 120, about 8 mi west of Tioga Pass entrance station.*

★ **Wawona Hotel.** In the southern tip of Yosemite, the park's first lodge was built in 1879. With a whitewashed exterior and wraparound verandas, this National Historic Landmark is a fine example of Victorian resort architecture—a blend of rusticity and elegance. The Wawona is an excellent place to stay or to stop for lunch when making the drive from the South entrance to the Valley, but be aware that the hotel is closed in January. ⊠ *Rte. 41, Wawona* ☎ *209/375–1425.*

WATERFALLS When the snow starts to melt (usually peaking in May), almost every rocky lip or narrow gorge becomes a spillway for streaming snowmelt churning down to meet the Merced River. But even in drier months, the waterfalls can be breathtaking. If you choose to hike any of the trails to or up the falls, be sure to wear shoes with good, no-slip soles; the rocks can be extremely slick. Stay on trails at all times.

Bridalveil Fall, a filmy fall of 620 feet that is often diverted as much as 20 feet one way or the other by the breeze, is the first marvelous view of Yosemite Valley you will see if you come in via Route 41.

Climb Mist Trail from Happy Isles for an up-close view of 594-foot **Nevada Fall,** the first major fall as the Merced River plunges out of the high country toward the eastern end of Yosemite Valley. If you don't want to hike, you can see it—distantly—from Glacier Point.

At 1,612 feet, **Ribbon Fall** is the highest single fall in North America. It's also the first valley waterfall to dry up in summer; the rainwater and melted snow that create the slender fall evaporate quickly at this height. Look just west of El Capitan from the Valley floor for the best view of the fall from the base of Bridalveil Fall.

Fern-covered black rocks frame 317-foot **Vernal Fall,** and rainbows play in the spray at its base. Take Mist Trail from Happy Isles to see it—or, if you'd rather not hike, go to Glacier Point for a distant view.

Fodor's Choice ★ **Yosemite Falls**—which form the highest waterfall in North America and the fifth-highest in the world—are actually three falls, one on top of another. The water from the top descends a total of 2,425 feet, and when the falls run hard, you can hear them thunder all across the Valley. When they dry up, as often happens in late summer, the Valley seems naked without the wavering tower of spray. To view the falls up close, head to their base on the trail from Camp 4.

SEQUOIA NATIONAL PARK

★ **Beetle Rock Family Nature Center.** At Beetle Rock Education Center, across the road from Giant Forest Museum, the Sequoia Natural History Association operates a nature center with interactive exhibits and a children's bookstore with science-oriented games, books, and toys. ⊠ *Generals Hwy., 4 mi south of Lodgepole Visitor Center* ☎ *559/565–4251* 🖭 *Free* ⊙ *July–Aug. 19, daily 10–4.*

★ **Crystal Cave.** Ten thousand feet of passageways in this marble cave were created from limestone that metamorphosed under tremendous heat and pressure. Formations are relatively undisturbed. The standard tour is 50 minutes in length. In summer Sequoia Natural History Association offers a four- to six-hour "wild cave" tour (reservations required) and a 90-minute discovery tour, a less-structured excursion with fewer people. Tickets are not available at the cave; purchase them by 2:30 PM, and at least 90 minutes in advance, from the Lodgepole or Foothills visitor center. ⊠ *Crystal Cave Rd., 6 mi west off Generals Hwy.* ☎ *559/565–3759* ⊕ *www.sequoiahistory.org* 🖭 *$10.95* ⊙ *Mid-May–mid-Oct., daily 10–4.*

Fodor's Choice ★ **General Sherman Tree.** This, the world's largest living tree, is estimated to be about 2,100 years old. ⊠ *Generals Hwy., Rte. 198, 2 mi south of Lodgepole Visitor Center.*

Fodor's Choice ★ **Generals Highway.** Connecting the two parks from Grant Grove to Giant Forest and the foothills to the south, this narrow, twisting road runs past Stony Creek, Lost Grove, Little Baldy, General Sherman Tree, Amphitheater Point, and Foothills Visitor Center. Stop to see the Giant Forest Museum, which focuses entirely on the ecology of the sequoia. Also stop at the Lodgepole Visitor Center, which has excellent exhibits and audiovisual programs describing the Sierra Nevada and the natural history of the area. Under normal conditions it takes two hours to complete the drive one way, but when parks are crowded in summer, traffic can slow to a crawl in some areas.

★ **Giant Forest Museum.** You can find outstanding exhibits on the ecology of the giant sequoia at the park's premier museum. Though housed in a historic building, it's entirely wheelchair-accessible. ⊠ *Generals Hwy.,*

4 mi south of Lodgepole Visitor Center ☎559/565–4480 ☜*Free* ⊙*Daily 8–5.*

Mineral King. This subalpine valley sits at 7,800 feet at the end of a steep, winding road. The trip from the park's entrance can take up to two hours. This is the highest point to which you can drive in the park. ⊠*End of Mineral King Rd., 25 mi east of Generals Hwy., Rte. 198, east of Three Rivers.*

> **STRANGE BUT TRUE**
>
> The majestic sequoia once grew throughout the Northern Hemisphere, until the trees were almost wiped out by glaciers. In fact, some of the fossils in Arizona's Petrified National Forest National Park are extinct sequoia species.

★ **Moro Rock.** Climb the steep 400-step staircase 300 feet to the top of this granite dome for spectacular views of the Great Western Divide and the western regions of the park. To the southwest you look down the Kaweah River to Three Rivers, Lake Kaweah, and—on clear days—the Central Valley and the Coast Range. To the northeast are views of the High Sierra. Thousands of feet below lies the middle fork of the Kaweah River. ⊠*Moro Rock–Crescent Meadow Rd., 2 mi east off Generals Hwy., Rte. 198, to parking area.*

KINGS CANYON NATIONAL PARK

Canyon View. The glacial history of the Kings River Canyon is evident from this viewpoint. Note the canyon's giant "U" shape, which sparked John Muir to compare it to Yosemite to the north. ⊠*Kings Canyon Scenic Byway, Rte. 180, 1 mi east of Cedar Grove turnoff.*

★ **Fallen Monarch.** No matter how tall you are, you could theoretically walk through the entire 100-foot length of this burned-out, fallen sequoia near the General Grant Tree. (In order to protect it, access to the log's interior is prohibited indefinitely.) Early explorers, cattle ranchers, and Native Americans used the log for shelter, and soldiers who began patrolling the area in the late 1880s used it to stable their horses. ⊠*Trailhead 1 mi north of Grant Grove Visitor Center.*

General Grant Tree. The nation's Christmas tree, this is also the world's third-largest living tree. ⊠*Trailhead 1 mi north of Grant Grove Visitor Center.*

Fodor'sChoice ★ **Kings Canyon Scenic Byway.** Winding alongside the powerful Kings River (the byway along Route 180, east of Grant Grove), drive below the towering granite cliffs and past two tumbling waterfalls in the Kings River Canyon. One mile past the Cedar Grove Village turnoff, the U-shape canyon becomes broader, and you can see evidence of its glacial past and the effects of wind and water on the granite. Four miles farther is Grand Sentinel Viewpoint, where you can see the 3,500-foot-tall granite monolith and some of the most interesting rock formations in the canyon. The drive dead-ends in the canyon, so you must double back. It's about one hour each way.

Fodor'sChoice ★ **Redwood Mountain Grove.** This is the largest grove of giant sequoias in the world. As you head south through Kings Canyon toward Sequoia on Generals Highway, several paved turnouts allow you to look out over the treetops. The grove itself is accessible only on foot or by horseback, but the drive to the trailhead, on a twisting, rutted dirt road down a steep gorge, is dramatic in itself. ⊠*Drive 5 mi south of Grant Grove on Generals Hwy., Rte. 198, then turn right at Quail Flat; follow it 1½ mi to Redwood Canyon trailhead.*

WHERE TO EAT

	WHAT IT COSTS				
	¢	$	¢¢	$$$	$$$$
RESTAURANTS	under $8	$8–$12	$13–$20	$21–$30	over $30

Restaurant prices are per person for a main course at dinner.

YOSEMITE NATIONAL PARK

$$$–$$$$

Fodor'sChoice

★

✕**Ahwahnee Hotel Dining Room.** This is the most dramatic dining room in Yosemite, if not California. The massive room has a 34-foot ceiling supported by immense sugar-pine beams, and floor-to-ceiling windows. In the evening everything glows with candlelight. Specialties on the often-changing menu highlight sustainable, organic produce and include salmon, duckling, and prime rib. Collared shirts and long pants (no jeans) are required for men at dinner. ⊠*Ahwahnee Hotel, Ahwahnee Rd., about ¾ mi east of Yosemite Valley Visitor Center, Yosemite Village* ☎*209/372–1489* ⌐*Reservations essential* ☰*AE, D, DC, MC, V.*

$$–$$$

★

✕**Mountain Room.** Though remarkably good, the food becomes secondary when you see Yosemite Falls through this dining room's wall of windows—almost every table has a view. The chef makes a point of using locally sourced, organic ingredients, so you can be assured of fresh salad and veggies here. Grilled trout and salmon, steak, pasta, and several children's dishes are also on the menu. ⊠*Yosemite Lodge, Northside Dr. about ¾ mi west of visitor center, Yosemite Village* ☎*209/372–1281* ⌐*Reservations essential* ☰*AE, D, DC, MC, V* ⊘*No lunch.*

$$–$$$

★

✕**Wawona Hotel Dining Room.** Watch deer graze on the meadow while you dine in the romantic, candlelighted dining room of the whitewashed Wawona Hotel, which dates from the late 1800s. The American-style cuisine favors fresh California ingredients and flavors; trout is a menu staple. There's also a Sunday brunch Easter through Thanksgiving, and a barbecue on the lawn Saturday evenings in summer. A jacket is required at dinner. ⊠*Wawona Hotel, Rte. 41, Wawona* ☎*209/375–1425* ⌐*Reservations essential* ☰*AE, D, DC, MC, V* ⊘*Closed Jan. and Feb.*

¢–$$

✕**Food Court at Yosemite Lodge.** Fast and convenient the food court serves simple fare, ranging from hamburgers and pizzas to pastas, carved roasted meats, and salads at lunch and dinner. There's also a selection of beer and wine. At breakfast you can get pancakes and eggs made any way you like. An espresso and smoothie bar near the entrance keeps longer hours. ⊠*Yosemite Lodge, about ¾ mi west of visitor center, Yosemite Village* ☎*209/372–1265* ☰*AE, D, DC, MC, V.*

SEQUOIA NATIONAL PARK

$–$$$ ✕ **Wuksachi Village Dining Room.** In the high-ceiling dining room at
★   Sequoia's only upscale restaurant, huge windows run the length of the
room, providing a view of the surrounding trees. The dinner menu lists
everything from sandwiches and burgers to steaks and pasta. Break-
fast and lunch are also served. ⊠ *Wuksachi Village* ☎ *559/565–4070*
⌂ *Reservations essential* ▤ *AE, D, DC, MC, V.*

¢   ✕ **Lodgepole Market and Snack Bar.** Visit the market for prepack-
aged sandwiches and salads to go or to assemble the components
of a picnic. In summer there's a deli for sandwiches and a snack bar
for breakfast, pizza, and hamburgers. ⊠ *Next to Lodgepole Visi-
tor Center* ☎ *559/565–3301* ▤ *AE, D, DC, MC, V* ⊙ *Closed early
Sept.–mid-Apr.*

KINGS CANYON NATIONAL PARK

$–$$$ ✕ **Grant Grove Restaurant.** Come here year-round for simple family-style
dining. The restaurant serves full breakfasts, and hot entrées and sand-
wiches for lunch and dinner. Take-out service is available. ⊠ *Grant
Grove Village* ☎ *559/335–5500* ▤ *AE, D, MC, V.*

¢–$ ✕ **Cedar Grove Market.** You can pick up sandwiches and salads to go at
this market, as well as a range of grocery items. It's open daily 8–8.
⊠ *Cedar Grove Village* ☎ *559/565–0100* ▤ *AE, D, MC, V* ⊙ *Closed
late Oct.–mid-Apr.*

WHERE TO STAY

WHAT IT COSTS				
¢	$	$$	$$$	$$$$
HOTELS	under $50	$50–$100	$101–$150	$151–$200	over $200
CAMPING	under $10	$10–$17	$18–$35	$36–$49	over $50

Hotel prices are per night for two people in a standard double room in high season, excluding taxes and service charges. Camping prices are for a standard (no
hookups, pit toilets, fire grates, picnic tables) campsite per night.

YOSEMITE NATIONAL PARK

$$$$ ✕ ▦ **The Ahwahnee.** This grand 1920s-era mountain lodge, a National
Fodor'sChoice   Historic Landmark, is constructed of rocks and sugar-pine logs. Guest
★   rooms have Native American design motifs; public spaces are decorated with art deco detailing, oriental rugs, and elaborate iron- and
woodwork. Some luxury hotel amenities, including turndown service
and guest bathrobes, are standard here. The Dining Room ($$$–$$$$;
reservations essential) is by far the most impressive restaurant in the
park, and one of the most beautiful rooms in California. If you stay in
a cottage room, be aware that each cottage has multiple guest rooms.
Each of the cushy cottages contains two nonadjoining guest rooms
with en suite bath. ⊠ *Ahwahnee Rd. north of Northside Dr., Yosemite
Village, 95389* ⊙ *Delaware North Reservations, 6771 N. Palm Ave.,
Fresno 93704* ☎ *559/252–4848* ⊕ *www.yosemitepark.com* ⇥ *99
lodge rooms, 4 suites, 24 cottage rooms* ⌂ *In-room: no a/c (some),*

ON THE WAY

Bodie State Historic Park: Old shacks and shops, abandoned mine shafts, a Methodist church, the mining village of Rattlesnake Gulch, and the remains of a small Chinatown are among the sights at this fascinating place, California's most authentic ghost town. It's about 40 mi east of Yosemite's Tuolumne Meadows. (Visit Bodie rather than the kitschy Calico Ghost Town, just outside Barstow.)

Mammoth Lakes: 30 mi south of Yosemite National Park on the eastern side, this fast-growing resort area boasts the stunning Panorama Gondola, which gives riders a great view of the dormant volcano that shaped the area. Time permitting, take the shuttle bus (summer and fall only) to Devils Postpile National Monument, where wacky rock formations resemble clumps of cooked spaghetti noodles.

Fresno: California's Central Valley, the rather bleak and smelly (eau de cow manure, anyone?) expanse between the Coastal and Sierra Madre mountain ranges, does have one city that's worth a quick visit (with several interesting museums and attractions). But don't take time away from the parks for a special visit!

refrigerator, Wi-Fi. In-hotel: restaurant, room service, bar, tennis court, pool, concierge ☐AE, D, DC, MC, V.

$$–$$$ ✕⌷**Wawona Hotel.** This 1879 National Historic Landmark sits at ★ Yosemite's southern end, near the Mariposa Grove of Big Trees. It's an old-fashioned New England–style estate, with whitewashed buildings, wraparound verandas, and pleasant, no-frills rooms decorated with period pieces. About half the rooms share bathrooms; those that do come equipped with robes. The romantic, candlelit dining room ($$–$$$) lies across the lobby from the cozy Victorian parlor, which has a fireplace, board games, and a piano, where a pianist plays ragtime most evenings. ⊠Hwy. 41, Wawona ⌂Delaware North Reservations, 6771 N. Palm Ave., Fresno 93704 ☎559/252–4848 ⊕www.yosemitepark. com ⌐104 rooms, 50 with bath △In-room: no a/c, no phone, no TV. In-hotel: restaurant, bar, golf course, tennis court, pool ☐AE, D, DC, MC, V ⊙Closed Jan. and Feb.

$$–$$$ ✕⌷**Yosemite Lodge at the Falls.** This lodge near Yosemite Falls, which ★ dates from 1915, looks like a 1960s motel-resort complex, with numerous brown, two-story buildings tucked beneath the trees around large parking lots. Motel-style rooms have two double beds, and larger rooms also have dressing areas and patios or balconies. A few have views of the falls. Of the lodge's eateries, the Mountain Room Restaurant ($$–$$$) is the most formal. The cafeteria-style Food Court (¢–$) serves three meals a day. Many park tours depart from the main building. ⊠Northside Dr. about ¾ mi west of visitor center, Yosemite Village ⌂Delaware North Reservations, 6771 N. Palm Ave., Fresno 93704 ☎559/252–4848 ⊕www.yosemitepark.com ⌐245 rooms △In-room: no a/c, Wi-Fi. In-hotel: 3 restaurants, bar, pool, bicycles, no-smoking rooms ☐AE, D, DC, MC, V.

$-$$ **Curry Village.** Opened in 1899 as a place where travelers could enjoy the beauty of Yosemite for a modest price, Curry Village has plain accommodations: standard motel rooms, cabins, and tent cabins, which have rough wood frames, canvas walls, and roofs. The tent cabins are a step up from camping, with linens and blankets provided (maid service upon request). Some have heat. Most of the cabins share shower and toilet facilities. ⊠ *South side of Southside Dr., Yosemite Valley* ⌕ *Delaware North Reservations, 6771 N. Palm Ave., Fresno 93704* ☎ *559/252–4848* ⊕ *www.yosemitepark.com* ⥵ *18 rooms; 183 cabins, 103 with bath; 427 tent cabins* ⌂ *In-room: no a/c, no phone, no TV. In-hotel: 3 restaurants, bar, pool, bicycles, no-smoking rooms* ⊟ *AE, D, DC, MC, V.*

CAMPGROUNDS & RV PARKS   Reservations are required at most of Yosemite's campgrounds, especially in summer. You can reserve a site up to five months in advance; bookings made more than 21 days in advance require prepayment. Unless otherwise noted, book your site through the central National Park Service reservations office. **National Park Reservation Service.** ⌕ *Box 1600, Cumberland, MD 21502* ☎ *800/436–7275* ⊕ *www.recreation. gov* ⊟ *D, MC, V* ⏰ *Daily 7–7.*

SEQUOIA NATIONAL PARK

$$$–$$$$ **Wuksachi Lodge.** These cedar-and-stone lodge buildings, which blend
Fodor'sChoice   with the landscape, house comfortable rooms with modern amenities. The village is 7,200 feet above sea level; many of the rooms have
★   spectacular views of the surrounding mountains. ⊠ *Wuksachi Village 93262* ☎ *559/565–4070 front desk, 559/253–2199, 888/252–5757 reservations* ⊟ *559/456–0542* ⊕ *www.visitsequoia.com* ⥵ *102 rooms* ⌂ *In-room: no a/c, refrigerator, dial-up, Wi-Fi. In-hotel: restaurant, bar, no-smoking rooms* ⊟ *AE, D, DC, MC, V.*

KINGS CANYON NATIONAL PARK

$$$ **John Muir Lodge.** This modern, timber-sided lodge is nestled in a
★   wooded area near Grant Grove Village. The rooms and suites all have queen beds and private baths, and there's a comfortable common room with low-pile carpeting and a stone fireplace where you can play cards and board games. The inexpensive, family-style Grant Grove Restaurant is a three-minute walk away. Though it's little more than a good motel, this is the finest place to stay in Grant Grove. ⊠ *Kings Canyon Scenic Byway, ¼ mi north of Grant Grove Village* ⌕ *Sequoia Kings Canyon Park Services Co., 5755 E. Kings Canyon Rd., Suite 101, Fresno 93727* ☎ *559/335–5500 or 866/522–6966* ⊟ *559/335–5507* ⊕ *www.sequoia-kingscanyon.com* ⥵ *24 rooms, 6 suites* ⌂ *In-room: no a/c, no TV* ⊟ *AE, D, MC, V.*

SPORTS & THE OUTDOORS

YOSEMITE NATIONAL PARK

Yosemite Bike Rentals. You can rent bikes by the hour ($7.50) or by day ($24.50) from either Yosemite Lodge or Curry Village bike stands. Bikes with child trailers, baby-jogger strollers, and wheelchairs are also available. ⊠ *Yosemite Lodge or Curry Village* ☎ *209/372–1208* ⊕ *www.yosemite*

park.com ✉$7.50 *(hr)/$24 (day)* ⏱*Apr.–Oct.*

★ **Yosemite Falls Trail.** This is the highest waterfall in North America. The upper fall (1,430 feet), the middle cascades (675 feet), and the lower fall (320 feet) combine for a total of 2,425 feet and, when viewed from the valley, appear as a single waterfall. The ¼-mi trail leads from the parking lot to the base of the falls. Upper Yosemite Fall Trail, a strenuous 3½-mi climb rising 2,700 feet, takes you above the top of the falls. ✉*Northside Dr. at Camp 4.*

★ **Mist Trail.** You can walk through rainbows when you visit 317-foot Vernal Fall. The hike to the bridge at the base of the fall is moderately strenuous and less than 1 mi long.

VITAL STATS

■ Twenty percent of California's plant species can be found in Yosemite National Park, which contains five major vegetation zones.

■ "The Nose" side of El Capitan was first climbed successfully in 1958. These days, climbers have about a 60% success rate, typically taking two or three days to complete the straight-up ascent.

■ Its roped section sometimes clogged with long lines, Half Dome is fully climbed by as many as 1,000 people a day. Since 1971, nine have died, including three in 2007.

It's another steep (and often wet) ¾-mi grind up to the top. From there, you can continue 2 mi to the top of Nevada Fall, a 594-foot cascade as the Merced River plunges out of the high country. The trail is open late spring to early fall, depending on snowmelt. ✉*Happy Isles.*

★ **Panorama Trail.** Starting at Glacier Point, the trail circles 8½ mi down through forest, past the secluded Illilouette Falls, to the top of Nevada Fall, where it connects with Mist Trail and the John Muir Trail. You'll pass Nevada, then Vernal Fall on your way down to the Valley floor for a total elevation loss of 3,200 feet. Arrange to take the early-morning hiker bus to Glacier Point, and allow a full day for this hike. ✉*Glacier Point.*

Fodor's Choice **John Muir Trail to Half Dome.** Ardent and courageous trekkers can con-
★ tinue on from the top of Nevada Fall, off Mist Trail, to the top of Half Dome. Some hikers attempt this entire 10- to 12-hour, 16¾-mi round-trip trek from Happy Isles in one day; if you're planning to do this, remember that the 4,800-foot elevation gain and the 8,842-foot altitude will cause shortness of breath. Another option is to hike to a campground in Little Yosemite Valley near the top of Nevada Fall the first day, then climb to the top of Half Dome and hike out the next day; it's highly recommended that you get your wilderness permit reservations at least a month in advance. Be sure to wear hiking boots and bring gloves. The last pitch up the back of Half Dome is very steep—the only way to climb this sheer rock face is to pull yourself up using the steel cable handrails, which are in place only from late spring to early fall. Those who brave the ascent will be rewarded with an unbeatable view of Yosemite Valley below and the high country beyond. Before

heading out, check conditions with rangers, and don't attempt the final ascent if there are any storm clouds overhead. ✉ *Happy Isles.*

SEQUOIA NATIONAL PARK

Big Trees Trail. The Giant Forest is known for its trails through sequoia groves. You can get the best views of the big trees from the meadows, where flowers are in full bloom by June or July. The 7/10-mi trail—the park's only wheelchair-accessible trail—circles Round Meadow. ✉ *Off Generals Hwy., Rte. 198, near Giant Forest Museum.*

★ **Congress Trail.** This easy 2-mi trail is a paved loop that begins near General Sherman Tree and winds through the heart of the sequoia forest. Watch for the groups of trees known as the House and Senate, and the individual trees called the President and McKinley. ✉ *Off Generals Hwy., Rte. 198, 2 mi north of Giant Forest.*

Fodor'sChoice **Crescent Meadow Trails.** John Muir reportedly called Crescent Meadow
★ the "gem of the Sierra." Brilliant wildflowers bloom here by midsummer, and a 1 8/10-mi trail loops around the meadow. A 1 6/10-mi trail begins at Crescent Meadow and leads to Tharp's Log, a cabin built from a fire-hollowed sequoia. ✉ *End of Moro Rock–Crescent Meadow Rd., 2 6/10 mi east off Generals Hwy., Rte. 198.*

KINGS CANYON NATIONAL PARK

Fodor'sChoice **Zumwalt Meadow Trail.** Walk beneath high granite walls and along
★ the meandering Kings River, en route to the lush Zumwalt Meadow. The 1½-mi trail involves a little rock-hopping but is otherwise easy. ✉ *Trailhead 4½ mi east of Cedar Grove Village turnoff from Kings Canyon Scenic Byway.*

★ **Redwood Canyon Trail.** Whether you hike the perimeter of two adjoining loops or take only one of them, this 6- or 10-mi trek in Redwood Canyon leads through the world's largest grove of sequoias. Take in the cascades, the quiet pools of Redwood Creek, and the mixed conifer forest on a day hike or overnight backpacking trip. ✉ *Drive 5 mi south of Grant Grove on Generals Hwy., Rte. 198, then turn right at Quail Flat; follow it 1½ mi to Redwood Canyon trailhead.*

VISITOR INFORMATION

Sequoia and Kings Canyon National Parks (✉ *47050 Generals Hwy. Rte. 198, Three River 93271–9651* ☎ *559/565–3341 or 559/565–3134* ⊕ *www.nps. gov/seki*).

Yosemite National Park (✉ *Information Office, Box 577, Yosemite National Park95389* ☎ *209/372–0200* ⊕ *www.nps.gov/yose*).

San Francisco

WITH THE CALIFORNIA WINE COUNTRY

Hyde Street Cable Car Line Russian Hill

WORD OF MOUTH

"San Francisco is about diversity. There's room for [those who like] the Wharf and Victorians and the Castro and North Beach and the Mission and Chinatown and even Union Square. Something for everyone."

—Catbert

EXPLORING SAN FRANCISCO

400 mi north of Los Angeles via I–5, I–580, and I–80; 570 mi northwest of Las Vegas via I–15, CA 58, CA 99, CA 46, I–5, I–580, and I–80; 800 mi south of Seattle via I–5, I–550, and I–80.

By Denise M. Leto

Snuggled on a 46½-square-mi tip of land between San Francisco Bay and the Pacific Ocean, San Francisco is a relatively small city of about 750,000 residents (4% fewer than during the dot-com heyday in 2000). San Franciscans cherish the city, partly for the same reasons so many visitors do: the proximity of the bay and its pleasures, rows of Victorian homes clinging precariously to the hillsides, the sun setting behind the Golden Gate Bridge. Longtime locals know the city's attraction goes much deeper, from the diversity of its neighborhoods and residents (trannies in the seedy Tenderloin, yuppie MBAs in the Marina, elderly Russians in the Richmond, working-class Latino families in the Mission) to the city's progressive free spirit (we voted to ban handguns, we embrace a photographer's project that involves naked people frolicking in trees on public land, our thirtysomething mayor poses for GQ and is seen out on the town with his soon-to-be-ex-wife, a former model). Take all these things together and you'll begin to understand why, despite the dizzying cost of living here, many San Franciscans can't imagine calling anyplace else home.

Just an hour or two away and a favorite getaway among locals, the wine country of Napa and Sonoma counties offer a bucolic setting, top-flight dining and lodging, and, of course, world-class wine.

WHO WILL ESPECIALLY LOVE THIS TRIP?

Foodies & oenophiles: San Franciscans are serious about food and wine. You can pop into an unassuming bistro in almost any neighborhood, and find an adventurous menu and surprising wine list. The Mission and SoMa offer particularly rich hunting grounds. And if it's vino you're after, the world-famous wine country of Napa and Sonoma counties won't disappoint.

People-Watchers: Few cities can touch San Francisco when it comes to enjoying the human parade. From towering trannies in the Tenderloin and the leather set haunting SoMa to homeless folks and street kids in Civic Center and the Haight, yuppies pushing kids and dogs in strollers in Noe Valley, and the old-money set in Pacific Heights, you could easily spend weeks (and no money) soaking up the vast diversity of this dynamic town.

Families with kids: You may not think of San Francisco as an urban center that welcomes children—and it's true that the city is sorely lacking in young families—but for visitors with tots, there's plenty to do here. Spend a day in Golden Gate Park drifting between the urban pleasures of the de Young Museum, the gorgeous Conservatory of Flowers, and the extraordinary California Academy of Sciences, and kid-friendly spots like the newly refurbished Koret Children's Quarter and the San Fran-

TOP 5 REASONS TO GO

Get out on the Bay: Take a simple and relatively cheap ferry ride, indulge in a dinner cruises, hop a kayak, or just take in the view strolling along the water, the way locals do.

Fabulous food & drink: From top-tier dining at destinations like Gary Danko and French Laundry to the burrito palaces of the Mission, this place is indeed foodie heaven. And many of the best wineries in America are just a short drive outside the city.

Golden Gate Bridge sunsets: Whether you walk the bridge with the sun glowing in the background or take in this one-of-a-kind vista from the bar at the Beach Chalet, it's an absolute don't-miss.

Alcatraz: Sure, everyone's heard the stories, but it's another thing altogether to experience the confinement and history of the Rock at the place itself; the revamped audio tour, with its gravelly voiced inmates and guards, is alone worth the price of admission, and the ferry ride is icing on the cake.

Cable cars: Another San Francisco cliché? Maybe, but don't sell it short: clacking down an impossibly steep hill with the bay sparkling in the distance is something everyone should experience at least once.

32

cisco Botanical Garden at the Strybing Arboretum. Or wander through the Presidio along its hiking paths, taking in fantastic Pacific vistas.

Amorous couples: Not many cities offer as many romantic places—with a heart-stopping view around every corner—as San Francisco. Hike up to Coit Tower and gaze at the bay; take the elevator up to the top of the St. Francis Hotel at Union Square and watch the evening lights come up; or cuddle up at Crissy Field under the Golden Gate Bridge. Lock fingers in one of the city's many candlelighted culinary treasures, and wander exotic alleys with foreign scents sweeping you far away. The city's stiff bay breeze, though cold, also encourages cuddling.

WHEN IS THE BEST TIME TO VISIT?

The best season to visit San Francisco is fall; September and October bring summer weather (the actual summer tends to be foggy and cool), perfect for strolling, alfresco dining, and exploring the city's natural wonders in relative warmth and comfort. A myriad of outdoor concerts and festivals are timed to take advantage of this prime weather. December and January tend to bring rain, and visitors are always wise to carry a sweater to protect against chilly bay breezes.

June's Lesbian, Gay, Bisexual and Transgender Pride Celebration is the biggest party of the year, drawing up to a million visitors from all over the world. Other favorites include the Chinese New Year celebration and parade, in February; and May's quirky Bay to Breakers race, where folks in wacky costumes (or utterly without) follow serious runners across town.

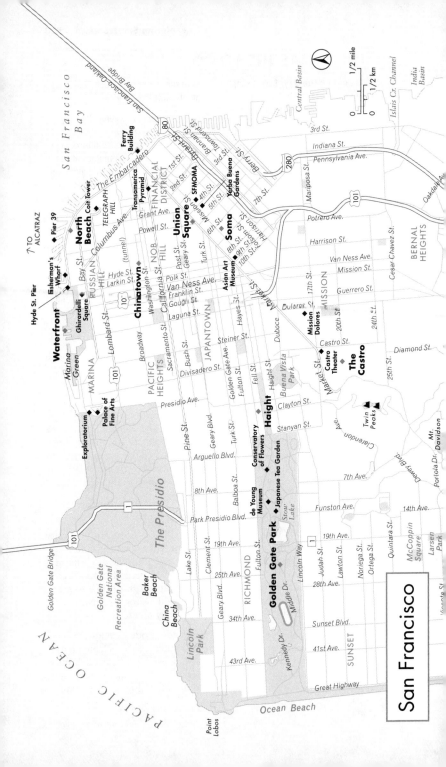

San Francisco

San Francisco Bay

San Francisco–Oakland Bay Bridge

80

TO ALCATRAZ

Pier 39

Coit Tower

Ferry Building

The Embarcadero

Transamerica Pyramid

FINANCIAL DISTRICT

TELEGRAPH HILL

North Beach

Columbus Ave.

Grant Ave.

Powell St.

Union Square

SFMOMA

Yerba Buena Gardens

Soma

3rd St.

Indiana St.

Pennsylvania Ave.

280

101

Mariposa St.

BERNAL HEIGHTS

Central Basin

Islais Cr. Channel

India Basin

3rd St.

Berry St.

Brannan St.

Townsend St.

1/2 mile

1/2 km

Fisherman's Wharf

Hyde St. Pier

Waterfront

Ghirardelli Square

Bay St.

RUSSIAN HILL

Hyde St.

Larkin St.

(tunnel)

Chinatown

NOB HILL

Washington St.

California St.

Van Ness Ave.

Polk St.

Franklin St.

Gough St.

Laguna St.

Asian Art Museum

Turk St.

Market St.

6th St.

7th St.

8th St.

9th St.

10th St.

Folsom St.

Harrison St.

Van Ness Ave.

Mission St.

Guerrero St.

Cesar Chavez St.

Potrero Ave.

Post St.

Geary St.

10

Marina Green

MARINA

Lombard St.

Broadway

PACIFIC HEIGHTS

Sacramento St.

Bush St.

JAPANTOWN

Steiner St.

Divisadero St.

Golden Gate Ave.

Fulton St.

Hayes St.

Fell St.

Haight St.

Buena Vista Park

MISSION

Mission Dolores

17th St.

20th St.

24th St.

Dolores St.

Duboce

Castro St.

Castro Theater

The Castro

Diamond St.

25th St.

101

Palace of Fine Arts

Exploratorium

Presidio Ave.

Pine St.

Geary Blvd.

Arguello Blvd.

Turk St.

Clayton St.

Stanyan St.

Haight

Conservatory of Flowers

Japanese Tea Garden

de Young Museum

Stow Lake

Clarendon Ave.

Twin Peaks

Mt. Davidson

Dewey Blvd.

Portola Dr.

7th Ave.

Funston Ave.

14th Ave.

Larsen Park

McCoppin Square

Quintara St.

The Presidio

1

Golden Gate Bridge

101

Golden Gate National Recreation Area

Baker Beach

China Beach

Lincoln Park

Point Lobos

8th Ave.

Balboa St.

Park Presidio Blvd.

Lake St.

Clement St.

19th Ave.

25th Ave.

34th Ave.

43rd Ave.

Geary Blvd.

RICHMOND

Fulton St.

Golden Gate Park

Kennedy Dr.

Middle Dr.

Lincoln Way

Judah St.

Lawton St.

Noriega St.

Ortega St.

19th Ave.

28th Ave.

Sunset Blvd.

41st Ave.

SUNSET

Great Highway

Ocean Beach

PACIFIC OCEAN

32

CLOSE UP

How to Snack

Like most California cities, San Francisco's dining scene reflects the rich diversity of its immigrant communities, past and present. Perhaps one of the most beloved—and certainly one of the most contested—meals in town is the burrito. An entire meal wrapped in a tortilla, the typical burrito includes beans (refried, pinto, or black), rice, meat (or not), salsa, cheese, and often sour cream and guacamole. Entire Web sites deconstruct which taqueria makes the best (the San Francisco Chronicle devotes at least one section a year to examining the same question), and every San Franciscan has a favorite.

Some of the best and cheapest burritos come from taco trucks; check out **El Norteño Tacos** (801 Bryant St., 415/756-1220), in SoMa, and **El Tonayense** (22nd and Harrison Sts, 415/550-9192), in the Mission. The Mission is thick with taquerias; consistent winners include **La Taqueria** (2889 Mission St., 415/285-7117), **Taqueria Cancun** (2288 Mission St.,

415/252-9560), and **Farolito Taqueria** (2950 24th St., 415/641-0758).

November heralds the eagerly anticipated opening of Dungeness crab season (it runs through June), when even locals head down to the food stalls around Fisherman's Wharf to enjoy this steaming delicacy. Add a round of sourdough from **Boudin Bakery** (160 Jefferson St., 415/928-1849), and you've got a true San Francisco feast.

Perhaps the grandfather of the small-plates movement, dim sum continues to be a popular San Francisco tradition. Find these snacks—savory and sweet, hot and cold—on nearly every block in Chinatown around lunchtime; standouts include **Great Eastern** (649 Jackson St., 415/986-2500) and the out-of-the-way **Hang Ah** (1 Pagoda Pl., at Stockton St., 415/982-5686), whose downstairs location makes it feel like a secret hideout. In the new Chinatown of the Richmond, folks crowd into **Ton Kiang** around noon to scoop up some of the best dim sum in the city.

HOW SHOULD I GET THERE?

DRIVING

Reaching San Francisco by car is simple—much simpler than navigating within the city and parking. From Los Angeles, take the I–5 north for almost 300 mi, then take the I–580 west to the I–80 west across the Bay Bridge and into town.

FLYING

San Francisco International Airport (SFO) is about 20 minutes south of the city without traffic. Just across the bay, Oakland International (OAK) is a viable alternative to SFO, worthwhile if you can book a cheaper flight in and out. From here, BART will take you into the city in about 25 minutes.

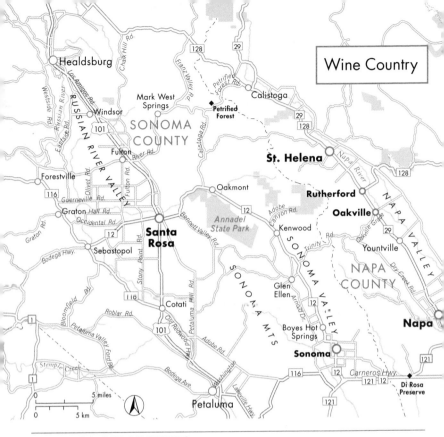

Wine Country

HOW DO I GET AROUND?

BY CAR

Driving in San Francisco can be an exercise in frustration for the unini-
tiated: the hills are steep; one-way streets are common; crossing main
arteries like Market Street can be difficult; and parking is notoriously
scarce and expensive. Happily, many of the city's top sights are clustered in a relatively small corner of town, and public transit reaches
almost all those places. Most visitors choose to forgo a rental while in
town. If you plan to visit wine country, you'll definitely want a car for
that easy drive—but pick it up at the end of your time in the city.

BY PUBLIC TRANSIT

City transit options include BART—a subway within San Francisco—
and Muni, which includes buses, trolleys, the historic streetcars of the
F-line, and cable cars. BART is useful for reaching the airport, the East
Bay, and far-flung neighborhoods from downtown. Most visitors stick
to the F-line and cable cars, which cover most of the top sights. Considering the price of riding a cable car—$5 a pop each way—seriously
think about investing in a 1-, 3-, or 7-day passport ($11, $18, and $24,
respectively), good for unlimited travel on all Muni options.

32

BY TAXI

Lots of locals get by without a car—parking space rent can be astronomical—and instead use public transit and taxi cabs to get around town. In San Francisco it costs $3.10 to drop the flag, and $2.25 per additional mile. Distances within town tend to be short—the city's only 7 mi by 7 mi, after all. Hail a cab on the street or, in Union Square, try your luck around the major hotels—listen for the ear-piercing whistles the doormen use to summon taxis.

WHERE SHOULD I FOCUS MY ENERGY?

If you're here for 1 day: Stick to downtown and soak up all you can: hoof it from Union Square through Chinatown and North Beach all the way to Fisherman's Wharf, then take a cable car back.

If you're here for 2 days: Walk the Embarcadero to the foodie mecca that is the Ferry Building, then explore the cultural hotspots of SoMa.

If you're here for 3 days: Head into the Mission to check out the confluence of hipster and Latino SF: fantastic mural art, funky retail therapy, cool watering holes, and destination taquerias.

If you're here for 4 days: Get out on the bay and explore notorious Alcatraz; the brief cruise with its city views is a great bonus.

If you're here for 5 days: Grab a hearty breakfast in the Haight, then head into Golden Gate Park and check out the glorious Conservatory of Flowers, Japanese Tea Garden, and the controversial de Young Museum, all clustered around the park's eastern end.

If you're here for 6 days: Add a day trip—or even better, a luxurious overnighter—to wine country.

If you're here for 7 days or more: Spend the morning walking the flamboyant Castro—a great brunch neighborhood—and then head north to the Presidio, the city's secret getaway. Have a picnic in the shadow of the Golden Gate Bridge or walk the 1.7-mi span all the way to photogenic Sausalito.

WHAT ARE THE TOP EXPERIENCES?

The Food: San Franciscans take their food seriously: no wonder when you consider the bounty of local organic produce, meats, artisanal breads and cheeses, and wine as well as the far-reaching influence of California cuisine. A whirlwind tour of culinary San Francisco has to include a visit to the gorgeously restored Ferry Building, on the Embarcadero at the foot of Market Street. Saturday's farmers' market positively hums with perfectly beautiful ingredients—many of the city's top chefs shop here. You won't find any bargains, but any day of the week you can enjoy fabulous bivalves at Hog Island Oyster Company, fantastic upscale Vietnamese cuisine at Slanted Door, or a superlative burger at Taylor's Refresher—or just gather delicious fixings for a waterfront picnic from Acme Bread and Cowgirl Creamery. Other don't-misses

CLAIM TO FAME

The City is famous worldwide for its cuisine; arguments rage in the newspapers as to whether it tops New York on the haute cuisine pyramid. Visitors plan entire trips around a table at Gary Danko, Chez Panisse in Berkeley, and French Laundry in Yountville, and locals lobby opinions about the city's dining options with vehemence. Even foodies with thin wallets can eat well anytime, and they share their thoughts in a rich variety of blogs, newspaper columns, and dining groups.

Another thing people see when they think of San Francisco are huge rainbow flags, in-your-face gay culture, television images of sequins, cut abs, and leather. This is a gay mecca, a Disneyland of LGBT culture. Visit the Castro—but not only the Castro—and you'll see couples of every stripe casually living their lives out loud. We're largely a politically progressive, live-and-let-live town, an attitude that sometimes shocks—but mostly enchants—visitors.

foodie stops include excellent, cheap Mexican food in the Mission; the Larkin Street corridor in the Tenderloin for Vietnamese, and pan-Asian restaurants—Chinese, Burmese, Indonesian—in the Richmond along Clement Street, Geary Boulevard, and Balboa Street.

The Bay: San Francisco Bay gives the city a constant stunning backdrop: sailboats bob on the tide, the sun dances off the water and glows red sinking below the Golden Gate Bridge. Out on the bay itself, many boat operators cater to visitors, from bay tours and dinner cruises to manned-sailboat rentals. Still, there are plenty of ways to enjoy the bay the way locals do. On a sunny day, simply hopping a ferry to Oakland or Sausalito and enjoying a beer among commuters is an inexpensive but exquisite pleasure.

Neighborhood strolls: San Francisco is a city of distinct neighborhoods, each with their own unique flavors and personality. Most folks hit the big-ticket areas: shopping at Union Square; an amble through densely packed, herb-, tea-, and trinket-shop-filled Chinatown, where produce stalls spill out onto the sidewalk; nibbles and wine or cappuccino in Italian-hued North Beach; and a walk through the gauntlet of souvenir shops and overprice waterfront restaurants in briny-smelling Fisherman's Wharf. These are all worthwhile, but also consider the smaller 'hoods that don't get as much airplay but reveal the true San Francisco: the in-your-face vibe of the stylish, still very gay Castro; the lively Latino-hipster stew in the mural-laden Mission; up-and-coming Hayes Valley, chockablock with cool galleries, cafés, a mix of watering holes, and one-of-a-kind boutiques; and low-key, family-friendly Noe Valley, whose main drag feels like a small town in itself.

Views & Hills: It's hard not to have a fantastic view in San Francisco: the bay pops up in the background from a million vantage points; rows of tightly packed Victorians line street after street; and the city bares itself from the hills. You'll stumble upon these as you wander town, but some of the best places to take in the cityscape are worth seeking out. Coit

Tower is an obvious vantage point—plus it has the added bonus of the glorious walk down the Filbert Steps. From Crissy Field, the view of the Golden Gate Bridge is tough to beat (but chilly at sunset). A cocktail at the Cliff House or the Beach Chalet gives stunning vistas of the Pacific surf. Take the elevator to the top floor of the St. Francis—even if you're not a guest—to watch the city lights come up in the evening. If you have a car, it's worth crossing the Bay Bridge to Treasure Island for a lovely cross-bay view of the city, especially at night, and to Grizzly Peak Boulevard in Berkeley, for a three-bridge view.

32

BEST BETS

SIGHTS AND TOURS

SAN FRANCISCO

TOURS **San Francisco City Guides** (☎ *415/557–4266* ⊕ *www.sfcityguides.org*). An outstanding free service supported by the San Francisco Public Library. Walking tour themes range from individual neighborhoods to local history (the Gold Rush, the 1906 quake, ghost walks) to architecture. Each May and October a slew of additional walks are added. Although the tours are free and the knowledgeable guides are volunteers, it's appropriate to make a $5 donation for these nonprofit programs. Tour schedules are available at library branches and the **San Francisco Visitor Information Center** (⊠ *Hallidie Plaza, lower level, Powell and Market Sts., Union Sq.* ☎ *415/391–2000, 415/392–0328 TDD* ⊕ *www.sfvisitor.org*).

★ **Alcatraz.** The boat ride to the island is brief (15 minutes) but affords beautiful views of the city, Marin County, and the East Bay. The audio tour, highly recommended, includes observations by guards and prisoners about life in one of America's most notorious penal colonies. Plan your schedule to allow at least three hours for the visit and boat rides combined. Buying your tickets in advance, even in the off season, is strongly recommended. ⊠ *Pier 33, Fisherman's Wharf* ☎ *415/981–7625* ⊕ *www.nps.gov/alca, www.parkconservancy.org/visit/alcatraz, www.alcatrazcruises.com* ✉ *$21.75, including audio tour; $28.75 evening tour, including audio* ⊘ *Ferry departs every 30–45 mins Sept.–late May, daily 9:30–2:15, 4:20 for evening tour Thurs.–Mon. only; late May–Aug., daily 9:30–4:15, 6:30 and 7:30 for evening tour.*

Fodor'sChoice **Cable Cars.** You've already seen them (on the big screen, in magazines, ★ and, admit it, on the Rice-a-Roni™ box). And considering a ticket costs $5 a pop, do you really need to ride a cable car? Yes, you do, at least once during your visit. Flag down a Powell-Hyde car along Powell Street, grab the pole, and clatter and jiggle up mansion-topped Nob Hill. Crest the hill, and hold on for the hair-raising descent to Fisherman's Wharf, with sun glittering off the bay and Alcatraz bobbing in the distance. Don't deny it—this would be a deal at twice the price. You can buy tickets on board (exact change isn't necessary) or at the kiosks at the cable-car turnarounds at Hyde and Beach streets and at Powell and Market streets. The heavily traveled Powell-Mason and Powell-Hyde lines begin at Powell and Market streets near Union Square and terminate at Fisherman's Wharf; lines for these routes can be long, especially in summer. The California Street line runs east and west from Market and California streets to Van Ness Avenue; there is often no wait to board this route. The Cable Cars are run by the **San Francisco Municipal Railway System** (*Muni* ☎ *415/673–6864* ⊕ *www. sfmuni.com*).

Fodor's Choice ★ **Chinatown.** A few blocks uphill from Union Square is the abrupt beginning of dense and insular Chinatown—the oldest such community in the country. When the street signs have Chinese characters, produce stalls crowd pedestrians off the sidewalk, and folks scurry by with telltale pink plastic shopping bags, you'll know you're there. (The neighborhood huddles together in the 17 blocks and 41 alleys bordered roughly by Bush, Kearny, and Powell streets and Broadway.) Chinatown has been attracting the curious for more than 100 years, and no neighborhood in the city absorbs as many tourists without seeming to forfeit its character. Join the flow and step into another world. Good-luck banners of crimson and gold hang beside dragon-entwined lampposts and pagoda roofs, while honking cars chime in with shoppers bargaining loudly in Cantonese or Mandarin.

★ **Coit Tower.** Whether you think it resembles a fire hose or something more, ahem, adult, this 210-foot tower is among San Francisco's most distinctive skyline sights. You can ride the elevator to the top of the tower—the only thing you have to pay for here—to enjoy the view of the Bay Bridge and the Golden Gate Bridge; due north is Alcatraz Island. Inside the tower, 19 Depression-era murals depict California's economic and political life. ⊠*Telegraph Hill Blvd. at Greenwich St. or Lombard St., North Beach* ☎*415/362–0808* 🎟*Free; elevator to top $3.75* ⊙*Daily 10–6.*

Fodor's Choice ★ **Ferry Building.** Renovated in 2003, the Ferry Building is the jewel of the Embarcadero. San Franciscans flock to the street-level Market Hall, stocking up on supplies from local favorites such as Acme Bread, Scharffen Berger Chocolate, and Cowgirl Creamery. Lucky diners claim a coveted table at Slanted Door, the city's beloved high-end Vietnamese restaurant. The seafood bars at Hog Island Oyster Company and Ferry Plaza Seafood have fantastic city panoramas—or you can take your purchases around to the building's bay side, where benches face views of the Bay Bridge. Extending from the piers on the north side of the building south to the Bay Bridge, the waterfront promenade is a favorite among joggers and picnickers. The Ferry Building also serves actual ferries: from behind the building they sail to Sausalito, Larkspur, Tiburon, and the East Bay. ⊠*Embarcadero at foot of Market St., Embarcadero* ⊕*www.ferrybuildingmarketplace.com.*

🄲 **Fisherman's Wharf.** It may be one of the city's best-known attractions, but the wharf is a no-go zone for most locals, who shy away from the difficult parking, overpriced food, and cheesy shops at third-rate shopping centers like the Cannery at Del Monte Square. If you just can't resist a

HISTORY YOU CAN SEE

Many remnants of the Spanish presence in early California remain in San Francisco, most notably in Mission San Francisco de Asís, aka Mission Dolores. The city's oldest standing structure—completed in 1791—is tiny and unassuming, with a lovely jumble of a graveyard out back. The Presidio itself originated as a Spanish military outpost; many of its lovely old Spanish-style buildings have been restored, and some are open to the public.

San Francisco turned boomtown when Sam Brannan's cry of "Gold!" echoed around the world in 1848 and transformed the country. Remnants of the Gold Rush remain buried beneath the city—including ships abandoned in harbor by Forty-Niners anxious to start panning. Catch a glimpse of these heady days at the free Wells Fargo Museum, where a stagecoach once used to shuttle gold to the city and cash to the miners presides over a collection of gold dust and miners' letters. For the full story, walk the Barbary Trail, a 3.8-mi path marked with bronze plaques that leads you through the most important Gold Rush neighborhoods—Jackson Square, parts of the Financial District, Chinatown, and Portsmouth Square—past remnants of a time when the entire city was drunk with vice, violence, and the possibility of riches.

visit here, come early to avoid the crowds and get a sense of the wharf's functional role—it's not just an amusement park replica. Most of the entertainment at the wharf is schlocky and overpriced, with one notable exception: the splendid **Musée Mécanique** (☎ *415/346–2000* ☉ *Weekdays 10–7, weekends 10–8*), a time-warped arcade with antique mechanical contrivances, including peep shows and nickelodeons. Admission is free, but you'll need quarters to bring the machines to life. ⊠ *Jefferson St. between Leavenworth St. and Pier 39, Fisherman's Wharf.*

Fodor'sChoice
★ **Golden Gate Bridge.** The suspension bridge that connects San Francisco with Marin County has long wowed sightseers with its simple but powerful art deco design. From the bridge's eastern-side walkway—the only side pedestrians are allowed on—you can take in the San Francisco skyline and the bay islands; look west for the wild hills of the Marin Headlands, the curving coast south to Land's End, and the Pacific Ocean. On sunny days, sailboats dot the water, and brave windsurfers test the often-treacherous tides beneath the bridge. ⊠ *Lincoln Blvd. near Doyle Dr. and Fort Point, Presidio* ☎ *415/921–5858* ⊕ *www.golden gatebridge.org* ☉ *Pedestrians Mar.–Oct., daily 5 AM–9 PM; Nov.–Apr., daily 5 AM–6:30 PM; hrs change with daylight savings time. Bicyclists daily 24 hrs.*

Fodor'sChoice
★ **Golden Gate Park.** It may be world famous, but first and foremost the park is the city's backyard. Come here any day of the week, and you can find a microcosm of San Francisco, from the Russian senior citizens feeding the pigeons at Stow Lake to the moms pushing strollers through the botanical gardens to the arts boosters checking out the latest at the de Young Museum. Be sure to visit the park's iconic treasures, including the serene Japanese Tea Garden and the beautiful Victorian Conserva-

tory of Flowers. If you have the time to venture farther into this urban oasis, you can discover less-accessible gems like the Beach Chalet and the wild western shores of Ocean Beach.

★ **Hyde Street Pier.** Cotton candy and souvenirs are all well and good, but if you want to get to the heart of the wharf—boats—there's no better place to do it than this pier, by far one of the wharf area's best bargains. Depending on the time of day, you might see boat builders at work or children pretending to man an early 1900s ship. Don't pass up the centerpiece collection of historic vessels, part of the **San Francisco Maritime National Historic Park,** almost all of which can be boarded. Across the street from the pier and almost a museum in itself is the San Francisco Maritime National Historic Park's **Visitor Center** (⊠ *499 Jefferson St., at Hyde St., Fisherman's Wharf* ☎ *415/447–5000* ⊗ *Memorial Day–Sept., daily 9:30–7; Oct.–Memorial Day, daily 9:30–5*), happily free of mind-numbing, text-heavy displays. Instead, fun, large-scale exhibits, such as a huge First Order Fresnel lighthouse lens and a shipwrecked boat, make this an engaging and relatively quick stop. ⊠ *Hyde and Jefferson Sts., Fisherman's Wharf* ☎ *415/561–7100* ⊕ *www.nps.gov/safr* ⊡ *Ships $5* ⊗ *Memorial Day–Sept., daily 9:30–5:30; Oct.–Memorial Day, daily 9:30–5.*

Fodor'sChoice **Palace of Fine Arts.** At first glance this stunning, rosy rococo palace seems
★ to be from another world, and indeed, it's the sole survivor of the many tinted-plaster structures (a temporary classical city of sorts) built for the 1915 Panama-Pacific International Exposition, the world's fair that celebrated San Francisco's recovery from the 1906 earthquake and fire. The expo buildings originally extended about a mile along the shore. Bernard Maybeck designed this faux Roman Classic beauty, which was reconstructed in concrete and reopened in 1967. ⊠ *Baker and Beach Sts., Marina* ☎ *415/561–0364 palace history tours* ⊕ *www.explorato rium.edu/palace* ⊡ *Free* ⊗ *Daily 24 hrs.*

★ **Union Square.** The heart of San Francisco's downtown since 1850, a 2½-acre square surrounded by department stores and the St. Francis Hotel, is about the only place you can sit for free in this part of town. The public responded to Union Square's 2002 redesign with a resounding shrug. With its pretty landscaping, easier street access, and the addition of a café (welcome, but nothing special), it's certainly an improvement over the old concrete wasteland, but no one's beating a path downtown to hang out here. Four globular lamp sculptures by the artist R. M. Fischer preside over the space; there's also an open-air stage, a visitor information booth, and a front-row seat to the cable-car tracks. And there's a familiar kaleidoscope of characters: office workers sunning and brown-bagging, street musicians, shoppers taking a rest, kids chasing pigeons, and a fair number of homeless people. At center stage, Robert Ingersoll Aitken's *Victory Monument* commemorates Commodore George Dewey's victory over the Spanish fleet at Manila in 1898. On the eastern edge of Union Square, **TIX Bay Area** (☎ *415/433–7827 info only* ⊕ *www.theatrebayarea.org*) provides half-price day-of-performance tickets (cash or traveler's checks only) to all types of performing-arts events, as well as regular full-price box-

32

STRANGE BUT TRUE

- There are more dogs in San Francisco today than children.

- In a town of big personalities, one of the most-recognized faces is Frank Chu, a middle-age guy in a frumpy suit who haunts the Financial District carrying a picket sign demanding the impeachment of politicians for keeping money from him and the citizens of the 12 galaxies.

- Each cable car costs $1 million to build, which makes the $5 fare a little more understandable.

- Armed with only helmets, safety harnesses, and painting equipment, a full-time crew of 38 painters keeps the Golden Gate Bridge clad in International Orange.

- At the border of Noe Valley and the Mission, you'll see a fire hydrant painted gold. This is the one hydrant that continued to pump water during and after the 1906 earthquake.

office services.Union Square covers a convenient but expensive four-level underground garage. ⊠*Bordered by Powell, Stockton, Post, and Geary Sts., Union Square.*

WINE COUNTRY

TOURS **Beau Wine Tours** (⊠*21707 8th St. E, Sonoma 95476* ☎*707/938–8001* ⊕*www.beauwinetours.com*) organizes personalized tours of Napa and Sonoma in their limos, vans, and shuttle buses. **Gray Line** (⊠*Pier 43½ Embarcadero, San Francisco 94131* ☎*415/434–8687 or 888/428–6937* ⊕*www.grayline.com*)has a tour that covers both southern Napa and Sonoma valleys in a single day, with a stop for lunch in Yountville. **Great Pacific Tour Co.** (⊠*518 Octavia St., Civic Center, San Francisco 94102* ☎*415/626–4499* ⊕*www.greatpacifictour.com*) operates full-day tours of Napa and Sonoma, including a restaurant or picnic lunch, in passenger vans that seat 14. In addition to renting bikes by the day, **Wine Country Bikes** (⊠*61 Front St., Healdsburg 95448* ☎*707/473–0610* ⊕*www.winecountrybikes.com*) organizes both one-day and mul-tiday trips throughout Sonoma County.

★ **Copia: The American Center for Wine, Food & the Arts,** named after the goddess of abundance, is a shrine to American food and wine. A permanent exhibit called "Forks in the Road" explores the American relationship to food and wine in past decades, from TV dinners to haute cuisine. All sorts of garden tours, video screenings, food- and wine tastings, and tours are scheduled daily (pick up a list from the information desk). ■**TIP→** Call in advance or check their Web site for information on wine-maker dinners and luncheon seminars. For an extra fee, you can get a fantastic opportunity to learn about the culinary arts from some of the area's best chefs and vintners. The adjacent Oxbow Public Market hosts a collection of artisanal food producers. ⊠*500 1st St., Napa* ☎*707/259–1600* ⊕*www.copia.org* 💲*$5* ⊙ *Wed.–Mon. 10–5.*

Fodor'sChoice **Frog's Leap** is the perfect place for wine novices to begin their educa-
★ tion. The owners, the Williams family, maintain a goofy sense of humor

about wine that translates into an entertaining yet informative experi-ence. Why resist a place that dubs one of its wines Leapfrögmilch? They also happen to produce some very fine zinfandel, cabernet sauvignon, merlot, and sauvignon blanc. They pride themselves on the sustain-ability of their operation, and the tour guides can tell you about their organic farming and solar power techniques. The winery includes a red barn built in 1884, an ecofriendly visitor center, and, naturally, a frog pond topped with lily pads. ⊠*8815 Conn Creek Rd., Ruther-ford* ☎*707/963–4704* ⊕*www.frogsleap.com* ⊠*Tasting and tour free* ⊗*Mon.–Sat. 10–4; tastings and tour by appointment.*

Fodor'sChoice The **Hess Collection Winery and Vineyards** is a delightful discovery on Mt.
★ Veeder 9 mi northwest of the city of Napa. (Don't give up; the road leading to the winery is long and winding.) The simple, rustic limestone structure, circa 1903, contains Swiss owner Donald Hess's personal art collection, including mostly large-scale works by such contemporary European and American artists as Robert Motherwell, Francis Bacon, and Frank Stella. Cabernet sauvignon is the real strength here, though Hess also produces some fine chardonnays. The winery and the art collection are open for self-guided tours (free) ⊠*4411 Redwood Rd., Napa, west of Rte. 29* ☎*707/255–1144* ⊕*www.hesscollection.com* ⊠*Tasting $10–$25* ⊗*Daily 10–5, tasting until 4.*

Fodor'sChoice The visitor center at beautiful **Matanzas Creek Winery** sets itself apart
★ with an understated Japanese aesthetic, with a tranquil fountain and a koi pond. Best of all, huge windows overlook a vast field of lavender plants. ■**TIP**➡ **The best time to visit is in June, when the lavender blooms and perfumes the air.** The winery specializes in three varietals—sauvi-gnon blanc, merlot, and chardonnay—though in 2005 they also started producing a popular dry rosé. After you taste the wines, ask for the self-guided garden-tour book before taking a stroll. ⊠*6097 Bennett Valley Rd., Santa Rosa* ☎*707/528–6464 or 800/590–6464* ⊕*www.matanzas creek.com* ⊠*Tasting $5, tour free* ⊗*Daily 10–4:30; tour weekdays at 10:30 and 2:30, Sat. at 10:30, by appointment.*

Fodor'sChoice The arch at the center of the sprawling Mission-style building at **Robert**
★ **Mondavi** perfectly frames the lawn and the vineyard behind, inviting a stroll under the lovely arcades. If you've never been on a winery tour before, the comprehensive 70- to 90-minute tour, followed by a seated tasting, is a good way to learn about oenology, as well as Robert Mon-davi's role in California wine making. You can also head straight for one of the two tasting rooms. Serious wine lovers should definitely con-sider springing for the $30 reserve-room tasting, where you can enjoy four generous tastes of Mondavi's top-of-the-line wines, including the reserve cabernet that cemented the winery's reputation. Concerts, mostly jazz and R&B, take place in summer on the lawn; call ahead for tickets. ⊠*7801 St. Helena Hwy. Rte. 29, Oakville* ☎*888/766–6328* ⊕*www.robertmondaviwinery.com* ⊠*Tasting $10–$30, tour $25* ⊗*Daily 10–5; tours daily on the hr 10–4.*

When visiting **Stony Hill Vineyard**, it's easy to imagine that this is what the Napa Valley was like 20 years ago, before many of the wineries started building glitzy visitor centers and charging tasting fees. When you call to make a reservation for a tour and tasting, you'll get directions for following the unmarked road that winds up the hill north of St. Helena to their secluded property. From this perch, you can have beautiful views of rolling hills in between stands of old oak and cypress trees. The tour is casual and conversational—the guide relies on questions from visitors instead of reciting a canned

spiel. The visit ends with a tasting of their excellent unoaked chardonnay. If you're lucky, you might get a nip of their dry gewürztraminer or Riesling, though they're often sold out. ⊠ *3331 St. Helena Hwy. N Rte. 29, St. Helena* ☎ *707/963–2636* ⊕ *www.stonyhillvineyard.com* ⌲ *Tasting and tour free* ☉ *Tasting and tour by appointment only.*

WHERE TO EAT

WHAT IT COSTS				
¢	$	$$	$$$	$$$$
AT DINNER under $10	$10–$14	$15–$22	$23–$29	over $30

Prices are per person for a typical main course or equivalent combination of smaller dishes. Note: if a restaurant offers only prix-fixe (set-price) meals, it has been given the price category that reflects the full prix-fixe price.

SAN FRANCISCO

$$$$
Fodor's Choice
★
AMERICAN
Embarcadero

Boulevard. Two of San Francisco's top restaurant celebrities—chef Nancy Oakes and designer Pat Kuleto—are responsible for this high-profile, high-price eatery in the magnificent 1889 Audiffred Building, a Parisian look-alike and one of the few downtown structures to survive the 1906 earthquake. Kuleto's belle epoque interior and Oakes's sophisticated American food with a French accent attract well-dressed locals and flush out-of-towners. The menu changes seasonally, but count on generous portions of dishes like sweetbreads saltimbocca with tender chanterelles, crisp-skinned pan-roasted squab with fresh figs, and flaky butterfish with shrimp-and-lobster-stuffed artichoke. Save room (and calories) for one of the dynamite desserts, such as the caramel brownie tart with raspberry coulis. There's counter seating for folks too hungry to wait for a table. ⊠ *1 Mission St., Embarcadero* ☎ *415/543–6084* ▭ *AE, D, DC, MC, V* ☉ *No lunch weekends.*

$$$$
Fodor's Choice
★
SEAFOOD
Union Sq.

Farallon. Sculpted jellyfish chandeliers, kelp-covered columns, and sea-urchin lights give this swanky Pat Kuleto–designed restaurant a decidedly quirky look. But there's nothing quirky about chef Mark Franz's impeccable seafood, which reels in serious diners from coast to coast. The menu changes daily, but rotating dishes include lobster bisque with oven-roasted mushrooms, bluenose bass with celery root puree and chanterelles, and seared rainbow trout with broccoli rabe. If you want to enjoy the surroundings but not pay the price, you can take a seat at the bar and fill up on lobster rolls, mussels and french fries, grilled squid, and more from the cheaper bar menu. ✉ *450 Post St., Union Sq.* ☎ *415/956–6969* ⊟ *AE, D, DC, MC, V* ⊘ *No lunch.*

$$$$ **Gary Danko.** Be prepared to wait your turn for a table behind chef Gary
Fodor's Choice Danko's legion of loyal fans, who typically keep the reservation book
★ chock-full here. The cost of a meal ($61–$92) is pegged to the number
NEW AMERICAN of courses, from three to five. The menu, which changes seasonally,
Fisherman's may include pancetta-wrapped frog legs, Moroccan squab with orange-
Wharf cumin carrots, and quail stuffed with wild mushrooms and foie gras. A diet-destroying chocolate soufflé with two sauces is usually among the desserts. The wine list is the size of a small-town phone book, and the banquette-lined room, with beautiful wood floors and stunning (but restrained) floral arrangements, is as memorable as the food. ✉ *800 N. Point St., Fisherman's Wharf* ☎ *415/749–2060* ⚖ *Reservations essential* ⊟ *D, DC, MC, V* ⊘ *No lunch.*

$$$ **Zuni Café.** After one bite of chef Judy Rodgers' succulent brick-oven-
Fodor's Choice roasted whole chicken with Tuscan bread salad, you'll understand
★ why she's a national star. Food is served here on two floors; the rabbit
MEDITERRANEAN warren of rooms on the second level includes a balcony overlooking
Hayes Valley the main dining room. The crowd is a disparate mix that reflects the make-up of the city: casual and dressy, young and old, hip and staid. At the long copper bar, trays of briny-fresh oysters on the half shell are dispensed along with cocktails and wine. The southern French–Italian menu changes daily (though the signature chicken, prepared for two, is a fixture). Rotating dishes include house-cured anchovies with Parmigiano-Reggiano, risotto with sorrel and prosciutto, and grilled duck breast with radicchio and sweet potatoes. Desserts are simple and satisfying and include crumbly crusted tarts and an addictive cream-laced coffee granita. ✉ *1658 Market St., Hayes Valley* ☎ *415/552–2522* ⊟ *AE, MC, V* ⊘ *Closed Mon.*

$$–$$$ **Delfina.** "Irresistible." That's how countless diehard fans describe Del-
Fodor's Choice fina. Such wild enthusiasm has made patience the critical virtue for
★ anyone wanting a reservation here. The interior is comfortable, with
ITALIAN hardwood floors, aluminum-top tables, a tile bar, and a casual, friendly
Mission atmosphere. The menu changes daily, but among the usual offerings are salt cod *mantecato* (whipped with olive oil) with fennel flatbread; grilled squid with warm white bean salad; gnocchi with rabbit sauce; and roast chicken with trumpet mushrooms. On warm nights, try for a table on the outdoor patio. The storefront next door is home to pint-size Pizzeria Delfina. ✉ *3621 18th St., Mission* ☎ *415/552–4055* ⚖ *Reservations essential* ⊟ *MC, V* ⊘ *No lunch.*

$$–$$$ **Slanted Door.** If you're looking for homey Vietnamese food served in a
VIETNAMESE down-to-earth dining room, *don't* stop here. Celebrated chef–owner
Embarcadero Charles Phan has mastered the upmarket, Western-accented Vietnamese menu. To showcase his cuisine, he chose a big space with sleek wooden tables and chairs, white marble floors, a cocktail lounge, a bar, and an enviable bay view. Among his popular dishes are green papaya salad, wood oven-roasted whole fish with ginger sauce, and shaking

32

ON THE WAY

Oakland: Take a pleasant ferry ride from the city to Jack London Square to get a tiny taste of Oakland; from here you can walk a few blocks to Oakland's densely packed, workaday Chinatown. Or hop BART to 19th Street and explore the burgeoning independent arts strip along Telegraph and Grand avenues.

Berkeley. Just across the Bay Bridge, this famed college town, best known as the birthplace of the Free Speech Movement of the 1960s, draws visitors for its liberal history, academic prowess, and offbeat shops and coffeehouses.

Muir Woods National Monument: Just outside San Francisco, you can wander through 550 acres filled with 250-foot tall redwoods—some more than 1,000 years old. To get here take U.S. 101 north across the Golden Gate Bridge to the Mill Valley/Stinson Beach exit, then follow the signs to Highway 1 north. *415/388–2595, www.nps.gov/muwo.*

beef (tender beef cubes with garlic and onion). To avoid the midday and evening crowds, stop in for the afternoon-tea menu (spring rolls, grilled pork over rice noodles), or visit Out the Door, Phan's take-out counter around the corner from the restaurant. Alas, the crush of fame has also brought some ragged service. ⊠ *Ferry Bldg., Embarcadero at Market St., Embarcadero* ☎ *415/861–8032* ⚓ *Reservations essential* ▭ *AE, MC, V.*

$–$$$
Fodor'sChoice
★
☺
CHINESE
Richmond

Ton Kiang. This restaurant introduced the lightly seasoned Hakka cuisine of southern China, rarely found in this country and even obscure to many Chinese. Salt-baked chicken, stuffed bean curd, steamed fresh bacon with dried mustard greens, chicken in wine sauce, and clay pots of meats and seafood are among the hallmarks of the Hakka kitchen, and all of them are done well here, as the tables packed with local Chinese families and others prove. Don't overlook the excellent seafood offerings like salt-and-pepper shrimp, catfish in black bean sauce, or stir-fried crab, for example. Some of the finest dim sum in the city brings in the noontime rush (a small selection is available at night, too). ⊠ *5821 Geary Blvd., Richmond* ☎ *415/387–8273* ▭ *MC, V.*

$–$$
Fodor'sChoice
★
☺
ITALIAN
North Beach

L'Osteria del Forno. A staff chattering in Italian and seductive aromas drifting from the open kitchen make customers who pass through the door of this modest storefront, with its sunny yellow walls and friendly waitstaff, feel as if they've stumbled into a homey trattoria in Italy. The kitchen produces small plates of simply cooked vegetables, a few pastas, some daily specials, milk-braised pork, a roast of the day, creamy polenta, and thin-crust pizzas—including a memorable "white" pie topped with porcini mushrooms and mozzarella. At lunch try one of North Beach's best focaccia sandwiches. ⊠ *519 Columbus Ave., North Beach* ☎ *415/982–1124* ▭ *No credit cards* ☯ *Closed Tues.*

¢–$$
Fodor'sChoice
★
SEAFOOD
Van Ness/Polk

Swan Oyster Depot. Here is old San Francisco at its best. Half fish market and half diner, this small, slim seafood operation, open since 1912, has no tables, only a narrow marble counter with about a dozen and a half stools. Most people come in to buy perfectly fresh salmon, halibut, crabs, and other seafood to take home. Everyone else—locals and out-of-towners—hops onto one of the rickety stools to enjoy a bowl of clam chowder—the only hot food served—a dozen oysters, half a cracked crab, a big shrimp salad, or a smaller shrimp cocktail. Come early or late to avoid a long wait. ⊠ *1517 Polk St., Van Ness/Polk* ☎ *415/673–1101* ▭ *No credit cards* ⊘ *Closed Sun. No dinner.*

WINE COUNTRY

$$$$ ✕ **French Laundry.** An old stone building houses the most acclaimed restaurant in Napa Valley—and, indeed, one of the most highly regarded in the country. The restaurant's two prix-fixe menus ($210), one of which is vegetarian, vary, but the "oysters and pearls," a silky sabayon of pearl tapioca with oysters and sevruga caviar, is a signature starter. Some courses rely on luxe ingredients like foie gras, while others take humble foods like fava beans and elevate them to art. Reservations at French Laundry are hard-won and not accepted more than two months in advance. ■TIP→ **Call two months ahead to the day at 10** AM **on the dot. Didn't get a reservation? Call on the day you'd like to dine here to be considered if there's a cancellation.** ⊠ *6640 Washington St., Yountville* ☎ *707/944–2380* ⊜ *Reservations essential* ▭ *AE, MC, V* ⊘ *Closed 1st 2 wks in Jan. No lunch Mon.–Thurs.*

FodorśChoice
★

VITAL STATS

■ The San Francisco city flag features the Phoenix, appropriate considering how many times the city has burned to the ground and been rebuilt.

■ The official city song, "I Left My Heart in San Francisco," was written by gay couple Douglass Cross and George Cory.

■ The first topless dance performance in the U.S. took place took place in 1964 at the Condor Club in North Beach.

■ The first death leap from the Golden Gate Bridge took place just three months after the bridge's completion in 1937.

WHERE TO STAY

	WHAT IT COSTS			
	¢	$	$$	$$$	$$$$
FOR 2 PEOPLE	under $90	$90–$149	$150–$199	$200–$249	over $250

Prices are for two people in a standard double room in high season, excluding 14% tax.

$$$$ ⊞ **Hotel Monaco.** A cheery 1910 beaux arts facade and snappily dressed doormen welcome you into the plush lobby, dominated by a French inglenook fireplace, vaulted ceilings featuring whimsical murals of hot-air balloons, and large metal baobab tree dedicated to hotelier Bill Kimpton. Rooms are full of flair, with vivid stripes and colors, Chinese-inspired armoires, canopy beds, and high-back upholstered chairs. Outer rooms have bay-window seats overlooking the bustling theater district. If you didn't bring a pet, request a "companion goldfish." Guests have cheered the hotel's staff for its "amazing service" and "attention to detail." The ornate Grand Café and Bar serves a

FodorśChoice
★

blend of French and Californian cuisine. You also receive complimentary access to the recently redone Equilibrium Spa, where you can soak, steam, or bake 6 AM–10 PM. ⊠ *501 Geary St., Union Square, 94102* 📞 *415/292–0100 or 866/622–5284* 📠 *415/292–0111* 🌐 *www. monaco-sf.com* 🛏 *181 rooms, 20 suites* ♿ *In-room: safe, VCR (some), dial-up, minibar, Wi-Fi. In-hotel: restaurant, room service, bar, gym, spa, concierge, laundry service, public Internet, parking (fee), no-smoking rooms, some pets allowed* 🚪 *AE, D, DC, MC, V.*

$$$$
Fodor's Choice
★

Mandarin Oriental. Two towers connected by glass-enclosed sky bridges compose the top 11 floors of San Francisco's third-tallest building. There are spectacular panoramas from every room, and windows open so you can hear the "ding ding" of the cable cars some 40 floors below. The recently renovated rooms, corridors, and lobby areas are decorated in rich hues of red, gold, and chocolate brown. The Mandarin Rooms have extra deep tubs next to picture windows so you can literally and figuratively soak up what one reader called "unbelievable views from the Golden Gate to the Bay Bridge and everything in between." Pamper yourself with luxurious Egyptian-cotton sheets, two kinds of robes (terry and waffle-weave), and terry slippers. A lovely complimentary tea and cookie tray delivered to your room upon your arrival indicates the hotel's commitment to service. The mezzanine-level restaurant, Silks, earns rave reviews for its innovative American cuisine with Asian touches. ⊠ *222 Sansome St., Financial District, 94104* 📞 *415/276–9600 or 800/622–0404* 📠 *415/276–9304* 🌐 *www.mandarinoriental.com/sanfrancisco* 🛏 *154 rooms, 4 suites* ♿ *In-room: safe, kitchen (some), VCR (some), dial-up, Wi-Fi. In-hotel: restaurant, room service, bar, gym, concierge, laundry service, public Internet, parking (fee), no-smoking rooms, some pets allowed (fee)* 🚪 *AE, D, DC, MC, V.*

$$$$
Fodor's Choice
★

Ritz-Carlton, San Francisco. This hotel, a stunning tribute to beauty and attentive, professional service, recently completed a $12.5 million renovation. Beyond the Ionic columns of the neoclassic facade, crystal chandeliers illuminate Georgian antiques and museum-quality 18th- and 19th-century paintings in the lobby. All rooms have featherbeds with 300-thread-count Egyptian cotton Frette sheets and down comforters. Club Level rooms include use of the Club Lounge, which has a dedicated concierge and several elaborate complimentary food presentations daily. The renowned Dining Room has a seasonal menu with modern French accents, and afternoon tea in the Lobby Lounge—overlooking the beautifully landscaped Terrace courtyard—is a San Francisco institution. ⊠ *600 Stockton St., at California St., Nob Hill, 94108* 📞 *415/296–7465* 📠 *415/291–0288* 🌐 *www.ritzcarlton.com/ hotels/san_francisco* 🛏 *276 rooms, 60 suites* ♿ *In-room: safe, refrigerator, VCR, dial-up, Wi-Fi. In-hotel: 2 restaurants, room service, bars, pool, gym, concierge, laundry service, executive floor, public Internet, parking (fee), no-smoking rooms, some pets allowed* 🚪 *AE, D, DC, MC, V.*

$$–$$$
Fodor's Choice
★

Hotel Rex. This stylish hotel, named for San Francisco Renaissance poet, translator and essayist Kenneth Rexroth, celebrates literary creativity. Shelves of antiquarian books line the library-theme lobby lounge, where book readings and roundtable discussions take place, and the adjacent study, decorated with a collection of vintage typewriters, has two high-tech workstations. Although the spacious rooms evoke the spirit of 1920s salon society with muted checkered bedspreads, striped carpets, and restored period furnishings, they also have modern touches such as CD players, and complimentary Aveda hair and skin products. Breakfast, lunch, and dinner featuring California cuisine and local wines are served in the petite bistro, Andrée. ⊠ *562 Sutter St., Union Square, 94102* ☎ *415/433–4434 or 800/433–4434* ☐ *415/433–3695* ⊕ *www.thehotelrex.com* ➴ *92 rooms, 2 suites* ⊘ *In-room: refrigerator, Wi-Fi. In-hotel: restaurant, room service, bar, concierge, laundry service, parking (fee), no-smoking rooms, public Internet* ☐ *AE, D, DC, MC, V.*

¢–$ Fodor'sChoice   ★   🏨 **Grant Plaza Hotel.** Amazingly low room rates and a prime location make this hotel a find for budget travelers wanting views of Chinatown's fascinating street life. Small, modern rooms are sparkling clean, with newer, slightly more expensive digs on the top floor and quieter quarters in the back. Even if you're not on the top floor, take the elevator up anyway to view two large, beautiful stained-glass windows. ⊠ *465 Grant Ave., Chinatown, 94108* ☎ *415/434–3883 or 800/472–6899* ☐ *415/434–3886* ⊕ *www.grantplaza.com* ➴ *71 rooms, 1 suite* ⊘ *In-room: no a/c, VCR (some), dial-up, Wi-Fi. In-hotel: public Internet, parking (fee), no-smoking rooms* ☐ *AE, D, DC, MC, V.*

NIGHTLIFE & THE ARTS

SAN FRANCISCO

Fodor'sChoice   ★   **Buena Vista Café.** Smack dab at the end of the Hyde Street cable-car line, the Buena Vista packs 'em in for its famous Irish coffee—which, according to the owners, was the first served stateside (in 1952). The place oozes nostalgia and draws devoted locals as well as out-of-towners relaxing after a day of sightseeing. It's narrow and can get crowded, but this place is a welcome respite from the overpriced, generic tourist joints nearby. ⊠ *2765 Hyde St., at Beach St., Fisherman's Wharf* ☎ *415/474–5044* ⊕ *www.thebuenavista.com.*

Fodor'sChoice   ★   **Castro Theatre.** Designed by art deco master Timothy Pfleuger and opened in 1922, the most dramatic movie theater in the city hosts revivals as well as foreign and independent engagements and the occasional sing-along movie musical. ⊠ *429 Castro St., near Market St., Castro* ☎ *415/621–6120* ⊕ *www.thecastrotheatre.com.*

San Francisco Symphony. One of America's top orchestras, the San Francisco Symphony performs from September through May, with additional summer performances of light classical music and show tunes; visiting artists perform here the rest of the year. ⊠ *Davies Symphony Hall, 201 Van Ness Ave., at Grove St., Civic Center* ☎ *415/864–6000* ⊕ *www.sfsymphony.org.*

Fodor'sChoice   ★   **Yoshi's.** The legendary Oakland club that has pulled in some of the world's best jazz musicians—Pat Martino, Branford Marsalis, and Kurt Elling in early 2007 alone—has opened a San Francisco location. The club has seating for 420 and, like Yoshi's in Oakland, serves Japanese food in an adjoining restaurant and at café tables in the club. And yes, the coupling of sushi and jazz *is* as elegant as it sounds. ✉*1300 Fillmore St., at Eddy St., Japantown* ☎*415/655-5600* ⊕*www.yoshis.com.*

SHOPPING

32

SAN FRANCISCO

Fodor$Choice ★ **Amoeba Music.** With more than 2.5 million new and used CDs, DVDs, and records, this warehouselike store (and the original Berkeley location) carries titles you can't find on Amazon at bargain prices. No niche is ignored—from electronica and hip-hop to jazz and classical—and the stock changes daily. Weekly in-store performances attract large crowds. ✉*1855 Haight St., between Stanyan and Shrader Sts., Haight* ☎*415/831-1200.*

Fodor$Choice ★ **City Lights Bookstore.** The city's most famous bookstore is where the Beat movement of the 1950s was born. Neal Cassady and Jack Kerouac hung out in the basement and now regulars and tourists while hours away in this well-worn space. The upstairs room highlights impressive poetry and Beat literature collections. Poet Lawrence Ferlinghetti, the owner, remains active in the workings of this three-story place. Since publishing Allen Ginsberg's *Howl* in 1956, City Lights' press continues to publish a dozen new titles each year. ✉*261 Columbus Ave., at Broadway, North Beach* ☎*415/362-8193.*

Fodor$Choice ★ **Ferry Plaza Farmers' Market.** The most upscale and expensive of the city's farmers' markets, in front of the restored Ferry Building, places baked goods and fancy pots of jam alongside organic basil and heirloom tomatoes. The Saturday market is the grandest, with about 100 vendors packed both in front of and behind the building. The Tuesday and Thursday markets are smaller. At the Sunday garden market, vegetable and ornamental plants crop up next to a small selection of food items. (The Thursday and Sunday markets don't operate in winter, generally December or January through March.) ■**TIP**➔ **On Saturday, don't miss the coffee at Blue Bottle—and yes, the line is worth it.** ✉*Ferry Plaza, Embarcadero at north end of Market St., Financial District* ☎*415/291-3276* ⊕*www.ferryplazafarmersmarket.com* ⊙*Tues. and Sun. 10–2, Thurs. 4–8, Sat. 8–2.*

WINE COUNTRY

★ The **Oakville Grocery** (✉*7856 St. Helena Hwy., Oakville; Rte. 29* ☎*707/944–8802*), built in 1881 as a general store, carries a surprisingly wide range of unusual and chichi groceries and prepared foods despite its tiny size. Despite the maddening crowds that pack the narrow aisles on weekends, it's still a fine place to sit on a bench out front and sip an espresso between winery visits.

SPORTS & THE OUTDOORS

Fodor$Choice ★ ♻ The **San Francisco Giants** (✉*AT&T Park, 24 Willie Mays Plaza, between 2nd and 3rd Sts., China Basin* ☎*415/972–2000 or 800/734–4268* ⊕*http://sanfrancisco.giants.mlb.com*) play in beautiful AT&T Park.

The **San Francisco Bicycle Coalition** (☎415/431–2453 ⊕www.sfbike.org) has extensive information about the policies and politics of riding a bicycle in the city and lists local events for cyclists on its Web site. You can also download (but not print) a PDF version of the *San Francisco Bike Map and Walking Guide.*

Blazing Saddles. This outfitter rents bikes for $7 an hour or $28 a day, and shares tips on sights to see along the paths. ✉2715 Hyde St., Fisherman's Wharf ✉465 Jefferson St., at Hyde St., Fisherman's Wharf ✉Pier 43½, near Taylor St., Fisherman's Wharf ✉Pier 41, at Powell St., Fisherman's Wharf ☎415/202–8888 ⊕www.blazingsaddles.com.

★ A former military garrison and a beautiful wildlife preserve, Angel Island has some steep roads and great views of the city and the bay. Bicycles must stay on roadways; there are no single-track trails on the island. A ferry operated by **Blue & Gold Fleet** (☎415/705–8200 ⊕www. blueandgoldfleet.com) runs to the island from Pier 41 at Fisherman's Wharf and takes about 20 minutes one way; the fare is $14.50 round-trip, which includes park admission. Ferries leave once a day at 10 AM weekdays and 10:30 AM weekends, returning at around 3:30 PM; schedules change, so call for up-to-date info. Twenty-five bicycles are permitted on-board on a first-come, first-served basis (you can also rent bikes on the island). The café is closed mid-November through February, so bring your own grub. ☎415/435–1915 ⊕www.angelisland.org.

Fodor's Choice The Presidio is part of **Golden Gate National Recreation Area (GGNRA)**
★ (☎415/561–4700 ⊕www.nps.gov/goga), which also encompasses the San Francisco coastline, the Marin Headlands, and Point Reyes National Seashore. It's veined with hiking trails, and guided walks are available. Current schedules are available at GGNRA visitor centers in the Presidio and Marin Headlands; you can also find them online at www.nps.gov/goga/parknews. For descriptions of each location within the recreation area—along with rich color photographs, hiking information, and maps—pick up a copy of *Guide to the Parks,* available in local bookstores or online from the **Golden Gate National Parks Conservancy** (☎415/561–3000 ⊕www.parksconservancy.org).

VISITOR INFORMATION

San Francisco Convention and Visitors Bureau (✉ 201 3rd St., Suite 900, San Francisco 94103 ☎415/391–2000, 415/392–0328 TDD ⊕www.onlyinsan francisco.com).

San Francisco Visitor Information Center (✉ Hallidie Plaza, lower level, Powell and Market Sts., Union Sq. ☎ 415/391–2000, 415/392–0328 TDD ⊕www. onlyinsanfrancisco.com).

Lake Tahoe

Lake Tahoe

WORD OF MOUTH

"Heavenly is by far the best resort to ski at and also closest to the casino resorts. The views of Lake Tahoe are outstanding. One thing that I like about Heavenly is that some of the easiest runs are at the top of the mountain . . . Once you get up there the top of the mountain has mostly green and blue runs."

–RBCal

EXPLORING LAKE TAHOE

189 mi northeast of San Francisco via I–80; 105 mi northeast of Sacramento via I–80; 61 mi southwest of Reno, NV, via I–80; 485 mi northeast of Los Angeles via I–5 and I–80; 635 mi southeast of Portland, OR, via I–5 and I–80

By Christine Vovakes

Snow creates stunning cobalt-blue Lake Tahoe's beauty: the ancient glaciers that formed it, the white-capped Sierra Nevada peaks that ring it, and the melting ice that feeds the largest alpine lake in North America. With its deep clear water that never freezes, the lake straddles the state line between California and Nevada and lies 6,225 feet above sea level.

If you come in winter, you can discover why Tahoe's ski resorts are almost as famous as its lake. Driving here in winter is no picnic, but even though icy tempests turn byways into skating rinks, they also send clarion calls to snow-lovers. When storms pelt the Tahoe Basin, skiers descend in droves like a conquering army. The rest of the year begs for an old-fashioned top-down driving tour. Putter around the lake's 72-mi loop, and dawdle in the small towns that dot the shore with names like Tahoma and Carnelian Bay. If you prefer solitude, you can escape to the many state parks, national forests, and protected tracts of wilderness that surround the 22-mi-long, 12-mi-wide lake. Or try your luck in the numerous never-closed casinos on the Nevada side.

WHO WILL ESPECIALLY LOVE THIS TRIP?

Sports Enthusiasts: Whether you're a daredevil who whooshes down the steepest slopes, or an angler who spends hours idling in a skiff, Tahoe has a sport to match every temperament in every season. Skiing, snowshoeing, and ice skating are the obvious choices in winter. Hiking easy trails, backpacking into the rugged wilderness, kayaking, swimming, river rafting, tennis, horseback riding, golf, and mountain biking are some of the best balmy weather pursuits. And it's easy to be active while you're here—many of the larger resorts are self-contained sports havens that provide access to numerous activities.

Anytime Revelers: With gaming tables that never close down, live music in the lounges, and dining to suit all tastes and budgets, the casinos on the Nevada side of Lake Tahoe draw people who love to party.

Nature Lovers: The mesmerizing beauty of Lake Tahoe turns almost every visitor into at least a temporary nature lover. Those who explore beyond the water's edge will find five national forests in the Tahoe Basin and a half-dozen state parks. Kids can take a simple trail and learn about spawning salmon at Lake Tahoe Visitor Center on Taylor Creek. Many areas of Desolation Wilderness (El Dorado National Forest Information Center, 530/644–6048, www.fs.fed.us/r5/eldorado) are for advanced hikers.

TOP 5 REASONS TO GO

The Lake: Deep, blue, and alpine pure, Lake Tahoe is far and away the main reason to visit this High Sierra paradise.

Snow, Snow, Snow: Daring black diamond runs or baby bunny bump—whether you're an expert, a beginner, or somewhere in between, there are slopes to suit your skills at numerous Tahoe area ski parks.

The Great Outdoors: A ring of national forests, recreation areas, and miles of trails make Tahoe a nature lover's bliss.

Dinner with a View: Dine in restaurants perched along the shore, or picnic lakeside at one of the state parks.

A Date with Lady Luck: Whether you want to roll dice, play some slots, or hope the blackjack dealer goes bust before you do, you can find nonstop action at the casinos on the Nevada side of the lake.

33

Foodies: Influenced by its proximity to the San Francisco Bay Area, Lake Tahoe's dining scene buzzes with innovative restaurants and top-notch chefs.

Families: While the casinos here provide adults-only entertainment, the rest of Lake Tahoe is a kid's playground. Almost all of the ski parks have children's learn-to-ski lessons. Heavenly Village in the heart of South Lake Tahoe entices the younger set with an ice rink, a cinema, and a gondola ride to the top of Heavenly Mountain. And for low-cost activities that will get your kids close to nature, pitch your tent in one of the lakeside campgrounds, such as the one at D.L. Bliss State Park.

WHEN IS THE BEST TIME TO VISIT?

A sapphire-blue lake shimmering deep in the center of an ice-white wonderland—that's Tahoe in winter. But snow means storms that often close roads and force chain requirements on the interstate. In summer the roads are open, but the lake and lodgings are clogged with visitors seeking respite from valley heat.

If you don't ski, opt for early fall and late spring visits. The crowds thin, prices dip, and you can count on Tahoe being beautiful year-round. Plus the casinos never close their doors.

Most Lake Tahoe accommodations, restaurants, and even a handful of parks are open year-round, but many visitor centers, mansions, state parks, and beaches are closed from November through May. During those months, multitudes of skiers and other winter-sports enthusiasts are attracted to Tahoe's downhill resorts and cross-country centers, North America's largest concentration of skiing facilities. Ski resorts try to open by Thanksgiving, if only with machine-made snow, and can operate through May or later. During the ski season, Tahoe's population swells on the weekends. If you're able to come midweek, you'll have the resorts and neighboring towns almost to yourself.

Lake Tahoe

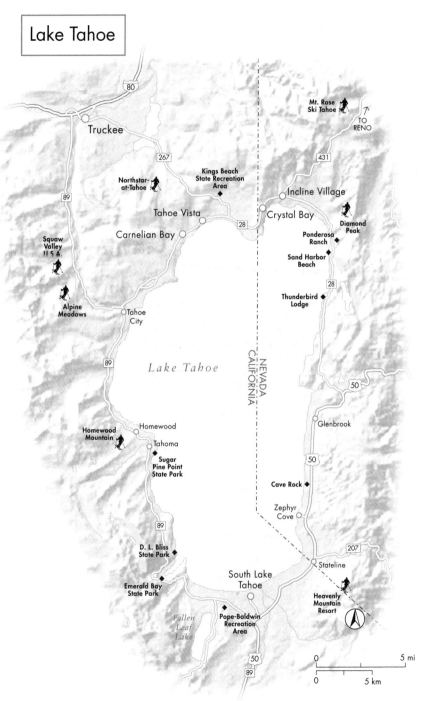

Truckee

Northstar-at-Tahoe

Kings Beach State Recreation Area

Tahoe Vista

Carnelian Bay

Incline Village

Crystal Bay

Mt. Rose Ski Tahoe

TO RENO

Diamond Peak

Ponderosa Ranch

Sand Harbor Beach

Squaw Valley USA

Alpine Meadows

Tahoe City

Thunderbird Lodge

Lake Tahoe

NEVADA
CALIFORNIA

Homewood Mountain

Homewood

Tahoma

Sugar Pine Point State Park

Glenbrook

Cave Rock

Zephyr Cove

D. L. Bliss State Park

Stateline

Emerald Bay State Park

South Lake Tahoe

Heavenly Mountain Resort

Fallen Leaf Lake

Pope-Baldwin Recreation Area

0   5 mi

0   5 km

How to Snack

33

After a chilly day on the slopes, you can find few sights more welcoming than the blazing fire pits outside numerous cafés and restaurants in the Tahoe area. Wedge into the group and warm your hands while sipping a hot drink at Marriott's Timber Lodge Fire and Ice Grill (4100 Lake Tahoe Blvd., South Lake Tahoe, 96150, 530/542-6650, www.fire-ice.com/locations/tahoe.html). For a quick pick-me-up, drop in at Mamasake (Village at Squaw Valley, 530/584-0110, www.mamasake.com) to enjoy the inexpensive afternoon special: a spicy-tuna or salmon handroll and a can of brew for five bucks (served between 3 and 5 PM). Grab bagels and pastries while you enjoy free Wi-Fi at Syd's Bagelry (550 N. Lake Tahoe Blvd., 530/583-2666), a popular local hangout in Tahoe City. If you get the munchies at 3 AM, head to the nearest casino where the grills, along with the gaming tables, never shut down. Try MontBleu's 20-Four (55 U.S. 50, Stateline, NV, 888/829-7630, www.montbleuresort.com/dining.php) for comfort food around the clock.

Nonskiers often find that Tahoe is most fun in summer, when it's cooler here than in the scorched Sierra Nevada foothills, the clean mountain air is bracingly crisp, and the surface temperature of Lake Tahoe is an invigorating 65°F to 70°F (compared with 40°F to 50°F in winter). This is also the time, however, when it may seem as if every tourist at the lake—100,000 on peak weekends—is in a car on the main road circling the shoreline. While the best strategy for avoiding the crush is to do as much as you can early in the day. September and October, when the throngs have dispersed but the weather is still pleasant, are among the most satisfying—and cheapest—months to visit. Christmas week and July 4 are the busiest times, and prices go through the roof; plan accordingly.

HOW SHOULD I GET THERE?

BY TRAIN
Train buffs chug through the Sierras via Amtak's California Zephyr line *(800/872-7245, www.amtrak.com)*, which runs from San Francisco to Chicago. It stops at Truckee, north of Lake Tahoe, and at Reno. Rental cars are available in both locations.

DRIVING
Lake Tahoe is 198 mi northeast of San Francisco, a drive of less than four hours in good weather. Avoid the heavy traffic leaving the San Francisco area for Tahoe on Friday afternoon and returning on Sunday afternoon. The major route is Interstate 80, which cuts through the Sierra Nevada about 14 mi north of the lake. From there Highway 89 and Highway 267 reach the west and north shores, respectively. U.S. 50 is the more direct route to the south shore, taking about two hours from Sacramento. From Reno you can get to the north shore by heading south on U.S. 395 for 10 mi, then west on Highway 431 for

25 mi. For the south shore, head south on U.S. 395 through Carson City, and then turn west on U.S. 50 (50 mi total).

Try to travel midweek; both routes are jammed on weekends in summer and winter.

FLYING

Reno's airport, the closest one to Lake Tahoe, is served by nearly a dozen airlines and all the major car-rental agencies. Tahoe Casino Express provides bus transportation from the Reno airport to South Lake Tahoe casinos *(775/325–8944 or 866/898–2463, www.south tahoeexpress.com)*. If your travel plans include a Bay Area tour or side trips to California's northern towns, fly into San Francisco, Oakland, or Sacramento.

> ### CLAIM TO FAME
>
> Tahoe is most famous for the lake itself, but skiing swooshes into contention as the second biggest draw. The 1960 Winter Olympics vaulted the area into a premier world-class ski destination, a reputation bolstered in recent years by the creation of numerous downhill resorts and cross-country centers. Known for some of the toughest skiing in the area, six-peaked Squaw Valley USA—the Olympics home base—became infamous as the locale of many of Warren Miller's extreme-skiing films. But that resort, along with all the others in the area, has devised multiple runs that attract skiers of all skill levels.

HOW DO I GET AROUND?

BY BOAT

Another option is to actually go out *on* the lake on the *Tahoe Queen (Ski Run Marina, off U.S. 50, South Lake Tahoe, 800/238–2463, www. laketahoecruises.com)*, a glass-bottom paddle wheeler, or on the 550-passenger M.S. *Dixie II (Zephyr Cove Marina, Zephyr Cove, 775/589–4906, www.laketahoecruises.com)*. Or, for the ultimate close-up view of the crystalline water, go kayaking.

BY BUS

Tahoe Area Regional Transit services the north shore, with one route to Truckee *(530/550–1212 or 800/736–6365; www.laketahoetransit. com)*. You can get around Tahoe's south shore via Blue Go *(530/541–7149, www.bluego.org)*.

BY CAR

The scenic 72-mi highway around the lake is marked Highway 89 on the southwest and west shores, Highway 28 on the north and northeast shores, and U.S. 50 on the east and southeast. Sections of Highway 89 sometimes close during snowy periods in winter, usually at Emerald Bay because of avalanche danger, which makes it impossible to complete the circular drive. Interstate 80, U.S. 50, and U.S. 395 are all-weather highways, but there may be delays as snow is cleared during major storms. (Note that Interstate 80 is a four-lane freeway; U.S. 50 is only two lanes with no center divider.) Carry tire chains from October through May, or rent a four-wheel-drive vehicle (most rental agencies do not allow tire chains to be used on their vehicles; ask when you book).

WHERE SHOULD I FOCUS MY ENERGY?

If you're here for 1 day: A leisurely one-day meander around the 72-mi road that circles the lake is an essential introduction to the Tahoe area.

■ In 1859 miners digging for gold struck silver instead, spawning the boom town of Virginia City to the east of Lake Tahoe.

If you're here for 2 days: Zip up South Lake Tahoe's Heavenly Gondola for a panoramic view of the lake and surrounding forested peaks.

■ The mail-carrying Pony Express made history in 1860 when it galloped from St. Joseph, Missouri, to Sacramento, California. The daring young riders on that eight-state circuit followed a path below Lake Tahoe that became Highway 50.

33

If you're here for 3 days: Hustle over the boundary into Stateline, Nevada, and check out the casino action.

If you're here for 4 days: Rent a kayak and paddle into Emerald Bay. Moor at the boat-in campground and hike the 1-mi trail to Vikingsholm Castle, a 1920s replica of an ancient Scandinavian castle.

■ Tracks for the First Transcontinental Railroad were laid through the Sierras just north of Lake Tahoe. The Amtrak California Zephyr still stops at the historic Truckee depot, which is now also a visitor center.

If you're here for 5 days: Tour Olympic Valley, focusing on Squaw Valley USA, the resort that hosted the 1960 Winter Olympics. Shop for souvenirs in the numerous stores housed in the resort's pedestrian mall.

If you're here for 6 days: Walk around old-town Truckee, then drive a few miles west on I–80 to explore the harrowing tale of starving pioneers at Donner State Memorial Park.

If you're here for 7 days or more: Wander through Tahoe's north shore communities and stop for a tour of Thunderbird Lodge, built in 1936. Or head east to Reno and check out the Biggest Little City in the World, known for its vibrant art scene and downtown river walk as well as its glitzy casinos.

WHAT ARE THE TOP EXPERIENCES?

The Views: No matter when you come to Lake Tahoe, Mother Nature welcomes you with open arms. Stand on the lookout over Emerald Bay and be awed by the bowl of deep blue alpine lake shimmering beneath you. Then stroll on Sand Harbor Beach, pull over at Zephyr Cove on the lake's Nevada side and watch the sunset, or scan the vista as you hike the Tahoe Rim Trail. While life in Tahoe can be pricey, the natural views are free—and unforgettable.

The Skiing: The 1960 Winter Olympics showcased Tahoe skiing, and hordes of downhill enthusiasts have been coming ever since. Squaw Valley USA played host to the world's best back then. Now the megaresort has runs for everyone from beginning skiers to experts. Family-friendly Northstar-at-Tahoe has six "Adventure Parks" for children, each with its own theme and kid-size ski thrills. Many vacationers prefer to stay in South Lake Tahoe, where Heavenly Resort's gondola whisks skiers from the town center up to the slopes. (It's also a great location for those who are less sports-inclined—Stateline, Nevada's casinos are just a few blocks away.)

The Casinos: Stateline's glitzy strip of Highway 50, with its high-rise casinos, is where you can find the most concentrated action at Lake Tahoe. Top-name entertainment jazzes up the South Shore Room at Harrah's Tahoe Hotel/Casino. Across the street, the rooms at Harveys Resort Hotel/Casino have great mountain- and lake views when you want to rest between bouts at the blackjack table. The casino scene at Mont-Bleu (*55 U.S. 50, Box 5800, 89449, 775/588–3515 or 800/648–3353, www.montbleuresort.com*) includes dancing to live bands in its club Blu. If you're looking for more refined surroundings, try the north shore's Hyatt Regency Lake Tahoe resort in ritzy Incline Village. It has 26 acres of prime lakeside property—and plenty of roulette wheels.

The Hiking: While gambling and skiing generate more buzz in Tahoe, outdoor enthusiasts quietly take to the hills to explore the area's beauty. Depending on your stamina, hike all or part of the Tahoe Rim Trail, a 165-mi ridgeline path that completely rings the lake. Trails also spool through granite-peaked Desolation Wilderness, a 63,960-acre preserve just west of Lake Tahoe. You can also track down trails of varying difficulty in D.L. Bliss, Emerald Bay, and Lake Tahoe-Nevada State Parks, and near the Lake Tahoe Visitor Center. The Pacific Crest Trail also runs along the Sierra Crest just west of the lake. A word of caution: be prepared for dramatic changes in weather—conditions can deteriorate rapidly in the Sierras.

> **LIKE A LOCAL**
>
> If you're new on the slopes, you should quickly learn the difference between a "bunny hill" and a "gulp-and-go chute." Snowboarders know an "airdog" rules the "superpipe," while a new boarder "biffs" most of the time.
>
> Hang around the casino's blackjack table, and you'll quickly learn that asking for a "hit" means you want another card. If you're at the roulette wheel, making an "inside" rather than an "outside" bet could cost you some bucks. Is poker your game? Kenny Rodgers wasn't kidding—you really do need to know when to hold 'em, and when to fold 'em.

BEST BETS

SIGHTS AND TOURS

D.L. Bliss State Park. At one time Duane LeRoy Bliss, a 19th-century lumber magnate, owned nearly 75% of Tahoe's lakefront, along with local steamboats, railroads, and banks. The park named in his honor shares 6 mi of shoreline with Emerald Bay State Park; combined the two parks cover 1,830 acres, 744 of which were donated to the state by the Bliss family in 1929. At the north end of Bliss is Rubicon Point, which overlooks one of the lake's deepest spots. Short trails lead to an old lighthouse and Balancing Rock, which weighs 250,000 pounds and balances on a fist of granite. A 4¼-mi trail—one of Tahoe's premier hikes—leads to Vikingsholm and provides stunning lake views. Two white-sand beaches front some of Tahoe's warmest water. ⊠*Hwy. 89; 3 mi north of Emerald Bay State Park* ☎*530/525–7277* ☎*$6 per vehicle, day use* ☉*Late May–Sept., daily dawn–dusk.*

VITAL STATS

■ State Capital: Sacramento, founded in 1849, is the oldest incorporated city in California.

■ State Motto: Eureka! The Greek word meaning, "I have found it," refers to—you guessed it—the 1848 discovery of gold at Sutter's Mill in Coloma.

■ State Fish: The California Golden Trout; found only in icy High Sierra streams, it isn't native to any other state.

■ State Tree: The California Redwood, found in the state's Coastal and Sierra provinces, is among the oldest of all living things in the world.

33

Fodor'sChoice ★ **Emerald Bay.** This 3-mi-long and 1-mi-wide fjordlike inlet on Lake Tahoe's shore was carved by a massive glacier millions of years ago. Famed for its jewel-like shape and colors, it surrounds Fannette, Tahoe's only island. Highway 89 curves high above the lake through Emerald Bay State Park; from the Emerald Bay lookout, the centerpiece of the park, you can survey the whole scene. This is one of the don't-miss views of Lake Tahoe. Come before the sun drops below the mountains to the west; the light is best in mid- to late mornings, when the bay's colors really pop.

A steep 1-mi-long trail from the lookout leads down to **Vikingsholm,** a 38-room estate completed in 1929. The original owner, Lora Knight, had this precise copy of a 1,200-year-old Viking castle built out of materials native to the area. ⊠*Hwy. 89; 4 mi west of Pope Baldwin Recreation Area* ☎*530/541–6498 summer, 530/525–7277 year-round* ⊕*www.vikingsholm.com* ☎*Day-use parking fee $6, mansion tour $5* ☉*Late May–mid-June, weekends, call for hrs; mid-June–Sept., daily 10–4.*

Fodor'sChoice ★ ☺ Whether you ski or not, you'll appreciate the impressive view of Lake Tahoe from the **Heavenly Gondola.** Its 138 eight-passenger cars travel from the middle of town 2½ mi up the mountain in 12 minutes. When the weather's fine, you can take one of three hikes around the mountaintop and then have lunch at Adventure Peak Grill. Heavenly also offers day care for children. ⊠*Downtown, South lake Tahoe* ☎*775/586–7000 or 800/432–8365* ⊕*www.skiheavenly.com* ☎*$28* ☉*Hrs vary; mid-Apr.–mid-Nov., daily 10–7; mid-Nov.–mid-Apr., daily 9–4.*

Lake Tahoe–Nevada State Park. Protecting much of the lake's eastern shore from development, Lake Tahoe–Nevada State Park comprises several sections that stretch from Incline Village to Zephyr Cove.

Beaches and trails provide access to a wilder side of the lake, whether you're into cross-country skiing, hiking, or just relaxing at a picnic. The east shore gets less snow and more sun than the west shore, making it a good early- or late-season outdoor destination. One of the most likable areas is **Sand Harbor Beach** (⊠ *Hwy. 28, 4 mi south of Incline Village* ☎ *775/831–0494* ⊕ *http://parks.nv.gov/lt.htm*). It's so popular that it's sometimes filled to capacity by 11 AM on summer weekends. Stroll the boardwalk and read the information signs for a good lesson in the local ecology.

The U.S. Forest Service operates the **Lake Tahoe Visitor Center,** on Taylor Creek. You can visit the site of a Washoe Indian settlement; walk self-guided trails through meadow, marsh, and forest; and inspect the Stream Profile Chamber, an underground underwater display with windows that afford views right into Taylor Creek (in fall you may see spawning kokanee salmon digging their nests). In summer U.S. Forest Service naturalists organize discovery walks and evening programs (call ahead). ⊠ *Hwy. 89, 3 mi north of junction with U.S. 50* ☎ *530/543–2674 June–Oct., 530/543–2600 year-round* ⊕ *www.fs.fed.us/r5/ltbmu* ☜ *Free* ☉ *Mid June–late Sept., daily 8–5:30; Memorial Day–mid-June, weekends 8–4:30.*

Fodor's Choice ★ George Whittell, a San Francisco socialite who once owned 40,000 acres of property along the lake, built the **Thunderbird Lodge** in 1936. You can tour the mansion and the grounds by reservation only, and though it's pricey, it provides a rare glimpse back to a time when only the very wealthy had homes at Tahoe. You can take a bus tour from the Incline Village Visitors Bureau, a 45-passenger catamaran tour from the Hyatt in Incline Village, or a 1950, 21-passenger wooden cruiser from Tahoe Keys Marina in South Lake Tahoe (which includes lunch). ⊠ *5000 Hwy. 28, Incline Village* ☎ *775/832–8750 lodge direct number; 800/468–2463, 775/832–1606 reservations; 775/588–1881, 888/867–6394 Tahoe Keys boat; 775/832–1234, 800/553–3288 Hyatt Incline Village boat* ⊕ *www.thunderbirdlodge.org* ☜ *$32 bus tour, $60–$110 boat tour* ☉ *May–Oct., call for tour times.*

WHERE TO EAT

WHAT IT COSTS				
¢	$	$$	$$$	$$$$
RESTAURANTS under $10	$10–$15	$16–$22	$23–$30	over $30

Restaurant prices are for a main course at dinner, excluding sales tax of 7¼%–7½% (depending on location).

$$$–$$$$
Fodor's Choice ★ ✕**PlumpJack Café.** The best restaurant at Olympic Valley is also the finest in the entire Tahoe Basin, the epitome of discreet chic and a must-visit for all serious foodies. The menu changes often, but look for tuna-tartare cones, seared diver scallops, Sonoma rabbit three ways, or grass-fed beef tenderloin. And rather than complicated, heavy sauces, the chef uses simple reductions to complement a dish. The result: clean,

ON THE WAY

Hangtown's Gold Bug Park & Mine: Placerville, known as raucous Hangtown during Gold Rush days, owns this fully lighted mine shaft that is open for self-guided tours. 1 mi north of U.S. 50 on Bedford Ave., Placerville, 530/642–5207, www.goldbugpark.org, $4.

National Automobile Museum: Love classic cars? Reno's auto museum has a Cadillac owned by Elvis Presley and the 1949 Mercury Coupe that James Dean drove in the movie Rebel Without a Cause. Mill and Lake Sts., Reno, NV, 775/333–9300, www.automuseum.org, $9

Old Truckee Jail Museum: This former lock-up opened its doors in 1875; it was the longest-operating jail in the state until 1964. 10143 Jibboom St., Truckee; 530/582–0893; http://truckeehistory.org.

33

dynamic, bright flavors. The wine list is exceptional for its variety and surprisingly low prices. If not for the view of the craggy mountains through the windows lining the cushy, 60-seat dining room, you might swear you were in San Francisco. A less expensive but equally adventurous menu is served at the bar. ✉ *1920 Squaw Valley Rd., Olympic Valley* ☎ *530/583–1578 or 800/323–7666* ✍ *Reservations essential* 🖃 *AE, D, MC, V.*

$$$ ✕**Evan's.** The top choice for high-end dining in South Lake, Evan's con-
★ temporary California menu includes such specialties as seared foie gras with pineapple and golden raisin compote, and venison in a blackberry-port demi-glace. The 40-seat dining room is intimate—some might find the tables a little close to each other—and the service and food are excellent and merit a special trip. ✉ *536 Emerald Bay Rd., South lake Tahoe* ☎ *530/542–1990* ✍ *Reservations essential* 🖃 *AE, D, MC, V* ⊘ *No lunch.*

$$–$$$ ✕**Soule Domain.** Rough-hewn wood beams and a vaulted wood ceiling
★ lend high romance to this cozy 1927 pine-log cabin, tucked beneath tall trees, next to the Tahoe Biltmore. On the eclectic menu, chef–owner Charles Soule's specialties include curried cashew chicken, lamb ravioli, rock shrimp with sea scallops, and a vegan sauté, but you can find the chef's current passion in the always-great roster of nightly specials. Some find it a little pricey, but if you're looking for someplace with a solid menu, where you can hold hands by candlelight, this is it. In winter request a table near the crackling fireplace. ✉ *9983 Cove Ave., ½ block up Stateline Rd. from Hwy. 28, Kings Beach* ☎ *530/546–7529* ✍ *Reservations essential* 🖃 *AE, MC, V* ⊘ *No lunch.*

¢ ✕**Fire Sign Café.** Watch the road carefully or you'll miss this great little
★ diner 2 mi south of Tahoe City on Highway 89. There's often a wait at the west shore's best spot for breakfast and lunch, but it's worth it. The pastries are made from scratch, the salmon is smoked in-house, the salsa is hand cut, and there's real maple syrup for the many flavors of pancakes and waffles. The eggs Benedict are delicious. ✉ *1785 W. Lake Blvd., Tahoe City* ☎ *530/583–0871* ✍ *Reservations not accepted* 🖃 *AE, MC, V* ⊘ *No dinner.*

WHERE TO STAY

	WHAT IT COSTS				
	¢	$	$$	$$$	$$$$
HOTELS	under $90	$90–$120	$121–$175	$176–$250	over $250

Hotel prices are for two people in a standard double room in high season, excluding service charges and 10%–14% tax.

$$$–$$$$ 🔲 **Black Bear Inn Bed and Breakfast.** South Lake Tahoe's most luxurious
Fodor'sChoice   inn feels like one of the grand old lodges of the Adirondacks. Its great
★   room has rough-hewn beams, plank floors, cathedral ceilings, Persian
rugs, and even an elk's head over the giant river-rock fireplace. Built
in the 1990s with meticulous attention to detail, the five inn rooms
and three cabins feature 19th-century American antiques, fine art, and
fireplaces; cabins also have kitchenettes. Never intrusive, the affable
innkeepers provide a sumptuous breakfast in the morning and wine
and cheese in the afternoon. ⊠ *1202 Ski Run Blvd., South Lake Tahoe
96150* 📠 *530/544–4451 or 877/232–7466* ⊕ *www.tahoeblackbear.
com* ➡ *5 rooms, 3 cabins* ⚭ *In-room: kitchen (some), VCR, DVD,
Wi-Fi. In-hotel: no elevator, public Wi-Fi, no kids under 16, no-smok-
ing rooms* ⊟ *AE, D, MC, V* ⊚| *BP.*

$$$–$$$$ ✕🔲 **Harrah's Tahoe Hotel/Casino.** Harrah's major selling point is that
every room has two full bathrooms, each with a television and tele-
phone, a boon if you're traveling with family. Top-name entertainment
is presented in the South Shore Room. Among the restaurants, the
romantic 16th-floor Summit ($$$$) is a standout, but bring a credit
card; there's also a buffet on the 18th floor. A tunnel runs under U.S.
50 to Harveys, which Harrah's now owns. Upper-floor rooms have
views of the lake or mountains, but if you really want the view, stay
at Harveys instead. Cheaper rates are available midweek. ⊠ *U.S. 50
at Stateline Ave., Stateline 89449* 📠 *775/588–6611 or 800/427–7247*
📠 *775/588–6607* ⊕ *www.harrahstahoe.com* ➡ *470 rooms, 62 suites*
⚭ *In-room: Ethernet, dial-up, Wi-Fi. In-hotel: 8 restaurants, room ser-
vice, pool, gym, spa, laundry service* ⊟ *AE, D, MC, V.*

$$$–$$$$ ✕🔲 **Hyatt Regency Lake Tahoe.** Once a dowdy casino hotel, the Hyatt
★   underwent a $60 million renovation between 2001 and 2003 and is
now a smart-looking, upmarket, full-service destination resort. On 26
acres of prime lakefront property, the resort has a nice range of luxu-
rious accommodations, from tower-hotel rooms to lakeside cottages.
The Lone Eagle Grille ($$–$$$$) serves steaks and seafood in one of
the north shore's most handsome lake-view dining rooms. There's also
a state-of-the-art spa and fitness center. Standard rates are very high,
but look for midweek or off-season discounts. ⊠ *Lakeshore and Country Club Drs., Incline Village 89450* 📠 *775/831–1111 or 888/899–
5019* 📠 *775/831–7508* ⊕ *www.laketahoe.hyatt.com* ➡ *422 rooms,
28 suites* ⚭ *In-room: safe, kitchen (some), refrigerator, Ethernet, dial-
up. In-hotel: 4 restaurants, room service, bars, pool, spa, beachfront,
bicycles, concierge, children's programs (ages 3–12), laundry service,
executive floor, public Wi-Fi, no-smoking rooms* ⊟ *AE, D, MC, V.*

33

$$$-$$$$ ⊡ **Northstar-at-Tahoe Resort.** The
★ area's most complete destination
resort is perfect for families, thanks
to its many sports activities—from
golf and tennis to skiing and snow-
shoeing—and its concentration
of restaurants, shops, recreation
facilities, and accommodations (the
Village Mall). Lodgings range from
hotel rooms to condos to private
houses, some with ski-in ski-out
access. The list continues to grow.
Northstar has been building lots of
new condos as well as a new Ritz-
Carlton (due to open in 2009).
Whatever lodging you book, you'll
receive free lift tickets and on-site
shuttle transportation and have
complimentary access to the Swim
and Racquet Club's swimming
pools, outdoor hot tubs, fitness cen-
ter, and teen center. ⊠ *Hwy. 267, 6*
mi southeast of Truckee, Box 129,

Truckee 96160 ☎ *530/562–1010 or 800/466–6784* ⊟ *530/562–2215*
⊕ *www.northstarattahoe.com* ⇆ *270 units* ♿ *In-room: no a/c (some),*
kitchen (some), VCR, dial-up (some). In-hotel: 6 restaurants, golf
course, tennis courts, bicycles, children's programs (ages 2–6), laundry
facilities, no-smoking rooms ⊟ *AE, D, MC, V.*

$$$-$$$$ ⊡ **PlumpJack Squaw Valley Inn.** If style and luxury are a must, make
Fodor'sChoice PlumpJack your first choice. The two-story, cedar-sided inn sits right
★ next to the cable car, and has a snappy, sophisticated look and laid-
back sensibility, perfect for the Bay Area cognoscenti who flock here
on weekends. All rooms have sumptuous beds with down comforters,
high-end bath amenities, and hooded terry robes to wear on your way
to the outdoor hot tubs. The bar is a happening après-ski destination,
and the namesake restaurant *(above)* superb. PlumpJack may not have
the bells and whistles of big luxury hotels, but the service—personable
and attentive—can't be beat. Not all rooms have tubs: if it matters,
request one. A complimentary buffet breakfast for two is included.
⊠ *1920 Squaw Valley Rd., Olympic Valley, 96146* ☎ *530/583–1576*
or 800/323–7666 ⊟ *530/583–1734* ⊕ *www.plumpjack.com* ⇆ *56*
rooms, 5 suites ♿ *In-room: no a/c, refrigerator, DVD, Wi-Fi. In-hotel:*
restaurant, bar, bicycles, concierge, public Wi-Fi, parking (no fee), no-
smoking rooms ⊟ *AE, D, MC, V* ⦾ *BP.*

$$-$$$$ ✕⊡ **Harveys Resort Hotel/Casino.** Harveys began as a cabin in 1944,
and now it's Tahoe's largest casino-hotel. Premium rooms have cus-
tom furnishings, oversize marble baths, minibars, and good lake views.
Although it was acquired by Harrah's and has lost some of its cachet,
Harveys remains a fine property. At Cabo Wabo ($–$$), an always-hop-
ping Baja-style cantina owned by Sammy Hagar, sip agave-style tequila

while munching on tapas and shouting across the table at your date. Harveys Cabaret is the hotel's showroom. ⊠ *U.S. 50, at Stateline Ave., Stateline 89449* ☎ *775/588–2411 or 800/648–3361* 🖷 *775/782–4889* ⊕ *www.harrahs.com* ⇆ *705 rooms, 38 suites* ⟁ *In-room: dial-up, Wi-Fi. In-hotel: 8 restaurants, room service, pool, gym, spa, concierge* ▤ *AE, D, MC, V.*

NIGHTLIFE & THE ARTS

NIGHTLIFE

Each of the major Stateline casinos has its own showroom, including Harrah's **South Shore Room** (☎ *775/588–6611*). The showrooms feature everything from comedy to magic acts to sexy floor shows to Broadway musicals. If you want to dance to DJ grooves and live bands, check out the scene at MontBleu's **Blu** (⊠ *55 U.S. 50* ☎ *775/588–3515*). At Harrah's, you can dance at **Vex** (⊠ *U.S. 50, at state line* ☎ *775/588–6611*). **Harveys Outdoor Summer Concert Series** (☎ *800/427–7247* ⊕ *www.harrahs.com*) presents outdoor concerts on weekends in summer with headliners such as the Eagles, Rascal Flatts, Stevie Wonder, and the Wallflowers. In all seasons, check out the nightly action at Harvey's **Cabo Wabo Cantina** (☎ *775/588–2411 or 800/648–3361* ⊕ *www.harrahs.com*)

THE ARTS

★ Fans of the Bard ought not to miss the **Lake Tahoe Shakespeare Festival** (☎ *775/832–1616 or 800/747–4697* ⊕ *www.laketahoeshakespeare. com*), which is held outdoors at Sand Harbor, with the lake as a stunning backdrop, from mid-July through August.

SHOPPING

At the base of the gondola the **Heavenly Village** is the centerpiece of South Lake Tahoe's efforts to reinvent itself and provide a focal point for tourism. Essentially a pedestrian mall, it includes some good shopping, a cinema, an arcade for kids, and the Heavenly Village Outdoor Ice Rink.

☾ The centerpiece of Olympic Valley is the **Village at Squaw Valley** (☎ *530/ 584–1000, 530/584–6205, 888/805–5022 for condo reservations* ⊕ *www. thevillageatsquaw.com*), a pedestrian mall at the base of several four-story ersatz Bavarian stone-and-timber buildings, where you can find restaurants, high-end condo rentals, boutiques, and cafés. The village often holds events and festivals.

SPORTS & THE OUTDOORS

KAYAKING

KAYAKING   **Kayak Tahoe** (⊠ *Timber Cove Marina; 3411 Lake Tahoe Blvd., behind Best Western Timber Cove Lodge* ☎ *530/544–2011* ⊕ *www.kayak tahoe.com*) has long been teaching people to kayak on Lake Tahoe and the Truckee River. Lessons and excursions (Emerald Bay, Cave Rock, Zephyr Cove) are offered June through September. You can also rent a kayak and paddle solo.

SKIING

Fodor's Choice ★ Straddling two states, vast **Heavenly Mountain Resort**—composed of nine peaks, two valleys, and four base-lodge areas, along with the largest snowmaking system in the western United States—has terrain for every skier. Beginners can choose wide, well-groomed trails, accessed from the California Lodge or the gondola from downtown South Lake Tahoe; kids have short and gentle runs in the Enchanted Forest area all to themselves. The Sky Express high-speed quad chair whisks intermediate and advanced skiers to the summit for wide cruisers or steep tree-skiing. Mott and Killebrew canyons draw experts to the Nevada side for steep chutes and thick-timber slopes. For snowboarders and tricksters, there are a whopping five terrain parks, including an enormous 22-foot super pipe. The ski school is big and offers everything from learn-to-ski packages to canyon-adventure tours. Call about ski and boarding camps. Skiing lessons are available for children ages 4 and up; there's day care for infants older than six weeks. ✉ *Ski Run Blvd., off Hwy. 89, U.S. 50, Stateline, NV* ☎ *775/586–7000 or 800/432–8365* ⊕ *www.skiheavenly.com* ✆ *91 trails on 4,800 acres, rated 20% beginner, 45% intermediate, 35% expert. Longest run 5½ mi, base 6,540 ft, summit 10,067 ft. Lifts: 30, including 1 aerial tram, 1 gondola, 2 high-speed 6-passenger lifts, and 6 high-speed quads.*

Northstar-at-Tahoe may be the best all-around family ski resort at Tahoe. With two tree-lined, northeast-facing, wind-protected bowls, it's the ideal place to ski in a storm. Hot-shot experts unfairly call the mountain "Flatstar," but the meticulous grooming and long cruisers make it an intermediate skier's paradise. Boarders are especially welcome, with an awesome terrain park, including a 400-foot-long super pipe, a half pipe, rails and boxes, and lots of kickers. Experts can ski the steeps and bumps off Lookout Mountain, where there's rarely a line for the high-speed quad. Northstar-at-Tahoe's cross-country center has 28 mi of groomed trails, including double-set tracks and skating lanes. The school has programs for skiers ages four and up, and day care is available for toilet-trained tots. The mountain gets packed on busy weekends (⇨ *"When to Go" section at the beginning of this chapter); to find alternatives on busy days.*but when there's room on the slopes, Northstar is loads of fun. ✉ *Hwy. 267, 6 mi southeast of Truckee* ☎ *530/562–1010, 530/562–1330 snow phone* 🖷 *530/562–2215* ⊕ *www.skinorthstar.com* ✆ *79 trails on 2,480 acres, rated 13% beginner, 62% intermediate, 25% advanced. Longest run 1.3 mi, base 6,330 ft, summit 8,610 ft. Lifts: 16, including a gondola and 5 high-speed quads.*

Fodor's Choice ★ Known for some of the toughest skiing in the Tahoe area, **Squaw Valley USA** was the centerpiece of the 1960 winter Olympics. Today it's the definitive North Tahoe ski resort and among the top-three megaresorts in California (the other two are Heavenly and Mammoth). Although Squaw has changed significantly since the Olympics, the skiing is still world-class and extends across vast bowls stretched between six peaks. Experts often head directly to the untamed terrain of the infamous KT-22 face, which has bumps, cliffs, and gulp-and-go chutes, or to the nearly vertical Palisades, where many famous Warren Miller extreme-skiing films have been shot. Fret not, beginners and intermediates: you have plenty of wide-open, groomed trails at High Camp (which sits at the *top* of the mountain) and around the more challenging Snow King Peak. Snowboarders and show-off skiers can tear up the three fantastic terrain parks, which include a giant super pipe. Lift prices include night skiing until 9 PM. Tickets for skiers 12 and under cost only $5. ⊠*1960 Squaw Valley Rd., off Hwy. 89, Olympic Valley, 5 mi northwest of Tahoe City* ☎*530/583–6985, 800/545–4350 reservations, 530/583–6955 snow phone* ⊕*www.squaw.com* ☞*100 trails on 4,000 acres, rated 25% beginner, 45% intermediate, 30% advanced. Longest run 3 mi, base 6,200 ft, summit 9,050 ft. Lifts: 33, including a gondola-style funitel, a cable car, 7 high-speed chairs, and 18 fixed-grip chairs.*

VISITOR INFORMATION

Lake Tahoe Incline Village/Crystal Bay Visitors Bureau (⊠*969 Tahoe Blvd., Incline Village, 89451* ☎*775/832–1606 or 800/468–2463* 🖷*775/832–1605* ⊕*www.gotahoe.com*).

Lake Tahoe Visitors Authority (⊠*1156 Ski Run Blvd., South Lake Tahoe, 96150* ☎*530/544–5050 or 800/288–2463* 🖷*530/544 2386* ⊕*www.bluelaketahoe. com*).

North Lake Tahoe Resort Association (✉*Box 1757, Tahoe City, 96145* ☎*530/583–3494 or 888/434–1262* 🖷*530/581–6904* ⊕*www.puretahoenorth. com*).

Truckee Donner Chamber of Commerce (⊠*10065 Donner Pass Rd., Truckee, CA, 96161* ☎*530/587–2757* ⊕*www.truckee.com*).

U.S. Forest Service (☎*530/587–2158 backcountry recording* ⊕*www.fs.fed. us/r5*).

Portland

WITH THE WILLAMETTE WINE COUNTRY & THE OREGON COAST

Multnomah Falls

WORD OF MOUTH

"You might consider doing Portland for at least a couple days—it is one of the most lively U.S. cities with lots to see and do—gardens, theater, great dining—staying in a downtown area hotel will let you step out your door and take free transportation on the street-cars, light rail, and buses in the downtown area. You can go up the gorge to Hood River on an easy day trip and loop back around Mt. Hood—or you could cross the river into Washington and visit Mt. St. Helens area too."

—norahs

EXPLORING PORTLAND

Portland is 175 mi south of Seattle via I-5; 635 mi north of San Francisco via I-80, I-505, and I-5; 550 mi southwest of Missoula, MT, via I-90, U.S. 395, and I-84; and 765 mi northeast of Salt Lake City via I-15 and I-84

By Andrew Collins

Often named in surveys and by lifestyle magazines as one of America's most livable cities, Portland has enjoyed an unprecedented growth in popularity since the late '90s, not only as a place to live but as a terrific getaway for visitors. Anchored by a compact, beautifully planned downtown fringed on one side by a river and another by soaring, wooded hills, the city also yields more than 90 diverse and distinct satellite neighborhoods, many of them rife with cool shops, top-notch restaurants, and hip music clubs and lounges.

Part of what makes this metropolis so special, however, is its embrace of such nonurban characteristics as greenery and parkland—Portland has some 250 parks, public gardens, and greenways, and the mild, if notoriously rainy, climate ensures the city's verdant appearance year-round. Portlanders are an outdoorsy lot, and they not only bike, hike, and jog around the city in astounding numbers, they also regularly take to the surrounding wilderness. Within a two-hour drive you can find 11,000-foot mountain peaks with year-round skiing, roaring whitewater rivers, and pristine Pacific Ocean beaches and bays.

Portland and the nearby Willamette Valley and Oregon coast form an easily navigated triangle that's easily explored. If you're here for more than a couple of days, it's well-worth venturing south for wine-tasting in the valley (revered for its pinot noirs) and west to the ocean.

WHO WILL ESPECIALLY LOVE THIS TRIP?

Cyclists: Portland has been named by Bicycling magazine as the nation's top city for cycling, in no small measure because of its copious and well-marked bike lanes, mild weather year-round, and beautiful waterfront. It's practicality for getting around aside—bike-rental shops thrive throughout the city and bike racks adorn the front of all local buses—cycling in Portland is also a vehicle for progressive politics and public service. Riders frequently gather to promote bicycling as an alternative to car travel.

Hipsters & Bar-Hoppers: With its many colleges and universities and a high number of savvy, educated, and culturally attuned twenty- and thirtysomething residents, Portland has become an emblem of coolness in recent years. Alternative music bands like Modest Mouse, Spoon, the Gossip, the Decemberists, and the Dandy Warhols either live or spend much of their time in Portland, and at the dozens of live-music clubs around town, you can see both emerging and established bands performing just about every night of the week. But the city also abounds with quirky coffeehouses, bustling gay bars, and swish hotel lounges packed with erudite and artsy hipsters of all ages and styles. Throw in the plethora of eclectic boutiques selling retro threads and decidedly

TOP 5 REASONS TO GO

The Music & Theater Scene: Excellent opera, symphony, and mainstream theater are draws, as are funky and inexpensive pub theaters. Clubs offering edgy, first-rate independent music also proliferate here—you may very well catch the next big alternative band here.

The Parks & Gardens: Home to the largest urban wilderness in the country (5,000-acre Forest Park), verdant Portland has dozens of other fine parks and gardens. Don't miss the Hoyt Arboretum, International Rose Test Garden, or Japanese Garden.

The Wineries: Just outside of Portland, the Willamette Valley contains an ever-growing concentration of wineries.

The Outdoor Recreation: Portland and the surrounding region appeal to just about anyone with a yen for sports and the outdoors. There are rivers and bays for kayaking, canoeing, and white-water rafting; miles of trails for biking and hiking; and snow-skiing and snowshoeing within an hour's drive of the city.

The Food: Portland has restaurants on a par with some of the finest and most celebrated eateries in Seattle and San Francisco, but at prices that won't break your budget. Known for regional Pacific Northwestern cuisine, along with fine Asian and Mediterranean restaurants, the Rose City has developed into a major foodie destination.

34

edgy clothing, and it's easy to see why Portland has become a favorite getaway of both high-end and budget-minded bon vivants, clubbers, and scenesters.

Food & Wine Connoisseurs: Right up until a decade ago, Portland might have been called a decent but somewhat provincial food city, punctuated by some especially good Thai and Vietnamese restaurants as well as a handful of trendy spots serving creative contemporary fare. But the city has undergone a culinary revolution over the past decade. And although the same could be said about many, if not most, major cities around the country, Portland stands out for its comparatively low prices and a tremendous devotion on the part of chefs and consumers to utilize local ingredients in innovative, often globally influenced ways. You can now find chefs earning national acclaim working not just downtown but in a number of off-the-beaten-path neighborhoods around town. And with Portland smack between the wine-producing regions of the Willamette Valley to the south and Washington's Columbia Valley to the east, it's easy to understand the city's vigorous embrace of wine, especially local pinot noirs. Even simple mom-and-pop cafés now frequently serve well-chosen, local wines.

Gardeners & Horticulturists: The "Rose City" has earned its nickname with good reason. With a relatively moderate climate and plenty of moisture year-round, Portland is one of the easiest cities in America to grow not only roses but flowers, shrubs, and trees of all kinds. Still, it's the roses that have put Portland on the horticultural map, and you can tour at the 4-acre International Rose Test Garden, just west of

Downtown Portland, The Pearl District & Old Town/Chinatown

downtown in Washington Park. You can find public gardens throughout the city, including Washington Park's other horticultural must, the Japanese Garden. Walk the 10 mi of trails at Hoyt Arboretum, and you can admire more than 1,000 species of plants. As you wander outside the city, you can find still more wonderful spots for garden-touring throughout the Willamette Valley, such as the 364,000-acre Forest Grove Educational Arboretum, the 240-acre Oregon Garden in Silverton, and—east of Salem—8,700-acre Silver Falls State Park, which contains a magnificent stand of Douglas firs and a forest floor carpeted with yellow violets.

WHEN IS THE BEST TIME TO VISIT?

Portland has a mild but rather wet climate, with the driest and sunniest months between June and September. Hotels fill up fast at this time, so book well ahead for summer visits. Spring and fall still often enjoy a mix of sunny and cloudy days and the city and its surrounding area

How to Snack

Take a cue from the locals and investigate the city's highly varied selection of food carts. Many are conveniently clustered near intersections. There's the parking lot at Southwest Alder and 9th streets, for instance, where you can find carts doling out everything from Russian sweet-and-sour borscht to Greek chicken gyros. A short walk away, at Southwest 5th and Oak streets, are purveyors of fiery Thai food curries, Vietnamese noodles, Mexican burritos, and more.

Another genre of snacking that scores high praise in Portland are coffeehouses—great ones have been percolating here just as long as they have in Seattle. You can find terrific local chains like **Coffee People** and **Stumptown Coffee Roasters**, with a handful of locations around the city. These places dole out not just hot mugs of java that will send a jolt of energy through your system—depending on the coffeehouse, they also proffer fresh baked treats, fresh-juice smoothies, gelato, and hot soups (not to mention, in many cases, free Wi-Fi). A few other coffeehouses of note here include **Vivace** (1400 N.W. 23rd Ave., 503/228–3667), which occupies a dashing gingerbread-style Victorian house in the courtly Nob Hill area; **Palio Coffee and Dessert House** (1996 S.E. Ladd St., 503/232–9412), which serves especially good sweets; and the loveably scruffy **Pied Cow** (3244 S.E. Belmont St., 503/230–4866), a low-key spot in a youthful, hip neighborhood.

Arguably the most famous and delicious spot for snacking around town is **Voodoo Doughnuts** (22 S.W. 3rd St., 503/241–4704), an offbeat late-night purveyor of tasty fried sweets. The doughnut flavors come with such bizarre toppings as crushed Butterfinger candy bars, pink marshmallow glaze, and Cocoa Puffs.

are less crowded, likely yielding better hotel and airfare deals. In winter Portland receives very little snow but can be inundated with rain and clouds for days, or even weeks, at a time. In the mountains around the city, however, you can expect plenty of snow.

Not surprisingly, Portland's top festivals and events take place in the warmer and more pleasant months, from late spring through early fall. Top picks include Cinco de Mayo in early May (Portland has a large population of transplants from Mexico), the Portland Rose Festival throughout the month of June (it's the most popular of the city's festivals), and the Oregon Brewer's Festival in July.

Outside the city, the Cannon Beach Sand Castle Contest brings folks out to the coast in June, the Mt. Hood Jazz Festival pulls in top entertainment in August, and the Oregon State Fair is always a major to-do in Salem.

HOW SHOULD I GET THERE?

DRIVING

Portland is connected to other Pacific Northwest and West Coast cities via I–5 and I–84, but other than Seattle, which is about a three-hour drive away, most large western cities are at least a day's drive away.

Willamette Valley & Wine Country

WASHINGTON

Columbia River

Astoria

30

26
101

Tillamook Head
Haystack Rock Seaside
Cannon Beach

53 TILLAMOOK
STATE FOREST

Hood
River

84

Nehalem Bay
Manzanita
Nehalem

26

Beaverton

Garibaldi
Tillamook

6

Tillamook Bay

Forest
Grove
Lake Oswego
Portland
Tigard

Mt. Hood ▲

26

Cape Lookout
State Park

Newberg
Dundee &
Yamhill

5

Oregon City

Government
Camp

McMinnville

Champoeg
State Park
Aurora

MT. HOOD
NATIONAL
FOREST

Pacific City

**Grand
Ronde** **Amity**

Silverton

Lincoln City

Depoe Bay

Otter Crest Loop
Yaquina Head

Salem

Silver Falls
State Park

Mt.
Jefferson ▲

Newport

101

20

Albany

214

22

Waldport

34

Corvallis

Brownsville

WILLAMETTE
NATIONAL
FOREST

20 126

Sisters

242

Yachats
Cape
Perpetua
Heceta Head

SIUSLAW
NATIONAL
FOREST

36

99E

**McKenzie
Bridge**

Eugene

Springfield

Florence

126

58

Mt.
Bachelor ▲

DESCHUTES
NATIONAL
FOREST

Winchester
Bay

Cottage
Grove

Oakridge

*Waldo
Lake*

OREGON DUNES
NAT'L REC. AREA

Reedsport

Drain

38

58

97

5

North Bend

Oakland

Steamboat

Charleston
Coos Bay

138

UMPQUA
NATIONAL
FOREST

CRATER LAKE
NATIONAL PARK

Roseburg

Bandon
Myrtle
Point

Winston

UMPQUA
VALLEY

42

Canyonville

*Crater
Lake*

97

Port Orford

Rogue River

Prospect

ROGUE
RIVER
NATIONAL
FOREST

Agness

Gold
Beach

Grants
Pass

101

SISKIYOU
NATIONAL
FOREST

199

*Upper
Klamath
Lake*

5

Medford

238

Pistol
River

Cave
Junction

Jacksonville

46

Klamath
Falls

Ashland

Harbor

Mt.
Ashland ▲

0   30 miles

0   30 kilometers

CALIFORNIA

PACIFIC OCEAN

That being said, the long drives up I–5 from California and along I–84 through eastern Oregon and Idaho offer plenty of stunning scenery.

PLANE

Portland International Airport (PDX) receives frequent praise as one of the nation's most efficient and pleasant facilities. It's served by all the major domestic airlines, plus such discount carriers as JetBlue and Southwest. There's also direct international service to Japan on Northwest Airlines and to Europe on Lufthansa and KLM. It's 20 to 40 minutes from the airport to downtown via light trail, shuttle bus, or taxi.

By Train Amtrak (800/872–7245, www.amtrak.com) stops in Portland each day during its Coast Starlight run from Los Angeles to Seattle.

34

HOW DO I GET AROUND?

BY BUS, LIGHT RAIL & STREETCAR

Portland has one of the best networks of public transportation of any city its size in the country. The city's TriMet (503/238–7433, www.trimet.org) system operates an extensive system of buses, a handy streetcar line through downtown and the Pearl District, and a three-line Light Rail network called MAX that connects downtown with several outlying neighborhoods and suburbs as well as the airport. Fares are free within a large downtown quadrant and quite reasonable for longer trips, and TriMet's Web site is extremely useful for finding the most effective strategy for getting around the city.

BY CAR

If you're going to be spending most of your time in downtown Portland, a car isn't necessary, although it's not an extreme liability, other than having to pay for parking at most hotels. To explore neighborhoods outside the city, a car is helpful but still not an absolute necessity, as Portland has a first-rate public transit system of buses, light rail, and streetcars. Outside of downtown, however, parking is easy to find and often free at hotels and restaurants, so a car can be a useful option. If you're planning trips to the wineries in the Willamette Valley or out to the coast, your best bet is to travel by car.

WHERE SHOULD I FOCUS MY ENERGY?

If you're here for 1 day: Spend the day exploring downtown, Nob Hill, and the Adjacent Pearl District. In the morning, check out the Portland Art Museum, Oregon History Center, and Pioneer Courthouse Square. Have lunch along Northwest 23rd Street in Nob Hill, and stroll along the riverfront in the afternoon, setting aside time to explore the Pearl District's shops and restaurants in the evening.

If you're here for 2 days: Use your second day to explore the northwest hills above Portland, stopping by Pittock Mansion, and spending time at the Japanese Garden and International Rose Garden in Washington Park.

If you're here for 3 days: Use your third day in town to check out some of the interesting neighborhoods and attractions east of the river in Portland, such as Hawthorne, the Alberta District, and the Mississippi District—great places to shop and eat abound in these areas. In the evening drive up to Mt. Tabor Park for Portland's best view of sunset.

If you're here for 4 days: Plan a day trip or even an overnight down the Willamette Valley a short ways, into the wine country around Newberg, Forest Grove, Dundee, and McMinnville (an excellent place to spend the night).

If you're here for 5 days: Take some time to see a bit more of the Willamette Valley, such as Oregon City's historic attractions, Lake Oswego's charming downtown, and Silverton's beautiful gardens and natural scenery. This is also a good time to visit the museums in Salem, the state capital.

If you're here for 6 days: Having spent a night or two in the Willamette Valley, proceed to the coast and take in a short stretch of this pristine oceanfront. If you're coming from McMinnville, drive west to Pacific City and make your way up past Cape Lookout State Park, Three Capes Loop, Cape Meares State Park, Manzanita, Tillamook, and the artsy community of Cannon Beach, before returning inland to Portland via U.S. 26.

If you're here for 7 days or more: With at least a week, you can travel farther down the Willamette Valley, perhaps dropping in on the intriguing college towns of Corvallis and Eugene, or perhaps explore a longer stretch of the coast, maybe spending a day in the charming city of Astoria. In Portland many additional attractions await those with more time to explore, such as the Classical Chinese Garden in Old Town, the Crystal Springs Rhododendron Garden, and Hoyt Arboretum. Also try to make your way out to Mt. Hood for some of the most stunning scenery in the region.

HISTORY YOU CAN SEE

It's just a 30-minute drive south of Portland to see the state's most history-rich community, Oregon City, which was the first incorporated city west of the Rocky Mountains. Today the city of 26,000 celebrates its heritage as the main terminus for the frontier families who embarked on great Oregon Trail from Missouri throughout the mid-19th century. The town's End of the Oregon Trail Interpretive Center tells the story of the city's early history, and throughout downtown you can find a number of historic homes and buildings, some of them now history museums.

WHAT ARE THE TOP EXPERIENCES?

The High Points: Portland itself is a hilly city with a number of areas that reward visitors with panoramic vistas, at least when the weather cooperates and the clouds clear. Downtown is backed to the west by a series of evergreen-studded hills—much of this area falls within the nation's largest urban wilderness, 5,000-acre Forest Park, which is laced with 70 mi of hiking trails. On the east side of town, Mt. Tabor is an extinct, albeit not particular tall, volcanic peak that's surrounded by a small, verdant park with great hiking trails—this is a nice spot to watch the sunset. But you can also find a number of lofty peaks outside of Portland, the most famous being 11,235-foot Mt. Hood, the tallest mountain in the state (and the only place in the lower 48 states with year-round snow skiing). Just across the border in Washington, you're also within a relatively short drive of volcanic Mt. St. Helens.

The Wineries: Oregon has developed a major cachet for its wineries over the past two decades, especially when it comes to pinot noir, the state grape of distinction. Many of the wineries in the Willamette Valley are open for tours, tastings, or both, and a number of the towns noted for this activity—such as Dundee and McMinnville—have sprouted fine restaurants, country inns, and shops to complement the numerous opportunities for vineyard touring. If you're short on time, Forest Grove, just south of Portland, has some excellent wineries that can be visited in just an afternoon.

The Beaches & Waterways: Water plays a distinct role in this part of Oregon. There's the winding Willamette River, which bisects Portland (the series of bridges traversing the river downtown make for a lovely photo-op) and makes its way down through the state, forming the agrarian and quite scenic Willamette Valley—you can find numerous opportunities for fishing, kayaking, and canoeing on the river, and there's great white-water rafting in some of the rivers that feed into the Willamette. On the north side of Portland, the Columbia River forms the border between Oregon and Washington—you can follow the river to the east, along I-84, into the rugged Columbia Gorge. And then, of course, there's the Oregon Coast. It takes a while to explore the entire shoreline, but the area just west of Portland, from Cannon Beach down to Pacific City, offers dramatic bays and headlands rife with marine wildlife—watch for seals, sea lions, dolphins, and whales.

The Shopping Districts: The swanky Nob Hill area, along Northwest 23rd and 21st streets, has a number of fine boutiques, as does the trendy Pearl District to the east, which is home to the world's largest shop of new and used books, Powell's City of Books. Across the river, on the east side of town, the Lloyd Center is another mall filled with appealing chain stores, but for a much more idiosyncratic shopping tour, stick with the city's offbeat retail districts, such as Sellwood (with many antiques stores), Hawthorne (perfect for vintage clothing and quirky boutiques), and Alberta (an avant-garde hub of art galleries and counter-culture). Finally, don't overlook the famed Portland Saturday Market, held downtown on weekends and offering a panoply of handcrafted items.

BEST BETS

SIGHTS AND TOURS

PORTLAND

Governor Tom McCall Waterfront Park. This broad and grassy park, with a fine ground-level view of downtown Portland's bridges and sky-line, hosts many events, among them the Rose Festival, classical and blues concerts, and the Oregon Brewers Festival. ⊠ *S. W. Naito Pkwy. (Front Ave.) from south of Hawthorne Bridge to Burnside Bridge, Downtown.*

★ **International Rose Test Garden.** Despite the name, these grounds are not an experimental greenhouse laboratory but three terraced gardens, set on 4 acres, where 10,000 bushes and 400 varieties of roses grow. The flowers, many of them new varieties, are at their peak in June, July, September, and October. ⊠ *400 S. W. Kingston Ave., Washington Park, 97221* ☎ *503/823–3636* ⊕ *www.portlandonline.com* ☜ *Free* ☉ *Daily dawn–dusk.*

Fodor's Choice   **Japanese Garden.** The most authentic Japanese garden outside Japan

★ is nestled among 5½ acres of Washington Park above the International Rose Test Garden. ⊠ *611 S. W. Kingston Ave., Washington Park, 97221* ☎ *503/223–1321* ⊕ *www.japanesegarden.com* ☜ *$6.75* ☉ *Oct.–Mar., Mon. noon–4, Tues.–Sun. 10–4; Apr.–Sept., Mon. noon–7, Tues.–Sun. 10–7.*

Oregon Historical Society. Impressive eight-story-high trompe l'oeil murals of Lewis and Clark and the Oregon Trail cover two sides of this down-town museum, which follows the state's story from prehistoric times to the present. ⊠ *1200 S. W. Park Ave., Downtown, 97205* ☎ *503/222–1741* ⊕ *www.ohs.org* ☜ *$10* ☉ *Mon.–Sat. 10–5, Sun. noon–5.*

★ **Oregon Museum of Science and Industry** *(OMSI).* Hundreds of hands-

☾ on exhibits draw families to this interactive science museum, which also has an Omnimax theater and the Northwest's largest planetarium. ⊠ *1945 S.E. Water Ave., south of Morrison Bridge, Under Hawthorne Bridge, 97214* ☎ *503/797–6674 or 800/955–6674* ⊕ *www.omsi.edu* ☜ *Full package $19, museum $9, planetarium $5.50, Omnimax $8.50, submarine $3.50* ☉ *Mid-June–Labor Day, daily 9:30–7; Labor Day–mid-June, daily 9:30–5.*

★ **Oregon Zoo.** This beautiful animal park in the West Hills is famous for

☾ its Asian elephants. Major exhibits include an African section with rhi-nos, hippos, zebras, and giraffes. Steller Cove, a state-of-the-art aquatic exhibit, has two Steller sea lions and a family of sea otters. In summer a 4-mi round-trip narrow-gauge train operates from the zoo, chugging through the woods to a station near the International Rose Test Gar-den and the Japanese Garden. ⊠ *4001 S. W. Canyon Rd., Washington Park, 97221* ☎ *503/226–1561* ⊕ *www.oregonzoo.org* ☜ *$9.75, $2 2nd Tues. of month* ☉ *Mid-Apr.–mid-Sept., daily 9–6; mid-Sept.–mid Apr., daily 9–4.*

Pioneer Courthouse Square. Considered by most to be the living room, public heart, and commercial soul of Downtown Portland, Pioneer Square is not entirely square but rather centered in this amphitheatrical brick piazza. Special seasonal, charitable, and festival-oriented events often take place in this premier people-watching venue. On Sunday **vintage trolley** (☎503/323–7363) cars run from the MAX station here to Lloyd Center, with free service every half hour between noon and 6 PM. Call to check on the current schedule. You can pick

> **STRANGE BUT TRUE**
>
> Mill Ends Park, in downtown Portland, at the intersection of Southwest Natio Parkway and Southwest Taylor Street, has been recognized in the Guinness Book of Records as being the smallest park in the world. Established in 1948, this "park" is little more than a cement planter with some pretty flowers poking out of it—it's circular, with an area of about 450 square inches.

34

up maps and literature about the city and the state here at the **Portland/Oregon Information Center** (☎503/275–8355 ⊕*www.pova.com* ⊘*Mar.–Oct., weekdays 8:30–5:30, Sat. 10–4, Sun. 10–2*). Directly across the street is one of downtown Portland's most familiar landmarks, the classically sedate **Pioneer Courthouse.** Built in 1869 it's the oldest public building in the Pacific Northwest. ⊠*701 S.W. 6th Ave., Downtown.*

★ **Portland Art Museum.** The treasures at the Pacific Northwest's oldest visual- and media-arts facility span 35 centuries of Asian, European, and American art. A high point is the Center for Native American Art, with regional and contemporary art from more than 200 tribes. ⊠*1219 S.W. Park Ave., Downtown, 97205* ☎*503/226–2811, 503/221–1156 film schedule* ⊕*www.pam.org* ☐*$10* ⊘*Tues., Wed., and Sat. 10–5, Thurs. and Fri. 10–8, Sun. noon–5.*

Fodor'sChoice **Portland Classical Chinese Garden.** This wonderland neighboring the Pearl
★ District and Old Town/Chinatown, the largest Suzhou-style garden outside China, has a large lake, bridged and covered walkways, koi- and water lily–filled ponds, rocks, bamboo, statues, waterfalls, and courtyards. ⊠*N.W. 3rd Ave. and Everett St., Old Town/Chinatown, 97209* ☎*503/228–8131* ⊕*www.portlandchinesegarden.org* ☐*$7* ⊘*Nov.–Mar., daily 10–5; Apr.–Oct., daily 9–6. Tours daily at noon and 1.*

WILLAMETTE VALLEY

★ Modest and whimsical touches at **Amity Vineyards** (⊠*18150 Amity Vineyards Rd. SE, Amity* ☎*503/835–2362* ⊕*www.amityvineyards.com*) underscore what seems to be Myron Redford's philosophy for winemaking: take your craft a lot more seriously than you take yourself.

Resembling three large covered wagons, the **End of the Oregon Trail Interpretive Center,** 19 mi south of Portland, is hard to miss. The history of the Oregon Trail is brought to life through theatrical shows, exhibits, and hands-on activities. ⊠*1726 Washington St., Oregon City* ☎*503/657–9336* ⊕*www.endoftheoregontrail.org* ☐*Store free, show $7* ⊘*Tues.–Sat. 11–4, Sun. noon–4.*

Fodor's Choice ★ The claim to fame of the **Evergreen Aviation Museum** is the Hughes (H-4) HK-1 Flying Boat, better known by its more sibilant nickname, the *Spruce Goose*, on permanent display here. If you can take your eyes off the Spruce Goose there are also more than 45 historic planes and replicas here from the early years of flight and World War II, as well as the postwar and modern eras. ✉ *500 N.E. Michael King Smith Way, McMinnville 97128* ☎ *503/434–4180* ⊕ *www.sprucegoose.org* 💲 *$13* ⊙ *Daily 9–5, closed holidays.*

Founded in 1970, **Ponzi Vineyards** (✉ *14665 S.W. Winery La., Beaverton, 97007* ☎ *503/628–1227* 🖨 *503/628–0354* ⊕ *www.ponziwines.com*) produces pinots and chardonnay, as well as Dolcetto and Arneis.

★ Hidden amid old-growth Douglas firs in the foothills of the Cascades, **Silver Falls State Park,** 26 mi east of Salem, is the largest state park in Oregon (8,700 acres). South Falls, roaring over the lip of a mossy basalt bowl into a deep pool 177 feet below, is the main attraction here, but 13 other waterfalls—half of them more than 100 feet high—are accessible to hikers. ✉ *20024 Silver Falls Hwy. SE, Sublimity* ☎ *503/873–8681 or 800/551–6949* ⊕ *www.oregonstateparks.org/park_211.php* 💲 *$3 per vehicle* ⊙ *Daily dawn–dusk.*

★ **Sokol Blosser** (✉ *5000 Sokol Blosser La., Dundee; 3 mi west of Dundee off Hwy. 99 W* ☎ *503/864–2282 or 800/582–6668* ⊕ *www.sokolblosser.com*), one of Oregon's oldest and largest wineries, has a tasting room and walk-through vineyard with a self-guided tour that explains the grape varieties—pinot noir and chardonnay, among others.

Originally built in 1887 the **Willamette Shore Trolley**—one standard and one double-decker trolley, both of museum quality—carries passengers on a 45-minute ride to Portland along a scenic 7-mi route, which you can travel one-way or round-trip; you'll take in Mt. Hood and the wooded banks of the Willamette River. ✉ *311 State St., Lake Oswego 97034* ☎ *503/697–7436* ⊕ *www.trainweb.org/oerhs/wst.htm* 💲 *$10 round-trip* ⊙ *Early May–Memorial Day, weekends; Memorial Day–Labor Day, Thurs.–Sun.; Labor Day–end of Sept., Fri.–Sun.; Oct., Sat.*

OREGON COAST

★ Towering over broad, sandy Cannon Beach is **Haystack Rock,** a 235-foot-high monolith that is one of the most-photographed natural wonders on the Oregon coast.

Established in 1974, **Nehalem Bay Winery** is known for its pinot noir, chardonnay, blackberry, and plum fruit wines. ⊠*34965 Hwy. 53, Nehalem, 97131* ☎*503/368–9463 or 888/368–9463* 🖷*503/368–5300* ⊕*www.nehalembaywinery.com* ⊙*Daily 9–6.*

★ More than 750,000 visitors annually journey through the **Tillamook County Creamery,** the largest cheese-making plant on the West Coast. ⊠*4175 U.S. 101 N, 2 mi north of Tillamook* ☎*503/815–1300* ⊕*www.tillamookcheese.com* ▱*Free* ⊙*Mid-Sept.–May, daily 8–6; June–mid-Sept., daily 8–8.*

WHERE TO EAT

WHAT IT COSTS				
¢	$	$$	$$$	$$$$
AT DINNER under $10	$10–$20	$21–$30	$31–$40	over $40

Restaurant prices are per person for a main course at dinner.

PORTLAND

$$$$
FodorśChoice
★
✕**Genoa.** Widely regarded as the finest restaurant in Portland, Genoa serves a seven-course prix-fixe menu focusing on authentic Italian cuisine, that changes every two weeks. Although the dining room is a bit drab, seating is limited to a few dozen diners, so service is excellent. Smoking is permitted in a separate sitting room. ⊠*2822 S.E. Belmont St., near Hawthorne District, 97214* ☎*503/238–1464* ⌔*Reservations essential* ▭*AE, D, DC, MC, V* ⊙*No lunch.*

$–$$
★
✕**The Heathman.** Chef Philippe Boulot revels in fresh ingredients of the Pacific Northwest. His menu changes with the season and includes entrées made with grilled and braised fish, fowl, veal, lamb, and beef. Among the chef's Northwest specialties are a delightful Dungeness crab, mango, and avocado salad, and seafood paella made with mussels, clams, shrimp, scallops, and chorizo. Equally creative choices are available for breakfast and lunch. The dining room, scented with wood smoke and adorned with Andy Warhol prints, is a favorite for special occasions. ⊠*Heathman Hotel, 1001 S.W. Broadway, Downtown, 97205* ☎*503/790–7752* ▭*AE, D, DC, MC, V.*

$–$$
FodorśChoice
★
✕**Higgins.** Chef Greg Higgins, former executive chef at the Heathman Hotel, focuses on ingredients from the Pacific Northwest and on organically grown herbs and produce while incorporating traditional French cooking styles and other international influences into his menu. Start with a salad of warm beets, asparagus, and artichokes or the country-style terrine of venison, chicken, and pork with dried sour cherries and roasted-garlic mustard. Main courses change seasonally and might include dishes made with Alaskan spot prawns, halibut, duck, or pork loin. Vegetarian items are available. A bistro menu is available in the adjoining bar, where comfortable leather booths and tables provide an alternative to the main dining room. ⊠*1239 S.W. Broadway, Downtown, 97205* ☎*503/222–9070* ▭*AE, D, DC, MC, V* ⊙*No lunch weekends.*

$–$$ ✕**Paley's Place.** This charming bistro serves French cuisine Pacific
Fodor'sChoice Northwest–style. Among the entrées are dishes with duck, New York
★ steak, chicken, pork tenderloin, and halibut. A vegetarian selection is
also available. There are two dining rooms and a classy bar. In warmer
months there's outdoor seating on the front porch and back patio.
⊠*1204 N.W. 21st Ave., Nob Hill, 97209* ☎*503/243–2403* ▭*AE,
MC, V* ⊗*No lunch.*

¢–$ ✕**Pambiche.** Locals know that you can drive by Pambiche any night
★ of the week and find it packed. With traditional Cuban fare including
plantains, roast pork, mojitos, and Cuban espresso, it's no surprise
why. If you have some time to wait for a table, you should stop by and
make an evening of it at this hopping neighborhood hot spot. Don't
miss out on the incredible dessert here; it's the sole reason why some
people make the trip. ⊠*2811 N.E. Glisan St., near Laurelhurst, 97232*
☎*503/233–0511* ⊿*Reservations not accepted* ▭*D, MC, V.*

WILLAMETTE VALLEY

$$ ✕**Tina's.** Chef–proprietors Tina and David Bergen share cooking duties
Fodor'sChoice here—Tina does the baking and is often on hand to greet you—and
★ David brings his experience as a former caterer and employee of nearby
Sokol Blosser Winery to the table, ensuring that you have the right glass
of wine—and there are many—to match your course. Fish and game
vie for attention on the country French menu—entrées might include
grilled Oregon salmon or Alaskan halibut, or a braised rabbit, local
lamb, or tenderloin. Avail yourself of any special soups, particularly if
there's corn chowder in the house. ⊠*760 Hwy. 99 W, Dundee 97115*
☎*503/538–8880* ⊗*No Lunch Sat.–Mon.* ▭*AE, D, MC, V* ⊕*www.
tinasdundee.com.*

$–$$ ✕**McCormick's Fish House & Bar.** The neighborhood feeling of this restau-
Fodor'sChoice rant belies its association with the national chain. Try creative seasonal
★ preparations such as macadamia-nut-crusted Alaskan halibut with
mango–beurre blanc sauce or salmon baked on a cedar plank. Mounted
fish are displayed on the ceiling of the rusty-brown main dining room.
The restaurant is popular with local families. ⊠*9945 S.W. Beaverton–
Hillsdale Hwy., Beaverton 97005* ☎*503/643–1322* ⊕*www.mccormick
andschmicks.com* ▭*AE, D, DC, MC, V* ⊗*No lunch Sun.*

WHERE TO STAY

WHAT IT COSTS					
	¢	$	$$	$$$	$$$$
FOR 2 PEOPLE	under $100	$100–$150	$151–$200	$201–$250	over $250

Hotel prices are for a standard double room, excluding room tax, which varies
6%–9½% depending on location.

PORTLAND

$$–$$$$ ⊞**Heathman Hotel.** Superior service, a renowned restaurant, a central
Fodor'sChoice downtown location (adjoining the Performing Arts Center), and swank
★ public areas have earned the Heathman its reputation for quality. From

ON THE WAY

Mt. Hood: Rising 11,235 above the Columbia River Gorge, Oregon's most dramatic peak is the only spot in the lower 48 states that offers skiing year-round, although many runs on lower slopes are used for biking in summer. There's much to do both on the mountain and in the vicinity, including superb hiking and mountaineering. And the Depression era Timberline Lodge is one of the West's great lodge hotels. 60 mi east of Portland, on north side of U.S. 26, 503/622-4822 or 888/622-4822, www.mthood.info.

Crater Lake National Park: If you're driving up to the Portland area from California, consider detouring to see the state's—and one of the West's—most spectacular national parks, Crater Lake. This rippling 21-square-mi lake was created 7,700 years ago after the eruption of Mt. Mazama. Rain and snowmelt fill the caldera, which is the deepest in the nation (and seventh deepest in the world). Off Hwy. 62, 75 mi northeast of I-5, 541/594-3100, www.nps.gov/crla. $10 per vehicle.

34

the teak-panel lobby hung with Warhol prints to the rosewood elevators and marble fireplaces, this hotel exudes refinement. The guest rooms provide the latest in customized comfort: a bed menu allows you to choose from orthopedic, European pillowtop, or European feather-bed mattresses for your resting pleasure, and the bathrooms have plenty of marble and mirrors. The second-floor mezzanine, with a small art gallery with works changing every several weeks and a small library (primarily filled with the works of notable Heathman guests), overlooks the high-ceiling Tea Court, a popular gathering spot in the evening. ⊠*1001 S.W. Broadway, Downtown, 97205* ☎*503/241-4100 or 800/551-0011* 🖷*503/790-7110* ⊕*www.heathmanhotel.com* 🛏*117 rooms, 33 suites* ⟨*In-room: dial-up, ethernet. In-hotel: public Wi-Fi, restaurant, room service, bar, gym, concierge, laundry service, parking (fee), no-smoking rooms, some pets allowed* ⊟*AE, D, DC, MC, V.*

$–$$$ 🏨**Benson Hotel.** Portland's grandest hotel was built in 1912. The hand-
★ carved Russian Circassian walnut paneling and the Italian white-marble staircase are among the noteworthy design touches in the public areas. In the guest rooms expect to find small crystal chandeliers and inlaid mahogany doors. Some even have the original ceilings. Extra touches include fully stocked private bars and bathrobes in every room. ⊠*309 S.W. Broadway, Downtown, 97205* ☎*503/228-2000 or 888/523-6766* 🖷*503/471-3920* ⊕*www.bensonhotel.com* 🛏*287 rooms* ⟨*In-room: refrigerator (some), dial-up. In-hotel: Wi-Fi, 2 restaurants, room service, bar, gym, concierge, laundry service, parking (fee), public Internet* ⊟*AE, D, DC, MC, V.*

$–$$ 🏨**Inn @ Northrup Station.** Bright colors, original artwork, retro designs,
★ and extremely luxurious suites fill this hotel in Nob Hill. Just moments from the shopping and dining on Northwest 21st Avenue, the inn looks like a stylish apartment building from the outside, with patios or balconies adjoining most of the suites, and a garden terrace for all guests to use. The striking colors and bold patterns found on bedspreads, arm-chairs, pillows, and throughout the halls and lobby manage to be charm-

ing, elegant, and fun, never falling into the kitsch that plagues many places that strive for "retro" decor. All rooms have full kitchens, two TVs, three phones, and large sitting areas. ⊠*2025 N.W. Northrup St., Nob Hill, 97209* ☎*503/224–0543 or 800/224–1180* 🖷*503/273–2102* ⊕*www.northrupstation.com* ☞*70 suites* ♿*In-room: kitchen. In-hotel: Wi-Fi, parking (no fee), no-smoking rooms* ⊟*AE, D, DC, MC, V* ℐⓄ*CP.*

WILLAMETTE VALLEY

$ 🖼**Mattey House Bed & Breakfast.**
Fodor'sChoice   Built in 1982 by English immigrant
★   Joseph Mattey, a local butcher, this Queen Anne Victorian mansion— on the National Register of Historic Places— has several cheerful areas that define it. A small balcony off the upstairs landing is perfect for sipping a glass of wine on a cool Yamhill Valley evening. The house, on 10 acres, is bound by an orchard and its own vineyard, which proprietors Jack and Denise maintain. Fine full breakfasts might include poached pears with raspberry sauce, frittatas, or Dutch-apple pancakes. ⊠*10221 N.E. Mattey La., off Hwy. 99 W, ¼ mi south of Lafayette, 97128* ☎*503/434–5058* 🖷*503/434–6667* ⊕*www.matteyhouse.com* ☞*4 rooms* ♿*In-room: no phone, no TV. In-hotel: no-smoking rooms* ⊟*AE, MC, V* ℐⓄ*BP.*

VITAL STATS

- State Capital: Salem, 45 mi south of Portland.
- State Motto: She Flies With Her Own Wings.
- State Nickname: The Beaver State.
- State Bird: Western meadowlark.
- State Tree: Douglas fir.
- State Flower: Oregon grape.
- State Nut: Hazelnut.
- State Fish: Chinook salmon.
- State Song: Oregon, My Oregon.

VISITOR INFORMATION

Portland Oregon Visitors Association (☎*503/275–9750 or 800/962–3700* ⊕*www.travelportland.com*).

Travel Oregon (☎*800/547–7842* ⊕*www.traveloregon.com*).

Seattle

WITH ORCAS ISLAND & THE NATIONAL PARKS

Pike Place Market

WORD OF MOUTH

"Walk along the waterfront (interesting parks and shops), then hike the stairs to the Pike Street Market, then, if there's time, walk down to the Aquarium or the other way to the Ferry Terminal and 'walk on' to Whidbey Island, or drive up to Snoqualmie Falls and have a wonderful breakfast."

—clarasong

EXPLORING SEATTLE

174 mi north of Portland, OR, via I–5; 504 mi northwest of Boise, ID, via I–84 and I–90; 475 mi west of Missoula, MT, via I–90

By Carissa
Bluestone

Gone are the days when Seattle was defined by flannel and fisherfolk—one tech boom and one tourism boom later (and much to locals' chagrin) the city is downright cosmopolitan. Seattle's restaurant scene has achieved national acclaim. The once-famous music scene that birthed Nirvana still thrives, and the city has added to its cultural resume with several multimillion-dollar projects, including a massive expansion of the Seattle Art Museum with the addition of a glorious sculpture park.

Beyond its attractive downtown—which sits astride Elliott Bay and Puget Sound, just two of the many beautiful bodies of water that define the region—the city is an amalgam of residential neighborhoods, each with its own distinct personality. Taken all together, Seattle can fit any mood, whether you want to sip espresso with hipsters in Capitol Hill or take a solitary stroll along a beachfront trail in Discovery Park.

On clear days you can see Mt. Rainier's snow-capped dome loom over the city. The San Juan Islands, of which Orcas Island is the most popular, are a ferry ride away from the city, and prime whale-watching territory. The North Cascades National Park, northeast of Seattle, has some of the state's most awe-inspiring trails and hidden valleys. And then there's Olympic National Park, on the Olympic Peninsula west of Seattle, with its combination of deserted beaches, rainforest walks, and craggy Olympic Mountain trails.

WHO WILL ESPECIALLY LOVE THIS TRIP?

Outdoorsy Types: A few hours outside Seattle, you hit real wilderness. If you've ever dreamed of being alone on a ridge surveying endless folds of mountains, head to North Cascades National Park. Mt. Rainier's 10-day Wonderland Trail is the ultimate commitment for Washington hikers. Or you can "settle" for strolling along beachfront trails in Discovery Park or kayaking past houseboats on Lake Union.

Foodies: Seattle's ever-expanding restaurant scene has everything from cheap Vietnamese soup to $40 steaks. But nothing's better than the regional cuisine that put the city on the culinary map, served up at spots like Matt's in the Market and Sitka & Spruce. What you choose to wash a meal down is no afterthought, either: the best coffee in the country is served up on virtually every street corner, and most restaurants have excellent wine lists showcasing Pacific Northwest vintages.

Culture Vultures: A burgeoning film scene percolates at Northwest Film Forum, while indie rock shakes the walls every night at Neumos. In addition to the great Seattle Art Museum and its outdoor branch the bayside Olympic Sculpture Park, Seattle has scads of galleries in its Belltown and Pioneer Square districts.

Families: It may seem at first glance that everyone in Seattle is single and between 25 and 35, but it's not just the nighthawks who love this

TOP 5 REASONS TO GO

Best of Both Worlds: Seattle has it all, from urban amenities to outdoor splendor. On the same day you can jog along a hushed forest trail, see cutting-edge art in a downtown gallery, take a kayak for a spin on massive Lake Union, and finish up with a five-star meal and a trip to the symphony.

Fresh, Local, Seasonal: So goes the mantra of Seattle's amazing chefs. Pacific Northwest cuisine is inventive, but fusion fireworks never overpower the amazing tastes of fresh regional seafood and produce.

Killer whales: Orcas visit the waters surrounding the San Juan Islands from April to October and can be viewed from a tour boat or kayak.

Rain Forest Treks: The Olympic Peninsula has the best examples of primeval temperate rain forest in the lower 48. Wander where giant trees are covered in mosses and ferns choke the ground.

Glacial Paces: Both Mt. Rainier and North Cascades national parks have impressive numbers of glaciers, which can be viewed up close on hikes through pristine wilderness.

35

pretty city. Among the many kid-friendly sights are the Seattle Aquarium, the Space Needle, and the Children's Museum at Seattle Center. All national parks have nature trails and ranger-led walks, and the unique features of the state from giant old trees to bald eagles soaring over beaches to adorable marmots waddling along trails will hold any kid's attention.

WHEN IS THE BEST TIME TO VISIT?

The best time to visit Seattle is July through September. Days are pleasant—often sunny and warm but not humid—while evenings are usually cool enough that very few residents bother to own air-conditioners. Late summer and early fall is also prime hiking season, the best time—and in many cases, only time—to hit the trails of the national parks. October can be beautiful, with scenic fall color driving tours through the North Cascades a favorite, but it can also be very wet. November through March can seem like one unending rainstorm. Spring has its charms, too (flowering trees in Seattle's residential neighborhoods and parks being one of them), but weather is unpredictable, and many trails aren't accessible until June.

Seattle doesn't have a huge number of festivals; the biggest and best-known are Bumbershoot, a huge music festival that takes over Seattle Center in September, and July's Seafair, Seattle's biggest festival of the year, which kicks off with a torchlight parade through Downtown, includes air shows by the Blue Angels, and culminates in hydroplane races on Lake Washington. Quirky neighborhood celebrations like the Fremont Summer Solstice Parade are tremendously fun and mostly take place in summer. Two of the city's best cultural festivals take place off-season: the Seattle International Film Festival in late May and the Earshot Jazz Festival in late October.

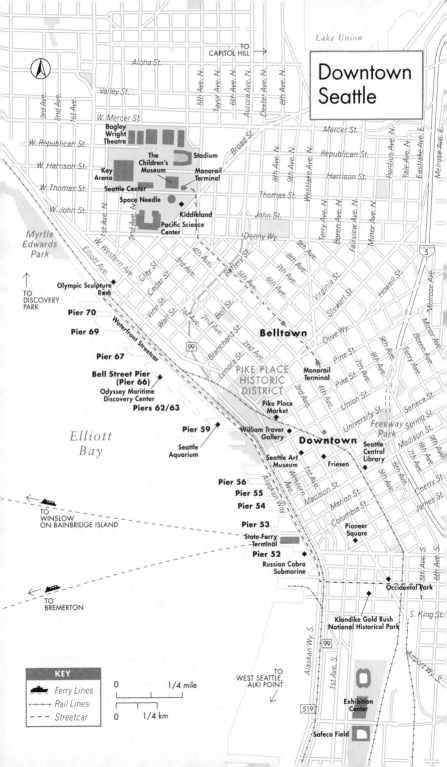

HOW SHOULD I GET THERE?

DRIVING

Literally cut in half by I–5, Seattle is a straight shot from Portland, San Francisco, and Vancouver, British Columbia. Interstate 90 connects the city to the eastern part of the state and to Idaho and Montana beyond. Off I–5, the James, Seneca, or Mercer street exits will take you into downtown. At the city of Olympia (60 mi southwest of Seattle), I–5 hooks up with U.S. 101, the fabled scenic coastal route that makes a loop around Olympic National Park before heading south to skirt the Pacific from Washington to Southern California.

FLYING

Seattle is a hub for regional air service. The major gateway is Seattle–Tacoma International Airport (SEA), known locally as Sea-Tac. The airport is south of the city and reasonably close to it—non-rush-hour trips to Downtown often take less than a half hour. There are plenty of car-rental facilities at Sea-Tac, but because of hefty airport concession fees, you're better off taking a cab into the city (around $30, not including tip) and renting a car Downtown—you'll save a lot of money doing so.

TRAIN

Amtrak has daily service to Seattle from the Midwest and California. The *Empire Builder* takes a northern route through Minnesota and Montana from Chicago to Spokane, from where separate legs continue to Seattle. The *Coast Starlight* begins in Los Angeles; makes stops throughout California, western Oregon, and Washington; and terminates in Seattle. Amtrak's *Cascades* trains travel between Seattle and Vancouver and among Seattle, Portland, and Eugene. Book Amtrak tickets at least a few days in advance, especially if you're traveling between Seattle and Portland on the weekend.

HOW DO I GET AROUND?

BY BUS

If you're only using the buses to travel around Downtown or east to Capitol Hill, you'll probably find navigating the system easy and quick. Traveling to the northern neighborhoods of Fremont and Ballard from Downtown is also easy, though your trip may involve transfers. Most buses, which are wheelchair-accessible, run until around midnight or 1 AM; some run all night, though in many cases taking a cab late at night is a much better solution than dealing with sporadic bus service. The visitor center at the Washington State Convention and Trade Center has maps and schedules or you can call Metro Transit directly (800/542–7876, 206/553–3000, 206/287–8463 for automated schedule line). Better yet, use the excellent trip-planner feature on Metro Transit's Web site, transit.metrokc.gov.

Fares at off-peak times are $1.25; during peak hours (6 AM–9 AM and 3 PM–6 PM), $1.50. Between 6 AM and 7 PM, city buses are free within the Metro Bus Ride Free Area (which encompasses much of the downtown

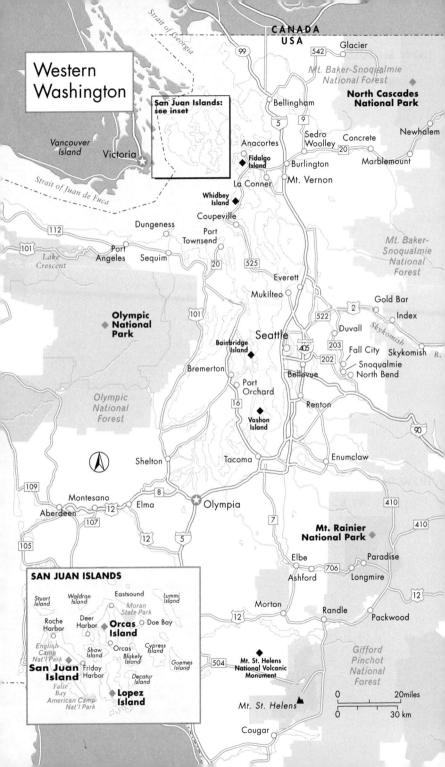

Western Washington

San Juan Islands:
see inset

CANADA
USA

North Cascades National Park

Mt. Baker-Snoqualmie National Forest

Glacier

542

99

5

9

Bellingham

Sedro Woolley

Concrete

Newhalem

20

Marblemount

Anacortes

Fidalgo Island

Burlington

La Conner

Mt. Vernon

Whidbey Island

Coupeville

Victoria

Vancouver Island

Strait of Georgia

Strait of Juan de Fuca

Dungeness

Port Townsend

Port Angeles

Sequim

112

101

Lake Crescent

Port Angeles

20

525

Everett

Mukilteo

Gold Bar

2

Index

Skykomish

Olympic National Park

101

522

Duvall

203

Fall City

Skykomish

Skykomish R.

Seattle

Bainbridge Island

405

202

Snoqualmie

North Bend

Bremerton

Bellevue

Port Orchard

Renton

16

Vashon Island

Olympic National Forest

90

Shelton

Tacoma

Enumclaw

109

Montesano

Elma

8

Olympia

410

410

Aberdeen

107

12

12

5

7

Mt. Rainier National Park

Elbe

706

Paradise

Ashford

Longmire

105

12

Morton

Randle

Packwood

Gifford Pinchot National Forest

504

Mt. St. Helens National Volcanic Monument

Mt. St. Helens

Cougar

0   20 miles
0   30 km

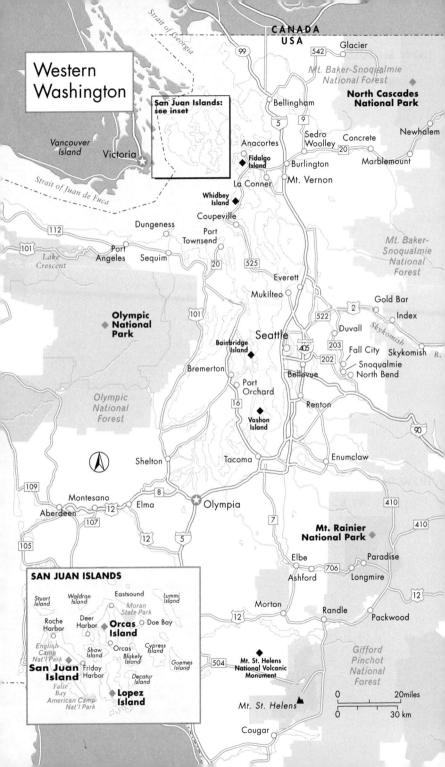

SAN JUAN ISLANDS

Stuart Island

Waldron Island

Eastsound

Lummi Island

Moran State Park

Roche Harbor

Deer Harbor

Orcas Island

Doe Bay

English Camp Nat'l Park

Orcas

Shaw Island

Cypress Island

San Juan Island

Friday Harbor

Blakely Island

Guemes Island

False Bay

Decatur Island

American Camp Nat'l Park

Lopez Island

How to Snack

The quintessential Seattle snack is a cup of strong-brewed, fair-trade coffee served up with a pastry brought in fresh each morning from one of the city's beloved bakeshops. **Café Vita, Caffe Fiore,** and **Tony's Coffee** are some of the best local grounds offered in coffeehouses throughout the city. In the pastry case, look for items from **Macrina Bakery, Great Harvest Bread Company, Essential Bakery,** and **Columbia City Bakery,** as well as delicious **Top Pot** or **Mighty-O** doughnuts.

The nighttime version of this is a glass of Pacific Northwest wine accompanied by cheeses and cured meats from Seattle's most-famous deli and charcuterie, **Salumi.** Wine bars like **Bricco, Poco** (1408 E. Pine St., Capitol Hill; 206/322-9463; www.pocowineroom.com), and **Purple Café** (1225 4th Ave., Downtown; 206/829-2280; www.thepurplecafe.com) all offer such tasting menus with their northwest vintages.

Seafood gets the royal treatment in most Seattle restaurants; **Union, Flying Fish** (2234 1st Ave, Belltown; 206/728-8595; www.flyingfishrestaurant.com), and **Matt's in the Market** are three musts. But you don't need a white tablecloth to tuck into the bounty of the sea: **Elliott's Oyster House** has the city's best shellfish bar (this is where you go to get that famous Dungeness crab and, of course, the five different types of local oysters). You can't get any simpler than **Steamers** (1201 Alaskan Way, Downtown; 206/267-0830) on Pier 56, where you can get clams, fish-and-chips, and local

seafood favorites at fast-food prices. Penn Cove mussels show up on many menus, too, and French eateries like **Le Pichet** (1933 1st Ave, Belltown; 206/256-1499; www.lepichetseattle.com) and its sister **Café Presse** offer some hearty preparations, such as sautéed with cider, bacon, and cream.

Seattle chefs' obsession with regional ingredients has gone far beyond the local farmers' markets—many now pay professional foragers to bring them the treasures from the deepest reaches of the state's forests. **Sitka and Spruce** and **Lark** (926 12th Ave, Capitol Hill; 206/323-5275; www.larkseattle.com) are particularly adept at incorporating foraged foods like miner's lettuce and other wild greens; wild mushrooms like morels, chanterelles, and boletes (fall); stinging nettles and fiddlehead ferns (spring); and huckleberries and blackberries (summer) into their daily changing menus.

Pike Place Market, the city's largest market, and the many wonderful Sunday neighborhood farmers' markets will give you plenty of access to local produce. Outside Seattle, keep your eyes peeled for roadside fruit stands, and look for seasonal berries, cherries, and doughnut peaches.

Uwajimaya (600 5th Ave S; 206/624-6248), the Japanese supergrocery in the International District, is the source of snacks you surely won't be able to find anywhere else. It also has a hoppin' food court offering a quick tour of Asian cuisines at lunch-counter prices, from sushi and teriyaki to Vietnamese spring rolls to Korean kim chi.

35

core). As you enter, you can see the fare posted on the fare box, which accepts both coins and bills.

BY CAR

Seattle has notorious traffic problems, partly because driving is often the most efficient way to get around the sprawling city, particularly to the quieter neighborhoods outside the downtown core. The best advice is to avoid driving during rush hour whenever possible. The worst tangles are on I–5, I–90, and any Downtown street that has a major on or off ramp to I–5. The Fremont Bridge and the 15th Avenue Bridge also get tied up. Aurora Avenue/99 gets very busy but often moves quickly enough. Other than that, you should find driving around Seattle a lot less anxiety-inducing than driving around other major cities. A car is absolutely necessary for side trips outside the city.

Parking is a headache and a half in Seattle. Street parking is only guaranteed in the quietest residential areas. The city has a good share of pay lots and garages in the central core of the city. Metered street parking exists in Downtown Seattle and the commercial stretches of Capitol Hill, but consider yourself lucky if you manage to snag a spot.

BY MONORAIL

Built for the 1962 World's Fair, the Seattle monorail is a quick, convenient link for tourists that travels an extremely short route between the Seattle Center and Downtown's Westlake Mall, at 4th Avenue and Pike Street. Making the 1-mi journey in 2 minutes, the monorail departs both points every 10 minutes from 11 AM to 9 PM daily. The round-trip fare is $4; children age four and under ride free. During weekends, Seattle Sonics basketball games, and the Folklife, Bite of Seattle, and Bumbershoot festivals—which all take place at the Seattle Center—you can park in the Macy's garage at 3rd Avenue and Stewart Street, take the monorail, and present your monorail ticket stub when you return for discounted parking rates of $5 on Friday and Saturday and $4 on Sunday and Monday.

BY TAXI

Seattle has a pretty small taxi fleet; taking a cab is not a major form of transportation in the city. Most people only take cabs to and from the airport and when they go out partying on weekends. You'll often be able to hail cabs on the street in Downtown, but anywhere else, you'll have to call. Expect long waits on Friday and Saturday nights.

Rides generally run about $2 per mile, and unless you're going a very short distance, the average cost of a cab ride in the city is $10–$12. The meter drop alone is $2.50, and you'll pay 50[cen] per minute stuck in traffic. The nice thing about Seattle metered cabs is that they almost always accept credit cards, and an automated system calls you on your cell phone to let you know that your cab has arrived.

WHERE SHOULD I FOCUS MY ENERGY?

If you're here for 1 day: Stick to the adjacent Downtown and Belltown neighborhoods, which together hold the majority of Seattle's sights.

If you're here for 2 days: Spend the next day in artsy Capitol Hill, which has parks, boutiques, and plenty of coffeeshops to chill out in.

CLAIM TO FAME

■ Washington State sure knows how to whet the palate. Seattle is the undisputed coffee capital of the country, and it's responsible for the java chain that conquered the world, Starbucks. Washington's wine country is only second in production to California—there are more than 200 wineries in the southern part of the state alone.

■ A healthier claim to fame is Washington's role in keeping the doctor away: more than half of the country's apples come from this state.

■ Seattle is perhaps best known for giving the world grunge, which was often referred to as "the Seattle Sound." Nirvana, Soundgarden, Alice in Chains, and Pearl Jam all got their start in the city's small music venues. Before the boys in flannel took over, Seattle's main music alum was Jimi Hendrix, whose grave is in Renton.

■ Seattle is also known as a mini Silicon Valley. Bill Gates, a Seattle native, built his Microsoft empire in the Eastside suburb of Redmond, and Amazon.com has its headquarters just south of the city, with plans to move the whole operation into the city proper in 2010.

35

If you're here for 3 days: Spend one day outside the city, hiking in Mt. Rainier National Park.

If you're here for 4 days: Tour the northern residential neighborhoods of Seattle, particularly Fremont and Ballard, which both have good shopping and dining.

If you're here for 5 days: Take the ferry to Orcas Island, and spend two days of your trip kayaking, whale-watching, or just relaxing.

If you're here for 6 days: Let Seattle-based adventures act as bookends to a trip to North Cascades National Park, where you can camp or stay in lodges.

If you're here for 7 days or more: Split your time between Seattle and the Olympic Peninsula; several days will allow you explore the extent of the national park and surrounding area, from rain forest to beaches.

WHAT ARE THE TOP EXPERIENCES?

The Food: Pacific Northwest dishes emphasize fresh, locally produced ingredients; even some of the fanciest restaurants in Seattle get their raw materials from the city's farmers' markets, Pike Place Market, and in some cases from their chef's own organic farms. These ingredients can be combined in straightforward ways—inventive takes on American comfort food—or fused with European and Asian influences. Best of all you don't have to spend big bucks for a taste: many bistros, bakeries, and cafés use local and organic ingredients as a matter of principle.

The Hiking: Washington State has so many beautiful trails, if there was ever a state sport, hiking would be it. There are enough trails in Mt. Rainier National Park alone to keep you busy (and awestruck) for

HISTORY YOU CAN SEE

In the late 1890s, Seattle quite surprisingly emerged as one of the country's crucial points of departure to the gold mines of the Klondike. Gold fever started in Seattle when the S.S. Portland docked near Pioneer Square carrying a ton of gold taken from the Yukon. When word came out that gold had been discovered in the Klondike River, western cities began to campaign in order to lure "stampeders" (prospectors) who were in need of lodging and equipment before heading north. After aggressively advertising its virtues as a staging area in publications and brochures all over the nation, Seattle managed to convince tens of thousands of gold seekers to use the city as their base. This part of the city's history is commemorating at the **Klondike Gold Rush National Historical Park** (319 2nd Ave S; 206/220–4240; www.nps.gov/klse) in Pioneer Square.

If you're interested in the general history of the city or amusing anecdotes about its early politicians and residents, you'll appreciate the **Underground Tour** (608 1st Ave; 206/682–4646; www.undergroundtour.com), which travels some of the subterranean passageways that were left behind when much of Pioneer Square was regraded after the Great Seattle Fire of 1889—storefronts that were once ground-level are now two stories below the street.

months. Between the three major parks the sheer variety of terrain is overwhelming. Share narrow ridge paths with mountain goats, scramble over boulders, conquer switchbacks that wind through old-growth forest, get your shoes wet on lingering snows in July, get your sleeves caught on huckleberry bushes, or just stroll through wildflower meadows on easy loop trails.

The Lazy Days: With storefronts full of outdoor gear and earnest cyclists slogging up the city's killer hills, it's hard to imagine Seattleites taking it easy—but if you need a little R&R, the city will oblige. Grab a paperback at Elliott Bay Book Company and head to a coffeehouse for an hour (or five). Fly a kite at Gasworks Park or just stake out a piece of green with a view of Lake Union and the skyline. There's not much happening on Orcas Island, but if you require even more solitude, take the ferry to rustic Lopez Island, affectionately called, "Slow-pez." And sure, you can sweat up as many switchbacks as you want in the North Cascades, but you can also opt to simply take a slow scenic drive along Highway 20 and continue on to Stehekin, a tiny valley community accessible only by boat or floatplane.

The Water: Seattle's dramatic position along the sparkling Puget Sound sets the tone of any Washington visit. The sound isn't the only blue water within city limits, either—Lake Union dominates the center of the city, and massive Lake Washington forms the eastern border. Craft of all size ply the Lake Washington Ship Canal, and you can get a close-up look at research boats, dinghies, and post yachts from the Ballard Locks. On hot days, the swimming rafts in Lake Washington turn into impromptu party barges, and serene kayak excursions can be had in any of the above spots. Orcas Island is famous for its great sea-kayaking trips, which often double as wildlife-spotting adventures. You can find waterfalls and mountain lakes in the North Cascades, and of course, a great stretch of coastline on the Olympic Peninsula—the water may be too cold for casual swimming but locals and visitors alike are usually content to simply gaze at the thundering Pacific for hours.

BEST BETS

SIGHTS AND TOURS

SEATTLE

★ **Capitol Hill.** With its mix of theaters and churches, coffeehouses and nightclubs, stately homes and student apartments, Capitol Hill still deserves its reputation as Seattle's most eclectic neighborhood. Seattle's youth culture, old money, gay scene, and everything in between all converge on the lively, if somewhat scuzzy stretch of Broadway E between E. Denny Way and E. Roy Street. Most of the good shopping, eating, and drinking is along the Pike–Pine corridor, which begins at the corners of Pike and Pine streets (which run parallel) and Melrose Avenue. High above the mansions of North Capitol Hill sits 45-acre Volunteer Park, a grassy expanse perfect for picnicking, sunbathing, reading, and strolling.

> **STRANGE BUT TRUE**
>
> ■ After the Great Seattle Fire of 1889, the city regraded the destroyed area to be two stories higher than the original streets. A big factor in this decision? Toilets. The toilets in the Pioneer Square district, which was built on tidelands that would often flood, would back up during high tide.
>
> ■ Six people have completed parachute jumps from the top of the Space Needle.
>
> ■ Three of the world's six floating bridges are in Washington State, including the longest floating pontoon bridge in the world—the Evergreen Point Floating Bridge, which connects Seattle with its suburbs on the east side of Lake Washington.

35

Fodor's Choice **Discovery Park.** Discovery Park is Seattle's largest park, and it has an ★ amazing variety of terrain: cool forest trails that can feel as secluded as mountain hikes lead to meadows, saltwater beaches, sand dunes, a lighthouse, and views that include Puget Sound, the Cascades, and the Olympics. ⊠*3801 W. Government Way, Magnolia* ✛*From Downtown Seattle to main entrance: take Elliott Ave. north until it becomes 15th Ave. NW. Take Dravus St. exit and turn left on Dravus at stoplight. Turn right on 20th Ave. W, which becomes Gilman Ave. W. Gilman eventually becomes W. Government Way; follow road into park* ☎*206/386–4236* ⊕*www.cityofseattle.net/parks* ⊡*Free* ☾*Park daily 6 AM–11 PM, visitor center Tues.–Sun. 8:30–5.*

★ **Fremont.** The neighborhood's small center is comprised of two short strips: Fremont Avenue heading north from the Fremont Bridge to N. 39th Street, and a few blocks of N. 36th Street as it veers west off Fremont Avenue toward Ballard. Both streets have an eclectic bunch of shops, cafés, bars, and small businesses. Beneath the Aurora Bridge at N.

36th Street lurks the 18-foot-tall *Fremont Troll,* clutching a Volkswagen Beetle in his massive left hand. Fremont's signature statue, *Waiting for the Interurban,* is a cast aluminum sculpture of five figures, one holding a small child. Residents enjoy dressing and ornamenting the figures for just about any joyful occasion, from retirements to birthdays to declarations of love. The sculpture's home is on N. 34th Street, just over the Fremont Bridge at Fremont Avenue. There's also a lovely stretch of the **Burke-Gilman Trail** along the canal on the west side of the Fremont Bridge.

Fodor'sChoice
★
Olympic Sculpture Park. The 9-acre open-air expanse nestled between Belltown and Elliott Bay is a scenic outdoor branch of the Seattle Art MuseumAround the grasses, blossoms, and water features are scattered an amazing variety of oversize, handmade pieces from some of the Northwest's notable visual artists. On clear days, you'll also get near-perfect views of the water with the jagged, snowcapped Olympic Mountains in the background. ⊠ *Western Ave. between Broad and Bay Sts., Belltown* ☎*206/645–3100* ⊕*www.seattleartmuseum.org* ☜*Free* ⊙*Park daily dawn–dusk. PACCAR Pavilion May–Sept., Tues.–Sun. 10–5, Fri. until 9; Oct.–Apr., Tues.–Sun. 10–4.*

Fodor'sChoice
★
Pike Place Market. Everyone visits the market, which means it's often infuriatingly crowded, especially when cruise ships are in port. During high season you might never find a quiet corner, but getting here early (around 8 AM) is probably your best bet. Booths sell seafood—which can be packed in dry ice for your flight home—produce, cheese, wine, spices, tea, coffee, and crafts; there are also several restaurants. The flower market is a must-see. ⊠*Pike Pl. at Pike St., west of 1st Ave., Downtown* ☎*206/682–7453* ⊕*www.pikeplacemarket.org* ⊙*Stall hrs vary: 1st-level shops Mon.–Sat. 10–6, Sun. 11–5; underground shops daily 11–5.*

Fodor'sChoice
★
Seattle Aquarium. The aquarium should call itself Otters R Us—you could spend hours just watching the delightful antics of the sea otters and their river cousins. The partially open-air Marine Mammal section also includes harbor seals and fur seals, and, unlike at some aquariums, you get unimpeded, close-up views of the animals from two levels—you can see them sleeping on the rocks or gliding around the water's surface and then go down a floor to watch them as they dive to the bottoms of their pools. ⊠*Pier 59 off Alaskan Way, Downtown* ☎*206/386–4300* ⊕*www.seattleaquarium.org* ☜*$12.50* ⊙*Daily 9:30–5.*

★ **Seattle Art Museum.** Long the pride of the city's art scene, SAM is now better than ever after a massive expansion that connects the iconic old building on University Street (where sculptor Jonathan Borofsky's several-stories-high *Hammering Man* still pounds away) to a sleek, light-filled high-rise space around the corner on 1st Avenue and Union Street. ⊠*1300 1st Ave., Downtown* ☎*206/654–3100* ⊕*www.seattleart museum.org* ☜*$13, free 1st Thurs. of month* ⊙*Tues., Wed., and weekends 10–5, Thurs. and Fri. 10–9, 1st Thurs. until midnight.*

★ **Space Needle.** The distinctive exterior of the 520-foot-high Space Needle is visible throughout much of the city—but the view from the inside out is even better. A 42-second elevator ride up to the circular observation deck yields 360-degree vistas of Elliott Bay, Queen Anne Hill, the

LIKE A LOCAL

■ The Seattle region has no end of baffling place names whose incorrect pronunciation will immediately peg you as a tourist. The best examples are the towns of Puyallup (pew-AL-up), Sequim (skwim), and Tacoma (Tah-CO-mah); the scenic stretch of Kalaloch (KLAY-loch) on the Olympic Peninsula; and Lake Chelan (sha-LAN) in the North Cascades region. Alki (AL-ki), as in Seattle's Alki Beach, rhymes with high. And the state's main mountain is pronounced Ray-NEAR not Rain-E-er. Giant Geoduck (GOOEY-duck) clams grown in Puget (PEW-jet) Sound are regional specialty, as are Dungeness (dun-jen-NESS) crabs.

■ In Seattle "the Ave" is the nearly official name for University Way, which is in the heart of the University District, known to everyone simply as the U District. (University of Washington is casually referred to as U Dub.) The Central District and International District are shortened to the C.D. and the I.D., respectively, and Capitol Hill is often just "the Hill." Seattle Art Museum is SAM. In fact, Seattleites tend to shorten the names of the city's most famous sights, often by stripping out specifics. Hence, we have the Needle, the aquarium, the locks (a necessary abbreviation of the Hiram M. Chittenden Locks in Ballard), and the Market (all the identification you'll need for Pike Place Market). The troll refers to the delightful larger-than-life troll sculpture under the Aurora Bridge in the Fremont neighborhood. Lastly, if you hear anyone refer to "riding the slut," don't blush too much—SLUT is a playful nickname some residents have bestowed on a new trolley system that serves the South Lake Union neighborhood.

■ Seattleites are not as militant about coffee lingo as you might expect, though you should know your sizes: short, tall, venti, grande. A few other pointers: a regular coffee (not espresso) is a "drip"; an "Americano" is an espresso diluted with water. (You might want to add "with room" when ordering either of those to ensure the barista doesn't fill the cup to the brim.) "Wet" or "dry" refers to what type of milk you want in a cappuccino (dry means foamed, wet means steamed).

35

University of Washington campus, and the Cascade Range. ✉*5th Ave. and Broad St., Queen Anne* ☎*206/905–2100* ⊕*www.spaceneedle.com* ✉*$16* ⊙*Sun.–Thurs. 9* AM*–11* PM*, Fri. and Sat. 9* AM*–midnight.*

OUTSIDE SEATTLE

Fodor's Choice
★
Mt. Rainier National Park. Two-and-a-half hours southeast of Seattle is majestic Mt. Rainier, the fifth-highest mountain in the contiguous United States. With more than two dozen major glaciers, the mountain holds the largest glacial system in the continental United States and the park offers 400 square mi of wilderness. ☎*360/569–2211* ⊕*www. nps.gov/mora* ✉*$15 per vehicle; $5 for motorcyclists or bicyclists.*

Fodor's Choice
★
North Cascades National Park. Countless snow-clad mountain spires dwarf glacial valleys and lowland, old-growth forests in North Cascades National Park. Considered by some the most spectacular mountain scenery in the lower 48 states, the untrammeled expanse covers 505,000 acres of rugged mountain land. ☎*360/856–5700* ⊕*www.nps.gov/noca* ✉*Free.*

Fodor'sChoice
★

Olympic National Park. One of the largest, most remote, and least-developed protected areas in the United States, Olympic National Park preserves 922,651 acres of the peninsula's magnificent, mountainous interior and wave-stung shoreline. ⊠*Headquarters: 600 E. Park Ave, Port Angeles* ☎*360/565–3130* ⊕*www.nps.gov/olym* ⊠*$10 per vehicle plus $5 per person.*

Fodor'sChoice
★

Orcas Island. Roads on flower-blossom–shape Orcas Island, the largest of the San Juan Islands, sweep through wide valleys and rise to gorgeous hilltop views. Farmers, fishermen, artists, retirees, and summer-home owners make up the population of about 4,500. Orcas is a favorite place for weekend getaways from the Seattle area. **Moran State Park** (⊠*Star Rte. 22; head northeast from Eastsound on Horseshoe Hwy. and follow signs* ☎*360/376–2326, 800/452–5678 for reservations*) comprises 5,000 acres of hilly, old-growth forests dotted with sparkling lakes, in the middle of which rises 2,400-foot-high Mt. Constitution, the tallest peak in the San Juans. A drive to the summit affords exhilarating views of the islands, the Cascades, the Olympics, and Vancouver Island. The ferries that make the rounds to Orcas also stop at **Lopez Island**, a broad, bay-encircled bit of terrain amid sparkling blue seas, a place where cabinlike homes are tucked into the woods, and boats are moored in lonely coves. Of the three San Juan islands with facilities to accommodate overnight visitors, it's the most rustic and least crowded during high season.

WHERE TO EAT

WHAT IT COSTS				
¢	$	$$	$$$	$$$$
AT DINNER	under $10	$10–$20	$20–$30	$30–$40	over $40

Prices are per person for a main course, excluding tax and tip.

SEATTLE

$$
✕**Matt's in the Market.** The crown jewel of the Market-area restaurants,
Fodor'sChoice
★
Matt's redefined intimate dining and personal service when it opened its 23-seat spot on the second floor of the Corner Market Building. A recent expansion nearly doubled the amount of seats, but the space is still tiny, and the basics remain: a lunch counter perfect for grabbing a delicious po'boy or cup of gumbo, an inviting space with simple adornments like clear glass vases filled with flowers from the market, a seasonal menu that synthesizes the best picks from the restaurant's neighbors, and an excellent wine list. At dinner, starters might include such delectable items as Manila clams steamed in beer, herbs, and chilies; entrées always include at least one catch of the day. ⊠*94 Pike St., Suite 32, Downtown* ☎*206/467–7909* ⊕*www.mattsinthemarket.com* ⊠*Reservations essential* ⊟*MC, V* ☉*Closed Sun.*

$$
★
✕**Union.** Dining at Union is a special experience, but everything about the place is so understated, the experience may take a while to process. Though from the street the restaurant looks very sleek and a little

ON THE WAY

Mt. St. Helens National Monument: In 1980 this volcano southwest of Mt. Rainier famously blew its top annihilating most of the life on its slopes. Today it's dormant and open for hikes; areas of amazing renewal are contrasted by lava tubes and lava-ravaged ancient forests. 360/449–7800 headquarters, 360/274–0962 visitor center; www.fs.fed.us/gpnf/mshnvm

Chateau Ste. Michelle Winery: One of the state's oldest wineries, Chateau Ste. Michelle is also the easiest to reach from Seattle at 20 mi northeast of the city proper. Tastings and tours are offered and you can picnic on the grounds which are on 87 wooded acres. 14111 N.E. 145th St., Woodinville; 425/488–1133 or 800/267–6793; www.ste-michelle.com

Lewis and Clark Interpretive Center, Cape Disappointment: In November 1805, Lewis and Clark, stood on this spot after a long journey along the Columbia River to a bluff above the Pacific. The center includes an illustrated timeline of the journey and an observation deck with panoramic views of the ocean and the river. Off U.S. 101, 75 mi south of Aberdeen (114 mi south of Olympia); 360/642–3078; www.parks.wa.gov/lcinterpctr.asp

35

standoffish (yes, there are an awful lot of red and gray accents), the space becomes very cozy once you settle in. Fresh ingredients come from Pike Place Market and the menu changes daily to accommodate what's available. Seafood is the strong point—no one cooks a scallop better than Union—but selections always include some type of pork dish, as well as fowl. Entrées are outstanding and reasonably priced, but you might opt to concoct a meal out of starters, which are more fun and inventive. The Dungeness crab salad with avocado and basil oil is always on the menu and it's a must. The wine list is excellent and servers are great at giving advice on which bottle to select. ⊠1400 1st Ave., Downtown ☎206/838–8000 ⊕www.unionseattle.com ⊟AE, MC, V ⊗No lunch.

$–$$ ✕**Elliott's Oyster House.** No place in Seattle serves better Dungeness crab or oysters than Elliott's, which has gotten the presentation of fresh seafood down to a fine art. You can't go wrong with the local rockfish or salmon. The dining room is bright, and there's a great view of Elliott Bay and of the harbor tour boats next door. The crowd is usually split 50–50 between tourists and locals, as Seattleites still fully embrace this place, especially the raw-bar happy hour. ⊠Pier 56 off Alaskan Way, Downtown ☎206/623–4340 ⊕http://elliottsoysterhouse.com ⊟AE, DC, MC, V.

$–$$ ✕**Shiro's.** Shiro Kashiba is the most famous sushi chef in Seattle; he's been in town for going on 40 years, and he still takes the time to helm the sushi bar at his popular restaurant. If you get a seat in front of Shiro, don't be shy—this is one place where ordering omakase (chef's choice) is almost a must. ⊠2401 2nd Ave., Belltown ☎206/443–9844 ⊕www.shiros.com ⊟AE, MC, V ⊗No lunch.

$ ✕**Sitka & Spruce.** Unceremoniously plunked in a strip mall in the decid-
Fodor'sChoice edly nontrendy Eastlake neighborhood is one of the city's best ambas-
★   sadors of regional cuisine. The menu changes daily, but of one thing
you can be sure—whatever's on your plate either came from Washington State or the Pacific Ocean next door. Seasonal treats like morels
and fiddlehead ferns are given lots of attention when available. Entrées,
which can range from fluke ceviche to organic tri-tip served with piles
of fresh greens, can be ordered as small plates to keep costs low and
sampling at a maximum. It's tiny, so waits can be long, and if you
don't score one of the five individual tables, you might end up making new friends at the communal table. ⊠*2238 Eastlake Ave E, Eastlake* ☎*206/324–0662 wwww.sitkaandspruce.com* ⚐*No reservations*
⊟*MC, V* ⊗*Closed Sun. No dinner Mon. and Tues.*

¢–$ ✕**Café Presse.** The owners of Le Pichet have brought their casual French
★ bistro food to the Hill, bestowing the city with a restaurant that is
at once trendy and laid-back, immensely satisfying and surprisingly
affordable. From the breakfast rush to the wee hours (it's open until 2
am daily), Presse serves up a simple menu of sandwiches (grilled or on
baguettes), pomme frites, soups, and salads; there are a few entrées, such
as Penn Cove mussels, roasted half chicken, and smoked pork chops for
anyone seeking a more complex sit-down meal. The space is Parisian hip
via the Northwest (check out the impressive wood-beam ceiling), with
the Hill's creative crowd adding to its indie cred. There's a casual dining
room with exposed brick walls in back, but the front of the house, with
its bustling bar area and floor-to-ceiling windows, is where the action is.
⊠*1117 12th Ave., Capitol Hill* ☎*206/709–7674* ⊟*MC, V.*

WHERE TO STAY

	WHAT IT COSTS				
	¢	$	$$	$$$	$$$$
FOR 2 PEOPLE	under $100	$100–$150	$150–$200	$200–$250	over $250

Price categories are assigned based on the range between the least and most
expensive standard double rooms in high season. Tax (17%) is extra.

SEATTLE

$$$$ 🏨**Alexis Hotel.** The Alexis occupies two historic buildings near the
★ waterfront. A 2007 refurbishment turned a worn-around-the-edges
property into one of the shining stars of the Downtown hotel scene.
Using slate grays, soft blues, taupes, and whites, the Alexis has updated
its look while maintaining a classic feel—the palette may be modern,
but the leather wing chairs in front of the wood-burning fireplaces
recall a different era. The Alexis has always had a focus on art (including a rotating collection of paintings selected by a Seattle Art Museum
curator in the corridor between wings) and that tradition continues
in the rooms as well—all have unique works of art. ⊠*1007 1st Ave.,
Downtown, 98104* ☎*206/624–4844 or 888/850–1155* ⊕*www.alexis
hotel.com* ⇱*88 rooms, 33 suites* ⚐*In-room: refrigerator, Wi-Fi. In-
hotel: restaurant, room service, bar, gym, spa, laundry service, con-*

cierge, public Wi-Fi, parking (fee), some pets allowed, no-smoking rooms ⊟AE, D, DC, MC, V.

$$$–$$$$
Fodor'sChoice
★
🏨**Hotel 1000.** Hotel 1000 is new to the scene, but all new luxury properties will have to answer to it. The centerpiece of the small lobby is a dramatically backlighted staircase (don't worry, there's an elevator) and glass sculpture that looks like crystallized stalks of bamboo. The small sitting room off the lobby, with its elegant fire pit surrounded by mid-century modern swiveling leather stools, looks as though it's been designed for leggy Scandinavian beauties and the men in black turtlenecks who love them. The designers wanted the hotel to have a distinctly Pacific Northwest feel

and they've succeeded greatly without being campy. The whole hotel is done in dark woods and deep earth tones with an occasional blue accent to represent the water. Rooms are full of surprising touches, including large tubs that fill from the ceiling, and Hotel 1000 is without a doubt the most high-tech hotel in the city. ⊠1000 1st Ave., Downtown, 98104 ☎206/932–3102 ⊕www.hotel1000seattle.com ⬐101 rooms, 19 suites ⌂In-room: safe, refrigerator, DVD, Wi-Fi. In-hotel: restaurant, room service, bar, gym, spa, laundry service, concierge, public Wi-Fi, parking (fee), some pets allowed, no-smoking rooms ⊟AE, MC, V.

$$$–$$$$
Fodor'sChoice
★
🏨**Inn at the Market.** For its views alone, the Inn at the Market would be worthy of a Fodor's Choice. But views alone don't make a hotel great—this one has all the pieces of the puzzle from friendly service to a great location (in the north end of Pike Place Market, but tucked away from the bustle of 1st Avenue) to simple, sophisticated guest rooms with Tempur-Pedic beds and bright, spacious bathrooms. All rooms have essentially the same decor and amenities; they're differentiated only by the types of views they offer. You certainly won't be disappointed with the Partial Water View rooms—some have small sitting areas arranged in front of the windows. The four Deluxe Water View rooms are really spectacular, though—708 and 710 are the ones to shoot for, as they share a large private sundeck. ⊠86 Pine St., Downtown, 98101 ☎206/443–3600 or 800/446–4484 ⊕www.innatthemarket.com ⬐60 rooms, 10 suites ⌂In-room: safe, refrigerator, Wi-Fi. In-hotel: 3 restaurants, room service, laundry service, concierge, public Wi-Fi, parking (fee), no-smoking rooms ⊟AE, D, DC, MC, V.

¢–$$
★
🏨**Ace Hotel.** The Ace is a dream come true for both penny-pinching hipsters and creative folks who appreciate the chic minimalist decor. Almost everything is white—except for the army surplus blankets on the beds and a few pieces of art on the walls (which include murals

from überhip street art luminary Shepard Fairey). The cheapest rooms share bathrooms, which are clean, stand-alone units with enormous showers. Suites are larger (some have leather couches) and have full private bathrooms hidden behind rotating walls. A small dining room hosts a continental breakfast and has a vending machine with unusual items like Japanese snacks. The Ace has guests of all ages, but if you're not soothed (or stimulated) by the stripped-down, almost austere quality of the rooms or not amused by finding a copy of the *Kama Sutra* where the Bible would be, you won't enjoy this place. ✉*2423 1st Ave., Belltown, 98121* ☎*206/448–4721* ⊕*www.theacehotel.com* ⤴*28 rooms* ♿*In-room: no a/c (some), refrigerator, Wi-Fi. In-hotel: laundry facilities, public Wi-Fi, parking (fee), some pets allowed, no-smoking rooms* ▭*AE, D, DC, MC, V.*

NIGHTLIFE & THE ARTS

MUSIC VENUES

Dimitriou's Jazz Alley (✉*2033 6th Ave., Downtown* ☎*206/441–9729* ⊕*www.jazzalley.com*) is where Seattleites dress up to see nationally known jazz artists.

★ **Neumo's** (✉*925 E. Pike St., Capitol Hill* ☎*206/709–9467* ⊕*www. neumos.com*) was one of the grunge era's iconic clubs (when it was Moe's), and it has managed to reclaim its status as a staple of the Seattle rock scene, despite being closed for a six-year stretch.

The Triple Door (✉*216 Union St., Downtown* ☎*206/838–4333* ⊕*www. thetripledoor.net*) has been referred to (perhaps not kindly) as a rock club for thirty- and fortysomethings. Although it's true that you can see more world music and jazz here than alternative music, the interesting lineup here often appeals to younger patrons, too.

SPORTS & THE OUTDOORS

Center for Wooden Boats (✉*1010 Valley St., Lake Union* ☎*206/382–2628* ⊕*www.cwb.org*). Seattle's free maritime heritage museum also rents classic wooden rowboats and sailboats for short trips around Lake Union.

Northwest Outdoor Center (✉*2100 Westlake Ave. N, Lake Union* ☎*206/281–9694* ⊕*www.nwoc.com*). This center on Lake Union's west side rents one- or two-person kayaks (it also has a few triples) by the hour or day, including equipment and basic or advanced instruction.

VISITOR INFORMATION

Seattle Convention and Visitor's Bureau (☎*206/461–5840 or 206/461–5888* ⊕ *www.visitseattle.org*).

Washington State Tourism (☎*800/544–1800* ⊕ *www.experiencewashington. com*).

Along the Way

Amarillo, Texas
Atlanta, Georgia
Baltimore, Maryland
Charlotte, North Carolina
Cheyenne, Wyoming
Cincinnati, Ohio
Cleveland, Ohio
Dallas, Texas
Detroit, Michigan
Houston, Texas
Jacksonville, Florida
Kansas City, Missouri
Milwaukee, Wisconsin
Pittsburgh, Pennsylvania
Providence, Rhode Island
Sacramento, California
St. Louis, Missouri

FODOR'S ESSENTIAL USA CONTAINS 35 of our favorite trips, and we undoubtedly left geographical gaps. What follows are quick overviews of a few of our favorite places to stop along the way—fantastic cities in their own right. For more information on what to see and do here—and across the county—visit our website, www.fodors.com.

AMARILLO, TEXAS

Amarillo is one of those legendary Old West towns where cowboys and Indians culture has morphed into a softer, more modern version of Western tenacity and hospitality. The people still hold on to their hardiness and homespun values and celebrate the rich mix of culture in the region, including a strong Tex-Mex feel. Folks are proud of their assorted histories and the city that settlers, businessmen, and railroads carved from this dry, flat grassland. Amarillo celebrates its rich historical themes with several museums, including the Panhandle–Plains Historical Museum, nicknamed by some "The Smithsonian of Texas."

DINING AND LODGING

✕ **Big Texan Steak Ranch.** The Big Texan is famous for its legendary 72-ounce slab o' beef. If you can consume the entire 4.5-pound fillet, you get it free—but note: 8,000 have succeeded, while 34,000 have tried and failed. ⌧ 7701 E. I–40 ☎ 800/657-7177 ▭ AE, D, MC, V.

✕ **La Fiesta Grande.** Meaning "the Big Party," this local Mexican favorite has a long menu (from chimichangas to chipotle shrimp), big portions, and cold margaritas that add up to a party-worthy experience. ⌧ 2201 S. Ross Ave. ☎ 806/374–3689 ▭ AE, D, DC, MC, V.

✕ **Zen 721.** A consistent smash with locals, 721 serves sumptuous Asian-style fare like tempura, several types of yakitori, and Ahi tuna, as well as non-Asian items like fish tacos, grilled beef, and barbecued quail. ⌧ 614 S. Polk St. ☎ 806/372–1909 ▭ AE, D, MC, V.

▦ **Ashmore Inn and Suites.** Spacious, clean, and friendly, the Ashmore is located off one of the main drags through town and is known for its great, free breakfast buffet. ⌧ 900 Sunland Park Dr. ☎ 915/833–2900 or 800/658–2744 ⊕ www.ashmoresuites-amarillo.com ⇗ 138 rooms ▭ AE, D, MC, V.

▦ **Big Texan Motel.** A little exaggerated but a lot of fun, this hotel takes the Texas spirit way past even the Texas-sized level. ⌧ 7701 E. I–40 ☎ 800/657–7177 ⊕ www.bigtexan.com ⇗ 50 rooms ▭ AE, D, MC, V.

▦ **Historical Parkview House Bed and Breakfast.** A wonderful example of an Old West home during the Victorian period, this B&B is crammed with antique knickknacks. ⌧ 1311 S. Jefferson St. ☎ 806/373–9464 ⊕ www.parkviewhousebb.com ⇗ 6 rooms ▭ AE, MC, V.

ATLANTA, GEORGIA

Atlanta's character has evolved from a mix of peoples: transplanted Northerners and those from elsewhere account for more than half the population and have undeniably affected the mood and character of the city. Irish immigrants had a major role in the city's early history, along with Germans and Austrians; the Hungarian-born Rich brothers founded Atlanta's principal department store. And the immigrants keep coming. In the past two decades Atlanta has seen spirited growth in its Asian and Latin-American communities. Related restaurants, shops, and institutions have become part of the city's texture.

DINING AND LODGING

✗**Aria.** The rustic heartiness of Chef Gerry Klaskala's entrées also appeals to the epicurean palate. His talent is best captured by his love of "slow foods"—braises, stews, roasts, and chops cooked over a roll-top French grill. ☒ *490 E. Paces Ferry Rd.* ☏ *404/233-7673* ⊟ *AE, D, DC, MC, V.*

✗**Bacchanalia.** Often called the city's best restaurant, Bacchanalia has been a special-occasion destination since it opened in Buckhead in 1993. The kitchen focuses on locally grown produce and seasonal ingredients. ☒ *1198 Howell Mill Rd.* ☏ *404/365-0410, Ext. 22* ⊟ *AE, DC, MC, V.*

✗**Flying Biscuit.** There's an hour-long wait on weekends for the big, fluffy biscuits served with cranberry-apple butter. Fancier dinners include roasted chicken and turkey meatloaf, as well as plenty of vegetarian options. ☒ *1655 McLendon Ave.* ☏ *404/687-8888* ⊟ *AE, MC, V*

🛏**Glenn Hotel.** This boutique hotel is a mix of New York sophistication and Miami sex appeal. Its rooms are small, but a thoughtful renovation makes the best of the space. ☒ *110 Marietta St. NW* ☏ *404/521-2250 or 866/404-5366* ⊕ *www.glennhotel.com* ⮑ *93 rooms, 16 suites* ⊟ *AE, D, DC, MC, V.*

🛏**Ritz-Carlton, Buckhead.** Decorated with 18th- and 19th-century antiques, this elegant hotel is a regular stopover for visiting celebrities. The spacious guestrooms are furnished with traditional reproductions. ☒ *3434 Peachtree Rd. NE* ☏ *404/237-2700 or 800/241-3333* ⊕ *www.ritzcarleton.com* ⮑ *524 rooms, 29 suites* ⊟ *AE, D, DC, V.*

🛏**Sheraton Midtown Atlanta Hotel at Colony Square.** Rooms are modern, with muted tones; those on higher floors have city views. ☒ *188 14th St.* ☏ *404/892-6000 or 800/422-7895* ⊕ *www.starwood.com* ⮑ *467 rooms, 32 suites* ⊟ *AE, D, DC, MV, V.*

BALTIMORE, MARYLAND

Baltimore is a city of neighborhoods. From the cobblestone streets of historic Fells Point and Federal Hill, up the wide avenues of elegant Mount Vernon, and across the countless modest blue-collar enclaves, the city wears many different faces. On the east and west sides, seamless blocks of the city's trademark redbrick row houses, each fronted by white marble steps, radiate outward from the modern towers of downtown Baltimore. Uptown, marble mansions, grand churches, and philanthropic institutions proudly bearing their founders' names mark the city's progress: fortunes earned on the harbor flowed north to create these monuments to wealth and power.

DINING AND LODGING

✕**Blue Sea Grill.** Start with a plate of raw oysters or a bowl of Maryland crab soup, then order from a selection of whole fishes—grilled, broiled, or panfried. The lobster macaroni and cheese is a favorite. ⊠ *614 Water St.* ☎*410/837–7300* ▤*AE, D, DC, MC, V.*

✕**Hamptons.** A panoramic view of the Inner Harbor competes with the restaurant's elegant interior. Expect carefully composed seasonal cuisine at once contemporary and classic: roasted pheasant with butternut squash and mushroom risotto in Madeira demi-glace, for instance. ⊠ *Harbor Court Hotel, 500 Light St.* ☎*410/347–9744* ▤*AE, D, MC, V.*

✕**Ixia.** From the food to the décor, Ixia sparkles. Service is top-notch, as are dishes such as tuna tartare, which features small, tender cubes of fish in an Asian chile vinaigrette and cucumber soup. ⊠ *518 N. Charles St.* ☎*410/727–1800* ▥ ▤*AE, D, DC, MC, V.*

▥**Baltimore Marriott Inner Harbor.** This 10-story hotel is a block away from Oriole Park at Camden Yards, Harborplace, and the convention center. ⊠*110 Eutaw St.* ☎*410/962–0202 or 800/228–9290* ⊕*www.marriott.com* ⤸*524 rooms, 2 suites* ▤*AE, D, DC, MC, V.*

▥**Hyatt Regency.** Rooms have rich gold and black-purple prints and cherrywood furniture; most rooms have views of the harbor or the city. ⊠*300 Light St.* ☎*410/528–1234 or 800/233-1234* ⊕*www.hyatt.com* ⤸*488 rooms, 26 suites* ▤*AE, D, DC, MC, V.*

▥**Renaissance Harbor Place Hotel.** The most conveniently located of the Inner Harbor hotels—across the street from the shopping pavilions. Guest rooms are light and cheerful; some have a view of the harbor, downtown, or the indoor courtyard. ⊠*202 E. Pratt St.* ☎*410/547–1200 or 800/468–3571* ⊕*www.renaissancehotels.com* ⤸*562 rooms, 60 suites* ▤*AE, D, DC, MC, V.*

CHARLOTTE, NORTH CAROLINA

Though Charlotte dates from Revolutionary War times (it is named for King George III's wife, Queen Charlotte), its Uptown is distinctively New South, with gleaming skyscrapers. Uptown encompasses all of downtown Charlotte, its business and cultural heart and soul. It's also home to the government center and some residential neighborhoods. And public art is keeping pace with the city's growing skyline. Examples of this are the sculptures at the four corners of Trade and Tryon streets. Erected at Independence Square, they symbolize Charlotte's beginnings: a gold miner (commerce), a mill worker (the city's textile heritage), an African-American railroad builder (transportation), and a mother holding her baby aloft (the future).

DINING AND LODGING

✕**Campania.** This Italian food here is as good as it gets outside Southern Italy. Try the excellent shrimp sautéed in garlic butter and herbs, smoked salmon with a cognac-tomato-cream sauce, or the veal chops. ⊠ *6414 Rea Rd.* ☎*704/541–8505* ▤*AE, D, MC, V.*

✕**College Place.** Expect simple down-home cooking—and plenty of it—at this cafeteria. Lunch has lots of vegetable dishes, homemade corn bread, and a soup and salad bar; big breakfasts are also served. ⊠ *300 S. College St.* ☎704/343–9268 ▭*No credit cards.*

✕**Mert's Heart and Soul.** Patrons will find large portions of Low Country and Gullah staples, such as fried chicken with greens, macaroni and cheese, and corn bread. Low Country specialties include shrimp-and-salmon omelets and red beans and rice. ⊠ *214 N. College St.* ☎704/342–4222 ▭*AE, MC, V.*

▦**Hilton Charlotte City Center.** In the Financial District, this hotel sits across the street from the Charlotte Convention Center. Guest rooms are large and comfortable; each has a nice view of the city. ⊠222 E. 3rd St. ☎704/377–1500 or 800 445 8667 ⊕www.hilton.com ⨼407 rooms, 25 suites ▭AE, D, MC, V.

▦**Morehead Inn.** Built in 1917, this grand colonial-revival home is in the Dilworth neighborhood. Rooms are filled with period antiques, including several with impressive four-poster beds. ⊠1122 E. Morehead St. ☎704/376–3357 or 888/667–3432 ⊕www.moreheadinn.com ⨼12 rooms ▭AE, DC, MC, V.

▦**Omni Charlotte Hotel.** This 16-story hotel is in the heart of Downtown, within walking distance of the Convention Center as well as many arts and sports venues. Many guest rooms have glass walls overlooking the skyline. ⊠132 E. Trade St. ☎704/377–0400 or 800/843–6664 ⊕www. omnicharlotte.com ⨼374 rooms, 33 suites ▭AE, D, MC, V.

36

CHEYENNE, WYOMING

Cheyenne is Wyoming's largest city, but at just over 50,000 people it is not a place where you'll have to fight traffic or wait in lines. Throughout the year it offers a decent variety of shopping, plus attractions ranging from art galleries to museums to parks. Cheyenne became the state capital in 1890, at a time when the rule of the cattle barons was beginning to weaken after harsh winter storms in the late 1880s and financial downturns in the national economy. But Cheyenne's link to ranching didn't fade, and the community launched its first Cheyenne Frontier Days in 1897, an event that continues to this day. During the late-July celebration—the world's largest outdoor rodeo extravaganza—the town is up to its neck in bucking broncs and bulls and joyful bluster. The parades, pageantry, and parties require the endurance of a cattle hand on a weeklong drive.

DINING AND LODGING

✕**The Albany.** Historic photographs of early Cheyenne set the tone for this downtown icon, a place that seems as old as the city itself (the structure was built circa 1900). It's a bit dark, and the booths are a bit shabby, but the American food is solid. ⊠1506 Capitol Ave. ☎307/638–3507 ▭AE, D, DC, MC, V.

✕**Little Bear Steakhouse.** Locals rave about this classic American steak house decorated with a Western theme. The seafood selections are diverse and well prepared. ✉ *1700 Little Bear Rd.* ☎ *307/634–3684* 🍴 *AE, D, DC, MC, V.*

✗ **Shadows.** This downtown spot in the historic Union Pacific Railroad Depot has its own brewery. Eat sandwiches, stone-oven pizzas, pasta, fresh fish, or steak in the bar or the adjacent restaurant. ✉ *115 W. 15th St., Suite 1* ☎ *307/634–7625* 🍴 *AE, D, MC, V.*

🏨 **Best Western Hitching Post Inn.** State legislators frequent this hotel, known to locals as "The Hitch." With its dark-wood walls, the hotel has an elegance not found elsewhere in Cheyenne. ✉ *1700 W. Lincolnway, 82001* ☎ *307/638–3301* 🌐 *www.hitchingpostinn.com* 🛏 *166 rooms* 🍴 *AE, D, DC, MC, V.*

🏨 **Little America Hotel and Resort.** An executive golf course and driving range are the highlights of this resort at the intersection of I–80 and I–25. ✉ *2800 W. Lincolnway, 82001* ☎ *307/775–8400 or 800/445–6945* 🌐 *www.littleamerica.com* 🛏 *188 rooms* 🍴 *AE, D, DC, MC, V.*

🏨 **Nagle Warren Mansion.** This delightful Victorian mansion B&B, built in 1888, has gorgeous woodwork, ornate staircases, and period furniture and wallpaper. Antiques furnish the lavish rooms, which are named for figures associated with the mansion's history; some rooms have gas fireplaces. ✉ *222 E. 17th St., 82001* ☎ *307/637–3333 or 800/811–2610* 🌐 *www.naglewarrenmansion.com* 🛏 *12 rooms* 🍴 *AE, MC, V.*

CINCINNATI, OHIO

A river's width from the South, Cincinnati resembles a southern city in many respects: Its summers are hot and humid, a result of being in a basin along the Ohio River, and its politics lean toward the conservative. This is just the first of several different identities, however. It's a river town, a sports town, a metropolis with architectural landmarks, and—since the opening of the $110 million National Underground Railroad Freedom Center in 2004—a history town. There are also a multitude of museums and one of the best zoos in the country. The rolling bluegrass-covered hills of Kentucky are just over the river, and the rural plains of Indiana and the meadow-marked countryside of Ohio are about a 30-minute drive away. If you want to sample a little bit of everything, consider Cincinnati your buffet.

DINING AND LODGING

✗ **Arnold's.** The oldest bar in Cincinnati, opened in 1861, caters to a diverse customer base and also serves a basic but solid Italian menu with such entrées as spaghetti and meatballs, eggplant marinara, Sicilian linguine, and sandwiches. ✉ *210 E. 8th St.* ☎ *513/421–6234* 🍴 *AE, D, MC, V.*

✗ **Graeter's.** This neighborhood ice cream parlor has multiple locations, including a dozen in Cincinnati and many others in Kentucky, Indiana, Dayton, and Columbus. Get in the inevitable line and start pondering your choices. ✉ *332 Ludlow Ave.* ☎ *513/281-4749* 🍴 *MC, V.*

✗ **Skyline Chili.** For many Cincinnati expatriates, the first stop on a hometown visit is the nearest Skyline Chili parlor. Whichever way they take it—three-way (chili with spaghetti and shredded cheddar cheese), four-way (chili with spaghetti, cheese, and onions), or cheese Coney (chili with shredded cheddar on a hot dog with bun)—people here are passionate about their chili. ⊠ *643 Vine St.* ☎*513/241-2020* ▭*AE, D, MC, V*

🏨**Cincinnatian Hotel.** A sedate 1882 French Second Empire-style hotel, the Cincinnatian offers contemporary elegance along with gracious personal service. It's not the largest hotel in Cincinnati, but it is the best. ⊠*601 Vine St.* ☎*513/381-3000 or 800/942-9000* ⊕*www.cincinnatianhotel.com* ⇗*147 rooms, 4 suites* ▭*AE, D, DC, MC, V.*

🏨**Hilton Cincinnati Netherland Plaza.** Downtown's grand art deco hotel is in the Carew Tower. The two-story lobby has bas-relief sculptures and dramatic fountains and light fixtures; guest rooms have 10-foot ceilings and soft pastel colors but tend to vary in size and configuration, with some rooms noticeably smaller and less grandly appointed. ⊠*35 W. 5th St.* ☎*513/421-9100* ⊕*www.hilton.com* ⇗*561 rooms* ▭*AE, D, DC, MC, V.*

🏨**Hyatt Regency.** One of the largest hotels in Cincinnati, this Downtown landmark has an atrium lobby with glass walls and ceiling, contemporary rooms in soft pastel colors, and first-rate service. It's connected by a skywalk to Saks Fifth Avenue and the Tower Place shopping center. ⊠*151 W. 5th St.* ☎*513/579-1234 or 800/233-1234* ⊕*www.hyatt.com* ⇗*488 rooms, 11 suites* ▭*AE, D, DC, MC, V.*

36

CLEVELAND, OHIO

Cleveland has the resilient, no-nonsense attitude of any hard-working, Upper Midwest city. It's rock and roll, football and beer, and polka and kielbasa. And although it hasn't blinked as some of the elements of its 1990s renaissance have faded a bit, the long-term trend is still toward improvement. While some efforts have failed, new restaurants and nightspots have joined old favorites to give the city an impressive variety of entertainment options and a cultural diversity that might come as a surprise to first-time visitors. Whatever the future holds, you can be sure that Cleveland will continue to change—for the better—defying expectations along the way.

DINING AND LODGING

✗**Frank Sterle's Slovenian Country House.** Meat loaf, Wiener schnitzel, made-from-scratch gravies, and a hint of grandma's tender loving care are staples at this Central European cafeteria-style restaurant on the near east side. ⊠ *1401 E. 55th St.* ☎*216/881-4181* ▭*AE, MC, V.*

✗**Heck's Café.** This publike eatery in historic Ohio City has an open kitchen and a glass garden atrium filled with plants. A Cleveland institution, Heck's has been around for more than 40 years and is known for its bouillabaisse and (arguably) the best burger in town. ⊠ *2927 Bridge Ave.* ☎*216/861-5464* ▭*AE, D, MC, V.*

✗**Tommy's.** A vegetarian institution, Tommy's serves hefty salads and sandwiches and embarrassingly large but delicious milk shakes made with Cleveland's own Pierre's ice cream. It's open daily for breakfast as well as for lunch and dinner. ⊠ *1824 Coventry Rd.* ☎*216/321-7757* ⊟*MC, V.*

⊡**Hilton Garden Inn Cleveland Downtown.** Just across the street from Jacobs Field in the Gateway District, the hotel lies within walking distance of Cleveland State University Convocation Center, Terminal Tower, and Quicken Loans Arena. ⊠*1100 Carnegie Ave.* ☎*216/658-6400* ⊕*www.hilton.com* ⤳*240 rooms, 8 suites* ⊟*AE, D, DC, MC, V.*

⊡**Renaissance Cleveland Hotel.** This grand 14-story 1851 hotel is within walking distance of the Cleveland Convention Center, the Flats, the Theater District, and the Rock and Roll Hall of Fame and Museum. ⊠*24 Public Sq.* ☎*216/696-5600* ⊕*www.renaissancehotels.com* ⤳*441 rooms, 50 suites* ⊟*AE, D, DC, MC, V.*

⊡**Wyndham Cleveland at Playhouse Square.** The 13-story Wyndham overlooks the bright lights of the vibrant theater district; some rooms have views of Playhouse Square. ⊠*1260 Euclid Ave.* ☎*216/615-7500* ⊕*www.wyndham.com* ⤳*205 rooms* ⊟*AE, D, DC, MC, V.*

DALLAS-FORT WORTH, TEXAS

These twin cities, separated by 30 miles of suburbs, are quite the odd couple. Dallas is glitzy and ritzy, a swelling, modernistic business metropolis whose inhabitants go to bed early and to church on Sunday. Fort Worth, sneered at as "Cowtown" by its neighbors, lives in the shadow of its wild history as a rip-roaring cowboy town, a place of gunfights and cattle drives—even though its cultural establishment is superior to Dallas's and it has seen a downtown rebirth in recent years. In Fort Worth that fellow in the faded jeans and cowboy hat could well be the president of the bank. In Dallas, people tend to be a bit more formal.

DINING AND LODGING

✗**Monica's Aca y Alla.** Everyday get-togethers feel like celebrations at this Deep Ellum favorite, which serves great food at inexpensive prices. Try the carne adobo (beef strips with a red salsa), Mexican lasagna, or Greene pasta (named for the owner). You can also find more standard Tex-Mex dishes. ⊠*2914 Main St., Dallas* ☎*214/748-2700* ⊟*AE, DC, MC, V.*

✗**Reata.** Diners get a modern spin on the Old West at this Fort Worth favorite. Specialties here include stacked enchiladas, tenderloin tacos, and bone-in ribeye steak. Portions are oversized; an order of the precariously stacked onion rings—thick, tall, and evenly-fried—could easily feed four. ⊠ *310 Houston St., Fort Worth* ☎*817/336-1009* ⊟*AE, D, MC, V.*

✗**Sonny Bryan's Smokehouse.** The original location has been dishing up smoky brisket and fall-off-the-bone pork ribs from the same ramshackle digs since 1958, attracting fans ranging from President George W. Bush to director Steven Spielberg. Locals know to get there early; when Sonny's is out of barbecue, you're out of luck. ⊠ *2202 Inwood Rd., Dallas* ☎*214/357-7120* ⊟*AE, MC, V.*

🏠**Rosewood Mansion on Turtle Creek.** Opulent rooms are appointed with antiques and original artwork. Guests have complimentary use of the property's Lexus vehicles, and a house car can also ferry guests to nearby destinations. The service here is legendary, as is the hotel restaurant. Count on finding Dallas-Fort Worth's most beautiful, celebrated, and powerful inside. ✉*2821 Turtle Creek Blvd., Dallas* ☎*214/559-2100* ⊕*www.mansiononturtlecreek.com* ↻*143 rooms* ▭*AE, D, DC, MC, V.*

🏠**Stockyards Hotel.** A storybook place that's seen more than its share of cowboys, rustlers, gangsters, and oil barons, this hotel has been used in many a movie. If you're visiting the Stockyards, take a moment to walk through the 1907 hotel's richly appointed lobby (even if you're not a guest). ✉*109 E. Exchange Ave., Fort Worth* ☎*817/625-6427 or 800/423-8471* ⊕*www.stockyardshotel.com* ↻*52 rooms* ▭*AE, D, DC, MC, V.*

🏠**W Dallas–Victory.** The first hotel in Dallas' burgeoning Victory Park makes a dramatic statement, altering the uptown skyline with a 33-story tower topped with glowing blue light. The crowd here is trend-conscious and pampered, and the décor is comfortable and minimalist—eggplant-colored walls, neutral bed linens, low-profile furniture. The W is just steps from the American Airlines Center—home to the NBA's Dallas Mavericks and the NHL's Dallas Stars—and minutes from downtown. ✉*2440 Victory Park Ln., Dallas* ☎*214/397-4100* ⊕*www.whotels.com* ↻*252 rooms* ▭*AE, D, DC, MC, V.*

DETROIT, MICHIGAN

Founded in 1701 as "la Ville d'Etroit"—the City at the Straits—Detroit is one of the Midwest's oldest cities. Originally a strategic Native American and French trading post, by the mid-19th century the city was compared to Paris because of its scenic parks and beautiful architecture. The 20th century saw Detroit's evolution into the modern Motor City, the city that put the world on wheels. Detroit is also one of the world's busiest inland ports and a major steel producer. The Detroit River is linked by steamship to more than 40 countries; vessels ranging from ocean-going freighters to private yachts dock in the city's protected harbor.

Metro Detroit is also notable for its ethnic diversity—visit Hamtramck for its excellent Polish bakeries, Dearborn for its thriving Middle Eastern community, or Mexicantown for its numerous restaurants. The city offers extensive opportunities for shopping, nightlife, and dining. First-time visitors are pleasantly surprised by Detroit's world-class museums, theaters, art galleries, downtown eateries and clubs, well-run parks, and enthusiastic sports-fan culture.

DINING AND LODGING

✗**Caucus Club.** A venerable Detroit institution, this spot recalls a time when elegant restaurants had boardroom decor, lots of oil paintings, and wood. The menu is of similar vintage: steaks, chops, Dover sole, and the club's famous baby back ribs. ⊠ *150 W. Congress St.* ☎ *313/965-4970* ⊟ *AE, D, DC, MC, V.*

✕ **Fishbone's Rhythm Kitchen Cafe.** This authentic New Orleans-style restaurant in the heart of Greektown is loud, brash, funky, and fun. The spicy creole fare on the seasonal menu includes gator, gumbo, crawfish, and gulf oysters on the half shell. The whiskey ribs are tops year-round. ⊠ *400 Monroe Ave.* ☎ *313/965-4600* ⊟ *AE, DC, MC, V.*

✕ **Traffic Jam & Snug.** The menu changes often, but you can count on wheatberry and other interesting breads, inventive salads, and daily specials like spinach lasagna and Caesar salad. Dessert is key: try the Five Chocolate Cake, a white-chocolate cheesecake topped with three chocolate layers, wrapped in chocolate fondant. ⊠ *511 W. Canfield St.* ☎ *313/831-9470* ⊟ *AE, D, MC, V.*

🏨 **Dearborn Inn–A Marriott Hotel.** Henry Ford built this hotel in 1931 to house foreign dignitaries and such inventors as Thomas Edison and Charles Lindbergh. The colonial-inspired property is across from the Henry Ford Museum and Greenfield Village; adjacent to the main building are five historic homes associated with such famous Americans as Patrick Henry, Edgar Allan Poe, and Walt Whitman. ⊠ *20301 Oakwood Blvd., Dearborn* ☎ *313/271-2700 or 800/228-9290* ⊕ *www.marriott.com* ↪ *222 rooms, 5 cottages* ⊟ *AE, D, DC, MC, V.*

🏨 **Hilton Windsor.** Most guest rooms in this downtown riverbank hotel have a view of Detroit's skyline and the shipping activity on the world's busiest inland waterway. ⊠ *277 Riverside Dr. W, Windsor, Ontario, Canada* ☎ *519/973-5555; 800/445-6667* ⊕ *www.hilton.com* ↪ *305 rooms* ⊟ *AE, D, DC, MC, V.*

🏨 **Hotel Pontchartrain.** The Pontch, as it is familiarly known, has light, airy rooms done in neutral shades accented by green-and-rose fabrics. Most rooms have wonderful views of the city and the river. Do not accept a room at the back of the hotel—which is across the street from a fire station—unless you are a very sound sleeper. ⊠ *Washington Blvd.* ☎ *313/965-0200* ⊕ *www.hotelpontch.com* ↪ *384 rooms* ⊟ *AE, D, DC, MC, V.*

HOUSTON, TEXAS

Unbridled energy has always been Houston's trademark. The forceful, wildcatter temperament that transformed what was once a swamp near the junction of the Buffalo and White Oak bayous into the nation's fourth-largest city also made the city a world energy center and pushed exploration into outer space—indeed, the first words spoken from the moon broadcast its name throughout the universe: "Houston, Tranquility Base here. The Eagle has landed." This same wild spirit (and a lack of zoning laws) explains much about the unrestricted growth that resulted in the city's patchwork layout: It's not unusual to find a luxury apartment complex next to a muffler repair shop, or a palm reader's storefront adjacent to a church. Magnificent glass and metal towers dominate the downtown corridor, but for the most part Houston's cityscape is characterized by random patches of impressive architecture interspersed with groomed greenbelts and lively neighborhoods.

DINING AND LODGING

✕**America's.** Dramatic South American rain forest decor may make you think you're in Peru while you dine on gulf snapper, roasted pork tenderloin, and, of course, plantains. ⊠ *1800 S. Post Oak Blvd.* ☎*713/961-1492* ⊟*AE, D, DC, MC, V.*

✕**Brennan's.** A cousin of New Orleans's Commander's Palace, Brennan's puts a Texas spin on creole cuisine. The landmark building's interiors are as charming as the hospitality is Southern-gracious. Chef Randy Evans' specialties, like turtle soup with sherry and pecan-crusted fish, repeatedly impress. Brunch in the peaceful courtyard is a memorable experience. ⊠ *3300 Smith St.* ☎*713/522-9711* ⊟*AE, D, DC, MC, V.*

✕**Goode Company Texas Bar-B-Q.** Down-home Texas barbecue is prepared ranch style—smoked and served with tasty red sauce. Patrons line up on the sidewalk to eat at picnic tables on the covered patio. A standard order is the chopped-beef brisket sandwich on jalapeño-cheese bread. Don't miss the celebrated pecan pie for dessert. ⊠ *5109 Kirby Dr.* ☎*713/522-2530* ⊟*AE, D, DC, MC, V.*

▥**Hilton Houston NASA Clear Lake.** On the shores of Clear Lake, Hilton Nassau Bay & Marina offers a number of water sports and easy access to NASA, which is across the street. ⊠*3000 NASA Pkwy.* ☎*281/333-9300* ⊕*www.hilton.com* ⬏*243 rooms* ⊟ *AE, D, DC, MC, V.*

▥**Hotel Derek.** This is the perfect choice for the cosmopolitan traveler. Mod furnishings grace the glossy-floored lobby and the sleek, contemporary rooms. ⊠*2525 W. Loop S* ☎*713/961-3000* ⊕*www.hotelderek.com* ⬏*314 rooms* ⊟*AE, D, DC, MC, V.*

▥**Houstonian Hotel, Club & Spa.** Spread over 18 acres in a wooded area near Memorial Park, the Houstonian has luxurious rooms and sports facilities galore—golf, tennis, a climbing wall, and indoor racket games. ⊠*111 N. Post Oak La.* ☎*713/680-2626 or 800/231-2759* ⊕*www.houstonian.com* ⬏*288 rooms* ⊟*AE, D, DC, MC, V.*

JACKSONVILLE, FLORIDA

One of Florida's oldest cities and — at 731 square mi—the largest city in the continental United States, Jacksonville offers an appealing downtown riverside area, handsome residential neighborhoods, a thriving arts scene, and, for football fans, the NFL Jaguars and the NCAA Gator Bowl. Remnants of the Old South flavor the city, especially in the Riverside/Avondale historic district, where moss-draped oak trees frame prairie-style bungalows and Tudor Revival mansions, and palm trees, Spanish bayonet, and azaleas populate the landscape.

DINING AND LODGING

✕**bb's.** The modern decor, which includes concrete floors and a stainless-steel wine bar (read: no hard liquor), provides an interesting backdrop for comfort food—inspired entrées and daily specials that might include char-grilled beef tenderloin, prosciutto-wrapped pork chops, or mushroom triangoli ravioli. On the lighter side, grilled pizzas, sandwiches, and salads, especially warm goat-cheese salad, are favorites. ⊠*1019 Hendricks Ave.* ☎*904/306–0100* ⊟*AE, D, DC, MC, V.*

✗**European Street Cafe.** The menu here has nearly 100 deli sandwiches and salads. Notable are raspberry almond chicken salad and the "Blue Max," with pastrami, corned beef, Swiss cheese, sauerkraut, hot mustard, and blue-cheese dressing. There are 20-plus beers on tap (plus more than 100 in bottles). ⊠*2753 Park St.* ☎*904/384–9999* ⊠*1704 San Marco Blvd.* ☎*904/398–9500* ⊠*5500 Beach Blvd.* ☎*904/398–1717* ▭*AE, D, MC, V.*

✗**Matthew's.** The menu changes nightly but might include lemon-roasted Amish chicken with honey-truffle spaghetti squash, or herb-roasted rack of lamb with mustard pistachio crust. Complement your meal with one of 450 wines, then dive into one of the warm soufflés for dessert. ⊠*2107 Hendricks Ave., San Marco* ☎*904/396–9922* ▭*AE, D, DC, MC, V.* ☺

🛏**Embassy Suites Hotel.** As the city's only full-service, all-suites hotel, the Embassy Suites gets high marks from travelers looking for comfortable accommodations at a reasonable price. ⊠*9300 Baymeadows Rd.* ☎*904/731–3555 or 800/362–2779* ⊕*www.embassysuitesjax.com* ⇨ *277 suites* ▭*AE, DC, MC, V.*

🛏**The Inn at Oak Street.** Built in 1902 as a private residence, the three-story, 6,000-square-foot Frame Vernacular–style building was restored and reopened as a bed-and-breakfast. Each room has a private bath—some with whirlpool tubs and others with double-head showers—and second-story rooms offer balconies. ⊠*2114 Oak St.* ☎*904/379–5525* ⊕*www.innatoakstreet.com* ⇨*6 rooms, 1 suite* ▭*AE, D, MC, V.*

🛏**Omni Jacksonville Hotel.** Further cementing its reputation as Jacksonville's most luxurious and glamorous hotel, the 16-story Omni underwent a multimillion-dollar makeover in 2006, including "downtown urban style" guest rooms (think neutral grays and creams, dark wood, stainless steel, and flat-screen TVs), which they claim are the largest in the city, and an expanded fitness center. ⊠*245 Water St.* ☎*904/355–6664 or 800/843–6664* 🖷*904/791–4812* ⊕*www.omnijacksonville.com* ⇨*326 rooms, 28 suites* ▭*AE, D, DC, MC, V.*

KANSAS CITY, MISSOURI

Kansas City bills itself as the "Heart of America." Within 250 mi of both the geographic and population centers of the nation, the city is famous for its stockyards, saxophone player Charlie "Bird" Parker and his Kansas City-style bebop, and some of the best barbecue in the world. The city has more boulevards than Paris and more working fountains (212 and counting) than any city but Rome. An unwritten rule dictates that a fountain be added to nearly every new commercial structure built, giving Kansas City its second nickname: "The City of Fountains."

DINING AND LODGING

✗**Arthur Bryant's.** Although there are more than 100 barbecue joints in Kansas City, Bryant's—low on decor but high on taste—tops the list for locals, who don't mind standing in long lines to order at the counter. ⊠ *1727 Brooklyn Ave.* ☎*816/231-1123* ▭*AE, D, MC, V.*

✕**Chappell's Restaurant and Sports Museum.** Just north of downtown, Chappell's is best known for meat entrées like the London broil and burgers, but it also serves lighter sandwiches and soups in an exceedingly casual, sports-bar environment. Chappell's houses the country's largest private collection of sports memorabilia displayed in a restaurant. ✉ *323 Armour Rd., North Kansas City* ☎ *816/421-0002* 🖃 *AE, D, DC, MC, V.*

✕**Plaza III.** Honored with the Wine Spectator Award of Excellence, this Plaza steakhouse prepares double-cut lamb chops that are just as succulent as its menu's many beef selections. All meat entrées are served with your choice of diable, béarnaise, or beef pan gravy, and accompaniments are offered à la carte. ✉ *4749 Pennsylvania* ☎ *816/753-0000* 🖃 *AE, D, DC, MC, V.*

🏨**Aladdin Holiday Inn Downtown Kansas City.** A 1925 building that's on the National Register of Historic Places, this hotel has rooms with lime green walls and retro, 1960s furniture and an art deco lobby. The Aladdin caters both to value-driven, family-oriented guests and appeals to those looking for something a little unusual. ✉ *1215 Wyandotte St.* ☎ *816/421-8888* 🌐 *www.ichotelsgroup.com* ⇲ *193 rooms* 🖃 *AE, D, DC, MC, V.*

🏨**Quarterage Hotel.** This intimate brick hotel, located close to Westport nightlife, still retains the 19th-century charm of its historic Westport neighborhood. It is a short drive from the Country Club Plaza, Downtown, and many other activities in the metropolitan area. ✉ *560 Westport Rd.* ☎ *816/931-0001 or 800/942-4233* 🌐 *www.quarteragehotel.com* ⇲ *123 rooms* 🖃 *AE, D, DC, MC, V.*

🏨**Westin Crown Center.** Part of the Crown Center complex, the Westin has a bustling lobby complete with a five-story waterfall and a natural limestone cliff. All rooms feature the chain's Heavenly Beds and nice views; the best face Crown Center Square to the east. ✉ *1 Pershing Rd.* ☎ *816/474-4400 or 800/228-3000* 🌐 *www.westin.com* ⇲ *729 rooms* 🖃 *AE, D, DC, MC, V.*

MILWAUKEE, WISCONSIN

A friendly Midwestern atmosphere prevails in Milwaukee, which is not so much a city as a large collection of neighborhoods situated on the shores of Lake Michigan. Wisconsin's largest city is an international seaport and the state's primary commercial and manufacturing center. Modern steel-and-glass high-rises occupy much of the downtown area, but they share the skyline with restored and well-kept 19th-century buildings from Milwaukee's early heritage. The city boomed in the 1840s with the arrival of German beer brewers, whose influence is still present. Milwaukee is known as a city of festivals, the biggest being Summerfest, held in late June and early July.

DINING AND LODGING

✕**Bartolotta's Lake Park Bistro.** On a bluff overlooking Lake Michigan, this bistro is renowned for its French-style Sunday brunch. The daily menu includes roast duck and seasonal seafood dishes with rich and buttery sauces. ⊠ *3133 E. Newberry Blvd.* ☎*414/962-6300* ▭*AE, D, DC, MC, V.*

✗**Elsa's on the Park.** Across from Cathedral Square Park, this chic but casual restaurant has frequently changing art exhibits and serves big, juicy hamburgers and pork-chop sandwiches. ⊠ *833 N. Jefferson St.* ☎*414/765-0615* ▭*AE, MC, V.*

✗**Polaris.** At this elegant, candlelit revolving restaurant—on the 22nd floor of the Hyatt Regency hotel—you can see Lake Michigan and nearly all of Milwaukee while you dine. Select from grilled beef tenderloin, duck with white bean cassoulet, and seared sea scallops. ⊠ *333 W. Kilbourn Ave.* ☎*414/270-6130* ▭*AE, D, DC, MC, V.*

▦**County Clare.** The guest rooms and pub at this inn—within walking distance of Lake Michigan and downtown—evoke Ireland, from the architecture to the stained-glass windows to the wood-burning fireplace. The pub prepares such Gaelic specialties as Irish stew and shepherd's pie. The cheery rooms have queen-size four-poster beds. ⊠*1234 N. Astor St.* ☎*414/272-5273* ⊕*www.countyclare-inn.com* ↩*29 rooms, 4 suites* ▭*AE, D, DC, MC, V.*

▦**Hilton Milwaukee City Center.** Kids can splash and slide year-round in the hotel's indoor water park. The brick hotel, adjacent to Milwaukee's convention center, was built in 1929 and its lobby is quite elegant. Lakefront attractions are a few blocks away. ⊠*509 W. Wisconsin Ave.* ☎*414/271-7250 or 800/445-8667* ⊕*www.hilton.com* ↩*730 rooms, 20 suites* ▭*AE, D, DC, MC, V.*

▦**Pfister Hotel.** Milwaukee's grandest old hotel dates from 1893. The lobby's long, high barrel-vaulted ceiling puts you in a Victorian frame of mind from the moment you step in. An English tea is served in the fern-shaded dining room most afternoons. ⊠*424 E. Wisconsin Ave.* ☎*414/273-8222 or 800/558-8222* ⊕*www.thepfisterhotel.com* ↩*307 rooms, 82 suites* ▭*AE, D, DC, MC, V.*

PITTSBURGH, PENNSYLVANIA

Pittsburgh has recast itself into a pleasing blend of turn-of-the-20th-century architectural masterpieces and modern skyscrapers, consistently ranked among the nation's most livable cities. Visitors will find that Pittsburgh has a real sense of fun, with outdoor activities on its rivers and parks, unique shopping downtown and in surrounding neighborhoods, and excellent dining in some of the state's most interesting locales. For the best view of Pittsburgh, take one of the city's two 19th-century cable cars and travel up Mt. Washington—the views are breathtaking from up here. You can see the rivers flowing together, appreciate the city's unique skyline, and take in PNC Park and Heinz Field, home to the Pittsburgh Pirates and Pittsburgh Steelers, respectively.

DINING AND LODGING

✗**Café du Jour.** Tucked between the cafés and raucous bars of East Carson Street is a secret garden where some of the city's best food is served. A narrow courtyard in the back of this café is a pleasant place to enjoy a Mediterranean-inspired menu that includes pork loin with thyme goat cheese timbale (a kind of custard or flan), roasted eggplant rolled with fresh mozzarella and sun-dried tomatoes, and tilapia with calamata olive tapenade. Bring your own wine or beer. ⊠ *1107 E. Carson St.* ☎*412/488-9695* ⊟*No credit cards*

✕**The Church Brew Works.** [This converted 1902 Catholic church offers a variety of brewed-on-site ales and lagers (the brewing equipment sits front-and-center, on what was once the altar) and a satisfying menu. The original stained-glass windows are still in place. Buffalo-and-wild-mushroom meat loaf, wood-fired pizzas, black pepper–glazed pork chops, and pierogies are on the menu. ⊠ *3525 Liberty Ave.* ☎*412/688-8200* ⊟*AE, D, MC, V.*

✕**Georgetowne Inn.** As with most restaurants that sit atop Mt. Washington, Georgetowne Inn overlooks the city. Candles and warm tones add to the rustic, romantic feel. Dishes include prime rib, swordfish, and veal and shrimp specials. ⊠ *1230 Grandview Ave.* ☎*412/481-4424* ⊟*AE, D, MC, V.*

⌂**Courtyard by Marriott–Pittsburgh Downtown.** One of a handful of newer, mid-range hotels in or near Downtown, this hotel occupies a former warehouse. The simple and comfortable rooms retain the high ceilings. ⊠*945 Penn Ave.* ☎*412/434-5551* ⊕*www.marriott.com* ☞*182 rooms* ⊟*AE, D, DC, MC, V.*

⌂**Omni William Penn.** Pittsburgh's grand hotel has a sumptuous lobby, where people relax with drinks under a coffered ceiling and crystal chandeliers. Many of the light-filled guest rooms are large enough for a couch and a wing chair. ⊠*Mellon Sq., 530 William Penn Pl.* ☎*412/281-7100 or 800/843-6664* ⊕*www.omnihotels.com* ☞*596 rooms* ⊟*AE, D, DC, MC, V.*

⌂**Sheraton Station Square.** This upscale chain hotel is in Station Square, a former railroad station reborn as a leisure destination across the river from Downtown. Some rooms have river views. ⊠*300 W. Station Square Dr.* ☎*412/261-2000 or 800/325-3535* ⊕*www.sheraton.com* ☞*399 rooms* ⊟*AE, D, DC, MC, V.*

PROVIDENCE, RHODE ISLAND

New England's second-largest city (with a population of 173,000, behind Boston) comes into the 21st century as a renaissance city. Once regarded, even by its own residents, as an awkward stepchild of greater Boston (50 mi to the north), Providence has metamorphosed from an area that empties out at the end of a workday to a clean, modern, cultural, and gastronomical hub. The focal point of the city these days is Waterplace Park, a series of footbridges, walkways, and green spaces that run along both sides of the Providence River, which flows through the heart of downtown.

DINING AND LODGING

✕**Al Forno.** Al Forno means "from the oven" in Italian. And from the oven comes an exceedingly popular wood-grilled pizza. Try roasted clams and spicy sausage in a tomato broth or bistro steak. ✉ *577 S. Main St.* ☎*401/273-9760* ▤*AE, DC, MC, V.*

✕**Neath's.** The large open dining room of this converted warehouse and the views of the Providence River are wonderful, but it's the food that has made this a hot spot. The menu showcases a blend of French and Asian cuisine, such as crisp Cambodian spring rolls with bean sprouts and grilled shrimp, and yellowfin tuna steak with a soy and ginger glaze over a soba noodle gallette. ✉ *262 S. Water St.* ☎*401/751-3700* ▤*AE, D, MC, V.*

✕**Union Station Brewery.** The historic brick building that houses this brewpub was once the freight house for the Providence Train Station. You can wash down tasty chicken enchiladas, an old-fashioned chicken potpie, classic meat loaf, or fish-and-chips with a pint of Providence cream ale or one of several other fine beers brewed here. If you can't decide on a beer, try a sampler tray. ✉ *36 Exchange Terr.* ☎*401/274-2739* ▤*AE, D, DC, MC, V.*

▥**Providence Biltmore.** Built in 1922, the Biltmore has a sleek art-deco exterior, an external glass elevator with delightful views of Providence, a grand ballroom, an Elizabeth Arden Red Door Spa, and an in-house Starbucks. The personal attentiveness of its staff, downtown location, and modern amenities make this hotel one of the city's best. ✉*Kennedy Plaza, Dorrance and Washington Sts.* ☎*401/421-0700 or 800/294-7709* ⊕*www.providencebiltmore.com* ⤴*291 rooms, 139 suites* ▤*AE, D, DC, MC, V.*

▥**Providence Marriott.** This modern, brick, six-story hotel near the capitol doesn't have the old-fashioned grandeur of the Providence Biltmore, but it has all the modern conveniences. ✉*1 Orms St.* ☎*401/272-2400 or 800/937-7768* ⊕*www.marriottprovidence.com* ⤴*346 rooms, 5 suites* ▤*AE, D, DC, MC, V.*

▥**Westin Providence.** The multi-turreted 25-story Westin towers over Providence's compact downtown, connected by skywalks to the city's gleaming convention center and the Providence Place mall. Its rooms have reproduction period furniture, and half have king-size beds; many have views of the city. ✉*1 W. Exchange St.* ☎*401/598-8000 or 800/937-8461* ⊕*www.westin.com* ⤴*364 rooms, 22 suites* ▤*AE, D, DC, MC, V.*

SACRAMENTO, CALIFORNIA

The gateway to California's Gold Country, the seat of state government (headed by Governor Arnold Schwarzenegger), and an agricultural hub, the city of Sacramento plays many important contemporary roles. The midtown area, just east of downtown, contains many of the city's best restaurants and quirkiest shops. An infusion of upscale, popular restaurants, nightclubs, and breweries is energizing the downtown scene (be aware that the pedestrians-only K Street Mall has a persistant panhandling problem). Sacramento contains more than 2,000 acres of natural and developed parkland. Grand old evergreens, deciduous and fruit-bearing trees (many lawns and even parks are littered with oranges in springtime), and giant palms give it a shady, lush quality. Genteel Victorian edifices sit side by side with art deco and postmodern skyscrapers.

DINING AND LODGING

✕**Biba.** Owner Biba Caggiano is a nationally recognized authority on Italian cuisine. ✉*2801 Capitol Ave.* ☎*916/455–2422* ⊕*www.biba-restaurant.com* ⌖*Reservations essential* ▭*AE, DC, MC, V.*

✕**Ernesto's Mexican Food.** Customers wait up to an hour for a table on Friday and Saturday evenings at this popular midtown restaurant. Fresh ingredients are stressed in the wide selection of entrées, and the margaritas are especially refreshing. ✉*16th and S Sts.* ☎*916/441–5850* ⊕*www.ernestosmexicanfood.com* ▭*AE, D, DC, MC, V.*

✕**The Firehouse.** Consistently ranked by local publications as one of the city's top 10 restaurants, this formal and historic restaurant has a full bar, courtyard seating (its signature attraction), and creative American cooking, such as rack of lamb marinated in olive oil and fresh herbs, served with Gorgonzola potato dauphinoise and port balsamic gastrique. ✉*1112 2nd St.* ☎*916/442–4772* ▭*AE, MC, V.*

▦**Amber House Bed & Breakfast Inn.** This B&B about a mile from the Capitol encompasses two homes. The original house is a Craftsman-style home with five bedrooms, and the second is an 1897 Dutch colonial-revival home. ✉*1315 22nd St.* ☎*916/444–8085 or 800/755–6526* ⊕*www.amberhouse.com* ⌖*10 rooms* ▭*AE, D, DC, MC, V.*

▦**Delta King.** This grand old riverboat, now permanently moored on Old Sacramento's waterfront, once transported passengers between Sacramento and San Francisco. ✉*1000 Front St.,* ☎*916/444–5464 or 800/825–5464* ⊕*www.deltaking.com* ⌖*44 rooms* ▭*AE, D, DC, MC, V.*

▦**Hyatt Regency Sacramento.** With a marble-and-glass lobby and luxurious rooms, this hotel across from the Capitol and adjacent to the convention center is arguably Sacramento's finest. The multitiered, glass-dominated hotel has a striking Mediterranean design. ✉*1209 L St.* ☎*916/443–1234 or 800/633–7313* ⊕*www.hyatt.com* ⌖*500 rooms, 24 suites* ▭*AE, D, DC, MC, V.*

36

ST. LOUIS, MISSOURI

St. Louis is known as the Gateway to the West. This was certainly the case for Lewis and Clark, who stopped here for provisions during their famous expedition. In the years that followed, the city became a manufacturing center for wagons, guns, blankets, saddles, and everything pioneers would need on their journeys west. Because of its size and location, St. Louis became a center for government and finance, and the 1904 World's Fair brought increasing growth and diversification to the local marketplace.

Today the city's educational institutions, including Washington University and St. Louis University, are global leaders in scientific and social research. Forest Park's Muny Opera is the largest open-air theater in the nation, and the St. Louis Art Museum is known throughout the world. But St. Louis is indisputably a baseball town, and a fanatic love of the sport—and specifically the Cardinals—is a way of life for many here.

DINING AND LODGING

✕**Blueberry Hill.** Order a burger, sip a locally brewed Rock 'n' Roll beer, and pop a quarter in the famous 2,000-tune jukebox to get the good times going. ⊠ *6504 Delmar Blvd.* ☎*314/727–0880* ☐ *AE, D, DC, MC, V.*

✕**Cunetto House of Pasta.** There's usually a wait at this popular Hill restaurant, but relaxing in the cocktail lounge is part of the experience. Once seated, you'll find plenty of veal and beef dishes, as well as more than 30 different pastas. ⊠ *5453 Magnolia Ave.* ☎*314/781–1135* ☐ *AE, D, DC, MC, V.*

✕**Mike Shannon's Steaks & Seafood.** This steak restaurant is packed with sports memorabilia and is a popular post-baseball game stop. It's owned by former Cardinal baseball great Mike Shannon. ⊠ *620 Market St.* ☎*314/421–1540* ☐ *AE, D, DC, MC, V.*

Cheshire Inn and Lodge. This Tudor-style hotel, built in 1969, is a romantic getaway within walking distance of Forest Park and the St. Louis Zoo and is a five-minute drive via I–40 from Downtown. ⊠ *6300 Clayton Rd.* ☎*314/647–7300 or 800/325–7378* ⊕*www.cheshire lodge.net* ⤴*92 rooms, 13 suites* ☐ *AE, DC, MC, V.*

Drury Inn–Union Station. Lead-glass windows and marble columns give historic charm to this former YMCA, which dates back to 1907. Convenient to the Gateway Arch, it is next to Union Station, St. Louis' turn-of-the-century rail hub morphed into a mall. ⊠ *201 S. 20th St.* ☎*314/231–3900* ⊕*www.druryhotels.com* ⤴*171 rooms, 6 suites* ☐ *AE, D, DC, MC, V.*

Millennium Hotel. Overlooking the Gateway Arch and on the Mississippi Riverfront, this hotel is a round high-rise with a revolving restaurant on the top floor. Some rooms have floor-to-ceiling windows with great views of the city. ⊠ *200 S. 4th St.* ☎*314/241–9500* ⊕*www.mil leniumhotels.com* ⤴*171 rooms, 6 suites* ☐ *AE, D, DC, MC, V .*

USA Essentials

PLANNING TOOLS, EXPERT INSIGHT, GREAT CONTACTS

There are planners and there are those who, excuse the pun, fly by the seat of their pants. We happily place ourselves among the planners. Our writers and editors try to anticipate all the issues you may face before and during any journey, and then they do their research. This section is the product of their efforts. Use it to get excited about your trip to Essential USA, to inform your travel planning, or to guide you on the road should the seat of your pants start to feel threadbare.

GETTING STARTED

We're really proud of our Web site: Fodors.com is a great place to begin any journey. Scan Travel Wire for suggested itineraries, travel deals, restaurant and hotel openings, and other up-to-the-minute info. Check out Booking to research prices and book plane tickets, hotel rooms, rental cars, and vacation packages. Head to Talk for on-the-ground pointers from travelers who frequent our message boards. You can also link to loads of other travel-related resources.

▮ RESOURCES

ONLINE TRAVEL TOOLS

Safety Transportation Security Administration (TSA ⊕ www.tsa.gov)

Time Zones Timeanddate.com (⊕ www.timeanddate.com/worldclock) can help you figure out the correct time anywhere.

Weather Accuweather.com (⊕ www.accuweather.com) is an independent weather-forecasting service with good coverage of hurricanes. **Weather.com** (⊕ www.weather.com) is the Web site for the Weather Channel.

▮ THINGS TO CONSIDER

GEAR

SHIPPING LUGGAGE AHEAD

Imagine traveling with only a carry-on in tow. Shipping your luggage in advance via an air-freight service is a great way to cut down on backaches, hassles, and stress—especially if your packing list includes strollers, car seats, etc. There are some things to be aware of, though.

First, research carry-on restrictions; if you absolutely need something that isn't practical to ship and isn't allowed in carry-ons, this strategy isn't for you. Second, plan to send your bags several days in advance. Third, plan to spend some money: it will cost at least $100 to send a small piece of luggage, a golf bag, or

a pair of skis to a domestic destination, much more to places overseas.

Some people use Federal Express to ship their bags, but this can cost even more than air-freight services. All these services insure your bag (for most, the limit is $1,000, but you should verify that amount); you can, however, purchase additional insurance for about $1 per $100 of value.

Contacts Luggage Concierge (☎800/288–9818 ⊕ www.luggageconcierge.com). **Luggage Express** (☎866/744–7224 ⊕ www.usxpluggageexpress.com). **Luggage Free** (☎800/361–6871 ⊕ www.luggagefree.com). **Sports Express** (☎800/357–4174 ⊕ www.sportsexpress.com) specializes in shipping golf clubs and other sports equipment. **Virtual Bellhop** (☎877/235–5467 ⊕ www.virtualbellhop.com).

TRIP INSURANCE

What kind of coverage do you honestly need? Do you even need trip insurance at all? Take a deep breath and read on.

We believe that comprehensive trip insurance is especially valuable if you're booking a very expensive or complicated trip (particularly to an isolated region) or if you're booking far in advance. Who knows what could happen six months down the road? But whether or not you get insurance has more to do with how comfortable you are assuming all that risk yourself.

Comprehensive travel policies typically cover trip-cancellation and interruption, letting you cancel or cut your trip short

Trip Insurance Resources

INSURANCE COMPARISON SITES		
Insure My Trip.com	800/487-4722	www.insuremytrip.com
Square Mouth.com	800/240-0369	www.quotetravelinsurance.com
COMPREHENSIVE TRAVEL INSURERS		
Access America	866/807-3982	www.accessamerica.com
CSA Travel Protection	800/873-9855	www.csatravelprotection.com
HTH Worldwide	610/254-8700 or 888/243-2358	www.hthworldwide.com
Travelex Insurance	888/457-4602	www.travelex-insurance.com
Travel Guard International	715/345-0505 or 800/826-4919	www.travelguard.com
Travel Insured International	800/243-3174	www.travelinsured.com
MEDICAL-ONLY INSURERS		
International Medical Group	800/628-4664	www.imglobal.com
International SOS	215/942-8000 or 713/521-7611	www.internationalsos.com
Wallach & Company	800/237-6615 or 504/687-3166	www.wallach.com

because of a personal emergency, illness, or, in some cases, acts of terrorism in your destination. Such policies also cover evacuation and medical care. Some also cover you for trip delays because of bad weather or mechanical problems as well as for lost or delayed baggage. Another type of coverage to look for is financial default—that is, when your trip is disrupted because a tour operator, airline, or cruise line goes out of business. Generally you must buy this when you book your trip or shortly thereafter, and it's only available to you if your operator isn't on a list of excluded companies.

Expect comprehensive travel insurance policies to cost about 4% to 7% or 8% of the total price of your trip (it's more like 8%–12% if you're over age 70). A medical-only policy may or may not be cheaper than a comprehensive policy. Always read the fine print of your policy to make sure that you are covered for the risks that are of most concern to you.

Compare several policies to make sure you're getting the best price and range of coverage available.

■ TIP→ OK. You know you can save a bundle on trips to warm-weather destinations by traveling in the rainy season. But there's also a chance that a severe storm will disrupt your plans. The solution? Look for hotels and resorts that offer storm/hurricane guarantees. Although they rarely allow refunds, most guarantees do let you rebook later if a storm strikes.

BOOKING YOUR TRIP

▌ WITH A TRAVEL AGENT

A knowledgeable brick-and-mortar travel agent can be a godsend if you're booking a cruise, a package trip that's not available to you directly, an air pass, or a complicated itinerary. What's more, travel agents that specialize in a destination may have exclusive access to certain deals and insider information on things such as charter flights. Agents who specialize in types of travelers (senior citizens, gays and lesbians, naturists) or types of trips (cruises, luxury travel, safaris) can also be invaluable.

▌TIP➔ Remember that Expedia, Traveloc-ity, and Orbitz are travel agents, not just booking engines. To resolve any problems with a reservation made through these companies, contact them first.

Complain about the surcharges all you like, but when things don't work out the way you'd hoped, it's nice to have an agent to put things right.

Agent Resources American Society of Travel Agents (☎703/739–2782 ⊕www. travelsense.org).

▌ ACCOMMODATIONS

BED & BREAKFASTS

Reservation Services Bed & Breakfast.com (☎512/322–2710 or 800/462–2632 ⊕www. bedandbreakfast.com) also sends out an online newsletter. Bed & Breakfast Inns Online (☎615/868–1946 or 800/215–7365 ⊕www. bbonline.com). BnB Finder.com (☎212/432–7693 or 888/547–8226 ⊕www.bnbfinder.com).

HOME EXCHANGES

Exchange Clubs Home Exchange.com (☎800/877–8723 ⊕www.homeexchange. com); $59.95 for a 1-year online listing. HomeLink International (☎800/638–3841 ⊕www.homelink.org); $90 yearly for Web-only membership; $140 includes Web access and two catalogs. Intervac U.S. (☎800/756–4663

⊕www.intervacus.com); $78.88 for Web-only membership; $126 includes Web access and a catalog.

▌ RENTAL CARS

When you reserve a car, ask about cancellation penalties, taxes, drop-off charges (if you're planning to pick up the car in one city and leave it in another), and surcharges (for being under or over a certain age, for additional drivers, or for driving across state or country borders or beyond a specific distance from your point of rental). All these things can add substantially to your costs. Request car seats and extras such as GPS when you book.

Rates are sometimes—but not always—better if you book in advance or reserve through a rental agency's Web site. There are other reasons to book ahead, though: for popular destinations, during busy times of the year, or to ensure that you get certain types of cars (vans, SUVs, exotic sports cars).

CAR-RENTAL INSURANCE

Everyone who rents a car wonders whether the insurance that the rental companies offer is worth the expense. No one—including us—has a simple answer. It all depends on how much regular insurance you have, how comfortable you are with risk, and whether or not money is an issue.

If you own a car and carry comprehensive car insurance for both collision and liability, your personal auto insurance will probably cover a rental, but read your policy's fine print to be sure. If you don't have auto insurance, then you should probably buy the collision- or loss-damage waiver (CDW or LDW) from the rental company. This eliminates your liability for damage to the car.

Online Booking Resources

AGGREGATORS		
Kayak	www.kayak.com	also looks at cruises and vacation packages.
Mobissimo	www.mobissimo.com	also looks at car-rental rates and activities.
Qixo	www.qixo.com	also compares cruises, vacation packages, and even travel insurance.
Sidestep	www.sidestep.com	also compares vacation packages and lists travel deals.
Travelgrove	www.travelgrove.com	also compares cruises and packages.
BOOKING ENGINES		
Cheap Tickets	www.cheaptickets.com	a discounter.
Expedia	www.expedia.com	a large online agency that charges a booking fee for airline tickets.
Hotwire	www.hotwire.com	a discounter.
Lastminute.com	www.lastminute.com	specializes in last-minute travel the main site is for the U.K., but it has a link to a U.S. site.
Luxury Link	www.luxurylink.com	has auctions (surprisingly good deals) as well as offers on the high-end side of travel.
Onetravel.com	www.onetravel.com	a discounter for hotels, car rentals, airfares, and packages.
Orbitz	www.orbitz.com	charges a booking fee for airline tickets, but gives a clear breakdown of fees and taxes before you book.
Priceline.com	www.priceline.com	a discounter that also allows bidding.
Travel.com	www.travel.com	allows you to compare its rates with those of other booking engines.
Travelocity	www.travelocity.com	charges a booking fee for airline tickets, but promises good problem resolution.
ONLINE ACCOMMODATIONS		
Hotelbook.com	www.hotelbook.com	focuses on independent hotels worldwide.
Hotel Club	www.hotelclub.net	good for major cities worldwide.
Hotels.com	www.hotels.com	a big Expedia-owned wholesaler that offers rooms in hotels all over the world.
Quikbook	www.quikbook.com	offers "pay when you stay" reservations that let you settle your bill at checkout, not when you book.
OTHER RESOURCES		
Bidding For Travel	www.biddingfortravel.com	a good place to figure out what you can get and for how much before you start bidding on, say, Priceline.

Online Booking Resources

CONTACTS		
Forgetaway		www.forgetaway.weather.com
Home Away	512/493–0382	www.homeaway.com
Interhome	954/791–8282 or 800/882–6864	www.interhome.us
Vacation Home Rentals Worldwide	201/767–9393 or 800/633–3284	www.vhrww.com
Villas International	415/499–9490 or 800/221–2260	www.villasintl.com

Some credit cards offer CDW coverage, but it's usually supplemental to your own insurance and rarely covers SUVs, minivans, luxury models, and the like. If your coverage is secondary, you may still be liable for loss-of-use costs from the car-rental company (again, read the fine print). But no credit-card insurance is valid unless you use that card for *all* transactions, from reserving to paying the final bill.

You may also be offered supplemental liability coverage; the car-rental company is required to carry a minimal level of liability coverage insuring all renters, but it's rarely enough to cover claims in a really serious accident if you're at fault. Your own auto-insurance policy will protect you if you own a car; if you don't, you have to decide whether you are willing to take the risk.

U.S. rental companies sell CDWs and LDWs for about $15 to $25 a day; supplemental liability is usually more than $10 a day. The car-rental company may offer you all sorts of other policies, but they're rarely worth the cost. Personal accident insurance, which is basic hospitalization coverage, is an especially egregious rip-off if you already have health insurance.

■TIP→ You can decline the insurance from the rental company and purchase it through a third-party provider such as Travel Guard (www.travelguard.com)—$9 per day for $35,000 of coverage. That's sometimes just under half the price of the CDW offered by some car-rental companies.

TRANSPORTATION

▌ BY AIR

▌**TIP→** If you travel frequently, look into the TSA's Registered Traveler program. The program, which is still being tested in several U.S. airports, is designed to cut down on gridlock at security checkpoints by allowing prescreened travelers to pass quickly through kiosks that scan an iris and/or a fingerprint. How sci-fi is that?

Airlines & Airports Airline and Airport Links.com (⊕www.airlineandairportlinks.com) has links to many of the world's airlines and airports.

Airline Security Issues Transportation Security Administration (⊕www.tsa.gov) has answers for almost every question that might come up.

Air Travel Resources in the USA

FLIGHTS

Airline Contacts **Alaska Airlines** (☎800/252-7522 or 206/433-3100 ⊕www.alaskaair.com). **American Airlines** (☎800/433-7300 ⊕www.aa.com). **ATA** (☎800/435-9282 or 317/282-8308 ⊕www.ata.com). **Continental Airlines** (☎800/523-3273 for U.S. and Mexico reservations, 800/231-0856 for international reservations ⊕www.continental.com). **Delta Airlines** (☎800/221-1212 for U.S. reservations, 800/241-4141 for international reservations ⊕www.delta.com). **jetBlue** (☎800/538-2583 ⊕www.jetblue.com). **Northwest Airlines** (☎800/225-2525 ⊕www.nwa.com). **Southwest Airlines** (☎800/435-9792 ⊕www.southwest.com). **Spirit Airlines** (☎800/772-7117 or 586/791-7300 ⊕www.spiritair.com). **United Airlines** (☎800/864-8331 for U.S. reservations, 800/538-2929 for international reservations ⊕www.united.com). **USAirways** (☎800/428-4322 for U.S. and Canada reservations, 800/622-1015 for international reservations ⊕www.usairways.com).

▌ BY BUS

Bus Information **Greyhound Lines, Inc.** (☎800/231-2222 ⊕www.greyhound.com).

Car-Rental Resources

AUTOMOBILE ASSOCIATIONS		
U.S.: American Automobile Association (AAA)	315/797-5000	www.aaa.com; most contact with the organization is through state and regional members.
National Automobile Club	650/294-7000	www.thenac.com; membership is open to California residents only.
MAJOR AGENCIES		
Alamo	800/462-5266	www.alamo.com.
Avis	800/331-1084	www.avis.com.
Budget	800/472-3325	www.budget.com.
Enterprise	800/261-7331	www.enterprise.com
Hertz	800/654-3001	www.hertz.com.
National Car Rental	800/227-7368	www.nationalcar.com.

FOR INTERNATIONAL TRAVELERS

CURRENCY

The dollar is the basic unit of U.S. currency. It has 100 cents. Coins are the penny (1¢); the nickel (5¢), dime (10¢), quarter (25¢), half-dollar (50¢), and the very rare golden $1 coin and even rarer silver $1. Bills are denominated $1, $5, $10, $20, $50, and $100, all mostly green and identical in size; designs and background tints vary. You may come across a $2 bill, but the chances are slim.

CUSTOMS

Information U.S. Customs and Border Protection (⊕www.cbp.gov).

DRIVING

Driving in the United States is on the right. Speed limits are posted in miles per hour (usually between 55 mph and 70 mph). Watch for lower limits in small towns and on back roads (usually 30 mph to 40 mph). Most states require front-seat passengers to wear seat belts; many states require children to sit in the back seat and to wear seat belts. In major cities rush hour is between 7 and 10 AM; afternoon rush hour is between 4 and 7 PM. To encourage carpooling, some freeways have special lanes, ordinarily marked with a diamond, for high-occupancy vehicles (HOV)—cars carrying two people or more.

Highways are well paved. Interstates—limited-access, multilane highways designated with an "I-" before the number—are fastest. Interstates with three-digit numbers circle urban areas, which may also have other limited-access expressways, freeways, and parkways. Tolls may be levied on limited-access highways. U.S. and state highways aren't necessarily limited-access, but may have several lanes.

Gas stations are plentiful. Most stay open late (24 hours along major highways and in big cities) except in rural areas, where Sunday hours are limited and where you may drive for long stretches without a refueling opportunity. Along larger highways, roadside stops with restrooms, fast-food restaurants,

and sundries stores are well spaced. State police and tow trucks patrol major highways. If your car breaks down on an interstate, pull onto the shoulder and wait for help, or have your passengers wait while you walk to an emergency phone (available in most states). If you carry a cell phone, dial *55, noting your location on the small green roadside mileage marker.

ELECTRICITY

The U.S. standard is AC, 110 volts/60 cycles. Plugs have two flat pins set parallel to each other.

EMBASSIES

Contacts Australia (☎202/797–3000 ⊕www.austemb.org). **Canada** (☎202/682–1740 ⊕www.canadianembassy.org). **United Kingdom** (☎202/588–7800 ⊕www.britainusa.com).

EMERGENCIES

For police, fire, or ambulance, dial 911 (0 in rural areas).

HOLIDAYS

New Year's Day (Jan. 1); Martin Luther King Day (3rd Mon. in Jan.); Presidents' Day (3rd Mon. in Feb.); Memorial Day (last Mon. in May); Independence Day (July 4); Labor Day (1st Mon. in Sept.); Columbus Day (2nd Mon. in Oct.); Thanksgiving Day (4th Thurs. in Nov.); Christmas Eve and Christmas Day (Dec. 24 and 25); and New Year's Eve (Dec. 31).

MAIL

You can buy stamps and aerograms and send letters and parcels in post offices. Stamp-dispensing machines can occasionally be found in airports, bus and train stations, office buildings, drugstores, and convenience stores. U.S. mail boxes are stout, dark blue steel bins; pickup schedules are posted inside the bin (pull down the handle to see them). Parcels weighing more than a pound must be mailed at a post office or at a private mailing center.

Within the United States a first-class letter weighing 1 ounce or less costs 41¢; each additional ounce costs 17¢. Postcards cost 26¢. Postcards or 1-ounce airmail letters to most countries costs 90¢; postcards or 1-ounce letters to Canada or Mexico cost 69¢.

To receive mail on the road, have it sent c/o General Delivery at your destination's main post office (use the correct five-digit ZIP code). You must pick up mail in person within 30 days, with a driver's license or passport for identification.

Contacts DHL (☎800/225–5345 ⊕www. dhl.com). **Federal Express** (☎800/463–3339 ⊕www.fedex.com). **Mail Boxes, Etc./ The UPS Store** (☎800/789–4623 ⊕www. mbe.com). **United States Postal Service** (⊕www.usps.com).

PASSPORTS & VISAS

Visitor visas aren't necessary for citizens of Australia, Canada, the United Kingdom, or most citizens of European Union countries coming for tourism and staying for fewer than 90 days. If you require a visa, the cost is $100, and waiting time can be substantial, depending on where you live. Apply for a visa at the U.S. consulate in your place of residence; check the U.S. State Department's special Visa Web site for further information.

Visa Information Destination USA (⊕www.unitedstatesvisas.gov).

PHONES

Numbers consist of a three-digit area code and a seven-digit local number. Within many local calling areas you dial only the seven digits; in others you dial "1" first and all 10 digits—just as you would for calls between area-code regions. The same is true for calls to numbers prefixed by "800," "888," "866," and "877"—all toll-free. For calls to numbers prefixed by "900" you must pay—usually dearly.

For international calls, dial "011" followed by the country code and the local number. For

help, dial "0" and ask for an overseas operator. Most phone books list country codes and U.S. area codes. The country code for Australia is 61, for New Zealand 64, for the United Kingdom 44. Calling Canada is the same as calling within the United States, whose country code, by the way, is 1.

For operator assistance, dial "0." For directory assistance, call 555–1212 or occasionally 411 (free at many public phones). You can reverse long-distance charges by calling "collect"; dial "0" instead of "1" before the 10-digit number.

Instructions are generally posted on pay phones. Usually you insert coins in a slot (usually 25¢–50¢ for local calls) and wait for a steady tone before dialing. On long-distance calls the operator tells you how much to insert; prepaid phone cards, widely available in various denominations, can be used from any phone. Follow the directions to activate the card (there's usually an access number, then an activation code), then dial your number.

CELL PHONES

The United States has several GSM (Global System for Mobile Communications) networks, so multiband mobiles from most countries (except for Japan) work here. Unfortunately, it's almost impossible to buy a pay-as-you-go mobile SIM card in the U.S.—which allows you to avoid roaming charges—without also buying a phone. That said, cell phones with pay-as-you-go plans are available for well under $100. The cheapest ones with decent national coverage are the GoPhone from Cingular and Virgin Mobile, which only offers pay-as-you-go service.

Contacts Cingular (☎888/333–6651 ⊕www.cingular.com). **Virgin Mobile** (☎No phone ⊕www.virginmobileusa.com).

ON THE GROUND

■ COMMUNICATIONS

INTERNET
Contacts **Cybercafes** (⊕www.cybercafes.
com) lists over 4,000 Internet cafés worldwide.

■ EATING OUT

RESERVATIONS & DRESS
Regardless of where you are, it's a good idea to make a reservation if you can. We only mention them specifically when reservations are essential (there's no other way you'll ever get a table) or when they are not accepted. For popular restaurants, book as far ahead as you can (often 30 days), and reconfirm as soon as you arrive.

Online reservation services make it easy to book a table before you even leave home. OpenTable covers most states, including 20 major cities, and has limited listings in Canada, Mexico, the United Kingdom, and elsewhere. DinnerBroker has restaurants throughout the United States as well as a few in Canada.

Contacts **OpenTable** (⊕*www.opentable.
com*). **DinnerBroker** (⊕*www.dinnerbro
ker.com*).

CREDIT CARDS
Throughout this guide, the following abbreviations are used: **AE**, American Express; **D**, Discover; **DC**, Diners Club; **MC**, MasterCard; and **V**, Visa.

It's a good idea to inform your credit-card company before you travel, especially if you're going abroad and don't travel internationally very often. Otherwise, the credit-card company might put a hold on your card owing to unusual activity—not a good thing halfway through your trip. Record all your credit-card numbers—as well as the phone numbers to call if your cards are lost or stolen—in a safe place, so you're prepared should something go wrong. Both MasterCard and Visa have general numbers you can call (collect if you're abroad) if your card is lost, but you're better off calling the number of your issuing bank, since MasterCard and Visa usually just transfer you to your bank; your bank's number is usually printed on your card.

Reporting Lost Cards **American Express** (☎800/528–4800 in U.S., 336/393–1111 collect from abroad ⊕www.americanexpress.
com). **Diners Club** (☎800/234–6377 in U.S., 303/799–1504 collect from abroad ⊕www.
dinersclub.com). **Discover** (☎800/347–2683 in U.S., 801/902–3100 collect from abroad ⊕www.discovercard.com). **MasterCard** (☎800/627–8372 in U.S., 636/722–7111 collect from abroad ⊕www.mastercard.com). **Visa** (☎800/847–2911 in U.S., 410/581–9994 collect from abroad ⊕www.visa.com).

TRAVELER'S CHECKS
Some consider this the currency of the cave man, and it's true that fewer establishments accept traveler's checks these days. Nevertheless, they're a cheap and secure way to carry extra money, particularly on trips to urban areas. Both Citibank (under the Visa brand) and American Express issue traveler's checks in the United States. Always keep track of all the serial numbers in case the checks are lost or stolen.

Contacts **American Express** (☎888/412–6945 in U.S., 801/945–9450 collect outside of U.S. to add value or speak to customer service ⊕www.americanexpress.com).

■ RESTROOMS

Find a Loo **The Bathroom Diaries** (⊕www.
thebathroomdiaries.com) is flush with unsanitized info on restrooms the world over—each one located, reviewed, and rated.

INDEX

Photo credits:

10, *Raymond Forbes/age fotostock*. 11, *Danny Warren/iStockphoto*. 12, *José Fuste Raga/age fotostock*. 13 (left), *Joy Brown/Shutterstock*. 13 (right), *Massachusetts Office of Tourism*. 15 (left), *Gary Moon/ age fotostock*. 15 (right), *Stuart Pearce/World Pictures/age fotostock*. 16, *Joe Viesti/viestiphoto.com*. 18, *Kord.com/age fotostock*. Chapter 1: The Maine Coast: 19, *Nancy Trueworthy/Aurora Photos*. Chapter 2: Boston: 37, *Jeff Greenberg/age fotostock*. Chapter 3: Cape Cod: 57, *Raymond Forbes/age fotostock*. Chapter 4: New York City: 75, *Renaud Visage/age fotostock*. Chapter 5: Niagara Falls: 101, *Kord.com/age fotostock*. Chapter 6: Philadelphia: 113, *Bob Krist/GPTMC*. Chapter 7: Washington, D.C.: 131, *San Rostro/age fotostock*. Chapter 8: North Carolina's Outer Banks: 153, *James Frank/ Aurora Photos*. Chapter 9: Charleston & Savannah: 167, *Walter Bibikow/age fotostock*. Chapter 10: Orlando & the Space Coast: 185, *Patrick Frilet/age fotostock*. Chapter 11: Miami & the Florida Keys: 203, *Jeff Greenberg/age fotostock*. Chapter 12: Kentucky Bluegrass Country: 221, *Jim Lane/Alamy*. Chapter 13: Tennessee: 233, *tbkmedia.de/Alamy*. Chapter 14: The Ozarks: 251, *Andre Jenny/Alamy*. Chapter 15: New Orleans: 265, *Ray Laskowitz/Alamy*. Chapter 16: The Texas Hill Country: 283, *Walter Bibikow/age fotostock*. Chapter 17: Chicago: 301, *Andre Jenny/Alamy*. Chapter 18: Minneapolis & St. Paul: 321, *K. Wothe/ARCO/age fotostock*. Chapter 19: South Dakota's Black Hills: 337, *nagelestock.com/Alamy*. Chapter 20: Western Montana: 351, *Dan Sherwood/age fotostock*. Chapter 21: Yellowstone National Park: 367, *John Warden/age fotostock*. Chapter 22: The Colorado Rockies: 383, *Stock Connection Distribution/Alamy*. Chapter 23: Santa Fe, Taos & Albuquerque: 401, *Sylvain Grandadam/age fotostock*. Chapter 24: Salt Lake City: 419, *Sylvain Grandadam/age fotostock*. Chapter 25: Southern Utah: 433, *P. Narayan/age fotostock*. Chapter 26: Grand Canyon National Park: 451, *National Park Service*. Chapter 27: Phoenix: 467, *Phillip Augustavo/Alamy*. Chapter 28: Las Vegas: 485, *Ken Ross/viestiphoto.com*. Chapter 29: The California Deserts: 507, *P. Michael Photoz/AKA/age fotostock*. Chapter 30: Los Angeles & San Diego: 525, *Richard Cummins/viestiphoto.com*. Chapter 31: Yosemite National Park: 553, *Yosemite Concession Services*. Chapter 32: San Francisco: 571: *Bill Brooks/Alamy*. Chapter 33: Lake Tahoe: 593, *SuperStock/age fotostock*. Chapter 34: Portland: *Jonathan Kingston/Aurora Photos*. Chapter 35: Seattle: 625: *Walter Bibikow/age fotostock*.

NOTES

NOTES

NOTES

NOTES

NOTES

ABOUT OUR WRITERS

Erin Byers Murray is the Boston editor for DailyCandy.com, where she spends her time uncovering the city's latest fashion, food, beauty, and travel finds. She's worked at *Boston* magazine and contributes regularly to the *Boston Globe*, *Boston* magazine, and *Fodor's*.

John Blodgett has spent so much time in Maine and Utah that he can't decide where he'd rather be. John had his first newspaper internship in the Maine mid-coast city of Brunswick, and these days he freelances in Salt Lake City.

A few years ago former *Fodor's* editor **Carissa Bluestone** peered at Seattle through a thick veil of rain and fell in love with the place. She's worked on freelance book projects ranging in subject matter from travel (including *Fodor's Seattle* and *Fodor's Pacific Northwest*) to sustainability to martial arts.

Former *Fodor's* staff editor and longtime contributor **Andrew Collins** grew up in New England and has written about it for *Fodor's Gay Guide to the USA*, several other *Fodor's* titles related to New England, and a number of newspapers and magazines. He has also contributed to *Fodor's New Mexico*, *Travel & Leisure*, *Out Traveler*, *Sunset*, and *New Mexico magazine*, and teaches a course on travel writing for New York City's Gotham Writers' Workshop.

Jennifer D'Anastasio enjoys promoting all the Twin Cities have to offer (beyond cold winter weather), and she continues to delight in discovering neighborhood eateries and local boutiques. She works as a financial writer and enjoys travel writing in her spare time.

Michelle Delio has lived in all five boroughs and now calls Manhattan home. A freelance writer who covers art, pop culture, photography, travel, and technology, Michelle contributes to Fodors.com, *Fodor's* guides to New York City and New Orleans, and *Fodor's Guide to the Da Vinci Code*.

Jessica Norman Dupuy is an Austin-based freelance writer specializing in food and travel. Raised in the Texas Hill Country, she enjoys the outdoors, savoring different cuisines, and any chance to travel abroad—or to the Rocky Mountains in a pinch. She is a contributor to *Texas Monthly* and other Texas publications.

T.D. Griffith has written or co-authored more than 40 books, and his travel writing has been featured in publications around the world. He has contributed to *Fodor's* for nearly two decades.

Amy Grisak is a freelancer specializing in Montana history, travel in her adopted home state, local food, and sustainable agriculture. She writes for several publications, including the *Great Falls Tribune*, *Montana Magazine*, *Mother Earth News*, and *Hobby Farms*.

MiChelle Jones has written numerous cultural and travel pieces about Nashville and the Southeast for several regional publications.

Veteran *Fodor's* writer and editor **Denise M. Leto** roams the backstreets of San Francisco for sheer love of the city, ferreting out its hidden treasures, reveling in its big-name attractions, and soaking up its special brand of quirkiness.

Piers Marchant is a Philadelphia-based writer and editor who has written extensively about film, travel, and the Pope. He is currently the editor-in-chief of *two.one.five* magazine, dedicated to spreading "phillyessence" throughout the world.

Snowbird **Susan MacCallum-Whitcomb** spends as much time as possible in the Sunshine State. A full-time freelancer, Susan also writes for *Fodor's Bermuda*, *Boston*, *Budapest*, *California*, and *Florida* guides, and contributes regularly to Fodors.com.

Writer and reporter Russell McCulley lived in New Orleans for the better part of two decades before moving back to his native Texas. His travel stories have appeared in *Islands magazine* and the *Miami Herald*, among other publications; he also contributes to *Fodor's New Orleans.*

Gary McKechnie knows a lot about his native Florida, having worked as a Walt Disney World ferrryboat pilot, Jungle Cruise skipper, steam-train conductor, and double-decker bus driver. He's the author of *Great American Motorcycle Tours.*

Freelance writer Leslie Mizzel, who lives in Greensboro, North Carolina, is always willing to stop at any roadside stand, shop, or museum because she believes it's not how fast you get there, it's the stories you have when you arrive.

Reed Parsell is a longtime travel writer who has worked as a copy editor for the *Sacramento Bee* since 1994 and as a contributing writer to *Sacramento* magazine since 2006; he's a regular contributor to *Fodor's California.*

Steve Pastorino finally put his journalism degree to work with this *Fodor's* assignment after a long career in sports management. He's now a regular contributor to the *Salt Lake Tribune.*

Michael Ream is a travel writer whose writing assignments have taken him to Tennessee, Mississippi, and Louisiana, where he wrote about recovery efforts in the wake of Hurricanes Katrina and Rita. He has also penned chapters for *Fodor's* on Memphis and East Texas.

Susan Reigler is the former restaurant critic and travel writer for the *Louisville Courier-Journal.* She is the author of *Fodor's Compass American Guide to Kentucky.* Her next book, *Kentucky State Parks: A Visitor's Companion,* will be published in 2009.

Sarah Richards, who updated the Niagara Falls chapter, has contributed to numerous *Fodor's* guides in the past covering such destinations as Scotland, Great Britain, Japan, Toronto, and Canada.

Eileen Robinson Smith has made Charleston her home base since 1982. She has also covered the Dominican Republic, Martinique, and Guadeloupe for *Fodor's* for some 15 years, and her byline has appeared in such publications as *Caribbean Travel & Life, Condé Nast Traveler,* and most Charleston publications.

Swain Scheps' unhealthy fascination with all things Vegas has led to contributions to *Kevin Blackwood's Casino Gambling for Dummies* and regular appearances in *Fodor's Las Vegas.* He's also the author of *Business Intelligence for Dummies.*

Perpetually in search of the newest, most exciting things Chicago has to offer, freelance writer Judy Sutton Taylor has spent the last 14 years scouring the shops and neighborhoods of her adopted hometown. Judy is also the kids editor for *Time Out Chicago.*

A freelance correspondent for the *Sacramento Bee,* Christine Vovakes regularly writes news and features about northern California. The *Washington Post,* the *Christian Science Monitor* and the *San Francisco Chronicle* are among the publications where her travel articles and photos have appeared.

Kyle Wagner wrote about restaurants and food in Denver for 14 years, first for the alternative weekly *Westword* and then for the *Denver Post,* before being named travel editor for the *Post* in 2005. Her work has also appeared in the *Rocky Mountain News* and *Sunset* magazine.

Bobbi Zane is a life-long Valley Girl. She grew up in Hollywood and now writes about the Palm Springs/Desert Resorts area, San Diego, and National Parks of the West for *Fodor's.* Her byline has also appeared in the *Los Angeles Times, Los Angeles Daily News, Westways,* and the *San Jose Mercury News.*